Rereading America

*Cultural Contexts for Critical
Thinking and Writing*

Rereading America

Cultural Contexts for Critical Thinking and Writing

Seventh Edition

Edited by

Gary Colombo
LOS ANGELES COMMUNITY COLLEGE DISTRICT

Robert Cullen
SAN JOSE STATE UNIVERSITY

Bonnie Lisle
UNIVERSITY OF CALIFORNIA, LOS ANGELES

Bedford/St. Martin's   Boston   •   New York

For Bedford / St. Martin's

Senior Developmental Editor: John Sullivan
Senior Production Editor: Lori Chong Roncka
Senior Production Supervisor: Nancy Myers
Marketing Manager: Karita dos Santos
Editorial Assistant: Jennifer Lyford
Production Assistant: Katherine Caruana
Copyeditor: Barbara Price
Cover Design: Donna Lee Dennison
Cover Art: Elena and Michel Gran, *American Flag.* Photo courtesy of Hollis Taggart Galleries, New York City and Albemarle Gallery, London. Painting courtesy of Elena and Michel Gran, © Elena and Michel Gran.
Composition: Stratford/TexTech
Printing and Binding: Haddon Craftsmen, Inc., an R. R. Donnelley & Sons Company

President: Joan E. Feinberg
Editorial Director: Denise B. Wydra
Editor in Chief: Karen S. Henry
Director of Marketing: Karen Melton Soeltz
Director of Editing, Design, and Production: Marcia Cohen
Managing Editor: Elizabeth M. Schaaf

Library of Congress Control Number: 2006940026

Preface for Instructors

About *Rereading America*

Designed for first-year writing and critical thinking courses, *Rereading America* anthologizes a diverse set of readings focused on the myths that dominate U.S. culture. This central theme brings together thought-provoking selections on a broad range of topics — family, education, success, gender roles, race, religion, and America seen from a global perspective — topics that raise controversial issues meaningful to college students of all backgrounds. We've drawn these readings from many sources, both within the academy and outside of it; the selections are both multicultural and cross-curricular and thus represent an unusual variety of voices, styles, and subjects.

The readings in this anthology speak directly to students' experiences and concerns. Every college student has had some brush with prejudice, and most have something to say about education, the family, or the gender stereotypes they see in films and on television. The issues raised here help students link their personal experiences with broader cultural perspectives and lead them to analyze, or "read," the cultural forces that have shaped and continue to shape their lives. By linking the personal and the cultural, students begin to recognize that they are not academic outsiders — they too have knowledge, assumptions, and intellectual frameworks that give them authority in academic culture. Connecting personal knowledge and academic discourse helps students see that they are able to think, speak, and write academically and that they don't have to absorb passively what the "experts" say.

Features of the Seventh Edition

A Cultural Approach to Critical Thinking   Like its predecessors, the seventh edition of *Rereading America* is committed to the premise that learning to think critically means learning to identify and see beyond dominant cultural myths — collective and often unconsciously held beliefs that influence our thinking, reading, and writing. Instead of treating cultural diversity as just another topic to be studied or "appreciated," *Rereading America* encourages students to grapple with the real differences in perspective that arise in a pluralistic society like ours. This method helps students to break through conventional assumptions and patterns of thought that hinder fresh critical responses and inhibit dialogue. It helps them recognize that even the most apparently "natural" fact or obvious idea results from a process of social construction. And it helps them to develop the intellectual independence essential to critical thinking, reading, and writing.

Classic and Conservative Perspectives To provide students with the historical context they often need, each chapter in this edition *of Rereading America* includes a "classic" expression of the myth under examination. Approaching the myth of success, for example, by way of Horatio Alger's *Ragged Dick* — or the myth of racial superiority by way of Thomas Jefferson's infamous diatribe against "race mixing" — gives students a better sense of the myth's origins and impact. We've also included at least one contemporary conservative revision of the myth in each chapter, so you'll find in this edition readings by cultural critics who stand to the right of center, writers like Rick Santorum, Shelby Steele, Ken Hamblin, Dinesh D'Sousa, and David Kupelian.

New Issues Today, tensions between secular and religious values continue to trouble communities across America. Not a year goes by without a case coming before the courts involving issues such as prayer in school, the display of the Ten Commandments, the public celebration of religious holidays, the teaching of evolution, or the inclusion of "God" in the Pledge of Allegiance. This edition of *Rereading America* offers a new chapter that invites students to reflect on the role of religion in American culture. "One Nation Under God: American Myths of Church and State" examines the current resurgence of religion in the United States and explores the myths of secularism and religious belief that frame our thinking about the meaning of faith. Authors in this chapter include Anne Lamott, David Kupelian, Bill McKibben, and Eric Marcus, who examine the foundations of personal belief and its force in a secular culture. The Visual Portfolio offers a pictorial meditation on the delicate balance between belief and intolerance in American society. Diana L. Eck and Maria Poggi Johnson explore religious diversity — and religious division — in contemporary America. The chapter closes with readings addressing the competing claims of church and state, with pieces from James Madison, Noah Feldman, and Sam Harris.

Timely New Readings To keep *Rereading America* up to date, we've worked hard to bring you the best new voices speaking on issues of race, gender, class, family, education, religion, and freedom. As in past editions, we've retained old favorites like Malcolm X, Richard Rodriguez, Shelby Steele, Jamaica Kincaid, Deborah Tannen, Jean Anyon, Toni Cade Bambara, Gary Soto, Judith Ortiz Cofer, and Mike Rose. But you'll also find a host of new selections by such authors as Evan Wolfson, Jonathan Kozol, Maysan Haydar, Deborah Rudacille, Sam Harris, and Harvey Mansfield. And like earlier versions, this edition of *Rereading America* includes a healthy mix of personal and academic writing, representing a wide variety of genres, styles, and rhetorical strategies.

Visual Portfolios   In addition to frontispieces and cartoons, we've included a Visual Portfolio of myth-related images in every chapter of *Rereading America*. These collections of photographs, advertisements, and reproductions of famous paintings invite students to examine how visual "texts" are constructed and how, like written texts, they are susceptible to multiple readings and rereadings. Each portfolio is accompanied by a series of questions that encourage critical analysis and connect portfolio images to ideas and themes in chapter reading selections. As in earlier editions, the visual frontispieces that open each chapter are integrated into the prereading assignments found in the chapter introductions. The cartoons, offered as a bit of comic relief and as opportunities for visual thinking, are paired with appropriate readings thoughout the text.

Focus on Media   We've continued the practice of including selections focusing on the media. Chapter Three includes a selection by Diana Kendall on the media's role in disseminating myths of material success. Chapter Four offers analyses of gender issues in the media, including Jean Kilbourne on images of women in advertising and Joan Morgan on black feminism and hip-hop culture. In our new chapter on religion, Chapter Six, David Kupelian argues that the media corrodes key religious values. And in Chapter Seven, Todd Gitlin examines the ways American popular culture influences societies throughout the world.

Focus on Struggle and Resistance   Most multicultural readers approach diversity in one of two ways: either they adopt a pluralist approach and conceive of American society as a kind of salad bowl of cultures, or, in response to recent worries about the lack of "objectivity" in the multicultural curriculum, they take what might be called the "talk show" approach and present American culture as a series of pro-and-con debates on a number of social issues. The seventh edition of *Rereading America*, like its predecessors, follows neither of these approaches. Pluralist readers, we feel, make a promise that's impossible to keep: no single text, and no single course, can do justice to the many complex cultures that inhabit the United States. Thus, the materials selected for *Rereading America* aren't meant to offer a taste of what "family" means for Native Americans, or the flavor of gender relations among immigrants. Instead, we've included selections like Melvin Dixon's "Aunt Ida Pieces a Quilt" or Harlon Dalton's "Horatio Alger," because they offer us fresh critical perspectives on the common myths that shape our ideas, values, and beliefs. Rather than seeing this anthology as a mosaic or kaleidoscope of cultural fragments that combine to form a beautiful picture, it's more accurate to think of *Rereading America* as a handbook that helps students explore the ways that the dominant culture shapes their ideas, values, and beliefs.

This notion of cultural dominance is studiously avoided in most recent multicultural anthologies. "Salad bowl" readers generally sidestep the issue of cultural dynamics: intent on celebrating America's cultural diversity, they offer a relatively static picture of a nation fragmented into a kind of cultural archipelago. "Talk show" readers admit the idea of conflict, but they distort the reality of cultural dynamics by presenting cultural conflicts as a matter of rational — and equally balanced — debate. All of the materials anthologized in *Rereading America* address the cultural struggles that animate American society — the tensions that result from the expectations established by our dominant cultural myths and the diverse realities that these myths often contradict.

Ultimately, *Rereading America* is about resistance. In this new edition we continue to include readings that offer positive alternatives to the dilemmas of cultural conflict. To make this commitment to resistance as visible as possible, we've tried to conclude every chapter of this new edition with a suite of readings offering creative and, we hope, empowering examples of Americans who work together to redefine our national myths.

Extensive Apparatus   *Rereading America* offers a wealth of features to help students hone their analytic abilities and to aid instructors as they plan class discussions, critical thinking activities, and writing assignments. These include:

- *A Comprehensive Introductory Essay*   The book begins with a comprehensive essay, "Thinking Critically, Challenging Cultural Myths," that introduces students to the relationships between thinking, cultural diversity, and the notion of dominant cultural myths, and shows how such myths can influence their academic performance. We've also included a section devoted to active reading, which offers suggestions for prereading, prewriting, note taking, text marking, and keeping a reading journal. Another section helps students work with the many visual images included in the book.

- *New "Fast Facts" Begin Each Chapter*   Several provocative statistics before each chapter introduction provide context for students and prompt discussion. For example, "Roughly 35 million Americans (one in eight) live below the government's official poverty line."

- *Detailed Chapter Introductions*   An introductory essay at the beginning of each chapter offers students a thorough overview of each cultural myth, placing it in historical context, raising some of the chapter's central questions, and orienting students to the chapter's internal structure.

- *Prereading Activities*   Following each chapter introduction you'll find prereading activities designed to encourage students to reflect on what they already know about the cultural myth in question. Often connected to the images that open every chapter, these prereading activities help students to engage the topic even before they begin to read.

- *Questions to Stimulate Critical Thinking*   Three groups of questions following each selection encourage students to consider the reading carefully in several contexts: "Engaging the Text" focuses on close reading of the selection itself; "Exploring Connections" puts the selection into dialogue with other selections throughout the book; "Extending the Critical Context" invites students to connect the ideas they read about here with sources of knowledge outside the anthology, including library research, personal experience, interviews, ethnographic-style observations, and so forth. As in past editions, we've included a number of questions linking readings with contemporary television shows and feature films for instructors who want to address the interplay of cultural myths and the mass media.

- *New "Further Connections" Close Each Chapter*   These questions and assignments help students make additional connections among readings. They also provide suggestions for exploring issues through research and include ideas for community projects.

- *An Extensive Instructor's Manual*   *Resources for Teaching* REREADING AMERICA provides detailed advice about ways to make the most of both the readings and the questions; it also offers further ideas for discussion, class activities, and writing assignments, as well as practical hints and suggestions that we've garnered from our own classroom experiences.

- *Online Resources*   The Top Links Web site for *Rereading America* contains annotated research links. For more information, visit bedford stmartins.com/rereadingamerica to explore this site and other helpful electronic resources for both students and instructors.

Acknowledgments

Critical thinking is always a collaborative activity, and the kind of critical thinking involved in the creation of an anthology like *Rereading America* represents collegial collaboration at its very best. Since publication of the last edition, we've heard from instructors across the country who have generously offered suggestions for new classroom activities and comments for further refinements and improvements. Among the many instructors who shared their insights with us as we reworked this edition, we'd particularly like to thank the following: José Amaya, Iowa State University; Michael A. Arnzen, Seton Hill University; Alvin Clarke, Iowa State University; Scott DeShong, Quinebaug Valley Community College; Stephen Evans, University of Kansas; Irene Faass, Iowa State University; Eileen Ferretti, Kingsborough Community College; Susan E. Howard, University of Houston, Downtown; Emily

Isaacs, Montclair State University; Laureen Katana, Community College of Philadelphia; Misty Krueger, University of Tennessee; Robb Kunz, Utah State University; Mark Lidman, Maple Woods Community College; Seri Luangphinith, University of Hawai'i at Hilo; Michael Morris, Eastfield College; Roxanne Munch, Joliet Junior College; Beverly Neiderman, Kent State University; Carol Nowotny-Young, University of Arizona; Ellen O'Brien, Roosevelt University; Ildiko Olasz, Michigan State University; Cecilia Ornelas, California State University, Fullerton; Ted Otteson, University of Missouri, Kansas City; Carol Perdue, Green River Community College; Evelyn Pezzulich, Bridgewater State College; Mary Anne Quick, Bristol Community College; Elizabeth Rich, Saginaw Valley State University; Therese Rizzo, University of Delaware; Carolyn Rubin-Trimble, University of Houston, Downtown; Lori Taylor, SUNY University at Buffalo; Linda Tucker, Southern Arkansas University; Phoebe Wiley, Frostburg State University; Malcolm Williams, University of Houston, Downtown; Elizabeth Wright, Pennsylvania State University, Hazleton.

For their help with the sixth edition, we'd like to thank Andrea Beaudin, Southern Connecticut State University; Nancy C. Botkin, Indiana University South Bend; Deborah Brink, Lower Columbia College; Blythe Creamer, University of California, Davis; Stephen F. Evans, University of Kansas; Kathy A. Fedorko, Middlesex County College; Julie Hirsch, University of Arizona, Tucson; Jennifer Lynn Holley, Southern Connecticut State University; Deborah Kirkman, University of Kentucky; Anna Leahy, Missouri Western State College; Kelly Mayhew, San Diego City College; Julie Nash, Merrimack College; Deirdre Neilen, SUNY Upstate Medical University; Hector Perez, University of the Incarnate Word; Josephine Perry, Los Medanos College; Margaret B. Racin, West Virginia University; Daniela Ragusa, University of Rhode Island; Marguerite Regan, Southwestern College; Elizabeth Rich, Saginaw Valley State University; Kim Robeson, MiraCosta Community College; Renée Ruderman, Metropolitan State College of Denver; Tereza M. Szeghi, University of Arizona; Karen Toloui, Diablo Valley College; Lisa Toner, University of Kentucky; Alberto S. Vitale, Indiana University South Bend; James Ray Watkins, Jr., Eastern Illinois University; James M. Welch, Wittenberg University; and Terry Williams, San Diego State University.

For their help with the fifth edition of *Rereading America,* we'd like to thank the following: Etta C. Abrahams, Michigan State University; Richard L. Arthur, Miami University of Ohio; Scott E. Ash, Nassau Community College; Michael Augsperger, University of Iowa; Larry Cain, Chabot College; Rosann M. Cook, Purdue University at Calumet; Mary Jean Corbett, Miami University of Ohio; Stephen Curley, Texas A&M University at Galveston; Ann M. DeDad, Cannon University; Florence Emch, California State University, Los Angeles; Juan F. Flores, Del Mar College; Nancy Gonchar, The College of New Rochelle; Tara Hart, Howard Community College; Sue Ellen Holbrook, Southern Connecticut State University; Stephen Horvath, Howard Community College; Irwin J. Koplik, Hofstra University; Michael

Lewis, University of Iowa; Linda Maitland, University of Houston; Doug Merrell, University of Washington; Robert Murray, St. Thomas Aquinas College; Kathleen O'Brien, Boston University; Renée Ruderman, Metropolitan State College of Denver; Karen Ryan-Engel, Gannon University; Amy Sileven, Southern Illinois University at Carbondale; Jane E. Simonsen, University of Iowa; Juliet Sloger, University of Rochester; Ken Smith, Indiana University South Bend; Judith A. Stainbrook, Gannon University; Douglas Steward, University of Kansas.

For their help with the fourth edition of *Rereading America*, we'd like to thank the following: Dan Armstrong, Lane Community College; H. Inness Asher, University of Louisiana, Lafayette; Margot Gayle Backis, St. John Fisher College; Marlow Belschner, Southern Illinois University; Nancy Botkin, Indiana University South Bend; Carol Brown, South Puget Sound Community College; William Carroll, Norfolk State University; Dolores Crim, Purdue University, Hammond; Linda L. Danielson, Lane Community College; Emily Detiner, Miami University; Kathy Doherty, Bentley College; Melinda M. Fiala, University of Missouri, Kansas City; Sara Gogol, Portland Community College; Joyce Huff, George Washington University; Kim Lang, Shippensburg University; Uvieja Leighton, The Union Institute; Elizabeth L. Lewis, Vermilion Community College; Jennifer Lowood, Vista Community College; Brij Lurine, University of New Mexico; Eunice M. Madison, Purdue University, Calumet; Kenneth K. Martin, Community College of Philadelphia; James McWard, University of Kansas; Kevin A. Moberg, University of North Dakota; John G. Morris, Cameron University; Craig J. Nauman, University of Wisconsin, Madison; Bruce Ouderkirk, University of Nebraska, Lincoln; E. Suzanne Owens, Lorain County Community College; Elizabeth Paulson, California State University; Amy Sapowith, University of California, Los Angeles; Jurgen Schlunk, West Virginia University; Tony Slagle, The Ohio State University; Penny L. Smith, Gannon University; Sharon Snyder, Purdue University, Calumet; Deborah Tenneg, Yale University; Ruthe Thompson, University of Arizona; Lorraine Threadgill, Community College of Philadelphia; Steve Turnwall, Los Medanos College; Riley Vann, West Virginia University; Nancy Wallace, Temple University; Ellen Weinauer, University of Southern Mississippi; Claudia L. Whitling, South Puget Sound Community College; Judy Wilkinson, Skyline College; Mark Wollarges, Vanderbilt University; Phyllis Zrzuay, Franklin Pierce College.

We are also grateful to those reviewers who helped shape previous editions.

As always, we'd also like to thank all the kind folks at Bedford/ St. Martin's, who do their best to make the effort of producing a book like this a genuine pleasure. Our publishers, former president Charles Christensen and president Joan Feinberg, deserve special praise for the support they've shown us over the years and for the wise counsel they've offered in the occasional hour of need. Our editor, John Sullivan, has been a true partner in the development of this edition and has again demonstrated the kind of style and grace we've come to expect from him as the consummate professional. We also want to thank Lori Chong Roncka, who served as production editor on this edition; Barbara Price, who expertly copyedited the manuscript; Donna Dennison, who produced our new cover; Sandy Schechter, for clearing text permissions; Linda Finnegan and Helane Prottas, for researching and tracking down art; and editorial assistant Jennifer Lyford, who helped out with many of the hundreds of details that go into a project such as this. Finally, we'd like to acknowledge our spouses, Elena Barcia, Liz Silver, and Roy Weitz.

Contents

2

Learning Power:
The Myth of Education and Empowerment   *113*

3

Money and Success: *The Myth of Individual Opportunity*　　259

4

True Women and Real Men:
Myths of Gender   *371*

> "The real crime of which white America is now most guilty is not racism. It is indifference. Understanding the difference between the two is a crucial step in liberating ourselves from the sterile and unproductive impasse that has characterized the dialogue on race relations in recent years."

> "Four basic conceptions of how ethnic or racial groups should relate to each other have been predominant in the history of American thought about group relations — ethnic hierarchy, one-way assimilation, cultural pluralism, and group separatism."

> "The migrant stumbles through the desert and I after him — he's on a pilgrimage and I'm in pursuit of him."

> "Mary Lynn wanted to have sex with any man other than her husband. . . . She was a Coeur d'Alene Indian married to a white man; she was a wife who wanted to have sex with an indigenous stranger."

> "Now a subtler form of discrimination has risen. . . . This discrimination does not aim at groups as a whole. Rather, it aims at the subset of the group that refuses to cover, that is, to assimilate to dominant norms. And for the most part, existing civil rights laws do not protect individuals against such covering demands."

> "I am a child of the Americas,
> a light-skinned mestiza of the Caribbean,
> A child of many diaspora, born into this continent at a crossroads."

Rereading America

*Cultural Contexts for Critical
Thinking and Writing*

Thinking Critically, Challenging Cultural Myths

Becoming a College Student

Beginning college can be a disconcerting experience. It may be the first time you've lived away from home and had to deal with the stresses and pleasures of independence. There's increased academic competition, increased temptation, and a whole new set of peer pressures. In the dorms you may find yourself among people whose backgrounds make them seem foreign and unapproachable. If you commute, you may be struggling against a feeling of isolation that you've never faced before. And then there are increased expectations. For an introductory history class you may read as many books as you covered in a year of high school coursework. In anthropology, you might be asked to conduct ethnographic research — when you've barely heard of an ethnography before, much less written one. In English you may tackle more formal analytic writing in a single semester than you've ever done in your life.

College typically imposes fewer rules than high school, but also gives you less guidance and makes greater demands — demands that affect the quality as well as the quantity of your work. By your first midterm exam, you may suspect that your previous academic experience is irrelevant, that nothing you've done in school has prepared you to think, read, or write in the ways your professors expect. Your sociology instructor says she doesn't care whether you can remember all the examples in the textbook as long as you can apply the theoretical concepts to real situations. In your composition class, the perfect five-paragraph essay you turn in for your first assignment is dismissed as "superficial, mechanical, and dull." Meanwhile, the lecturer in your political science or psychology course is rejecting ideas about country, religion, family, and self that have always been a part of your deepest beliefs. How can you cope with these new expectations and challenges?

There is no simple solution, no infallible five-step method that works for everyone. As you meet the personal challenges of college, you'll grow as a human being. You'll begin to look critically at your old habits, beliefs, and values, to see them in relation to the new world you're entering. You may have to re-examine your relationships to family, friends, neighborhood, and heritage. You'll have to sort out your strengths from your weaknesses and make tough choices about who you are and who you want to become. Your academic work demands the same process of serious self-examination. To excel in college work you need to grow intellectually — to become a critical thinker.

What Is Critical Thinking?

What do instructors mean when they tell you to think critically? Most would say that it involves asking questions rather than memorizing information. Instead of simply collecting the "facts," a critical thinker probes them, looking for underlying assumptions and ideas. Instead of focusing on dates and events in history or symptoms in psychology, she probes for motives, causes — an explanation of how these things came to be. A critical thinker cultivates the ability to imagine and value points of view different from her own — then strengthens, refines, enlarges, or reshapes her ideas in light of those other perspectives. She is at once open and skeptical: receptive to new ideas yet careful to test them against previous experience and knowledge. In short, a critical thinker is an active learner, someone with the ability to shape, not merely absorb, knowledge.

All this is difficult to put into practice, because it requires getting outside your own skin and seeing the world from multiple perspectives. To see why critical thinking doesn't come naturally, take another look at the cover of this book. Many would scan the title, *Rereading America,* take in the surface meaning — to reconsider America — and go on to page one. There isn't much to question here; it just "makes sense." But what happens with the student who brings a different perspective? For example, a student from El Salvador might justly complain that the title reflects an ethnocentric view of what it means to be an American. After all, since America encompasses all the countries of North, South, and Central America, he lived in "America" long before arriving in the United States. When this student reads the title, then, he actually does *reread* it; he reads it once in the "commonsense" way but also from the perspective of someone who has lived in a country dominated by U.S. intervention and interests. This double vision or double perspective frees him to look beyond the "obvious" meaning of the book and to question its assumptions.

Of course, you don't have to be bicultural to become a proficient critical thinker. You can develop a genuine sensitivity to alternative perspectives even if you've never lived outside your hometown. But to do so you need to recognize that there are no "obvious meanings." The automatic equation that the native-born student makes between "America" and the United States seems to make sense only because our culture has traditionally endorsed the idea that the United States *is* America and, by implication, that other countries in this hemisphere are somehow inferior — not the genuine article. We tend to accept this equation and its unfortunate implications because we are products of our culture.

The Power of Cultural Myths

Culture shapes the way we think; it tells us what "makes sense." It holds people together by providing us with a shared set of customs, values, ideas, and beliefs, as well as a common language. We live enmeshed in this cultural web: it influences the way we relate to others, the way we look, our tastes, our habits; it enters our dreams and desires. But as culture binds us together it also selectively blinds us. As we grow up, we accept ways of looking at the world, ways of thinking and being that might best be characterized as cultural frames of reference or cultural myths. These myths help us understand our place in the world — our place as prescribed by our culture. They define our relationships to friends and lovers, to the past and future, to nature, to power, and to nation. Becoming a critical thinker means learning how to look beyond these cultural myths and the assumptions embedded in them.

You may associate the word "myth" primarily with the myths of the ancient Greeks. The legends of gods and heroes like Athena, Zeus, and Oedipus embodied the central ideals and values of Greek civilization — notions like civic responsibility, the primacy of male authority, and humility before the gods. The stories were "true" not in a literal sense but as reflections of important cultural beliefs. These myths assured the Greeks of the nobility of their origins; they provided models for the roles that Greeks would play in their public and private lives; they justified inequities in Greek society; they helped the Greeks understand human life and destiny in terms that "made sense" within the framework of that culture.

Our cultural myths do much the same. Take, for example, the American dream of success. Since the first European colonists came to the "New World" some four centuries ago, America has been synonymous with the idea of individual opportunity. For generations, immigrants have been lured across the ocean to make their fortunes in a land where the streets were said to be paved with gold. Of course, we don't always agree on what success means or how it should be measured. Some calculate the meaning of success in terms of multidigit salaries or the acreage of their country estates. Others discover success in the attainment of a dream — whether it's graduating from college, achieving excellence on the playing field, or winning new rights and opportunities for less fortunate fellow citizens. For some Americans, the dream of success is the very foundation of everything that's right about life in the United States. For others, the American dream is a cultural mirage that keeps workers happy in low-paying jobs while their bosses pocket the profits of an unfair system. But whether you embrace or reject the dream of success, you can't escape its influence. As Americans, we are steeped in a culture that prizes individual achievement; growing up in the United States, we are told again and again by parents, teachers, advertisers, Hollywood writers, politicians, and opinion makers that we, too, can achieve our dream — that we, too, can "Just Do It" if we try. You might aspire to become an Internet tycoon, or you might rebel and opt for a simple life, but you can't ignore the impact of the myth. We each define success in our own way, but, ultimately, the myth of success defines who we are and what we think, feel, and believe.

Cultural myths gain such enormous power over us by insinuating themselves into our thinking before we're aware of them. Most are learned at a deep, even unconscious level. Gender roles are a good example. As children we get gender role models from our families, our schools, our churches, and other important institutions. We see them acted out in the relationships between family members or portrayed on television, in the movies, or in song lyrics. Before long, the culturally determined roles we see for women and men appear to us as "self-evident": it seems "natural" for a man to be strong, responsible, competitive, and heterosexual, just as it may seem "unnatural" for a man to shun competitive activity or to take a romantic interest in other men. Our most dominant cultural myths shape the way we perceive the world and blind us to alternative ways of seeing and being. When something violates the expectations that such myths create, it may even be called unnatural, immoral, or perverse.

Cultural Myths as Obstacles to Critical Thinking

Cultural myths can have more subtle effects as well. In academic work they can reduce the complexity of our reading and thinking. A few years ago, for example, a professor at Los Angeles City College noted that he and his students couldn't agree in their interpretations of the following poem by Theodore Roethke:

My Papa's Waltz

The whiskey on your breath
Could make a small boy dizzy;
But I hung on like death:
Such waltzing was not easy.

We romped until the pans
Slid from the kitchen shelf;
My mother's countenance
Could not unfrown itself.

The hand that held my wrist
Was battered on one knuckle;
At every step you missed
My right ear scraped a buckle.

You beat time on my head
With a palm caked hard by dirt,
Then waltzed me off to bed
Still clinging to your shirt.

The instructor read this poem as a clear expression of a child's love for his blue-collar father, a rough-and-tumble man who had worked hard all his life ("a palm caked hard by dirt"), who was not above taking a drink of whiskey to ease his mind, but who also found the time to "waltz" his son off to bed. The students didn't see this at all. They saw the poem as a story about an abusive father and heavy drinker. They seemed unwilling to look beyond the father's roughness and the whiskey on his breath, equating these with drunken violence. Although the poem does suggest an element of fear mingled with the boy's excitement ("I hung on like death"), the class ignored its complexity — the mixture of fear, love, and boisterous fun that colors the son's memory of his father. It's possible that some students might overlook the positive traits in the father in this poem because they have suffered child abuse themselves. But this couldn't be true for all the students in the class. The difference between these interpretations lies, instead, in the influence of cultural myths. After all, in a culture now dominated by images of the family that emphasize "positive" parenting, middle-class values, and sensitive fathers, it's no wonder that students refused to see this father sympathetically. Our culture simply doesn't associate good, loving families with drinking or with even the suggestion of physical roughness.

Years of acculturation — the process of internalizing cultural values — leave us with a set of rigid categories for "good" and "bad" parents, narrow conceptions of how parents should look, talk, and behave toward their children. These cultural categories work like mental pigeonholes: they help us sort out and evaluate our experiences rapidly, almost before we're consciously aware of them. They give us a helpful shorthand for interpreting the world; after all, we can't stop to ponder every new situation we meet as if it were a puzzle or a philosophical problem. But while cultural categories help us make practical decisions in everyday life, they also impose their inherent rigidity on our thinking and thus limit our ability to understand the complexity of our experience. They reduce the world to dichotomies — simplified either/or choices: either women or men, either heterosexuals or homosexuals, either nature or culture, either animal or human, either "alien" or American, either them or us.

Rigid cultural beliefs can present serious obstacles to success for first-year college students. In a psychology class, for example, students' cultural myths may so color their thinking that they find it nearly impossible to comprehend Freud's ideas about infant sexuality. Ingrained assumptions about childhood innocence and sexual guilt may make it impossible for them to see children as sexual beings — a concept absolutely basic to an understanding of the history of psychoanalytic theory. Yet college-level critical inquiry thrives on exactly this kind of revision of common sense: academics prize the unusual, the subtle, the ambiguous, the complex — and expect students to appreciate them as well. Good critical thinkers in all academic disciplines welcome the opportunity to challenge conventional ways of seeing the world;

they seem to take delight in questioning everything that appears clear and self-evident.

Questioning: The Basis of Critical Thinking

By questioning the myths that dominate our culture, we can begin to resist the limits they impose on our vision. In fact, they invite such questioning. Often our personal experience fails to fit the images the myths project: a young woman's ambition to be a test pilot may clash with the ideal of femininity our culture promotes; a Cambodian immigrant who has suffered from racism in the United States may question our professed commitment to equality; a student in the vocational track may not see education as the road to success that we assume it is; and few of our families these days fit the mythic model of husband, wife, two kids, a dog, and a house in the suburbs.

Moreover, because cultural myths serve such large and varied needs, they're not always coherent or consistent. Powerful contradictory myths coexist in our society and our own minds. For example, while the myth of "the melting pot" celebrates equality, the myth of individual success pushes us to strive for inequality — to "get ahead" of everyone else. Likewise, our attitudes toward education are deeply paradoxical: on one level Americans tend to see schooling as a valuable experience that unites us in a common culture and helps us bring out the best in ourselves; yet at the same time we suspect that formal classroom instruction stifles creativity and chokes off natural intelligence and enthusiasm. These contradictions infuse our history, literature, and popular culture; they're so much a part of our thinking that we tend to take them for granted, unaware of their inconsistencies.

Learning to recognize contradictions lies at the very heart of critical thinking, for intellectual conflict inevitably generates questions. Can both (or all) perspectives be true? What evidence do I have for the validity of each? Is there some way to reconcile them? Are there still other alternatives? Questions like these represent the beginning of serious academic analysis. They stimulate the reflection, discussion, and research that are the essence of good scholarship. Thus, whether we find contradictions between myth and lived experience, or between opposing myths, the wealth of powerful, conflicting material generated by our cultural mythology offers a particularly rich context for critical inquiry.

The Structure of *Rereading America*

We've designed this book to help you develop the habits of mind you'll need to become a critical thinker — someone who recognizes the way that cultural myths shape thinking and can move beyond them to evaluate issues from multiple perspectives. Each of the book's seven chapters addresses one of the dominant myths of American culture. We begin with the myth that's literally closest to home — the myth of the model family. In "Harmony at Home" we look at the impact that the idea of the nuclear family has had on generations of Americans, including those who don't fit comfortably within its limitations. We also present some serious challenges to this time-honored definition of American family life. Next we turn to a topic that every student should have a lot to say about — the myth of educational empowerment. "Learning Power" gives you the chance to reflect on how the "hidden curriculum" of schooling has shaped your own attitudes toward learning. We begin our exploration of American cultural myths by focusing on home and education because most students find it easy to make personal connections with these topics and because they both involve institutions — families and schools — that are surrounded by a rich legacy of cultural stories and myths. These two introductory chapters are followed by consideration of what is perhaps the most famous of all American myths, the American Dream. Chapter Three, "Money and Success," addresses the idea of unlimited personal opportunity that brought millions of immigrants to our shores and set the story of America in motion. It invites you to weigh some of the human costs of the dream and to reconsider your own definition of a successful life.

The second portion of the book focuses on four cultural myths that offer greater intellectual and emotional challenges, in part because they are so intertwined with every American's personal identity and because they touch on highly charged social issues. "True Women and Real Men" considers the socially constructed categories of gender — the traditional roles that enforce differences between women and men. This chapter also explores the perspectives of Americans who defy conventional gender boundaries. The book's fifth chapter, "Created Equal," examines two myths that have powerfully shaped racial and ethnic relations in the United States: the myth of the melting pot, which celebrates cultural homogenization, and the myth of racial and ethnic superiority, which promotes separateness and inequality. This chapter probes the nature of prejudice, explores the ways that prejudicial attitudes are created, and examines ethnic identities within a race-divided society. Each of these two chapters questions how our culture divides and defines our world, how it artificially channels our experience into oppositions like black and white, male and female, straight and gay. The book's sixth chapter, "One Nation Under God," addresses one of the most compelling issues to emerge in contemporary U.S. culture — the place of religious belief in American society. Framed against the recent resurgence of faith in American public life, this new chapter explores some of the central myths surrounding the notion of America as a secular state, and questions whether deeply held religious beliefs are compatible with the values of an open, pluralistic society. The book concludes by addressing a subject that has assumed critical importance in the past few years — America's meaning in a changing world. The events of September 11, 2001, have forced us to reassess our relationships with other countries and to consider what we as a nation represent to people the world over. In "Land of Liberty" we examine how one of our most prized cultural ideals, the myth of freedom, has shaped our sense of national destiny and how our belief in our own "exceptionalism" as a nation has contributed to growing anti-Americanism in other lands. This final chapter also invites you to consider whether the ideal of individual liberty can survive in a world that is increasingly obsessed with security and dominated by powerful political and economic forces.

The Selections

Our identities — who we are and how we relate to others — are deeply entangled with the cultural values we have internalized since infancy. Cultural myths become so closely identified with our personal beliefs that rereading them actually means rereading ourselves, rethinking the way we see the world. Questioning long-held assumptions can be an exhilarating experience, but it can be distressing too. Thus, you may find certain selections in *Rereading America* difficult, controversial, or even downright offensive. They are meant to challenge you and to provoke classroom debate. But as you discuss the ideas you encounter in this book, remind yourself that your classmates may bring with them very different, and equally profound, beliefs. Keep an open mind, listen carefully, and treat other perspectives with the same respect you'd expect other people to show for your own. It's by encountering new ideas and engaging with others in open dialogue that we learn to grow.

Because *Rereading America* explores cultural myths that shape our thinking, it doesn't focus on the kind of well-defined public issues you might expect to find in a traditional composition anthology. You won't be reading arguments for and against affirmative action, bilingual education, or the death penalty here. Although we do include conservative as well as liberal — and even radical — perspectives, we've deliberately avoided the traditional pro-and-con approach because we want you to aim deeper than that; we want you to focus on the subtle cultural beliefs that underlie, and frequently determine, the debates that are waged on public issues. We've also steered clear of the "issues approach" because we feel it reinforces simplistic either/or thinking. Polarizing American culture into a series of debates doesn't encourage you to examine your own beliefs or explore how they've been shaped by the cultures you're part of. To begin to appreciate the influence of your own cultural myths, you need new perspectives: you need to stand outside the ideological machinery that makes American culture run to begin to appreciate its power. That's why we've included many strongly dissenting views: there are works by community activists, gay-rights activists, socialists, libertarians, and more. You may find that their views confirm your own experience of what it means to be an American, or you may find that you bitterly disagree with them. We only hope that you will use the materials here to gain some insight into the values and beliefs that shape our thinking and our national identity. This book is meant to complicate the mental categories that our cultural myths have established for us. Our intention is not to present a new "truth" to replace the old but to expand the range of ideas you bring to all your reading and writing in college. We believe that learning to see and value other perspectives will enable you to think more critically — to question, for yourself, the truth of any statement.

You may also note that several selections in *Rereading America* challenge the way you think writing is supposed to look or sound. You won't find many "classic" essays in this book, the finely crafted reflective essays on general topics that are often held up as models of "good writing." It's not that we reject this type of essay in principle. It's just that most writers who stand outside mainstream culture seem to have little use for it.

Our selections, instead, come from a wide variety of sources: professional books and journals from many disciplines, popular magazines, college textbooks, autobiographies, oral histories, and literary works. We've included this variety partly for the very practical reason that you're likely to encounter texts like these in your college coursework. But we also see textual diversity, like ethnic and political diversity, as a way to multiply perspectives and stimulate critical analysis. For example, an academic article like Jean Anyon's study of social class and school curriculum might give you a new way of understanding Mike Rose's personal narrative about his classroom experiences. On the other hand, you may find that some of the teachers Rose encounters don't neatly fit Anyon's theoretical model. Do such discrepancies mean that Anyon's argument is invalid? That her analysis needs to be modified to account for these teachers? That the teachers are simply exceptions to the rule? You'll probably want to consider your own classroom experience as you wrestle with such questions. Throughout the book, we've chosen readings that "talk to each other" in this way and that draw on the cultural knowledge you bring with you. These readings invite you to join the conversation; we hope they raise difficult questions, prompt lively discussion, and stimulate critical inquiry.

The Power of Dialogue

Good thinking, like good writing and good reading, is an intensely social activity. Thinking, reading, and writing are all forms of relationship — when you read, you enter into dialogue with an author about the subject at hand; when you write, you address an imaginary reader, testing your ideas against probable responses, reservations, and arguments. Thus, you can't become an accomplished writer simply by declaring your right to speak or by criticizing as an act of principle: real authority comes when you enter into the discipline of an active exchange of opinions and interpretations. Critical thinking, then, is always a matter of dialogue and debate — discovering relationships between apparently unrelated ideas, finding parallels between your own experiences and the ideas you read about, exploring points of agreement and conflict between yourself and other people.

We've designed the readings and questions in this text to encourage you to make just these kinds of connections. You'll notice, for example, that we often ask you to divide into small groups to discuss readings, and we frequently suggest that you take part in projects that require you to collaborate with your classmates. We're convinced that the only way you can learn critical reading, thinking, and writing is by actively engaging others in an intellectual exchange. So we've built into the text many opportunities for listening, discussion, and debate.

The questions that follow each selection should guide you in critical thinking. Like the readings, they're intended to get you started, not to set limits; we strongly recommend that you also devise your own questions and pursue them either individually or in study groups. We've divided our questions into three categories. Here's what to expect from each:

- Those labeled "Engaging the Text" focus on the individual selection they follow. They're designed to highlight important issues in the reading, to help you begin questioning and evaluating what you've read, and sometimes to remind you to consider the author's choices of language, evidence, structure, and style.

- The questions labeled "Exploring Connections" will lead you from the selection you've just finished to one or more other readings in this book. It's hard to make sparks fly from just one stone; if you think hard about these connecting questions, though, you'll see some real collisions of ideas and perspectives, not just polite and predictable "differences of opinion."

- The final questions for each reading, "Extending the Critical Context," invite you to extend your thinking beyond the book — to your family, your community, your college, the media, or the more traditional research environment of the library. The emphasis here is on creating new knowledge by applying ideas from this book to the world around you and by testing these ideas in your world.

Active Reading

You've undoubtedly read many textbooks, but it's unlikely that you've had to deal with the kind of analytic, argumentative, and scholarly writing you'll find in college and in *Rereading America*. These different writing styles require a different approach to reading as well. In high school you probably read to "take in" information, often for the sole purpose of reproducing it later on a test. In college you'll also be expected to recognize larger issues, such as the author's theoretical slant, her goals and methods, her assumptions, and her relationship to other writers and researchers. These expectations can be especially difficult in the first two years of college, when you take introductory courses that survey large, complex fields of knowledge. With all these demands on your attention, you'll need to read actively to keep your bearings. Think of active reading as a conversation between you and the text: instead of listening passively as the writer talks, respond to what she says with questions and comments of your own. Here are some specific techniques you can practice to become a more active reader.

Prereading and Prewriting

It's best with most college reading to "preread" the text. In prereading, you briefly look over whatever information you have on the author and the selection itself. Reading chapter introductions and headnotes like those provided in this book can save you time and effort by giving you information about the author's background and concerns, the subject or thesis of the selection, and its place in the chapter as a whole. Also take a look at the title and at any headings or subheadings in the piece. These will give you further clues about an article's general scope and organization. Next, quickly skim the entire selection, paying a bit more attention to the first few paragraphs and the conclusion. Now you should have a pretty good sense of the author's position — what she's trying to say in this piece of writing.

At this point you may do one of several things before you settle down to in-depth reading. You may want to jot down in a few lines what you think the author is doing. Or you may want to make a list of questions you can ask about this topic based on your prereading. Or you may want to freewrite a page or so on the subject. Informally writing out your own ideas will prepare you for more in-depth reading by recalling what you already know about the topic.

We emphasize writing about what you've read because reading and writing are complementary activities: being an avid reader will help you as a writer by familiarizing you with a wide range of ideas and styles to draw on; likewise, writing about what you've read will give you a deeper understanding of your reading. In fact, the more actively you "process" or reshape what you've read, the better you'll comprehend and remember it. So you'll learn more effectively by marking a text as you read than by simply reading; taking notes as you read is even more effective than marking, and writing about the material for your own purposes (putting it in your own words and connecting it with what you already know) is better still.

Marking the Text and Taking Notes

After prereading and prewriting, you're ready to begin critical reading in earnest. As you read, be sure to highlight ideas and phrases that strike you as especially significant — those that seem to capture the gist of a particular paragraph or section, or those that relate directly to the author's purpose or argument. While prereading can help you identify central ideas, you may find that you need to reread difficult sections or flip back and skim an earlier passage if you feel yourself getting lost. Many students think of themselves as poor readers if they can't whip through an article at high speed without pausing. However, the best readers read recursively — that is, they shuttle back and forth, browsing, skimming, and rereading as necessary, depending on their interest, their familiarity with the subject, and the difficulty of the material. This shuttling actually parallels what goes on in your mind when you read actively, as you alternately recall prior knowledge or experience and predict or look for clues about where the writer is going next.

Keep a record of your mental shuttling by writing comments in the margins as you read. It's often useful to gloss the contents of each paragraph or section, to summarize it in a word or two written alongside the text. This note will serve as a reminder or key to the section when you return to it for further thinking, discussion, or writing. You may also want to note passages that puzzled you. Or you may want to write down personal reactions or questions stimulated by the reading. Take time to ponder why you felt confused or annoyed or affirmed by a particular passage. Let yourself wonder "out loud" in the margins as you read.

The following section illustrates one student's notes on a few stanzas of Inés Hernández-Ávila's "Para Teresa" (p. 206). In this example, you can see that the reader puts glosses or summary comments to the left of the poem and questions or personal responses to the right. You should experiment and create your own system of note taking, one that works best for the way you read. Just remember that your main goals in taking notes are to help you understand the author's overall position, to deepen and refine your responses to the selection, and to create a permanent record of those responses.

Para Teresa[1]

INÉS HERNÁNDEZ-ÁVILA

This poem explores and attempts to resolve an old conflict between its speaker and her schoolmate, two Chicanas at "Alamo which-had-to-be-its-name" Elementary School who have radically different ideas about what education means and does. Inés Hernández-Ávila (b. 1947) is an associate professor of Native American Studies at the University of California, Davis. This poem appeared in her collection Con Razón, Corazón *(1987).*

---

[1]*Para Teresa:* For Teresa. [All notes are the author's.]

Writes to Teresa

A tí-Teresa — *Why in Spanish?*
Te dedico las palabras estás
que (explotan) de mi corazón[2] — *Why do her words explode?*

The day of their confrontation

That day during lunch hour
at <u>Alamo which-had-to-be-its-name</u> *!Why?*
Elementary
my <u>dear raza</u> — *Feels close to T. (?)*
That day in the bathroom
Door guarded
Myself cornered
I was accused by you, Teresa
Tú y las demás de tus amigas
Pachucas todas
Eran Uds. cinco.[3]

T.'s accusation

Me gritaban que porque me creía tan grande[4]
<u>What was I trying to do, you growled</u>
<u>Show you up?</u>
Make the teachers like me, pet me, — *Teachers must be white / Anglo.*
Tell me what <u>a credit (to my people)</u> I was?
<u>I was playing right into their hands,</u> you challenged
And you would have none of it.
I was to stop.

Speaker is a "good student."

Keeping a Reading Journal

You may also want (or be required) to keep a reading journal in response to the selections you cover in *Rereading America*. In such a journal you'd keep all the freewriting that you do either before or after reading. Some students find it helpful to keep a double-entry journal, writing initial responses on the left side of the page and adding later reflections and reconsiderations on the right. You may want to use your journal as a place to explore personal reactions to your reading. You can do this by writing out imaginary dialogues — between two writers who address the same subject, between yourself and the writer of the selection, or between two parts of yourself. You can use the journal as a place to rewrite passages from a poem or essay in your own voice and from your own point of view. You can write letters to an author you particularly like or dislike or to a character in a story or poem. You might even draw a cartoon that comments on one of the reading selections.

Many students don't write as well as they could because they're afraid to take risks. They may have been repeatedly penalized for breaking "rules" of

---

[2]*A . . . corazón:* To you, Teresa, I dedicate these words that explode from my heart.
[3]*Tú . . . cinco:* You and the rest of your friends, all Pachucas, there were five of you.
[4]*Me . . . grande:* You were screaming at me, asking me why I thought I was so hot.

grammar or essay form; their main concern in writing becomes avoiding trouble rather than exploring ideas or experimenting with style. But without risk and experimentation, there's little possibility of growth. One of the benefits of journal writing is that it gives you a place to experiment with ideas, free from worries about "correctness." Here are two examples of student journal entries, in response to "Para Teresa" (we reprint the entries as they were written):

Entry 1: Internal Dialogue

Me 1: I agree with Inés Hernández-Ávila's speaker. Her actions were justifiable in a way that if you can't fight 'em, join 'em. After all, Teresa is just making the situation worse for her because not only is she sabotaging the teacher-student relationship, she's also destroying her chance for a good education.

Me 2: Hey, Teresa's action was justifiable. Why else would the speaker admit at the end of the poem that what Teresa did was fine thus she respects Teresa more?

Me 1: The reason the speaker respected Teresa was because she (Teresa) was still keeping her culture alive, although through different means. It wasn't her action that the speaker respected, it was the representation of it.

Me 2: The reason I think Teresa acted the way she did was because she felt she had something to prove to society. She wanted to show that no one could push her people around; that her people were tough.

Entry 2: Personal Response

"Con cố gắng học giỏi, cho Bá Má,
Rồi sau nây dời sống cua con sẽ thõai mái lắm."[5]
What if I don't want to?
What if I can't?
Sometimes I feel my parents don't understand what
I'm going through.
To them, education is money.
And money is success.
They don't see beyond that.
Sometimes I want to fail my classes purposely to
See their reaction, but that is too cruel.
They have taught me to value education.
Education makes you a person, makes you somebody, they say.
I agree.
They are proud I am going to UCLA.
They brag to their friends, our Vietnamese community, people
I don't even know.

. . .

They believe in me, but I doubt myself. . . .

[5]"Con . . . lám": "Daughter, study hard (for us, your Mom and Dad), so your future will be bright and easy."

You'll notice that neither of these students talks directly about "Para Teresa" as a poem. Instead, each uses it as a point of departure for her own reflections on ethnicity, identity, and education. Although we've included a number of literary works in *Rereading America,* we don't expect you to do literary analysis. We want you to use these pieces to stimulate your own thinking about the cultural myths they address. So don't feel you have to discuss imagery in Inés Hernández-Ávila's "Para Teresa" or characterization in Toni Cade Bambara's "The Lesson" in order to understand and appreciate them.

Working with Visual Images

The myths we examine in *Rereading America* make their presence felt not only in the world of print — essays, stories, poems, memoirs — but in every aspect of our culture. Consider, for example, the myth of "the American family." If you want to design a minivan, a restaurant, a cineplex, a park, a synagogue, a personal computer, or a tax code, you had better have some idea of what families are like and how they behave. Most important, you need a good grasp of what Americans *believe* about families, about the mythology of the American family. The Visual Portfolio in each chapter, while it maintains our focus on myths, also carries you beyond the medium of print and thus lets you practice your analytical skills in a different arena.

Although we are all surrounded by visual stimuli, we don't always think critically about what we see. Perhaps we are numbed by constant exposure to a barrage of images on TV, in magazines and newspapers, in video games and films. In any case, here are a few tips on how to get the most out of the images we have collected for this book. Take the time to look at the images carefully; first impressions are important, but many of the photographs contain details that might not strike you immediately. Once you have noted the immediate impact of an image, try focusing on separate elements such as background, foreground, facial expressions, and body language. Read any text that appears in the photograph, even if it's on a T-shirt or a belt buckle. Remember that many photographs are carefully *constructed,* no matter how "natural" they may look. In a photo for a magazine advertisement, for example, everything is meticulously chosen and arranged: certain actors or models are cast for their roles; they wear makeup; their clothes are really costumes; the location or setting of the ad is designed to reinforce its message; lighting is artificial; and someone is trying to sell you something.

Also be sure to consider the visual images contextually, not in isolation. How does each resemble or differ from its neighbors in the portfolio? How does it reinforce or challenge cultural beliefs or stereotypes? Put another way, how can it be understood in the context of the myths examined in *Rereading America*? Each portfolio is accompanied by a few questions to help you begin this type of analysis. You can also build a broader context for our visual images by collecting your own, then working in small groups to create a portfolio or collage.

Finally, remember that both readings and visual images are just starting points for discussion. You have access to a wealth of other perspectives and ideas among your family, friends, classmates; in your college library; in your personal experience; and in your imagination. We urge you to consult them all as you grapple with the perspectives you encounter in this text.

1

Harmony at Home

The Myth of the Model Family

The Donna Reed Show.

FAST FACTS

1. A large majority of Americans live in households with at least one other member of their family. Of these "household families," 76% are headed by a married couple, 18% are headed by a woman with no husband present, and 6% are headed by a man with no wife present.

2. Data on same-sex couples are inexact, but the 2000 Census estimated that there were approximately 594,000 households headed by same-sex partners. Roughly 33% of lesbian households and 22% of male couples had children under 18 years of age in the home. One state, Massachusetts, recognizes same-sex marriages.

3. Experts estimate that 40% to 50% of existing marriages will end in divorce.

4. The number of childless households has increased dramatically since 1970, from 55% to 68% of all households.

5. More than 400,000 children are born in the United States each year to women younger than 20 years old; nearly 1.5 million children are born annually to unmarried women.

Source: U.S. Census Bureau, *Census 2000.*

WHAT WOULD AN AMERICAN POLITICAL CAMPAIGN be without wholesome photographs of the candidates kissing babies and posing with their loving families? Politicians understand the cultural power of these symbols; they appreciate the family as one of our most sacred American institutions. The vision of the ideal nuclear family — Dad, Mom, a couple of kids, maybe a dog, and a spacious suburban home — is a cliché but also a potent myth, a dream that millions of Americans work to fulfill. The image is so compelling that it's easy to forget what a short time it's been around, especially compared with the long history of the family itself.

In fact, what we call the "traditional" family, headed by a breadwinner-father and a housewife-mother, has existed for little more than two hundred years, and the suburbs only came into being in the 1950s. But the family as a social institution was legally recognized in Western culture at least as far back as the Code of Hammurabi, created in ancient Mesopotamia some four thousand years ago. To appreciate how profoundly concepts of family life have changed, consider the absolute power of the Mesopotamian father, the patriarch: the law allowed him to use any of his dependents, including his wife, as collateral for loans or even to sell family members outright to pay his debts.

Although patriarchal authority was less absolute in Puritan America, fathers remained the undisputed heads of families. Seventeenth-century Connecticut, Massachusetts, and New Hampshire enacted laws condemning rebellious children to severe punishment and, in extreme cases, to death. In the early years of the American colonies, as in Western culture stretching back to Hammurabi's time, unquestioned authority within the family served as both the model for and the basis of state authority. Just as family members owed complete obedience to the father, so all citizens owed unquestioned loyalty to the king and his legal representatives. In his influential volume *Democracy in America* (1835), French aristocrat Alexis de Tocqueville describes the relationship between the traditional European family and the old political order:

> Among aristocratic nations, social institutions recognize, in truth, no one in the family but the father; children are received by society at his hands; society governs him, he governs them. Thus, the parent not only has a natural right, but acquires a political right to command them; he is the author and the support of his family; but he is also its constituted ruler.

By the mid-eighteenth century, however, new ideas about individual freedom and democracy were stirring the colonies. And by the time Tocqueville visited the United States in 1831, they had evidently worked a revolution in the family as well as in the nation's political structure: he observes, "When the condition of society becomes democratic, and men adopt as their general principle that it is good and lawful to judge of all things for one's self, . . . the power which the opinions of a father exercise over those of his sons diminishes, as well as his legal power." To Tocqueville, this shift away from strict patriarchal rule signaled a change in the emotional climate of families: "as manners and laws become more democratic, the relation of father and son becomes more intimate and more affectionate; rules and authority are less talked of, confidence and tenderness are oftentimes increased, and it would seem that the natural bond is drawn closer." In his view, the American family heralded a new era in human relations. Freed from the rigid hierarchy of the past, parents and children could meet as near equals, joined by "filial love and fraternal affection."

This vision of the democratic family — a harmonious association of parents and children united by love and trust — has mesmerized popular culture in the United States. From the nineteenth century to the present, popular novels, magazines, music, and advertising images have glorified the comforts of loving domesticity. In recent years, we've probably absorbed our strongest impressions of the ideal family from television situation comedies. In the 1950s we had the Andersons on *Father Knows Best,* the Stones on *The Donna Reed Show,* and the real-life Nelson family on *The Adventures of Ozzie & Harriet.* Over the next three decades, the model stretched to include single parents, second marriages, and interracial adoptions on *My Three Sons, The Brady Bunch,* and *Diff'rent Strokes,* but the underlying ideal of wise, loving parents and harmonious, happy families remained unchanged. But today, America has begun to worry about the health of its families: even the families on TV no longer reflect the domestic tranquility of the Anderson clan. America is becoming increasingly ambivalent about the future of family life, and perhaps with good reason. The myth of the family scarcely reflects the complexities of modern American life. High divorce rates, the rise of the single-parent household, the national debate about same-sex marriage, and a growing frankness about domestic violence are transforming the way we see family life.

This chapter examines the myth of the model family and explores alternative visions of family life. It opens with three paintings by Norman Rockwell that express the meaning of "family values" circa 1950, an era some consider the heyday of American family life. The subsequent readings immediately challenge the ideal of the harmonious nuclear family. In "Looking for Work," Gary Soto recalls his boyhood desire to live the myth and recounts his humorous attempts to transform his working-class Chicano family into a facsimile of the Cleavers on *Leave It to Beaver*. Stephanie Coontz then takes a close analytical look at the 1950s family, explaining its lasting appeal to some Americans but also documenting its dark side.

The next selections blend narrative, analytical, and visual approaches to understanding the meanings of family. "Aunt Ida Pieces a Quilt," a short poem by Melvin Dixon, tells the story of an extended African American family helping one another cope with the loss of Ida's nephew to AIDS. In "An Indian Story," Roger Jack paints a warm, magical portrait of the bond between a Native American boy and his caretaker aunt. The reading by Judy Root Aulette moves us from individual experience to broad sociological patterns, as she meticulously examines how the dynamics of race, class, and gender — key issues throughout *Rereading America* — play out within the American family. Extending themes introduced by Aulette, the chapter's Visual Portfolio offers you a chance to practice your hand at interpreting images; the photographs in this collection suggest some of the complex ways the contemporary American family intersects with gender, ethnicity, and social status.

The chapter concludes with two readings from the national debate on same-sex marriage. In "It Takes a Family," former Republican senator Rick Santorum argues that the best structure for raising children is the traditional mom-and-pop nuclear family. The chapter ends with Evan Wolfson's "What Is Marriage?" — a powerful argument that gay and lesbian Americans deserve the same rights to civil marriages that all other citizens (including felons) enjoy.

Sources

Gerda Lerner, *The Creation of Patriarchy.* New York: Oxford University Press, 1986.

Steven Mintz and Susan Kellogg, *Domestic Revolutions: A Social History of American Family Life.* New York: Free Press, 1988.

Alexis de Tocqueville, *Democracy in America*. 1835; New York: Vintage Books, 1990.

BEFORE READING

- Spend ten minutes or so jotting down every word, phrase, or image you associate with the idea of "family." Write as freely as possible, without censoring your thoughts or worrying about grammatical correctness. Working in small groups, compare lists and try to categorize your responses. What assumptions about families do they reveal?

- Draw a visual representation of your family. This could take the form of a graph, chart, diagram, map, cartoon, symbolic picture, or literal portrait. Don't worry if you're not a skillful artist: the main point is to convey an idea, and even stick figures can speak eloquently. When you're finished, write a journal entry about your drawing. Was it easier to depict some feelings or ideas visually than it would have been to describe them in words? Did you find some things about your family difficult or impossible to convey visually? Does your drawing "say" anything that surprises you?

- Do a brief freewrite about the television family — from *The Donna Reed Show* — pictured on the title page of this chapter (p. 17). What can you tell about their relationship? What does this image suggest to you about the ideals and realities of American family life?

A *Family Tree, Freedom from Want,* and *Freedom from Fear*

NORMAN ROCKWELL

The first "reading" for this book consists of three paintings by Norman Rockwell (1894–1978), one of America's most prolific and popular artists. Together they capture what the idea of family meant to the nation half a century ago, a time some consider the golden age of American family life. A Family Tree (1959) is an oil painting that, like hundreds of Rockwell's images, became cover art for the Saturday Evening Post. Freedom from Want *and* Freedom from Fear *are part of Rockwell's* Four Freedoms *series (1943). Their appearance in the* Saturday Evening Post, *along with* Freedom of Speech *and* Freedom of Worship, *generated millions of requests for reprints.*

A Family Tree, by Norman Rockwell.

Freedom from Want, by Norman Rockwell.

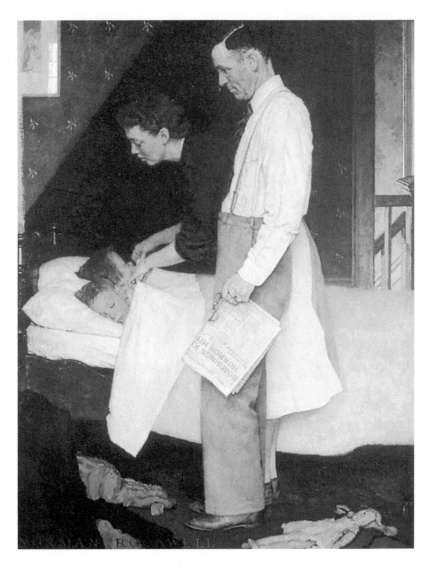

Freedom from Fear, by Norman Rockwell.

ENGAGING THE TEXT

1. What is the usual purpose of family trees? Why do you think they are important to many Americans? How significant is a family tree to you or others in your family?

2. Discuss the details of *A Family Tree* and their significance. For example, identify each figure and explain what it contributes to Rockwell's composite picture of America.

3. How does Rockwell's painting differ from a typical family tree? What are its basic messages about American families and marriages? What does it "say" about U.S. history, race relations, and occupations?

4. What is the appeal of *Freedom from Want*? What ideas about family does it assume or promote? What is your own reaction to Rockwell's image? Support your answers with reference to details of the painting.

5. Rockwell's Four Freedoms paintings allude to Franklin D. Roosevelt's 1941 State of the Union address, which described "four essential human freedoms." Roosevelt defined freedom from want as "economic understandings which will secure to every nation a healthy peacetime life for its inhabitants — everywhere in the world." To what extent does Rockwell's *Freedom from Want* reflect FDR's definition, and what meanings does it add or alter?

6. In *Freedom from Fear,* why did Rockwell choose this moment to paint? What can you guess about the relationships within the family? What about its relationship to the rest of the world?

7. In his speech before Congress, Roosevelt said that freedom from fear, "translated into world terms, means a worldwide reduction of armaments to such a point and in such a thorough fashion that no nation will be in a position to commit an act of physical aggression against any neighbor — anywhere in the world." Compare FDR's ideas to those expressed in Rockwell's *Freedom from Fear.* To what extent can the differences be explained by the shift from Roosevelt's preparing the nation for war in early 1941 to our full engagement in World War II when Rockwell's paintings appeared?

EXPLORING CONNECTIONS

8. Compare Rockwell's paintings to the frontispiece photo for this chapter (p. 17). How does Rockwell's vision of family life differ from that depicted by the photo?

EXTENDING THE CRITICAL CONTEXT

9. Research your family tree and make your own drawing of it. How does it compare to the family tree Rockwell has created? Write a journal entry or short essay about your family tree.

10. Discuss how well the idea of a tree can represent what you know about families. Are there ways in which the tree image or metaphor might be misleading or inaccurate? What other analogies or metaphors can you

suggest for depicting family histories? Draw either an updated version of Rockwell's family tree or an image based on a fresh metaphor or analogy.

11. What might pictures entitled *Freedom from Want* and *Freedom from Fear* look like if they were painted today? Describe in detail a scene or image to fit each of these titles; if possible, draw, paint, or photograph your image.

12. Millions of Americans "consumed" the images Rockwell produced for the *Saturday Evening Post*. What images are we consuming today? What ideas about family and marriage appear in today's mass culture — advertisements, song lyrics, cereal boxes, sitcoms, reality shows, talk radio, junk mail, and similar cultural products?

Looking for Work

GARY SOTO

"Looking for Work" is the narrative of a nine-year-old Mexican American boy who wants his family to imitate the "perfect families" he sees on TV. Much of the humor in this essay comes from the author's perspective as an adult looking back at his childhood self, but Soto also respects the child's point of view. In the marvelous details of this midsummer day, Soto captures the interplay of seductive myth and complex reality. Gary Soto (b. 1952) grew up "on the industrial side of Fresno, right smack against a junkyard and the junkyard's cross-eyed German shepherd." Having discovered poetry almost by chance in a city college library, he has now published several volumes of his own; his New and Selected Poems (1995) was a finalist for both the Los Angeles Times Book Award and the National Book Award. He has also published novels, short stories, memoirs, books for children and young adults, and the libretto for an opera titled Nerdlandia.

One July, while killing ants on the kitchen sink with a rolled newspaper, I had a nine-year-old's vision of wealth that would save us from ourselves. For weeks I had drunk Kool-Aid and watched morning reruns of *Father Knows Best*, whose family was so uncomplicated in its routine that I very much wanted to imitate it. The first step was to get my brother and sister to wear shoes at dinner.

"Come on, Rick — come on, Deb," I whined. But Rick mimicked me and the same day that I asked him to wear shoes he came to the dinner table in only his swim trunks. My mother didn't notice, nor did my sister, as we sat to eat our beans and tortillas in the stifling heat of our kitchen. We all gleamed like cellophane, wiping the sweat from our brows with the backs of our hands as we talked about the day: Frankie our neighbor was beat up by Faustino; the swimming pool at the playground would be closed for a day because the pump was broken.

Such was our life. So that morning, while doing-in the train of ants which arrived each day, I decided to become wealthy, and right away! After downing a bowl of cereal, I took a rake from the garage and started up the block to look for work.

We lived on an ordinary block of mostly working class people: warehousemen, egg candlers,[1] welders, mechanics, and a union plumber. And there were many retired people who kept their lawns green and the gutters uncluttered of the chewing gum wrappers we dropped as we rode by on our bikes. They bent down to gather our litter, muttering at our evilness.

At the corner house I rapped the screen door and a very large woman in a muu-muu answered. She sized me up and then asked what I could do.   5

"Rake leaves," I answered smiling.

"It's summer, and there ain't no leaves," she countered. Her face was pinched with lines; fat jiggled under her chin. She pointed to the lawn, then the flower bed, and said: "You see any leaves there — or there?" I followed her pointing arm, stupidly. But she had a job for me and that was to get her a Coke at the liquor store. She gave me twenty cents, and after ditching my rake in a bush, off I ran. I returned with an unbagged Pepsi, for which she thanked me and gave me a nickel from her apron.

I skipped off her porch, fetched my rake, and crossed the street to the next block where Mrs. Moore, mother of Earl the retarded man, let me weed a flower bed. She handed me a trowel and for a good part of the morning my fingers dipped into the moist dirt, ripping up runners of Bermuda grass. Worms surfaced in my search for deep roots, and I cut them in halves, tossing them to Mrs. Moore's cat who pawed them playfully as they dried in the sun. I made out Earl whose face was pressed to the back window of the house, and although he was calling to me I couldn't understand what he was trying to say. Embarrassed, I worked without looking up, but I imagined his contorted mouth and the ring of keys attached to his belt — keys that jingled with each palsied step. He scared me and I worked quickly to finish the flower bed. When I did finish Mrs. Moore gave me a quarter and two peaches from her tree, which I washed there but ate in the alley behind my house.

I was sucking on the second one, a bit of juice staining the front of my T-shirt, when Little John, my best friend, came walking down the alley with a baseball bat over his shoulder, knocking over trash cans as he made his way toward me.

Little John and I went to St. John's Catholic School, where we sat   10 among the "stupids." Miss Marino, our teacher, alternated the rows of good

[1]*egg candler:* One who inspects eggs by holding them up to a light.

students with the bad, hoping that by sitting side-by-side with the bright students the stupids might become more intelligent, as though intelligence were contagious. But we didn't progress as she had hoped. She grew frustrated when one day, while dismissing class for recess, Little John couldn't get up because his arms were stuck in the slats of the chair's backrest. She scolded us with a shaking finger when we knocked over the globe, denting the already troubled Africa. She muttered curses when Leroy White, a real stupid but a great softball player with the gift to hit to all fields, openly chewed his host[2] when he made his First Communion; his hands swung at his sides as he returned to the pew looking around with a big smile.

Little John asked what I was doing, and I told him that I was taking a break from work, as I sat comfortably among high weeds. He wanted to join me, but I reminded him that the last time he'd gone door-to-door asking for work his mother had whipped him. I was with him when his mother, a New Jersey Italian who could rise up in anger one moment and love the next, told me in a polite but matter-of-fact voice that I had to leave because she was going to beat her son. She gave me a homemade popsicle, ushered me to the door, and said that I could see Little John the next day. But it was sooner than that. I went around to his bedroom window to suck my popsicle and watch Little John dodge his mother's blows, a few hitting their mark but many whirring air.

It was midday when Little John and I converged in the alley, the sun blazing in the high nineties, and he suggested that we go to Roosevelt High School to swim. He needed five cents to make fifteen, the cost of admission, and I lent him a nickel. We ran home for my bike and when my sister found out that we were going swimming, she started to cry because she didn't have the fifteen cents but only an empty Coke bottle. I waved for her to come and three of us mounted the bike — Debra on the cross bar, Little John on the handle bars and holding the Coke bottle which we would cash for a nickel and make up the difference that would allow all of us to get in, and me pumping up the crooked streets, dodging cars and pot holes. We spent the day swimming under the afternoon sun, so that when we got home our mom asked us what was darker, the floor or us? She feigned a stern posture, her hands on her hips and her mouth puckered. We played along. Looking down, Debbie and I said in unison, "Us."

That evening at dinner we all sat down in our bathing suits to eat our beans, laughing and chewing loudly. Our mom was in a good mood, so I took a risk and asked her if sometime we could have turtle soup. A few days before I had watched a television program in which a Polynesian tribe killed a large turtle, gutted it, and then stewed it over an open fire. The turtle, basted in a sugary sauce, looked delicious as I ate an afternoon bowl of cereal, but my sister, who was watching the program with a glass of Kool-Aid between her knees, said, "Caca."

---

[2]*his host:* The wafer that embodies, in the Catholic sacrament of Communion, the bread of the Last Supper and the body of Christ.

My mother looked at me in bewilderment. "Boy, are you a crazy Mexican. Where did you get the idea that people eat turtles?"

"On television," I said, explaining the program. Then I took it a step 15
further. "Mom, do you think we could get dressed up for dinner one of these days? David King does."

"*Ay, Dios,*" my mother laughed. She started collecting the dinner plates, but my brother wouldn't let go of his. He was still drawing a picture in the bean sauce. Giggling, he said it was me, but I didn't want to listen because I wanted an answer from Mom. This was the summer when I spent the mornings in front of the television that showed the comfortable lives of white kids. There were no beatings, no rifts in the family. They wore bright clothes; toys tumbled from their closets. They hopped into bed with kisses and woke to glasses of fresh orange juice, and to a father sitting before his morning coffee while the mother buttered his toast. They hurried through the day making friends and gobs of money, returning home to a warmly lit living room, and then dinner. *Leave It to Beaver* was the program I replayed in my mind:

"May I have the mashed potatoes?" asks Beaver with a smile.

"Sure, Beav," replies Wally as he taps the corners of his mouth with a starched napkin.

The father looks on in his suit. The mother, decked out in earrings and a pearl necklace, cuts into her steak and blushes. Their conversation is politely clipped.

"Swell," says Beaver, his cheeks puffed with food. 20

Our own talk at dinner was loud with belly laughs and marked by our pointing forks at one another. The subjects were commonplace.

"Gary, let's go to the ditch tomorrow," my brother suggests. He explains that he has made a life preserver out of four empty detergent bottles strung together with twine and that he will make me one if I can find more bottles. "No way are we going to drown."

"Yeah, then we could have a dirt clod fight," I reply, so happy to be alive.

Whereas the Beaver's family enjoyed dessert in dishes at the table, our mom sent us outside, and more often than not I went into the alley to peek over the neighbor's fences and spy out fruit, apricots or peaches.

I had asked my mom and again she laughed that I was a crazy *chavalo*[3] 25
as she stood in front of the sink, her arms rising and falling with suds, face glistening from the heat. She sent me outside where my brother and sister were sitting in the shade that the fence threw out like a blanket. They were talking about me when I plopped down next to them. They looked at one another and then Debbie, my eight-year-old sister, started in.

"What's this crap about getting dressed up?"

She had entered her *profanity* stage. A year later she would give up such words and slip into her Catholic uniform, and into squealing on my brother and me when we "cussed this" and "cussed that."

---

[3]*chavalo:* Kid.

I tried to convince them that if we improved the way we looked we might get along better in life. White people would like us more. They might invite us to places, like their homes or front yards. They might not hate us so much.

My sister called me a "craphead," and got up to leave with a stalk of grass dangling from her mouth. "They'll never like us."

My brother's mood lightened as he talked about the ditch — the white   30
water, the broken pieces of glass, and the rusted car fenders that awaited our knees. There would be toads, and rocks to smash them.

David King, the only person we knew who resembled the middle class, called from over the fence. David was Catholic, of Armenian and French descent, and his closet was filled with toys. A bear-shaped cookie jar, like the ones on television, sat on the kitchen counter. His mother was remarkably kind while she put up with the racket we made on the street. Evenings, she often watered the front yard and it must have upset her to see us — my brother and I and others — jump from trees laughing, the unkillable kids of the very poor, who got up unshaken, brushed off, and climbed into another one to try again.

David called again. Rick got up and slapped grass from his pants. When I asked if I could come along he said no. David said no. They were two years older so their affairs were different from mine. They greeted one another with foul names and took off down the alley to look for trouble.

I went inside the house, turned on the television, and was about to sit down with a glass of Kool-Aid when Mom shooed me outside.

"It's still light," she said. "Later you'll bug me to let you stay out longer. So go on."

I downed my Kool-Aid and went outside to the front yard. No one was   35
around. The day had cooled and a breeze rustled the trees. Mr. Jackson, the plumber, was watering his lawn and when he saw me he turned away to wash off his front steps. There was more than an hour of light left, so I took advantage of it and decided to look for work. I felt suddenly alive as I skipped down the block in search of an overgrown flower bed and the dime that would end the day right.

ENGAGING THE TEXT

1. Why is the narrator attracted to the kind of family life depicted on TV? What, if anything, does he think is wrong with his life? Why do his desires apparently have so little impact on his family?

2. Why does the narrator first go looking for work? How has the meaning of work changed by the end of the story, when he goes out again "in search of an overgrown flower bed and the dime that would end the day right"? Explain.

3. As Soto looks back on his nine-year-old self, he has a different perspective on things than he had as a child. How would you characterize the mature Soto's thoughts about his childhood family life? (Was it "a good family"?

What was wrong with Soto's thinking as a nine-year-old?) Back up your remarks with specific references to the narrative.

4. Review the story to find each mention of food or drink. Explain the role these references play.

5. Review the cast of "supporting characters" in this narrative — the mother, sister, brother, friends, and neighbors. What does each contribute to the story and in particular to the meaning of family within the story?

EXPLORING CONNECTIONS

6. Read Roger Jack's "An Indian Story" (p. 51) and compare Soto's family to the one Roger Jack describes. In particular, consider gender roles, the household atmosphere, and the expectations placed on children and parents.

7. Compare and contrast the relationship of school and family in this narrative to that described by Mike Rose (p. 161), Richard Rodriguez (p. 193), or Inés Hernández-Ávila (p. 206).

8. Like Soto's story, the cartoon on page 35 attests to the power of the media to shape our ideas about family. Write a journal entry describing the media family that most accurately reflects your image of family life. Discuss these entries, and the impact of media on your image of the family, with your classmates.

EXTENDING THE CRITICAL CONTEXT

9. Write a journal entry about a time when you wished your family were somehow different. What caused your dissatisfaction? What did you want your family to be like? Was your dissatisfaction ever resolved?

10. "Looking for Work" is essentially the story of a single day. Write a narrative of one day when you were eight or nine or ten; use details as Soto does to give the events of the day broader significance.

What We Really Miss About the 1950s

STEPHANIE COONTZ

Popular myth has it that the 1950s were the ideal decade for the American family. In this example of academic writing at its best, Stephanie Coontz provides a clear, well-documented, and insightful analysis of what was really going on and suggests that our nostalgia for the 1950s could mislead us today. Stephanie Coontz teaches history and family studies at the Evergreen State College in Olympia, Washington. An award-winning writer and nationally recognized expert on the family, she has published her work in books, popular magazines, and academic journals; she has also testified before a House Select Committee on families and appeared in several television documentaries. Her most recent book, honored as one of the best books of 2005 by the Washington Post, *is entitled* Marriage, A History: From Obedience to Intimacy, or How Love Conquered Marriage. *"What We Really Miss About the 1950s" is excerpted from an earlier work,* The Way We Really Are: Coming to Terms with America's Changing Families *(1997).*

In a 1996 poll by the Knight-Ridder news agency, more Americans chose the 1950s than any other single decade as the best time for children to grow up.[1] And despite the research I've done on the underside of 1950s families, I don't think it's crazy for people to feel nostalgic about the period. For one thing, it's easy to see why people might look back fondly to a decade when real wages grew more in any single year than in the entire ten years of the 1980s combined, a time when the average 30-year-old man could buy a median-priced home on only 15–18 percent of his salary.[2]

But it's more than just a financial issue. When I talk with modern parents, even ones who grew up in unhappy families, they associate the 1950s with a yearning they feel for a time when there were fewer complicated choices for kids or parents to grapple with, when there was more predictability in how people formed and maintained families, and when there was a coherent "moral order" in their community to serve as a reference point for family norms. Even people who found that moral order grossly unfair or repressive often say that its presence provided them with something concrete to push against.

I can sympathize entirely. One of my most empowering moments occurred the summer I turned 12, when my mother marched down to the library with me to confront a librarian who'd curtly refused to let me check out a book that was "not appropriate" for my age. "Don't you *ever* tell my daughter what she can and can't read," fumed my mom. "She's a mature young lady and she can make her own choices." In recent years I've often thought back to the gratitude I felt toward my mother for that act of trust in

[1]Steven Thomma, "Nostalgia for '50s Surfaces," *Philadelphia Inquirer*, Feb. 4, 1996. [All notes are the author's.]

[2]Frank Levy, *Dollars and Dreams: The Changing American Income Distribution* (New York: Russell Sage, 1987), p. 6; Frank Levy, "Incomes and Income Inequality," in Reynolds Farley, ed., *State of the Union: America in the 1990s*, vol. 1 (New York: Russell Sage, 1995), pp. 1–57; Richard May and Kathryn Porter, "Poverty and Income Trends, 1994," Washington, D.C.: Center on Budget and Policy Priorities, March 1996; Rob Nelson and Jon Cowan, "Buster Power," *USA Weekend*, October 14–16, 1994, p. 10.

me. I wish I had some way of earning similar points from my own son. But much as I've always respected his values, I certainly wouldn't have walked into my local video store when he was 12 and demanded that he be allowed to check out absolutely anything he wanted!

Still, I have no illusions that I'd actually like to go back to the 1950s, and neither do most people who express such occasional nostalgia. For example, although the 1950s got more votes than any other decade in the Knight-Ridder poll, it did not win an outright majority: 38 percent of respondents picked the 1950s; 27 percent picked the 1960s or the 1970s. Voters between the ages of 50 and 64 were most likely to choose the 1950s, the decade in which they themselves came of age, as the best time for kids; voters under 30 were more likely to choose the 1970s. African Americans differed over whether the 1960s, 1970s, or 1980s were best, but all age groups of blacks agreed that later decades were definitely preferable to the 1950s.

Nostalgia for the 1950s is real and deserves to be taken seriously, but it usually shouldn't be taken literally. Even people who *do* pick the 1950s as the best decade generally end up saying, once they start discussing their feelings in depth, that it's not the family arrangements in and of themselves that they want to revive. They don't miss the way women used to be treated, they sure wouldn't want to live with most of the fathers they knew in their neighborhoods, and "come to think of it" — I don't know how many times I've recorded these exact words — "I communicate with my kids *much* better than my parents or grandparents did." When Judith Wallerstein recently interviewed 100 spouses in "happy" marriages, she found that only five "wanted a marriage like their parents'." The husbands "consciously rejected the role models provided by their fathers. The women said they could never be happy living as their mothers did."[3]

People today understandably feel that their lives are out of balance, but they yearn for something totally *new* — a more equal distribution of work, family, and community time for both men and women, children and adults. If the 1990s are lopsided in one direction, the 1950s were equally lopsided in the opposite direction.

What most people really feel nostalgic about has little to do with the internal structure of 1950s families. It is the belief that the 1950s provided a more family-friendly economic and social environment, an easier climate in which to keep kids on the straight and narrow, and above all, a greater feeling of hope for a family's long-term future, especially for its young. The contrast between the perceived hopefulness of the fifties and our own misgivings about the future is key to contemporary nostalgia for the period. Greater optimism *did* exist then, even among many individuals and groups who were in terrible circumstances. But if we are to take people's sense of loss

5

[3]Judith Wallerstein and Sandra Blakeslee, *The Good Marriage: How and Why Love Lasts* (Boston: Houghton Mifflin, 1995), p. 15.

seriously, rather than merely to capitalize on it for a hidden political agenda, we need to develop a historical perspective on where that hope came from.

Part of it came from families comparing their prospects in the 1950s to their unstable, often grindingly uncomfortable pasts, especially the two horrible decades just before. In the 1920s, after two centuries of child labor and income insecurity, and for the first time in American history, a bare majority of children had come to live in a family with a male breadwinner, a female homemaker, and a chance at a high school education. Yet no sooner did the ideals associated with such a family begin to blossom than they were buried by the stock market crash of 1929 and the Great Depression of the 1930s. During the 1930s domestic violence soared; divorce rates fell, but informal separations jumped; fertility plummeted. Murder rates were higher in 1933 than they were in the 1980s. Families were uprooted or torn apart. Thousands of young people left home to seek work, often riding the rails across the country.[4]

World War II brought the beginning of economic recovery, and people's renewed interest in forming families resulted in a marriage and childbearing boom, but stability was still beyond most people's grasp. Postwar communities were rocked by racial tensions, labor strife, and a right-wing backlash against the radical union movement of the 1930s. Many women resented being fired from wartime jobs they had grown to enjoy. Veterans often came home to find that they had to elbow their way back into their families, with wives and children resisting their attempts to reassert domestic authority. In one recent study of fathers who returned from the war, four times as many reported painful, even traumatic, reunions as remembered happy ones.[5]

By 1946 one in every three marriages was ending in divorce. Even   10
couples who stayed together went through rough times, as an acute housing shortage forced families to double up with relatives or friends. Tempers frayed and generational relations grew strained. "No home is big enough to house two families, particularly two of different generations, with opposite theories on child training," warned a 1948 film on the problems of modern marriage.[6]

So after the widespread domestic strife, family disruptions, and violence of the 1930s and the instability of the World War II period, people were ready to try something new. The postwar economic boom gave them the chance. The 1950s was the first time that a majority of Americans could even *dream* of creating a secure oasis in their immediate nuclear families.

[4]Donald Hernandez, *America's Children: Resources from Family, Government and the Economy* (New York: Russell Sage, 1993), pp. 99, 102; James Morone, "The Corrosive Politics of Virtue," *American Prospect* 26 (May–June 1996), p. 37; "Study Finds U.S. No. 1 in Violence," *Olympian*, November 13, 1992. See also Stephen Mintz and Susan Kellogg, *Domestic Revolutions: A Social History of American Family Life* (New York: The Free Press, 1988).

[5]William Tuttle, Jr., *"Daddy's Gone to War": The Second World War in the Lives of America's Children* (New York: Oxford University Press, 1993).

[6]"Marriage and Divorce," *March of Time*, film series 14 (1948).

ROGER REALIZES A CHERISHED CHILDHOOD MEMORY IS ACTUALLY A SCENE FROM AN OLD MOVIE.

There they could focus their emotional and financial investments, reduce obligations to others that might keep them from seizing their own chance at a new start, and escape the interference of an older generation of neighbors or relatives who tried to tell them how to run their lives and raise their kids. Oral histories of the postwar period resound with the theme of escaping from in-laws, maiden aunts, older parents, even needy siblings.

The private family also provided a refuge from the anxieties of the new nuclear age and the cold war, as well as a place to get away from the political witch-hunts led by Senator Joe McCarthy and his allies. When having the wrong friends at the wrong time or belonging to any "suspicious" organization could ruin your career and reputation, it was safer to pull out of groups you might have joined earlier and to focus on your family. On a more positive note, the nuclear family was where people could try to satisfy their long-pent-up desires for a more stable marriage, a decent home, and the chance to really enjoy their children.

The 1950s Family Experiment

The key to understanding the successes, failures, and comparatively short life of 1950s family forms and values is to understand the period as one of *experimentation* with the possibilities of a new kind of family, not as the expression of some longstanding tradition. At the end of the 1940s, the divorce rate, which had been rising steadily since the 1890s, dropped sharply; the age of marriage fell to a 100-year low; and the birth rate soared. Women who had worked during the Depression or World War II quit their jobs as soon as they became pregnant, which meant quite a few women were specializing in child raising; fewer women remained childless during the 1950s than in any decade since the late nineteenth century. The timing and spacing of childbearing became far more compressed, so that young mothers were likely to have two or more children in diapers at once, with no older sibling to help in their care. At the same time, again for the first time in 100 years, the educational gap between young middle-class women and men increased, while job segregation for working men and women seems to have peaked. These demographic changes increased the dependence of women on marriage, in contrast to gradual trends in the opposite direction since the early twentieth century.[7]

The result was that family life and gender roles became much more predictable, orderly, and settled in the 1950s than they were either twenty years earlier or would be twenty years later. Only slightly more than one in four marriages ended in divorce during the 1950s. Very few young people spent any extended period of time in a nonfamily setting: They moved from their parents' family into their own family, after just a brief experience with independent living, and they started having children soon after marriage. Whereas two-thirds of women aged 20 to 24 were not yet married in 1990, only 28 percent of women this age were still single in 1960.[8]

---

[7]Arlene Skolnick and Stacey Rosencrantz, "The New Crusade for the Old Family," *American Prospect*, Summer 1994, p. 65; Hernandez, *America's Children*, pp. 128–32; Andrew Cherlin, "Changing Family and Household: Contemporary Lessons from Historical Research," *Annual Review of Sociology* 9 (1983), pp. 54–58; Sam Roberts, *Who We Are: A Portrait of America Based on the Latest Census* (New York: Times Books, 1995), p. 45.

[8]Levy, "Incomes and Income Inequality," p. 20; Arthur Norton and Louisa Miller, *Marriage, Divorce, and Remarriage in the 1990s*, Current Population Reports Series P23-180 (Washington, D.C.: Bureau of the Census, October 1992); Roberts, *Who We Are* (1995 ed.), pp. 50–53.

Ninety percent of all the households in the country were families in the 15
1950s, in comparison with only 71 percent by 1990. Eighty-six percent of all
children lived in two-parent homes in 1950, as opposed to just 72 percent in
1990. And the percentage living with both biological parents — rather than,
say, a parent and stepparent — was dramatically higher than it had been at
the turn of the century or is today: seventy percent in 1950, compared with
only 50 percent in 1990. Nearly 60 percent of kids — an all-time high —
were born into male breadwinner-female homemaker families; only a
minority of the rest had mothers who worked in the paid labor force.[9]

If the organization and uniformity of family life in the 1950s were new,
so were the values, especially the emphasis on putting all one's emotional
and financial eggs in the small basket of the immediate nuclear family.
Right up through the 1940s, ties of work, friendship, neighborhood, ethnicity, extended kin, and voluntary organizations were as important a source of
identity for most Americans, and sometimes a *more* important source of
obligation, than marriage and the nuclear family. All this changed in the
postwar era. The spread of suburbs and automobiles, combined with the
destruction of older ethnic neighborhoods in many cities, led to the decline
of the neighborhood social club. Young couples moved away from parents
and kin, cutting ties with traditional extrafamilial networks that might compete for their attention. A critical factor in this trend was the emergence of
a group of family sociologists and marriage counselors who followed Talcott
Parsons in claiming that the nuclear family, built on a sharp division of labor
between husband and wife, was the cornerstone of modern society.

The new family experts tended to advocate views such as those first
raised in a 1946 book, *Their Mothers' Sons*, by psychiatrist Edward
Strecker. Strecker and his followers argued that American boys were infan-
tilized and emasculated by women who were old-fashioned "moms" instead
of modern "mothers." One sign that you might be that dreaded "mom,"
Strecker warned women, was if you felt you should take your aging parents
into your own home, rather than putting them in "a good institution . . .
where they will receive adequate care and comfort." Modern "mothers"
placed their parents in nursing homes and poured all their energies into
their nuclear family. They were discouraged from diluting their wifely and
maternal commitments by maintaining "competing" interests in friends,
jobs, or extended family networks, yet they were also supposed to cheerfully
grant early independence to their (male) children — an emotional double

---

[9]Dennis Hogan and Daniel Lichter, "Children and Youth: Living Arrangements and Welfare," in Farley, ed., *State of the Union*, vol. 2, p. 99; Richard Gelles, *Contemporary Families: A
Sociological View* (Thousand Oaks, Calif.: Sage, 1995), p. 115; Hernandez, *America's Children*,
p. 102. The fact that only a small percentage of children had mothers in the paid labor force,
though a full 40 percent did not live in male breadwinner-female homemaker families, was
because some children had mothers who worked, unpaid, in farms or family businesses, or
fathers who were unemployed, or the children were not living with both parents.

bind that may explain why so many women who took this advice to heart ended up abusing alcohol or tranquilizers over the course of the decade.[10]

The call for young couples to break from their parents and youthful friends was a consistent theme in 1950s popular culture. In *Marty*, one of the most highly praised TV plays and movies of the 1950s, the hero almost loses his chance at love by listening to the carping of his mother and aunt and letting himself be influenced by old friends who resent the time he spends with his new girlfriend. In the end, he turns his back on mother, aunt, and friends to get his new marriage and a little business of his own off to a good start. Other movies, novels, and popular psychology tracts portrayed the dreadful things that happened when women became more interested in careers than marriage or men resisted domestic conformity.

Yet many people felt guilty about moving away from older parents and relatives; "modern mothers" worried that fostering independence in their kids could lead to defiance or even juvenile delinquency (the recurring nightmare of the age); there was considerable confusion about how men and women could maintain clear breadwinner-homemaker distinctions in a period of expanding education, job openings, and consumer aspirations. People clamored for advice. They got it from the new family education specialists and marriage counselors, from columns in women's magazines, from government pamphlets, and above all from television. While 1950s TV melodramas warned against letting anything dilute the commitment to getting married and having kids, the new family sitcoms gave people nightly lessons on how to make their marriage or rapidly expanding family work — or, in the case of *I Love Lucy*, probably the most popular show of the era, how *not* to make their marriage and family work. Lucy and Ricky gave weekly comic reminders of how much trouble a woman could get into by wanting a career or hatching some hare-brained scheme behind her husband's back.

At the time, everyone knew that shows such as *Donna Reed, Ozzie and Harriet, Leave It to Beaver,* and *Father Knows Best* were not the way families really were. People didn't watch those shows to see their own lives reflected back at them. They watched them to see how families were *supposed* to live — and also to get a little reassurance that they were headed in the right direction. The sitcoms were simultaneously advertisements, etiquette manuals, and how-to lessons for a new way of organizing marriage and child raising. I have studied the scripts of these shows for years, since I often use them in my classes on family history, but it wasn't until I became a parent that I felt their extraordinary pull. The secret of their appeal, I suddenly realized, was that they offered 1950s viewers, wracked with the same feelings of parental inadequacy as was I, the promise that there were easy answers and surefire techniques for raising kids.

20

[10]Edward Strecker, *Their Mothers' Sons: The Psychiatrist Examines an American Problem* (Philadelphia: J. B. Lippincott, 1946), p. 209.

Ever since, I have found it useful to think of the sitcoms as the 1950s equivalent of today's beer ads. As most people know, beer ads are consciously aimed at men who *aren't* as strong and sexy as the models in the commercials, guys who are uneasily aware of the gap between the ideal masculine pursuits and their own achievements. The promise is that if the viewers on the couch will just drink brand X, they too will be able to run 10 miles without gasping for breath. Their bodies will firm up, their complexions will clear up, and maybe the Swedish bikini team will come over and hang out at their place.

Similarly, the 1950s sitcoms were aimed at young couples who had married in haste, women who had tasted new freedoms during World War II and given up their jobs with regret, veterans whose children resented their attempts to reassert paternal authority, and individuals disturbed by the changing racial and ethnic mix of postwar America. The message was clear: Buy these ranch houses, Hotpoint appliances, and child-raising ideals; relate to your spouse like this; get a new car to wash with your kids on Sunday afternoons; organize your dinners like that — and you too can escape from the conflicts of race, class, and political witch hunts into harmonious families where father knows best, mothers are never bored or irritated, and teenagers rush to the dinner table each night, eager to get their latest dose of parental wisdom.

Many families found it possible to put together a good imitation of this way of living during the 1950s and 1960s. Couples were often able to construct marriages that were much more harmonious than those in which they had grown up, and to devote far more time to their children. Even when marriages were deeply unhappy, as many were, the new stability, economic security, and educational advantages parents were able to offer their kids counted for a lot in people's assessment of their life satisfaction. And in some matters, ignorance could be bliss: The lack of media coverage of problems such as abuse or incest was terribly hard on the casualties, but it protected more fortunate families from knowledge and fear of many social ills.[11]

There was tremendous hostility to people who could be defined as "others": Jews, African Americans, Puerto Ricans, the poor, gays or lesbians, and "the red menace." Yet on a day-to-day basis, the civility that prevailed in homogeneous neighborhoods allowed people to ignore larger patterns of racial and political repression. Racial clashes were ever-present in the 1950s, sometimes escalating into full-scale antiblack riots, but individual homicide rates fell to almost half the levels of the 1930s. As nuclear families moved into the suburbs, they retreated from social activism but entered

---

[11]For discussion of the discontents, and often searing misery, that were considered normal in a "good-enough" marriage in the 1950s and 1960s, see Lillian Rubin, *Worlds of Pain: Life in the Working-Class Family* (New York: Basic Books, 1976); Mirra Komarovsky, *Blue Collar Marriage* (New Haven, Conn.: Vintage, 1962); Elaine Tyler May, *Homeward Bound: American Families in the Cold War Era* (New York: Basic Books, 1988).

voluntary relationships with people who had children the same age; they became involved in PTAs together, joined bridge clubs, went bowling. There does seem to have been a stronger sense of neighborly commonalities than many of us feel today. Even though this local community was often the product of exclusion or repression, it sometimes looks attractive to modern Americans whose commutes are getting longer and whose family or work patterns give them little in common with their neighbors.[12]

The optimism that allowed many families to rise above their internal   25
difficulties and to put limits on their individualistic values during the 1950s came from the sense that America was on a dramatically different trajectory than it had been in the past, an upward and expansionary path that had already taken people to better places than they had ever seen before and would certainly take their children even further. This confidence that almost everyone could look forward to a better future stands in sharp contrast to how most contemporary Americans feel, and it explains why a period in which many people were much worse off than today sometimes still looks like a better period for families than our own.

Throughout the 1950s, poverty was higher than it is today, but it was less concentrated in pockets of blight existing side-by-side with extremes of wealth, and, unlike today, it was falling rather than rising. At the end of the 1930s, almost two-thirds of the population had incomes below the poverty standards of the day, while only one in eight had a middle-class income (defined as two to five times the poverty line). By 1960, a majority of the population had climbed into the middle-income range.[13]

Unmarried people were hardly sexually abstinent in the 1950s, but the age of first intercourse was somewhat higher than it is now, and despite a tripling of nonmarital birth rates between 1940 and 1958, more than

---

[12]See Robert Putnam, "The Strange Disappearance of Civic America," *American Prospect*, Winter 1996. For a glowing if somewhat lopsided picture of 1950s community solidarities, see Alan Ehrenhalt, *The Lost City: Discovering the Forgotten Virtues of Community in the Chicago of the 1950s* (New York: Basic Books, 1995). For a chilling account of communities uniting against perceived outsiders, in the same city, see Arnold Hirsch, *Making the Second Ghetto: Race and Housing in Chicago, 1940–1960* (Cambridge, Mass.: Harvard University Press, 1983). On homicide rates, see "Study Finds United States No. 1 in Violence," *Olympian*, November 13, 1992; *New York Times*, November 13, 1992, p. A9; and Douglas Lee Eckberg, "Estimates of Early Twentieth-Century U.S. Homicide Rates: An Econometric Forecasting Approach," *Demography* 32 (1995), p. 14. On lengthening commutes, see "It's Taking Longer to Get to Work," *Olympian*, December 6, 1995.

[13]The figures in this and the following paragraph come from Levy, "Incomes and Income Inequality," pp. 1–57; May and Porter, "Poverty and Income Trends, 1994"; Reynolds Farley, *The New American Reality: Who We Are, How We Got Here, Where We Are Going* (New York: Russell Sage, 1996), pp. 83–85; Gelles, *Contemporary Families*, p. 115; David Grissmer, Sheila Nataraj Kirby, Mark Berends, and Stephanie Williamson, *Student Achievement and the Changing American Family*, Rand Institute on Education and Training (Santa Monica, Calif.: Rand, 1994), p. 106.

70 percent of nonmarital pregnancies led to weddings before the child was born. Teenage birth rates were almost twice as high in 1957 as in the 1990s, but most teen births were to married couples, and the effect of teen pregnancy in reducing further schooling for young people did not hurt their life prospects the way it does today. High school graduation rates were lower in the 1950s than they are today, and minority students had far worse test scores, but there were jobs for people who dropped out of high school or graduated without good reading skills — jobs that actually had a future. People entering the job market in the 1950s had no way of knowing that they would be the last generation to have a good shot at reaching middle-class status without the benefit of postsecondary schooling.

Millions of men from impoverished, rural, unemployed, or poorly educated family backgrounds found steady jobs in the steel, auto, appliance, construction, and shipping industries. Lower-middle-class men went further on in college during the 1950s than they would have been able to expect in earlier decades, enabling them to make the transition to secure white-collar work. The experience of shared sacrifices in the Depression and war, reinforced by a New Deal–inspired belief in the ability of government to make life better, gave people a sense of hope for the future. Confidence in government, business, education, and other institutions was on the rise. This general optimism affected people's experience and assessment of family life. It is no wonder modern Americans yearn for a similar sense of hope.

But before we sign on to any attempts to turn the family clock back to the 1950s we should note that the family successes and community solidarities of the 1950s rested on a totally different set of political and economic conditions than we have today. Contrary to widespread belief, the 1950s was not an age of laissez-faire government and free market competition. A major cause of the social mobility of young families in the 1950s was that federal assistance programs were much more generous and widespread than they are today.

In the most ambitious and successful affirmative action program ever adopted in America, 40 percent of young men were eligible for veterans' benefits, and these benefits were far more extensive than those available to Vietnam-era vets. Financed in part by a federal income tax on the rich that went up to 87 percent and a corporate tax rate of 52 percent, such benefits provided quite a jump start for a generation of young families. The GI bill paid most tuition costs for vets who attended college, doubling the percentage of college students from prewar levels. At the other end of the life span, Social Security began to build up a significant safety net for the elderly, formerly the poorest segment of the population. Starting in 1950, the federal government regularly mandated raises in the minimum wage to keep pace with inflation. The minimum wage may have been only $1.40 as late as 1968, but a person who worked for that amount full-time, year-round, earned 118 percent of the poverty figure for a family of three. By 1995, a full-time minimum-wage worker could earn only 72 percent of the poverty level.[14]

An important source of the economic expansion of the 1950s was that public works spending at all levels of government comprised nearly 20 percent of total expenditures in 1950, as compared to less than 7 percent in 1984. Between 1950 and 1960, nonmilitary, nonresidential public construction rose by 58 percent. Construction expenditures for new schools (in dollar amounts adjusted for inflation) rose by 72 percent; funding on sewers and waterworks rose by 46 percent. Government paid 90 percent of the costs of building the new Interstate Highway System. These programs opened up suburbia to growing numbers of middle-class Americans and created secure, well-paying jobs for blue-collar workers.[15]

Government also reorganized home financing, underwriting low down payments and long-term mortgages that had been rejected as bad business by private industry. To do this, government put public assets behind housing lending programs, created two new national financial institutions to facilitate home loans, allowed veterans to put down payments as low as a dollar on a house, and offered tax breaks to people who bought homes. The National Education Defense Act funded the socioeconomic mobility of thousands of young men who trained themselves for well-paying jobs in such fields as engineering.[16]

Unlike contemporary welfare programs, government investment in 1950s families was not just for immediate subsistence but encouraged long-term asset development, rewarding people for increasing their investment in homes and education. Thus it was far less likely that such families or individuals would ever fall back to where they started, even after a string of bad luck. Subsidies for higher education were greater the longer people stayed in school and the more expensive the school they selected. Mortgage deductions got bigger as people traded up to better houses.[17]

[14]William Chafe, *The Unfinished Journey: America Since World War II* (New York: Oxford University Press, 1986), pp. 113, 143; Marc Linder, "Eisenhower-Era Marxist-Confiscatory Taxation: Requiem for the Rhetoric of Rate Reduction for the Rich," *Tulane Law Review* 70 (1996), p. 917; Barry Bluestone and Teresa Ghilarducci, "Rewarding Work: Feasible Antipoverty Policy," *American Prospect* 28 (1996), p. 42; Theda Skocpol, "Delivering for Young Families," *American Prospect* 28 (1996), p. 67.

[15]Joel Tarr, "The Evolution of the Urban Infrastructure in the Nineteenth and Twentieth Centuries," in Royce Hanson, ed., *Perspectives on Urban Infrastructure* (Washington, D.C.: National Academy Press, 1984); Mark Aldrich, *A History of Public Works Investment in the United States*, report prepared by the CPNSAD Research Corporation for the U.S. Department of Commerce, April 1980.

[16]For more information on this government financing, see Kenneth Jackson, *Crabgrass Frontier: The Suburbanization of the United States* (New York: Oxford University Press, 1985); and *The Way We Never Were*, chapter 4.

[17]John Cook and Laura Sherman, "Economic Security Among America's Poor: The Impact of State Welfare Waivers on Asset Accumulation," Center on Hunger, Poverty, and Nutrition Policy, Tufts University, May 1996.

These social and political support systems magnified the impact of the postwar economic boom. "In the years between 1947 and 1973," reports economist Robert Kuttner, "the median paycheck more than doubled, and the bottom 20 percent enjoyed the greatest gains." High rates of unionization meant that blue-collar workers were making much more financial progress than most of their counterparts today. In 1952, when eager home buyers flocked to the opening of Levittown, Pennsylvania, the largest planned community yet constructed, "it took a factory worker one day to earn enough money to pay the closing costs on a new Levittown house, then selling for $10,000." By 1991, such a home was selling for $100,000 or more, and it took a factory worker *eighteen weeks* to earn enough money for just the closing costs.[18]

The legacy of the union struggle of the 1930s and 1940s, combined   35
with government support for raising people's living standards, set limits on corporations that have disappeared in recent decades. Corporations paid 23 percent of federal income taxes in the 1950s, as compared to just 9.2 percent in 1991. Big companies earned higher profit margins than smaller firms, partly due to their dominance of the market, partly to America's postwar economic advantage. They chose (or were forced) to share these extra earnings, which economists call "rents," with employees. Economists at the Brookings Institution and Harvard University estimate that 70 percent of such corporate rents were passed on to workers at all levels of the firm, benefiting secretaries and janitors as well as CEOs. Corporations routinely retained workers even in slack periods, as a way of ensuring workplace stability. Although they often received more generous tax breaks from communities than they gave back in investment, at least they kept their plants and employment offices in the same place. AT&T, for example, received much of the technology it used to finance its postwar expansion from publicly funded communications research conducted as part of the war effort, and, as current AT&T Chairman Robert Allen puts it, there "used to be a lifelong commitment on the employee's part and on our part." Today, however, he admits, "the contract doesn't exist anymore."[19]

Television trivia experts still argue over exactly what the fathers in many 1950s sitcoms did for a living. Whatever it was, though, they obviously didn't have to worry about downsizing. If most married people stayed in

[18]Robert Kuttner, "The Incredible Shrinking American Paycheck," *Washington Post National Weekly Edition*, November 6–12, 1995, p. 23; Donald Bartlett and James Steele, *America: What Went Wrong?* (Kansas City: Andrews McMeel, 1992), p. 20.

[19]Richard Barnet, "Lords of the Global Economy," *Nation*, December 19, 1994, p. 756; Clay Chandler, "U.S. Corporations: Good Citizens or Bad?" *Washington Post National Weekly Edition*, May 20–26, 1996, p. 16; Steven Pearlstein, "No More Mr. Nice Guy: Corporate America Has Done an About-Face in How It Pays and Treats Employees," *Washington Post National Weekly Edition*, December 18–24, 1995, p. 10; Robert Kuttner, "Ducking Class Warfare," *Washington Post National Weekly Edition*, March 11–17, 1996, p. 5; Henry Allen, "Ha! So Much for Loyalty," *Washington Post National Weekly Edition*, March 4–10, 1996, p. 11.

long-term relationships during the 1950s, so did most corporations, sticking with the communities they grew up in and the employees they originally hired. Corporations were not constantly relocating in search of cheap labor during the 1950s; unlike today, increases in worker productivity usually led to increases in wages. The number of workers covered by corporate pension plans and health benefits increased steadily. So did limits on the work week. There is good reason that people look back to the 1950s as a less hurried age: The average American was working a shorter workday in the 1950s than his or her counterpart today, when a quarter of the workforce puts in 49 or more hours a week.[20]

So politicians are practicing quite a double standard when they tell us to return to the family forms of the 1950s while they do nothing to restore the job programs and family subsidies of that era, the limits on corporate relocation and financial wheeling-dealing, the much higher share of taxes paid by corporations then, the availability of union jobs for noncollege youth, and the subsidies for higher education such as the National Defense Education Act loans. Furthermore, they're not telling the whole story when they claim that the 1950s was the most prosperous time for families and the most secure decade for children. Instead, playing to our understandable nostalgia for a time when things seemed to be getting better, not worse, they engage in a tricky chronological shell game with their figures, diverting our attention from two important points. First, many individuals, families, and groups were excluded from the economic prosperity, family optimism, and social civility of the 1950s. Second, the all-time high point of child well-being and family economic security came not during the 1950s but *at the end of the 1960s.*

We now know that 1950s family culture was not only nontraditional; it was also not idyllic. In important ways, the stability of family and community life during the 1950s rested on pervasive discrimination against women, gays, political dissidents, non-Christians, and racial or ethnic minorities, as well as on a systematic cover-up of the underside of many families. Families that were harmonious and fair of their own free will may have been able to function more easily in the fifties, but few alternatives existed for members of discordant or oppressive families. Victims of child abuse, incest, alcoholism, spousal rape, and wife battering had no recourse, no place to go, until well into the 1960s.[21]

At the end of the 1950s, despite ten years of economic growth, 27.3 percent of the nation's children were poor, including those in white "underclass" communities such as Appalachia. Almost 50 percent of married-couple

[20]Ehrenhalt, *The Lost City*, pp. 11–12; Jeremy Rifken, *The End of Work: The Decline of the Global Labor Force and the Dawn of the Post-Market Era* (New York: G. P. Putnam's Sons, 1995), pp. 169, 170, 231; Juliet Schorr, *The Overworked American: The Unexpected Decline of Leisure* (New York: Basic Books, 1991).

[21]For documentation that these problems existed, see chapter 2 of *The Way We Never Were.*

African-American families were impoverished — a figure far higher than today. It's no wonder African Americans are not likely to pick the 1950s as a golden age, even in comparison with the setbacks they experienced in the 1980s. When blacks moved north to find jobs in the postwar urban manufacturing boom they met vicious harassment and violence, first to prevent them from moving out of the central cities, then to exclude them from public space such as parks or beaches.

In Philadelphia, for example, the City of Brotherly Love, there were   40
more than 200 racial incidents over housing in the first six months of 1955 alone. The Federal Housing Authority, such a boon to white working-class families, refused to insure homes in all-black or in racially mixed neighborhoods. Two-thirds of the city dwellers evicted by the urban renewal projects of the decade were African Americans and Latinos; government did almost nothing to help such displaced families find substitute housing.[22]

Women were unable to take out loans or even credit cards in their own names. They were excluded from juries in many states. A lack of options outside marriage led some women to remain in desperately unhappy unions that were often not in the best interests of their children or themselves. Even women in happy marriages often felt humiliated by the constant messages they received that their whole lives had to revolve around a man. "You are not ready when he calls — miss one turn," was a rule in the Barbie game marketed to 1950s girls; "he criticizes your hairdo — go to the beauty shop." Episodes of *Father Knows Best* advised young women: "The worst thing you can do is to try to beat a man at his own game. You just beat the women at theirs." One character on the show told women to always ask themselves, "Are you after a job or a man? You can't have both."[23]

The Fifties Experiment Comes to an End

The social stability of the 1950s, then, was a response to the stick of racism, sexism, and repression as well as to the carrot of economic opportunity and government aid. Because social protest mounted in the 1960s and unsettling challenges were posed to the gender roles and sexual mores of the previous decade, many people forget that families continued to make gains throughout the 1960s and into the first few years of the 1970s. By 1969, child poverty was down to 14 percent, its lowest level ever; it hovered just above that marker until 1975, when it began its steady climb up to contemporary

[22]The poverty figures come from census data collected in *The State of America's Children Yearbook, 1996* (Washington, D.C.: Children's Defense Fund, 1996), p. 77. See also Hirsch, *Making the Second Ghetto;* Raymond Mohl, "Making the Second Ghetto in Metropolitan Miami, 1940–1960," *Journal of Urban History* 25 (1995), p. 396; Micaela di Leonardo, "Boys on the Hood," *Nation,* August 17–24, 1992, p. 180; Jackson, *Crabgrass Frontier,* pp. 226–227.

[23]Susan Douglas, *Where the Girls Are: Growing Up Female with the Mass Media* (New York: Times Books, 1994), pp. 25, 37.

figures (22 percent in 1993; 21.2 percent in 1994). The high point of health and nutrition for poor children was reached in the early 1970s.[24]

So commentators are being misleading when they claim that the 1950s was the golden age of American families. They are disregarding the number of people who were excluded during that decade and ignoring the socio-economic gains that continued to be made through the 1960s. But they are quite right to note that the improvements of the 1950s and 1960s came to an end at some point in the 1970s (though not for the elderly, who continued to make progress).

Ironically, it was the children of those stable, enduring, supposedly idyllic 1950s families, the recipients of so much maternal time and attention, that pioneered the sharp break with their parents' family forms and gender roles in the 1970s. This was not because they were led astray by some youthful Murphy Brown in her student rebel days or inadvertently spoiled by parents who read too many of Dr. Spock's child-raising manuals.

Partly, the departure from 1950s family arrangements was a logical extension of trends and beliefs pioneered in the 1950s, or of inherent contradictions in those patterns. For example, early and close-spaced childbearing freed more wives up to join the labor force, and married women began to flock to work. By 1960, more than 40 percent of women over the age of 16 held a job, and working mothers were the fastest growing component of the labor force. The educational aspirations and opportunities that opened up for kids of the baby boom could not be confined to males, and many tight-knit, male-breadwinner, nuclear families in the 1950s instilled in their daughters the ambition to be something other than a homemaker.[25]

Another part of the transformation was a shift in values. Most people would probably agree that some changes in values were urgently needed: the extension of civil rights to racial minorities and to women; a rejection of property rights in children by parents and in women by husbands; a reaction against the political intolerance and the wasteful materialism of 1950s culture. Other changes in values remain more controversial: opposition to American intervention abroad; repudiation of the traditional sexual double standard; rebellion against what many young people saw as the hypocrisy of parents who preached sexual morality but ignored social immorality such as racism and militarism.

Still other developments, such as the growth of me-first individualism, are widely regarded as problematic by people on all points along the political spectrum. It's worth noting, though, that the origins of antisocial

---

[24]*The State of America's Children Yearbook, 1966*, p. 77; May and Porter, "Poverty and Income Trends: 1994," p. 23; Sara McLanahan et al., *Losing Ground: A Critique*, University of Wisconsin Institute for Research on Poverty, Special Report No. 38, 1985.

[25]For studies of how both middle-class and working-class women in the 1950s quickly departed from, or never quite accepted, the predominant image of women, see Joanne Meyerowitz, ed., *Not June Cleaver: Women and Gender in Postwar America, 1945–1960* (Philadelphia: Temple University Press, 1994).

individualism and self-indulgent consumerism lay at least as much in the family values of the 1950s as in the youth rebellion of the 1960s. The marketing experts who never allowed the kids in *Ozzie and Harriet* sitcoms to be shown drinking milk, for fear of offending soft-drink companies that might sponsor the show in syndication, were ultimately the same people who slightly later invested billions of dollars to channel sexual rebelliousness and a depoliticized individualism into mainstream culture.

There were big cultural changes brewing by the beginning of the 1970s, and tremendous upheavals in social, sexual, and family values. And yes, there were sometimes reckless or simply laughable excesses in some of the early experiments with new gender roles, family forms, and personal expression. But the excesses of 1950s gender roles and family forms were every bit as repellent and stupid as the excesses of the sixties: Just watch a dating etiquette film of the time period, or recall that therapists of the day often told victims of incest that they were merely having unconscious oedipal fantasies.

Ultimately, though, changes in values were not what brought the 1950s family experiment to an end. The postwar family compacts between husbands and wives, parents and children, young and old, were based on the postwar social compact between government, corporations, and workers. While there was some discontent with those family bargains among women and youth, the old relations did not really start to unravel until people began to face the erosion of the corporate wage bargain and government broke its tacit societal bargain that it would continue to invest in jobs and education for the younger generation.

In the 1970s, new economic trends began to clash with all the social   50
expectations that 1950s families had instilled in their children. That clash, not the willful abandonment of responsibility and commitment, has been the primary cause of both family rearrangements and the growing social problems that are usually attributed to such family changes, but in fact have *separate* origins.

ENGAGING THE TEXT

1. According to Coontz, what do we really miss about the 1950s? In addition, what *don't* we miss?

2. In Coontz's view, what was the role of the government in making the 1950s in America what they were? What part did broader historical forces or other circumstances play?

3. Although she concentrates on the 1950s, Coontz also describes the other decades from the 1920s to the 1990s, when she wrote this piece. Use her information to create a brief chart naming the key characteristics of each decade. Then consider your own family history and see how well it fits the pattern Coontz outlines. Discuss the results with classmates or write a journal entry reflecting on what you learn.

4. Consider the most recent ten years of American history. What events or trends (for example, the 9/11 attacks, same-sex marriage legislation) do you think a sociologist or cultural historian might consider important for understanding our current mythologies of family? How do you think our ideas about family have changed in this decade?

EXPLORING CONNECTIONS

5. Compare Norman Rockwell's enormously popular portrayals of family life (pp. 22–24) with the account provided by Coontz. Do you think she would call Rockwell's paintings "nostalgic"? What do we mean by this word?
6. Review "Looking for Work" by Gary Soto (p. 26). How does this narrative evoke nostalgia for a simpler, better era for families? Does it reveal any of the problems with the 1950s that Coontz describes?

EXTENDING THE CRITICAL CONTEXT

7. Coontz suggests that an uninformed nostalgia for the 1950s could promote harmful political agendas. (See, for example, paras. 7 and 37.) Do you see any evidence in contemporary media of nostalgia for the 1950s? Do you agree with Coontz that such nostalgia can be dangerous? Why or why not?
8. Watch an episode of a 1950s sitcom (if possible, record it) such as *Father Knows Best, The Donna Reed Show, Leave It to Beaver,* or *I Love Lucy.* Analyze the extent to which it reveals both positive and negative aspects of the 1950s that Coontz discusses (for example, an authoritarian father figure, limited roles for wives, economic prosperity, or a sense of a secure community).

Aunt Ida Pieces a Quilt
MELVIN DIXON

This is an extraordinary poem about AIDS, love, and family life. Its author, Melvin Dixon (b. 1950), received his Ph.D. from Brown University; in addition to teaching English at Queens College in New York, he published poetry, literary criticism, translations, and two novels. "Aunt Ida" appeared in Brother to Brother: New Writings by Black Gay Men *(1991). Dixon died of complications from AIDS in 1992.*

You are right, but your patch isn't big enough.
— JESSE JACKSON

*When a cure is found and the last panel is
sewn into place, the Quilt will be displayed
in a permanent home as a national monument
to the individual, irreplaceable people lost to AIDS —
and the people who knew and loved them most.*
— CLEVE JONES, *founder,* THE NAMES *Project*

They brought me some of his clothes. The hospital gown,
those too-tight dungarees, his blue choir robe
with the gold sash. How that boy could sing!
His favorite color in a necktie. A Sunday shirt.
What I'm gonna do with all this stuff?   5
I can remember Junie without this business.
My niece Francine say they quilting all over the country.
So many good boys like her boy, gone.

At my age I ain't studying no needle and thread.
My eyes ain't so good now and my fingers lock in a fist,   10
they so eaten up with arthritis. This old back
don't take kindly to bending over a frame no more.
Francine say ain't I a mess carrying on like this.
I could make two quilts the time I spend running my mouth.

Just cut his name out the cloths, stitch something nice   15
about him. Something to bring him back. You can do it,
Francine say. Best sewing our family ever had.
Quilting ain't that easy, I say. Never was easy.
Y'all got to help me remember him good.

Most of my quilts was made down South. My mama   20
And my mama's mama taught me. Popped me on the tail
if I missed a stitch or threw the pattern out of line.
I did "Bright Star" and "Lonesome Square" and "Rally Round,"
what many folks don't bother with nowadays. Then Elmo and me
married and came North where the cold in Connecticut   25
cuts you like a knife. We was warm, though.
We had sackcloth and calico and cotton, 100% pure.
What they got now but polyester rayon. Factory made.

Let me tell you something. In all my quilts there's a secret
nobody knows. Every last one of them got my name Ida   30
stitched on the back side in red thread.
That's where Junie got his flair. Don't let nobody fool you.
When he got the Youth Choir standing up and singing
the whole church would rock. He'd throw up his hands

from them wide blue sleeves and the church would hush   35
right down to the funeral parlor fans whisking the air.
He'd toss his head back and holler and we'd all cry holy.

And nevermind his too-tight dungarees.
I caught him switching down the street one Saturday night,
and I seen him more than once. I said, Junie,   40
you ain't got to let the world know all your business.
Who cared where he went when he wanted to have fun.
He'd be singing his heart out come Sunday morning.

When Francine say she gonna hang this quilt in the church
I like to fall out. A quilt ain't no showpiece,   45
it's to keep you warm. Francine say it can do both.
Now I ain't so old-fashioned I can't change,
but I made Francine come over and bring her daughter
Belinda. We cut and tacked his name, *JUNIE*.
Just plain and simple, "*JUNIE, our boy.*"   50
Cut the *J* in blue, the *U* in gold. *N* in dungarees
just as tight as you please. The *I* from the hospital gown
and the white shirt he wore First Sunday. Belinda
put the necktie in *E* in the cross stitch I showed her.

Wouldn't you know we got to talking about Junie.   55
We could smell him in the cloth.
Underarm. Afro Sheen pomade.[1] Gravy stains.
I forgot all about my arthritis.
When Francine left me to finish up, I swear
I heard Junie giggling right along with me   60
as I stitched Ida on the back side in red thread.

Francine say she gonna send this quilt to Washington
like folks doing from all 'cross the country,
so many good people gone. Babies, mothers, fathers
and boys like our Junie. Francine say   65
they gonna piece this quilt to another one,
another name and another patch
all in a larger quilt getting larger and larger.

Maybe we all like that, patches waiting to be pieced.
Well, I don't know about Washington.   70
We need Junie here with us. And Maxine,
she cousin May's husband's sister's people,
she having a baby and here comes winter already.
The cold cutting like knives. Now where did I put that needle?

---

[1]*Afro Sheen pomade:* Hair-care product for African Americans.

ENGAGING THE TEXT

1. Identify all of the characters and their relationships in the poem. Then retell the story of the poem in your own words.
2. Discuss the movement of Aunt Ida's mind and her emotions as we move from stanza to stanza. What happens to Aunt Ida in the poem? What is the dominant feeling at the end of the poem?
3. Junie's clothes take on symbolic weight in the quilt and, of course, in the poem as well. What do the hospital gown, the dungarees, the choir robe, and the white shirt and necktie represent?
4. What is Aunt Ida about to make at the end of the poem, and what is its significance?

EXPLORING CONNECTIONS

5. Look at the paintings by Norman Rockwell (pp. 22–24) and the photographs in this chapter's Visual Portfolio (p. 81). Discuss how you might tell the story of "Aunt Ida Pieces a Quilt" visually instead of verbally — for example, as a painting, a mural, a photograph, or a photo essay. Sketch or draw an image based on the poem and share it with classmates.
6. What roles do women play in "Aunt Ida Pieces a Quilt"? Compare these roles to those played by women in the Rockwell paintings (pp. 22–24), Gary Soto's "Looking for Work" (p. 26), and "What We Really Miss About the 1950s" by Stephanie Coontz (p. 31). Based on these examples, would it be fair to conclude that Americans see "the family" as predominantly a woman's responsibility?

EXTENDING THE CRITICAL CONTEXT

7. Write a screenplay or dramatic script to "translate" the story of "Aunt Ida Pieces a Quilt" into dramatic form. Time permitting, organize a group to read or perform the piece for the class.
8. Watch the documentary *Common Threads: Stories from the Quilt* and write a poem based on the life of one of the people profiled in this film.

An Indian Story

ROGER JACK

This narrative concerns growing up away from one's father in one of the Indian cultures of the Pacific Northwest. It's also an intimate view of a non-nuclear family; the author is interested in the family not as a static set of defined relationships but as a social network that adapts to the ever-changing circumstances and needs of its members. Roger Jack works as a counselor and instructor for the American Indian Studies Program at Eastern Washington University. His work has been published in several journals and anthologies, including Spawning the Medicine River, Earth Power Coming, *and* The Clouds Threw This Light. *"An Indian Story" appeared in* Dancing on the Rim of the World: An Anthology of Contemporary Northwest Native American Writing *(1990), edited by Andrea Lerner.*

Aunt Greta was always a slow person. Grandpa used to say she was like an old lady out of the old days who never hurried herself for anything, no matter what. She was only forty-five, heavyset, dark-complexioned, and very knowledgeable of the old ways, which made her seem even older. Most of the time she wore her hair straight up or in a ponytail that hung below her beltline. At home she wore pants and big, baggy shirts, but at ritual gatherings she wore her light blue calico dress, beaded moccasins, hair braided and clasped with beaded barrettes. Sometimes she wore a scarf on her head like ladies older than she. She said we emulate those we love and care for. I liked seeing her dressed for ceremonials. Even more, I liked seeing her stand before crowds of tribal members and guests translating the old language to the new for our elders, or speaking on behalf of the younger people who had no understanding of the Indian language. It made me proud to be her nephew and her son.

My mom died when I was little. Dad took care of me as best he could after that. He worked hard and earned good money as an accountant at the agency. But about a year after Mom died he married a half-breed Indian and this made me feel very uncomfortable. Besides, she had a child of her own who was white. We fought a lot — me and Jeffrey Pine — and then I'd get into trouble because I was older and was supposed to know better than to misbehave.

I ran away from home one day when everyone was gone — actually, I walked to Aunt Greta's and asked if I could move in with her since I had already spent so much time with her anyway. Then after I had gone to bed that night, Dad came looking for me and Aunt Greta told him what I had told her about my wanting to move in with her. He said it would be all right for a while, then we would decide what to do about it later. That was a long time ago. Now I am out of high school and going to college. Meanwhile, Jeffrey Pine is a high-school dropout and living with the folks.

Aunt Greta was married a long time ago. She married a guy named Mathew who made her very happy. They never had children, but when persistent people asked either of them what was wrong, they would simply reply they were working on it. Then Mathew died during their fifth year of marriage. No children. No legacy. After that Aunt Greta took care of Grandpa, who had moved in with them earlier when Grandma died. Grandpa wasn't too old, but sometimes he acted like it. I guess it came from that long, drawn-out transition from horse riding and breeding out in the wild country to reservation life in buggies, dirt roads, and cars. He walked slowly everywhere he went; he and Aunt Greta complemented each other that way.

Eventually, Aunt Greta became interested in tribal politics and threatened to run for tribal council, so Grandpa changed her Indian name from Little Girl Heart to Old Woman Walking, which he had called Grandma when she was alive. Aunt Greta didn't mind. In fact, she was proud of her new name. Little Girl Heart was her baby name, she said. When Grandpa died a couple of years later she was all alone. She decided tribal politics wasn't for her but began teaching Indian culture and language classes. That's when I walked into her life like a newborn Mathew or Grandpa or the baby she never had. She had so much love and knowledge to share, which she passed on to me naturally and freely; she received wages for teaching others. But that was gesticulation, she said.

My home and academic life improved a lot after I had moved in with Aunt Greta. Dad and his wife had a baby boy, and then a girl, but I didn't see too much of them. It was like we were strangers living a quarter mile from one another. Aunt Greta and I went on vacations together from the time I graduated from the eighth grade. We were trailblazers, she said, because our ancestors never traveled very far from the homeland.

The first year we went to Maryhill, Washington, which is about a tenhour drive from our reservation home in Park City, and saw the imitation Stonehenge Monument. We arrived there late in the evening because we had to stop off in every other town along the road to eat, whether or not we were hungry, because that was Aunt Greta's way and Grandma's and all the other old ladies of the tribe. You have to eat to survive, they would say. It was almost dark when we arrived at the park. We saw the huge outlines of the massive hewn stones placed in a circular position and towering well over our heads. We stood small and in awe of their magnificence, especially seeing darkness fall upon us. Stars grew brighter and we saw them more keenly as time passed. Then they started falling, dropping out of the sky to meet us where we stood. I could see the power of Aunt Greta protruding through her eyes; if I had power I wouldn't have to explore, physically, the sensation I imagined her feeling. She said nothing for a long time. Then, barely audible, she murmured something like, "I have no teepee. I need no cover. This moment has been waiting for me here all this time." She paused. Then, "I wasn't sure what I would find here, but I'm glad we came. I was going to say something goofy like 'we should have brought the teepee and we could call upon Coyote to come and knock over these poles so we could drape our canvas over the skeleton and camp!' But I won't. I'm just glad we came here."

"Oh no, you aren't flipping out on me, are you?" I ribbed her. She always said good Indians remember two things: their humor and their history. These are the elements that dictate our culture and our survival in this crazy world. If these are somehow destroyed or forgotten, we would be doomed to extinction. Our power gone. And she had the biggest, silliest grin on her face. She said, "I want to camp right here!" and I knew she was serious.

We camped in the car, in the parking lot, that night. But neither of us slept until nearly daybreak. She told me Coyote stories and Indian stories and asked me what I planned to do with my life. "I want to be like you," I told her. Then she reminded me that I had a Dad to think about, too, and that maybe I should think about taking up his trade. I thought about a lot of stories I had heard about boys following in their father's footsteps — good or bad — and I told Aunt Greta that I wasn't too sure about living on the reservation and working at the agency all my life. Then I tried to sleep, keeping in mind everything we had talked about. I was young, but my Indian memory was good and strong.

On our way home from Maryhill we stopped off at Coyote's Sweat-house down by Soap Lake. I crawled inside the small cavernous stone structure and Aunt Greta said to make a wish for something good. She tossed a coin inside before we left the site. Then we drove through miles of desert country and basalt cliffs and canyons, but we knew we were getting closer to home when the pine trees started weeding out the sagebrush, and the mountains overrode the flatland.

Our annual treks after that brought us to the Olympic Peninsula on the coast and the Redwood Forest in northern California; Yellowstone National Park in Wyoming and Glacier Park in Montana; and the Crazy Horse/ Mount Rushmore Monuments in South Dakota. We were careful in coordinating our trips with pow-wows too. Then we talked about going all the way to Washington, D.C., and New York City to see the sights and how the other half lived, but we never did.

After high-school graduation we went to Calgary for a pow-wow and I got into trouble for drinking and fighting with some local Indians I had met. They talked me into it. The fight occurred when a girlfriend of one of the guys started acting very friendly toward me. Her boyfriend got jealous and started pushing me around and calling me names; only after I defended myself did the others join in the fight. Three of us were thrown into the tribe's makeshift jail. Aunt Greta was not happy when she came to pay my bail. As a matter of fact, I had never seen her angry before. Our neighbors at the campground thought it was funny that I had been arrested and thrown into jail and treated the incident as an everyday occurrence. I sat in the car imagining my own untimely death. I was so sick.

After dropping the ear poles, I watched Aunt Greta take down the rest of the teepee with the same meticulousness with which we had set it up. She went around the radius of the teepee removing wooden stakes from the ground that held fast the teepee's body to the earth. Then she stood on a folding chair to reach the pins that held the face of the teepee together. She folded the teepee into halves as it hung, still, on the center pole. She folded

10

it again and again until it grew clumsy and uneven, then she motioned for me to come and drop the pole so she could untie the fastener that made the teepee our home. Meanwhile, I had to drop all skeletal poles from the sky and all that remained were a few holes in the ground and flattened patches of grass that said we had been there. I stood looking over the crowd. Lots of people had come from throughout Canada and the northern states for the pow-wow. Hundreds of people sat watching the war dance. Other people watched the stick-games and card games. But what caught my attention were the obvious drunks in the crowd. I was "one of them" now.

Aunt Greta didn't talk much while we drove home. It was a long, lonely drive. We stopped only twice to eat cold, tasteless meals. Once in Canada and once stateside. When we finally got home, Aunt Greta said, "Good night," and went to bed. It was only eight o'clock in the evening. I felt a heavy calling to go talk to Dad about what had happened. So I did.

He was alone when I arrived at his house. As usual I walked through the 15 front door without knocking, but immediately heard him call out, "Son?"

"Yeah," I said as I went to sit on a couch facing him. "How did you know it was me?"

He smiled, said hello, and told me a father is always tuned in to his son. Then he sensed my hesitation to speak and asked, "What's wrong?"

"I got drunk in Calgary." My voice cracked. "I got into a fight and thrown in jail too. Aunt Greta had to bail me out. Now she's mad at me. She hasn't said much since we packed to come home."

"Did you tell her you were sorry for screwing up?" Dad asked.

"Yeah. I tried to tell her. But she clammed up on me." 20

"I wouldn't worry about it," Dad said. "This was bound to happen sooner or later. You really feel guilty when you take that first drink and get caught doing it. Hell, when I got drunk the first time, my Mom and Dad took turns preaching to me about the evils of drinking, fornication, and loose living. It didn't stop me though. I was one of those smart asses who had to have his own way. What you have to do is come up with some sort of reparation. Something that will get you back on Greta's good side."

"I guess that's what got to me. She didn't holler or preach to me. All the while I was driving I could feel her staring at me." My voice strengthened, "But she wouldn't say anything."

"Well, Son. You have to try to imagine what's going through her mind too. As much as I love you, you have been Greta's boy since you were knee-high to a grasshopper. She has done nothing but try to provide all the love and proper caring that she can for you. Maybe she thinks she has done something wrong in your upbringing. She probably feels more guilty about what happened than you. Maybe she hasn't said anything because she isn't handling this very well either." Dad became a little less serious before adding, "Of course, Greta's been around the block a time or two herself."

Stunned, I asked, "What do you mean?"

"Son, as much as Greta's life has changed, there are some of us who   25
remember her younger days. She liked drinking, partying, and loud music
along with war dancing, stick-games, and pow-wows. She got along wherever she went looking for a good time. She was one of the few who could do
that. The rest of us either took to drinking all the time, or we hit the pow-
wow circuit all straight-faced and sober, never mixing up the two. Another
good thing about Greta was that when she found her mate and decided to
settle down, she did it right. After she married Mathew she quit running
around." Dad smiled, "Of course, Mathew may have had some influence on
her behavior, since he worked for the alcohol program."

"I wonder why she never remarried?" I asked.

"Some women just don't," Dad said authoritatively. "But she never had
a shortage of men to take care of. She had your Grandpa — and YOU!" We
laughed. Then he continued, "Greta could have had her pick of any man on
the reservation. A lot of men chased after her before she married, and a lot
of them chased after her after Mathew died. But she never had time for
them."

"I wonder if she would have gotten married again if I hadn't moved in
on her?"

"That's a question only Greta can answer. You know, she may work in
tribal programs and college programs, but if she had to give it all up for one
reason in the world, it would be you." Dad became intent, "You are her
bloodline. You know that? Otherwise I wouldn't have let you stay with her
all these years. The way her family believes is that two sisters coming from
the same mother and father are the same. Especially blood. After your
Mother died and you asked to go and live with your Aunt, that was all right.
As a matter of fact, according to her way, we were supposed to have gotten
married after our period of mourning was over."

"You — married to Aunt Greta!" I half-bellowed and again we laughed.   30

"Yeah. We could have made a hell of a family, don't you think?" Dad
tried steadying his mood. "But, you know, maybe Greta's afraid of losing
you too. Maybe she's afraid that you're entering manhood and that you'll be
leaving her. Like when you go away to college. You are still going to college,
aren't you?"

"Yeah. But I never thought of it as leaving her. I thought it more like
going out and doing what's expected of me. Ain't I supposed to strike out on
my own one day?"

"Yeah. Your leaving your family and friends behind may be expected,
but like I said, 'you are everything to Greta,' and maybe she has other plans
for you." Dad looked down to the floor and I caught a glimpse of graying
streaks of hair on top of his head. Then he asked me which college I
planned on attending.

"One in Spokane," I answered. "I ain't decided which one yet."

Then we talked about other things and before we knew it his missus   35
and the kids were home. Junior was nine, Anna Lee eight; they had gone to

the last day of the tribe's celebration and carnival in Nespelem, which was what Aunt Greta and I had gone to Calgary to get away from for once. I sat quietly and wondered what Aunt Greta must have felt for my wrongdoing. The kids got louder as they told Dad about their carnival rides and games and prizes they had won. They shared their goodies with him and he looked to be having a good time eating popcorn and cotton candy.

I remembered a time when Mom and Dad brought me to the carnival. Grandpa and Grandma were with us. Mom and Dad stuck me on a big, black merry-go-round horse with flaming red nostrils and fiery eyes. Its long, dangling tongue hung out of its mouth. I didn't really want to ride that horse, but I felt I had to because Grandpa kept telling Mom and Dad that I belonged on a real horse and not some wooden thing. I didn't like the horse, when it hit certain angles it jolted and scared me even more. Mom and Dad offered me another ride on it, but I refused.

"Want some cotton candy?" Junior brought me back to reality. "We had fun going on the rides and trying to win some prizes. Here, you can have this one." He handed me one of his prizes. And, "Are you gonna stay with us tonight?"

I didn't realize it was after eleven o'clock.

"You can sleep in my bed," Junior offered.

"Yeah. Maybe I will, Little Brother." Junior smiled. I bade everyone   40
good night and went to his room and pulled back his top blanket revealing his Star Wars sheets. I chuckled at the sight of them before lying down and trying to sleep on them. This would be my first time sleeping away from Aunt Greta in a long time. I still felt tired from my drinking and the long drive home, but I was glad to have talked to Dad. I smiled in thinking that he said he loved me, because Indian men hardly ever verbalize their emotions. I went to sleep thinking how alone Aunt Greta must have felt after I had left home and promised myself to return there as early as I could.

I ate breakfast with the family before leaving. Dad told me one last thing that he and Aunt Greta had talked about sometime before. "You know, she talked about giving you an Indian name. She asked me if you had one and I said 'no.' She talked about it and I thought maybe she would go ahead and do it too, but her way of doing this is: boys are named for their father's side and girls are named for their mother's. Maybe she's still waiting for me to give you a name. I don't know."

"I remember when Grandpa named her, but I never thought of having a name myself. What was the name?" I asked.

"I don't remember. Something about stars."

Aunt Greta was sitting at the kitchen table drinking coffee and listening to an Elvis album when I got home. Elvis always made her lonesome for the old days or it cheered her up when she felt down. I didn't know what to say, but showed her the toy totem pole Junior had given me.

"That's cute," she said. "So you spent the night at the carnival?"   45

"No. Junior gave it to me," I explained. "I camped at Dad's."

"Are you hungry?" she was about to get up from the table.

"No. I've eaten." I saw a stack of pancakes on the stove. I hesitated another moment before asking, "What's with Elvis?"

"He's dead!" she said and smiled, because that's what I usually said to her. "Oh well, I just needed a little cheering up, I guess."

I remember hearing a story about Aunt Greta that happened a long time ago. She was a teenager when the Elvis craze hit the reservation. Back then hardly any families had television sets, so they couldn't see Elvis. But when his songs hit the airwaves on the radio the girls went crazy. The guys went kind of crazy too — but they were pissed off crazy. A guy can't be that good looking and talented too, they claimed. They were jealous of Elvis. Elvis had a concert in Seattle and my Mom and Aunt Greta and a couple other girls went to it. Legend said that Elvis kissed Aunt Greta on the cheek during his performance and she took to heart the old "ain't never going to wash that cheek again" promissory and never washed her cheek for a long time and it got chapped and cracked until Grandpa and Grandma finally had to order her to go to the clinic to get some medicine to clean up her face. She hated them for a while, still swearing Elvis would be her number one man forever.

"How's your Dad?"

"He's all right. The kids were at the carnival when I got to his house, so we had a nice, long visit." I paused momentarily before adding, "And he told me some stories about you too."

"Oh?" she acted concerned even though her crow's feet showed.

"Yeah. He said you were quite a fox when you were young. And he said you probably could have had any man you wanted before you married Uncle Mathew, and you could have had any man after Uncle Mathew died. So, how come you never snagged yourself another husband?"

Aunt Greta sat quietly for a moment. I could see her slumping into the old way of doing things which said you thought things through before saying them. "I suppose I could have had my pick of the litter. It's just that after my old man died I didn't want anyone else. He was so good to me that I didn't think I could find any better. Besides, I had you and Grandpa to care for, didn't I? Have I ever complained about that?"

"Yeah," I persisted, "but haven't you ever thought about what might have happened if you had gotten married again? You might have done like Dad and started a whole new family. Babies, even!"

Aunt Greta was truly embarrassed. "Will you get away from here with talk like that. I don't need babies. Probably won't be long now and you'll be bringing them home for me to take care of anyhow."

Now I was embarrassed. We got along great after that initial conversation. It was like we had never gone to Calgary and I had never gotten on to her wrong side at all. We were like kids rediscovering what it was worth to have a real good friend go away for a while and then come back. To be appreciative of each other, I imagined Aunt Greta might have said.

Our trip to Calgary happened in July. August and September found me dumbfounded as to what to do with myself college-wise. I felt grateful that Indian parents don't throw out their offspring when they reach a certain age. Aunt Greta said it was too late for fall term and that I should rest my brain for a while and think about going to college after Christmas. So I explored different schools in the area and talked to people who had gone to them. Meanwhile, some of my friends were going to Haskell Indian Junior College in Kansas. Aunt Greta frowned upon my going there. She said it was too far away from home, people die of malaria there, and if you're not drunk, you're just crazy. So I stuck with the Spokane plan.

That fall Aunt Greta was invited to attend a language seminar in Port-   60
land. She taught Indian language classes when asked to. So we decided to take a side trip to our old campsite at Stonehenge. This time we arrived early in the morning and it was foggy and drizzling rain. The sight of the stones didn't provide the feeling we had experienced earlier. To us, the sight seemed to be just a bunch of rocks standing, overlooking the Columbia River, a lot of sagebrush, and two state highways. It didn't offer us feelings of mysticism and power anymore. Unhappy with the mood, Aunt Greta said we might as well leave; her words hung heavy on the air.

We stayed in Portland for a week and then made it a special point to leave late in the afternoon so we could stop by Stonehenge again at dusk. So with careful planning we arrived with just enough light to take a couple pictures and then darkness began settling in. We sat in the car eating baloney sandwiches and potato chips and drinking pop because we were tired of restaurant food and we didn't want people staring at us when we ate. That's where we were when an early evening star fell. Aunt Greta's mouth fell open, potato chip crumbs clung to the sides of her mouth. "This is it!" she squealed in English, Indian, and English again. "Get out of the car, Son," and she half pushed me out the door. "Go and stand in the middle of the circle and pray for something good to happen to you." I ran out and stood waiting and wondering what was supposed to happen. I knew better than to doubt Aunt Greta's wishes or superstitions. Then the moment came to pass.

"Did you feel it?" she asked as she led me back to the car.

"I don't know," I told her because I didn't think anything had happened.

"I guess it just takes some people a little longer to realize," she said.

I never quite understood what was supposed to have happened that   65
day. A couple months later I was packing up to move to Spokane. I decided to go into the accounting business, like Dad. Aunt Greta quizzed me hourly before I was to leave whether I was all right and if I would be all right in the city. "Yeah, yeah," I heard myself repeating. So by the time I really was to leave she clued me in on her new philosophy: it wasn't that I was leaving her, it was just that she wouldn't be around to take care of me much anymore. She told me, "Good Indians stick together," and that I should search out our people who were already there, but not forget those who were still at home.

After I arrived in Spokane and settled down I went home all too frequently to actually experience what Aunt Greta and everyone told me. Then my studies got so intense that I didn't think I could travel home as much anymore. So I stayed in Spokane a lot more than before. Finally it got so I didn't worry as much about the folks at home. I would be out walking in the evening and know someone's presence was with me. I never bothered telephoning Dad at his office at the agency; and I never knew where or when Aunt Greta worked. She might have been at the agency or school. Then one day Dad telephoned me at school. After asking how I was doing, he told me why he was calling. "Your Aunt Greta is sick. The doctors don't know what's wrong with her yet. They just told me to advise her family of the possibility that it could be serious." I only half heard what he was saying, "Son, are you there?"

"Yeah."

"Did you hear me? Did you hear what I said?"

"Yeah. I don't think you have to worry about Aunt Greta though. She'll be all right. Like the old timers used to say, 'she might go away for a while, but she'll be back,'" and I hung up the telephone unalarmed.

ENGAGING THE TEXT

1. Give specific examples of how the narrator's extended family or kinship structure works to solve family problems. What problems does it seem to create or make worse?

2. What key choices does the narrator make in this story? How are these choices influenced by family members or family considerations?

3. Is the family portrayed here matriarchal, patriarchal, egalitarian, or something else? Explain. To what extent is parenting influenced by gender roles?

4. What events narrated in this story might threaten the survival of a nuclear family? How well does the extended family manage these crises?

5. How strong an influence does the narrator's father have on him? How can you explain the father's influence given how rarely the two see each other?

6. How do you interpret the narrator's reaction when he hears about Aunt Greta's failing health? What is implied in the story's closing lines?

EXPLORING CONNECTIONS

7. Compare and contrast "Looking for Work" (p. 26) and "An Indian Story" in terms of what each narrator learns about family and how they learn it. Do they learn the same things they would likely learn in a traditional nuclear family headed by a father? Explain.

8. Compare the family dynamics in "Aunt Ida Pieces a Quilt" (p. 48) and "An Indian Story." In each case, how does the family seem to define itself? Who makes the decisions? How — and how well — does each family handle the crises it faces?

EXTENDING THE CRITICAL CONTEXT

9. This story celebrates the power of stories to connect people and to shape or affirm one's identity. Throughout, the narrator relates family stories about his father and his aunt that give him a clearer sense of himself and his relationship to those he loves. In a journal entry or essay, relate one or two family stories that are important to you and explain how they help you define who you are.

From *Changing American Families*
JUDY ROOT AULETTE

Imagine you had spent several years reading about the relationship of family to race, gender roles, and social class. Many of the key things you would have learned are summarized in this selection. Author Judy Root Aulette synthesizes the conclusions of dozens of studies by other researchers, offering an extremely informative overview of how American families both reflect and help maintain social stratification according to race, class, and gender. Aulette teaches at the University of North Carolina at Charlotte, in the Department of Sociology and Anthropology. This reading is taken from her book Changing American Families *(2002).*

Social Class, Race Ethnicity, and Gender and Family Life

The stratification systems of class, race ethnicity, and gender constitute a major feature of the macro level of social organization in our society. They exist beyond the control of any individual and are so pervasive they sometimes become invisible. But they weave in and out of our lives, sometimes overlapping, and sometimes contradicting each other, but always defining and shaping our lives and our relationships with others.

In this section, we will examine the way in which class, race, and gender create different experiences within families. The emphasis will be on the effect that the macro organization of our society, which includes these three systems of stratification, has on the micro level of society, the everyday experience of families. We will also observe the ways in which families respond to the macro system by helping to preserve inequality, attempting to survive in spite of inequality, and creating ways in which to resist inequality and thereby alter the institutions of inequality.

This section investigates different social classes and racial ethnic groups. Gender is also covered, as the section discusses how women and men relate to each other in families in various social classes and racial ethnic groups.

Upper-Class Families: Gatekeepers

Life in an upper-class family is not often open to scrutiny by the public or by researchers. As a result, less is known about the private lives of the members of this social class than of others. Rich people, however, know a lot about each other. Their preoccupation with maintaining boundaries between themselves and others has been noted by a number of scholars who have studied the elite (Domhoff, 1970; Eitzen, 1985; Mills, 1956). Families are a key way in which "membership" is identified. Being from a "good family" is essential and sometimes even overrides financial status. For example, when one of the "best families" loses its fortune, family members may be still counted as upper class, at least for a time, because of their ancestry (Bedard, 1992).

Georg Simmel (1907/1978) wrote that "Aristocrats would get to know   5
each other better in an evening than the middle class would in a month." He meant that wealthy people identify themselves by membership and background, while middle-class people identify themselves by individual achievement. Therefore, a person who knows the meaning of various memberships and connections among the upper class can draw a complete picture of a person. An essential piece of information in determining membership is family lineage.

Families play a critical role in keeping an individual in the upper class:

> The most important single predictor of a son's occupational status is his father's occupational status. A man born into the top 5% of family income had a 63% chance of earning over $25,000 a year in 1976 (being in the top 17.8% of family income). But a man born into the bottom 10% of family income had only a 1% chance of attaining this level (Braun, 1991).

Women in elite families play a special role in maintaining boundaries. "Women serve as gatekeepers of many of the institutions of the very rich. They launch children, serve as board members at private schools, run clubs, and facilitate marriage pools through events like debuts and charity balls" (Rapp, 1982).

Families also help maintain an individual's social standing among the wealthy class by teaching family members how to maintain their class position. For example, upper-class children learn not to "spend down capital" (Millman, 1991). This means that they should use only the interest, not the principal, of an inherited estate. The wealth that has been accumulated may have taken generations to acquire and is thought of as belonging to the family line, not to individuals.

Tax laws reinforce the idea that wealth belongs to all generations of a family rather than to individuals. Inheritance taxes can be reduced if the inheritance of an estate skips generations. When the inheritance is claimed only every other generation, taxes must be paid only every other generation. For example, if a wealthy person wills his or her estate to grandchildren rather than to children, one tax is paid rather than two (Millman, 1991). This increases the motivation to teach children to live on the interest and not to touch the principal and that the family fortune should be shared only within a small circle of kin.

Volunteer work is an especially important activity in the production and   10
maintenance of social status (Daniels, 1988). Susan Ostrander (1984) interviewed thirty-six upper-class women about their activities "to uphold the power and privilege of their class in the social order of things" (Ostrander, 1984, p. 3).

Marriage was one issue about which they spoke. One woman explained, "A compatible marriage first and foremost is a marriage within one's class" (Ostrander, 1984, p. 86). The women talked about debuts as critical events to ensure that their children met the proper prospective mates. Social clubs were also cited as places to keep themselves away from those the women referred to as "anybodies."

Athletic games and activities were also mentioned as important. The women believed that these activities enhanced the ability of their children to stay in their class. They spoke of the lessons of "discipline, confidence, competition, and a sense of control" (Ostrander, 1984, p. 94).

A good education in a prestigious upper-class school was another goal because of both the academic training and the social networks it afforded their children. The women spent much time planning and orchestrating all of these activities.

Upper-class families are largely responsible for maintaining their own position within the stratification system. They pass wealth down within families. They teach their children how to maintain their position, and they bring their children into the social institutions such as elite schools and clubs that further reinforce their membership in the class. Women play a special role in maintaining the class and especially the boundaries around the class.

Along with the maintenance of individual families within the class or   15
the maintenance of the class itself is the maintenance of the system of inequality. In a system of finite resources where some have control over a large proportion of those resources, others have control over less. Resources are not distributed equally. Families are essential to the constant work of retaining those resources and creating relationships of difference and inequality between themselves and other classes. "The family as an institution ensures the continuity of the have-nots as well as entrenching the power and privilege of the haves" (Morgan, 1985, p. 214).

Middle-Class Families

Four factors characterize middle-class families: (1) geographical mobility resulting in residence away from kin; (2) replacement of kin with other institutions for economic support; (3) reliance on friendship rather than kinship for affective support and exchange; and (4) investment of resources lineally (Rapp, 1982).

In order to maintain their income, middle-class families may have to move around. For example, people in middle-class occupations are frequently asked to move when their company needs them to work at another site. Middle-class professionals may find that to get a raise or further their career they must take a job with another company in another state.

These moves remove them from extended family ties, and when economic help is needed middle-class people may rely on nonfamily sources. For example, a middle-class family that needs money for a down payment on a house would go to a bank for a loan. Both upper-class and working-class families might be more likely to seek assistance from their kin.

Middle-class families may also replace kin with friends in seeking emotional and social support. In the discussion of working-class families that follows, we will see how working-class people convert friends into kin in order to facilitate sharing material goods (Stack, 1974). Rayna Rapp (1982) argues that middle-class people do just the opposite. She states that middle-class people refrain from sharing with extended kin and maintain friendships that do not include sharing resources. In this way, middle-class families are better able to accumulate material wealth rather than dispersing it. Middle-class families stress upward mobility based on not sharing what they have accumulated (Millman, 1991).

The wealth that each relatively independent middle-class household is able to accumulate is invested lineally — between parents and children — rather than laterally among extended family and close friends, as is the case in working-class households. Investing in education for their children and in extravagant wedding gifts are examples of the ways middle-class families share lineally (Rapp, 1982).

Geographic Mobility. Americans have always been a mobile community, although today we are somewhat less mobile than in previous years. In the nineteenth century, 50 to 75 percent of the residents in any given town were likely to not be there ten years later. People born in the twentieth century were more likely to live near their birthplace than people born in the nineteenth century (Coontz, 1992). Nevertheless, one of the sources of the independence and isolation of contemporary middle-class families is the geographic mobility that accompanies their occupations. Every year about 45 million Americans move. More than half of these moves are for a job. Of interstate moves, 22 percent are for a job transfer, 19 percent are for a new job, 6 percent are to look for a job, and 3 percent are for what the Census Bureau calls "unspecified employment related reasons" (Hendershott, 1995).

Most researchers have looked at this issue as it exists in families where the husband needs to move because men are much more likely than women, especially married women, to move for work. The "typical" relocated corporate employee is a thirty-seven-year-old married man who owns his home, has two children, and works in sales and marketing (Hendershott, 1995).

These moves are experienced differently for women and men in families. The moves enhance the career of the husband for whom the move is being made, and many men seem to feel that moving is not a problem. Almost half of the men in one survey said that family ties pose no obstacle to their possible relocation (Harrison, 1991). When a man must move because his wife has found another job, however, his response is somewhat different. Research shows that a man will follow his wife only if she earns 25 percent to 40 percent more than he does (Lee, 1986). Although the moves are rewarding for men and the household they support, they also create hardship for wives and children. "Very few women do not suffer some losses as the result of a family move. These may include giving up friends, community and sense of self-worth and identity, close contact with relatives and often, a job or career possibility" (Gaylord, 1984). Children, especially those between the ages of three and five and the ages of fourteen and sixteen, also report emotional difficulties with moving (Seidenberg, 1973).

Much of the research on the "trailing wife" and the difficulty that relocation for a man's job causes for his family was done in the 1970s and 1980s. Hendershott (1995) reviewed relocation policies and surveys of more than five hundred companies in the 1990s and found that some factors have been altered more recently. She found that moving is not without stress, but that the focus of the older research on the disruption and loss caused by relocation overshadows the ways in which mobility creates improved economic opportunities for the moving families and at times even for the trailing spouse and children. In addition to the greater opportunities of the new job, some companies offer incentives for the move itself. For example, the FBI has given 25 percent cost-of-living increases and $20,000 bonuses to agents who move (Hendershott, 1995).

Hendershott (1995) also compared relocaters with "stayers," people who did not agree to relocate. She found that the stress of declining an opportunity that involved moving can be equal to the stress of accepting a move.

Another area of change Hendershott (1995) observed was an increase in the importance of elder care concerns. In a large 1993 survey of corporations, 25 percent said they believed that concern for employees about their older parents was growing in importance in decisions about relocation.

The Black Middle Class.   Black middle-class families are similar to white ones in the focus of their lives on home and family (Bedard, 1992). Charles Willie's (1983) research on black middle-class families shows them to be achievement oriented, upwardly mobile, immersed in work, and with little time for leisure. Education, hard work, and thrift are perceived to be the means to achievement.

There are also some interesting differences between black middle-class and working-class families and white middle-class and working-class families. Attitudes about education are one example. Middle-class and working-class black families place an enormous amount of emphasis on education for their children because they perceive education to be the road to success and a way to overcome racial discrimination (Wilkinson, 1984). Lower-middle-class black families prioritize education and encourage their daughters to choose education over marriage (Higgenbotham, 1981).

In contrast working-class white families are more ambivalent and sometimes even negative about education for their children (Willie, 1985). They "worry that highly educated children will no longer honor family customs and maintain cohesion with their relatives" (Anderson, 1988, p. 177).

A second racial ethnic difference is the perception by black middle-class families of cultivating community responsibility:

> Middle-class black parents insist that their children get a good education not only to escape possible deprivations but to serve as symbols of achievement for the family as well as for the race. Each generation is expected to stand on the shoulders of the past generation and to do more. All achievement by members in black middle-class families is for the purpose of group advancement as well as individual enhancement. (Willie, 1988, p. 183)

In contrast, white families emphasize freedom, autonomy, and individualism. The negative feature of this emphasis is that individualism can shatter family solidarity and can lead individuals to display narcissistic attitudes and hedonistic behavior (Willie, 1988).

In the black middle-class family, "Individual fulfillment is seen as self-centered activity and therefore is less valued. What counts in the black middle class is how the family is faring" (Willie, 1988, p. 184). The down side of the emphasis on solidarity is that it stifles experimentation. Risk-taking is discouraged, and individuals may hesitate to try more experimental and creative activities.

Willie (1988) concludes that blacks and whites can learn from each other on this question. "Too much creativity has been stifled in middle-class blacks who have been trained to put family needs above personal needs. And too many individuals have drifted aimlessly in middle-class white families who have been taught to put individual freedom before collective concern" (Willie, 1988, p. 184).

The third difference concerns the question of gender equality. A number of studies have found a greater level of equality between husbands and wives in black families than in white families (Morgan, 1985; Middleton & Putney, 1960; Willie, 1983, 1985, 1988; TenHouten, 1970; Mack, 1978). . . .

Black women are more likely to have been in the labor force than white women. Egalitarian ideologies are stronger among blacks than whites (Hunter & Sellers, 1998). Black men are more likely to share in housework and child care than white men (Anderson, 1988). Willie (1988) asserts that gender equality is a worthy goal and that black families have been pioneers in this effort. Therefore, he concludes, "the egalitarian family form is a major contribution by blacks to American society" (Willie, 1988, p. 186).

Working-Class White Families

White working-class families are characterized by three factors: (1) the ideological commitment to marry for love, not money; (2) the importance of extended kin and other networks to economic and emotional survival; and (3) the appearance of separation of work and family. Within each of these factors is a contrast between what people believe and what they really experience (Rapp, 1982).

Working-class couples marry for love. Person after person in Lillian Rubin's (1976) interviews of blue-collar couples said they had married for love and that love provided a way to escape from the difficulties of their parents' homes. One young woman recalled: "We just knew right away that we were in love. We met at a school dance, and that was it. I knew who he was before. He was real popular; everybody liked him. I was so excited when he asked me to dance, I just melted" (Rubin, 1976, p. 52).

In contrast, upper-class couples recognize their marriages as a way to preserve their class identity (Millman, 1991). Upper-class couples may marry for love, but they are conscious that love should only occur between themselves and others of their class. Middle-class people may also marry for love, but as we saw in the discussion above of middle-class families, the overriding task of middle-class families is also an economic one, to enhance the earning power of the breadwinner.

Working-class people are also affected by the economic realities of their lives. Working-class families must operate as economic units. The economic tasks of families are less a part of their dreams about marriage than they are a part of the reality of their married lives. "The economic realities that so quickly confronted the young working-class couples of this study ricocheted through the marriage dominating every aspect of experience, coloring every facet of their early adjustment. The women finding their dreams disappointed felt somehow that their men had betrayed the promise implicit in their union" (Rubin, 1976, p. 75).

The second characteristic of working-class families is the reliance on extended kin and others "to bridge the gap between what a household's resources really are and what a family's position is supposed to be" (Rapp, 1982, p. 175). Rapp (1982) says that working-class families are normatively nuclear. By this she means that they believe that independent autonomous families are the best form and that for the most part their families are independent and autonomous.

Observations of their real behavior, however, reveal much sharing of   40
baby-sitting, meals, and small amounts of money, especially among
extended kin (Rubin, 1976; Stacey, 1990). Sometimes these extended kin
relationships became problematic, and half of the women Rubin (1976)
interviewed said that the struggle over who comes first, a man's wife or his
mother, was a source of contention between themselves and their husbands.
For example, one woman told Rubin: "He used to stop off there at his
mother's house on his way home from work and that used to make me furious. On top of that they eat supper earlier than we do, so a lot of times, he'd
eat with them. Then he'd come home and I'd have a nice meal fixed, and
he'd say he wasn't hungry. Boy did that make me mad" (Rubin, 1976, p. 88).

The third characteristic of working-class families is the appearance that
work and family are completely separate. Blue-collar jobs do not include
bringing work home, and one's occupation does not carry over into one's
identity in the way a middle-class professional's might. But work and family
are not entirely separate in the working class, where work affects family life
and family affects the workplace. . . .

Working-Class African American Families: The Moynihan Report and Its Historical Context

. . . From the days of slavery up to the middle of the twentieth
century . . . black families were a focus of the struggle of African Americans
for equality. During slavery, African American people fought plantation
owners and the slave system for the right to marry and live with their
spouses and children. During the sharecropping period, black families
struggled for the right for wives and mothers to devote time to their families
instead of working for whites. As industrialization developed, African
American women moved from the farms to the cities to take jobs as domes-
tics. Here they challenged their employers for the right to work shorter
hours to spend time with their husbands and children.

In the last half of the twentieth century and into the twenty-first,
African American families continue to be a volatile political issue. Some
have blamed African American families for a myriad of urban problems. . . .
Advocates of African American families have fought back, expressing an
alternative point of view. They argue that black families have been scapegoats and are not to blame for poverty and civil unrest. Furthermore, they
argue, black families have been the victims of poverty and inequality caused
by structural problems.

One important event in this history was the publication of a U.S. Labor
Department report entitled *The Negro Family: A Case for National Action*
(Moynihan, 1965), commonly called the Moynihan Report after its author,
Daniel Patrick Moynihan, the senator from the state of New York.

The 1950s and 1960s were an important period in American history   45
because of one of the most significant social movements in the twentieth
century, the Civil Rights Movement, which protested the unequal treatment

of African Americans in the United States. Civil rights activists argued that socially powerful institutions like the legal system, government, schools, businesses, and landlords had created poverty and injustice in the black community. In 1965 the Moynihan Report appeared with an alternative point of view.

The Moynihan Report blamed the dilapidated housing, poverty, unemployment, and inferior education experienced by African Americans on the organization of black families. Where the civil rights movement saw these same problems and found their cause in the racism of the most powerful sectors of society, Moynihan blamed the victims.

Moynihan argued that black families were disorganized and female dominated. He maintained that black men were humiliated and emasculated by domineering black women. According to Moynihan, the only hope for saving the black family and therefore the community was to reestablish black men as the rightful heads of their families (Giddings, 1984). Moynihan wrote: "Ours is a society which presumes male leadership in private and public affairs; a subculture such as that of the Negro American, in which this is not the pattern, is placed at a distinct disadvantage" (quoted in Gresham, 1989, p. 118). In order to overcome this disadvantage, the Moynihan Report advised "that jobs had primacy and the government should not rest until every able-bodied Negro man was working even if it meant that some women's jobs had to be redesigned to enable men to fulfill them" (Giddings, 1984, p. 328).

The Moynihan Report also suggested that if black men were to take their rightful place as head of the family and community, they would need to bolster their skills in behaving in a properly masculine manner. Moynihan suggested they join the army: "There is another special quality about military service for Negro men: it is an utterly masculine world. Given the strains of the disorganized and matrifocal family life in which so many Negro youth come of age, the Armed Forces are a dramatic and desperately needed change: a world away from women, a world run by strong men of unquestioned authority" (Moynihan, 1965, p. 42).

Moynihan reframed the debate around civil rights so that the opposing sides were no longer African Americans versus an unrepresentative government or poor people versus the power structure. New lines were drawn by the Moynihan Report between black men and black women over who would have access to scarce jobs and who would dominate in families.

Several scholars and the African American community in general reacted critically to the Moynihan Report. People like Joyce Ladner (1971), Andrew Billingsley (1968), and William Ryan (1971) led the debate against Moynihan's assertions (Giddings, 1984; Rainwater & Yancey, 1967).

One of the most controversial features of the report concerned the so-called "black matriarchy." The term *matriarchy* means rule by the mother. At the core of Moynihan's argument was the characterization of African American women as dominant authoritarian figures, matriarchs.

Robert Staples (1981) actively attacked this idea, calling black matriarchy a myth. He asked, if black women are so dominant and powerful, why do we not see great numbers of black women in Congress, and why do we continue to see black women earning less than white men and women and black men?

Staples argued, furthermore, that when we see black women actively working to ensure that their children are fed and when we see black women fighting shoulder to shoulder with black men for integration, education, and civil rights, we should be proud, not critical. Staples commented: "While white women have entered the history books for making flags and engaging in social work, black women have participated in the total black liberation struggle" (Staples, 1981, p. 32).

Carol Stack (1974), an anthropologist, decided to systematically investigate Moynihan's thesis by doing fieldwork in a low-income black neighborhood she called the Flats. Her work became one of the most influential alternative views of poor black families (Katz, 1989).

The Flats.   Were African American families in the Flats disorganized matriarchies? This was the question with which Stack began her research. After two years of observing and interviewing the residents of the Flats, Stack (1974) concluded that the families there were neither nuclear nor male dominated. Nor were they disintegrating, nonexistent, or matriarchal. Instead, Stack found families that were complex organized networks characterized by five factors: (1) kin and nonkin membership, (2) swapping, (3) shared child raising, (4) fluid physical boundaries, and (5) domestic authority of women.

Networks were composed of both kin and nonkin — parents, siblings, cousins, aunts, uncles, and grandparents, as well as nonkin who became "like family" because of their extended interaction and support of network members. After living in the Flats for two years and sharing rides and child care, even Carol Stack was integrated into the network as a member of the family and began to be called sister by one of the women in the Flats. When people change friends into family, as the people in the Flats did with Carol Stack, sociologists call them fictive kin (Gittens, 1998).

The stereotypical middle-class white family is bound together through blood or legal relationships of marriage and adoption. In the Flats, people recognized these ties. More importantly, however, familial networks in the Flats were also bound together by social relationships based on swapping.

Swapping.   *Swapping* refers to the borrowing and trading of resources, possessions, and services. In times of need, a member of the network could rely on other members for money, food, clothes, a ride, or child care. In return the member was obligated to share what he or she had with those in need. Because resources were scarce, people in the Flats constantly redistributed them in order to survive.

Stack describes an example of a swapping network. The description illustrates the many different kinds of resources that are swapped and the complex system that keeps those resources moving in an efficient and fair manner:

> Cecil (35) lives in the Flats with his mother Willie Mae, his oldest sister and her two children, and his younger brother. Cecil's younger sister Lily lives with their mother's sister Bessie. Bessie has three children and Lily has two. Cecil and his mother have part-time jobs in a cafe and Lily's children are on aid. In July of 1970 Cecil and his mother had just put together enough money to cover their rent. Lily paid her utilities, but she did not have enough money to buy food stamps for herself and her children. Cecil and Willie Mae knew that after they paid their rent they would not have any money for food for the family. They helped Lily by buying her food stamps, and then the two households shared meals together until Willie Mae was paid two weeks later. A week later Lily received her second ADC check and Bessie got some spending money from her boyfriends. They gave some of this money to Cecil and Willie Mae to pay their rent, and gave Willie Mae money to cover her insurance and pay a small sum on a living room suite at the local furniture store. Willie Mae reciprocated later on by buying dresses for Bessie and Lily's daughters and by caring for all the children when Bessie got a temporary job. (Stack, 1974, p. 37)

Bloodmothers and Other Mothers.   Child keeping is a special form of swapping in the Flats and other black communities (Collins, 1990). Poverty makes it difficult for parents to care for children alone. In addition, the value of community responsibility is historically rooted in the culture of West Africa and the slave community of the South. Sharing child care in the black community is common, with various adults in addition to the parents sharing or entirely taking over the responsibility for raising a child.

Sometimes child keeping may be shared among parents and other adults for a short time. In other cases it may be for an extended period of years. Sometimes the child lives with one adult at a time. In other cases the child is literally shared, staying in one residence one night and another the next, or eating with one adult and sleeping in the home of another.

Children do not see this as being without a real parent but rather as having a number of real parents. Adults, likewise, do not treat their children differently depending on whether they are their natural children or network children. Rather, among many African Americans, adults feel a sense of responsibility for all children in the community (Collins, 1990).

Household and Family.   The domestic networks that comprise the families in the Flats are often spread over several addresses. On the other hand, people who are not nuclear family members may "double up" within a household. Where people sleep and eat and where they contribute money for the rent or spend their time is not necessarily concentrated in one physical location. The physical boundaries of families in the Flats are fluid. They range over several addresses; they change; and they overlap.

In middle-class nuclear families, in contrast, households and families tend to be the same. Nuclear family members live in a single family home, and other people do not live with them. A person who assumes that nuclear families are the only possible way in which to organize a family might look at families in the Flats and conclude that no family existed. A more careful examination, however, reveals that a family form does exist, although it is quite different from that of the middle-class nuclear family.

Extended Network Families in Racial Ethnic Communities. Child sharing among an extended network family is not unique to African American communities. John Red Horse (1980) describes this kind of family organization in some Native American societies. He explains: "An Indian family, therefore, is an active kinship system inclusive of parents, children, aunts, uncles, cousins and grandparents and is accompanied by the incorporation of significant non-kin who become family members" (Red Horse, 1980, p. 463).

Red Horse notes that sharing in the Native American community is sometimes informal, as it is for African Americans in the Flats, but also may be formally marked by naming rituals. In naming ceremonies, which may occur immediately after birth or later in a child's life, the child is given a name and an adult is chosen as the namesake. After the ceremony, the adult is responsible for the child and is obligated to set a good example and to help care for the child or to take over child care completely if the parent is unable to care for the child.

In the Chicano community, a similar system of shared child raising occurs, called *compadrazgo* (Dill, 1986). Many parents designate nonkin, *compadres,* as godparents *(padrinos* and *madrinas).* Godparents celebrate holidays and important rites of passage like first communion and marriage with their godchildren. They are also relied on for economic and social support in times of need to substitute in case of the death of a parent (Camarillo, 1979).

Asian American families, especially those that are recent immigrants to the United States, also rely on networks of kin and nonkin (Hein, 1993; Lockery, 1998). Jon Matsuoka (1990) explains that among Vietnamese and other Southeast Asian immigrants, a quickly expanding population, extended family includes not only those who are currently alive but ancestors and families of the future. Children are taught that their primary duty is to their family lineage. The dominant American ideology that emphasizes the individual and his or her place in a nuclear family has been problematic for Asian immigrants who believe that one's connections are much broader (Kitano & Daniels, 1988). Asian families illustrate the way in which child sharing not only implies a broad range of people who are responsible for children but also a range of people to whom children are obligated.

Women's Domestic Authority. This description of life in the Flats indicates that Moynihan's (1965) portrayal of the black community as one in which families were disrupted or chaotic was false. The families in the Flats were quite different from the stereotypical middle-class white family. But

65

they were highly organized and provided a source of survival in an impoverished community.

Moynihan (1965) also proposed that black families were matriarchal.
Stack (1974) investigated this issue as well and concluded that women in
the Flats were not matriarchal.

In a matriarchal society, power over households and the community as   70
a whole is controlled by older women. . . . The Flats was not matriarchal
because women were not powerful in the community. Power in the Flats
was wielded by landlords, employers, and especially the government
through the welfare office.

Stack found that women in the Flats also did not have matriarchal relationships with the men in their network families. Women had more authority relative to men than women in white middle-class, male-dominated
nuclear families. But decisions in the Flats tended to be made by groups of
people that included both women and men in the network. In more general
overviews of the question of the black matriarchy, no empirical data have
been shown to support its existence (McAdoo, 1988).

Immigrant Families

The percentage of the population living in the United States that was
born in another country was highest, about 14 percent, at the turn of the
nineteenth century. It fell steadily to a low of about 4.5 percent in 1970,
when it began to rise, reaching 8 percent in 1990. The proportion has never
been huge, but immigrants have been and continue to be an important part
of our population.

Earlier in the century, most immigrants came from Europe. Today
most come from Latin America and Asia. Mexico represents the largest
source country, with 13 percent of immigrants. It is followed by the Philippines (7 percent), Vietnam (6 percent), Dominican Republic (5 percent),
China (5 percent), and India (5 percent). Most immigrants are concentrated
in the following states: California (23 percent), New York (18 percent),
Florida (9 percent), Texas (7 percent), New Jersey (6 percent), and Illinois
(5 percent) (Littman, 1998).

Mexican Americans.   Until the middle of the nineteenth century, the
areas that we now call the states of New Mexico, California, Nevada, Utah,
Arizona, as well as most of Texas, half of Colorado, and a little bit of Oklahoma, Kansas, and Wyoming were part of Mexico. The Texas War of Independence and the Mexican-American War resulted in 814,145 square miles
of land becoming part of the Untied States (Russell, 1994). The people who
lived in those areas included many Mexicans and Native Americans as well
as Anglos who had migrated there before annexation. Since then, many
Mexican people born in the currently Mexican area have migrated into the
formerly Mexican area.

. . . Through births and continued immigration, the proportion of the   75
population that is Hispanic is predicted to grow from about 12.5 in 2000 to

about 25 percent in 2050. These data include people from many other Latin American nations besides Mexico, but ... Mexican Americans make up a significant percentage of the total Latino population.

Immigrant families face special kinds of problems. Julia Rodriguez (1988; see also Zavella, 1987) studied women who came north both to follow their husbands who were seeking work and to find jobs themselves. Their emigration from Mexico depended on their ability to obtain support from relatives and friends in Mexico who could help them obtain documents, pay for travel, and arrange for child care. In addition, some had to find child care for children they left temporarily in Mexico while they moved to the United States.

Once they arrived in the United States, the women quickly worked to become familiar with their new communities and to establish new networks to exchange goods. They also needed to establish information networks because of their special needs as new immigrants or undocumented workers so as to find employment, housing, health care, and schools in a new environment.

This kind of migration, which takes place in steps with some members following others, is called family stage migration (Hondagneu-Sotelo, 1997). Hondagneu-Sotelo (1997) has found that the process of migration creates change in gender relations within families. She reviews two periods of migration: pre-1965 and post-1965. In the 1950s and 1960s, ideas about what is properly masculine gave men the authority to act autonomously to decide to migrate. Gender expectations also told men that they were supposed to be good providers and therefore had to choose to leave their families. Properly gendered women had to accept their husband's decision, remain chaste, and stay behind to take care of the children despite their fears of becoming *mujer abandonada* (an abandoned woman) or being unable to handle the financial and social burdens of raising a family alone. After the 1970s, expectations about gender changed, and women were more likely to follow their husbands rather than stay behind.

Before 1965, men had come mostly unaccompanied and had stayed for long periods of time in bachelor communities in which many men shared households. Men learned to do work that had been reserved for women, like cooking, cleaning, and shopping. One man explained:

> Back in Mexico, I didn't know how to prepare food, iron a shirt, or wash my clothes. I only knew how to work, how to harvest. But when I found myself with certain urgencies here, I learned how to do everything that a woman can do to keep a man comfortable. And the custom stayed with me. . . . I now know how to prepare American food and Mexican food, while back in my country I didn't know to cook at all. Necessity forced me to do things which I had previously ignored. (Hondagneu-Sotelo, 1997, p. 480)

The men expressed pride in their newfound talents and continued to share these tasks when their wives joined them. At the same time, the long periods during which wives had been forced to take charge while their

MORE NONTRADITIONAL FAMILY UNITS

Guy, Chair, Three-Way Lamp

A Woman, Her Daughter, Forty-four
My Little Ponies

The Troy Triplets and Their
Personal Trainer

Two Guys, Two Gals, Two Phones,
a Fax, and a Blender

R. Chast

husbands were away changed them as well, making them more assertive and less subservient. One woman explained:

> When he came here [to the United States], everything changed. It was different. It was me who took the responsibility for putting food on the table, for keeping the children clothed, for tending the animals. I did all of these things alone, and in this way, I discovered my capacities. And do you know, these accomplishments gave me satisfaction. (Hondagneu-Sotelo, 1997, p. 479)

In households where the men had migrated after 1965 and their wives 　80 had quickly joined them, these kind of gender transitions had not occurred. The pre-1965 migrants' households were strikingly more egalitarian than the post-1965 households (Hondagneu-Sotelo, 1997).

Vietnamese Immigrant Families.   Vietnamese families have described similar experiences (Kibria, 1996). Traditional Vietnamese families were modeled on Confucian principles that organized extended families around a patriarch. Young brides joined their husbands' households, where they had little status and were subordinate and dependent on their husbands (Kandiyoti, 1988). If the wife lived long enough, however, she could expect in her old age to take her place at a higher level in the household hierarchy and enjoy deference and allegiance from younger members. This model began to change in Vietnam in the 1950s and 1960s as a result of the war.

Migration to the United States further challenged the traditional model for two reasons. First, Vietnamese women were more likely to find employment in the United States than men were, which created a shift in power that benefited women. Second, women began to organize social networks to help them survive in their new communities. They exchanged food, information, and strategies to use to negotiate institutions like social services, hospitals, and schools. The networks also became useful ways to control men inside households. For example, if men were abusive or tried to keep their wives from working outside the home, network members would intervene by mobilizing community opinion against them.

Kibria (1996) argues that these changes altered the patriarchal relations but did not transform them. Gender inequality remained intact despite immigration, although it was renegotiated. Access to economic resources improved for women, but such resources were too limited to provide independence. In addition, women themselves often wanted to maintain the old system because it allotted authority over children to them in their old age, which they did not wish to give up.

References

Anderson, Margaret. 1988. *Thinking about women: Sociological perspectives on sex and gender.* 2d ed. New York: Macmillan.

Bedard, Marcia. 1992. *Breaking with tradition: Diversity, conflict and change in contemporary American families.* Dix Hills, NY: General Hall.

Billingsley, Andrew. 1968. *Black families in white America.* Englewood Cliffs, NJ: Prentice-Hall.

Braun, Denny. 1991. *The rich get richer: The rise of income inequality in the U.S. and the world.* Chicago: Nelson Hall.

Camarillo, Albert. 1979. *Chicanos in a changing society: From Mexican pueblos to American barrios in Santa Barbara and Southern California, 1848–1930.* Cambridge, MA: Harvard University Press.

Collins, Patricia Hill. 1990. *Black feminist thought: Knowledge, consciousness and the politics of empowerment.* New York: Harper Collins.

Coontz, Stephanie. 1992. *The way we never were: American families and the nostalgia trap.* New York: Basic Books.

Dill, Bonnie Thornton. 1986. *Our mother's grief: Racial ethnic women and the maintenance of families.* Memphis, TN: MSU Center for Research on Women.

Domhoff, William. 1970. *The higher circles: The governing class in America.* New York: Random House.

Eitzen, D. Stanley. 1985. *In conflict and order: Understanding society.* 3d ed. Boston: Allyn and Bacon.

Gaylord, Maxine. 1984. Relocation and the corporate family. In R. Voydanoff (ed.), *Work and family: Changing roles of women and men* (pp. 144–152). Palo Alto, CA: Mayfield.

Giddings, Paula. 1984. *When and where I enter: The impact of black women on race and sex in America.* New York: Bantam Books.

Gittens, Diane. 1998. The family in question: Is it universal? In S. Ferguson (ed.), *Shifting the center: Understanding contemporary families* (pp. 1–12). Mountain View, CA: Mayfield.

Gresham, Jewell. 1989. White patriarchal supremacy: The politics of family in America. *Nation* 249 (4):116–121.

Harrison, Lee. 1991. California report. *Personnel Journal* 70 (October):26.

Hein, Jeremy. 1993. *States and international migrants: The incorporation of Indochinese refugees in the U.S. and France.* San Francisco: Westview.

Hendershott, Anne. 1995. *Moving for work: The sociology of relocating in the 1990s.* New York: University Press of America.

Higgenbotham, Elizabeth. 1981. Is marriage a priority? Class differences in marital options of educated black women. In P. Stein (ed.), *Single life: Unmarried adults in social context* (pp. 259–267). New York: St. Martin's Press.

Hondagneu-Sotelo, Pierrette. 1997. Overcoming patriarchal constraints: The reconstruction of gender relations among Mexican immigrant women and men. In M. Baca Zinn, P. Hondagneu-Sotelo, and M. Messner (eds.), *Through the prism of difference: Readings on sex and gender* (pp. 477–485). Boston: Allyn and Bacon.

Hunter, Andrea, and Sherrill Sellers. 1998. Feminist attitudes among African American women and men. *Gender and Society* 12 (1):81–99.

Kandiyoti, D. 1988. Bargaining with patriarchy. *Gender and Society* 2:274–291.

Katz, Michael. 1989. *The undeserving poor: From the war on poverty to the war on welfare.* New York: Pantheon.

Kibria, Nazli. 1996. Power, patriarchy and gender conflict in the Vietnamese immigrant community. In E. Chow, D. Wilkinson, and M. Baca Zinn (eds.),

Race, class and gender: Common bonds, different voices (pp. 206–222). Thousand Oaks, CA: Sage.

Kitano, Harry, and Roger Daniels. 1988. *Asian Americans: Emerging minorities.* Englewood Cliffs, NJ: Prentice Hall.

Ladner, Joyce. 1971. *Tomorrow's tomorrow: The black woman.* Garden City, NY: Doubleday.

Lee, Dwight. 1986. Government policy and the distortions in family housing. In J. Peden and F. Glahe (eds.), *American family and the state* (pp. 310–320). San Francisco: Pacific Research Institute.

Littman, Mark, ed. 1998. *Statistical portrait of U.S.: Social conditions and trends, 1998.* Lanham, MD: Bernan Press.

Lockery, Shirley. 1998. Caregiving among racial and ethnic minority elders: Family and social supports. In E. Stanford and F. Torres-Gil (eds.), *Diversity: New approaches to ethnic minority aging* (pp. 113–122). Amityville, NY: Baywood.

Mack, Delores. 1978. The power relations in black families and white families. In R. Staples (ed.), *The black family* (pp. 144–149). Belmont, CA: Wadsworth.

Matsuoka, Jon. 1990. Differential acculturation among Vietnamese refugees. *Social Work* 35:341–345.

McAdoo, John. 1988. Roles of black fathers in the socialization of black children. In H. McAdoo (ed.), *Black families.* Newbury Park, CA: Sage.

Middleton, R., and S. Putney. 1960. Dominance in decisions in the family: Race and class differences. *American Journal of Sociology* 65 (6):605–609.

Millman, Marcia. 1991. *Warm hearts and cold cash: The intimate dynamics of families and money.* New York: Free Press.

Mills, C. Wright. 1956. *The power elite.* London: Oxford University Press.

Morgan, David. 1985. *The family, politics and social theory.* Boston: Routledge and Kegan Paul.

Moynihan, Daniel. 1965. *The Negro family: The case for national action.* Office of Policy Planning and Research, U.S. Department of Labor. Washington, DC: GPO.

Ostrander, Susan. 1984. *Women of the upper class.* Philadelphia: Temple University Press.

Rainwater, Lee, and William Yancey. 1967. *The Moynihan Report and the politics of the controversy.* Cambridge, MA: MIT Press.

Rapp, Rayna. 1982. Family and class in contemporary America: Notes toward an understanding of ideology. In B. Thorne with M. Yalom (eds.), *Rethinking the family: Some feminist questions* (pp. 168–187). New York: Longman.

Red Horse, John. 1980. Family structure and value orientation in American Indians. *Social Casework: The Journal of Contemporary Social Work* 59:462–467.

Rodriguez, Julia. 1988. Labor migration and familial responsibilities: Experience of Mexican women. In M. Melville (ed.), *Mexicanas at work in the U.S.* (pp. 47–63). Houston: University of Houston Press.

Rubin, Lillian. 1976. *Worlds of pain: Life in working class families.* New York: Basic Books.

Russell, James. 1994. *After the fifth sun: Class and race in North America.* Englewood Cliffs, NJ: Prentice Hall.

Ryan, William. 1971. *Blaming the victim.* New York: Random House.

Seidenberg, R. 1973. *Corporate wives — corporate casualties?* New York: Amacon.

Simmel, Georg. (1907/1978). *The philosophy of money.* London: Routledge and Kegan Paul.

Stacey, Judith. 1990. *Brave new families: Stories of domestic upheaval in late twentieth century America.* New York: Basic Books.

Stack, Carol. 1974. *All our kin: Strategies for survival in the black community.* New York: Harper and Row.

Staples, Robert. 1981. The myth of the black matriarchy. *Black Scholar,* December, 32.

TenHouten, W. 1970. The black family: Myth and reality. *Psychiatry* 25:145–173.

Wilkinson, Doris. 1984. Afro-American women and their families. *Marriage and Family Review* 7 (Fall): 459–467.

Willie, Charles. 1983. *Race, ethnicity and socioeconomic status: A theoretical analysis of their interrelationship.* Dix Hills, NY: General Hall.

Willie, Charles. 1985. *Black and white families: A study in complementarity.* Bayside, NY: General Hall.

Willie, Charles. 1988. *A new look at black families.* 3d ed. Bayside, NY: General Hall.

Zavella, Patricia. 1987. *Women's work and Chicano families: Cannery workers of the Santa Clara Valley.* Ithaca: Cornell University Press.

ENGAGING THE TEXT

1. Review the distinguishing characteristics Aulette associates with upper-class families — for example, volunteering and learning not to spend down capital. Explain how these practices function to mark and maintain social status. Also discuss how well these characteristics match your own impressions of upper-class families — based on personal experience or on portrayals of the wealthy in books, TV, and movies.

2. In paragraph 16, Aulette associates four factors with middle-class American families. If possible, test these four factors against the family histories of your classmates. For example, do you find "geographical mobility resulting in residences away from kin"? Taken as a whole, does the students' experience support the significance of the four factors Aulette identifies?

3. Working in groups, make a large version of the chart below and fill in the rows and columns with the characteristics Aulette says researchers have discovered.

	Middle Class	*Working Class*
White Families	(**Example**) Huge emphasis on education	Ambivalence about education
Black Families		

What evidence can you find in your reading or personal experience to support or challenge these generalizations? What useful purpose, if any, is served by such generalizations about family, class, and race?

4. Describe the significance of the Moynihan Report, and summarize the problems or errors Aulette identifies in the report. (Note in particular Aulette's extensive summary of research carried out by Carol Stack in "the Flats.") Then discuss how Moynihan's analysis of black families could be so influential if it was indeed so seriously flawed.

EXPLORING CONNECTIONS

5. Review Aulette's discussion of African American families and reread "Aunt Ida Pieces a Quilt" (p. 48). Discuss what social class Aunt Ida's family seems to belong to and consider how Aulette might view the actions of the women in the poem. To what extent do the authors seem to share similar perspectives on black families?

6. Review "An Indian Story" (p. 51). Cite specific ways in which the family described in Roger Jack's narrative fits or fails to fit Aulette's brief description of Native American families (paras. 64–65). Does the family in "An Indian Story" show any of the characteristics Aulette associates with working-class African American families (pp. 68–73)? How would you account for the differences and similarities you see?

7. Look at the photo "Affluence" on page 259. List a dozen or more details that Aulette would say marks the man's upper-class status. To what extent can you connect these details to the man's family life?

EXTENDING THE CRITICAL CONTEXT

8. Aulette describes many family types in the selection above. Which type or types offer the best fit to your own family? Explain how Aulette's generalizations reflect your individual family, and describe any ways in which your family is unlike the patterns researchers see.

Visual Portfolio
Reading Images of American Families

HDTV. It's A Joy.

Simply from Samsung. For the digital generation. High-Definition Television. The ultimate viewing experience from the world leader in extrasensory reception. Picture and sound so clear, you won't believe your eyes and ears. Samsung's Tantus HDTV is the finest high-definition (1080i resolution), 55" widescreen (16:9 display design), fully-integrated system you can buy. Samsung circuitry transforms your regular television signal into absolute clarity. And the 45-watt Dolby Digital* system makes it sound-sational. A dreamlike experience: reality will never seem the same. Tantus HDTV. The beginning of a new era in home entertainment. For more information on Samsung's full line of digital televisions, call 1 800 SAMSUNG or visit our web site at www.samsungdigital.com

SAMSUNG
DIGITAL

Visual Portfolio

READING IMAGES OF AMERICAN FAMILIES

1. The first image in the portfolio shows a family posing for a group photograph. What might be the occasion for this photo? Who do you think the people are, and what are their relationships? What impressions do you get about them from their facial expressions, their clothing, and the room and its furnishings? In terms of its messages about family, how closely does this image resemble those painted by Norman Rockwell that appear on pages 22–24?

2. The photograph of Thomas Jefferson's descendants is clearly posed. Explain in detail why you think photographer Erica Burger constructed the image as she did.

3. The photograph on page 82 encompasses more than 250 years of American history, from Thomas Jefferson's birth in 1743 to 1999. What parts of American history can you link to specific details in the photo? What does the photo say to you about the next century of American history?

4. What ideas and emotions do you think are most strongly projected by the image of the gay fathers on page 83, and what specific elements of the photograph help convey these ideas and emotions? Do you think the image is constructed to advocate same-sex parenting? Finally, compare the image to "Freedom from Fear" by Norman Rockwell (p. 24) in terms of its portrayal of marriage and parenting.

5. First, describe your initial reaction to the photograph of the lesbian brides; for example, did it surprise you or work against your expectations? Next, tell the story of this picture: discuss what's happening and find out if your classmates "read" the photo in the same way you do. Explain the significance of as many details in the image as possible — for example, gowns, facial expression, setting, and background. This photograph was published with the caption, "Love and Marriage"; explain why you think it is or is not a good title for the image.

6. What is the emotional impact of the photograph of a woman bathing her child in a washtub in the kitchen? What do you feel when you see this image, and why? Why does the photographer consider this moment worthy of our attention?

7. One of Samsung's objectives (p. 86) is to grab your attention with a dramatic and unusual image: you have presumably never seen a 55-inch TV atop a baby carriage. But why does the company choose, of all things in the world, a baby carriage? Analyze Samsung's strategy and explain what the image and the strategy imply about the American family. Also discuss the caption, "HDTV. It's A Joy."

8. Compare any of these contemporary images to one or more of the Norman Rockwell paintings that opened this chapter (pp. 22–24). What questions does this comparison raise?

It Takes a Family: Conservatism and the Common Good

RICK SANTORUM

According to former U.S. senator Rick Santorum, the traditional ideal American family — husband, wife, and kids in a stable and loving environment — should be the desired norm in American culture; supporting the traditional nuclear family should be a goal actively pursued by government, business, religion, communities, and individuals. Drawing on extensive sociological research, Santorum argues that two-parent families function best and that the best communities have many such families. From this vantage point, liberal legislators, judges, and media have hurt American society by making divorce too easy, by tolerating or encouraging cohabitation before marriage, and by endorsing gay and lesbian marriage. Rick Santorum represented Pennsylvania in the U.S. Senate from 1995 to 2007 and is a prominent conservative spokesman on family issues. The selection reprinted here is from his book It Takes a Family: Conservatism and the Common Good *(2005).*

Families and the Common Good

It is an open and shut case: the best place for kids to grow up is with a happily married mom and dad, and the more of these families there are in a community, the better it is for everyone.

Crime, for example, is directly related to family structure. We should *know* this from common sense and our own life experiences. But for those who need a study to prove what is obvious, I have a bunch. In one study of more than 6,000 young men ages 14 to 22, it was found that boys who grew up without a married mother and father were more than *twice* as likely to end up in jail as boys who did. This proved true even after taking into account factors such as a mother's education level, race, family income, and community unemployment rates and median income.

Other studies have shown that broken homes can increase the delinquency in a community by 10 to 15 percent, and the proportion of single-parent households in a community predicts the rate of violent crime and burglary much better than a community's level of poverty.

Recent research has also shown that healthy communities and healthy families support each other and make it more likely that kids will do well. Good communities are more able to benefit from the value of healthy families, and healthy families are more able to benefit from the value of good communities. For example, teenage boys who come from strong families living in a good neighborhood are less likely to get into fights than boys who come from a good family or a good neighborhood but not from both.

Having said all that, I have to say two more things. First, lots of single 5
parents do a wonderful job raising children. It's not only possible that
children can experience positive outcomes growing up in a single-parent
household; depending on the neighborhood and the single parent's own
family history, it is more likely than not. But, as Dr. Wade Horn, an assistant
secretary at the U.S. Department of Health and Human Services and
one of the Bush administration's foremost experts on family life, points
out, the risks for children are simply greater when they grow up in a single-
parent home. Dr. Horn often compares it to two airplanes. One nearly
always gets you to your destination safely. The other gets you there most of
the time, but significantly less often than the first. Both planes offer at least
pretty good odds, but every one of us would choose the first plane. Well,
when it comes to children, the first plane is a family headed by a mother
and father in a healthy marriage. The second plane is the single-parent
home.

Second, I want to be sure that we avoid the trap of somehow presenting
father absence as an inner-city, minority problem. It is not. In absolute
numbers, there are more white than black children growing up without
fathers today. And father absence isn't just about men who get women
pregnant and then abandon them. It is about emotional detachment as well:
middle-class men whose lives center around work and the golf course
instead of around their wives and children, for example. And as I just said,
it's about divorce: very much about divorce. Divorce leads to father abandonment much more often than people recognize, despite the constant
attempts by the popular culture to paint a picture of the "happily" divorced.
(I don't mean to browbeat divorced men and women, but I do think that
they will agree that at the heart of every divorce there is a tragedy — one
which the popular culture pretends does not exist.) In a childless marriage,
it is conceivable that the No-Fault Freedom caveat may be true (i.e., "as
long as no gets hurt"), but this is virtually impossible when children are
involved. In disrupted families, only about one child in six sees his father as
much as once a week. Ten years after a marriage breaks up, research has
shown that approximately two-thirds of children report that they haven't
seen their father for over a year.

I have met with my share of fatherhood-rights groups, so I know that
the divorce courts are often not kind to fathers. I also know that divorced
wives can make it difficult for the fathers of their children to visit. Personally, I cannot imagine the pain of not being able to be a part of my children's formative years. But fathers, let's be honest with ourselves: decisions
have consequences — for us, and for our children.

Marriage matters because children matter. Without marriage, children
suffer. There is simply no better investment parents can make in their children's future than a healthy marriage. For my wife Karen and me, marriage
is a sacred vocation. We give ourselves to each other: mind, body, and soul.
Nothing in this world is more important to me than the happiness and well-
being of my wife and children. It is my most important job. All of my

strength comes from my love for them and God's love for me. When children live with parents who love each other, sacrifice for each other, and are committed to each other, they are given a real head start on life.

Children living outside of wedlock get hurt. And here are some more hard numbers:

One study analyzing the outcomes of over one million children ages   10
one to four found that children born to unmarried parents are at greater risk of dying from an injury, even after taking into account differences in income, education, race, and age.

Children living in single-parent homes are as much as twice as likely to suffer physical, emotional, or educational neglect. The overall rate of child abuse and neglect in single-parent homes is 27.3 per 1,000 children, while in two-parent households it is 15.5 per 1,000. It is lower still in two-parent *married* households.

According to one large national study, teenagers in single-parent households or households with a stepparent are at 1.5 to 2.5 times the risk of using illegal drugs as are teens living with their mother and father.

Children who live with only one parent have poorer grades, poorer attendance records, and higher dropout rates at school than students who come home to a two-parent household.

Finally, children in single-mother families are 1.5 to 2 times more likely to have behavioral or emotional problems than kids living with a married mother and father.

I could go on. The research making this point could fill a book bigger   15
than this one. Every statistic that I am aware of — and I would be eager to hear if there is even *one* on the other side — indicates that marriage is better for children, and usually by a very large margin. Back in the 1960s and 1970s when the village elders[1] pressed to make divorce easier through no-fault divorce laws and championed the legitimacy of "alternative lifestyles," we didn't really have evidence about the effect of these revolutions on children. Now we *know*.

That's why there should really be no family "debate," no marriage "debate." The social science evidence, four thousand years of human history, and common sense have long settled the question. In a decent society, every child should have the best shot at growing up to be a healthy and successful adult. That opportunity is found in healthy, married, mom-and-dad families. The traditional family is not about some "special interest." It's about the rights of parents and children, and ultimately it's about the common good.

There should be no argument that a married mother-and-father household is the best place for raising kids. The problem is, we don't do anything about it. And part of the problem is that our government and many social

---

[1]*village elders:* Santorum's term for "the liberal elite" who want to order society by imposing control through large institutions such as the government.

service agencies often do a lousy job of supporting healthy marriages and repairing unhealthy ones.

The common myth is that the reason high percentages of children in low-income, minority communities are living without a father is because men get women pregnant and, if the women are not convinced by the fathers and their peers to abort the children, the men disappear from their lives. But the truth is more complicated. Eighty-two percent of urban, low-income fathers and mothers are in a romantic relationship at the time their child is born. The vast majority of these expect that they will get married. One major study of urban parents found that, of those who were not living together but were romantically involved at the time their baby was born, more than 80 percent of both the mothers and the fathers expected that they would marry or, at the least though certainly not as good, live together. But a year later, in this study, just 11 percent of these couples had actually married. We know that over time, fathers who are not married to their children's mother begin to disappear. So what is happening here? What is going wrong so that couples that have a baby, who want to get married and think they will get married, end up not getting married?

"When low-income couples have a child out of wedlock and they are considering marriage, they are met with a deafening silence from the existing social services delivery network," is how Dr. Horn explains it. "Instead of a social services system that supports and encourages them to pursue their choice of marriage, they are told that, rather, the goal is for the father to simply sign a paternity establishment paper."

In other words, the government in the form of the social worker   20
communicates loud and clear that it doesn't believe low-income, minority couples can maintain a marriage. It effectively says: don't bother trying, just be sure the father establishes paternity so we can come after him for child support. But where are the churches, the civic groups, and community organizations? Have they given up hope as well? Sadly, the answer is, with a few notable exceptions, yes. We've gone from the days of shotgun marriage (which I'm not sure in some cases was all that bad) to the days of shotgun paternity establishment. As communities facing out-of-wedlock pregnancy, we've gone from common concern to common indifference.

Jason Krofsky works for Families Northwest, a pro-family organization based in Washington State and founded by former pro football player Jeff Kemp. Jason heads up the work they do in communities throughout the Pacific Northwest to build partnerships among government, businesses, religious institutions, and community- and faith-based organizations to support healthy families and strong marriages. Invariably, he says, he finds that most religious leaders are just as guilty as the government when it comes to believing the institution of marriage is beyond repair, especially in inner-city communities.

Further evidence that our society is somehow having a terrible effect on family ties comes in a study of the experience of immigrant Latino families versus Latino families who have been in this country more than one generation. Immigrant Latino teenagers — that is, youth who came to this country with their families — are less likely to engage in unhealthy risk behaviors, such as violence and fighting, than Latino teenagers who were born in this country. This is true even though immigrant Latino teenagers tend to live in families and neighborhoods that are poorer than those of later-generation Latino youths.

Why is this? What does this country do to families that chips away, even tears down, the foundation that kids need to grow up healthy and secure? I think the answer lies in the erosion of the kinds of capital[2] I discussed earlier. A society rich in social, cultural, and moral capital — like America in previous generations — supports and nurtures families. A society in which those kinds of capital have eroded creates something like a vacuum, sucking the life out of families.

We've wasted decades and countless lives under the direction of the village elders trying to build bureaucracies to aid the poor and marginal in our society, while ignoring the central importance of the traditional family. We must stop pretending that the health of the mom-and-dad family isn't really important. Conservatives always knew this was a mistake, but, to be quite candid, failed to offer an alternative vision; now, thanks to the social science evidence, we *all* know that this was a mistake. We need to spend the coming decades working to build up traditional families. What is it that stands against us in this effort? The village elders and their well-funded special interests — and they will not go away quietly.

The Meaning of Family

I have been talking about the "traditional" family. By that, I mean a   25
family constituted by a mother and a father who have committed themselves to each other in lifelong marriage, together with their children. This is "traditional," but the reason it is a traditional relationship is because it is fundamentally *natural*. But it is just there that the village elders dig in their heels and cry "Foul!" To the liberal mind, such a definition is "restrictive." It limits our "freedom" to choose who and how we will love. It "excludes" what liberals like to think of as simply "different kinds of families," no better and no worse than the natural family. Liberals get nervous at the very word *natural*, since nature is what we are as human beings, which we cannot change or choose otherwise.

---

[2]*capital:* According to Santorum, the "five pillars of American civilization" are social capital (trust, mutual responsibility, and connectedness), economic capital (financially secure families), moral capital (virtue, proper conduct, and respect for human life), cultural capital (the stories, images, songs, and arts that explain who we are), and intellectual capital (our traditions of education and schooling).

In the tradition of my own faith community, the Catholic Church, we speak about the *natural law*, which we might think of as the operating instructions for human beings. The promise of the natural law is that we will be happiest, and freest, when we follow the law built into our nature as men and women. For liberals, however, *nature* is too confining, and thus is the enemy of *freedom.* Consequently, when liberals think about society, they see only "individuals" — *not* men and women and children. Men and women and children have natures, but liberal "individuals" are abstractions, free to choose anything at all and unconfined by purportedly illusory factors like gender. At first, the liberal vision may sound attractive — because freedom is attractive. The only problem is that it is a false vision, because nature is nature, and the freedom to choose against the natural law is not really freedom at all.

That all sounds pretty philosophical. But take cohabitation, or living together outside of marriage, as an example. Today's conventional wisdom holds that it is better than harmless, that it is a healthy way for a couple to "test drive" marriage. Some even say that cohabitation is better than marriage, since people should be together only when they are in love with one another, and we can never know how and whom we will love in the future: a vow of lifelong love, they say, is unrealistic. Today, the majority of men and women under the age of 30 believe that living together before marriage is a good way to avoid an eventual divorce. About half of all unmarried women between the ages of 25 and 39 have lived with a man whom they were not married to at some point in the past, and about one-quarter are currently living with a man without the benefit of marriage.

The problem is that the myth that living together leads to better marriages is wrong. The opposite is true. One study found that marriages preceded by cohabitation have nearly a 50 percent greater chance of ending in divorce than marriages that were not preceded by cohabitation. Furthermore, children born to parents who are just living together instead of married do not fare very well. Teenagers, for example, growing up with unmarried, cohabiting parents have more emotional and behavioral problems than do teenagers living with their married mother and father.

Despite all the evidence, as a society today we will go to almost any length to avoid telling ourselves, and others, the truth: marriage is better than living together. Too few of us dare say living together without the benefit of marriage is *wrong.* We are afraid to make any such "value judgment." But that is exactly what we need to do. We parents owe it to our children to be honest, to give them a vision of the highest good. Failure to affirm a moral vision to our children is a form of *abandonment* by parents and by society. It leaves our children defenseless against the endless parade of influences the popular culture has in store for them.

And we need to be honest about the latest liberal assault on our marriage tradition as well. Even a year or two ago, few Americans imagined that we would be facing the issue of same-sex marriage today. Thanks to a few 30 activist justices on the U.S. Supreme Court and to even more activist judges[3] in Massachusetts, however, America is on the verge of undergoing a social revolution simply without any historical precedent. There are few places where the clash between what freedom means and its impact on families is clearer than when it comes to transforming the definition of marriage.

Liberals believe that the traditional family is neither natural nor vital, that it's an antiquated social convention which has not only outlived its usefulness, but is now inherently discriminatory and repressive toward legitimate alternative "families." As the Massachusetts high court said to the legislature of Massachusetts concerning the *Goodrich* case, "For no rational reason the marriage laws of the Commonwealth discriminate against a defined class (homosexuals); no amount of tinkering with language will eradicate that stain." So traditional marriage is a stain on the fabric of America that needs to be "Shouted out." How have we come to this?

It may come as a shock to some, but marriage is not, and never has been, just about the sex life of consenting adults. However, given the self-centeredness of our popular culture, it is not surprising that many adults today see marriage as about them being happy as *individuals.* This is one of the reasons our divorce rate is so high. Since marriage has become more and more about adult happiness, and less and less about children and their well-being, it is no wonder other groups in society want to use marriage for the same purpose. In fact, one of the criticisms I often hear when I speak with proponents of same-sex marriage is that heterosexuals have so deconstructed marriage through no-fault divorce that today marriage is only about adults, so why shouldn't it include them too? Touché! But do I need to say in response that two wrongs don't make a right?

Society's interest in protecting marriage goes beyond the public recognition of a romantic relationship and making people feel accepted. I've made the case that the reason our society has such a strong interest in strengthening the institution of marriage is because marriage as we traditionally understood it is far and away the best place for raising children — who happen to be the future of any society. All of the "legal incidents" of marriage built up over the years aim to secure a stable family in which to welcome children. Every known society has some form of marriage. And it's always about bringing together a male and female into the kind of sexual union where the interests of children under the care of their own mother and father are protected. Marriage is the word for the way in which we connect a man, a woman, and their children into one loving family. It represents our best attempt to see that every child receives his or her birthright:

---

[3]*activist justices . . . activist judges:* "Activist" is used pejoratively here to critique judges who use the power of the court to shape public policy; in contrast, many liberals praise "activist" decisions such as *Brown v. Topeka Board of Education* (1954), which ruled the racial segregation of public schools unconstitutional.

the right to know and be known by, to love and be loved by, his or her own mother and father.

When liberals, through unelected judges, order us to change this understanding of marriage into something radically different, the result is likely to be dangerous for children and for society. When the state declares two men marrying is just as valuable to society as the union of husband and wife, this is not neutrality, it is radical social engineering. It commits the government to the position that family structure does not matter; that children don't need fathers (or mothers for that matter), just abstract individual "caregivers." It shifts marriage further away from its core purpose of protecting the needs of (and the need for) children. It would transform our public understanding of marriage so that marriage would mean something like mere cohabitation, an adult relationship to be formed as adults please, rather than as children need.

Do we need to confuse future generations of Americans even more   35 about the role and importance of an institution that is so critical to the common good? It is because children have a right to a faithfully married mother and father that we must oppose this radical redefinition — not because we are mean-spirited.

Moreover, once the government commits to same-sex marriage as a civil right, it will use the power of the state to enforce this new vision of marriage. Public schools will teach it, of course. But the logic of same-sex marriage will lead inevitably to even more government intrusion on the freedom of people and faith communities who continue to define marriage as the union of husbands and wives. What do I mean? When in *Loving v. Virginia* the Supreme Court ruled that state laws banning interracial marriage were unconstitutional, that ruling seemed at first to affect only private individuals. But sixteen years later, the IRS ruled that religious groups that opposed interracial marriage could be stripped of their tax-exempt status, because they were not operating for the public good. The Supreme Court ruled furthermore that the First Amendment's protection of the free exercise of religion provided no defense. Of course, I agree that laws against interracial marriage were unjust. My point is this: If we apply the logic of a civil right to same-sex marriage, people who believe children need mothers and fathers will be treated in the public square like racists, and churches that persist in teaching the traditional norm will risk the loss of their tax-exempt status. In other words, such churches will be treated as outlaws. How can we turn boys into good family men in a society that treats the idea that fathers matter as a form of bigotry?

Same-sex marriage is really "liberal marriage." That is, the "right" of homosexuals to "marry" one another is a logical result of what *must* happen to the definition of marriage if we view society as composed of nothing but abstract, autonomous *individuals*, rather than of men and women with their given natures. Abstract individuals, after all, are completely interchangeable and completely "free" to define who and what they are. To the liberal mind, therefore, there is no "rational basis" for limiting marriage only to people of opposite sexes: and that is what the four left-wing judges in Massachusetts held. Our village elders now declare that those holding to the traditional understanding of marriage are simply irrational.

But there is one more thing about these abstract, autonomous individuals that the left say are the real basis of society. Call it the liberal's marriage paradox. Individuals are free to do anything they want, including to redefine marriage, gender, and basic social institutions in pursuit of individual desire and preference. There is only one thing that individuals cannot do if they are to remain autonomous: they cannot commit themselves permanently to another human being. To do so would be a kind of slavery. As a result, the left's view of any marriage contract is that it is really only a kind of cohabitation, the choice of two people, each day, to continue together, but always with the perfect freedom to leave whenever either chooses. Of course, all too many marriages today end in divorce, and to most Americans that is a tragedy. But in "liberal marriage," there can never be any real expectation of permanence. In a society in which the liberal understanding of marriage becomes the law of the land, divorce would not only be the norm rather than the exception, but the institution of marriage would disappear altogether.

Bibliographical Note

First of all, at various points in the book there are extended quotations from individuals, usually social entrepreneurs such as Scott Syphax or Jeremy Nowak. Unless otherwise indicated, these are taken from interviews conducted either by myself or by Jeffrey Rosenberg. There are also numerous quotations from American founding fathers. These can be found in *The Founders' Constitution* (five volumes), Philip B. Kurland and Ralph Lerner, eds. (Indianapolis: Liberty Fund, 2000) or in *The Founders' Almanac,* Matthew Spalding, ed. (Washington, DC: Heritage Foundation, 2001). Sometimes I have also briefly quoted from journalistic sources: in nearly every case, these quotations can be found on the Internet.

In Part One ("It Takes a Family"), I cite Russell Kirk's notion of conservatism as "stewardship of a patrimony," and this becomes a major theme in the book. Kirk's most famous work is *The Conservative Mind* (Chicago: Henry Regnery, 1953), but a more accessible illustration of the stewardship approach to political and social questions is offered in the essays collected in Kirk's *Redeeming the Time* (Wilmington, DE: ISI Books, 1999). I also cite Mary Eberstadt's *Home-Alone America* (New York: Sentinel, 2004).

This first section is swarming with statistics, and unfortunately, these come from a swarm of sources. Among the important sources for comparative data on outcomes for children in various family forms, I have learned in particular from work by Sara McLanahan. For example, her book, with Gary Sandefur, *Growing Up with a Single Parent: What Hurts, What Helps* (Cambridge, MA: Harvard University Press, 1994). Also her study, with several coauthors, "The Fragile Families and Child Wellbeing Study Baseline

National Report," and her study, with Cynthia Harper, "Father Absence and Youth Incarceration," both prepared for the Center for Research on Child Wellbeing at Princeton. Other statistics first appeared in L. Edwards Wells and Joseph H. Rankin, "Families and Delinquency: A Meta-Analysis of the Impact of Broken Homes," *Social Problems* 38 (1): 71–93; Douglas A. Smith and G. Roger Jarjoura, "Social Structure and Criminal Victimization," *Journal of Research in Crime and Delinquency* (February 1988): 27–52; Kathleen M. Roche, et al., "Neighborhood Variations in the Salience of Family Support to Boys' Fighting," *Journal of Adolescent & Family Health* 3 (2): 55–64; Seth J. Scholer, Edward F. Mitchel Jr., and Wayne A. Ray, "Predictors of Injury Mortality in Early Childhood," *Pediatrics* 100 (1997): 342–47; and John P. Hoffmann and Robert A. Johnson, "A National Portrait of Family Structure and Adolescent Drug Use," *Journal of Marriage and the Family* 60: 633–45.

Data on cohabitation comes from work by the Center for Research on Child Wellbeing, the Urban Institute in Washington, D.C., and the National Marriage Project in Piscataway, New Jersey—and from Larry Bumpass and L. Hsien-Hen, "Trends in Cohabitation and Implications for Children's Family Contexts in the U.S.," *Population Studies* 54: 29–41; and Alfred DeMaris and K. Baninadha Rao, "Premarital Cohabitation and Subsequent Marital Stability in the United States: A Reassessment," *Journal of Marriage and the Family* 54: 178–90.

Engaging the Text

1. Santorum writes that it's an "open and shut case" that "the best place for kids to grow up is with a happily married mom and dad" (para. 1). List the main claims he makes to back up this assertion; then evaluate his reasoning and evidence for each claim. Explain why you agree or disagree that it's an open and shut case.

2. How do government laws and policies influence what is sometimes considered the "private sphere" of family life? What do you think is the proper role of government in promoting or discouraging particular modes of family life or in regulating marriage, divorce, custody of children, and cohabitation? To what extent should civil law reflect "natural law" as described by Santorum in paragraphs 25–26?

3. Santorum critiques religious leaders for doing too little to defend traditional marriage (para. 21). What do you think is the proper role of organized religion in shaping public policy on families? To what extent do religious leaders in your community influence public opinion or public policy on issues like divorce and same-sex marriage?

4. Analyze Dr. Wade Horn's metaphor comparing a single-parent household to an airplane that doesn't always reach its destination safely (para. 5).

5. Debate the last sentence of the excerpt: "In a society in which the liberal understanding of marriage becomes the law of the land, divorce would not

only be the norm rather than the exception, but the institution of marriage would disappear altogether."

EXPLORING CONNECTIONS

6. How might Santorum evaluate the families in "Looking for Work" by Gary Soto (p. 26) and "Aunt Ida Pieces a Quilt" by Melvin Dixon (p. 48)? What effects does "father absence" (para. 6) have on these families? How important is father absence compared with other factors in their lives such as ethnicity, education, and social class?

7. Review the images of the gay and lesbian couples in this chapter's Visual Portfolio (pp. 83, 84). Explain how the images themselves might be said to "argue" against Santorum's views. To extend the assignment, write a letter from one of the couples to the senator.

8. How might Roger Jack or one of the people he portrays in "An Indian Story" (p. 51) respond to Santorum's arguments? What relevance, if any, do these issues have for Native Americans and for tribal cultures?

EXTENDING THE CRITICAL CONTEXT

9. Devise a simple anonymous survey to test for a correlation between family structure and "positive outcomes" for kids (para. 5). Administer it in your own class or more widely and discuss the results. How would you expect the results to differ if you surveyed a representative cross-section of your state?

10. Consider marriage and divorce as portrayed in popular culture (for example, movies, TV shows, ads, popular songs, billboards, comic strips). Cite specific examples to support or challenge Santorum's assertions that there are "constant attempts by popular culture to paint a picture of the 'happily' divorced" (para. 6) and that children may be "defenseless against the endless parade of influences the popular culture has in store for them" (para. 29).

What Is Marriage?

EVAN WOLFSON

Marriage involves a legally binding contract, a moral commitment, a change in familial ties, and in some cases, a religious rite. Evan Wolfson explores the nature of this complex yet familiar state in the following selection. Wolfson, named by Time *magazine in 2004 as among the 100 most powerful and influential people in the world, has had a distinguished and diverse career. Educated at Yale College and Harvard Law School, he spent two years in the Peace Corps, participated in the investigation of the Iran-*

*Contra scandal that rocked the Reagan presidency, and appeared before the
U.S. Supreme Court in* Boy Scouts of America v. James Dale. *He is currently executive director of* Freedom to Marry, *a gay and nongay partner-
ship seeking equal marriage rights for all Americans. The excerpt reprinted
here is from his book* Why Marriage Matters: America, Equality, and Gay
People's Right to Marry *(2004).*

> Civil marriage is at once a deeply personal commitment to another
> human being and a highly public celebration of the ideals of mutuality,
> companionship, intimacy, fidelity, and family.
>
> — MASSACHUSETTS SUPREME JUDICIAL COURT,
> *Goodridge v. Department of Public Health* (2003)[1]

> How the world can change,
> It can change like that,
> Due to one little word:
> "Married."
> — JOHN KANDER AND FRED EBB,
> "Married," *Cabaret* (1966)

Depending on which linguistic expert you ask, there are anywhere from
two thousand to seven thousand different languages spoken in the world
today. That's a huge number to put your mind around — even for someone
who lives in Manhattan, where seemingly hundreds of those languages can
be heard on the subway on any given day. Still, I'm willing to bet that each
of these languages has something in common with the others: a word that
means marriage.

No matter what language people speak — from Arabic to Yiddish, from
Chinook to Chinese — marriage is what we use to describe a specific relationship of love and dedication to another person. It is how we explain the
families that are united because of that love. And it universally signifies a
level of self-sacrifice and responsibility and a stage of life unlike any other.

Now of course, different cultures and times have had many different
conceptions of marriage, different rules and different ways of regarding
those who are married — not to mention different treatment for married
men and married women. . . . But with all this variety and all the changes
that have occurred in marriage over time and in different places, including

---

[1]*Goodridge v. Department of Public Health*, 440 Mass. 309 (Massachusetts Supreme
Judicial Court, 2003). [Editors' note: This is the case that effectively legalized same-sex marriage in Massachusetts; the Court ruled that "barring an individual from the protections, benefits, and obligations of civil marriage solely because that person would marry a person of the
same sex violates the Massachusetts Constitution."]

our country and within our lifetime, it is clear that marriage has been a defining institution in virtually every society throughout history. Given its variety and omnipresence, it is not surprising that when people talk about marriage, they often mean different things.

Consider all the different dimensions of marriage in the United States alone. First, marriage is a personal commitment and an important choice that belongs to couples in love. In fact, many people consider their choice of partner the most significant choice they will ever make. It is a relationship between people who are, hopefully, in love and an undertaking that most couples hope will endure.

Marriage is also a social statement, preeminently describing and defin-   5
ing a person's relationships and place in society. Marital status, along with what we do for a living, is often one of the first pieces of information we give to others about ourselves. It's so important, in fact, that most married people wear a symbol of their marriage on their hand.

Marriage is also a relationship between a couple and the government. Couples need the government's participation to get into and out of a marriage. Because it is a legal or "civil" institution, marriage is the legal gateway to a vast array of protections, responsibilities, and benefits — most of which cannot be replicated in any other way, no matter how much forethought you show or how much you are able to spend on attorneys' fees and assembling proxies and papers.

The tangible legal and economic protections and responsibilities that come with marriage include access to health care and medical decision making for your partner and your children; parenting and immigration rights; inheritance, taxation, Social Security, and other government benefits; rules for ending a relationship while protecting both parties; and the simple ability to pool resources to buy or transfer property without adverse tax treatment. In 1996, the federal government cataloged more than 1,049 ways in which married people are accorded special status under federal law; in a 2004 report, the General Accounting Office bumped up those federal effects of marriage to at least 1,138. Add in the state-level protections and the intangible as well as tangible privileges marriage brings in private life, and it's clear that the legal institution of marriage is one of the major safety nets in life, both in times of crisis and in day-to-day living.

Marriage uniquely permits couples to travel and deal with others in business or across borders without playing a game of "now you're legally next of kin; now you're legally not." It is a known commodity; no matter how people in fact conduct their marriages, there is a clarity, security, and automatic level of respect and legal status when someone gets to say, "That's my husband" or "I love my wife."

Marriage has spiritual significance for many of us and familial significance for nearly all of us. Family members inquire when one is going to get married, often to the point of nagging. Many religions perform marriage ceremonies, many consider marriage holy or a sacrament within their faith,

and the majority of American couples get married in a religious setting —
although the percentage of those having a purely civil ceremony is at nearly
40 percent and growing. As far as the law is concerned, however, what
counts is not what you do at the altar or whether you march down the aisle,
but that you get a civil marriage license from the government and sign a
legal document in the vestibule of the church, synagogue, temple, or
mosque — or at city hall, a court, or a clerk's office. As a legal matter, what
the priest, minister, rabbi, or other clergy member does is *witness* the couple's commitment and attest to their conformity with the requirements for a
civil marriage license.

As ubiquitous and varied as the institution is, the word *marriage* and its   10
myriad translations throughout the world also have a unique meaning that
children often use in making a joke. Who doesn't remember taunting
friends with a question like this: "If you love candy so much, why don't you
marry it?" Of course we know now — and I suppose we must have known
then — that the punch line was in the question itself. The joke shows that
though they may well "go together like a horse and carriage," *marriage* is
different from *love*. *Love* is a word that can be applied to anything from
your favorite song and your best-fitting pair of Levi's to your parents, your
roommate, or your boyfriend, while *marriage* signifies an unequaled commitment. And, as the childhood taunt illustrates, that's a distinction most of
us have understood since we were kids.

Still, marriage is now the vocabulary we use to talk of love, family, dedication, self-sacrifice, and stages of life. Marriage is a language of love, equality, and inclusion. While recognizing that marriage should not be the sole
criterion for benefits and support — nor the only family form worthy of
respect — most of us take marriage seriously and most of us do marry.

None of this is to say that marriage is the right choice for everybody. One
need only meet a happy single or divorced person to know that many people
are pleased with their decision to avoid matrimony. And, of course, we've all
been to weddings where we wonder how *she* could marry *him*. As splendid as
the institution is in the abstract, and as revered as marriage is in virtually
every society, one need only look at the divorce rate to know that there are
bad marriages and marriages that, without fault, have ceased to work.

There is clearly a difference between *marriage* and *marriages*, between
the institution and the choices and conduct of real couples in their commitment. For better or for worse, marriage is about choice, whether it be the
choice to "make it official" with your beloved and to accept the protections
and the responsibilities that accompany that decision; the choice to work
at your marriage and make it rewarding and good; the choice to betray
or divorce a spouse; or the choice to avoid the institution of marriage
altogether.

But marriage hasn't always been about choice. In fact, . . . it has historically been a battlefield, the site of collisions within and between governments and religions over who should regulate it. But marriage has weathered

centuries of skirmishes and change. It has evolved from an institution that was imposed on some people and denied to others, to the loving union of companionship, commitment, and caring between equal partners that we think of today.[2]

In ancient Rome, for example, a man was not considered a citizen until   15
he was married, and in many countries today, people, no matter how old, live under the roof, and remain under the control, of their parents until they wed — often a powerful incentive to marry (and a far cry from our idea of marriage as a choice made out of love). And you might be surprised to learn that, for example, the Catholic Church had nothing to do with marriage during the church's first one thousand years; marriage was not yet recognized officially as a Catholic sacrament, nor were weddings then performed in churches. Rather, marriage was understood as a dynastic or property arrangement for families and the basic social unit, *households* (then often extended families or kin, often including servants and even slaves). Family life and law in past centuries, let alone marriage, were very different from anything we'd recognize in the United States today.

[2]Hendrik Hartog, "What Gay Marriage Teaches About the History of Marriage," History News Network, April 5, 2004, http://hnn.us/articles/4400.html (lecture by author of *Man and Wife in America: A History* to Organization of American Historians tracing evolution of marriage and past battles).

Battles over marriage have taken place in America, too. . . . There was a time when our country excluded African-Americans from marriage altogether, prohibited people from marrying a partner of the "wrong" race, denied married people the use of contraception, and stripped women of their rights and even personhood — essentially making them chattel — at the altar. It took decades and decades of fighting to change these injustices. And change still needs to take place in the hearts of many, not to mention the law. As recently as 1998 in South Carolina and 2000 in Alabama, 40 percent of the voters in each state voted to keep offensive language barring interracial marriage in their respective state constitutions.

But fortunately, the general story of our country is movement toward inclusion and equality. The majority of Americans are fair. They realize that exclusionary conceptions of marriage fly in the face of our national commitment to freedom as well as the personal commitment made by loving couples. Americans have been ready again and again to make the changes needed to ensure that the institution of marriage reflects the values of love, inclusion, interdependence, and support.

Such a change came about as recently as 1987, when a group of Americans who had been denied the freedom to marry came before the U.S. Supreme Court. Before the justices issued an opinion in the case, *Turner v. Safley,* they had to determine what role marriage plays in American society. Or, more precisely, what role marriage plays in American law.

After careful consideration, the justices outlined four "important attributes" of marriage: First, they said, marriage represents an opportunity to make a public statement of commitment and love to another person, and an opportunity to receive public support for that commitment. Second, the justices said, marriage has for many people an important spiritual or religious dimension. Third, marriage offers the prospect of physical "consummation," which of course most of us call something else. And fourth, the justices said, marriage in the United States is the unique and indispensable gateway, the "precondition," for a vast array of protections, responsibilities, and benefits — public and private, tangible and intangible, legal and economic — that have real importance for real people.

The Supreme Court of course understood, as we discussed above, that 20 marriage has other purposes and aspects in the religious sphere, in business, and in people's personal lives. The justices knew, for example, that for many people, marriage is also important as a structure in which they can have and raise children. But when examined with the U.S. Constitution in mind, these four attributes or interests identified by the Court are the ones that have the legal weight. And after weighing these attributes, the justices ruled — in a unanimous decision — that marriage is such an important choice that it may not be arbitrarily denied by the government. Accordingly, they ordered that the government stop refusing marriage licenses to the group of Americans who had brought the case.

That group of Americans was prisoners.

Seventeen years after the Supreme Court recognized that the choice to marry is so important that it cannot be arbitrarily denied to convicted felons, one group of Americans is still denied the freedom to marry. No matter how long they have been together as a couple, no matter how committed and loving their relationship, and no matter how much they need the basic tools and support that come with marriage, lesbian and gay Americans in this country are excluded from the legal right to obtain a civil marriage license and marry the person they love.

Who are these same-sex couples and how does the exclusion from marriage harm them and their families?

They include Maureen Kilian and Cindy Meneghin of Butler, New Jersey, a committed couple ever since they met more than thirty years ago during their junior year in high school. Maureen works part-time as a parish administrator for Christ Church in nearby Pompton Lakes, where her job includes entering the names of married couples into the church registry. Cindy, meanwhile, is the director of Web services at Montclair State University. The women wish that one of them could stay at home full-time to help care for their two children, Josh and Sarah. But because they aren't married, neither of them is eligible for family health insurance through her employer, so both of them have to leave the kids in order to stay insured.

"We are good citizens, we pay our taxes, and we are caring parents — but we don't have the same equality as other Americans," Maureen told the *New York Times*. "We're tired of having to explain our relationship. When you say you're married, everyone understands that." More than anything, Maureen and Cindy told the *Times*, they want spousal inheritance rights, so that if one of them dies, the other one can stay in their home without having to pay crippling estate taxes to the Internal Revenue Service. That security comes with marriage.[3]

Alicia Heath-Toby and Saundra Toby-Heath also live in New Jersey and have been a couple for more than fifteen years. Alicia is a deacon and Saundra an usher in the Liberation in Truth Unity Fellowship Church, an African-American congregation, and they regularly participate in church cookouts, picnics, dances, and family activities as well as services. The women have children and grandchildren, bought a home together in Newark, and pay taxes. When Alicia had surgery, Saundra took weeks off from her work as a FedEx dispatcher to take care of her. Denied access to family health insurance and required to pay two deductibles instead of one because they are not married, Saundra and Alicia want to enter a legal commitment to match the religious one they already celebrated in their church.

"If two complete strangers met each other last week and got legally married today, they would have more rights under the law than our relationship has after fifteen years of being together. That's not fair," Saundra and Alicia

25

---

[3] Andrew Jacobs, "More Than Mere Partners," *New York Times*, December 19, 2003, p. B1.

told their lawyers at Lambda Legal Defense & Education Fund. "We pay first-class taxes, but we're treated like second-class citizens."[4] They worry about their kids and each other, and they want the best legal and economic protection they can get for their family. That protection comes with marriage.

Tony Eitnier and Thomas Arnold have been life partners for more than ten years, but until recently they were faced every day with the fear that it would be their last together. That's because Tony is from the United States and Thomas is from Germany. Unlike most of America's close allies, such as Canada and the United Kingdom, our country discriminates with policies that do not allow gay citizens to remain together with committed partners from other countries under the family unification principles that normally apply in immigration. "It [is] a mental battle not to go crazy, never knowing if your partner is going to have to leave tomorrow," Tony told the Associated Press. "You become paranoid."[5]   30

Because Germany is one of more than fifteen countries with an immigration policy that treats binational same-sex couples equally, Tony and Thomas moved to Berlin, where they can live together without fear of a forced separation. That's little comfort for Tony's family in San Diego, California, though. "I'm very close to my family, and it was extremely traumatic to have to leave," Tony said. "My parents are bitter at the government."[6] The couple holds on to the hope that they can return to the U.S. and live openly and legally as a couple in Tony's own country, America, the land of the free. That right comes with marriage.

Chris Lodewyks and Craig Hutchison of Pompton Lakes, New Jersey, have been committed partners since they met when they were freshmen in college, more than thirty years ago. As is the case for many middle-aged couples, Chris and Craig have spent a good part of the past decade looking after their aging parents. When Chris's mom was battling cancer at the end of her life, Craig took time off from work to help care for her. And now that Chris is retired, he can spend time helping Craig's elderly mother. The men also are active in the community. Chris has spearheaded a town cleanup day, with businesses donating prizes to hundreds of volunteers, and Craig serves on the board of a YMCA camp. "Gay and lesbian topics are in the news every day," Chris told New Jersey's *Bergen County Record.* "This is an emotional time, and some people may be looking at this like it's going too fast. But it's not going too fast. It's time for us to have the same civil rights as everyone else."[7]

---

[4]"New Black Group to Fight for Marriage Equality," *Blacklight,* National Black Justice Coalition, March 24, 2004, http://www.blacklightonline.com/fma.html.

[5]David Cray, "Painful Choices Face Many Same-sex Couples When One is American, the Other Foreign," Associated Press, November 23, 2003.

[6]Cray, "Painful Choices."

[7]John Chadwick, "White House Working on Law to Block Gay Marriage," *Bergen County (N.J.) Record,* July 31, 2003, p. A1.

Chris and Craig have shown the personal commitment to each other, have done the work, and have undertaken on their own many of the family responsibilities of a married couple, including caring for each other's parents. Now they want the full legal responsibilities and protections that the government bestows on married couples. "After thirty years of commitment and responsibility the government treats our accomplishments together as worthless," Craig said.[8] Full protections and legal responsibility come with marriage.

Julie and Hillary Goodridge of Jamaica Plain, Massachusetts, have been in a committed relationship for sixteen years and are raising a young daughter together. One day the women played the Beatles song "All You Need Is Love" for their daughter, Annie, who was five years old at the time. When Hillary asked Annie if she knew any people who loved each other, Annie named several of her mothers' married friends. "What about Mommy and Ma?" Hillary asked. "Well," Annie replied, "if you loved each other you'd get married." At that point, Hillary later told *Newsweek* magazine, "My heart just dropped."[9]

It wasn't the first time that the freedom to marry would have helped clarify the Goodridges' family relationship for the people around them. The most dramatic illustration of how exclusion from marriage harms their family took place after Julie's caesarean delivery of Annie, when Hillary was denied entry into the ICU to see her newborn daughter. "They said, 'Only immediate family,' and I had a fit," Hillary told *People* magazine.[10]

Who wouldn't have a fit? And who should have to go through an ordeal like that, especially at such an important, trying, and hopefully joyous time as the birth of a child? The Goodridges want assurance that they won't encounter similar obstacles the next time Julie, Hillary, or Annie is hospitalized or in need. That assurance comes with marriage.

In fact, exclusion from the freedom to marry unfairly punishes committed same-sex couples and their families by depriving them of critical assistance, security, and obligations in virtually every area of life, including, yes, even death and taxes:

- Death: If a couple is not married and one partner dies, the other partner is not entitled to get bereavement leave from work, to file wrongful death claims, to draw the Social Security payments of the deceased partner, or to automatically inherit a shared home, assets, or personal items in the absence of a will.
- Debts: Unmarried partners do not generally have responsibility for each other's debt.

[8]Lambda Legal, "New Jersey Family Profiles," March 24, 2004, http://www.lambdalegal.org/cgibin/iowa/documents/record?record=1068.
[9]Evan Thomas, "The War Over Gay Marriage," *Newsweek,* July 7, 2003, p. 38.
[10]Richard Jerome, "State of the Union," *People,* August 18, 2003, p. 100.

- Divorce: Unmarried couples do not have access to the courts or to the legal and financial guidelines in times of breakup, including rules for how to handle shared property, child support, and alimony, or to protect the weaker party and the kids.

- Family leave: Unmarried couples are often not covered by laws and policies that permit people to take medical leave to care for a sick spouse or for the kids.

- Health: Unlike spouses, unmarried partners are usually not considered next of kin for the purposes of hospital visitation and emergency medical decisions. In addition, they can't cover their families on their health plans without paying taxes on the coverage, nor are they eligible for Medicare and Medicaid coverage.

- Housing: Denied marriage, couples of lesser means are not recognized as a family and thus can be denied or disfavored in their applications for public housing.

- Immigration: U.S. residency and family unification are not available to an unmarried partner from another country.

- Inheritance: Unmarried surviving partners do not automatically inherit property should their loved one die without a will, nor do they get legal protection for inheritance rights such as elective share or to bypass the hassles and expenses of probate court.

- Insurance: Unmarried partners can't always sign up for joint home and auto insurance. In addition, many employers don't cover domestic partners or their biological or nonbiological children in their health insurance plans.

- Parenting: Unmarried couples are denied the automatic right to joint parenting, joint adoption, joint foster care, and visitation for nonbiological parents. In addition, the children of unmarried couples are denied the guarantee of child support and an automatic legal relationship to both parents, and are sometimes sent a wrong-headed but real negative message about their own status and family.

- Portability: Unlike marriages, which are honored in all states and countries, domestic partnerships and other alternative mechanisms only exist in a few states and countries, are not given any legal acknowledgment in most, and leave families without the clarity and security of knowing what their legal status and rights will be.

- Privilege: Unmarried couples are not shielded against having to testify against each other in judicial proceedings, and are also usually denied the coverage in crime-victims counseling and protection programs afforded married couples.

- Property: Unmarried couples are excluded from special rules that permit married couples to buy and own property together under favorable terms, rules that protect married couples in their shared homes, and rules regarding the distribution of property in the event of death or divorce.

- Retirement: In addition to being denied access to shared or spousal benefits through Social Security as well as coverage under Medicare and other programs, unmarried couples are denied withdrawal rights and protective tax treatment given to spouses with regard to IRAs and other retirement plans.
- Taxes: Unmarried couples cannot file joint tax returns and are excluded from tax benefits and claims specific to marriage. In addition, they are denied the right to transfer property to each other and pool the family's resources without adverse tax consequences.

And, again, virtually all of these critical, concrete legal incidents of marriage cannot be arranged by shelling out money for an attorney or writing up private agreements, even if the couple has lots of forethought to discuss all the issues in advance and then a bunch of extra cash to throw at lawyers.

It's not just same-sex couples who are harmed by society's refusal to respect their personal commitment and human desire for the protections and statement of marriage. Going back to that juvenile quip, "If you love it, why don't you marry it," let me tell you one of my earliest memories of when I realized I was gay.

I am lucky to have a very close and loving family, and grew up living with my parents, sister, and two brothers. One night — I couldn't have been more than eleven or twelve — my mother and I were watching something on TV and talking. Dad was out on his weekly bowling night and the other kids must have already gone off to sleep. I remember saying to my mom, in what must have seemed an out-of-the-blue declaration, "I don't think I'll get married." I don't remember if, or how, my mom responded. But I do remember that I realized I might be excluded from the joys of married life, and felt there was something in the picture society showed me that I didn't fit into, before I could tell my mom or even fully understand that I was gay.

Many gay kids, even before they hear the word *gay* and associate it with themselves, and even before they fully understand how their own lives will take shape, do understand that they are different from their friends. For the most part, of course, gay kids grow up in the nongay world — raised by nongay parents; surrounded by mostly nongay siblings, friends, relatives, and teachers; exposed to nongay images and expectations everywhere, from church, television, and popular music. And yet, until now our society has also sent those kids the message that the dream of romantic love, of commitment, of family, of marriage is not for them. America tells its children that the dream of "first comes love, then comes marriage" is not for you if you're gay.

This is wrong and has to change.

Unlike the members of most other minority groups, we gay people are   40
not usually born into our own identity or community, or into families that share or understand our sense of self; we have to find our way largely on our own, often after working through negative messages about homosexuality, or a lack of understanding from family members, peers, churches, and the

other institutions that people rely on for self-identification, solidarity, and support.

When I told my mother I didn't think I'd get married, I was not rejecting marriage; I was working out my own sense of difference in a world that said I could not have what marriage signifies — life as a couple with the person you choose, legal recognition, acceptance — given the restrictions placed both on marriage and on people like me.

Again, I was lucky. I never doubted that my parents loved me and would love me, even if and when they found out I was gay. That doesn't mean it was easy for my parents. When, years later, I told them I am gay, it meant there were some differences in the life they imagined for me, differences they in turn had to accept as part of their unconditional love for me.

Even with loving parents and personal self-confidence, as a young child not even knowing the word *gay,* I was led to believe that I had to reject a pattern of life that didn't seem to be available for me with the kind of partner I could truly love, someone of the same sex. In a childish way, I thought it was "marriage" I didn't fit into, when, in fact, the love and commitment marriage signifies were perfectly appropriate dreams for me. It was exclusion, rejection, and the denial of the freedom to marry that were and are unnecessary, harsh, harmful, and wrong.

Notice here that I'm not using terms like "gay marriage" or "same-sex marriage." That's because these terms imply that same-sex couples are asking for rights and privileges that married couples do not have, or for rights that are something lesser or different than what nongay couples have. In fact, we don't want "gay marriage," we want marriage — the same freedom to marry, with the same duties, dignity, security, and expression of love and equality as our nongay brothers and sisters have.

Gay people have the same mix of reasons for wanting the freedom to marry as nongay people: emotional and economic, practical and personal, social and spiritual. The inequities and the legal and cultural second-class status that exclusion from marriage reinforces affect all gay people, but the denial of marriage's safety net falls hardest on the poor, the less educated, and the otherwise vulnerable. And the denial of the freedom to marry undermines young gay people's sense of self and their dreams of a life together with a partner. 45

Of course our country needs to find ways other than marriage to support and welcome all kids, all families, and all communities. Marriage is not, need not, and should not be the only means of protecting oneself and a loving partner or family. But like other Americans, same-sex couples need the responsibilities and support marriage offers legally and economically to families dealing with parenting, property, Social Security, finances, and the like, especially in times of crisis, health emergency, divorce, and death. And gay people, like all human beings, love and want to declare love, want inclusion in the community and the equal choices and possibilities that belong to us all as Americans.

Marriage equality is the precondition for these rights, these protections, this inclusion, this full citizenship. The freedom to marry is important in building strong families and strong communities. What sense does it make to deny that freedom to Maureen and Cindy, Alicia and Saundra, Tony and Thomas, Chris and Craig, or Julie and Hillary?

How many more young people have to grow up believing that they are alone, that they are not welcome, that they are unequal and second-class, that their society does not value their love or expect them to find permanence and commitment?

How many nongay parents and family members have to worry or feel pain for their gay loved ones? What mother doesn't want the best for all her kids, or want to be able to dance at her lesbian daughter's wedding just as she did at her other child's?

As Americans have done so many times in the past, it's time we learn   50
from our mistakes and acknowledge that lesbian and gay Americans — like people the world around — speak the vocabulary of marriage, live the personal commitment of marriage, do the hard work of marriage, and share the responsibilities we associate with marriage. It's time to allow them the same freedom every other American has — the freedom to marry.

Engaging the Text

1. Banning legally recognized marriage for lesbian and gay couples does not mean they are not establishing families and raising children in countless American communities. Why is the formal legal recognition of same-sex marriage a crucial issue for Wolfson? Why is there such strong opposition to his views?

2. Wolfson begins this reading (and thus Chapter One of his book) with an extended definition of marriage (paras. 2–13). Why does he make this his first task, and what are the key elements of his definition? Do you find his definition fair and sensible, or is it somehow slanted, incomplete, or illogical? Explain.

3. Review the examples of real-life couples Wolfson describes in paragraphs 24–32. For each couple, explain why Wolfson chose to include them in his book. How does each example contribute to his argument?

4. Wolfson is writing for a broad audience, but he hasn't set aside his legal expertise. Discuss how both the "content" and the form of "What Is Marriage?" reflect his background in the law.

5. Review how Wolfson uses the court case *Turner v. Safley* (paras. 18–21), which ruled that Missouri could not arbitrarily deny marriage rights to prisoners. What is his rhetorical strategy in this section, and how effective do you judge it? Discuss whether *Turner v. Safley* is relevant to the issue of same-sex marriage.

EXPLORING CONNECTIONS

6. Write or role-play a discussion between Wolfson and Rick Santorum (p. 88).

7. Re-examine the images of gay couples in the Visual Portfolio (pp. 83, 84). How has your own understanding of the images developed through your reading of Wolfson and Rick Santorum (p. 88)?

EXTENDING THE CRITICAL CONTEXT

8. The Massachusetts Supreme Judicial Court did not reach a unanimous decision in *Goodridge v. Department of Public Health,* the 2003 case that legalized same-sex marriages in Massachusetts. Debate these two key points made in dissenting opinions:

> [The issue of gay marriage] is one deeply rooted in social policy [and the] decision must be made by the Legislature, not the court.
> — Dissent filed by JUSTICE ROBERT J. CORDY

> It is rational for the Legislature to postpone any redefinition of marriage that would include same-sex couples until such time as it is certain that redefinition will not have unintended and undesirable social consequences.
> — Dissent filed by JUSTICE MARTHA B. SOSMAN

 How do you think Wolfson might respond to these arguments?

9. If you live in any state other than Massachusetts, which permits same-sex marriage, research and report on the status of same-sex marriages and civil unions in your state. Start by finding out what the law currently says; to extend the research you may wish to learn about relevant court cases, proposed new legislation, and political action by gay and lesbian rights organizations.

10. Throughout this chapter, families have been portrayed through a variety of metaphors: they have appeared as a nuclear unit, a family tree, a network of relationships, and a quilt with many parts. What are the implications of each of these metaphors? How do they affect our view of family? What other metaphors might capture your vision of American family life?

FURTHER CONNECTIONS

1. Family relationships are a frequent subject for novels and films, perhaps because these extended forms can take the time to explore the complexities of family dynamics. Making substantial use of at least one reading in this chapter, write an essay analyzing the portrayal of family in a single novel or film.

2. Review the "Fast Facts" that appear near the beginning of this chapter (p. 18). Can you now interpret any of these facts in new ways? Discuss the benefits and shortcomings of amassing data on American families.

3. Tolstoy wrote that all happy families are alike, but that each unhappy family is unhappy in its own way. Taking into account your own experience and the readings in this chapter, write a journal entry or an essay articulating your views of what makes families happy or unhappy, and assessing your own experiences of family up to this point in your life.

2

Learning Power

The Myth of Education and Empowerment

Skeptical Student, photo by Charles Agel.

FAST FACTS

1. The average annual earnings of workers with a high school diploma, a bachelor's degree, and an advanced degree in 2006 were, respectively, $27,915, $51,206, and $71,602.

2. Students who do not complete high school can expect to earn $18,734 per year, are more likely to be unemployed, and are less likely than their peers to be in good health throughout their lifetimes.

3. According to the Bill and Melinda Gates Foundation's Graduation Project, only one out of three U.S. high school students was expected to graduate in 2006, with urban schools in low-income areas graduating as few as 26% of the total students in their senior classes.

4. One fourth of all African Americans in the Midwest and Northeast attend "apartheid schools" — institutions that have virtually no white student populations.

5. Thirty-one percent of all undergraduate students attended two-year colleges in 2006, and 50% of all full-time college students held jobs.

6. The percentage of white, Asian, Latino, and black college students who graduate in four years or less is, respectively, 37.6%, 38.8%, 21.3%, and 28.9%.

7. In 2003, American eighth graders ranked fifteenth in terms of mathematics achievement, coming in behind their peers in Singapore, the Republic of Korea, Hong Kong, Chinese Taipei, Japan, Belgium, the Netherlands, Estonia, Hungary, Malaysia, Latvia, the Russian Federation, the Slovak Republic, and Australia.

Sources: (1) U.S. Census Bureau; (2) National Center for Educational Statistics; (3) Editorial Projects in Education Research Center; (4) Harvard University's Civil Rights Project; (5) U.S. Census Bureau; (6) UCLA Higher Education Research Institute; (7) National Center for Educational Statistics.

Broke out of Chester gaol,[1] last night, one James Rockett, a very short well set fellow, pretends to be a schoolmaster, of a fair complexion, and smooth fac'd; Had on when he went away, a light colored camblet coat, a blue cloth jacket, without sleeves, a check shirt, a pair of old dy'd leather breaches, gray worsted stockings, a pair of half worn pumps, and an almost new beaver hat; his hair is cut off, and wears a cap; he is a great taker of snuff, and very apt to get drunk; he has with him two certificates, one from some inhabitants in Burlington county, Jersey, which he will no doubt produce as a pass. Who ever takes up and secures said Rockett in any gaol, shall have two Pistoles reward, paid by October 27, 1756. — SAMUEL SMITH, Gaoler

— Advertisement for a "runaway schoolmaster"
Pennsylvania Gazette, November 25, 1756

AMERICANS HAVE ALWAYS HAD mixed feelings about schooling. Today, most Americans tend to see education as something intrinsically valuable or important. After all, education is the engine that drives the American Dream. The chance to learn, better oneself, and gain the skills that pay off in upward mobility has sustained the hope of millions of Americans. As a nation we look up to figures like Abraham Lincoln and Frederick Douglass, who learned to see beyond poverty and slavery by learning to read. Education tells us that the American Dream can work for everyone. It reassures us that we are, in fact, "created equal" and that the path to achievement lies through individual effort and hard work, not blind luck or birth.

But as the advertisement quoted above suggests, American attitudes toward teachers and teaching haven't always been overwhelmingly positive. The Puritans who established the Massachusetts Bay Colony viewed education with respectful skepticism. Schooling in Puritan society was a force for spiritual rather than worldly advancement. Lessons were designed to reinforce moral and religious training and to teach children to read the Bible for themselves. Education was important to the Puritan "Divines" because it was a source of order, control, and discipline. But when education aimed at more worldly goals or was undertaken for self-improvement, it was seen as a menacing, sinful luxury. Little wonder, then, that the Puritans often viewed teaching as something less than an ennobling profession. In fact, teachers in the early colonies were commonly treated as menial employees by the families and communities they served. The following list of the "Duties of a Schoolmaster" gives you some idea of the status of American educators in the year 1661:

1. Act as court-messenger
2. Serve summonses
3. Conduct certain ceremonial church services
4. Lead Sunday choir

[1]*gaol:* Jail.

5. Ring bell for public worship
6. Dig graves
7. Take charge of school
8. Perform other occasional duties

Colonial American teachers were frequently indentured servants who had sold themselves for five to ten years, often for the price of passage to the New World. Once here, they drilled their masters' children in spiritual exercises until they earned their freedom — or escaped.

The reputation of education in America began to improve with the onset of the Revolutionary War. Following the overthrow of British rule, leaders sought to create a spirit of nationalism that would unify the former colonies. Differences were to be set aside, for, as George Washington pointed out, "the more homogeneous our citizens can be made ... the greater will be our prospect of permanent union." The goal of schooling became the creation of uniformly loyal, patriotic Americans. In the words of Benjamin Rush, one of the signers of the Declaration of Independence, "Our schools of learning, by producing one general and uniform system of education, will render the mass of people more homogeneous and thereby fit them more easily for uniform and peaceable government."

Thomas Jefferson saw school as a training ground for citizenship and democratic leadership. Recognizing that an illiterate and ill-informed population would be unable to assume the responsibilities of self-government, Jefferson laid out a comprehensive plan in 1781 for public education in the state of Virginia. According to Jefferson's blueprint, all children would be eligible for three years of free public instruction. Of those who could not afford further schooling, one promising "genius" from each school was to be "raked from the rubbish" and given six more years of free education. At the end of that time, ten boys would be selected to attend college at public expense. Jeffersonian Virginia may have been the first place in the United States where education so clearly offered the penniless boy a path to self-improvement. However, this path was open to very few, and Jefferson, like Washington and Rush, was more concerned with benefiting the state than serving the individual student: "We hope to avail the state of those talents which nature has sown as liberally among the poor as the rich, but which perish without use, if not sought for and cultivated." For leaders of the American Revolution, education was seen as a tool for nation-building, not personal development.

Perhaps that's why Native American leaders remained lukewarm to the idea of formal education despite its growing popularity with their colonial neighbors. When, according to Ben Franklin's report, the government of Virginia offered to provide six American Indian youths with the best college education it could afford in 1744, the tribal leaders of the Six Nations politely declined, pointing out that our ideas of this kind of education happen not to be the same with yours. We have had some experience of it; several of our young people were formerly brought up at the colleges of the northern provinces; they were instructed in all your sciences; but when they came back to us, they were bad runners; ignorant of every means of living in the woods; unable to bear either cold or hunger; knew neither how to build a cabin, take a deer, or kill an enemy; spoke our language imperfectly; were therefore neither fit for hunters, warriors, or counselors: they were totally good for nothing.

It's not surprising that these tribal leaders saw American education as useless. Education works to socialize young people — to teach them the values, beliefs, and skills central to their society; the same schooling that prepared students for life in Anglo-American culture made them singularly unfit for tribal life. As people who stood outside the dominant society, Native Americans were quick to realize education's potential as a tool for enforcing cultural conformity. But despite their resistance, by the 1880s the U.S. government had established special "Indian schools" dedicated to assimilating Indian children into Anglo-American culture and destroying tribal knowledge and tribal ways.

In the nineteenth century two great historical forces — industrialization and immigration — combined to exert even greater pressure for the "homogenization" of young Americans. Massive immigration from Ireland and Eastern and Central Europe led to fears that "non-native" peoples would undermine the cultural identity of the United States. Many saw school as the first line of defense against this perceived threat, a place where the children of "foreigners" could become Americanized. In a meeting of educators in 1836, one college professor stated the problem as bluntly as possible:

> Let us now be reminded, that unless we educate our immigrants, they will be our ruin. It is no longer a mere question of benevolence, of duty, or of enlightened self-interest, but the intellectual and religious training of our foreign population has become essential to our own safety; we are prompted to it by the instinct of self-preservation.

Industrialization gave rise to another kind of uniformity in nineteenth-century public education. Factory work didn't require the kind of educational preparation needed to transform a child into a craftsman or merchant. So, for the first time in American history, school systems began to categorize students into different educational "tracks" that offered qualitatively different kinds of education to different groups. Some — typically students from well-to-do homes — were prepared for professional and managerial positions. But most were consigned to education for life "on the line." Increasing demand for factory workers put a premium on young people who were obedient and able to work in large groups according to fixed schedules. As a result, leading educators in 1874 proposed a system of schooling that would meet the needs of the "modern industrial community" by stressing "punctuality, regularity, attention, and silence, as habits necessary through life." History complicates the myth of education as a source of personal empowerment. School can bind as effectively as it can liberate; it can enforce conformity and limit life chances as well as foster individual talent.

But history also supplies examples of education serving the idealistic goals of democracy, equality, and self-improvement. Nineteenth-century educator and reformer Horace Mann worked to expand educational opportunity to all Americans. Mann believed that genuine democratic self-government would become a reality only if every citizen were sufficiently educated to make reasoned judgments about even the thorniest public issues. "Education," according to Mann, "must prepare our citizens to become municipal officers, intelligent jurors, honest witnesses, legislators, or competent judges of legislation — in fine, to fill all the manifold relations of life." In Mann's conception, the "common school," offering educational opportunity to anyone with the will to learn, would make good on the central promise of American democracy; it would become "the great equalizer of the conditions of men."

At the turn of the century, philosopher and educational theorist John Dewey made even greater claims for educational empowerment. A fierce opponent of the kind of "tracking" associated with industrial education, Dewey proposed that schools should strive to produce thinking citizens rather than obedient workers. As members of a democracy, all men and women, according to Dewey, are entitled to an education that helps them make the best of their natural talents and enables them to participate as fully as possible in the life of their community: "only by being true to the full growth of the individuals who make it up, can society by any chance be true to itself." Most of our current myths of education echo the optimism of Mann and Dewey. Guided by their ideas, most Americans still believe that education leads to self-improvement and can help us empower ourselves — and perhaps even transform our society.

Does education empower us? Or does it stifle personal growth by squeezing us into prefabricated cultural molds? This chapter takes a critical look at American education: what it can do and how it shapes or enhances our identities. The first set of readings provides a starting point for exploring the myth of educational empowerment. We begin with a classic statement of the goals of American education — Horace Mann's 1848 "Report of the Massachusetts Board of Education." Mann's optimistic view of education as a means of social mobility in a democratic state provides a clear statement of the myth of personal empowerment through education. For a quick update on where we stand a century and a half later, we turn to documentary filmmaker Michael Moore's scathing assessment of the current state of American education in "Idiot Nation."

Next, in "Against School," veteran teacher and libertarian John Taylor Gatto offers his own provocative analysis of how public education "cripples our kids." In "'I Just Wanna Be Average,'" Mike Rose provides a moving personal account of the dream of educational success and pays tribute to an inner-city teacher who never loses sight of what can be achieved in a class-room. An excerpt from Jean Anyon's "Social Class and the Hidden Curriculum of Work" rounds off the section by suggesting that schools virtually program students for success or failure according to their socioeconomic status.

Following these initial readings, the chapter's Visual Portfolio presents three paintings by Norman Rockwell that reflect some of America's most hallowed cultural memories of the classroom experience. The reproductions include *The Spirit of Education, The Graduate,* and Rockwell's famous civil-rights-movement portrait of Ruby Bridges as she was escorted to the schoolhouse door. They offer you the chance to consider the place of education in America's cultural mythology and to imagine how a contemporary artist might update the story of educational success for the twenty-first century.

The next group of readings offers a closer look at the tensions experienced by so-called nontraditional students as they struggle with the complexities — and prejudices — of a deeply traditional educational system. The section begins with a classic autobiographical selection by Richard Rodriguez, which raises questions about the ambivalent role schooling plays in the lives of many Americans who come from families new to the world of higher education. In her dramatic narrative poem "Para Teresa," Inés Hernández-Ávila asks whether academic achievement demands cultural conformity or whether it can become a form of protest against oppression and racism. "Learning to Read" closes the section with the moving story of Malcolm X's spiritual and political rebirth through his self-made and highly untraditional education in prison.

We end our examination of American education with two readings that raise questions about the current state of U.S. classrooms. Deborah Tannen's "The Roots of Debate in Education and the Hope of Dialogue" suggests that the combative intellectual style of American higher education works against the interests of female students. In "Still Separate, Still Unequal," long-time educational activist Jonathan Kozol issues a warning about the "re-segregation" of schools across the nation and the negative impact of recent education reforms.

Sources

John Hardin Best and Robert T. Sidwell, eds., *The American Legacy of Learning: Readings in the History of Education.* Philadelphia: J. B. Lippincott Co., 1966.

Sol Cohen, ed., *Education in the United States: A Documentary History*, 5 vols. New York: Random House, 1974.

John Dewey, "The School and Society" (1899) and "My Pedagogic Creed" (1897). In *John Dewey on Education*. New York: Modern Library, 1964.

Benjamin Franklin, "Remarks Concerning the Savages of North America." In *The Works of Dr. Benjamin Franklin*. Hartford: S. Andrus and Son, 1849.

Thomas Jefferson, *Notes on the State of Virginia*. Chapel Hill: University of North Carolina Press, 1955.

Lorraine Smith Pangle and Thomas L. Pangle, *The Learning of Liberty: The Educational Ideas of the American Founders*. Lawrence: University Press of Kansas, 1993.

Leonard Pitt, *We Americans*, vol. 2, 3rd ed. Dubuque: Kendall/Hunt, 1987.

Edward Stevens and George H. Wood, *Justice, Ideology, and Education: An Introduction to the Social Foundations of Education*. New York: Random House, 1987.

Elizabeth Vallance, "Hiding the Hidden Curriculum: An Interpretation of the Language of Justification in Nineteenth-Century Educational Reform." *Curriculum Theory Network*, vol. 4. no. 1 (1973–74), pp. 5–21.

Robert B. Westbrook, "Public Schooling and American Democracy." In *Democracy, Education, and the Schools*, Roger Soder, ed. San Francisco: Jossey-Bass Publishers, 1996.

BEFORE READING

- Freewrite for fifteen or twenty minutes about your best and worst educational experiences. Then, working in groups, compare notes to see if you can find recurring themes or ideas in what you've written. What aspects of school seem to stand out most clearly in your memories? Do the best experiences have anything in common? How about the worst? What aspects of your school experience didn't show up in the freewriting?

- Work in small groups to draw a collective picture that expresses your experience of high school or college. Don't worry about your drawing skill — just load the page with imagery, feelings, and ideas. Then show your work to other class members and let them try to interpret it.

- Write a journal entry from the point of view of the girl pictured on the title page of this chapter (p. 113). Try to capture the thoughts that are going through her head. What has her day in school been like? What is she looking forward to? What is she dreading? Share your entries with your classmates and discuss your responses.

From *Report of the Massachusetts Board of Education, 1848*

HORACE MANN

If you check a list of schools in your home state, you'll probably discover at least a few dedicated to the memory of Horace Mann. We memorialize Mann today in school systems across the country because he may have done more than any other American to codify the myth of empowerment through education. Born on a farm in Franklin, Massachusetts, in 1796, Mann raised himself out of rural poverty to a position of national eminence through hard work and study. His first personal educational experiences, however, were far from pleasurable: the ill-trained and often brutal schoolmasters he first encountered in rural Massachusetts made rote memorization and the power of the rod the focus of their educational approach. After graduating from Brown University in 1819, Mann pursued a career in law and politics and eventually served as president of the Massachusetts State Senate. Discouraged by the condition of the state's public schools, Mann abandoned his political career to become secretary of the Massachusetts Board of Education in 1837. Mann's vision of "the common school," the centerpiece of his approach to democratic education, grew out of research he conducted on the Prussian school system during his tour of Europe in 1843. Presented originally as an address to the Massachusetts State Legislature, the report of 1848 has had a lasting impact on the goals and content of American education.

Without undervaluing any other human agency, it may be safely affirmed that the common school, improved and energized as it can easily be, may become the most effective and benignant of all the forces of civilization. Two reasons sustain this position. In the first place, there is a universality in its operation, which can be affirmed of no other institution whatever. If administered in the spirit of justice and conciliation, all the rising generation may be brought within the circle of its reformatory and elevating influences. And, in the second place, the materials upon which it operates are so pliant and ductile as to be susceptible of assuming a greater variety of forms than any other earthly work of the Creator. The inflexibility and ruggedness of the oak, when compared with the lithe sapling or the tender germ, are but feeble emblems to typify the docility of childhood when contrasted with the obduracy and intractableness of man. It is these inherent advantages of the common school, which, in our own State, have produced results so striking, from a system so imperfect, and an administration so feeble. In teaching the blind and the deaf and dumb, in kindling the latent spark of intelligence that lurks in an idiot's mind, and in the more holy work of reforming abandoned and outcast children, education has proved what it can do by glorious experiments. These wonders it has done in its infancy, and with the lights of a limited experience; but when its faculties shall be fully developed, when it shall be trained to wield its mighty energies for the protection of society against the giant vices which now invade and torment it, — against intemperance, avarice, war, slavery, bigotry, the woes of want, and the wickedness of waste, — then there will not be a height to which these enemies of the race can escape which it will not scale, nor a Titan among them all whom it will not slay.

I proceed, then, in endeavoring to show how the true business of the schoolroom connects itself, and becomes identical, with the great interests of society. The former is the infant, immature state of those interests; the latter their developed, adult state. As "the child is father to the man," so may the training of the schoolroom expand into the institutions and fortunes of the State.

Physical Education

In the worldly prosperity of mankind, health and strength are indispensable ingredients. . . .

Leaving out, then, for the present purpose, all consideration of the pains of sickness and the anguish of bereavement, the momentous truth still remains, that sickness and premature death are positive evils for the statesman and political economist to cope with. The earth, as a hospital for the diseased, would soon wear out the love of life; and, if but the half of mankind were sick, famine, from non-production, would speedily threaten the whole.

Now, modern science has made nothing more certain than that both good and ill health are the direct result of causes mainly within our own control. In other words, the health of the race is dependent upon the conduct of the race. The health of the individual is determined primarily by his parents, secondarily by himself. The vigorous growth of the body, its strength and its activity, its powers of endurance, and its length of life, on the one hand; and dwarfishness, sluggishness, infirmity, and premature death on the other, — are all the subjects of unchangeable laws. These laws are ordained of God; but the knowledge of them is left to our diligence, and the observance of them to our free agency. . . .

My general conclusion, then, under this head, is, that it is the duty of all the governing minds in society — whether in office or out of it — to diffuse a knowledge of these beautiful and beneficent laws of health and life throughout the length and breadth of the State; to popularize them; to make them, in the first place, the common acquisition of all, and, through education and custom, the common inheritance of all, so that the healthful habits naturally growing out of their observance shall be inbred in the people, exemplified in the personal regimen of each individual, incorporated into the economy of every household, observable in all private dwellings, and in all public edifices, especially in those buildings which are erected by capitalists for the residence of their work-people, or for renting to the poorer classes; obeyed, by supplying cities with pure water; by providing public baths, public walks, and public squares; by rural cemeteries; by the drainage and sewerage of populous towns, and by whatever else may promote the general salubrity of the atmosphere: in fine, by a religious observance of all those sanitary regulations with which modern science has blessed the world.

For this thorough diffusion of sanitary intelligence, the common school is the only agency. It is, however, an adequate agency. . . .

Intellectual Education as a Means of Removing Poverty, and Securing Abundance

. . . According to the European theory, men are divided into classes, — some to toil and earn, others to seize and enjoy. According to the Massachusetts theory, all are to have an equal chance for earning, and equal security in the enjoyment of what they earn. The latter tends to equality of condition; the former, to the grossest inequalities. . . .

But is it not true that Massachusetts, in some respects, instead of adhering more and more closely to her own theory, is becoming emulous of the baneful examples of Europe? The distance between the two extremes of society is lengthening, instead of being abridged. With every generation, fortunes increase on the one hand, and some new privation is added to poverty on the other. We are verging towards those extremes of opulence and of penury, each of which unhumanizes the human mind. A perpetual struggle for the bare necessaries of life, without the ability to obtain them, makes men wolfish. Avarice, on the other hand, sees, in all the victims of misery around it, not objects for pity and succor, but only crude materials to be worked up into more money.

I suppose it to be the universal sentiment of all those who mingle any   10
ingredient of benevolence with their notions on political economy, that vast and overshadowing private fortunes are among the greatest dangers to which the happiness of the people in a republic can be subjected. Such fortunes would create a feudalism of a new kind, but one more oppressive and unrelenting than that of the middle ages. The feudal lords in England and on the Continent never held their retainers in a more abject condition of servitude than the great majority of foreign manufacturers and capitalists hold their operatives and laborers at the present day. The means employed are different; but the similarity in results is striking. What force did then, money does now. The villein of the middle ages had no spot of earth on which he could live, unless one were granted to him by his lord. The operative or laborer of the present day has no employment, and therefore no

bread, unless the capitalist will accept his services. The vassal had no shelter but such as his master provided for him. Not one in five thousand of English operatives or farm-laborers is able to build or own even a hovel; and therefore they must accept such shelter as capital offers them. The baron prescribed his own terms to his retainers: those terms were peremptory, and the serf must submit or perish. The British manufacturer or farmer prescribes the rate of wages he will give to his work-people; he reduces these wages under whatever pretext he pleases; and they, too, have no alternative but submission or starvation. In some respects, indeed, the condition of the modern dependant is more forlorn than that of the corresponding serf class in former times. Some attributes of the patriarchal relation did spring up between the lord and his lieges to soften the harsh relations subsisting between them. Hence came some oversight of the condition of children, some relief in sickness, some protection and support in the decrepitude of age. But only in instances comparatively few have kindly offices smoothed the rugged relation between British capital and British labor. The children of the work-people are abandoned to their fate; and notwithstanding the privations they suffer, and the dangers they threaten, no power in the realm has yet been able to secure them an education; and when the adult laborer is prostrated by sickness, or eventually worn out by toil and age, the poor-house, which has all along been his destination, becomes his destiny....

Now, surely nothing but universal education can counterwork this tendency to the domination of capital and servility of labor. If one class possesses all the wealth and the education, while the residue of society is ignorant and poor, it matters not by what name the relation between them may be called: the latter, in fact and in truth, will be the servile dependants and subjects of the former. But, if education be equably diffused, it will draw property after it by the strongest of all attractions, for such a thing never did happen, and never can happen, as that an intelligent and practical body of men should be permanently poor. Property and labor in different classes are essentially antagonistic; but property and labor in the same class are essentially fraternal. The people of Massachusetts have, in some degree, appreciated the truth, that the unexampled prosperity of the State — its comfort, its competence, its general intelligence and virtue — is attributable to the education, more or less perfect, which all its people have received: but are they sensible of a fact equally important; namely, that it is to this same education that two-thirds of the people are indebted for not being today the vassals of as severe a tyranny, in the form of capital, as the lower classes of Europe are bound to in the form of brute force?

Education, then, beyond all other devices of human origin, is the great equalizer of the conditions of men, — the balance-wheel of the social machinery. I do not here mean that it so elevates the moral nature as to make men disdain and abhor the oppression of their fellow-men. This idea pertains to another of its attributes. But I mean that it gives each man the independence and the means by which he can resist the selfishness of other men. It does better than to disarm the poor of their hostility towards the rich: it prevents being poor. Agrarianism is the revenge of poverty against wealth. The wanton destruction of the property of others — the burning of hay-ricks and corn-ricks, the demolition of machinery because it supersedes hand-labor, the sprinkling of vitriol on rich dresses — is only agrarianism run mad. Education prevents both the revenge and the madness. On the other hand, a fellow-feeling for one's class or caste is the common instinct of hearts not wholly sunk in selfish regards for person or for family. The spread of education, by enlarging the cultivated class or caste, will open a wider area over which the social feelings will expand; and, if this education should be universal and complete, it would do more than all things else to obliterate factitious distinctions in society. . . .

For the creation of wealth, then, — for the existence of a wealthy people and a wealthy nation, — intelligence is the grand condition. The number of improvers will increase as the intellectual constituency, if I may call it, increases. In former times, and in most parts of the world even at the present day, not one man in a million has ever had such a development of mind as made it possible for him to become a contributor to art or science. Let this development precede, and contributions, numberless, and of inestimable value, will be sure to follow. That political economy, therefore, which busies itself about capital and labor, supply and demand, interest and rents, favorable and unfavorable balances of trade, but leaves out of account the element of a widespread mental development, is nought but stupendous folly. The greatest of all the arts in political economy is to change a consumer into a producer; and the next greatest is to increase the producer's producing power, — an end to be directly attained by increasing his intelligence. For mere delving, an ignorant man is but little better than a swine, whom he so much resembles in his appetites, and surpasses in his powers of mischief. . . .

Political Education

The necessity of general intelligence, — that is, of education (for I use the terms as substantially synonymous, because general intelligence can never exist without general education, and general education will be sure to produce general intelligence), — the necessity of general intelligence under a republican form of government, like most other very important truths, has become a very trite one. It is so trite, indeed, as to have lost much of its force by its familiarity. Almost all the champions of education seize upon this argument first of all, because it is so simple as to be understood by the ignorant, and so strong as to convince the sceptical. Nothing would be easier than to follow in the train of so many writers, and to demonstrate by logic, by history, and by the nature of the case, that a republican form of government, without intelligence in the people, must be, on a vast scale, what a madhouse, without superintendent or keepers, would be on a small one, — the despotism of a few succeeded by universal anarchy, and anarchy by despotism, with no change but from bad to worse. . . .

However elevated the moral character of a constituency may be, how- 15 ever well informed in matters of general science or history, yet they must, if citizens of a republic, understand something of the true nature and functions of the government under which they live. That any one, who is to participate in the government of a country when he becomes a man, should receive no instruction respecting the nature and functions of the government he is afterwards to administer, is a political solecism. In all nations, hardly excepting the most rude and barbarous, the future sovereign receives some training which is supposed to fit him for the exercise of the powers and duties of his anticipated station. Where, by force of law, the government devolves upon the heir while yet in a state of legal infancy, some regency, or other substitute, is appointed to act in his stead until his arrival at mature age; and, in the mean time, he is subjected to such a course of study and discipline as will tend to prepare him, according to the political theory of the time and the place, to assume the reins of authority at the appointed age. If in England, or in the most enlightened European monarchies, it would be a proof of restored barbarism to permit the future sovereign to grow up without any knowledge of his duties, — and who can doubt that it would be such a proof? — then, surely, it would be not less a proof of restored or of never-removed barbarism amongst us to empower any individual to use the elective franchise without preparing him for so momentous a trust. Hence the Constitution of the United States, and of our own State, should be made a study in our public schools. The partition of the powers of government into the three co-ordinate branches, — legislative, judicial, and executive — with the duties appropriately devolving upon each; the mode of electing or of appointing all officers, with the reasons on which it was founded; and, especially, the duty of every citizen, in a government of laws, to appeal to the courts for redress in all cases of alleged wrong, instead of undertaking to vindicate his own rights by his own arm; and, in a government where the people are the acknowledged sources of power, the duty of changing laws and rulers by an appeal to the ballot, and not by rebellion, — should be taught to all the children until they are fully understood.

Had the obligations of the future citizen been sedulously inculcated upon all the children of this Republic, would the patriot have had to mourn over so many instances where the voter, not being able to accomplish his purpose by voting, has proceeded to accomplish it by violence; where, agreeing with his fellow-citizens to use the machinery of the ballot, he makes a tacit reservation, that, if that machinery does not move according to his pleasure, he will wrest or break it? If the responsibleness and value of the elective franchise were duly appreciated, the day of our state and national elections would be among the most solemn and religious days in the calendar. Men would approach them, not only with preparation and solicitude, but with the sobriety and solemnity with which discreet and religious-minded men meet the great crises of life. No man would throw away his vote through caprice or wantonness, any more than he would throw away his estate, or sell his family into bondage. No man would cast his vote through malice or revenge, any more than a good surgeon would amputate a limb, or a good navigator sail through perilous straits, under the same criminal passions.

But perhaps it will be objected, that the Constitution is subject to different readings, or that the policy of different administrations has become the subject of party strife; and, therefore, if any thing of constitutional or political law is introduced into our schools, there is danger that teachers will be chosen on account of their affinities to this or that political party, or that teachers will feign affinities which they do not feel in order that they may be chosen; and so each schoolroom will at length become a miniature political club-room, exploding with political resolves, or flaming out with political addresses, prepared by beardless boys in scarcely legible hand-writing and in worse grammar.

With the most limited exercise of discretion, all apprehensions of this kind are wholly groundless. There are different readings of the Constitution, it is true; and there are partisan topics which agitate the country from side to side: but the controverted points, compared with those about which there is no dispute, do not bear the proportion of one to a hundred. And, what is more, no man is qualified, or can be qualified, to discuss the disputable questions, unless previously and thoroughly versed in those questions about which there is no dispute. In the terms and principles common to all, and recognized by all, is to be found the only common medium of language and of idea by which the parties can become intelligible to each other; and there, too, is the only common ground whence the arguments of the disputants can be drawn. . . .

. . . Thus may all the children of the Commonwealth receive instruction in all the great essentials of political knowledge, — in those elementary ideas without which they will never be able to investigate more recondite and debatable questions; thus will the only practicable method be adopted for discovering new truths, and for discarding, instead of perpetuating, old errors; and thus, too, will that pernicious race of intolerant zealots, whose whole faith may be summed up in two articles, — that they themselves are always infallibly right, and that all dissenters are certainly wrong, — be extinguished, — extinguished, not by violence, nor by proscription, but by the more copious inflowing of the light of truth.

Moral Education

Moral education is a primal necessity of social existence. The unrestrained passions of men are not only homicidal, but suicidal; and a community without a conscience would soon extinguish itself. Even with a natural conscience, how often has evil triumphed over good! From the beginning of time, wrong has followed right, as the shadow the substance. . . .

But to all doubters, disbelievers, or despairers in human progress, it may still be said, there is one experiment which has never yet been tried. It is an experiment, which, even before its inception, offers the highest authority for its ultimate success. Its formula is intelligible to all; and it is as legible as though written in starry letters on an azure sky. It is expressed in these few and simple words: *"Train up a child in the way he should go; and, when he is old, he will not depart from it."* This declaration is positive. If the conditions are complied with, it makes no provision for a failure. Though pertaining to morals, yet, if the terms of the direction are observed, there is no more reason to doubt the result than there would be in an optical or a chemical experiment.

But this experiment has never yet been tried. Education has never yet been brought to bear with one-hundredth part of its potential force upon the natures of children, and, through them, upon the character of men and of the race. In all the attempts to reform mankind which have hitherto been made, whether by changing the frame of government, by aggravating or softening the severity of the penal code, or by substituting a government-created for a God-created religion, — in all these attempts, the infantile and youthful mind, its amenability to influences, and the enduring and self-operating character of the influences it receives, have been almost wholly unrecognized. Here, then, is a new agency, whose powers are but just beginning to be understood, and whose mighty energies hitherto have been but feebly invoked; and yet, from our experience, limited and imperfect as it is, we do know, that, far beyond any other earthly instrumentality, it is comprehensive and decisive. . . .

. . . So far as human instrumentalities are concerned, we have abundant means for surrounding every child in the State with preservative and moral influences as extensive and as efficient as those under which the present industrious, worthy, and virtuous members of the community were reared. And as to all those things in regard to which we are directly dependent upon the divine favor, have we not the promise, explicit and unconditional, that the men SHALL NOT depart from the way in which they should go, if the children are trained up in it? It has been overlooked that this promise is not restricted to parents, but seems to be addressed indiscriminately to all, whether parents, communities, states, or mankind. . . .

Religious Education

But it will be said that this grand result in practical morals is a consummation of blessedness that can never be attained without religion, and that no community will ever be religious without a religious education. Both these propositions I regard as eternal and immutable truths. Devoid of religious principles and religious affections, the race can never fall so low but that it may sink still lower; animated and sanctified by them, it can never rise so high but that it may ascend still higher. And is it not at least as presumptuous to expect that mankind will attain to the knowledge of truth, without being instructed in truth, and without that general expansion and development of faculty which will enable them to recognize and comprehend truth in any other department of human interest as in the department of religion? ...

... That our public schools are not theological seminaries, is admitted. 25 That they are debarred by law from inculcating the peculiar and distinctive doctrines of any one religious denomination amongst us, is claimed; and that they are also prohibited from ever teaching that what they do teach is the whole of religion, or all that is essential to religion or to salvation, is equally certain. But our system earnestly inculcates all Christian morals; it founds its morals on the basis of religion; it welcomes the religion of the Bible; and, in receiving the Bible, it allows it to do what it is allowed to do in no other system, — *to speak for itself*. But here it stops, not because it claims to have compassed all truth, but because it disclaims to act as an umpire between hostile religious opinions.

The very terms "public school" and "common school" bear upon their face that they are schools which the children of the entire community may attend. Every man not on the pauper-list is taxed for their support; but he is not taxed to support them as special religious institutions: if he were, it would satisfy at once the largest definition of a religious establishment. But he is taxed to support them as a *preventive* means against dishonesty, against fraud, and against violence, on the same principle that he is taxed to support criminal courts as a *punitive* means against the same offences. He is taxed to support schools, on the same principle that he is taxed to support paupers, — because a child without education is poorer and more wretched than a man without bread. He is taxed to support schools, on the same principle that he would be taxed to defend the nation against foreign invasion, or against rapine committed by a foreign foe, — because the general prevalence of ignorance, superstition, and vice, will breed Goth and Vandal at home more fatal to the public well-being than any Goth or Vandal from abroad. And, finally, he is taxed to support schools, because they are the most effective means of developing and training those powers and faculties in a child, by which, when he becomes a man, he may understand what his highest interests and his highest duties are, and may be in fact, and not in name only, a free agent. The elements of a political education are not bestowed upon any school child for the purpose of making him vote with this or that political party when he becomes of age, but for the purpose of enabling him to choose for himself with which party he will vote. So the religious education which a child receives at school is not imparted to him for the purpose of making him join this or that denomination when he arrives at years of discretion, but for the purpose of enabling him to judge for himself, according to the dictates of his own reason and conscience, what his religious obligations are, and whither they lead. ...

Such, then, in a religious point of view, is the Massachusetts system of common schools. Reverently it recognizes and affirms the sovereign rights of the Creator, sedulously and sacredly it guards the religious rights of the creature; while it seeks to remove all hinderances, and to supply all furtherances, to a filial and paternal communion between man and his Maker. In a social and political sense, it is a *free* school-system. It knows no distinction of rich and poor, of bond and free, or between those, who, in the imperfect light of this world, are seeking, through different avenues, to reach the gate of heaven. Without money and without price, it throws open its doors, and spreads the table of its bounty, for all the children of the State. Like the sun, it shines not only upon the good, but upon the evil, that they may become good; and, like the rain, its blessings descend not only upon the just, but upon the unjust, that their injustice may depart from them, and be known no more.

ENGAGING THE TEXT

1. What is Mann's view of the powers of education? What does he see as education's role in society? To what extent would you agree that education successfully carries out these functions today?

2. What does Mann mean by "sanitary intelligence" (para. 7)? Why did he feel that the development of this kind of intelligence was such an important aspect of schooling? In what ways has your own education stressed the development of sanitary intelligence? How valuable has this nonacademic instruction been?

3. How does Mann view the role of education in relation to wealth and poverty? How do you think such views would be received today if advocated by a school-board candidate or contender for the presidency? In your estimation, how effective has education been in addressing economic differences in American society?

4. Mann suggests that education plays a special role in preparing citizens to become active participants in a republican form of government. In what ways has your education prepared you to participate in democratic decision making? How effective has this preparation been? What could be done to improve the way that schools currently prepare students for their role as citizens?

5. What, according to Mann, is the proper relationship of public education to issues of morality and religion? What specific moral or ethical principles should public schools attempt to teach?

EXPLORING CONNECTIONS

6. Read "Class in America — 2003" by Gregory Mantsios (p. 307), and "Stephen Cruz" by Studs Terkel (p. 353), and write an essay in which you discuss how class differences in American society complicate the educational program outlined by Mann.

IF ALL THE "EDUCATION REFORMS" HAPPENED AT ONCE,

7. Review the cartoon "If All the 'Education Reforms' Happened at Once," which appears at the top of this page. As a class, debate whether or not American education is trying to do too much today.

EXTENDING THE CRITICAL CONTEXT

8. Research recent court decisions and legislative initiatives on the issue of prayer in school. How do prevailing views of the separation of church and state compare with the ideas presented in Mann's assessment of the goals of public education in 1848? Then, as a class, debate the proper role of moral and religious instruction in public education.

9. Working in small groups, draft a list of what you think the proper goals of public education in a democracy should be. Exchange these lists, then compare and discuss your results. How does your class's view of the powers of education differ from that offered by Mann?

Idiot Nation

MICHAEL MOORE

When Michael Moore (b. 1954) held up his Oscar for best documentary during the 2002 Academy Awards show and shouted "Shame on you, Mr. Bush" to a chorus of boos from the audience, no one who knew his work would have been shocked. A social gadfly and cinematic activist without equal for the past two decades, Moore isn't the type to shy away from telling the president what he thinks of him on national TV; nor is he the type to disguise his contempt for the general level of idiocy he sees in American society. In this selection from Stupid White Men . . . and Other Sorry Excuses for the State of the Nation, *his best-selling 2002 diatribe against our collective cluelessness, Moore zeroes in on the sorry state of American education. Serving up generous examples from his own less-than-stellar educational career, Moore takes us on a tour of the failings of America's schoolrooms — from libraries without books to commanders in chief who can't distinguish between countries and continents. Along the way, he touches on topics like the cultural illiteracy of television talk show hosts, the growing movement for educational "accountability," and the corporate takeover of America's classrooms. He even offers a list of things every student can do to fight back against educational subservience. Before winning the Oscar in 2002 for his* Bowling for Columbine, *Moore directed* Roger and Me (1989), *which chronicled his attempts to question then-General-Motors-chairman Roger Smith about a series of factory closures that devastated the economy of Flint, Michigan, Moore's hometown. He is also the creator of* Fahrenheit 9/11, *a controversial documentary film exploring the Bush Administration's response to the 9/11 terrorist attacks.*

Do you feel like you live in a nation of idiots?

I used to console myself about the state of stupidity in this country by repeating this to myself: *Even if there are two hundred million stone-cold idiots in this country, that leaves at least eighty million who'll get what I'm saying — and that's still more than the populations of the United Kingdom and Iceland combined!*

Then came the day I found myself sharing an office with the ESPN game show *Two-Minute Drill*. This is the show that tests your knowledge of not only who plays what position for which team, but who hit what where in a 1925 game between Boston and New York, who was rookie of the year in 1965 in the old American Basketball Association, and what Jake Wood had for breakfast the morning of May 12, 1967.

I don't know the answer to any of those questions — but for some reason I do remember Jake Wood's uniform number: 2. Why on earth am I retaining that useless fact?

I don't know, but after watching scores of guys waiting to audition for that ESPN show, I think I do know something about intelligence and the American mind. Hordes of these jocks and lunkheads hang out in our hallway awaiting their big moment, going over hundreds of facts and statistics in their heads and challenging each other with questions I can't see why anyone would be able to answer other than God Almighty Himself. To look at these testosterone-loaded bruisers you would guess that they were a bunch of illiterates who would be lucky if they could read the label on a Bud.

In fact, they are geniuses. They can answer all thirty obscure trivia questions in less than 120 seconds. That's four seconds a question — including the time used by the slow-reading celebrity athletes who ask the questions.

I once heard the linguist and political writer Noam Chomsky say that if you want proof the American people aren't stupid, just turn on any sports talk radio show and listen to the incredible retention of facts. It is amazing — and it's proof that the American mind is alive and well. It just isn't challenged with anything interesting or exciting. *Our* challenge, Chomsky said, was to find a way to make politics as gripping and engaging as sports. When we do that, watch how Americans will do nothing but talk about who did what to whom at the WTO.[1]

But first, they have to be able to read the letters *WTO*.

There are forty-four million Americans who cannot read and write above a fourth-grade level — in other words, who are functional illiterates.

How did I learn this statistic? Well, I *read* it. And now you've read it. So we've already eaten into the mere 99 hours a *year* an average American adult spends reading a book — compared with 1,460 hours watching television.

I've also read that only 11 percent of the American public bothers to *read* a daily newspaper, beyond the funny pages or the used car ads.

So if you live in a country where forty-four million can't read — and perhaps close to another two hundred million can read but usually don't — well, friends, you and I are living in one very scary place. A nation that not only churns out illiterate students BUT GOES OUT OF ITS WAY TO REMAIN IGNORANT AND STUPID is a nation that should not be running the world — at least not until a majority of its citizens can locate Kosovo[2] (or any other country it has bombed) on the map.

It comes as no surprise to foreigners that Americans, who love to revel in their stupidity, would "elect" a president who rarely reads *anything* — including his own briefing papers — and thinks Africa is a nation, not a continent. An idiot leader of an idiot nation. In our glorious land of plenty, less is always more when it comes to taxing any lobe of the brain with the intake

---

[1]*WTO:* World Trade Organization.

[2]*Kosovo:* Province that precipitated the 1999 NATO invasion of Serbia after it demanded increased autonomy.

of facts and numbers, critical thinking, or the comprehension of anything
that isn't . . . well, sports.

Our Idiot-in-Chief does nothing to hide his ignorance — he even brags
about it. During his commencement address to the Yale Class of 2001,
George W. Bush spoke proudly of having been a mediocre student at Yale.
"And to the C students, I say you, too, can be President of the United
States!" The part where you also need an ex-President father, a brother as
governor of a state with missing ballots, and a Supreme Court full of your
dad's buddies must have been too complicated to bother with in a short
speech.

As Americans, we have quite a proud tradition of being represented by   15
ignorant high-ranking officials. In 1956 President Dwight D. Eisenhower's
nominee as ambassador to Ceylon (now Sri Lanka) was unable to identify
either the country's prime minister or its capital during his Senate confirmation hearing. Not a problem — Maxwell Gluck was confirmed anyway. In
1981 President Ronald Reagan's nominee for deputy secretary of state,
William Clark, admitted to a wide-ranging lack of knowledge about foreign
affairs at his confirmation hearing. Clark had no idea how our allies in Western Europe felt about having American nuclear missiles based there, and
didn't know the names of the prime ministers of South Africa or Zimbabwe.
Not to worry — he was confirmed, too. All this just paved the way for Baby
Bush, who hadn't quite absorbed the names of the leaders of India or Pakistan, two of the seven nations that possess the atomic bomb.

And Bush went to Yale *and* Harvard.

Recently a group of 556 seniors at fifty-five prestigious American universities (e.g., Harvard, Yale, Stanford) were given a multiple-choice test
consisting of questions that were described as "high school level." Thirty-
four questions were asked. These top students could only answer 53 percent
of them correctly. And only one student got them all right.

A whopping 40 percent of these students did not know when the Civil
War took place — even when given a wide range of choices: A. 1750–1800;
B. 1800–1850; C. 1850–1900; D. 1900–1950; or E. after 1950. (*The answer
is C, guys.*) The two questions the college seniors scored highest on were
(1) Who is Snoop Doggy Dog? (98 percent got that one right), and (2) Who
are Beavis and Butt-head? (99 percent knew). For my money, Beavis and
Butt-head represented some of the best American satire of the nineties, and
Snoop and his fellow rappers have much to say about America's social ills,
so I'm not going down the road of blaming MTV.

What I *am* concerned with is why politicians like Senators Joe Lieberman of Connecticut and Herbert Kohl of Wisconsin want to go after MTV
when *they* are the ones responsible for the massive failure of American education. Walk into any public school, and the odds are good that you'll find
overflowing classrooms, leaking ceilings, and demoralized teachers. In 1 out

of 4 schools, you'll find students "learning" from textbooks published in the 1980s — or earlier.

Why is this? Because the political leaders — and the people who vote   20
for them — have decided it's a bigger priority to build another bomber than to educate our children. They would rather hold hearings about the depravity of a television show called *Jackass* than about their own depravity in neglecting our schools and children and maintaining our title as Dumbest Country on Earth.

I hate writing these words. I *love* this big lug of a country and the crazy people in it. But when I can travel to some backwater village in Central America, as I did back in the eighties, and listen to a bunch of twelve-year-olds tell me their concerns about the World Bank, I get the feeling that *something* is lacking in the United States of America.

Our problem isn't just that our kids don't know nothin' but that the adults who pay their tuition are no better. I wonder what would happen if we tested the U.S. Congress to see just how much our representatives know. What if we were to give a pop quiz to the commentators who cram our TVs and radios with all their nonstop nonsense? How many would *they* get right?

A while back, I decided to find out. It was one of those Sunday mornings when the choice on TV was the *Parade of Homes* real estate show or *The McLaughlin Group*. If you like the sound of hyenas on Dexedrine, of course, you go with *McLaughlin*. On this particular Sunday morning, perhaps as my punishment for not being at Mass, I was forced to listen to magazine columnist Fred Barnes (now an editor at the right-wing *Weekly Standard* and co-host of the Fox News show *The Beltway Boys*) whine on and on about the sorry state of American education, blaming the teachers and their evil union for why students are doing so poorly.

"These kids don't even know what *The Iliad* and *The Odyssey* are!" he bellowed, as the other panelists nodded in admiration at Fred's noble lament.

The next morning I called Fred Barnes at his Washington office.   25
"Fred," I said, "tell me what *The Iliad* and *The Odyssey* are."

He started hemming and hawing. "Well, they're . . . uh . . . you know . . . uh . . . okay, fine, you got me — I don't know what they're about. Happy now?"

No, not really. You're one of the top TV pundits in America, seen every week on your own show and plenty of others. You gladly hawk your "wisdom" to hundreds of thousands of unsuspecting citizens, gleefully scorning others for their ignorance. Yet you and your guests know little or nothing yourselves. Grow up, get some books, and go to your room.

Yale and Harvard. Princeton and Dartmouth. Stanford and Berkeley. Get a degree from one of those universities, and you're set for life. So what if, on that test of the college seniors I previously mentioned, 70 percent of the students at those fine schools had never heard of the Voting Rights

Act[3] or President Lyndon Johnson's Great Society initiatives?[4] Who needs to know stuff like that as you sit in your Tuscan villa watching the sunset and checking how well your portfolio did today?

So what if *not one* of these top universities that the ignorant students attend requires that they take even one course in American history to graduate? Who needs history when you are going to be tomorrow's master of the universe?

Who cares if 70 percent of those who graduate from America's colleges   30
are not required to learn a foreign language? Isn't the rest of the world speaking English now? And if they aren't, hadn't all those damn foreigners better GET WITH THE PROGRAM?

And who gives a rat's ass if, out of the seventy English Literature programs at seventy major American universities, only twenty-three now require English majors to take a course in Shakespeare? Can somebody please explain to me what Shakespeare and English have to do with each other? What good are some moldy old plays going to be in the business world, anyway?

Maybe I'm just jealous because I don't have a college degree. Yes, I, Michael Moore, am a college dropout.

Well, I never *officially* dropped out. One day in my sophomore year, I drove around and around the various parking lots of our commuter campus in Flint, searching desperately for a parking space. There simply was no place to park — every spot was full, and no one was leaving. After a frustrating hour spent circling around in my '69 Chevy Impala, I shouted out the window, "That's it, I'm dropping out!" I drove home and told my parents I was no longer in college.

"Why?" they asked.

"Couldn't find a parking spot," I replied, grabbing a Redpop and mov-   35
ing on with the rest of my life. I haven't sat at a school desk since.

My dislike of school started somewhere around the second month of first grade. My parents — and God Bless Them Forever for doing this — had taught me to read and write by the time I was four. So when I entered St. John's Elementary School, I had to sit and feign interest while the other kids, like robots, sang, "A-B-C-D-E-F-G . . . Now I know my ABCs, tell me what you think of me!" Every time I heard that line, I wanted to scream out, "Here's what I think of you — quit singing that damn song! Somebody get me a Twinkie!"

I was bored beyond belief. The nuns, to their credit, recognized this, and one day Sister John Catherine took me aside and said that they had

---

[3]*Voting Rights Act:* 1965 legislation that guaranteed equal voting rights for African Americans.

[4]*Lyndon Johnson's Great Society initiatives:* 1964–65 program of economic and social welfare legislation designed by Lyndon Johnson, thirty-sixth president of the United States, to eradicate poverty.

decided to skip me up to second grade, effective immediately. I was thrilled. When I got home I excitedly announced to my parents that I had already advanced a grade in my first month of school. They seemed underwhelmed by this new evidence of my genius. Instead they let out a "WHAT THE — ," then went into the kitchen and closed the door. I could hear my mother on the phone explaining to the Mother Superior that there was *no way* her little Michael was going to be attending class with kids bigger and older than him, so please, Sister, put him back in first grade.

I was crushed. My mother explained to me that if I skipped first grade I'd always be the youngest and littlest kid in class all through my school years (well, inertia and fast food eventually proved her wrong on that count). There would be no appeals to my father, who left most education decisions to my mother, the valedictorian of her high school class. I tried to explain that if I was sent back to first grade it would appear that I'd *flunked* second grade on my first day — putting myself at risk of having the crap beaten out of me by the first graders I'd left behind with a rousing "See ya, suckers!" But Mom wasn't falling for it; it was then I learned that the only person with higher authority than Mother Superior was Mother Moore.

The next day I decided to ignore all instructions from my parents to go back to first grade. In the morning, before the opening bell, all the students had to line up outside the school with their classmates and then march into the building in single file. Quietly, but defiantly, I went and stood in the second graders' line, praying that God would strike the nuns blind so they wouldn't see which line I was in. The bell rang — and no one had spotted me! The second grade line started to move, and I went with it. *Yes!* I thought. *If I can pull this off, if I can just get into that second grade classroom and take my seat, then nobody will be able to get me out of there.* Just as I was about to enter the door of the school, I felt a hand grab me by the collar of my coat. It was Sister John Catherine.

"I think you're in the wrong line, Michael," she said firmly. "You are now in first grade again." I began to protest: my parents had it "all wrong," or "those weren't *really* my parents," or . . . 40

For the next twelve years I sat in class, did my work, and remained constantly preoccupied, looking for ways to bust out. I started an underground school paper in fourth grade. It was shut down. I started it again in sixth. It was shut down. In eighth grade I not only started the paper again, I convinced the good sisters to let me write a play for our class to perform at the Christmas pageant. The play had something to do with how many rats occupied the parish hall and how all the rats in the country had descended on St. John's Parish Hall to have their annual "rat convention." The priest put a stop to that one — and shut down the paper again. Instead, my friends and I were told to go up on stage and sing three Christmas carols and then leave the stage without uttering a word. I organized half the class to go up there and utter nothing. So we stood there and refused to sing the carols, our silent protest against censorship. By the second song, intimidated by the stern looks from their parents in the audience, most of the protesters joined in on the singing — and by the third song, I too, had capitulated, joining in on "O Holy Night," and promising myself to live to fight another day.

High school, as we all know, is some sort of sick, sadistic punishment of kids by adults seeking vengeance because they can no longer lead the responsibility-free, screwing-around-24/7 lives young people enjoy. What other explanation could there be for those four brutal years of degrading comments, physical abuse, and the belief that you're the only one not having sex?

As soon as I entered high school — and the public school system — all the grousing I'd done about the repression of the Sisters of St. Joseph was forgotten; suddenly they all looked like scholars and saints. I was now walking the halls of a two-thousand-plus-inmate holding pen. Where the nuns had devoted their lives to teaching for no earthly reward, those running the public high school had one simple mission: "Hunt these little pricks down like dogs, then cage them until we can either break their will or ship them off to the glue factory!" Do this, don't do that, tuck your shirt in, wipe that smile off your face, where's your hall pass, THAT'S THE WRONG PASS! *YOU — DETENTION!!*

One day I came home from school and picked up the paper. The headline read: "26th Amendment Passes — Voting Age Lowered to 18." Below that was another headline: "School Board President to Retire, Seat Up for Election."

Hmm. I called the county clerk.   45

"Uh, I'm gonna be eighteen in a few weeks. If I can vote, does that mean I can also run for office?"

"Let me see," the lady replied. "That's a new question!"

She ruffled through some papers and came back on the phone. "Yes," she said, "you can run. All you need to do is gather twenty signatures to place your name on the ballot."

Twenty signatures? That's it? I had no idea running for elective office required so little work. I got the twenty signatures, submitted my petition, and started campaigning. My platform? "Fire the high school principal and the assistant principal!"

Alarmed at the idea that a high school student might actually find a   50 legal means to remove the very administrators he was being paddled by, five local "adults" took out petitions and got themselves added to the ballot, too.

Of course, they ended up splitting the older adult vote five ways — and I won, getting the vote of every single stoner between the ages of eighteen and twenty-five (who, though many would probably never vote again, relished the thought of sending their high school wardens to the gallows).

The day after I won, I was walking down the hall at school (I had one more week to serve out as a student), and I passed the assistant principal, my shirt tail proudly untucked.

"Good morning, Mr. Moore," he said tersely. The day before, my name had been "Hey-You!" Now I was his boss.

Within nine months after I took my seat on the school board, the principal and assistant principal had submitted their "letters of resignation," a face-saving device employed when one is "asked" to step down. A couple of years later the principal suffered a heart attack and died.

I had known this man, the principal, for many years. When I was eight 55 years old, he used to let me and my friends skate and play hockey on this little pond beside his house. He was kind and generous, and always left the door to his house open in case any of us needed to change into our skates or if we got cold and just wanted to get warm. Years later, I was asked to play bass in a band that was forming, but I didn't own a bass. He let me borrow his son's.

I offer this to remind myself that all people are actually good at their core, and to remember that someone with whom I grew to have serious disputes was also someone with a free cup of hot chocolate for us shivering little brats from the neighborhood.

Teachers are now the politicians' favorite punching bag. To listen to the likes of Chester Finn, a former assistant secretary of education in Bush the Elder's administration, you'd think all that has crumbled in our society can be traced back to lax, lazy, and incompetent teachers. "If you put out a Ten-Most-Wanted list of who's killing American education, I'm not sure who you would have higher on the list: the teachers' union or the education school faculties," Finn said.

Sure, there are a lot of teachers who suck, and they'd be better suited to making telemarketing calls for Amway. But the vast majority are dedicated educators who have chosen a profession that pays them less than what some of their students earn selling Ecstasy, and for that sacrifice we seek to punish them. I don't know about you, but I want the people who have the direct attention of my child more hours a day than I do treated with tender loving care. Those are my kids they're "preparing" for this world, so why on earth would I want to piss them off?

You would think society's attitude would be something like this:

Teachers, thank you so much for devoting your life to my child. Is there ANYTHING I can do to help you? Is there ANYTHING you need? I am here for you. Why? Because you are helping my child — MY BABY — learn and grow. Not only will you be largely responsible for her ability to make a living, but your influence will greatly affect how she views the world, what she knows about other people in this world, and how she will feel about herself. I want her to believe she can attempt anything — that no doors are closed and that no dreams are too distant. I am entrusting the most valuable person in my life to you for seven hours each day. You are thus one of the most important people in my life! Thank you.

No, instead, this is what teachers hear: 60

- "You've got to wonder about teachers who claim to put the interests of children first — and then look to milk the system dry through wage hikes." (*New York Post*, 12/26/00)
- "Estimates of the number of bad teachers range from 5 percent to 18 percent of the 2.6 million total." (Michael Chapman, *Investor's Business Daily*, 9/21/98)
- "Most education professionals belong to a closed community of devotees . . . who follow popular philosophies rather than research on what works." (Douglas Carminen, quoted in the *Montreal Gazette*, 1/6/01)
- "Teachers unions have gone to bat for felons and teachers who have had sex with students, as well as those who simply couldn't teach." (Peter Schweizen, *National Review*, 8/17/98)

What kind of priority do we place on education in America? Oh, it's on the funding list — somewhere down between OSHA[5] and meat inspectors. The person who cares for our child every day receives an average of $41,351 annually. A Congressman who cares only about which tobacco lobbyist is taking him to dinner tonight receives $145,100.

Considering the face-slapping society gives our teachers on a daily basis, is it any wonder so few choose the profession? The national teacher shortage is so big that some school systems are recruiting teachers outside the United States. Chicago recently recruited and hired teachers from twenty-eight foreign countries, including China, France, and Hungary. By the time the new term begins in New York City, seven thousand veteran teachers will have retired — and 60 percent of the new teachers hired to replace them are uncertified.

But here's the kicker for me: 163 New York City schools opened the 2000–2001 school year *without a principal!* You heard right — school, with *no one in charge.* Apparently the mayor and the school board are experimenting with chaos theory — throw five hundred poor kids into a crumbling building, and watch nature take its course! In the city from which most of the wealth in the world is controlled, where there are more millionaires per square foot than there is gum on the sidewalk, we somehow can't find the money to pay a starting teacher more than $31,900 a year. And we act surprised when we can't get results.

And it's not just teachers who have been neglected — American schools are *literally* falling apart. In 1999 one-quarter of U.S. public schools reported that the condition of at least one of their buildings was inadequate. In 1997 the entire Washington, D.C., school system had to delay the start of school for three weeks because nearly *one-third* of the schools were found to be unsafe.

[5]*OSHA:* Occupational Safety and Health Administration.

Almost 10 percent of U.S. public schools have enrollments that are   65
more than 25 percent greater than the capacity of their permanent buildings. Classes have to be held in the hallways, outdoors, in the gym, in the
cafeteria; one school I visited even held classes in a janitor's closet. It's not
as if the janitor's closets are being used for anything related to cleaning,
anyway — in New York almost 15 percent of the eleven hundred public
schools are without full-time custodians, forcing teachers to mop their own
floors and students to do without toilet paper. We already send our kids
out into the street to hawk candy bars so their schools can buy band
instruments — what's next? Car washes to raise money for toilet paper?

Further proof of just how special our little offspring are is the number
of public and even school libraries that have been shut down or had their
hours cut back. The last thing we need is a bunch of kids hanging out
around a bunch of books!

Apparently "President" Bush agrees: in his first budget he proposed cutting federal spending on libraries by $39 million, down to $168 million — a
nearly 19 percent reduction. Just the week before, his wife, former school
librarian Laura Bush, kicked off a national campaign for America's libraries,
calling them "community treasure chests, loaded with a wealth of information available to everyone, equally." The President's mother, Barbara Bush,
heads the Foundation for Family Literacy. Well, there's nothing like having
firsthand experience with illiteracy in the family to motivate one into acts
of charity.

For kids who are exposed to books at home, the loss of a library is sad.
But for kids who come from environments where people don't read, the loss
of a library is a tragedy that might keep them from ever discovering the joys
of reading — or from gathering the kind of information that will decide
their lot in life. Jonathan Kozol, for decades an advocate for disadvantaged
children, has observed that school libraries "remain the clearest window to a
world of noncommercial satisfactions and enticements that most children in
poor neighborhoods will ever know."

Kids deprived of access to good libraries are also being kept from developing the information skills they need to keep up in workplaces that are
increasingly dependent on rapidly changing information. The ability to conduct research is "probably the most essential skill [today's students] can have,"
says Julie Walker, executive director of the American Association of School
Librarians. "The knowledge [students] acquire in school is not going to serve
them throughout their lifetimes. Many of them will have four to five careers
in a lifetime. It will be their ability to navigate information that will matter."

Who's to blame for the decline in libraries? Well, when it comes to   70
school libraries, you can start by pointing the finger (yes, *that* finger) at
Richard Nixon. From the 1960s until 1974, school libraries received specific
funding from the government. But in 1974 the Nixon administration
changed the rules, stipulating that federal education money be doled out in
"block grants" to be spent by states however they chose. Few states chose to

spend the money on libraries, and the downslide began. This is one reason that materials in many school libraries today date from the 1960s and early 1970s, before funding was diverted. ("No, Sally, the Soviet Union isn't our enemy. The Soviet Union has been kaput for ten years. . . .")

This 1999 account by an *Education Week* reporter about the "library" at a Philadelphia elementary school could apply to any number of similarly neglected schools:

> Even the best books in the library at T. M. Pierce Elementary School are dated, tattered, and discolored. The worst — many in a latter state of disintegration — are dirty and fetid and leave a moldy residue on hands and clothing. Chairs and tables are old, mismatched, or broken. There isn't a computer in sight. . . . Outdated facts and theories and offensive stereotypes leap from the authoritative pages of encyclopedias and biographies, fiction and nonfiction tomes. Among the volumes on these shelves a student would find it all but impossible to locate accurate information on AIDS or other contemporary diseases, explorations of the moon and Mars, or the past five U.S. presidents.

The ultimate irony in all of this is that the very politicians who refuse to fund education in America adequately are the same ones who go ballistic over how our kids have fallen behind the Germans, the Japanese, and just about every other country with running water and an economy not based on the sale of Chiclets. Suddenly they want "accountability." They want the teachers held responsible and to be tested. And they want the kids to be tested — over and over and over.

There's nothing terribly wrong with the concept of using standardized testing to determine whether kids are learning to read and write and do math. But too many politicians and education bureaucrats have created a national obsession with testing, as if everything that's wrong with the educational system in this country would be magically fixed if we could just raise those scores.

The people who really should be tested (besides the yammering pundits) are the so-called political leaders. Next time you see your state representative or congressman, give him this pop quiz — and remind him that any future pay raises will be based on how well he scores:

1. What is the annual pay of your average constituent?
2. What percent of welfare recipients are children?
3. How many known species of plants and animals are on the brink of extinction?
4. How big is the hole in the ozone layer?
5. Which African countries have a lower infant mortality rate than Detroit?
6. How many American cities still have two competing newspapers?

7. How many ounces in a gallon?

8. Which do I stand a greater chance of being killed by: a gun shot in school or a bolt of lightning?

9. What's the only state capital without a McDonald's?

10. Describe the story of either *The Iliad* or *The Odyssey*.

Answers

1. $28,548

2. 67 percent

3. 11,046

4. 10.5 million square miles

5. Libya, Mauritius, Seychelles

6. 34

7. 128 ounces

8. You're twice as likely to be killed by lightning as by a gun shot in school.

9. Montpelier, Vermont

10. *The Iliad* is an ancient Greek epic poem by Homer about the Trojan War. *The Odyssey* is another epic poem by Homer recounting the ten-year journey home from the Trojan War made by Odysseus, the king of Ithaca.

Chances are, the genius representing you in the legislature won't score 50 percent on the above test. The good news is that you get to flunk him within a year or two.

There is one group in the country that isn't just sitting around carping about all them lamebrain teachers — a group that cares deeply about what kinds of students will enter the adult world. You could say they have a vested interest in this captive audience of millions of young people . . . or in the billions of dollars they spend each year. (Teenagers alone spent more than $150 billion last year.) Yes, it's Corporate America, whose generosity to our nation's schools is just one more example of their continuing patriotic service.

Just how committed are these companies to our children's schools?

According to numbers collected by the Center for the Analysis of Commercialism in Education (CACE), their selfless charity has seen a tremendous boom since 1990. Over the past ten years, school programs and activities have seen corporate sponsorship increase by 248 percent. In exchange for this sponsorship, schools allow the corporation to associate its name with the events.

For example, Eddie Bauer sponsors the final round of the National Geography Bee. Book covers featuring Calvin Klein and Nike ads are distributed to students. Nike and other shoemakers, looking for early access to tomorrow's stars, sponsor inner-city high school basketball teams.

Pizza Hut set up its "Book-It!" program to encourage children to read.   80
When students meet the monthly reading goal, they are rewarded with a
certificate for a Pizza Hut personal pan pizza. At the restaurant, the store
manager personally congratulates the children and gives them each a sticker
and a certificate. Pizza Hut suggests school principals place a "Pizza Hut
Book-It!" honor roll list in the school for everyone to see.

General Mills and Campbell's Soup thought up a better plan. Instead
of giving free rewards, they both have programs rewarding schools for getting parents to buy their products. Under General Mills's "Box Tops for
Education" program, schools get ten cents for each box top logo they send
in, and can earn up to $10,000 a year. That's 100,000 General Mills prod-
ucts sold. Campbell's Soup's "Labels for Education" program is no better. It
touts itself as "Providing America's children with FREE school equipment!"
Schools can earn one "free" Apple iMac computer for only 94,950 soup
labels. Campbell's suggests setting a goal of a label a day from each student.
With Campbell's conservative estimate of five labels per week per child, all
you need is a school of 528 kids to get that free computer.

It's not just this kind of sponsorship that brings these schools and corporations together. The 1990s saw a phenomenal 1,384 percent increase in
exclusive agreements between schools and soft-drink bottlers. Two hundred
and forty school districts in thirty-one states have sold exclusive rights to
one of the big three soda companies (Coca-Cola, Pepsi, Dr. Pepper) to push
their products in schools. Anybody wonder why there are more overweight
kids than ever before? Or more young women with calcium deficiencies
because they're drinking less milk? And even though federal law prohibits
the sale of soft drinks in schools until lunch periods begin, in some overcrowded schools "lunch" begins in midmorning. Artificially flavored carbonated sugar water — the breakfast of champions! (In March 2001 Coke
responded to public pressure, announcing that it would add water, juice,
and other sugar-free, caffeine-free, and calcium-rich alternatives to soda to
its school vending machines.)

I guess they can afford such concessions when you consider their deal
with the Colorado Springs school district. Colorado has been a trailblazer
when it comes to tie-ins between the schools and soft drink companies. In
Colorado Springs, the district will receive $8.4 million over ten years from
its deal with Coca-Cola — and more if it exceeds its "requirement" of selling
seventy thousand cases of Coke products a year. To ensure the levels are
met, school district officials urged principals to allow students unlimited
access to Coke machines and allow students to drink Coke in the classroom.

But Coke isn't alone. In the Jefferson County, Colorado, school district
(home of Columbine High School), Pepsi contributed $1.5 million to help
build a new sports stadium. Some county schools tested a science course,
developed in part by Pepsi, called "The Carbonated Beverage Company."
Students taste-tested colas, analyzed cola samples, watched a video tour of a
Pepsi bottling plant, and visited a local plant.

The school district in Wylie, Texas, signed a deal in 1996 that shared the rights to sell soft drinks in the schools between Coke and Dr. Pepper. Each company paid $31,000 a year. Then, in 1998, the county changed its mind and signed a deal with Coke worth $1.2 million over fifteen years. Dr. Pepper sued the county for breach of contract. The school district bought out Dr. Pepper's contract, costing them $160,000 — plus another $20,000 in legal fees.

It's not just the companies that sometimes get sent packing. Students who lack the proper corporate school spirit do so at considerable risk. When Mike Cameron wore a Pepsi shirt on "Coke Day" at Greenbrier High School in Evans, Georgia, he was suspended for a day. "Coke Day" was part of the school's entry in a national "Team Up With Coca-Cola" contest, which awards $10,000 to the high school that comes up with the best plan for distributing Coke discount cards. Greenbrier school officials said Cameron was suspended for "being disruptive and trying to destroy the school picture" when he removed an outer shirt and revealed the Pepsi shirt as a photograph was being taken of students posed to spell out the word *Coke.* Cameron said the shirt was visible all day, but he didn't get in trouble until posing for the picture. No slouch in the marketing department, Pepsi quickly sent the high school senior a box of Pepsi shirts and hats.

If turning the students into billboards isn't enough, schools and corporations sometimes turn the school itself into one giant neon sign for corporate America. Appropriation of school space, including scoreboards, rooftops, walls, and textbooks, for corporate logos and advertising is up 539 percent.

Colorado Springs, not satisfied to sell its soul only to Coca-Cola, has plastered its school buses with advertisements for Burger King, Wendy's, and other big companies. Free book covers and school planners with ads for Kellogg's Pop-Tarts and pictures of FOX TV personalities were also handed out to the students.

After members of the Grapevine-Colleyville Independent School District in Texas decided they didn't want advertisements in the classrooms, they allowed Dr. Pepper and 7-Up logos to be painted on the rooftops of two high schools. The two high schools, not coincidentally, lie under the Dallas airport flight path.

The schools aren't just looking for ways to advertise; they're also concerned with the students' perceptions of various products. That's why, in some schools, companies conduct market research in classrooms during school hours. Education Market Resources of Kansas reports that "children respond openly and easily to questions and stimuli" in the classroom setting. (Of course, that's what they're *supposed* to be doing in a classroom — but for their own benefit, not that of some corporate pollsters.) Filling out marketing surveys instead of learning, however, is probably *not* what they should be doing.

Companies have also learned they can reach this confined audience by "sponsoring" educational materials. This practice, like the others, has exploded as well, increasing 1,875 percent since 1990.

Teachers have shown a Shell Oil video that teaches students that the way to experience nature is by driving there — after filling your Jeep's gas tank at a Shell station. ExxonMobil prepared lesson plans about the flourishing wildlife in Prince William Sound, site of the ecological disaster caused by the oil spill from the Exxon *Valdez*. A third-grade math book features exercises involving counting Tootsie Rolls. A Hershey's-sponsored curriculum used in many schools features "The Chocolate Dream Machine," including lessons in math, science, geography — and nutrition.

In a number of high schools, the economics course is supplied by General Motors. GM writes and provides the textbooks and the course outline. Students learn from GM's example the benefits of capitalism and how to operate a company — like GM.

And what better way to imprint a corporate logo on the country's children than through television and the Internet beamed directly into the classroom. Electronic marketing, where a company provides programming or equipment to schools for the right to advertise to their students, is up 139 percent.

One example is the ZapMe! Corporation, which provides schools with a free computer lab and access to pre-selected Web sites. In return, schools must promise that the lab will be in use at least four hours a day. The catch? The ZapMe! Web browser has constantly scrolling advertisements — and the company gets to collect information on students' browsing habits, information they can then sell to other companies. ⁹⁵

Perhaps the worst of the electronic marketers is Channel One Television. Eight million students in 12,000 classrooms watch Channel One, an in-school news *and advertising* program, every day. (That's right: EVERY day.) Kids are spending the equivalent of six full school days a year watching Channel One in almost 40 percent of U.S. middle and high schools. Instructional time lost to the ads alone? One entire day per year. That translates into an annual cost to taxpayers of more than $1.8 billion.

Sure, doctors and educators agree that our kids can never watch enough TV. And there's probably a place in school for some television programs — I have fond memories of watching astronauts blasting off on the television rolled into my grade school auditorium. But out of the daily twelve-minute Channel One broadcasts, only 20 percent of the airtime is devoted to stories about politics, the economy, and cultural and social issues. That leaves a whopping 80 percent for advertising, sports, weather, features, and Channel One promotions.

Channel One is disproportionately shown in schools in low income communities with large minority populations, where the least money is available for education, and where the least amount is spent on textbooks and other academic materials. Once these districts receive corporate handouts, government's failure to provide adequate school funding tends to remain unaddressed.

For most of us, the only time we enter an American high school is to vote at our local precinct. (There's an irony if there ever was one — going to participate in democracy's sacred ritual while two thousand students in the same building live under some sort of totalitarian dictatorship.) The halls are packed with burned-out teenagers shuffling from class to class, dazed and confused, wondering what the hell they're doing there. They learn how to regurgitate answers the state wants them to give, and any attempt to be an individual is now grounds for being suspected to be a member of the trench coat mafia.[6] I visited a school recently, and some students asked me if I noticed that they and the other students in the school were all wearing white or some neutral color. Nobody dares wear black, or anything else wild and distinct. That's a sure ticket to the principal's office — where the school psychologist will be waiting to ascertain whether that Limp Bizkit shirt you have on means that you intend to shoot up Miss Nelson's fourth hour geometry class.

So the kids learn to submerge any personal expression. They learn that   100
it's better to go along so that you get along. They learn that to rock the boat could get them rocked right out of the school. Don't question authority. Do as you're told. Don't think, just do as I say.

Oh, and have a good and productive life as an active, well-adjusted participant in our thriving democracy!

Are You a Potential School Shooter?

The following is a list of traits the FBI has identified as "risk factors" among students who may commit violent acts. Stay away from any student showing signs of:

- Poor coping skills
- Access to weapons
- Depression
- Drug and alcohol abuse
- Alienation
- Narcissism
- Inappropriate humor
- Unlimited, unmonitored television and Internet use

Since this includes all of you, drop out of school immediately. Home schooling is not a viable option, because you must also stay away from yourself.

---

[6]*trench coat mafia:* Name of a self-styled group of students that included Columbine High School shooters Eric Harris and Dylan Klebold; hence, any potentially violent group of students.

How to Be a Student Subversive Instead of a Student Subservient

There are many ways you can fight back at your high school — and have fun while doing it. The key thing is to learn what all the rules are, and what your rights are by law and by school district policy. This will help to prevent you getting in the kinds of trouble you don't need.

It may also get you some cool perks. David Schankula, a college student who has helped me on this book, recalls that when he was in high school in Kentucky, he and his buddies found some obscure state law that said any student who requests a day off to go to the state fair must be given the day off. The state legislature probably passed this law years ago to help some farm kid take his prize hog to the fair without being penalized at school. But the law was still on the books, and it gave any student the right to request the state fair day off — regardless of the reason. So you can imagine the look on the principal's face when David and his city friends submitted their request for their free day off from school — and there was nothing the principal could do.

Here's a few more things you can do:

1. Mock the Vote.

Student council and class elections are the biggest smokescreen the school throws up, fostering the illusion that you actually have any say in the running of the school. Most students who run for these offices either take the charade too seriously — or they just think it'll look good on their college applications. [105]

So why not run yourself? Run just to ridicule the whole ridiculous exercise. Form your own party, with its own stupid name. Campaign on wild promises: *If elected, I'll change the school mascot to an amoeba,* or *If elected, I'll insist that the principal must first eat the school lunch each day before it is fed to the students.* Put up banners with cool slogans: "Vote for me — a real loser!"

If you get elected, you can devote your energies to accomplishing things that will drive the administration crazy, but help out your fellow students (demands for free condoms, student evaluations of teachers, less homework so you can get to bed by midnight, etc).

2. Start a School Club.

You have a right to do this. Find a sympathetic teacher to sponsor it. The Pro-Choice Club. The Free Speech Club. The Integrate Our Town Club. Make every member a "president" of the club, so they all can claim it on their college applications. One student I know tried to start a Feminist Club, but the principal wouldn't allow it because then they'd be obliged to give equal time to a Male Chauvinist Club. That's the kind of idiot thinking you'll encounter, but don't give up. (Heck, if you find yourself in that situation, just say *fine* — and suggest that the principal could sponsor the Chauvinist Club.)

3. Launch Your Own Newspaper or Webzine.

You have a constitutionally protected right to do this. If you take care not to be obscene, or libelous, or give them any reason to shut you down, this can be a great way to get the truth out about what's happening at your school. Use humor. The students will love it.

4. Get Involved in the Community.

Go to the school board meetings and inform them what's going on in 110 the school. Petition them to change things. They will try to ignore you or make you sit through a long, boring meeting before they let you speak, but they have to let you speak. Write letters to the editor of your local paper. Adults don't have a clue about what goes on in your high school. Fill them in. More than likely you'll find someone there who'll support you.

Any or all of this will raise quite a ruckus, but there's help out there if you need it. Contact the local American Civil Liberties Union if the school retaliates. Threaten lawsuits — school administrators HATE to hear that word. Just remember: there's no greater satisfaction than seeing the look on your principal's face when you have the upper hand. Use it.

And Never Forget This:

There Is No Permanent Record!

ENGAGING THE TEXT

1. What evidence does Moore offer to support his contention that America is a nation of idiots? To what extent would you agree with this blunt assessment of American intelligence? Why? What limitations, if any, do you see in the "question/answer" approach that Moore takes to gauging intelligence?

2. Moore shares a number of personal experiences in this selection to dramatize his disgust with formal education. How do your own elementary and high school memories compare with Moore's school experiences? Overall, how would you characterize his attitude toward schools and schooling? To what extent would you agree with him?

3. How accurate is the grim picture of American schools that Moore offers in this selection? Would you agree with his assessment of the typical class room, the quality of the average school library, and the general ability of American teachers and of the staff who support them?

4. Who, in Moore's view, is responsible for the sorry state of America's schools? To what extent would you agree? What reforms do you think Moore would like to see, and what changes, if any, would you recommend?

5. How does Moore feel about corporate involvement in public education? Why? What possible conflicts of interest or ethical questions do you see arising in relation to the following kinds of corporate/school collaboration:

- Sponsorship of sports teams and clubs
- Exclusive contracts for soda and snack vending machines
- Fast-food franchise "food courts"
- Sponsorship of libraries, computer labs, etc.
- Commercial instruction via cable TV
- Free books with inserted advertising
- Free courses on history or economics with business or corporate content
- Volunteer "teachers" and tutors from corporate ranks

What role, if any, do you think corporations should play in support of American public schools? Why?

6. What does Moore suggest that individual students do to "fight back" against the deadening effects of the educational system? What did you do when you were in elementary and secondary school to make your own experience more meaningful? Now that you're in college, what can you do to be a "student subversive instead of a student subservient"?

EXPLORING CONNECTIONS

7. How does Moore's portrayal of the current state of American education compare with the image of the American school as described by Horace Mann (p. 121)? What seems to be the mission or goal of public schooling, according to Moore? How would you expect him to react to the goals that Mann envisions for the school? Why? Would you agree with Moore?

8. To what extent does Moore's depiction of the idiocy of schools support or challenge John Taylor Gatto's critique of American public education in "Against School" (p. 152)? Do you think that Moore would agree with Gatto's claim that mandatory public schooling has turned us into a nation of children?

EXTENDING THE CRITICAL CONTEXT

9. Test Moore's central thesis about the idiocy of the average American by working in groups to devise and administer your own general information test. You can borrow questions from the many bits of information that Moore offers throughout this selection, or simply pool your own knowledge supplemented with additional library research. Administer your questionnaire to groups of fellow students, professors, family, friends, or members of the community at large. Then compare your results to see if Americans really are as uninformed as Moore suggests.

10. As Moore suggests, even some top American universities no longer require students to take basic courses in subjects like history or foreign language. How comprehensive are the general education requirements at your college? Do you think that they provide the average student with a well-rounded education? What additional courses or requirements, if any, would you include? Why?

From *School Is Hell*. Copyright © 1987 Matt Groening. All rights reserved. Reprinted by permission of Pantheon Books, a division of Random House, Inc., New York. Courtesy of Acme Features Syndicate.

Against School

JOHN TAYLOR GATTO

The official mission statements of most American schools brim with good intentions. On paper, schools exist to help students realize their full potential, to equip them with the skills they'll need to achieve success and contribute to society, or to foster the development of independence, critical thinking, and strong ethical values. But as John Taylor Gatto (b. 1935) sees it, public schools actually exist to fulfill six covert functions meant to "cripple our kids." The frightening thing is that Gatto might know what he's talking about. An award-winning educator and ardent libertarian, Gatto has taught in New York public schools for more than two decades. In 1989, 1990, and 1991, he was named New York City Teacher of the Year, and in 1991 he was also honored as New York State Teacher of the Year. His publications include Dumbing Us Down: The Hidden Curriculum of Compulsory Schooling *(1992),* A Different Kind of Teacher *(2000), and* The Underground History of American Education *(2001). This selection originally appeared in* Harper's Magazine.

I taught for thirty years in some of the worst schools in Manhattan, and in some of the best, and during that time I became an expert in boredom. Boredom was everywhere in my world, and if you asked the kids, as I often did, *why* they felt so bored, they always gave the same answers: They said the work was stupid, that it made no sense, that they already knew it. They said they wanted to be doing something real, not just sitting around. They said teachers didn't seem to know much about their subjects and clearly weren't interested in learning more. And the kids were right: their teachers were every bit as bored as they were.

Boredom is the common condition of schoolteachers, and anyone who has spent time in a teachers' lounge can vouch for the low energy, the whining, the dispirited attitudes, to be found there. When asked why *they* feel bored, the teachers tend to blame the kids, as you might expect. Who wouldn't get bored teaching students who are rude and interested only in grades? If even that. Of course, teachers are themselves products of the same twelve-year compulsory school programs that so thoroughly bore their students, and as school personnel they are trapped inside structures even more rigid than those imposed upon the children. Who, then, is to blame?

We all are. My grandfather taught me that. One afternoon when I was seven I complained to him of boredom, and he batted me hard on the head. He told me that I was never to use that term in his presence again, that if I was bored it was my fault and no one else's. The obligation to amuse and instruct myself was entirely my own, and people who didn't know that were childish people, to be avoided if possible. Certainly not to be trusted. That episode cured me of boredom forever, and here and there over the years I was able to pass on the lesson to some remarkable student. For the most part, however, I found it futile to challenge the official notion that boredom and childishness were the natural state of affairs in the classroom. Often I had to defy custom, and even bend the law, to help kids break out of this trap.

The empire struck back, of course; childish adults regularly conflate opposition with disloyalty. I once returned from a medical leave to discover that all evidence of my having been granted the leave had been purposely destroyed, that my job had been terminated, and that I no longer possessed even a teaching license. After nine months of tormented effort I was able to retrieve the license when a school secretary testified to witnessing the plot unfold. In the meantime my family suffered more than I care to remember. By the time I finally retired in 1991, I had more than enough reason to think of our schools — with their long-term, cell-block-style, forced confinement of both students and teachers — as virtual factories of childishness. Yet I honestly could not see *why* they had to be that way. My own experience had revealed to me what many other teachers must learn along the way, too, yet keep to themselves for fear of reprisal: if we wanted to we could easily and inexpensively jettison the old, stupid structures and help kids *take* an education rather than merely *receive* a schooling. We could encourage the best qualities of youthfulness — curiosity, adventure, resilience, the capacity for surprising insight — simply by being more flexible about time, texts, and tests, by introducing kids to truly competent adults, and by giving each student what autonomy he or she needs in order to take a risk every now and then.

But we don't do that. And the more I asked why not, and persisted in thinking about the "problem" of schooling as an engineer might, the more I missed the point: What if there is no "problem" with our schools? What if they are the way they are, so expensively flying in the face of common sense and long experience in how children learn things, not because they are doing something wrong but because they are doing something right? Is it possible that George W. Bush accidentally spoke the truth when he said we would "leave no child behind"? Could it be that our schools are designed to make sure not one of them ever really grows up? 5

Do we really need school? I don't mean education, just forced schooling: six classes a day, five days a week, nine months a year, for twelve years. Is this deadly routine really necessary? And if so, for what? Don't hide behind reading, writing, and arithmetic as a rationale, because 2 million happy homeschoolers have surely put that banal justification to rest. Even if they hadn't, a considerable number of well-known Americans never went through the twelve-year wringer our kids currently go through, and they turned out all right. George Washington, Benjamin Franklin, Thomas Jefferson, Abraham Lincoln? Someone taught them, to be sure, but they were not products of a school *system,* and not one of them was ever "graduated" from a secondary school. Throughout most of American history, kids generally didn't go to high school, yet the unschooled rose to be admirals, like Farragut;[1] inventors, like Edison; captains of industry, like Carnegie[2] and Rockefeller;[3] writers, like Melville and Twain and Conrad;[4] and even scholars, like Margaret Mead.[5] In fact, until pretty recently people who reached the age of thirteen weren't looked upon as children at all. Ariel Durant, who co-wrote an enormous, and very good, multivolume history of the world with her husband, Will, was happily married at fifteen, and who could reasonably claim that Ariel Durant[6] was an uneducated person? Unschooled, perhaps, but not uneducated.

We have been taught (that is, schooled) in this country to think of "success" as synonymous with, or at least dependent upon, "schooling," but historically that isn't true in either an intellectual or a financial sense. And plenty of people throughout the world today find a way to educate themselves without resorting to a system of compulsory secondary schools that all too often resemble prisons. Why, then, do Americans confuse education with just such a system? What exactly is the purpose of our public schools?

Mass schooling of a compulsory nature really got its teeth into the United States between 1905 and 1915, though it was conceived of much earlier and pushed for throughout most of the nineteenth century. The reason given for this enormous upheaval of family life and cultural traditions was, roughly speaking, threefold:

1. To make good people.
2. To make good citizens.
3. To make each person his or her personal best.

These goals are still trotted out today on a regular basis, and most of us accept them in one form or another as a decent definition of public education's mission, however short schools actually fall in achieving them. But we are dead wrong. Compounding our error is the fact that the national literature

---

[1]*Farragut:* Admiral David Glasgow Farragut (1801–1870), American naval officer who won several important victories for the North in the Civil War, including the capture of the port of New Orleans in 1862.

[2]*Carnegie:* Andrew Carnegie (1835–1919), American businessman and philanthropist who made his enormous fortune in the steel industry.

[3]*Rockefeller:* John D. Rockefeller (1839–1937), American industrialist who founded Standard Oil and who was for a time the richest man in the world.

[4]*Melville and Twain and Conrad:* Herman Melville (1819–1891), American novelist best known as the author of *Moby-Dick* (1851); Mark Twain, the pen name of American writer Samuel Langhorne Clemens (1835–1910), author of *Adventures of Huckleberry Finn* (1884); and Polish-born writer Joseph Conrad (1857–1924), best known for the novella "Heart of Darkness" (1899).

[5]*Margaret Mead:* American anthropologist (1901–1978) and author of the groundbreaking book *Coming of Age in Samoa* (1928).

[6]*Ariel Durant:* With husband Will (1885–1981), Ariel (1898–1981) won the Pulitzer Prize for literature for volume ten of their eleven-volume *The Story of Civilization,* published from 1935 to 1975.

holds numerous and surprisingly consistent statements of compulsory schooling's true purpose. We have, for example, the great H. L. Mencken,[7] who wrote in *The American Mercury* for April 1924 that the aim of public education is not

> to fill the young of the species with knowledge and awaken their intelligence. . . . Nothing could be further from the truth. The aim . . . is simply to reduce as many individuals as possible to the same safe level, to breed and train a standardized citizenry, to put down dissent and originality. That is its aim in the United States . . . and that is its aim everywhere else.

Because of Mencken's reputation as a satirist, we might be tempted to dismiss this passage as a bit of hyperbolic sarcasm. His article, however, goes on to trace the template for our own educational system back to the now vanished, though never to be forgotten, military state of Prussia. And although he was certainly aware of the irony that we had recently been at war with Germany, the heir to Prussian thought and culture, Mencken was being perfectly serious here. Our educational system really is Prussian in origin, and that really is cause for concern.

    The odd fact of a Prussian provenance for our schools pops up again and again once you know to look for it. William James[8] alluded to it many times at the turn of the century. Orestes Brownson,[9] the hero of Christopher Lasch's[10] 1991 book, *The True and Only Heaven*, was publicly denouncing the Prussianization of American schools back in the 1840s. Horace Mann's[11] "Seventh Annual Report" to the Massachusetts State Board of Education in 1843 is essentially a paean to the land of Frederick the Great[12] and a call for its schooling to be brought here. That Prussian culture loomed large in America is hardly surprising given our early association with that utopian state. A Prussian served as Washington's aide during the Revolutionary War, and so many German-speaking people had settled here by 1795 that Congress considered publishing a German-language edition of the federal laws. But what shocks is that we should so eagerly have adopted one of the very worst aspects of Prussian culture: an educational system deliberately designed to produce mediocre intellects, to hamstring the inner life, to deny

10

[7]*H. L. Mencken:* American social critic and commentator known for his satiric wit (1880–1956).

[8]*William James:* American psychologist and philosopher (1842–1910).

[9]*Orestes Brownson:* American philosopher and essayist (1803–1876).

[10]*Christopher Lasch:* American historian and social critic (1932–1994), probably best known for *The Culture of Narcissism: American Life in an Age of Diminished Expectations* (1979) and *The Revolt of the Elites: And the Betrayal of Democracy* (1994).

[11]*Horace Mann:* Secretary of the State Board of Education in Massachusetts. See the excerpt from *Report of the Massachusetts Board of Education, 1848* (p. 121).

[12]*Frederick the Great:* King of Prussia (now part of present-day Germany), who reigned from 1740 to 1786.

students appreciable leadership skills, and to ensure docile and incomplete citizens — all in order to render the populace "manageable."

It was from James Bryant Conant — president of Harvard for twenty years, World War I poison-gas specialist, World War II executive on the atomic-bomb project, high commissioner of the American zone in Germany after World War II, and truly one of the most influential figures of the twentieth century — that I first got wind of the real purposes of American schooling. Without Conant, we would probably not have the same style and degree of standardized testing that we enjoy today, nor would we be blessed with gargantuan high schools that warehouse 2,000 to 4,000 students at a time, like the famous Columbine High[13] in Littleton, Colorado. Shortly after I retired from teaching I picked up Conant's 1959 book-length essay, *The Child, the Parent, and the State,* and was more than a little intrigued to see him mention in passing that the modern schools we attend were the result of a "revolution" engineered between 1905 and 1930. A revolution? He declines to elaborate, but he does direct the curious and the uninformed to Alexander Inglis's 1918 book, *Principles of Secondary Education,* in which "one saw this revolution through the eyes of a revolutionary."

Inglis, for whom a lecture in education at Harvard is named, makes it perfectly clear that compulsory schooling on this continent was intended to be just what it had been for Prussia in the 1820s: a fifth column[14] into the burgeoning democratic movement that threatened to give the peasants and the proletarians a voice at the bargaining table. Modern, industrialized, compulsory schooling was to make a sort of surgical incision into the prospective unity of these underclasses. Divide children by subject, by age-grading, by constant rankings on tests, and by many other more subtle means, and it was unlikely that the ignorant mass of mankind, separated in childhood, would ever re-integrate into a dangerous whole.

Inglis breaks down the purpose — the *actual* purpose — of modern schooling into six basic functions, any one of which is enough to curl the hair of those innocent enough to believe the three traditional goals listed earlier:

1. The *adjustive* or *adaptive* function. Schools are to establish fixed habits of reaction to authority. This, of course, precludes critical judgment completely. It also pretty much destroys the idea that useful or interesting material should be taught, because you can't test for *reflexive* obedience until you know whether you can make kids learn, and do, foolish and boring things.

2. The *integrating* function. This might well be called "the conformity function," because its intention is to make children as alike as possible. People who conform are predictable, and this is of great use to those who wish to harness and manipulate a large labor force.

[13]*Columbine High:* Site of April 20, 1999, massacre by students Eric Harris and Dylan Klebold, who killed twelve and wounded twenty-four others before killing themselves.

[14]*a fifth column:* Secret group of infiltrators who undermine a nation's defenses.

3. The *diagnostic and directive* function. School is meant to determine each student's proper social role. This is done by logging evidence mathematically and anecdotally on cumulative records. As in "your permanent record." Yes, you do have one.

4. The *differentiating* function. Once their social role has been "diagnosed," children are to be sorted by role and trained only so far as their destination in the social machine merits — and not one step further. So much for making kids their personal best.

5. The *selective* function. This refers not to human choice at all but to Darwin's theory of natural selection as applied to what he called "the favored races." In short, the idea is to help things along by consciously attempting to improve the breeding stock. Schools are meant to tag the unfit — with poor grades, remedial placement, and other punishments — clearly enough that their peers will accept them as inferior and effectively bar them from the reproductive sweepstakes. That's what all those little humiliations from first grade onward were intended to do: wash the dirt down the drain.

6. The *propaedeutic* function. The societal system implied by these rules will require an elite group of caretakers. To that end, a small fraction of the kids will quietly be taught how to manage this continuing project, how to watch over and control a population deliberately dumbed down and declawed in order that government might proceed unchallenged and corporations might never want for obedient labor.

That, unfortunately, is the purpose of mandatory public education in this country. And lest you take Inglis for an isolated crank with a rather too cynical take on the educational enterprise, you should know that he was hardly alone in championing these ideas. Conant himself, building on the ideas of Horace Mann and others, campaigned tirelessly for an American school system designed along the same lines. Men like George Peabody, who funded the cause of mandatory schooling throughout the South, surely understood that the Prussian system was useful in creating not only a harmless electorate and a servile labor force but also a virtual herd of mindless consumers. In time a great number of industrial titans came to recognize the enormous profits to be had by cultivating and tending just such a herd via public education, among them Andrew Carnegie and John D. Rockefeller.

There you have it. Now you know. We don't need Karl Marx's conception of a grand warfare between the classes to see that it is in the interest of complex management, economic or political, to dumb people down, to demoralize them, to divide them from one another, and to discard them if they don't conform. Class may frame the proposition, as when Woodrow Wilson, then president of Princeton University, said the following to the New York City School Teachers Association in 1909: "We want one class of persons to have a liberal education, and we want another class of persons, a very much larger class, of necessity, in every society, to forgo the privileges of a liberal education and fit themselves to perform specific difficult manual tasks." But the motives behind the disgusting decisions that bring about these ends need not be class-based at all. They can stem purely from fear, or from the by now familiar belief that "efficiency" is the paramount virtue, rather than love, liberty, laughter, or hope. Above all, they can stem from simple greed.

There were vast fortunes to be made, after all, in an economy based on mass production and organized to favor the large corporation rather than the small business or the family farm. But mass production required mass consumption, and at the turn of the twentieth century most Americans considered it both unnatural and unwise to buy things they didn't actually need. Mandatory schooling was a godsend on that count. School didn't have to train kids in any direct sense to think they should consume nonstop, because it did something even better: it encouraged them not to think at all. And that left them sitting ducks for another great invention of the modern era — marketing.

Now, you needn't have studied marketing to know that there are two groups of people who can always be convinced to consume more than they need to: addicts and children. School has done a pretty good job of turning our children into addicts, but it has done a spectacular job of turning our children into children. Again, this is no accident. Theorists from Plato to Rousseau[15] to our own Dr. Inglis knew that if children could be cloistered with other children, stripped of responsibility and independence, encouraged to develop only the trivializing emotions of greed, envy, jealousy, and fear, they would grow older but never truly grow up. In the 1934 edition of his once well-known book *Public Education in the United States*, Ellwood P. Cubberley detailed and praised the way the strategy of successive school enlargements had extended childhood by two to six years, and forced schooling was at that point still quite new. This same Cubberley — who was dean of Stanford's School of Education, a textbook editor at Houghton Mifflin, and Conant's friend and correspondent at Harvard — had written the following in the 1922 edition of his book *Public School Administration:* "Our schools are . . . factories in which the raw products (children) are to be shaped and fashioned. . . . And it is the business of the school to build its pupils according to the specifications laid down."

It's perfectly obvious from our society today what those specifications were. Maturity has by now been banished from nearly every aspect of our lives. Easy divorce laws have removed the need to work at relationships; easy credit has removed the need for fiscal self-control; easy entertainment has removed the need to learn to entertain oneself; easy answers have removed the need to ask questions. We have become a nation of children, happy to surrender our judgments and our wills to political exhortations and commercial

---

[15]*Plato to Rousseau:* Plato (c. 427–c. 347 B.C.E.), extraordinarily influential Greek philosopher. Jean-Jacques Rousseau, Swiss philosopher and writer (1712–1778).

blandishments that would insult actual adults. We buy televisions, and then we buy the things we see on the television. We buy computers, and then we buy the things we see on the computer. We buy $150 sneakers whether we need them or not, and when they fall apart too soon we buy another pair. We drive SUVs and believe the lie that they constitute a kind of life insurance, even when we're upside-down in them. And, worst of all, we don't bat an eye when Ari Fleischer[16] tells us to "be careful what you say," even if we remember having been told somewhere back in school that America is the land of the free. We simply buy that one too. Our schooling, as intended, has seen to it.

Now for the good news. Once you understand the logic behind modern schooling, its tricks and traps are fairly easy to avoid. School trains children to be employees and consumers; teach your own to be leaders and adventurers. School trains children to obey reflexively; teach your own to think critically and independently. Well-schooled kids have a low threshold for boredom; help your own to develop an inner life so that they'll never be bored. Urge them to take on the serious material, the *grown-up* material, in history, literature, philosophy, music, art, economics, theology — all the stuff schoolteachers know well enough to avoid. Challenge your kids with plenty of solitude so that they can learn to enjoy their own company, to conduct inner dialogues. Well-schooled people are conditioned to dread being alone, and they seek constant companionship through the TV, the computer, the cell phone, and through shallow friendships quickly acquired and quickly abandoned. Your children should have a more meaningful life, and they can.

First, though, we must wake up to what our schools really are: laborato-   20
ries of experimentation on young minds, drill centers for the habits and attitudes that corporate society demands. Mandatory education serves children only incidentally; its real purpose is to turn them into servants. Don't let your own have their childhoods extended, not even for a day. If David Farragut could take command of a captured British warship as a preteen, if Thomas Edison could publish a broadsheet at the age of twelve, if Ben Franklin could apprentice himself to a printer at the same age (then put himself through a course of study that would choke a Yale senior today), there's no telling what your own kids could do. After a long life, and thirty years in the public school trenches, I've concluded that genius is as common as dirt. We suppress our genius only because we haven't yet figured out how to manage a population of educated men and women. The solution, I think, is simple and glorious. Let them manage themselves.

Engaging the Text

1. Why does Gatto think that school is boring and childish? How does Gatto's depiction of school compare with your own elementary and secondary school experience?

[16]*Ari Fleischer:* Press secretary for George W. Bush from 2001 to 2003 (b. 1960).

2. What, according to Gatto, are the six unstated purposes of public schooling? To what extent does your own prior educational experience support this bleak view of American education?

3. To what extent would you agree that we really don't need to go to school? Given the current state of technology and a globalizing economy, do you think most people would gain the abilities they need to survive and thrive through homeschooling?

4. How would you go about teaching your own children to be "leaders and adventurers," to think "critically and independently," and to "develop an inner life so that they'll never be bored"? How many parents, in your estimation, have the time, experience, and resources to make Gatto's ideal education a reality?

EXPLORING CONNECTIONS

5. Compare Horace Mann's view of the purpose of public education (p. 121) with Gatto's analysis of the hidden purposes of compulsory schooling. Which of these depictions of public education does your own experience of schooling support?

6. Look ahead to Jean Anyon's excerpt from *Social Class and the Hidden Curriculum of Work* (p. 173) and compare Anyon's analysis of the real agenda of American public education with that described by Gatto. To what extent does Anyon's class-based analysis of education in America support Gatto's description of the unspoken purposes of public schooling?

7. How does Gatto's general assessment of his fellow Americans compare with that advanced by Henry David Thoreau (p. 836)? Do you think Americans as a group are more or less independent and self-reliant today than they were back in 1849 when Thoreau wrote "Civil Disobedience"?

EXTENDING THE CRITICAL CONTEXT

8. Working in groups, write a proposal for a school that wouldn't be boring or childish and that would create the kind of independent, critical, active thinkers that Gatto prizes. What would a day in such a school be like? What would the students do? What would they learn? Who would teach them?

9. Research the state of Prussia and Frederick the Great to learn more about Prussian history and culture. How might your findings change your response to Gatto's argument? Would you agree that the Prussian influence on American schooling is really a "cause for concern"? Why? What other nineteenth-century nation might have offered a better model?

"I Just Wanna Be Average"

MIKE ROSE

Mike Rose is anything but average: he has published poetry, scholarly research, a textbook, and two widely praised books on education in America. A professor in the School of Education at UCLA, Rose (b. 1944) has won awards from the National Academy of Education, the National Council of Teachers of English, and the John Simon Guggenheim Memorial Foundation.

Below you'll read the story of how this highly successful teacher and writer started high school in the "vocational education" track, learning dead-end skills from teachers who were often underprepared or incompetent. Rose shows that students whom the system has written off can have tremendous unrealized potential, and his critique of the school system specifies several reasons for the "failure" of students who go through high school belligerent, fearful, stoned, frustrated, or just plain bored. This selection comes from Lives on the Boundary *(1989), Rose's exploration of America's educationally underprivileged. His most recent book,* Possible Lives *(1996), offers a nation-wide tour of creative classrooms and innovative educational programs. Rose is currently a professor at the UCLA Graduate School of Education and Information Studies.*

It took two buses to get to Our Lady of Mercy. The first started deep in South Los Angeles and caught me at midpoint. The second drifted through neighborhoods with trees, parks, big lawns, and lots of flowers. The rides were long but were livened up by a group of South L.A. veterans whose parents also thought that Hope had set up shop in the west end of the county. There was Christy Biggars, who, at sixteen, was dealing and was, according to rumor, a pimp as well. There were Bill Cobb and Johnny Gonzales, grease-pencil artists extraordinaire, who left Nembutal-enhanced[1] swirls of "Cobb" and "Johnny" on the corrugated walls of the bus. And then there was Tyrrell Wilson. Tyrrell was the coolest kid I knew. He ran the dozens[2] like a metric halfback, laid down a rap that outrhymed and outpointed Cobb, whose rap was good but not great — the curse of a moderately soulful kid trapped in white skin. But it was Cobb who would sneak a radio onto the bus, and thus underwrote his patter with Little Richard, Fats Domino, Chuck Berry, the Coasters, and Ernie K. Doe's[3] mother-in-law, an awful woman who was "sent from down below." And so it was that Christy and Cobb and Johnny G. and Tyrrell and I and assorted others picked up along the way passed our days in the back of the bus, a funny mix brought together by geography and parental desire.

Entrance to school brings with it forms and releases and assessments. Mercy relied on a series of tests, mostly the Stanford-Binet,[4] for placement, and somehow the results of my tests got confused with those of another student named Rose. The other Rose apparently didn't do very well, for I was placed in the vocational track, a euphemism for the bottom level. Neither I

---

[1]*Nembutal:* Trade name for pentobarbital, a sedative drug.

[2]*the dozens:* A verbal game of African origin in which competitors try to top each other's insults.

[3]*Little Richard, Fats Domino, Chuck Berry, the Coasters, and Ernie K. Doe:* Popular black musicians of the 1950s.

[4]*Stanford-Binet:* An IQ test.

nor my parents realized what this meant. We had no sense that Business Math, Typing, and English-Level D were dead ends. The current spate of reports on the schools criticizes parents for not involving themselves in the education of their children. But how would someone like Tommy Rose, with his two years of Italian schooling, know what to ask? And what sort of pressure could an exhausted waitress apply? The error went undetected, and I remained in the vocational track for two years. What a place.

My homeroom was supervised by Brother Dill, a troubled and unstable man who also taught freshman English. When his class drifted away from him, which was often, his voice would rise in paranoid accusations, and occasionally he would lose control and shake or smack us. I hadn't been there two months when one of his brisk, face-turning slaps had my glasses sliding down the aisle. Physical education was also pretty harsh. Our teacher was a stubby ex-lineman who had played old-time pro ball in the Midwest. He routinely had us grabbing our ankles to receive his stinging paddle across our butts. He did that, he said, to make men of us. "Rose," he bellowed on our first encounter; me standing geeky in line in my baggy shorts. "'Rose'? What the hell kind of name is that?"

"Italian, sir," I squeaked.

"Italian! Ho. Rose, do you know the sound a bag of shit makes when it   5 hits the wall?"

"No, sir."

"Wop!"[5]

Sophomore English was taught by Mr. Mitropetros. He was a large, bejeweled man who managed the parking lot at the Shrine Auditorium. He would crow and preen and list for us the stars he'd brushed against. We'd ask questions and glance knowingly and snicker, and all that fueled the poor guy to brag some more. Parking cars was his night job. He had little training in English, so his lesson plan for his day work had us reading the district's required text, *Julius Caesar,* aloud for the semester. We'd finished the play way before the twenty weeks was up, so he'd have us switch parts again and again and start again: Dave Snyder, the fastest guy at Mercy, muscling through Caesar to the breathless squeals of Calpurnia, as interpreted by Steve Fusco, a surfer who owned the school's most envied paneled wagon. Week ten and Dave and Steve would take on new roles, as would we all, and render a water-logged Cassius and a Brutus that are beyond my powers of description.

Spanish I — taken in the second year — fell into the hands of a new recruit. Mr. Montez was a tiny man, slight, five foot six at the most, soft-spoken and delicate. Spanish was a particularly rowdy class, and Mr. Montez was as prepared for it as a doily maker at a hammer throw. He would tap his pencil to a room in which Steve Fusco was propelling spitballs from his heavy lips, in which Mike Dweetz was taunting Billy Hawk, a half-Indian,

---

[5]*Wop:* Derogatory term for Italian.

half-Spanish, reed-thin, quietly explosive boy. The vocational track at Our
Lady of Mercy mixed kids traveling in from South L.A. with South Bay
surfers and a few Slavs and Chicanos from the harbors of San Pedro. This
was a dangerous miscellany: surfers and hodads[6] and South-Central blacks
all ablaze to the metronomic tapping of Hector Montez's pencil.

One day Billy lost it. Out of the corner of my eye I saw him strike   10
out with his right arm and catch Dweetz across the neck. Quick as a spasm,
Dweetz was out of his seat, scattering desks, cracking Billy on the side of
the head, right behind the eye. Snyder and Fusco and others broke it up,
but the room felt hot and close and naked. Mr. Montez's tenuous authority
was finally ripped to shreds, and I think everyone felt a little strange about
that. The charade was over, and when it came down to it, I don't think any
of the kids really wanted it to end this way. They had pushed and pushed
and bullied their way into a freedom that both scared and embarrassed
them.

Students will float to the mark you set. I and the others in the vocational classes were bobbing in pretty shallow water. Vocational education
has aimed at increasing the economic opportunities of students who do not
do well in our schools. Some serious programs succeed in doing that, and
through exceptional teachers — like Mr. Gross in *Horace's Compromise*[7] —
students learn to develop hypotheses and troubleshoot, reason through a
problem, and communicate effectively — the true job skills. The vocational
track, however, is most often a place for those who are just not making it, a
dumping ground for the disaffected. There were a few teachers who worked
hard at education; young Brother Slattery, for example, combined a stern
voice with weekly quizzes to try to pass along to us a skeletal outline of
world history. But mostly the teachers had no idea of how to engage the
imaginations of us kids who were scuttling along at the bottom of the pond.

And the teachers would have needed some inventiveness, for none of
us was groomed for the classroom. It wasn't just that I didn't know things —
didn't know how to simplify algebraic fractions, couldn't identify different
kinds of clauses, bungled Spanish translations — but that I had developed
various faulty and inadequate ways of doing algebra and making sense of
Spanish. Worse yet, the years of defensive tuning out in elementary school
had given me a way to escape quickly while seeming at least half alert. During my time in Voc. Ed., I developed further into a mediocre student and a
somnambulant problem solver, and that affected the subjects I did have the
wherewithal to handle: I detested Shakespeare; I got bored with history. My
attention flitted here and there. I fooled around in class and read my books
indifferently — the intellectual equivalent of playing with your food. I did
what I had to do to get by, and I did it with half a mind.

[6]*hodads:* Nonsurfers.
[7]*Horace's Compromise:* A book on American education by Theodore Sizer.

But I did learn things about people and eventually came into my own socially. I liked the guys in Voc. Ed. Growing up where I did, I understood and admired physical prowess, and there was an abundance of muscle here. There was Dave Snyder, a sprinter and halfback of true quality. Dave's ability and his quick wit gave him a natural appeal, and he was welcome in any clique, though he always kept a little independent. He enjoyed acting the fool and could care less about studies, but he possessed a certain maturity and never caused the faculty much trouble. It was a testament to his independence that he included me among his friends — I eventually went out for track, but I was no jock. Owing to the Latin alphabet and a dearth of *R*s and *S*s, Snyder sat behind Rose, and we started exchanging one-liners and became friends.

There was Ted Richard, a much-touted Little League pitcher. He was chunky and had a baby face and came to Our Lady of Mercy as a seasoned street fighter. Ted was quick to laugh and he had a loud, jolly laugh, but when he got angry he'd smile a little smile, the kind that simply raises the corner of the mouth a quarter of an inch. For those who knew, it was an eerie signal. Those who didn't found themselves in big trouble, for Ted was very quick. He loved to carry on what we would come to call philosophical discussions: What is courage? Does God exist? He also loved words, enjoyed picking up big ones like *salubrious* and *equivocal* and using them in our conversations — laughing at himself as the word hit a chuckhole rolling off his tongue. Ted didn't do all that well in school — baseball and parties and testing the courage he'd speculated about took up his time. His textbooks were *Argosy* and *Field and Stream,* whatever newspapers he'd find on the bus stop — from the *Daily Worker* to pornography — conversations with uncles or hobos or businessmen he'd meet in a coffee shop, *The Old Man and the Sea.* With hindsight, I can see that Ted was developing into one of those rough-hewn intellectuals whose sources are a mix of the learned and the apocryphal, whose discussions are both assured and sad.

And then there was Ken Harvey. Ken was good-looking in a puffy way 15 and had a full and oily ducktail and was a car enthusiast . . . a hodad. One day in religion class, he said the sentence that turned out to be one of the most memorable of the hundreds of thousands I heard in those Voc. Ed. years. We were talking about the parable of the talents, about achievement, working hard, doing the best you can do, blah-blah-blah, when the teacher called on the restive Ken Harvey for an opinion. Ken thought about it, but just for a second, and said (with studied, minimal affect), "I just wanna be average." That woke me up. Average? Who wants to be average? Then the athletes chimed in with the clichés that make you want to laryngectomize them, and the exchange became a platitudinous melee. At the time, I thought Ken's assertion was stupid, and I wrote him off. But his sentence has stayed with me all these years, and I think I am finally coming to understand it.

Ken Harvey was gasping for air. School can be a tremendously disorienting place. No matter how bad the school, you're going to encounter notions that don't fit with the assumptions and beliefs that you grew up with — maybe you'll hear these dissonant notions from teachers, maybe from the other students, and maybe you'll read them. You'll also be thrown in with all kinds of kids from all kinds of backgrounds, and that can be unsettling — this is especially true in places of rich ethnic and linguistic mix, like the L.A. basin. You'll see a handful of students far excel you in courses that sound exotic and that are only in the curriculum of the elite: French, physics, trigonometry. And all this is happening while you're trying to shape an identity, your body is changing, and your emotions are running wild. If you're a working-class kid in the vocational track, the options you'll have to deal with this will be constrained in certain ways: you're defined by your school as "slow"; you're placed in a curriculum that isn't designed to liberate you but to occupy you, or, if you're lucky, train you, though the training is for work the society does not esteem; other students are picking up the cues from your school and your curriculum and interacting with you in particular ways. If you're a kid like Ted Richard, you turn your back on all this and let your mind roam where it may. But youngsters like Ted are rare. What Ken and so many others do is protect themselves from such suffocating madness by taking on with a vengeance the identity implied in the vocational track. Reject the confusion and frustration by openly defining yourself as the Common Joe. Champion the average. Rely on your own good sense. Fuck this bullshit. Bullshit, of course, is everything you — and the others — fear is beyond you: books, essays, tests, academic scrambling, complexity, scientific reasoning, philosophical inquiry.

The tragedy is that you have to twist the knife in your own gray matter to make this defense work. You'll have to shut down, have to reject intellectual stimuli or diffuse them with sarcasm, have to cultivate stupidity, have to convert boredom from a malady into a way of confronting the world. Keep your vocabulary simple, act stoned when you're not or act more stoned than you are, flaunt ignorance, materialize your dreams. It is a powerful and effective defense — it neutralizes the insult and the frustration of being a vocational kid and, when perfected, it drives teachers up the wall, a delightful secondary effect. But like all strong magic, it exacts a price.

My own deliverance from the Voc. Ed. world began with sophomore biology. Every student, college prep to vocational, had to take biology, and unlike the other courses, the same person taught all sections. When teaching the vocational group, Brother Clint probably slowed down a bit or omitted a little of the fundamental biochemistry, but he used the same book and more or less the same syllabus across the board. If one class got tough, he could get tougher. He was young and powerful and very handsome, and looks and physical strength were high currency. No one gave him any trouble.

I was pretty bad at the dissecting table, but the lectures and the textbook were interesting: plastic overlays that, with each turned page, peeled away skin, then veins and muscle, then organs, down to the very bones that Brother Clint, pointer in hand, would tap out on our hanging skeleton.

Dave Snyder was in big trouble, for the study of life — versus the living of it — was sticking in his craw. We worked out a code for our multiple-choice exams. He'd poke me in the back: once for the answer under *A*, twice for *B*, and so on; and when he'd hit the right one, I'd look up to the ceiling as though I were lost in thought. Poke: cytoplasm. Poke, poke: methane. Poke, poke, poke: William Harvey. Poke, poke, poke, poke: islets of Langerhans. This didn't work out perfectly, but Dave passed the course, and I mastered the dreamy look of a guy on a record jacket. And something else happened. Brother Clint puzzled over this Voc. Ed. kid who was racking up 98s and 99s on his tests. He checked the school's records and discovered the error. He recommended that I begin my junior year in the College Prep program. According to all I've read since, such a shift, as one report put it, is virtually impossible. Kids at that level rarely cross tracks. The telling thing is how chancy both my placement into and exit from Voc. Ed. was; neither I nor my parents had anything to do with it. I lived in one world during spring semester, and when I came back to school in the fall, I was living in another.

Switching to College Prep was a mixed blessing. I was an erratic 20 student. I was undisciplined. And I hadn't caught onto the rules of the game: why work hard in a class that didn't grab my fancy? I was also hopelessly behind in math. Chemistry was hard; toying with my chemistry set years before hadn't prepared me for the chemist's equations. Fortunately, the priest who taught both chemistry and second-year algebra was also the school's athletic director. Membership on the track team covered me; I knew I wouldn't get lower than a C. U.S. history was taught pretty well, and I did okay. But civics was taken over by a football coach who had trouble reading the textbook aloud — and reading aloud was the centerpiece of his pedagogy. College Prep at Mercy was certainly an improvement over the vocational program — at least it carried some status — but the social science curriculum was weak, and the mathematics and physical sciences were simply beyond me. I had a miserable quantitative background and ended up copying some assignments and finessing the rest as best I could. Let me try to explain how it feels to see again and again material you should once have learned but didn't.

You are given a problem. It requires you to simplify algebraic fractions or to multiply expressions containing square roots. You know this is pretty basic material because you've seen it for years. Once a teacher took some time with you, and you learned how to carry out these operations. Simple versions, anyway. But that was a year or two or more in the past, and these are more complex versions, and now you're not sure. And this, you keep telling yourself, is ninth- or even eighth-grade stuff.

Next it's a word problem. This is also old hat. The basic elements are as familiar as story characters: trains speeding so many miles per hour or shadows of buildings angling so many degrees. Maybe you know enough, have sat through enough explanations, to be able to begin setting up the problem: "If one train is going this fast . . ." or "This shadow is really one line of a triangle..." Then: "Let's see..." "How did Jones do this?" "Hmmmm." "No." "No, that won't work." Your attention wavers. You wonder about other things: a football game, a dance, that cute new checker at the market. You try to focus on the problem again. You scribble on paper for a while, but the tension wins out and your attention flits elsewhere. You crumple the paper and begin daydreaming to ease the frustration.

The particulars will vary, but in essence this is what a number of students go through, especially those in so-called remedial classes. They open their textbooks and see once again the familiar and impenetrable formulas and diagrams and terms that have stumped them for years. There is no excitement here. *No* excitement. Regardless of what the teacher says, this is not a new challenge. There is, rather, embarrassment and frustration and, not surprisingly, some anger in being reminded once again of long-standing inadequacies. No wonder so many students finally attribute their difficulties to something inborn, organic: "That part of my brain just doesn't work." Given the troubling histories many of these students have, it's miraculous that any of them can lift the shroud of hopelessness sufficiently to make deliverance from these classes possible.

Through this entire period, my father's health was deteriorating with cruel momentum. His arteriosclerosis progressed to the point where a simple nick on his shin wouldn't heal. Eventually it ulcerated and widened. Lou Minton would come by daily to change the dressing. We tried renting an oscillating bed — which we placed in the front room — to force blood through the constricted arteries in my father's legs. The bed hummed through the night, moving in place to ward off the inevitable. The ulcer continued to spread, and the doctors finally had to amputate. My grandfather had lost his leg in a stockyard accident. Now my father too was crippled. His convalescence was slow but steady, and the doctors placed him in the Santa Monica Rehabilitation Center, a sun-bleached building that opened out onto the warm spray of the Pacific. The place gave him some strength and some color and some training in walking with an artificial leg. He did pretty well for a year or so until he slipped and broke his hip. He was confined to a wheelchair after that, and the confinement contributed to the diminishing of his body and spirit.

I am holding a picture of him. He is sitting in his wheelchair and smiling 25
at the camera. The smile appears forced, unsteady, seems to quaver, though it is frozen in silver nitrate. He is in his mid-sixties and looks eighty. Late in my junior year, he had a stroke and never came out of the resulting coma. After that, I would see him only in dreams, and to this day that is how I join him. Sometimes the dreams are sad and grisly and primal: my father lying in a bed soaked with his suppuration,[8] holding me, rocking me. But sometimes the dreams bring him back to me healthy: him talking to me on an empty street, or buying some pictures to decorate our old house, or transformed somehow into someone strong and adept with tools and the physical.

---

[8]*suppuration:* Discharge from wounds.

Jack MacFarland couldn't have come into my life at a better time. My father was dead, and I had logged up too many years of scholastic indifference. Mr. MacFarland had a master's degree from Columbia and decided, at twenty-six, to find a little school and teach his heart out. He never took any credentialing courses, couldn't bear to, he said, so he had to find employment in a private system. He ended up at Our Lady of Mercy teaching five sections of senior English. He was a beatnik who was born too late. His teeth were stained, he tucked his sorry tie in between the third and fourth buttons of his shirt, and his pants were chronically wrinkled. At first, we couldn't believe this guy, thought he slept in his car. But within no time, he had us so startled with work that we didn't much worry about where he slept or if he slept at all. We wrote three or four essays a month. We read a book every two to three weeks, starting with the *Iliad* and ending up with Hemingway. He gave us a quiz on the reading every other day. He brought a prep school curriculum to Mercy High.

MacFarland's lectures were crafted, and as he delivered them he would pace the room jiggling a piece of chalk in his cupped hand, using it to scribble on the board the names of all the writers and philosophers and plays and novels he was weaving into his discussion. He asked questions often, raised everything from Zeno's paradox to the repeated last line of Frost's "Stopping by Woods on a Snowy Evening." He slowly and carefully built up our knowledge of Western intellectual history — with facts, with connections, with speculations. We learned about Greek philosophy, about Dante, the Elizabethan world view, the Age of Reason, existentialism. He analyzed poems with us, had us reading sections from John Ciardi's *How Does a Poem Mean?*, making a potentially difficult book accessible with his own explanations. We gave oral reports on poems Ciardi didn't cover. We imitated the styles of Conrad, Hemingway, and *Time* magazine. We wrote and talked, wrote and talked. The man immersed us in language.

Even MacFarland's barbs were literary. If Jim Fitzsimmons, hung over and irritable, tried to smart-ass him, he'd rejoin with a flourish that would spark the indomitable Skip Madison — who'd lost his front teeth in a hapless tackle — to flick his tongue through the gap and opine, "good chop," drawing out the single "o" in stinging indictment. Jack MacFarland, this tobacco-stained intellectual, brandished linguistic weapons of a kind I hadn't encountered before. Here was this *egghead*, for God's sake, keeping some pretty difficult people in line. And from what I heard, Mike Dweetz and Steve Fusco and all the notorious Voc. Ed. crowd settled down as well when MacFarland took the podium. Though a lot of guys groused in the school-yard, it just seemed that giving trouble to this particular teacher was a silly thing to do. Tomfoolery, not to mention assault, had no place in the world he was trying to create for us, and instinctively everyone knew that. If nothing else, we all recognized MacFarland's considerable intelligence and respected the hours he put into his work. It came to this: the troublemaker would look foolish rather than daring. Even Jim Fitzsimmons was reading *On the Road* and turning his incipient alcoholism to literary ends.

There were some lives that were already beyond Jack MacFarland's ministrations, but mine was not. I started reading again as I hadn't since elementary school. I would go into our gloomy little bedroom or sit at the dinner table while, on the television, Danny McShane was paralyzing Mr. Moto with the atomic drop, and work slowly back through *Heart of Darkness*, trying to catch the words in Conrad's sentences. I certainly was not MacFarland's best student; most of the other guys in College Prep, even my fellow slackers, had better backgrounds than I did. But I worked very hard, for MacFarland had hooked me. He tapped my old interest in reading and creating stories. He gave me a way to feel special by using my mind. And he provided a role model that wasn't shaped on physical prowess alone, and something inside me that I wasn't quite aware of responded to that. Jack MacFarland established a literacy club, to borrow a phrase of Frank Smith's, and invited me — invited all of us — to join.

There's been a good deal of research and speculation suggesting that the   30 acknowledgment of school performance with extrinsic rewards — smiling faces, stars, numbers, grades — diminishes the intrinsic satisfaction children experience by engaging in reading or writing or problem solving. While it's certainly true that we've created an educational system that encourages our best and brightest to become cynical grade collectors and, in general, have developed an obsession with evaluation and assessment, I must tell you that venal though it may have been, I loved getting good grades from MacFarland. I now know how subjective grades can be, but then they came tucked in the back of essays like bits of scientific data, some sort of spectroscopic readout that said, objectively and publicly, that I had made something of value. I suppose I'd been mediocre for too long and enjoyed a public redefinition. And I suppose the workings of my mind, such as they were, had been private for too long. My linguistic play moved into the world; . . . these papers with their circled, red B-pluses and A-minuses linked my mind to something outside it. I carried them around like a club emblem.

One day in the December of my senior year, Mr. MacFarland asked me where I was going to go to college. I hadn't thought much about it. Many of the students I teach today spent their last year in high school with a physics text in one hand and the Stanford catalog in the other, but I wasn't even aware of what "entrance requirements" were. My folks would say that they wanted me to go to college and be a doctor, but I don't know how seriously I ever took that; it seemed a sweet thing to say, a bit of supportive family chatter, like telling a gangly daughter she's graceful. The reality of higher education wasn't in my scheme of things: no one in the family had gone to college; only two of my uncles had completed high school. I figured I'd get a night job and go to the local junior college because I knew that Snyder and Company were going there to play ball. But I hadn't even prepared for that. When I finally said, "I don't know," MacFarland looked down at me — I was seated in his office — and said, "Listen, you can write."

My grades stank. I had A's in biology and a handful of B's in a few English and social science classes. All the rest were C's — or worse. MacFarland said I would do well in his class and laid down the law about doing well in the others. Still, the record for my first three years wouldn't have been acceptable to any four-year school. To nobody's surprise, I was turned down flat by USC and UCLA. But Jack MacFarland was on the case. He had received his bachelor's degree from Loyola University, so he made calls to old professors and talked to somebody in admissions and wrote me a strong letter. Loyola finally accepted me as a probationary student. I would be on trial for the first year, and if I did okay, I would be granted regular status. MacFarland also intervened to get me a loan, for I could never have afforded a private college without it. Four more years of religion classes and four more years of boys at one school, girls at another. But at least I was going to college. Amazing.

In my last semester of high school, I elected a special English course fashioned by Mr. MacFarland, and it was through this elective that there arose at Mercy a fledgling literati. Art Mitz, the editor of the school newspaper and a very smart guy, was the kingpin. He was joined by me and by Mark Dever, a quiet boy who wrote beautifully and who would die before he was forty. MacFarland occasionally invited us to his apartment, and those visits became the high point of our apprenticeship: we'd clamp on our training wheels and drive to his salon.

He lived in a cramped and cluttered place near the airport, tucked away in the kind of building that architectural critic Reyner Banham calls a *dingbat*. Books were all over: stacked, piled, tossed, and crated, underlined and dog eared, well worn and new. Cigarette ashes crusted with coffee in saucers or spilling over the sides of motel ashtrays. The little bedroom had, along two of its walls, bricks and boards loaded with notes, magazines, and oversized books. The kitchen joined the living room, and there was a stack of German newspapers under the sink. I had never seen anything like it: a great flophouse of language furnished by City Lights and Café le Metro. I read every title. I flipped through paperbacks and scanned jackets and memorized names: Gogol, *Finnegans Wake*, Djuna Barnes, Jackson Pollock, *A Coney Island of the Mind*, F. O. Matthiessen's *American Renaissance*, all sorts of Freud, *Troubled Sleep*, Man Ray, *The Education of Henry Adams*, Richard Wright, *Film as Art*, William Butler Yeats, Marguerite Duras, *Redburn*, *A Season in Hell*, *Kapital*. On the cover of Alain-Fournier's *The Wanderer* was an Edward Gorey drawing of a young man on a road winding into dark trees. By the hotplate sat a strange Kafka novel called *Amerika*, in which an adolescent hero crosses the Atlantic to find the Nature Theater of Oklahoma. Art and Mark would be talking about a movie or the school newspaper, and I would be consuming my English teacher's library. It was heady stuff. I felt like a Pop Warner[9] athlete on steroids.

Art, Mark, and I would buy stogies and triangulate from MacFarland's   35
apartment to the Cinema, which now shows X-rated films but was then L.A.'s

---

[9]*Pop Warner:* A nationwide youth athletics organization.

premier art theater, and then to the musty Cherokee Bookstore in Hollywood to hobnob with beatnik homosexuals — smoking, drinking bourbon and coffee, and trying out awkward phrases we'd gleaned from our mentor's bookshelves. I was happy and precocious and a little scared as well, for Hollywood Boulevard was thick with a kind of decadence that was foreign to the South Side. After the Cherokee, we would head back to the security of MacFarland's apartment, slaphappy with hipness.

Let me be the first to admit that there was a good deal of adolescent passion in this embrace of the avant-garde: self-absorption, sexually charged pedantry, an elevation of the odd and abandoned. Still it was a time during which I absorbed an awful lot of information: long lists of titles, images from expressionist paintings, new wave shibboleths,[10] snippets of philosophy, and names that read like Steve Fusco's misspellings — Goethe, Nietzsche, Kierkegaard. Now this is hardly the stuff of deep understanding. But it was an introduction, a phrase book, a Baedeker[11] to a vocabulary of ideas, and it felt good at the time to know all these words. With hindsight I realize how layered and important that knowledge was.

It enabled me to do things in the world. I could browse bohemian bookstores in far-off, mysterious Hollywood; I could go to the Cinema and see events through the lenses of European directors; and, most of all, I could share an evening, talk that talk, with Jack MacFarland, the man I most admired at the time. Knowledge was becoming a bonding agent. Within a year or two, the persona of the disaffected hipster would prove too cynical, too alienated to last. But for a time it was new and exciting: it provided a critical perspective on society, and it allowed me to act as though I were living beyond the limiting boundaries of South Vermont.[12]

ENGAGING THE TEXT

1. Describe Rose's life in Voc. Ed. What were his teachers like? Have you ever had experience with teachers like these?

2. What did Voc. Ed. do to Rose and his fellow students? How did it affect them intellectually, emotionally, and socially? Why was it subsequently so hard for Rose to catch up in math?

3. Why is high school so disorienting to students like Ken Harvey? How does he cope with it? What other strategies do students use to cope with the pressures and judgments they encounter in school?

4. What does Jack MacFarland offer Rose that finally helps him learn? Do you think it was inevitable that someone with Rose's intelligence would eventually succeed?

[10]*new wave shibboleths:* Trendy phrases or jargon.
[11]*Baedeker:* Travel guide.
[12]*South Vermont:* A street in an economically depressed area of Los Angeles.

EXPLORING CONNECTIONS

5. To what extent do Rose's experiences challenge or confirm John Taylor Gatto's critique of public education in "Against School" (p. 152)? How might Gatto account for the existence of truly remarkable teachers like Rose's Jack McFarland?

6. How does Michael Moore's assessment of the general state of intelligence in America in "Idiot Nation" (p. 132) help to explain the attitudes of Rose's friends toward education? How would you account for the fact that many American teens seem to feel it's OK to be "average" intellectually even as they strive for other kinds of excellence?

7. Draw a Groening-style cartoon (see pp. 151 and 160) or comic strip of Rose in the vocational track, or of Rose before and after his liberation from Voc. Ed.

8. Read Gregory Mantsios's "Class in America — 2003" (p. 307) and write an imaginary dialogue between Rose and Mantsios about why some students, like Rose, seem to be able to break through social class barriers and others, like Dave Snyder, Ted Richard, and Ken Harvey, do not.

EXTENDING THE CRITICAL CONTEXT

9. Rose explains that high school can be a "tremendously disorienting place" (para. 16). What, if anything, do you find disorienting about college? What steps can students at your school take to lessen feelings of disorientation? What could the college do to help them?

10. Review one or more of Rose's descriptions of his high school classmates; then write a description of one of your own high school classmates, trying to capture in a nutshell how that person coped or failed to cope with the educational system.

11. Watch on videotape any one of the many films that have been made about charismatic teachers (for example, *Dangerous Minds, Renaissance Man, Stand and Deliver,* or *Dead Poets Society*) and compare Hollywood's depiction of a dynamic teacher to Rose's portrayal of Jack MacFarland. What do such charismatic teachers offer their students personally and intellectually? Do you see any disadvantages to classes taught by teachers like these?

From *Social Class and the Hidden Curriculum of Work*

JEAN ANYON

It's no surprise that schools in wealthy communities are better than those in poor communities, or that they better prepare their students for desirable jobs. It may be shocking, however, to learn how vast the differences in schools are — not so much in resources as in teaching methods and philosophies of education. Jean Anyon observed five elementary schools over the course of a full school year and concluded that fifth graders of different economic backgrounds are already being prepared to occupy particular rungs on the social ladder. In a sense, some whole schools are on the vocational education track, while others are geared to produce future doctors, lawyers, and business leaders. Anyon's main audience is professional educators, so you may find her style and vocabulary challenging, but, once you've read her descriptions of specific classroom activities, the more analytic parts of the essay should prove easier to understand. Anyon is chairperson of the Department of Education at Rutgers University, Newark. Her most recent book is Ghetto Schooling: A Political Economy of Urban Educational Reform *(1997). This essay first appeared in the* Journal of Education *in 1980.*

Scholars in political economy and the sociology of knowledge have recently argued that public schools in complex industrial societies like our own make available different types of educational experience and curriculum knowledge to students in different social classes. Bowles and Gintis,[1] for example, have argued that students in different social-class backgrounds are rewarded for classroom behaviors that correspond to personality traits allegedly rewarded in the different occupational strata — the working classes for docility and obedience, the managerial classes for initiative and personal assertiveness. Basil Bernstein, Pierre Bourdieu, and Michael W. Apple,[2] focusing on school knowledge, have argued that knowledge and skills leading to social power and regard (medical, legal, managerial) are made available to the advantaged social groups but are withheld from the working classes, to whom a more "practical" curriculum is offered (manual skills, clerical knowledge). While there has been considerable argumentation of these points regarding education in England, France, and North America, there has been little or no attempt to investigate these ideas empirically in elementary or secondary schools and classrooms in this country.[3]

This article offers tentative empirical support (and qualification) of the above arguments by providing illustrative examples of differences in student *work* in classrooms in contrasting social-class communities. The examples

[1]S. Bowles and H. Gintis, *Schooling in Capitalist America: Educational Reform and the Contradictions of Economic Life* (New York: Basic Books, 1976). [All notes are the author's, except 4 and 11.]

[2]B. Bernstein, *Class, Codes and Control*, Vol. 3. *Towards a Theory of Educational Transmission*, 2d ed. (London: Routledge & Kegan Paul, 1977); P. Bourdieu and J. Passeron, *Reproduction in Education, Society and Culture* (Beverly Hills, Calif.: Sage, 1977); M. W. Apple, *Ideology and Curriculum* (Boston: Routledge & Kegan Paul, 1979).

[3]But see, in a related vein, M. W. Apple and N. King, "What Do Schools Teach?" *Curriculum Inquiry* 6 (1977): 341-58; R. C. Rist, *The Urban School: A Factory for Failure* (Cambridge, Mass.: MIT Press, 1973).

were gathered as part of an ethnographical[4] study of curricular, pedagogical, and pupil evaluation practices in five elementary schools. The article attempts a theoretical contribution as well and assesses student work in the light of a theoretical approach to social-class analysis. . . . It will be suggested that there is a "hidden curriculum" in schoolwork that has profound implications for the theory — and consequence — of everyday activity in education. . . .

The Sample of Schools

. . . The social-class designation of each of the five schools will be identified, and the income, occupation, and other relevant available social characteristics of the students and their parents will be described. The first three schools are in a medium-sized city district in northern New Jersey, and the other two are in a nearby New Jersey suburb.

The first two schools I will call *working-class schools*. Most of the parents have blue-collar jobs. Less than a third of the fathers are skilled, while the majority are in unskilled or semiskilled jobs. During the period of the study (1978–1979), approximately 15 percent of the fathers were unemployed. The large majority (85 percent) of the families are white. The following occupations are typical: platform, storeroom, and stockroom workers; foundrymen, pipe welders, and boilermakers; semiskilled and unskilled assemblyline operatives; gas station attendants, auto mechanics, maintenance workers, and security guards. Less than 30 percent of the women work, some part-time and some full-time, on assembly lines, in storerooms and stockrooms, as waitresses, barmaids, or sales clerks. Of the fifth-grade parents, none of the wives of the skilled workers had jobs. Approximately 15 percent of the families in each school are at or below the federal "poverty" level;[5] most of the rest of the family incomes are at or below $12,000, except some of the skilled workers whose incomes are higher. The incomes of the majority of the families in these two schools (at or below $12,000) are typical of 38.6 percent of the families in the United States.[6]

The third school is called the *middle-class school,* although because of   5
neighborhood residence patterns, the population is a mixture of several social classes. The parents' occupations can be divided into three groups: a small group of blue-collar "rich," who are skilled, well-paid workers such as printers, carpenters, plumbers, and construction workers. The second group is composed of parents in working-class and middle-class white-collar

[4]*ethnographical:* Based on an anthropological study of cultures or subcultures — the "cultures" in this case being the five schools observed.

[5]The U.S. Bureau of the Census defines *poverty* for a nonfarm family of four as a yearly income of $6,191 a year or less. U.S. Bureau of the Census, *Statistical Abstract of the United States: 1978* (Washington, D.C.: U.S. Government Printing Office, 1978), 465, table 754.

[6]U.S. Bureau of the Census, "Money Income in 1977 of Families and Persons in the United States," *Current Population Reports* Series P-60, no. 118 (Washington, D.C.: U.S. Government Printing Office, 1979), p. 2, table A.

jobs: women in office jobs, technicians, supervisors in industry, and parents employed by the city (such as firemen, policemen, and several of the school's teachers). The third group is composed of occupations such as personnel directors in local firms, accountants, "middle management," and a few small capitalists (owners of shops in the area). The children of several local doctors attend this school. Most family incomes are between $13,000 and $25,000, with a few higher. This income range is typical of 38.9 percent of the families in the United States.[7]

The fourth school has a parent population that is at the upper income level of the upper middle class and is predominantly professional. This school will be called the *affluent professional school.* Typical jobs are: cardiologist, interior designer, corporate lawyer or engineer, executive in advertising or television. There are some families who are not as affluent as the majority (the family of the superintendent of the district's schools, and the one or two families in which the fathers are skilled workers). In addition, a few of the families are more affluent than the majority and can be classified in the capitalist class (a partner in a prestigious Wall Street stock brokerage firm). Approximately 90 percent of the children in this school are white. Most family incomes are between $40,000 and $80,000. This income span represents approximately 7 percent of the families in the United States.[8]

In the fifth school the majority of the families belong to the capitalist class. This school will be called the *executive elite school* because most of the fathers are top executives (for example, presidents and vice-presidents) in major United States–based multinational corporations — for example, AT&T, RCA, Citibank, American Express, U.S. Steel. A sizable group of fathers are top executives in financial firms on Wall Street. There are also a number of fathers who list their occupations as "general counsel" to a particular corporation, and these corporations are also among the large multinationals. Many of the mothers do volunteer work in the Junior League, Junior Fortnightly, or other service groups; some are intricately involved in town politics; and some are themselves in well-paid occupations. There are no minority children in the school. Almost all the family incomes are over $100,000, with some in the $500,000 range. The incomes in this school represent less than 1 percent of the families in the United States.[9]

Since each of the five schools is only one instance of elementary education in a particular social-class context, I will not generalize beyond the sample. However, the examples of schoolwork which follow will suggest

[7]Ibid.

[8]This figure is an estimate. According to the Bureau of the Census, only 2.6 percent of families in the United States have money income of $50,000 or over. U.S. Bureau of the Census, *Current Population Reports* Series P-60. For figures on income at these higher levels, see J. D. Smith and S. Franklin, "The Concentration of Personal Wealth, 1922–1969," *American Economic Review* 64 (1974): 162–67.

[9]Smith and Franklin, "The Concentration of Personal Wealth."

characteristics of education in each social setting that appear to have theoretical and social significance and to be worth investigation in a larger number of schools. . . .

The Working-Class Schools

In the two working-class schools, work is following the steps of a procedure. The procedure is usually mechanical, involving rote behavior and very little decision making or choice. The teachers rarely explain why the work is being assigned, how it might connect to other assignments, or what the idea is that lies behind the procedure or gives it coherence and perhaps meaning or significance. Available textbooks are not always used, and the teachers often prepare their own dittos or put work examples on the board. Most of the rules regarding work are designations of what the children are to do; the rules are steps to follow. These steps are told to the children by the teachers and are often written on the board. The children are usually told to copy the steps as notes. These notes are to be studied. Work is often evaluated not according to whether it is right or wrong but according to whether the children followed the right steps.

The following examples illustrate these points. In math, when two-digit   10
division was introduced, the teacher in one school gave a four-minute lecture on what the terms are called (which number is the divisor, dividend, quotient, and remainder). The children were told to copy these names in their notebooks. Then the teacher told them the steps to follow to do the problems, saying, "This is how you do them." The teacher listed the steps on the board, and they appeared several days later as a chart hung in the middle of the front wall: "Divide, Multiply, Subtract, Bring Down." The children often did examples of two-digit division. When the teacher went over the examples with them, he told them what the procedure was for each problem, rarely asking them to conceptualize or explain it themselves: "Three into twenty-two is seven; do your subtraction and one is left over." During the week that two-digit division was introduced (or at any other time), the investigator did not observe any discussion of the idea of grouping involved in division, any use of manipulables, or any attempt to relate two-digit division to any other mathematical process. Nor was there any attempt to relate the steps to an actual or possible thought process of the children. The observer did not hear the terms *dividend, quotient,* and so on, used again. The math teacher in the other working-class school followed similar procedures regarding two-digit division and at one point her class seemed confused. She said, "You're confusing yourselves. You're tensing up. Remember, when you do this, it's the same steps over and over again — and that's the way division always is." Several weeks later, after a test, a group of her children "still didn't get it," and she made no attempt to explain the concept of dividing things into groups or to give them manipulables for their own investigation. Rather, she went over the steps with them again and told them that they "needed more practice."

In other areas of math, work is also carrying out often unexplained fragmented procedures. For example, one of the teachers led the children through a series of steps to make a 1-inch grid on their paper *without* telling them that they were making a 1-inch grid or that it would be used to study scale. She said, "Take your ruler. Put it across the top. Make a mark at every number. Then move your ruler down to the bottom. No, put it across the bottom. Now make a mark on top of every number. Now draw a line from . . ." At this point a girl said that she had a faster way to do it and the teacher said, "No, you don't; you don't even know what I'm making yet. Do it this way or it's wrong." After they had made the lines up and down and across, the teacher told them she wanted them to make a figure by connecting some dots and to measure that, using the scale of 1 inch equals 1 mile. Then they were to cut it out. She said, "Don't cut it until I check it."

In both working-class schools, work in language arts is mechanics of punctuation (commas, periods, question marks, exclamation points), capitalization, and the four kinds of sentences. One teacher explained to me, "Simple punctuation is all they'll ever use." Regarding punctuation, either a teacher or a ditto stated the rules for where, for example, to put commas. The investigator heard no classroom discussion of the aural context of punctuation (which, of course, is what gives each mark its meaning). Nor did the investigator hear any statement or inference that placing a punctuation mark could be a decision-making process, depending, for example, on one's intended meaning. Rather, the children were told to follow the rules. Language arts did not involve creative writing. There were several writing assignments throughout the year, but in each instance the children were given a ditto, and they wrote answers to questions on the sheet. For example, they wrote their "autobiography" by answering such questions as "Where were you born?" "What is your favorite animal?" on a sheet entitled "All About Me."

In one of the working-class schools, the class had a science period several times a week. On the three occasions observed, the children were not called upon to set up experiments or to give explanations for facts or concepts. Rather, on each occasion the teacher told them in his own words what the book said. The children copied the teacher's sentences from the board. Each day that preceded the day they were to do a science experiment, the teacher told them to copy the directions from the book for the procedure they would carry out the next day and to study the list at home that night. The day after each experiment, the teacher went over what they had "found" (they did the experiments as a class, and each was actually a class demonstration led by the teacher). Then the teacher wrote what they "found" on the board, and the children copied that in their notebooks. Once or twice a year there are science projects. The project is chosen and assigned by the teacher from a box of 3-by-5-inch cards. On the card the teacher has written the question to be answered, the books to use, and how much to write. Explaining the cards to the observer, the teacher said, "It tells them exactly what to do, or they couldn't do it."

Social studies in the working-class schools is also largely mechanical, rote work that was given little explanation or connection to larger contexts. In one school, for example, although there was a book available, social studies work was to copy the teacher's notes from the board. Several times a week for a period of several months the children copied these notes. The fifth grades in the district were to study United States history. The teacher used a booklet she had purchased called "The Fabulous Fifty States." Each day she put information from the booklet in outline form on the board and the children copied it. The type of information did not vary: the name of the state, its abbreviation, state capital, nickname of the state, its main products, main business, and a "Fabulous Fact" ("Idaho grew twenty-seven billion potatoes in one year. That's enough potatoes for each man, woman, and . . ."). As the children finished copying the sentences, the teacher erased them and wrote more. Children would occasionally go to the front to pull down the wall map in order to locate the states they were copying, and the teacher did not dissuade them. But the observer never saw her refer to the map; nor did the observer ever hear her make other than perfunctory remarks concerning the information the children were copying. Occasionally the children colored in a ditto and cut it out to make a stand-up figure (representing, for example, a man roping a cow in the Southwest). These were referred to by the teacher as their social studies "projects."

Rote behavior was often called for in classroom work. When going over math and language arts skills sheets, for example, as the teacher asked for the answer to each problem, he fired the questions rapidly, staccato, and the scene reminded the observer of a sergeant drilling recruits: above all, the questions demanded that you stay at attention: "The next one? What do I put here? . . . Here? Give us the next." Or "How many commas in this sentence? Where do I put them . . . The next one?" 15

The four fifth-grade teachers observed in the working-class schools attempted to control classroom time and space by making decisions without consulting the children and without explaining the basis for their decisions. The teacher's control thus often seemed capricious. Teachers, for instance, very often ignored the bells to switch classes — deciding among themselves to keep the children after the period was officially over to continue with the work or for disciplinary reasons or so they (the teachers) could stand in the hall and talk. There were no clocks in the rooms in either school, and the children often asked, "What period is this?" "When do we go to gym?" The children had no access to materials. These were handed out by teachers and closely guarded. Things in the room "belonged" to the teacher: "Bob, bring me my garbage can." The teachers continually gave the children orders. Only three times did the investigator hear a teacher in either working-class school preface a directive with an unsarcastic "please," or "let's," or "would you." Instead, the teachers said, "Shut up," "Shut your mouth," "Open your books," "Throw your gum away — if you want to rot your teeth, do it on your own time." Teachers made every effort to control the movement of the children, and often shouted, "Why are you out of your seat??!!" If the children got permission to leave the room, they had to take a written pass with the date and time. . . .

Middle-Class School

In the middle-class school, work is getting the right answer. If one accumulates enough right answers, one gets a good grade. One must follow the directions in order to get the right answers, but the directions often call for some figuring, some choice, some decision making. For example, the children must often figure out by themselves what the directions ask them to do and how to get the answer: what do you do first, second, and perhaps third? Answers are usually found in books or by listening to the teacher. Answers are usually words, sentences, numbers, or facts and dates; one writes them on paper, and one should be neat. Answers must be given in the right order, and one cannot make them up.

The following activities are illustrative. Math involves some choice: one may do two-digit division the long way or the short way, and there are some math problems that can be done "in your head." When the teacher explains how to do two-digit division, there is recognition that a cognitive process is involved; she gives you several ways and says, "I want to make sure you understand what you're doing — so you get it right"; and, when they go over the homework, she asks the *children* to tell how they did the problem and what answer they got.

In social studies the daily work is to read the assigned pages in the textbook and to answer the teacher's questions. The questions are almost always designed to check on whether the students have read the assignment and understood it: who did so-and-so; what happened after that; when did it happen, where, and sometimes, why did it happen? The answers are in the book and in one's understanding of the book; the teacher's hints when one doesn't know the answers are to "read it again" or to look at the picture or at the rest of the paragraph. One is to search for the answer in the "context," in what is given.

Language arts is "simple grammar, what they need for everyday life." The language arts teacher says, "They should learn to speak properly, to write business letters and thank-you letters, and to understand what nouns and verbs and simple subjects are." Here, as well, actual work is to choose the right answers, to understand what is given. The teacher often says, "Please read the next sentence and then I'll question you about it." One teacher said in some exasperation to a boy who was fooling around in class, "If you don't know the answers to the questions I ask, then you can't stay in this *class!* [pause] You *never* know the answers to the questions I ask, and it's not fair to me — and certainly not to you!"

Most lessons are based on the textbook. This does not involve a critical perspective on what is given there. For example, a critical perspective in social studies is perceived as dangerous by these teachers because it may

20

lead to controversial topics; the parents might complain. The children, however, are often curious, especially in social studies. Their questions are tolerated and usually answered perfunctorily. But after a few minutes the teacher will say, "All right, we're not going any farther. Please open your social studies workbook." While the teachers spend a lot of time explaining and expanding on what the textbooks say, there is little attempt to analyze how or why things happen, or to give thought to how pieces of a culture, or, say, a system of numbers or elements of a language fit together or can be analyzed. What has happened in the past and what exists now may not be equitable or fair, but (shrug) that is the way things are and one does not confront such matters in school. For example, in social studies after a child is called on to read a passage about the pilgrims, the teacher summarizes the paragraph and then says, "So you can see how strict they were about everything." A child asks, "Why?" "Well, because they felt that if you weren't busy you'd get into trouble." Another child asks, "Is it true that they burned women at the stake?" The teacher says, "Yes, if a woman did anything strange, they hanged them. [*sic*] What would a woman do, do you think, to make them burn them? [*sic*] See if you can come up with better answers than my other [social studies] class." Several children offer suggestions, to which the teacher nods but does not comment. Then she says, "Okay, good," and calls on the next child to read.

Work tasks do not usually request creativity. Serious attention is rarely given in school work on *how* the children develop or express their own feelings and ideas, either linguistically or in graphic form. On the occasions when creativity or self-expression is requested, it is peripheral to the main activity or it is "enrichment" or "for fun." During a lesson on what similes are, for example, the teacher explains what they are, puts several on the board, gives some other examples herself, and then asks the children if they can "make some up." She calls on three children who give similes, two of which are actually in the book they have open before them. The teacher does not comment on this and then asks several others to choose similes from the list of phrases in the book. Several do so correctly, and she says, "Oh good! You're picking them out! See how good we are?" Their homework is to pick out the rest of the similes from the list.

Creativity is not often requested in social studies and science projects, either. Social studies projects, for example, are given with directions to "find information on your topic" and write it up. The children are not supposed to copy but to "put it in your own words." Although a number of the projects subsequently went beyond the teacher's direction to find information and had quite expressive covers and inside illustrations, the teacher's evaluative comments had to do with the amount of information, whether they had "copied," and if their work was neat.

The style of control of the three fifth-grade teachers observed in this school varied from somewhat easygoing to strict, but in contrast to the working-class schools, the teachers' decisions were usually based on external rules and regulations — for example, on criteria that were known or available to the children. Thus, the teachers always honor the bells for changing classes, and they usually evaluate children's work by what is in the textbooks and answer booklets.

There is little excitement in schoolwork for the children, and the assignments are perceived as having little to do with their interests and feelings. As one child said, what you do is "store facts up in your head like cold storage — until you need it later for a test or your job." Thus, doing well is important because there are thought to be *other*, likely rewards: a good job or college.[10]

Affluent Professional School

In the affluent professional school, work is creative activity carried out independently. The students are continually asked to express and apply ideas and concepts. Work involves individual thought and expressiveness, expansion and illustration of ideas, and choice of appropriate method and material. (The class is not considered an open classroom, and the principal explained that because of the large number of discipline problems in the fifth grade this year they did not departmentalize. The teacher who agreed to take part in the study said she is "more structured" this year than she usually is.) The products of work in this class are often written stories, editorials and essays, or representations of ideas in mural, graph, or craft form. The products of work should not be like everybody else's and should show individuality. They should exhibit good design, and (this is important) they must also fit empirical reality. Moreover, one's work should attempt to interpret or "make sense" of reality. The relatively few rules to be followed regarding work are usually criteria for, or limits on, individual activity. One's product is usually evaluated for the quality of its expression and for the appropriateness of its conception to the task. In many cases, one's own satisfaction with the product is an important criterion for its evaluation. When right answers are called for, as in commercial materials like SRA (Science Research Associates) and math, it is important that the children decide on an answer as a result of thinking about the idea involved in what they're being asked to do. Teacher's hints are to "think about it some more."

The following activities are illustrative. The class takes home a sheet requesting each child's parents to fill in the number of cars they have, the number of television sets, refrigerators, games, or rooms in the house, and so on. Each child is to figure the average number of a type of possession owned by the fifth grade. Each child must compile the "data" from all the sheets. A calculator is available in the classroom to do the mechanics of finding the average. Some children decide to send sheets to the fourth-grade families for

---

[10]A dominant feeling, expressed directly and indirectly by teachers in this school, was boredom with their work. They did, however, in contrast to the working-class schools, almost always carry out lessons during class times.

comparison. Their work should be "verified" by a classmate before it is handed in.

Each child and his or her family has made a geoboard. The teacher asks the class to get their geoboards from the side cabinet, to take a handful of rubber bands, and then to listen to what she would like them to do. She says, "I would like you to design a figure and then find the perimeter and area. When you have it, check with your neighbor. After you've done that, please transfer it to graph paper and tomorrow I'll ask you to make up a question about it for someone. When you hand it in, please let me know whose it is and who verified it. Then I have something else for you to do that's really fun. [pause] Find the average number of chocolate chips in three cookies. I'll give you three cookies, and you'll have to *eat* your way through, I'm afraid!" Then she goes around the room and gives help, suggestions, praise, and admonitions that they are getting noisy. They work sitting, or standing up at their desks, at benches in the back, or on the floor. A child hands the teacher his paper and she comments, "I'm not accepting this paper. Do a better design." To another child she says, "That's fantastic! But you'll never find the area. Why don't you draw a figure inside [the big one] and subtract to get the area?"

The school district requires the fifth grade to study ancient civilization (in particular, Egypt, Athens, and Sumer). In this classroom, the emphasis is on illustrating and re-creating the culture of the people of ancient times. The following are typical activities: the children made an 8mm film on Egypt, which one of the parents edited. A girl in the class wrote the script, and the class acted it out. They put the sound on themselves. They read stories of those days. They wrote essays and stories depicting the lives of the people and the societal and occupational divisions. They chose from a list of projects, all of which involved graphic representations of ideas: for example, "Make a mural depicting the division of labor in Egyptian society."

Each child wrote and exchanged a letter in hieroglyphics with a fifth grader in another class, and they also exchanged stories they wrote in cuneiform. They made a scroll and singed the edges so it looked authentic. They each chose an occupation and made an Egyptian plaque representing that occupation, simulating the appropriate Egyptian design. They carved their design on a cylinder of wax, pressed the wax into clay, and then baked the clay. Although one girl did not choose an occupation but carved instead a series of gods and slaves, the teacher said, "That's all right, Amber, it's beautiful." As they were working the teacher said, "Don't cut into your clay until you're satisfied with your design." 30

Social studies also involves almost daily presentation by the children of some event from the news. The teacher's questions ask the children to expand what they say, to give more details, and to be more specific. Occasionally she adds some remarks to help them see connections between events.

The emphasis on expressing and illustrating ideas in social studies is accompanied in language arts by an emphasis on creative writing. Each child wrote a rebus story for a first grader whom they had interviewed to see what kind of story the child liked best. They wrote editorials on pending decisions by the school board and radio plays, some of which were read over the school intercom from the office and one of which was performed in the auditorium. There is no language arts textbook because, the teacher said, "The principal wants us to be creative." There is not much grammar, but there is punctuation. One morning when the observer arrived, the class was doing a punctuation ditto. The teacher later apologized for using the ditto. "It's just for review," she said. "I don't teach punctuation that way. We use their language." The ditto had three unambiguous rules for where to put commas in a sentence. As the teacher was going around to help the children with the ditto, she repeated several times, "Where you put commas depends on how you say the sentence; it depends on the situation and what you want to say." Several weeks later the observer saw another punctuation activity. The teacher had printed a five-paragraph story on an oak tag and then cut it into phrases. She read the whole story to the class from the book, then passed out the phrases. The group had to decide how the phrases could best be put together again. (They arranged the phrases on the floor.) The point was not to replicate the story, although that was not irrelevant, but to "decide what you think the best way is." Punctuation marks on cardboard pieces were then handed out, and the children discussed and then decided what mark was best at each place they thought one was needed. At the end of each paragraph the teacher asked, "Are you satisfied with the way the paragraphs are now? Read it to yourself and see how it sounds." Then she read the original story again, and they compared the two.

Describing her goals in science to the investigator, the teacher said, "We use ESS (Elementary Science Study). It's very good because it gives a hands-on experience — so they can make *sense* out of it. It doesn't matter whether it [what they find] is right or wrong. I bring them together and there's value in discussing their ideas."

The products of work in this class are often highly valued by the children and the teacher. In fact, this was the only school in which the investigator was not allowed to take original pieces of the children's work for her files. If the work was small enough, however, and was on paper, the investigator could duplicate it on the copying machine in the office.

The teacher's attempt to control the class involves constant negotiation. 35 She does not give direct orders unless she is angry because the children have been too noisy. Normally, she tries to get them to foresee the consequences of their actions and to decide accordingly. For example, lining them up to go see a play written by the sixth graders, she says, "I presume you're lined up by someone with whom you want to sit. I hope you're lined up by someone you won't get in trouble with." . . .

One of the few rules governing the children's movement is that no more than three children may be out of the room at once. There is a school rule that anyone can go to the library at any time to get a book. In the fifth grade I observed, they sign their name on the chalkboard and leave. There are no passes. Finally, the children have a fair amount of officially sanctioned say over what happens in the class. For example, they often negotiate what work is to be done. If the teacher wants to move on to the next subject, but the children say they are not ready, they want to work on their present projects some more, she very often lets them do it.

Executive Elite School

In the executive elite school, work is developing one's analytical intellectual powers. Children are continually asked to reason through a problem, to produce intellectual products that are both logically sound and of top academic quality. A primary goal of thought is to conceptualize rules by which elements may fit together in systems and then to apply these rules in solving a problem. Schoolwork helps one to achieve, to excel, to prepare for life.

The following are illustrative. The math teacher teaches area and perimeter by having the children derive formulas for each. First she helps them, through discussion at the board, to arrive at $A = W \times L$ as a formula (not *the* formula) for area. After discussing several, she says, "Can anyone make up a formula for perimeter? Can you figure that out yourselves? [pause] Knowing what we know, can we think of a formula?" She works out three children's suggestions at the board, saying to two, "Yes, that's a good one," and then asks the class if they can think of any more. No one volunteers. To prod them, she says, "If you use rules and good reasoning, you get many ways. Chris, can you think up a formula?"

She discusses two-digit division with the children as a decision-making process. Presenting a new type of problem to them, she asks, "What's the *first* decision you'd make if presented with this kind of example? What is the first thing you'd *think*? Craig?" Craig says, "To find my first partial quotient." She responds, "Yes, that would be your first decision. How would you do that?" Craig explains, and then the teacher says, "OK, we'll see how that works for you." The class tries his way. Subsequently, she comments on the merits and shortcomings of several other children's decisions. Later, she tells the investigator that her goals in math are to develop their reasoning and mathematical thinking and that, unfortunately, "there's no *time* for manipulables."

While right answers are important in math, they are not "given" by the book or by the teacher but may be challenged by the children. Going over some problems in late September the teacher says, "Raise your hand if you do not agree." A child says, "I don't agree with sixty-four." The teacher responds, "OK, there's a question about sixty-four. [to class] Please check it. Owen, they're disagreeing with you. Kristen, they're checking yours." The teacher emphasized this repeatedly during September and October with statements like "Don't be afraid to say you disagree. In the last [math] class, somebody disagreed, and they were right. Before you disagree, check yours, 40 and if you still think we're wrong, then we'll check it out." By Thanksgiving, the children did not often speak in terms of right and wrong math problems but of whether they agreed with the answer that had been given.

There are complicated math mimeos with many word problems. Whenever they go over the examples, they discuss how each child has set up the problem. The children must explain it precisely. On one occasion the teacher said, "I'm more — just as interested in *how* you set up the problem as in what answer you find. If you set up a problem in a good way, the answer is *easy* to find."

Social studies work is most often reading and discussion of concepts and independent research. There are only occasional artistic, expressive, or illustrative projects. Ancient Athens and Sumer are, rather, societies to analyze. The following questions are typical of those that guide the children's independent research. "What mistakes did Pericles make after the war?" "What mistakes did the citizens of Athens make?" "What are the elements of a civilization?" "How did Greece build an economic empire?" "Compare the way Athens chose its leaders with the way we choose ours." Occasionally the children are asked to make up sample questions for their social studies tests. On an occasion when the investigator was present, the social studies teacher rejected a child's question by saying, "That's just fact. If I asked you that question on a test, you'd complain it was just memory! Good questions ask for concepts."

In social studies — but also in reading, science, and health — the teachers initiate classroom discussions of current social issues and problems. These discussions occurred on every one of the investigator's visits, and a teacher told me, "These children's opinions are important — it's important that they learn to reason things through." The classroom discussions always struck the observer as quite realistic and analytical, dealing with concrete social issues like the following: "Why do workers strike?" "Is that right or wrong?" "Why do we have inflation, and what can be done to stop it?" "Why do companies put chemicals in food when the natural ingredients are available?" and so on. Usually the children did not have to be prodded to give their opinions. In fact, their statements and the interchanges between them struck the observer as quite sophisticated conceptually and verbally, and well-informed. Occasionally the teachers would prod with statements such as, "Even if you don't know [the answers], if you think logically about it, you can figure it out." And "I'm asking you [these] questions to help you think this through."

Language arts emphasizes language as a complex system, one that should be mastered. The children are asked to diagram sentences of complex grammatical construction, to memorize irregular verb conjugations (he lay, he has lain, and so on ...), and to use the proper participles, conjunctions, and interjections in their speech. The teacher (the same one who teaches social studies) told them, "It is not enough to get these right on tests; you must use what you learn [in grammar classes] in your written and oral work. I will grade you on that."

Most writing assignments are either research reports and essays for   45
social studies or experiment analyses and write-ups for science. There is only
an occasional story or other "creative writing" assignment. On the occasion
observed by the investigator (the writing of a Halloween story), the points
the teacher stressed in preparing the children to write involved the structural
aspects of a story rather than the expression of feelings or other ideas. The
teacher showed them a filmstrip, "The Seven Parts of a Story," and lectured
them on plot development, mood setting, character development, consistency, and the use of a logical or appropriate ending. The stories they subsequently wrote were, in fact, well-structured, but many were also personal
and expressive. The teacher's evaluative comments, however, did not refer to
the expressiveness or artistry but were all directed toward whether they had
"developed" the story well.

Language arts work also involved a large amount of practice in presentation of the self and in managing situations where the child was expected to
be in charge. For example, there was a series of assignments in which each
child had to be a "student teacher." The child had to plan a lesson in grammar, outlining, punctuation, or other language arts topic and explain the
concept to the class. Each child was to prepare a worksheet or game and a
homework assignment as well. After each presentation, the teacher and
other children gave a critical appraisal of the "student teacher's" performance. Their criteria were: whether the student spoke clearly, whether the
lesson was interesting, whether the student made any mistakes, and
whether he or she kept control of the class. On an occasion when a child did
not maintain control, the teacher said, "When you're up there, you have
authority and you have to use it. I'll back you up." . . .

The executive elite school is the only school where bells do not demar-
cate the periods of time. The two fifth-grade teachers were very strict about
changing classes on schedule, however, as specific plans for each session
had been made. The teachers attempted to keep tight control over the children during lessons, and the children were sometimes flippant, boisterous,
and occasionally rude. However, the children may be brought into line by
reminding them that "It is up to you," "You must control yourself," "You are
responsible for your work," you must "set your own priorities." One teacher
told a child, "You are the only driver of your car — and only you can regulate your speed." A new teacher complained to the observer that she had
thought "these children" would have more control.

While strict attention to the lesson at hand is required, the teachers
make relatively little attempt to regulate the movement of the children at
other times. For example, except for the kindergartners the children in this
school do not have to wait for the bell to ring in the morning; they may go to
their classroom when they arrive at school. Fifth graders often came early to
read, to finish work, or to catch up. After the first two months of school, the
fifth-grade teachers did not line the children up to change classes or to go to
gym, and so on, but, when the children were ready and quiet, they were
told they could go — sometimes without the teachers.

In the classroom, the children could get materials when they needed them and took what they needed from closets and from the teacher's desk. They were in charge of the office at lunchtime. During class they did not have to sign out or ask permission to leave the room; they just got up and left. Because of the pressure to get work done, however, they did not leave the room very often. The teachers were very polite to the children, and the investigator heard no sarcasm, no nasty remarks, and few direct orders. The teachers never called the children "honey" or "dear" but always called them by name. The teachers were expected to be available before school, after school, and for part of their lunchtime to provide extra help if needed. . . .

The foregoing analysis of differences in schoolwork in contrasting social-class contexts suggests the following conclusion: the "hidden curriculum" of schoolwork is tacit preparation for relating to the process of production in a particular way. Differing curricular, pedagogical, and pupil evaluation practices emphasize different cognitive and behavioral skills in each social setting and thus contribute to the development in the children of certain potential relationships to physical and symbolic capital,[11] to authority, and to the process of work. School experience, in the sample of schools discussed here, differed qualitatively by social class. These differences may not only contribute to the development in the children in each social class of certain types of economically significant relationships and not others but would thereby help to *reproduce* this system of relations in society. In the contribution to the reproduction of unequal social relations lies a theoretical meaning and social consequence of classroom practice.   50

The identification of different emphases in classrooms in a sample of contrasting social-class contexts implies that further research should be conducted in a large number of schools to investigate the types of work tasks and interactions in each to see if they differ in the ways discussed here and to see if similar potential relationships are uncovered. Such research could have as a product the further elucidation of complex but not readily apparent connections between everyday activity in schools and classrooms and the unequal structure of economic relationships in which we work and live.

ENGAGING THE TEXT

1. Examine the ways any single subject is taught in the four types of schools Anyon describes. What differences in teaching methods and in the student-teacher relationship do they reflect? What other differences do you note in the schools? What schools in your geographic region would closely approximate the working-class, middle-class, affluent professional, and executive elite schools of her article?

[11]*physical and symbolic capital:* Elsewhere Anyon defines *capital* as "property that is used to produce profit, interest, or rent"; she defines *symbolic capital* as the knowledge and skills that "may yield social and cultural power."

2. What attitudes toward knowledge and work are the four types of schools teaching their students? What kinds of jobs are students being prepared to do? Do you see any evidence that the schools in your community are producing particular kinds of workers?

3. What is the "hidden curriculum" of Anyon's title? How is this curriculum taught, and what social, cultural, or political purposes does it serve?

EXPLORING CONNECTIONS

4. Which of the four types of schools that Anyon describes do you think Michael Moore attended, given the experiences he offers from his own education in "Idiot Nation" (p. 132)? Why? Do you think his attitude toward the state of schooling in America would be different if he had attended a different kind of school?

5. How might Anyon explain the boredom, absurdity, and childishness that John Taylor Gatto (p. 152) associates with compulsory public education? To what extent do Anyon and Gatto seem to agree about the relationship between school and social class?

6. Draw a Groening-like (see pp. 151 and 160) cartoon or comic strip about a classroom situation in a working-class, middle-class, professional, or elite school (but do not identify the type of school explicitly). Pool all the cartoons from the class. In small groups, sort the comics according to the type of school they represent.

7. Analyze the teaching styles that Mike Rose encounters at Our Lady of Mercy (p. 161). Which of Anyon's categories would they fit best? Do Rose's experiences at his high school tend to confirm or complicate Anyon's analysis?

EXTENDING THE CRITICAL CONTEXT

8. Should all schools be run like professional or elite schools? What would be the advantages of making these schools models for all social classes? Do you see any possible disadvantages?

9. Choose a common elementary school task or skill that Anyon does not mention. Outline four ways it might be taught in the four types of schools.

Visual Portfolio

READING IMAGES OF EDUCATION AND EMPOWERMENT

The Spirit of Education (1934), by Norman Rockwell.

The Graduate (1959), by Norman Rockwell.

The Problem We All Live With (1964), by Norman Rockwell.

Visual Portfolio

READING IMAGES OF EDUCATION
AND EMPOWERMENT

1. What is happening in *The Spirit of Education?* What is Norman Rockwell saying about the situation — and about education — through the attitudes of the boy and the seated woman?

2. What meaning can you find in the elements that make up the boy's costume? What significance is there in the book, the torch, the laurel crown, the toga and sandals? What are these symbols supposed to suggest about education? If you were to costume someone to represent education today, how would you do it?

3. In *The Graduate*, why has Rockwell chosen to place his subject in front of a newspaper? To what extent are the headlines of the paper relevant? What is Rockwell suggesting through the young man's posture and attitude?

4. Plan an updated version of the portrait on page 191, featuring a twenty-first-century graduate and a more contemporary background.

5. What is the setting of *The Problem We All Live With?* What event does it commemorate? How do you interpret the painting's title?

6. What does Rockwell suggest about the relationship of education, society, power, and violence through the visual details included in this painting? What significance do you see, for example, in the absence of the men's faces, the position of their hands and arms, the rhythm of their strides, the smallness of the girl, her attitude, the materials she carries, and so forth?

The Achievement of Desire

RICHARD RODRIGUEZ

Hunger of Memory, *the autobiography of Richard Rodriguez and the source of the following selection, set off a storm of controversy in the Chicano community when it appeared in 1981. Some hailed it as an uncompromising portrayal of the difficulties of growing up between two cultures; others condemned it because it seemed to blame Mexican Americans for the difficulties they encountered assimilating into mainstream American society. Rodriguez was born in 1944 into an immigrant family outside San Francisco. Though he was unable to speak English when he entered school, his educational career can only be described as brilliant: undergraduate work at Stanford University, graduate study at Berkeley and Columbia, a Fulbright fellowship to study English literature in London, a subsequent grant from the National Endowment for the Humanities. In this selection, Rodriguez analyzes the motives that led him to abandon his study of Renaissance literature and return to live with his parents. He is currently an associate editor with the* Pacific News Service *in San Francisco, an essayist for the* Newshour with Jim Lehrer, *and a contributing editor for* Harper's *magazine and for the* Opinion *section of the* Los Angeles Times. *His other books include* Mexico's Children *(1991),* Days of Obligation: An Argument with My Mexican Father *(1993), which was nominated for the Pulitzer Prize in nonfiction, and* Brown: The Last Discovery of America *(2002).*

I stand in the ghetto classroom — "the guest speaker" — attempting to lecture on the mystery of the sounds of our words to rows of diffident students. "Don't you hear it? Listen! The music of our words. '*Sumer is i-cumen in.*[1] . . .' And songs on the car radio. We need Aretha Franklin's voice to fill plain words with music — her life." In the face of their empty stares, I try to create an enthusiasm. But the girls in the back row turn to watch some boy passing outside. There are flutters of smiles, waves. And someone's mouth elongates heavy, silent words through the barrier of glass. Silent words — the lips straining to shape each voiceless syllable: "*Meet meee late errr.*" By the door, the instructor smiles at me, apparently hoping that I will be able to spark some enthusiasm in the class. But only one student seems to be listening. A girl, maybe fourteen. In this gray room her eyes shine with ambition. She keeps nodding and nodding at all that I say; she even takes notes. And each time I ask a question, she jerks up and down in her desk like a marionette, while her hand waves over the bowed heads of her classmates. It is myself (as a boy) I see as she faces me now (a man in my thirties).

The boy who first entered a classroom barely able to speak English, twenty years later concluded his studies in the stately quiet of the reading room in the British Museum. Thus with one sentence I can summarize my academic career. It will be harder to summarize what sort of life connects the boy to the man.

With every award, each graduation from one level of education to the next, people I'd meet would congratulate me. Their refrain always the same: "Your parents must be very proud." Sometimes then they'd ask me how I managed it — my "success." (How?) After a while, I had several quick answers to give in reply. I'd admit, for one thing, that I went to an excellent grammar school. (My earliest teachers, the nuns, made my success their ambition.) And my brother and both my sisters were very good students. (They often brought home the shiny school trophies I came to want.) And

[1]*Sumer is i-cumen in:* Opening line of a Middle English poem ("Summer has come").

my mother and father always encouraged me. (At every graduation they were behind the stunning flash of the camera when I turned to look at the crowd.)

As important as these factors were, however, they account inadequately for my academic advance. Nor do they suggest what an odd success I managed. For although I was a very good student, I was also a very bad student. I was a "scholarship boy," a certain kind of scholarship boy. Always successful, I was always unconfident. Exhilarated by my progress. Sad. I became the prized student — anxious and eager to learn. Too eager, too anxious — an imitative and unoriginal pupil. My brother and two sisters enjoyed the advantages I did, and they grew to be as successful as I, but none of them ever seemed so anxious about their schooling. A second-grade student, I was the one who came home and corrected the "simple" grammatical mistakes of our parents. ("Two negatives make a positive.") Proudly I announced — to my family's startled silence — that a teacher had said I was losing all trace of a Spanish accent. I was oddly annoyed when I was unable to get parental help with a homework assignment. The night my father tried to help me with an arithmetic exercise, he kept reading the instructions, each time more deliberately, until I pried the textbook out of his hands, saying, "I'll try to figure it out some more by myself."

When I reached the third grade, I outgrew such behavior. I became   5
more tactful, careful to keep separate the two very different worlds of my day. But then, with ever-increasing intensity, I devoted myself to my studies. I became bookish, puzzling to all my family. Ambition set me apart. When my brother saw me struggling home with stacks of library books, he would laugh, shouting: "Hey, Four Eyes!" My father opened a closet one day and was startled to find me inside, reading a novel. My mother would find me reading when I was supposed to be asleep or helping around the house or playing outside. In a voice angry or worried or just curious, she'd ask: "What do you see in your books?" It became the family's joke. When I was called and wouldn't reply, someone would say I must be hiding under my bed with a book.

(How did I manage my success?)

What I am about to say to you has taken me more than twenty years to admit: A *primary reason for my success in the classroom was that I couldn't forget that schooling was changing me and separating me from the life I enjoyed before becoming a student.* That simple realization! For years I never spoke to anyone about it. Never mentioned a thing to my family or my teachers or classmates. From a very early age, I understood enough, just enough about my classroom experiences to keep what I knew repressed, hidden beneath layers of embarrassment. Not until my last months as a graduate student, nearly thirty years old, was it possible for me to think much about the reasons for my academic success. Only then. At the end of my schooling, I needed to determine how far I had moved from my past. The adult finally confronted, and now must publicly say, what the child shuddered from knowing and could never admit to himself or to those many faces that smiled at his every success. ("Your parents must be very proud. . . .")

At the end, in the British Museum (too distracted to finish my dissertation) for weeks I read, speed-read, books by modern educational theorists, only to find infrequent and slight mention of students like me. (Much more is written about the more typical case, the lower-class student who barely is helped by his schooling.) Then one day, leafing through Richard Hoggart's *The Uses of Literacy,* I found, in his description of the scholarship boy, myself. For the first time I realized that there were other students like me, and so I was able to frame the meaning of my academic success, its consequent price — the loss.

Hoggart's description is distinguished, at least initially, by deep understanding. What he grasps very well is that the scholarship boy must move between environments, his home and the classroom, which are at cultural extremes, opposed. With his family, the boy has the intense pleasure of intimacy, the family's consolation in feeling public alienation. Lavish emotions texture home life. *Then,* at school, the instruction bids him to trust lonely reason primarily. Immediate needs set the pace of his parents' lives. From his mother and father the boy learns to trust spontaneity and nonrational ways of knowing. *Then,* at school, there is mental calm. Teachers emphasize the value of a reflectiveness that opens a space between thinking and immediate action.

Years of schooling must pass before the boy will be able to sketch the 10
cultural differences in his day as abstractly as this. But he senses those differences early. Perhaps as early as the night he brings home an assignment from school and finds the house too noisy for study.

> He has to be more and more alone, if he is going to "get on." He will have, probably unconsciously, to oppose the ethos[2] of the hearth, the intense gregariousness of the working-class family group. Since everything centres upon the living-room, there is unlikely to be a room of his own; the bedrooms are cold and inhospitable, and to warm them or the front room, if there is one, would not only be expensive, but would require an imaginative leap — out of the tradition — which most families are not capable of making. There is a corner of the living-room table. On the other side Mother is ironing, the wireless is on, someone is singing a snatch of song or Father says intermittently whatever comes into his head. The boy has to cut himself off mentally, so as to do his homework, as well as he can.[3]

The next day, the lesson is as apparent at school. There are even rows of desks. Discussion is ordered. The boy must rehearse his thoughts and

[2]*ethos:* The fundamental spirit or character of a thing.
[3]All quotations are from Richard Hoggart, *The Uses of Literacy* (London: Chatto and Windus, 1957), Chapter 10. [Author's note]

raise his hand before speaking out in a loud voice to an audience of class-mates. And there is time enough, and silence, to think about ideas (big ideas) never considered at home by his parents.

Not for the working-class child alone is adjustment to the classroom difficult. Good schooling requires that any student alter early childhood habits. But the working-class child is usually least prepared for the change. And, unlike many middle-class children, he goes home and sees in his parents a way of life not only different but starkly opposed to that of the classroom. (He enters the house and hears his parents talking in ways his teachers discourage.)

Without extraordinary determination and the great assistance of others — at home and at school — there is little chance for success. Typi-cally most working-class children are barely changed by the classroom. The exception succeeds. The relative few become scholarship students. Of these, Richard Hoggart estimates, most manage a fairly graceful transition. Somehow they learn to live in the two very different worlds of their day. There are some others, however, those Hoggart pejoratively terms "scholar-ship boys," for whom success comes with special anxiety. Scholarship boy: good student, troubled son. The child is "moderately endowed," intellectu-ally mediocre, Hoggart supposes — though it may be more pertinent to note the special qualities of temperament in the child. High-strung child. Brooding. Sensitive. Haunted by the knowledge that one *chooses* to become a student. (Education is not an inevitable or natural step in growing up.) Here is a child who cannot forget that his academic success distances him from a life he loved, even from his own memory of himself.

Initially, he wavers, balances allegiance. ("The boy is himself [until he reaches, say, the upper forms[4]] very much of *both* the worlds of home and school. He is enormously obedient to the dictates of the world of school, but emotionally still strongly wants to continue as part of the family circle.") Gradually, necessarily, the balance is lost. The boy needs to spend more and more time studying, each night enclosing himself in the silence permitted and required by intense concentration. He takes his first step toward acade-mic success, away from his family.

From the very first days, through the years following, it will be with his parents — the figures of lost authority, the persons toward whom he feels deepest love — that the change will be most powerfully measured. A sepa-ration will unravel between them. Advancing in his studies, the boy notices that his mother and father have not changed as much as he. Rather, when he sees them, they often remind him of the person he once was and the life he earlier shared with them. He realizes what some Romantics[5] also know

15

---

[4]*upper forms:* Upper grades or classes in British secondary schools.
[5]*Romantics:* Adherents of the principles of romanticism — a literary and philosophical movement that emphasized the imagination, freedom, nature, the return to a simple life, and the ordinary individual.

when they praise the working class for the capacity for human closeness, qualities of passion and spontaneity, that the rest of us experience in like measure only in the earliest part of our youth. For the Romantic, this doesn't make working-class life childish. Working-class life challenges precisely because it is an *adult* way of life.

The scholarship boy reaches a different conclusion. He cannot afford to admire his parents. (How could he and still pursue such a contrary life?) He permits himself embarrassment at their lack of education. And to evade nostalgia for the life he has lost, he concentrates on the benefits education will bestow upon him. He becomes especially ambitious. Without the support of old certainties and consolations, almost mechanically, he assumes the procedures and doctrines of the classroom. The kind of allegiance the young student might have given his mother and father only days earlier, he transfers to the teacher, the new figure of authority. "[The scholarship boy] tends to make a father-figure of his form-master,"[6] Hoggart observes.

But Hoggart's calm prose only makes me recall the urgency with which I came to idolize my grammar school teachers. I began by imitating their accents, using their diction, trusting their every direction. The very first facts they dispensed, I grasped with awe. Any book they told me to read, I read — then waited for them to tell me which books I enjoyed. Their every casual opinion I came to adopt and to trumpet when I returned home. I stayed after school "to help" — to get my teacher's undivided attention. It was the nun's encouragement that mattered most to me. (She understood exactly what — my parents never seemed to appraise so well — all my achievements entailed.) Memory gently caressed each word of praise bestowed in the classroom so that compliments teachers paid me years ago come quickly to mind even today.

The enthusiasm I felt in second-grade classes I flaunted before both my parents. The docile, obedient student came home a shrill and precocious son who insisted on correcting and teaching his parents with the remark: "My teacher told us. . . ."

I intended to hurt my mother and father. I was still angry at them for having encouraged me toward classroom English. But gradually this anger was exhausted, replaced by guilt as school grew more and more attractive to me. I grew increasingly successful, a talkative student. My hand was raised in the classroom; I yearned to answer any question. At home, life was less noisy than it had been. (I spoke to classmates and teachers more often each day than to family members.) Quiet at home, I sat with my papers for hours each night. I never forgot that schooling had irretrievably changed my family's life. That knowledge, however, did not weaken ambition. Instead, it strengthened resolve. Those times I remembered the loss of my past with regret, I quickly reminded myself of all the things my teachers could give

---

[6]*form-master:* A teacher in a British secondary school.

me. (They could make me an educated man.) I tightened my grip on pencil and books. I evaded nostalgia. Tried hard to forget. But one does not forget by trying to forget. One only remembers. I remembered too well that education had changed my family's life. I would not have become a scholarship boy had I not so often remembered.

Once she was sure that her children knew English, my mother would 20 tell us, "You should keep up your Spanish." Voices playfully groaned in response. "*¡Pochos!*"[7] my mother would tease. I listened silently.

After a while, I grew more calm at home. I developed tact. A fourth-grade student, I was no longer the show-off in front of my parents. I became a conventionally dutiful son, politely affectionate, cheerful enough, even — for reasons beyond choosing — my father's favorite. And much about my family life was easy then, comfortable, happy in the rhythm of our living together: hearing my father getting ready for work; eating the breakfast my mother had made me; looking up from a novel to hear my brother or one of my sisters playing with friends in the backyard; in winter, coming upon the house all lighted up after dark.

But withheld from my mother and father was any mention of what most mattered to me: the extraordinary experience of first-learning. Late afternoon: in the midst of preparing dinner, my mother would come up behind me while I was trying to read. Her head just over mine, her breath warmly scented with food. "What are you reading?" Or, "Tell me about your new courses." I would barely respond, "Just the usual things, nothing special." (A half smile, then silence. Her head moving back in the silence. Silence! Instead of the flood of intimate sounds that had once flowed smoothly between us, there was this silence.) After dinner, I would rush to a bedroom with papers and books. As often as possible, I resisted parental pleas to "save lights" by coming to the kitchen to work. I kept so much, so often, to myself. Sad. Enthusiastic. Troubled by the excitement of coming upon new ideas. Eager. Fascinated by the promising texture of a brand-new book. I hoarded the pleasures of learning. Alone for hours. Enthralled. Nervous. I rarely looked away from my books — or back on my memories. Nights when relatives visited and the front rooms were warmed by Spanish sounds, I slipped quietly out of the house.

It mattered that education was changing me. It never ceased to matter. My brother and sisters would giggle at our mother's mispronounced words. They'd correct her gently. My mother laughed girlishly one night, trying not to pronounce *sheep* as *ship*. From a distance I listened sullenly. From that distance, pretending not to notice on another occasion, I saw my father looking at the title pages of my library books. That was the scene on my mind when I walked home with a fourth-grade companion and heard him say that his parents read to him every night. (A strange-sounding book — *Winnie the*

---

[7]*Pocho:* A derogatory Spanish word for a Mexican American who has adopted the attitudes, values, and lifestyle of Anglo culture.

Pooh.) Immediately, I wanted to know, "What is it like?" My companion, however, thought I wanted to know about the plot of the book. Another day, my mother surprised me by asking for a "nice" book to read. "Something not too hard you think I might like." Carefully I chose one, Willa Cather's[8] *My Ántonia.* But when, several weeks later, I happened to see it next to her bed unread except for the first few pages, I was furious and suddenly wanted to cry. I grabbed up the book and took it back to my room and placed it in its place, alphabetically on my shelf.

"Your parents must be very proud of you." People began to say that to me about the time I was in sixth grade. To answer affirmatively, I'd smile. Shyly I'd smile, never betraying my sense of the irony: I was not proud of my mother and father. I was embarrassed by their lack of education. It was not that I ever thought they were stupid, though stupidly I took for granted their enormous native intelligence. Simply, what mattered to me was that they were not like my teachers.

But, "Why didn't you tell us about the award?" my mother demanded,   25
her frown weakened by pride. At the grammar school ceremony several weeks after, her eyes were brighter than the trophy I'd won. Pushing back the hair from my forehead, she whispered that I had "shown" the *gringos.*[9] A few minutes later, I heard my father speak to my teacher and felt ashamed of his labored, accented words. Then guilty for the shame. I felt such contrary feelings. (There is no simple roadmap through the heart of the scholarship boy.) My teacher was so soft-spoken and her words were edged sharp and clean. I admired her until it seemed to me that she spoke too carefully. Sensing that she was condescending to them, I became nervous. Resentful. Protective. I tried to move my parents away. "You both must be very proud of Richard," the nun said. They responded quickly. (They were proud.) "We are proud of all our children." Then this afterthought: "They sure didn't get their brains from us." They all laughed. I smiled.

In fourth grade I embarked upon a grandiose reading program. "Give me the names of important books," I would say to startled teachers. They soon found out that I had in mind "adult books." I ignored their suggestion of anything I suspected was written for children. (Not until I was in college, as a result, did I read *Huckleberry Finn* or *Alice's Adventures in Wonderland.*) Instead, I read *The Scarlet Letter* and Franklin's *Autobiography.* And whatever I read I read for extra credit. Each time I finished a book, I reported the achievement to a teacher and basked in the praise my effort earned. Despite my best efforts, however, there seemed to be more and more books I needed to read. At the library I would literally tremble as I came upon whole shelves of books I hadn't read. So I read and I read and I read: *Great Expectations;*

---

[8]*Willa Cather:* American novelist (1876–1947).
[9]*gringos:* Anglos.

all the short stories of Kipling; *The Babe Ruth Story;* the entire first volume of the *Encyclopaedia Britannica* (A–ANSTEY); the *Iliad; Moby Dick; Gone with the Wind; The Good Earth; Ramona; Forever Amber; The Lives of the Saints; Crime and Punishment; The Pearl.* . . . Librarians who initially frowned when I checked out the maximum ten books at a time started saving books they thought I might like. Teachers would say to the rest of the class, "I only wish the rest of you took reading as seriously as Richard obviously does."

But at home I would hear my mother wondering, "What do you see in your books?" (Was reading a hobby like her knitting? Was so much reading even healthy for a boy? Was it the sign of "brains"? Or was it just a convenient excuse for not helping around the house on Saturday mornings?) Always, "What do you see . . . ?"

What *did* I see in my books? I had the idea that they were crucial for my academic success, though I couldn't have said exactly how or why. In the sixth grade I simply concluded that what gave a book its value was some major idea or theme it contained. If that core essence could be mined and memorized, I would become learned like my teachers. I decided to record in a notebook the themes of the books that I read. After reading *Robinson Crusoe,* I wrote that its theme was "the value of learning to live by oneself." When I completed *Wuthering Heights,* I noted the danger of "letting emotions get out of control." Rereading these brief moralistic appraisals usually left me disheartened. I couldn't believe that they were really the source of reading's value. But for many more years, they constituted the only means I had of describing to myself the educational value of books.

I entered high school having read hundreds of books. My habit of reading made me a confident speaker and writer of English. Reading also enabled me to sense something of the shape, the major concerns, of Western thought. (I was able to say something about Dante[10] and Descartes[11] and Engels[12] and James Baldwin[13] in my high school term papers.) In these various ways, books brought me academic success as I hoped that they would. But I was not a good reader. Merely bookish, I lacked a point of view when I read. Rather, I read in order to acquire a point of view. I vacuumed books for epigrams, scraps of information, ideas, themes — anything to fill the hollow within me and make me feel educated. When one of my teachers suggested to his drowsy tenth-grade English class that a person could not have a "complicated idea" until he had read at least two thousand books, I heard the remark without detecting either its irony or its very complicated truth. I merely determined to compile a list of all the books I had ever read.

---

[10]*Dante:* Dante Alighieri, Italian poet (1265–1321); author of *The Divine Comedy.*

[11]*Descartes:* René Descartes, French philosopher and mathematician (1596–1650).

[12]*Engels:* Friedrich Engels, German socialist (1820–1895); coauthor with Karl Marx of *The Communist Manifesto* in 1848.

[13]*James Baldwin:* American novelist and essayist (1924–1987).

Harsh with myself, I included only once a title I might have read several times. (How, after all, could one read a book more than once?) And I included only those books over a hundred pages in length. (Could anything shorter be a book?)

There was yet another high school list I compiled. One day I came 30 across a newspaper article about the retirement of an English professor at a nearby state college. The article was accompanied by a list of the "hundred most important books of Western Civilization." "More than anything else in my life," the professor told the reporter with finality, "these books have made me all that I am." That was the kind of remark I couldn't ignore. I clipped out the list and kept it for the several months it took me to read all of the titles. Most books, of course, I barely understood. While reading Plato's *Republic,* for instance, I needed to keep looking at the book jacket comments to remind myself what the text was about. Nevertheless, with the special patience and superstition of a scholarship boy, I looked at every word of the text. And by the time I reached the last word, relieved, I con-vinced myself that I had read *The Republic.* In a ceremony of great pride, I solemnly crossed Plato off my list.

. . . The scholarship boy does not straddle, cannot reconcile, the two great opposing cultures of his life. His success is unromantic and plain. He sits in the classroom and offers those sitting beside him no calming reassur-ance about their own lives. He sits in the seminar room — a man with brown skin, the son of working-class Mexican immigrant parents. (Address-ing the professor at the head of the table, his voice catches with nervous-ness.) There is no trace of his parents' accent in his speech. Instead he approximates the accents of teachers and classmates. Coming from *him* those sounds seem suddenly odd. Odd too is the effect produced when *he* uses academic jargon — bubbles at the tip of his tongue: "*Topos* . . . negative capability . . . vegetation imagery in Shakespearean comedy."[14] He lifts an opinion from Coleridge, takes something else from Frye or Empson or Leavis.[15] He even repeats exactly his professor's earlier comment. All his ideas are clearly borrowed. He seems to have no thought of his own. He chatters while his listeners smile — their look one of disdain.

When he is older and thus when so little of the person he was sur-vives, the scholarship boy makes only too apparent his profound lack of *self-*confidence. This is the conventional assessment that even Richard Hoggart repeats:

> [The scholarship boy] tends to over-stress the importance of examina-tions, of the piling-up of knowledge and of received opinions. He dis-covers a technique of apparent learning, of the acquiring of facts rather than of the handling and use of facts. He learns how to receive a

---

[14]*topos . . . negative capability . . . :* Technical terms associated with the study of literary criticism.
[15]*Coleridge . . . Frye . . . Empson . . . Leavis:* Important literary critics.

purely literate education, one using only a small part of the personality
and challenging only a limited area of his being. He begins to see life
as a ladder, as a permanent examination with some praise and some
further exhortation at each stage. He becomes an expert imbiber and
doler-out; his competence will vary, but will rarely be accompanied by
genuine enthusiasms. He rarely feels the reality of knowledge, of other
men's thoughts and imaginings, on his own pulses.... He has something of the blinkered pony about him....

But this is criticism more accurate than fair. The scholarship boy is a
very bad student. He is the great mimic; a collector of thoughts, not a
thinker; the very last person in class who ever feels obliged to have an opinion of his own. In large part, however, the reason he is such a bad student is
because he realizes more often and more acutely than most other
students — than Hoggart himself — that education requires radical self-
reformation. As a very young boy, regarding his parents, as he struggles with
an early homework assignment, he knows this too well. That is why he lacks
self-assurance. He does not forget that the classroom is responsible for
remaking him. He relies on his teacher, depends on all that he hears in the
classroom and reads in his books. He becomes in every obvious way the
worst student, a dummy mouthing the opinions of others. But he would not
be so bad — nor would he become so successful, a *scholarship* boy — if he
did not accurately perceive that the best synonym for primary "education" is
"imitation."

Like me, Hoggart's imagined scholarship boy spends most of his years
in the classroom afraid to long for his past. Only at the very end of his
schooling does the boy-man become nostalgic. In this sudden change of
heart, Richard Hoggart notes:

> He longs for the membership he lost, "he pines for some Nameless
> Eden where he never was." The nostalgia is the stronger and the more
> ambiguous because he is really "in quest of his own absconded self yet
> scared to find it." He both wants to go back and yet thinks he has gone
> beyond his class, feels himself weighted with knowledge of his own
> and their situation, which hereafter forbids him the simpler pleasures
> of his father and mother....

According to Hoggart, the scholarship boy grows nostalgic because he   35
remains the uncertain scholar, bright enough to have moved from his past,
yet unable to feel easy, a part of a community of academics.

This analysis, however, only partially suggests what happened to me in
my last years as a graduate student. When I traveled to London to write a
dissertation on English Renaissance literature, I was finally confident of
membership in a "community of scholars." But the pleasure that confidence
gave me faded rapidly. After only two or three months in the reading room

of the British Museum, it became clear that I had joined a lonely community. Around me each day were dour faces eclipsed by large piles of books. There were the regulars, like the old couple who arrived every morning, each holding a loop of the shopping bag which contained all their notes. And there was the historian who chattered madly to herself. ("Oh dear! Oh! Now, what's this? What? Oh, my!") There were also the faces of young men and women worn by long study. And everywhere eyes turned away the moment our glance accidentally met. Some persons I sat beside day after day, yet we passed silently at the end of the day, strangers. Still, we were united by a common respect for the written word and for scholarship. We did form a union, though one in which we remained distant from one another.

More profound and unsettling was the bond I recognized with those writers whose books I consulted. Whenever I opened a text that hadn't been used for years, I realized that my special interests and skills united me to a mere handful of academics. We formed an exclusive — eccentric! — society, separated from others who would never care or be able to share our concerns. (The pages I turned were stiff like layers of dead skin.) I began to wonder: Who, beside my dissertation director and a few faculty members, would ever read what I wrote? and: Was my dissertation much more than an act of social withdrawal? These questions went unanswered in the silence of the Museum reading room. They remained to trouble me after I'd leave the library each afternoon and feel myself shy — unsteady, speaking simple sentences at the grocer's or the butcher's on my way back to my bed-sitter.[16]

Meanwhile my file cards accumulated. A professional, I knew exactly how to search a book for pertinent information. I could quickly assess and summarize the usability of the many books I consulted. But whenever I started to write, I knew too much (and not enough) to be able to write anything but sentences that were overly cautious, timid, strained brittle under the heavy weight of footnotes and qualifications. I seemed unable to dare a passionate statement. I felt drawn by professionalism to the edge of sterility, capable of no more than pedantic, lifeless, unassailable prose.

Then nostalgia began.

After years spent unwilling to admit its attractions, I gestured nostalgi- 40
cally toward the past. I yearned for that time when I had not been so alone. I became impatient with books. I wanted experience more immediate. I feared the library's silence. I silently scorned the gray, timid faces around me. I grew to hate the growing pages of my dissertation on genre[17] and Renaissance literature. (In my mind I heard relatives laughing as they tried to make sense of its title.) I wanted something — I couldn't say exactly what. I told myself that I wanted a more passionate life. And a life less thoughtful. And above all, I wanted to be less alone. One day I heard some Spanish academics whispering back and forth to each other, and their sounds seemed ghostly voices recalling my life. Yearning became preoccupation then. Boyhood memories beckoned,

---

[16]*bed-sitter:* A one-room apartment.
[17]*genre:* A class or category of artistic work; e.g., the genre of poetry.

flooded my mind. (Laughing intimate voices. Bounding up the front steps of the porch. A sudden embrace inside the door.)

For weeks after, I turned to books by educational experts. I needed to learn how far I had moved from my past — to determine how fast I would be able to recover something of it once again. But I found little. Only a chapter in a book by Richard Hoggart ... I left the reading room and the circle of faces.

I came home. After the year in England, I spent three summer months living with my mother and father, relieved by how easy it was to be home. It no longer seemed very important to me that we had little to say. I felt easy sitting and eating and walking with them. I watched them, nevertheless, looking for evidence of those elastic, sturdy strands that bind generations in a web of inheritance. I thought as I watched my mother one night: of course a friend had been right when she told me that I gestured and laughed just like my mother. Another time I saw for myself: my father's eyes were much like my own, constantly watchful.

But after the early relief, this return, came suspicion, nagging until I realized that I had not neatly sidestepped the impact of schooling. My desire to do so was precisely the measure of how much I remained an academic. *Negatively* (for that is how this idea first occurred to me): my need to think so much and so abstractly about my parents and our relationship was in itself an indication of my long education. My father and mother did not pass their time thinking about the cultural meanings of their experience. It was I who described their daily lives with airy ideas. And yet, *positively:* the ability to consider experience so abstractly allowed me to shape into desire what would otherwise have remained indefinite, meaningless longing in the British Museum. If, because of my schooling, I had grown culturally separated from my parents, my education finally had given me ways of speaking and caring about that fact.

My best teachers in college and graduate school, years before, had tried to prepare me for this conclusion, I think, when they discussed texts of aristocratic pastoral literature. Faithfully, I wrote down all that they said. I memorized it: "The praise of the unlettered by the highly educated is one of the primary themes of 'elitist' literature." But, "the importance of the praise given the unsolitary, richly passionate and spontaneous life is that it simultaneously reflects the value of a reflective life." I heard it all. But there was no way for any of it to mean very much to me. I was a scholarship boy at the time, busily laddering my way up the rungs of education. To pass an examination, I copied down exactly what my teachers told me. It would require many more years of schooling (an inevitable miseducation) in which I came to trust the silence of reading and the habit of abstracting from immediate experience — moving away from a life of closeness and immediacy I remembered with my parents, growing older — before I turned unafraid to desire the past, and thereby achieved what had eluded me for so long — the end of education.

ENGAGING THE TEXT

1. How does education affect Rodriguez's relationship to his family, his past, and his culture? Do you agree with him that education requires "radical self-reformation" (para. 33)?
2. What is a "scholarship boy"? Why does Rodriguez consider himself a bad student despite his academic success?
3. What happens to Rodriguez in London? Why does he ultimately abandon his studies there?
4. What drives Rodriguez to succeed? What does education represent to him? To his father and mother?
5. What is Rodriguez's final assessment of what he has gained and lost through his education? Do you agree with his analysis?

EXPLORING CONNECTIONS

6. Compare Rodriguez's attitude toward education and success with that of Mike Rose (p. 161) in "'I Just Wanna Be Average.'"
7. To what extent do Rodriguez's experiences as a "scholarship boy" confirm or complicate Jean Anyon's analysis (p. 173) of the relationship between social class, education, and success?
8. Read "Stephen Cruz" (p. 353) and compare his attitudes toward education and success with those of Rodriguez.

EXTENDING THE CRITICAL CONTEXT

9. What are your personal motives for academic success? How do they compare with those of Rodriguez?
10. Today many college students find that they're following in the footsteps of family members — not breaking ground as Rodriguez did. What special difficulties do such second- or third-generation college students face?

Para Teresa[1]

INÉS HERNÁNDEZ-ÁVILA

This poem explores and attempts to resolve an old conflict between its speaker and her schoolmate, two Chicanas at "Alamo which-had-to-be-its-name" Elementary School who have radically different ideas about what

[1]*Para Teresa:* For Teresa. [All notes are the author's.]

education means and does. Inés Hernández-Ávila (b. 1947) is an associate professor of Native American studies at the University of California, Davis. This poem appeared in her collection Con Razón, Corazón *(1987).*

A tí-Teresa
Te dedico las palabras estás
que explotan de mi corazón[2]

That day during lunch hour
at Alamo which-had-to-be-its-name   5
Elementary
my dear raza
That day in the bathroom
Door guarded
Myself cornered   10
I was accused by you, Teresa
Tú y las demás de tus amigas
Pachucas todas
Eran Uds. cinco.[3]

Me gritaban que porque me creía tan grande[4]   15
What was I trying to do, you growled
Show you up?
Make the teachers like me, pet me,
Tell me what a credit to my people I was?
I was playing right into their hands, you challenged   20
And you would have none of it.
I was to stop.

I was to be like you
I was to play your game of deadly defiance
Arrogance, refusal to submit.   25
The game in which the winner takes nothing
Asks for nothing
Never lets his weaknesses show.

But I didn't understand.
My fear salted with confusion   30
Charged me to explain to you
I did nothing *for the teachers*.
I studied for my parents and for my grandparents
Who cut out honor roll lists

[2]*A . . . corazón:* To you, Teresa, I dedicate these words that explode from my heart.
[3]*Tú . . . cinco:* You and the rest of your friends, all Pachucas, there were five of you.
[4]*Me . . . grande:* You were screaming at me, asking me why I thought I was so hot.

Whenever their nietos'[5] names appeared   35
For my shy mother who mastered her terror
to demand her place in mother's clubs
For my carpenter-father who helped me patiently with my math.
For my abuelos que me regalaron lápices en la Navidad[6]
And for myself.   40

Porque reconocí en aquel entonces
una verdad tremenda
que me hizo a mi un rebelde
Aunque tú no te habías dadocuenta[7]
We were not inferior   45
You and I, y las demás de tus amigas
Y los demás de nuestra gente[8]
I knew it the way I knew I was alive
We were good, honorable, brave
Genuine, loyal, strong   50
And smart.
Mine was a deadly game of defiance, also.
My contest was to prove
beyond any doubt
that we were not only equal but superior to them.   55
That was why I studied.
If I could do it, we all could.

You let me go then.
Your friends unblocked the way
I who-did-not-know-how-to-fight   60
was not made to engage with you-who-grew-up-fighting
Tu y yo,[9] Teresa
We went in different directions
Pero fuimos juntas.[10]

In sixth grade we did not understand   65
Uds. with the teased, dyed-black-but-reddening hair,
Full petticoats, red lipsticks
and sweaters with the sleeves
pushed up
Y yo conformándome con lo que deseaba mi mamá[11]   70

---

[5]*nietos'*: Grandchildren's.

[6]*abuelos . . . Navidad:* Grandparents who gave me gifts of pencils at Christmas.

[7]*Porque . . . dadocuenta:* Because I recognized a great truth then that made me a rebel, even though you didn't realize it.

[8]*Y . . . gente:* And the rest of your friends / And the rest of our people.

[9]*Tu y yo:* You and I.

[10]*Pero fuimos juntas:* But we were together.

[11]*Y . . . mamá:* And I conforming to my mother's wishes.

Certainly never allowed to dye, to tease, to paint myself
I did not accept your way of anger,
Your judgements
You did not accept mine.

But now in 1975, when I am twenty-eight   75
Teresa
I remember you.
Y sabes —
Te comprendo,
Es más, te respeto.   80
Y si me permites,
Te nombro — "hermana."[12]

ENGAGING THE TEXT

1. The speaker says that she didn't understand Teresa at the time of the incident she describes. What didn't she understand, and why? How have her views of Teresa and of herself changed since then? What seems to have brought about this change?

2. What attitudes toward school and the majority culture do Teresa and the speaker represent? What about the speaker's family? In what way are both girls playing a game of "deadly defiance"? What arguments can you make for each form of rebellion?

3. Why do you think Hernández-Ávila wrote this poem in both Spanish and English? What does doing so say about the speaker's life? About her change of attitude toward Teresa?

EXPLORING CONNECTIONS

4. Compare the speaker's attitude toward school and family with those of Richard Rodriguez (p. 193). What motivates each of them? What tensions do they feel?

5. Write a dialogue between the speaker of this poem, who wants to excel, and Ken Harvey, the boy whom Mike Rose said just wanted to be average (p. 161). Explore the uncertainties, pressures, and desires that these students felt. In what ways are these two apparently contrasting students actually similar?

EXTENDING THE CRITICAL CONTEXT

6. Was there a person or group you disliked, feared, or fought with in elementary school? Has your understanding of your adversary or of your own motives changed since then? If so, what brought about this change?

---

[12]*Y sabes . . . "hermana":* And do you know what, I understand you. Even more, I respect you. And, if you permit me, I name you my sister.

Learning to Read

MALCOLM X

Born Malcolm Little on May 19, 1925, Malcolm X was one of the most articulate and powerful leaders of black America during the 1960s. A street hustler convicted of robbery in 1946, he spent seven years in prison, where he educated himself and became a disciple of Elijah Muhammad, founder of the Nation of Islam. In the days of the civil rights movement, Malcolm X emerged as the leading spokesman for black separatism, a philosophy that urged black Americans to cut political, social, and economic ties with the white community. After a pilgrimage to Mecca, the capital of the Muslim world, in 1964, he became an orthodox Muslim, adopted the Muslim name El Hajj Malik El-Shabazz, and distanced himself from the teachings of the black Muslims. He was assassinated in 1965. In the following excerpt from his autobiography (1965), coauthored with Alex Haley and published the year of his death, Malcolm X describes his self-education.

It was because of my letters that I happened to stumble upon starting to acquire some kind of a homemade education.

I became increasingly frustrated at not being able to express what I wanted to convey in letters that I wrote, especially those to Mr. Elijah Muhammad.[1] In the street, I had been the most articulate hustler out there — I had commanded attention when I said something. But now, trying to write simple English, I not only wasn't articulate, I wasn't even functional. How would I sound writing in slang, the way I would *say* it, something such as, "Look, daddy, let me pull your coat about a cat, Elijah Muhammad — "

Many who today hear me somewhere in person, or on television, or those who read something I've said, will think I went to school far beyond the eighth grade. This impression is due entirely to my prison studies.

It had really begun back in the Charlestown Prison, when Bimbi[2] first made me feel envy of his stock of knowledge. Bimbi had always taken charge of any conversations he was in, and I had tried to emulate him. But every book I picked up had few sentences which didn't contain anywhere from one to nearly all of the words that might as well have been in Chinese. When I just skipped those words, of course, I really ended up with little idea of what the book said. So I had come to the Norfolk Prison Colony still

---

[1]*Elijah Muhammad:* American clergyman (1897–1975); leader of the Nation of Islam, 1935–1975.

[2]*Bimbi:* A fellow inmate whose encyclopedic learning and verbal facility greatly impressed Malcolm X.

going through only book-reading motions. Pretty soon, I would have quit even these motions, unless I had received the motivation that I did.

I saw that the best thing I could do was get hold of a dictionary — to study, to learn some words. I was lucky enough to reason also that I should try to improve my penmanship. It was sad. I couldn't even write in a straight line. It was both ideas together that moved me to request a dictionary along with some tablets and pencils from the Norfolk Prison Colony school.

I spent two days just riffling uncertainly through the dictionary's pages. I'd never realized so many words existed! I didn't know *which* words I needed to learn. Finally, just to start some kind of action, I began copying.

In my slow, painstaking, ragged handwriting, I copied into my tablet everything printed on that first page, down to the punctuation marks.

I believe it took me a day. Then, aloud, I read back, to myself, everything I'd written on the tablet. Over and over, aloud, to myself, I read my own handwriting.

I woke up the next morning, thinking about those words — immensely proud to realize that not only had I written so much at one time, but I'd written words that I never knew were in the world. Moreover, with a little effort, I also could remember what many of these words meant. I reviewed the words whose meanings I didn't remember. Funny thing, from the dictionary first page right now, that "aardvark" springs to my mind. The dictionary had a picture of it, a long-tailed, long-eared, burrowing African mammal, which lives off termites caught by sticking out its tongue as an anteater does for ants.

I was so fascinated that I went on — I copied the dictionary's next page. And the same experience came when I studied that. With every succeeding page, I also learned of people and places and events from history. Actually the dictionary is like a miniature encyclopedia. Finally the dictionary's A section had filled a whole tablet — and I went on into the B's. That was the way I started copying what eventually became the entire dictionary. It went a lot faster after so much practice helped me to pick up handwriting speed. Between what I wrote in my tablet, and writing letters, during the rest of my time in prison I would guess I wrote a million words.

I suppose it was inevitable that as my word-base broadened, I could for the first time pick up a book and read and now begin to understand what the book was saying. Anyone who has read a great deal can imagine the new world that opened. Let me tell you something: from then until I left that prison, in every free moment I had, if I was not reading in the library, I was reading on my bunk. You couldn't have gotten me out of books with a wedge. Between Mr. Muhammad's teachings, my correspondence, my visitors, . . . and my reading of books, months passed without my even thinking about being imprisoned. In fact, up to then, I never had been so truly free in my life.

The Norfolk Prison Colony's library was in the school building. A variety of classes was taught there by instructors who came from such places as

Harvard and Boston universities. The weekly debates between inmate teams were also held in the school building. You would be astonished to know how worked up convict debaters and audiences would get over subjects like "Should Babies Be Fed Milk?"

Available on the prison library's shelves were books on just about every general subject. Much of the big private collection that Parkhurst[3] had willed to the prison was still in crates and boxes in the back of the library — thousands of old books. Some of them looked ancient: covers faded, old-time parchment-looking binding. Parkhurst . . . seemed to have been principally interested in history and religion. He had the money and the special interest to have a lot of books that you wouldn't have in a general circulation. Any college library would have been lucky to get that collection.

As you can imagine, especially in a prison where there was heavy emphasis on rehabilitation, an inmate was smiled upon if he demonstrated an unusually intense interest in books. There was a sizable number of well-read inmates, especially the popular debaters. Some were said by many to be practically walking encyclopedias. They were almost celebrities. No university would ask any student to devour literature as I did when this new world opened to me, of being able to read and *understand*.

I read more in my room than in the library itself. An inmate who was   15 known to read a lot could check out more than the permitted maximum number of books. I preferred reading in the total isolation of my own room.

When I had progressed to really serious reading, every night at about ten P.M. I would be outraged with the "lights out." It always seemed to catch me right in the middle of something engrossing.

Fortunately, right outside my door was a corridor light that cast a glow into my room. The glow was enough to read by, once my eyes adjusted to it. So when "lights out" came, I would sit on the floor where I could continue reading in that glow.

At one-hour intervals at night guards paced past every room. Each time I heard the approaching footsteps, I jumped into bed and feigned sleep. And as soon as the guard passed, I got back out of bed onto the floor area of that light-glow, where I would read for another fifty-eight minutes until the guard approached again. That went on until three or four every morning. Three or four hours of sleep a night was enough for me. Often in the years in the streets I had slept less than that.

The teachings of Mr. Muhammad stressed how history had been "whitened" — when white men had written history books, the black man simply had been left out. Mr. Muhammad couldn't have said anything that would have struck me much harder. I had never forgotten how when my

[3]*Parkhurst:* Charles Henry Parkhurst (1842–1933); American clergyman, reformer, and president of the Society for the Prevention of Crime.

class, me and all of those whites, had studied seventh-grade United States history back in Mason, the history of the Negro had been covered in one paragraph, and the teacher had gotten a big laugh with his joke, "Negroes' feet are so big that when they walk, they leave a hole in the ground."

This is one reason why Mr. Muhammad's teachings spread so swiftly all over the United States, among *all* Negroes, whether or not they became followers of Mr. Muhammad. The teachings ring true — to every Negro. You can hardly show me a black adult in America — or a white one, for that matter — who knows from the history books anything like the truth about the black man's role. In my own case, once I heard of the "glorious history of the black man," I took special pains to hunt in the library for books that would inform me on details about black history. 20

I can remember accurately the very first set of books that really impressed me. I have since bought that set of books and I have it at home for my children to read as they grow up. It's called *Wonders of the World*. It's full of pictures of archeological finds, statues that depict, usually, non-European people.

I found books like Will Durant's[4] *Story of Civilization.* I read H. G. Wells'[5] *Outline of History. Souls of Black Folk* by W. E. B. Du Bois[6] gave me a glimpse into the black people's history before they came to this country. Carter G. Woodson's[7] *Negro History* opened my eyes about black empires before the black slave was brought to the United States, and the early Negro struggles for freedom.

J. A. Rogers'[8] three volumes of *Sex and Race* told about race-mixing before Christ's time; and Aesop being a black man who told fables; about Egypt's Pharaohs; about the great Coptic Christian Empire;[9] about Ethiopia, the earth's oldest continuous black civilization, as China is the oldest continuous civilization.

Mr. Muhammad's teaching about how the white man had been created led me to *Findings in Genetics*, by Gregor Mendel.[10] (The dictionary's G section was where I had learned what "genetics" meant.) I really studied this book by the Austrian monk. Reading it over and over, especially certain sections, helped me to understand that if you started with a black man, a

---

[4]*Will Durant:* American author and historian (1885–1981). Durant, with his wife Ariel (1898–1981), won the Pulitzer Prize for literature for volume ten of their eleven-volume *The Story of Civilization,* published from 1935 to 1975.

[5]*H. G. Wells:* English novelist and historian (1866–1946).

[6]*W. E. B. Du Bois:* William Edward Burghardt Du Bois, distinguished black scholar, author, and activist (1868–1963). Du Bois was the first director of the NAACP and was an important figure in the Harlem Renaissance; his best-known book is *Souls of Black Folk.*

[7]*Carter G. Woodson:* Distinguished African American historian (1875–1950); considered the father of black history.

[8]*J. A. Rogers:* African American historian and journalist (1883–1965).

[9]*Coptic Christian Empire:* The domain of the Coptic Church, a native Egyptian Christian church that retains elements of its African origins.

[10]*Gregor Mendel:* Austrian monk, botanist, and pioneer in genetic research (1822–1884).

white man could be produced; but starting with a white man, you never could produce a black man — because the white chromosome is recessive. And since no one disputes that there was but one Original Man, the conclusion is clear.

During the last year or so, in the *New York Times,* Arnold Toynbee[11] used the word "bleached" in describing the white man. His words were: "White (i.e., bleached) human beings of North European origin. . . ." Toynbee also referred to the European geographic area as only a peninsula of Asia. He said there was no such thing as Europe. And if you look at the globe, you will see for yourself that America is only an extension of Asia. (But at the same time Toynbee is among those who have helped to bleach history. He has written that Africa was the only continent that produced no history. He won't write that again. Every day now, the truth is coming to light.)

I never will forget how shocked I was when I began reading about slavery's total horror. It made such an impact upon me that it later became one of my favorite subjects when I became a minister of Mr. Muhammad's. The world's most monstrous crime, the sin and the blood on the white man's hands, are almost impossible to believe. Books like the one by Frederick Olmsted[12] opened my eyes to the horrors suffered when the slave was landed in the United States. The European woman, Fanny Kemble,[13] who had married a Southern white slaveowner, described how human beings were degraded. Of course I read *Uncle Tom's Cabin.*[14] In fact, I believe that's the only novel I have ever read since I started serious reading.

Parkhurst's collection also contained some bound pamphlets of the Abolitionist[15] Anti-Slavery Society of New England. I read descriptions of atrocities, saw those illustrations of black slave women tied up and flogged with whips; of black mothers watching their babies being dragged off, never to be seen by their mothers again; of dogs after slaves, and of the fugitive slave catchers, evil white men with whips and clubs and chains and guns. I read about the slave preacher Nat Turner, who put the fear of God into the white slavemaster. Nat Turner wasn't going around preaching pie-in-the-sky and "non-violent" freedom for the black man. There in Virginia one night in 1831, Nat and seven other slaves started out at his master's home and through the night they went from one plantation "big house" to the next, killing, until by the next morning 57 white people were dead and Nat had about 70 slaves following him. White people, terrified for their lives, fled from their homes, locked themselves up in public buildings, hid in the woods, and some even left the state. A small army of soldiers took two

[11]*Arnold Toynbee:* English historian (1889–1975).

[12]*Frederick Olmsted:* Frederick Law Olmsted (1822–1903), American landscape architect, city planner, and opponent of slavery.

[13]*Fanny Kemble:* Frances Anne Kemble, English actress and author (1809–1893); best known for her autobiographical *Journal of a Residence on a Georgia Plantation,* published in 1863 to win support in Britain for the abolitionist cause.

[14]*Uncle Tom's Cabin:* Harriet Beecher Stowe's 1852 antislavery novel.

[15]*Abolitionist:* Advocating the prohibition of slavery.

months to catch and hang Nat Turner. Somewhere I have read where Nat Turner's example is said to have inspired John Brown[16] to invade Virginia and attack Harpers Ferry nearly thirty years later, with thirteen white men and five Negroes.

I read Herodotus,[17] "the father of History," or, rather, I read about him. And I read the histories of various nations, which opened my eyes gradually, then wider and wider, to how the whole world's white men had indeed acted like devils, pillaging and raping and bleeding and draining the whole world's non-white people. I remember, for instance, books such as Will Durant's *The Story of Oriental Civilization*, and Mahatma Gandhi's[18] accounts of the struggle to drive the British out of India.

Book after book showed me how the white man had brought upon the world's black, brown, red, and yellow peoples every variety of the suffering of exploitation. I saw how since the sixteenth century, the so-called "Christian trader" white man began to ply the seas in his lust for Asian and African empires, and plunder, and power. I read, I saw, how the white man never has gone among the non-white peoples bearing the Cross in the true manner and spirit of Christ's teachings — meek, humble, and Christlike.

I perceived, as I read, how the collective white man had been actually   30 nothing but a piratical opportunist who used Faustian machinations[19] to make his own Christianity his initial wedge in criminal conquests. First, always "religiously," he branded "heathen" and "pagan" labels upon ancient non-white cultures and civilizations. The stage thus set, he then turned upon his non-white victims his weapons of war.

I read how, entering India — half a *billion* deeply religious brown people — the British white man, by 1759, through promises, trickery, and manipulations, controlled much of India through Great Britain's East India Company. The parasitical British administration kept tentacling out to half of the sub-continent. In 1857, some of the desperate people of India finally mutinied — and, excepting the African slave trade, nowhere has history recorded any more unnecessary bestial and ruthless human carnage than the British suppression of the non-white Indian people.

Over 115 million African blacks — close to the 1930s population of the United States — were murdered or enslaved during the slave trade. And I read how when the slave market was glutted, the cannibalistic white powers of Europe next carved up, as their colonies, the richest areas of the black continent. And Europe's chancelleries for the next century played a chess game of naked exploitation and power from Cape Horn to Cairo.

---

[16]*John Brown:* American abolitionist (1800–1859); leader of an attack on Harpers Ferry, West Virginia, in 1859.

[17]*Herodotus:* Early Greek historian (484?–425? B.C.).

[18]*Mahatma Gandhi:* Hindu religious leader, social reformer, and advocate of nonviolence (1869–1948).

[19]*Faustian machinations:* Evil plots or schemes. Faust was a legendary character who sold his soul to the devil for knowledge and power.

Ten guards and the warden couldn't have torn me out of those books. Not even Elijah Muhammad could have been more eloquent than those books were in providing indisputable proof that the collective white man had acted like a devil in virtually every contact he had with the world's collective non-white man. I listen today to the radio, and watch television, and read the headlines about the collective white man's fear and tension concerning China. When the white man professes ignorance about why the Chinese hate him so, my mind can't help flashing back to what I read, there in prison, about how the blood forebears of this same white man raped China at a time when China was trusting and helpless. Those original white "Christian traders" sent into China millions of pounds of opium. By 1839, so many of the Chinese were addicts that China's desperate government destroyed twenty thousand chests of opium. The first Opium War[20] was promptly declared by the white man. Imagine! Declaring *war* upon someone who objects to being narcotized! The Chinese were severely beaten, with Chinese-invented gunpowder.

The Treaty of Nanking made China pay the British white man for the destroyed opium; forced open China's major ports to British trade; forced China to abandon Hong Kong; fixed China's import tariffs so low that cheap British articles soon flooded in, maiming China's industrial development.

After a second Opium War, the Tientsin Treaties legalized the ravaging opium trade, legalized a British-French-American control of China's customs. China tried delaying that Treaty's ratification; Peking was looted and burned.

"Kill the foreign white devils!" was the 1901 Chinese war cry in the Boxer Rebellion.[21] Losing again, this time the Chinese were driven from Peking's choicest areas. The vicious, arrogant white man put up the famous signs, "Chinese and dogs not allowed."

Red China after World War II closed its doors to the Western white world. Massive Chinese agricultural, scientific, and industrial efforts are described in a book that *Life* magazine recently published. Some observers inside Red China have reported that the world never has known such a hate-white campaign as is now going on in this non-white country where, present birth-rates continuing, in fifty more years Chinese will be half the earth's population. And it seems that some Chinese chickens will soon come home to roost, with China's recent successful nuclear tests.

Let us face reality. We can see in the United Nations a new world order being shaped, along color lines — an alliance among the non-white nations. America's U.N. Ambassador Adlai Stevenson[22] complained not long ago

35

[20]*Opium War:* 1839–1842 war between Britain and China that ended with China's cession of Hong Kong to British rule.

[21]*Boxer Rebellion:* The 1898–1900 uprising by members of a secret Chinese society who opposed foreign influence in Chinese affairs.

[22]*Adlai Stevenson:* American politician (1900–1965); Democratic candidate for the presidency in 1952 and 1956.

that in the United Nations "a skin game"[23] was being played. He was right. He was facing reality. A "skin game" *is* being played. But Ambassador Stevenson sounded like Jesse James accusing the marshal of carrying a gun. Because who in the world's history ever has played a worse "skin game" than the white man?

Mr. Muhammad, to whom I was writing daily, had no idea of what a new world had opened up to me through my efforts to document his teachings in books.

When I discovered philosophy, I tried to touch all the landmarks of philosophical development. Gradually, I read most of the old philosophers, Occidental and Oriental. The Oriental philosophers were the ones I came to prefer; finally, my impression was that most Occidental philosophy had largely been borrowed from the Oriental thinkers. Socrates, for instance, traveled in Egypt. Some sources even say that Socrates was initiated into some of the Egyptian mysteries. Obviously Socrates got some of his wisdom among the East's wise men.

I have often reflected upon the new vistas that reading opened to me. I knew right there in prison that reading had changed forever the course of my life. As I see it today, the ability to read awoke inside me some long dormant craving to be mentally alive. I certainly wasn't seeking any degree, the way a college confers a status symbol upon its students. My homemade education gave me, with every additional book that I read, a little bit more sensitivity to the deafness, dumbness, and blindness that was afflicting the black race in America. Not long ago, an English writer telephoned me from London, asking questions. One was, "What's your alma mater?" I told him, "Books." You will never catch me with a free fifteen minutes in which I'm not studying something I feel might be able to help the black man.

Yesterday I spoke in London, and both ways on the plane across the Atlantic I was studying a document about how the United Nations proposes to insure the human rights of the oppressed minorities of the world. The American black man is the world's most shameful case of minority oppression. What makes the black man think of himself as only an internal United States issue is just a catch-phrase, two words, "civil rights." How is the black man going to get "civil rights" before first he wins his *human* rights? If the American black man will start thinking about his *human* rights, and then start thinking of himself as part of one of the world's great peoples, he will see he has a case for the United Nations.

I can't think of a better case! Four hundred years of black blood and sweat invested here in America, and the white man still has the black man begging for what every immigrant fresh off the ship can take for granted the minute he walks down the gangplank.

But I'm digressing. I told the Englishman that my alma mater was books, a good library. Every time I catch a plane, I have with me a book that

40

---

[23]*skin game:* A dishonest or fraudulent scheme, business operation, or trick, with the added reference in this instance to skin color.

I want to read — and that's a lot of books these days. If I weren't out here every day battling the white man, I could spend the rest of my life reading, just satisfying my curiosity — because you can hardly mention anything I'm not curious about. I don't think anybody ever got more out of going to prison than I did. In fact, prison enabled me to study far more intensively than I would have if my life had gone differently and I had attended some college. I imagine that one of the biggest troubles with colleges is there are too many distractions, too much panty-raiding, fraternities, and boola-boola and all of that. Where else but in a prison could I have attacked my ignorance by being able to study intensely sometimes as much as fifteen hours a day?

ENGAGING THE TEXT

1. What motivated Malcolm X to educate himself?
2. What kind of knowledge did Malcolm X gain by learning to read? How did this knowledge free or empower him?
3. Would it be possible for public schools to empower students in the way that Malcolm X's self-education empowered him? If so, how? If not, why not?
4. Some readers are offended by the strength of Malcolm X's accusations and by his grouping of all members of a given race into "collectives." Given the history of racial injustice he recounts here, do you feel he is justified in taking such a position?

EXPLORING CONNECTIONS

5. Compare and contrast Malcolm X's views on the meaning and purpose of education — or on the value and nature of reading — with those of Richard Rodriguez (p. 193). How can you account for the differences in their attitudes?
6. Imagine that John Taylor Gatto (p. 152), Mike Rose (p. 161), Richard Rodriguez (p. 193), and Malcolm X have been appointed to redesign American education. Working in groups, role-play a meeting in which the committee attempts to reach consensus on its recommendations. Report to the class the results of the committee's deliberations and discuss them.

THE BOONDOCKS   **by AARON MCGRUDER**

7. What does the *Boondocks* cartoon (p. 218) suggest about the possibility of teaching and learning "revolutionary" ideas within the setting of a public school system?

Extending the Critical Context

8. Survey some typical elementary or secondary school textbooks to test the currency of Malcolm X's charge that the educational establishment presents a "whitened" view of America. What view of America is presently being projected in public school history and social science texts?

9. Go to the library and read one page of the dictionary chosen at random. Study the meanings of any unfamiliar words and follow up on the information on your page by consulting encyclopedias, books, or articles. Let yourself be guided by chance and by your interests. After you've tried this experiment, discuss in class the benefits and drawbacks of an unsystematic self-education like Malcolm X's.

The Roots of Debate in Education and the Hope of Dialogue

Deborah Tannen

From the perspective of the twenty-first century, it's hard to imagine a time when women were excluded from institutions of higher education. Although many American colleges began admitting women in significant numbers little more than a century ago, female students now outnumber males on almost every coeducational campus in the nation. But as Deborah Tannen reminds us, the history of higher education stretches back far earlier than the founding of the United States. The college as an institution grew up in the male-dominated cultures of ancient Greece and medieval Europe and continues to this day to value an "agonistic," or conflict-based, mode of intellectual inquiry that, in Tannen's view, undermines the performance of many female students. A professor of linguistics at Georgetown University and a regular guest and commentator on television news shows, Tannen (b. 1945) has authored sixteen books on issues of interpersonal and cross-gender communication. Her publications include That's Not What I Meant: How Conversational Style Makes or Breaks Relationships *(1986),* You Just Don't Understand: Women and Men in Conversation *(1990), and the source of this selection,* The Argument Culture: Stopping America's War of Words *(1999). Tannen's most recent publication is* You're Wearing That?: Understanding Mothers and Daughters in Conversation *(2006).*

The teacher sits at the head of the classroom, feeling pleased with herself and her class. The students are engaged in a heated debate. The very noise level reassures the teacher that the students are participating, taking responsibility for their own learning. Education is going on. The class is a success.

But look again, cautions Patricia Rosof, a high school history teacher who admits to having experienced that wave of satisfaction with herself and the job she is doing. On closer inspection, you notice that only a few students are participating in the debate; the majority of the class is sitting silently, maybe attentive but perhaps either indifferent or actively turned off. And the students who are arguing are not addressing the subtleties, nuances, or complexities of the points they are making or disputing. They do not have that luxury because they want to win the argument — so they must go for the most gross and dramatic statements they can muster. They will not concede an opponent's point, even if they can see its validity, because that would weaken their position. Anyone tempted to synthesize the varying views would not dare to do so because it would look like a "cop-out," an inability to take a stand.

One reason so many teachers use the debate format to promote student involvement is that it is relatively easy to set up and the rewards are quick and obvious: the decibel level of noise, the excitement of those who are taking part. Showing students how to integrate ideas and explore subtleties and complexities is much harder. And the rewards are quieter — but more lasting.

Our schools and universities, our ways of doing science and approaching knowledge, are deeply agonistic. We all pass through our country's educational system, and it is there that the seeds of our adversarial culture are planted. Seeing how these seeds develop, and where they came from, is a key to understanding the argument culture and a necessary foundation for determining what changes we would like to make.

Roots of the Adversarial Approach to Knowledge

The argument culture, with its tendency to approach issues as a polarized debate, and the culture of critique, with its inclination to regard criticism and attack as the best if not the only type of rigorous thinking, are deeply rooted in Western tradition, going back to the ancient Greeks.[1] This point is made by Walter Ong, a Jesuit professor at Saint Louis University, in his book *Fighting for Life*. Ong credits the ancient Greeks with a fascination

5

[1]This does not mean it goes back in an unbroken chain. David Noble, in *A World Without Women*, claims that Aristotle was all but lost to the West during the early Christian era and was rediscovered in the medieval era, when universities were first established. This is significant for his observation that many early Christian monasteries welcomed both women and men who could equally aspire to an androgynous ideal, in contrast to the Middle Ages, when the female was stigmatized, unmarried women were consigned to convents, priests were required to be celibate, and women were excluded from spiritual authority. [All notes are the author's, except 6, 15, 18, 20, and 21.]

with adversativeness in language and thought.[2] He also connects the adversarial tradition of educational institutions to their all-male character. To attend the earliest universities, in the Middle Ages, young men were torn from their families and deposited in cloistered environments where corporal, even brutal, punishment was rampant. Their suffering drove them to bond with each other in opposition to their keepers — the teachers who were their symbolic enemies. Similar in many ways to puberty rites in traditional cultures, this secret society to which young men were confined also had a private language, Latin, in which students read about military exploits. Knowledge was gleaned through public oral disputation and tested by combative oral performance, which carried with it the risk of public humiliation. Students at these institutions were trained not to discover the truth but to argue either side of an argument — in other words, to debate. Ong points out that the Latin term for school, *ludus,* also referred to play or games, but it derived from the military sense of the word — training exercises for war.

If debate seems self-evidently the appropriate or even the only path to insight and knowledge, says Ong, consider the Chinese approach. Disputation was rejected in ancient China as "incompatible with the decorum and harmony cultivated by the true sage."[3] During the Classical periods in both China and India, according to Robert T. Oliver, the preferred mode of rhetoric was exposition rather than argument. The aim was to "enlighten an inquirer," not to "overwhelm an opponent." And the preferred style reflected "the earnestness of investigation" rather than "the fervor of conviction." In contrast to Aristotle's trust of logic and mistrust of emotion, in ancient Asia intuitive insight was considered the superior means of perceiving truth. Asian rhetoric was devoted not to devising logical arguments but to explicating widely accepted propositions. Furthermore, the search for

---

[2]There is a fascinating parallel in the evolution of the early Christian Church and the Southern Baptist Church: Noble shows that the early Christian Church regarded women as equally beloved of Jesus and equally capable of devoting their lives to religious study, so women comprised a majority of early converts to Christianity, some of them leaving their husbands — or bringing their husbands along — to join monastic communities. It was later, leading up to the medieval period, that the clerical movement gained ascendancy in part by systematically separating women, confining them in either marriage or convents, stigmatizing them, and barring them from positions of power within the church. Christine Leigh Heyrman, in *Southern Cross: The Beginnings of the Bible Belt,* shows that a similar trajectory characterized the Southern Baptist movement. At first, young Baptist and Methodist preachers (in the 1740s to 1830s) preached that both women and blacks were equally God's children, deserving of spiritual authority — with the result that the majority of converts were women and slaves. To counteract this distressing demography, the message was changed: antislavery rhetoric faded, and women's roles were narrowed to domesticity and subservience. With these shifts, the evangelical movement swept the South. At the same time, Heyrman shows, military imagery took over: The ideal man of God was transformed from a "willing martyr" to a "formidable fighter" led by "warrior preachers."

[3]Ong, *Fighting for Life,* p. 122. Ong's source, on which I also rely, is Oliver, *Communication and Culture in Ancient India and China.* My own quotations from Oliver are from p. 259.

abstract truth that we assume is the goal of philosophy, while taken for granted in the West, was not found in the East, where philosophy was concerned with observation and experience.

If Aristotelian philosophy, with its emphasis on formal logic, was based on the assumption that truth is gained by opposition, Chinese philosophy offers an alternative view. With its emphasis on harmony, says anthropologist Linda Young, Chinese philosophy sees a diverse universe in precarious balance that is maintained by talk. This translates into methods of investigation that focus more on integrating ideas and exploring relations among them than on opposing ideas and fighting over them.

Onward, Christian Soldiers

The military-like culture of early universities is also described by historian David Noble, who describes how young men attending medieval universities were like marauding soldiers: The students — all seminarians — roamed the streets bearing arms, assaulting women, and generally creating mayhem. Noble traces the history of Western science and of universities to joint origins in the Christian Church. The scientific revolution, he shows, was created by religious devotees setting up monastery-like institutions devoted to learning. Early universities were seminaries, and early scientists were either clergy or devoutly religious individuals who led monk-like lives. (Until as recently as 1888, fellows at Oxford were expected to be unmarried.)

That Western science is rooted in the Christian Church helps explain why our approach to knowledge tends to be conceived as a metaphorical battle: The Christian Church, Noble shows, has origins and early forms rooted in the military. Many early monks had actually been soldiers before becoming monks.[4] Not only were obedience and strict military-like discipline required, but monks saw themselves as serving "in God's knighthood," warriors in a battle against evil. In later centuries, the Crusades brought actual warrior-monks.

The history of science in the Church holds the key to understanding   10 our tradition of regarding the search for truth as an enterprise of oral disputation in which positions are propounded, defended, and attacked without regard to the debater's personal conviction. It is a notion of truth as objective, best captured by formal logic, that Ong traces to Aristotle. Aristotle regarded logic as the only trustworthy means for human judgment; emotions get in the way: "The man who is to judge would not have his judgment warped by speakers arousing him to anger, jealousy, or compassion. One

---

[4]Pachomius, for example, "the father of communal monasticism . . . and organizer of the first monastic community, had been a soldier under Constantine" and modeled his community on the military, emphasizing order, efficiency, and military obedience. Cassian, a fourth-century proselytizer, "'likened the monk's discipline to that of the soldier,' and Chrysostom, another great champion of the movement, 'sternly reminded the monks that Christ had armed them to be soldiers in a noble fight'" (Noble, *A World Without Women*, p. 54).

might as well make a carpenter's tool crooked before using it as a measure."[5]

This assumption explains why Plato wanted to ban poets from education in his ideal community. As a lover of poetry, I can still recall my surprise and distress on reading this in *The Republic*[6] when I was in high school. Not until much later did I understand what it was all about.[7] Poets in ancient Greece were wandering bards who traveled from place to place performing oral poetry that persuaded audiences by moving them emotionally. They were like what we think of as demagogues: people with a dangerous power to persuade others by getting them all worked up. Ong likens this to our discomfort with advertising in schools, which we see as places where children should learn to think logically, not be influenced by "teachers" with ulterior motives who use unfair persuasive tactics.

Sharing Time: Early Training in School

A commitment to formal logic as the truest form of intellectual pursuit remains with us today. Our glorification of opposition as the path to truth is related to the development of formal logic, which encourages thinkers to regard truth seeking as a step-by-step alternation of claims and counterclaims.[8] Truth, in this schema, is an abstract notion that tends to be taken out of context. This formal approach to learning is taught in our schools, often indirectly.

Educational researcher James Wertsch shows that schools place great emphasis on formal representation of knowledge. The common elementary school practice of "sharing time" (or, as it used to be called, "show-and-tell") is a prime arena for such training. Wertsch gives the example of a kindergarten pupil named Danny who took a piece of lava to class.[9] Danny told his classmates, "My mom went to the volcano and got it." When the teacher asked what he wanted to tell about it, he said, "I've always been taking care of it." This placed the rock at the center of his feelings and his family: the rock's connection to his mother, who gave it to him, and the attention and care he has lavished on it. The teacher reframed the children's interest in the rock as informational: "Is it rough or smooth?" "Is it heavy or light?" She also suggested they look up "volcano" and "lava" in the dictionary. This is not to imply that the teacher harmed the child; she built on his personal attachment to the rock to teach him a new way of thinking about it. But the

[5]Aristotle, quoted in Oliver, *Communication and Culture in Ancient India and China,* p. 259.

[6]*The Republic:* Plato's utopian vision of the ideal state.

[7]I came to understand the different meaning of "poet" in Classical Greece from reading Ong and also *Preface to Plato* by Eric Havelock. These insights informed many articles I wrote about oral and literate tradition in Western culture, including "Oral and Literate Strategies in Spoken and Written Narratives" and "The Oral/Literate Continuum in Discourse."

[8]Moulton, "A Paradigm of Philosophy"; Ong, *Fighting for Life.*

[9]The example of Danny and the lava: Wertsch, *Voices of the Mind,* pp. 113–14.

example shows the focus of education on formal rather than relational knowledge — information about the rock that has meaning out of context, rather than information tied to the context: Who got the rock for him? How did she get it? What is his relation to it?

Here's another example of how a teacher uses sharing time to train children to speak and think formally. Sarah Michaels spent time watching and tape-recording in a first-grade classroom. During sharing time, a little girl named Mindy held up two candles and told her classmates, "When I was in day camp we made these candles. And I tried it with different colors with both of them but one just came out, this one just came out blue and I don't know what this color is." The teacher responded, "That's neat-o. Tell the kids how you do it from the very start. Pretend we don't know a thing about candles. OK, what did you do first? What did you use?" She continued to prompt: "What makes it have a shape?" and "Who knows what the string is for?" By encouraging Mindy to give information in a sequential manner, even if it might not seem the most important to her and if the children might already know some of it, the teacher was training her to talk in a focused, explicit way.

The tendency to value formal, objective knowledge over relational, intuitive knowledge grows out of our notion of education as training for debate. It is a legacy of the agonistic heritage. There are many other traces as well. Many Ph.D. programs still require public "defenses" of dissertations or dissertation proposals, and oral performance of knowledge in comprehensive exams. Throughout our educational system, the most pervasive inheritance is the conviction that issues have two sides, that knowledge is best gained through debate, that ideas should be presented orally to an audience that does its best to poke holes and find weaknesses, and that to get recognition, one has to "stake out a position" in opposition to another. 15

Integrating Women in the Classroom Army

If Ong is right, the adversarial character of our educational institutions is inseparable from their all-male heritage. I wondered whether teaching techniques still tend to be adversarial today and whether, if they are, this may hold a clue to a dilemma that has received much recent attention: that girls often receive less attention and speak up less in class.[10] One term I taught a large lecture class of 140 students and decided to take advantage of this army (as it were) of researchers to answer these questions. Becoming observers in their own classrooms, my students found plenty of support for Ong's ideas.

I asked the students to note how relatively adversarial the teaching methods were in their other classes and how the students responded. Gabrielle DeRouen-Hawkins's description of a theology class was typical:

[10]See David and Myra Sadker, *Failing at Fairness.*

The class is in the format of lecture with class discussion and participation. There are thirteen boys and eleven girls in the class.[11] In a fifty-minute class:

> Number of times a male student spoke: 8
> Number of times a female student spoke: 3

... In our readings, theologians present their theories surrounding G-D, life, spirituality, and sacredness. As the professor (a male) outlined the main ideas about the readings, he posed questions like "And what is the fault with / Smith's / basis that the sacred is individualistic?" The only hands that went up were male. Not one female <u>dared</u> challenge or refute an author's writings. The only questions that the females asked (and all female comments were questions) involved a problem they had with the content of the reading. The males, on the other hand, openly questioned, criticized, and refuted the readings on five separate occasions. The three other times that males spoke involved them saying something like: "/ Smith / is very vague in her theory of XX. Can you explain it further?" They were openly argumentative.

This description raises a number of fascinating issues. First, it gives concrete evidence that at least college classrooms proceed on the assumption that the educational process should be adversarial: The teacher invited students to criticize the reading. (Theology, a required course at Georgetown, was a subject where my students most often found adversarial methods — interestingly, given the background I laid out earlier.) Again, there is nothing inherently wrong with using such methods. Clearly, they are very effective in many ways. However, among the potential liabilities is the risk that women students may be less likely to take part in classroom discussions that are framed as arguments between opposing sides — that is, debate — or as attacks on the authors — that is, critique. (The vast majority of students' observations revealed that men tended to speak more than women in their classes — which is not to say that individual women did not speak more than individual men.)

Gabrielle commented that since class participation counted for 10 percent of students' grades, it might not be fair to women students that the agonistic style is more congenial to men. Not only might women's grades suffer because they speak up less, but they might be evaluated as less intelligent or prepared because when they did speak, they asked questions rather than challenging the readings.

I was intrigued by the student's comment "/ Smith / is very vague in her theory of XX. Can you explain it further?" It could have been phrased "I didn't understand the author's theory. Can you explain it to me?" By beginning "The author is vague in her theory," the questioner blamed the author for his failure to understand. A student who asks a question in class risks

20

---

[11]Although my colleagues and I make efforts to refer to our students — all over the age of eighteen — as "women" and "men" and some students in my classes do the same, the majority refer to each other and themselves as "girls" and "boys" or "girls" and "guys."

appearing ignorant. Prefacing the question this way was an excellent way to minimize that risk.

In her description of this class, Gabrielle wrote that not a single woman "<u>dared</u> challenge or refute" an author. She herself underlined the word "dared." But in reading this I wondered whether "dared" was necessarily the right word. It implies that the women in the class wished to challenge the author but did not have the courage. It is possible that not a single woman *cared* to challenge the author. Criticizing or challenging might not be something that appealed to them or seemed worth their efforts. Going back to the childhoods of boys and girls, it seems possible that the boys had had more experiences, from the time they were small, that encouraged them to challenge and argue with authority figures than the girls had.

This is not to say that classrooms are more congenial to boys than girls in every way. Especially in the lowest grades, the requirement that children sit quietly in their seats seems clearly to be easier for girls to fulfill than boys, since many girls frequently sit fairly quietly for long periods of time when they play, while most boys' idea of play involves at least running around, if not also jumping and roughhousing. And researchers have pointed out that some of the extra attention boys receive is aimed at controlling such physical exuberance. The adversarial aspect of educational traditions is just one small piece of the pie, but it seems to reflect boys' experiences and predilections more than girls'.

A colleague commented that he had always taken for granted that the best way to deal with students' comments is to challenge them; he took it to be self-evident that this technique sharpens their minds and helps them develop debating skills. But he noticed that women were relatively silent in his classes. He decided to try beginning discussion with relatively open questions and letting comments go unchallenged. He found, to his amazement and satisfaction, that more women began to speak up in class.

Clearly, women can learn to perform in adversarial ways. Anyone who doubts this need only attend an academic conference in the field of women's studies or feminist studies — or read Duke University professor Jane Tompkins's essay showing how a conference in these fields can be like a Western shoot-out. My point is rather about the roots of the tradition and the tendency of the style to appeal initially to more men than women in the Western cultural context. Ong and Noble show that the adversarial culture of Western science and its exclusion of women were part and parcel of the same historical roots — not that individual women may not learn to practice and enjoy agonistic debate or that individual men may not recoil from it. There are many people, women as well as men, who assume a discussion must be contentious to be interesting. Author Mary Catherine Bateson recalls that when her mother, the anthropologist Margaret Mead, said, "I had an argument with" someone, it was a positive comment. "An argument," to her, meant a spirited intellectual interchange, not a rancorous conflict. The same assumption emerged in an obituary for Diana Trilling, called "one of the very last of the great midcentury New York intellectuals."[12] She and her friends had tried to live what they called "a life of significant contention" — the contention apparently enhancing rather than undercutting the significance.

Learning by Fighting

Although there are patterns that tend to typify women and men in a   25
given culture, there is an even greater range among members of widely divergent cultural backgrounds. In addition to observing adversarial encounters in their current classrooms, many students recalled having spent a junior year in Germany or France and commented that American classrooms seemed very placid compared to what they had experienced abroad. One student, Zach Tyler, described his impressions this way:

> I have very vivid memories of my junior year of high school, which I spent in Germany as an exchange student. The classroom was very debate-oriented and agonistic. One particular instance I remember well was in physics class, when a very confrontational friend of mine had a heated debate with the teacher about solving a problem. My friend ran to the board and scribbled out how he would have solved the problem, completely different from the teacher's, which also gave my friend the right answer and made the teacher wrong.
>
> STUDENT: "You see! This is how it should be, and you are wrong!"
> TEACHER: "No! No! No! You are absolutely wrong in every respect! Just look at how you did this!" (He goes over my friend's solution and shows that it does not work.) "Your solution has no base, as I just showed you!"
> STUDENT: "You can't prove that. Mine works just as well!"
> TEACHER: "My God, if the world were full of technical idiots like yourself! Look again!" (And he clearly shows how my friend's approach was wrong, after which my friend shut up.)

In Zach's opinion, the teacher encouraged this type of argument. The student learned he was wrong, but he got practice in arguing his point of view.

This incident occurred in high school. But European classrooms can be adversarial even at the elementary school level, according to another student, Megan Smyth, who reported on a videotape she saw in her French class:

> Today in French class we watched an excerpt of a classroom scene of fifth-graders. One at a time, each student was asked to stand up and recite a poem that they were supposed to have memorized. The teacher screamed at the students if they forgot a line or if they didn't

[12]Jonathan Alter, "The End of the Journey," *Newsweek*, Nov. 4, 1996, p. 61. Trilling died at the age of ninety-one.

speak with enough emotion. They were reprimanded and asked to repeat the task until they did it perfectly and passed the "oral test."

There is probably little question about how Americans would view this way of teaching, but the students put it into words:

> After watching this scene, my French teacher asked the class what our opinion was. The various responses included: French schools are very strict, the professor was "mean" and didn't have respect for the students, and there's too much emphasis on memorization, which is pointless.

If teaching methods can be more openly adversarial in European than American elementary and high schools, academic debate can be more openly adversarial there as well. For example, Alice Kaplan, a professor of French at Duke University, describes a colloquium on the French writer Céline that she attended in Paris:

> After the first speech, people started yelling at each other. "Are you suggesting that Céline was fascist!" "You call that evidence!" "I will not accept ignorance in the place of argument!" I was scared.[13]

These examples dramatize that many individuals can thrive in an adversarial atmosphere. And those who learn to participate effectively in any verbal game eventually enjoy it, if nothing else than for the pleasure of exercising that learned skill. It is important to keep these examples in mind in order to avoid the impression that adversarial tactics are always destructive. Clearly, such tactics sometimes admirably serve the purpose of intellectual inquiry. In addition to individual predilection, cultural learning plays a role in whether or not someone enjoys the game played this way.

Graduate School as Boot Camp

Although the invective Kaplan heard at a scholarly meeting in Paris is more extreme than what is typical at American conferences, the assumption that challenge and attack are the best modes of scholarly inquiry is pervasive in American scholarly communities as well. Graduate education is a training ground not only for teaching but also for scientific research. Many graduate programs are geared to training young scholars in rigorous thinking, defined as the ability to launch and field verbal attacks.

Communications researchers Karen Tracy and Sheryl Baratz tapped into some of the ethics that lead to this atmosphere in a study of weekly symposia attended by faculty and graduate students at a major research university. When they asked participants about the purpose of the symposia, they were told it was to "trade ideas" and "learn things." But it didn't take too much discussion to uncover the participants' deeper concern: to be seen

[13]Kaplan, *French Lessons*, p. 119.

as intellectually competent. And here's the rub: to be seen as competent, a student had to ask "tough and challenging questions."

One faculty member commented, when asked about who participated actively in a symposium,

> Among the graduate students, the people I think about are Jess, Tim, uh let's see, Felicia will ask a question but it'll be a nice little supportive question.[14]

"A nice little supportive question" diminished the value of Felicia's participation and her intelligence — the sort of judgment a student would wish to avoid. Just as with White House correspondents, there is value placed on asking "tough questions." Those who want to impress their peers and superiors (as most, if not all, do) are motivated to ask the sorts of questions that gain approval.

Valuing attack as a sign of respect is part of the argument culture of 30 academia — our conception of intellectual interchange as a metaphorical battle. As one colleague put it, "In order to play with the big boys, you have to be willing to get into the ring and wrestle with them." Yet many graduate students (and quite a few established scholars) remain ambivalent about this ethic, especially when they are on the receiving rather than the distribution end. Sociolinguist Winnie Or tape-recorded a symposium at which a graduate student presented her fledgling research to other students and graduate faculty. The student later told Or that she left the symposium feeling that a truck had rolled over her. She did not say she regretted having taken part; she felt she had received valuable feedback. But she also mentioned that she had not looked at her research project once since the symposium several weeks before. This is telling. Shouldn't an opportunity to discuss your research with peers and experts fire you up and send you back to the isolation of research renewed and reinspired? Isn't something awry if it leaves you not wanting to face your research project at all?

This young scholar persevered, but others drop out of graduate school, in some cases because they are turned off by the atmosphere of critique. One woman who wrote to me said she had been encouraged to enroll in graduate school by her college professors, but she lasted only one year in a major midwest university's doctoral program in art history. This is how she described her experience and her decision not to continue.

> Grad school was the nightmare I never knew existed. . . . Into the den of wolves I go, like a lamb to slaughter. . . . When, at the end of my first year (masters) I was offered a job as a curator for a private collection, I jumped at the chance. I wasn't cut out for academia — better try the "real world."

Reading this I thought, is it that she was not cut out for academia, or is it that academia as it was practiced in that university is not cut out for people

---

[14]Tracy and Baratz, "Intellectual Discussion in the Academy as Situated Discourse," p. 309.

like her. It is cut out for those who enjoy, or can tolerate, a contentious environment.

(These examples remind us again of the gender dynamic. The graduate student who left academia for museum work was a woman. The student who asked a "nice little supportive question" instead of a "tough, challenging one" was a woman. More than one commentator has wondered aloud if part of the reason women drop out of science courses and degree programs is their discomfort with the agonistic culture of Western science. And Lani Guinier[15] has recently shown that discomfort with the agonistic procedures of law school is partly responsible for women's lower grade point averages in law school, since the women arrive at law school with records as strong as the men's.)

The Culture of Critique: Attack in the Academy

The standard way of writing an academic paper is to position your work in opposition to someone else's, which you prove wrong. This creates a *need* to make others wrong, which is quite a different matter from reading something with an open mind and discovering that you disagree with it. Students are taught that they must disprove others' arguments in order to be original, make a contribution, and demonstrate their intellectual ability. When there is a *need* to make others wrong, the temptation is great to oversimplify at best, and at worst to distort or even misrepresent others' positions, the better to refute them — to search for the most foolish statement in a generally reasonable treatise, seize upon the weakest examples, ignore facts that support your opponent's views, and focus only on those that support yours. Straw men spring up like scarecrows in a cornfield.

Sometimes it seems as if there is a maxim driving academic discourse that counsels, "If you can't find something bad to say, don't say anything." As a result, any work that gets a lot of attention is immediately opposed. There is an advantage to this approach: Weaknesses are exposed, and that is surely good. But another result is that it is difficult for those outside the field (or even inside) to know what is "true." Like two expert witnesses hired by opposing attorneys, academics can seem to be canceling each other out. In the words of policy analysts David Greenberg and Philip Robins:

> The process of scientific inquiry almost ensures that competing sets of results will be obtained. . . . Once the first set of findings are published, other researchers eager to make a name for themselves must come up with different approaches and results to get their studies published.[16]

How are outsiders (or insiders, for that matter) to know which "side" to believe? As a result, it is extremely difficult for research to influence public policy.

---

[15]*Lani Guinier:* Legal scholar (b. 1950) whose 1993 nomination to the Supreme Court was defeated in Congress.

[16]Greenberg and Robins, "The Changing Role of Social Experiments in Policy Analysis," p. 350.

A leading researcher in psychology commented that he knew of two   35
young colleagues who had achieved tenure by writing articles attacking him.
One of them told him, in confidence, that he actually agreed with him, but
of course he could not get tenure by writing articles simply supporting
someone else's work; he had to stake out a position in opposition. Attacking
an established scholar has particular appeal because it demonstrates origi-
nality and independence of thought without requiring true innovation. After
all, the domain of inquiry and the terms of debate have already been established. The critic has only to say, like the child who wants to pick a fight, "Is
not!" Younger or less prominent scholars can achieve a level of attention
otherwise denied or eluding them by stepping into the ring with someone
who has already attracted the spotlight.

The young psychologist who confessed his motives to the established
one was unusual, I suspect, only in his self-awareness and willingness to
articulate it. More commonly, younger scholars, or less prominent ones,
convince themselves that they are fighting for truth, that they are among the
few who see that the emperor has no clothes. In the essay mentioned earlier, Jane Tompkins describes how a young scholar-critic can work herself
into a passionate conviction that she is morally obligated to attack, because
she is fighting on the side of good against the side of evil. Like the reluctant
hero in the film *High Noon,* she feels she has no choice but to strap on her
holster and shoot. Tompkins recalls that her own career was launched by an
essay that

> began with a frontal assault on another woman scholar. When I wrote
> it I felt the way the hero does in a Western. Not only had this critic
> argued *a, b,* and *c,* she had held *x, y,* and *z!* It was a clear case of outra-
> geous provocation.[17]

Because her attack was aimed at someone with an established career
("She was famous and I was not. She was teaching at a prestigious university
and I was not. She had published a major book and I had not."), it was a
"David and Goliath situation" that made her feel she was "justified in hitting
her with everything I had." (This is analogous to what William Safire[18]
describes as his philosophy in the sphere of political journalism: "Kick 'em
when they're up.")[19]

The claim of objectivity is belied by Tompkins's account of the spirit in
which attack is often launched: the many motivations, other than the search
for truth, that drive a critic to pick a fight with another scholar. Objectivity
would entail a disinterested evaluation of all claims. But there is nothing
disinterested about it when scholars set out with the need to make others
wrong and transform them not only into opponents but into villains.

[17]These and other quotes from Tompkins appear in her essay "Fighting Words,"
pp. 588–89.

[18]*William Safire:* Political commentator (b. 1929).

[19]Safire is quoted in Howard Kurtz, "Safire Made No Secret of Dislike for Inman," *The
Washington Post,* Jan. 19, 1994, p. A6.

In academia, as in other walks of life, anonymity breeds contempt. Some of the nastiest rhetoric shows up in "blind" reviews — of articles submitted to journals or book proposals submitted to publishers. "Peer review" is the cornerstone of academic life. When someone submits an article to a journal, a book to a publisher, or a proposal to a funding institution, the work is sent to established scholars for evaluation. To enable reviewers to be honest, they remain anonymous. But anonymous reviewers often take a tone of derision such as people tend to use only when talking about someone who is not there — after all, the evaluation is not addressed to the author. But authors typically receive copies of the evaluations, especially if their work is rejected. This can be particularly destructive to young scholars just starting out. For example, one sociolinguist wrote her dissertation in a firmly established tradition: She tape-recorded conversations at the company where she worked part-time. Experts in our field believe it is best to examine conversations in which the researcher is a natural participant, because when strangers appear asking to tape-record, people get nervous and may change their behavior. The publisher sent the manuscript to a reviewer who was used to different research methods. In rejecting the proposal, she referred to the young scholar "using the audiotaped detritus from an old job." Ouch. What could justify the sneering term "detritus"? What is added by appending "old" to "job," other than hurting the author? Like Heathcliff,[20] the target hears only the negative and — like Heathcliff — may respond by fleeing the field altogether.

One reason the argument culture is so widespread is that arguing is so easy to do. Lynne Hewitt, Judith Duchan, and Erwin Segal came up with a fascinating finding: Speakers with language disabilities who had trouble taking part in other types of verbal interaction were able to participate in arguments. Observing adults with mental retardation who lived in a group home, the researchers found that the residents often engaged in verbal conflicts as a means of prolonging interaction. It was a form of sociability. Most surprising, this was equally true of two residents who had severe language and comprehension disorders yet were able to take part in the verbal disputes, because arguments have a predictable structure.

Academics, too, know that it is easy to ask challenging questions without listening, reading, or thinking very carefully. Critics can always complain about research methods, sample size, and what has been left out. To study anything, a researcher must isolate a piece of the subject and narrow the scope of vision in order to focus. An entire tree cannot be placed under a microscope; a tiny bit has to be separated to be examined closely. This gives critics the handle of a weapon with which to strike an easy blow: They can point out all the bits that were not studied. Like family members or

40

[20]*Heathcliff:* The male protagonist of Emily Brontë's nineteenth-century novel *Wuthering Heights.* He overreacts when he hears the novel's heroine criticize him.

partners in a close relationship, anyone looking for things to pick on will have no trouble finding them.

All of this is not to imply that scholars should not criticize each other or disagree. In the words of poet William Blake,[21] "Without contraries is no progression."[22] The point is to distinguish constructive ways of doing so from nonconstructive ones. Criticizing a colleague on empirical grounds is the beginning of a discussion; if researchers come up with different findings, they can engage in a dialogue: What is it about their methods, data, or means of analysis that explains the different results? In some cases, those who set out to disprove another's claims end up proving them instead — something that is highly unlikely to happen in fields that deal in argumentation alone.

A stunning example in which opponents attempting to disprove a heretical claim ended up proving it involves the cause and treatment of ulcers. It is now widely known and accepted that ulcers are caused by bacteria in the stomach and can be cured by massive doses of antibiotics. For years, however, the cure and treatment of ulcers remained elusive, as all the experts agreed that ulcers were the classic psychogenic illness caused by stress. The stomach, experts further agreed, was a sterile environment: No bacteria could live there. So pathologists did not look for bacteria in the stomachs of ailing or deceased patients, and those who came across them simply ignored them, in effect not seeing what was before their eyes because they did not believe it could be there. When Dr. Barry Marshall, an Australian resident in internal medicine, presented evidence that ulcers are caused by bacteria, no one believed him. His findings were ultimately confirmed by researchers intent on proving him wrong.[23]

The case of ulcers shows that setting out to prove others wrong can be constructive — when it is driven by genuine differences and when it motivates others to undertake new research. But if seeking to prove others wrong becomes a habit, an end in itself, the sole line of inquiry, the results can be far less rewarding.

Believing as Thinking

"The doubting game" is the name English professor Peter Elbow gives   45
to what educators are trained to do. In playing the doubting game, you approach others' work by looking for what's wrong, much as the press corps follows the president hoping to catch him stumble or an attorney pores over an opposing witness's deposition looking for inconsistencies that can be challenged on the stand. It is an attorney's job to discredit opposing witnesses, but is it a scholar's job to approach colleagues like an opposing attorney?

---

[21]*William Blake:* English Romantic poet (1757–1827).

[22]I've borrowed the William Blake quote from Peter Elbow, who used it to open his book *Embracing Contraries.*

[23]Terence Monmaney, "Marshall's Hunch," *The New Yorker,* Sept. 20, 1993, pp. 64–72.

Elbow recommends learning to approach new ideas, and ideas different from your own, in a different spirit — what he calls a "believing game." This does not mean accepting everything anyone says or writes in an unthinking way. That would be just as superficial as rejecting everything without thinking deeply about it. The believing game is still a game. It simply asks you to give it a whirl: Read *as if* you believed, and see where it takes you. Then you can go back and ask whether you want to accept or reject elements in the argument or the whole argument or idea. Elbow is not recommending that we stop doubting altogether. He is telling us to stop doubting exclusively. We need a systematic and respected way to detect and expose strengths, just as we have a systematic and respected way of detecting faults.

Americans need little encouragement to play the doubting game because we regard it as synonymous with intellectual inquiry, a sign of intelligence. In Elbow's words, "We tend to assume that the ability to criticize a claim we disagree with counts as more serious intellectual work than the ability to enter into it and temporarily assent."[24] It is the believing game that needs to be encouraged and recognized as an equally serious intellectual pursuit.

Although criticizing is surely part of critical thinking, it is not synonymous with it. Again, limiting critical response to critique means not doing the other kinds of critical thinking that could be helpful: looking for new insights, new perspectives, new ways of thinking, new knowledge. Critiquing relieves you of the responsibility of doing integrative thinking. It also has the advantage of making the critics feel smart, smarter than the ill-fated author whose work is being picked apart like carrion. But it has the disadvantage of making them less likely to learn from the author's work.

The Socratic Method — or Is It?

Another scholar who questions the usefulness of opposition as the sole path to truth is philosopher Janice Moulton. Philosophy, she shows, equates logical reasoning with the Adversary Paradigm, a matter of making claims and then trying to find, and argue against, counterexamples to that claim. The result is a debate between adversaries trying to defend their ideas against counterexamples and to come up with counterexamples that refute the opponent's ideas. In this paradigm, the best way to evaluate someone's work is to "subject it to the strongest or most extreme opposition."[25]

But if you parry individual points — a negative and defensive enterprise — you never step back and actively imagine a world in which a different system of ideas could be true — a positive act. And you never ask how larger systems of thought relate to each other. According to Moulton, our devotion to the Adversary Paradigm has led us to misinterpret the type of argumentation that Socrates favored: We think of the Socratic method as

50

[24]Elbow, *Embracing Contraries,* p. 258.
[25]Moulton, "A Paradigm of Philosophy," p. 153.

systematically leading an opponent into admitting error. This is primarily a way of showing up an adversary as wrong. Moulton shows that the original Socratic method — the *elenchus* — was designed to convince others, to shake them out of their habitual mode of thought and lead them to new insight. Our version of the Socratic method — an adversarial public debate — is unlikely to result in opponents changing their minds. Someone who loses a debate usually attributes that loss to poor performance or to an adversary's unfair tactics. . . .

Getting Beyond Dualism

At the heart of the argument culture is our habit of seeing issues and ideas as absolute and irreconcilable principles continually at war. To move beyond this static and limiting view, we can remember the Chinese approach to yin and yang. They are two principles, yes, but they are conceived not as irreconcilable polar opposites but as elements that coexist and should be brought into balance as much as possible. As sociolinguist Suzanne Wong Scollon notes, "Yin is always present in and changing into yang and vice versa."[26] How can we translate this abstract idea into daily practice?

To overcome our bias toward dualism, we can make special efforts not to think in twos. Mary Catherine Bateson, an author and anthropologist who teaches at George Mason University, makes a point of having her class compare *three* cultures, not two. If students compare two cultures, she finds, they are inclined to polarize them, to think of the two as opposite to each other. But if they compare three cultures, they are more likely to think about each on its own terms.[27]

As a goal, we could all try to catch ourselves when we talk about "both sides" of an issue — and talk instead about "all sides." And people in any field can try to resist the temptation to pick on details when they see a chance to score a point. If the detail really does not speak to the main issue, bite your tongue. Draw back and consider the whole picture. After asking, "Where is this wrong?" make an effort to ask, "What is right about this?" — not necessarily *instead*, but *in addition*. . . .

Perhaps, too, it is time to question our glorification of debate as the best, if not the only, means of inquiry. The debate format leads us to regard those doing different kinds of research as belonging to warring camps. There is something very appealing about conceptualizing differing approaches in this way, because dichotomies appeal to our sense of how knowledge should be organized.

Well, what's wrong with that?   55

What's wrong is that it obscures aspects of disparate work that overlap and can enlighten each other.

[26]Suzanne Wong Scollon, personal communication.
[27]Mary Catherine Bateson, personal communication.

What's wrong is that it obscures the complexity of research. Fitting ideas into a particular camp requires you to oversimplify them. Again, disinformation and distortion can result. Less knowledge is gained, not more. And time spent attacking an opponent or defending against attacks is not spent doing something else — like original research.

What's wrong is that it implies that only one framework can apply, when in most cases many can. As a colleague put it, "Most theories are wrong not in what they assert but in what they deny."[28] Clinging to the elephant's leg, they loudly proclaim that the person describing the elephant's tail is wrong. This is not going to help them — or their readers — understand an elephant. Again, there are parallels in personal relationships. I recall a man who had just returned from a weekend human-development seminar. Full of enthusiasm, he explained the main lesson he had learned: "I don't have to make others wrong to prove that I'm right." He experienced this revelation as a liberation; it relieved him of the burden of trying to prove others wrong.

If you limit your view of a problem to choosing between two sides, you inevitably reject much that is true, and you narrow your field of vision to the limits of those two sides, making it unlikely you'll pull back, widen your field of vision, and discover the paradigm shift that will permit truly new understanding.

In moving away from a narrow view of debate, we need not give up   60
conflict and criticism altogether. Quite the contrary, we can develop more varied — and more constructive — ways of expressing opposition and negotiating disagreement.

We need to use our imaginations and ingenuity to find different ways to seek truth and gain knowledge, and add them to our arsenal — or, should I say, to the ingredients for our stew. It will take creativity to find ways to blunt the most dangerous blades of the argument culture. It's a challenge we must undertake, because our public and private lives are at stake.

References

Bateson, Mary Catherine. *With a Daughter's Eye: A Memoir of Margaret Mead and Gregory Bateson* (New York: William Morrow, 1984).

Elbow, Peter. *Embracing Contraries: Explorations in Learning and Teaching* (New York and Oxford: Oxford University Press, 1986).

Greenberg, David H., and Philip K. Robins. "The Changing Role of Social Experiments in Policy Analysis." *Journal of Policy Analysis and Management* 5:2 (1986), pp. 340–62.

Guinier, Lani, Michelle Fine, and Jane Balin, with Ann Bartow and Deborah Lee Stachel. "Becoming Gentlemen: Women's Experiences at One Ivy League Law School." 143 *University of Pennsylvania Law Review* (Nov. 1994), pp. 1–110.

Havelock, Eric A. *Preface to Plato* (Cambridge, Mass.: Belknap Press, Harvard University Press, 1963).

[28]I got this from A. L. Becker, who got it from Kenneth Pike, who got it from . . .

Hewitt, Lynne E., Judith F. Duchan, and Erwin M. Segal. "Structure and Function of Verbal Conflicts Among Adults with Mental Retardation." *Discourse Processes* 16(4) (1993), pp. 525–43.

Heyrman, Christine Leigh. *Southern Cross: The Beginnings of the Bible Belt* (New York: Knopf, 1997).

Kaplan, Alice. *French Lessons: A Memoir* (Chicago: University of Chicago Press, 1993).

Kurtz, Howard. *Hot Air: All Talk, All the Time* (New York: Times Books, 1996).

Michaels, Sarah. "'Sharing Time': Children's Narrative Styles and Differential Access to Literacy." *Language in Society* 10:3 (1981), pp. 423–42.

Moulton, Janice. "A Paradigm of Philosophy: The Adversary Method." In *Discovering Reality*, Sandra Harding and Merrill B. Hintikka, eds. (Dordrecht, Holland: Reidel, 1983), pp. 149–64.

Noble, David. A *World Without Women: The Christian Clerical Culture of Western Science* (New York and Oxford: Oxford University Press, 1992).

Oliver, Robert T. *Communication and Culture in Ancient India and China* (Syracuse, N.Y.: Syracuse University Press, 1971).

Ong, Walter J. *Fighting for Life: Contest, Sexuality, and Consciousness* (Ithaca, N.Y.: Cornell University Press, 1981).

Or, Winnie Wing Fung. "Agonism in Academic Discussion." Paper presented at the 96th Annual Meeting of the American Anthropological Association, Nov. 19–23, 1997, Washington, D.C.

Rosof, Patricia J. F. "Beyond Rhetoric." *The History Teacher* 26(4) (1993), pp. 493–97.

Sadker, Myra, and David Sadker. *Failing at Fairness: How America's Schools Cheat Girls* (New York: Scribner's, 1994).

Tompkins, Jane. "Fighting Words: Unlearning to Write the Critical Essay." *Georgia Review* 42 (1988), pp. 585–90.

Tracy, Karen, and Sheryl Baratz. "Intellectual Discussion in the Academy as Situated Discourse." *Communication Monographs* 60 (1993), pp. 300–20.

Wertsch, James V. *Voices of the Mind: A Sociocultural Approach to Mediated Action* (Cambridge, Mass.: Harvard University Press, 1991).

Young, Linda W. L. *Crosswalk and Culture in Sino-American Communication* (Cambridge, England: Cambridge University Press, 1994).

ENGAGING THE TEXT

1. How, according to Tannen, do today's classrooms reflect their origin in Greek philosophy and the Christian universities of the medieval era? What relationship does Tannen see between the thinking of the early Christian Church and Western science?

2. Explain the distinction that Tannen makes between "formal, objective knowledge" and "relational, intuitive knowledge" (paras. 12–15). How, according to Tannen, do these different understandings of knowledge affect the experiences of male and female students in contemporary college classrooms?

3. What is the "culture of critique" that, in Tannen's view, dominates higher education? To what extent does your experience of schooling support the claim that critical, or Socratic, thinking is taught within an "Adversary

Paradigm" in American colleges? Do you agree that "the argument culture" has become so widespread in our society because arguing is "easy to do"?

4. What's wrong, according to Tannen, with the argumentative, or "agonistic," intellectual culture of higher education? How does Tannen suggest we move beyond it? Does Tannen herself move beyond an argumentative approach to critical thinking in this analysis of higher education?

EXPLORING CONNECTIONS

5. In examining the educational cultures of schools serving students from differing social classes, Jean Anyon (p. 173) describes a "hidden curriculum" that reinforces social class position. Compare Anyon's notion of a hidden curriculum with the one revealed by Tannen in her analysis of education's culture of argument.

6. Explain the *Doonesbury* cartoon on this page in terms of Tannen's discussion of the male-centeredness of American education.

EXTENDING THE CRITICAL CONTEXT

7. Replicate the informal research Tannen assigns her students by observing how frequently adversarial teaching methods are employed in the other classes you are taking. In your observations, describe the type of conflict involved as well as the way that students respond to it. Do your conclusions support or challenge Tannen's analysis of the culture of higher education?

8. In recent years, there has been growing interest in returning to same-sex schooling at all educational levels. Working in groups, debate the advantages and disadvantages of same-sex schools.

9. Read "Girls Rule" by Christina Hoff Sommers in the May 2000 issue of the *Atlantic Monthly* magazine, an article that disputes the claim that the culture of American classrooms encourages educational inequality. Report to the class on Sommers's objections to the position that schools and teachers tend to favor boys over girls. To what extent do you think that teachers and teaching styles generally favor either male or female students in American schools?

Doonesbury   BY GARRY TRUDEAU

Doonesbury © 1992 G. B. Trudeau. Reprinted with permission of Universal Press Syndicate.

Still Separate, Still Unequal

Jonathan Kozol

In Brown v. Board of Education *(1954), the U.S. Supreme Court overturned its ruling in* Plessy v. Ferguson *(1896), which had sanctioned "separate but equal" facilities for blacks and whites throughout the South for more than half a century. The Court's decision in* Brown *ended the deliberate segregation of U.S. schools and promised to usher in a new era of equality in American education. But according to longtime educational critic Jonathan Kozol, American schools today may be more segregated than at any time since 1954. And the "educational apartheid" that Kozol sees in U.S. schools isn't just about color. Kozol associates the "resegregation" of public education with a deterioration of classroom conditions and teaching practices that threatens an entire generation of Americans.*

After graduating from Harvard with a degree in literature and studying as a Rhodes Scholar at Oxford University, Kozol (b. 1936) took his first job teaching in an inner-city elementary school near Boston. His account of that experience, Death at an Early Age: The Destruction of the Hearts and Minds of Negro Children in the Boston Public Schools *(1967) won national acclaim and established him as one of the country's foremost educational activists and social reformers. Since then, his work with poor children and their families has resulted in a dozen books, including* Free Schools *(1972),* Illiterate America *(1980),* On Being a Teacher *(1981),* Rachael and Her Children: Homeless Families in America *(1988),* Savage Inequalities *(1991), and* The Shame of the Nation: The Restoration of Apartheid Schooling in America *(2005), the source of this selection.*

Many Americans who live far from our major cities and who have no firsthand knowledge of the realities to be found in urban public schools seem to have the rather vague and general impression that the great extremes of racial isolation that were matters of grave national significance some thirty-five or forty years ago have gradually but steadily diminished in more recent years. The truth, unhappily, is that the trend, for well over a decade now, has been precisely the reverse. Schools that were already deeply segregated twenty-five or thirty years ago are no less segregated now, while thousands of other schools around the country that had been integrated either voluntarily or by the force of law have since been rapidly resegregating.

In Chicago, by the academic year 2002–2003, 87 percent of public-school enrollment was black or Hispanic; less than 10 percent of children in the schools were white. In Washington, D.C., 94 percent of children were black or Hispanic; less than 5 percent were white. In St. Louis, 82 percent of the student population were black or Hispanic; in Philadelphia and Cleveland, 79 percent; in Los Angeles, 84 percent, in Detroit, 96 percent; in Baltimore, 89 percent. In New York City, nearly three quarters of the students were black or Hispanic.

Even these statistics, as stark as they are, cannot begin to convey how deeply isolated children in the poorest and most segregated sections of these cities have become. In the typically colossal high schools of the Bronx, for instance, more than 90 percent of students (in most cases, more than 95 percent) are black or Hispanic. At John F. Kennedy High School in 2003, 93 percent of the enrollment of more than 4,000 students were black and Hispanic; only 3.5 percent of students at the school were white. At Harry S. Truman High School, black and Hispanic students represented 96 percent of the enrollment of 2,700 students; 2 percent were white. At Adlai Stevenson High School, which enrolls 3,400 students, blacks and Hispanics made up 97 percent of the student population; a mere eight-tenths of one percent were white.

A teacher at P.S. 65 in the South Bronx once pointed out to me one of the two white children I had ever seen there. His presence in her class was something of a wonderment to the teacher and to the other pupils. I asked how many white kids she had taught in the South Bronx in her career. "I've been at this school for eighteen years," she said. "This is the first white student I have ever taught."

One of the most disheartening experiences for those who grew up in the   5
years when Martin Luther King Jr. and Thurgood Marshall[1] were alive is to visit public schools today that bear their names, or names of other honored leaders of the integration struggles that produced the temporary progress that took place in the three decades after *Brown v. Board of Education,*[2] and to find out how many of these schools are bastions of contemporary segregation. It is even more disheartening when schools like these are not in deeply segregated inner-city neighborhoods but in racially mixed areas where the integration of a public school would seem to be most natural, and where, indeed, it takes a conscious effort on the part of parents or school officials in these districts to avoid the integration option that is often right at their front door.

In a Seattle neighborhood that I visited in 2002, for instance, where approximately half the families were Caucasian, 95 percent of students at the Thurgood Marshall Elementary School were black, Hispanic, Native American, or of Asian origin. An African-American teacher at the school told me — not with bitterness but wistfully — of seeing clusters of white parents and their children each morning on the corner of a street close to the school, waiting for a bus that took the children to a predominantly white school.

---

[1]*Thurgood Marshall:* First African American justice on the Supreme Court (1908–1993).

[2]*Brown v. Board of Education:* 1954 Supreme Court case outlawing public school segregation. The court ruled, "Separate educational facilities are inherently unequal."

"At Thurgood Marshall," according to a big wall poster in the school's lobby, "the dream is alive." But school-assignment practices and federal court decisions that have countermanded long-established policies that previously fostered integration in Seattle's schools make the realization of the dream identified with Justice Marshall all but unattainable today. In San Diego there is a school that bears the name of Rosa Parks in which 86 percent of students are black and Hispanic and only some 2 percent are white. In Los Angeles there is a school that bears the name of Dr. King that is 99 percent black and Hispanic, and another in Milwaukee in which black and Hispanic children also make up 99 percent of the enrollment. There is a high school in Cleveland that is named for Dr. King in which black students make up 97 percent of the student body, and the graduation rate is only 35 percent. In Philadelphia, 98 percent of children at a high school named for Dr. King are black. At a middle school named for Dr. King in Boston, black and Hispanic children make up 98 percent of the enrollment. . . .

There is a well-known high school named for Martin Luther King Jr. in New York City too. This school, which I've visited repeatedly in recent years, is located in an upper-middle-class white neighborhood, where it was built in the belief — or hope — that it would draw large numbers of white students by permitting them to walk to school, while only their black and Hispanic classmates would be asked to ride the bus or come by train. When the school was opened in 1975, less than a block from Lincoln Center in Manhattan, "it was seen," according to the *New York Times*, "as a promising effort to integrate white, black and Hispanic students in a thriving neighborhood that held one of the city's cultural gems." Even from the start, however, parents in the neighborhood showed great reluctance to permit their children to enroll at Martin Luther King, and, despite "its prime location and its name, which itself creates the highest of expectations," notes the *Times*, the school before long came to be a destination for black and Hispanic students who could not obtain admission into more successful schools. It stands today as one of the nation's most visible and problematic symbols of an expectation rapidly receding and a legacy substantially betrayed.

Perhaps most damaging to any serious effort to address racial segregation openly is the refusal of most of the major arbiters of culture in our northern cities to confront or even clearly name an obvious reality they would have castigated with a passionate determination in another section of the nation fifty years before — and which, moreover, they still castigate today in retrospective writings that assign it to a comfortably distant and allegedly concluded era of the past. There is, indeed, a seemingly agreed-upon convention in much of the media today not even to use an accurate descriptor like "racial segregation" in a narrative description of a segregated school. Linguistic sweeteners, semantic somersaults, and surrogate vocabularies are repeatedly employed. Schools in which as few as 3 or 4 percent of students may be white or Southeast Asian or of Middle Eastern origin, for instance — and where *every other child* in the building is black or Hispanic — are referred to as "diverse." Visitors to schools like these discover quickly the eviscerated meaning of the word, which is no longer a proper adjective but a euphemism for a plainer word that has apparently become unspeakable.

School systems themselves repeatedly employ this euphemism in describing the composition of their student populations. In a school I visited in the fall of 2004 in Kansas City, Missouri, for example, a document distributed to visitors reports that the school's curriculum "addresses the needs of children from diverse backgrounds." But as I went from class to class, I did not encounter any children who were white or Asian — or Hispanic, for that matter — and when I was later provided with precise statistics for the demographics of the school, I learned that 99.6 percent of students there were African American. In a similar document, the school board of another district, this one in New York State, referred to "the diversity" of its student population and "the rich variations of ethnic backgrounds." But when I looked at the racial numbers that the district had reported to the state, I learned that there were 2,800 black and Hispanic children in the system, 1 Asian child, and 3 whites. Words, in these cases, cease to have real meaning; or, rather, they mean the opposite of what they say.

High school students whom I talk with in deeply segregated neighborhoods and public schools seem far less circumspect than their elders and far more open in their willingness to confront these issues. "It's more like being hidden," said a fifteen-year-old girl named Isabel[3] I met some years ago in Harlem, in attempting to explain to me the ways in which she and her classmates understood the racial segregation of their neighborhoods and schools. "It's as if you have been put in a garage where, if they don't have room for something but aren't sure if they should throw it out, they put it there where they don't need to think of it again."

I asked her if she thought America truly did not "have room" for her or other children of her race. "Think of it this way," said a sixteen-year-old girl sitting beside her. "If people in New York woke up one day and learned that we were gone, that we had simply died or left for somewhere else, how would they feel?"

"How do you think they'd feel?" I asked.

"I think they'd be relieved," this very solemn girl replied.

Many educators make the argument today that given the demographics of large cities like New York and their suburban areas, our only realistic goal should be the nurturing of strong, empowered, and well-funded schools in segregated neighborhoods. Black school officials in these situations have sometimes conveyed to me a bitter and clear-sighted recognition that they're

---

[3]The names of children mentioned in this article have been changed to protect their privacy. [Notes 3, 6, and 8 are Kozol's.]

being asked, essentially, to mediate and render functional an uncontested separation between children of their race and children of white people living sometimes in a distant section of their town and sometimes in almost their own immediate communities. Implicit in this mediation is a willingness to set aside the promises of *Brown* and — though never stating this or even thinking of it clearly in these terms — to settle for the promise made more than a century ago in *Plessy v. Ferguson,* the 1896 Supreme Court ruling in which "separate but equal" was accepted as a tolerable rationale for the perpetuation of a dual system in American society.

Equality itself — equality alone — is now, it seems, the article of faith to which most of the principals of inner-city public schools subscribe. And some who are perhaps most realistic do not even dare to ask for, or expect, complete equality, which seems beyond the realm of probability for many years to come, but look instead for only a sufficiency of means — "adequacy" is the legal term most often used today — by which to win those practical and finite victories that appear to be within their reach. Higher standards, higher expectations, are repeatedly demanded of these urban principals, and of the teachers and students in their schools, but far lower standards — certainly in ethical respects — appear to be expected of the dominant society that isolates these children in unequal institutions.

"Dear Mr. Kozol," wrote the eight-year-old, "we do not have the things you have. You have Clean things. We do not have. You have a clean bathroom. We do not have that. You have Parks and we do not have Parks. You have all the thing and we do not have all the thing. Can you help us?"

The letter, from a child named Alliyah, came in a fat envelope of twenty-seven letters from a class of third-grade children in the Bronx. Other letters that the students in Alliyah's classroom sent me registered some of the same complaints. "We don't have no gardens," "no Music or Art," and "no fun places to play," one child said. "Is there a way to fix this Problem?" Another noted a concern one hears from many children in such overcrowded schools: "We have a gym but it is for lining up. I think it is not fair." Yet another of Alliyah's classmates asked me, with a sweet misspelling, if I knew the way to make her school into a "good" school — "like the other kings have" — and ended with the hope that I would do my best to make it possible for "all the kings" to have good schools.

The letter that affected me the most, however, had been written by a child named Elizabeth. "It is not fair that other kids have a garden and new things. But we don't have that," said Elizabeth. "I wish that this school was the most beautiful school in the whole why world."

20

"The whole why world" stayed in my thoughts for days. When I later met Elizabeth, I brought her letter with me, thinking I might see whether, in reading it aloud, she'd change the "why" to "wide" or leave it as it was. My visit to her class, however, proved to be so pleasant, and the children seemed so eager to bombard me with their questions about where I lived, and why I lived there rather than in New York, and who I lived with, and how many dogs I had, and other interesting questions of that sort, that I decided not to interrupt the nice reception they had given me with questions about usages and spelling. I left "the whole why world" to float around unedited and unrevised in my mind. The letter itself soon found a resting place on the wall above my desk.

In the years before I met Elizabeth, I had visited many other schools in the South Bronx and in one northern district of the Bronx as well. I had made repeated visits to a high school where a stream of water flowed down one of the main stairwells on a rainy afternoon and where green fungus molds were growing in the office where the students went for counseling. A large blue barrel was positioned to collect rainwater coming through the ceiling. In one makeshift elementary school housed in a former skating rink next to a funeral establishment in yet another nearly all-black-and-Hispanic section of the Bronx, class size rose to thirty-four and more; four kindergarten classes and a sixth-grade class were packed into a single room that had no windows. The air was stifling in many rooms, and the children had no place for recess because there was no outdoor playground and no indoor gym.

In another elementary school, which had been built to hold 1,000 children but was packed to bursting with some 1,500, the principal poured out his feelings to me in a room in which a plastic garbage bag had been attached somehow to cover part of the collapsing ceiling. "This," he told me, pointing to the garbage bag, then gesturing around him at the other indications of decay and disrepair one sees in ghetto schools much like it elsewhere, "would not happen to white children."

Libraries, once one of the glories of the New York City school system, were either nonexistent or, at best, vestigial in large numbers of the elementary schools. Art and music programs had also for the most part disappeared. "When I began to teach in 1969," the principal of an elementary school in the South Bronx reported to me, "every school had a full-time licensed art and music teacher and librarian." During the subsequent decades, he recalled, "I saw all of that destroyed."

School physicians also were removed from elementary schools during these years. In 1970, when substantial numbers of white children still attended New York City's public schools, 400 doctors had been present to address the health needs of the children. By 1993 the number of doctors had been cut to 23, most of them part-time — a cutback that affected most severely children in the city's poorest neighborhoods, where medical facilities were most deficient and health problems faced by children most extreme. Teachers told me of asthmatic children who came into class with chronic wheezing and who at any moment of the day might undergo more serious attacks, but in the schools I visited there were no doctors to attend to them.

In explaining these steep declines in services, political leaders in New York tended to point to shifting economic factors, like a serious budget   25 crisis in the middle 1970s, rather than to the changing racial demographics of the student population. But the fact of economic ups and downs from year to year, or from one decade to the next, could not convincingly explain the permanent shortchanging of the city's students, which took place routinely in good economic times and bad. The bad times were seized upon politically to justify the cuts, and the money was never restored once the crisis years were past.

"If you close your eyes to the changing racial composition of the schools and look only at budget actions and political events," says Noreen Connell, the director of the nonprofit Educational Priorities Panel in New York, "you're missing the assumptions that are underlying these decisions." When minority parents ask for something better for their kids, she says, "the assumption is that these are parents who can be discounted. These are kids who just don't count — children we don't value."

This, then, is the accusation that Alliyah and her classmates send our way: "You have . . . We do not have." Are they right or are they wrong? Is this a case of naive and simplistic juvenile exaggeration? What does a third-grader know about these big-time questions of fairness and justice? Physical appearances apart, how in any case do you begin to measure something so diffuse and vast and seemingly abstract as having more, or having less, or not having at all?

Around the time I met Alliyah in the school year 1997–1998, New York's Board of Education spent about $8,000 yearly on the education of a third-grade child in a New York City public school. If you could have scooped Alliyah up out of the neighborhood where she was born and plunked her down in a fairly typical white suburb of New York, she would have received a public education worth about $12,000 a year. If you were to lift her up once more and set her down in one of the wealthiest white suburbs of New York, she would have received as much as $18,000 worth of public education every year and would likely have had a third-grade teacher paid approximately $30,000 more than her teacher in the Bronx was paid.

The dollars on both sides of the equation have increased since then, but the discrepancies between them have remained. The present per-pupil spending level in the New York City schools is $11,700, which may be compared with a per-pupil spending level in excess of $22,000 in the well-to-do suburban district of Manhasset, Long Island. The present New York City level is, indeed, almost exactly what Manhasset spent per pupil eighteen years ago, in 1987, when that sum of money bought a great deal more in services and salaries than it can buy today. In dollars adjusted for inflation, New York City has not yet caught up to where its wealthiest suburbs were a quarter-century ago. . . .

As racial isolation deepens and the inequalities of education finance remain unabated and take on new and more innovative forms, the principals of many inner-city schools are making choices that few principals in public schools that serve white children in the mainstream of the nation ever need to contemplate. Many have been dedicating vast amounts of time and effort to create an architecture of adaptive strategies that promise incremental gains within the limits inequality allows.

New vocabularies of stentorian determination, new systems of incentive, and new modes of castigation, which are termed "rewards and sanctions," have emerged. Curriculum materials that are alleged to be aligned with governmentally established goals and standards and particularly suited to what are regarded as "the special needs and learning styles" of low-income urban children have been introduced. Relentless emphasis on raising test scores, rigid policies of nonpromotion and nongraduation, a new empiricism and the imposition of unusually detailed lists of named and numbered "outcomes" for each isolated parcel of instruction, an oftentimes fanatical insistence upon uniformity of teachers in their management of time, an openly conceded emulation of the rigorous approaches of the military and a frequent use of terminology that comes out of the world of industry and commerce — these are just a few of the familiar aspects of these new adaptive strategies.

Although generically described as "school reform," most of these practices and policies are targeted primarily at poor children of color; and although most educators speak of these agendas in broad language that sounds applicable to all, it is understood that they are valued chiefly as responses to perceived catastrophe in deeply segregated and unequal schools.

"If you do what I tell you to do, how I tell you to do it, when I tell you to do it, you'll get it right," said a determined South Bronx principal observed by a reporter for the *New York Times*. She was laying out a memorizing rule for math to an assembly of her students. "If you don't, you'll get it wrong." This is the voice, this is the tone, this is the rhythm and didactic certitude one hears today in inner-city schools that have embraced a pedagogy of direct command and absolute control. "Taking their inspiration from the ideas of B. F. Skinner[4] . . ." says the *Times*, proponents of scripted rote-and-drill curricula articulate their aim as the establishment of "faultless communication" between "the teacher, who is the stimulus," and "the students, who respond."

The introduction of Skinnerian approaches (which are commonly employed in penal institutions and drug-rehabilitation programs), as a way of altering the attitudes and learning styles of black and Hispanic children, is provocative, and it has stirred some outcries from respected scholars. To actually go into a school where you know some of the children very, very well and see the way that these approaches can affect their daily lives and thinking processes is even more provocative.

On a chilly November day four years ago in the South Bronx, I entered   35
P.S. 65, a school I had been visiting since 1993. There had been major

---

[4]*B. F. Skinner:* American psychologist (1904–1990) known for his theories on stimulus and response.

changes since I'd been there last. Silent lunches had been instituted in the cafeteria, and on days when children misbehaved, silent recess had been introduced as well. On those days the students were obliged to sit in rows and maintain perfect silence on the floor of a small indoor room instead of going out to play. The words SUCCESS FOR ALL, the brand name of a scripted curriculum — better known by its acronym, SFA — were prominently posted at the top of the main stairway and, as I would later find, in almost every room. Also frequently displayed within the halls and classrooms were a number of administrative memos that were worded with unusual didactic absoluteness. "Authentic Writing," read a document called "Principles of Learning" that was posted in the corridor close to the principal's office, "is driven by curriculum and instruction." I didn't know what this expression meant. Like many other undefined and arbitrary phrases posted in the school, it seemed to be a dictum that invited no interrogation.

I entered the fourth grade of a teacher I will call Mr. Endicott, a man in his mid-thirties who had arrived here without training as a teacher, one of about a dozen teachers in the building who were sent into this school after a single summer of short-order preparation. Now in his second year, he had developed a considerable sense of confidence and held the class under a tight control.

As I found a place to sit in a far corner of the room, the teacher and his young assistant, who was in her first year as a teacher, were beginning a math lesson about building airport runways, a lesson that provided children with an opportunity for measuring perimeters. On the wall behind the teacher, in large letters, was written: "Portfolio Protocols: 1. You are responsible for the selection of [your] work that enters your portfolio. 2. As your skills become more sophisticated this year, you will want to revise, amend, supplement, and possibly replace items in your portfolio to reflect your intellectual growth." On the left side of the room: "Performance Standards Mathematics Curriculum: M-5 Problem Solving and Reasoning. M-6 Mathematical Skills and Tools . . ."

My attention was distracted by some whispering among the children sitting to the right of me. The teacher's response to this distraction was immediate: his arm shot out and up in a diagonal in front of him, his hand straight up, his fingers flat. The young co-teacher did this, too. When they saw their teachers do this, all the children in the classroom did it, too.

"Zero noise," the teacher said, but this instruction proved to be unneeded. The strange salute the class and teachers gave each other, which turned out to be one of a number of such silent signals teachers in the school were trained to use, and children to obey, had done the job of silencing the class.

"Active listening!" said Mr. Endicott. "Heads up! Tractor beams!" 40 which meant, "Every eye on me."

On the front wall of the classroom, in handwritten words that must have taken Mr. Endicott long hours to transcribe, was a list of terms that could be used to praise or criticize a student's work in mathematics. At

Level Four, the highest of four levels of success, a child's "problem-solving strategies" could be described, according to this list, as "systematic, complete, efficient, and possibly elegant," while the student's capability to draw conclusions from the work she had completed could be termed "insightful" or "comprehensive." At Level Two, the child's capability to draw conclusions was to be described as "logically unsound"; at Level One, "not present." Approximately 50 separate categories of proficiency, or lack of such, were detailed in this wall-sized tabulation.

A well-educated man, Mr. Endicott later spoke to me about the form of classroom management that he was using as an adaptation from a model of industrial efficiency. "It's a kind of 'Taylorism'[5] in the classroom," he explained, referring to a set of theories about the management of factory employees introduced by Frederick Taylor in the early 1900s. "Primitive utilitarianism" is another term he used when we met some months later to discuss these management techniques with other teachers from the school. His reservations were, however, not apparent in the classroom. Within the terms of what he had been asked to do, he had, indeed, become a master of control. It is one of the few classrooms I had visited up to that time in which almost nothing even hinting at spontaneous emotion in the children or the teacher surfaced while I was there.

The teacher gave the "zero noise" salute again when someone whispered to another child at his table. "In two minutes you will have a chance to talk and share this with your partner." Communication between children in the class was not prohibited but was afforded time slots and, remarkably enough, was formalized in an expression that I found included in a memo that was posted on the wall beside the door. "An opportunity . . . to engage in Accountable Talk."

Even the teacher's words of praise were framed in terms consistent with the lists that had been posted on the wall. "That's a Level Four suggestion," said the teacher when a child made an observation other teachers might have praised as simply "pretty good" or "interesting" or "mature."

There was, it seemed, a formal name for every cognitive event within   45
this school: "Authentic Writing," "Active Listening," "Accountable Talk." The ardor to assign all items of instruction or behavior a specific name was unsettling me. The adjectives had the odd effect of hyping every item of endeavor. "Authentic Writing" was, it seemed, a more important act than what the children in a writing class in any ordinary school might try to do. "Accountable Talk" was something more self-conscious and significant than merely useful conversation.

Since that day at P.S. 65, I have visited nine other schools in six different cities where the same Skinnerian curriculum is used. The signs on the

---

[5]*Taylorism:* Approach to management named after American engineer and business school professor Frederick Taylor. His *Principles of Scientific Management* (1911) sought to increase efficiency and productivity.

walls, the silent signals, the curious salute, the same insistent naming of all cognitive particulars, became familiar as I went from one school to the next.

"Meaningful Sentences," began one of the many listings of proficiencies expected of the children in the fourth grade of an inner-city elementary school in Hartford (90 percent black, 10 percent Hispanic) that I visited a short time later. "Noteworthy Questions," "Active Listening," and other designations like these had been posted elsewhere in the room. Here, too, the teacher gave the kids her outstretched arm, with hand held up, to reestablish order when they grew a little noisy, but I noticed that she tried to soften the effect of this by opening her fingers and bending her elbow slightly so it did not look quite as forbidding as the gesture Mr. Endicott had used. A warm and interesting woman, she later told me she disliked the regimen intensely.

Over her desk, I read a "Mission Statement," which established the priorities and values for the school. Among the missions of the school, according to the printed statement, which was posted also in some other classrooms of the school, was "to develop productive citizens" who have the skills that will be needed "for successful global competition," a message that was reinforced by other posters in the room. Over the heads of a group of children at their desks, a sign anointed them BEST WORKERS OF 2002.

Another signal now was given by the teacher, this one not for silence but in order to achieve some other form of class behavior, which I could not quite identify. The students gave exactly the same signal in response. Whatever the function of this signal, it was done as I had seen it done in the South Bronx and would see it done in other schools in months to come. Suddenly, with a seeming surge of restlessness and irritation — with herself, as it appeared, and with her own effective use of all the tricks that she had learned — she turned to me and said, "I can do this with my dog." . . .

50

In some inner-city districts, even the most pleasant and old-fashioned class activities of elementary schools have now been overtaken by these ordering requirements. A student teacher in California, for example, wanted to bring a pumpkin to her class on Halloween but knew it had no ascertainable connection to the California standards. She therefore had developed what she called "The Multi-Modal Pumpkin Unit" to teach science (seeds), arithmetic (the size and shape of pumpkins, I believe — this detail wasn't clear), and certain items she adapted out of language arts, in order to position "pumpkins" in a frame of state proficiencies. Even with her multi-modal pumpkin, as her faculty adviser told me, she was still afraid she would be criticized because she knew the pumpkin would not really help her children to achieve expected goals on state exams.

Why, I asked a group of educators at a seminar in Sacramento, was a teacher being placed in a position where she'd need to do preposterous curricular gymnastics to enjoy a bit of seasonal amusement with her kids on Halloween? How much injury to state-determined "purpose" would it do to let the children of poor people have a pumpkin party once a year for no other reason than because it's something fun that other children get to do on autumn days in public schools across most of America?

"Forcing an absurdity on teachers does teach something," said an African-American professor. "It teaches acquiescence. It breaks down the will to thumb your nose at pointless protocols — to call absurdity 'absurd.'" Writing out the standards with the proper numbers on the chalkboard has a similar effect, he said; and doing this is "terribly important" to the principals in many of these schools. "You *have* to post the standards, and the way you know the children know the standards is by asking them to *state* the standards. And they *do* it — and you want to be quite certain that they do it if you want to keep on working at that school."

In speaking of the drill-based program in effect at P.S. 65, Mr. Endicott told me he tended to be sympathetic to the school administrators, more so at least than the other teachers I had talked with seemed to be. He said he believed his principal had little choice about the implementation of this program, which had been mandated for all elementary schools in New York City that had had rock-bottom academic records over a long period of time. "This puts me into a dilemma," he went on, "because I love the kids at P.S. 65." And even while, he said, "I know that my teaching SFA is a charade . . . if I don't do it I won't be permitted to teach these children."

Mr. Endicott, like all but two of the new recruits at P.S. 65 — there were about fifteen in all — was a white person, as were the principal and most of the administrators at the school. As a result, most of these neophyte instructors had had little or no prior contact with the children of an inner-city neighborhood; but, like the others I met, and despite the distancing between the children and their teachers that resulted from the scripted method of instruction, he had developed close attachments to his students and did not want to abandon them. At the same time, the class- and race-specific implementation of this program obviously troubled him. "There's an expression now," he said. "'The rich get richer, and the poor get SFA.'" He said he was still trying to figure out his "professional ethics" on the problem that this posed for him.

White children made up "only about one percent" of students in the New York City schools in which this scripted teaching system was imposed,[6] according to the *New York Times,* which also said that "the prepackaged lessons" were intended "to ensure that all teachers — even novices or the most inept" — would be able to teach reading. As seemingly pragmatic and hardheaded as such arguments may be, they are desperation strategies that come out of the acceptance of inequity. If we did not have a deeply segregated system in which more experienced instructors teach the children of the privileged and the least experienced are sent to teach the children of minorities, these practices would not be needed and could not be so

[6]SFA has since been discontinued in the New York City public schools, though it is still being used in 1,300 U.S. schools, serving as many as 650,000 children. Similar scripted systems are used in schools (overwhelmingly minority in population) serving several million children.

convincingly defended. They are confections of apartheid,[7] and no matter by what arguments of urgency or practicality they have been justified, they cannot fail to further deepen the divisions of society.

There is no misery index for the children of apartheid education. There ought to be; we measure almost everything else that happens to them in their schools. Do kids who go to schools like these enjoy the days they spend in them? Is school, for most of them, a happy place to be? You do not find the answers to these questions in reports about achievement levels, scientific methods of accountability, or structural revisions in the modes of governance. Documents like these don't speak of happiness. You have to go back to the schools themselves to find an answer to these questions. You have to sit down in the little chairs in first and second grade, or on the reading rug with kindergarten kids, and listen to the things they actually say to one another and the dialogue between them and their teachers. You have to go down to the basement with the children when it's time for lunch and to the playground with them, if they have a playground, when it's time for recess, if they still have recess at their school. You have to walk into the children's bathrooms in these buildings. You have to do what children do and breathe the air the children breathe. I don't think that there is any other way to find out what the lives that children lead in school are really like.

High school students, when I first meet them, are often more reluctant than the younger children to open up and express their personal concerns; but hesitation on the part of students did not prove to be a problem when I visited a tenth-grade class at Fremont High School in Los Angeles. The students were told that I was a writer, and they took no time in getting down to matters that were on their minds.

"Can we talk about the bathrooms?" asked a soft-spoken student named Mireya.

In almost any classroom there are certain students who, by the force of their directness or the unusual sophistication of their way of speaking, tend to capture your attention from the start. Mireya later spoke insightfully about some of the serious academic problems that were common in the school, but her observations on the physical and personal embarrassments she and her schoolmates had to undergo cut to the heart of questions of essential dignity that kids in squalid schools like this one have to deal with all over the nation.

Fremont High School, as court papers filed in a lawsuit against the state   60
of California document, has fifteen fewer bathrooms than the law requires. Of the limited number of bathrooms that are working in the school, "only one or two . . . are open and unlocked for girls to use." Long lines of girls are "waiting to use the bathrooms," which are generally "unclean" and "lack basic supplies," including toilet paper. Some of the classrooms, as court

---

[7]*Apartheid:* Literally "apartness," the policy of racial segregation and discrimination in South Africa, restricting the rights of nonwhites, which ended in 1990.

papers also document, "do not have air conditioning," so that students, who attend school on a three-track schedule that runs year-round, "become red-faced and unable to concentrate" during "the extreme heat of summer." The school's maintenance records report that rats were found in eleven classrooms. Rat droppings were found "in the bins and drawers" of the high school's kitchen, and school records note that "hamburger buns" were being "eaten off [the] bread-delivery rack."

No matter how many tawdry details like these I've read in legal briefs or depositions through the years, I'm always shocked again to learn how often these unsanitary physical conditions are permitted to continue in the schools that serve our poorest students — even after they have been vividly described in the media. But hearing of these conditions in Mireya's words was even more unsettling, in part because this student seemed so fragile and because the need even to speak of these indignities in front of me and all the other students was an additional indignity.

"The problem is this," she carefully explained. "You're not allowed to use the bathroom during lunch, which is a thirty-minute period. The only time that you're allowed to use it is between your classes." But "this is a huge building," she went on. "It has long corridors. If you have one class at one end of the building and your next class happens to be way down at the other end, you don't have time to use the bathroom and still get to class before it starts. So you go to your class and then you ask permission from your teacher to go to the bathroom and the teacher tells you, 'No. You had your chance between the periods...'

"I feel embarrassed when I have to stand there and explain it to a teacher."

"This is the question," said a wiry-looking boy named Edward, leaning forward in his chair. "Students are not animals, but even animals need to relieve themselves sometimes. We're here for eight hours. What do they think we're supposed to do?"

"It humiliates you," said Mireya, who went on to make the interesting statement that "the school provides solutions that don't actually work," and this idea was taken up by several other students in describing course requirements within the school. A tall black student, for example, told me that she hoped to be a social worker or a doctor but was programmed into "Sewing Class" this year. She also had to take another course, called "Life Skills," which she told me was a very basic course — "a retarded class," to use her words — that "teaches things like the six continents," which she said she'd learned in elementary school.

When I asked her why she had to take these courses, she replied that she'd been told they were required, which as I later learned was not exactly so. What was required was that high school students take two courses in an area of study called "The Technical Arts," and which the Los Angeles Board of Education terms "Applied Technology." At schools that served the middle class or upper-middle class, this requirement was likely to be met by courses that had academic substance and, perhaps, some relevance to college prepara-

tion. At Beverly Hills High School, for example, the technical-arts requirement could be fulfilled by taking subjects like residential architecture, the
designing of commercial structures, broadcast journalism, advanced computer
graphics, a sophisticated course in furniture design, carving and sculpture, or
an honors course in engineering research and design. At Fremont High, in
contrast, this requirement was far more often met by courses that were basically vocational and also obviously keyed to low-paying levels of employment.

Mireya, for example, who had plans to go to college, told me that she
had to take a sewing class last year and now was told she'd been assigned to
take a class in hairdressing as well. When I asked her teacher why Mireya
could not skip these subjects and enroll in classes that would help her to
pursue her college aspirations, she replied, "It isn't a question of what students want. It's what the school may have available. If all the other elective
classes that a student wants to take are full, she has to take one of these
classes if she wants to graduate."

A very small girl named Obie, who had big blue-tinted glasses tilted up
across her hair, interrupted then to tell me with a kind of wild gusto that
she'd taken hairdressing *twice*! When I expressed surprise that this was possible, she said there were two levels of hairdressing offered here at Fremont
High. "One is in hairstyling," she said. "The other is in braiding."

Mireya stared hard at this student for a moment and then suddenly
began to cry. "I don't *want* to take hairdressing. I did not need sewing
either. I knew how to sew. My mother is a seamstress in a factory. I'm trying
to go to college. I don't need to sew to go to college. My mother sews. I
hoped for something else."

"What would you rather take?" I asked.   70

"I wanted to take an AP class," she answered.

Mireya's sudden tears elicited a strong reaction from one of the boys
who had been silent up till now: a thin, dark-eyed student named Fortino,
who had long hair down to his shoulders. He suddenly turned directly to
Mireya and spoke into the silence that followed her last words.

"Listen to me," he said. "The owners of the sewing factories need laborers. Correct?"

"I guess they do," Mireya said.

"It's not going to be their own kids. Right?"   75

"Why not?" another student said.

"So they can grow beyond themselves," Mireya answered quietly. "But
we remain the same."

"You're ghetto," said Fortino, "so we send you to the factory." He sat
low in his desk chair, leaning on one elbow, his voice and dark eyes loaded
with a cynical intelligence. "You're ghetto — so you sew!"

"There are higher positions than these," said a student named Samantha.

"You're ghetto," said Fortino unrelentingly, "So sew!"   80

Admittedly, the economic needs of a society are bound to be reflected
to some rational degree within the policies and purposes of public schools.

But, even so, there must be *something* more to life as it is lived by six-year-olds or ten-year-olds, or by teenagers, for that matter, than concerns about "successful global competition." Childhood is not merely basic training for utilitarian adulthood. It should have some claims upon our mercy, not for its future value to the economic interests of competitive societies but for its present value as a perishable piece of life itself.

Very few people who are not involved with inner-city schools have any real idea of the extremes to which the mercantile distortion of the purposes and character of education have been taken or how unabashedly proponents of these practices are willing to defend them. The head of a Chicago school, for instance, who was criticized by some for emphasizing rote instruction that, his critics said, was turning children into "robots," found no reason to dispute the charge. "Did you ever stop to think that these robots will never burglarize your home?" he asked, and "will never snatch your pocketbooks. . . . These robots are going to be producing taxes."

Corporate leaders, when they speak of education, sometimes pay lip-service to the notion of "good critical and analytic skills," but it is reasonable to ask whether they have in mind the critical analysis of *their* priorities. In principle, perhaps some do; but, if so, this is not a principle that seems to have been honored widely in the schools I have been visiting. In all the various business-driven inner-city classrooms I have observed in the past five

years, plastered as they are with corporation brand names and managerial vocabularies, I have yet to see the two words "labor unions." Is this an oversight? How is that possible? Teachers and principals themselves, who are almost always members of a union, seem to be so beaten down that they rarely even question this omission.

It is not at all unusual these days to come into an urban school in which the principal prefers to call himself or herself "building CEO" or "building manager." In some of the same schools teachers are described as "classroom managers."[8] I have never been in a suburban district in which principals were asked to view themselves or teachers in this way. These terminologies remind us of how wide the distance has become between two very separate worlds of education. . . .

ENGAGING THE TEXT

1. Compare notes in class on your own elementary and secondary school experiences. How do the schools you attended compare with the public schools Kozol describes, both in terms of physical condition and teaching approach?

2. What evidence have you seen of reluctance on the part of politicians, educators, and the media to talk about the segregated state of America's public schools? Would you agree that the current state of public education in the United States amounts to "resegregation" and is, in fact, evidence of "apartheid" in American society?

3. Who is to blame for the current resegregation of American public schools, according to Kozol? Whom — or what — would you blame? To what extent would you agree that the state of inner-city schools represents a "moral failure" in America? Why might it be so important to Kozol to see this issue in moral — and not simply in political or social — terms?

[8]A school I visited three years ago in Columbus, Ohio, was littered with "Help Wanted" signs. Starting in kindergarten, children in the school were being asked to think about the jobs that they might choose when they grew up. In one classroom there was a poster that displayed the names of several retail stores: J. C. Penney, Wal-Mart, Kmart, Sears, and a few others. "It's like working in a store," a classroom aide explained. "The children are learning to pretend they're cashiers." At another school in the same district, children were encouraged to apply for jobs in their classrooms. Among the job positions open to the children in this school, there was an "Absence Manager" and a "Behavior Chart Manager," a "Form Collector Manager," a "Paper Passer Outer Manager," a "Paper Collecting Manager," a "Paper Returning Manager," an "Exit Ticket Manager," even a "Learning Manager," a "Reading Corner Manager," and a "Score Keeper Manager." I asked the principal if there was a special reason why those two words "management" and "manager" kept popping up throughout the school. "We want every child to be working as a manager while he or she is in this school," the principal explained. "We want to make them understand that, in this country, companies will give you opportunities to work, to prove yourself, no matter what you've done." I wasn't sure what she meant by "no matter what you've done," and asked her if she could explain it. "Even if you have a felony arrest," she said, "we want you to understand that you can be a manager someday."

EXPLORING CONNECTIONS

4. Compare Mike Rose's account of his own school experience during the 1950s and 1960s (p. 161) with the contemporary urban classrooms described by Kozol in this selection. How might Rose assess the teaching methods that dominate the school reforms Kozol describes? Do you think a Jack McFarland would succeed in today's inner-city schools? Why or why not?

5. Compare what Kozol, Michael Moore (p. 132), and John Taylor Gatto (p. 152) have to say about the impact of corporate America on U.S. schools. To what extent does your own prior educational experience suggest that corporate influence is undermining American education?

6. How well do the schools that Kozol describes fit any of the four categories of schools presented by Jean Anyon (p. 173)? To what extent do you think it would be possible to adapt the approaches and methods used in Anyon's professional or elite schools more broadly?

EXTENDING THE CRITICAL CONTEXT

7. Working in groups, sample news and magazine stories published in the last year to determine if Kozol is correct when he says that the media are reluctant to discuss the "segregation" of American public education. How many of the articles you identify address the idea of segregation? Of the inequalities of public education?

8. Learn more about the "No Child Left Behind Act" and other aspects of the accountability reform movement in education. What kinds of accountability reforms have been implemented in your area? What evidence do you find that these measures have worked? To what extent would you agree that accountability reforms have turned children into robots and reduced teaching to mechanical drill?

9. Over the past few years, a number of states have begun requiring high school students to take standardized "exit" exams to guarantee that they meet minimum academic standards before graduation. Research this educational reform to find out more about its impact on students, and then debate its merits in class. Would you support recent proposals that would require a similar nationwide test for college students before they receive their degrees? Why or why not?

FURTHER CONNECTIONS

1. In the United States, the notion of schooling as the road to success has always been balanced by a pervasive distrust of education. This phenomenon, known as "American anti-intellectualism" grew out of the first settlers' suspicion of anything that reminded them of the "corrupting" influences of European sophistication. American anti-intellectualism often shows up most vividly in pop-cultural portrayals of school, students, and educators. Working in groups, survey recent treatments of school on television, in films, and on Internet blogs and Web sites. How is schooling treated in the mass media and by popular bloggers on the left and the right? Overall, how powerful does anti-intellectualism seem to be in American culture today?

2. Over the past few years, educational critics across the political spectrum have voiced concern about declining success rates for males in America's schools and colleges. During the last decade, for example, the number of women in America's colleges and universities has steadily increased until, today, women outnumber men in almost every academic field outside the so-called hard sciences. Research this issue to learn more about how males are faring in America's schools. Do you think, as some critics claim, that school in America has become a "feminized" institution that is particularly hostile to boys? What other reasons might explain declines in male educational achievement over the past two decades?

3. In his recent book on the impact of globalization, *The World Is Flat: A Brief History of the 21st Century* (2005), journalist and social commentator Thomas Friedman argues that America's schools are failing to equip students with the essential math, science, and language skills they'll need to compete in a global world economy. Compare notes with your classmates about how well you feel your own school experiences have prepared you for competition in the global marketplace. How much math and science did you study in high school? How would you rate your own ability in math and science? How much did you learn about other cultures and languages? In general, do you feel that America's schools today are preparing most students to compete successfully in a globalizing world?

4. Working in groups, research the educational systems in other countries to see how they compare with secondary education in the United States. For example, how is secondary school education handled in countries like England, France, Germany, Denmark, Japan, China, Cuba, and Russia? What role do testing and the rote memorization of facts play in the educational system

(continued on next page)

you select to study? To what extent does this system emphasize creativity, personal expression, and critical thinking? Overall, how effective is this nation's educational system in terms of preparing students for a productive and successful life? What, if anything, might we as a nation learn from this approach to secondary education?

5. Educational researchers estimate that 25 percent to 60 percent of the ninth graders in America's urban public schools will drop out before graduation. Do additional research on the "dropout crisis" to learn more about the scope and causes of this problem. Why are so many Americans opting out of school today? Which groups are most in danger of leaving school before graduation? What can be done to encourage young Americans to stay in school?

6. Under the principle of affirmative action, American colleges and universities were permitted to consider the racial background of applicants in admissions decision making. As a result, the percentage of minority students in America's colleges and universities increased steadily from 1965 until the late 1990s when several states reversed or seriously weakened earlier affirmative action admissions policies. Since then, the diversity of many college campuses across the country has declined significantly. Research the history of the college systems in your state. How has the decline of affirmative action affected college enrollments? What are the arguments for and against the consideration of race as an element of college admissions?

3

Money and Success

The Myth of Individual Opportunity

Affluence, photo by Steven Weinrebe.

FAST FACTS

1. The top 1% of American households own approximately 40% of the nation's wealth, roughly the same share as the bottom 95%.

2. Roughly 35 million Americans (one in eight) live below the government's official poverty line.

3. From 1995 to 2001, the net worth of the typical non-Hispanic white household increased from $88,500 to $120,900. The household net worth of people of color declined from $18,300 to $17,100.

4. Between 1968 and 2000, U.S. credit card debt (adjusted for inflation) increased from less than $10 billion to more than $600 billion.

5. About 13.5% of U.S. workers are unionized.

6. Among full-time workers with bachelor's degrees, women will earn $900,000 less over a forty-year career than men; men with professional degrees will earn approximately $2 million more (yes, $2 million each) than their female counterparts with the same degrees.

7. The network of food programs coordinated by America's Second Harvest assists approximately 25 million Americans annually. Of these, 36% are under age 18, 8% are under age 5, and 10% are elderly. Approximately 44 million American adults are obese, with associated health-care costs of $75 billion.

Sources: (1) Holly Sklar, "Imagine a Country — 2003" in Paula S. Rothenberg, ed., *Race, Class, and Gender in the United States: An Integrated Study* (New York: Worth Publishers, 2004), p. 276; (2) U.S. Census Bureau, *Current Population Reports*, P60-226, p. 9; (3) U.S. Census Bureau, *2006 Statistical Abstract of the United States,* Table 702; (4) Stephen J. McNamee and Robert K. Miller Jr., *The Meritocracy Myth* (New York: Rowman & Littlefield, 2004), p. 201; (5) Sklar, pp. 278–79; (6) U.S. Census Bureau, education press release, July 18, 2002; (7) America's Second Harvest (www.secondharvest.org) and the American Medical Association, *National Summit on Obesity, 2004: Executive Summary,* p. 1.

AMERICANS CHERISH THE NOTION that the United States is a land of unequaled opportunity, where hard work and smart choices yield big rewards, where no one is stuck on the lower rungs of the economic ladder. Yet statistically speaking, upward mobility is no easier here than in England and France, and it is harder here than in Canada and some Scandinavian countries. Moreover, it is extraordinarily difficult to escape poverty if you've "chosen" the wrong parents: 95 percent of children born to poor parents will themselves be poor all their lives. And while the rich are indeed getting richer, maintaining the comfortable lifestyle of the middle class seems increasingly dependent not on hard work but on global economic forces like the price of crude oil and the migration of American jobs overseas.

Despite the profound effects of money, or the lack thereof, on our daily lives, most Americans dislike talking about social class. For example, both our rich and our poor shun those terms. When we do talk about money and success, most of us favor a "meritocracy," a fair competition for success that's not rigged according to race, gender, or family history. A wealth of data relating success to education, ethnicity, gender, and inheritance, however, suggests that our reality falls short of our ideals; no individual is guaranteed success or doomed to failure, but the odds are stacked against women, people of color, and those born into poverty.

Our current cultural myths about success have deep roots and a long history. Indeed, the dream of individual opportunity has been at home in America since Europeans discovered a "new world" in the Western hemisphere. Early immigrants like J. Hector St. John de Crèvecoeur extolled the freedom and opportunity to be found in this new land. His glowing descriptions of a classless society where anyone could attain success through honesty and hard work fired the imaginations of many European readers: in *Letters from an American Farmer* (1782) he wrote, "We are all animated with the spirit of an industry which is unfettered and unrestrained, because each person works for himself. . . . We have no princes, for whom we toil, starve, and bleed: we are the most perfect society now existing in the world." The promise of a land where "the rewards of [a man's] industry follow with equal steps the progress of his labor" drew poor immigrants from Europe and fueled national expansion into the western territories.

Our national mythology abounds with illustrations of the American success story. There's Benjamin Franklin, the very model of the self-educated, self-made man, who rose from modest origins to become a renowned scientist, philosopher, and statesman. In the nineteenth century, Horatio Alger, a writer of pulp fiction for young boys — fiction that you will get to sample below — became America's best-selling author with rags-to-riches tales like *Struggling Upward* (1886) and *Bound to Rise* (1873). The notion of success haunts us: we spend millions every year reading about the rich and famous, learning how to "make a fortune in real estate with no money down," and "dressing for success." The myth of success has even invaded our personal relationships: today it's as important to be "successful" in marriage or parenthood as it is to come out on top in business.

But dreams easily turn into nightmares. Every American who hopes to "make it" also knows the fear of failure, because the myth of success inevitably implies comparison between the haves and the have-nots, the achievers and the drones, the stars and the anonymous crowd. Under pressure of the myth, we become engrossed in status symbols: we try to live in the "right" neighborhoods, wear the "right" clothes, eat the "right" foods.

These emblems of distinction assure us and others that we are different, that we stand out from the crowd. It is one of the great paradoxes of our culture that we believe passionately in the fundamental equality of all yet strive as hard as we can to separate ourselves from our fellow citizens. This separation is particularly true of our wealthiest citizens, who have increasingly isolated themselves from everyone else with gated communities, exclusive schools, and private jets.

Steeped in a Puritan theology that vigorously preached the individual's responsibility to the larger community, colonial America balanced the drive for individual gain with concern for the common good. To Franklin, the way to wealth lay in practicing the virtues of honesty, hard work, and thrift: "Without industry and frugality nothing will do, and with them every thing. He that gets all he can honestly, and saves all he gets ... will certainly become RICH" ("Advice to a Young Tradesman," 1748). And Alger's heroes were as concerned with moral rectitude as they were with financial gain: a benefactor advises Ragged Dick, "If you'll try to be somebody, and grow up into a respectable member of society, you will. You may not become rich, — it isn't everybody that becomes rich, you know, — but you can obtain a good position and be respected." But in the twentieth century the mood of the myth changed.

In the 1970s, Robert Ringer's enormously popular *Looking Out for Number One* urged readers to "forget foundationless traditions, forget the 'moral' standards others may have tried to cram down your throat ... and, most important, think of yourself — Number One.... You and you alone will be responsible for your success or failure." The myth of success may have been responsible for making the United States what it is today, but it also seems to be pulling us apart. Can we exist as a living community if our greatest value can be summed up by the slogan "Me first"?

The chapter opens with a pair of strongly contrasting narratives about young people learning about money and opportunity. The first, an excerpt from Horatio Alger's classic rags-to-riches novel *Ragged Dick*, unambiguously promotes the myth of individual success. The second, Toni Cade Bambara's "The Lesson," dramatizes economic inequality through the eyes of a group of Harlem kids who travel uptown to see how the rich live and spend. Next, in "Horatio Alger," Harlon Dalton examines the cultural meanings of such storytelling and finds the myth Alger popularized not just misleading but "socially destructive." Ken Hamblin's "The Black Avenger," the chapter's conservative selection, reasserts the value of the American Dream and argues further that it is "truly accessible to all black citizens."

The next pair of readings, Barbara Ehrenreich's "Serving in Florida" and Gregory Mantsios's "Class in America — 2003," offer a wealth of hard facts about social class, from two very different perspectives. Ehrenreich investigates the daily grind of working-class life by recounting her personal experience of struggling to make ends meet on waitressing wages. Mantsios, taking a broad sociological view and citing numerous compelling statistics, offers a stark portrayal of a social and economic system that serves the powerful and wealthy.

The chapter next turns to visual, poetic, and pop-culture riffs on money and success. The Visual Portfolio explores dreams of success, the cost of failure, and the relationship of opportunity to race, gender, and education. Dana Gioia's clever poem "Money" highlights our obsession with the language of cold, hard cash; a darker poem by Sharon Olds, "From Seven Floors Up," measures the distance between affluence and homelessness as revealed in a simple glance out a window. The chapter's media selection — Diana Kendall's "Framing Class" — studies how TV tends to distort our view of economic inequalities, for example by treating poverty as individual misfortune rather than systematic oppression.

The chapter concludes with narratives about two people who have moved beyond pursuing money to ways of life they find more rewarding. The oral history of Stephen Cruz, a successful Mexican American engineer, reveals a man pursuing the American Dream but gradually becoming disillusioned with it. The American Dream is radically redefined in Anne Witte Garland's "Good Noise: Cora Tucker," which presents the story of an African American activist who measures success in terms of lives saved instead of dollars spent.

Sources

Peter Baida, *Poor Richard's Legacy: American Business Values from Benjamin Franklin to Donald Trump.* New York: William Morrow, 1990.

Correspondents of the New York Times, *Class Matters.* New York: Times Books / Henry Holt and Company, 2005.

Stephen J. McNamee and Robert K. Miller Jr., *The Meritocracy Myth.* New York: Rowman & Littlefield, 2004.

J. Hector St. John de Crèvecoeur, *Letters from an American Farmer.* New York: Dolphin Books, 1961. First published in London, 1782.

BEFORE READING

- Working alone or in groups, make a list of people who best represent your idea of success. (You may want to consider public and political figures, leaders in government, entertainment, sports, education, or other fields.) List the specific qualities or accomplishments that make these people successful. Compare notes with your classmates, then freewrite about the meaning of success: What does it mean to you? To the class as a whole? Keep your list and your definition. As you work through this chapter, reread and reflect on what you've written, comparing your ideas with those of the authors included here.

- Write a journal entry that captures the thoughts of the man pictured in the photo at the beginning of this chapter (p. 259). What feelings or attitudes can you read in his expression, his dress, and his body language? How do you think he got where he is today? How easy or difficult is it to "read" social class in the dress, speech, possessions, and behavior of people you see at school, work, or other environments?

From *Ragged Dick*

HORATIO ALGER

The choice of Horatio Alger to exemplify the myth of individual opportunity is almost automatic. Alger's rags-to-riches stories have become synonymous with the notion that anyone can succeed — even to generations of Americans who have never read one of the books that were best-sellers a century ago. The excerpt below is typical of Alger's work in that it focuses on a young man's progress from a poor background toward "fame and fortune." Alger (1832–1899) published over a hundred such stories; most observers agree that their popularity depended less on their literary accomplishments than on the promises they made about opportunity in America and the rewards of hard work.

Dick now began to look about for a position in a store or counting-room. Until he should obtain one he determined to devote half the day to blacking boots, not being willing to break in upon his small capital. He found that he could earn enough in half a day to pay all his necessary expenses, including the entire rent of the room. Fosdick desired to pay his half; but Dick steadily refused, insisting upon paying so much as compensation for his friend's services as instructor.

It should be added that Dick's peculiar way of speaking and use of slang terms had been somewhat modified by his education and his intimacy with Henry Fosdick. Still he continued to indulge in them to some extent, especially when he felt like joking, and it was natural to Dick to joke, as my readers have probably found out by this time. Still his manners were considerably improved, so that he was more likely to obtain a situation than when first introduced to our notice.

Just now, however, business was very dull, and merchants, instead of hiring new assistants, were disposed to part with those already in their employ. After making several ineffectual applications, Dick began to think he should be obliged to stick to his profession until the next season. But about this time something occurred which considerably improved his chances of preferment.

This is the way it happened.

As Dick, with a balance of more than a hundred dollars in the savings bank, might fairly consider himself a young man of property, he thought himself justified in occasionally taking a half holiday from business, and going on an excursion. On Wednesday afternoon Henry Fosdick was sent by his employer on an errand to that part of Brooklyn near Greenwood Cemetery. Dick hastily dressed himself in his best, and determined to accompany him.

The two boys walked down to the South Ferry, and, paying their two cents each, entered the ferry-boat. They remained at the stern, and stood by the railing, watching the great city, with its crowded wharves, receding from view. Beside them was a gentleman with two children, — a girl of eight and a little boy of six. The children were talking gayly to their father. While he was pointing out some object of interest to the little girl, the boy managed to creep, unobserved, beneath the chain that extends across the boat, for the protection of passengers, and, stepping incautiously to the edge of the boat, fell over into the foaming water.

At the child's scream, the father looked up, and, with a cry of horror, sprang to the edge of the boat. He would have plunged in, but, being unable to swim, would only have endangered his own life, without being able to save his child.

"My child!" he exclaimed in anguish, — "who will save my child? A thousand — ten thousand dollars to any one who will save him!"

There chanced to be but few passengers on board at the time, and nearly all these were either in the cabins or standing forward. Among the few who saw the child fall was our hero.

Now Dick was an expert swimmer. It was an accomplishment which he had possessed for years, and he no sooner saw the boy fall than he resolved to rescue him. His determination was formed before he heard the liberal offer made by the boy's father. Indeed, I must do Dick the justice to say that, in the excitement of the moment, he did not hear it at all, nor would it have stimulated the alacrity with which he sprang to the rescue of the little boy.

Little Johnny had already risen once, and gone under for the second time, when our hero plunged in. He was obliged to strike out for the boy, and this took time. He reached him none too soon. Just as he was sinking for the third and last time, he caught him by the jacket. Dick was stout and strong, but Johnny clung to him so tightly, that it was with great difficulty he was able to sustain himself.

"Put your arms round my neck," said Dick.

The little boy mechanically obeyed, and clung with a grasp strengthened by his terror. In this position Dick could bear his weight better. But the ferry-boat was receding fast. It was quite impossible to reach it. The father, his face pale with terror and anguish, and his hands clasped in suspense, saw the brave boy's struggles, and prayed with agonizing fervor that he might be successful. But it is probable, for they were now midway of the river, that both Dick and the little boy whom he had bravely undertaken to rescue would have been drowned, had not a row-boat been fortunately near. The two men who were in it witnessed the accident, and hastened to the rescue of our hero.

"Keep up a little longer," they shouted, bending to their oars, "and we will save you."

Dick heard the shout, and it put fresh strength into him. He battled   15
manfully with the treacherous sea, his eyes fixed longingly upon the approaching boat.

"Hold on tight, little boy," he said. "There's a boat coming."

The little boy did not see the boat. His eyes were closed to shut out the fearful water, but he clung the closer to his young preserver. Six long, steady strokes, and the boat dashed along side. Strong hands seized Dick and his youthful burden, and drew them into the boat, both dripping with water.

"God be thanked!" exclaimed the father, as from the steamer he saw the child's rescue. "That brave boy shall be rewarded, if I sacrifice my whole fortune to compass it."

"You've had a pretty narrow escape, young chap," said one of the boat-men to Dick. "It was a pretty tough job you undertook."

"Yes," said Dick. "That's what I thought when I was in the water. If it   20
hadn't been for you, I don't know what would have 'come of us."

"Anyhow you're a plucky boy, or you wouldn't have dared to jump into the water after this little chap. It was a risky thing to do."

"I'm used to the water," said Dick, modestly. "I didn't stop to think of the danger, but I wasn't going to see that little fellow drown without tryin' to save him."

The boat at once headed for the ferry wharf on the Brooklyn side. The captain of the ferry-boat, seeing the rescue, did not think it necessary to stop his boat, but kept on his way. The whole occurrence took place in less time than I have occupied in telling it.

The father was waiting on the wharf to receive his little boy, with what feeling of gratitude and joy can be easily understood. With a burst of happy tears he clasped him to his arms. Dick was about to withdraw modestly, but the gentleman perceived the movement, and, putting down the child, came forward, and, clasping his hand, said with emotion, "My brave boy, I owe you a debt I can never repay. But for your timely service I should now be plunged into an anguish which I cannot think of without a shudder."

Our hero was ready enough to speak on most occasions, but always felt   25
awkward when he was praised.

"It wasn't any trouble," he said, modestly. "I can swim like a top."

"But not many boys would have risked their lives for a stranger," said the gentleman. "But," he added with a sudden thought, as his glance rested on Dick's dripping garments, "both you and my little boy will take cold in wet clothes. Fortunately I have a friend living close at hand, at whose house you will have an opportunity of taking off your clothes, and having them dried."

Dick protested that he never took cold; but Fosdick, who had now joined them, and who, it is needless to say, had been greatly alarmed at

Dick's danger, joined in urging compliance with the gentleman's proposal, and in the end our hero had to yield. His new friend secured a hack, the driver of which agreed for extra recompense to receive the dripping boys into his carriage, and they were whirled rapidly to a pleasant house in a side street, where matters were quickly explained, and both boys were put to bed.

"I aint used to goin' to bed quite so early," thought Dick. "This is the queerest excursion I ever took."

Like most active boys Dick did not enjoy the prospect of spending half a day in bed; but his confinement did not last as long as he anticipated.

In about an hour the door of his chamber was opened, and a servant appeared, bringing a new and handsome suit of clothes throughout.

"You are to put on these," said the servant to Dick; "but you needn't get up till you feel like it."

"Whose clothes are they?" asked Dick.

"They are yours."

"Mine! Where did they come from?"

"Mr. Rockwell sent out and bought them for you. They are the same size as your wet ones."

"Is he here now?"

"No. He bought another suit for the little boy, and has gone back to New York. Here's a note he asked me to give you."

Dick opened the paper, and read as follows, —

"Please accept this outfit of clothes as the first instalment of a debt which I can never repay. I have asked to have your wet suit dried, when you can reclaim it. Will you oblige me by calling to-morrow at my counting room, No. —, Pearl Street.

"Your friend,
"JAMES ROCKWELL."

When Dick was dressed in his new suit, he surveyed his figure with pardonable complacency. It was the best he had ever worn, and fitted him as well as if it had been made expressly for him.

"He's done the handsome thing," said Dick to himself; "but there wasn't no 'casion for his givin' me these clothes. My lucky stars are shinin' pretty bright now. Jumpin' into the water pays better than shinin' boots; but I don't think I'd like to try it more'n once a week."

About eleven o'clock the next morning Dick repaired to Mr. Rockwell's counting-room on Pearl Street. He found himself in front of a large and handsome warehouse. The counting-room was on the lower floor. Our hero entered, and found Mr. Rockwell sitting at a desk. No sooner did that gentleman see him than he arose, and, advancing, shook Dick by the hand in the most friendly manner.

"My young friend," he said, "you have done me so great a service that I wish to be of some service to you in return. Tell me about yourself, and what plans or wishes you have formed for the future."

Dick frankly related his past history, and told Mr. Rockwell of his 45 desire to get into a store or counting-room, and of the failure of all his applications thus far. The merchant listened attentively to Dick's statement, and, when he had finished, placed a sheet of paper before him, and, handing him a pen, said, "Will you write your name on this piece of paper?"

Dick wrote, in a free, bold hand, the name Richard Hunter. He had very much improved his penmanship, as has already been mentioned, and now had no cause to be ashamed of it.

Mr. Rockwell surveyed it approvingly.

"How would you like to enter my counting-room as clerk, Richard?" he asked.

Dick was about to say "Bully," when he recollected himself, and answered, "Very much."

"I suppose you know something of arithmetic, do you not?" 50

"Yes, sir."

"Then you may consider yourself engaged at a salary of ten dollars a week. You may come next Monday morning."

"Ten dollars!" repeated Dick, thinking he must have misunderstood.

"Yes; will that be sufficient?"

"It's more than I can earn," said Dick, honestly. 55

"Perhaps it is at first," said Mr. Rockwell, smiling; "but I am willing to pay you that. I will besides advance you as fast as your progress will justify it."

Dick was so elated that he hardly restrained himself from some demonstration which would have astonished the merchant; but he exercised self-control, and only said, "I'll try to serve you so faithfully, sir, that you won't repent having taken me into your service."

"And I think you will succeed," said Mr. Rockwell, encouragingly. "I will not detain you any longer, for I have some important business to attend to. I shall expect to see you on Monday morning."

Dick left the counting-room, hardly knowing whether he stood on his head or his heels, so overjoyed was he at the sudden change in his fortunes. Ten dollars a week was to him a fortune, and three times as much as he had expected to obtain at first. Indeed he would have been glad, only the day before, to get a place at three dollars a week. He reflected that with the stock of clothes which he had now on hand, he could save up at least half of it, and even then live better than he had been accustomed to do; so that his little fund in the savings bank, instead of being diminished, would be steadily increasing. Then he was to be advanced if he deserved it. It was indeed a bright prospect for a boy who, only a year before, could neither read nor write, and depended for a night's lodging upon the chance hospitality of an alley-way or old wagon. Dick's great ambition to "grow up 'spectable" seemed likely to be accomplished after all.

"I wish Fosdick was as well off as I am," he thought generously. But he   60
determined to help his less fortunate friend, and assist him up the ladder as
he advanced himself.

When Dick entered his room on Mott Street, he discovered that some
one else had been there before him, and two articles of wearing apparel
had disappeared.

"By gracious!" he exclaimed; "somebody's stole my Washington coat
and Napoleon pants. Maybe it's an agent of Barnum's, who expects to make
a fortun' by exhibitin' the valooable wardrobe of a gentleman of fashion."

Dick did not shed many tears over his loss, as, in his present circumstances, he never expected to have any further use for the well-worn garments. It may be stated that he afterwards saw them adorning the figure of
Micky Maguire; but whether that estimable young man stole them himself,
he never ascertained. As to the loss, Dick was rather pleased that it had
occurred. It seemed to cut him off from the old vagabond life which he
hoped never to resume. Henceforward he meant to press onward, and rise as
high as possible.

Although it was yet only noon, Dick did not go out again with his brush.
He felt that it was time to retire from business. He would leave his share of
the public patronage to other boys less fortunate than himself. That evening
Dick and Fosdick had a long conversation. Fosdick rejoiced heartily in his
friend's success, and on his side had the pleasant news to communicate that
his pay had been advanced to six dollars a week.

"I think we can afford to leave Mott Street now," he continued. "This   65
house isn't as neat as it might be, and I should like to live in a nicer quarter
of the city."

"All right," said Dick. "We'll hunt up a new room tomorrow. I shall
have plenty of time, having retired from business. I'll try to get my reg'lar
customers to take Johnny Nolan in my place. That boy hasn't any enterprise. He needs somebody to look out for him."

"You might give him your box and brush, too, Dick."

"No," said Dick; "I'll give him some new ones, but mine I want to keep,
to remind me of the hard times I've had, when I was an ignorant boot-black,
and never expected to be anything better."

"When, in short, you were 'Ragged Dick.' You must drop that name,
and think of yourself now as" —

"Richard Hunter, Esq.," said our hero, smiling.   70

"A young gentleman on the way to fame and fortune," added Fosdick.

ENGAGING THE TEXT

1. List the values, characteristics, and actions that help Ragged Dick succeed.
   How valuable do you consider these today? How important is virtue
   compared to good luck — in the story and in your own experience?

2. Skim the Alger selection to find as many mentions of money as you can. How frequent are they? What seem to be Alger's ideas about money, wealth, salaries, and other financial issues?

3. By the time we reach the end of this story, quite a few things have changed from the time Dick "was an ignorant boot-black, and never expected to be anything better" (para. 68). Working in small groups, list as many changes as you can. What seems to be Alger's attitude toward them?

4. Why is Alger careful to note that Dick does not hear Mr. Rockwell's offer of $10,000 to whoever would save Little Johnny? Is Dick being short-changed by getting a job and clothes but not a $10,000 reward?

EXPLORING CONNECTIONS

5. Look ahead to "Horatio Alger" by Harlon L. Dalton later in this chapter (p. 278). Does Dalton's analysis of the Alger myth change your understanding of this excerpt? Explain. What elements in this story might Dalton cite to support his claims?

6. Read "Looking for Work" by Gary Soto (p. 26). Compare and contrast Alger's ideas about work, money, and aspiration to those found in Soto's narrative.

EXTENDING THE CRITICAL CONTEXT

7. Dick considers himself a "young man of property" when he has $100 in the bank. Talk to classmates and see if you can reach any consensus about what it would take today to be a "young man or woman of property." Similarly, see if you can agree on what a good starting salary would be for a recent college graduate, or on what levels of wealth and income define the poor, the middle class, and the upper class in the United States today. Write a note summarizing your conclusions and keep it for reference as you read the rest of this chapter.

8. If you did the first "Before Reading" assignment on page 263, compare and contrast the qualities that made the people on your list successful with the qualities Alger gives to Ragged Dick.

The Lesson

TONI CADE BAMBARA

"The Lesson" looks at wealth through the eyes of a poor black girl whose education includes a field trip to one of the world's premier toy stores. The story speaks to serious social issues with a comic, energetic, and utterly engaging voice. Toni Cade Bambara (1939–1995) grew up in the Harlem and

Bedford-Stuyvesant areas of New York City. Trained at Queens College and City College of New York in dance, drama, and literature, she is best known for her collections of stories, Gorilla, My Love *(1972) and* The Seabirds Are Still Alive and Other Stories *(1977), and for her novels,* If Blessing Comes *(1987) and* The Salt Eaters *(1980), winner of the American Book Award. Her novel* Those Bones Are Not My Child, *edited by Toni Morrison, was published posthumously in 1999. "The Lesson" is taken from* Gorilla, My Love.

Back in the days when everyone was old and stupid or young and foolish and me and Sugar were the only ones just right, this lady moved on our block with nappy hair and proper speech and no makeup. And quite naturally we laughed at her, laughed the way we did at the junk man who went about his business like he was some big-time president and his sorry-ass horse his secretary. And we kinda hated her too, hated the way we did the winos who cluttered up our parks and pissed on our handball walls and stank up our hallways and stairs so you couldn't halfway play hide-and-seek without a goddamn gas mask. Miss Moore was her name. The only woman on the block with no first name. And she was black as hell, cept for her feet, which were fish-white and spooky. And she was always planning these boring-ass things for us to do, us being my cousin, mostly, who lived on the block cause we all moved North the same time and to the same apartment then spread out gradual to breathe. And our parents would yank our heads into some kinda shape and crisp up our clothes so we'd be presentable for travel with Miss Moore, who always looked like she was going to church, though she never did. Which is just one of the things the grownups talked about when they talked behind her back like a dog. But when she came calling with some sachet[1] she'd sewed up or some gingerbread she'd made or some book, why then they'd all be too embarrassed to turn her down and we'd get handed out all spruced up. She'd been to college and said it only right that she should take responsibility for the young ones' education, and she not even related by marriage or blood. So they'd go for it. Specially Aunt Gretchen. She was the main gofer in the family. You got some ole dumb shit foolishness you want somebody to go for, you send for Aunt Gretchen. She been screwed into the go-along for so long, it's a blood-deep natural thing with her. Which is how she got saddled with me and Sugar and Junior in the first place while our mothers were in a la-de-da apartment up the block having a good ole time.

So this one day Miss Moore rounds us all up at the mailbox and it's puredee hot and she's knockin herself out about arithmetic. And school suppose to let up in summer I heard, but she don't never let up. And the

---

[1]*sachet:* A small bag filled with a sweet-smelling substance. Sachets are often placed in drawers to scent clothes.

starch in my pinafore scratching the shit outta me and I'm really hating this nappy-head bitch and her goddamn college degree. I'd much rather go to the pool or to the show where it's cool. So me and Sugar leaning on the mailbox being surly, which is a Miss Moore word. And Flyboy checking out what everybody brought for lunch. And Fat Butt already wasting his peanut-butter-and-jelly sandwich like the pig he is. And Junebug punchin on Q.T.'s arm for potato chips. And Rosie Giraffe shifting from one hip to the other waiting for somebody to step on her foot or ask her if she from Georgia so she can kick ass, preferably Mercedes'. And Miss Moore asking us do we know what money is, like we a bunch of retards. I mean real money, she say, like it's only poker chips or monopoly papers we lay on the grocer. So right away I'm tired of this and say so. And would much rather snatch Sugar and go to the Sunset and terrorize the West Indian kids and take their hair ribbons and their money too. And Miss Moore files that remark away for next week's lesson on brotherhood, I can tell. And finally I say we oughta get to the subway cause it's cooler and besides we might meet some cute boys. Sugar done swiped her mama's lipstick, so we ready.

So we heading down the street and she's boring us silly about what things cost and what our parents make and how much goes for rent and how money ain't divided up right in this country. And then she gets to the part about we all poor and live in the slums, which I don't feature. And I'm ready to speak on that, but she steps out in the street and hails two cabs just like that. Then she hustles half the crew in with her and hands me a five-dollar bill and tells me to calculate 10 percent tip for the driver. And we're off. Me and Sugar and Junebug and Flyboy hangin out the window and hollering to everybody, putting lipstick on each other cause Flyboy a faggot anyway, and making farts with our sweaty armpits. But I'm mostly trying to figure how to spend this money. But they all fascinated with the meter ticking and Junebug starts laying bets as to how much it'll read when Flyboy can't hold his breath no more. Then Sugar lays bets as to how much it'll be when we get there. So I'm stuck. Don't nobody want to go for my plan, which is to jump out at the next light and run off to the first bar-b-que we can find. Then the driver tells us to get the hell out cause we are there already. And the meter reads eighty-five cents. And I'm stalling to figure out the tip and Sugar say give him a dime. And I decide he don't need it bad as I do, so later for him. But then he tries to take off with Junebug foot still in the door so we talk about his mama something ferocious. Then we check out that we on Fifth Avenue[2] and everybody dressed up in stockings. One lady in a fur coat, hot as it is. White folks crazy.

"This is the place," Miss Moore say, presenting it to us in the voice she uses at the museum. "Let's look in the windows before we go in."

---

[2]*Fifth Avenue:* The street in New York most famous for its expensive stores.

"Can we steal?" Sugar asks very serious like she's getting the ground   5
rules square away before she plays. "I beg your pardon," say Miss Moore,
and we fall out. So she leads us around the windows of the toy store and me
and Sugar screamin, "This is mine, that's mine, I gotta have that, that was
made for me, I was born for that," till Big Butt drowns us out.

"Hey, I'm goin to buy that there."

"That there? You don't even know what it is, stupid."

"I do so," he say punchin on Rosie Giraffe. "It's a microscope."

"Whatcha gonna do with a microscope, fool?"

"Look at things."   10

"Like what, Ronald?" ask Miss Moore. And Big Butt ain't got the first
notion. So here go Miss Moore gabbing about the thousands of bacteria in a
drop of water and the somethinorother in a speck of blood and the million
and one living things in the air around us is invisible to the naked eye. And
what she say that for? Junebug go to town on that "naked" and we rolling.
Then Miss Moore ask what it cost. So we all jam into the window smudgin it
up and the price tag say $300. So then she ask how long'd take for Big Butt
and Junebug to save up their allowances. "Too long," I say. "Yeh," adds
Sugar, "outgrown it by that time." And Miss Moore say no, you never out-
grow learning instruments. "Why, even medical students and interns and,"
blah, blah, blah. And we ready to choke Big Butt for bringing it up in the
first damn place.

"This here costs four hundred eighty dollars," say Rosie Giraffe. So we
pile up all over her to see what she pointin out. My eyes tell me it's a chunk
of glass cracked with something heavy, and different-color inks dripped into
the splits, then the whole thing put into a oven or something. But for $480 it
don't make sense.

"That's a paperweight made of semi-precious stones fused together
under tremendous pressure," she explains slowly, with her hands doing the
mining and all the factory work.

"So what's a paperweight?" asks Rosie Giraffe.

"To weigh paper with, dumbbell," say Flyboy, the wise man from the   15
East.

"Not exactly," say Miss Moore, which is what she say when you warm or
way off too. "It's to weigh paper down so it won't scatter and make your
desk untidy." So right away me and Sugar curtsy to each other and then to
Mercedes who is more the tidy type.

"We don't keep paper on top of the desk in my class," say Junebug, figuring Miss Moore crazy or lyin one.

"At home, then," she say. "Don't you have a calendar and a pencil case
and a blotter and a letter-opener on your desk at home where you do your
homework?" And she know damn well what our homes look like cause she
nosys around in them every chance she gets.

"I don't even have a desk," say Junebug. "Do we?"

"No. And I don't get no homework neither," say Big Butt.   20

"And I don't even have a home," say Flyboy like he do at school to keep the white folks off his back and sorry for him. Send this poor kid to camp posters, is his speciality.

"I do," say Mercedes. "I have a box of stationery on my desk and a picture of my cat. My godmother bought the stationery and the desk. There's a big rose on each sheet and the envelopes smell like roses."

"Who want to know about your smelly-ass stationery," say Rosie Giraffe fore I can get my two cents in.

"It's important to have a work area all your own so that . . ."

"Will you look at this sailboat, please," say Flyboy, cuttin her off and pointin to the thing like it was his. So once again we tumble all over each other to gaze at this magnificent thing in the toy store which is just big enough to maybe sail two kittens across the pond if you strap them to the posts tight. We all start reciting the price tag like we in assembly. "Handcrafted sailboat of fiberglass at one thousand one hundred ninety-five dollars."

"Unbelievable," I hear myself say and am really stunned. I read it again for myself just in case the group recitation put me in a trance. Same thing. For some reason this pisses me off. We look at Miss Moore and she lookin at us, waiting for I dunno what.

"Who'd pay all that when you can buy a sailboat set for a quarter at Pop's, a tube of glue for a dime, and a ball of string for eight cents? It must have a motor and a whole lot else besides," I say. "My sailboat cost me about fifty cents."

"But will it take water?" say Mercedes with her smart ass.

"Took mine to Alley Pond Park once," say Flyboy. "String broke. Lost it. Pity."

"Sailed mine in Central Park and it keeled over and sank. Had to ask my father for another dollar."

"And you got the strap," laugh Big Butt. "The jerk didn't even have a string on it. My old man wailed on his behind."

Little Q.T. was staring hard at the sailboat and you could see he wanted it bad. But he too little and somebody'd just take it from him. So what the hell. "This boat for kids, Miss Moore?"

"Parents silly to buy something like that just to get all broke up," say Rosie Giraffe.

"That much money it should last forever," I figure.

"My father'd buy it for me if I wanted it."

"Your father, my ass," say Rosie Giraffe getting a chance to finally push Mercedes.

"Must be rich people shop here," say Q.T.

"You are a very bright boy," say Flyboy. "What was your first clue?" And he rap him on the head with the back of his knuckles, since Q.T. the only one he could get away with. Though Q.T. liable to come up behind you years later and get his licks in when you half expect it.

"What I want to know is," I says to Miss Moore though I never talk to her, I wouldn't give the bitch that satisfaction, "is how much a real boat costs? I figure a thousand'd get you a yacht any day."

"Why don't you check that out," she says, "and report back to the group?" Which really pains my ass. If you gonna mess up a perfectly good swim day least you could do is have some answers. "Let's go in," she say like she got something up her sleeve. Only she don't lead the way. So me and Sugar turn the corner to where the entrance is, but when we get there I kinda hang back. Not that I'm scared, what's there to be afraid of, just a toy store. But I feel funny, shame. But what I got to be shamed about? Got as much right to go in as anybody. But somehow I can't seem to get hold on the door, so I step away for Sugar to lead. But she hangs back too. And I look at her and she looks at me and this is ridiculous. I mean, damn, I have never ever been shy about doing nothing or going nowhere. But then Mercedes steps up and then Rosie Giraffe and Big Butt crowd in behind and shove, and next thing we all stuffed into the doorway with only Mercedes squeezing past us, smoothing out her jumper and walking right down the aisle. Then the rest of us tumble in like a glued-together jigsaw done all wrong. And people lookin at us. And it's like the time me and Sugar crashed into the Catholic church on a dare. But once we got in there and everything so hushed and holy and the candles and the bowin and the handkerchiefs on all the drooping heads, I just couldn't go through with the plan. Which was for me to run up to the altar and do a tap dance while Sugar played the nose flute and messed around in the holy water. And Sugar kept givin me the elbow. Then later teased me so bad I tied her up in the shower and turned it on and locked her in. And she'd be there till this day if Aunt Gretchen hadn't finally figured I was lying about the boarder takin a shower.

Same thing in the store. We all walkin on tiptoe and hardly touchin the games and puzzles and things. And I watched Miss Moore who is steady watchin us like she waitin for a sign. Like Mama Drewery watches the sky and sniffs the air and takes note of just how much slant is in the bird formation. Then me and Sugar bump smack into each other, so busy gazing at the toys, 'specially the sailboat. But we don't laugh and go into our fat-lady bump-stomach routine. We just stare at that price tag. Then Sugar run a finger over the whole boat. And I'm jealous and want to hit her. Maybe not her, but I sure want to punch somebody in the mouth.

"Watcha bring us here for, Miss Moore?"

"You sound angry, Sylvia. Are you mad about something?" Give me one of them grins like she tellin a grown-up joke that never turns out to be funny. And she's lookin very closely at me like maybe she plannin to do my portrait from memory. I'm mad, but I won't give her that satisfaction. So I slouch around the store bein very bored and say, "Let's go."

Me and Sugar at the back of the train watchin' the tracks whizzin by large then small then gettin gobbled up in the dark. I'm thinkin about this tricky toy I saw in the store. A clown that somersaults on a bar then does chin-ups just cause you yank lightly at his leg. Cost $35. I could see me askin my mother for a $35 birthday clown. "You wanna who that costs what?" she'd say, cockin her head to the side to get a better view of the hole in my head. Thirty-five dollars could buy new bunk beds for Junior and Gretchen's boy. Thirty-five dollars and the whole household could go visit Granddaddy Nelson in the country. Thirty-five dollars would pay for the rent and the piano bill too. Who are these people that spend that much for performing clowns and $1,000 for toy sailboats? What kinda work they do and how they live and how come we ain't in on it? Where we are is who we are, Miss Moore always pointin out. But it don't necessarily have to be that way, she always adds then waits for somebody to say that poor people have to wake up and demand their share of the pie and don't none of us know what kind of pie she talkin about in the first damn place. But she ain't so smart cause I still got her four dollars from the taxi and she sure ain't gettin it. Messin up my day with this shit. Sugar nudges me in my pocket and winks.

Miss Moore lines us up in front of the mailbox where we started from, 45 seem like years ago, and I got a headache for thinkin so hard. And we lean all over each other so we can hold up under the draggy-ass lecture she always finishes us off with at the end before we thank her for borin us to tears. But she just looks at us like she readin tea leaves. Finally she say, "Well, what did you think of F.A.O. Schwarz?"[3]

Rosie Giraffe mumbles, "White folks crazy."

"I'd like to go in there again when I get my birthday money," says Mercedes, and we shove her out the pack so she has to lean on the mailbox by herself.

"I'd like a shower. Tiring day," say Flyboy.

Then Sugar surprises me by saying, "You know, Miss Moore, I don't think all of us here put together eat in a year what that sailboat costs." And Miss Moore lights up like somebody goosed her. "And?" she say, urging Sugar on. Only I'm standin on her foot so she don't continue.

"Imagine for a minute what kind of society it is in which some people 50 can spend on a toy what it would cost to feed a family of six or seven. What do you think?"

"I think," say Sugar pushing me off her feet like she never done before, cause I whip her ass in a minute, "that this is not much of a democracy if you ask me. Equal chance to pursue happiness means an equal crack at the dough, don't it?" Miss Moore is besides herself and I am disgusted with Sugar's treachery. So I stand on her foot one more time to see if she'll shove me. She shuts up, and Miss Moore looks at me, sorrowfully I'm thinkin. And somethin weird is going on, I can feel it in my chest.

"Anybody else learn anything today?" lookin dead at me. I walk away

---

[3]*F.A.O. Schwarz:* The name and the toy store are real. The store, in fact, has become a tourist attraction.

and Sugar has to run to catch up and don't even seem to notice when I shrug her arm off my shoulder.

"Well, we got four dollars anyway," she says.

"Uh hunh."

"We could go to Hascombs and get half a chocolate layer and then go   55 to the Sunset and still have plenty money for potato chips and ice-cream sodas."

"Uh hunh."

"Race you to Hascombs," she say.

We start down the block and she gets ahead which is O.K. by me cause I'm goin to the West End and then over to the Drive to think this day through. She can run if she want to and even run faster. But ain't nobody gonna beat me at nuthin.

ENGAGING THE TEXT

1. What is the lesson Miss Moore is trying to teach in this story? How well is it received by Mercedes, Sugar, and the narrator, Sylvia? Why does the narrator react differently from Sugar, and what is the meaning of her last line in the story, "But ain't nobody gonna beat me at nuthin"?

2. Why did Bambara write the story from Sylvia's point of view? How would the story change if told from Miss Moore's perspective? From Sugar's? How would it change if the story were set today as opposed to three decades ago?

3. The story mentions several expensive items: a fur coat, a microscope, a paperweight, a sailboat, and a toy clown. Why do you think the author chose each of these details? If the story were set in the present instead of circa 1970, what items might serve the same purposes?

4. In paragraph 44 Sylvia says, "Where we are is who we are, Miss Moore always pointin out. But it don't necessarily have to be that way." What does Miss Moore mean by this? Do you agree? What does Miss Moore expect the children to do to change the situation?

EXPLORING CONNECTIONS

5. Both Sylvia and Ragged Dick (p. 264) can be seen as trying to find their place in the world of money and social status. Compare their situations and their attitudes about class and upward mobility. How do Bambara's ideas about money and opportunity differ from Alger's?

6. "The Lesson" describes education outside of the schoolroom. How might John Taylor Gatto (p. 152) or Jean Anyon (p. 173) assess the effectiveness of Miss Moore's teaching? Do you think Miss Moore's lessons directly challenge the children's classroom learning? Explain.

7. Compare Sylvia and Sugar's relationship here with that of Teresa and the speaker of the poem in "Para Teresa" (p. 206). Which girls stand the better chance of achieving success? Why?

EXTENDING THE CRITICAL CONTEXT

8. For the next class meeting, browse the Internet or magazines, newspapers, and catalogs to find the most overpriced, unnecessary item you can. Spend a few minutes swapping examples, then discuss the information you've gathered: Are there any lessons to be learned here about wealth, success, and status?

9. The opening lines of "The Lesson" suggest that Sylvia is now a mature woman looking back on her youth. Working in groups, write a brief biography explaining what has happened to Sylvia since the day of "The Lesson." What has she done? Who has she become? Read your profiles aloud to the class and explain your vision of Sylvia's development.

Horatio Alger

HARLON L. DALTON

The first selection in this chapter dramatizes the American Dream coming true in an uncomplicated if rather contrived way: the ambitious young "Ragged Dick" determines to improve himself, works hard, seizes his opportunity, and quickly makes his way to "fame and fortune." This piece by Harlon L. Dalton (b. 1947) questions that myth, calling it not only false, but worse — "socially destructive." Using Alger as his prime example, Dalton systematically explains how the rags-to-riches myth can conceal important social realities like race and class. A professor at Yale Law School, Harlon L. Dalton specializes in the relationship of law to theology, psychology, and race theory. He has served on the board of directors for the American Civil Liberties Union and was a member of the National Commission on AIDS. "Horatio Alger" is taken from his book Racial Healing: Confronting the Fear Between Blacks and Whites *(1995).*

Ah, Horatio Alger, whose name more than any other is associated with the classic American hero. A writer of mediocre fiction, Alger had a formula for commercial success that was simple and straightforward: his lead characters, young boys born into poverty, invariably managed to transcend their station in life by dint of hard work, persistence, initiative, and daring.[1] Nice story line. There is just one problem — it is a myth. Not just in the sense

[1]Edwin P. Hoyt, *Horatio's Boys: The Life and Works of Horatio Alger, Jr.* (Radnor, Penn.: Chilton Book Company, 1974). [All notes are Dalton's.]

that it is fictional, but more fundamentally because the lesson Alger conveys is a false one. To be sure, many myths are perfectly benign, and more than a few are salutary, but on balance Alger's myth is socially destructive.

The Horatio Alger myth conveys three basic messages: (1) each of us is judged solely on her or his own merits; (2) we each have a fair opportunity to develop those merits; and (3) ultimately, merit will out. Each of them is, to be charitable, problematic. The first message is a variant on the rugged individualism ethos. . . . In this form, it suggests that success in life has nothing to do with pedigree, race, class background, gender, national origin, sexual orientation — in short, with anything beyond our individual control. Those variables may exist, but they play no appreciable role in how our actions are appraised.

This simply flies in the face of reality. There are doubtless circumstances — the hiring of a letter carrier in a large metropolitan post office, for example — where none of this may matter, but that is the exception rather than the rule. Black folk certainly know what it is like to be favored, disfavored, scrutinized, and ignored all on the basis of our race. Sometimes we are judged on a different scale altogether. Stephen Carter has written movingly about what he calls "the best black syndrome," the tendency of White folk to judge successful Black people only in relation to each other rather than against all comers. Thus, when Carter earned the second-highest score in his high school on the National Merit Scholarship qualifying test, he was readily recognized as "the best Black" around, but somehow not seen as one of the best students, period.[2]

Although I would like to think that things are much different now, I know better. Not long ago a student sought my advice regarding how to deal with the fact that a liberal colleague of mine (and of Stephen Carter's) had written a judicial clerkship recommendation for her in which he described her as the best Black student to have ever taken his class. Apparently the letter caused a mild stir among current law clerks in several courthouses, one of whom saw fit to inform the student. "What was the professor [whom she declined to name] thinking of?" she wondered aloud. "What does his comment mean? What is a judge supposed to make of it? 'If for some reason you think you have to hire one of them, then she's the way to go'? I could understand if he said I was one of the top ten students or even the top thousand, but what does the 'best Black' mean?"

Black folk also know what it is like to be underestimated because of the   5
color of their skin. For example, those of us who communicate in standard English are often praised unduly for how well we speak. This is, I might add, an experience all too familiar to Asian-Americans, including those born and bred in the U.S.A. And we know what it is like to be feared, pitied, admired, and scorned on account of our race, before we even have a chance

---

[2]Stephen L. Carter, *Reflections of an Affirmative Action Baby* (New York: Basic Books, 1991), 47–49.

to say boo! We, in turn, view White people through the prism of our own race-based expectations. I honestly am surprised every time I see a White man who can play basketball above the rim, just as Puerto Ricans and Cubans tend to be surprised to discover "Americans" who salsa truly well. All of which is to say that the notion that every individual is judged solely on personal merit, without regard for sociological wrapping, is mythical at best.

The second message conveyed by Horatio Alger is that we all have a shot at reaching our true potential. To be fair, neither Alger nor the myth he underwrote suggests that we start out equal. Nor does the myth necessarily require that we be given an equal opportunity to succeed. Rather, Alger's point is that each of us has the power to create our own opportunities. That turns out to be a difficult proposition to completely disprove, for no matter what evidence is offered up to show that a particular group of people have not fared well, it can always be argued that they did not try hard enough, or that they spent too much time wallowing in their predicament and not enough figuring out how to rise above it. Besides, there are always up-by-the-bootstraps examples to point to, like Colin Powell, whose name has so frequently been linked with that of Horatio Alger's that he must think they are related.[3] Nevertheless, it is by now generally agreed that there is a large category of Americans — some have called it the underclass — for whom upward mobility is practically impossible without massive changes in the structure of the economy and in the allocation of public resources.

As for the notion that merit will out, it assumes not only a commitment to merit-based decision making but also the existence of standards for measuring merit that do not unfairly favor one individual over another. Such standards, of course, must come from somewhere. They must be decided upon by somebody. And that somebody is rarely without a point of view. Ask a devotee of West Coast basketball what skills you should look for in recruiting talent and near the top of his list will be the ability to "get out on the break," to "be creative in the open court," and "to finish the play." On the other hand, ask someone who prefers East Coast basketball and her list will rank highly the ability "to d-up [play defense]," "to board [rebound]," and "to maintain focus and intensity."

Or, to take another example, what makes a great Supreme Court justice? Brains to spare? Common sense? Proper judicial temperament? Political savvy? Extensive lawyering experience? A well-developed ability to

---

[3]Sandy Grady, "Will He or Won't He?: Win or Lose, Presidential Pursuit by Colin Powell Would Do America a Necessary Service," *Kansas City Star*, 24 April 1995; Thomas B. Edsall, "For Powell, Timing Could be Crucial: As Gulf War Hero Hints at 1996 Bid, Associates Look into Details," *Washington Post*, 6 April 1995; J. F. O. McAllister, "The Candidate of Dreams," *Time*, 13 March 1995; Deroy Murdock, "Colin Powell: Many Things to Many People," *Washington Times*, 16 January 1995; Doug Fischer, "U.S. Politics: War Hero Well-Placed to Become First Black President," *Ottawa Citizen*, 8 October 1994; "General Nice Guy: Profile Colin Powell," *Sunday Telegraph*, 25 September 1994; Otto Kreisher, "As a Civilian, Powell's Options Are Enviable," *San Diego Union-Tribune*, 26 September 1993.

THE BOONDOCKS   by **AARON MCGRUDER**

abstract? Vision? Well-honed rhetorical skills? A reverence for our rich legal heritage? The capacity to adapt to changing times? Even if one is tempted to say "all of the above," how should these (or any other set of characteristics) be ranked? Measured? Evaluated?

The answers depend in part on whom you ask. Practicing lawyers, for example, are probably likely to rank extensive lawyering experience more highly than, say, brains. They are also likely to pay close attention to judicial temperament, which for them means whether the prospective justice would be inclined to treat them with respect during a court appearance. Sitting judges are also likely to rank judicial temperament highly, meaning whether the prospective justice would be a good colleague. In choosing among the other characteristics, they might each favor the ones that they happen to possess in abundance. Politicians might well see more merit in political savvy than would, say, academics, who could be expected to favor brains, the ability to abstract, and perhaps rhetorical skills.

All of these relevant actors might be honestly trying to come up with   10 appropriate standards for measuring merit, but they would arrive at markedly different results. And any given result would screen out people who would succeed under another, equally plausible set of standards. Thus, if there is a genuine commitment to merit-based decision making it is possible that merit will out, but only for those who have the right kind of merit.

Which brings us to the prior question: is merit all we care about in deciding who gets what share of life's goodies? Clearly not. Does anyone, for example, honestly believe that any Supreme Court justice in recent memory was nominated solely on the basis of merit (however defined)? Any President? Any member of Congress? Does anyone believe that America's health-care resources are distributed solely on merit? That tax breaks are distributed solely on merit? That baseball club owners are selected solely on merit?

As I suggested earlier, the mere fact that a myth is based on false premises or conveys a false image of the world does not necessarily make it undesirable. Indeed, I place great stock in the idea that some illusions are, or at least can be, positive. As social psychologist Shelley Taylor has observed, "[normal] people who are confronted with the normal rebuffs of everyday life seem to construe their experience [so] as to develop and maintain an exaggeratedly positive view of their own attributes, an unrealistic optimism about the future, and a distorted faith in their ability to control what goes on around them."[4] Taylor's research suggests that, up to a point, such self-aggrandizement actually improves one's chances of worldly success.[5]

This may well explain the deep appeal of the Horatio Alger myth. True or not, it can help to pull people in the direction they want to go. After all, in order to succeed in life, especially when the odds are stacked against you, it is often necessary to first convince yourself that there is a reason to get up in the morning. So what is my beef? Where is the harm?

In a nutshell, my objection to the Alger myth is that it serves to maintain the racial pecking order. It does so by mentally bypassing the role of race in American society. And it does so by fostering beliefs that themselves serve to trivialize, if not erase, the social meaning of race. The Alger myth encourages people to blink at the many barriers to racial equality (historical, structural, and institutional) that litter the social landscape. Yes, slavery was built on the notion that Africans were property and not persons; yes, even after that "peculiar institution" collapsed, it continued to shape the life prospects of those who previously were enslaved; yes, the enforced illiteracy and cultural disruption of slavery, together with the collapse of Reconstruction, virtually assured that the vast majority of "freedmen" and "freedwomen" would not be successfully integrated into society; yes, Jim Crow laws, segregation, and a separate and unequal social reality severely undermined the prospects for Black achievement; yes, these and other features of our national life created a racial caste system that persists to this day; yes, the short-lived civil rights era of the 1950s and 1960s was undone by a broad and sustained White backlash; yes, the majority of Black people in America are mired in poverty; yes, economic mobility is not what it used to be, given the decline in our manufacturing and industrial base; yes, the siting of the illicit drug industry in our inner cities has had pernicious effects on Black and Latino neighborhoods; yes, yes, yes, BUT (drumroll) "all it takes to make it in America is initiative, hard work, persistence, and pluck." After all, just look at Colin Powell!

There is a fundamental tension between the promise of opportunity enshrined in the Alger myth and the realities of a racial caste system. The main point of such a system is to promote and maintain inequality. The main point of the Alger myth is to proclaim that everyone can rise above her station in life. Despite this tension, it is possible for the myth to coexist with social reality. To quote Shelley Taylor once again:

> [T]he normal human mind is oriented toward mental health and . . . at every turn it construes events in a manner that promotes benign fictions about the self, the world, and the future. The mind is, with some

15

---

[4]Shelley E. Taylor, *Positive Illusions: Creative Self-Deception and the Healthy Mind* (New York: Basic Books, 1989), xi.

[5]Ibid., xi, 7, 228–46.

significant exceptions, intrinsically adaptive, oriented toward overcoming rather than succumbing to the adverse events of life. . . . At one level, it constructs beneficent interpretations of threatening events that raise self-esteem and promote motivation; yet at another level, it recognizes the threat or challenge that is posed by these events.[6]

Not surprisingly, then, there are lots of Black folk who subscribe to the Alger myth and at the same time understand it to be deeply false. They live with the dissonance between myth and reality because both are helpful and healthful in dealing with "the adverse events of life." Many Whites, however, have a strong interest in resolving the dissonance in favor of the myth. Far from needing to be on guard against racial "threat[s] or challenge[s]," they would just as soon put the ugliness of racism out of mind. For them, the Horatio Alger myth provides them the opportunity to do just that.[7]

Quite apart from the general way in which the myth works to submerge the social realities of race, each of the messages it projects is also incompatible with the idea of race-based advantage or disadvantage. If, as the myth suggests, we are judged solely on our individual merits, then caste has little practical meaning. If we all can acquire the tools needed to reach our full potential, then how important can the disadvantage of race be? If merit will eventually carry the day, then shouldn't we be directing our energies toward encouraging Black initiative and follow-through rather than worrying about questions of power and privilege?

By interring the myth of Horatio Alger, or at least forcing it to coexist with social reality, we can accomplish two important goals. First, we can give the lie to the idea that Black people can simply lift themselves up by their own bootstraps. With that pesky idea out of the way, it is easier to see why White folk need to take joint ownership of the nation's race problem. Second, the realization that hard work and individual merit, while certainly critical, are not guarantors of success should lead at least some White people to reflect on whether their own achievements have been helped along by their preferred social position.

Finally, quite apart from race, it is in our national interest to give the Horatio Alger myth a rest, for it broadcasts a fourth message no less false than the first three — that we live in a land of unlimited potential. Although that belief may have served us well in the past, we live today in an era of diminished possibilities. We need to make a series of hard choices, followed by yet more hard choices regarding how to live with the promise of less. Confronting that reality is made that much harder by a mythology that assures us we can have it all.

[6]Ibid., xi.
[7]Robert T. Carter, et al., "White Racial Identity Development and Work Values," *Journal of Vocational Behavior, Special Issue: Racial Identity and Vocational Behavior* 44, no. 2 (April 1994): 185–97.

ENGAGING THE TEXT

1. The first message communicated by the Alger myth, according to Dalton, is that "each of us is judged solely on her or his own merits" (para. 2). What does this message mean to Dalton, and why does he object to it? How does he make his case against it, and what kind of evidence does he provide? Explain why you agree or disagree with his claim that this first message "simply flies in the face of reality" (para. 3).

2. Dalton says it is "generally agreed," but do *you* agree that "there is a large category of Americans . . . for whom upward mobility is practically impossible" (para. 6)? Why or why not?

3. How persuasive do you find Dalton's claims that American society is far from operating as a strictly merit-based system?

4. Why does Dalton believe that the Alger myth is destructive? Do you think the power of the American Dream to inspire or motivate people is outweighed by the negative effects Dalton cites, or vice versa? Write a journal entry explaining your position.

EXPLORING CONNECTIONS

5. Test Dalton's claims against the actual excerpt from Horatio Alger's *Ragged Dick* (p. 264). For example, does the novel seem to match the formula Dalton summarizes in his first paragraph? Similarly, can you find in the novel any examples of the three messages Dalton identifies in his second paragraph? On balance, does the excerpt from Alger seem to promote ideas that you consider socially destructive? Why or why not?

6. How do you think Dalton would assess the chances for success of Sylvia and her friends in "The Lesson" (p. 270)? Explain why you think he would praise or critique Miss Moore's attempts to educate the children about social class and money.

7. What ideas and attitudes about success are expressed in the cartoon by Aaron McGruder on page 281? How do they compare with those of Ragged Dick (p. 264) and the children in "The Lesson" (p. 270)? How might Harlon Dalton explain the humor of the cartoon?

EXTENDING THE CRITICAL CONTEXT

8. Pick a few contemporary cultural icons like Sean Combs, Jennifer Lopez, Gloria Estefan, Bruce Lee, Tiger Woods and Oprah Winfrey. Conduct a minipoll about what their success means to race relations in the United States. Do the responses you get support Dalton's contention that such figures encourage people "to blink at the many barriers to racial equality" (para. 14)?

9. Dalton argues that the Alger myth should be buried, or, to use his word, "interred." Supposing for the moment that you agree, how could that be accomplished? How is a cultural myth challenged, revised, or robbed of its mythic power?

The Black Avenger

KEN HAMBLIN

If radio talk show hosts are paid to be controversial, Ken Hamblin earned his money. He refers to young black women who bear children out of wedlock as "brood mares"; most of their children were sired, he writes, by "black thugs." One of Hamblin's main themes is the vitality of the American Dream and, in particular, his belief that black Americans should embrace that dream, quit whining about white racism, forget affirmative action, and make successes of themselves in the best country on earth. "The Black Avenger" touches on many of Hamblin's most provocative ideas. It is excerpted from his book Pick a Better Country: An Unassuming Colored Guy Speaks His Mind about America *(1996). Hamblin has himself lived a version of the American Dream. Raised in a poor area of Brooklyn by West Indian immigrant parents, Hamblin has himself experienced elements of the American Dream: his work in varied media fields (photojournalism, cinematography, TV production, newspapers) culminated in a nationally syndicated talk radio show. In 1999 he published* Plain Talk and Common Sense from the Black Avenger.

Broad brushstrokes have been used over the last couple of years to paint a simplistic picture of the serious grievances emanating from middle America.

This picture painted and broadcast by the mainstream media is far different from the complex white backlash that I see and fear, however. The mainstream media have reduced nearly every political and social phenomenon I have written about in this book to a simple sound bite and a three-word headline: "Angry White Men."

The premise is that the black race and the white race are moving farther and farther apart because these angry white men are coming together in a collective backlash against the benefits afforded blacks through civil rights over the last three decades.

The evidence frequently cited is that these men, who for years held an unfair advantage in the workplace and in society in general, now are attacking programs such as affirmative action, which were designed to give minorities the edge to compensate for the years they were not treated as equals.

The predominantly liberal media report that these white men make up   5 the core of the growing conservative audience of talk radio. As a nationally syndicated talk radio host who is on the air for three hours five days a week, I guess this means that I should be among the first to hear from these guys.

But in actuality, that misconception is shattered regularly on *The Ken Hamblin Show*. The most interesting evidence against the stereotype comes in call after call, day after day, from white men, white southern men in particular, whom I hear crying uncle in this tired debate about race.

They are not crying uncle in the sense that they are rolling over.

What they are saying is: "Look, I personally didn't do it. I've gone through the family Bible. I haven't found one instance where we owned slaves. But I'll admit that at one time in America an injustice was committed against people of color — against black people, African Americans, Negroes. And as a white person, I am willing to atone for that."

In January of 1994 my local Denver radio program was broadcast live on C-Span and then repeated several times over the following week. On that show I addressed this guilt factor among white Americans and, as a spoof, offered to send my listeners and my viewers a copy of my very own "Certificate of Absolution."

Some months earlier, a man had called me on the air, identified himself   10
as white, and told me with candor and some degree of desperation that he was tired of feeling guilty about "my people."

That prompted me to come up with an official pardon in the form of a certificate, which only a clear-thinking black American would be authorized to issue. Soon after that, a Denver printer named Rex Kniss, who listened to my show, called and said he would be willing to print the certificate.

Rex added some "certificate" language to my thoughts and we ended up with the following:

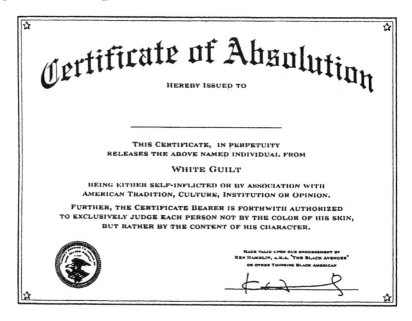

I signed the Certificate "The Black Avenger," a moniker that I use particularly with my radio listeners. The idea behind the name was that I wanted to avenge the lies and the disinformation that more than thirty years of liberalism have brought about in this country. More to the point, I wanted to present myself as living proof that America works for black people too. As the Black Avenger, I was a living, breathing challenge to the well-honed Myth of the Hobbled Black.[1]

"The Black Avenger" caught on among my fans in 1993 while I was on a local Denver radio station that also carried Rush Limbaugh. Limbaugh was hyping his newsletter by promoting an appearance in Colorado after one of his callers from Fort Collins, a man named Dan, said his wife wouldn't let him spend the money to buy a subscription. Limbaugh said he'd personally come out to Fort Collins if Dan would organize a bake sale to raise money for the subscription. The result was "Dan's Bake Sale," which drew Limbaugh fans from all over the country and raised money not only for Dan's newsletter but also for charity.

My local station got behind the event by lining up buses to take our Limbaugh fans fifty miles north to Fort Collins.   15

Meanwhile, I had just gotten back into motorcycles — a couple of years late, I might add. As I tell my wife and all of my male friends circa fifty years of age, it's a male rite of passage to buy a motorcycle when you turn fifty. I was fifty-two, pushing fifty-three, and hadn't ridden one since I had a Honda 150 in the late 1960s.

A fellow motorcyclist called my show and said he didn't want to go to Dan's Bake Sale by bus, but that he and I should go on our scoots. That prompted a lot of on-air bravado, and I ended up leading a cavalcade of some forty bikes in front of that many more buses to Fort Collins. On the ride, I was dressed in black leather from head to toe and wearing a black helmet with a tinted face guard — exhibiting some resemblance to Darth Vader or — you got it — the Black Avenger. After that trip, the Black Avenger moniker stuck.

Over time, when asked why I called myself the Black Avenger, I must admit I started answering a bit flippantly, mocking the comic book characters of my youth: "Truth, justice, and the American way . . . honey."[2]

I added "honey" after a black caller, in all seriousness, challenged me, claiming that "truth, justice, and the American way" were not "black" values because these American principles weren't afforded to black people. He further insinuated that I was trying to "act white." Of course, I stood my ground.

I am an American first, I replied. Don't ask me to choose between this Republic and the color of my skin. If you're a Pan-Africanist or a black nationalist, you won't like that answer.   20

After thinking about the absurdity of this man trying to discount blacks as beneficiaries of the American Way, I decided to add "honey" with an

---

[1]*Myth of the Hobbled Black:* Hamblin's name for the notions that African Americans are helplessly victimized by past and present racial discrimination, that few blacks are successful in America, that blacks can't make it without special assistance.

[2]*Truth, justice, and the American way:* The values that Superman stands for.

ethnic ghetto drawl for the sole purpose of messing with self-righteous African Americans like him who still feed off the Myth of the Hobbled Black.

As a result of my appearance on C-Span, I received nearly 8,000 pieces of mail, more than 5,000 of them requesting the Certificate of Absolution. To this day I hear from people from all over America who remember the program, and my staff continues to fill orders for the certificate every week.

Needless to say, it warms my heart to know that so many white people are sleeping better at night, no longer writhing in pain brought about by their white guilt.

All joking aside, the extent of white guilt in this country is immense. It directly correlates with the endless depiction by the mass media of the profound pain that black people purportedly still suffer as a result of the years they were excluded from America's mainstream.

The constant reports of this pain and suffering that are broadcast   25 through the media, combined with the "blame whitey" syndrome that emanates from the black-trash[3] welfare culture, have caused some white Americans to suffer such a high degree of guilt that they have an almost fanatic desire to undo the injustices of slavery, perhaps beginning with guilt about not having delivered the forty acres and a mule promised to every Negro after the Civil War.

The greater majority of white Americans have passed on a nagging sense of social obligation from one generation to the next. After four or five generations, however, mass amnesia has set in. The people who are haunted by this guilt — the white majority, mainstream Americans obsessed with undoing this injustice — have forgotten exactly what their crime was. In fact, they have no idea what their particular crime was.

As is the case with my southern callers, most Americans can't trace their family tree back to the equivalent of Tara, the fictitious plantation in *Gone With the Wind,* or to the ownership of slaves. So the guilt no longer arises from having once personally owned slaves, be they black people or indentured Irishmen. The guilt now is imposed just because of a lack of melanin in their skin, just because they are white. Simply by virtue of the birth of a white child, another guilty American is created. It's as if we were talking about the burden of the national debt. That baby inherits the guilt of slavery, the guilt of an injustice of long, long ago.

Because of this guilt and the ongoing stories of black oppression, white people have been conditioned to accept just about any level of black rage and the illogical demands resulting from it.

All of which brings us back around to modern-day African-American revolutionaries like welfare queen Dorothy King.

---

[3]*black-trash:* Hamblin's counterpart to "white trash," these are black Americans who, in his words, are "unskilled and unemployed" and who "tend to be socially inept, possess limited education and few salable job skills."

Despite her crassness, in some ways King is very sophisticated. She   30
knowingly touches a little secret in white people who have been conditioned by years of hearing about black hardships — the little secret that they
are glad, they are relieved, to have been born white rather than a disen-
franchised minority. These white middle-class citizens — especially the
thirty- and forty-something crowd — have been inundated from the cradle
with news reports about the dreadful burden of being black in America —
reports of suffering the hardships of poverty, racism, and second-class
citizenship.

While going through college, these white folks saw liberal administrators and professors excuse low test scores from black students because of
these inherent hardships. They felt sorry for affirmative action students who
obviously must have been scared, because they refused to compete. And
though clearly this discrimination was self-imposed by the blacks themselves, they watched black students segregate themselves at all levels of
campus life — from African-American studies to African-American student
unions to African-American graduations — in essence implementing a
post–civil rights version of "white only" and "colored" sections.

These white people graduated, got married, and began family life in
comfortable suburbs . . . and bingo! They see Dorothy King on the nightly
TV news, cataloging all the black hardships they have been conditioned to
believe exist.

So when King makes absurd demands, like "give me" a house, these
guilt-ridden white people shy away from standing up to her with what
should be the logical American response: "Heavens no, we won't give you a
house. Go out and work for it."

Nope. They stay out of it. Because they fear that X-ray vision might dis-
cern their little secret — the secret that they are eternally thankful they are
white, and just having that thought makes them racists.

I have heard white Americans express so much racial guilt that, being   35
the old Catholic that I am, on some days I feel as though my radio show has
become a confessional.

Because of the earnestness with which these people come to my show,
it has dawned on me that if we as minority people, as black Americans, can't
cut a deal with these average white Americans who are sitting at the table
apologizing for the past, then we are a flawed and a lost people.

Or we are a disingenuous people who demand to prolong the negotiation with no intention of ever ending the strife and the separation, with no
intention of ever doing our part to fill up the moat between the races or of
getting on with the business of continuing to build a strong America that
will benefit all of us.

I have a bigger, more selfish reason for wanting to avenge white guilt,
however, a reason that goes beyond relieving the strain on white America.
Guilt almost certainly inspires pity for the injured party — in this case black
Americans. I contend that we can never stand tall as a people and expect to

be treated as equals so long as we allow ourselves to be patronized in this fashion.

I also hear from white people across the country who call my radio show and say essentially, "Get over it."

They respond to the poverty pimps' demands for more and more repa- 40 rations for black people by asking what credit they get for all the taxes they have paid to support decades of Great Society programs that benefited black recipients. They want consideration for the years of affirmative action that gave black Americans a pass to automatically step to the front of the employment line.

Those kinds of queries undoubtedly contribute to the notion that there are angry white men. And I am certain there are, in fact, some white men who are angry, perhaps even racist. But the truth is that, as a black man, I ask some of the same questions, albeit from a different perspective.

When will black people recognize that we are able and willing to stand on our own? When will we acknowledge that we are able and willing to stand side by side with other Americans to compete for jobs and our piece of the American Dream? When will we get over that ugly and unjust period in our American history and evolve into healthy citizens of this great country?

I don't perceive that the majority of white Americans I talk to are say- ing "Get over it" sarcastically in order to dismiss the subject or to lobby for a return to the days of yore.

Rather, I think they are saying to black Americans: "Get over it, because even if we haven't paid the bill in full, we certainly have made enough of an effort to make amends that you should acknowledge some sin- cerity on our part."

Personally, I heartily second the call to get over it. 45

I am absolutely convinced that if we black Americans unequivocally throw in our lot with mainstream America today, we have much more to gain in the future than we have lost in the past. We have more to gain by putting our energies into the pursuit of the American Dream than we have to gain by continuing to whine about being compensated for having been kept out of the game in the past. We have an opportunity to realize all the benefits of being an American in the name of all of those who came before us, those Negroes who were kept unfairly from the full potential of this great country.

I would go so far as to say that we *owe* it to our forefathers to seize the opportunity that they helped to make available to us by their own stalwart faith in the American Dream. I know that all of my life I have felt I owed it to my mother and her sisters to make something of myself, to achieve the level of success that they only dreamed would be possible in their new homeland.

Today mainstream America has opened its full society and culture to us. The white majority has supported legislation that makes the American Dream truly accessible to all black citizens.

Oh, sure, there's still the old-guard club or the snooty neighborhood where the members or residents may look down their noses at black newcomers. But I would wager that those scenarios are few and far between.

And I am also willing to bet that in most cases the feelings of discrimination and exclusion are self-imposed by xenophobic quota blacks.

In fact, some of today's cries of racism have become downright ludicrous.

I wrote a column in the *Denver Post* in the summer of 1994 about a group of Denver area black women who claimed that a white shopkeeper in a Western Slope mountain town "stripped away our dignity, making us feel frustrated and powerless" by making an offhand remark when they walked into his store.

It seems one of the women was complaining about the heat, and the shopkeeper responded, "Hey! Watermelon's not served until one o'clock."

When he realized the ladies were seriously offended, he reportedly tried to make light of the situation, but alas, the oppressed travelers bustled out the door and followed up by writing a critical letter to the editor of the local newspaper.

I wrote that had I been presented with the watermelon-serving schedule, I promptly would have inquired about the cantaloupe.

I don't doubt there are some angry white men. I'm still unconvinced that this shopkeeper was one of them, however.

More important is the fact that I am one black man who refuses to be shamed or made to feel powerless anymore by white bigots and racists. White folks can no longer intimidate me. I know better.

What I am constantly amazed at is how thin-skinned, how delicate, and how utterly afraid the beneficiaries of Dr. Martin Luther King's proud march for liberation have become.

Furthermore, as a black American, I am shamed by the Myth of the Hobbled Black. I am shamed that so many of my people have allowed themselves in one way or another to become part of the sham.

Someone must have the courage to kill this myth. Someone has to be embarrassed that, with the opportunities available to us today, so many black Americans remain in a declining state of existence in Dark Town. Someone has to be embarrassed for the great number of middle-class black Americans who live in seclusion, apparently afraid to celebrate their success as educated and sophisticated Americans.

Someone must speak out to avenge the mythical disability of the Hobbled Black, and I think it's only logical that successful middle-class black Americans take the lead to meet this challenge.

White liberals won't do it because they continue to feed off the myth in order to further their own political and social agenda. White conservatives who speak out about ending the welfare culture have no credibility. They are summarily labeled racists.

And so I have lobbed a loud salvo by declaring myself the Black Avenger, standing tall to dispel the Myth of the Hobbled Black. I am standing up to put an end to the decades of liberal propaganda which deny that today opportunity exists for any American man or woman willing to pursue it.

I fully understand that it's not easy to be black and publicly refute the Myth of the Hobbled Black, because the quota blacks, the poverty pimps, the African Americans, will do all in their collective power to try to de-black you: "You ain't black no more. You don't understand the pain and suffering. You forgot your roots, boy."

But their admonishments have nothing to do with pain and suffering.   65
The real reason they are trying to de-black me and people like me is that we are telling the truth. And the truth is that being poor and black does not give you an excuse to gang-bang, to ruin a city, to make parks unsafe, to terrorize senior citizens, and to denounce the American Dream.

I am not a mean person. But I have run the gauntlet of ghetto life, and I have survived. I understand the value of life. And I understand that being poor is never an excuse to become a mugger or a killer.

Like a lot of black babies, I started out on the lowest social rung. I was raised by women. I grew up on welfare. I lived on the toughest streets of New York.

But I was not raised to be black trash or to be a victim. I never went through a drug rehab center. I have never been a guest of the government beyond my enlistment in the service. I have never believed — because I was never told — that because of the color of my skin I could never get the fullest measure of opportunity in America.

When you are poor, you may be so busy trying to survive that you miss the opportunity to smell the roses. You may miss the pure joy of watching your children grow up. But none of that gives you a valid reason to disregard what's right and what's wrong.

I am one American who is saying no to the myth that all people of color are   70
weak, illiterate, potentially violent, and substandard in their expectations for themselves and their children as contributors to the community.

Despite the attempted intimidation emanating from the black-trash welfare culture, every day I hear from more and more healthy black Americans — and guilt-free white Americans — who are joining the crusade to tell the truth about black people and their good fortune to be Americans.

My personal adventure in America is at its pinnacle today because I am able to talk every day on my radio show with so many people from coast to coast and from all walks of life. I hear personally from hundreds more Americans off the air every day through the Internet and via letters to the editors of newspapers that carry my column.

And every day I am reassured that the heartbeat of America remains strong. I am reassured that the great majority of Americans maintain the true American spirit, the spirit that ultimately will make it possible for us to prevail.

I draw my strength from that heartbeat of America; it gives me the power to be the Black Avenger.

ENGAGING THE TEXT

1. Working in groups, summarize the central claims Hamblin makes about the United States and the American Dream. To what extent do you agree or disagree with these assertions, and why?

2. Assess Hamblin's assertion that some white Americans "suffer such a high degree of guilt that they have an almost fanatic desire to undo the injustices of slavery" (para. 25). Have you seen evidence of such a compulsion in the media, in your education or reading, in your community? Discuss.

3. Hamblin often uses language that is rhetorically daring, to say the least — language that is pointedly *not* politically correct. What do you think he means by the terms listed below? What effect does such language have on you as a reader?

   welfare queen (para. 29)
   poverty pimp (para. 40)
   quota blacks (para. 50)
   Dark Town (para. 60)

4. Review Hamblin's account of how he assumed his alias, "The Black Avenger" (paras. 13–18); note the various components of this persona, including the motorcycle and motorcycle outfit, the Darth Vader connection, the Superman/comic books connection, and his ghetto pronunciation of "honey." What impression do you think Hamblin is trying to create? How well do you think he succeeds?

EXPLORING CONNECTIONS

5. How closely do Hamblin's ideas about success mirror those of Horatio Alger in "Ragged Dick" (p. 264)? Brainstorm the kind of inspirational novel or screenplay Hamblin might write today — more than a century after Alger established the rags-to-riches genre.

6. How might Harlon Dalton (p. 278) or Toni Cade Bambara (p. 270) critique Hamblin's assertions about opportunities for African Americans?

7. Review these readings from Chapter Two, "Learning Power":

   Mike Rose, "I Just Wanna Be Average" (p. 161)
   Jean Anyon, from *Social Class and the Hidden Curriculum of Work* (p. 173)
   John Taylor Gatto, "Against School," (p. 152)

   How do these writers attempt to complicate or refute Hamblin's notions about success in contemporary America?

EXTENDING THE CRITICAL CONTEXT

8. In paragraph 31, Hamblin offers a brief description of black students segregating themselves on college campuses. How well would his description fit

your campus today? To what extent are ethnic groups segregated or self-segregated?

9. Choose the genre of current television you know best (for example, prime-time dramas, soap operas, reality TV, news, comedy shows, music videos, sports broadcasts) and discuss how it typically portrays how easy or difficult it is for African Americans to achieve success. Do you find evidence of "white guilt," the "Myth of the Hobbled Black," or the "'blame whitey' syndrome"? Overall, do you think current media representations of black success and failure are complex and realistic, or simplistic and biased?

Serving in Florida

Barbara Ehrenreich

If you're considering dropping out of college and settling into a comfy minimum-wage job (or two), please read this excerpt first. As a journalist preparing to write about working-class life, Barbara Ehrenreich decided to take a series of unglamorous jobs — waitressing, housecleaning, retail sales — and to live on the meager wages these jobs paid. In this narrative, Ehrenreich describes trying to make ends meet by adding a second waitressing job (at "Jerry's") to her eight-hour shift at "The Hearthside," having discovered that $2.43 an hour plus tips doesn't add up as fast as her rent and other bills. The full account of Ehrenreich's "plunge into poverty" may be found in the New York Times *best-seller* Nickel and Dimed: On (Not) Getting By in America *(2001). Ehrenreich (b. 1941) has published articles in many of America's leading magazines and newspapers. The most recent of her thirteen books is* Bait and Switch: The (Futile) Pursuit of the American Dream *(2005).*

Picture a fat person's hell, and I don't mean a place with no food. Instead there is everything you might eat if eating had no bodily consequences — the cheese fries, the chicken-fried steaks, the fudge-laden desserts — only here every bite must be paid for, one way or another, in human discomfort. The kitchen is a cavern, a stomach leading to the lower intestine that is the garbage and dishwashing area, from which issue bizarre smells combining the edible and the offal: creamy carrion, pizza barf, and that unique and enigmatic Jerry's[1] scent, citrus fart. The floor is slick with

---

[1]*Jerry's:* Not the real name of the restaurant where Ehrenreich worked; the restaurant was part of a "well-known national chain."

spills, forcing us to walk through the kitchen with tiny steps, like Susan McDougal in leg irons.[2] Sinks everywhere are clogged with scraps of lettuce, decomposing lemon wedges, water-logged toast crusts. Put your hand down on any counter and you risk being stuck to it by the film of ancient syrup spills, and this is unfortunate because hands are utensils here, used for scooping up lettuce onto the salad plates, lifting out pie slices, and even moving hash browns from one plate to another. The regulation poster in the single unisex rest room admonishes us to wash our hands thoroughly, and even offers instructions for doing so, but there is always some vital substance missing — soap, paper towels, toilet paper — and I never found all three at once. You learn to stuff your pockets with napkins before going in there, and too bad about the customers, who must eat, although they don't realize it, almost literally out of our hands.

The break room summarizes the whole situation: there is none, because there are no breaks at Jerry's. For six to eight hours in a row, you never sit except to pee. Actually, there are three folding chairs at a table immediately adjacent to the bathroom, but hardly anyone ever sits in this, the very rectum of the gastroarchitectural system. Rather, the function of the peri-toilet area is to house the ashtrays in which servers and dishwashers leave their cigarettes burning at all times, like votive candles, so they don't have to waste time lighting up again when they dash back here for a puff. Almost everyone smokes as if their pulmonary well-being depended on it — the multinational mélange of cooks; the dishwashers, who are all Czechs here; the servers, who are American natives — creating an atmosphere in which oxygen is only an occasional pollutant. My first morning at Jerry's, when the hypoglycemic shakes set in, I complain to one of my fellow servers that I don't understand how she can go so long without food. "Well, I don't understand how *you* can go so long without a cigarette," she responds in a tone of reproach. Because work is what you do for others; smoking is what you do for yourself. I don't know why the antismoking crusaders have never grasped the element of defiant self-nurturance that makes the habit so endearing to its victims — as if, in the American workplace, the only thing people have to call their own is the tumors they are nourishing and the spare moments they devote to feeding them.

Now, the Industrial Revolution is not an easy transition, especially, in my experience, when you have to zip through it in just a couple of days. I have gone from craft work straight into the factory, from the air-conditioned morgue of the Hearthside[3] directly into the flames. Customers arrive in human waves, sometimes disgorged fifty at a time from their tour buses, puckish and whiny. Instead of two "girls" on the floor at once, there can be as many as six of us running around in our brilliant pink-and-orange Hawaiian

[2]*Susan McDougal in leg irons:* McDougal refused to testify against President Bill Clinton and Hillary Clinton before the Whitewater grand jury in 1996; she spent almost twenty-two months in various prisons and eventually received a presidential pardon in 2001.

[3]*Hearthside:* The other restaurant where Ehrenreich worked.

shirts. Conversations, either with customers or with fellow employees, seldom last more than twenty seconds at a time. On my first day, in fact, I am hurt by my sister servers' coldness. My mentor for the day is a supremely competent, emotionally uninflected twenty-three-year-old, and the others, who gossip a little among themselves about the real reason someone is out sick today and the size of the bail bond someone else has had to pay, ignore me completely. On my second day, I find out why. "Well, it's good to see *you* again," one of them says in greeting. "Hardly anyone comes back after the first day." I feel powerfully vindicated — a survivor — but it would take a long time, probably months, before I could hope to be accepted into this sorority.

I start out with the beautiful, heroic idea of handling the two jobs at once, and for two days I almost do it: working the breakfast/lunch shift at Jerry's from 8:00 till 2:00, arriving at the Hearthside a few minutes late, at 2:10, and attempting to hold out until 10:00. In the few minutes I have between jobs, I pick up a spicy chicken sandwich at the Wendy's drive-through window, gobble it down in the car, and change from khaki slacks to black, from Hawaiian to rust-colored polo. There is a problem, though. When, during the 3:00–4:00 o'clock dead time, I finally sit down to wrap silver, my flesh seems to bond to the seat. I try to refuel with a purloined cup of clam chowder, as I've seen Gail and Joan do dozens of times, but Stu[4] catches me and hisses "No *eating!*" although there's not a customer around to be offended by the sight of food making contact with a server's lips. So I tell Gail I'm going to quit, and she hugs me and says she might just follow me to Jerry's herself.

But the chances of this are minuscule. She has left the flophouse and her annoying roommate and is back to living in her truck. But, guess what, she reports to me excitedly later that evening, Phillip has given her permission to park overnight in the hotel parking lot, as long as she keeps out of sight, and the parking lot should be totally safe since it's patrolled by a hotel security guard! With the Hearthside offering benefits like that, how could anyone think of leaving? This must be Phillip's theory, anyway. He accepts my resignation with a shrug, his main concern being that I return my two polo shirts and aprons.

Gail would have triumphed at Jerry's, I'm sure, but for me it's a crash course in exhaustion management. Years ago, the kindly fry cook who trained me to waitress at a Los Angeles truck stop used to say: Never make an unnecessary trip; if you don't have to walk fast, walk slow; if you don't have to walk, stand. But at Jerry's the effort of distinguishing necessary from unnecessary and urgent from whenever would itself be too much of an energy drain. The only thing to do is to treat each shift as a one-time-only emergency: you've got fifty starving people out there, lying scattered on the

5

---

[4]*Gail, Joan, Stu:* Waitress, hostess, and assistant manager at the Hearthside restaurant. Phillip, mentioned in the subsequent paragraph, is the top manager.

battlefield, so get out there and feed them! Forget that you will have to do this again tomorrow, forget that you will have to be alert enough to dodge the drunks on the drive home tonight — just burn, burn, burn! Ideally, at some point you enter what servers call a "rhythm" and psychologists term a "flow state," where signals pass from the sense organs directly to the muscles, bypassing the cerebral cortex, and a Zen-like emptiness sets in. I'm on a 2:00–10:00 P.M. shift now, and a male server from the morning shift tells me about the time he "pulled a triple" — three shifts in a row, all the way around the clock — and then got off and had a drink and met this girl, and maybe he shouldn't tell me this, but they had sex right then and there and it was like *beautiful*.

But there's another capacity of the neuromuscular system, which is pain. I start tossing back drugstore-brand ibuprofens as if they were vitamin C, four before each shift, because an old mouse-related repetitive-stress injury in my upper back has come back to full-spasm strength, thanks to the tray carrying. In my ordinary life, this level of disability might justify a day of ice packs and stretching. Here I comfort myself with the Aleve commercial where the cute blue-collar guy asks: If you quit after working four hours, what would your boss say? And the not-so-cute blue-collar guy, who's lugging a metal beam on his back, answers: He'd fire me, that's what. But fortunately, the commercial tells us, we workers can exert the same kind of authority over our painkillers that our bosses exert over us. If Tylenol doesn't want to work for more than four hours, you just fire its ass and switch to Aleve.

True, I take occasional breaks from this life, going home now and then to catch up on e-mail and for conjugal visits (though I am careful to "pay" for everything I eat here, at $5 for a dinner, which I put in a jar), seeing *The Truman Show*[5] with friends and letting them buy my ticket. And I still have those what-am-I-doing-here moments at work, when I get so homesick for the printed word that I obsessively reread the six-page menu. But as the days go by, my old life is beginning to look exceedingly strange. The e-mails and phone messages addressed to my former self come from a distant race of people with exotic concerns and far too much time on their hands. The neighborly market I used to cruise for produce now looks forbiddingly like a Manhattan yuppie emporium. And when I sit down one morning in my real home to pay bills from my past life, I am dazzled by the two- and three-figure sums owed to outfits like Club Body Tech and Amazon.com.

Management at Jerry's is generally calmer and more "professional" than at the Hearthside, with two exceptions. One is Joy, a plump, blowsy woman in her early thirties who once kindly devoted several minutes of her time to instructing me in the correct one-handed method of tray carrying but whose moods change disconcertingly from shift to shift and even within

---

[5]*The Truman Show*: 1998 film (directed by Peter Weir and starring Jim Carrey) about a man who discovers his whole life is actually a TV show.

one. The other is B.J., aka B.J. the Bitch, whose contribution is to stand by the kitchen counter and yell, "Nita, your order's up, move it!" or "Barbara, didn't you see you've got another table out there? Come *on*, girl!" Among other things, she is hated for having replaced the whipped cream squirt cans with big plastic whipped-cream-filled baggies that have to be squeezed with both hands — because, reportedly, she saw or thought she saw employees trying to inhale the propellant gas from the squirt cans, in the hope that it might be nitrous oxide. On my third night, she pulls me aside abruptly and brings her face so close that it looks like she's planning to butt me with her forehead. But instead of saying "You're fired," she says, "You're doing fine." The only trouble is I'm spending time chatting with customers: "That's how they're getting you." Furthermore I am letting them "run me," which means harassment by sequential demands: you bring the catsup and they decide they want extra Thousand Island; you bring that and they announce they now need a side of fries, and so on into distraction. Finally she tells me not to take her wrong. She tries to say things in a nice way, but "you get into a mode, you know, because everything has to move so fast."[6]

I mumble thanks for the advice, feeling like I've just been stripped   10
naked by the crazed enforcer of some ancient sumptuary law:[7] No chatting for *you*, girl. No fancy service ethic allowed for the serfs. Chatting with customers is for the good-looking young college-educated servers in the downtown carpaccio and ceviche joints, the kids who can make $70–$100 a night. What had I been thinking? My job is to move orders from tables to kitchen and then trays from kitchen to tables. Customers are in fact the major obstacle to the smooth transformation of information into food and food into money — they are, in short, the enemy. And the painful thing is that I'm beginning to see it this way myself. There are the traditional ass-hole types — frat boys who down multiple Buds and then make a fuss because the steaks are so emaciated and the fries so sparse — as well as the variously impaired — due to age, diabetes, or literacy issues — who require patient nutritional counseling. The worst, for some reason, are the Visible Christians — like the ten-person table, all jolly and sanctified after Sunday night service, who run me mercilessly and then leave me $1 on a $92 bill. Or the guy with the crucifixion T-shirt (SOMEONE TO LOOK UP TO) who complains that his baked potato is too hard and his iced tea too icy (I cheer-fully fix both) and leaves no tip at all. As a general rule, people wearing crosses or WWJD? ("What Would Jesus Do?") buttons look at us disapprovingly no matter what we do, as if they were confusing waitressing with Mary Magdalene's original profession.

---

[6]In *Workers in a Lean World: Unions in the International Economy* (Verso, 1997), Kim Moody cites studies finding an increase in stress-related workplace injuries and illness between the mid-1980s and the early 1990s. He argues that rising stress levels reflect a new system of "management by stress" in which workers in a variety of industries are being squeezed to extract maximum productivity, to the detriment of their health. [Ehrenreich's note.]

[7]*sumptuary laws:* Laws which regulate personal behavior on moral or religious grounds.

I make friends, over time, with the other "girls" who work my shift: Nita, the tattooed twenty-something who taunts us by going around saying brightly, "Have we started making money yet?" Ellen, whose teenage son cooks on the graveyard shift and who once managed a restaurant in Massachusetts but won't try out for management here because she prefers being a "common worker" and not "ordering people around." Easygoing fiftyish Lucy, with the raucous laugh, who limps toward the end of the shift because of something that has gone wrong with her leg, the exact nature of which cannot be determined without health insurance. We talk about the usual girl things — men, children, and the sinister allure of Jerry's chocolate peanut-butter cream pie — though no one, I notice, ever brings up anything potentially expensive, like shopping or movies. As at the Hearthside, the only recreation ever referred to is partying, which requires little more than some beer, a joint, and a few close friends. Still, no one is homeless, or cops to it anyway, thanks usually to a working husband or boyfriend. All in all, we form a reliable mutual-support group: if one of us is feeling sick or overwhelmed, another one will "bev" a table or even carry trays for her. If one of us is off sneaking a cigarette or a pee, the others will do their best to conceal her absence from the enforcers of corporate rationality.[8]

But my saving human connection — my oxytocin receptor, as it were — is George, the nineteen-year-old Czech dishwasher who has been in this country exactly one week. We get talking when he asks me, tortuously, how much cigarettes cost at Jerry's. I do my best to explain that they cost over a dollar more here than at a regular store and suggest that he just take one from the half-filled packs that are always lying around on the break table. But that would be unthinkable. Except for the one tiny earring signaling his allegiance to some vaguely alternative point of view, George is a perfect straight arrow — crew-cut, hardworking, and hungry for eye contact. "Czech Republic," I ask, "or Slovakia?" and he seems delighted that I know the difference. "Vaclav Havel," I try, "Velvet Revolution, Frank Zappa?" "Yes, yes, 1989," he says, and I realize that for him this is already history.

My project is to teach George English. "How are you today, George?" I say at the start of each shift. "I am good, and how are you today, Barbara?" I learn that he is not paid by Jerry's but by the "agent" who shipped him

---

[8]Until April 1998, there was no federally mandated right to bathroom breaks. According to Marc Linder and Ingrid Nygaard, authors of *Void Where Prohibited: Rest Breaks and the Right to Urinate on Company Time* (Cornell University Press, 1997), "The right to rest and void at work is not high on the list of social or political causes supported by professional or executive employees, who enjoy personal workplace liberties that millions of factory workers can only dream about.... While we were dismayed to discover that workers lacked an acknowledged right to void at work, [the workers] were amazed by outsiders' naïve belief that their employers would permit them to perform this basic bodily function when necessary.... A factory worker, not allowed a break for six-hour stretches, voided into pads worn inside her uniform; and a kindergarten teacher in a school without aides had to take all twenty children with her to the bathroom and line them up outside the stall door while she voided." [Ehrenreich's note.]

over — $5 an hour, with the agent getting the dollar or so difference between that and what Jerry's pays dishwashers. I learn also that he shares an apartment with a crowd of other Czech "dishers," as he calls them, and that he cannot sleep until one of them goes off for his shift, leaving a vacant bed. We are having one of our ESL sessions late one afternoon when B.J. catches us at it and orders "Joseph" to take up the rubber mats on the floor near the dishwashing sinks and mop underneath. "I thought your name was George," I say loud enough for B.J. to hear as she strides off back to the counter. Is she embarrassed? Maybe a little, because she greets me back at the counter with "George, Joseph — there are so many of them!" I say nothing, neither nodding nor smiling, and for this I am punished later, when I think I am ready to go and she announces that I need to roll fifty more sets of silverware, and isn't it time I mixed up a fresh four-gallon batch of blue-cheese dressing? May you grow old in this place, B.J., is the curse I beam out at her when I am finally permitted to leave. May the syrup spills glue your feet to the floor.

I make the decision to move closer to Key West. First, because of the drive. Second and third, also because of the drive: gas is eating up $4–$5 a day, and although Jerry's is as high-volume as you can get, the tips average only 10 percent, and not just for a newbie like me. Between the base pay of $2.15 an hour and the obligation to share tips with the busboys and dish-washers, we're averaging only about $7.50 an hour. Then there is the $30 I had to spend on the regulation tan slacks worn by Jerry's servers — a set-back it could take weeks to absorb. (I had combed the town's two downscale department stores hoping for something cheaper but decided in the end that these marked-down Dockers, originally $49, were more likely to survive a daily washing.) Of my fellow servers, everyone who lacks a working husband or boyfriend seems to have a second job: Nita does something at a computer eight hours a day; another welds. Without the forty-five-minute commute, I can picture myself working two jobs and still having the time to shower between them.

So I take the $500 deposit I have coming from my landlord, the $400 I have earned toward the next month's rent, plus the $200 reserved for emer-gencies, and use the $1,100 to pay the rent and deposit on trailer number

15

46 in the Overseas Trailer Park, a mile from the cluster of budget hotels that constitute Key West's version of an industrial park. Number 46 is about eight feet in width and shaped like a barbell inside, with a narrow region — because of the sink and the stove — separating the bedroom from what might optimistically be called the "living" area, with its two-person table and half-sized couch. The bathroom is so small my knees rub against the shower stall when I sit on the toilet, and you can't just leap out of the bed, you have to climb down to the foot of it in order to find a patch of floor space to stand on. Outside, I am within a few yards of a liquor store, a bar that advertises "free beer tomorrow," a convenience store, and a Burger King — but no supermarket or, alas, Laundromat. By reputation, the Overseas park is a nest of crime and crack, and I am hoping at least for some vibrant multicultural street life. But desolation rules night and day, except for a thin stream of pedestrians heading for their jobs at the Sheraton or the 7-Eleven. There are not exactly people here but what amounts to canned labor, being preserved between shifts from the heat.

In line with my reduced living conditions, a new form of ugliness arises at Jerry's. First we are confronted — via an announcement on the computers through which we input orders — with the new rule that the hotel bar, the Driftwood, is henceforth off-limits to restaurant employees. The culprit, I learn through the grapevine, is the ultraefficient twenty-three-year-old who trained me — another trailer home dweller and a mother of three. Something had set her off one morning, so she slipped out for a nip and returned to the floor impaired. The restriction mostly hurts Ellen, whose habit it is to free her hair from its rubber band and drop by the Driftwood for a couple of Zins[9] before heading home at the end of her shift, but all of us feel the chill. Then the next day, when I go for straws, I find the dry-storage room locked. It's never been locked before; we go in and out of it all day — for napkins, jelly containers, Styrofoam cups for takeout. Vic, the portly assistant manager who opens it for me, explains that he caught one of the dishwashers attempting to steal something and, unfortunately, the miscreant will be with us until a replacement can be found — hence the locked door. I neglect to ask what he had been trying to steal but Vic tells me who he is — the kid with the buzz cut and the earring, you know, he's back there right now.

I wish I could say I rushed back and confronted George to get his side of the story. I wish I could say I stood up to Vic and insisted that George be given a translator and allowed to defend himself or announced that I'd find a lawyer who'd handle the case pro bono.[10] At the very least I should have testified as to the kid's honesty. The mystery to me is that there's not much worth stealing in the dry-storage room, at least not in any fenceable quantity: "Is Gyorgi here, and am having 200 — maybe 250 — catsup packets. What do you say?" My guess is that he had taken — if he had taken anything at

[9]*Zins:* Glasses of zinfandel wine.
[10]*pro bono:* Free of charge.

all — some Saltines or a can of cherry pie mix and that the motive for taking
it was hunger.

So why didn't I intervene? Certainly not because I was held back by the
kind of moral paralysis that can mask as journalistic objectivity. On the contrary, something new — something loathsome and servile — had infected
me, along with the kitchen odors that I could still sniff on my bra when I
finally undressed at night. In real life I am moderately brave, but plenty
of brave people shed their courage in POW camps, and maybe something
similar goes on in the infinitely more congenial milieu of the low-wage
American workplace. Maybe, in a month or two more at Jerry's, I might
have regained my crusading spirit. Then again, in a month or two I might
have turned into a different person altogether — say, the kind of person
who would have turned George in.

But this is not something I was slated to find out. When my month-long
plunge into poverty was almost over, I finally landed my dream job —
housekeeping. I did this by walking into the personnel office of the only
place I figured I might have some credibility, the hotel attached to Jerry's,
and confiding urgently that I had to have a second job if I was to pay my
rent and, no, it couldn't be front-desk clerk. "All *right*," the personnel lady
fairly spits, "so it's *housekeeping*," and marches me back to meet Millie, the
housekeeping manager, a tiny, frenetic Hispanic woman who greets me as
"babe" and hands me a pamphlet emphasizing the need for a positive attitude. The pay is $6.10 an hour and the hours are nine in the morning till
"whenever," which I am hoping can be defined as a little before two. I don't
have to ask about health insurance once I meet Carlotta, the middle-aged
African American woman who will be training me. Carlie, as she tells me to
call her, is missing all of her top front teeth.

On that first day of housekeeping and last day — although I don't yet   20
know it's the last — of my life as a low-wage worker in Key West, Carlie is in a
foul mood. We have been given nineteen rooms to clean, most of them
"checkouts," as opposed to "stay-overs," and requiring the whole enchilada of
bed stripping, vacuuming, and bathroom scrubbing. When one of the rooms
that had been listed as a stay-over turns out to be a checkout, she calls Millie to
complain, but of course to no avail. "So make up the motherfucker," she orders
me, and I do the beds while she sloshes around the bathroom. For four hours
without a break I strip and remake beds, taking about four and a half minutes
per queen-sized bed, which I could get down to three if there were any reason
to. We try to avoid vacuuming by picking up the larger specks by hand, but
often there is nothing to do but drag the monstrous vacuum cleaner — it
weighs about thirty pounds — off our cart and try to wrestle it around the
floor. Sometimes Carlie hands me the squirt bottle of "Bam" (an acronym for
something that begins, ominously, with "butyric" — the rest of it has been
worn off the label) and lets me do the bathrooms. No service ethic challenges
me here to new heights of performance. I just concentrate on removing the
pubic hairs from the bathtubs, or at least the dark ones that I can see.

I had looked forward to the breaking-and-entering aspect of cleaning the stay-overs, the chance to examine the secret physical existence of strangers. But the contents of the rooms are always banal and surprisingly neat — zipped-up shaving kits, shoes lined up against the wall (there are no closets), flyers for snorkeling trips, maybe an empty wine bottle or two. It is the TV that keeps us going, from Jerry to Sally to *Hawaii Five-O* and then on to the soaps. If there's something especially arresting, like "Won't Take No for an Answer" on Jerry, we sit down on the edge of a bed and giggle for a moment, as if this were a pajama party instead of a terminally dead-end job. The soaps are the best, and Carlie turns the volume up full blast so she won't miss anything from the bathroom or while the vacuum is on. In Room 503, Marcia confronts Jeff about Lauren. In 505, Lauren taunts poor cheated-on Marcia. In 511, Helen offers Amanda $10,000 to stop seeing Eric, prompting Carlie to emerge from the bathroom to study Amanda's troubled face. "You take it, girl," she advises. "I would for sure."

The tourists' rooms that we clean and, beyond them, the far more expensively appointed interiors in the soaps begin after a while to merge. We have entered a better world — a world of comfort where every day is a day off, waiting to be filled with sexual intrigue. We are only gate-crashers in this fantasy, however, forced to pay for our presence with backaches and perpetual thirst. The mirrors, and there are far too many of them in hotel rooms, contain the kind of person you would normally find pushing a shopping cart down a city street — bedraggled, dressed in a damp hotel polo shirt two sizes too large, and with sweat dribbling down her chin like drool. I am enormously relieved when Carlie announces a half-hour meal break, but my appetite fades when I see that the bag of hot dog rolls she has been carrying around on our cart is not trash salvaged from a checkout but what she has brought for her lunch.

Between the TV and the fact that I'm in no position, as a first dayer, to launch new topics of conversation, I don't learn much about Carlie except that she hurts, and in more than one way. She moves slowly about her work, muttering something about joint pain, and this is probably going to doom her, since the young immigrant housekeepers — Polish and Salvadoran — like to polish off their rooms by two in the afternoon, while she drags the work out till six. It doesn't make any sense to hurry, she observes, when you're being paid by the hour. Already, management has brought in a woman to do what sounds like time-motion studies and there's talk about switching to paying by the room.[11] She broods, too, about all the little evidences of disrespect that come her way, and not only from management. "They don't care about us," she tells me of the hotel guests; in fact, they don't notice us at all unless something gets stolen from a room — "then they're all over you." We're eating our lunch side by side in the break room

<hr>

[11]A few weeks after I left, I heard ads on the radio for housekeeping jobs at this hotel at the amazing rate of "up to $9 an hour." When I inquired, I found out that the hotel had indeed started paying by the room, and I suspect that Carlie, if she lasted, was still making the equivalent of $6 an hour or quite a bit less. [Ehrenreich's note.]

when a white guy in a maintenance uniform walks by and Carlie calls out, "Hey you," in a friendly way, "what's your name?"

"Peter Pan," he says, his back already to us.

"That wasn't funny," Carlie says, turning to me. "That was no kind of   25
answer. Why did he have to be funny like that?" I venture that he has an attitude, and she nods as if that were an acute diagnosis. "Yeah, he got a attitude all right."

"Maybe he's a having a bad day," I elaborate, not because I feel any obligation to defend the white race but because her face is so twisted with hurt.

When I request permission to leave at about 3:30, another housekeeper warns me that no one has so far succeeded in combining housekeeping with serving at Jerry's: "Some kid did it once for five days, and you're no kid." With that helpful information in mind, I rush back to number 46, down four Advils (the name brand this time), shower, stooping to fit into the stall, and attempt to compose myself for the oncoming shift. So much for what Marx termed the "reproduction of labor power," meaning the things a worker has to do just so she'll be ready to labor again. The only unforeseen obstacle to the smooth transition from job to job is that my tan Jerry's slacks, which had looked reasonably clean by 40-watt bulb last night when I hand washed my Hawaiian shirt, prove by daylight to be mottled with catsup and ranch-dressing stains. I spend most of my hour-long break between jobs attempting to remove the edible portions of the slacks with a sponge and then drying them over the hood of my car in the sun.

I can do this two-job thing, is my theory, if I can drink enough caffeine and avoid getting distracted by George's ever more obvious suffering.[12] The first few days after the alleged theft, he seemed not to understand the trouble he was in, and our chirpy little conversations had continued. But the last couple of shifts he's been listless and unshaven, and tonight he looks like the ghost we all know him to be, with dark half-moons hanging from his eyes. At one point, when I am briefly immobilized by the task of filling little paper cups with sour cream for baked potatoes, he comes over and looks as if he'd like to explore the limits of our shared vocabulary, but I am called to the floor for a table. I resolve to give him all my tips that night, and to hell with the experiment in low-wage money management. At eight, Ellen and I grab a snack together standing at the mephitic end of the kitchen counter, but I can only manage two or three mozzarella sticks, and lunch had been a mere handful of McNuggets. I am not tired at all, I assure myself, though it may be that there is simply no more "I" left to do the tiredness monitoring. What I would see if I were more alert to the situation is that the forces of

[12]In 1996 the number of persons holding two or more jobs averaged 7.8 million, or 6.2 percent of the workforce. It was about the same rate for men and for women (6.1 versus 6.2). About two-thirds of multiple jobholders work one job full-time and the other part-time. Only a heroic minority — 4 percent of men and 2 percent of women — work two full-time jobs simultaneously (John F. Stinson Jr., "New Data on Multiple Jobholding Available from the CPS," *Monthly Labor Review,* March 1997). [Ehrenreich's note.]

destruction are already massing against me. There is only one cook on duty, a young man named Jesus ("Hay-Sue," that is), and he is new to the job. And there is Joy, who shows up to take over in the middle of the shift dressed in high heels and a long, clingy white dress and fuming as if she'd just been stood up in some cocktail bar.

Then it comes, the perfect storm. Four of my tables fill up at once. Four tables is nothing for me now, but only so long as they are obligingly staggered. As I bev table 27, tables 25, 28, and 24 are watching enviously. As I bev 25, 24 glowers because their bevs haven't even been ordered. Twenty-eight is four yuppyish types, meaning everything on the side and agonizing instructions as to the chicken Caesars. Twenty-five is a middle-aged black couple who complain, with some justice, that the iced tea isn't fresh and the tabletop is sticky. But table 24 is the meteorological event of the century: ten British tourists who seem to have made the decision to absorb the American experience entirely by mouth. Here everyone has at least two drinks — iced tea *and* milk shake, Michelob *and* water (with lemon slice in the water, please) — and a huge, promiscuous orgy of break-fast specials, mozz sticks, chicken strips, quesadillas, burgers with cheese and without, sides of hash browns with cheddar, with onions, with gravy, seasoned fries, plain fries, banana splits. Poor Jesus! Poor me! Because when I arrive with their first tray of food — after three prior trips just to refill bevs — Princess Di refuses to eat her chicken strips with her pancake and sausage special since, as she now reveals, the strips were meant to be an appetizer. Maybe the others would have accepted their meals, but Di, who is deep into her third Michelob, insists that everything else go back while they work on their starters. Meanwhile, the yuppies are waving me down for more decaf and the black couple looks ready to summon the NAACP.

Much of what happens next is lost in the fog of war. Jesus starts going under. The little printer in front of him is spewing out orders faster than he can rip them off, much less produce the meals. A menacing restlessness rises from the tables, all of which are full. Even the invincible Ellen is ashen from stress. I take table 24 their reheated main courses, which they imme-diately reject as either too cold or fossilized by the microwave. When I return to the kitchen with their trays (three trays in three trips) Joy con-fronts me with arms akimbo: "What *is* this?" She means the food — the plates of rejected pancakes, hash browns in assorted flavors, toasts, burgers, sausages, eggs. "Uh, scrambled with cheddar," I try, "and that's — " "*No,*" she screams in my face, "is it a traditional, a super-scramble, an eye-opener?" I pretend to study my check for a clue, but entropy has been up to its tricks, not only on the plates but in my head, and I have to admit that the original order is beyond reconstruction. "You don't know an eye-opener from a traditional?" she demands in outrage. All I know, in fact, is that my legs have lost interest in the current venture and have announced their intention to fold. I am saved by a yuppie (mercifully not one of mine) who chooses this moment to charge into the kitchen to bellow that his food is twenty-five minutes late. Joy screams at him to get the hell out of her

30

kitchen, *please,* and then turns on Jesus in a fury, hurling an empty tray across the room for emphasis.

I leave. I don't walk out, I just leave. I don't finish my side work or pick up my credit card tips, if any, at the cash register or, of course, ask Joy's permission to go. And the surprising thing is that you *can* walk out without permission, that the door opens, that the thick tropical night air parts to let me pass, that my car is still parked where I left it. There is no vindication in this exit, no fuck-you surge of relief, just an overwhelming dank sense of failure pressing down on me and the entire parking lot. I had gone into this venture in the spirit of science, to test a mathematical proposition, but somewhere along the line, in the tunnel vision imposed by long shifts and relentless concentration, it became a test of myself, and clearly I have failed. Not only had I flamed out as a housekeeper/server, I had forgotten to give George my tips, and, for reasons perhaps best known to hardworking, generous people like Gail and Ellen, this hurts. I don't cry, but I am in a position to realize, for the first time in many years, that the tear ducts are still there and still capable of doing their job.

When I moved out of the trailer park, I gave the key to number 46 to Gail and arranged for my deposit to be transferred to her. She told me that Joan was still living in her van and that Stu had been fired from the Hearthside. According to the most up-to-date rumors, the drug he ordered from the restaurant was crack and he was caught dipping into the cash register to pay for it. I never found out what happened to George.

Engaging the Text

1. What's the point of Ehrenreich's experiment? What do you think she was hoping to learn by stepping down the economic ladder, and what can you learn as her reader? Explain why you find her approach more or less effective than one that provides economic data and analysis.

2. Throughout this selection Ehrenreich seeks not merely to narrate facts but to elicit emotional and other responses from her readers. For one or more of the passages listed below, explain what response you think Ehrenreich is after and what *specific* methods she uses to evoke it:

    the opening description of Jerry's (paras. 1–2)

    the description of customers (para. 10)

    George's story (paras. 12–13, 16–18)

    the description of trailer number 46 (para. 15)

    the footnotes throughout the narrative

3. Ehrenreich ordinarily lives much more comfortably than she did as a waitress, and of course she had an escape hatch from her experiment — she would not serve food or clean rooms forever and could have gone back to her usual life if necessary at any time. Explain the effect her status as a "tourist" in working-class culture has on you as a reader.

4. Write a journal entry about your worst job. How did your experience of being "nickeled and dimed" compare with Ehrenreich's? What was the worst aspect of this work experience for you?

EXPLORING CONNECTIONS

5. What, if anything, do you think Gail, Ellen, and George could do to substantially improve their material and economic well-being? What are the greatest barriers they face? What advice might Horatio Alger (p. 264) or Ken Hamblin (p. 285) give them, and how do you think it would be received?
6. Using Gail, Ellen, or George as a rough model for your central character, write a detailed plot summary for a novel that would be the anti–*Ragged Dick*, a story in which someone pursues the American Dream and fails. How plausible is your story line compared to the one Horatio Alger created for Ragged Dick (p. 264)?

EXTENDING THE CRITICAL CONTEXT

7. Ehrenreich made $6.10 per hour as a housekeeper. Working in groups, sketch out a monthly budget based on this salary for (a) an individual, (b) a single parent with a preteen child, and (c) a family of four in which one adult is ill or has been laid off. Be sure to include money for basics like rent, utilities, food, clothing, transportation, and medical care.
8. Check local want ads and shop windows to identify some of the least promising job prospects in your community. Talk to potential employers and learn as much as you can about such issues as wages, working conditions, hours, drug screening, and healthcare, retirement, or other benefits.
9. Order a meal at whichever restaurant in your community is most like "Jerry's." Study the working conditions in the restaurant, paying special attention to the kinds of problems Ehrenreich faced on her shifts. Write up an informal journal entry from the imagined point of view of a server at the restaurant.

Class in America — 2003

GREGORY MANTSIOS

Which of these gifts might a high school graduate in your family receive — a corsage, a savings bond, or a BMW? The answer indicates your social class, a key factor in American lives that many of us conspire to ignore. The selection below, however, makes it hard to deny class distinctions and their nearly universal influence on our lives. The essay juxtaposes myths and realities: Mantsios (b. 1950) outlines four widely held beliefs about class in the United States and then systematically refutes them with statistical evidence. Even if your eyes are already open to the existence of classes in the United States, some of the numbers the author cites are likely to surprise you. Mantsios is director of the Labor Resource Center at Queens College of the City University of New York and editor of A New Labor Movement for the New Century *(1998). The essay reprinted below appeared in* Race, Class, and Gender in the United States: An Integrated Study, *edited by Paula S. Rothenberg (2004).*

People in the United States don't like to talk about class. Or so it would seem. We don't speak about class privileges, or class oppression, or the class nature of society. These terms are not part of our everyday vocabulary, and in most circles they are associated with the language of the rhetorical fringe. Unlike people in most other parts of the world, we shrink from using words that classify along economic lines or that point to class distinctions: phrases like "working class," "upper class," and "ruling class" are rarely uttered by Americans.

For the most part, avoidance of class-laden vocabulary crosses class boundaries. There are few among the poor who speak of themselves as lower class; instead, they refer to their race, ethnic group, or geographic location. Workers are more likely to identify with their employer, industry, or occupational group than with other workers, or with the working class.[1]

Neither are those at the other end of the economic spectrum likely to use the word "class." In her study of thirty-eight wealthy and socially prominent women, Susan Ostrander asked participants if they considered themselves members of the upper class. One participant responded, "I hate to use the word 'class.' We are responsible, fortunate people, old families, the people who have something."

Another said, "I hate [the term] upper class. It is so non–upper class to use it. I just call it 'all of us,' those who are wellborn."[2]

It is not that Americans, rich or poor, aren't keenly aware of class 5 differences — those quoted above obviously are; it is that class is not in the domain of public discourse. Class is not discussed or debated in public because class identity has been stripped from popular culture. The institu-

---

[1] See Jay MacLead, *Ain't No Makin' It: Aspirations and Attainment in a Lower-Income Neighborhood* (Boulder, CO: Westview Press, 1995); Benjamin DeMott, *The Imperial Middle* (New York: Morrow, 1990); Ira Katznelson, *City Trenches: Urban Politics and Patterning of Class in the United States* (New York: Pantheon Books, 1981); Charles W. Tucker, "A Comparative Analysis of Subjective Social Class: 1945–1963," *Social Forces*, no. 46, June 1968, pp. 508–514; Robert Nisbet, "The Decline and Fall of Social Class," *Pacific Sociological Review*, vol. 2, Spring 1959, pp. 11–17; and Oscar Glantz, "Class Consciousness and Political Solidarity," *American Sociological Review*, vol. 23, August 1958, pp. 375–382.

[2] Susan Ostander, "Upper-Class Women: Class Consciousness as Conduct and Meaning," in G. William Domhoff, *Power Structure Research* (Beverly Hills, CA: Sage Publications, 1980, pp. 78–79). Also see Stephen Birmingham, *America's Secret Aristocracy* (Boston: Little Brown, 1987).

tions that shape mass culture and define the parameters of public debate have avoided class issues. In politics, in primary and secondary education, and in the mass media, formulating issues in terms of class is unacceptable, perhaps even un-American.

There are, however, two notable exceptions to this phenomenon. First, it is acceptable in the United States to talk about "the middle class." Interestingly enough, such references appear to be acceptable precisely because they mute class differences. References to the middle class by politicians, for example, are designed to encompass and attract the broadest possible constituency. Not only do references to the middle class gloss over differences, but these references also avoid any suggestion of conflict or exploitation.

This leads us to the second exception to the class-avoidance phenomenon. We are, on occasion, presented with glimpses of the upper class and the lower class (the language used is "the wealthy" and "the poor"). In the media, these presentations are designed to satisfy some real or imagined voyeuristic need of "the ordinary person." As curiosities, the ground-level view of street life and the inside look at the rich and the famous serve as unique models, one to avoid and one to aspire to. In either case, the two models are presented without causal relation to each other: one is not rich because the other is poor.

Similarly, when social commentators or liberal politicians draw attention to the plight of the poor, they do so in a manner that obscures the class structure and denies class exploitation. Wealth and poverty are viewed as one of several natural and inevitable states of being: differences are only differences. One may even say differences are the American way, a reflection of American social diversity.

We are left with one of two possibilities: either talking about class and recognizing class distinctions are not relevant to U.S. society, or we mistakenly hold a set of beliefs that obscure the reality of class differences and their impact on people's lives.

Let us look at four common, albeit contradictory, beliefs about the   10 United States.

Myth 1: The United States is fundamentally a classless society. Class distinctions are largely irrelevant today, and whatever differences do exist in economic standing, they are — for the most part — insignificant. Rich or poor, we are all equal in the eyes of the law, and such basic needs as health care and education are provided to all regardless of economic standing.

Myth 2: We are, essentially, a middle-class nation. Despite some variations in economic status, most Americans have achieved relative affluence in what is widely recognized as a consumer society.

Myth 3: We are all getting richer. The American public as a whole is steadily moving up the economic ladder, and each generation propels itself to greater economic well-being. Despite some fluctuations, the U.S. position in the global economy has brought previously unknown prosperity to most, if not all, Americans.

Myth 4: Everyone has an equal chance to succeed. Success in the United States requires no more than hard work, sacrifice, and perseverance:

"In America, anyone can become a millionaire; it's just a matter of being in the right place at the right time."

In trying to assess the legitimacy of these beliefs, we want to ask several 15 important questions. Are there significant class differences among Americans? If these differences do exist, are they getting bigger or smaller, and do these differences have a significant impact on the way we live? Finally, does everyone in the United States really have an equal opportunity to succeed?

The Economic Spectrum

Let's begin by looking at difference. An examination of available data reveals that variations in economic well-being are, in fact, immense. Consider the following:

- The wealthiest 1 percent of the American population holds 38 percent of the total national wealth. That is, they own well over one-third of all the consumer durables (such as houses, cars, and stereos) and financial assets (such as stocks, bonds, property, and savings accounts). The richest 20 percent of Americans hold 83 percent of the total household wealth in the country.[3]
- Approximately 241,000 Americans, or approximately three quarters of 1 percent of the adult population, earn more than $1 million *annually*, with many of these individuals earning over $10 million and some earning over $100 million. It would take the average American, earning $34,000 per year, more than 65 *lifetimes* to earn $100 million.[4]

Affluence and prosperity are clearly alive and well in certain segments of the U.S. population. However, this abundance is in contrast to the poverty and despair that is also prevalent in the United States. At the other end of the spectrum:

- Approximately 12 percent of the American population — that is, nearly one of every eight people in this country — live below the official poverty line (calculated in 2001 at $9,214 for an individual and $17,960 for a family of four).[5] Among the poor are over 2.3 million homeless, including nearly 1 million homeless children.[6]

---

[3] Lawrence Mishel, Jared Bernstein, and Heather Boushey, *The State of Working America: 2002–03* (Ithaca, NY: ILR Press, Cornell University Press, 2003, p. 277).

[4] The number of individuals filing tax returns showing a gross adjusted income of $1 million or more in 2000 was 241,068 (Tax Stats at a Glance, Internal Revenue Service, U.S. Treasury Department, available at www.irs.ustreas.gov/taxstats/article/0,,id=102886,99. html).

[5] Bernadette D. Proctor and Joseph Dalaker, "U.S. Census Bureau, Current Population Reports," *Poverty in the United States: 2001* (Washington, DC: U.S. Government Printing Office, 2002, pp. 1–5).

[6] Martha Burt, "A New Look at Homelessness in America" (Washington, DC: The Urban Institute, February 2000).

- Approximately one out of every five children in the United States under the age of six lives in poverty.[7]

The contrast between rich and poor is sharp, and with nearly one-third of the American population living at one extreme or the other, it is difficult to argue that we live in a classless society. Big-payoff reality shows, celebrity salaries, and multimillion dollar lotteries notwithstanding, evidence suggests that the level of inequality in the United States is getting higher. Census data show the gap between the rich and the poor to be the widest since the government began collecting information in 1947[8] and that this gap is continuing to grow. While four out of five households in the United States saw their share of net worth fall between 1992 and 2000, households in the top fifth of the population saw their share increase from 59 percent to 63 percent.[9]

Nor is such a gap between rich and poor representative of the rest of the industrialized world. In fact, the United States has by far the most unequal distribution of household income.[10] The income gap between rich and poor in the United States (measured as the percentage of total income held by the wealthiest 20 percent of the population versus the poorest 20 percent) is approximately 11 to 1, one of the highest ratios in the industrialized world. The ratio in Japan and Germany, by contrast, is 4 to 1.[11]

Reality 1:   There are enormous differences in the economic standing   20
of American citizens. A sizable proportion of the U.S. population occupies opposite ends of the economic spectrum. In the middle range of the economic spectrum:

- Sixty percent of the American population holds less than 6 percent of the nation's wealth.[12]
- While the real income of the top 1 percent of U.S. families skyrocketed by 59 percent during the economic boom of the late 1990s, the income of the middle fifth of the population grew only slightly and its share of income (15 percent of the total compared to 48 percent of the total for the wealthiest fifth), actually declined during this same period.[13]
- Regressive changes in governmental tax policies and the weakening of labor unions over the last quarter century have led to a significant

---

[7] Proctor and Dalaker, op. cit., p. 4.

[8] Mishel et al., op. cit., p. 53.

[9] Mishel et al., ibid., p. 280.

[10] Based on a comparison of 19 industrialized states: Mishel et al., ibid., pp. 411–412.

[11] See The Center on Budget and Policy Priorities, Economic Policy Institute, "Pulling Apart: State-by-State Analysis of Income Trends," January 2000, fact sheet; "Current Population Reports: Consumer Income" (Washington, DC: U.S. Department of Commerce, 1993); The World Bank, "World Development Report: 1992" (Washington, DC: International Bank for Reconstruction and Development, 1992); The World Bank, "World Development Report 1999/2000," pp. 238–239.

[12] Derived from Mishel et al., op. cit., p. 281.

[13] Mishel et al., ibid., p. 54.

rise in the level of inequality between the rich and the middle class. Between 1979 and 2000, the gap in household income between the top fifth and middle fifth of the population rose by 31 percent.[14] During the economic boom of the 1990s, four out of five Americans saw their share of net worth decline, while the top fifth saw their share increase from 59 percent to 63 percent.[15] One prominent economist described economic growth in the United States as a "spectator sport for the majority of American families."[16] Economic decline, on the other hand, is much more "inclusive," with layoffs impacting hardest on middle- and lower-income families — those with fewer resources to fall back on.

The level of inequality is sometimes difficult to comprehend fully by looking at dollar figures and percentages. To help his students visualize the distribution of income, the well-known economist Paul Samuelson asked them to picture an income pyramid made of children's blocks, with each layer of blocks representing $1,000. If we were to construct Samuelson's pyramid today, the peak of the pyramid would be much higher than the Eiffel Tower, yet almost all of us would be within six feet of the ground.[17] In other words, the distribution of income is heavily skewed; a small minority of families take the lion's share of national income, and the remaining income is distributed among the vast majority of middle-income and low-income families. Keep in mind that Samuelson's pyramid represents the distribution of income, not wealth. The distribution of wealth is skewed even further.

Reality 2:   The middle class in the United States holds a very small share of the nation's wealth and that share is declining steadily. The gap between rich and poor and between rich and the middle class is larger than it has ever been.

American Life-Styles

At last count, nearly 33 million Americans across the nation lived in unrelenting poverty.[18] Yet, as political scientist Michael Harrington once commented, "America has the best dressed poverty the world has ever known."[19] Clothing disguises much of the poverty in the United States, and this may explain, in part, its middle-class image. With increased mass marketing of "designer" clothing and with shifts in the nation's economy from blue-collar (and often better-paying) manufacturing jobs to white-collar and pink-collar jobs in the service sector, it is becoming increasingly difficult to

[14] Mishel et al., ibid., p. 70.

[15] Mishel et al., ibid., p. 280.

[16] Alan Blinder, quoted by Paul Krugman, in "Disparity and Despair," *U.S. News and World Report,* March 23, 1992, p. 54.

[17] Paul Samuelson, *Economics,* 10th ed. (New York: McGraw-Hill, 1976, p. 84).

[18] Joseph Dalaker, "U.S. Census Bureau, Current Population Reports, series P60–207," *Poverty in the United States: 1998* (Washington, DC: U.S. Government Printing Office, 1999, p. v).

[19] Michael Harrington, *The Other America* (New York: Macmillan, 1962, pp. 12–13).

distinguish class differences based on appearance.[20] The dress-down environment prevalent in the high-tech industry (what one author refers to as the "no-collars movement") has reduced superficial distinctions even further.[21]

Beneath the surface, there is another reality. Let's look at some "typical" and not-so-typical life-styles.

American Profile

Name:	Harold S. Browning
Father:	manufacturer, industrialist
Mother:	prominent social figure in the community
Principal child-rearer:	governess
Primary education:	an exclusive private school on Manhattan's Upper East Side *Note:* a small, well-respected primary school where teachers and administrators have a reputation for nurturing student creativity and for providing the finest educational preparation *Ambition:* "to become President"
Supplemental tutoring:	tutors in French and mathematics
Summer camp:	sleep-away camp in northern Connecticut *Note:* camp provides instruction in the creative arts, athletics, and the natural sciences
Secondary education:	a prestigious preparatory school in Westchester County *Note:* classmates included the sons of ambassadors, doctors, attorneys, television personalities, and well-known business leaders *After-school activities:* private riding lessons *Ambition:* "to take over my father's business" *High-school graduation gift:* BMW
Family activities:	theater, recitals, museums, summer vacations in Europe, occasional winter trips to the Caribbean *Note:* as members of and donors to the local art museum, the Brownings and their children attend private receptions and exhibit openings at the invitation of the museum director
Higher education:	an Ivy League liberal arts college in Massachusetts *Major:* economics and political science *After-class activities:* debating club, college newspaper, swim team *Ambition:* "to become a leader in business"

---

[20] Stuart Ewen and Elizabeth Ewen, *Channels of Desire: Mass Images and the Shaping of American Consciousness* (New York: McGraw-Hill, 1982).

[21] Andrew Ross, *No-Collar: The Humane Work Place and Its Hidden Costs* (New York: Basic Books, 2002).

First full-time job (age 23):	assistant manager of operations, Browning Tool and Die, Inc. (family enterprise)
Subsequent employment:	*3 years* — executive assistant to the president, Browning Tool and Die
	Responsibilities included: purchasing (materials and equipment), personnel, and distribution networks
	4 years — advertising manager, Lackheed Manufacturing (home appliances)
	3 years — director of marketing and sales, Comerex, Inc. (business machines)
Present employment (age 38):	executive vice president, SmithBond and Co. (digital instruments)
	Typical daily activities: review financial reports and computer printouts, dictate memoranda, lunch with clients, initiate conference calls, meet with assistants, plan business trips, meet with associates
	Transportation to and from work: chauffeured company limousine
	Annual salary: $315,000
	Ambition: "to become chief executive officer of the firm, or one like it, within the next five to ten years"
Present residence:	eighteenth-floor condominium on Manhattan's Upper West Side, eleven rooms, including five spacious bedrooms and terrace overlooking river
	Interior: professionally decorated and accented with elegant furnishings, valuable antiques, and expensive artwork
	Note: building management provides doorman and elevator attendant; family employs au pair for children and maid for other domestic chores
Second residence:	farm in northwestern Connecticut, used for weekend retreats and for horse breeding (investment/ hobby)
	Note: to maintain the farm and cater to the family when they are there, the Brownings employ a part-time maid, groundskeeper, and horse breeder

Harold Browning was born into a world of nurses, maids, and governesses. His world today is one of airplanes and limousines, five-star restaurants, and luxurious living accommodations. The life and life-style of Harold Browning is in sharp contrast to that of Bob Farrell.   25

American Profile

Name:	Bob Farrell
Father:	machinist
Mother:	retail clerk
Principal child-rearer:	mother and sitter
Primary education:	a medium-size public school in Queens, New York, characterized by large class size, outmoded physical facilities, and an educational philosophy emphasizing basic skills and student discipline *Ambition:* "to become President"
Supplemental tutoring:	none
Summer camp:	YMCA day camp *Note:* emphasis on team sports, arts and crafts
Secondary education:	large regional high school in Queens *Note:* classmates included the sons and daughters of carpenters, postal clerks, teachers, nurses, shopkeepers, mechanics, bus drivers, police officers, salespersons *After-school activities:* basketball and handball in school park *Ambition:* "to make it through college" *High-school graduation gift:* $500 savings bond
Family activities:	family gatherings around television set, bowling, an occasional trip to the movie theater, summer Sundays at the public beach
Higher education:	a two-year community college with a technical orientation *Major:* electrical technology *After-school activities:* employed as a part-time bagger in local supermarket *Ambition:* "to become an electrical engineer"
First full-time job (age 19):	service-station attendant *Note:* continued to take college classes in the evening
Subsequent employment:	mail clerk at large insurance firm, manager trainee, large retail chain
Present employment (age 38):	assistant sales manager, building supply firm *Typical daily activities:* demonstrate products, write up product orders, handle customer complaints, check inventory *Transportation to and from work:* city subway *Annual salary:* $39,261 *Ambition:* "to open up my own business" *Additional income:* $6,100 in commissions

	from evening and weekend work as salesman in local men's clothing store
President residence:	the Farrells own their own home in a working-class neighborhood in Queens

Bob Farrell and Harold Browning live very differently: the life-style of one is privileged; that of the other is not so privileged. The differences are class differences, and these differences have a profound impact on the way they live. They are differences between playing a game of handball in the park and taking riding lessons at a private stable; watching a movie on television and going to the theater; and taking the subway to work and being driven in a limousine. More important, the difference in class determines where they live, who their friends are, how well they are educated, what they do for a living, and what they come to expect from life.

Yet, as dissimilar as their life-styles are, Harold Browning and Bob Farrell have some things in common; they live in the same city, they work long hours, and they are highly motivated. More important, they are both white males.

Let's look at someone else who works long and hard and is highly motivated. This person, however, is black and female.

American Profile

Name:	Cheryl Mitchell
Father:	janitor
Mother:	waitress
Principal child-rearer:	grandmother
Primary education:	large public school in Ocean Hill-Brownsville, Brooklyn, New York *Note:* rote teaching of basic skills and emphasis on conveying the importance of good attendance, good manners, and good work habits; school patrolled by security guards *Ambition:* "to be a teacher"
Supplemental tutoring:	none
Summer camp:	none
Secondary education:	large public school in Ocean Hill-Brownsville *Note:* classmates included sons and daughters of hairdressers, groundskeepers, painters, dressmakers, dishwashers, domestics *After-school activities:* domestic chores, part-time employment as babysitter and housekeeper

	Ambition: "to be a social worker"
	High-school graduation gift: corsage
Family activities:	church-sponsored socials
Higher education:	one semester of local community college
	Note: dropped out of school for financial reasons
First full-time job (age 17):	counter clerk, local bakery
Subsequent employment:	file clerk with temporary-service agency, supermarket checker
Present employment (age 38):	nurse's aide at a municipal hospital
	Typical daily activities: make up hospital beds, clean out bedpans, weigh patients and assist them to the bathroom, take temperature readings, pass out and collect food trays, feed patients who need help, bathe patients, and change dressings
	Annual salary: $15,820
	Ambition: "to get out of the ghetto"
Present residence:	three-room apartment in the South Bronx, needs painting, has poor ventilation, is in a high-crime area
	Note: Cheryl Mitchell lives with her four-year-old son and her elderly mother

When we look at the lives of Cheryl Mitchell, Bob Farrell, and Harold Browning, we see life-styles that are very different. We are not looking, however, at economic extremes. Cheryl Mitchell's income as a nurse's aide puts her above the government's official poverty line.[22] Below her on the income pyramid are 33 million poverty-stricken Americans. Far from being poor, Bob Farrell has an annual income as an assistant sales manager that puts him well above the median income level — that is, more than 50 percent of the U.S. population earns less money than Bob Farrell.[23] And while Harold Browning's income puts him in a high-income bracket, he stands only a fraction of the way up Samuelson's income pyramid. Well above him are the 241,000 individuals whose annual salary exceeds $1 million. Yet Harold Browning spends more money on his horses than Cheryl Mitchell earns in a year.

[22] Based on a poverty threshold for a family of three in 2003 of $15,260.

[23] The median income in 2001 was $38,275 for men, $29,214 for women, and $42,228 for households. Carmen DeNavas-Walt and Robert Cleveland, "U.S. Census Bureau, Current Population Reports," *Money Income in the United States; 2001* (Washington, DC: U.S. Government Printing Office, 2002, p. 4).

Reality 3:   Even ignoring the extreme poles of the economic spec-   30
trum, we find enormous class differences in the life-styles among the haves,
the have-nots, and the have-littles.

Class affects more than life-style and material well-being. It has a significant impact on our physical and mental well-being as well.

Researchers have found an inverse relationship between social class
and health. Lower-class standing is correlated to higher rates of infant mortality, eye and ear disease, arthritis, physical disability, diabetes, nutritional
deficiency, respiratory disease, mental illness, and heart disease.[24] In all
areas of health, poor people do not share the same life chances as those in
the social class above them. Furthermore, lower-class standing is correlated
with a lower quality of treatment for illness and disease. The results of poor
health and poor treatment are borne out in the life expectancy rates within
each class. Researchers have found that the higher your class standing, the
higher your life expectancy. Conversely, they have also found that within
each age group, the lower one's class standing, the higher the death rate; in
some age groups, the figures are as much as two and three times as high.[25]

Reality 4:   From cradle to grave, class standing has a significant
impact on our chances for survival.

The lower one's class standing, the more difficult it is to secure appropriate housing, the more time is spent on the routine tasks of everyday life,
the greater is the percentage of income that goes to pay for food and other
basic necessities, and the greater is the likelihood of crime victimization.[26]
Class can accurately predict chances for both survival and success.

Class and Educational Attainment

School performance (grades and test scores) and educational attain-   35
ment (level of schooling completed) also correlate strongly with economic
class. Furthermore, despite some efforts to make testing fairer and school-

---

[24] E. Pamuk, D. Makuc, K. Heck, C. Reuben, and K. Lochner, *Socioeconomic Status and Health Chartbook, Health, United States, 1998* (Hyattsville, MD: National Center for Health Statistics, 1998, pp. 145–159); Vincente Navarro, "Class, Race, and Health Care in the United States," in Bersh Berberoglu, *Critical Perspectives in Sociology,* 2nd ed. (Dubuque, IA: Kendall/Hunt, 1993, pp. 148–156); Melvin Krasner, *Poverty and Health in New York City* (New York: United Hospital Fund of New York, 1989). See also U.S. Dept. of Health and Human Services, *Health Status of Minorities and Low Income Groups,* 1985; and Dan Hughes, Kay Johnson, Sara Rosenbaum, Elizabeth Butler, and Janet Simons, *The Health of America's Children* (The Children's Defense Fund, 1988).

[25] E. Pamuk et al., op. cit., Kenneth Neubeck and Davita Glassberg, *Sociology; A Critical Approach* (New York: McGraw-Hill, 1996, pp. 436–438); Aaron Antonovsky, "Social Class, Life Expectancy, and Overall Mortality," in *The Impact of Social Class* (New York: Thomas Crowell, 1972, pp. 467–491). See also Harriet Duleep, "Measuring the Effect of Income on Adult Mortality Using Longitudinal Administrative Record Data," *Journal of Human Resources,* vol. 21, no. 2, Spring 1986.

[26] E. Pamuk et al., op. cit., fig. 20; Dennis W. Roncek, "Dangerous Places: Crime and Residential Environment," *Social Forces,* vol. 60, no. 1, September 1981, pp. 74–96.

ing more accessible, current data suggest that the level of inequity is staying the same or getting worse.

In his study for the Carnegie Council on Children twenty-five years ago, Richard De Lone examined the test scores of over half a million students who took the College Board exams (SATs). His findings were consistent with earlier studies that showed a relationship between class and scores on standardized tests; his conclusion: "the higher the student's social status, the higher the probability that he or she will get higher grades."[27] Fifteen years after the release of the Carnegie report, College Board surveys reveal data that are no different: test scores still correlate strongly with family income.

Average Combined Scores by Income (400 to 1600 scale)[28]

FAMILY INCOME	MEDIAN SCORE
More than $100,000	1130
$80,000 to $100,000	1082
$70,000 to $80,000	1058
$60,000 to $70,000	1043
$50,000 to $60,000	1030
$40,000 to $50,000	1011
$30,000 to $40,000	986
$20,000 to $30,000	954
$10,000 to $20,000	907
less than $10,000	871

These figures are based on the test results of 1,302,903 SAT takers in 1999.

A little more than twenty years ago, researcher William Sewell showed a positive correlation between class and overall educational achievement. In comparing the top quartile (25 percent) of his sample to the bottom quartile, he found that students from upper-class families were twice as likely to obtain training beyond high school and four times as likely to attain a postgraduate degree. Sewell concluded: "Socioeconomic background . . . operates independently of academic ability at every stage in the process of educational attainment."[29]

Today, the pattern persists. There are, however, two significant changes. On the one hand, the odds of getting into college have improved for the bottom quartile of the population, although they still remain relatively low compared to the top. On the other hand, the chances of completing a

[27] Richard De Lone, *Small Futures* (New York: Harcourt Brace Jovanovich, 1978, pp. 14–19).

[28] Derived from The College Entrance Examination Board, "1999, A Profile of College Bound Seniors: SAT Test Takers;" available at www.collegeboard.org/sat/cbsenior/yr1999/NAT/natbk499.html#income.

[29] William H. Sewell, "Inequality of Opportunity for Higher Education," *American Sociological Review*, vol. 36, no. 5, 1971, pp. 793–809.

college degree have deteriorated markedly for the bottom quartile. Researchers estimate the chances of completing a four-year college degree (by age 24) to be nineteen times as great for the top 25 percent of the population as it is for the bottom 25 percent.[30]

Reality 5:   Class standing has a significant impact on chances for educational achievement.

Class standing, and consequently life chances, are largely determined at birth. Although examples of individuals who have gone from rags to riches abound in the mass media, statistics on class mobility show these leaps to be extremely rare. In fact, dramatic advances in class standing are relatively infrequent. One study showed that fewer than one in five men surpass the economic status of their fathers.[31] For those whose annual income is in six figures, economic success is due in large part to the wealth and privileges bestowed on them at birth. Over 66 percent of the consumer units with incomes of $100,000 or more have inherited assets. Of these units, over 86 percent reported that inheritances constituted a substantial portion of their total assets.[32]

Economist Harold Wachtel likens inheritance to a series of Monopoly games in which the winner of the first game refuses to relinquish his or her cash and commercial property for the second game. "After all," argues the winner, "I accumulated my wealth and income by my own wits." With such an arrangement, it is not difficult to predict the outcome of subsequent games.[33]

Reality 6:   All Americans do not have an equal opportunity to succeed. Inheritance laws ensure a greater likelihood of success for the offspring of the wealthy.

Spheres of Power and Oppression

When we look at society and try to determine what it is that keeps most people down — what holds them back from realizing their potential as healthy, creative, productive individuals — we find institutional forces that are largely beyond individual control. Class domination is one of these forces. People do not choose to be poor or working class; instead, they are limited and confined by the opportunities afforded or denied them by a social and economic system. The class structure in the United States is a function of its economic system: capitalism, a system that is based on private rather than public ownership and control of commercial enterprises. Under capitalism, these enterprises are governed by the need to produce a profit for the owners, rather than to fulfill collective needs. Class divisions arise from the differences between those who own and control corporate enterprise and those who do not.

[30] The Mortenson Report on Public Policy Analysis of Opportunity for Postsecondary Education, "Postsecondary Education Opportunity" (Iowa City, IA: September 1993, no. 16).

[31] De Lone, op. cit., pp. 14–19.

[32] Howard Tuchman, *Economics of the Rich* (New York: Random House, 1973, p. 15).

[33] Howard Wachtel, *Labor and the Economy* (Orlando, FL: Academic Press, 1984, pp. 161–162).

Racial and gender domination are other forces that hold people down. Although there are significant differences in the way capitalism, racism, and sexism affect our lives, there are also a multitude of parallels. And although class, race, and gender act independently of each other, they are at the same time very much interrelated.

On the one hand, issues of race and gender cut across class lines. 45 Women experience the effects of sexism whether they are well-paid professionals or poorly paid clerks. As women, they face discrimination and male domination, as well as catcalls and stereotyping. Similarly, a wealthy black man faces racial oppression, is subjected to racial slurs, and is denied opportunities because of his color. Regardless of their class standing, women and members of minority races are constantly dealing with institutional forces that are holding them down precisely because of their gender, the color of their skin, or both.

On the other hand, the experiences of women and minorities are differentiated along class lines. Although they are in subordinate positions vis-à-vis white men, the particular issues that confront women and minorities may be quite different depending on their position in the class structure.

Power is incremental, and class privileges can accrue to individual women and to individual members of a racial minority. At the same time, class-oppressed men, whether they are white or black, have privileges afforded them as men in a sexist society. Similarly, class-oppressed whites, whether they are men or women, benefit from white privilege in a racist society. Spheres of power and oppression divide us deeply in our society, and the schisms between us are often difficult to bridge.

Whereas power is incremental, oppression is cumulative, and those who are poor, black, and female are often subject to all of the forces of class, race, and gender discrimination simultaneously. This cumulative situation is what is meant by the double and triple jeopardy of women and minorities.

Furthermore, oppression in one sphere is related to the likelihood of oppression in another. If you are black and female, for example, you are much more likely to be poor or working class than you would be as a white male. Census figures show that the incidence of poverty varies greatly by race and gender.

Chances of Being Poor in America[34]

WHITE MALE/ FEMALE	WHITE FEMALE HEAD*	HISPANIC MALE/ FEMALE	HISPANIC FEMALE HEAD*	BLACK MALE/ FEMALE	BLACK FEMALE HEAD*
1 in 10	1 in 5	1 in 5	1 in 3	1 in 5	1 in 3

*Persons in families with female householder, no husband present.

In other words, being female and being nonwhite are attributes in our   50
society that increase the chances of poverty and of lower-class standing.

Reality 7:   Racism and sexism significantly compound the effects of class in society.

ENGAGING THE TEXT

1. Reexamine the four myths Mantsios identifies (paras. 10–14). What does Mantsios say is wrong about each myth, and what evidence does he provide to critique each? How persuasive do you find his evidence and reasoning?

2. Does the essay make a case that the wealthy are exploiting the poor? Does it simply assume this? Are there other possible interpretations of the data Mantsios provides? Explain your position, taking into account the information in "Class in America — 2003."

[34] Derived from Proctor and Dalaker, op. cit., p. 3.

3. Work out a rough budget for a family of three with an annual income of $15,260, the "poverty threshold" for 2003. Be sure to include costs for food, clothing, housing, transportation, healthcare, and other unavoidable expenses. Do you think this is a reasonable "poverty line," or is it too high or too low?

4. Imagine that you are Harold S. Browning, Bob Farrell, or Cheryl Mitchell. Write an entry for this person's journal after a tough day on the job. Compare and contrast your entry with those written by other students.

5. In this essay, Mantsios does not address solutions to the problems he cites. What changes do you imagine Mantsios would like to see? What changes, if any, would you recommend?

EXPLORING CONNECTIONS

6. Working in small groups, discuss which class each of the following would belong to and how this class affiliation would shape the life chances of each:

> Gary Soto in "Looking for Work" (p. 26)
>
> George in "Serving in Florida" (p. 294)
>
> The narrator of "An Indian Story" (p. 51)
>
> Stephen Cruz (p. 353)
>
> Sylvia in "The Lesson" (p. 270)
>
> Cora Tucker (p. 358)
>
> C. P. Ellis (p. 519)
>
> Mike Rose (p. 161)
>
> Richard Rodriguez (p. 193)

7. Although Mantsios does not focus on the Horatio Alger myth as does Harlon Dalton (p. 278), both authors concern themselves with seeing beyond myths of success to underlying realities. Compare the ways these two writers challenge the American mythology of success. Do the two readings complement one another, or do you see fundamental disagreements between the two authors? Whose approach do you find more persuasive, insightful, or informative, and why?

8. How might "Black Avenger" Ken Hamblin (p. 285) respond to Mantsios's analysis of class in America? How can a belief in individual opportunity be maintained in the face of Mantsios's statistics on social class and life chances?

9. Compare this essay by Mantsios to the selection from *Changing American Families* by Judy Root Aulette (p. 61). What similarities or differences do you see in the ways they understand and write about social class, wealth, and poverty?

EXTENDING THE CRITICAL CONTEXT

10. Mantsios points out, "Inheritance laws ensure a greater likelihood of success for the offspring of the wealthy" (para. 42). Explain why you think this

is or is not a serious problem. Keeping in mind the difference between wealth and income, discuss how society might attempt to remedy this problem and what policies you would endorse.

11. Skim through a few recent issues of a financial magazine like *Forbes* or *Money*. Who is the audience for these publications? What kind of advice is offered, what kinds of products and services are advertised, and what levels of income and investment are discussed?

12. Study the employment pages of a major newspaper in your area. Roughly what percentage of the openings would you consider upper class, middle class, and lower class? On what basis do you make your distinctions? What do the available jobs suggest about the current levels of affluence in your area?

With a Simmons® Beautyrest® or BackCare,® you are bound to wake up feeling better rested and more refreshed. And there couldn't be a better time to check one out than now. Because you can win up to $1 million instantly in our "Million Dollar Mattress Test." Just stop by your local participating Simmons dealer and try out a Beautyrest or BackCare. These sleep systems are designed to give you a better night's sleep. Something 80% of Americans aren't getting these days. For a Simmons dealer near you, call 1-800-SIMMONS. It could be well worth the trip.

Better Sleep Through Science?

www.simmons.com

©1999 Simmons Company. No purchase necessary. Void where prohibited. Game ends 12/31/99. Full rules available at participating retailers. Grand prize paid $25,000 per year over 40 years. Those who wish to request a free game piece may send a self-addressed, stamped #10 envelope to MDMT Request, P.O. Box 19418, Atlanta, GA 31126, postmarked by 12/31/99.

Getty Images.

Visual Portfolio
READING IMAGES OF INDIVIDUAL OPPORTUNITY

1. When do you think the photo of the father giving cash to his family was taken, and what ideas about money, social class, family, and gender was it meant to convey at that time? Explain why you think it was or was not meant to be humorous. What meanings does the image convey to you today? Compare this photograph with Norman Rockwell's *Freedom from Fear* (p. 24) in terms of cultural messages and visual composition or structure.

2. Explain the appeal of the Simmons mattress ad. Consider in particular the different ways the idea of money is being used to sell mattresses. Also discuss such details of the photograph as its overhead perspective, the woman's posture and facial expression, and the amount of money actually pictured.

3. What's happening in the photograph of the bank meeting? Discuss such elements of the photo as the setting, the bankers' clothes, their facial expressions, and the framed portraits on the wall. What does this image tell you about money and success? Compare the women in this photo to the other females in this portfolio — the mother and daughter getting their allowance, and the woman with a million dollars. Considered as a group, what do these images say about women and money in American culture?

4. How does the urban scene with the TV fit into a portfolio of images about money and success? What ideas and emotions does it trigger in you? Explain the prominence of the broken TV: Why is a portion of the image framed by a TV rather than by one of countless alternatives (picture frame, doorway, window, etc.)?

5. In the photograph of a man repairing novelty items during vocational training, what else is going on? What is the man thinking? What is his relationship to his work, to the toys, and to his coworkers? What do you make of the slogan on his T-shirt, "Freedom by any means necessary"?

6. Working in small groups, take a close look at the design of whatever coins, paper money, and bank cards you have handy. What information is being conveyed in their words, images, and physical design?

Money
DANA GIOIA

Money and poetry are strange bedfellows: we rarely think of them together. Dana Gioia (b. 1950) is well suited to couple them, however; he did graduate study in both comparative literature and business administration, and even when he worked as a product manager for Kool-Aid, he set aside two hours a day for reading and writing poetry. Gioia has served as chair of the National Endowment for the Arts since 2003. His most recent book of poetry, Interrogations at Noon *(2001) was honored with the American Book Award, and he has also published translations, critical works, and an opera libretto. In this poem, published in* Forbes *(1999), he invites us to think about the ways we talk about money.*

> Money is a kind of poetry.
> — WALLACE STEVENS

Money, the long green,
cash, stash, rhino, jack
or just plain dough.

Chock it up, fork it over,
shell it out. Watch it   5
burn holes through pockets.

To be made of it! To have it
to burn! Greenbacks, double eagles,
megabucks and Ginnie Maes.

It greases the palm, feathers a nest,   10
holds heads above water,
makes both ends meet.

Money breeds money.
Gathering interest, compounding daily.
Always in circulation   15

Money. You don't know where it's been,
but you put it where your mouth is.
And it talks.

ENGAGING THE TEXT

1. Which words and phrases in the poem are familiar to you, which unfamiliar? Work with classmates to clarify the meanings of as many words and phrases as possible. As you do so, try to associate each word or phrase with one or more particular settings where it might be used (for example, banks, casinos, Wall Street, drug deals) and with any particular ideas about money it expresses.

2. What is the dominant attitude about money expressed in the poem? To what extent do you share this attitude?

3. The brevity of the last line and its placement at the poem's conclusion give it special emphasis. Why do you think Gioia ends his poem this way?

EXPLORING CONNECTIONS

4. Compare this poem with the one by Sharon Olds below. Think about the tone of each poem, about each poem's speaker or voice, and about the ways each poem tries to appeal to you.

EXTENDING THE CRITICAL CONTEXT

5. An ordinary dictionary may not help you much with understanding synonyms for money like "rhino" and "jack." How might you find out more about the meanings of these words, and perhaps about their derivation or history? In other words, what resources beyond your dictionary are available to you for learning about language? Consult some of these resources and see what you can find out about the vocabulary in this poem.

6. Gioia constructs his poem by using many words and phrases either meaning "money" or associated with money. Write your own poem using the same strategy, but with a different main topic — food, music, friendship, TV, or a topic of your choice. A dictionary of quotations and a thesaurus might help you.

From Seven Floors Up
SHARON OLDS

This short poem uses one of the simplest but most effective artistic methods ever devised — dramatic contrast. The figures compared here are a homeless man and the comfortable poet who observes him; the differences between the two invite you to consider why poverty and affluence coexist and what determines who succeeds. Sharon Olds (b. 1942) is author of several books of poetry, including Satan Says *(1980),* The Dead and the Living *(1983, winner of the National Book Critics Circle Award),* The Gold Cell *(1987),* The Father *(1992), and* Blood, Tin, Straw *(1999). Olds was honored as poet laureate of New York State for 1998–2000; she teaches at New York University. Her most recent volume of poetry,* The Unswept Room *(2002), was a National Book Award finalist.*

He is pushing a shopping cart up the ramp
out of the park.[1] He owns, in the world,
only what he has there — no sink, no water, no
heat. When we'd come out of the wilderness,

---

[1] *up the ramp / out of the park:* This suggests Central Park in New York City.

after the week in the desert, in tents,   5
and on the river, by canoe, and when I had my own
motel-room, I cried for humble, dreading
joy in the shower, I kneeled and put
my arms around the cold, clean
toilet. From up here, his profile looks like   10
Che Guevara's,[2] in the last picture,
the stitches like marks on a butcher's chart.
Suddenly I see that I have thought that it could not
happen to me, homelessness
— like death, by definition it would not happen.   15
And he shoulders his earth, his wheeled hovel,
north, the wind at his back — November,
the trees coming bare in earnest. November,
month of my easy birth.

ENGAGING THE TEXT

1. Why do you think Olds chose the title "From Seven Floors Up"? Why is this detail important enough to become the poem's title?

2. Take a few moments to visualize each image in the poem. Identify those you consider most powerful or interesting.

3. What is the dominant feeling about homelessness expressed in this poem? Does it express any of your own feelings about poverty? Explain.

4. What does the speaker mean when she says that hers was an "easy birth"? The speaker seems to think she could become homeless; how likely does this seem to you?

5. Do you think homelessness could ever happen to you? Explain why or why not.

EXPLORING CONNECTIONS

6. Write a conversation among three or more of these figures as they discuss what determines success versus failure:

   the speaker of the poem "From Seven Floors Up"

   the homeless man in "From Seven Floors Up"

   Gregory Mantsios, author of "Class in America — 2003" (p. 307)

   Barbara Ehrenreich, author of "Serving in Florida" (p. 294)

7. Like this poem, Barbara Ehrenreich's "Serving in Florida" (p. 294) is based on a relatively privileged woman's observation of those less fortunate. Compare the relationship of this poem's speaker and the homeless man to that of Ehrenreich and her coworkers. For example, to what extent are the ideas of each piece shaped by the observer's nearness to or distance from

[2]*Che Guevara:* Ernesto Guevara, Argentina-born Cuban revolutionary (1928–1967).

the people she is observing? Explain the effect each author's approach has on you as a reader.

EXTENDING THE CRITICAL CONTEXT

8. Write a brief poem from the point of view of the homeless man, imagining him looking seven stories up and seeing someone gazing down at him.

Framing Class, Vicarious Living, and Conspicuous Consumption

DIANA KENDALL

Diana Kendall, a professor of sociology at Baylor University, has performed an extensive study of how newspapers and TV have portrayed social class in the last half-century. She concludes that the media shape public opinions about the upper, middle, working, and poverty classes by "framing" their stories and their programming in a relatively small number of patterned, predictable, and misleading ways. For example, "the media glorify the upper classes, even when they are accused of wrongdoing." In the selection, excerpted from her book Framing Class: Media Representations of Wealth and Poverty in America *(2005), she analyzes how several common media frames communicate cultural messages about social class. Her other publications include* The Power of Good Deeds: Privileged Women and the Social Reproduction of the Upper Class *(2002) and the textbooks* Sociology in Our Times *(2003) and* Social Problems in a Diverse Society *(2006).*

"The Simple Life 2" — the second season of the reality show, on which the celebutante Paris Hilton and her Best Friend Forever, the professional pop-star-daughter Nicole Richie, are set on a cross-country road trip — *once again takes the heaviest of topics and makes them as weightless as a social X-ray.*[1]

This statement by television critic Choire Sicha, in her review of FOX TV's reality-based entertainment show *The Simple Life*, sums up a recurring theme of *Framing Class:* The media typically take "the heaviest of topics," such as class and social inequality, and trivialize it. Rather than providing a

[1]Choire Sicha, "They'll Always Have Paris," *New York Times,* June 13, 2004, AR31 [emphasis added].

meaningful analysis of inequality and showing realistic portrayals of life in various social classes, the media either play class differences for laughs or sweep the issue of class under the rug so that important distinctions are rendered invisible. By ignoring class or trivializing it, the media involve themselves in a social construction of reality that rewards the affluent and penalizes the working class and the poor. In real life, Paris Hilton and Nicole Richie are among the richest young women in the world; however, in the world of *The Simple Life,* they can routinely show up somewhere in the city or the country, pretend they are needy, and rely on the kindness of strangers who have few economic resources.

The Simple Life is only one example of many that demonstrate how class is minimized or played for laughs by the media. [Below] I have provided many examples of how class is framed in the media and what messages those framing devices might convey to audiences. In this chapter, I will look at the sociological implications of how framing contributes to our understanding of class and how it leads to vicarious living and excessive consumerism by many people. I will also discuss reasons why prospects for change in how journalists and television writers portray the various classes are limited. First, we look at two questions: How do media audiences understand and act upon popular culture images or frames? Is class understood differently today because of these frames?

Media Framing and the Performance of Class in Everyday Life

In a mass-mediated culture such as ours, the media do not simply mirror society; rather, they help to shape it and to create cultural perceptions.[2] The blurring between what is real and what is not real encourages people to emulate the upper classes and shun the working class and the poor. Television shows, magazines, and newspapers sell the idea that the only way to get ahead is to identify with the rich and powerful and to live vicariously through them. From sitcoms to reality shows, the media encourage ordinary people to believe that they may rise to fame and fortune; they too can be the next American Idol. Constantly bombarded by stories about the lifestyles of the rich and famous, viewers feel a sense of intimacy with elites, with whom they have little or no contact in their daily lives.[3] According to the social critic bell hooks, we overidentify with the wealthy, because the media socialize us to believe that people in the upper classes are better than

---

[2]Tim Delaney and Allene Wilcox, "Sports and the Role of the Media," in *Values, Society and Evolution,* ed. Harry Birx and Tim Delaney, 199–215 (Auburn, N.Y.: Legend, 2002).

[3]bell hooks [Gloria Watkins], *Where We Stand: Class Matters* (New York: Routledge, 2000), 73.

we are. The media also suggest that we need have no allegiance to people in our own class or to those who are less fortunate.[4]

Vicarious living — watching how other individuals live rather than experiencing life for ourselves — through media representations of wealth and success is reflected in many people's reading and viewing habits and in their patterns of consumption. According to hooks, television promotes hedonistic consumerism:

> Largely through marketing and advertising, television promoted the myth of the classless society, offering on one hand images of an American dream fulfilled wherein any and everyone can become rich and on the other suggesting that the lived experience of this lack of class hierarchy was expressed by our *equal right to purchase anything we could afford.*[5]

As hooks suggests, equality does not exist in contemporary society, but media audiences are encouraged to view themselves as having an "equal right" to purchase items that somehow will make them equal to people above them in the social class hierarchy. However, the catch is that we must actually be able to afford these purchases. Manufacturers and the media have dealt with this problem by offering relatively cheap products marketed by wealthy celebrities. Paris Hilton, an heir to the Hilton Hotel fortune, has made millions of dollars by marketing products that give her fans a small "slice" of the good life she enjoys. Middle- and working-class people can purchase jewelry from the Paris Hilton Collection — sterling silver and Swarovski crystal jewelry ranging in price from fifteen to a hundred dollars — and have something that is "like Paris wears." For less than twenty dollars per item, admirers can purchase the Paris Hilton Wall Calendar; a "Paris the Heiress" Paper Doll Book; Hilton's autobiography, *Confessions of an Heiress;* and even her dog's story, *The Tinkerbell Hilton Diaries: My Life Tailing Paris Hilton.* But Hilton is only one of thousands of celebrities who make money by encouraging unnecessary consumerism among people who are inspired by media portrayals of the luxurious and supposedly happy lives of rich celebrities. The title of Hilton's television show, *The Simple Life,* appropriates the image of simple people, such as the working class and poor, who might live happy, meaningful lives, and transfers this image to women whose lives are anything but simple as they flaunt designer clothing and spend collectively millions of dollars on entertainment, travel, and luxuries that can be afforded only by the very wealthy.[6]

How the media frame stories about class *does* make a difference in what we think about other people and how we spend our money. Media frames constitute a mental shortcut (schema) that helps us formulate our thoughts.

5

[4]hooks, *Where We Stand,* 77.
[5]hooks, *Where We Stand,* 71 [emphasis added].
[6]hooks, *Where We Stand,* 72.

The Upper Classes: Affluence and Consumerism for All

Although some media frames show the rich and famous in a negative manner, they still glorify the material possessions and lifestyles of the upper classes. Research has found that people who extensively watch television have exaggerated views of how wealthy most Americans are and what material possessions they own. Studies have also found that extensive television viewing leads to higher rates of spending and to lower savings, presumably because television stimulates consumer desires.[7]

For many years, most media framing of stories about the upper classes has been positive, ranging from *consensus framing* that depicts members of the upper class as being like everyone else, to *admiration framing* that portrays them as generous, caring individuals. The frame most closely associated with rampant consumerism is *emulation framing*, which suggests that people in all classes should reward themselves with a few of the perks of the wealthy, such as buying a piece of Paris's line of jewelry. The writers of television shows such as ABC's *Life of Luxury*, E!'s *It's Good to Be* . . . [a wealthy celebrity, such as Nicole Kidman], and VH1's *The Fabulous Life* rely heavily on admiration and price-tag framing, by which the worth of a person is measured by what he or she owns and how many assistants constantly cater to that person's whims. On programs like FOX's *The O.C.* and *North Shore* and NBC's *Las Vegas*, the people with the most expensive limousines, yachts, and jet aircraft are declared the winners in life. Reality shows like *American Idol*, *The Billionaire*, *For Love or Money*, and *The Apprentice* suggest that anyone can move up the class ladder and live like the rich if he or she displays the best looks, greatest talent, or sharpest entrepreneurial skills. It is no wonder that the economist Juliet B. Schor finds that the overriding goal of children age ten to thirteen is to get rich. In response to the statement "I want to make a lot of money when I grow up," 63 percent of the children in Schor's study agreed, whereas only 7 percent disagreed.[8]

Many adults who hope to live the good life simply plunge farther into debt. Many reports show that middle- and working-class American consumers are incurring massive consumer debts as they purchase larger houses, more expensive vehicles, and many other items that are beyond their means. According to one analyst, media portrayals of excessive consumer spending and a bombardment of advertisements by credit-card companies encourage people to load up on debt.[9] With the average U.S. household now spending 13 percent of its after-tax income to *service* debts (not pay off the

---

[7]Juliet B. Schor, *Born to Buy: The Commercialized Child and the New Consumer Culture* (New York: Scribner, 2004).

[8]Schor, *Born to Buy*.

[9]Joseph Nocera, *A Piece of the Action: How the Middle Class Joined the Money Class* (New York: Simon and Schuster, 1994).

principal!), people with average incomes who continue to aspire to lives of luxury like those of the upper classes instead may find themselves spending their way into the "poor house" with members of the poverty class.

The Poor and Homeless: "Not Me!" — Negative Role Models in the Media

The sharpest contrasts in media portrayals are between depictions of   10 people in the upper classes and depictions of people at the bottom of the class structure. At best, the poor and homeless are portrayed as deserving of our sympathy on holidays or when disaster strikes. In these situations, those in the bottom classes are depicted as being temporarily down on their luck or as working hard to get out of their current situation but in need of public assistance. At worst, however, the poor are blamed for their own problems; stereotypes of the homeless as bums, alcoholics, and drug addicts, caught in a hopeless downward spiral because of their *individual* pathological behavior, are omnipresent in the media.

For the most part, people at the bottom of the class structure remain out of sight and out of mind for most media audiences. *Thematic framing* depicts the poor and homeless as "faceless" statistics in reports on poverty. *Episodic framing* highlights some problems of the poor but typically does not link their personal situations [and] concerns to such larger societal problems as limited educational opportunities, high rates of unemployment, and jobs that pay depressingly low wages.

The poor do not fare well on television entertainment shows, where writers typically represent them with one-dimensional, bedraggled characters standing on a street corner holding cardboard signs that read "Need money for food." When television writers tackle the issue of homelessness, they often portray the lead characters (who usually are white and relatively affluent) as helpful people, while the poor and homeless are depicted as deviants who might harm themselves or others. Hospital and crime dramas like *E.R., C.S.I.,* and *Law & Order* frequently portray the poor and homeless as "crazy," inebriated in public, or incompetent to provide key information to officials. Television reality shows like *Cops* go so far as to advertise that they provide "footage of debris from the bottom tiers of the urban social order."[10] Statements such as this say a lot about the extent to which television producers, directors, and writers view (or would have us view) the lower classes.

From a sociological perspective, framing of stories about the poor and homeless stands in stark contrast to framing of stories about those in the upper classes, and it suggests that we should distance ourselves from "those people." We are encouraged to view the poor and homeless as the *Other*,

---

[10]Karen De Coster and Brad Edmonds, "TV Nation: The Killing of American Brain Cells," Lewrockwell.com, 2004, www.lewrockwell.com/decoster/decoster78.html (accessed July 7, 2004).

the outsider; in the media we find little commonality between our lives and the experiences of people at the bottom of the class hierarchy. As a result, it is easy for us to buy into the dominant ideological construction that views poverty as a problem of individuals, not of the society as a whole, and we may feel justified in our rejection of such people.[11]

The Working Class: Historical Relics and Jokes

The working class and the working poor do not fare much better than the poor and homeless in media representations. The working class is described as "labor," and people in this class are usually nothing more than faces in a crowd on television shows. The media portray people who *produce* goods and services as much less interesting than those who *excessively consume* them, and this problem can only grow worse as more of the workers who produce the products are thousands of miles away from us, in nations like China, very remote from the typical American consumer.[12]

Contemporary media coverage carries little information about the work- 15
ing class or its problems. Low wages, lack of benefits, and hazardous working conditions are considered boring and uninteresting topics, except on the public broadcasting networks or an occasional television "news show" such as *60 Minutes* or *20/20*, when some major case of worker abuse has recently been revealed. The most popular portrayal of the working class is *caricature framing*, which depicts people in negative ways, such as being dumb, white trash, buffoons, bigots, or slobs. Many television shows featuring working-class characters play on the idea that the clothing, manners, and speech patterns of the working class are not as good as those of the middle or upper classes. For example, working-class characters (such as Roseanne, the animated Homer Simpson, and *The King of Queens*' Doug) may compare themselves to the middle and upper classes by saying that they are not as "fancy as the rich people." Situation comedy writers have perpetuated working-class stereotypes, and now a number of reality shows, such as *The Swan* and *Extreme Makeover*, try to take "ordinary" working-class people and "improve" them through cosmetic surgery, new clothing, and different hairstyles.

Like their upper-class celebrity counterparts, so-called working-class comedians like Jeff Foxworthy have ridiculed the blue-collar lifestyle. They

---

[11]Judith Butler ("Performative Acts and Gender Constitution: An Essay in Phenomenology and Feminist Theory," in *Performing Feminisms: Feminist Critical Theory and Theatre*, ed. Sue-Ellen Case [Baltimore: Johns Hopkins University Press, 1990], 270) has described gender identity as performative, noting that social reality is not a given but is continually created as an illusion "through language, gesture, and all manner of symbolic social sign." In this sense, class might also be seen as performative, in that people act out their perceived class location not only in terms of their own class-related identity but in regard to how they treat other people, based on their perceived class position.

[12]See Thomas Ginsberg, "Union Hopes to Win Over Starbucks Shop Workers," *Austin American-Statesman*, July 2, 2004, D6.

also have marketed products that make fun of the working class. Foxworthy's website, for example, includes figurines ("little statues for *inside* the house"), redneck cookbooks, Games Rednecks Play, and calendars that make fun of the working class generally. Although some people see these items as humorous ("where's yore sense of humor?"), the real message is that people in the lower classes lack good taste, socially acceptable manners, and above all, middle-class values. If you purchase "redneck" merchandise, you too can make fun of the working class and clearly distance yourself from it.

Middle-Class Framing and Kiddy-Consumerism

Media framing of stories about the middle class tells us that this economic group is the value center and backbone of the nation. *Middle-class values framing* focuses on the values of this class and suggests that they hold the nation together. Early television writers were aware that their shows needed to appeal to middle-class audiences, who were the targeted consumers for the advertisers' products, and middle-class values of honesty, integrity, and hard work were integral ingredients of early sitcoms. However, some contemporary television writers spoof the middle class and poke fun at values supposedly associated with people in this category. The writers of FOX's *Malcolm in the Middle* and *Arrested Development,* for example, focus on the dysfunctions in a fictional middle-class family, including conflicts between husband and wife, between parents and children, and between members of the family and outsiders.

Why do these shows make fun of the middle class? Because corporations that pay for the advertisements want to capture the attention of males between ages eighteen and thirty-nine, and individuals in this category are believed to enjoy laughing at the uptight customs of conventional middle-class families. In other shows, as well, advertisers realize the influence that their programs have on families. That is why they are happy to spend billions of dollars on product placements (such as a Diet Coke can sitting on a person's desk) in the shows and on ads during commercial breaks. In recent research, Schor examined why very young children buy into the consumerism culture and concluded that extensive media exposure to products was a key reason. According to Schor, "More children [in the United States] than anywhere else believe that their clothes and brands describe who they are and define their social status. American kids display more brand affinity than their counterparts anywhere else in the world; indeed, experts describe them as increasingly 'bonded to brands.'"[13]

Part of this bonding occurs through constant television watching and Internet use, as a steady stream of ads targets children and young people. Schor concludes that we face a greater problem than just excessive

[13]Schor, *Born to Buy,* 13.

consumerism. A child's well-being is undermined by the consumer culture: "High consumer involvement is a significant cause of depression, anxiety, low self-esteem, and psychosomatic complaints."[14] Although no similar studies have been conducted to determine the effects of the media's emphasis on wealth and excessive consumerism among adults, it is likely that today's children will take these values with them into adulthood if our society does not first reach the breaking point with respect to consumer debt.

The issue of class in the United States is portrayed in the media not through a realistic assessment of wealth, poverty, or inequality but instead through its patterns of rampant consumerism. The general message remains, one article stated, "We pledge allegiance to the mall."[15]

Media Framing and Our Distorted View of Inequality

Class clearly permeates media culture and influences our thinking on social inequality. How the media frame stories involving class constitutes a *socially constructed reality* that is not necessarily an accurate reflection of the United States. Because of their pervasive nature, the media have the symbolic capacity to define the world for other people. In turn, readers and viewers gain information from the media that they use to construct a picture of class and inequality — a picture that becomes, at least to them, a realistic representation of where they stand in the class structure, what they should (or should not) aspire to achieve, and whether and why they should view other people as superior, equal, or inferior to themselves.

Because of the media's power to socially construct reality, we must make an effort to find out about the objective nature of class and evaluate social inequality on our own terms. Although postmodern thinkers believe that it is impossible to distinguish between real life and the fictionalized version of reality that is presented by the media, some sociologists argue that we can learn the difference between media images of reality and the actual facts pertaining to wealth, poverty, and inequality. The more we become aware that we are not receiving "raw" information or "just" entertainment from the media, the more we are capable of rationally thinking about how we are represented in media portrayals and what we are being encouraged to do (engage in hedonistic consumerism, for example) by these depictions. The print and electronic media have become extremely adept at framing issues of class in a certain manner, but we still have the ability to develop alternative frames that better explain who we are and what our nation is truly like in regard to class divisions.

[14]Schor, *Born to Buy,* 167.
[15]Louis Uchitelle, "We Pledge Allegiance to the Mall," *New York Times,* December 6, 2004, C12.

The Realities of Class

What are the realities of inequality? The truth is that the rich are get-ting richer and that the gulf between the rich and the poor continues to widen in the United States. Since the 1990s, the poor have been more likely to stay poor, and the affluent have been more likely to stay affluent. How do we know this? Between 1991 and 2001, the income of the top one-fifth of U.S. families increased by 31 percent; during the same period, the income of the bottom one-fifth of families increased by only 10 percent.[16] The chasm is even wider across racial and ethnic categories; African Americans and Latinos/Latinas are overrepresented among those in the bottom income levels. Over one-half of African American and Latino/Latina households fall within the lowest income categories.

Wealth inequality is even more pronounced. The super-rich (the top 0.5 percent of U.S. households) own 35 percent of the nation's wealth, with net assets averaging almost nine million dollars. The very rich (the next 0.5 percent of households) own about 7 percent of the nation's wealth, with net assets ranging from $1.4 million to $2.5 million. The rich (9 percent of households) own 30 percent of the wealth, with net assets of a little over four hundred thousand dollars. Meanwhile, everybody else (the bottom 90 percent of households) owns only 28 percent of the nation's wealth. Like income, wealth disparities are greatest across racial and ethnic categories. According to the Census Bureau, the net worth of the average white house-hold in 2000 was more than ten times that of the average African American household and more than eight times that of the average Latino/Latina household. Moreover, in 2002, almost thirty-five million people lived below the official government poverty level of $18,556 for a family of four, an increase of more than one million people in poverty since 2001.[17]

The Realities of Hedonistic Consumerism

Consumerism is a normal part of life; we purchase the things that we   25
need to live. However, hedonistic consumerism goes beyond all necessary and meaningful boundaries. As the word *hedonism* suggests, some people are so caught up in consumerism that this becomes the main reason for their existence, the primary thing that brings them happiness. Such people engage in the self-indulgent pursuit of happiness through what they buy. An example of this extreme was recently reported in the media. When Antoinette Millard was sued by American Express for an allegedly past-due

---

[16]Carmen DeNavas-Walt and Robert W. Cleveland, "Income in the United States: 2002," *U.S. Census Bureau: Current Population Reports*, P60–221 (Washington, D.C.: U.S. Govern-ment Printing Office, 2003).

[17]Bernadette D. Proctor and Joseph Dalaker, "Poverty in the United States: 2002," *U.S. Census Bureau: Current Population Reports*, P60–222 (Washington, D.C.: U.S. Government Printing Office, 2003).

account, she filed a counterclaim against American Express for having provided her with a big-spender's credit card that allowed her to run up bills of nearly a million dollars in luxury stores in New York.[18] Using the "victim defense," Millard claimed that, based on her income, the company should not have solicited her to sign up for the card. Although this appears to be a far-fetched defense (especially in light of some of the facts),[19] it may be characteristic of the lopsided thinking of many people who spend much more money than they can hope to earn. Recent studies have shown that the average American household is carrying more than eight thousand dollars in credit-card debt and that (statistically speaking) every fifteen seconds a person in the United States goes bankrupt.[20] Although fixed costs (such as housing, food, and gasoline) have gone up for most families over the past thirty years, these debt-and-bankruptcy statistics in fact result from more people buying items that are beyond their means and cannot properly use anyway. Our consumer expectations for ourselves and our children have risen as the media have continued to attractively portray the "good life" and to bombard us with ads for something else that we *must* have.

Are we Americans actually interested in learning about class and inequality? Do we want to know where we really stand in the U.S. class structure? Although some people may prefer to operate in a climate of denial, media critics believe that more people are finally awakening to biases in the media, particularly when they see vast inconsistencies between media portrayals of class and their everyday lives. According to the sociologists Robert Perrucci and Earl Wysong, "It is apparent that increasing experiences with and knowledge about class-based inequalities among the nonprivileged is fostering a growing awareness of and concerns about the nature and extent of superclass interests, motives, and power in the economic and political arenas."[21] Some individuals are becoming aware of the effect that media biases can have on what they read, see, and hear. A recent Pew Research Center poll, for example, reflects that people in the working

---

[18]Antoinette Millard, also known as Lisa Walker, allegedly was so caught up in hedonistic consumerism that she created a series of false identities (ranging from being a Saudi princess to being a lawyer, a model, and a wealthy divorcee) and engaged in illegal behavior (such as trying to steal $250,000 from an insurance company by reporting that certain jewelry had been stolen, when she actually had sold it). See Vanessa Grigoriadis, "Her Royal Lie-ness: The So-Called Saudi Princess Was Only One of the Many Identities Lisa Walker Tried On Like Jewelry," *New York Metro*, www.newyorkmetro.com/nymetro/news/people/columns/intelligencer/n_10418 (accessed December 18, 2004); Samuel Maull, "Antoinette Millard Countersues American Express for $2 Million for Allowing Her to Charge $951,000," creditsuit.org/credit.php/blog/comments/antoinette_millard_countersues_american_express_for_2_million_for_allowing (accessed December 18, 2004).

[19]Steve Lohr, "Maybe It's Not All Your Fault," *New York Times*, December 5, 2004, WR1.

[20]Lohr, "Maybe It's Not All Your Fault."

[21]Robert Perrucci and Earl Wysong, *The New Class Society*, 2nd ed. (Lanham, Md.: Rowman & Littlefield, 2003), 199.

class do not unquestioningly accept media information and commentary that preponderantly support the status quo.[22]

Similarly, Perrucci and Wysong note that television can have a paradoxical effect on viewers: It can serve both as a pacifier and as a source of heightened class consciousness. Programs that focus on how much money the very wealthy have may be a source of entertainment for nonelites, but they may also produce antagonism among people who work hard and earn comparatively little, when they see people being paid so much for doing so little work (e.g., the actress who earns seventeen million dollars per film or the sports star who signs a hundred-million-dollar multiyear contract). Even more egregious are individuals who do not work at all but are born into the "right family" and inherit billions of dollars.

Although affluent audiences might prefer that the media industry work to "reinforce and disguise privileged-class interests,"[23] there is a good chance that the United States will become more class conscious and that people will demand more accurate assessments of the problems we face if more middle- and working-class families see their lifestyles continue to deteriorate in the twenty-first century.

Is Change Likely? Media Realities Support the Status Quo

Will journalists and entertainment writers become more cognizant of class-related issues in news and in television shows? Will they more accurately portray those issues in the future? It is possible that the media will become more aware of class as an important subject to address, but several trends do not bode well for more accurate stories and portrayals of class. Among these are the issues of media ownership and control.

Media Ownership and Senior Management

Media ownership has become increasingly concentrated in recent decades. Massive mergers and acquisitions involving the three major television networks (ABC, CBS, and NBC) have created three media "behemoths" — Viacom, Disney, and General Electric — and the news and entertainment divisions of these networks now constitute only small elements of much larger, more highly diversified corporate structures. Today, these media giants control most of that industry, and a television network is viewed as "just another contributor to the bottom line."[24] As the media scholar Shirley Biagi states, "The central force driving the media business in America is the desire to make money. American media are businesses, vast

30

---

[22]Perrucci and Wysong, *The New Class Society.*

[23]Perrucci and Wysong, *The New Class Society,* 284.

[24]Committee of Concerned Journalists, "The State of the News Media 2004," www .journalism.org (accessed June 17, 2004).

businesses. The products of these businesses are information and entertainment.... But American media are, above all, profit-centered."[25]

Concentration of media ownership through chains, broadcast networks, cross-media ownership, conglomerates, and vertical integration (when one company controls several related aspects of the same business) are major limitations to change in how class is represented in the news and entertainment industry. Social analysts like Greg Mantsios[26] are pessimistic about the prospects for change, because of the upper-class-based loyalties of media corporate elites:

> It is no wonder Americans cannot think straight about class. The mass media is neither objective, balanced, independent, nor neutral. Those who own and direct the mass media are themselves part of the upper class, and neither they nor the ruling class in general have to conspire to manipulate public opinion. Their interest is in preserving the status quo, and their view of society as fair and equitable comes naturally to them. But their ideology dominates our society and justifies what is in reality a perverse social order — one that perpetuates unprecedented elite privilege and power on the one hand and widespread deprivation on the other.[27]

According to Mantsios, wealthy media shareholders, corporate executives, and political leaders have a vested interest in obscuring class relations not only because these elites are primarily concerned about profits but because — being among the "haves" themselves — they do not see any reason to stir up class-related animosities. Why should they call attention to the real causes of poverty and inequality and risk the possibility of causing friction among the classes?

Media executives do not particularly care if the general public criticizes the *content* of popular culture as long as audiences do not begin to question the superstructure of media ownership and the benefits these corporations derive from corporate-friendly public policies. According to the sociologist Karen Sternheimer,

> Media conglomerates have a lot to gain by keeping us focused on the popular culture "problem," lest we decide to close some of the corporate tax loopholes to fund more social programs.... In short, the news media promote media phobia because it doesn't threaten the bottom line. Calling for social programs to reduce inequality and poverty would.[28]

---

[25]Shirley Biagi, *Media Impact: An Introduction to Mass Media* (Belmont, Calif.: Wadsworth, 2003), 21.

[26] *Mantsios:* See "Class in America — 2003" (p. 307). [Editors' note]

[27]Gregory Mantsios, "Media Magic: Making Class Invisible," in *Privilege: A Reader*, ed. Michael S. Kimmel and Abby L. Ferber, 99–109 (Boulder, Colo.: Westview, 2003), 108.

[28]Karen Sternheimer, *It's Not the Media: The Truth about Pop Culture's Influence on Children* (Boulder, Colo.: Westview, 2003), 211.

Although the corporate culture of the media industry may be set by shareholders and individuals in the top corporate ranks, day-to-day decisions often rest in the hands of the editor-in-chief (or a person in a similar role) at a newspaper or a television executive at a local station. Typically, the goals of these individuals reflect the profit-driven missions of their parent companies and the continual need to generate the right audiences (often young males between eighteen and thirty-five years of age) for advertisers. Television commentator Jeff Greenfield acknowledges this reality: "The most common misconception most people have about television concerns its product. To the viewer, the product is the programming. To the television executive, the product is the audience."[29] The profits of television networks and stations come from selling advertising, not from producing programs that are accurate reflections of social life.

Recent trends in the media industry — including concentration of ownership, a focus on increasing profits, and a move toward less regulation of the media by the federal government — do not offer reassurance that media representations of class (along with race, gender, age, and sexual orientation) will be of much concern to corporate shareholders or executives at the top media giants — unless, of course, this issue becomes related to the bottom line or there is public demand for change, neither of which seems likely. However, it does appear that there is a possibility for change among some journalists and entertainment writers.

Journalists: Constraints and Opportunities

Some analysts divide journalists into the "big time" players — reporters and journalists who are rich, having earned media salaries in the millions and by writing best-selling books (e.g., ABC's Peter Jennings) — and the "everyday" players, who are primarily known in their local or regional media markets.[30] Elite journalists in the first category typically are employed by major television networks (ABC, CBS, and NBC), popular cable news channels (such as CNN and FOX News), or major national newspapers such as the *Wall Street Journal, New York Times,* or *USA Today.* These journalists may be influential in national media agenda-setting, whereas the everyday media players, beat reporters, journalists, and middle- to upper-level managers at local newspapers or television stations at best can influence local markets.

[29]Quoted in Biagi, *Media Impact,* 170.

[30]One study identified the "typical journalist" as "a white Protestant male who has a bachelor's degree from a public college, is married, 36 years old, earns about $31,000 a year, has worked in journalism for about 12 years, does not belong to a journalism association, and works for a medium-sized (42 journalists), group-owned daily newspaper" (Weaver and Wilhoit 1996). Of course, many journalists today are white women, people of color, non-Protestants, and individuals who are between the ages of 45 and 54 (Committee of Concerned Journalists, "The State of the News Media 2004").

Some of these individuals — at either level — are deeply concerned about the state of journalism in this country, as one recent Pew Research Center for the People and the Press study of 547 national and local reporters, editors, and executives found.[31] One of the major concerns among these journalists was that the economic behavior of their companies was eroding the quality of journalism in the United States. By way of example, some journalists believe that business pressures in the media industry are making the news "thinner and shallower."[32] Journalists are also concerned that the news media pay "too little attention . . . to complex issues."[33] However, a disturbing finding in the Pew study was that some journalists believe that news content is becoming more shallow because that is what the public *wants*. This cynical view may become a self-fulfilling prophecy that leads journalists to produce a shallower product, based on the mistaken belief that the public cannot handle anything else.[34]

Despite all this, some opportunities do exist in the local and national news for *civic journalism* — "a belief that journalism has an obligation to public life — an obligation that goes beyond just telling the news or unloading lots of facts."[35] Civic journalism is rooted in the assumption that journalism has the ability either to empower a community or to help disable it. Based on a civic journalism perspective, a news reporter gathering information for a story has an opportunity to introduce other voices beyond those of the typical mainstream spokesperson called upon to discuss a specific issue such as the loss of jobs in a community or the growing problem of homelessness. Just as more journalists have become aware of the importance of fair and accurate representations of people based on race, gender, age, disability, and sexual orientation, it may be possible to improve media representations of class. Rather than pitting the middle class against the working class and the poor, for example, the media might frame stories in such a way as to increase people's awareness of their shared concerns in a nation where the upper class typically is portrayed as more important and more deserving than the average citizen.

The process of civic journalism encourages journalists to rethink their use of frames. Choosing a specific frame for a story is "the most powerful decision a journalist will make."[36] As journalists become more aware that

[31]Pew Center for Civic Journalism, "Finding Third Places: Other Voices, Different Stories," 2004, www.pewcenter.org/doingcj/videos/thirdplaces.html (accessed July 6, 2004).

[32]Bill Kovach, Tom Rosenstiel, and Amy Mitchell, "A Crisis of Confidence: A Commentary on the Findings," Pew Research Center for the People and the Press, 2004, www.stateofthenewsmedia.org/prc.pdf (accessed July 6, 2004), 27.

[33]Kovach, Rosenstiel, and Mitchell, "A Crisis of Confidence," 29.

[34]Kovach, Rosenstiel, and Mitchell, "A Crisis of Confidence."

[35]Pew Center for Civic Journalism, "Finding Third Places."

[36]Steve Smith, "Developing New Reflexes in Framing Stories," Pew Center for Civic Journalism, 1997, www.pewcenter.org/doingcj/civiccat/displayCivcat.php?id=97 (accessed July 3, 2004).

the media are more than neutral storytelling devices, perhaps more of them will develop alternative frames that look deeply into a community of interest (which might include the class-based realities of neighborhoods) to see "how the community interacts with, interrelates to, and potentially solves a pressing community problem." By asking "What is the essence of this story?" rather than "What is the conflict value of this story?" journalists might be less intent, for example, on pitting the indigenous U.S. working class against more recent immigrants or confronting unionized workers with their nonunionized counterparts. Stories that stress conflict have winners and losers, victors and villains; they suggest that people must compete, rather than cooperate, across class lines.[37] An exploration of other types of framing devices might produce better results in showing how social mobility does or does not work in the U.S. stratification system — highlighting, for example, what an individual's real chances are for moving up the class ladder (as is promised in much of the jargon about the rich and famous).

Advocates of civic journalism suggest that two practices might help journalists do a better job of framing in the public interest: *public listening* and *civic mapping*. Public listening refers to "the ability of journalists to listen with open minds and open ears; to understand what people are really saying."[38] Journalists engaged in public listening would be less interested in getting "superficial quotes or sound bites" and instead would move more deeply into the conversations that are actually taking place. Journalists would use open-ended questions in their interviews, by which they could look more deeply into people's hopes, fears, and values, rather than asking closed-ended questions to which the only allowable response choices are "yes/no" or "agree/disagree" — answers that in effect quickly (and superficially) gauge an individual's opinion on a topic. When journalists use civic mapping, they seek out underlying community concerns through discussions with people. They attempt to look beneath the surface of current public discourse on an issue. Mapping helps journalists learn about the ideas, attitudes, and opinions that really exist among diverse groups of people, not just "public opinion" or politicians' views of what is happening.

By seeking out *third places* where they can find "other voices" and hear "different stories," journalists may learn more about people from diverse backgrounds and find out what they are actually thinking and experiencing.[39] A "third place" is a location where people gather and often end up talking about things that are important to them. According to the sociologist Ray Oldenburg, the third place is "a great variety of public places that host the regular, voluntary, informal, and happily anticipated gatherings of

40

---

[37]Richard Harwood, "Framing a Story: What's It Really About?" Pew Center for Civic Journalism, 2004, www.pewcenter.org/doingcj/videos/framing.html (accessed July 3, 2004).

[38]Smith, "Developing New Reflexes in Framing Stories."

[39]Pew Center for Civic Journalism, "Finding Third Places."

individuals beyond the realms of home and work."[40] If the first place is the home, and the second place is the work setting, then the third place includes such locations as churches, community centers, cafes, coffee shops, bookstores, bars, and other places where people informally gather. As journalists join in the conversation, they can learn what everyday people are thinking about a social issue such as tax cuts for the wealthy. They can also find out what concerns people have and what they think contributes to such problems as neighborhood deterioration.

In addition to listening to other voices and seeking out different stories in third places, journalists might look more systematically at how changes in public policies — such as in tax laws, welfare initiatives, or policies that affect publicly funded child care or public housing — might affect people in various class locations. What are the political and business pressures behind key policy decisions like these? How do policies affect the middle class? The working class? Others? For example, what part does class play in perceptions about local law enforcement agencies? How are police officers viewed in small, affluent incorporated cities that have their own police departments, as compared to low-income neighborhoods of the bigger cities? While wealthy residents in the smaller cities may view police officers as "employees" who do their bidding (such as prohibiting the "wrong kind of people" from entering their city limits at night), in some low-income sectors of larger cities the police may be viewed as "oppressors" or as "racists" who contribute to, rather than reduce, problems of lawlessness and crime in the community. Journalists who practice civic journalism might look beyond typical framing devices to tell a more compelling story about how the intersections of race *and* class produce a unique chemistry between citizens and law enforcement officials. In this way, journalists would not be using taken-for-granted framing devices that have previously been employed to "explain" what is happening in these communities.

Given current constraints on the media, including the fact that much of the new investment in journalism today is being spent on disseminating the news rather than on collecting it,[41] there is room for only cautious optimism that some journalists will break out of the standard reflexive mode to explore the microscopic realities of class at the level where people live, and at the macroscopic level of society, where corporate and governmental elites make important decisions that affect everyone else.

Some media analysts believe that greater awareness of class-related realities in the media would strengthen the democratic process in the United States. According to Mantsios, "A mass media that did not have its own class interests in preserving the status quo would acknowledge that inordinate

[40]Ray Oldenburg, *The Great Good Place: Cafés, Coffee Shops, Bookstores, Bars, Hair Salons and Other Hangouts at the Heart of a Community* (New York: Marlowe, 1999), 16.

[41]Committee of Concerned Journalists, "The State of the News Media 2004."

wealth and power undermine democracy and that a 'free market' economy can ravage a people and their communities."[42] It remains to be seen, however, whether organizations like the Project for Excellence in Journalism and the Committee of Concerned Journalists will be successful in their efforts to encourage journalists to move beyond the standard reflexive mode so that they will use new frames that more accurately reflect class-based realities.

Like journalists, many television entertainment writers could look for better ways to frame stories. However, these writers are also beleaguered by changes in the media environment, including new threats to their economic security from reality shows that typically do not employ in-house or freelance writers like continuing series do. As a result, it has become increasingly difficult for entertainment writers to stay gainfully employed, let alone bring new ideas into television entertainment.[43]

We cannot assume that most journalists and television writers are in a   45 position to change media portrayals of class and inequality; however, in the final analysis, the responsibility rests with each of us to evaluate the media and to treat it as only one, limited, source of information and entertainment in our lives. For the sake of our children and grandchildren, we must balance the perspectives we gain from the media with our own lived experiences and use a wider sociological lens to look at what is going on around us in everyday life. Some analysts believe that the media amuse and lull audiences rather than stimulating them to think, but we must not become complacent, thinking that everything is all right as our society and world become increasingly divided between the "haves" and the "have nots."[44] If the media industry persists in retaining the same old frames for class, it will behoove each of us as readers and viewers to break out of those frames and more thoroughly explore these issues on our own.

Bibliography

Biagi, Shirley. *Media Impact: An Introduction to Mass Media,* Belmont, Calif.: Wadsworth, 2003.

Butler, Judith. "Performative Acts and Gender Constitution: An Essay in Phenomenology and Feminist Theory." In *Performing Feminisms: Feminist Critical Theory and Theatre.* Edited by Sue-Ellen Case. Baltimore: Johns Hopkins University Press, 1990.

Committee of Concerned Journalists. "The State of the News Media 2004." www.journalism.org (accessed June 17, 2004).

De Coster, Karen, and Brad Edmonds. Lewrockwell.com, 2003. "TV Nation: The Killing of American Brain Cells." www.lewrockwell.com/decoster/decoster78.html (accessed July 7, 2004).

---

[42]Mantsios, "Media Magic," 108.

[43]"So You Wanna Be a Sitcom Writer?" soyouwanna.com, 2004, www.soyouwanna.com/site/syws/sitcom/sitcom.html (accessed July 7, 2004).

[44]Sternheimer, *It's Not the Media.*

Delaney, Tim, and Allene Wilcox. "Sports and the Role of the Media." In *Values, Society and Evolution,* edited by Harry Birx and Tim Delaney, 199–215. Auburn, N.Y. Legend, 2002.

DeNavas-Walt, Carmen, and Robert W. Cleveland. "Income in the United States: 2002." *U.S. Census Bureau: Current Population Reports,* P60-221. Washington, D.C.: U.S. Government Printing Office, 2003.

Ginsberg, Thomas. "Union Hopes to Win Over Starbucks Shop Workers." *Austin American-Statesman,* July 2, 2004, D6.

Grigoriadis, Vanessa. "Her Royal Lie-ness: The So-Called Saudi Princess Was Only One of the Many Identities Lisa Walker Tried On Like Jewelry." *New York Metro.* www.newyorkmetro.com/nymetro/news/people/columns/intelligencer/n_10418 (accessed December 18, 2004).

Harwood, Richard. "Framing a Story: What's It Really About?" Pew Center for Civic Journalism, 2004. www.pewcenter.org/doingcj/videos/framing.html (accessed July 3, 2004).

hooks, bell [Gloria Watkins]. *Where We Stand: Class Matters.* New York: Routledge, 2000.

Kovach, Bill, Tom Rosenstiel, and Amy Mitchell. "A Crisis of Confidence: A Commentary on the Findings." Pew Research Center for the People and the Press, 2004. www.stateofthenewsmedia.org/prc.pdf (accessed July 6, 2004).

Mantsios, Gregory. "Media Magic: Making Class Invisible." In *Privilege: A Reader,* edited by Michael S. Kimmel and Abby L. Ferber, 99–109. Boulder, Colo.: Westview, 2003.

Maull, Samuel. "Antoinette Millard Countersues American Express for $2 Million for Allowing Her to Charge $951,000." creditsuit.org/credit.php/blog/comments/antoinette_millard_countersues_american_express_for_2_million_for_allowing (accessed December 18, 2004).

Nocera, Joseph. *A Piece of the Action: How the Middle Class Joined the Money Class.* New York: Simon and Schuster, 1994.

Oldenburg, Ray. *The Great Good Place: Cafés, Coffee Shops, Bookstores, Bars Hair Salons and Other Hangouts at the Heart of a Community.* New York: Marlowe, 1999.

Perrucci, Robert, and Earl Wysong. *The New Class Society.* 2nd edition. Lanham, Md.: Rowman & Littlefield, 2003.

Pew Center for Civic Journalism. 2004, "Finding Third Places: Other Voices, Different Stories." www.pewcenter.org/doingcj/videos/thirdplaces.html (accessed July 6, 2004).

Proctor, Bernadette D., and Joseph Dalaker. "Poverty in the United States: 2002." *U.S. Census Bureau: Current Population Reports,* P60-22. Washington, D.C.: U.S. Government Printing Office, 2003.

Schor, Juliet B. *Born to Buy: The Commercialized Child and the New Consumer Culture.* New York: Scribner, 2004.

Sicha, Choire. "They'll Always Have Paris." *New York Times,* June 13, 2004, AR31, AR41.

Smith, Steve. "Developing New Reflexes in Framing Stories." Pew Center for Civic Journalism, 1997. www.pewcenter.org/doingcj/civiccat/displayCivcat.php?id=97 (accessed July 3, 2004).

"So You Wanna Be a Sitcom Writer?" soyouwanna.com, 2004. www.soyouwanna.com/site/syws/sitcom/sitcom.html (accessed July 7, 2004).

Sternheimer, Karen. *It's Not the Media: The Truth about Pop Culture's Influence on Children.* Boulder, Colo.: Westview, 2003.

Uchitelle, Louis. "We Pledge Allegiance to the Mall." *New York Times,* December 6, 2004, C12.

Weaver, David H., and G. Cleveland Wilhoit. *The American Journalist in the 1990s.* Mahwah, N.J.: Lawrence Erlbaum, 1996.

ENGAGING THE TEXT

1. Debate Kendall's assertion that "the media do not simply mirror society; rather, they help to shape it and to create cultural perceptions" (para. 3). Do you agree with Kendall's claim that the media distort our perceptions of social inequality? Do you think that watching TV inclines Americans to run up credit card debt?

2. Review Kendall's explanation of why middle- and working-class people sometimes buy items beyond their means, particularly items associated with wealthy celebrities. Do you agree that this behavior is best understood as "vicarious living" and "unnecessary consumerism"? In small groups, brainstorm lists of purchases you think exemplify hedonistic or unnecessary consumerism. How does hedonistic consumerism appear in a college setting?

3. Kendall says the media use "thematic framing" and "episodic framing" in portraying poor Americans. Define these terms in your own words and discuss whether the media typically portray the poor as "deviant" or "Other."

4. According to Kendall, how do media representations of the working class and the middle class differ? Do you see evidence of this difference in the shows she mentions or in others you are familiar with?

5. What does Kendall mean by "civic journalism" (para. 37)? Why is she pessimistic about the future of civic journalism in national news organizations? Do you see any evidence of such journalism in your local news outlets?

EXPLORING CONNECTIONS

6. Imagine what "Looking for Work" (p. 26) or "The Lesson" (p. 270) might look like if it were turned into a TV episode. Keeping Kendall's observations in mind, how do you think TV might frame these stories about social class?

7. Re-examine the images in the Visual Portfolio (p. 325). Discuss them in terms of how they "frame" issues. That is, consider how they provide "mental shortcuts" to help us understand class in particular ways.

EXTENDING THE CRITICAL CONTEXT

8. Watch an episode of *The Simple Life* to test Kendall's claims about that program; report your findings to the class.

9. Review Kendall's definitions of consensus framing, admiration framing, emulation framing, and price-tag framing. Then watch one of the TV shows she mentions in paragraph 8 or a similar current show and look for evidence of these framing devices. Discuss with classmates how prominent these frames seem to be in contemporary TV programs.

Stephen Cruz

STUDS TERKEL

The speaker of the following oral history is Stephen Cruz, a man who at first glance seems to be living the American Dream of success and upward mobility. He is never content, however, and he comes to question his own values and the meaning of success in the world of corporate America. Studs Terkel (b. 1912) is the best-known practitioner of oral history in the United States. Over the course of a long career he has compiled several books by interviewing widely varying people — ordinary people for the most part — about important subjects like work, race, faith, and the Great Depression. The edited versions of these interviews are often surprisingly powerful crystallizations of American social history: Terkel's subjects give voice to the frustrations and hopes of whole generations of Americans. Terkel won a Pulitzer Prize in 1985 for "The Good War": An Oral History of World War II. *His most recent book is* And They All Sang: Adventures of an Eclectic Disc Jockey *(2005). This selection first appeared in his* American Dreams: Lost and Found *(1980).*

He is thirty-nine.

"The family came in stages from Mexico. Your grandparents usually came first, did a little work, found little roots, put together a few bucks, and brought the family in, one at a time. Those were the days when controls at the border didn't exist as they do now."

You just tried very hard to be whatever it is the system wanted of you. I was a good student and, as small as I was, a pretty good athlete. I was well liked, I thought. We were fairly affluent, but we lived down where all the trashy whites were. It was the only housing we could get. As kids, we never understood why. We did everything right. We didn't have those Mexican accents, we were never on welfare. Dad wouldn't be on welfare to save his soul. He woulda died first. He worked during the Depression. He carries that pride with him, even today.

Of the five children, I'm the only one who really got into the business world. We learned quickly that you have to look for opportunities and add things up very quickly. I was in liberal arts, but as soon as Sputnik[1] went up, well, golly, hell, we knew where the bucks were. I went right over to the registrar's office and signed up for engineering. I got my degree in '62. If you had a master's in business as well, they were just paying all kinds of bucks. So that's what I did. Sure enough, the market was super. I had fourteen job offers. I could have had a hundred if I wanted to look around.

---

[1] *Sputnik:* Satellite launched by the Soviet Union in 1957; this launch signaled the beginning of the "space race" between the United States and the USSR.

I never once associated these offers with my being a minority. I was   5
aware of the Civil Rights Act of 1964, but I was still self-confident enough
to feel they wanted me because of my abilities. Looking back, the reason I
got more offers than the other guys was because of the government edict.
And I thought it was because I was so goddamned brilliant. (Laughs.) In
1962, I didn't get as many offers as those who were less qualified. You have
a tendency to blame the job market. You just don't want to face the issue of
discrimination.

I went to work with Procter & Gamble. After about two years, they told
me I was one of the best supervisors they ever had and they were gonna
promote me. Okay, I went into personnel. Again, I thought it was because I
was such a brilliant guy. Now I started getting wise to the ways of the American
Dream. My office was glass-enclosed, while all the other offices were
enclosed so you couldn't see into them. I was the visible man.

They made sure I interviewed most of the people that came in. I just
didn't really think there was anything wrong until we got a new plant manager,
a southerner. I received instructions from him on how I should interview
blacks. Just check and see if they smell, okay? That was the beginning
of my training program. I started asking: Why weren't we hiring more
minorities? I realized I was the only one in a management position.

I guess as a Mexican I was more acceptable because I wasn't really
black. I was a good compromise. I was visibly good. I hired a black secretary,
which was *verboten*. When I came back from my vacation, she was
gone. My boss fired her while I was away. I asked why and never got a good
reason.

Until then, I never questioned the American Dream. I was convinced if
you worked hard, you could make it. I never considered myself different.
That was the trouble. We had been discriminated against a lot, but I never
associated it with society. I considered it an individual matter. Bad people,
my mother used to say. In '68 I began to question.

I was doing fine. My very first year out of college, I was making twelve   10
thousand dollars. I left Procter & Gamble because I really saw no opportunity.
They were content to leave me visible, but my thoughts were not really
solicited. I may have overreacted a bit, with the plant manager's attitude,
but I felt there's no way a Mexican could get ahead here.

I went to work for Blue Cross. It's 1969. The Great Society[2] is in full
swing. Those who never thought of being minorities before are being
turned on. Consciousness raising is going on. Black programs are popping
up in universities. Cultural identity and all that. But what about the one
issue in this country: economics? There were very few management jobs for
minorities, especially blacks.

---

[2]*The Great Society:* President Lyndon B. Johnson's term for the American society he
hoped to establish through social reforms, including an antipoverty program.

The stereotypes popped up again. If you're Oriental, you're real good in mathematics. If you're Mexican, you're a happy guy to have around, pleasant but emotional. Mexicans are either sleeping or laughing all the time. Life is just one big happy kind of event. *Mañana.* Good to have as part of the management team, as long as you weren't allowed to make decisions.

I was thinking there were two possibilities why minorities were not making it in business. One was deep, ingrained racism. But there was still the possibility that they were simply a bunch of bad managers who just couldn't cut it. You see, until now I believed everything I was taught about the dream: the American businessman is omnipotent and fair. If we could show these turkeys there's money to be made in hiring minorities, these businessmen — good managers, good decision makers — would respond. I naively thought American businessmen gave a damn about society, that given a choice they would do the right thing. I had that faith.

I was hungry for learning about decision-making criteria. I was still too far away from top management to see exactly how they were working. I needed to learn more. Hey, just learn more and you'll make it. That part of the dream hadn't left me yet. I was still clinging to the notion of work your ass off, learn more than anybody else, and you'll get in that sphere.

During my fifth year at Blue Cross, I discovered another flaw in the American Dream. Minorities are as bad to other minorities as whites are to minorities. The strongest weapon the white manager had is the old divide and conquer routine. My mistake was thinking we were all at the same level of consciousness. 15

I had attempted to bring together some blacks with the other minorities. There weren't too many of them anyway. The Orientals never really got involved. The blacks misunderstood what I was presenting, perhaps I said it badly. They were on the cultural kick: a manager should be crucified for saying "Negro" instead of "black." I said as long as the Negro or the black gets the job, it doesn't mean a damn what he's called. We got into a huge hassle. Management, of course, merely smiled. The whole struggle fell flat on its face. It crumpled from divisiveness. So I learned another lesson. People have their own agenda. It doesn't matter what group you're with, there is a tendency to put the other guy down regardless.

The American Dream began to look so damn complicated, I began to think: Hell, if I wanted, I could just back away and reap the harvest myself. By this time, I'm up to twenty-five thousand dollars a year. It's beginning to look good, and a lot of people are beginning to look good. And they're saying: "Hey, the American Dream, you got it. Why don't you lay off?" I wasn't falling in line.

My bosses were telling me I had all the "ingredients" for top management. All that was required was to "get to know our business." This term comes up all the time. If I could just warn all minorities and women whenever you hear "get to know our business," they're really saying "fall in line." Stay within that fence, and glory can be yours. I left Blue Cross disillusioned. They offered me a director's job at thirty thousand dollars before I quit.

All I had to do was behave myself. I had the "ingredients" of being a good Chicano, the equivalent of the good nigger. I was smart. I could articulate well. People didn't know by my speech patterns that I was of Mexican heritage. Some tell me I don't look Mexican, that I have a certain amount of Italian, Lebanese, or who knows. (Laughs.)

One could easily say: "Hey, what's your bitch? The American Dream   20 has treated you beautifully. So just knock it off and quit this crap you're spreading around." It was a real problem. Every time I turned around, America seemed to be treating me very well.

Hell, I even thought of dropping out, the hell with it. Maybe get a job in a factory. But what happened? Offers kept coming in. I just said to myself: God, isn't this silly? You might as well take the bucks and continue looking for the answer. So I did that. But each time I took the money, the conflict in me got more intense, not less.

Wow, I'm up to thirty-five thousand a year. This is a savings and loan business. I have faith in the executive director. He was the kind of guy I was looking for in top management: understanding, humane, also looking for the formula. Until he was up for consideration as executive v.p. of the entire organization. All of a sudden everything changed. It wasn't until I saw this guy flip-flop that I realized how powerful vested interests are. Suddenly he's saying: "Don't rock the boat. Keep a low profile. Get in line." Another disappointment.

Subsequently, I went to work for a consulting firm. I said to myself: Okay, I've got to get close to the executive mind. I need to know how they work. Wow, a consulting firm.

Consulting firms are saving a lot of American businessmen. They're doing it in ways that defy the whole notion of capitalism. They're not allowing these businesses to fail. Lockheed was successful in getting U.S. funding guarantees because of the efforts of consulting firms working on their behalf, helping them look better. In this kind of work, you don't find minorities. You've got to be a proven success in business before you get there.

The American Dream, I see now, is governed not by education, oppor-   25 tunity, and hard work, but by power and fear. The higher up in the organization you go, the more you have to lose. The dream is *not losing*. This is the notion pervading America today: don't lose.

When I left the consulting business, I was making fifty thousand dollars a year. My last performance appraisal was: you can go a long way in this business, you can be a partner, but you gotta know our business. It came up again. At this point, I was incapable of being disillusioned any more. How easy it is to be swallowed up by the same set of values that governs the top guy. I was becoming that way. I was becoming concerned about losing that fifty grand or so a year. So I asked other minorities who had it made. I'd go up and ask 'em: "Look, do you owe anything to others?" The answer was:

"We owe nothing to anybody." They drew from the civil rights movement but felt no debt. They've quickly forgotten how it happened. It's like I was when I first got out of college. Hey, it's really me, I'm great. I'm great. I'm as angry with these guys as I am with the top guys.

Right now, it's confused. I've had fifteen years in the business world as "a success." Many Anglos would be envious of my progress. Fifty thousand dollars a year puts you in the one or two top percent of all Americans. Plus my wife making another thirty thousand. We had lots of money. When I gave it up, my cohorts looked at me not just as strange, but as something of a traitor. "You're screwing it up for all of us. You're part of our union, we're the elite, we should govern. What the hell are you doing?" So now I'm looked at suspiciously by my peer group as well.

I'm teaching at the University of Wisconsin at Platteville. It's nice. My colleagues tell me what's on their minds. I got a farm next-door to Platteville. With farm prices being what they are (laughs), it's a losing proposition. But with university work and what money we've saved, we're gonna be all right.

The American Dream is getting more elusive. The dream is being governed by a few people's notion of what the dream is. Sometimes I feel it's a small group of financiers that gets together once a year and decides all the world's issues.

It's getting so big. The small-business venture is not there any more. Business has become too big to influence. It can't be changed internally. A counterpower is needed.   30

ENGAGING THE TEXT

1. As Cruz moves up the economic ladder, he experiences growing conflict that keeps him from being content and proud of his accomplishments. To what do you attribute his discontent? Is his "solution" one that you would recommend?

2. Cruz says that the real force in America is the dream of "not losing" (para. 25). What does he mean by this? Do you agree?

3. What, according to Stephen Cruz, is wrong with the American Dream? Write an essay in which you first define and then either defend or critique his position.

4. Imagine a continuation of Stephen Cruz's life in which he gives up his teaching job and returns to the business world. What might his career have been like over the last thirty years? How would you expect Cruz to react to the business environment today?

EXPLORING CONNECTIONS

5. Compare Stephen Cruz to "Ragged Dick" (p. 264) and to "Black Avenger" Ken Hamblin (p. 285) in terms of the American Dream and individual success. What goals, beliefs, or values do they share, and what distinguishes Cruz from the others?

6. Compare Stephen Cruz to Richard Rodriguez (p. 193), Gary Soto (p. 26), and Mike Rose (p. 161) in terms of their attitudes toward education and success.

EXTENDING THE CRITICAL CONTEXT

7. According to Cruz, in 1969 few management positions were open to members of minority groups. Working in small groups, go to the library and look up current statistics on minorities in business (for example, the number of large minority-owned companies; the number of minority chief executives among major corporations; the distribution of minorities among top management, middle management, supervisory, and clerical positions). Compare notes with classmates and discuss.

Good Noise: Cora Tucker

ANNE WITTE GARLAND

When most people think about the American Dream, they don't visualize a factory job and a cluttered house right next to the railroad tracks. As you read this selection about community activist Cora Tucker, however, think about the connection of her life to core American values like democracy, progress, and individual rights. Author Anne Witte Garland is a freelance writer covering environmental, public health, consumer, and women's issues. She is the author of The Way We Grow: Good-Sense Solutions for Protecting Our Families from Pesticides in Food *(1993). This selection comes from her 1988 book* Women Activists: Challenging the Abuse of Power.

Cora Tucker's house is so close to the railroad tracks that at night when trains thunder by, the beds shake. The house and furniture are modest, and in the kitchen there's a lingering smell of the lard Cora cooks with. There are traces of Virginia red clay on the kitchen floor, and piled up on the bedroom floor are cardboard boxes overflowing with newspaper clippings and other papers.

Cora admits she doesn't like housekeeping anymore. The plaques and photographs hanging in the kitchen and living room attest to what she does enjoy; alongside religious pictures and photos of her children and grandchildren, there are several citizenship awards, certificates acknowledging her work in civil rights, and photos of her — a pretty, smiling black woman — with various politicians. One framed picture in the kitchen was handmade for Cora by some of the inmates in a nearby prison, whom Cora has visited and helped. In it, Old English letters made of foil spell out, "God grant me the serenity to accept the things I cannot change, the courage to change the things I can, and wisdom to know the difference." Cora has plenty of all three virtues, although "serene" probably isn't the first adjective a stranger would pin on her. But then, there isn't much that Cora would say she can't change, either.

Cora Tucker is something of an institution in Halifax County, Virginia, a rural county bordering North Carolina. In more than a dozen years, she has missed only a handful of the county board of supervisors' monthly meetings. Her name appears in the letters columns of the two daily newspapers several times a week — either signed onto her own letter or, almost as often, vilified in someone else's. She seems to know and be known by every black person on the street, in the post offices, and in stores and restaurants. And she is known by white and black people alike as having taken on many of the local, white-controlled institutions. Her main concern is simply fighting for the underdog, which she does in many ways — from social work–like visits to the elderly and invalids, to legal fights against racial discrimination, registering people to vote, and lobbying on issues like health care and the environment.

Cora was born in 1941 ten miles from where she lives now, near the Halifax county seat, in the small town of South Boston. Her father was a school teacher and later a railway porter. He died when Cora was three, and her mother and the nine children became sharecroppers on white men's farms. It was as a sharecropper, Cora says, that she learned how to do community organizing. She started by trying to help other sharecroppers to get things like better heating and food stamps. "I didn't call it 'organizing,' then," she says. "I just called it 'being concerned.' When you do sharecropping, you move around a lot. So I got to know everybody in the county, and to know what people's problems were.

"Sharecropping is the worst form of drudgery; it's slavery really. You   5
work on a man's farm, supposedly for half the profit on the crops you grow. That's what the contract says. But you pay for all the stuff that goes into the crop — seeds, fertilizer, and all. You get free housing, but most sharecroppers' housing is dilapidated and cold. It isn't insulated — it's just shacks, really. Sharecroppers are poor. I know of a family of twelve who grew fifteen acres of tobacco, and at the end of the year, they had earned just fifty dollars. And I know sharecroppers who needed food and applied for food stamps, but couldn't get them because they supposedly made too much money; the boss went to the food stamp office, and said they made such and such, so they couldn't qualify."

Cora went to work very young, planting and plowing with the others in the family. Her mother taught her to cook when she was six; Cora remembers having to stand on a crate to reach the kitchen counter. She was a curious and intelligent child who loved school and was unhappy when she had to stay out of school to clean house for the white woman on the farm where they lived.

Cora always adored her mother. Bertha Plenty Moesley was a "chief stringer" — a step in tobacco processing that involves picking the green tobacco leaves from the plants one at a time, and stringing them together three leaves to a stick, so that they can be hung to dry and cure. "My mama worked hard," Cora says. "She would plow and do all the things the men did. She was independent; she raised her children alone for eighteen years. When I was little, I felt so bad that she had to work that hard just so we could survive. There was welfare out there — all kinds of help, if only some-body had told her how to go about getting it. She had very little education, and didn't know to go down to the welfare office for help. As I got older, I was upset by that and made up my mind, when I was about eight or nine years old, that if I ever got grown, I'd make sure that everybody knew how to get everything there was to get. And I really meant it. I learned early how to get things done, and I learned it would take initiative to get what I wanted."

By the time Cora learned about welfare, her mother wouldn't take advantage of it. She was proud, and she told the children to have self-respect. "We didn't have anything else," Cora's mother says. "The kids had only themselves to be proud of." Cora took the advice to heart. There's a story she tells about growing up that has found a permanent place in community-organizing lore. In her high school, which was segregated at the time (Halifax County schools didn't integrate until 1969, under court order), Cora entered an essay contest on the topic of "what America means to me." She was taken by surprise when her bitter essay about growing up black in the South won a statewide award. But on awards night she was in for another surprise. The winners were to have their essays read, and then shake hands with the Virginia governor. Cora's mother was in the audience beaming, along with Cora's friends and teachers. But when her essay was read, Cora didn't recognize it — it had been rewritten, and the less critical sentiments weren't hers at all. She refused to greet the governor. "I disappointed everyone — my mother even cried."

The only person who supported her that night, she says, was a high school literature teacher, whom she credits as an important influence on her. "He spent a lot of time with me, encouraging me. Every time an issue came up that I felt strongly about, he'd have me write about it — letters to the editor that never got printed. He told me, 'Nobody can make you a second-class citizen but you. You should be involved in what's going on around you.'"

Instead, at seventeen she dropped out of high school to get married. As she describes it, the next several years were consumed with housekeeping and having children — six of them in rapid succession. She and her husband adopted a seventh. At first, Cora says, she threw herself enthusiastically into her new role. "I just wanted to be married. My father-in-law used to tease

10

me about making myself so busy just being married. He'd say, 'You ain't going to keep this up for long.' But I'd say yes I would. Every morning, I put clean sheets on our beds — washed and ironed them. I ironed every diaper. I read all the housekeeping magazines; my house was immaculate. But I was beginning to find myself so bored, even then. My husband was farming then, sharecropping, and he'd get up early; I'd get up too, and feed him and the kids, and then do the cleaning. But when you clean every day, there just isn't that much to do, so I'd be finished by ten in the morning! I joined a book club, so that I would get a book every month — but I would get bored in between. I would read the book in two days — I tried to savor it, but I couldn't make it last any longer. Then, when the kids started growing up and going to school, that would occupy me a little more. I'd feed them, then take them to school, and come back and clean and then start making lunch. But just as soon as my baby started school, I went out and got a job."

Halifax County has several textile and garment factories, and Cora went to work as a seamstress for one of the largest, a knit sportswear manufacturer. It was a fairly new operation, and the mostly women employees were expected to do everything, from lifting fabric bolts weighing forty or fifty pounds each, to sitting at sewing machines for eight hour stretches. There was no union; the county boasts in promotional material that less than 5 percent of the county's workforce is unionized. "Every time I used to talk to the girls there, my boss thought I was trying to get a union started. And I sure thought there *should* be a union; there were lots of health hazards, and people were always getting hurt. People got back injuries, two people even had heart attacks in the factory, because of the working conditions. I once got a woman to come down from Baltimore to talk about forming a union, but people got frightened because the bosses warned us that if there was any union activity, we'd lose our jobs."

Cora worked at the factory for seven years. The first thing she did with the money she was earning was to buy land for a house. "We had lived in places where we were so cold," she says. "We'd have no windows, and no wood. My dream was always to grow up and build me a house — my own house, out of brick. My husband never really wanted one; he was just as happy moving around. But after I had the babies and went to work at the factory, I told him I was going to build me a house. So the first year I worked, I saved a thousand dollars. The next year I saved another thousand, and then borrowed some from the company, to buy some land. Then I started saving again, for the house. But when I went to the FHA, they said I couldn't get a house without my husband's permission. At first, he said he wasn't going to have anything to do with it, so I said I'd buy a trailer instead. When he found out, he figured I might just as well put the money into a house, so he signed the papers. We built the house; it was the first time any of us had been inside a new house. I was crazy about it; we could sit down and say exactly where we wanted things. And while I was working, I bought every stick of furniture in it."

In 1976 Cora hurt her back and had to leave her job. Over the next few years she underwent surgery several times — first for her back, and then for cancer (for which she has had to have periodic treatments ever since). In the meantime, she had become active in the community. In the 1960s, she had participated in organizations like the National Association for the Advancement of Colored People, and another group called the Assemblies, but they moved too slowly for her tastes. ("They weren't really interested in taking on the power structure," she complains.) She had also organized her own letter-writing campaign in support of the federal Voting Rights Act to make it easier for blacks to vote. She had gone around to local churches, speaking to people and encouraging them to write to their representatives in Washington. She also took advantage of knowing women who ran beauty parlors — she provided the paper and pens, so that women could write letters while they sat under the hair dryers. "People would say to me, 'What good will it do?' But I think politicians have to be responsive if enough pressure can be brought to bear on them. You can complain, I can complain, but that's just two people. A politician needs to get piles of letters saying vote for this bill, because if you don't, you won't be in office much longer!" Cora was responsible for generating about five hundred letters supporting the voting law.

She takes voting very seriously. In 1977, she campaigned for a populist candidate for Virginia governor. She was undergoing cancer treatments at the time, but they made her tired, so she stopped the treatments in order to register people to vote. She had taught herself to drive, and personally rode around the county from house to house, filling her car with everyone there who was of voting age, driving them to the court house to register, and then home again. She's credited with having registered over one thousand people this way, and on election day, she personally drove many of them to the polling place.

While Cora was growing up, her mother's house was always filled with people — besides her own family, several cousins lived with them, and aunts and uncles who had moved up north and came back to visit would stay with Cora's mother. Cora's own house was the same way — always filled with neighborhood teenagers, white and black. Cora became a confidante for the young people, and she encouraged them to read about black history, and to be concerned about the community. One of the things that upset the teenagers was the fate of a county recreation center. Halifax had no recreation facilities, and the county had applied for money from the federal Department of Housing and Urban Development (HUD) to build a center. When HUD awarded the county $500,000, however, the county turned it down because, as Cora puts it, there were "too many strings attached" — meaning it would have to be integrated. At home because of her back trouble and cancer, Cora took it on herself to help steer the teenagers' anger toward research into community problems. "When I heard about the recreation center, I went to the county board meeting and raised hell," she says. "But they went ahead and did what they wanted anyway. What I realized then was that if I had had all those kids come with me to the meeting, there would have been some changes. You need warm bodies — persons present and accounted for — if you want to get things done."

In 1975, Cora founded her own organization, Citizens for a Better America. CBA's first project was a study of black spending and employment patterns in the county. The study was based on a survey of three hundred people; it took two years to complete, with Cora's teenage friends doing much of the legwork. The findings painted a clear picture of inequality. Blacks made up nearly half the county population, and according to the survey, spent a disproportionate share of their salaries on food, cars, and furniture. But, as the study pointed out, there were very few black employees at the grocery stores where the money was spent, not a single black salesperson in the furniture stores, and no black salesperson at the auto dealerships. Blacks weren't represented at all on newspaper or radio station staffs.

Cora saw to it that the survey results were published in the local newspaper. The next step was to act on the results. The survey had uncovered problems with hiring practices and promotions of blacks in the school system, so Cora complained to the school board. After waiting in vain for the board to respond, CBA filed a complaint with what was then the federal Department of Health, Education, and Welfare. An HEW investigation confirmed the problems, and the agency threatened to cut off federal education funds to the county if the discrimination wasn't corrected. The county promised that the next principals it hired would be black.

CBA then took on other aspects of the county government. The survey had found that of all the county employees, only 7 percent were black — chiefly custodial workers or workers hired with federal Comprehensive Employment Training Administration (CETA) funds. Only one black person in the county government made over $20,000 a year. When the county refused to negotiate with Cora's organization about their hiring practices, CBA filed a complaint with the federal revenue sharing program. A Virginia state senator was successful in getting a federal investigation into the complaint stalled, but Cora went over his head, to the congressional Black Caucus and Maryland's black congressman, Parren Mitchell. Mitchell contacted Senator Edward Kennedy's office, which pressed to have the investigation completed. The findings confirmed CBA's, and the county was told to improve its hiring practices or stand to lose federal revenues.

CBA also initiated a boycott of local businesses that didn't hire minorities — Cora avoided the term "boycott," and instead called the action the "Spend Your Money Wisely Campaign." Leaflets were distributed listing the stores that hired black employees, and urging people, "Where Blacks are not HIRED, Blacks should not buy!"

Cora was developing a reputation. She started having frequent contact with the congressional Black Caucus, and would be called occasionally to   20 testify in Washington on welfare issues. "They don't usually get people like me to testify; they get all these 'experts' instead. But every once in a while, it's good for them to hear from someone who isn't a professional, whose English isn't good, and who talks from a grassroots level."

It wasn't just in Washington that her reputation was growing, but back home, too. "I have a lot of enemies," she says. "There are derogatory things in the papers about me all the time. And the county government doesn't like me, because I keep going to all those board meetings and raising hell about what they do. When I go sometimes, they say, 'Yes, what do you want now, Ms. Tucker?' But I don't care what they think — I just tell them what I want. So a lot of the white power structure don't really like me. They think I'm a troublemaker, but I'm not really. I just believe what I believe in. Then there are black people too, who think that I want too much too soon. But when you think about it, black people have been in America 360-some years, so when is the time ever going to be right? The time doesn't *get* right; you make it right. So I'm not offended by what anybody says about me."

Sometimes the problem isn't just what people say; it's what they do. Cora has had many experiences with harassment. At first it was phone calls, from people threatening to burn her house down or telling her to "go back to Africa." Once she wrote a letter to the editor saying, "This is an open letter to all the people who call me and ask, what do you niggers want now? and hang up before I can tell them. . . .

"Blacks and poor people want to share in the economic progress of Halifax County, and when we get our children educated and motivated we would like them to come back to Halifax County and do something other than push mops and brooms. And a few of us would like our grandchildren to grow up near us, and if our children decide to make their home elsewhere it will be due to choice and not an economic necessity."

The harassment has taken other forms as well. Cora was followed and run off the highway one night, and had all four tires slashed one day when her car was parked in town. Once she was in the post office and a man recognized her, walked over, and spit on her; another time a car with out-of-state license plates pulled up next to her car as if to ask directions, and the man spat into her face. She came home from a meeting one night to find that someone had broken into her home and drenched her bed with gasoline. But Cora views the abuses with amazing equanimity: "If you stop doing things because somebody says something bad about you or does something to you," she says, "then you'll never get *anything* done."

And she wasn't making only enemies; she was also gaining a following. 25
One woman, who now works in the local legal aid office where Cora stops in frequently to get answers to legal questions, tells how she first met Cora. The woman had been born in Halifax, but had moved to New Jersey when she was a young girl. The civil rights movement progressed, and when the woman was finished with school, she moved back to Virginia, thinking that

things there would be much better than they *had* been for blacks. But she found that any progress had been superficial only. When she started looking for work, she discovered that there were no blacks in responsible positions. She wore her hair in an Afro, and in hindsight thinks that it cost her jobs: at one point, it seemed she would be offered a position with the county, but when the man who was to be her boss saw her, he didn't give her the job. Another prospective employer turned her down with the flat statement that he didn't want any union people around.

She became disillusioned, and was shocked at the complacency around her. About that time, she saw Cora Tucker's name in the paper. She was impressed, and started asking around about Cora. Not too long afterwards, she went to a community action program meeting, and noticed that Cora was scheduled to speak. "I was excited. I thought, finally, I'm going to meet a black person who's alive!" But she was initially disappointed. "I had pictured her as a towering woman — a fiery, eloquent speaker, like Barbara Jordan. Instead, there she was, short, and not that articulate."

But she quickly got drawn to Cora's strengths. "Cora wouldn't be happy at home, doing housekeeping," she says. "She's just not cut out for that. She's cut out for doing exactly what she's doing — getting out and raising hell about issues that affect people. She keeps pushing. When I get burned, I back off. But when Cora gets burned, she just blows out the fire and goes on."

Even people who don't like Cora give her credit: "I'm not a Cora Tucker fan," says one South Boston resident. "But I admit that she might just be the most informed person on political issues in this county." People credit Cora with having stamina and with inspiring others. An old friend of hers who runs a corner grocery says, "She keeps people fired up; she won't let us get lazy. It's because of her that I even watch the news!" One woman who was in school with Cora and now works for the county government says, "She was always making noise at school. We knew she'd grow up noisy. But it's *good* noise. When Cora talks, she knows what she's talking about."

And although Cora thinks she'll never be much of a public speaker, others disagree. One man who has worked with Cora for several years described a dinner ceremony sponsored by a human rights coalition in Richmond. "They had asked Cora to come and be a featured speaker. The woman who spoke before her gave this very polished speech. And then Cora got up, and gave her very unpolished speech. But it was moving to everyone in the room, because it was so much from the heart. It was the contrast of day and night between her and the previous speaker. What she had to say was so honest and down to earth, that people were very touched by it. And that's just the way she is."

Cora is very religious. "I believe in God, and in the providence of 30 prayer. I go to church regularly." The churches in her area are still segregated; she attends the Crystal Hill Baptist Church, which, she points out with a chuckle, is brick-colored, while the white congregation down the road painted their brick church white. In an essay called "Halifax County and Blacks," under a subtitle "Things Blacks Must Do to Succeed," Cora once wrote, "First, blacks must go to church. The church is the backbone of black progress." Every summer for several years Cora has organized a "Citizenship Day of Prayer" on the lawn of the county courthouse in South Boston, which attracts hundreds of people who probably wouldn't gather if the event were called a rally. At the event a list of grievances is always read off — including complaints about such things as how people are treated by the welfare system, unfair employment practices, or disproportionate suspensions of black pupils in the schools.

Problems like that — and what to do about them — are raised regularly at Citizens for a Better America meetings, held the fourth Friday of each month at a local funeral home. CBA has several hundred members, and with help from friends, Cora publishes a monthly one-page newsletter, which she decorates with American flag stickers and short religious sayings. The newsletter is a hodgepodge of useful information, including notices of food stamp law changes, regular updates on what the Virginia General Assembly is considering, board of supervisors' actions, community news, and news about other subjects that Cora is currently concerned with. One issue might have an essay on education, something on federal budget cutbacks and poor people, and a paragraph on the dangers of uranium mining. In 1986, when the federal government was considering southern Virginia, including part of Halifax County, as a possible site for a high-level nuclear waste dump, Cora and CBA fought back, using a section of the federal law requiring that the siting consideration take Indians and other minorities into account. Among other things, CBA found that blacks owned more farmland in Halifax County than in any other county in the country, and that historically, the first black-owned businesses and land in the country were on the site that would be affected by the nuclear waste dump.

Cora learns facts quickly; she can attend a meeting on the problems of family farmers one day, and the next, go to another meeting and be able to reel off facts and figures about farm foreclosures, the cost of fertilizers, trends in agribusiness, and the harmful effect of various pesticides. She reads constantly — newspapers, books, anything on an issue that interests her. "I save newspaper clippings — especially statements from politicians. That way, five years from now when they say, 'I'm definitely against that,' I can go back and say, 'But on such and such a date, you said *this*.'"

Cora stays extremely busy. Several years ago, she went back and got her graduate equivalency diploma, and took some courses at the community college. She thought she might want her degree: "I used to think I wanted to be a social worker. But I changed my mind, because you can't do as much inside the system as you can on the outside. There are so many people who become social workers, and then sit there with their hands tied. What people really need is somebody on the outside who's going to go and raise hell for them about laws and regulations."

Besides CBA gatherings, meetings of the county board of supervisors, and her usual rounds to the legal aid office and the county office building, Cora still visits elderly people, helps women without cars to do their shopping, reads and explains people's mail about food stamps and social security to them, and answers frequent letters. She takes every letter seriously. One, for instance, addressed simply to "Cora Tucker, Halifax, Virginia," read, "Dear Mrs. Tucker, Please don't let the county send us to be experimented on. We heard that they are going to take people on welfare to be experimented on." Cora remembered that there had been separate articles in the newspaper recently, on the "workfare" program to employ welfare recipients, and on a county decision to allow dogs from the animal pound to be used for medical experiments. Cora concluded that the person who wrote the letter had gotten the two issues confused — but she wasn't satisfied until she had called the county administrator and had gotten him to pledge to do a better job of explaining the issues publicly.

Cora's work goes far beyond Halifax. CBA itself has chapters in several   35
other places, including one started in Baltimore by one of Cora's sisters. In addition, when a new coalition group, Virginia Action, was started in the state in 1980, Cora was on the founding committee and was elected its first president. She also became active on the board of its national affiliate, Citizen Action. And in 1981, on top of everything else she was doing, this woman who as a girl had refused to shake the governor's hand was talked into running as a write-in protest candidate for governor by several black groups. She didn't get many votes, but her campaign was covered in the press, and she thinks that she raised issues about black people's concerns that otherwise would have been ignored.

Cora hasn't received much support in her work from her family, except from her mother. She and her husband are estranged, and her children haven't taken an active interest in Cora's work. Cora visits her mother often, in an old house several miles away that has woodburning stoves for heat, religious pictures in the downstairs room, and, hanging in the stairway, a plastic placemat depicting Martin Luther King's tomb. Cora's mother is clearly proud of her; she emphasizes what a smart girl Cora was, and is, and how courageous.

Others agree. As a man who works with Cora at Virginia Action puts it, "All of the issues Cora has taken on — like voting rights and employment discrimination — had been problems in Halifax County for decades. But nobody was willing to fight. And the reason was that it's very, very hard to be somebody going against the mainstream in a small rural community. It's a hell of a lot easier to play the role of the gadfly when you live in an urban environment, where you have your own community of friends, and you don't have to worry about the world. In a small rural community, your community *is* your world. And it's hard to fight the people you have to face every single day. Cora's able to do it because she's got guts. There's just nothing else to it but courage. In a small community those people writing nasty letters to the editor about you are people you're going to run into at the grocery, or whose kids go to school with yours. In addition, being black in a southern rural community, and being a woman, make it that much harder. She hasn't even had the active support of a large part of the black community — they feel threatened by her; she's stolen a lot of their fire. And she's always fighting back as opposed to the blacks who always cooperate with the white power structure. She just reached a point where she decided that slow-moving efforts weren't enough for the things that needed doing — things that were clear in her mind. She recognized the dangers that would be involved, but went ahead because she knew she was right."

ENGAGING THE TEXT

1. How might Cora Tucker define success? To what extent has she achieved it?

2. What motivates Cora Tucker? How do you explain her courage and commitment? Can you think of any ways to encourage more people to emulate some of her virtues?

3. What has her experience taught Cora Tucker about "organizing"? What are her strategies for getting things done?

4. Do you think people in small towns or rural communities are better able than urban dwellers to influence political decisions that affect them? Why or why not?

EXPLORING CONNECTIONS

5. Review the pieces by Horatio Alger (p. 264), Ken Hamblin (p. 285), and Studs Terkel (p. 353) to refresh in your mind their perspectives on the American Dream. What does Cora Tucker have in common with any of the others, and how does she differ from them?

6. In "Class in America — 2003" (p. 307), Gregory Mantsios writes, "When we look at society and try to determine what it is that keeps most people down — what holds them back from realizing their potential as healthy, creative, productive individuals — we find institutional forces that are largely beyond individual control." How do you think Cora Tucker might respond to this statement? Does her story challenge this or other claims by Mantsios?

EXTENDING THE CRITICAL CONTEXT

7. Research grass-roots organizations like Citizens for a Better America in your community. Choose one, attend a meeting, and interview members of the organization. Report to the class on its goals, strategies, accomplishments, and current objectives and challenges.

8. In May 2000, the American Association of Retired Persons (AARP) released "Money and the American Family," a report based on nationwide inter-

views. The report contains several interesting findings — for example, that 11 percent of Americans are "wealth-averse" and, like Cora Tucker, don't particularly crave money. Consult the AARP report and summarize what you find for the class. If you have Internet access, visit the AARP Web site at www.aarp.org or the *Rereading America* site: www.bedfordstmartins.com/ rereadingamerica.

FURTHER CONNECTIONS

1. How would you expect your county to compare with other counties in your state in terms of wealth? How would you expect your state to compare with other states? Research state and county data from the U.S. Census Bureau Web site (www.census.gov) and present or write up your findings. To what extent do you think you have had advantages or disadvantages because of where you were born or grew up?

2. The Merriam Webster Online Dictionary defines "wage slave" as "a person dependent on wages or a salary for a livelihood." Are you a wage slave now, and do you expect to be one in the future? Discuss the connotations of this term, and explain why you think the term is or is not a useful one in contemporary America. What are the alternatives to wage slavery?

3. Sketch out a rough plan of what you might try to accomplish in the five years after you receive your college diploma. How much do your career or educational plans reflect a desire to earn a high salary or to be considered "successful" in some other way? Do you see significant barriers or challenges in attaining these tentative goals? To extend this exercise, talk to a career counselor about your plans, or interview someone working in the field you are considering pursuing.

4. This chapter of *Rereading America* has been criticized by conservatives for undermining the work ethic of American college students. Rush Limbaugh, for example, claimed that the chapter "presents America as a stacked deck," thus "robbing people of the ability to see the enormous opportunities directly in front of them." Do you agree? Write a journal entry or essay in which you explain how these readings have influenced your attitudes toward work and success.

4

True Women and Real Men

Myths of Gender

Bree Scott-Hartland as Delphinia Blue, photo by Carolyn Jones. (From *Living Proof*, Abbeville Press, 1994.)

FAST FACTS

1. Women hold 50.3% of all management and professional positions. Yet, only 7.9% of *Fortune* 500 top earners and 1.4 % of *Fortune* 500 CEOs are women.

2. In 2003, women constituted 14.5% of the U.S. House of Representatives and 14% of the Senate; in Rwanda, women made up 48.8% of the lower house and 30% of the upper house.

3. Every year approximately 4 million American women are victims of serious assault by their husbands or partners.

4. Gay and lesbian teenagers are about four times more likely than their heterosexual classmates to be threatened with a weapon at school and are five times more likely to skip school because they feel unsafe.

5. Among men aged 15–44, 76.3% agree or strongly agree with the statement, "It is more important for a man to spend a lot of time with his family than to be successful at his career."

6. Some 59.6% of men and 63.7% of women aged 15–44 disagree or strongly disagree with the statement, "It is much better for everyone if the man earns the main living and the woman takes care of the home and family."

7. Some 73% of college and university faculty and 74% of students describe the climate of their campus as homophobic.

8. In thirty-four states employers may legally fire employees based on their sexual orientation; in forty-four states they may fire employees based on gender identity.

Sources: (1) Catalyst (www.catalyst.org), "Women 'Take Care,' Men 'Take Charge,'" 2005; (2) Judith Lorber, *Breaking the Bowls: Degendering and Feminist Change* (New York: Norton, 2005); (3) The National Domestic Violence Hotline (www.ndvh.org), "Abuse in America"; (4) ACLU (www.aclu.org), "Doing the Math: What the Numbers Say About Harassment of Gay, Lesbian, Bisexual, and Trans-gendered Students"; (5, 6) CDC National Center for Health Statistics, "Fertility, Contraception, and Fatherhood," May 2006; (7) Susan R. Rankin, *Campus Climate for Gay, Lesbian, Bisexual, and Transgender People: A National Perspective* (New York: The National Gay and Lesbian Task Force Policy Institute, 2003); (8) Human Rights Campaign (www.hrc.org), "GLBT Workplace Issues."

COMMON SENSE TELLS US that there are obvious differences between females and males: after all, biology, not culture, determines whether you're able to bear children. But culture and cultural myths do shape the roles men and women play in our public and private relationships: we may be born female and male, but we are made women and men. Sociologists distinguish between sex and gender — between one's biological identity and the conventional patterns of behavior we learn to associate with each sex. While biological sex remains relatively stable, the definition of "appropriate" gender behavior varies dramatically from one cultural group or historical period to the next. The variations show up markedly in the way we dress. For example, in Thailand, men who act and dress like women are not only socially accepted but encouraged to participate in popular, male-only beauty pageants; in contemporary Anglo-American culture, on the other hand, cross-dressers are usually seen as deviant or ridiculous. Male clothing in late-seventeenth- and early-eighteenth-century England would also have failed our current "masculinity" tests: in that period, elaborate laces, brocades, wigs, and even makeup signaled wealth, status, and sexual attractiveness for men and women alike.

History shows us how completely our gender derives from cultural myths about what is proper for men and women to think, enjoy, and do. And history is replete with examples of how the apparent "naturalness" of gender has been used to regulate political, economic, and personal relations between the sexes.

Many nineteenth-century scientists argued that it was "unnatural" for women to attend college; rigorous intellectual activity, they asserted, would draw vital energy away from a woman's reproductive organs and make her sterile. According to this line of reasoning, women who sought higher education threatened the natural order by jeopardizing their ability to bear children and perpetuate the species. Arguments based on nature were likewise used to justify women's exclusion from political life. In his classic 1832 treatise on American democracy, for instance, James Fenimore Cooper remarked that women's domestic role and "necessary" subordination to men made them unsuitable for participation in public affairs. Thus, he argued, denying women the right to vote was perfectly consistent with the principles of American democracy:

> In those countries where the suffrage is said to be universal, exceptions exist, that arise from the necessity of things. . . . The interests of women being thought to be so identified with those of their male relatives as to become, in a great degree, inseparable, females are, almost generally, excluded from the possession of political rights. There can be no doubt that society is greatly the gainer, by thus excluding one half its members, and the half that is best adapted to give a tone to its domestic happiness, from the strife of parties, and the fierce struggles of political controversies. . . . These exceptions, however, do not very materially affect the principle of political equality. (*The American Democrat*)

Resistance to gender equality has been remarkably persistent in the United States. It took over seventy years of hard political work by both black and white women's organizations to win the right to vote. But while feminists gained the vote for women in 1920 and the legal right to equal educational and employment opportunities in the 1970s, attitudes change even more slowly than laws. Contemporary antifeminist campaigns voice some of the same anxieties as their nineteenth-century counterparts over the "loss" of femininity and domesticity.

Women continue to suffer economic inequities based on cultural assumptions about gender. What's defined as "women's work" — nurturing, feeding, caring for family and home — is devalued and pays low wages or none at all. When women enter jobs traditionally held by men, they often encounter discrimination, harassment, or "glass ceilings" that limit their advancement. But men, too, pay a high price for their culturally imposed roles. Psychological research shows higher rates of depression among people of both sexes who adhere closely to traditional roles than among those who do not. Moreover, studies of men's mental and physical health suggest that social pressure to "be a man" (that is, to be emotionally controlled, powerful, and successful) can contribute to isolation, anxiety, stress, and illness, and may be partially responsible for men's shorter life spans. As sociologist Margaret Andersen observes, "traditional gender roles limit the psychological and social possibilities for human beings."

Even our assumption that there are "naturally" only two genders is a cultural invention that fails to accommodate the diversity of human experience. Some cultures have three or more gender categories. One of the best-known third genders is the American Indian *berdache*, a role that is found in as many as seventy North and South American tribes. The berdache is a biological male who takes the social role of a woman, does women's work (or in some cases both women's and men's work), and often enjoys high status in the society; the berdache has sex with men who are not themselves berdaches and in some cultures may also marry a man. Euro-American culture, by contrast, offers no socially acceptable alternative gender roles. As a result, gay men, lesbians, bisexuals, transsexuals, cross-dressers, and other gender rebels confront pervasive and often legally sanctioned discrimination similar to that once experienced by women. Just as many Americans in the past considered it "unnatural" and socially destructive for women to vote or go to college, many now consider it "unnatural" and socially destructive for gays and lesbians to marry, bear or adopt children, serve in the military, lead scout groups, or teach school.

This chapter focuses on cultural myths of gender and the influence they wield over human development and personal identity. The first three selections examine how dominant American culture defines female and male gender roles — and how those roles may define us. In "How the Americans Understand the Equality of the Sexes," Alexis de Tocqueville describes the status of American women in the early years of the Republic. Jamaica Kincaid's "Girl," a story framed as a mother's advice to her daughter, presents a more contemporary take on what it means to be raised a woman. Aaron H. Devor's "Becoming Members of Society" examines gender as a socially constructed category and discusses the psychological processes that underlie gender role acquisition.

Next, two personal narratives and a Visual Portfolio offer contemporary rereadings of conventional gender roles. Judith Ortiz Cofer's personal reflection, "The Story of My Body," traces the shifting meanings of gender and identity for a woman of color who moves among different social and cultural contexts. In "Veiled Intentions," Maysan Haydar reflects on her decision, as a feminist, to wear the traditional Muslim headscarf; in the process, she questions mainstream assumptions about what it means to be "free" or "oppressed" as a woman. The portfolio presents both conventional and unconventional images of women and men that provide an opportunity to think about the ways that we "read" gender visually.

The second half of the chapter opens with two essays that examine the power of the media to reflect our attitudes and shape our behavior as women and men. Jean Kilbourne's " 'Two Ways a Woman Can Get Hurt': Advertising and Violence" argues that the objectification of women in ads constitutes a form of cultural abuse. In "From Fly-Girls to Bitches and Hos," self-described "hip-hop feminist" Joan Morgan takes a different approach to analyzing the depiction of women in popular culture: she maintains that it's necessary to look behind the violent misogyny of many rap lyrics in order to understand and heal the pain of the African American men who compose and perform the songs. In counterpoint, political scientist Harvey Mansfield weighs the pros and cons of shifting gender roles in "The Manliness of Men," an essay that is at once critical of and nostalgic for the old-fashioned "manly man."

The final two essays challenge the very idea that there are only two obvious, clearly defined sexes or gender identities. Deborah Rudacille's "The Hands of God" introduces us to the Chevalier d'Eon, an eighteenth-century French diplomat and spy who lived for nearly fifty years as a man and for over thirty as a woman, serving his country in both roles. D'Eon, like other transgendered and intersexual people, illustrates the inadequacy of binary thinking about gender and sex. "Appearances," by Carmen Vázquez, documents the penalties — from verbal harassment to murder — paid by both gay and straight people who commit "gender betrayal" by daring to cross conventional gender lines. Vázquez, and the chapter as a whole, end with a plea to recognize that "the dignity of each person is worthy of celebration and protection."

Sources

Margaret L. Andersen, *Thinking About Women: Sociological Perspectives on Gender*, 3rd ed. New York: Macmillan, 1993.

James Fenimore Cooper, *The American Democrat*. N.p.: Minerva Press, 1969.

Marilyn French, *Beyond Power: On Women, Men, and Morals*. New York: Ballantine Books, 1985.

Paula Giddings, *When and Where I Enter: The Impact of Black Women on Race and Sex in America.* New York: Bantam Books, 1984.

Ruth Hubbard, *The Politics of Women's Biology.* New Brunswick, NJ: Rutgers University Press, 1990.

Judith Lorber, *Paradoxes of Gender.* New Haven and London: Yale University Press, 1994.

James D. Weinrich and Walter L. Williams, "Strange Customs, Familiar Lives: Homosexualities in Other Cultures." *Homosexuality: Research Implications for Public Policy.* Ed. John C. Gonsiorek and James D. Weinrich. Newbury Park, CA: Sage, 1991.

BEFORE READING

- Imagine for a moment that you were born female (if you're a man) or male (if you're a woman). How would your life be different? Would any of your interests and activities change? How about your relationships with other people? Write a journal entry describing your past, present, and possible future in this alternate gender identity.

- Collect and bring to class images of girls and boys, women and men taken from popular magazines and newspapers. Working in groups, make a collage of either male or female gender images; then compare and discuss your results. What do these media images tell you about what it means to be a woman or a man in this culture?

- Do a brief freewrite focusing on the performer in the frontispiece to this chapter (p. 371). How would you describe this person's gender? In what ways does this image challenge traditional ideas about maleness and femaleness?

How the Americans Understand the Equality of the Sexes

ALEXIS DE TOCQUEVILLE

In 1831, Alexis de Tocqueville (1805–1859), a French aristocrat, left Europe to study the American penal system. The young democracy that he observed in the United States left a deep impression on Tocqueville, and in 1835 he published his reflections on this new way of life in Democracy in America — *a work that has since become the point of departure for many studies of American culture. In the following passage from* Democracy in

America, Tocqueville compares the social condition of American women to that of their European counterparts. Tocqueville's concept of equality and assumptions about women can seem foreign to modern readers, so it would be a good idea to take your time as you read this short passage.

I have shown how democracy destroys or modifies the different inequalities which originate in society; but is that all? or does it not ultimately affect that great inequality of man and woman which has seemed, up to the present day, to be eternally based in human nature? I believe that the social changes which bring nearer to the same level the father and son, the master and servant, and, in general, superiors and inferiors, will raise woman, and make her more and more the equal of man. But here, more than ever, I feel the necessity of making myself clearly understood; for there is no subject on which the coarse and lawless fancies of our age have taken a freer range.

There are people in Europe who, confounding together the different characteristics of the sexes, would make man and woman into beings not only equal, but alike. They would give to both the same functions, impose on both the same duties, and grant to both the same rights; they would mix them in all things, — their occupations, their pleasures, their business. It may readily be conceived, that, by thus attempting to make one sex equal to the other, both are degraded; and from so preposterous a medley of the works of nature, nothing could ever result but weak men and disorderly women.

It is not thus that the Americans understand that species of democratic equality which may be established between the sexes. They admit that, as nature has appointed such wide differences between the physical and moral constitution of man and woman, her manifest design was to give a distinct employment to their various faculties; and they hold that improvement does not consist in making beings so dissimilar do pretty nearly the same things, but in causing each of them to fulfil their respective tasks in the best possible manner. The Americans have applied to the sexes the great principle of political economy which governs the manufactures of our age, by carefully dividing the duties of man from those of woman, in order that the great work of society may be the better carried on.

In no country has such constant care been taken as in America to trace two clearly distinct lines of action for the two sexes, and to make them keep pace one with the other, but in two pathways which are always different. American women never manage the outward concerns of the family, or conduct a business, or take a part in political life; nor are they, on the other hand, ever compelled to perform the rough labor of the fields, or to make any of those laborious exertions which demand the exertion of physical strength. No families are so poor as to form an exception to this rule. If, on the one hand, an American woman cannot escape from the quiet circle of domestic employments, she is never forced, on the other, to go beyond it. Hence it is, that the women of America, who often exhibit a masculine strength of understanding and a manly energy, generally preserve great delicacy of personal appearance, and always retain the manners of women, although they sometimes show that they have the hearts and minds of men.

Nor have the Americans ever supposed that one consequence of democratic principles is the subversion of marital power, or the confusion of the natural authorities in families. They hold that every association must have a head in order to accomplish its object, and that the natural head of the conjugal association is man. They do not therefore deny him the right of directing his partner; and they maintain that, in the smaller association of husband and wife, as well as in the great social community, the object of democracy is to regulate and legalize the powers which are necessary, and not to subvert all power.

This opinion is not peculiar to one sex, and contested by the other: I never observed that the women of America consider conjugal authority as a fortunate usurpation of their rights, nor that they thought themselves degraded by submitting to it. It appeared to me, on the contrary, that they attach a sort of pride to the voluntary surrender of their own will, and make it their boast to bend themselves to the yoke, — not to shake it off. Such, at least, is the feeling expressed by the most virtuous of their sex; the others are silent; and, in the United States, it is not the practice for a guilty wife to clamor for the rights of women, whilst she is trampling on her own holiest duties.[1]

It has often been remarked, that in Europe a certain degree of contempt lurks even in the flattery which men lavish upon women: although a European frequently affects to be the slave of woman, it may be seen that he never sincerely thinks her his equal. In the United States, men seldom compliment women, but they daily show how much they esteem them. They constantly display an entire confidence in the understanding of a wife, and a profound respect for her freedom; they have decided that her mind is just as fitted as that of a man to discover the plain truth, and her heart as firm to embrace it; and they have never sought to place her virtue, any more than his, under the shelter of prejudice, ignorance, and fear.

It would seem that, in Europe, where man so easily submits to the despotic sway of women, they are nevertheless deprived of some of the greatest attributes of the human species, and considered as seductive but imperfect beings; and (what may well provoke astonishment) women ultimately

---

[1]Allusion to Mary Wollstonecraft (1759–1797), English radical, political theorist, and author of *Vindication of the Rights of Woman*, who argued that women should enjoy complete political, economic, and sexual freedom; Wollstonecraft scandalized the "polite" society of her day by living according to her feminist principles.

look upon themselves in the same light, and almost consider it as a privilege that they are entitled to show themselves futile, feeble, and timid. The women of America claim no such privileges.

Again, it may be said that in our morals we have reserved strange immunities to man; so that there is, as it were, one virtue for his use, and another for the guidance of his partner; and that, according to the opinion of the public, the very same act may be punished alternately as a crime, or only as a fault. The Americans know not this iniquitous division of duties and rights; amongst them, the seducer is as much dishonored as his victim.

It is true that the Americans rarely lavish upon women those eager   10
attentions which are commonly paid them in Europe; but their conduct to women always implies that they suppose them to be virtuous and refined; and such is the respect entertained for the moral freedom of the sex, that in the presence of a woman the most guarded language is used, lest her ear should be offended by an expression. In America, a young unmarried woman may, alone and without fear, undertake a long journey.

The legislators of the United States, who have mitigated almost all the penalties of criminal law, still make rape a capital offence, and no crime is visited with more inexorable severity by public opinion. This may be accounted for; as the Americans can conceive nothing more precious than a woman's honor, and nothing which ought so much to be respected as her independence, they hold that no punishment is too severe for the man who deprives her of them against her will. In France, where the same offence is visited with far milder penalties, it is frequently difficult to get a verdict from a jury against the prisoner. Is this a consequence of contempt of decency, or contempt of women? I cannot but believe that it is a contempt of both.

Thus, the Americans do not think that man and woman have either the duty or the right to perform the same offices, but they show an equal regard for both their respective parts; and though their lot is different, they consider both of them as beings of equal value. They do not give to the courage of woman the same form or the same direction as to that of man; but they never doubt her courage: and if they hold that man and his partner ought not always to exercise their intellect and understanding in the same manner, they at least believe the understanding of the one to be as sound as that of the other, and her intellect to be as clear. Thus, then, whilst they have allowed the social inferiority of woman to subsist, they have done all they could to raise her morally and intellectually to the level of man; and in this respect they appear to me to have excellently understood the true principle of democratic improvement.

As for myself, I do not hesitate to avow, that, although the women of the United States are confined within the narrow circle of domestic life, and their situation is, in some respects, one of extreme dependence, I have nowhere seen woman occupying a loftier position; and if I were asked, now that I am drawing to the close of this work, in which I have spoken of so many important things done by the Americans, to what the singular prosperity and growing strength of that people ought mainly to be attributed, I should reply, To the superiority of their women.

Engaging the Text

1. What roles does Tocqueville assume are natural and appropriate for women? For men? Which of his assumptions, if any, seem contemporary? Which ones seem antiquated, and why?

2. How do American and European attitudes toward women differ, according to Tocqueville? In what ways does he suggest that American democracy is enabling women to become "more and more the equal of man" (para. 1)?

3. By the time Tocqueville wrote this selection, the first feminist manifesto, Wollstonecraft's *Vindication of the Rights of Woman* (1792), had been read and discussed in Europe for over forty years. Which parts of Tocqueville's essay seem to be intended as a response to feminist arguments for women's equality?

4. Tocqueville finds some forms of equality between women and men more desirable than others. Which forms does he approve of, which does he disapprove of, and why?

Exploring Connections

5. Read the selection by Aaron H. Devor (p. 383); how and why does Devor's understanding of gender roles differ from Tocqueville's assumption that the "great inequality of man and woman" appears to be "eternally based in human nature" (para. 1)?

6. Both Tocqueville and Thomas Jefferson (p. 486) attempt to justify or rationalize a particular form of inequality. What strategies does each writer use to build his case for the subjection of women or for the enslavement of blacks? Which of their arguments appear least effective to you as a modern reader, and why?

Extending the Critical Context

7. Work in groups to list the specific tasks involved in maintaining a household in the 1830s (keep in mind that electricity, indoor plumbing, ready-made clothing, and prepared foods were not available). How credible is Tocqueville's claim that no American woman is "ever compelled . . . to make any of those laborious exertions which demand the exertion of physical strength" (para. 4)? How do you explain his failure to acknowledge the hard physical labor routinely performed by many women during this time?

Girl

JAMAICA KINCAID

Although she now lives in New England, Jamaica Kincaid (b. 1949) retains strong ties, including citizenship, to her birthplace — the island of Antigua in the West Indies. After immigrating to the United States to attend college, she ended up educating herself instead, eventually becoming a staff writer for The New Yorker, *the author of several critically acclaimed books, and an instructor at Harvard University. About the influence of parents on children she says, "The magic is they carry so much you don't know about. They know you in a way you don't know yourself." Some of that magic is exercised in the story "Girl," which was first published in* The New Yorker *and later appeared in Kincaid's award-winning collection* At the Bottom of the River *(1983). She has written and edited many volumes of nonfiction on subjects ranging from colonialism to gardening and has published four novels:* Annie John *(1985),* Lucy *(1990),* The Autobiography of My Mother *(1996), and* Mr. Potter *(2002).*

Wash the white clothes on Monday and put them on the stone heap; wash the color clothes on Tuesday and put them on the clothesline to dry; don't walk barehead in the hot sun; cook pumpkin fritters[1] in very hot sweet oil; soak your little clothes right after you take them off; when buying cotton to make yourself a nice blouse, be sure that it doesn't have gum[2] on it, because that way it won't hold up well after a wash; soak salt fish overnight before you cook it; is it true that you sing benna[3] in Sunday school?; always eat your food in such a way that it won't turn someone else's stomach; on Sundays try to walk like a lady and not like the slut you are so bent on becoming; don't sing benna in Sunday school; you mustn't speak to wharf-rat boys, not even to give directions; don't eat fruits on the street — flies will follow you; *but I don't sing benna on Sundays at all and never in Sunday school;* this is how to sew on a button; this is how to make a buttonhole for the button you have just sewed on; this is how to hem a dress when you see the hem coming down and so to prevent yourself from looking like the slut I know you are so bent on becoming; this is how you iron your father's khaki shirt so that it doesn't have a crease; this is how you iron your father's khaki pants so that they don't have a crease; this is how you grow okra[4] — far from the house,

---

[1]*fritters:* Small fried cakes of batter, often containing vegetables, fruit, or other fillings.
[2]*gum:* Plant residue on cotton.
[3]*sing benna:* Sing popular music (not appropriate for Sunday school).
[4]*okra:* A shrub whose pods are used in soups, stews, and gumbo.

because okra tree harbors red ants; when you are growing dasheen,[5] make sure it gets plenty of water or else it makes your throat itch when you are eating it; this is how you sweep a corner; this is how you sweep a whole house; this is how you sweep a yard; this is how you smile to someone you don't like too much; this is how you smile to someone you don't like at all; this is how you smile to someone you like completely; this is how you set a table for tea; this is how you set a table for dinner; this is how you set a table for dinner with an important guest; this is how you set a table for lunch; this is how you set a table for breakfast; this is how to behave in the presence of men who don't know you very well, and this way they won't recognize immediately the slut I have warned you against becoming; be sure to wash every day, even if it is with your own spit; don't squat down to play marbles — you are not a boy, you know; don't pick people's flowers — you might catch something; don't throw stones at blackbirds, because it might not be a blackbird at all; this is how to make a bread pudding; this is how to make doukona;[6] this is how to make pepper pot;[7] this is how to make a good medicine for a cold; this is how to make a good medicine to throw away a child before it even becomes a child; this is how to catch a fish; this is how to throw back a fish you don't like, and that way something bad won't fall on you; this is how to bully a man; this is how a man bullies you; this is how to love a man, and if this doesn't work there are other ways, and if they don't work don't feel too bad about giving up; this is how to spit up in the air if you feel like it, and this is how to move quick so that it doesn't fall on you; this is how to make ends meet; always squeeze bread to make sure it's fresh; *but what if the baker won't let me feel the bread?;* you mean to say that after all you are really going to be the kind of woman who the baker won't let near the bread?

ENGAGING THE TEXT

1. What are your best guesses as to the time and place of the story? Who is telling the story? What does this dialogue tell you about the relationship between the characters, their values and attitudes? What else can you surmise about these people (for instance, ages, occupation, social status)? On what evidence in the story do you base these conclusions?

2. Why does the story juxtapose advice on cooking and sewing, for example, with the repeated warning not to act like a slut?

3. Explain the meaning of the last line of the story: "you mean to say that after all you are really going to be the kind of woman who the baker won't let near the bread?"

---

[5]*dasheen:* The taro plant, cultivated, like the potato, for its edible tuber.
[6]*doukona:* Plaintain pudding; the plaintain fruit is similar to the banana.
[7]*pepper pot:* A spicy West Indian stew.

4. What does the story tell us about male-female relationships? According to the speaker, what roles are women and men expected to play? What kinds of power, if any, does the speaker suggest that women may have?

EXPLORING CONNECTIONS

5. To what extent would Tocqueville approve of the behaviors and attitudes that the mother is trying to teach her daughter in this selection?
6. What does it mean to be a successful mother in "Girl"? How does this compare to being a good mother or parent in "An Indian Story" (p. 51) or "Looking for Work" (p. 26)? Of all the parents in these narratives, which do you consider most successful, which least, and why?

EXTENDING THE CRITICAL CONTEXT

7. Write an imitation of the story. If you are a woman, record some of the advice or lessons your mother or another woman gave you; if you are a man, put down advice received from your father or from another male. Read what you have written aloud in class, alternating between male and female speakers, and discuss the results: How does parental guidance vary according to gender?
8. Write a page or two recording what the daughter might be thinking as she listens to her mother's advice; then compare notes with classmates.

Becoming Members of Society: Learning the Social Meanings of Gender

AARON H. DEVOR

Gender is the most transparent of all social categories: we acquire gender roles so early in life and so thoroughly that it's hard to see them as the result of lessons taught and learned. Maleness and femaleness seem "natural," not the product of socialization. In this wide-ranging scholarly essay, Aaron H. Devor suggests that many of our notions of what it means to be female or male are socially constructed. He also touches on the various ways that different cultures define gender. A professor of sociology and Dean of Graduate Studies at the University of Victoria in British Columbia, Devor is a member of the International Academy of Sex Research and author of FTM: Female-to-Male Transsexuals in Society *(1997). Born Holly Devor in 1951,*

Devor announced in 2003 his decision to live as a man and to adopt the name Aaron H. Devor. This selection is taken from his groundbreaking book, Gender Blending: Confronting the Limits of Duality *(1989).*

The Gendered Self

The task of learning to be properly gendered members of society only begins with the establishment of gender identity. Gender identities act as cognitive filtering devices guiding people to attend to and learn gender role behaviors appropriate to their statuses. Learning to behave in accordance with one's gender identity is a lifelong process. As we move through our lives, society demands different gender performances from us and rewards, tolerates, or punishes us differently for conformity to, or digression from, social norms. As children, and later adults, learn the rules of membership in society, they come to see themselves in terms they have learned from the people around them.

Children begin to settle into a gender identity between the age of eighteen months and two years.[1] By the age of two, children usually understand that they are members of a gender grouping and can correctly identify other members of their gender.[2] By age three they have a fairly firm and consistent concept of gender. Generally, it is not until children are five to seven years old that they become convinced that they are permanent members of their gender grouping.[3]

Researchers test the establishment, depth, and tenacity of gender identity through the use of language and the concepts mediated by language. The language systems used in populations studied by most researchers in this field conceptualize gender as binary and permanent. All persons are either male or female. All males are first boys and then men; all females are first girls and then women. People are believed to be unable to change genders without sex change surgery, and those who do change sex are considered to be both disturbed and exceedingly rare.

This is by no means the only way that gender is conceived in all cultures. Many aboriginal cultures have more than two gender categories and accept the idea that, under certain circumstances, gender may be changed without changes being made to biological sex characteristics. Many North and South American native peoples had a legitimate social category for

---

[1]Much research has been devoted to determining when gender identity becomes solidified in the sense that a child knows itself to be unequivocally either male or female. John Money and his colleagues have proposed eighteen months of age because it is difficult or impossible to change a child's gender identity once it has been established around the age of eighteen months. Money and Ehrhardt, p. 243. [All notes are Devor's except 12, 20, and 21.]

[2]Mary Driver Leinbach and Beverly I. Fagot, "Acquisition of Gender Labels: A Test for Toddlers," *Sex Roles* 15 (1986), pp. 655–66.

[3]Maccoby, pp. 225–29; Kohlberg and Ullian, p. 211.

persons who wished to live according to the gender role of another sex. Such people were sometimes revered, sometimes ignored, and occasionally scorned. Each culture had its own word to describe such persons, most commonly translated into English as "berdache." Similar institutions and linguistic concepts have also been recorded in early Siberian, Madagascan, and Polynesian societies, as well as in medieval Europe.[4]

Very young children learn their culture's social definitions of gender 5 and gender identity at the same time that they learn what gender behaviors are appropriate for them. But they only gradually come to understand the meaning of gender in the same way as the adults of their society do. Very young children may learn the words which describe their gender and be able to apply them to themselves appropriately, but their comprehension of their meaning is often different from that used by adults. Five-year-olds, for example, may be able to accurately recognize their own gender and the genders of the people around them, but they will often make such ascriptions on the basis of role information, such as hair style, rather than physical attributes, such as genitals, even when physical cues are clearly known to them. One result of this level of understanding of gender is that children in this age group often believe that people may change their gender with a change in clothing, hair style, or activity.[5]

The characteristics most salient to young minds are the more culturally specific qualities which grow out of gender role prescriptions. In one study, young school age children, who were given dolls and asked to identify their gender, overwhelmingly identified the gender of the dolls on the basis of attributes such as hair length or clothing style, in spite of the fact that the dolls were anatomically correct. Only 17 percent of the children identified the dolls on the basis of their primary or secondary sex characteristics.[6] Children five to seven years old understand gender as a function of role rather than as a function of anatomy. Their understanding is that gender (role) is supposed to be stable but that it is possible to alter it at will. This demonstrates that although the standard social definition of gender is based on genitalia, this is not the way that young children first learn to distinguish gender. The process of learning to think about gender in an adult fashion is one prerequisite to

---

[4]See Susan Baker, "Biological Influences on Human Sex and Gender," in *Women: Sex and Sexuality*, ed. Catherine R. Stimpson and Ethel S. Person (Chicago: University of Chicago Press, 1980), p. 186; Evelyn Blackwood, "Sexuality and Gender in Certain Native American Tribes: The Case of Cross-Gender Females," *Signs* 10 (1984), pp. 27–42; Vern L. Bullough, "Transvestites in the Middle Ages," *American Journal of Sociology* 79 (1974), 1381–89; J. Cl. DuBois, "Transsexualisme et Anthropologie Culturelle," *Gynecologie Practique* 6 (1969), pp. 431–40; Donald C. Forgey, "The Institution of Berdache among the North American Plains Indians," *Journal of Sex Research* 11 (Feb. 1975), pp. 1–15; Walter L. Williams, *The Spirit and the Flesh: Sexual Diversity in American Indian Culture* (Boston: Beacon, 1986).

[5]Maccoby, p. 255.

[6]Ibid., p. 227.

becoming a full member of society. Thus, as children grow older, they learn to think of themselves and others in terms more like those used by adults.

Children's developing concepts of themselves as individuals are necessarily bound up in their need to understand the expectations of the society of which they are a part. As they develop concepts of themselves as individuals, they do so while observing themselves as reflected in the eyes of others. Children start to understand themselves as individuals separate from others during the years that they first acquire gender identities and gender roles. As they do so, they begin to understand that others see them and respond to them as particular people. In this way they develop concepts of themselves as individuals, as an "I" (a proactive subject) simultaneously with self-images of themselves as individuals, as a "me" (a member of society, a subjective object). Children learn that they are both as they see themselves and as others see them.[7]

To some extent, children initially acquire the values of the society around them almost indiscriminately. To the degree that children absorb the generalized standards of society into their personal concept of what is correct behavior, they can be said to hold within themselves the attitude of the "generalized other."[8] This "generalized other" functions as a sort of monitoring or measuring device with which individuals may judge their own actions against those of their generalized conceptions of how members of society are expected to act. In this way members of society have available to them a guide, or an internalized observer, to turn the more private "I" into the object of public scrutiny, the "me." In this way, people can monitor their own behavioral impulses and censor actions which might earn them social disapproval or scorn. The tension created by the constant interplay of the personal "I" and the social "me" is the creature known as the "self."

But not all others are of equal significance in our lives, and therefore not all others are of equal impact on the development of the self. Any person is available to become part of one's "generalized other," but certain individuals, by virtue of the sheer volume of time spent in interaction with someone, or by virtue of the nature of particular interactions, become more significant in the shaping of people's values. These "significant others" become prominent in the formation of one's self-image and one's ideals and goals. As such they carry disproportionate weight in one's personal "generalized other."[9] Thus, children's individualistic impulses are shaped into a socially acceptable form both by particular individuals and by a more generalized pressure to conformity exerted by innumerable faceless members of society. Gender identity is one of the most central portions of that developing sense of self. . . .

---

[7]George Herbert Mead, "Self," in *The Social Psychology of George Herbert Mead*, ed. Anselm Strauss (Chicago: Phoenix Books, 1962, 1934), pp. 212–60.

[8]G. H. Mead.

[9]Hans Gerth and C. Wright Mills, *Character and Social Structure: The Psychology of Social Institutions* (New York: Harcourt, Brace and World, 1953), p. 96.

Gender Role Behaviors and Attitudes

The clusters of social definitions used to identify persons by gender are   10
collectively known as femininity and masculinity. Masculine characteristics
are used to identify persons as males, while feminine ones are used as signi-
fiers for femaleness. People use femininity or masculinity to claim and communicate their membership in their assigned, or chosen, sex or gender.
Others recognize our sex or gender more on the basis of these characteristics than on the basis of sex characteristics, which are usually largely
covered by clothing in daily life.

These two clusters of attributes are most commonly seen as mirror
images of one another with masculinity usually characterized by dominance
and aggression, and femininity by passivity and submission. A more evenhanded description of the social qualities subsumed by femininity and masculinity might be to label masculinity as generally concerned with egoistic
dominance and femininity as striving for cooperation or communion.[10]
Characterizing femininity and masculinity in such a way does not portray
the two clusters of characteristics as being in a hierarchical relationship to
one another but rather as being two different approaches to the same
question, that question being centrally concerned with the goals, means,
and use of power. Such an alternative conception of gender roles captures
the hierarchical and competitive masculine thirst for power, which can, but
need not, lead to aggression, and the feminine quest for harmony and
communal well-being, which can, but need not, result in passivity and
dependence.

Many activities and modes of expression are recognized by most members of society as feminine. Any of these can be, and often are, displayed by
persons of either gender. In some cases, cross gender behaviors are ignored
by observers, and therefore do not compromise the integrity of a person's
gender display. In other cases, they are labeled as inappropriate gender role
behaviors. Although these behaviors are closely linked to sexual status in the
minds and experiences of most people, research shows that dominant persons of either gender tend to use influence tactics and verbal styles usually
associated with men and masculinity, while subordinate persons, of either
gender, tend to use those considered to be the province of women.[11] Thus it

[10]Egoistic dominance is a striving for superior rewards for oneself or a competitive striving to reduce the rewards for one's competitors even if such action will not increase one's own
rewards. Persons who are motivated by desires for egoistic dominance not only wish the best
for themselves but also wish to diminish the advantages of others whom they may perceive as
competing with them. See Maccoby, p. 217.

[11]Judith Howard, Philip Blumstein, and Pepper Schwartz, "Sex, Power, and Influence Tactics in Intimate Relationships," *Journal of Personality and Social Psychology* 51 (1986),
pp. 102–09; Peter Kollock, Philip Blumstein, and Pepper Schwartz, "Sex and Power in Interaction: Conversational Privileges and Duties," *American Sociological Review* 50 (1985), pp. 34–46.

seems likely that many aspects of masculinity and femininity are the result, rather than the cause, of status inequalities.

Popular conceptions of femininity and masculinity instead revolve around hierarchical appraisals of the "natural" roles of males and females. Members of both genders are believed to share many of the same human characteristics, although in different relative proportions; both males and females are popularly thought to be able to do many of the same things, but most activities are divided into suitable and unsuitable categories for each gender class. Persons who perform the activities considered appropriate for another gender will be expected to perform them poorly; if they succeed adequately, or even well, at their endeavors, they may be rewarded with ridicule or scorn for blurring the gender dividing line.

The patriarchal gender schema[12] currently in use in mainstream North American society reserves highly valued attributes for males and actively supports the high evaluation of any characteristics which might inadvertently become associated with maleness. The ideology which the schema grows out of postulates that the cultural superiority of males is a natural outgrowth of the innate predisposition of males toward aggression and dominance, which is assumed to flow inevitably from evolutionary and biological sources. Female attributes are likewise postulated to find their source in innate predispositions acquired in the evolution of the species. Feminine characteristics are thought to be intrinsic to the female facility for childbirth and breastfeeding. Hence, it is popularly believed that the social position of females is biologically mandated to be intertwined with the care of children and a "natural" dependency on men for the maintenance of mother-child units. Thus the goals of femininity and, by implication, of all biological females are presumed to revolve around heterosexuality and maternity.[13]

Femininity, according to this traditional formulation, "would result in warm and continued relationships with men, a sense of maternity, interest in caring for children, and the capacity to work productively and continuously in female occupations."[14] This recipe translates into a vast number of proscriptions and prescriptions. Warm and continued relations with men and an interest in maternity require that females be heterosexually oriented. A heterosexual orientation requires women to dress, move, speak, and act in ways that men will find attractive. As patriarchy has reserved active expressions of power as a masculine attribute, femininity must be expressed through modes of dress, movement, speech, and action which

15

---

[12]*schema:* A mental framework, scheme, or pattern that helps us make sense of experience.
[13]Chodorow, p. 134.
[14]Jon K. Meyer and John E. Hoopes, "The Gender Dysphoria Syndromes: A Position Statement on So-Called 'Transsexualism'," *Plastic and Reconstructive Surgery* 54 (Oct. 1974), pp. 444–51.

communicate weakness, dependency, ineffectualness, availability for sexual or emotional service, and sensitivity to the needs of others.

Some, but not all, of these modes of interrelation also serve the demands of maternity and many female job ghettos. In many cases, though, femininity is not particularly useful in maternity or employment. Both mothers and workers often need to be strong, independent, and effectual in order to do their jobs well. Thus femininity, as a role, is best suited to satisfying a masculine vision of heterosexual attractiveness.

Body postures and demeanors which communicate subordinate status and vulnerability to trespass through a message of "no threat" make people appear to be feminine. They demonstrate subordination through a minimizing of spatial use: people appear feminine when they keep their arms closer to their bodies, their legs closer together, and their torsos and heads less vertical then do masculine-looking individuals. People also look feminine when they point their toes inward and use their hands in small or childlike gestures. Other people also tend to stand closer to people they see as feminine, often invading their personal space, while people who make frequent appeasement gestures, such as smiling, also give the appearance of femininity. Perhaps as an outgrowth of a subordinate status and the need to avoid conflict with more socially powerful people, women tend to excel over men at the ability to correctly interpret, and effectively display, nonverbal communication cues.[15]

Speech characterized by inflections, intonations, and phrases that convey nonaggression and subordinate status also make a speaker appear more feminine. Subordinate speakers who use more polite expressions and ask more questions in conversation seem more feminine. Speech characterized by sounds of higher frequencies are often interpreted by listeners as feminine, childlike, and ineffectual.[16] Feminine styles of dress likewise display subordinate status through greater restriction of the free movement of the body, greater exposure of the bare skin, and an emphasis on sexual characteristics. The more gender distinct the dress, the more this is the case.

Masculinity, like femininity, can be demonstrated through a wide variety of cues. Pleck has argued that it is commonly expressed in North American society through the attainment of some level of proficiency at some, or all, of the following four main attitudes of masculinity. Persons who display success and high status in their social group, who exhibit "a manly air of toughness, confidence, and self-reliance" and "the aura of aggression, violence, and

---

[15]Erving Goffman, *Gender Advertisements* (New York: Harper Colophon Books, 1976); Judith A. Hall, *Non-Verbal Sex Differences: Communication Accuracy and Expressive Style* (Baltimore: Johns Hopkins University Press, 1984); Nancy M. Henley, *Body Politics: Power, Sex and Non-Verbal Communication* (Englewood Cliffs, New Jersey: Prentice Hall, 1979); Marianne Wex, *"Let's Take Back Our Space": "Female" and "Male" Body Language as a Result of Patriarchal Structures* (Berlin: Frauenliteraturverlag Hermine Fees, 1979).

[16]Karen L. Adams, "Sexism and the English Language: The Linguistic Implications of Being a Woman," in *Women: A Feminist Perspective*, 3rd edition, ed. Jo Freeman (Palo Alto, Calif.: Mayfield, 1984), pp. 478–91; Hall, pp. 37, 130–37.

daring," and who conscientiously avoid anything associated with femininity are seen as exuding masculinity.[17] These requirements reflect the patriarchal ideology that masculinity results from an excess of testosterone, the assumption being that androgens supply a natural impetus toward aggression, which in turn impels males toward achievement and success. This vision of masculinity also reflects the ideological stance that ideal maleness (masculinity) must remain untainted by female (feminine) pollutants.

Masculinity, then, requires of its actors that they organize themselves and their society in a hierarchical manner so as to be able to explicitly quantify the achievement of success. The achievement of high status in one's social group requires competitive and aggressive behavior from those who wish to obtain it. Competition which is motivated by a goal of individual achievement, or egoistic dominance, also requires of its participants a degree of emotional insensitivity to feelings of hurt and loss in defeated others, and a measure of emotional insularity to protect oneself from becoming vulnerable to manipulation by others. Such values lead those who subscribe to them to view feminine persons as "born losers" and to strive to eliminate any similarities to feminine people from their own personalities. In patriarchally organized societies, masculine values become the ideological structure of the society as a whole. Masculinity thus becomes "innately" valuable and femininity serves a contrapuntal function to delineate and magnify the hierarchical dominance of masculinity.

Body postures, speech patterns, and styles of dress which demonstrate and support the assumption of dominance and authority convey an impression of masculinity. Typical masculine body postures tend to be expansive and aggressive. People who hold their arms and hands in positions away from their bodies, and who stand, sit, or lie with their legs apart — thus maximizing the amount of space that they physically occupy — appear most physically masculine. Persons who communicate an air of authority or a readiness for aggression by standing erect and moving forcefully also tend to appear more masculine. Movements that are abrupt and stiff, communicating force and threat rather than flexibility and cooperation, make an actor look masculine. Masculinity can also be conveyed by stern or serious facial expressions that suggest minimal receptivity to the influence of others, a characteristic which is an important element in the attainment and maintenance of egoistic dominance.[18]

Speech and dress which likewise demonstrate or claim superior status are also seen as characteristically masculine behavior patterns. Masculine speech patterns display a tendency toward expansiveness similar to that found in masculine body postures. People who attempt to control the direction of conversations seem more masculine.[19] Those who tend to speak more loudly, use less polite and more assertive forms, and tend to interrupt

20

[17]Elizabeth Hafkin Pleck, *Domestic Tyranny: The Making of Social Policy Against Family Violence from Colonial Times to the Present* (Cambridge: Oxford University Press, 1989), p. 139.

[18]Goffman, *Gender Advertisements;* Hall; Henley; Wex.

[19]Adams; Hall, pp. 37, 130–37.

"We don't believe in pressuring the children. When the time is right, they'll choose the appropriate gender."

the conversations of others more often also communicate masculinity to others. Styles of dress which emphasize the size of upper body musculature, allow freedom of movement, and encourage an illusion of physical power and a look of easy physicality all suggest masculinity. Such appearances of strength and readiness to action serve to create or enhance an aura of aggressiveness and intimidation central to an appearance of masculinity. Expansive postures and gestures combine with these qualities to insinuate that a position of secure dominance is a masculine one.

Gender role characteristics reflect the ideological contentions underlying the dominant gender schema in North American society. That schema leads us to believe that female and male behaviors are the result of socially directed hormonal instructions which specify that females will want to have children and will therefore find themselves relatively helpless and dependent on males for support and protection. The schema claims that males are innately aggressive and competitive and therefore will dominate over females. The social hegemony[20] of this ideology ensures that we are all raised to practice gender roles which will confirm this vision of the nature of the sexes. Fortunately, our training to gender roles is neither complete nor

[20]*hegemony:* System of preponderant influence, authority, or dominance.

uniform. As a result, it is possible to point to multitudinous exceptions to, and variations on, these themes. Biological evidence is equivocal about the source of gender roles; psychological androgyny[21] is a widely accepted concept. It seems most likely that gender roles are the result of systematic power imbalances based on gender discrimination.[22]

Engaging the Text

1. Devor charges that most languages present gender as "binary and permanent" (para. 3). Has this been your own view? How does Devor challenge this idea — that is, what's the alternative to gender being binary and permanent — and how persuasive do you find his evidence?

2. How, according to Devor, do children "acquire" gender roles? What are the functions of the "generalized other" and the "significant other" in this process?

3. Explain the distinction Devor makes between the "I" and the "me" (paras. 7 and 8). Write a journal entry describing some of the differences between your own "I" and "me."

4. Using examples from Devor and from other reading or observation, list some "activities and modes of expression" (para. 12) that society considers characteristically female and characteristically male. Which are acceptable cross-gender behaviors, and which are not? Search for a "rule" that defines what types of cross-gender behaviors are tolerated.

5. Do some aspects of the traditional gender roles described by Devor seem to be changing? If so, which ones, and how?

Exploring Connections

6. To what extent do Alexis de Tocqueville's views of women and men (p. 376) reflect the "patriarchal gender schema" as Devor defines it?

7. Drawing on Devor's discussion of gender role formation, analyze the difference between the "I" and the "me" of the girl in Jamaica Kincaid's story (p. 381).

8. How would Devor explain the humor of the cartoon on page 391? How do the details of the cartoon — the setting, the women's appearance, the three pictures on the coffee table — contribute to its effect?

Extending the Critical Context

9. As a class, identify at least half a dozen men living today who are widely admired in American culture. To what extent do they embody the "four main attitudes of masculinity" outlined by Devor (para. 19)?

10. Write an essay or journal entry analyzing your own gender role socialization. To what extent have you been pressured to conform to conventional roles? To what extent have you resisted them? What roles have "generalized others" and "significant others" played in shaping your identity?

[21]*androgyny:* The state of having both male and female characteristics.
[22]Howard, Blumstein, and Schwartz; Kollock, Blumstein, and Schwartz.

The Story of My Body
JUDITH ORTIZ COFER

Accepting the idea that gender roles are socially constructed might not be too difficult, but it may come as a shock to realize that even the way we see our bodies is filtered through the lens of social values and beliefs. In this personal essay, Judith Ortiz Cofer reflects on the different roles her own body has assumed in different contexts and cultures — the ways that different societies have "read" the meanings of her physical appearance. The story of her body becomes, to some extent, the story of her life, and woven into the tale are intriguing comments on gender and on cross-cultural perception. A native of Puerto Rico, Ortiz Cofer (b. 1952) is the Franklin Professor of English and Creative Writing at the University of Georgia. Her publications include three novels and many collections of poetry and prose, including Silent Dancing: A Partial Remembrance of a Puerto Rican Childhood *(1990),* An Island Like You: Stories of the Barrio *(1995),* Woman in Front of the Sun: On Becoming a Writer *(2000), and most recently,* A Love Story Beginning in Spanish: Poems *(2005). "The Story of My Body" appeared in* The Latin Deli *(1993).*

> Migration is the story of my body.
> — VICTOR HERNÁNDEZ CRUZ

Skin

I was born a white girl in Puerto Rico but became a brown girl when I came to live in the United States. My Puerto Rican relatives called me tall; at the American school, some of my rougher classmates called me Skinny Bones, and the Shrimp because I was the smallest member of my classes all through grammar school until high school, when the midget Gladys was given the honorary post of front row center for class pictures and score-keeper, bench warmer, in P.E. I reached my full stature of five feet in sixth grade.

I started out life as a pretty baby and learned to be a pretty girl from a pretty mother. Then at ten years of age I suffered one of the worst cases of chicken pox I have ever heard of. My entire body, including the inside of my ears and in between my toes, was covered with pustules which in a fit of panic at my appearance I scratched off my face, leaving permanent scars. A cruel school nurse told me I would always have them — tiny cuts that looked as if a mad cat had plunged its claws deep into my skin. I grew my hair long and hid behind it for the first years of my adolescence. This was when I learned to be invisible.

Color

In the animal world it indicates danger: the most colorful creatures are often the most poisonous. Color is also a way to attract and seduce a mate. In the human world color triggers many more complex and often deadly reactions. As a Puerto Rican girl born of "white" parents, I spent the first years of my life hearing people refer to me as *blanca*, white. My mother insisted that I protect myself from the intense island sun because I was more prone to sunburn than some of my darker, *trigueño*[1] playmates. People were always commenting within my hearing about how my black hair contrasted so nicely with my "pale" skin. I did not think of the color of my skin consciously except when I heard the adults talking about complexion. It seems to me that the subject is much more common in the conversation of mixed-race peoples than in mainstream United States society, where it is a touchy and sometimes even embarrassing topic to discuss, except in a political context. In Puerto Rico I heard many conversations about skin color. A pregnant woman could say, "I hope my baby doesn't turn out *prieto*" (slang for "dark" or "black") "like my husband's grandmother, although she was a good-looking *negra*[2] in her time." I am a combination of both, being olive-skinned — lighter than my mother yet darker than my fair-skinned father. In America, I am a person of color, obviously a Latina. On the Island I have been called everything from a *paloma blanca*,[3] after the song (by a black suitor), to *la gringa*.[4]

My first experience of color prejudice occurred in a supermarket in Paterson, New Jersey. It was Christmastime, and I was eight or nine years old. There was a display of toys in the store where I went two or three times a day to buy things for my mother, who never made lists but sent for milk, cigarettes, a can of this or that, as she remembered from hour to hour. I enjoyed being trusted with money and walking half a city block to the new, modern grocery store. It was owned by three good-looking Italian brothers. I liked the younger one with the crew-cut blond hair. The two older ones watched me and the other Puerto Rican kids as if they thought we were going to steal something. The oldest one would sometimes even try to hurry me with my purchases, although part of my pleasure in these expeditions came from looking at everything in the well-stocked aisles. I was also teaching myself to read English by sounding out the labels on packages: L&M cigarettes, Borden's homogenized milk, Red Devil potted ham, Nestle's chocolate mix, Quaker oats, Bustelo coffee, Wonder bread, Colgate toothpaste, Ivory soap, and Goya (makers of products used in Puerto Rican dishes) everything — these are some of the brand names that taught me nouns. Several times this man had come up to me, wearing his blood-stained butcher's apron, and towering over

[1]*trigueño:* Brown-skinned.
[2]*negra:* Black.
[3]*paloma blanca:* White dove.
[4]*la gringa:* A white, non-Latina woman.

me had asked in a harsh voice whether there was something he could help me find. On the way out I would glance at the younger brother who ran one of the registers and he would often smile and wink at me.

It was the mean brother who first referred to me as "colored." It was a   5 few days before Christmas, and my parents had already told my brother and me that since we were in Los Estados[5] now, we would get our presents on December 25 instead of Los Reyes, Three Kings Day, when gifts are exchanged in Puerto Rico. We were to give them a wish list that they would take to Santa Claus, who apparently lived in the Macy's store downtown — at least that's where we had caught a glimpse of him when we went shopping. Since my parents were timid about entering the fancy store, we did not approach the huge man in the red suit. I was not interested in sitting on a stranger's lap anyway. But I did covet Susie, the talking schoolteacher doll that was displayed in the center aisle of the Italian brothers' supermarket. She talked when you pulled a string on her back. Susie had a limited repertoire of three sentences: I think she could say: "Hello, I'm Susie Schoolteacher," "Two plus two is four," and one other thing I cannot remember. The day the older brother chased me away, I was reaching to touch Susie's blond curls. I had been told many times, as most children have, not to touch anything in the store that I was not buying. But I had been looking at Susie for weeks. In my mind, she was my doll. After all, I had put her on my Christmas wish list. The moment is frozen in my mind as if there were a photograph of it on file. It was not a turning point, a disaster, or an earth-shaking revelation. It was simply the first time I considered — if naively — the meaning of skin color in human relations.

I reached to touch Susie's hair. It seems to me that I had to get on tiptoe, since the toys were stacked on a table and she sat like a princess on top of the fancy box she came in. Then I heard the booming "Hey, kid, what do you think you're doing!" spoken very loudly from the meat counter. I felt caught, although I knew I was not doing anything criminal. I remember not looking at the man, but standing there, feeling humiliated because I knew everyone in the store must have heard him yell at me. I felt him approach, and when I knew he was behind me, I turned around to face the bloody butcher's apron. His large chest was at my eye level. He blocked my way. I started to run out of the place, but even as I reached the door I heard him shout after me: "Don't come in here unless you gonna buy something. You PR kids put your dirty hands on stuff. You always look dirty. But maybe dirty brown is your natural color." I heard him laugh and someone else too in the back. Outside in the sunlight I looked at my hands. My nails needed a little cleaning as they always did, since I liked to paint with watercolors, but I took a bath every night. I thought the man was dirtier than I was in his stained apron. He was also always sweaty — it showed in big yellow circles under his shirt-sleeves. I sat on the front steps of the apartment building

---

[5]*Los Estados:* "The States" — that is, the United States.

where we lived and looked closely at my hands, which showed the only skin I could see; since it was bitter cold and I was wearing my quilted play coat, dungarees, and a knitted navy cap of my father's. I was not pink like my friend Charlene and her sister Kathy, who had blue eyes and light brown hair. My skin is the color of the coffee my grandmother made, which was half milk, *leche con café* rather than *café con leche*.[6] My mother is the opposite mix. She has a lot of café in her color. I could not understand how my skin looked like dirt to the supermarket man.

I went in and washed my hands thoroughly with soap and hot water, and borrowing my mother's nail file, I cleaned the crusted watercolors from underneath my nails. I was pleased with the results. My skin was the same color as before, but I knew I was clean. Clean enough to run my fingers through Susie's fine gold hair when she came home to me.

Size

My mother is barely four feet eleven inches in height, which is average for women in her family. When I grew to five feet by age twelve, she was amazed and began to use the word tall to describe me, as in "Since you are tall, this dress will look good on you." As with the color of my skin, I didn't consciously think about my height or size until other people made an issue of it. It is around the preadolescent years that in America the games children play for fun become fierce competitions where everyone is out to "prove" they are better than others. It was in the playground and sports fields that my size-related problems began. No matter how familiar the story is, every child who is the last chosen for a team knows the torment of waiting to be called up. At the Paterson, New Jersey, public schools that I attended, the volleyball or softball game was the metaphor for the battle-field of life to the inner city kids — the black kids versus the Puerto Rican kids, the whites versus the blacks versus the Puerto Rican kids; and I was 4F,[7] skinny, short, bespectacled, and apparently impervious to the blood thirst that drove many of my classmates to play ball as if their lives depended on it. Perhaps they did. I would rather be reading a book than sweating, grunting, and running the risk of pain and injury. I simply did not see the point in competitive sports. My main form of exercise then was walking to the library, many city blocks away from my barrio.

Still, I wanted to be wanted. I wanted to be chosen for the team. Physical education was compulsory, a class where you were actually given a grade. On my mainly all A report card, the C for compassion I always received from the P.E. teachers shamed me the same as a bad grade in a real class. Invariably, my father would say: "How can you make a low grade

---

[6]*leche con café . . . café con leche:* Milk with coffee (light brown) . . . coffee with milk (dark brown).

[7]*4F:* Draft-board classification meaning "unfit for military service;" hence, not physically fit.

for *playing games?*" He did not understand. Even if I had managed to make a hit (it never happened) or get the ball over that ridiculously high net, I already had a reputation as a "shrimp," a hopeless nonathlete. It was an area where the girls who didn't like me for one reason or another — mainly because I did better than they on academic subjects — could lord it over me; the playing field was the place where even the smallest girl could make me feel powerless and inferior. I instinctively understood the politics even then; how the *not* choosing me until the teacher forced one of the team captains to call my name was a coup of sorts — there, you little show-off, tomorrow you can beat us in spelling and geography, but this afternoon you are the loser. Or perhaps those were only my own bitter thoughts as I sat or stood in the sidelines while the big girls were grabbed like fish and I, the little brown tadpole, was ignored until Teacher looked over in my general direction and shouted, "Call Ortiz," or, worse, "Somebody's *got* to take her."

No wonder I read Wonder Woman comics and had Legion of Super   10 Heroes daydreams. Although I wanted to think of myself as "intellectual," my body was demanding that I notice it. I saw the little swelling around my once-flat nipples, the fine hairs growing in secret places; but my knees were still bigger than my thighs, and I always wore long- or half-sleeve blouses to hide my bony upper arms. I wanted flesh on my bones — a thick layer of it. I saw a new product advertised on TV. Wate-On. They showed skinny men and women before and after taking the stuff, and it was a transformation like the ninety-seven-pound-weakling-turned-into-Charles-Atlas ads that I saw on the back covers of my comic books. The Wate-On was very expensive. I tried to explain my need for it in Spanish to my mother, but it didn't translate very well, even to my ears — and she said with a tone of finality, eat more of my good food and you'll get fat — anybody can get fat. Right. Except me. I was going to have to join a circus someday as Skinny Bones, the woman without flesh.

Wonder Woman was stacked. She had a cleavage framed by the spread wings of a golden eagle and a muscular body that has become fashionable with women only recently. But since I wanted a body that would serve me in P.E., hers was my ideal. The breasts were an indulgence I allowed myself. Perhaps the daydreams of bigger girls were more glamorous, since our ambitions are filtered through our needs, but I wanted first a powerful body. I daydreamed of leaping up above the gray landscape of the city to where the sky was clear and blue, and in anger and self-pity, I fantasized about scooping my enemies up by their hair from the playing fields and dumping them on a barren asteroid. I would put the P.E. teachers each on their own rock in space too, where they would be the loneliest people in the universe, since I knew they had no "inner resources," no imagination, and in outer space, there would be no air for them to fill their deflated volleyballs with. In my mind all P.E. teachers have blended into one large spiky-haired woman with a whistle on a string around her neck and a volleyball under one arm. My Wonder Woman fantasies of revenge were a source of comfort to me in my early career as a shrimp.

I was saved from more years of P.E. torment by the fact that in my sophomore year of high school I transferred to a school where the midget, Gladys, was the focal point of interest for the people who must rank according to size. Because her height was considered a handicap, there was an unspoken rule about mentioning size around Gladys, but of course, there was no need to say anything. Gladys knew her place: front row center in class photographs. I gladly moved to the left or to the right of her, as far as I could without leaving the picture completely.

Looks

Many photographs were taken of me as a baby by my mother to send to my father, who was stationed overseas during the first two years of my life. With the army in Panama when I was born, he later traveled often on tours of duty with the navy. I was a healthy, pretty baby. Recently, I read that people are drawn to big-eyed round-faced creatures, like puppies, kittens, and certain other mammals and marsupials, koalas, for example, and, of course, infants. I was all eyes, since my head and body, even as I grew older, remained thin and small-boned. As a young child I got a lot of attention from my relatives and many other people we met in our barrio. My mother's beauty may have had something to do with how much attention we got from strangers in stores and on the street. I can imagine it. In the pictures I have seen of us together, she is a stunning young woman by Latino standards: long, curly black hair, and round curves in a compact frame. From her I learned how to move, smile, and talk like an attractive woman. I remember going into a bodega[8] for our groceries and being given candy by the proprietor as a reward for being *bonita,* pretty.

I can see in the photographs, and I also remember, that I was dressed in the pretty clothes, the stiff, frilly dresses, with layers of crinolines underneath, the glossy patent leather shoes, and, on special occasions, the skull-hugging little hats and the white gloves that were popular in the late fifties and early sixties. My mother was proud of my looks, although I was a bit too thin. She could dress me up like a doll and take me by the hand to visit relatives, or go to the Spanish mass at the Catholic church and show me off. How was I to know that she and the others who called me "pretty" were representatives of an aesthetic that would not apply when I went out into the mainstream world of school?

In my Paterson, New Jersey, public schools there were still quite a few   15 white children, although the demographics of the city were changing rapidly. The original waves of Italian and Irish immigrants, silk-mill workers, and laborers in the cloth industries had been "assimilated." Their children were now the middle-class parents of my peers. Many of them moved their children to the Catholic schools that proliferated enough to have

---

[8]*bodega:* Market.

leagues of basketball teams. The names I recall hearing still ring in my ears: Don Bosco High versus St. Mary's High, St. Joseph's versus St. John's. Later I too would be transferred to the safer environment of a Catholic school. But I started school at Public School Number 11. I came there from Puerto Rico, thinking myself a pretty girl, and found that the hierarchy for popularity was as follows: pretty white girl, pretty Jewish girl, pretty Puerto Rican girl, pretty black girl. Drop the last two categories; teachers were too busy to have more than one favorite per class, and it was simply understood that if there was a big part in the school play, or any competition where the main qualification was "presentability" (such as escorting a school visitor to or from the principal's office), the classroom's public address speaker would be requesting the pretty and/or nice-looking white boy or girl. By the time I was in the sixth grade, I was sometimes called by the principal to represent my class because I dressed neatly (I knew this from a progress report sent to my mother, which I translated for her) and because all the "presentable" white girls had moved to the Catholic schools (I later surmised this part). But I was still not one of the popular girls with the boys. I remember one incident where I stepped out into the playground in my baggy gym shorts and one Puerto Rican boy said to the other: "What do you think?" The other one answered: "Her face is OK, but look at the toothpick legs." The next best thing to a compliment I got was when my favorite male teacher, while handing out the class pictures, commented that with my long neck and delicate features I resembled the movie star Audrey Hepburn. But the Puerto Rican boys had learned to respond to a fuller figure: long necks and a perfect little nose were not what they looked for in a girl. That is when I decided I was a "brain." I did not settle into the role easily. I was nearly devastated by what the chicken pox episode had done to my self-image. But I looked into the mirror less often after I was told that I would always have scars on my face, and I hid behind my long black hair and my books.

After the problems at the public school got to the point where even nonconfrontational little me got beaten up several times, my parents enrolled me at St. Joseph's High School. I was then a minority of one among the Italian and Irish kids. But I found several good friends there — other girls who took their studies seriously. We did our homework together and talked about the Jackies. The Jackies were two popular girls, one blonde and the other red-haired, who had women's bodies. Their curves showed even in the blue jumper uniforms with straps that we all wore. The blonde Jackie would often let one of the straps fall off her shoulder, and although she, like all of us, wore a white blouse underneath, all the boys stared at her arm. My friends and I talked about this and practiced letting our straps fall off our shoulders. But it wasn't the same without breasts or hips.

My final two and a half years of high school were spent in Augusta, Georgia, where my parents moved our family in search of a more peaceful environment. There we became part of a little community of our army-connected relatives and friends. School was yet another matter. I was enrolled in a huge school of nearly two thousand students that had just that year been forced to integrate. There were two black girls and there was me. I did extremely well academically. As to my social life, it was, for the most part, uneventful—yet it is in my memory blighted by one incident. In my junior year, I became wildly infatuated with a pretty white boy. I'll call him Ted. Oh, he was pretty: yellow hair that fell over his forehead, a smile to die for—and he was a great dancer. I watched him at Teen Town, the youth center at the base where all the military brats gathered on Saturday nights. My father had retired from the navy, and we had all our base privileges— one other reason we moved to Augusta. Ted looked like an angel to me. I worked on him for a year before he asked me out. This meant maneuvering to be within the periphery of his vision at every possible occasion. I took the long way to my classes in school just to pass by his locker, I went to football games, which I detested, and I danced (I too was a good dancer) in front of him at Teen Town—this took some fancy footwork, since it involved subtly moving my partner toward the right spot on the dance floor. When Ted finally approached me, "A Million to One" was playing on the jukebox, and when he took me into his arms, the odds suddenly turned in my favor. He asked me to go to a school dance the following Saturday. I said yes, breathlessly. I said yes, but there were obstacles to surmount at home. My father did not allow me to date casually. I was allowed to go to major events like a prom or a concert with a boy who had been properly screened. There was such a boy in my life, a neighbor who wanted to be a Baptist missionary and was practicing his anthropological skills on my family. If I was desperate to go somewhere and needed a date, I'd resort to Gary. This is the type of religious nut that Gary was: when the school bus did not show up one day, he put his hands over his face and prayed to Christ to get us a way to get to school. Within ten minutes a mother in a station wagon, on her way to town, stopped to ask why we weren't in school. Gary informed her that the Lord had sent her just in time to find us a way to get there in time for roll call. He assumed that I was impressed. Gary was even good-looking in a bland sort of way, but he kissed me with his lips tightly pressed together. I think Gary probably ended up marrying a native woman from wherever he may have gone to preach the Gospel according to Paul. She probably believes that all white men pray to God for transportation and kiss with their mouths closed. But it was Ted's mouth, his whole beautiful self, that concerned me in those days. I knew my father would say no to our date, but I planned to run away from home if necessary. I told my mother how important this date was. I cajoled and pleaded with her from Sunday to Wednesday. She listened to my arguments and must have heard the note of desperation in my voice. She said very gently to me: "You better be ready for disappointment." I did not ask what she meant. I did not want her fears for me to taint my happiness. I asked her to tell my father about my date. Thursday at breakfast my father looked at me across the table with his eyebrows together. My mother looked at him with her mouth set in a straight line. I looked down at my bowl of cereal. Nobody said anything. Friday I tried on every dress in my closet. Ted would be picking me up at six on Saturday: dinner and then the sock hop at school. Friday night I was in my room doing my nails or something else in preparation for Saturday (I know I groomed myself nonstop all week) when the telephone rang. I ran to get it. It was Ted. His voice sounded funny when he said my name, so funny that I felt compelled to ask: "Is something wrong?" Ted blurted it all out without a preamble. His father had asked who he was going out with. Ted had told him my name. "Ortiz? That's Spanish, isn't it?" the father had asked. Ted had told him yes, then shown him my picture in the yearbook. Ted's father had shaken his head. No. Ted would not be taking me out. Ted's father had known Puerto Ricans in the army. He had lived in New York City while studying architecture and had seen how the spics lived. Like rats. Ted repeated his father's words to me as if I should understand *his* predicament when I heard why he was breaking our date. I don't remember what I said before hanging up. I do recall the darkness of my room that sleepless night and the heaviness of my blanket in which I wrapped myself like a shroud. And I remember my parents' respect for my pain and their gentleness toward me that weekend. My mother did not say "I warned you," and I was grateful for her understanding silence.

In college, I suddenly became an "exotic" woman to the men who had survived the popularity wars in high school, who were not practicing to be worldly: they had to act liberal in their politics, in their lifestyles, and in the women they went out with. I dated heavily for a while, then married young. I had discovered that I needed stability more than social life. I had brains for sure and some talent in writing. These facts were a constant in my life. My skin color, my size, and my appearance were variables — things that were judged according to my current self-image, the aesthetic values of the time, the places I was in, and the people I met. My studies, later my writing, the respect of people who saw me as an individual person they cared about, these were the criteria for my sense of self-worth that I would concentrate on in my adult life.

ENGAGING THE TEXT

1. Ortiz Cofer writes a good deal about how people perceived her and about how their perceptions changed according to time and place. Trace the stages Ortiz Cofer lived through, citing examples from the text, and discuss in each instance how her self-image was affected by people around her. What main point(s) do you think Ortiz Cofer may be trying to make with the narrative?

2. Which of the difficulties Ortiz Cofer faces are related specifically to gender (or made more serious by gender)? Do boys face comparable problems?

3. In your opinion, did Ortiz Cofer make the right decisions throughout her story? Is there anything she or her parents could have done to avoid or resist the various mistreatments she describes?

4. What role do media images play in Ortiz Cofer's story?

5. Does everyone have a story similar to Ortiz Cofer's, or not? Other people may be overweight, wear braces, mature very early or very late, have big noses or unusual voices, and so on. What, if anything, sets Ortiz Cofer's experience apart from the usual "traumas" of childhood?

EXPLORING CONNECTIONS

6. Review Aaron H. Devor's "Becoming Members of Society" (p. 383). How do Ortiz Cofer's experiences support and/or complicate Devor's explanation of gender role socialization?

7. Like Ortiz Cofer, Maysan Haydar (below) must find ways to define her identity within two different cultures. What problems do both women face, what strengths or advantages do they find within each culture, and what strategies do they adopt to negotiate the tensions that arise among conflicting cultural values?

8. Compare the childhood experiences of Ortiz Cofer and Gary Soto (p. 26). To what extent do their relationships, concerns, and behavior appear to be influenced by gender? What other social forces shape their lives?

EXTENDING THE CRITICAL CONTEXT

9. In her self-analysis, Ortiz Cofer discusses the "variables" in her physical appearance — the socially determined values that influence her perception of her body. She also reflects on personal "facts" or "constants" — more durable features, like her writing and her need for stability — that contribute to her identity. Write a series of journal entries that tell the story of your own body. What "variables" have influenced your perception of your appearance? What "facts" about yourself have become "constants"?

Veiled Intentions: Don't Judge a Muslim Girl by Her Covering
MAYSAN HAYDAR

A love for heavy metal probably isn't the first thing you'd expect of a nice Muslim girl, but according to a friend's Web site, "Maysan Haydar has always been cool.... She got a tongue ring before everyone else. She was the first person I knew to dye her hair purple." In this essay Haydar (b. 1977) examines some of the "seeming contradictions of my life" as an outspoken feminist who chooses to wear the traditional hijab, *or headscarf, of an observant*

Muslim woman. A native of Flint, Michigan, Haydar now lives in New York City, where she is a social worker. Her articles have appeared in a variety of publications ranging from The Nation *and* Spin *to* Venus Zine, HUES (Hear Us Emerging Sisters), *and* CMJ (College Music Journal). *"Veiled Intentions" appeared in* Body Outlaws: Rewriting the Rules of Beauty and Body Image *(2003), edited by Ophira Edut.*

> O Prophet! Tell thy wives and daughters and the believing women that they should cast their outer garments over their persons. That is most convenient that they should be known and not be molested.
> — THE QURAN, Chapter 33, Verse 59

> And say to the believing women that they should lower their gaze and guard their modesty: that they should not display their beauty and ornaments except what ordinarily appears thereof; that they should draw their veils over their bosoms and not display their beauty . . .
> — THE QURAN, Chapter 24, Verse 30–31

I have a confession to make.

I've been covering my hair, as is prescribed for Muslim women, since I was twelve years old. And while there are many good reasons for doing so, I wasn't motivated by a desire to be different, to honor tradition, or to make a political statement.

I wanted the board game Girl Talk.

When girls from our small, Midwestern Muslim community donned their first *hijab* (headscarf), their families rewarded them with parties and monetary gifts. At twelve, I wasn't nearly as physically developed as a Muslim girl is supposed to be when she starts covering, but I desperately wanted Girl Talk. I knew that if I announced my intention to begin veiling in the board game aisle at Kmart, I could ask for anything and receive it.

My choice of Girl Talk as reward for taking on a religious responsibility 5
is amusing to me now, because it's so antithetical to what veiling is supposed to represent. Girl Talk was the ultimate slumber party game, where players performed gags or revealed embarrassing secrets, then got to choose from four kinds of fortune cards as a prize. My favorite cards hooked me up with the class president, the football captain, or a hunky lifeguard who saved me from drowning. And I still have a sheet of "zit stickers," which were meant to punish gamers who failed to share their dirt.

Now that I'm twenty-five and have worn a veil for more than half my life, I can admit to this shallow beginning, which is so far from my reason for veiling today. As an adult, I embrace the veil's modesty, which allows me to be seen as a whole person instead of a twenty-piece chicken dinner. In spite of the seeming contradictions of my life — I'm married to a white man who was raised Catholic, I love heavy metal, I consider myself a feminist, and I sport a few well-disguised piercings — I follow my religion's standard of modesty and appearance. It's only now, after comparing my turbulent teen experiences with those of other women, that I can fully appreciate how much of a saving grace this small piece of cloth was.

Much to my chagrin, many Americans see veiling as an oppressive tool forced on Muslim women by the men in our culture. Yet, the practice of covering hair and body is a choice for many women — and it is not specific to Islam. All the monotheistic religions (Christianity, Judaism, and Islam) advocate modesty in dress, though the interpretation of "modesty" varies greatly. Ironically, the population that spends millions on beauty products, plastic surgery, and self-help guides is the same one that takes pity on me for being so "helpless" and "oppressed." On a New York City bus a couple weeks ago, I sat with another woman, also veiled, but wearing a traditional *jilbab* (a cloak that women wear over their clothing). A girl two seats over remarked to her friend, while flipping her hair for effect, that she couldn't understand how we could dress this way. "Me, I got to be *free*."

To my eyes, her idea of freedom involved a complicated hairstyle, loads of makeup and jeans she probably had to sew herself into. If anything, I would find that ensemble more caging, more oppressive and more painful than clothes that allow me to walk in front of construction sites confidently, with minimal risk of harassment. (Construction workers may feel obligated to say something to every passing woman, but I often get things like "I like your skirt!" or "Girl, I would marry you!" — harmless compared to the degradation I've heard many women complain about.)

As for freedom, my parents have a healthy understanding of Islam, especially the Quranic verse "Let there be no compulsion in religion" (2:256). Having been raised in religiously different homes themselves (Mom: very liberal, European-minded, not so religious; Dad: religious, culturally structured gender roles and expectations), they only practiced traditions that they understood, accepted, and believed. Thus, my mother knew the best way to introduce veiling to me was to emphasize its feminist, forward-thinking reasons: Covering removes that first level of being judged, of being assessed based on my measurements, and it absolves me of the need or desire to be wanted solely for my looks. My choice of Girl Talk didn't showcase a deep understanding of that idea. But reflecting back, I see that wearing a scarf greatly influenced how people viewed me and my goals, before I could ever appreciate that it was having that effect.

In high school, my interactions with the opposite sex were different than the norm. If I hadn't yet been inclined to deal with boys in an unpressured, ungiggly, un-made-up way, the scarf shoved me in that direction. So, without being given handbooks or informative flyers about how they should curb their posturing and come-ons, guys sensed that they should treat me with respect.

I didn't watch boys and girls learn about each other from the sidelines. I have many rich friendships with men, and over the years a good number of them have made a go at becoming "more than friends." I didn't participate in

10

dating games, but I was flattered by the attention, especially since I knew I was being liked for who I was beyond my body. What made me attractive was my ability to relate to everyone in a very natural way, without all the confusing sexual pressure. The weirdness that normally clouds boy-girl interactions was lifted, because most guys automatically assumed I wasn't available for dating. Of course, girls deserve to be treated with respect no matter what they wear. But since we live in a world of mixed messages, I got to bypass a lot of damaging experiences.

The veil bestowed other experiences upon me that I wouldn't quite classify as negative, but definitely educational. Like anyone else who's visibly different from the norm, I encountered ridiculous ideas about what a covered person should be, do, and enjoy. If someone overheard me talking about my interests, which included karate and skateboarding, I grew to enjoy their disbelief and shock. I didn't pick my hobbies to prove that stereotypes are often false, but it was nice to make people reconsider their notions of a Muslim girl.

Moving to New York City right after college and living alone was the most affirming thing I've done to solidify my resolve and truly understand what veiling means. Here, for the first time, people believed that I was wearing a scarf because I wanted to, not because my family coerced me into it. On the other hand, New York exemplifies what's wrong with our image-obsessed society. I worked for a couple of magazines and saw the way women acted out to draw attention to themselves. It was especially apparent at my anything-goes dot-com job, where women showed up to work in backless halter tops and were fawned over by male coworkers.

And now, as I write this, I can watch women subjugate themselves on reality dating shows. On a show about aspiring models I heard a woman say that her greatest goal would be to appear in *Stuff* magazine. I can't imagine centering my life on something as fleeting and meaningless as being admired simply for my body.

You might assume that because Muslim women traditionally don't display our bodies, we don't hold them as important or feel connected to them — or that we don't value ourselves as sexual beings. Guess again. While our degree of modesty is high, the value Muslim women place on the bodies underneath our veils is higher. In Sunday school, girls are taught that our bodies are beautiful ("God is beautiful and loves beauty" is a *hadith,* or saying, of the prophet Muhammad) and that they're so valuable that they're only meant to be shared in an intimate relationship: husband and wife, mother and baby, among women, and in clinical or safe spaces (for example, with your doctor, among family members). Historically, the most severe-looking coverings used to be limited to the richest women in Arab society; being swathed in so much cloth was regarded as a sign of status.

People who have written about being in the secluded quarters of Arab homes or at their parties often express surprise at the degree to which these cloaked women maintain themselves via fitness, style, and decadent rituals.

(Let's not even get started on the body hair–removal process in the Middle East.) I'm not one for creams and blushes, but I understand that there are women who enjoy the beauty process, and I see no harm in indulging it for the right reasons. Feminist author Geraldine Brooks, in her book *Nine Parts of Desire,* quotes women across the Middle East who extol the virtues of prettying up for their loved ones. To me, this demonstrates that Western priorities are out of line: American women spend hours getting ready for strangers to see them but don't give the same effort to those who see them in intimate settings.

As for the variation in Muslim women's dress, it demonstrates the wide-ranging interpretations of modesty. I often get asked what the most "right" version is: the Afghani *burqah,* the Iranian *chador,* the Pakistani *salwar kameez,*[1] the Arab *jilbab,* or a sweatshirt and jeans. The short answer is that the recommendations for modesty are to be interpreted and applied at the discretion of the woman picking her clothes.

All through high school, I wore a *jilbab* exclusively, because I didn't have to spend any effort worrying about what was in season or what I would be expected to wear to fit in. I now cover my hair, but generally wear jeans and a long-sleeved shirt. My once-strict interpretation of modesty has been adapted to my urban lifestyle. Is wearing an *abaya* (the head-to-toe gown that completely covers the wearer) and a face veil a good idea in New York City? Probably not, since the *abaya* would likely get stuck in a subway door or pick up the dust off any floor you glide across. But not wearing an *abaya* in Saudi Arabia would probably make getting around very difficult for a woman.

It's utopic and ridiculous to assert that looks don't matter and that by veiling I'm avoiding the messiness — particularly after September 11th. Now some people hold their breath a bit longer, assuming I'm a fundamentalist or wondering if I'm there to cause them harm. I sense people studying me on the trains, reading the cover of the book in my hand and trying to gauge if I'm one of "us" or one of "them." I grapple with the frustration that I can't reassure everyone individually that my goals have everything to do with social justice and nothing to do with holy war. But I have seen suspicions fade in the eyes of the pregnant woman to whom I've given my subway seat, or the Hasidic[2] man whose elbow I've taken to help him up the stairs.

Though many of the stereotypes and incorrect assumptions people had while I was growing up still prevail (that Muslim equals backwards/oppressed/fundamentalist/terrorist), current events have pedestrians describ- 20

---

[1]*burqah . . . salwar kameez:* The *burqah* covers a women from head to toe, with a mesh strip in front of the eyes to allow some vision; the *chador* also drapes the head and body, but not the face; the *salwar kameez* is a tunic-and-trouser set.

[2]*Hasidic:* Hasidism is a form of Jewish mysticism; Hasidic men typically wear long black coats and wide-brimmed black hats, while women cover their hair and wear long skirts and long sleeves for modesty.

ing their secondhand "expertise" of Islam — the history of Wahhabi Islam,[3] the export of Sayyid Qutb[4] and the Muslim Brotherhood's[5] ideas — or trying to argue that the Quranic requirements for modesty don't include veiling. It's much harder to explain why I cover to those who think they have a full understanding of the culture and the faith than those whose "knowledge" of the Middle East is limited to *Aladdin* and *hummus*.

I do appreciate the status Islam and the Middle East have in the news these days — the interest has generated new scholarship on Arabia's history and anthropology and on Islamic law, all of which I'm interested in and am relieved is being researched. This research includes a pool of female scholars reexamining Islamic texts with a feminist lens, and separating actual religious commands from their long-held, culturally laden interpretations, which often smack of patriarchy.

Forcing women to veil or unveil usually has the opposite effect. When I attended elementary school in Saudi Arabia and flew home to Michigan each summer, a parade of women swathed in black *abayas* would head to the airplane bathrooms once we were safely in the air and emerge wearing short, tight ensembles. Conversely, banning the veil in Syria and Turkey sparked a resurgence in its popularity.

The question of veiling comes up once someone finds out that I've married into a family that celebrates Christmas, with my full participation. "If you have a daughter, what will she wear?" they ask. I haven't yet cracked a pregnancy or parenting book, but I hope that my policy will be similar to the egalitarian way I was raised. If she wants to, she can; if she doesn't want to, then she won't. It's far more important for her to respect herself, her body, and her life.

At the heart of my veiling is personal freedom. I dress this way because it has made it easier to get through adolescent phases and New York City streets with no self-loathing, body hang-ups, or sexual harassment. I wish more women emerged unscathed; no one should suffer for what they look like or what they wear.

ENGAGING THE TEXT

1. List the advantages and disadvantages that Haydar associates with covering. Do you agree that her *hijab* enables her "to be seen as a whole person" (para. 6)? Why or why not?

---

[3]*Wahhabi Islam:* A Sunni fundamentalist form of Islam founded by Muhammad ibn Abdel al Wahhab (1703–1792), Wahhabism is the majority faith of Saudi Arabia and Qatar.

[4]*Sayyid Qutb:* Egyptian writer and intellectual (1906–1966) who condemned western values and promoted the idea of a fundamentalist Islamic state; affiliated with the Muslim Brotherhood.

[5]*Muslim Brotherhood:* Worldwide movement, founded in Egypt in 1928, that advocates government imposition of strict Islamic law.

2. What compromises does Haydar make between religious observance and modern, secular culture? Do her stated reasons for wearing the *hijab* seem more religious, more practical, or both?

3. Examine the interactions with others that Haydar describes in her essay. How would you explain the different responses to her appearance? To what extent do they reflect assumptions about her as a Muslim, as a religious person, or as a modest woman?

4. How do Haydar's definitions of "freedom" and "oppression" of women differ from those assumed by the girl on the bus (para. 7)? Debate which forms of oppression harm women more, which types of freedom are most important to preserve, and why.

5. Working in groups, brainstorm several ways, besides veiling, that an adolescent girl might avoid "the weirdness that normally clouds boy-girl interactions" (para. 11). Share your ideas with the class and discuss the pros and cons of each.

EXPLORING CONNECTIONS

6. Review Aaron H. Devor's discussion of gender role socialization (p. 383), and compare the influence of "generalized others" and "significant others" in the experiences of Haydar and Judith Ortiz Cofer (p. 393). What tension does each woman feel between her "I" and her "me"? How does she resolve it?

7. Read Diana Eck's discussion of stereotyping and discrimination against people whose religious dress makes them "visibly different" (p. 693). To what extent does Haydar experience or avoid the consequences of such stereotypes? How does she actively counter them?

EXTENDING THE CRITICAL CONTEXT

8. Write a journal entry in which you envision how your own life would change if you chose to wear some distinctively religious article of clothing.

9. Design and conduct a brief survey to gauge attitudes toward veiling on your campus or in your community.

Visual Portfolio

Reading Images of Gender

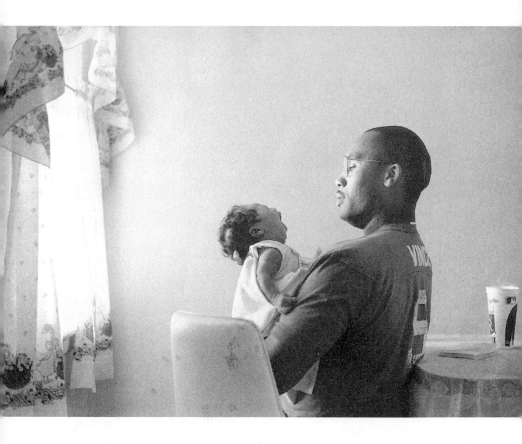

Visual Portfolio
READING IMAGES OF GENDER

1. Write a brief story to accompany the image of the woman vacuuming. When and where does this take place? Who is the woman? Why is she vacuuming? What accounts for her expression and body language? Share your stories in class: How do the interpretations differ? What elements of the image support each narrative?

2. Working in pairs or groups, develop an interpretation of the photo of the young woman looking in the mirror. Take into account the framing of the photo, the setting, the young woman's outfit, her posture and expression, the direction of her gaze, and the fragmented reflection. Present these interpretations in class and evaluate the persuasiveness of each.

3. Based on your discussions of the first two images in the portfolio, write an imaginary dialogue between the two women in which they talk about what it means to them to be female.

4. Imagine that you are one of the people in the picture of the four teens and freewrite about what is happening (or what has just happened). What are you thinking and feeling at this moment, and why? Compare your responses to those of classmates: Does the gender of the "character" you adopt affect your interpretation of the image? If so, how and why?

5. What does the photo of the victorious boxer suggest about her feelings at that moment? About her opponent's response to his loss? What other messages — about sports or gender or competition, for example — does the picture convey to you? Point to particular visual details that support your interpretations.

6. To what extent does each of the two sprinters on page 413 conform or resist conforming to conventional gender roles? How might Aaron H. Devor and Maysan Haydar interpret this image?

7. How would you describe the mood or feeling the photographer has captured in the picture of the father and child? How do the light, the setting, the stance, and the expression of each figure contribute to this impression?

8. Do you think that "Masculinity" would be an appropriate title for the picture of the man and child? Why or why not? Eli Reed, the photographer, titles the photo simply, "Mississippi, 1991"; why do you think he chose to identify it by place and time rather than by theme?

9. Brainstorm a list of familiar media images — from books, movies, TV, magazines, and so forth — that may have influenced the clothing styles of the father and daughter pictured on page 415. What gender characteristics or stereotypes do you associate with each style of dress? To what extent does the photo itself reinforce or subvert these stereotypes?

"Two Ways a Woman Can Get Hurt": Advertising and Violence

JEAN KILBOURNE

*Most of us like to think of ourselves as immune to the power of ads —
we know that advertisers use sex to get our attention and that they make
exaggerated claims about a product's ability to make us attractive, popular,
and successful. Because we can see through these subtle or not-so-subtle
messages, we assume that we're too smart to be swayed by them. But Jean
Kilbourne argues that ads affect us in far more profound and potentially
damaging ways. The way that ads portray bodies — especially women's
bodies — as objects conditions us to see each other in dehumanizing ways,
thus "normalizing" attitudes that can lead to sexual aggression. Kilbourne
(b. 1946) has spent most of her professional life teaching and lecturing about
the world of advertising. She has produced award-winning documentaries
on images of women in ads (*Killing Us Softly, Slim Hopes*) *and tobacco
advertising (*Pack of Lies*). She has also been a member of the National
Advisory Council on Alcohol Abuse and Alcoholism and has twice served as
an adviser to the surgeon general of the United States. Currently she serves
on the Massachusetts Governor's Commission on Sexual and Domestic
Abuse and teaches at Wellesley College. This selection is taken from her
1999 book,* Can't Buy My Love: How Advertising Changes the Way We
Think and Feel *(formerly titled* Deadly Persuasion).*

Sex in advertising is more about disconnection and distance than connection and closeness. It is also more often about power than passion, about
violence than violins. The main goal, as in pornography, is usually power
over another, either by the physical dominance or preferred status of men
or what is seen as the exploitative power of female beauty and female sexuality. Men conquer and women ensnare, always with the essential aid of a
product. The woman is rewarded for her sexuality by the man's wealth, as in
an ad for Cigarette boats in which the woman says, while lying in a man's
embrace clearly after sex, "Does this mean I get a ride in your Cigarette?"

Sex in advertising is pornographic because it dehumanizes and objecti-
fies people, especially women, and because it fetishizes products, imbues
them with an erotic charge — which dooms us to disappointment since
products never can fulfill our sexual desires or meet our emotional needs.
The poses and postures of advertising are often borrowed from pornography, as are many of the themes, such as bondage, sadomasochism, and the
sexual exploitation of children. When a beer ad uses the image of a man

Two Ways A Woman Can Get Hurt.

(Heartbreaker)

(Soap and water shave)

Skintimate Shave Gel Ultra Protection formula contains 75% moisturizers, including vitamin E, to protect your legs from nicks, cuts and razor burn. So while guys may continue to be a pain, shaving most definitely won't.

SKINTIMATE®SHAVE GEL
LOVE YOUR LEGS

licking the high-heeled boot of a woman clad in leather, when bondage is used to sell neckties in the *New York Times,* perfume in *The New Yorker,* and watches on city buses, and when a college magazine promotes an S&M Ball, pornography can be considered mainstream.

The right tie can make even the most casual evening more memorable

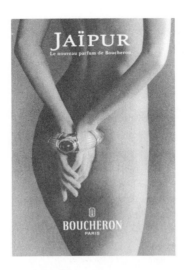

Most of us know all this by now and I suppose some consider it kinky good fun. Pornography is more dangerously mainstream when its glorification of rape and violence shows up in mass media, in films and television shows, in comedy and music videos, and in advertising. Male violence is subtly encouraged by ads that encourage men to be forceful and dominant, and to value sexual intimacy more than emotional intimacy. "Do you want to be the one she tells her deep, dark secrets to?" asks a three-page ad for men's cologne. "Or do you want to be her deep, dark secret?" The last page advises men, "Don't be such a good boy." There are two identical women looking adoringly at the man in the ad, but he isn't looking at either one of them. Just what is the deep, dark secret? That he's sleeping with both of them? Clearly the way to get beautiful women is to ignore them, perhaps mistreat them.

"Two ways a woman can get hurt," says an ad for shaving gel, featuring a razor and a photo of a handsome man. My first thought is that the man is a

batterer or date rapist, but the ad informs us that he is merely a "heart-breaker." The gel will protect the woman so that "while guys may continue to be a pain, shaving most definitely won't." Desirable men are painful — heartbreakers at best.

Wouldn't it be wonderful if, realizing the importance of relationships in all of our lives, we could seek to learn relational skills from women and to help men develop these strengths in themselves? In fact, we so often do the opposite. The popular culture usually trivializes these abilities in women, mocks men who have real intimacy with women (it is almost always married men in ads and cartoons who are jerks), and idealizes a template for relationships between men and women that is a recipe for disaster: a template that views sex as more important than anything else, that ridicules men who are not in control of their women (who are "pussy-whipped"), and that disparages fidelity and commitment (except, of course, to brand names).

Indeed the very worst kind of man for a woman to be in an intimate relationship with, often a truly dangerous man, is the one considered most sexy and desirable in the popular culture. And the men capable of real intimacy (the ones we tell our deep, dark secrets to) constantly have their very masculinity impugned. Advertising often encourages women to be attracted to hostile and indifferent men while encouraging boys to become these men. This is especially dangerous for those of us who have suffered from "condemned isolation" in childhood: like heat-seeking missiles, we rush inevitably to mutual destruction.

Men are also encouraged to never take no for an answer. Ad after ad implies that girls and women don't really mean "no" when they say it, that women are only teasing when they resist men's advances. "NO" says an ad showing a man leaning over a woman against a wall. Is she screaming or laughing? Oh, it's an ad for deodorant and the second word, in very small

print, is "sweat." Sometimes it's "all in good fun," as in the ad for Possession shirts and shorts featuring a man ripping the clothes off a woman who seems to be having a good time.

And sometimes it is more sinister. A perfume ad running in several teen magazines features a very young woman, with eyes blackened by makeup or perhaps something else, and the copy, "Apply generously to your neck so he can smell the scent as you shake your head 'no.'" In other words,

IF YOUR DATE WON'T LISTEN TO REASON, TRY A VELVET HAMMER.

Sip exotic cocktails, dine and dance to Swing Era music at Georgetown's top nightspot. 1232 36th St., NW. Reservations, call 342-0009. Free valet parking. Jackets required.

F. SCOTT'S

he'll understand that you don't really mean it and he can respond to the scent like any other animal.

Sometimes there seems to be no question but that a man should force a woman to have sex. A chilling newspaper ad for a bar in Georgetown features a closeup of a cocktail and the headline, "If your date won't listen to reason, try a Velvet Hammer." A vodka ad pictures a wolf hiding in a flock of sheep, a hideous grin on its face. We all know what wolves do to sheep. A campaign for Bacardi Black rum features shadowy figures almost obliterated by darkness and captions such as "Some people embrace the night because the rules of the day do not apply." What it doesn't say is that people who are above the rules do enormous harm to other people, as well as to themselves.

These ads are particularly troublesome, given that between one-third and three-quarters of all cases of sexual assault involve alcohol consumption by the perpetrator, the victim, or both.[1] "Make strangers your friends, and your friends a lot stranger," says one of the ads in a Cuervo campaign that uses colorful cartoon beasts and emphasizes heavy drinking. This ad is especially disturbing when we consider the role of alcohol in date rape, as is another ad in the series that says, "The night began with a bottle of Cuervo and ended with a vow of silence." Over half of all reported rapes on college campuses occur when either the victim or the assailant has been drinking.[2] Alcohol's role has different meaning for men and women, however. If a man is drunk when he commits a rape, he is considered less responsible. If a woman is drunk (or has had a drink or two or simply met the man in a bar), she is considered more responsible.

10

---

[1]Wilsnack, Plaud, Wilsnack, and Klassen, 1997, 262. [All notes are the author's, except 5, 9, 15, and 18.]

[2]Abbey, Ross, and McDuffie, 1991. Also Martin, 1992, 230–37.

In general, females are still held responsible and hold each other responsible when sex goes wrong — when they become pregnant or are the victims of rape and sexual assault or cause a scandal. Constantly exhorted to be sexy and attractive, they discover when assaulted that that very sexiness is evidence of their guilt, their lack of "innocence." Sometimes the ads play on this by "warning" women of what might happen if they use the product. "Wear it but beware it," says a perfume ad. Beware what exactly? Victoria's Secret tempts young women with blatantly sexual ads promising that their lingerie will make them irresistible. Yet when a young woman accused William Kennedy Smith of raping her, the fact that she wore Victoria's Secret panties was used against her as an indication of her immorality. A jury acquitted Smith, whose alleged history of violence against women was not permitted to be introduced at trial.

It is sadly not surprising that the jury was composed mostly of women. Women are especially cruel judges of other women's sexual behavior, mostly because we are so desperate to believe we are in control of what happens to us. It is too frightening to face the fact that male violence against women is irrational and commonplace. It is reassuring to believe that we can avoid it by being good girls, avoiding dark places, staying out of bars, dressing "innocently." An ad featuring two young women talking intimately at a coffee shop says, "Carla and Rachel considered themselves open-minded and non-judgmental people. Although they did agree Brenda was a tramp." These terrible judgments from other women are an important part of what keeps all women in line.

If indifference in a man is sexy, then violence is sometimes downright erotic. Not surprisingly, this attitude too shows up in advertising. "Push my buttons," says a young woman, "I'm looking for a man who can totally floor me." Her vulnerability is underscored by the fact that she is in an elevator, often a dangerous place for women. She is young, she is submissive (her eyes are downcast), she is in a dangerous place, and she is dressed provocatively. And she is literally asking for it.

"Wear it out and make it scream," says a jeans ad portraying a man sliding his hands under a woman's transparent blouse. This could be a seduction, but it could as easily be an attack. Although the ad that ran in the Czech version of *Elle* portraying three men attacking a woman seems unambiguous, the terrifying image is being used to sell jeans *to women*. So someone must think that women would find this image compelling or attractive. Why would we? Perhaps it is simply designed to get our attention, by shocking us

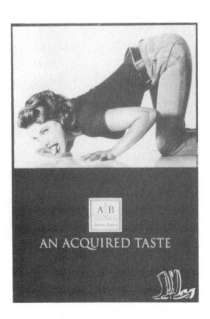

AN ACQUIRED TASTE

and by arousing unconscious anxiety. Or perhaps the intent is more subtle and it is designed to play into the fantasies of domination and even rape that some women use in order to maintain an illusion of being in control (we are the ones having the fantasies, after all, we are the directors).

A camera ad features a woman's torso wrapped in plastic, her hands   15 tied behind her back. A smiling woman in a lipstick ad has a padlocked chain around her neck. An ad for MTV shows a vulnerable young woman, her breasts exposed, and the simple copy "Bitch." A perfume ad features a man shadowboxing with what seems to be a woman.

Sometimes women are shown dead or in the process of being killed. "Great hair never dies," says an ad featuring a female corpse lying on a bed, her breasts exposed. An ad in the Italian version of *Vogue* shows a man aiming a gun at a nude woman wrapped in plastic, a leather briefcase covering her face. And an ad for Bitch skateboards, for God's sake, shows a cartoon

La Borsa è la Vita

bitch skateboards

version of a similar scene, this time clearly targeting young people. We believe we are not affected by these images, but most of us experience visceral shock when we pay conscious attention to them. Could they be any less shocking to us on an unconscious level?

Most of us become numb to these images, just as we become numb to the daily litany in the news of women being raped, battered, and killed. According to former surgeon general Antonia Novello, battery is the single greatest cause of injury to women in America, more common than automobile accidents, muggings, and stranger rapes combined, and more than one-third of women slain in this country die at the hands of husbands or boyfriends.[3] Throughout the world, the biggest problem for most women is simply surviving at home. The Global Report on Women's Human Rights concluded that "Domestic violence is a leading cause of female injury in almost every country in the world and is typically ignored by the state or only erratically punished."[4] Although usually numb to these facts on a conscious level, most women live in a state of subliminal terror, a state that, according to Mary Daly,[5] keeps us divided both from each other and from our most passionate, powerful, and creative selves.[6]

Ads don't directly cause violence, of course. But the violent images contribute to the state of terror. And objectification and disconnection create a climate in which there is widespread and increasing violence. Turning a human being into a thing, an object, is almost always the first step toward justifying violence against that person. It is very difficult, perhaps impossible, to be violent to someone we think of as an equal, someone we have empathy with, but it is very easy to abuse a thing. We see this with racism,

---

[3]Novello, 1991. Also Blumenthal, 1995.
[4]Wright, 1995, A2.
[5]*Mary Daly:* Radical feminist scholar and author (b. 1928).
[6]Weil, 1999, 21.

with homophobia. The person becomes an object and violence is inevitable. This step is already taken with women. The violence, the abuse, is partly the chilling but logical result of the objectification.

An editorial in *Advertising Age* suggests that even some advertisers are concerned about this: "Clearly it's time to wipe out sexism in beer ads; for the brewers and their agencies to wake up and join the rest of America in realizing that sexism, sexual harassment, and the cultural portrayal of women in advertising are inextricably linked."[7] Alas, this editorial was written in 1991 and nothing has changed.

It is this link with violence that makes the objectification of women a   20 more serious issue than the objectification of men. Our economic system constantly requires the development of new markets. Not surprisingly, men's bodies are the latest territory to be exploited. Although we are growing more used to it, in the beginning the male sex object came as a surprise. In 1994 a "gender bender" television commercial in which a bevy of women office workers gather to watch a construction worker doff his shirt to quaff a Diet Coke led to so much hoopla that you'd have thought women were mugging men on Madison Avenue.[8]

There is no question that men are used as sex objects in ads now as never before. We often see nude women with fully clothed men in ads (as in art), but the reverse was unheard of, until recently. These days some ads do feature clothed and often aggressive women with nude men. And women sometimes blatantly objectify men, as in the Metroliner ad that says, "'She's reading Nietzsche,' Harris noted to himself as he walked towards the café car for a glass of cabernet. And as he passed her seat, Maureen looked up from her book and thought, 'Nice buns.'"

[7]Brewers can help fight sexism, 1991, 28.
[8]Kilbourne, 1994, F13.

Although these ads are often funny, it is never a good thing for human beings to be objectified. However, there is a world of difference between the objectification of men and that of women. The most important difference is that there is no danger for most men, whereas objectified women are always at risk. In the Diet Coke ad, for instance, the women are physically separated from the shirtless man. He is the one in control. His body is powerful, not passive. Imagine a true role reversal of this ad: a group of businessmen gather to leer at a beautiful woman worker on her break, who removes her shirt before drinking her Diet Coke. This scene would be frightening, not funny, as the Diet Coke ad is. And why is the Diet Coke ad funny? Because we know it doesn't describe any truth. However, the ads featuring images of male violence against women do describe a truth, a truth we are all aware of, on one level or another.

When power is unequal, when one group is oppressed and discriminated against *as a group,* when there is a context of systemic and historical oppression, stereotypes and prejudice have different weight and meaning. As Anna Quindlen[9] said, writing about "reverse racism": "Hatred by the powerful, the majority, has a different weight — and often very different effects — than hatred by the powerless, the minority."[10] When men objectify women, they do so in a cultural context in which women are constantly objectified and in which there are consequences — from economic discrimination to violence — to that objectification.

For men, though, there are no such consequences. Men's bodies are not routinely judged and invaded. Men are not likely to be raped, harassed, or beaten (that is to say, men presumed to be heterosexual are not, and very few men are abused in these ways by women). How many men are frightened to be alone with a woman in an elevator? How many men cross the street when a group of women approaches? Jackson Katz, who writes and lectures on male violence, often begins his workshops by asking men to describe the things they do every day to protect themselves from sexual assault. The men are surprised, puzzled, sometimes amused by the question. The women understand the question easily and have no trouble at all coming up with a list of responses. We don't list our full names in the phone directory or on our mailboxes, we try not to be alone after dark, we carry our keys in our hands when we approach our cars, we always look in the back seat before we get in, we are wary of elevators and doorways and bushes, we carry pepper sprays, whistles, Mace.

Nonetheless, the rate of sexual assault in the United States is the highest of any industrialized nation in the world.[11] According to a 1998 study by the federal government, one in five of us has been the victim of rape or   25

---

[9]*Anna Quindlen:* Novelist and Pulitzer Prize-winning journalist who often writes about women's issues (b. 1953).

[10]Quindlen, 1992, E17.

[11]Blumenthal, 1995, 2.

where women are women
and men are
roadkill.

harley-davidson motorclothes

attempted rape, most often before our seventeenth birthday. And more than half of us have been physically assaulted, most often by the men we live with. In fact, three of four women in the study who responded that they had been raped or assaulted as adults said the perpetrator was a current or former husband, a cohabiting partner or a date.[12] The article reporting the results of this study was buried on page twenty-three of my local newspaper, while the front page dealt with a long story about the New England Patriots football team.

A few summers ago, a Diet Pepsi commercial featured Cindy Crawford being ogled by two boys (they seemed to be about twelve years old) as she got out of her car and bought a Pepsi from a machine. The boys made very suggestive comments, which in the end turned out to be about the Pepsi's can rather than Ms. Crawford's. There was no outcry: the boys' behavior was acceptable and ordinary enough for a soft-drink commercial.

Again, let us imagine the reverse: a sexy man gets out of a car in the countryside and two preteen girls make suggestive comments, seemingly about his body, especially his buns. We would fear for them and rightly so. But the boys already have the right to ogle, to view women's bodies as property to be looked at, commented on, touched, perhaps eventually hit and raped. The boys have also learned that men ogle primarily to impress other men (and to affirm their heterosexuality). If anyone is in potential danger in this ad, it is the woman (regardless of the age of the boys). Men are not seen as *property* in this way by women. Indeed if a woman does whistle at a man

---

[12]Tjaden and Thoennes, 1998.

or touches his body or even makes direct eye contact, it is still *she* who is at risk and the man who has the power.

"I always lower my eyes to see if a man is worth following," says the woman in an ad for men's pants. Although the ad is offensive to everyone, the woman is endangering only herself.

"Where women are women and men are roadkill," says an ad for motorcycle clothing featuring an angry-looking African-American woman.

Women are sometimes hostile and angry in ads these days, especially women of color who are often seen as angrier and more threatening than white women. But, regardless of color, we all know that women are far more likely than men to end up as roadkill — and, when it happens, they are blamed for being on the road in the first place.

Even little girls are sometimes held responsible for the violence against them. In 1990 a male Canadian judge accused a three-year-old girl of being "sexually aggressive" and suspended the sentence of her molester, who was then free to return to his job of baby-sitter.[13] The deeply held belief that all women, regardless of age, are really temptresses in disguise, nymphets, sexually insatiable and seductive, conveniently transfers all blame and responsibility onto women.

All women are vulnerable in a culture in which there is such widespread objectification of women's bodies, such glorification of disconnection, so much violence against women, and such blaming of the victim. When everything and everyone is sexualized, it is the powerless who are most at risk. Young girls, of course, are especially vulnerable. In the past twenty years or so, there have been several trends in fashion and advertising that could be seen as cultural reactions to the women's movement, as perhaps unconscious fear of female power. One has been the obsession with

30

[13]Two men and a baby, 1990, 10.

thinness. Another has been an increase in images of violence against women. Most disturbing has been the increasing sexualization of children, especially girls. Sometimes the little girl is made up and seductively posed. Sometimes the language is suggestive. "Very cherry," says the ad featuring a sexy little African-American girl who is wearing a dress with cherries all over it. A shocking ad in a gun magazine features a smiling little girl, a toddler, in a bathing suit that is tugged up suggestively in the rear. The copy beneath the photo says, "short BUTTS from FLEMING FIREARMS."[14] Other times girls are juxtaposed with grown women, as in the ad for underpants that says "You already know the feeling."

This is not only an American phenomenon. A growing national obsession in Japan with schoolgirls dressed in uniforms is called "Loli-con," after Lolita.[15] In Tokyo hundreds of "image clubs" allow Japanese men to act out their fantasies with make-believe schoolgirls. A magazine called *V-Club* featuring pictures of naked elementary-school girls competes with another called *Anatomical Illustrations of Junior High School Girls.*[16] Masao Miyamoto, a male psychiatrist, suggests that Japanese men are turning to girls because they feel threatened by the growing sophistication of older women.[17]

In recent years, this sexualization of little girls has become even more disturbing as hints of violence enter the picture. A three-page ad for Prada clothing features a girl or very young woman with a barely pubescent body,

[14]Herbert, 1999, WK 17.

[15]*Lolita:* The title character of Vladimir Nabokov's 1955 novel, Lolita is a young girl who is sexually pursued by her stepfather.

[16]Schoolgirls as sex toys, 1997, 2E.

[17]Ibid.

clothed in what seem to be cotton panties and perhaps a training bra, viewed through a partially opened door. She seems surprised, startled, worried, as if she's heard a strange sound or glimpsed someone watching her. I suppose this could be a woman awaiting her lover, but it could as easily be a girl being preyed upon.

The 1996 murder of six-year-old JonBenet Ramsey[18] was a gold mine for the media, combining as it did child pornography and violence. In November of 1997 *Advertising Age* reported in an article entitled "JonBenet keeps hold on magazines" that the child had been on five magazine covers in October, "Enough to capture the Cover Story lead for the month. The pre-adolescent beauty queen, found slain in her home last Christmas, garnered 6.5 points. The case earned a *triple play* [italics mine] in the *National Enquirer*, and one-time appearances on *People* and *Star*."[19] Imagine describing a six-year-old child as "pre-adolescent."

Sometimes the models in ads are children, other times they just look like children. Kate Moss was twenty when she said of herself, "I look twelve."[20] She epitomized the vacant, hollow-cheeked look known as "heroin chic" that was popular in the mid-nineties. She also often looked vulnerable, abused, and exploited. In one ad she is nude in the corner of a huge sofa, cringing as if braced for an impending sexual assault. In another she is lying nude on her stomach, pliant, available, androgynous enough to appeal to all kinds of pedophiles. In a music video she is dead and bound to a chair while Johnny Cash sings "Delia's Gone."

[18]*JonBenet Ramsey:* Six-year-old beauty-pageant winner who was sexually molested and murdered in her Boulder, Colorado, home in 1996.
[19]Johnson, 1997, 42.
[20]Leo, 1994, 27.

It is not surprising that Kate Moss models for Calvin Klein, the fashion designer who specializes in breaking taboos and thereby getting himself public outrage, media coverage, and more bang for his buck. In 1995 he brought the federal government down on himself by running a campaign that may have crossed the line into child pornography.[21] Very young models (and others who just seemed young) were featured in lascivious print ads and in television commercials designed to mimic child porn. The models were awkward, self-conscious. In one commercial, a boy stands in what seems to be a finished basement. A male voiceover tells him he has a great body and asks him to take off his shirt. The boy seems embarrassed but he complies. There was a great deal of protest, which brought the issue into national consciousness but which also gave Klein the publicity and free media coverage he was looking for. He pulled the ads but, at the same time, projected that his jeans sales would almost double from $115 million to $220 million that year, partly because of the free publicity but also because the controversy made his critics seem like prudes and thus positioned Klein as the daring rebel, a very appealing image to the majority of his customers.

Having learned from this, in 1999 Klein launched a very brief advertising campaign featuring very little children frolicking in their underpants, which included a controversial billboard in Times Square.[22] Although in some ways this campaign was less offensive than the earlier one and might have gone unnoticed had the ads come from a department store catalog rather than from Calvin Klein, there was the expected protest and Klein quickly withdrew the ads, again getting a windfall of media coverage. In my

[21]Sloan, 1996, 27.
[22]Associated Press, 1999, February 18, A7.

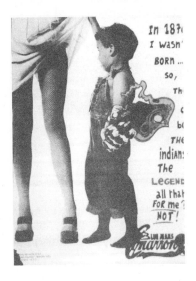

opinion, the real obscenity of this campaign is the whole idea of people buying designer underwear for their little ones, especially in a country in which
at least one in five children doesn't have enough to eat.

Although boys are sometimes sexualized in an overt way, they are more
often portrayed as sexually precocious, as in the Pepsi commercial featuring
the young boys ogling Cindy Crawford or the jeans ad portraying a very little boy looking up a woman's skirt. It may seem that I am reading too much
into this ad, but imagine if the genders were reversed. We would fear for a
little girl who was unzipping a man's fly in an ad (and we would be shocked,
I would hope). Boys are vulnerable to sexual abuse too, but cultural attitudes make it difficult to take this seriously. As a result, boys are less likely
to report abuse and to get treatment.

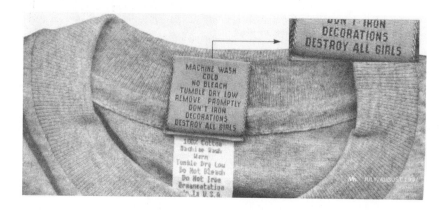

Many boys grow up feeling that they are unmanly if they are not always "ready for action," capable of and interested in sex with any woman who is available. Advertising doesn't cause this attitude, of course, but it contributes to it. A Levi Strauss commercial that ran in Asia features the shock of a schoolboy who discovers that the seductive young woman who has slipped a note into the jeans of an older student is his teacher. And an ad for BIC pens pictures a young boy wearing X-ray glasses while ogling the derriere of an older woman. Again, these ads would be unthinkable if the genders were reversed. It is increasingly difficult in such a toxic environment to see children, boys or girls, as *children.*

In the past few years there has been a proliferation of sexually 40 grotesque toys for boys, such as a Spider Man female action figure whose exaggerated breasts have antennae coming out of them and a female Spawn figure with carved skulls for breasts. Meantime even children have easy access to pornography in video games and on the World Wide Web, which includes explicit photographs of women having intercourse with groups of men, with dogs, donkeys, horses, and snakes; photographs of women being raped and tortured; some of these women made up to look like little girls.

It is hard for girls not to learn self-hatred in an environment in which there is such widespread and open contempt for women and girls. In 1997 a company called Senate distributed clothing with inside labels that included, in addition to the usual cleaning instructions, the line "Destroy all girls." A Senate staffer explained that he thought it was "kind of cool."[23] Given all this, it's not surprising that when boys and girls were asked in a recent study to write an essay on what it would be like to be the other gender, many boys wrote they would rather be dead. Girls had no trouble writing essays about activities, power, freedom, but boys were often stuck, could think of nothing.

---

[23]Wire and *Times* staff reports, 1997, D1.

It is also not surprising that, in such an environment, sexual harassment is considered normal and ordinary. According to an article in the journal *Eating Disorders:*

> In our work with young women, we have heard countless accounts of this contempt being expressed by their male peers: the girls who do not want to walk down a certain hallway in their high school because they are afraid of being publicly rated on a scale of one to ten; the girls who are subjected to barking, grunting and mooing calls and labels of "dogs, cows, or pigs" when they pass by groups of male students; those who are teased about not measuring up to buxom, bikini-clad [models]; and the girls who are grabbed, pinched, groped, and fondled as they try to make their way through the school corridors.
>
> Harassing words do not slide harmlessly away as the taunting sounds dissipate.... They are slowly absorbed into the child's identity and developing sense of self, becoming an essential part of who she sees herself to be. Harassment involves the use of words as weapons to inflict pain and assert power. Harassing words are meant to instill fear, heighten bodily discomfort, and diminish the sense of self.[24]

It is probably difficult for those of us who are older to understand how devastating and cruel and pervasive this harassment is, how different from the "teasing" some of us might remember from our own childhoods (not that that didn't hurt and do damage as well). A 1993 report by the American Association of University Women found that 76 percent of female students in grades eight to eleven and 56 percent of male students said they had been sexually harassed in school.[25] One high-school junior described a year of torment at her vocational school: "The boys call me slut, bitch. They call me a ten-timer, because they say I go with ten guys at the same time. I put up with it because I have no choice. The teachers say it's because the boys think I'm pretty."[26]

High school and junior high school have always been hell for those who were different in any way (gay teens have no doubt suffered the most, although "overweight" girls are a close second), but the harassment is more extreme and more physical these days. Many young men feel they have the right to judge and touch young women and the women often feel they have no choice but to submit. One young woman recalled that "the guys at school routinely swiped their hands across girls' legs to patrol their shaving prowess and then taunt them if they were slacking off. If I were running late, I'd protect myself by faux shaving — just doing the strip between the bottom of my jeans and the top of my cotton socks."[27]

[24]Larkin, Rice, and Russell, 1996, 5–26.
[25]Daley and Vigue, 1999, A12.
[26]Hart, 1998, A12.
[27]Mackler, 1998, 56.

Sexual battery, as well as inappropriate sexual gesturing, touching, and   45
fondling, is increasing not only in high schools but in elementary and
middle schools as well.[28] There are reports of sexual assaults by students on
other students as young as eight. A fifth-grade boy in Georgia repeatedly
touched the breasts and genitals of one of his fellow students while saying,
"I want to get in bed with you" and "I want to feel your boobs." Authorities
did nothing, although the girl complained and her grades fell. When her
parents found a suicide note she had written, they took the board of education to court.[29]

A high-school senior in an affluent suburban school in the Boston area
said she has been dragged by her arms so boys could look up her skirt and
that boys have rested their heads on her chest while making lewd comments. Another student in the same school was pinned down on a lunch
table while a boy simulated sex on top of her. Neither student reported any
of the incidents, for fear of being ostracized by their peers.[30] In another
school in the Boston area, a sixteen-year-old girl, who had been digitally
raped by a classmate, committed suicide.[31]

According to Nan Stein, a researcher at Wellesley College:

> Schools may in fact be training grounds for the insidious cycle of
> domestic violence. . . . The school's hidden curriculum teaches young
> women to suffer abuse privately, that resistance is futile. When they
> witness harassment of others and fail to respond, they absorb a differ-
> ent kind of powerlessness — that they are incapable of standing up to
> injustice or acting in solidarity with their peers. Similarly, in schools
> boys receive permission, even training, to become batterers through
> the practice of sexual harassment.[32]

This pervasive harassment of and contempt for girls and women constitute a kind of abuse. We know that addictions for women are rooted in
trauma, that girls who are sexually abused are far more likely to become
addicted to one substance or another. I contend that all girls growing up in
this culture are sexually abused — abused by the pornographic images of
female sexuality that surround them from birth, abused by all the violence
against women and girls, and abused by the constant harassment and threat
of violence. Abuse is a continuum, of course, and I am by no means implying that cultural abuse is as terrible as literally being raped and assaulted.
However, it hurts, it does damage, and it sets girls up for addictions and
self-destructive behavior. Many girls turn to food, alcohol, cigarettes, and
other drugs in a misguided attempt to cope.

As Marian Sandmaier said in *The Invisible Alcoholics: Women and
Alcohol Abuse in America*, "In a culture that cuts off women from many of

---

[28]Daley and Vigue, 1999, A1, A12.
[29]Shin, 1999, 32.
[30]Daley and Vigue, 1999, A12.
[31]Daley and Abraham, 1999, B6.
[32]Stein, 1993, 316–17.

their own possibilities before they barely have had a chance to sense them, that pain belongs to all women. Outlets for coping may vary widely, and may be more or less addictive, more or less self-destructive. But at some level, all women know what it is to lack access to their own power, to live with a piece of themselves unclaimed."[33]

Today, every girl is endangered, not just those who have been physically and sexually abused. If girls from supportive homes with positive role models are at risk, imagine then how vulnerable are the girls who have been violated. No wonder they so often go under for good — ending up in abusive marriages, in prison, on the streets. And those who do are almost always in the grip of one addiction or another. More than half of women in prison are addicts and most are there for crimes directly related to their addiction. Many who are there for murder killed men who had been battering them for years. Almost all of the women who are homeless or in prisons and mental institutions are the victims of male violence.[34]

Male violence exists within the same cultural and sociopolitical context that contributes to addiction. Both can be fully understood only within this context, way beyond individual psychology and family dynamics. It is a context of systemic violence and oppression, including racism, classism, heterosexism, weightism, and ageism, as well as sexism, all of which are traumatizing in and of themselves. Advertising is only one part of this cultural context, but it is an important part and thus is a part of what traumatizes.

Sources

Abbey, A., Ross, L., and McDuffie, D. (1991). Alcohol's role in sexual assault. In Watson, R., ed. *Addictive behaviors in women.* Totowa, NJ: Humana Press.

Associated Press (1999, February 18). Calvin Klein retreats on ad. *Boston Globe,* A7.

Blumenthal, S. J. (1995, July). *Violence against women.* Washington, DC: Department of Health and Human Services.

Brewers can help fight sexism (1991, October 28). *Advertising Age,* 28.

Daley, B., and Vigue, D. I. (1999, February 4). Sex harassment increasing amid students, officials say. *Boston Globe,* A1, A12.

Hart, J. (1998, June 8). Northampton confronts a crime, cruelty. *Boston Globe,* A1, A12.

Herbert, B. (1999, May 2). America's littlest shooters. *New York Times,* WK 17.

Johnson, J. A. (1997, November 10). JonBenet keeps hold on magazines. *Advertising Age,* 42.

Kilbourne, J. (1994, May 15). 'Gender bender' ads: Same old sexism. *New York Times,* F13.

Larkin, J., Rice, C., and Russell, V. (1996, Spring). Slipping through the cracks: Sexual harassment. *Eating Disorders: The Journal of Treatment and Prevention,* vol. 4, no. 1, 5–26.

Leo, J. (1994, June 13). Selling the woman-child. *U. S. News and World Report,* 27.

---

[33]Sandmaier, 1980, xviii.
[34]Snell, 1991.

Mackler, C. (1998). Memoirs of a (sorta) ex-shaver. In Edut, O., ed. (1998). *Adios, Barbie*. Seattle, WA: Seal Press, 55–61.

Novello, A. (1991, October 18). Quoted by Associated Press, AMA to fight wife-beating. *St. Louis Post Dispatch*, 1, 15.

Quindlen, A. (1992, June 28). All of these you are. *New York Times*, E17.

Sandmaier, M. (1980). *The invisible alcoholics: Women and alcohol abuse in America*. New York: McGraw-Hill.

Schoolgirls as sex toys. *New York Times* (1997, April 16), 2E.

Shin, A. (1999, April/May). Testing Title IX. *Ms.*, 32.

Sloan, P. (1996, July 8). Underwear ads caught in bind over sex appeal. *Advertising Age*, 27.

Snell, T. L. (1991). *Women in prison*. Washington, DC: U.S. Department of Justice.

Stein, N. (1993). No laughing matter: Sexual harassment in K-12 schools. In Buchwald, E., Fletcher, P. R., and Roth, M. (1993). *Transforming a rape culture*. Minneapolis, MN: Milkweed Editions, 311–31.

Tjaden, R., and Thoennes, N. (1998, November). *Prevalence, incidence, and consequences of violence against women: Findings from the National Violence Against Women Survey*. Washington, DC: U.S. Department of Justice.

Two men and a baby (1990, July/August). *Ms.*, 10.

Vigue, D. J., and Abraham, Y. (1999, February 7). Harassment a daily course for students. *Boston Globe*, B1, B6.

Weil, L. (1999, March). Leaps of faith. *Women's Review of Books*, 21.

Wilsnack, S. C., Plaud, J. J., Wilsnack, R. W., and Klassen, A. D. (1997). Sexuality, gender, and alcohol use. In Wilsnack, R. W., and Wilsnack, S. C., eds. *Gender and alcohol: Individual and social perspectives*. New Brunswick, N.J.: Rutgers Center of Alcohol Studies, 262.

Wire and Times Staff Reports (1997, May 20). Orange County skate firm's 'destroy all girls' tags won't wash. *Los Angeles Times*, D1.

Wright, R. (1995, September 10). Brutality defines the lives of women around the world. *Boston Globe*, A2.

ENGAGING THE TEXT

1. What parallels does Kilbourne see between advertising and pornography? How persuasive do you find the evidence she offers? Do the photos of the ads she describes strengthen her argument? Why or why not?

2. Why is it dangerous to depict women and men as sex objects, according to Kilbourne? Why is the objectification of women *more* troubling, in her view? Do you agree?

3. How does Kilbourne explain the appeal of ads that allude to bondage, sexual aggression, and rape — particularly for female consumers? How do you respond to the ads reproduced in her essay?

4. What does Kilbourne mean when she claims that the depiction of women in advertising constitutes "cultural abuse"? How does she go about drawing connections between advertising images and social problems like sexual violence, harassment, and addiction? Which portions of her analysis do you find most and least persuasive, and why?

EXPLORING CONNECTIONS

5. Media images constitute part of the "generalized other" — the internalized
   sense of what is socially acceptable and unacceptable — described by
   Aaron H. Devor (p. 383). In addition to the violent and sexualized images
   Kilbourne examines, what other images or messages about gender do you
   encounter regularly in the media? Which ones have been most influential
   in the development of your "generalized other"?

6. Drawing on the essays by Kilbourne, Joan Morgan (below), and Carmen
   Vázquez (p. 472), write an essay exploring the power of media to promote
   or curb violence.

EXTENDING THE CRITICAL CONTEXT

7. Kilbourne claims that popular culture idealizes dangerous, exploitative, or
   dysfunctional relationships between women and men. Working in small
   groups, discuss the romantic relationships depicted in movies you've seen
   recently. Does her critique seem applicable to those films? List the evidence you find for and against her argument and compare your results with
   those of other groups.

8. In her analysis of two ads (the Diet Pepsi commercial featuring Cindy
   Crawford and the Diet Coke ad with the shirtless construction worker),
   Kilbourne applies a gender reversal test in order to demonstrate the existence of a double standard. Try this test yourself on a commercial or ad that
   relies on sexual innuendo. Write a journal entry describing the ad and
   explaining the results of your test.

9. Working in pairs or small groups, survey the ads in two magazines — one
   designed to appeal to a predominantly female audience and one aimed at a
   largely male audience. What differences, if any, do you see in the kinds of
   images and appeals advertisers use in the two magazines? How often do
   you see the kinds of "pornographic" ads Kilbourne discusses? Do you find
   any ads depicting the "relational skills" that she suggests are rarely emphasized in popular culture?

From Fly-Girls to Bitches and Hos

JOAN MORGAN

*As a music writer and fan of hip-hop, Joan Morgan loves the power of
rap. As a feminist, she is troubled by the pervasive sexism of its lyrics. The
misogyny of rap, she argues, is a symptom of crisis in the black community;
it must be confronted and understood, not simply condemned, as a step*

toward healing the pain that it both expresses and inflicts. This passage comes from her collection of essays, When Chickenheads Come Home to Roost... My Life as a Hip-Hop Feminist *(1999). Formerly the executive editor of* Essence, *she has also written for* The Village Voice, Vibe, Ms., *and* Spin.

> Feminist criticism, like many other forms of social analysis, is widely considered part of a hostile white culture. For a black feminist to chastise misogyny in rap publicly would be viewed as divisive and counterproductive. There is a widespread perception in the black community that public criticism of black men constitutes collaborating with a racist society....
>
> — MICHELE WALLACE, "When Black Feminism
> Faces the Music, and the Music Is Rap,"
> *The New York Times*[1]

Lord knows our love jones for hip-hop is understandable. Props given to rap music's artistic merits, its irrefutable impact on pop culture, its ability to be alternately beautiful, poignant, powerful, strong, irreverent, visceral, and mesmerizing — homeboy's clearly got it like that. But in between the beats, booty shaking, and hedonistic abandon, I have to wonder if there isn't something inherently unfeminist in supporting a music that repeatedly reduces me to tits and ass and encourages pimping on the regular. While it's human to occasionally fall deep into the love thang with people or situations that simply aren't good for you, feminism alerted me long ago to the dangers of romancing a misogynist (and ridiculously fine, brilliant ones with gangsta leans are no exception). Perhaps the nonbelievers were right, maybe what I'd been mistaking for love and commitment for the last twenty years was really nothing but a self-destructive obsession that made a mockery of my feminism....

I guess it all depends on how you define the f-word. My feminism places the welfare of black women and the black community on its list of priorities. It also maintains that black-on-black love is essential to the survival of both.

We have come to a point in our history, however, when black-on-black love — a love that's survived slavery, lynching, segregation, poverty, and racism — is in serious danger. The stats usher in this reality like taps before the death march: According to the U.S. Census Bureau, the number of black two-parent households has decreased from 74 percent to 48 percent since 1960. The leading cause of death among black men ages fifteen to

---

[1]Michele Wallace, "When Black Feminism Faces the Music, and the Music Is Rap," *The New York Times*, July 29, 1990. [All notes are Morgan's.]

twenty-four is homicide. The majority of them will die at the hands of other black men.[2]

Women are the unsung victims of black-on-black crime. A while back, a friend of mine, a single mother of a newborn (her "babyfather" — a brother — abdicated responsibility before their child was born) was attacked by a pit bull while walking her dog in the park. The owner (a brother) trained the animal to prey on other dogs and the flesh of his fellow community members.

A few weeks later my mom called, upset, to tell me about the murder of   5
a family friend. She was a troubled young woman with a history of substance abuse, aggravated by her son's murder two years ago. She was found beaten and burned beyond recognition. Her murderers were not "skinheads," "The Man," or "the racist white power structure." More likely than not, they were brown men whose faces resembled her own.

Clearly, we are having a very difficult time loving one another.

Any feminism that fails to acknowledge that black folks in nineties America are living and trying to love in a war zone is useless to our struggle against sexism. Though it's often portrayed as part of the problem, rap music is essential to that struggle because it takes us straight to the battlefield.

My decision to expose myself to the sexism of Dr. Dre, Ice Cube, Snoop Dogg, or the Notorious B.I.G. is really my plea to my brothers to tell me who they are. I need to know why they are so angry at me. Why is disrespecting me one of the few things that make them feel like men? What's the haps, what are you going through on the daily that's got you acting so foul?

As a black woman and a feminist I listen to the music with a willingness to see past the machismo in order to be clear about what I'm *really* dealing with. What I hear frightens me. On booming track after booming track, I hear brothers talking about spending each day high as hell on malt liquor and Chronic. Don't sleep. What passes for "40 and a blunt" good times in most of hip-hop is really alcoholism, substance abuse, and chemical dependency. When brothers can talk so cavalierly about killing each other and then reveal that they have no expectation to see their twenty-first birthday, that is straight-up depression *masquerading* as machismo.

Anyone curious about the processes and pathologies that form the psy-   10
che of the young, black, and criminal-minded needs to revisit our dearly departed Notorious B.I.G.'s first album, *Ready to Die*. Chronicling the life and times of the urban "soldier," the album is a blues-laden soul train that took us on a hustler's life journey. We boarded with the story of his birth, strategically stopped to view his dysfunctional, warring family, his first robbery, his first stint in jail, murder, drug-dealing, getting paid, partying, sexin', rap-pin', mayhem, and death. Biggie's player persona might have

---

[2]Joan Morgan, "Real Love," *Vibe*, April 1996, p. 38.

momentarily convinced the listener that he was livin' phat without a care in the world but other moments divulged his inner hell. The chorus of "Everyday Struggle": *I don't wanna live no more / Sometimes I see death knockin' at my front door* revealed that "Big Poppa" was also plagued with guilt, regret, and depression. The album ultimately ended with his suicide.

The seemingly impenetrable wall of sexism in rap music is really the complex mask African-Americans often wear both to hide and express the pain. At the close of this millennium, hip-hop is still one of the few forums in which young black men, even surreptitiously, are allowed to express their pain.

When it comes to the struggle against sexism and our intimate relationships with black men, some of the most on-point feminist advice I've received comes from sistas like my mother, who wouldn't dream of using the term. During our battle to resolve our complicated relationships with my equally wonderful and errant father, my mother presented me with the following gem of wisdom, "One of the most important lessons you will ever learn in life and love, is that you've got to love people for what they are — not for who you would like them to be."

This is crystal clear to me when I'm listening to hip-hop. Yeah, sistas are hurt when we hear brothers calling us bitches and hos. But the real crime isn't the name-calling, it's their failure to love us — to be our brothers in the way that we commit ourselves to being their sistas. But recognize: Any man who doesn't truly love himself is incapable of loving us in the healthy way we need to be loved. It's extremely telling that men who can only see us as "bitches" and "hos" refer to themselves only as "niggas."

In the interest of our emotional health and overall sanity, black women have got to learn to love brothers realistically, and that means differentiating between who they are and who we'd like them to be. Black men are engaged in a war where the real enemies — racism and the white power structure — are masters of camouflage. They've conditioned our men to believe the enemy is brown. The effects of this have been as wicked as they've been debilitating. Being in battle with an enemy that looks just like you makes it hard to believe in the basics every human being needs. For too many black men there is no trust, no community, no family. Just self.

Since hip-hop is the mirror in which so many brothers see themselves, it's significant that one of the music's most prevalent mythologies is that black boys rarely grow into men. Instead, they remain perpetually postadolescent or die. For all the machismo and testosterone in the music, it's frighteningly clear that many brothers see themselves as powerless when it comes to facing the evils of the larger society, accepting responsibility for their lives, or the lives of their children.   15

So, sista friends, we gotta do what any rational, survivalist-minded person would do after finding herself in a relationship with someone whose pain makes him abusive. We've gotta continue to give up the love but *from a distance that's safe.* Emotional distance is a great enabler of unconditional love and support because it allows us to recognize that the attack, the "bitch, ho" bullshit — isn't personal but part of the illness.

And the focus of black feminists has got to change. We can't afford to keep expending energy on banal discussions of sexism in rap when sexism is only part of a huge set of problems. Continuing on our previous path is akin to demanding that a fiending, broke crackhead not rob you blind because it's *wrong* to do so.

If feminism intends to have any relevance in the lives of the majority of black women, if it intends to move past theory and become functional it has to rescue itself from the ivory towers of academia. Like it or not, hip-hop is not only the dominion of the young, black, and male, it is also the world in which young black women live and survive. A functional game plan for us, one that is going to be as helpful to Shequanna on 142nd as it is to Samantha at Sarah Lawrence, has to recognize hip-hop's ability to articulate the pain our *community* is in and use that knowledge to create a redemptive, healing space.

Notice the emphasis on "community." Hip-hop isn't only instrumental in exposing black men's pain, it brings the healing sistas need right to the surface. Sad as it may be, it's time to stop ignoring the fact that rappers meet "bitches" and "hos" daily — women who reaffirm their depiction of us on vinyl. Backstage, the road, and the 'hood are populated with women who would do anything to be with a rapper sexually for an hour if not a night. It's time to stop fronting like we don't know who rapper Jeru the Damaja was talking about when he said:

> Now a queen's a queen but a stunt's a stunt
> You can tell who's who by the things they want

Sex has long been the bartering chip that women use to gain protection, material wealth, and the vicarious benefits of power. In the black community, where women are given less access to all of the above, "trickin'" becomes a means of leveling the playing field. Denying the justifiable anger of rappers — men who couldn't get the time of day from these women before a few dollars and a record deal — isn't empowering and strategic. Turning a blind eye and scampering for moral high ground diverts our attention away from the young women who are being denied access to power and are suffering for it.

It might've been more convenient to direct our sistafied rage attention to "the sexist representation of women" in those now infamous Sir Mix-A-Lot videos, to fuss over *one* sexist rapper, but wouldn't it have been more productive to address the failing self-esteem of the 150 or so half-naked young women who were willing, unpaid participants? And what about how flip we are when it comes to using the b-word to describe each other? At some point we've all been the recipients of competitive, unsisterly, "bitchiness," particularly when vying for male attention.

Since being black and a woman makes me fluent in both isms, I sometimes use racism as an illuminating analogy. Black folks have finally gotten to the point where we recognize that we sometimes engage in oppressive behaviors that white folks have little to do with. Complexion prejudices and classism are illnesses which have their *roots* in white racism but the perpetrators are certainly black.

Similarly, sistas have to confront the ways we're complicit in our own oppression. Sad to say it, but many of the ways in which men exploit our images and sexuality in hip-hop is done with our permission and cooperation. We need to be as accountable to each other as we believe "race traitors" (i.e., one hundred or so brothers in blackface cooning in a skinhead's music video) should be to our community. To acknowledge this doesn't deny our victimization but it does raise the critical issue of whose responsibility it is to end our oppression. As a feminist, I believe it is too great a responsibility to leave to men.

A few years ago, on an airplane making its way to Montego Bay, I received another gem of girlfriend wisdom from a sixty-year-old self-declared nonfeminist. She was meeting her husband to celebrate her thirty-fifth wedding anniversary. After telling her I was twenty-seven and very much single, she looked at me and shook her head sadly. "I feel sorry for your generation. You don't know how to have relationships, especially the women." Curious, I asked her why she thought this was. "The women of your generation, you want to be right. The women of my generation, we didn't care about being right. We just wanted to win."

Too much of the discussion regarding sexism and the music focuses on being right. We feel we're *right* and the rappers are wrong. The rappers feel it's their *right* to describe their "reality" in any way they see fit. The store owners feel it's their *right* to sell whatever the consumer wants to buy. The consumer feels it's his *right* to be able to decide what he wants to listen to. We may be the "rightest" of the bunch but we sure as hell ain't doing the winning.

I believe hip-hop can help us win. Let's start by recognizing that its illuminating, informative narration and its incredible ability to articulate our collective pain is an invaluable tool when examining gender relations. The information we amass can help create a redemptive, healing space for brothers and sistas.

We're all winners when a space exists for brothers to honestly state and explore the roots of their pain and subsequently their misogyny, sans judgment. It is criminal that the only space our society provided for the late Tupac Shakur to examine the pain, confusion, drug addiction, and fear that led to his arrest and his eventual assassination was in a prison cell. How can we win if a prison cell is the only space an immensely talented but troubled young black man could dare utter these words: "Even though I'm not guilty of the charges they gave me, I'm not innocent in terms of the way I was acting. I'm just as guilty for not doing things. Not with this case but with my

life. I had a job to do and I never showed up. I was so scared of this responsibility that I was running away from it."[3] We have to do better than this for
our men.

And we have to do better for ourselves. We desperately need a space to
lovingly address the uncomfortable issues of our failing self-esteem, the
ways we sexualize and objectify ourselves, our confusion about sex and love
and the unhealthy, unloving, unsisterly ways we treat each other. Commitment to developing these spaces gives our community the potential for
remedies based on honest, clear diagnoses.

As I'm a black woman, I am aware that this doubles my workload —
that I am definitely going to have to listen to a lot of shit I won't like — but
without these candid discussions, there is little to no hope of exorcising the
illness that hurts and sometimes kills us.

ENGAGING THE TEXT

1. What qualities of rap music and rap artists does Morgan admire or appreciate? What fears does she have for rap's female fans and for the artists
   themselves? To what extent do you agree with Morgan's assessment of the
   misogyny, anger, and despair expressed by rap?

2. What evidence does Morgan offer that "black folks in nineties America
   are living and trying to love in a war zone"? How does she explain the causes
   of the violence she describes? How persuasive do you find her analysis,
   and why?

3. How do you interpret Morgan's call for establishing "a redemptive, healing
   space" for confronting the pain expressed by rap? What kind of "space" is
   she talking about, and how would you go about establishing it?

4. What audience is Morgan addressing and what persuasive strategies — of
   both argument and style — does she use to appeal to that audience? What
   do you find effective or ineffective about her approach?

5. While Morgan asserts that we need to examine the lives of rappers like
   Notorious B.I.G. to understand the roots of their misogyny, critics might
   counter that she is simply making excuses for intolerable attitudes. Write
   an essay explaining why you agree or disagree with Morgan's argument.

EXPLORING CONNECTIONS

6. Compare Jean Kilbourne's analysis of sexism and violence in advertising
   (p. 417) to Morgan's discussion of the same themes in rap. What are the
   causes and consequences of "pornographic" depictions of women in
   popular culture according to each writer? Do you think Kilbourne would
   concur with Morgan about how we should respond to these images? Why
   or why not?

---

[3]Kevin Powell, "The Vibe Q: Tupac Shakur, Ready to Live," *Vibe*, April 11, 1995, p. 52.

7. Look ahead to "The Manliness of Men" (below) and compare Harvey Mansfield's depiction of manliness to the images of masculinity portrayed by rap artists.

EXTENDING THE CRITICAL CONTEXT

8. Survey the current issues of several magazines aimed at fans of rap music. What images do they present of women, men, and human relationships? How often do they reflect the themes that Morgan discusses? What other themes and patterns do you find, if any, and how do you explain their significance?

9. Examine the lyrics of several female rappers and compare them to those of the male rappers Morgan mentions. What similarities and differences do you find in the subjects they address and the feelings they express? If you're not a fan of rap, you may want to consult an online hip-hop dictionary for help in decoding some of the language (www.rapdict.org).

The Manliness of Men
HARVEY MANSFIELD

Harvey Mansfield is William R. Kenan, Jr., Professor of Government at Harvard University, where he chaired the Department of Government from 1973 to 1977. In fact, his Web page notes that he "has hardly left Harvard since his first arrival in 1949" as an undergraduate. Mansfield has also served as president of the New England Political Science Association and won a National Humanities Medal in 2004. He has published extensively on Machiavelli and Burke, and collaborated on a new translation of Alexis de Tocqueville's Democracy in America. *"The Manliness of Men" appeared in 2003 in* The American Enterprise. *Mansfield's ideas are worked out more comprehensively in his latest book,* Manliness *(2006).*

Today the very word "manliness" seems obsolete.

There are other words, such as "courage," "frankness," or "confidence," that convey the good side of manliness without naming a sex. But to use them in place of "manliness" begs the question of whether moral or psychological qualities specific to each sex exist. Our society today denies that such differences are real, and seeks to abolish all signs of such qualities in our language. To the extent that feminism recognizes gender differences at all, it presents them as bad, and as the fault of men.

The women's revolution has succeeded to an amazing degree. Our society has adopted, quite without realizing the magnitude of the change, a practice of equality between the sexes never before known in human history. My intent is not to stand in the way of this change. Women are not going to be herded back into the kitchen by men. But we need to recognize that there have been both gains and losses in this revolution.

Manliness can be heroic. But it can also be vainly boastful, prone to meaningless scuffling, and unfriendly. It jeers at those who do not seem to measure up, and asks men to continually prove themselves. It defines turf and fights for it — sometimes to defend precious rights, sometimes for no good reason. Manliness has always been under a cloud of doubt — raised by men who may not have the time or taste for it.

But such doubts about manliness can hardly be found in today's femi-   5
nism. Contemporary feminists, and the women they influence, have essentially a single problem with manliness: that it excludes women. Betty Friedan's feminist classic *The Feminine Mystique* is not an attack on manliness, but on femininity. It insists women should be strong and aggressive — like men.

Though the word is scarce in use, there is an abundance of manliness in action in America today. Young males still pick fights, often with deadly weapons. What we suffer from today, is a lack of intelligent criticism of manliness. Feminism has undermined, if not destroyed, the counterpart to manliness — femininity — and with it the basis on which half the population could be skeptical of the excesses of manliness.

Of course, women are still women. While they want men to be sensitive to women, they don't necessarily want them to be sensitive in general. That's why the traditional manly male — who is protective of women, but a sorry flop when it comes to sensitivity — is far from a disappearing species.

Manliness offers gallantry to women. But is gallantry fundamentally insincere because it always contains an element of disdain? The man who opens a door for a woman makes a show of being stronger than she, one could say. At the same time, the woman does go first. Manly men are romantic about women; unmanly men are sympathetic. Which is better for women?

The "sensitive male" who mimics many female emotions and interests, while discarding the small favors men have traditionally done for women, is mostly just a creation of contemporary feminists who are irritated with the ways of men, no longer tolerant of their foibles, and demanding new behavior that would pave the way for ambitious women. Feminists insist that men must work harder to appreciate women. Yet they never ask women to be more understanding of men.

Manliness is a quality that causes individuals to stand up for something.   10
It is a quality that calls private persons into public life. In the past such people have been predominantly male, and it is no accident that those who possess this quality have often ended up as political rulers and leaders.

Manly men defend their turf, just as other male mammals do. The analogy to animals obviously suggests something animalistic about manliness. But manliness is specifically human as well.

Manly men defend not just their turf but their country. Manliness is best shown in war, the defense of one's country at its most difficult and dangerous. In Greek, the word for manliness, *andreia,* is also the word for courage.

For good and for ill, males impelled by their manliness have dominated all politics of which we know. Is there something inevitable about this domination or are we free to depart from it? With more and more countries moving toward democracy and peace, perhaps manliness will become less necessary.

Yet there might also be a democratic manliness. In democracies, Tocqueville said, a manly frankness prevails — an open and fearless stance of "man to man" in which all are equal. Does democracy, then, tend to produce, and require, manliness?

Feminists find all sexual roles objectionable. They are insulted by the idea that nature has determined different social parts and purposes for the sexes. They have largely forced the abandonment of any idea of sexual nature in favor of the feminist notion of "choice." A woman today has the choice of every occupation that used to be reserved for men, plus traditional women's roles. Inevitably, "choice" for women opens up choices for men too. What happens when men are no longer pressed to face the duties that used to go with being a man? Traditionally, the performance of a man's duties has required him to protect and support his family. To be a man means to support dependents, not merely yourself.

But the modern woman above all does not want to be a dependent. She may not have thought about what her independence does to the manliness of men (it might make men more selfish). And she may not have considered carefully whether the protection she does without will be replaced by sensitivity, or by neglect. The statistics on male abandonment of their children in our day are not heartwarming.

According to feminists, any traditional notion that the different sexes complement each other serves merely to justify the inferiority of women. On its face, complementarity suggests real equality — each sex is superior in its place. But if you are sure that the best positions have been the men's, and that women have been the "second sex," then in order to achieve equality you must go for full interchangeability of the sexes. You must deny any natural preponderance of one quality or another in men and women.

Do men and women have different natures that justify different social roles? Or are these natures just "socially constructed"? If women can conclude that their roles have been designed artificially by society, then they are free to remake themselves without constraint. But the latest science suggests that being a man or a woman is much more than having certain bodily equipment. . . . Perhaps men and women are characterized more by how they think than by their sexual organs.

While maleness is partly just a fact of biology, in humans it is linked to thinking and reason in ways that make manliness something much more than mere aggression. In humans, masculinity is more than just defense of one's own; it has been extended to require noble sacrifice for a cause beyond oneself.

Certainly, women reason and sacrifice too, and they are not devoid   20 of aggressiveness. But their participation in these things is not "equal." As Aristotle said, men find it easier to be courageous — and women find it easier to be moderate. Of course, you cannot avoid Aristotle's qualifier, "for the most part."

For the most part, men will always have more manliness than women have, and it is up to both sexes to fashion this fact into something good.

ENGAGING THE TEXT

1. What "gains and losses" (para. 3) does Mansfield attribute to the growing equality of women?

2. Mansfield contrasts the "manly" man to the "sensitive" man; do you agree with his assumption that manliness and sensitivity are incompatible? Why or why not?

3. According to Mansfield, why have political leaders been overwhelmingly male until recently? Working with classmates, brainstorm and evaluate other possible explanations. Compare your conclusions with those of other groups.

4. Mansfield asks, "Is gallantry fundamentally insincere because it always contains an element of disdain?" (para. 8). How would you answer his question?

5. Write a journal entry responding to one of the following claims by Mansfield:

> "Feminism has undermined, if not destroyed . . . femininity" (para. 6)
> "A woman today has the choice of every occupation that used to be
>   reserved for men, plus traditional women's roles" (para. 15)
> Women's independence "might make men more selfish" (para. 26)
> "Men find it easier to be courageous — and women find it easier to be
>   moderate" (para. 20)

What evidence do you see that supports or challenges his assertions? Compare your response to those of your classmates: how much or how little consensus do you find about either the claims themselves or the evidence you've cited?

EXPLORING CONNECTIONS

6. How do Mansfield's views of men's and women's roles compare to those of Tocqueville (p. 376) and Devor (p. 383)?

7. Examine the images in the Visual Portfolio (p. 409); to what extent does each photo reflect or contest Mansfield's ideas about men, women, and contemporary relationships between them?

8. Write or role-play an imaginary conversation among Mansfield, Jean Kilbourne (p. 417) and Joan Morgan (p. 443) in which they discuss his contention that "Feminists insist that men must work harder to appreciate women. Yet they never ask women to be more understanding of men" (para. 9).

EXTENDING THE CRITICAL CONTEXT

9. As a class, construct a collage of images that illustrate Mansfield's description of "manly men"; then create individual collages that reflect your personal views of male identity. Write a journal entry reflecting on the similarities and differences you see between the Mansfield collage and your own.

10. Working with the individual collages the class created (see above), divide them into two groups: those constructed by women and by men. Do you detect any gender differences in the ways that men and women depict masculine identity? If so, how do you explain those differences?

11. Drawing on current media images as well as your own observations, write an essay discussing Mansfield's assertion that women are attracted to "the traditional manly male — who is protective of women, but a sorry flop when it comes to sensitivity" (para. 7).

The Hands of God

DEBORAH RUDACILLE

Deborah Rudacille (b. 1958) began to research transgender issues when she learned that a close friend planned to make the transition from female to male: "I was concerned and confused and I soon learned that I was not alone. Nearly everyone I spoke with about the subject was as confused as I was, and in some cases far more judgmental." A few months later, the murder of a male-to-female transsexual in her own neighborhood gave even more urgency to Rudacille's inquiry. In The Riddle of Gender: Science, Activism, and Transgender Rights *(2005), from which this selection is taken, she investigates the history, science, politics, and lived experience of transgender identity; her hope, she writes in the introduction, is to "promote greater understanding and acceptance of a group (or groups) of people who typically want nothing more than to live their lives in peace and be able to enjoy the same civil status and protections granted to others." A science writer at Johns Hopkins University, Rudacille is also the author of* The Scalpel and the Butterfly: The Conflict Between Animal Research and Animal Protection *(2001).*

I certify that Chevalier d'Éon lived with me for approximately three years, that I always considered him to be a woman; however, after his death and upon observation of the corpse discovered that he was a man. My wife certifies the same.

— WILLIAM BOUNING, London, 1810[1]

I began the research for this book in the way that I approach every scientific subject that interests me, by searching the literature. I soon discovered that far from being a product of the modern world, gender variance has been documented across cultures and in every epoch of history.[2] Male-bodied persons dressing and living as women and female-bodied persons dressing and living as men were known in ancient Greece and Rome, among Native American tribes prior to the arrival of Europeans, on the Indian subcontinent, in Africa, in Siberia, in eastern Europe, and in nearly every other indigenous society studied by anthropologists. According to historian Vern Bullough, "gender crossing is so ubiquitous, that genitalia by itself has never been a universal nor essential insignia of a lifelong gender."[3] In some of these cultures, cross-gendered persons were considered shamans gifted with extraordinary psychic powers, and they assumed special ceremonial roles. In many religions, the gods themselves can transform their sex at will, cross-dress, or are androgynous. Our Judeo-Christian heritage, founded on a belief in an exclusively male deity, has frowned on such gender fluidity; nonetheless, throughout the Middle Ages and even into the modern era, cross-dressing has been permitted and indeed celebrated at festivals, in clubs, and on the stage.

Moreover, the deathbed discovery of a gender reversal is a far more common occurrence in Western history than one might suspect. Many (though not all) of the persons whose names and stories are known to us today were born female and lived some or all of their lives as men. A few of the better-known individuals in this category include James Barry, British army physician and Inspector-General, died 1865; Charles Durkee Pankhurst, California stage-coach driver, died 1879; Murray Hall, Tammany Hall politician, died 1901; Jack Bee Garland, soldier in the Spanish-American War, died 1936; and Billy Tipton, jazz trumpeter, died 1989. Some of these people were married to women, who publicly expressed shock and amazement when their partners

---

[1]Quoted in Magnus Hirschfeld, *Transvestites: The Erotic Urge to Cross Dress*, trans. by Michael A. Lombardi-Nash (Buffalo, N.Y.: Prometheus Books, 1991), 341–42.

[2]See, for example, *Third Sex, Third Gender: Beyond Sexual Dimorphism in Culture*, Gilbert Herdt, ed. (New York: Zone Books, 1994); "Mythological, Historical, and Cross-Cultural Aspects of Transsexualism," in *Transsexualism and Sex Reassignment*, ed. Richard Green, M.D., and John Money, Ph.D. (Baltimore: Johns Hopkins University Press, 1969), chap. 1; Part I, "Cultural and Historical Background" in Vern L. Bullough and Bonnie Bullough, *Cross Dressing, Sex, and Gender* (Philadelphia: University of Pennsylvania Press, 1993); and Leslie Feinberg, *Transgender Warriors* (Boston: Beacon Press, 1996).

[3]Bullough and Bullough, *Cross Dressing, Sex, and Gender*, 5.

died and were found to be other than what friends and neighbors assumed them to be. It is impossible to know if this shock was real or was feigned for the benefit of a public that was not prepared to accept the alternative explanation — that the widow had lived happily with a female-bodied person who saw himself and was accepted by others (including his wife) as a man. The case of the Chevalier d'Éon, an eighteenth-century aristocrat whose gender was a source of considerable controversy during his lifetime, is a bit more complex, and because it became a public scandal, I will recount it more fully here.

Born in France in 1728, Charles-Geneviève Louis-Auguste-André-Timothée d'Éon de Beaumont lived forty-nine years as a man and thirty-four as a woman. Aristocrat, diplomat, soldier, and spy, d'Éon worked for the French government in both male and female roles, exhibiting such a chameleon-like ability to change from man to woman and back again that contemporary historians remain just as baffled as d'Éon's peers by the chevalier's metamorphoses. Traditional accounts suggest that d'Éon was dispatched on his first diplomatic mission to Russia in female garb to infiltrate the social circle of the Empress Elizabeth. After successfully carrying out this mission, d'Éon returned to France and assumed an unambiguously male role, becoming a captain of dragoons and fighting valiantly in the Seven Years' War. Wounded in battle, d'Éon was named a Knight of St. Louis, and in 1762 was offered a diplomatic assignment at the British royal court. In a letter, the French king Louis XV congratulated the chevalier on his new post and wrote, "You have served me just as well in women's clothing as you have in the clothes you are now wearing."[4]

While d'Éon was serving as minister plenipotentiary in London, his slight build and pretty features led many to believe that he was in fact a cross-dressed woman. People in England and France began placing wagers on his sex. The London Stock Exchange took bets on his gender,[5] and the amount of money wagered on the chevalier purportedly rose to nearly two hundred thousand pounds in England alone. The fear of kidnapping began to haunt the chevalier, who suspected that those who had wagered large sums of money on the shape of his genitalia might seek to resolve the question by kidnapping and forced exposure. To avert a diplomatic crisis, King Louis XV of France sent a letter to George III of England, stating that d'Éon was a woman. Rather than calming public doubts, this letter created an even greater frenzy. Lawsuits were filed by losing bettors, doctors were called in to testify, and d'Éon was officially declared a woman by an English court. The chevalier responded to this public humiliation with dignity and defiance, writing to a friend, "I am what the hands of God have made me."[6]

---

[4]Letter quoted in ibid., 337.

[5]Marjorie Garber, *Vested Interests: Cross-Dressing and Cultural Anxiety* (New York: Routledge, 1992), 260.

[6]Letter to the Count de Broglio, February 10, 1775, quoted in Garber, *Vested Interests*, 264.

In exchange for d'Éon's agreement to live quietly as a woman, the   5
French government granted the chevalier a generous pension. Although
agreeing to abandon military dress, d'Éon requested permission to continue
wearing the Cross of St. Louis, which as he wrote in a letter to the king "has
always been a reward for bravery on the battlefield. Many officers have
become priests or politicians and have worn this distinction over their new
apparel. Therefore, I do not believe that a brave woman, who was raised in
men's clothing by her family, can be denied this right after she has carried
out the dangerous duties in a praiseworthy fashion."[7] This request was
granted and Mademoiselle d'Éon spent much of the remainder of her life
residing in London with a female companion. When d'Éon died in 1810,
five men who had known d'Éon were asked to examine the body and record
their observations in order to settle definitively the question of d'Éon's sex.
All five witnesses testified that the body was anatomically male. The
deceased's female companion of many years professed herself shocked to
discover that Mademoiselle d'Éon was not the woman she had always
assumed her to be.

A generation after the Chevalier d'Éon's death, a group of French doctors examined another puzzling corpse — that of a thirty-year-old railroad
employee who had committed suicide in a squalid attic room in Paris. Abel
Barbin, known for twenty-four years as Adelaide Herculine Barbin (and
called Alexina), had been born with a body that appeared female. She was
raised in a convent and became a teacher at an all-girl boarding school.
Severe pain in her lower abdomen caused Alexina to seek medical assistance while employed at the school. The results of the doctor's examination
changed her life forever. "His hand was already slipping under my sheet
and coming to a stop at the sensitive place. It pressed upon it several times,
as if to find there the solution to a difficult problem. It did not leave off at
that point!!! He had found the explanation that he was looking for! But it
was easy to see that it exceeded all his expectations!"[8]

The doctor had discovered Alexina's undescended testicles and small
penis, though he did not reveal this information to either Alexina or her
employer, and instead advised the headmistress of the school to terminate
the young schoolmistress. Alexina sought the advice of her bishop, who sent
her to a second physician, a researcher, who prepared "a voluminous report,
a masterpiece in the medical style, intended to ensure before the courts a
petition for rectification." In June 1860, the birth register in Barbin's home
district was amended, and the female Alexina became the male Abel —
by an act of law, not surgery. Though the body remained the same, the legal
person was transformed from female to male. The scandal that ensued

---

[7]Letter quoted in Hirschfeld, *Transvestites,* 339.

[8]Herculine Barbin, *Herculine Barbin: Being the Recently Discovered Memoirs of a
Nineteenth-Century French Hermaphrodite,* trans. Richard McDougall (New York: Pantheon,
1980), 68–69.

when the newspapers and the public discovered that a man had been teaching in an all-girl boarding school condemned Abel to "abandonment, to cold isolation.[9] His life as a man began in pain and confusion and plummeted rapidly into despair. He attempted to make a fresh start in Paris, but, impoverished and alone in a city that granted anonymity if not happiness, Abel was unable to make the transition from convent-bred woman to working man. He committed suicide at the age of thirty, overcome by feelings of isolation and desolation, the sense that he was absolutely alone in the world.

In his journal, Abel predicted that after his death his anomalous body would become a teaching tool and an exemplar of oddity. "When that day comes a few doctors will make a little stir around my corpse; they will shatter all the extinct mechanisms of its impulses, will draw new information from it, will analyze all the mysterious sufferings that were heaped up on a single human being."[10] This premonition was fulfilled as Abel's body was autopsied and the genitals and internal organs probed, studied, and sketched for the edification of future physicians pondering the riddle of "hermaphrodites," individuals whose bodies did not conform to traditional notions of male and female anatomy.

Though the Chevalier d'Éon and Abel Barbin are perhaps the best-known cases of presurgical "sex changes" in Western history, physically intersexual people such as Herculine Barbin and neurologically intersexual people such as the Chevalier d'Éon have always existed. Gender variance thus appears to be a "natural" phenomenon, an example of biological diversity. Professor Milton Diamond of the University of Hawaii, who has studied the phenomenon of intersexuality for more than half a century, argues persuasively that gender variance should be considered neither an anomaly nor a pathology, but a simple variation. "Variety is Nature's way," he told an audience at the International Foundation for Gender Education (IFGE) in March 2003. "How many of us in this room are the same height, weight? We're all part of a great experiment."[11] Unfortunately, society doesn't view gender variance with the same benevolence that it views differences in height and (less benevolently today) weight. "Difference is a dirty word to many," Diamond pointed out.

As contemporary historians and writers have worked to uncover the hidden history of homosexuality, some long-dead individuals who adopted cross-gendered dress and lifestyles have been lauded as gay pioneers. The most famous such case is that of Alan Hart (née Alberta Lucille), a Portland

10

---

[9]Ibid., 87.

[10]Ibid., 103.

[11]Milton Diamond, at the annual meeting of the International Foundation for Gender Education, March 21, 2003, Philadelphia, Pa.

physician who began living as a man after a hysterectomy in 1917.[12] The historian Jonathan Ned Katz identified Hart on the basis of a case study published by the physician who oversaw, and encouraged, Hart's metamorphosis. Katz and the larger gay community promptly proclaimed Hart (who was married to a woman) a lesbian pioneer, and explained Hart's decision to live as a man as an accommodation to social prejudices and coercion by a homophobic physician.

Among gays as well as straights, the complex relationship between sexual orientation and gender identity has thus sometimes been reduced to a simple formula with four variables: male or female, gay or straight. This perspective is shared by members of the (straight) public who believe that a man who wears dresses can't possibly be heterosexual, even if he sleeps with women only, just as some gay Americans believe that a female-bodied person who dresses like a man must be a masculine lesbian. Both gays and straights have a hard time believing that both of these individuals might in fact be heterosexual men. That idea challenges everything that we think we know about sex, gender, and sexual orientation. "Some men are born in female bodies," said Katherine (Kit) Rachlin — a clinical psychologist who has worked with transgendered clients for more than fifteen years — at a conference I attended while beginning research on this book. Like many Americans, gay and straight, I received this statement with certain skepticism. But after having met numerous men born in female bodies and women born in male bodies, I no longer doubt that it is true.

Sexual orientation is invisible, but gender identity is difficult to hide. It's evident in the way we walk, the way we talk, the way we dress, the way we cut our hair. My identity as a woman is clearly visible in hundreds of small and large ways. When you pass me on the street, your brain registers my long hair, makeup, skirt, pocketbook, and painted nails, and renders the verdict "female." Even if I cut my hair short, skipped makeup, and wore jeans and a T-shirt, you would still identify me as a woman by my physique, by my gait, and by the way I related to you, my fellow pedestrian, as I walked by. But what if, when you passed me on the street, you felt a moment of confusion? What if you felt it necessary to turn around and stare

---

[12]Hart underwent analysis with a Portland, Oregon, psychiatrist, J. Allen Gilbert, who, in 1917, helped Hart obtain a hysterectomy and begin living as a man. In *Gay American History: Lesbians and Gay Men in the U.S.A.* (New York: Thomas Y. Crowell Company, 1976), historian Jonathan Ned Katz identifies Hart on the basis of a paper Gilbert wrote about the case, hails Hart as a lesbian foremother, and harshly criticizes Gilbert for the course of treatment he recommended. In *Sex Changes: The Politics of Transgenderism* (San Francisco: Cleis Press, 1997), Pat Califia takes Katz and other gay historians to task for their tendency to view early transmen such as Hart as self-hating lesbians. "Unfortunately, since Katz's work has appeared in print, other gay and lesbian historians have also promoted the myth that all 'passing women' are lesbian elders. . . . The task of sorting out the dykes from the transgendered men, or at least the task of recognizing that both tendencies are present in the histories of 'passing women,' still remains to be done" (Califia, 155).

at me as I walked away from you? What if you turned to your companion and said, "Was that a guy or a girl?" Would you be reacting to sexual orientation or gender expression?

Many people infer the former from the latter, and believe that "masculine" women and "feminine" men are invariably gay. Feminine males and masculine females are often subject to scorn and derision, as anyone who has spent time on a playground can testify. A boy who rejects rough play and sports, who walks or talks in a way considered effeminate by his peers, is verbally and sometimes physically abused. The rules for girls are a bit looser in childhood. But by middle school, girls who are deemed inappropriately masculine by their peers are also teased and harassed. These prejudices carry through into adult life, and the all-purpose word used by many people to enforce gender conformity is "gay" — even when they are referring not to the person's choice of partner, but to the way he or she expresses gender. It is worth noting that though an increasing number of cities and states have added "sexual orientation" to civil rights legislation, fewer have added riders protecting people whose gender expression makes them targets of discrimination or violence. This lapse is a sign of our continuing failure to understand and acknowledge the distinction between sexual orientation and gender identity, and it has major consequences.

Jillian Weiss, an attorney who has published several articles about the legal issues confronting transgendered and transsexual people, notes that "gender identity is subject to scrutiny in a way that sexual identity [orientation] is not."[13] The letter M or F affixed to one's birth certificate "publicly identifies us in every area of life, whether it be a license to drive or conduct business, proof of citizenship required to obtain employment, a benefit program such as social security, or filing of income taxes." Biological sex (and therefore gender identity) is thus regulated by the state in a way that sexual orientation is not. Citizens of the United States and most other nations are not required to announce their sexual orientation or to affirm it in legal documents. If you are a woman who decides to begin sleeping with women, it is no one's business but your own. But if you (a female-bodied or intersexual person assigned as female at birth) decide that you are a man and wish to live and be recognized as a man in the world, then you must petition the authorities to *approve* that change. In effect, you must ask the state's permission to live as a man — and present a legitimate (medical) reason for your desire to do so.

Law is based on custom. Deeply rooted assumptions about our bodies   15
keep us locked into the belief that there are only two sexes — male and female — and that the sex of the body is always consistent with the sex of the brain. The equations work like this: Born with a vagina, female. Born

[13]Jillian Todd Weiss, "The Gender Caste System: Identity, Privacy, and Heteronormativity," *Law and Sexuality* 10 (2002): 131.

with a penis, male. It seems incomprehensible that a child born with a penis could grow up with the certain knowledge that she is a girl, or that a child born with a vagina could be equally convinced that he is a boy. Many people are unwilling to accept that "the hands of God" or Nature could have fashioned human beings whose sense of self is at war with their flesh, or whose gender identity falls somewhere in between the poles of male and female.

Because we live in a culture that expects science to settle questions based in the body, we look to science to tell us what it means to be male and female, how gender identity is formed, and why it is that the sex of the body sometimes seems to be at odds with the sex of the mind. But despite our sophisticated tests, science can still offer no definitive answer to this question, only tantalizing clues. When the governments of England and France attempted to solve the riddle of the Chevalier d'Éon's sex, they called in two doctors to examine the chevalier's body. From the evidence of their eyes (the chevalier appeared to have breasts), the doctors concluded that a woman stood before them. Only at death were the chevalier's genitals examined, and they told a different story. Today our tools are vastly more powerful, yet they are no more accurate in predicting gender identity in certain cases than the eyeball test that established the Chevalier d'Éon's or Herculine Barbin's anatomical sex.

"Ordinarily, the purpose of scientific investigation is to bring more clarity, more light into fields of obscurity. Modern researchers, however, delving into 'the riddle of sex,' have actually produced — so far — more obscurity, more complexity. Instead of the two conventional sexes with their anatomical differences, there may be up to ten or more separate concepts and manifestations of sex and each could be of vital importance to the individual," the pioneering sexologist Harry Benjamin wrote in 1966. "Here are some of the kinds of sex I have in mind: chromosomal, genetic, anatomical, legal, gonadal, germinal, endocrine (hormonal), psychological and also the social sex, usually based on the sex of rearing."[14]

Benjamin's understanding of the multiplicity of factors that contribute to a person's gender identity, and his ability to see that a lack of agreement among these components is a source of considerable anguish for some people, remains rare. Most people do not consider gender a riddle. Most do not make a distinction between anatomical sex and gender identity. Nor do they realize that it is possible for a person to have XY chromosomes yet female-body morphology and genitals as a result of androgen insensitivity syndrome (AIS), or XX chromosomes yet male-body morphology and genitals as a result of congenital adrenal hyperplasia (CAH). Those are only two of a number of genetic and endocrine conditions that can create anatomically intersexual people. Once these persons were called hermaphrodites, after the intersexual offspring of the gods Hermes and Aphrodite. As that

[14]Harry Benjamin, *The Transsexual Phenomenon* (New York: Ace Books, 1966), p. 5.

myth indicates, in some cultures, intersexual and transgendered persons have been viewed with reverence and respect.

Our own culture has not been so kind. Intersexual people have been forced to undergo physically and psychologically traumatic surgeries to "normalize" their genitalia. The medicalization of intersex conditions has caused tremendous suffering. However, it has also granted intersexual people legitimacy in the eyes of the medical profession, lawmakers, and the public. No one accuses intersexual persons of being mentally ill. Their gender variance is inscribed on their bodies, in their gonads, genitals, or chromosomes — and so seems "real" because it is a material, measurable entity. The same is not true of transgendered and transsexual persons, who present a baffling enigma to their families, physicians, and themselves.

Take for example a genitally female, genetically XX girl who tells her   20
mother at age three that she is a boy, and from her earliest childhood spurns girlish activities, clothing, and behavior. "My whole life I'm telling my mom, 'I'm not a girl, I'm not a girl, I'm not a girl' and thinking what the hell is going on here?" says Brad,[15] one of the first employees of the city of San Francisco to take advantage of the new policy of insurance reimbursement for sex reassignment surgery for city employees.[16] "When you are little, you're kind of androgynous. Both little boys and little girls are running around, taking their shirts off, jumping in mud, throwing dirtballs. So if you are a little aggressive and gened as female, they say you're just a tomboy. But once you get up to a certain age, like six or seven, it starts separating. And I was like, 'You're pushing me the wrong way. I'm supposed to be over there with the boys; why are you making me go over here with the girls?' You look at your body and you are in the wrong body, and it's a nightmare. You wake up in this nightmare every day and you have to deal with it. And you keep thinking, When am I gonna wake up?"

[15]Author interview with "Brad" [source requested anonymity for family reasons], San Francisco, Calif., August 31, 2001.

[16]On Monday, April 30, 2001, the Board of Supervisors passed a measure making the city the first in the nation to pay for its transgendered employees' surgical and medical needs related to sex correction. The coverage does not extend to cosmetic procedures, only to hormones, genital reconstruction, and hysterectomies and mastectomies for FTMs. Employees must work for the city for a year to become eligible for the benefits. If using a doctor within the city's health network, employees have to pay 15 percent out of pocket; if using a doctor outside the network, employees are responsible for 50 percent of the costs. An article by Margie Mason for the Associated Press said that the city had identified fourteen transgendered employees out of its thirty-seven thousand workers. Margie Mason, "Sex-Change Benefits Approved in San Francisco," Associated Press, April 30, 2001. Brad told me, "In the city there are thirteen of us. Half of those have already had the surgery; out of the other seven, three don't want surgery. So I would say that there are only four people. Hello? There are not going to be droves of people coming out here. There aren't that many city jobs, and you've got to wait a year anyway. This year they've got one point seven million dollars set aside for the thirty-five surgeries they thought were gonna happen. They said that they overestimated, because they wanted to err on the side of more, but they are way overestimating."

Brad's description of his early life was echoed by many of the transgendered and transsexual people I interviewed for this book, who struggled for many years to understand their suffering and confusion without being able to put a name on what they were experiencing. Gender variance is not a widely discussed subject, even in medical schools, and as a consequence many physicians, like the general public, know very little about the subject other than what they are able to glean from sensationalist media accounts of cross-dressing and transsexuality. Gender variance still seems to be considered a more suitable topic for late-night talk show jokes than for journals of public health and public policy, even though a recent needs assessment survey in Washington, D.C., estimated that the median life expectancy of a transgendered person in the nation's capital is only thirty-seven years.[17] Poverty, substance abuse, HIV infection, violence, and inadequate health care are the factors behind this statistic. Of the 252 transgendered people surveyed in the district, 29 percent reported no source of income, and another 31 percent reported annual incomes of under ten thousand dollars per year. Half the participants did not have health insurance and 39 percent did not have a doctor, though 52 percent had taken sex hormones at some time in their lives and 36 percent were taking hormones at the time of the study. A number of the respondents were working, or had worked, as commercial sex workers — a consequence of the persistent employment discrimination experienced by many transgendered people.

Though many are far better off materially than the subjects of the Washington, D.C., study, transgendered and transsexual people of every social class and at every income level share many of the same vulnerabilities. Public prejudices make it difficult for visibly transgendered or transsexual people to gain an education, employment, housing, or health care, and acute gender dysphoria leaves people at high risk for drug abuse, depression, and suicide. "You do everything you can possibly do to check out, to get away," says Brad, who at forty-six has been sober for sixteen years. When I asked if his drinking and drug abuse were tied to his confusion about his gender and related traumas, he replied, "Absolutely. Because I couldn't be who I was after so many years of hiding from myself. At that point I didn't really know who I was. It's very much a catch-22, and you're just like, 'Fuck it. I'll just take more drugs. I'll just do more drinking. I'll just do whatever because I can't deal with this.'" Brad began his transition after nearly a decade of sobriety. "Without being clean and sober, I would never have gotten to this point," he says. "I would have been dead."

Though the first scientific study of gender variance was published in Germany nearly a century ago, scientific understanding of the causes of what are today classified as "gender identity disorders" remains sketchy.

---

[17]Jessica Xavier, "Final report of the Washington Transgender Needs Assessment Survey," Washington, D.C., Administration for HIV and AIDS, District of Columbia Department of Health.

Did transvestites (people who wear the clothes and sometimes adopt the lifestyle of the other sex) exist before the German sexologist Magnus Hirschfeld introduced them into the clinical literature in 1910? Undoubtedly. But prior to Hirschfeld, transvestites were believed to be a kind of homosexual — a category that itself had been only recently created. (Hirschfeld was the first to note that transvestites were usually heterosexual.) Similarly, though Hirschfeld included case studies of people born male who clearly expressed female gender identities, he didn't identify transsexuals as a separate diagnostic category. British sexologist Havelock Ellis, who had experience with both transvestites and transsexuals, wanted to call members of both groups "eonists," after the Chevalier d'Éon, a nomenclature that never caught on. It remained for the American physician Harry Benjamin to clarify the distinction between transvestism (today called crossdressing) and transsexuality in his 1966 book, *The Transsexual Phenomenon,* and for a professional organization in Benjamin's name to establish Standards of Care for treatment of transsexuality, in 1980.

More recently, "gender identity disorder" has been created to replace "transsexualism" as a diagnosis in the American Psychiatric Association's *Diagnostic and Statistical Manual of Mental Disorders* (DSM). But science is no more certain today why some people feel so acutely uncomfortable in the sex they were assigned at birth than it was in Hirschfeld's time — nor why their number seems to be increasing. Statistics on transsexualism and transgenderism are notoriously unreliable; in the case of transgenderism (a broad and variously defined category) they are mere guesswork. However, it is possible to track the number of people requesting sex-reassignment surgery and to make some general estimates of prevalence (the number of cases of a given condition present in a given population during a given time) based on those figures.

According to the fourth edition of the DSM (DSM-IV), about 1 in 10,000 people seek sex-reassignment surgery (SRS) in the United States every year, and approximately 1 in 30,000 men and 1 in 100,000 women will undergo SRS at some point during their lives. This is believed to be a very conservative estimate, based on SRS statistics that are decades old. Professor Lynn Conway of the University of Michigan suggests that the DSM-IV figures are off by at least two orders of magnitude and that "the prevalence of SRS in the U.S. is at least on the order of 1:2500, and may be as much as twice that value. Therefore, the intrinsic prevalence of MtF transsexualism here must be on the order of ~1:500 and may be even larger than that."[18] A group of researchers in the Netherlands recently estimated the prevalence of transsexuality to be 1 in 11,900 males and 1 in 30,400 females; this estimate was based on the number of Dutch citizens seeking services compared with the general population.[19]

25

[18]Lynn Conway, "How Frequently Does Transsexualism Occur," available online at http://www.lynnconway.com.

[19]P. L. E. Eklund, L. J. G. Gooren, and P. D. Bezemer, "Prevalence of Transsexualism in the Netherlands," *British Journal of Psychiatry* 152 (1988): 638–40.

Legal scholar Jillian Weiss has pointed out that "gender identity disorders" are probably far more common than previously suspected,[20] on the basis of four general observations. First, unrecognized gender problems are occasionally diagnosed when patients are seen with anxiety, depression, substance abuse, and other psychiatric conditions, which often serve to mask the underlying gender issue. Second, many individuals who meet the diagnostic criteria for "gender identity disorder" never present themselves for treatment (this category includes the great majority of cross-dressers, professional female impersonators, and gender-variant gay people). Third, the intensity of some people's feelings of gender-related discomfort fluctuates throughout their lifetimes, and does not always achieve a sustained "clinical threshold" requiring treatment. Finally, gender-variant behavior among female-bodied persons is "invisible" in a way that gender-variant behavior in male-bodied persons is not. On the most basic level, this is exemplified by the relative ease with which women can don men's clothing.

The number of people self-identifying as transgendered or transsexual and seeking services (hormone therapy and/or surgery) has certainly risen in every decade since Christine Jorgensen brought the issue to the public's attention, in 1952. Gunter Dorner, a German endocrinologist who has devoted his career to studying the effects of hormones on the brain, has postulated a fourfold increase in the incidence of transsexualism over the past forty years in the former East Germany.[21] Is Dorner correct? No one knows. But if various forms of gender variance are indeed on the increase, as seems to be the case, what might be the cause of this phenomenon? Dr. Paul

[20]Weiss, "Gender Caste System," 129 (n. 9).

[21]G. Dorner, F. Gotz, W. Rohde, et al., "Genetic and Epigenetic Effects on Sexual Brain Organization Mediated by Sex Hormones," *Neuroendocrinology Letters* 22 (2001): 403–409. See also G. Dorner, I. Poppe, F. Stahl, et al., "Gene and Environment-Dependent Neuroendocrine Etiogenesis of Homosexuality and Transsexualism," *Experimental and Clinical Endocrinology* 98, no. 2 (1991): 141–50; G. Dorner, "Neuroendocrine Response to Estrogen and Brain Differentiation in Heterosexuals, Homosexuals, and Transsexuals, *Archives of Sexual Behavior* 17, no. 1 (February 1988): 57–75; G. Dorner, "Sex Hormone Dependent Brain Differentiation and Sexual Behavior," *Experimental Brain Research* suppl. 3 (1981): 238–45; G. Dorner, F. Docke, F. Gotz, et al., "Sexual Differentation of Gonadotrophin Secretion, Sexual Orientation and Gender Role Behavior," *Journal of Steroid Biochemistry* 27, no. 4–6 (1987): 1081–87.

Dorner has published extensively on the organizational effects of hormones on the brain, and possible implications for sexual orientation and transsexualism. Earlier in his career, Dorner's theories on the somatic basis of homosexuality and gender variance were considered reactionary, but since 1987, the biological school has rebounded. "By the early 1980s, endocrinological theories of sexual orientation seemed to have reached a low point of credibility, and those who still espoused them were considered the 'bad guys' who were on a mission to eliminate homosexuality by a technical fix. In Dorner's case the label was well deserved." Simon LeVay, *Queer Science: The Use and Abuse of Research into Homosexuality* (Cambridge and London: MIT Press, 1996), 120. Later, in a discussion of Dorner's hypothesis that prenatal stress might play a role in the development of homosexuality in men, LeVay says that "to give Dorner his due, his theory does have one thing going for it: it is based on a solid body of research conducted on animals." *Queer Science*, 164.

McHugh, former chief of psychiatry at Johns Hopkins School of Medicine and a noted opponent of sex reassignment surgery, believes that gender variance is a fad or a "craze" driven by the media and the Internet. McHugh's views are the flip side of the postmodern "performativity" argument that gender is a cultural construction and that the body is a text upon which individuals are free to inscribe their gender of choice.[22] In this view, gender-queer people are revolutionaries helping to dismantle an oppressive system — and their numbers are increasing, as more and more people challenge the tyranny of the gender binary.

Others believe that greater public tolerance and acceptance, combined with the increased ability to connect with others online and in person, is responsible for the increasing visibility and political activism of gender-variant people. "Twenty or forty or fifty years ago, you couldn't have had a meeting like this one," Professor Milton Diamond told me at the 2003 annual meeting of the International Foundation for Gender Education. The majority of the meeting's participants were cross-dressed men, a group that remains the most heavily closeted of sexual minorities and the most persecuted. "A meeting like this would have been broken up by the police," Diamond said. Then too, he pointed out, "Many of these individuals think that they are the only ones in the world, and they don't think that there is a solution, and when they find a solution or find a safe haven somewhere, they utilize it. Many of these activities are like support groups in their own way. They don't call them that, but that's what they are."

Without denying the influence of social factors in helping more people come out, as a science writer I can't help being interested in biological explanations for what seems to be a pronounced increase in the number of gender-variant people in the world today. An enormous quantity of man-made chemicals has been released into the environment since the chemical revolution began after World War II. According to researchers who have studied their effects, "many of these chemicals can disturb development of the endocrine system and of the organs that respond to endocrine signals in organisms indirectly exposed during prenatal and/or early postnatal life; effects of exposure during development are permanent and irreversible."[23] Some scientists and transpeople argue that the buildup of these endocrine-disrupting chemicals in the environment has begun to produce the same kind of effects on human sexual differentiation that have already been observed in wildlife and laboratory animals.[24] In this view, a previously rare

[22]See Judith Butler, *Gender Trouble: Feminism and the Subversion of Identity* (New York: Routledge, 1999) and *Bodies That Matter: On the Discursive Limits of Sex* (New York: Routledge, 1993).

[23]World Health Organization, "Global Assessment of the State of the Science of Endocrine Disruptors," retrieved from http://www.who.int/pcs/emerg_site/edc/global_edc_TOC.htm, July 31, 2002.

[24]See Theo Colborn, Dianne Dumanoski, and John Peterson Myers, *Our Stolen Future* (New York: Dutton, 1996).

collection of endocrine-mediated anomalies is becoming more common as a result of the bioaccumulation of these chemicals, many of which are stored in fat and transmitted to the developing fetus through the placenta in pregnancy.

The strongest evidence for a possible biological basis for gender variance comes from research on the effects of the drug diethylstilbestrol (DES). DES is a synthetic estrogen developed in 1938. Between 1945 and 1970, DES and other synthetic hormones were prescribed to millions of pregnant women in the mistaken belief that they would help prevent miscarriages. DES was even included in vitamins given to pregnant women, and in animal feed. Use of DES during pregnancy was discontinued in the United States in 1971, when seven young women whose mothers had taken DES during pregnancy were found to be suffering from a rare vaginal cancer. Since then, research on animals and human epidemiological studies have proved that DES causes myriad health problems in both males and females exposed to the drug in the womb, including structural damage to the reproductive system. Animal research has also shown that DES and other estrogenic chemicals affect the development of sex-dimorphic brain structures and behavior in animals.[25] Laboratory animals exposed to hormones at critical stages of development in utero exhibited behaviors associated with the other sex after birth. Only in recent years have some researchers begun to note higher-than-expected rates of transgenderism in DES sons and daughters. The moderators of an online discussion group for the XY children of DES mothers surveyed subscribers in 2002 and discovered that 36.5 percent of the forum's members were either preoperative or postoperative transsexuals, while another 14.3 percent defined themselves as transgendered.[26] An update taken on the five-year anniversary of the group showed that since 1999, between one-quarter and one-third of the members of the DES Sons Network had indicated that gender identity and/or sexuality issues were among their most significant concerns. These data have not yet found their way into the scientific literature, however, and the combined cohort studies of DES children have thus far failed to ask a single question related to gender identity. This epidemiologic failure baffles DES "sons" who are now daughters and who are aware of the increasing public health concerns about chemicals that bind to the estrogen receptor in humans and animals.

30

[25]See J. A. McLachlan, R. R. Newbold, and B. Bullock, "Reproductive Tract Lesions in Male Mice Exposed Prenatally to Diethylstilbestrol," *Science* 190 (1975): 991–92; R. R. Newbold, B. Bullock, and J. A. McLachlan, "Mullerian Remnants of Male Mice Exposed Prenatally to Diethylstilbestrol," *Teratog. Carcinog. Mutagen.* 7 (1987): 377–89; W. B. Gill, G. F. Schumacher, M. Bibbo, et al., "Association of Diethylstilbestrol in Utero with Cryptorchidism, Testicular Hypoplasia and Semen Abnormalities," *Journal of Urology* 122 (1979): 36–39; J. A. Visser, A. McLuskey, M. Verhoef-Post, et al., "Effect of Prenatal Exposure to Diethylstilbestrol on Mullerian Duct Development in Fetal Male Mice," *Endocrinology* 139 (1998): 4244–251.

[26]Scott Kerlin and Dana Beyer, M.D., "The DES Sons Online Discussion Network: Critical Issues and the Need for Further Research," unpublished paper, August 2002.

"There are millions of us who were exposed to DES. And millions more exposed to DDT, DDE, dioxin, and god knows whatever else is out there that is estrogenic," says Dr. Dana Beyer, a transgendered physician who serves as co-moderator of the DES Sons Network.[27] "You look at DES and say, 'If that can mimic estrogen, there must be other things out there. What are people eating? What are they exposed to in the water supply? Five million people were exposed to DES in this country alone. Globally, there are many millions more. And we're still alive and kicking and suffering from the effects. Plus there probably will be third-generation effects and maybe fourth- and fifth-generation effects."

Efforts to establish the etiology, or cause, of transsexuality and other forms of gender variance have most often focused on psychological rather than organic causes — this is not surprising, since gender identity disorders are classified as psychiatric, not medical, conditions. Many psychiatrists have attempted to root gender nonconformity in an unstable home environment, abusive or disturbed parents, gender confusion in the family, and other social factors. This line of research has not been very successful, however, as relatively few individuals who grow up in disturbed circumstances of any kind exhibit gender anomalies. As early as 1973, a psychologist working with cross-gendered clients noted that "there is no more psychopathology in the transsexual population than in the population at large, although societal response to the transsexual does impose almost insurmountable problems."[28]

For that reason many transgendered people reject "pathologization" and would like to see the gender identity disorders removed from the *Diagnostic and Statistical Manual of Mental Disorders* in the same way that homosexuality was removed from the DSM. Others argue that this step would have disastrous effects for transsexual people. Rusty Moore, a professor at Hofstra University, in New York, says that transsexuality is "a part of human variation just like having a clubfoot is human variation. So people have surgery to correct clubfeet or cleft palate and that gets paid for by medical reimbursement. But in the meantime, until that medical reclassification takes place, our biggest legal protection is what we already have, the DSM. Because that's the only thing that stops the people that are out to get us."[29]

Some who believe that transgenderism and transsexuality are biologically based argue that the condition known as "gender identity disorder" ought to be removed from the DSM and reclassified as a congenital endocrinological disorder. "Somewhere the hormones that are secreted

---

[27]Author interview with Dana Beyer, Bethesda, Md., September 27, 2002.

[28]This was noted as early as 1973. "The psychodynamic histories of transsexuals do not yield any consistent differentiation characteristics from the rest of the population." Marie C. Mehl, Ph.D., "Transsexualism: A Perspective" in *Proceedings of the Second Interdisciplinary Symposium on Gender Dysphoria Syndrome,* ed. Donald R. Laub, M.D., and Patrick S. Gandy, M.S., Stanford University Medical Center, February 2–4, 1973, 15.

[29]Author interview with Rusty Moore, New York City, July 1, 2001.

either by the brain or by the testes in response to the brain — the fetal hormonal system — are messed up. The end result is the morphological phenomenon, the brain anatomy or hypothalamic anatomy," says Dr. Dana Beyer.[30] For that reason, "we're thinking of trying to push a new name for this: Benjamin's disorder. So that when a baby is born or when a child is growing up and comes and says, 'You know, Mommy says that I'm a boy, but I think I'm a girl,' the doctor would say, 'Okay, let's rule out Benjamin's disorder.' Let's figure out what's going on here, rather than telling the parents the kid is crazy, delusional. The assumption is that you are psychotic or have some kind of mental abnormality. That's the problem with the DSM. If we can make this a congenital anomaly just like cleft palate and cleft lip, or any of the physical intersex conditions, that shifts everybody's perspective."

In *The Normal and the Pathological*, a study that traces the develop-   35
ment of the concept of pathology in medicine, the historian of science Georges Canguilhem pointed out that "an anomaly or mutation is not in itself pathological."[31] Canguilhem carefully delineated the distinction between anomaly and pathology. "An anomaly is a fact of individual variation which prevents two beings from being able to take the place of each other completely," he writes. "But diversity is not disease; the *anomalous* is not the pathological." This concept was articulated in various ways by many of the transgendered people with whom I have spoken over the past three years.

"There's an idea that people have subconsciously inculcated about how gender and the body work, and when someone says, 'I'm doing it a little differently,' it's like 'No, you're wrong.' But no, we're just doing it differently than you," says historian Susan Stryker.[32] "It's a privilege to not have to think about how you are embodied," she says, comparing gender privilege to race privilege and pointing out that normatively gendered people don't have to think about gender "in the same way that white people never have to think about race." According to Stryker, transgendered people must question basic assumptions about what it means to be male or female, and the relation of gender to the body, in the same way that other minority groups must examine and reject the assumptions that create their oppression. "I didn't have the privilege of having my body communicate who I am to other people without some kind of interventions. Transsexuals are subject to a double standard. People say, 'You're essentializing gender because you think it's all in the genitals.' Well, no, I don't. It's about my sense of self, and being able to communicate my sense of self to other people the way everybody else does."

The concept of "gender" as applied to human beings is itself a fairly

---

[30]Author interview with Beyer.

[31]Georges Canguilhem, *The Normal and the Pathological* (New York: Zone Books, 1991), 137.

[32]Author interview with Susan Stryker, San Francisco Calif., September 4, 2001.

new concept. Until the middle of the twentieth century, scientists recognized only biological sex, and though a determination of "sex" was usually based on the appearance of the genitals at birth, scientific discoveries complicated this simple picture as early as the eighteenth century. In cases of ambiguous genitalia, the gonads (testicles or ovaries) were used to establish sex until the discovery of Barr bodies (inactivated X chromosomes in female cells) in the mid-twentieth century. Then chromosomes became the new litmus test for sex — but by that point, it had become increasingly clear that there were persons, rare though they might be, whose sense of themselves as men or women was in distinct contrast to the results of chromosome testing. The terms "gender role" and "gender identity" as descriptions of a person's innate sense of self were born in the 1950s, and very quickly the word "gender" became a synonym for sex, although transgendered people today (and throughout history) have made it clear that this is a misconception. Sometimes, they say, the body lies.

ENGAGING THE TEXT

1. What does Rudacille mean by "the sex of the brain" (para. 15)? How does the story of the Chevalier d'Éon illustrate this concept?

2. Define and distinguish among the terms "intersexual," "transgendered," and "transsexual." Why are these distinctions important, according to Rudacille?

3. Rudacille reviews several explanations — both social and biological — for the growing number of transgendered and transsexual people today. Which of these explanations seem most persuasive, and why?

4. Why do some advocates argue that transgenderism and transsexuality should be reclassified as biological rather than psychological disorders? Why do others maintain that they should not be seen as disorders at all? What are the advantages and disadvantages of each position?

5. Some readers would be put off by Rudacille's subject matter. What rhetorical strategies does she use to engage readers' interest and to appeal for greater understanding of gender variation?

EXPLORING CONNECTIONS

6. What is the source of the humor in the cartoon on p. 471? Is it making fun of the man who's speaking, of rigidly defined sexual identities, of modern families, or something else?

7. Rudacille points out that civil rights legislation often fails to protect transgendered people from discrimination. Read Kenji Yoshino's discussion of civil rights law and "covering" (p. 598), and discuss whether or not his concept of a "liberty-based approach to civil rights" would offer more effective protection than legislation based on group rights.

"I have two children from a previous sexuality."

EXTENDING THE CRITICAL CONTEXT

8. Research the lives of Billy Tipton and at least one of the other people
    Rudacille lists as examples of gender reversal (para. 2). What did they gain
    and lose by assuming a different gender identity? How were they regarded
    during their lifetimes? Did that perception change after the revelation of
    their biological sex? If so, how?

9. Look up one of the historical figures Rudacille mentions in *The Encyclope-
    dia of Lesbian, Gay, Bisexual, and Transgender History in America* and in
    another, more general reference work like Encarta. If the two accounts dif-
    fer, how do you explain the differences?

10. Watch a film that features a central character who is transgendered
    (e.g., *TransAmerica, Boys Don't Cry, Normal, Hedwig and the Angry
    Inch*). Does the movie depict gender identity as primarily psychological
    or biological? To what extent is the central character's identity portrayed
    as a problem for himself or herself, and to what extent a problem for
    others? Is he or she presented as a tragic, comic, heroic, or mundane
    figure?

Appearances
CARMEN VÁZQUEZ

Have you ever gone for a walk in the evening, ridden a city bus, or gone out dancing? Did these activities make you fear for your life? In this essay, Vázquez writes about what can happen in such everyday situations when the pedestrian, commuter, or dancer is perceived as gay or lesbian. She also discusses some possible causes of homophobia, and she pleads for change. Vázquez (b. 1949) was born in Bayamon, Puerto Rico, and grew up in Harlem, New York. She has been active in the lesbian/gay movement for many years and was a founding member of the New York State Lesbian and Gay Health and Human Services Network; currently she serves as deputy executive director of Empire State Pride Agenda. She has published essays and book reviews in a number of publications. "Appearances" comes from an anthology titled Homophobia: How We All Pay the Price *(1992).*

North of Market Street and east of Twin Peaks, where you can see the white fog mushroom above San Francisco's hills, is a place called the Castro. Gay men, lesbians, and bisexuals stroll leisurely up and down the bustling streets. They jaywalk with abandon. Night and day they fill the cafés and bars, and on weekends they line up for a double feature of vintage classics at their ornate and beloved Castro theater.

The 24 bus line brings people into and out of the Castro. People from all walks of life ride the electric-powered coaches. They come from the opulence of San Francisco's Marina and the squalor of Bayview projects. The very gay Castro is in the middle of its route. Every day, boys in pairs or gangs from either end of the city board the bus for a ride through the Castro and a bit of fun. Sometimes their fun is fulfilled with passionately obscene derision: "Fucking cocksucking faggots." "Dyke cunts." "Diseased butt fuckers." Sometimes, their fun is brutal.

Brian boarded the 24 Divisadero and handed his transfer to the driver one late June night. Epithets were fired at him the moment he turned for a seat. He slid his slight frame into an empty seat next to an old woman with silver blue hair who clutched her handbag and stared straight ahead. Brian stuffed his hands into the pockets of his worn brown bomber jacket and stared with her. He heard the flip of a skateboard in the back. The taunting shouts grew louder. "Faggot!" From the corner of his eye, he saw a beer bottle hurtling past the window and crash on the street. A man in his forties, wearing a Giants baseball cap and warmup jacket, yelled at the driver to stop the bus and get the hoodlums off. The bus driver ignored him and pulled out.

Brian dug his hands deeper into his pockets and clenched his jaw. It was just five stops to the top of the hill. When he got up to move toward the exit, the skateboard slammed into his gut and one kick followed another until every boy had got his kick in. Despite the plea of the passengers, the driver never called the police.

Brian spent a week in a hospital bed, afraid that he would never walk again. A lawsuit filed by Brian against the city states, "As claimant lay crumpled and bleeding on the floor of the bus, the bus driver tried to force claimant off the bus so that the driver could get off work and go home. Claimant was severely beaten by a gang of young men on the #24 Divisadero Bus who perceived that he was gay."

On the south side of Market Street, night brings a chill wind and rough trade. On a brisk November night, men with sculptured torsos and thighs wrapped in leather walked with precision. The clamor of steel on the heels of their boots echoed in the darkness. Young men and women walked by the men in leather, who smiled in silence. They admired the studded bracelets on Mickey's wrists, the shine of his flowing hair, and the rise of his laughter. They were, each of them, eager to be among the safety of like company where they could dance with abandon to the pulse of hard rock, the hypnotism of disco, or the measured steps of country soul. They looked forward to a few drinks, flirting with strangers, finding Mr. or Ms. Right or, maybe, someone to spend the night with.

At the end of the street, a lone black street lamp shone through the mist. The men in leather walked under the light and disappeared into the next street. As they reached the corner, Mickey and his friends could hear the raucous sounds of the Garden spill onto the street. They shimmied and rocked down the block and through the doors.

The Garden was packed with men and women in sweat-stained shirts. Blue smoke stung the eyes. The sour and sweet smell of beer hung in the air. Strobe lights pulsed over the dancers. Mickey pulled off his wash-faded black denim jacket and wrapped it around his waist. An iridescent blue tank top hung easy on his shoulders. Impatient with the wait for a drink, Mickey steered his girlfriend onto the crowded dance floor.

Reeling to the music and immersed in the pleasure of his rhythms, Mickey never saw the ice pick plunge into his neck. It was just a bump with a drunk yelling, "Lame-assed faggot." "Faggot. Faggot. Faggot. Punk faggot." Mickey thought it was a punch to the neck. He ran after the roaring drunk man for seven steps, then lurched and fell on the dance floor, blood gushing everywhere. His girlfriend screamed. The dance floor spun black.

Mickey was rushed to San Francisco General Hospital, where thirty-six stitches were used by trauma staff to close the wound on his neck. Doctors said the pick used in the attack against him was millimeters away from his spinal cord. His assailant, charged with attempted murder, pleaded innocent.

Mickey and Brian were unfortunate stand-ins for any gay man. Mickey was thin and wiry, a great dancer clad in black denim, earrings dangling from his ear. Brian was slight of build, wore a leather jacket, and boarded a bus in the Castro. Dress like a homo, dance like a homo, must be a homo.

The homophobic fury directed at lesbians, gay men, and bisexuals in America most often finds its target. Ironclad evidence of sexual orientation, however, is not necessary for someone to qualify as a potential victim of deadly fury. Appearances will do.

The incidents described above are based on actual events reported to the San Francisco Police and Community United Against Violence (CUAV), an agency serving victims of antilesbian and antigay violence where I worked for four years. The names of the victims have been changed. Both men assaulted were straight.

Incidents of antilesbian and antigay violence are not uncommon or limited to San Francisco. A *San Francisco Examiner* survey estimates that over one million hate-motivated physical assaults take place each year against lesbians, gays, and bisexuals. The National Gay and Lesbian Task Force conducted a survey in 1984 that found that 94 percent of all lesbians and gay men surveyed reported being physically assaulted, threatened, or harassed in an antigay incident at one time or another. The great majority of these incidents go unreported.

To my knowledge, no agency other than CUAV keeps track of incidents of antigay violence involving heterosexuals as victims. An average of 3 percent of the over three hundred victims seen by CUAV each year identify as heterosexuals. This may or may not be an accurate gauge of the actual prevalence of antigay violence directed at heterosexuals. Most law enforcement agencies, including those in San Francisco, have no way of documenting this form of assault other than under a generic "harassment" code. The actual incidence of violence directed at heterosexuals that is motivated by homophobia is probably much higher than CUAV's six to nine victims a year. Despite the official paucity of data, however, it is a fact that incidents of antigay and antilesbian violence in which straight men and women are victimized do occur. Shelters for battered women are filled with stories of lesbian baiting of staff and of women whose husbands and boyfriends repeatedly called them "dykes" or "whores" as they beat them.[1] I have personally experienced verbal abuse while in the company of a straight friend, who was assumed to be my lover.

Why does it happen? I have no definitive answers to that question.   15
Understanding homophobic violence is no less complex than understanding racial violence. The institutional and ideological reinforcements of homophobia are myriad and deeply woven into our culture. I offer one perspective that I hope will contribute to a better understanding of how homophobia works and why it threatens all that we value as humane.

At the simplest level, looking or behaving like the stereotypical gay man or lesbian is reason enough to provoke a homophobic assault. Beneath the

---

[1]See Suzanne Pharr, *Homophobia: A Weapon of Sexism* (Inverness, Calif.: Chardon, 1988). [All notes are Vázquez's.]

veneer of the effeminate gay male or the butch dyke, however, is a more basic trigger for homophobic violence. I call it *gender betrayal.*

The clearest expression I have heard of this sense of gender betrayal comes from Doug Barr, who was acquitted of murder in an incident of gay bashing in San Francisco that resulted in the death of John O'Connell, a gay man. Barr is currently serving a prison sentence for related assaults on the same night that O'Connell was killed. He was interviewed for a special report on homophobia produced by ABC's *20/20* (10 April 1986). When asked what he and his friends thought of gay men, he said, "We hate homosexuals. They degrade our manhood. We was brought up in a high school where guys are football players, mean and macho. Homosexuals are sissies who wear dresses. I'd rather be seen as a football player."

Doug Barr's perspective is one shared by many young men. I have made about three hundred presentations to high school students in San Francisco, to boards of directors and staff of nonprofit organizations, and at conferences and workshops on the topic of homophobia or "being lesbian or gay." Over and over again, I have asked, "Why do gay men and lesbians bother you?" The most popular response to the question is, "Because they act like girls," or, "Because they think they're men." I have even been told, quite explicitly, "I don't care what they do in bed, but they shouldn't act like that."

They shouldn't act like that. Women who are not identified by their relationship to a man, who value their female friendships, who like and are knowledgeable about sports, or work as blue-collar laborers and wear what they wish are very likely to be "lesbian baited" at some point in their lives. Men who are not pursuing sexual conquests of women at every available opportunity, who disdain sports, who choose to stay at home and be a house-husband, who are employed as hairdressers, designers, or house-cleaners, or who dress in any way remotely resembling traditional female attire (an earring will do) are very likely to experience the taunts and sometimes the brutality of "fag bashing."

The straitjacket of gender roles suffocates many lesbians, gay men, and 20 bisexuals, forcing them into closets without an exit and threatening our very existence when we tear the closet open. It also, however, threatens all heterosexuals unwilling to be bound by their assigned gender identity. Why, then, does it persist?

Suzanne Pharr's examination of homophobia as a phenomenon based in sexism and misogyny offers a succinct and logical explanation for the virulence of homophobia in Western civilization:

> It is not by chance that when children approach puberty and increased sexual awareness they begin to taunt each other by calling these names: "queer," "faggot," "pervert." It is at puberty that the full force of society's pressure to conform to heterosexuality and prepare for marriage is brought to bear. Children know what we have taught them, and we have given clear messages that those who deviate from standard expectations are to be made to get back in line. . . .

To be named as lesbian threatens all women, not just lesbians, with great loss. And any woman who steps out of role risks being called a lesbian. To understand how this is a threat to all women, one must understand that any woman can be called a lesbian and there is no real way she can defend herself: there is no real way to credential one's sexuality. (*The Children's Hour*, a Lillian Hellman play, makes this point when a student asserts two teachers are lesbians and they have no way to disprove it.) She may be married or divorced, have children, dress in the most feminine manner, have sex with men, be celibate — but there are lesbians who do all these things. *Lesbians look like all women and all women look like lesbians.*[2]

I would add that gay men look like all men and all men look like gay men. There is no guaranteed method for identifying sexual orientation. Those small or outrageous deviations we sometimes take from the idealized mystique of "real men" and "real women" place all of us — lesbians, gay men, bisexuals, and heterosexuals alike — at risk of violence, derision, isolation, and hatred.

It is a frightening reality. Dorothy Ehrlich, executive director of the Northern California American Civil Liberties Union (ACLU), was the victim of a verbal assault in the Castro several years ago. Dorothy lives with her husband, Gary, and her two children, Jill and Paul, in one of those worn and comfortable Victorian homes that grace so many San Francisco neighborhoods. Their home is several blocks from the Castro, but Dorothy recalls the many times she and Gary could hear, from the safety of their bedroom, shouts of "faggot" and men running in the streets.

When Jill was an infant, Gary and Dorothy had occasion to experience for themselves how frightening even the threat of homophobic violence can be. One foggy, chilly night they decided to go for a walk in the Castro. Dorothy is a small woman whom some might call petite; she wore her hair short at the time and delights in the comfort of jeans and oversized wool jackets. Gary is very tall and lean, a bespectacled and bearded cross between a professor and a basketball player who wears jean jackets and tweed jackets with the exact same slouch. On this night they were crossing Castro Street, huddled close together with Jill in Dorothy's arms. As they reached the corner, their backs to the street, they heard a truck rev its engine and roar up Castro, the dreaded "faggot" spewing from young men they could not see in the fog. They looked around them for the intended victims, but there was no one else on the corner with them. They were the target that night: Dorothy and Gary and Jill. They were walking on "gay turf," and it was reason enough to make them a target. "It was so frightening," Dorothy said. "So frightening and unreal."

[2]Ibid., 17–19.

But it is real. The *20/20* report on homophobia ends with the story of Tom and Jan Matarrase, who are married, have a child, and lived in Brooklyn, New York, at the time of their encounter with homophobic violence. On camera, Tom and Jan are walking down a street in Brooklyn lined with brown townhouses and black wrought-iron gates. It is snowing, and, with hands entwined, they walk slowly down the street where they were assaulted. Tom is wearing a khaki trenchcoat, slacks, and loafers. Snowflakes melt into the tight dark curls on his head. Jan is almost his height, her short bobbed hair moving softly as she walks. She is wearing a black leather jacket, a red scarf, and burnt orange cords. The broadness of her hips and softness of her face belie the tomboy flavor of her carriage and clothes, and it is hard to believe that she was mistaken for a gay man. But she was.

They were walking home, holding hands and engrossed with each 25 other. On the other side of the street, Jan saw a group of boys moving toward them. As the gang approached, Jan heard a distinct taunt meant for her and Tom: "Aw, look at the cute gay couple." Tom and Jan quickened their step, but it was too late. Before they could say anything, Tom was being punched in the face and slammed against a car. Jan ran toward Tom and the car, screaming desperately that Tom was her husband. Fists pummeled her face as well. Outnumbered and in fear for their lives, Tom yelled at Jan to please open her jacket and show their assailants that she was a woman. The beating subsided only when Jan was able to show her breasts.

For the *20/20* interview, Jan and Tom sat in the warmth of their living room, their infant son in Jan's lap. The interviewer asked them how they felt when people said they looked like a gay couple. "We used to laugh," they said. "But now we realize how heavy the implications are. Now we know what the gay community goes through. We had no idea how widespread it was. It's on every level."

Sadly, it *is* on every level. Enforced heterosexism and the pressure to conform to aggressive masculine and passive feminine roles place fag bashers and lesbian baiters in the same psychic prison with their victims, gay or straight. Until all children are free to realize their full potential, until all women and men are free from the stigma, threats, alienation, or violence that come from stepping outside their roles, we are all at risk.

The economic and ideological underpinnings of enforced heterosexism and sexism or any other form of systematic oppression are formidable foes and far too complex for the scope of this essay. It is important to remember, however, that bigots are natural allies and that poverty or the fear of it has the power to seduce us all into conformity. In Castro graffiti, *faggot* appears right next to *nigger* and *kike*. Race betrayal or any threat to the sanctimony of light-skinned privilege engenders no less a rage than gender betrayal, most especially when we have a great stake in the elusive privilege of proper gender roles or the right skin color. *Queer lover* and *fag hag* are cut from the same mold that gave us *nigger lover*, a mold forged by fears of change and a loss of privilege.

Unfortunately, our sacrifices to conformity rarely guarantee the privilege or protection we were promised. Lesbians, gay men, and bisexuals who have tried to pass know that. Heterosexuals who have been perceived to be gay know that. Those of us with a vision of tomorrow that goes beyond tolerance to a genuine celebration of humanity's diversity have innumerable fronts to fight on. Homophobia is one of them.

But how will this front be won? With a lot of help, and not easily. Challenges to homophobia and the rigidity of gender roles must go beyond the visible lesbian and gay movement. Lesbians, gay men, and bisexuals alone cannot defuse the power of stigmatization and the license it gives to frighten, wound, or kill. Literally millions of us are needed on this front, straight and gay alike. We invite any heterosexual unwilling to live with the damage that "real men" or "real women" messages wreak on them, on their children, and on lesbians, gay men, and bisexuals to join us. We ask that you not let queer jokes go unchallenged at work, at home, in the media, or anywhere. We ask that you foster in your children a genuine respect for themselves and their right to be who and what they wish to be, regardless of their gender. We ask that you embrace your daughter's desire to swing a bat or be a carpenter, that you nurture your son's efforts to express affection and sentiment. We ask that you teach your children how painful and destructive words like *faggot* or *bulldyke* are. We ask that you invite your lesbian, gay, and bisexual friends and relatives into the routine of your lives without demanding silence or discretion from them. We invite you to study our history, read the literature written by our people, patronize our businesses, come into our homes and neighborhoods. We ask that you give us your vote when we need it to protect our privacy or to elect open lesbians, gay men, and bisexuals to office. We ask that you stand with us in public demonstrations to demand our right to live as free people, without fear. We ask that you respect our dignity by acting to end the poison of homophobia.

Until individuals are free to choose their roles and be bound only by the limits of their own imagination, *faggot, dyke,* and *pervert* will continue to be playground words and adult weapons that hurt and limit far many more people than their intended victims. Whether we like it or not, the romance of virile men and dainty women, of Mother, Father, Dick, Jane, Sally, and Spot is doomed to extinction and dangerous in a world that can no longer meet the expectations conjured by history. There is much to be won and so little to lose in the realization of a world where the dignity of each person is worthy of celebration and protection. The struggle to end homophobia can and must be won, for all our sakes. Personhood is imminent.

30

ENGAGING THE TEXT

1. Do you think violent events like the ones described above are fairly common or quite rare? How aware of this problem are people in your community? How much attention have you seen paid to gay-bashing in the newspapers, on TV, in books or films, or in everyday conversation?

2. Vázquez waits a while to disclose that "Brian" and "Mickey" were actually straight men, but she *does* disclose this fact. Why does she wait? Why does she disclose it? Does the issue of antigay violence change in any way when we recognize that sometimes its victims are heterosexual?

3. Vázquez cites "gender betrayal" as a possible cause of antigay violence. Explain gender betrayal in your own words; discuss how it works and how well it explains the violence described in the narratives Vázquez recounts.

4. According to Vázquez, Suzanne Pharr links homophobia to misogyny, the hatred of women: the "lesbian" label, she says, can be used to threaten all women. Review and discuss this argument; then discuss how well it can be applied to men, as Vázquez suggests it might be.

5. Besides the threat of physical violence, how does homophobia place us *all* "at risk," according to Vázquez?

EXPLORING CONNECTIONS

6. To what extent does Vázquez's concept of "gender betrayal" (para. 16) explain the attitudes and behavior encountered by Kathleen Boatwright (p. 676)?

7. Vázquez suggests that we are imprisoned by "enforced heterosexism and the pressure to conform to aggressive masculine and passive feminine roles" (para. 27). How might advertising images contribute to this problem, according to the analysis of Jean Kilbourne (p. 417). What evidence, if any, do you find of ads working against conventional gender identities?

EXTENDING THE CRITICAL CONTEXT

8. Vázquez writes that "the institutional and ideological reinforcements of homophobia are myriad and deeply woven into our culture" (para. 15). Over a period of days, keep track of all references to gays, lesbians, or homosexuality in casual conversations, news reports, TV programs, and other media. To what extent do you agree with Vázquez that homophobia is deeply ingrained in our culture?

9. San Francisco, the city in which some of the incidents described took place, is known as one of the most tolerant in the United States. Research your own community's history of assaults on gay and lesbian people. You might begin by talking to gay and lesbian organizations; police or public health departments may also have pertinent information. Report to the class or write a formal paper presenting your findings.

10. Near the end of her essay, Vázquez lists a variety of ways that individuals can combat homophobia (para. 30). Write a journal entry assessing how easy or how difficult it would be for you to follow each of her suggestions, and why.

FURTHER CONNECTIONS

1. Compare the rhetorical strategies and effectiveness of any two of the selections in this chapter. What is each writer's purpose and what audience is he or she addressing? To what extent and how does each author appeal to readers' reason and emotions? What kind of persona does each writer project? What kinds of evidence does each author rely on? How persuasive or compelling do you find each selection, and why?

2. Research the issue of domestic violence. How is it defined? How prevalent is domestic violence nationwide, in your state, and in your community? What are the risk factors for abusers and their victims? Investigate the resources in your community that offer assistance to victims of domestic abuse: hotlines, shelters, organizations, and government agencies that provide counseling or legal aid. Do these services focus on punishing abusers or "curing" them? Write a paper evaluating the effectiveness of different approaches to protecting victims from abusive partners.

3. Research the status of women in the field or profession you plan to pursue. Are women's salaries and compensation comparable to those of men with similar credentials and experience? What is the ratio of women to men in the field as a whole, in entry-level positions, and in executive or high-status positions? Interview at least one woman in this line of work: In what ways, if any, does she feel that her work experience has differed from a man's? Report your findings to the class.

4. Title IX, the law mandating equal funding for women's sports at publicly funded schools, has been praised for opening new opportunities for women athletes and criticized for siphoning money away from some popular men's sports. Research the impact of Title IX on athletics programs at your college or university: How has the picture of women's and men's sports changed since 1972, the year Title IX was enacted? Have women's and men's athletics attained equality at your school?

5. Some religious groups argue that laws and policies that prohibit harassment of or discrimination against homosexuals infringe on their religious freedom. Investigate a specific case in which a religious organization has made this claim. What arguments have been advanced on both sides of the case? What values and assumptions underlie these arguments? What rights and freedoms are at stake for each party in the dispute?

5

Created Equal

The Myth of the Melting Pot

Antiracism March, photo by Eli Reed.

FAST FACTS

1. From colonial times to the Civil War, American governments derived more revenue from slave taxes than from any other source.

2. A white male born in 2003 has an average life expectancy of 75.3 years; a black male born in the same year has an average life expectancy of 69 years; the average lifespan for white and black women is 80.5 and 76.1 years, respectively.

3. In 2002, nearly three-quarters (74.5%) of white households and less than half of black (47.3%) and Latino (48.2%) households owned their own homes.

4. Nationally, 86% of whites live in neighborhoods where minorities make up less than 1% of the population.

5. Between 1980 and 2003, the number of interracial marriages in the United States more than tripled, to approximately 2.1 million.

6. As of the year 2005, more than 12% of Americans are foreign-born and over 19% speak a language other than English at home.

Sources: (1) Kevin Outterson, "Slave Taxes," in *Should America Pay? Slavery and the Raging Debate on Reparations*, ed. Raymond A. Winbush (New York: Amistad/Harper Collins, 2003), p. 135; (2) U.S. Department of Health and Human Services/CDC, *National Vital Statistics Reports* 54.14 (April 19, 2006); (3) U.S. Census Bureau, *Housing Vacancies and Home Ownership, 2002*; (4) PBS (www.pbs.org), "Race — The Power of an Illusion" — Background Readings; (5) Vincent N. Parrillo, *Diversity in America*, 2nd ed. (Thousand Oaks, CA: Pine Forge Press, 2005), p. 186; (6) U.S. Census Bureau, *2005 American Community Survey.*

THE MYTH OF THE MELTING POT predates the drafting of the U.S. Constitution. In 1782, a year before the Peace of Paris formally ended the Revolutionary War, J. Hector St. John de Crèvecoeur envisioned the young American republic as a crucible that would forge its disparate immigrant population into a vigorous new society with a grand future:

> What, then, is the American, this new man? He is neither an European, or the descendant of an European. . . . He is an American, who leaving behind him all his ancient prejudices and manners, receives new ones from the new mode of life he has embraced, the new government he obeys, and the new rank he holds. . . . Here individuals of all nations are melted into a new race of men, whose labours and posterity will one day cause great changes in the world.

Crèvecoeur's metaphor has remained a powerful ideal for many generations of American scholars, politicians, artists, and ordinary citizens.

Ralph Waldo Emerson, writing in his journal in 1845, celebrated the national vitality produced by the mingling of immigrant cultures: "In this continent — asylum of all nations, — the energy of . . . all the European tribes, — of the Africans, and of the Polynesians — will construct a new race, a new religion, a new state, a new literature." An English Jewish writer named Israel Zangwill, himself an immigrant, popularized the myth in his 1908 drama, *The Melting Pot.* In the play, the hero rhapsodizes, "Yes East and West, and North and South, the palm and the pine, the pole and the equator, the crescent and the cross — how the great Alchemist melts and fuses them with his purging flame! Here shall they all unite to build the Republic of Man and the Kingdom of God." The myth was perhaps most vividly dramatized, though, in a pageant staged by Henry Ford in the early 1920s. Decked out in the costumes of their native lands, Ford's immigrant workers sang traditional songs from their homelands as they danced their way into an enormous replica of a cast-iron pot. They then emerged from the other side wearing identical "American" business suits, waving minia-ture American flags, and singing "The Star-Spangled Banner."

The drama of becoming an American has deep roots: immigrants take on a new identity — and a new set of cultural myths — because they want to become members of the community, equal members with all the rights, responsibilities, and opportunities of their fellow citizens. The force of the melting pot myth lies in this implied promise that all Americans are indeed "created equal." However, the myth's promises of openness, harmony, unity, and equality were deceptive from the beginning. Crèvecoeur's exclu-sive concern with the mingling of *European* peoples (he lists the "English, Scotch, Irish, French, Dutch, Germans, and Swedes") utterly ignored the presence of some three-quarters of a million Africans and African Ameri-cans who then lived in this country, as well as the tribal peoples who had lived on the land for thousands of years before European contact. Crèvecoeur's vision of a country embracing "all nations" clearly applied only to northern European nations. Benjamin Franklin, in a 1751 essay, was more blunt: since Africa, Asia, and most of America were inhabited by dark-skinned people, he argued, the American colonies should consciously try to increase the white population and keep out the rest: "Why increase the Sons of Africa, by Planting them in America, where we have so fair an opportunity, by excluding Blacks and Tawneys, of increasing the lovely White . . . ?" If later writers like Emerson and Zangwill saw a more inclusive cultural mix as a source of hope and renewal for the United States, others throughout this country's history have, even more than Franklin, feared that mix as a threat.

The fear of difference underlies another, equally powerful American myth — the myth of racial supremacy. This is the negative counterpart of the melting pot ideal: instead of the equal and harmonious blending of cultures, it proposes a racial and ethnic hierarchy based on the "natural superiority" of Anglo-Americans. Under the sway of this myth, differences become signs of inferiority, and "inferiors" are treated as childlike or even subhuman. This myth has given rise to some of the most shameful passages in our national life: slavery, segregation, and lynching; the near extermination of tribal peoples and cultures; the denial of citizenship and constitutional rights to African Americans, American Indians, Chinese and Japanese immigrants; the brutal exploitation of Mexican and Asian laborers. The catalog of injustices is long and painful. The melting pot ideal itself has often masked the myth of racial and ethnic superiority. "Inferiors" are expected to "melt" into conformity with Anglo-American behavior and values. Henry Ford's pageant conveys the message that ethnic identity is best left behind — exchanged for something "better," more uniform, less threatening.

This chapter explores the interaction between these two related cultural myths: the myth of unity and the myth of difference and hierarchy. It examines how the categories of race and ethnicity are defined and how they operate to divide us. These issues become crucial as the population of the United States grows increasingly diverse. The selections here challenge you to reconsider the fate of the melting pot myth as we enter the era of multi-ethnic, multicultural America. Can we learn to accept and honor our differences?

The first half of the chapter focuses on the origins and lingering consequences of racism. It opens with a selection by Thomas Jefferson that unambiguously expresses the myth of racial superiority. Pondering the future of freed slaves, Jefferson concludes that because blacks "are inferior to whites in the endowments both of body and mind," they should be prevented from intermarrying and "staining the blood" of the superior race. Ellis Cose, in "Discharging a Debt," takes on the politically charged issue of reparations: he recounts two incidents from the 1920s in which white residents destroyed thriving black neighborhoods in their communities and details recent efforts to win restitution for the victims of these crimes. This prologue leads to a larger discussion of the argument that America owes a debt to blacks for the economic and psychic damage they have suffered as a result of 400 years of racial oppression. Surveying the most common psychological and sociological theories of prejudice, Vincent N. Parrillo provides a series of frameworks for understanding the roots of racial conflict. Studs Terkel's oral history "C. P. Ellis" at once reminds us of the persistence of racist beliefs and offers hope for change: this remarkable first-person account of Ellis's transformation from Klansman to union activist examines racism from the inside and shows how one man conquered his own bigotry. Next, two essays consider the difficulty — and the necessity — of dealing with race in our daily interactions. In "I'm Black, You're White, Who's Innocent?" Shelby Steele argues that the psychological need to feel innocent on the highly charged issue of race keeps us from honest dialogue; he proposes that African Americans take the initiative by ceasing to blame whites for the injustices of the past and by refusing to play the victim. Psychotherapist Paul L. Wachtel offers a different perspective, arguing that we must all directly face the problems of race in order to solve them, but that to do so we need a more nuanced vocabulary for discussing racial issues. A Visual Portfolio gives individual faces to abstractions like race and discrimination; the images challenge us to ponder the centrality of race in American culture and to rethink ways we "read" identity.

The second half of the chapter addresses the emerging myth of the "new melting pot." First, George M. Fredrickson presents an overview of ethnic relations in American history, showing how concepts of ethnic hierarchy, assimilation, pluralism, and separatism have shaped group identities and interactions over time. Rubén Martínez probes the personal, cultural, and political significance of the U.S.-Mexican border in "The Crossing," which focuses on his encounter with a seriously ill undocumented immigrant in the Sonoran desert of New Mexico. In his pointedly funny short story "Assimilation," Sherman Alexie introduces us to an American Indian woman who begins to question the meaning of her marriage to a white man. Legal scholar Kenji Yoshino challenges the "judicial bias toward assimilation" in American law; he argues that, for example, a court decision upholding a workplace ban on braided hair constitutes a subtle form of discrimination. Finally, in her poem "Child of the Americas," Aurora Levins Morales affirms both the value of her multicultural roots and the enduring power of the melting pot myth.

Sources

John Hope Franklin, *Race and History: Selected Essays*, 1938–1988. Baton Rouge: Louisiana State University Press, 1989, pp. 321–31.
Milton M. Gordon, *Assimilation in American Life: The Role of Race, Religion, and National Origins*. New York: Oxford University Press, 1964.
Itabari Njeri, "Beyond the Melting Pot." *Los Angeles Times*, January 13, 1991, pp. E1, E8–9.
Leonard Pitt, *We Americans*, vol. 2, 3rd ed. Dubuque: Kendall/Hunt, 1987.
Ronald Takaki, "Reflections on Racial Patterns in America." In *From Different Shores: Perspectives on Race and Ethnicity in America*, Ronald Takaki, ed. New York: Oxford University Press, 1987, pp. 26–37.

BEFORE READING

- Survey images in the popular media (newspapers, magazines, TV shows, movies, and pop music) for evidence of the myth of the melting pot. Do you find any figures in popular culture who seem to endorse the idea of a "new melting pot" in the United States? How closely do these images reflect your understanding of your own and other ethnic and racial groups? Explore these questions in a journal entry, then discuss in class.

- Alternatively, you might investigate the metaphors that are being used to describe racial and ethnic group relations or interactions between members of different groups on your campus and in your community. Consult local news sources and campus publications, and keep your ears open for conversations that touch on these issues. Do some freewriting about what you discover and compare notes with classmates.

- The frontispiece photo on page 481 was taken at an antiracism march. Why do you think that these people and this particular moment of the march caught the photographer's eye? What do the positions and expressions of the four main figures suggest about their feelings and concerns and about the cause they are marching for? Jot down your impressions and note the visual details that support your "reading" of the picture. Then compare your responses in small groups: How much consistency or variation do you find in your interpretations?

From *Notes on the State of Virginia*

THOMAS JEFFERSON

Thomas Jefferson is probably best known as the author of the Declaration of Independence. As third president of the United States (1801–1809), Thomas Jefferson (1743–1826) promoted westward expansion in the form of the Louisiana Purchase and the Lewis and Clark Expedition. In addition to his political career he was a scientist, architect, city planner (Washington, D.C.), and founder of the University of Virginia. This passage from his Notes on the State of Virginia *(1785) reveals a very different and, for many readers, shocking side of Jefferson's character — that of a slave owner and defender of white supremacy. Here he proposes that the new state of Virginia gradually phase out slavery rather than abolish it outright. He also recommends that all newly emancipated slaves be sent out of the state to form separate colonies, in part to prevent racial conflict and in part to prevent intermarriage with whites. Jefferson was not the first and was far from the last politician to advocate solving the nation's racial problems by removing African Americans from its boundaries. In 1862, the Great Emancipator himself, Abraham Lincoln, called a delegation of black leaders to the White House to enlist their support in establishing a colony for African Americans in Central America. Congress had appropriated money for this project, but it was abandoned after the governments of Honduras, Nicaragua, and Costa Rica protested the plan.*

Many of the laws which were in force during the monarchy being relative merely to that form of government, or inculcating principles inconsistent with republicanism, the first assembly which met after the establishment of the commonwealth appointed a committee to revise the whole code, to reduce it into proper form and volume, and report it to the assembly. This work has been executed by three gentlemen,[1] and reported. . . . The following are the most remarkable alterations proposed:

To change the rules of descent, so as that the lands of any person dying intestate shall be divisible equally among all his children, or other representatives, in equal degree.

To make slaves distributable among the next of kin, as other movables. . . .

To emancipate all slaves born after the passing [of] the act. The bill reported by the revisers does not itself contain this proposition; but an amendment containing it was prepared, to be offered to the legislature whenever the bill should be taken up, and farther directing, that they should continue with their parents to a certain age, then to be brought up, at the public expense, to tillage, arts, or sciences, according to their geniuses, till the females should be eighteen, and the males twenty-one years of age, when they should be colonized to such place as the circumstances of the time should render most proper, sending them out with arms, implements of household and of the handicraft arts, seeds, pairs of the useful domestic animals, &c., to declare them a free and independent people, and extend to them our alliance and protection, till they have acquired strength; and to send vessels at the same time to other parts of the world for an equal number of white inhabitants; to induce them to migrate hither, proper encouragements were to be proposed. It will probably be asked, Why not retain and incorporate the blacks into the State, and thus save the expense of supplying by importation of white settlers, the vacancies they will leave? Deep-rooted prejudices entertained by the whites; ten thousand recollections, by the blacks, of the injuries they have sustained; new provocations; the real distinctions which nature has made; and many other circumstances, will divide us into parties, and produce convulsions, which will probably never end but in the extermination of the one or the other race. To these objections, which are political, may be added others, which are physical and moral. The first difference which strikes us is that of color. Whether the black of the negro resides in the reticular membrane between the skin and scarf-skin, or in the scarf-skin itself; whether it proceeds from the color of the blood, the color of the bile, or from that of some other secretion, the difference is fixed in nature, and is as real as if its seat and cause were better known to us. And is this difference of no importance? Is it not the foundation of a greater or less share of beauty in the two races? Are not the fine mixtures of red and white, the expressions of every passion by greater or less suffusions of color in the one, preferable to that eternal monotony, which reigns in the countenances,

[1]*executed by three gentlemen:* Jefferson was one of the three men who wrote this set of proposed revisions to the legal code of Virginia.

that immovable veil of black which covers the emotions of the other race? Add to these, flowing hair, a more elegant symmetry of form, their own judgment in favor of the whites, declared by their preference of them, as uniformly as is the preference of the Oranootan[2] for the black woman over those of his own species. The circumstance of superior beauty, is thought worthy of attention in the propagation of our horses, dogs, and other domestic animals; why not in that of man? Besides those of color, figure, and hair, there are other physical distinctions proving a difference of race. They have less hair on the face and body. They secrete less by the kidneys, and more by the glands of the skin, which gives them a very strong and disagreeable odor. This greater degree of transpiration, renders them more tolerant of heat, and less so of cold than the whites. Perhaps, too, a difference of structure in the pulmonary apparatus, which a late ingenious experimentalist has discovered to be the principal regulator of animal heat, may have disabled them from extricating, in the act of inspiration, so much of that fluid from the outer air, or obliged them in expiration, to part with more of it. They seem to require less sleep. A black after hard labor through the day, will be induced by the slightest amusements to sit up till midnight, or later, though knowing he must be out with the first dawn of the morning. They are at least as brave, and more adventuresome. But this may perhaps proceed from a want of forethought, which prevents their seeing a danger till it be present. When present, they do not go through it with more coolness or steadiness than the whites. They are more ardent after their female; but love seems with them to be more an eager desire, than a tender delicate mixture of sentiment and sensation. Their griefs are transient. Those numberless afflictions, which render it doubtful whether heaven has given life to us in mercy or in wrath, are less felt, and sooner forgotten with them. In general, their existence appears to participate more of sensation than reflection. To this must be ascribed their disposition to sleep when abstracted from their diversions, and unemployed in labor. An animal whose body is at rest, and who does not reflect, must be disposed to sleep of course. Comparing them by their faculties of memory, reason, and imagination, it appears to me that in memory they are equal to the whites; in reason much inferior, as I think one could scarcely be found capable of tracing and comprehending the investigations of Euclid; and that in imagination they are dull, tasteless, and anomalous. It would be unfair to follow them to Africa for this investigation. We will consider them here, on the same stage with the whites, and where the facts are not apochryphal on which a judgment is to be formed. It will be right to make great allowances for the difference of condition, of education, of conversation, of the sphere in which they move. Many millions of them have been brought to, and born in America. Most of them, indeed, have been confined to tillage, to their own homes, and their own society; yet many have

[2]*Oranootan:* Orangutan.

been so situated, that they might have availed themselves of the conversation of their masters; many have been brought up to the handicraft arts, and from that circumstance have always been associated with the whites. Some have been liberally educated, and all have lived in countries where the arts and sciences are cultivated to a considerable degree, and all have had before their eyes samples of the best works from abroad. The Indians, with no advantages of this kind, will often carve figures on their pipes not destitute of design and merit. They will crayon out an animal, a plant, or a country, so as to prove the existence of a germ in their minds which only wants cultivation. They astonish you with strokes of the most sublime oratory; such as prove their reason and sentiment strong, their imagination glowing and elevated. But never yet could I find that a black had uttered a thought above the level of plain narration; never saw even an elementary trait of painting or sculpture. In music they are more generally gifted than the whites with accurate ears for tune and time, and they have been found capable of imagining a small catch.[3] Whether they will be equal to the composition of a more extensive run of melody, or of complicated harmony, is yet to be proved. Misery is often the parent of the most affecting touches in poetry. Among the blacks is misery enough, God knows, but no poetry. Love is the peculiar œstrum of the poet. Their love is ardent, but it kindles the senses only, not the imagination. Religion, indeed, has produced a Phyllis Whately [*sic*];[4] but it could not produce a poet. The compositions published under her name are below the dignity of criticism. The heroes of the Dunciad[5] are to her, as Hercules to the author of that poem. Ignatius Sancho[6] has approached nearer to merit in composition; yet his letters do more honor to the heart than the head. They breathe the purest effusions of friendship and general philanthropy, and show how great a degree of the latter may be compounded with strong religious zeal. He is often happy in the turn of his compliments, and his style is easy and familiar, except when he affects a Shandean[7] fabrication of words. But his imagination is wild and extravagant, escapes incessantly from every

---

[3]The instrument proper to them is the Banjar, which they brought hither from Africa, and which is the original of the guitar, its chords being precisely the four lower chords of the guitar. [Author's note]

[4]*Phyllis Whately:* Phillis Wheatley (175?–1784) was born in Africa but transported to the United States and sold as a slave when she was a young child. Her *Poems on Various Subjects, Religious and Moral* (1773) was the first book of poetry to be published by an African American.

[5]*the heroes of the Dunciad:* In the mock epic poem *The Dunciad* (1728), English satirist Alexander Pope (1688–1744) lampoons his literary rivals as fools and dunces.

[6]*Ignatius Sancho:* Born on a slave ship, Ignatius Sancho (1729–1780) became a servant in the homes of several English aristocrats, where he educated himself and became acquainted with some of the leading writers and artists of the period. He later became a grocer in London and devoted himself to writing. His letters were collected and published in 1782.

[7]*Shandean:* In the style of Laurence Sterne's comic novel, *The Life and Opinions of Tristram Shandy* (1758–1766). Sancho admired Sterne's writing and corresponded regularly with him.

restraint of reason and taste, and, in the course of its vagaries, leaves a tract of thought as incoherent and eccentric, as is the course of a meteor through the sky. His subjects should often have led him to a process of sober reasoning; yet we find him always substituting sentiment for demonstration. Upon the whole, though we admit him to the first place among those of his own color who have presented themselves to the public judgment, yet when we compare him with the writers of the race among whom he lived and particularly with the epistolary class in which he has taken his own stand, we are compelled to enroll him at the bottom of the column. This criticism supposes the letters published under his name to be genuine, and to have received amendment from no other hand; points which would not be of easy investigation. The improvement of the blacks in body and mind, in the first instance of their mixture with the whites, has been observed by every one, and proves that their inferiority is not the effect merely of their condition of life. . . .

The opinion that they are inferior in the faculties of reason and imagi-   5
nation, must be hazarded with great diffidence. To justify a general conclusion, requires many observations, even where the subject may be submitted to the anatomical knife, to optical glasses, to analysis by fire or by solvents. How much more then where it is a faculty, not a substance, we are examining; where it eludes the research of all the senses; where the conditions of its existence are various and variously combined; where the effects of those which are present or absent bid defiance to calculation; let me add too, as a circumstance of great tenderness, where our conclusion would degrade a whole race of men from the rank in the scale of beings which their Creator may perhaps have given them. To our reproach it must be said, that though for a century and a half we have had under our eyes the races of black and of red men, they have never yet been viewed by us as subjects of natural history. I advance it, therefore, as a suspicion only, that the blacks, whether originally a distinct race, or made distinct by time and circumstances, are inferior to the whites in the endowments both of body and mind. It is not against experience to suppose that different species of the same genus, or varieties of the same species, may possess different qualifications. Will not a lover of natural history then, one who views the gradations in all the races of animals with the eye of philosophy, excuse an effort to keep those in the department of man as distinct as nature has formed them? This unfortunate difference of color, and perhaps of faculty, is a powerful obstacle to the emancipation of these people. Many of their advocates, while they wish to vindicate the liberty of human nature, are anxious also to preserve its dignity and beauty. Some of these, embarrassed by the question, "What further is to be done with them?" join themselves in opposition with those who are actuated by sordid avarice only. Among the Romans emancipation required but one effort. The slave, when made free, might mix with, without staining the blood of his master. But with us a second is necessary, unknown to history. When freed, he is to be removed beyond the reach of mixture.

ENGAGING THE TEXT

1. Jefferson proposes colonizing — that is, sending away — all newly emancipated slaves and declaring them "a free and independent people" (para. 4). In what ways would their freedom and independence continue to be limited, according to this proposal?

2. Jefferson predicts that racial conflict in the United States "will probably never end but in the extermination of the one or the other race" (para. 4). Which of the divisive issues he mentions, if any, are still sources of conflict today? Given the history of race relations from Jefferson's time to our own, do you think his pessimism was justified? Why or why not?

3. Jefferson presents what seems on the surface to be a systematic and logical catalog of the differences he sees between blacks and whites; he then attempts to demonstrate the "natural" superiority of whites based on these differences. Working in pairs or small groups, look carefully at his observations and the conclusions he draws from them. What flaws do you find in his analysis?

EXPLORING CONNECTIONS

4. Consider the picture of Jefferson's descendants on page 82. Write a journal entry or essay comparing the image of Jefferson you received in American history classes to the impression you get from the photo and from the passage above. How do you account for the differences?

5. Working in groups, write scripts for an imaginary meeting between Jefferson and Malcolm X (p. 210) and present them to the class. After each group has acted out its scenario, compare the different versions of the meeting. What does each script assume about the motives and character of the two men?

EXTENDING THE CRITICAL CONTEXT

6. Read the Declaration of Independence and compare Jefferson's most famous document to the lesser-known passage reprinted here. How do the purposes of the two texts differ? What ideas and principles, if any, do they have in common, and where do they conflict? (The text of the Declaration is reprinted as an appendix in most unabridged dictionaries and is available online at http://lcweb2.loc.gov/const/declar.html.)

7. Write a letter to Jefferson responding to this selection and explaining your point of view. What would you tell him about how and why attitudes have changed between his time and ours?

8. Influenced by the heroic image of Jefferson as a champion of freedom and democracy, civic leaders have named libraries, schools, and other public institutions after him for the last two hundred years. Debate whether or not it is appropriate to honor Jefferson in this way given the opinions expressed in this passage.

Discharging a Debt

ELLIS COSE

In the years following the Civil War, Congress debated many proposals that would have taken land from large southern plantations and redistributed it to former slaves as compensation for their unpaid labor under slavery. None of these plans was adopted. In a few states, such land grants were initially made, only to be quickly rescinded by the federal government. Since then, activists have mounted a number of unsuccessful attempts to win economic restitution for the former slaves and their descendants. The reparations movement has generated intense controversy: critics contend that the quest for reparations is too late and too divisive to be worthwhile; proponents debate what form restitution might take and how it could be fairly administered.

In his most recent book, Bone to Pick: Of Forgiveness, Reconciliation, Reparation, and Revenge *(2004), Ellis Cose places slavery reparations in a global context, discussing Germany's payment of restitution to victims of the Holocaust, New Zealand's attempts to compensate the native Maori population for broken treaties and confiscated lands, and South Africa's reconciliation movement following the demise of racial apartheid. In this selection from the book, Cose examines American precedents for reparations: the successful campaign by Japanese Americans for restitution and a government apology for their internment during World War II and the belated acknowledgement of two devastating attacks on African American communities in Tulsa, Oklahoma, and Rosewood, Florida, during the 1920s. Cose (b. 1951), an award-winning journalist, has been a contributing editor at* Newsweek *for over twenty years. His other books on race include* The Envy of the World *(2002),* Color-Blind: Seeing Beyond Race in a Race-Obsessed World *(1997), and* The Rage of a Privileged Class *(1994). He also authored the Rockefeller Foundation report,* Beyond Brown v. Board: The Final Battle for Excellence in American Education *(2004) and published a history of American immigration,* A Nation of Strangers *(1992).*

The truth of what happened to Japanese Americans during World War II was never much in dispute. Some 120,000 were arrested in 1942 and held in concentration camps, supposedly in the national interest. Supreme Court Associate Justice William O. Douglas, concurring in *Kiyoshi Hirabayashi v. U.S.*,[1] 1943, bluntly made the case:

---

[1]*Kiyoshi Hirabayashi v. U.S.*: U.S. Supreme Court case decided in June 1943, which upheld the use of wartime curfews against American citizens of Japanese descent.

After the disastrous bombing of Pearl Harbor the military had a grave problem on its hands. The threat of Japanese invasion of the west coast was not fanciful but real. The presence of many thousands of aliens and citizens of Japanese ancestry in or near to the key points along that coastline aroused special concern in those charged with the defense of the country. . . . If the military were right in their belief that among citizens of Japanese ancestry there was an actual or incipient fifth column, we were indeed faced with the imminent threat of a dire emergency. We must credit the military with as much good faith in that belief as we would any other public official acting pursuant to his duties. We cannot possibly know all the facts which lay behind that decision.

As the war wound down, the country realized its mistake. In December 1944, with a Supreme Court decision on the question pending, the military reversed itself and declared that detainees, as of January 1945, could return home. The last of the camps was shut down in 1946. But nearly half a century elapsed before the U.S. Congress made amends.

Like the Holocaust victims and the Maori treaty claimants, the Japanese Americans benefited from a change in attitude and from the rise of a human rights culture. They also benefited from the civil rights movement, which as Mitchell Maki et al. observed in *Achieving the Impossible Dream,* "taught the lessons, provided the energy, and instilled the inspiration through which the modern redress struggle emerged."

Throughout the 1970s, as activists made the case to various constituencies, support grew for the idea of restitution. Yvonne Braithwaite Burke, chair of the Congressional Black Caucus, pledged her support to the efforts in 1975. The Japanese American Citizens League announced its Reparations Campaign Committee the following year.

Rather than pursue reparations directly, advocates and their congressional allies decided to proceed in stages. They came up with legislation to create a Commission on Wartime Relocation and Internment of Civilians to study the issue. The legislation passed in 1980, and President Jimmy Carter signed it into law. The commission's report, issued in February 1983, was an indictment of U.S. treatment of Japanese Americans during the war:

> This policy of exclusion, removal, and detention was executed against 120,000 people without individual review, and exclusion was continued virtually without regard for their demonstrated loyalty to the United States. . . .
>
> All this was done despite the fact that not a single documented act of espionage, sabotage, or fifth column activity was committed by an American citizen of Japanese ancestry or by a resident Japanese alien on the West Coast. . . .
>
> The broad historical causes which shaped these decisions were race prejudice, war hysteria, and a failure of political leadership. Widespread ignorance of Japanese-Americans contributed to a policy conceived in haste and executed in an atmosphere of fear and anger at Japan.

A grave injustice was done to American citizens and resident aliens of Japanese ancestry who, without individual review or any probative evidence against them, were excluded, removed, and detained by the United States during World War II.

Payments began in October 1990 at an emotionally charged ceremony, featuring Attorney General Richard Thornburgh, in the Great Hall of Justice.

"By finally admitting a wrong, a nation does not destroy its integrity, but rather reinforces the sincerity of its commitment to the Constitution, and hence to its people. In forcing us to reexamine our history, you have made us only stronger and more proud," declared Thornburgh at the ceremony as he handed out $20,000 checks and a letter of apology from President George Bush.

There was "more than a tinge of irony to the letters — and a special urgency to yesterday's ceremony," wrote *Washington Post* reporter Michael Isikoff, who went on to observe: "Since President Ronald Reagan signed the law more than two years ago, funding for the reparations has wound slowly through the congressional appropriations process and money became available only with the start of the new fiscal year last week. In the meantime, 1,600 survivors of the camps have died and thousands more are ailing, unable to enjoy the funds they are slated to receive."

Congressman Robert Matsui, who was six months old when he was interned along with his parents, believes the process that led to the payment of reparations was beneficial in itself. "There was . . . a catharsis in the community that grew from the very process of strategizing the redress legislation and seeing it through to fruition. Japanese Americans in their sixties, seventies, and eighties and some even older — many of whom had never voted — got involved in testifying, letter writing, and lobbying. Many of them had never been able to talk about their agonizing experiences, even with one another, let alone air their pain in public," wrote Matsui in the foreword to *Achieving the Impossible Dream.*

Matsui also confided that he had only realized as an adult that he still 10 carried scars from his incarceration — scars that cut to the core of his being, scars that as a child had made him ashamed to acknowledge what his family had endured. He saw the restitution, and the acknowledgment and apology that came with it, as society's way of "liberating future generations" from the trauma and shame that he had borne.

Survivors of another American tragedy, similarly shrouded in silence, have recently told their story to the world. But unlike the story of Japanese internment, which was widely known and always recognized as part of the chronicle of World War II, the tragedy that struck Tulsa, Oklahoma, was until recently largely unknown. That incident had been swept into a corner of historical neglect and lost in the muddle of misremembered things to which shameful episodes are so often consigned.

Thanks to a recent bounty of articles and books, and a formal investigation by the Oklahoma Commission to Study the Tulsa Race Riot of 1921, the major facts are no longer in question. On the morning of May 31, 1921, Tulsa had a thriving black community called Greenwood — a community so prosperous that it was known as the Black Wall Street of America, one of the few places in America where blacks could dream of success on a grand scale. By the time the sun went down the following evening, Black Wall Street was a smoldering mass of burned-out houses, dead bodies, and devastated dreams. Between seventy-five and three hundred people were killed; the true number will probably never be known because of the cover-up that followed. More than one thousand homes were razed. "A mob destroyed thirty-five square blocks of the African-American community during the evening of May 31, through the afternoon of June 1, 1921. It was a tragic, infamous moment in Oklahoma and the nation's history. The worst civil disturbance since the Civil War," wrote State Representative Don Ross in the Tulsa riot commission report.

For years, the episode was essentially forgotten, left out of America's history books and purged from the nation's collective memory, not so much out of shame but because, from the perspective of white Tulsa, it was all so unseemly — and so bad for the city's image.

The series of events began with an apparently bogus complaint that a black man had attempted to assault a white woman in an elevator. The young man was arrested and an inflammatory newspaper article appeared. "Negro Assaults a White Girl!" was the headline. Perhaps there was also an angry editorial. It remains unclear if the editorial, supposedly headlined "To Lynch a Negro Tonight," was actually published, since the editorials from that day's *Tulsa Tribune*, presumably in a bid to salvage the paper's reputation, were systematically destroyed.

Mobilized by reports of the assault, whites showed up outside the jail   15 en masse, amid much talk of lynching. Armed blacks, fearful that yet another lynching was about to take place, headed downtown, intent on protecting the young man in custody. The sheriff pledged not to give the man to the mob and convinced the anxious blacks to return home. The whites, incensed at the blacks' temerity in coming downtown *armed no less,* worked themselves into a frenzy. They grabbed whatever weapons they could find. Some broke into and raided gun shops. Armed with rifles, shotguns, pistols, kerosene, even machine guns, and fueled by liquor and rage, they laid siege to Greenwood. The National Guard was called in and became the rioters' military auxiliary. At one point airplanes appeared in the sky. As James Hirsch reported in *Riot and Remembrance:*

> Exactly what they did has been debated ever since but numerous black witnesses have said the aircraft were used to assault Greenwood: pilots either dropped incendiary devices like "turpentine balls" and dynamite or used rifles to strafe people from the sky. If true, Tulsa was the first

U.S. city to suffer an aerial assault. But police officials say the planes were used only to monitor the fires and to locate refugees. . . . Even if the planes were not used for offensive purposes, their presence emphasized the total-war atmosphere of the raid and seared another harrowing image into many blacks' memories.

Greenwood's residents fought heroically to save their homes; but they never stood a chance. The mob burned their community to the ground. As Tim Madigan reported in *The Burning,* "Panoramic photographs of the decimation bore a haunting resemblance to those from Nagasaki and Hiroshima a quarter-century later: Thirty-five square blocks of the Negro community lay almost completely in ruin, save for hundreds of outhouses and a few isolated residences. As the whites had moved north on June 1, they put the torch to more than 1,115 Negro homes (314 more were looted, but not burned), five hotels, thirty-one restaurants, four drugstores, eight doctors' offices, the new Dunbar School, two dozen grocery stores, the Negro hospital, the public library, and even a dozen churches, including the community's most magnificent new edifice, Mount Zion Baptist Church." And later, when the smoke cleared, city officials charged the blacks with inciting the riot.

Subsequently, black property owners filed some $4 million in claims. All were denied. Over a hundred lawsuits filed by blacks following the disturbance were also dismissed by Oklahoma courts. Nothing was provided for the destruction of the community, though the city did approve two claims exceeding $5,000 to white gun shop owners for ammunition and weaponry stolen in the heat of the riot.

The cover-up that followed the massacre is almost as mind-boggling as the riot itself. For much of Oklahoma, life quickly went back to normal. People pretended the upheaval had never happened; and over time most people convinced themselves that it had not. When the riot commission's report was released in February 2001, there was a sense that Tulsa was finally ready to acknowledge what had happened and to make appropriate amends. The report itself contained an unabashed endorsement of reparations.

"The riot proclaimed that there were two Oklahomas; that one claimed the right to push down, push out, and push under the other; and that it had the power to do so," proclaimed the report, before delivering the kicker to the sermon:

> That is what the Tulsa race riot has been all about for so long afterwards, why it has lingered not as a past event but lived as a present entity. It kept on saying that there remained two Oklahomas; that one claimed the right to be dismissive of, ignorant of, and oblivious to the other; and that it had the power to do that.
>
> That is why the Tulsa race riot can be about something else. It can be about making two Oklahomas one — but only if we understand that this is what reparation is all about. Because the riot is both symbolic and singular, reparations become both singular and symbolic, too. Compelled not legally by courts but extended freely by choice, they

say that individual acts of reparation will stand as symbols that fully acknowledge and finally discharge a collective responsibility.

Because we must face it: There is no way but by government to represent the collective, and there is no way but by reparations to make real the responsibility.

Does this commission have specific recommendations about whether or not reparations can or should be made and the appropriate methods? Yes, it surely does. . . .

Reparations are the right thing to do.

In the prologue he penned to the commission's report, Ross was even   20 more forceful:

> There was murder, false imprisonment, forced labor, a cover-up, and local precedence for restitution. . . . The preponderance of the information demands what was promised. Whether it was Ku Klux Klan instigated, land speculators' conspiracy, inspired by yellow journalism, or random acts, it happened. Justice demands a closure as it did with Japanese Americans and Holocaust victims of Germany. It is a moral obligation. Tulsa was likely the first city in the [nation] to be bombed from the air. There was a precedent of payments to at least two white victims of the riot. The issue today is what government entity should provide financial repair to the survivors and the condemned community that suffered under vigilante violence? The Report tells the story, let justice point the finger and begin the reconciliation!

In *Riot and Remembrance,* published in 2002, author James Hirsch anticipated a happy ending. He congratulated the city on breaking the "culture of silence" and called Tulsa "a model of how a city sought redemption."

Not quite. Not yet.

As I write these words, in August 2003, survivors of the Tulsa riot and descendants who lost property have filed a lawsuit against the State of Oklahoma, the City of Tulsa, Tulsa's Police Department, and Tulsa's police chief. They hope that lawsuit will win them the compensation the city and state did not see fit to pay. The lawyers' complaint takes note of the recommendations of the commission and of the widespread expectation that those recommendations would be followed: "Instead, it appears that despite the concurrence in and acknowledgment of the facts establishing their complicity in the Riot and its consequences, the state and municipality have decided to wait for the survivors, all of them in excess of eighty years old, to die off so that the problem will 'silently' pass away."

Don Ross, the state representative who was instrumental in the creation of the riot commission, retired in 2002, after twenty years in the state legislature. When we spoke in July 2003, he was not at all happy with how things had turned out. The city, he said, had dug in its heels "and the prevailing attitude about the riot is as it was in 1921 — to ignore it, for it to go away, to do nothing." He was once hopeful that things would not be so, that there would, at the very least, be a memorial museum commemorating the losses of the riot. There was even a bond issue that he thought might fund the museum. But that was before lawmakers relying on polling data decided that the public — at least the white public — was not particularly in favor of the idea. He accuses the city of using the threat of the survivors' lawsuit as an excuse for digging in: "There's no positive sign that anything's going to be done. . . . I saw [the commission report] as a way to bring the two communities together." But Tulsa, as he sees it, responded with: "We won't give them anything."

Michael Hausfeld, a partner in the Washington law firm Cohen, Milstein, 25 Hausfeld & Toll, is working with an array of lawyers — most notably Charles Ogletree, a famous civil rights and defense attorney who teaches at Harvard Law School — to make sure that "We won't" is not Tulsa's final answer. Compact, balding, with wire-rimmed glasses, Hausfeld projects intensity and intelligence. The suit against Tulsa and Oklahoma, he acknowledged, faced "formidable legal obstacles." The statute of limitations, in particular, would be difficult to get around.

Such statutes are designed to ensure that people don't do precisely what Hausfeld had done: walk into court with a claim decades after the fact when memories have faded, witnesses have died, and the likelihood of establishing liability is all but nil. Nonetheless, Hausfeld felt there were compelling reasons — just as there were with the Holocaust restitution cases — that the claims should go forward.

The essence of the argument is that Oklahoma was not disposed to entertain such suits from blacks at the time the suits ideally should have been filed. The black community well understood the futility of trying to fight the system in the 1920s. How could they expect justice from a grand jury that had already blamed "bad Negroes" for the riot, a grand jury that was on record ridiculing in racist language the idea that Negroes had the same rights as whites? It would have been not only futile to argue the case back then but also dangerous. "The entire community had been obliterated." There could not possibly have been a more hostile or "intimidating environment." In the wake of the massacre, the victims were understandably not particularly inclined to try to exercise their supposed — yet elusive — rights, certainly not before the very people and institutions that had just tried to destroy them. They were more concerned with trying to pull their lives together as they sought safety in invisibility.

Even those who had the faith and the courage to bring claims, argued Hausfeld, faced yet another hurdle: "fraudulent concealment." There was a wholesale cover-up on the part of the state, a decision to destroy, deny, or tamper with the evidence claimants would need to wage a successful legal fight.

Hausfeld had yet another argument for why the statute of limitations should not apply: "With mass tragedies, time gives you more information, not less." The Greenwood massacre was not just a random, violent incident; it was the destruction of an entire community, of a culture, of a way of life.

Such a titanic trauma could not be assessed as if it were some ordinary event. Memories did not necessarily fade over time. Nor did evidence evaporate. Indeed, history brought a certain clarity and perspective to such atrocities. So the very rationale for the statute of limitations became significantly less compelling when confronted with the reality of a Greenwood.

Hausfeld was confident the legal arguments were strong; he was less   30 certain about the political will to do right. He found it strange and disturbing that, even when faced with a suit, Tulsa was dragging its heels. "No one has sat down with us to say, 'What do you really want?'" Hausfeld said, just before he hopped on a plane to Tulsa in late summer 2003.

Oklahoma's response was in stark contrast to that of Florida, which also saw a black community destroyed by a frenzied white mob. A small all-black town of about two hundred people in north Florida, Rosewood was attacked in January 1923 after (what else?) an unidentified black man supposedly sexually assaulted a white woman. Not only were several residents killed, but the community was also totally destroyed. The homes were torched, property was stolen, and the inhabitants were chased into the wilderness. Following the rampage, Rosewood's black residents disappeared, leaving their burned-out homes and land behind. As in Tulsa, officials found no reason to prosecute any rioters. And, as in Tulsa, the entire shameful episode was forgotten as Rosewood, already destroyed, literally vanished from history — until 1982, when a reporter for the *St. Petersburg Times* stumbled upon the story. The resulting article spurred some national notice. And a decade later a group of survivors approached the state legislature, demanding a memorial and restitution.

The story of a vengeance-crazed white mob destroying a black town struck many Floridians as an outrageous fabrication. The legislature commissioned a study from a team of researchers at Florida universities to get to the truth. That report, released in December 1993, was a hard-hitting denunciation of Florida officials and an unabashed brief for the Rosewood survivors:

> We believe that Sheriff Walker failed to control local events and to request proper assistance from Governor Hardee when events moved beyond his control. While Hardee condemned the violence and ordered a special prosecutor to conduct a grand jury investigation, he did so (more than a month had passed) only after black residents were forced to leave Rosewood and their property was destroyed.
>
> The failure of elected white officials to take forceful actions to protect the safety and property of local black residents was part of a pattern in the state and throughout the region. . . .
>
> Like the racial violence in Ocoee, Perry, and numerous other communities throughout Florida and the South during this era, Rosewood was a tragedy of American democracy and the American legal system. In all these incidents, alleged assaults against white women were sufficient to warrant the abandonment of the American justice system. The need to protect southern white women was seen as sufficient to

justify racial violence and oppression. When black resistance was added to an alleged assault upon a white woman then elements of southern society believed retribution against the entire black community was warranted. Far too many whites believed an example had to be set so that other black communities throughout Florida understood that such resistance to southern racial mores would not be tolerated. We conclude that by their failure to restrain the mob and to uphold the legal due process, the white leaders of the state and country were willing to tolerate such behavior by white citizens.

With the report in hand, legislators passed the Rosewood Compensation Act, which provided for scholarships and awarded nine survivors of the so-called Rosewood massacre $150,000 apiece. In 1997, director John Singleton released a movie chronicling the massacre. . . .

If success in winning reparations for historical wrongs is largely about politics, then what about the efforts of Americans to get reparations for slavery and its aftermath?

The basic argument is clear as rainwater: *Slavery was a crime as*   35
horrible as any imaginable. People were tortured, enslaved, and unfairly deprived of the fruits of their labor. They were denied the right to hand down any appreciable assets. And their descendants, who were promised freedom and forty acres, were lynched, segregated, discriminated against, and in virtually every way excluded from enjoying the full fruits of freedom. They never got their land. And they only recently have been given the opportunity to earn anything approximating fair compensation. Hence a debt is owed.

It is the argument that Martin Lurther King Jr. made in a *Playboy* magazine interview in 1965: "Can any fair-minded citizen deny that the Negro has been deprived? Few people reflect that for two centuries the Negro was enslaved, and robbed of any wages — potential accrued wealth which would have been the legacy of his descendants. *All* of America's wealth today could not adequately compensate its Negroes for his centuries of exploitation and humiliation."

Some are now saying that time has finally arrived to begin paying off that debt. Raymond A. Winbush, director of the Institute for Urban Research at Morgan State University, notes that this is not the first era in which the demand has been made. It was made shortly after the Civil War, and with the dawn of Marcus Garvey's brand of Black Nationalism, in the early part of the twentieth century.

"Why is it that Japanese Americans received an apology and compensatory measures . . . but Black Americans in all but a few instances have been unsuccessful in their efforts for remedies to the crimes inflicted upon them? Why do Jews continue to litigate successfully for and receive billions of dollars from nations and corporations nearly sixty years after the Holocaust . . . yet African Americans are subjected to paternalistic rejections of their movement for reparations for 350 years of enslavement and domestic apartheid?

I believe it is because the history of Black/white relations in this country is so long and sordid that reparations for damages done . . . would call for an enormous upheaval of the social fabric of the United States unmatched even by *Brown v. Board*," writes Winbush in *Should America Pay?*

Every year since 1989, Congressman John Conyers has introduced legislation asking, so far without success, for creation of a commission to study the question of reparations for African Americans. The commission, similar in concept to the body that recommended redress for Japanese Americans interned during World War II, would be charged with documenting the lingering impact of the institution that Conyers believes continues to wreak havoc on black life.

In *Black Wealth/White Wealth* social scientist Melvin L. Oliver and   40 Thomas M. Shapiro provide a glimpse of what such an exhaustive study might show. After reviewing reams of historical and economic data, they conclude that whites, at every income level, possess several times more wealth than blacks. They believe that the majority of the difference — perhaps three-quarters of it — can be explained by America's history of discrimination and "racialized" policies, beginning with the slave trade: "Slaves were by law not able to own property or accumulate assets. In contrast, no matter how poor whites were, they had the right — if they were males, that is . . . to buy land, enter into contracts, own businesses, and develop wealth assets that could build equity and economic self-sufficiency for themselves and their families." Blacks, who could not accumulate such riches, also "confronted a world that systematically thwarted any attempts to economically better their lives." This "inheritance of accumulated disadvantages over generations," argue the authors, continues to undermine the economic well-being of African Americans. They see a strong (though not politically plausible) case for reparations for black Americans. . . .

No country, no people, no regime willingly accepts the blame for having done horrible things, along with the responsibility for trying to repair damaged lives and replace confiscated or stolen goods. And once race enters the room, what was already a difficult conversation becomes virtually impossible. While one side wants to talk about how to settle a debt, the other is denying that any debt is due: *I didn't own slaves, why should I pay? My ancestors weren't even in this country when your people were enslaved. Wouldn't you have been worse off without slavery? At least you are now a citizen of the United States. Yes, some bad things happened, but that was long, long ago: Can't you just get over it?*

"To correct a historical wrong — be it for slavery, or segregation, for discrimination or exclusion — is to drive a wedge even more deeply between angry blacks who demand compensation for their losses and indignant whites who disavow any responsibility. The Tulsa race riot lasted less than sixteen hours, but its search for closure overlapped America's own struggle to make peace with a painful past," wrote James Hirsch in *Riot and Remembrance*.

In some things, it seems, there is something of a historical statute of limitations. Shakespeare apparently had it backward. What he no doubt should have written was: "The good that men do lives after them; the evil is interred with their bones." So the same son of the South who clings so tightly to his Confederate flag, who argues for its continued relevance, dismisses slavery as insignificant in terms of modern problems. The same patriot who believes heroic acts of World War I and World War II are worthy of celebration does not believe shameful acts from those same eras are worthy of condemnation. There are people who arrived in America less than a decade ago who — through their payment of taxes, through their participation in the American political process — assume responsibility for myriad things they personally had nothing to do with. They pay off debts incurred by past presidents; accept treaty obligations negotiated by long-departed diplomats; but they also, for the most part, accept an argument that says, in effect, "Racial wrongs, and any responsibility to atone for them, do not persist beyond a generation."

Why do so many of us live in such segregated communities? Why did the O. J. Simpson case cast such a polarizing shadow? Why are the statistics of socioeconomic well-being so divergent for people of different hues? Part of the answer lies in history: in decisions sanctioned and carried out by the state that elevated one set of people above another.

The plea for American reparations is, as much as anything, a plea to   45
learn or to reconsider that history — and to reconsider, as well, the assumption that the way the world is — with one racial group significantly better off than another — is simply the natural state of things. In *Paying for the Past,* Christian Pross observes, "The reparations program set the stage for a change in consciousness and for a transformation . . . in the way German society dealt with the Nazi past." The hope of many of those in America who support reparations is that the educational process that accompanies the debate will spark a similar transformation.

Tim Madigan holds himself out as an example of how immersion in previously forbidden history can deeply change perceptions. The research he did for *The Burning* was "a life-changing odyssey. Early in the process, I began to suspect that a crucial piece remained missing from America's long attempts at racial reconciliation. Too many in this country remained as ignorant as I was. Too many were just as oblivious to some of the darkest moments in our history, a legacy of which Tulsa is both a tragic example and a shameful metaphor. How can we heal when we don't know what we're healing from?" . . .

The argument for reparations is essentially an argument about keeping promises and restoring a damaged community, about giving people restitution for what was taken, about providing opportunities that were denied. The problem is not that black Americans never got forty acres (and a mule); it is that so much was taken and so little given that impoverishment and despair became self-perpetuating. To correct that, one need not arrive at a figure of precisely what was taken, or calculate the present value of forty acres and write a check. One need not, in fact, talk about reparations at all. One need only make a decision that a damaged community, whatever the cost, must be restored.

. . . It is possible to provide a community with jobs, with better schooling, with economic development without labeling it payment of a debt for the sins of the Fathers. And, indeed, if we ever reach the point when America is prepared to do that, there will be no reason to talk reparations. Instead we will simply be asking: What must we do to provide all Americans with the wherewithal to achieve whatever it is they deserve?

Bibliography

Hirsch, James S. *Riot and Remembrance* (Boston, New York: Houghton Mifflin Company, 2002).

Madigan, Tim. *The Burning* (New York: St. Martin's Press, 2001).

Maki, Mitchell T., Harr H. L. Kitano, and Meagan Berthold. *Achieving the Impossible Dream* (Urbana and Chicago: University of Illinois Press, 1999).

Oklahoma Commission to Study the Tulsa Race Riot of 1921, *Tulsa Race Riot* (State of Oklahoma, 2001).

Oliver, Melvin L., and Thomas M. Shapiro. *Black Wealth/White Wealth* (New York, London: Routledge, 1997).

Pross, Christian. *Paying for the Past* (Baltimore and London: The Johns Hopkins University Press, 1998).

Winbush, Raymond A., ed. *Should America Pay?* (New York: HarperCollins, 2003).

Engaging the Text

1. Cose discusses several historical precedents for slavery reparations. In what ways are the cases of the Japanese internment, the Tulsa riots, and the destruction of Rosewood similar to or different from the case of slavery? How does Cose use each of these events to develop and support his argument in favor of slavery reparations?

2. According to Cose, why are an official investigation, apology, and restitution important to the victims of great historic injustices or to their descendants? Why is this process important to society as a whole?

3. Outline the economic justification for reparations: What measurable monetary losses have African Americans suffered as a result of slavery and discrimination? Are there losses that cannot be measured in economic terms? If so, how might they be redressed?

4. Examine Cose's argument that the statute of limitations should not apply in cases like the Tulsa Riots and the enslavement of African Americans. What evidence does he present to support his contention that African Americans today still feel the effects of slavery? How persuasive do you find his reasoning?

EXPLORING CONNECTIONS

5. To what extent does Steele's notion of "seeing for innocence" (p. 530) account for the persistent silence and denial of the white community concerning the destruction of the black neighborhoods in Tulsa and Rosewood? How might Steele respond to Cose's call for reparations?

6. Compare Cose's discussion of white resistance to the idea of reparations and Paul L. Wachtel's (p. 541) analysis of white indifference to the problems of African Americans. How do these writers explain the reactions of whites to blacks' demands for recognition or social change? What solutions do they offer? In your view, how workable are these solutions, and why?

EXTENDING THE CRITICAL CONTEXT

7. Do some further research into the comparative status of white and black Americans: income, home ownership, education, and so forth. To what extent do your findings support Cose's contention that the inheritance of slavery, segregation, and discrimination "continues to undermine the economic well-being of African Americans" (para. 40)?

8. Research the debate about reparations for slavery. Summarize the arguments you find both for and against reparations for slavery as well as some of the specific proposals for how reparations might be distributed. In class, stage a congressional hearing on the issue, taking the roles of a variety of experts who offer testimony to the Committee on Reparations. Then write an essay evaluating the testimony and explaining how you would vote on the issue, and why.

9. Cose mentions that as of 2003, the victims of the Tulsa riot still had not received any compensation for their losses. Research the status of the lawsuit against Tulsa and the state of Oklahoma: Has the case been resolved? If so, do you think justice has been served? What does this case suggest about the possibility of slavery reparations?

Causes of Prejudice

VINCENT N. PARRILLO

What motivates the creation of racial categories? In the following selection, Vincent Parrillo reviews several theories that seek to explain the motives for prejudiced behavior—from socialization theory to economic competition. As Parrillo indicates, prejudice cannot be linked to any single cause: a whole network of forces and frustrations underlies this complex set of feelings and behaviors. Parrillo (b. 1938) chairs the Department of Sociology at William Paterson College in New Jersey. His books include Rethinking Today's Minorities *(1991),* Diversity in America *(1996), and* Understanding Race and Ethnic Relations *(2002). He has also written and produced two award-winning documentaries for PBS television. This excerpt originally appeared in* Strangers to These Shores *(1999, 6th ed.).*

Prejudicial attitudes may be either positive or negative. Sociologists primarily study the latter, however, because only negative attitudes can lead to turbulent social relations between dominant and minority groups. Numerous writers, therefore, have defined *prejudice* as an attitudinal "system of negative beliefs, feelings, and action-orientations regarding a certain group or groups of people."[1] The status of the strangers is an important factor in the development of a negative attitude. Prejudicial attitudes exist among members of both dominant and minority groups. Thus, in the relations between dominant and minority groups, the antipathy felt by one group for another is quite often reciprocated.

Psychological perspectives on prejudice — whether behaviorist, cognitive, or psychoanalytic — focus on the subjective states of mind of individuals. In these perspectives, a person's prejudicial attitudes may result from imitation or conditioning (behaviorist), perceived similarity–dissimilarity of beliefs (cognitive), or specific personality characteristics (psychoanalytic). In contrast, sociological perspectives focus on the objective conditions of society as the social forces behind prejudicial attitudes and behind racial and ethnic relations. Individuals do not live in a vacuum; social reality affects their states of mind.

Both perspectives are necessary to understand prejudice. As psychologist Gordon Allport argued, besides needing a close study of habits, perceptions, motivation, and personality, we need an analysis of social settings, situational forces, demographic and ecological variables, and legal and economic trends.[2] Psychological and sociological perspectives complement each other in providing a fuller explanation about intergroup relations.

The Psychology of Prejudice

We can understand more about prejudice among individuals by focusing on four areas of study: levels of prejudice, self-justification, personality, and frustration.

[1]Reported by Daniel Wilner, Rosabelle Price Walkley, and Stuart W. Cook, "Residential Proximity and Intergroup Relations in Public Housing Projects," *Journal of Social Issues* 8 (1) (1952): 45. See also James W. Vander Zanden, *American Minority Relations,* 3d ed. (New York: Ronald Press, 1972), p. 21. [All notes are the author's.]

[2]Gordon W. Allport, "Prejudice: Is It Societal or Personal?" *Journal of Social Issues* 18 (1962): 129–30.

Levels of Prejudice.   Bernard Kramer suggests that prejudice exists on   5
three levels: cognitive, emotional, and action orientation.[3] The **cognitive
level of prejudice** encompasses a person's beliefs and perceptions of a
group as threatening or nonthreatening, inferior or equal (e.g., in terms of
intellect, status, or biological composition), seclusive or intrusive, impulse-
gratifying, acquisitive, or possessing other positive or negative characteristics. Mr. X's cognitive beliefs are that Jews are intrusive and acquisitive.
Other illustrations of cognitive beliefs are that the Irish are heavy drinkers
and fighters. African Americans are rhythmic and lazy, and the Poles are
thick-headed and unintelligent. Generalizations shape both ethnocentric
and prejudicial attitudes, but there is a difference. **Ethnocentrism** is a generalized rejection of all outgroups on the basis of an ingroup focus, whereas
prejudice is a rejection of certain people solely on the basis of their membership in a particular group.

In many societies, members of the majority group may believe that
a particular low-status minority group is dirty, immoral, violent, or law-
breaking. In the United States, the Irish, Italians, African Americans,
Mexicans, Chinese, Puerto Ricans, and others have at one time or another
been labeled with most, if not all, of these adjectives. In most European
countries and in the United States, the group lowest on the socioeconomic
ladder has often been depicted in caricature as also lowest on the evolutionary ladder. The Irish and African Americans in the United States and
the peasants and various ethnic groups in Europe have all been depicted in
the past as apelike:

> The Victorian images of the Irish as "white Negro" and simian Celt, or
> a combination of the two, derived much of its force and inspiration
> from physiognomical beliefs . . . [but] every country in Europe had its
> equivalent of "white Negroes" and simianized men, whether or not
> they happened to be stereotypes of criminals, assassins, political radi-
> cals, revolutionaries, Slavs, gypsies, Jews, or peasants.[4]

The **emotional level of prejudice** refers to the feelings that a minority group arouses in an individual. Although these feelings may be based on
stereotypes from the cognitive level, they represent a more intense stage of
personal involvement. The emotional attitudes may be negative or positive,
such as fear/envy, distrust/trust, disgust/admiration, or contempt/empathy.
These feelings, based on beliefs about the group, may be triggered by social
interaction or by the possibility of interaction. For example, whites might
react with fear or anger to the integration of their schools or neighborhoods,
or Protestants might be jealous of the lifestyle of a highly successful
Catholic business executive.

---

[3]Bernard M. Kramer, "Dimensions of Prejudice," *Journal of Psychology* 27 (April 1949):
389–451.

[4]L. Perry Curtis, Jr., *Apes and Angels: The Irishman in Victorian Caricature* (Washington, D.C.: Smithsonian Press, 1971).

An **action-orientation level of prejudice** is the positive or negative predisposition to engage in discriminatory behavior. A person who harbors strong feelings about members of a certain racial or ethnic group may have a tendency to act for or against them — being aggressive or nonaggressive, offering assistance or withholding it. Such an individual would also be likely to want to exclude or include members of that group both in close, personal social relations and in peripheral social relations. For example, some people would want to exclude members of the disliked group from doing business with them or living in their neighborhood. Another manifestation of the action-orientation level of prejudice is the desire to change or maintain the status differential or inequality between the two groups, whether the area is economic, political, educational, social, or a combination. Note that an action orientation is a predisposition to act, not the action itself.

Self-Justification.   **Self-justification** involves denigrating a person or group to justify maltreatment of them. In this situation, self-justification leads to prejudice and discrimination against members of another group.

Some philosophers argue that we are not so much rational creatures as   10
we are rationalizing creatures. We require reassurance that the things we do and the lives we live are proper, that good reasons for our actions exist. If we can convince ourselves that another group is inferior, immoral, or dangerous, we may feel justified in discriminating against its members, enslaving them, or even killing them.

History is filled with examples of people who thought their maltreatment of others was just and necessary: As defenders of the "true faith," the Crusaders killed "Christ-killers" (Jews) and "infidels" (Moslems). Participants in the Spanish Inquisition imprisoned, tortured, and executed "heretics," "the disciples of the Devil." Similarly, the Puritans burned witches, whose refusal to confess "proved they were evil"; pioneers exploited or killed Native Americans who were "heathen savages"; and whites mistreated, enslaved, or killed African Americans, who were "an inferior species." According to U.S. Army officers, the civilians in the Vietnamese village of My Lai were "probably" aiding the Vietcong; so in 1968 U.S. soldiers fighting in the Vietnam War felt justified in slaughtering over 300 unarmed people there, including women, children, and the elderly.

Some sociologists believe that self-justification works the other way around. That is, instead of self-justification serving as a basis for subjugating others, the subjugation occurs first and the self-justification follows, resulting in prejudice and continued discrimination.[5] The evolution of racism as a concept after the establishment of the African slave trade would seem to support this idea. Philip Mason offers an insight into this view:

> A specialized society is likely to defeat a simpler society and provide a lower tier still of enslaved and conquered peoples. The rulers and organizers sought security for themselves and their children; to perpetuate the power, the esteem, and the comfort they had achieved, it was necessary not only that the artisans and labourers should work contentedly but that the rulers should sleep without bad dreams. No one can say with certainty how the myths originated, but it is surely relevant that when one of the founders of Western thought set himself to frame an ideal state that would embody social justice, he — like the earliest city dwellers — not only devised a society stratified in tiers but believed it would be necessary to persuade the traders and workpeople that, by divine decree, they were made from brass and iron, while the warriors were made of silver and the rulers of gold.[6]

Another example of self-justification serving as a source of prejudice is the dominant group's assumption of an attitude of superiority over other groups. In this respect, establishing a prestige hierarchy — ranking the status of various ethnic groups — results in differential association. To enhance or maintain self-esteem, a person may avoid social contact with groups deemed inferior and associate only with those identified as being of high status. Through such behavior, self-justification may come to intensify the social distance between groups.... *Social distance* refers to the degree to which ingroup members do not engage in social or primary relationships with members of various outgroups.

---

[5]See Marvin B. Scott and Stanford M. Lyman, "Accounts," *American Sociological Review* 33 (February 1968): 40–62.

[6]Philip Mason, *Patterns of Dominance* (New York: Oxford University Press, 1970), p. 7. See also Philip Mason, *Race Relations* (New York: Oxford University Press, 1970), pp. 17–29.

Personality. In 1950, in *The Authoritarian Personality,* T. W. Adorno and his colleagues reported a correlation between individuals' early childhood experiences of harsh parental discipline and their development of an **authoritarian personality** as adults.[7] If parents assume an excessively domineering posture in their relations with a child, exercising stern measures and threatening to withdraw love if the child does not respond with weakness and submission, the child tends to be insecure and to nurture much latent hostility against the parents. When such children become adults, they may demonstrate **displaced aggression,** directing their hostility against a powerless group to compensate for their feelings of insecurity and fear. Highly prejudiced individuals tend to come from families that emphasize obedience.

The authors identified authoritarianism by the use of a measuring   15 instrument called an F scale (the *F* standing for potential fascism). Other tests included the A-S (anti-Semitism) and E (ethnocentrism) scales, the latter measuring attitudes toward various minorities. One of their major findings was that people who scored high on authoritarianism also consistently showed a high degree of prejudice against all minority groups. These highly prejudiced persons were characterized by rigidity of viewpoint, dislike for ambiguity, strict obedience to leaders, and intolerance of weakness in themselves and others.

No sooner did *The Authoritarian Personality* appear than controversy began. H. H. Hyman and P. B. Sheatsley challenged the methodology and analysis.[8] Solomon Asch questioned the assumptions that the F scale responses represented a belief system and that structural variables (such as ideologies, stratification, and mobility) do not play a role in shaping personality.[9] E. A. Shils argued that the authors were interested only in measuring authoritarianism of the political right while ignoring such tendencies in those at the other end of the political spectrum.[10] Other investigators sought alternative explanations for the authoritarian personality. D. Stewart and T. Hoult extended the framework beyond family childhood experiences to include other social factors.[11] H. C. Kelman and Janet Barclay pointed out that substantial evidence exists showing that lower intelligence and less education also correlate with high authoritarianism scores on the F scale.[12]

[7]T. W. Adorno, Else Frankel-Brunswik, Daniel J. Levinson, and R. Nevitt Sanford, *The Authoritarian Personality* (New York: Harper & Row, 1950).

[8]H. H. Hyman and P. B. Sheatsley, "The Authoritarian Personality: A Methodological Critique," in R. Christie and M. Jahoda (eds.), *Studies in the Scope and Method of "The Authoritarian Personality"* (Glencoe, Ill.: Free Press, 1954).

[9]Solomon E. Asch, *Social Psychology* (Englewood Cliffs, N.J.: Prentice-Hall, 1952), p. 545.

[10]E. A. Shils, "Authoritarianism: Right and Left," in *Studies in the Scope and Method of "The Authoritarian Personality."*

[11]D. Stewart and T. Hoult, "A Social-Psychological Theory of 'The Authoritarian Personality.'" *American Journal of Sociology* 65 (1959): 274.

[12]H. C. Kelman and Janet Barclay, "The F Scale as a Measure of Breadth of Perspective," *Journal of Abnormal and Social Psychology* 67 (1963): 608–15.

Despite the critical attacks, the underlying conceptions of *The Authoritarian Personality* were important, and research into personality as a factor in prejudice has continued. Subsequent investigators refined and modified the original study. Correcting scores for response bias, they conducted cross-cultural studies. Respondents in Germany and Near East countries, where more authoritarian social structures exist, scored higher on authoritarianism and social distance between groups. In Japan, Germany, and the United States, authoritarianism and social distance were moderately related. Other studies suggested that an inverse relationship exists between social class and F scale scores: the higher the social class, the lower the authoritarianism.[13]

Although studies of authoritarian personality have helped us understand some aspects of prejudice, they have not provided a causal explanation. Most of the findings in this area show a correlation, but the findings do not prove, for example, that harsh discipline of children causes them to become prejudiced adults. Perhaps the strict parents were themselves prejudiced, and the child learned those attitudes from them. Or as George Simpson and J. Milton Yinger say:

> One must be careful not to assume too quickly that a certain tendency — rigidity of mind, for example — that is correlated with prejudice necessarily causes that prejudice. . . . The sequence may be the other way around. . . . It is more likely that both are related to more basic factors.[14]

For some people, prejudice may indeed be rooted in subconscious childhood tensions, but we simply do not know whether these tensions directly cause a high degree of prejudice in the adult or whether other powerful social forces are the determinants. Whatever the explanation, authoritarianism is a significant phenomenon worthy of continued investigation. Recent research, however, has stressed social and situational factors, rather than personality, as primary causes of prejudice and discrimination.[15]

Yet another dimension of the personality component is that people with   20
low self-esteem are more prejudiced than those who feel good about themselves. Some researchers have argued that individuals with low self-esteem deprecate others to enhance their feelings about themselves.[16] One study

---

[13]For an excellent summary of authoritarian studies and literature, see John P. Kirscht and Ronald C. Dillehay, *Dimensions of Authoritarianism: A Review of Research and Theory* (Lexington: University of Kentucky Press, 1967).

[14]George E. Simpson and J. Milton Yinger, *Racial and Cultural Minorities: An Analysis of Prejudice and Discrimination* (New York: Harper & Row, 1953), p. 91.

[15]Ibid., pp. 62–79.

[16]Howard J. Ehrlich, *The Social Psychology of Prejudice* (New York: Wiley, 1974); G. Sherwood, "Self-Serving Biases in Person Perception," *Psychological Bulletin* 90 (1981): 445–59; T. A. Wills, "Downward Comparison Principles in Social Psychology," *Psychological Bulletin* 90 (1981): 245–71.

asserts that "low self-esteem individuals seem to have a generally negative view of themselves, their ingroup, outgroups, and perhaps the world," and thus their tendency to be more prejudiced is not due to rating the outgroup negatively in comparison to their ingroup.[17]

Frustration.   Frustration is the result of relative deprivation in which expectations remain unsatisfied. **Relative deprivation** is a lack of resources, or rewards, in one's standard of living in comparison with those of others in the society. A number of investigators have suggested that frustrations tend to increase aggression toward others.[18] Frustrated people may easily strike out against the perceived cause of their frustration. However, this reaction may not be possible because the true source of the frustration is often too nebulous to be identified or too powerful to act against. In such instances, the result may be displaced aggression; in this situation, the frustrated individual or group usually redirects anger against a more visible, vulnerable, and socially sanctioned target, one unable to strike back. Minorities meet these criteria and are thus frequently the recipients of displaced aggression by the dominant group.

Blaming others for something that is not their fault is known as **scapegoating.** The term comes from the ancient Hebrew custom of using a goat during the Day of Atonement as a symbol of the sins of the people. In an annual ceremony, a priest placed his hands on the head of a goat and listed the people's sins in a symbolic transference of guilt; he then chased the goat out of the community, thereby freeing the people of sin.[19] Since those times, the powerful group has usually punished the scapegoat group rather than allowing it to escape.

There have been many instances throughout world history of minority groups serving as scapegoats, including the Christians in ancient Rome, the Huguenots in France, the Jews in Europe and Russia, and the Puritans and Quakers in England. Gordon Allport suggests that certain characteristics are necessary for a group to become a suitable scapegoat. The group must be (1) highly visible in physical appearance or observable customs and actions; (2) not strong enough to strike back; (3) situated within easy access of the dominant group and, ideally, concentrated in one area; (4) a past

---

[17]Jennifer Crocker and Ian Schwartz, "Prejudice and Ingroup Favoritism in a Minimal Intergroup Situation: Effects of Self-Esteem," *Personality and Social Psychology Bulletin* 11 (4) (December 1985): 379–86.

[18]John Dollard, Leonard W. Doob, Neal E. Miller, O. H. Mowrer, and Robert P. Sears, *Frustration and Aggression* (New Haven, Conn.: Yale University Press, 1939); A. F. Henry and J. F. Short, Jr., *Suicide and Homicide* (New York: Free Press, 1954); Neal Miller and Richard Bugelski, "Minor Studies in Aggression: The Influence of Frustration Imposed by the Ingroup on Attitudes Expressed Toward Out-Groups," *Journal of Psychology* 25 (1948): 437–42; Stuart Palmer, *The Psychology of Murder* (New York: T. Y. Crowell, 1960); Brenden C. Rule and Elizabeth Percival, "The Effects of Frustration and Attack on Physical Aggression," *Journal of Experimental Research on Personality* 5 (1971): 111–88.

[19]Leviticus 16:5–22.

target of hostility for whom latent hostility still exists; and (5) the symbol of an unpopular concept.[20]

Some groups fit this typology better than others, but minority racial and ethnic groups have been a perennial choice. Irish, Italians, Catholics, Jews, Quakers, Mormons, Chinese, Japanese, Blacks, Puerto Ricans, Chicanos, and Koreans have all been treated, at one time or another, as the scapegoat in the United States. Especially in times of economic hardship, societies tend to blame some group for the general conditions, which often leads to aggressive action against the group as an expression of frustration. For example, a study by Carl Hovland and Robert Sears found that, between 1882 and 1930, a definite correlation existed between a decline in the price of cotton and an increase in the number of lynchings of Blacks.[21]

In several controlled experiments, social scientists have attempted to 25 measure the validity of the scapegoat theory. Neal Miller and Richard Bugelski tested a group of young men aged eighteen to twenty who were working in a government camp about their feelings toward various minority groups. The young men were reexamined about these feelings after experiencing frustration by being obliged to take a long, difficult test and being denied an opportunity to see a film at a local theater. This group showed some evidence of increased prejudicial feelings, whereas a control group, which did not experience any frustration, showed no change in prejudicial attitudes.[22]

Donald Weatherley conducted an experiment with a group of college students to measure the relationship between frustration and aggression against a specific disliked group.[23] After identifying students who were or were not highly anti-Semitic and subjecting them to a strongly frustrating experience, he asked the students to write stories about pictures shown to them. Some of the students were shown pictures of people who had been given Jewish names; other students were presented with pictures of unnamed people. When the pictures were unidentified, the stories of the anti-Semitic students did not differ from those of other students. When the pictures were identified, however, the anti-Semitic students wrote stories reflecting much more aggression against the Jews in the pictures than did the other students.

For over twenty years, Leonard Berkowitz and his associates studied and experimented with aggressive behavior. They concluded that, confronted with equally frustrating situations, highly prejudiced individuals are more likely to seek scapegoats than are nonprejudiced individuals. Another intervening variable is that personal frustrations (marital failure, injury, or

---

[20]Gordon W. Allport, *The Nature of Prejudice* (Cambridge, Mass.: Addison-Wesley, 1954), pp. 13–14.

[21]Carl I. Hovland and Robert R. Sears, "Minor Studies of Aggression: Correlation of Lynchings with Economic Indices," *Journal of Psychology* 9 (Winter 1940): 301–10.

[22]Miller and Bugelski, "Minor Studies in Aggression," pp. 437–42.

[23]Donald Weatherley, "Anti-Semitism and the Expression of Fantasy Aggression," *Journal of Abnormal and Social Psychology* 62 (1961): 454–57.

mental illness) make people more likely to seek scapegoats than do shared frustrations (dangers of flood or hurricane).[24]

Some experiments have shown that aggression does not increase if the frustration is understandable.[25] Other experiments have found that people become aggressive only if the aggression directly relieves their frustration.[26] Still other studies have shown that anger is a more likely result if the person responsible for the frustrating situation could have acted otherwise.[27] Clearly, the results are mixed, depending on the variables within a given social situation.

Frustration-aggression theory, although helpful, is not completely satisfactory. It ignores the role of culture and the reality of actual social conflict and fails to show any causal relationship. Most of the responses measured in these studies were of people already biased. Why did one group rather than another become the object of the aggression? Moreover, frustration does not necessarily precede aggression, and aggression does not necessarily flow from frustration.

The Sociology of Prejudice

Sociologist Talcott Parsons provided one bridge between psychology and sociology by introducing social forces as a variable in frustration–aggression theory. He suggested that both the family and the occupational structure may produce anxieties and insecurities that create frustration.[28] According to this view, the growing-up process (gaining parental affection and approval, identifying with and imitating sexual role models, and competing with others in adulthood) sometimes involves severe emotional strain. The result is an adult personality with a large reservoir of repressed aggression that becomes *free-floating* — susceptible to redirection against convenient scapegoats. Similarly, the occupational system is a source of frustration: its emphasis on competitiveness and individual achievement, its function of conferring status, its requirement that people inhibit their natural impulses at work, and its ties to the state of the economy are among the factors that generate emotional

30

---

[24]See Leonard Berkowitz, "Whatever Happened to the Frustration-Aggression Hypothesis?" *American Behavioral Scientist* 21 (1978): 691–708; L. Berkowitz, *Aggression: A Social Psychological Analysis* (New York: McGraw-Hill, 1962).

[25]D. Zillman, *Hostility and Aggression* (Hillsdale, N.J.: Laurence Erlbaum, 1979); R. A. Baron, *Human Aggression* (New York: Plenum Press, 1977); N. Pastore, "The Role of Arbitrariness in the Frustration-Aggression Hypothesis," *Journal of Abnormal and Social Psychology* 47 (1952): 728–31.

[26]A. H. Buss, "Instrumentality of Aggression, Feedback, and Frustration as Determinants of Physical Aggression," *Journal of Personality and Social Psychology* 3 (1966): 153–62.

[27]J. R. Averill, "Studies on Anger and Aggression: Implications for Theories of Emotion," *American Psychologist* 38 (1983): 1145–60.

[28]Talcott Parsons, "Certain Primary Sources and Patterns of Aggression in the Social Structure of the Western World," in *Essays in Sociological Theory* (New York: Free Press, 1964), pp. 298–322.

anxieties. Parsons pessimistically concluded that minorities fulfill a functional "need" as targets for displaced aggression and therefore will remain targets.[29]

Perhaps most influential in staking out the sociological position on prejudice was Herbert Blumer, who suggested that prejudice always involves the "sense of group position" in society. Agreeing with Kramer's delineation of three levels of prejudice, Blumer argued that prejudice can include beliefs, feelings, and a predisposition to action, thus motivating behavior that derives from the social hierarchy.[30] By emphasizing historically established group positions and relationships, Blumer shifted his focus away from the attitudes and personality compositions of individuals. As a social phenomenon, prejudice rises or falls according to issues that alter one group's position vis-à-vis that of another group.

Socialization. In the **socialization process,** individuals acquire the values, attitudes, beliefs, and perceptions of their culture or subculture, including religion, nationality, and social class. Generally, the child conforms to the parents' expectations in acquiring an understanding of the world and its people. Being impressionable and knowing of no alternative conceptions of the world, the child usually accepts these concepts without questioning. We thus learn the prejudices of our parents and others, which then become part of our values and beliefs. Even when based on false stereotypes, prejudices shape our perceptions of various peoples and influence our attitudes and actions toward particular groups. For example, if we develop negative attitudes about Jews because we are taught that they are shrewd, acquisitive, and clannish — all-too-familiar stereotypes — as adults we may refrain from business or social relationships with them. We may not even realize the reason for such avoidance, so subtle has been the prejudice instilled within us.

People may learn certain prejudices because of their pervasiveness. The cultural screen that we develop and through which we view the surrounding world is not always accurate, but it does permit transmission of shared values and attitudes, which are reinforced by others. Prejudice, like cultural values, is taught and learned through the socialization process. The prevailing prejudicial attitudes and actions may be deeply embedded in custom or law (e.g., the **Jim Crow laws** of the 1890s and the early twentieth century establishing segregated public facilities throughout the South, which subsequent generations accepted as proper, and maintained in their own adult lives).

Although socialization explains how prejudicial attitudes may be transmitted from one generation to the next, it does not explain their origin or

---

[29]For an excellent review of Parsonian theory in this area, see Stanford M. Lyman, *The Black American in Sociological Thought: A Failure of Perspective* (New York: Putnam, 1972), pp. 145–69.

[30]Herbert Blumer, "Race Prejudice as a Sense of Group Position," *Pacific Sociological Review* 1 (1958): 3–7.

why they intensify or diminish over the years. These aspects of prejudice must be explained in another way.

Economic Competition. People tend to be more hostile toward others   35
when they feel that their security is threatened; thus many social scientists conclude that economic competition and conflict breed prejudice. Certainly, considerable evidence shows that negative stereotyping, prejudice, and discrimination increase markedly whenever competition for available jobs increases.

An excellent illustration relates to the Chinese sojourners in the nineteenth-century United States. Prior to the 1870s, the transcontinental railroad was being built, and the Chinese filled many of the jobs made available by this project in the sparsely populated West. Although they were expelled from the region's gold mines and schools and could obtain no redress of grievances in the courts, they managed to convey to some Whites the image of being a clean, hard-working, law-abiding people. The completion of the railroad, the flood of former Civil War soldiers into the job market, and the economic depression of 1873 worsened their situation. The Chinese became more frequent victims of open discrimination and hostility. Their positive stereotype among some Whites was widely displaced by a negative one: They were now "conniving," "crafty," "criminal," "the yellow menace." Only after they retreated into Chinatowns and entered specialty occupations that minimized their competition with Whites did the intense hostility abate.

One pioneer in the scientific study of prejudice, John Dollard, demonstrated how prejudice against the Germans, which had been virtually nonexistent, arose in a small U.S. industrial town when times got bad:

> Local Whites largely drawn from the surrounding farms manifested considerable direct aggression toward the newcomers. Scornful and derogatory opinions were expressed about the Germans, and the native Whites had a satisfying sense of superiority toward them. . . . The chief element in the permission to be aggressive against the Germans was rivalry for jobs and status in the local woodenware plants. The native Whites felt definitely crowded for their jobs by the entering German groups and in case of bad times had a chance to blame the Germans who by their presence provided more competitors for the scarcer jobs. There seemed to be no traditional pattern of prejudice against Germans unless the skeletal suspicion of all out-groupers (always present) be invoked in this place.[31]

Both experimental studies and historical analyses have added credence to the economic-competition theory. Muzafer Sherif directed several experiments showing how intergroup competition at a boys' camp

---

[31]John Dollard, "Hostility and Fear in Social Life," *Social Forces* 17 (1938): 15–26.

led to conflict and escalating hostility.[32] Donald Young pointed out that, throughout U.S. history, in times of high unemployment and thus intense job competition, nativist movements against minorities have flourished.[33] This pattern has held true regionally — against Asians on the West Coast, Italians in Louisiana, and French Canadians in New England — and nationally, with the antiforeign movements always peaking during periods of depression. So it was with the Native American Party in the 1830s, the Know-Nothing Party in the 1850s, the American Protective Association in the 1890s, and the Ku Klux Klan after World War I. Since the passage of civil rights laws on employment in the twentieth century, researchers have consistently detected the strongest antiblack prejudice among working-class and middle-class Whites who feel threatened by Blacks entering their socioeconomic group in noticeable numbers.[34] It seems that any group applying the pressure of job competition most directly on another group becomes a target of its prejudice.

Once again, a theory that offers some excellent insights into prejudice — in particular, that adverse economic conditions correlate with increased hostility toward minorities — also has some serious shortcomings. Not all groups that have been objects of hostility (e.g., Quakers and Mormons) have been economic competitors. Moreover, why is hostility against some groups greater than against others? Why do the negative feelings in some communities run against groups whose numbers are so small that they cannot possibly pose an economic threat? Evidently values besides economic ones cause people to be antagonistic to a group perceived as an actual or potential threat.

Social Norms.   Some sociologists have suggested that a relationship   40
exists between prejudice and a person's tendency to conform to societal expectations.[35] **Social norms** — the norms of one's culture — form the generally shared rules defining what is and is not proper behavior. By learning and automatically accepting the prevailing prejudices, an individual is simply conforming to those norms.

---

[32]Muzafer Sherif, O. J. Harvey, B. Jack White, William Hood, and Carolyn Sherif, *Intergroup Conflict and Cooperation: The Robbers Cave Experiment* (Norman: University of Oklahoma Institute of Intergroup Relations, 1961). See also M. Sherif, "Experiments in Group Conflict," *Scientific American* 195 (1956): 54–58.

[33]Donald Young, *Research Memorandum on Minority Peoples in the Depression* (New York: Social Science Research Council, 1937), pp. 133–41.

[34]Andrew Greeley and Paul Sheatsley, "The Acceptance of Desegregation Continues to Advance," *Scientific American* 210 (1971): 13–19; T. F. Pettigrew, "Three Issues in Ethnicity: Boundaries, Deprivations, and Perceptions," in M. Yinger and S. J. Cutler (eds.), *Major Social Issues: A Multidisciplinary View* (New York: Free Press, 1978); R. D. Vanneman and T. F. Pettigrew, "Race and Relative Deprivation in the United States," *Race* 13 (1972): 461–86.

[35]See Harry H. L. Kitano, "Passive Discrimination in the Normal Person," *Journal of Social Psychology* 70 (1966): 23–31.

This theory holds that a direct relationship exists between degree of conformity and degree of prejudice. If so, people's prejudices should decrease or increase significantly when they move into areas where the prejudicial norm is lesser or greater. Evidence supports this view. Thomas Pettigrew found that Southerners in the 1950s became less prejudiced against Blacks when they interacted with them in the army, where the social norms were less prejudicial.[36] In another study, Jeanne Watson found that people moving into an anti-Semitic neighborhood in New York City became more anti-Semitic.[37]

John Dollard's study, *Caste and Class in a Southern Town* (1937), provides an in-depth look at the emotional adjustment of Whites and Blacks to rigid social norms.[38] In his study of the processes, functions, and maintenance of accommodation, Dollard detailed the "carrot-and-stick" method social groups employed. Intimidation — sometimes even severe reprisals for going against social norms — ensured compliance. However, reprisals usually were unnecessary. The advantages Whites and Blacks gained in psychological, economic, or behavioral terms served to perpetuate the caste order. These gains in personal security and stability set in motion a vicious circle. They encouraged a way of life that reinforced the rationale of the social system in this community.

Two 1994 studies provided further evidence of the powerful influence of social norms. Joachim Krueger and Russell W. Clement found that consensus bias persisted despite the availability of statistical data and knowledge about such bias.[39] Michael R. Leippe and Donna Eisenstadt showed that induced compliance can change socially significant attitudes and that the change generalizes to broader beliefs.[40]

Although the social-norms theory explains prevailing attitudes, it does not explain either their origins or the reasons why new prejudices develop when other groups move into an area. In addition, the theory does not explain why prejudicial attitudes against a particular group rise and fall cyclically over the years.

Although many social scientists have attempted to identify the causes of prejudice, no single factor provides an adequate explanation. Prejudice is a

45

[36]Thomas Pettigrew, "Regional Differences in Anti-Negro Prejudice," *Journal of Abnormal and Social Psychology* 59 (1959): 28–36.

[37]Jeanne Watson, "Some Social and Psychological Situations Related to Change in Attitude," *Human Relations* 3 (1950): 15–56.

[38]John Dollard, *Caste and Class in a Southern Town,* 3d ed. (Garden City, N.Y.: Doubleday Anchor Books, 1957).

[39]Joachim Krueger and Russell W. Clement, "The Truly False Consensus Effect: An Ineradicable and Egocentric Bias in Social Perception," *Journal of Personality and Social Psychology* 67 (1994): 596–610.

[40]Michael R. Leippe and Donna Eisenstadt, "Generalization of Dissonance Reduction: Decreasing Prejudice through Induced Compliance," *Journal of Personality and Social Psychology* 67 (1994): 395–414.

complex phenomenon, and it is most likely the product of more than one causal agent. Sociologists today tend either to emphasize multiple-cause explanations or to stress social forces encountered in specific and similar situations — forces such as economic conditions, stratification, and hostility toward an outgroup.

ENGAGING THE TEXT

1. Review Parrillo's discussion of the cognitive, emotional, and action-oriented levels of prejudice. Do you think it's possible for an individual to hold prejudiced beliefs that do *not* affect her feelings and actions? Why or why not?

2. How can prejudice arise from self-justification? Offer some examples of how a group can assume an attitude of superiority in order to justify ill-treatment of others.

3. How, according to Parrillo, might personal factors like authoritarian attitudes, low self-esteem, or frustration promote the growth of prejudice?

4. What is the "socialization process," according to Parrillo? In what different ways can socialization instill prejudice?

5. What is the relationship between economic competition and prejudice? Do you think prejudice would continue to exist if everyone had a good job with a comfortable income?

EXPLORING CONNECTIONS

6. Which of the theories Parrillo outlines, if any, might help to explain the attitudes toward blacks expressed by Thomas Jefferson (p. 486)? Which apply most clearly to the life story of C. P. Ellis (p. 519)?

7. Read or review Carmen Vázquez's "Appearances" (p. 472). How useful are the theories presented by Parrillo in analyzing prejudice against gays and lesbians? To what extent can concepts like levels of prejudice, self-justification, frustration, socialization, and economic competition help us understand antigay attitudes?

8. Which of the causes of prejudice that Parrillo describes are reflected in the comments about immigrants in Darrin Bell's cartoon (p. 508)? What is Bell saying about the nature of anti-immigrant attitudes in U.S. history? What does he suggest about immigrants themselves?

EXTENDING THE CRITICAL CONTEXT

9. List the various groups that you belong to (racial, economic, cultural, social, familial, and so forth) and arrange them in a status hierarchy. Which groups were you born into? Which groups did you join voluntarily? Which have had the greatest impact on your socialization? Which groups isolate you the most from contact with outsiders?

10. Working in small groups, research recent news stories for examples of incidents involving racism or prejudice. Which of the theories described by Parrillo seem most useful for analyzing the motives underlying these events?

C. P. Ellis
STUDS TERKEL

The following oral history brings us uncomfortably close to unambiguous, deadly prejudice: C. P. Ellis is a former Ku Klux Klan member who claims to have overcome his racist (and sexist) attitudes; he speaks here as a union leader who feels an alliance to other workers, including blacks and women. Studs Terkel (b. 1912) is probably the best-known practitioner of oral history in the United States. He has compiled several books by interviewing dozens of widely varying people — ordinary people for the most part — about important subjects like work, social class, race, the Great Depression, and aging. The edited versions of these interviews are often surprisingly powerful crystallizations of American social history: Terkel's subjects give voice to the frustrations and hopes of whole generations of Americans. Terkel won a Pulitzer Prize in 1985 for "The Good War": An Oral History of World War II, *and in 1997 he received a National Humanities Medal from President Bill Clinton. Currently he serves as Distinguished Scholar-In-Residence at the Chicago Historical Society.* "C. P. Ellis" *first appeared in* American Dreams: Lost and Found *(1980).*

We're in his office in Durham, North Carolina. He is the business manager of the International Union of Operating Engineers. On the wall is a plaque: "Certificate of Service, in recognition to C. P. Ellis, for your faithful service to the city in having served as a member of the Durham Human Relations Council. February 1977."

At one time, he had been president (exalted cyclops) of the Durham chapter of the Ku Klux Klan. . . .

He is fifty-two years old.

My father worked in a textile mill in Durham. He died at forty-eight years old. It was probably from cotton dust. Back then, we never heard of brown lung. I was about seventeen years old and had a mother and sister depending on somebody to make a livin'. It was just barely enough insurance to cover his burial. I had to quit school and go to work. I was about eighth grade when I quit.

My father worked hard but never had enough money to buy decent clothes. When I went to school, I never seemed to have adequate clothes to wear. I always left school late afternoon with a sense of inferiority. The other kids had nice clothes, and I just had what Daddy could buy. I still got some of those inferiority feelin's now that I have to overcome once in a while.

I loved my father. He would go with me to ball games. We'd go fishin' together. I was really ashamed of the way he'd dress. He would take this money and give it to me instead of putting it on himself. I always had the feeling about somebody looking at him and makin' fun of him and makin' fun of me. I think it had to do somethin' with my life.

My father and I were very close, but we didn't talk about too many intimate things. He did have a drinking problem. During the week, he would work every day, but weekends he was ready to get plastered. I can understand when a guy looks at his paycheck and looks at his bills, and he's worked hard all the week, and his bills are larger than his paycheck. He'd done the best he could the entire week, and there seemed to be no hope. It's an illness thing. Finally you just say: "The heck with it. I'll just get drunk and forget it."

My father was out of work during the depression, and I remember going with him to the finance company uptown, and he was turned down. That's something that's always stuck.

My father never seemed to be happy. It was a constant struggle with him just like it was for me. It's very seldom I'd see him laugh. He was just tryin' to figure out what he could do from one day to the next.

After several years pumping gas at a service station, I got married. We   10 had to have children. Four. One child was born blind and retarded, which was a real additional expense to us. He's never spoken a word. He doesn't know me when I go to see him. But I see him, I hug his neck. I talk to him, tell him I love him. I don't know whether he knows me or not, but I know he's well taken care of. All my life, I had work, never a day without work, worked all the overtime I could get and still could not survive financially. I began to say there's somethin' wrong with this country. I worked my butt off and just never seemed to break even.

I had some real great ideas about this great nation. (Laughs.) They say to abide by the law, go to church, do right and live for the Lord, and everything'll work out. But it didn't work out. It just kept gettin' worse and worse.

I was workin' a bread route. The highest I made one week was seventy-five dollars. The rent on our house was about twelve dollars a week. I will never forget: outside of this house was a 265-gallon oil drum, and I never did get enough money to fill up that oil drum. What I would do every night, I would run up to the store and buy five gallons of oil and climb up the ladder and pour it in that 265-gallon drum. I could hear that five gallons when it hits the bottom of that oil drum, splatters, and it sounds like it's nothin' in there. But it would keep the house warm for the night. Next day you'd have to do the same thing.

I left the bread route with fifty dollars in my pocket. I went to the bank and borrowed four thousand dollars to buy the service station. I worked seven days a week, open and close, and finally had a heart attack. Just about two months before the last payments of that loan. My wife had done the best she could to keep it runnin'. Tryin' to come out of that hole, I just couldn't do it.

I really began to get bitter. I didn't know who to blame. I tried to find somebody. I began to blame it on black people. I had to hate somebody. Hatin' America is hard to do because you can't see it to hate it. You gotta have somethin' to look at to hate. (Laughs.) The natural person for me to hate would be black people, because my father before me was a member of the Klan. As far as he was concerned, it was the savior of the white people. It was the only organization in the world that would take care of the white people. So I began to admire the Klan.

I got active in the Klan while I was at the service station. Every Monday   15
night, a group of men would come by and buy a Coca-Cola, go back to the car, take a few drinks, and come back and stand around talkin'. I couldn't help but wonder: Why are these dudes comin' out every Monday? They said they were with the Klan and have meetings close-by. Would I be interested? Boy, that was an opportunity I really looked forward to! To be part of some-thin'. I joined the Klan, went from member to chaplain, from chaplain to vice-president, from vice-president to president. The title is exalted cyclops.

The first night I went with the fellas, they knocked on the door and gave the signal. They sent some robed Klansmen to talk to me and give me some instructions. I was led into a large meeting room, and this was the time of my life! It was thrilling. Here's a guy who's worked all his life and struggled all his life to be something, and here's the moment to be some-thing. I will never forget it. Four robed Klansmen led me into the hall. The lights were dim, and the only thing you could see was an illuminated cross. I knelt before the cross. I had to make certain vows and promises. We promised to uphold the purity of the white race, fight communism, and pro-tect white womanhood.

After I had taken my oath, there was loud applause goin' throughout the building, musta been at least four hundred people. For this one little ol' person. It was a thrilling moment for C. P. Ellis.

It disturbs me when people who do not really know what it's all about are so very critical of individual Klansmen. The majority of 'em are low-income whites, people who really don't have a part in something. They have been shut out as well as the blacks. Some are not very well educated either. Just like myself. We had a lot of support from doctors and lawyers and police officers.

Maybe they've had bitter experiences in this life and they had to hate somebody. So the natural person to hate would be the black person. He's beginnin' to come up, he's beginnin' to learn to read and start votin' and run for political office. Here are white people who are supposed to be superior to them, and we're shut out.

I can understand why people join extreme right-wing or left-wing   20
groups. They're in the same boat I was. Shut out. Deep down inside, we want to be part of this great society. Nobody listens, so we join these groups.

At one time, I was state organizer of the National Rights party. I orga-nized a youth group for the Klan. I felt we were getting old and our generation's gonna die. So I contacted certain kids in schools. They were havin' racial problems. On the first night, we had a hundred high school students. When they came in the door, we had "Dixie" playin'. These kids were just thrilled to death. I begin to hold weekly meetin's with 'em, teachin' the principles of the Klan. At that time, I believed Martin Luther King had Communist connections. I began to teach that Andy Young[1] was affiliated with the Communist party.

I had a call one night from one of our kids. He was about twelve. He said: "I just been robbed downtown by two niggers." I'd had a couple of drinks and that really teed me off. I go downtown and couldn't find the kid. I got worried. I saw two young black people. I had the .32 revolver with me. I said: "Nigger, you seen a little young white boy up here? I just got a call from him and was told that some niggers robbed him of fifteen cents." I pulled my pistol out and put it right at his head. I said: "I've always wanted to kill a nigger and I think I'll make you the first one." I nearly scared the kid to death, and he struck off.

This was the time when the civil rights movement was really beginnin' to peak. The blacks were beginnin' to demonstrate and picket downtown stores. I never will forget some black lady I hated with a purple passion. Ann Atwater. Every time I'd go downtown, she'd be leadin' a boycott. How I hated — pardon the expression, I don't use it much now — how I just hated the black nigger. (Laughs.) Big, fat, heavy woman. She'd pull about eight demonstrations, and first thing you know they had two, three blacks at the checkout counter. Her and I have had some pretty close confrontations.

I felt very big, yeah. (Laughs.) We're more or less a secret organization. We didn't want anybody to know who we were, and I began to do some thinkin'. What am I hidin' for? I've never been convicted of anything in my life. I don't have any court record. What am I, C. P. Ellis, as a citizen and a member of the United Klansmen of America? Why can't I go to the city council meeting and say: "This is the way we feel about the matter? We don't want you to purchase mobile units to set in our schoolyards. We don't want niggers in our schools."

We began to come out in the open. We would go to the meetings, and the blacks would be there and we'd be there. It was a confrontation every time. I didn't hold back anything. We began to make some inroads with the city councilmen and county commissioners. They began to call us friend. Call us at night on the telephone: "C. P., glad you came to that meeting last night." They didn't want integration either, but they did it secretively, in order to get elected. They couldn't stand up openly and say it, but they were glad somebody was sayin' it. We visited some of the city leaders in their

25

[1]*Andy Young:* Andrew Jackson Young, Jr. (b. 1932), prominent black leader and politician. Young was a friend and adviser of Martin Luther King, Jr., and served as President Jimmy Carter's ambassador to the United Nations. In the 1980s, he was twice elected mayor of Atlanta.

home and talked to 'em privately. It wasn't long before councilmen would call me up: "The blacks are comin' up tonight and makin' outrageous demands. How about some of you people showin' up and have a little balance?" I'd get on the telephone. "The niggers is comin' to the council meeting tonight. Persons in the city's called me and asked us to be there."

We'd load up our cars and we'd fill up half the council chambers, and the blacks the other half. During these times, I carried weapons to the meetings, outside my belt. We'd go there armed. We would wind up just hollerin' and fussin' at each other. What happened? As a result of our fightin' one another, the city council still had their way. They didn't want to give up control to the blacks nor the Klan. They were usin' us.

I began to realize this later down the road. One day I was walkin' downtown and a certain city council member saw me comin'. I expected him to shake my hand because he was talkin' to me at night on the telephone. I had been in his home and visited with him. He crossed the street. Oh shit, I began to think, somethin's wrong here. Most of 'em are merchants or maybe an attorney, an insurance agent, people like that. As long as they kept low-income whites and low-income blacks fightin', they're gonna maintain control.

I began to get that feeling after I was ignored in public. I thought: Bullshit, you're not gonna use me any more. That's when I began to do some real serious thinkin'.

The same thing is happening in this country today. People are being used by those in control, those who have all the wealth. I'm not espousing communism. We got the greatest system of government in the world. But those who have it simply don't want those who don't have it to have any part of it. Black and white. When it comes to money, the green, the other colors make no difference. (Laughs.)

I spent a lot of sleepless nights. I still didn't like blacks. I didn't want to   30
associate with 'em. Blacks, Jews, or Catholics. My father said: "Don't have anything to do with 'em." I didn't until I met a black person and talked with him, eyeball to eyeball, and met a Jewish person and talked to him, eyeball to eyeball. I found out they're people just like me. They cried, they cussed, they prayed, they had desires. Just like myself. Thank God, I got to the point where I can look past labels. But at that time, my mind was closed.

I remember one Monday night Klan meeting. I said something was wrong. Our city fathers were using us. And I didn't like to be used. The reactions of the others was not too pleasant: "Let's just keep fightin' them niggers."

I'd go home at night and I'd have to wrestle with myself. I'd look at a black person walkin' down the street, and the guy'd have ragged shoes or his clothes would be worn. That began to do somethin' to me inside. I went through this for about six months. I felt I just had to get out of the Klan. But I wouldn't get out.

Then something happened. The state AFL–CIO[2] received a grant from the Department of HEW,[3] a $78,000 grant: how to solve racial problems in the school system. I got a telephone call from the president of the state AFL–CIO. "We'd like to get some people together from all walks of life." I said: "All walks of life? Who you talkin' about?" He said: "Blacks, whites, liberals, conservatives, Klansmen, NAACP[4] people."

I said: "No way am I comin' with all those niggers. I'm not gonna be associated with those type of people." A White Citizens Council guy said: "Let's go up there and see what's goin' on. It's tax money bein' spent." I walk in the door, and there was a large number of blacks and white liberals. I knew most of 'em by face 'cause I seen 'em demonstratin' around town. Ann Atwater was there. (Laughs.) I just forced myself to go in and sit down.

The meeting was moderated by a great big black guy who was bushy-headed. (Laughs.) That turned me off. He acted very nice. He said: "I want you all to feel free to say anything you want to say." Some of the blacks stand up and say it's white racism. I took all I could take. I asked for the floor and cut loose. I said: "No, sir, it's black racism. If we didn't have niggers in the schools, we wouldn't have the problems we got today." 35

I will never forget. Howard Clements, a black guy, stood up. He said: "I'm certainly glad C. P. Ellis come because he's the most honest man here tonight." I said: "What's that nigger tryin' to do?" (Laughs.) At the end of that meeting, some blacks tried to come up shake my hand, but I wouldn't do it. I walked off.

Second night, same group was there. I felt a little more easy because I got some things off my chest. The third night, after they elected all the committees, they want to elect a chairman. Howard Clements stood up and said: "I suggest we elect two co-chairpersons." Joe Beckton, executive director of the Human Relations Commission, just as black as he can be, he nominated me. There was a reaction from some blacks. Nooo. And, of all things, they nominated Ann Atwater, that big old fat black gal that I had just hated with a purple passion, as co-chairman. I thought to myself: Hey, ain't no way I can work with that gal. Finally, I agreed to accept it, 'cause at this point, I was tired of fightin', either for survival or against black people or against Jews or against Catholics.

A Klansman and a militant black woman, co-chairmen of the school committee. It was impossible. How could I work with her? But after about two or three days, it was in our hands. We had to make it a success. This give me another sense of belongin', a sense of pride. This helped this inferi-

---

[2]*AFL–CIO:* American Federation of Labor and Congress of Industrial Organizations — a huge federation of independent labor unions in the United States, Canada, Mexico, Panama, and elsewhere.

[3]*HEW:* Health, Education, and Welfare — at the time, a department of the federal government.

[4]*NAACP:* National Association for the Advancement of Colored People.

ority feelin' I had. A man who has stood up publicly and said he despised black people, all of a sudden he was willin' to work with 'em. Here's a chance for a low-income white man to be somethin'. In spite of all my hatred for blacks and Jews and liberals, I accepted the job. Her and I began to reluctantly work together. (Laughs.) She had as many problems workin' with me as I had workin' with her.

One night, I called her: "Ann, you and I should have a lot of differences and we got 'em now. But there's somethin' laid out here before us, and if it's gonna be a success, you and I are gonna have to make it one. Can we lay aside some of these feelin's?" She said: "I'm willing if you are." I said: "Let's do it."

My old friends would call me at night: "C. P., what the hell is wrong   40
with you? You're sellin' out the white race." This begin to make me have guilt feelin's. Am I doin' right? Am I doin' wrong? Here I am all of a sudden makin' an about-face and tryin' to deal with my feelin's, my heart. My mind was beginnin' to open up. I was beginnin' to see what was right and what was wrong. I don't want the kids to fight forever.

We were gonna go ten nights. By this time, I had went to work at Duke University, in maintenance. Makin' very little money. Terry Sanford give me this ten days off with pay. He was president of Duke at the time. He knew I was a Klansman and realized the importance of blacks and whites getting along.

I said: "If we're gonna make this thing a success, I've got to get to my kind of people." The low-income whites. We walked the streets of Durham, and we knocked on doors and invited people. Ann was goin' into the black community. They just wasn't respondin' to us when we made these house calls. Some of 'em were cussin' us out. "You're sellin' us out, Ellis, get out of my door. I don't want to talk to you." Ann was gettin' the same response from blacks. "What are you doin' messin' with that Klansman?"

One day, Ann and I went back to the school and we sat down. We began to talk and just reflect. Ann said: "My daughter came home cryin' every day. She said her teacher was makin' fun of me in front of the other kids." I said: "Boy, the same thing happened to my kid. White liberal teacher was makin' fun of Tim Ellis's father, the Klansman. In front of other peoples. He came home cryin'." At this point — (he pauses, swallows hard, stifles a sob) — I begin to see, here we are, two people from the far ends of the fence, havin' identical problems, except hers bein' black and me bein' white. From that moment on, I tell ya, that gal and I worked together good. I begin to love the girl, really. (He weeps.)

The amazing thing about it, her and I, up to that point, had cussed each other, bawled each other, we hated each other. Up to that point, we didn't know each other. We didn't know we had things in common.

We worked at it, with the people who came to these meetings. They   45
talked about racism, sex education, about teachers not bein' qualified. After seven, eight nights of real intense discussion, these people, who'd never talked to each other before, all of a sudden came up with resolutions. It was really somethin', you had to be there to get the tone and feelin' of it.

At that point, I didn't like integration, but the law says you do this and I've got to do what the law says, okay? We said: "Let's take these resolutions to the school board." The most disheartening thing I've ever faced was the school system refused to implement any one of these resolutions. These were recommendations from the people who pay taxes and pay their salaries. (Laughs.)

I thought they were good answers. Some of 'em I didn't agree with, but I been in this thing from the beginning, and whatever comes of it, I'm gonna support it. Okay, since the school board refused, I decided I'd just run for the school board.

I spent eighty-five dollars on the campaign. The guy runnin' against me spent several thousand. I really had nobody on my side. The Klan turned against me. The low-income whites turned against me. The liberals didn't particularly like me. The blacks were suspicious of me. The blacks wanted to support me, but they couldn't muster up enough to support a Klansman on the school board. (Laughs.) But I made up my mind that what I was doin' was right, and I was gonna do it regardless what anybody said.

It bothered me when people would call and worry my wife. She's always supported me in anything I wanted to do. She was changing, and my boys were too. I got some of my youth corps kids involved. They still followed me.

I was invited to the Democratic women's social hour as a candidate.   50 Didn't have but one suit to my name. Had it six, seven, eight years. I had it cleaned, put on the best shirt I had and a tie. Here were all these high-class wealthy candidates shakin' hands. I walked up to the mayor and stuck out my hand. He give me that handshake with that rag type of hand. He said: "C. P., I'm glad to see you." But I could tell by his handshake he was lyin' to me. This was botherin' me. I know I'm a low-income person. I know I'm not wealthy. I know they were sayin': "What's this little ol' dude runnin' for school board?" Yet they had to smile and make like they're glad to see me. I begin to spot some black people in that room. I automatically went to 'em and that was a firm handshake. They said: "I'm glad to see you, C. P." I knew they meant it — you can tell about a handshake.

Every place I appeared, I said I will listen to the voice of the people. I will not make a major decision until I first contacted all the organizations in the city. I got 4,640 votes. The guy beat me by two thousand. Not bad for eighty-five bucks and no constituency.

The whole world was openin' up, and I was learnin' new truths that I had never learned before. I was beginnin' to look at a black person, shake hands with him, and see him as a human bein'. I hadn't got rid of all this stuff, I've still got a little bit of it. But somethin' was happenin' to me.

It was almost like bein' born again. It was a new life. I didn't have these sleepless nights I used to have when I was active in the Klan and slippin' around at night. I could sleep at night and feel good about it. I'd rather live now than at any other time in history. It's a challenge.

Back at Duke, doin' maintenance, I'd pick up my tools, fix the commode, unstop the drains. But this got in my blood. Things weren't right in this country, and what we done in Durham needs to be told. I was so miserable at Duke, I could hardly stand it. I'd go to work every morning just hatin' to go.

My whole life had changed. I got an eighth-grade education, and I 55 wanted to complete high school. Went to high school in the afternoons on a program called PEP — Past Employment Progress. I was about the only white in class, and the oldest. I begin to read about biology. I'd take my books home at night, 'cause I was determined to get through. Sure enough, I graduated. I got the diploma at home.

I come to work one mornin' and some guy says: "We need a union." At this time I wasn't pro-union. My daddy was anti-labor, too. We're not gettin' paid much, we're havin' to work seven days in a row. We're all starvin' to death. The next day, I meet the international representative of the Operating Engineers. He give me authorization cards. "Get these cards out and we'll have an election." There was eighty-eight for the union and seventeen no's. I was elected chief steward for the union.

Shortly after, a union man come down from Charlotte and says we need a full-time rep. We've got only two hundred people at the two plants here. It's just barely enough money comin' in to pay your salary. You'll have to get out and organize more people. I didn't know nothin' about organizin' unions, but I knew how to organize people, stir people up. (Laughs.) That's how I got to be business agent for the union.

When I began to organize, I began to see far deeper. I began to see people again bein' used. Blacks against whites. I say this without any hesitancy: management is vicious. There's two things they want to keep: all the money and all the say-so. They don't want these poor workin' folks to have none of that. I begin to see management fightin' me with everything they had. Hire anti-union law firms, badmouth unions. The people were makin' a dollar ninety-five an hour, barely able to get through weekends. I worked as a business rep for five years and was seein' all this.

Last year, I ran for business manager of the union. He's elected by the workers. The guy that ran against me was black, and our membership is seventy-five percent black. I thought: Claiborne, there's no way you can beat that black guy. People know your background. Even though you've made tremendous strides, those black people are not gonna vote for you. You know how much I beat him? Four to one. (Laughs.)

The company used my past against me. They put out letters with a 60 picture of a robe and a cap: would you vote for a Klansman? They wouldn't deal with the issues. I immediately called for a mass meeting. I met with the ladies at an electric component plant. I said: "Okay, this is Claiborne Ellis. This is where I come from. I want you to know right now, you black ladies here, I was at one time a member of the Klan. I want you to know, because they'll tell you about it."

I invited some of my old black friends. I said: "Brother Joe, Brother Howard, be honest now and tell these people how you feel about me." They done it. (Laughs.) Howard Clements kidded me a little bit. He said: "I don't know what I'm doin' here, supportin' an ex-Klansman." (Laughs.) He said: "I know what C. P. Ellis come from. I knew him when he was. I knew him as he grew, and growed with him. I'm tellin' you now: follow, follow this Klansman." (He pauses, swallows hard.) "Any questions?" "No," the black ladies said. "Let's get on with the meeting, we need Ellis." (He laughs and weeps.) Boy, black people sayin' that about me. I won one thirty-four to forty-one. Four to one.

It makes you feel good to go into a plant and butt heads with professional union busters. You see black people and white people join hands to defeat the racist issues they use against people. They're tryin' the same things with the Klan. It's still happenin' today. Can you imagine a guy who's got an adult high school diploma runnin' into professional college graduates who are union busters? I gotta compete with 'em. I work seven days a week, nights and on Saturday and Sunday. The salary's not that great, and if I didn't care, I'd quit. But I care and I can't quit. I got a taste of it. (Laughs.)

I tell people there's a tremendous possibility in this country to stop wars, the battles, the struggles, the fights between people. People say: "That's an impossible dream. You sound like Martin Luther King." An ex-Klansman who sounds like Martin Luther King. (Laughs.) I don't think it's an impossible dream. It's happened in my life. It's happened in other people's lives in America.

I don't know what's ahead of me. I have no desire to be a big union official. I want to be right out here in the field with the workers. I want to walk through their factory and shake hands with that man whose hands are dirty. I'm gonna do all that one little ol' man can do. I'm fifty-two years old, and I ain't got many years left, but I want to make the best of 'em.

When the news came over the radio that Martin Luther King was assassinated, I got on the telephone and begin to call other Klansmen. We just had a real party at the service station. Really rejoicin' 'cause that son of a bitch was dead. Our troubles are over with. They say the older you get, the harder it is for you to change. That's not necessarily true. Since I changed, I've set down and listened to tapes of Martin Luther King. I listen to it and tears come to my eyes 'cause I know what he's sayin' now. I know what's happenin'.

POSTSCRIPT:
The phone rings. A conversation.
"This was a black guy who's director of Operation Breakthrough in Durham. I had called his office. I'm interested in employin' some young black person who's interested in learnin' the labor movement. I want somebody who's never had an opportunity, just like myself. Just so he can read and write, that's all."

ENGAGING THE TEXT

1. How does Ellis battle the racism he finds in himself? What gives him the motivation and strength to change? What specific changes does he undergo, and how successful is he in abandoning racist attitudes?

2. Would Ellis say that economic class is more important than race in determining job placement and occupational mobility? Find specific passages that reveal Ellis's beliefs about the connections between economic class, race, and success in American society. What do you believe?

3. How well does Ellis seem to understand himself, his feelings, his motives? Give evidence for your assertions.

4. What is Terkel's role in this selection? Is he unconsciously helping to rationalize or justify the actions of the Ku Klux Klan?

5. Does Ellis's story offer a credible way of overcoming misunderstanding and hatred between races? Do you think such a "solution" would be workable on a large scale? Why or why not?

EXPLORING CONNECTIONS

6. To what extent does Ellis's experience illustrate the theories of prejudice described by Vincent N. Parrillo in the previous selection (p. 504)? Which of these theories best account for Ellis's racism and for his eventual transformation?

7. Review the account of Malcolm X's self-education (p. 210). How does the dramatic self-transformation he experiences compare with C. P. Ellis's rebirth? What relationships can you find between the circumstances that led to their initial attitudes, the conditions or events that fostered their transformations, and the effects that these transformations had on their characters?

EXTENDING THE CRITICAL CONTEXT

8. Interview a friend, family member, or fellow student in another class to create your own oral history on the subject of racial attitudes. Ask your subject to describe a time when he or she was forced to re-evaluate his or her thoughts or feelings about someone from a different racial or ethnic group. Try to include as many relevant details as possible in your retelling of the story. Share and edit these oral histories in small groups, and then assemble them into a class anthology.

I'm Black, You're White, Who's Innocent?

SHELBY STEELE

This essay comes from one of the most controversial American books of the 1980s — The Content of Our Character: A New Vision of Race in America. *Shelby Steele (b. 1946) believes that black Americans have failed to seize opportunities that would lead to social equality; he is also an outspoken critic of affirmative action, arguing that instead of promoting equality it locks its recipients into second-class status. Critics have accused him of underestimating the power of racism, of blaming victims for their predicament, of being a traitor to his race. In this selection, Steele offers his observations on why black and white Americans have not been able to sustain the kind of dialogue that would make mutual understanding possible. Steele's second book,* A Dream Deferred: The Second Betrayal of Black Freedom in America *(1998), elaborates the critique of innocence and guilt laid out in this essay. In his new work, Steele argues that programs — like affirmative action — that were devised to reduce racial inequality have actually harmed rather than helped most African Americans, and have benefitted only guilty white liberals and a black "grievance elite." He further develops this theme in his most recent book,* White Guilt: How Blacks and Whites Together Destroyed the Promise of the Civil Rights Era *(2006). Steele's essays have garnered a number of awards and have appeared in* Harper's, The American Scholar, The New Republic, *and many other journals and magazines. He is a research fellow at the Hoover Institution, Stanford University.*

It is a warm, windless California evening, and the dying light that covers the redbrick patio is tinted pale orange by the day's smog. Eight of us, not close friends, sit in lawn chairs sipping chardonnay. A black engineer and I (we had never met before) integrate the group. A psychologist is also among us, and her presence encourages a surprising openness. But not until well after the lovely twilight dinner has been served, when the sky has turned to deep black and the drinks have long since changed to scotch, does the subject of race spring awkwardly upon us. Out of nowhere the engineer announces, with a coloring of accusation in his voice, that it bothers him to send his daughter to a school where she is one of only three black children. "I didn't realize my ambition to get ahead would pull me into a world where my daughter would lose touch with her blackness," he says.

Over the course of the evening we have talked about money, past and present addictions, child abuse, even politics. Intimacies have been revealed, fears named. But this subject, race, sinks us into one of those shaming silences where eye contact terrorizes. Our host looks for something in the bottom of his glass. Two women stare into the black sky as if to locate the Big Dipper and point it out to us. Finally, the psychologist seems to gather herself for a challenge, but it is too late. "Oh, I'm sure she'll be just fine," says our hostess, rising from her chair. When she excuses herself to get the coffee, the psychologist and two sky gazers offer to help.

With four of us now gone, I am surprised to see the engineer still silently holding his ground. There is a willfulness in his eyes, an inner pride. He knows he has said something awkward, but he is determined not to give a damn. His unwavering eyes intimidate even me. At last the host's head snaps erect. He has an idea. "The hell with coffee," he says. "How about some of the smoothest brandy you've ever tasted?" An idea made exciting by the escape it offers. Gratefully, we follow him back into the house, quickly drink his brandy, and say our good-byes.

An autopsy of this party might read: death induced by an abrupt and lethal injection of the American race issue. An accurate if superficial assessment. Since it has been my fate to live a rather integrated life, I have often witnessed sudden deaths like this. The threat of them, if not the reality, is a part of the texture of integration. In the late 1960s, when I was just out of college, I took a delinquent's delight in playing the engineer's role, and actually developed a small reputation for playing it well. Those were the days of flagellatory white guilt: it was such great fun to pinion some professor or housewife or, best of all, a large group of remorseful whites, with the knowledge of both their racism and their denial of it. The adolescent impulse to sneer at convention, to startle the middle-aged with doubt, could be indulged under the guise of racial indignation. And how could I lose? My victims — earnest liberals for the most part — could no more crawl out from under my accusations than Joseph K. in Kafka's *Trial*[1] could escape the amorphous charges brought against him. At this odd moment in history the world was aligned to facilitate my immaturity.

About a year of this was enough: the guilt that follows most cheap thrills caught up to me, and I put myself in check. But the impulse to do it faded more slowly. It was one of those petty talents that is tied to vanity, and when there were ebbs in my self-esteem the impulse to use it would come alive again. In integrated situations I can still feel the faint itch. But then there are many youthful impulses that still itch and now, just inside the door of midlife, this one is least precious to me.

5

In the literature classes I teach I often see how the presence of whites all but seduces some black students into provocation. When we come to a novel by a black writer, say Toni Morrison, the white students can easily discuss the human motivations of the black characters. But, inevitably, a black student, as if by reflex, will begin to set in relief the various racial problems

---

[1]*Kafka's* Trial: Czech writer Franz Kafka (1883–1924) is famous for his dreamlike and ominous stories. In his novel *The Trial*, the character known only as Joseph K. battles an intricate legal and police system that never specifies his alleged crime.

that are the background of these characters' lives. This student's tone will carry a reprimand: the class is afraid to confront the reality of racism. Classes cannot be allowed to die like dinner parties, however. My latest strategy is to thank that student for his or her moral vigilance and then appoint the young man or woman as the class's official racism monitor. But even if I get a laugh — I usually do, but sometimes the student is particularly indignant, and it gets uncomfortable — the strategy never quite works. Our racial division is suddenly drawn in neon. Overcaution spreads like spilled paint. And, in fact, the black student who started it all does become a kind of monitor. The very presence of this student imposes a new accountability on the class.

I think those who provoke this sort of awkwardness are operating out of a black identity that obliges them to badger white people about race almost on principle. Content hardly matters. (For example, it made little sense for the engineer to expect white people to anguish terribly much over his decision to send his daughter to school with *white* children.) Race indeed remains a source of white shame; the goal of these provocations is to put whites, no matter how indirectly, in touch with this collective guilt. In other words, these provocations I speak of are *power* moves, little shows of power that try to freeze the "enemy" in self-consciousness. They gratify and inflate the provocateur. They are the underdog's bite. And whites, far more secure in their power, respond with self-contained and tolerant silence that is itself a show of power. What greater power than that of nonresponse, the power to let a small enemy sizzle in his own juices, to even feel a little sad at his frustration just as one is also complimented by it. Black anger always, in a way, flatters white power. In America, to know that one is not black is to feel an extra grace, a little boost of impunity.

I think the real trouble between the races in America is that the races are not just races but competing power groups — a fact that is easily minimized, perhaps because it is so obvious. What is not so obvious is that this is true quite apart from the issue of class. Even the well-situated middle-class (or wealthy) black is never completely immune to that peculiar contest of power that his skin color subjects him to. Race is a separate reality in American society, an entity that carries its own potential for power, a mark of fate that class can soften considerably but not eradicate.

The distinction of race has always been used in American life to sanction each race's pursuit of power in relation to the other. The allure of race as a human delineation is the very shallowness of the delineation it makes. Onto this shallowness — mere skin and hair — men can project a false depth, a system of dismal attributions, a series of malevolent or ignoble stereotypes that skin and hair lack the substance to contradict. These dark projections then rationalize the pursuit of power. Your difference from me makes you bad, and your badness justifies, even demands, my pursuit of power over you — the oldest formula for aggression known to man. Whenever much importance is given to race, power is the primary motive.

But the human animal almost never pursues power without first 10 convincing himself that he is *entitled* to it. And this feeling of entitlement has its own precondition: to be entitled one must first believe in one's innocence, at least in the area where one wishes to be entitled. By innocence I mean a feeling of essential goodness in relation to others and, therefore, superiority to others. Our innocence always inflates us and deflates those we seek power over. Once inflated we are entitled; we are in fact licensed to go after the power our innocence tells us we deserve. In this sense, *innocence is power.* Of course, innocence need not be genuine or real in any objective sense, as the Nazis demonstrated not long ago. Its only test is whether or not we can convince ourselves of it.

I think the racial struggle in America has always been primarily a struggle for innocence. White racism from the beginning has been a claim of white innocence and therefore of white entitlement to subjugate blacks. And in the sixties, as went innocence so went power. Blacks used the innocence that grew out of their long subjugation to seize more power, while whites lost some of their innocence and so lost a degree of power over blacks. Both races instinctively understand that to lose innocence is to lose power (in relation to each other). To be innocent someone else must be guilty, a natural law that leads the races to forge their innocence on each other's backs. The inferiority of the black always makes the white man superior; the evil might of whites makes blacks good. This pattern means that both races have a hidden investment in racism and racial disharmony despite their good intentions to the contrary. Power defines their relations, and power requires innocence, which, in turn, requires racism and racial division.

I believe it was his hidden investment that the engineer was protecting when he made his remark — the white "evil" he saw in a white school "depriving" his daughter of her black heritage confirmed his innocence. Only the logic of power explained his emphasis — he bent reality to show that he was once again a victim of the white world and, as a victim, innocent. His determined eyes insisted on this. And the whites, in their silence, no doubt protected their innocence by seeing him as an ungracious troublemaker, his bad behavior underscoring their goodness. What none of us saw was the underlying game of power and innocence we were trapped in, or how much we needed a racial impasse to play that game.

When I was a boy of about twelve, a white friend of mine told me one day that his uncle, who would be arriving the next day for a visit, was a racist. Excited by the prospect of seeing such a man, I spent the following afternoon hanging around the alley behind my friend's house, watching from a distance as this uncle worked on the engine of his Buick. Yes, here was evil and I was compelled to look upon it. And I saw evil in the sharp angle of his elbow as he pumped his wrench to tighten nuts. I saw it in the blade-sharp crease of his chinos, in the pack of Lucky Strikes that threatened to slip from his shirt pocket as he bent, and in the way his concentration seemed to shut out the human world. He worked neatly and efficiently, wiping his hands constantly, and I decided that evil worked like this.

I felt a compulsion to have this man look upon me so that I could see evil — so that I could see the face of it. But when he noticed me standing beside his toolbox, he said only, "If you're looking for Bobby, I think he went up to the school to play baseball." He smiled nicely and went back to work. I was stunned for a moment, but then I realized that evil could be sly as well, could smile when it wanted to trick you.

Need, especially hidden need, puts a strong pressure on perception, and my need to have this man embody white evil was stronger than any contravening evidence. As a black person you always hear about racists but rarely meet any who will let you know them as such. And I needed to incarnate this odious category of humanity, those people who hated Martin Luther King, Jr., and thought blacks should "go slow" or not at all. So, in my mental dictionary, behind the term "white racist," I inserted this man's likeness. I would think of him and say to myself, "There is no reason for him to hate black people. Only evil explains unmotivated hatred." And this thought soothed me; I felt innocent. If I hated white people, which I did not, at least I had a reason. His evil commanded me to assert in the world the goodness he made me confident of in myself. 15

In looking at this man I was *seeing for innocence* — a form of seeing that has more to do with one's hidden need for innocence (and power) than with the person or group one is looking at. It is quite possible, for example, that the man I saw that day was not a racist. He did absolutely nothing in my presence to indicate that he was. I invested an entire afternoon in seeing not the man but in seeing my innocence through the man. *Seeing for innocence* is, in this way, the essence of racism — the use of others as a means to our own goodness and superiority.

The loss of innocence has always to do with guilt, Kierkegaard[2] tells us, and it has never been easy for whites to avoid guilt where blacks are concerned. For whites, *seeing for innocence* means seeing themselves and blacks in ways that minimize white guilt. Often this amounts to a kind of white revisionism,[3] as when President Reagan declared himself "colorblind" in matters of race. The President, like many of us, may have aspired to racial color blindness, but few would grant that he ever reached this sublimely guiltless state. His statement clearly revised reality, moved it forward into some heretofore unknown America where all racial determinism would have vanished. I do not think that Ronald Reagan was a racist, as that term is commonly used, but neither do I think that he was capable of seeing color without making attributions, some of which may have been negative — nor am I, or anyone else I've ever met.

---

[2]*Kierkegaard:* Danish philosopher and religious thinker Søren Kierkegaard (1813–1855).
[3]*revisionism:* The reinterpretation or revising of reality to suit one's current purposes.

So why make such a statement? I think Reagan's claim of color blindness with regard to race was really a claim of racial innocence and guiltlessness — the preconditions for entitlement and power. This was the claim that grounded Reagan's campaign against special entitlement programs — affirmative action, racial quotas, and so on — that black power had won in the sixties. Color blindness was a strategic assumption of innocence that licensed Reagan's use of government power against black power. . . .

Black Americans have had to find a way to handle white society's presumption of racial innocence whenever they have sought to enter the American mainstream. Louis Armstrong's[4] exaggerated smile honored the presumed innocence of white society — *I will not bring you your racial guilt if you will let me play my music.* Ralph Ellison[5] calls this "masking"; I call it bargaining. But whatever it's called, it points to the power of white society to enforce its innocence. I believe this power is greatly diminished today. Society has reformed and transformed — Miles Davis[6] never smiles. Nevertheless, this power has not faded altogether and blacks must still contend with it.

Historically, blacks have handled white society's presumption of inno- 20
cence in two ways: they have bargained with it, granting white society its innocence in exchange for entry into the mainstream, or they have challenged it, holding that innocence hostage until their demand for entry (or other concessions) was met. A bargainer says, *I already believe you are innocent (good, fair-minded) and have faith that you will prove it.* A challenger says, *If you are innocent, then prove it.* Bargainers *give* in hope of receiving; challengers *withhold* until they receive. Of course, there is risk in both approaches, but in each case the black is negotiating his own self-interest against the presumed racial innocence of the larger society.

Clearly, the most visible black bargainer on the American scene today is Bill Cosby. His television show has been a perfect formula for black bargaining in the eighties. The remarkable Huxtable family — with its doctor/lawyer parent combination, its drug-free, college-bound children, and its wise yet youthful grandparents — is a blackface version of the American dream. Cosby is a subscriber to the American identity, and his subscription confirms his belief in its fair-mindedness. His vast audience knows this, knows that Cosby will never assault their innocence with racial guilt. Racial controversy is all but banished from the show. The Huxtable family never discusses affirmative action.

The bargain Cosby offers his white viewers — *I will confirm your racial innocence if you accept me* — is a good deal for all concerned. Not only

---

[4]*Louis Armstrong:* American jazz trumpet virtuoso and singer (1900–1971).
[5]*Ralph Ellison:* American novelist (1914–1994), best known for *Invisible Man,* the account of a nameless black youth coming of age in a hostile society.
[6]*Miles Davis:* Jazz musician and trumpeter (1926–1991).

does it allow whites to enjoy Cosby's humor with no loss of innocence, but it actually enhances their innocence by implying that race is not the serious problem for blacks that it once was. If anything, the success of this handsome, affluent black family points to the fair-mindedness of whites who, out of their essential goodness, changed society so that black families like the Huxtables could succeed. Whites can watch *The Cosby Show* and feel complimented on a job well done.

The power that black bargainers wield is the power of absolution. On Thursday nights, Cosby, like a priest, absolves his white viewers, forgives and forgets the sins of the past. And for this he is rewarded with an almost sacrosanct[7] status. Cosby benefits from what might be called the gratitude factor. His continued number-one rating may have something to do with the (white) public's gratitude at being offered a commodity so rare in our time; he tells his white viewers each week that they are okay, and that this black man is not going to challenge them.

When a black bargains, he may invoke the gratitude factor and find himself cherished beyond the measure of his achievement; when he challenges, he may draw the dark projections of whites and become a source of irritation to them. If he moves back and forth between these two options, as I think many blacks do today, he will likely baffle whites. It is difficult for whites either to accept or reject such blacks. It seems to me that Jesse Jackson is such a figure — many whites see Jackson as a challenger by instinct and a bargainer by political ambition. They are uneasy with him, more than a little suspicious. His powerful speech at the 1984 Democratic Convention was a masterpiece of bargaining. In it he offered a King-like[8] vision of what America could be, a vision that presupposed Americans had the fair-mindedness to achieve full equality — an offer in hope of a return. A few days after this speech, looking for rest and privacy at a lodge in Big Sur,[9] he and his wife were greeted with standing ovations three times a day when they entered the dining room for meals. So much about Jackson is deeply American — this underdog striving, his irrepressible faith in himself, the daring of his ambition, and even his stubbornness. These qualities point to his underlying faith that Americans can respond to him despite race, and this faith is a compliment to Americans, an offer of innocence.

But Jackson does not always stick to the terms of his bargain as Cosby does on TV. When he hugs Arafat,[10] smokes cigars with Castro,[11] refuses to repudiate Farrakhan,[12] threatens a boycott of major league baseball, or,   25

---

[7]*sacrosanct:* Sacred.

[8]*King-like:* Like that of Martin Luther King, Jr.

[9]*Big Sur:* Section of the California coast known for its natural beauty.

[10]*Arafat:* Yasir Arafat (1929–2004), leader of the Palestine Liberation Organization, or PLO.

[11]*Castro:* Fidel Castro (b. 1926), president of Cuba.

[12]*Farrakhan:* Louis Farrakhan (b. 1933), Nation of Islam leader, often accused of making anti-Semitic remarks. Many African American politicians carefully distance themselves from Farrakhan.

more recently, talks of "corporate barracudas," "pension-fund socialism," and "economic violence," he looks like a challenger in bargainer's clothing, and his positions on the issues look like familiar protests dressed in white-paper formality. At these times he appears to be revoking the innocence so much else about him seems to offer. The old activist seems to come out of hiding once again to take white innocence hostage until whites prove they deserve to have it. In his candidacy there is a suggestion of protest, a fierce insistence on his *right* to run, that sends whites a message that he may secretly see them as a good bit less than innocent. His dilemma is to appear the bargainer while his campaign itself seems to be a challenge.

There are, of course, other problems that hamper Jackson's bid for the Democratic presidential nomination. He has held no elective office, he is thought too flamboyant and opportunistic by many, there are rather loud whispers of "character" problems. As an individual, he may not be the best test of a black man's chances for winning so high an office. Still, I believe it is the aura of challenge surrounding him that hurts him most. Whether it is right or wrong, fair or unfair, I think no black candidate will have a serious chance at his party's nomination, much less the presidency, until he can convince white Americans that he can be trusted to preserve their sense of racial innocence. Such a candidate will have to use his power of absolution; he will have to flatly forgive and forget. He will have to bargain with white innocence out of genuine belief that it really exists. There can be no faking it. He will have to offer a vision that is passionately raceless, a vision that strongly condemns any form of racial politics. This will require the most courageous kind of leadership, leadership that asks all the people to meet a new standard.

Now the other side of America's racial impasse: how do blacks lay claim to their racial innocence?

The most obvious and unarguable source of black innocence is the victimization that blacks endured for centuries at the hands of a race that insisted on black inferiority as a means to its own innocence and power. Like all victims, what blacks lost in power they gained in innocence — innocence that, in turn, entitled them to pursue power. This was the innocence that fueled the civil rights movement of the sixties and that gave blacks their first real power in American life — victimization metamorphosed into power via innocence. But this formula carries a drawback that I believe is virtually as devastating to blacks today as victimization once was. It is a formula that binds the victim to his victimization by linking his power to his status as a victim. And this, I'm convinced, is the tragedy of black power in America today. It is primarily a victim's power, grounded too deeply in the entitlement derived from past injustice and in the innocence that Western/Christian tradition has always associated with poverty.

Whatever gains this power brings in the short run through political action, it undermines in the long run. Social victims may be collectively entitled, but they are all too often individually demoralized. Since the social victim has been oppressed by society, he comes to feel that his individual

FEIFFER®

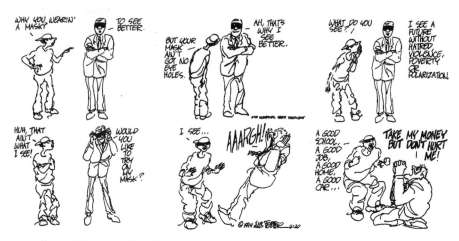

life will be improved more by changes in society than by his own initiative. Without realizing it, he makes society rather than himself the agent of change. The power he finds in his victimization may lead him to collective action against society, but it also encourages passivity within the sphere of his personal life.

Not long ago, I saw a television documentary that examined life in   30
Detroit's inner city on the twentieth anniversary of the riots there in which forty-three people were killed. A comparison of the inner city then and now showed a decline in the quality of life. Residents feel less safe, drug trafficking is far worse, crimes by blacks against blacks are more frequent, housing remains substandard, and the teenage pregnancy rate has skyrocketed. Twenty years of decline and demoralization, even as opportunities for blacks to better themselves have increased. This paradox is not peculiar to Detroit. By many measures, the majority of blacks — those not yet in the middle class — are further behind whites today than before the victories of the civil rights movement. But there is a reluctance among blacks to examine this paradox, I think, because it suggests that racial victimization is not our real problem. If conditions have worsened for most of us as racism has receded, then much of the problem must be of our own making. To admit this fully would cause us to lose the innocence we derive from our victimization. And we would jeopardize the entitlement we've always had to challenge society. We are in the odd and self-defeating position in which taking responsibility for bettering ourselves feels like a surrender to white power.

So we have a hidden investment in victimization and poverty. These distressing conditions have been the source of our own real power, and

there is an unconscious sort of gravitation toward them, a complaining celebration of them. One sees evidence of this in the near happiness with which
certain black leaders recount the horror of Howard Beach,[13] Bensonhurst,[14]
and other recent instances of racial tension. As one is saddened by these
tragic events, one is also repelled at the way some black leaders — agitated
to near hysteria by the scent of victim power inherent in them — leap forward to exploit them as evidence of black innocence and white guilt. It is as
though they sense the decline of black victimization as a loss of standing and
dive into the middle of these incidents as if they were reservoirs of pure
black innocence swollen with potential power.

Seeing for innocence pressures blacks to focus on racism and to neglect
the individual initiative that would deliver them from poverty — the only
thing that finally delivers *anyone* from poverty. With our eyes on innocence
we see racism everywhere and miss opportunity even as we stumble over it.
About 70 percent of black students at my university[15] drop out before
graduation — a flight from opportunity that racism cannot explain. It is an
injustice that whites can see for innocence with more impunity than blacks
can. The price whites pay is a certain blindness to themselves. Moreover,
for whites seeing for innocence continues to engender the bad faith of a
long-disgruntled minority. But the price blacks pay is an ever-escalating
poverty that threatens to make the worst off a permanent underclass. Not
fair, but real.

Challenging works best for the collective, while bargaining is more the
individual's suit. From this point on, the race's advancement will come from
the efforts of its individuals. True, some challenging will be necessary for a
long time to come. But bargaining is now — today — a way for the black
individual to *join* the larger society, to make a place for himself or herself.

"Innocence is ignorance," Kierkegaard says, and if this is so, the claim
of innocence amounts to an insistence on ignorance, a refusal to know. In
their assertions of innocence both races carve out very functional areas of
ignorance for themselves — territories of blindness that license a misguided
pursuit of power. Whites gain superiority by not knowing blacks; blacks gain
entitlement by not seeing their own responsibility for bettering themselves.
The power each race seeks in relation to the other is grounded in a double-
edged ignorance of the self as well as of the other.

The original sin that brought us to an impasse at the dinner party I   35
mentioned occurred centuries ago, when it was first decided to exploit racial
difference as a means to power. It was a determinism that flowed karmically
from this sin that dropped over us like a net that night. What bothered me
most was our helplessness. Even the engineer did not know how to go

---

[13]*Howard Beach:* Scene in Queens, New York, of a December 1986 racial confrontation
in which several young African American men were severely beaten and one died.

[14]*Bensonhurst:* Location in Brooklyn, New York, where the racially motivated murder of
sixteen-year-old Yusuf Hawkins took place in August 1989.

[15]*my university:* Refers to San Jose State University where Steele was then teaching.

forward. His challenge hadn't worked, and he'd lost the option to bargain. The marriage of race and power depersonalized us, changed us from eight people to six whites and two blacks. The easiest thing was to let silence blanket our situation, our impasse. . . .

What both black and white Americans fear are the sacrifices and risks that true racial harmony demands. This fear is the measure of our racial chasm. And though fear always seeks a thousand justifications, none is ever good enough, and the problems we run from only remain to haunt us. It would be right to suggest courage as an antidote to fear, but the glory of the word might only intimidate us into more fear. I prefer the word *effort* — relentless effort, moral effort. What I like most about this word are its connotations of everydayness, earnestness, and practical sacrifice. No matter how badly it might have gone for us that warm summer night, we should have talked. We should have made the effort.

ENGAGING THE TEXT

1. What does Steele mean by "innocence" and by "seeing for innocence"? How does he apply these terms to racial conflict and struggles for power in the United States? How do blacks and whites claim innocence through racial conflict? What does Steele mean when he says "innocence is power"?

2. According to Steele, what strategies have African Americans employed to handle "white society's presumption of racial innocence" (para. 19)? How does he account for public reactions to figures like Bill Cosby and Jesse Jackson in terms of these strategies? Are there other possible explanations of their appeal?

3. Steele believes that "bargaining is now — today — a way for the black individual to *join* the larger society" (para. 33). Do you agree? Is bargaining an available and acceptable alternative for all African Americans?

4. Steele writes that when the issue of race comes up in classes, "overcaution spreads like spilled paint" (para. 6). If you have observed this phenomenon in class or in other circumstances, write a journal entry describing one such incident and analyzing the behavior of the people involved.

EXPLORING CONNECTIONS

5. How might Ken Hamblin (p. 285), Vincent N. Parrillo (p. 504), George M. Fredrickson (p. 561), and Paul L. Wachtel (p. 541) evaluate Steele's assertion that racism grows out of the desire to claim "innocence"? Imagine that they are all participating in a panel discussion and role-play the conversation that would ensue.

6. Write an imaginary conversation among C. P. Ellis (p. 519), Malcolm X (p. 210), and Steele on American racism. What might they each say about the causes of racist thinking and behavior? About the chances for curbing racism? How would they respond to each other's ideas and strategies for change?

7. What does Jules Feiffer's cartoon (p. 540) suggest about the ways that black and white Americans see the world? How does Feiffer's view of the psychology of race compare to Steele's?

EXTENDING THE CRITICAL CONTEXT

8. At the end of this essay, Steele writes, "No matter how badly it might have gone for us . . . we should have talked. We should have made the effort." Working in groups, role-play the conversation that might have occurred that night. How might you initiate such conversations on your campus? Is talk the only or best solution to the kinds of tensions Steele describes?

Talking About Racism: How Our Dialogue Gets Short-Circuited

PAUL L. WACHTEL

In the following selection, eminent psychotherapist Paul L. Wachtel suggests that racial conflicts are often aggravated by problems of communication. African Americans' legitimate grievances need to be heard and addressed by whites, who often resist listening. In an effort to break through this resistance, blacks may hurl charges of racism that make whites even more defensive, which in turn shuts down conversation. In order to address America's race problem, Wachtel argues, we must learn to break these unproductive patterns of behavior. Wachtel (b. 1940) is CUNY Distinguished Professor in clinical psychology at City University of New York Graduate Center and at City College of New York, where he also served as Acting Director of the Colin Powell Center for Policy Studies. He has written and edited many books on psychotherapy and has applied his psychological training to the analysis of social issues in such well-received works as The Poverty of Affluence *(1983),* Action and Insight *(1987), and* Race in the Mind of America *(1999), from which this passage is taken.*

Racism: A Term with a Host of Meanings

Consider the following scenarios — some tragic and dramatic, some mundane, but all sadly recognizable features of the racial landscape in America:

-   A KKK mob burns a cross on the lawn of a black family that has moved into a formerly white neighborhood.

- A white person crosses the street to avoid encountering several black teenagers walking toward him.
- A black couple looking for an apartment is told that it is rented, but a white couple sent by a civil rights group to test for discrimination is shown the apartment an hour later and told it is available.
- A white person says he supports fair housing laws because he believes it is unfair and unjust to discriminate on the basis of race, but confesses that he himself would be afraid to live in a neighborhood that was not mostly white.
- A professor claims he has data proving that blacks are inferior in intelligence.
- A sports commentator comments that blacks are more naturally gifted as athletes.
- A white resident in an expensive co-op makes a friendly comment to a black woman riding in the elevator with her, but the comment makes it clear she has erroneously assumed that the black woman, who is in fact editor of a leading magazine, is a maid.
- The owner of a jewelry store does not buzz in a well-dressed black man for fear he is a robber.
- Two middle-class whites discuss their annoyance when a black youth passes by with a boom box loudly blaring rap music, saying, "Kids like that have no consideration; they think they own the streets."
- An employer interviewed by a researcher says that he has experienced repeatedly that blacks are more frequently late to work and tend to have an "attitude."
- A museum holds an exhibit of leading contemporary artists and none of the artists chosen are black.
- A literature survey course on the greatest works of world literature from Homer to the present has no black authors on the reading list.
- A candidate for office states that this country was founded as a white Christian nation and that is how it should remain.
- A high school institutes a writing requirement for graduation that requires mastery of standard English.
- A test is given for a civil service job and whites score higher on the test than blacks.
- A search committee for a faculty job at a prestigious university refuses to modify its criteria in considering a black applicant who has published few papers in leading professional journals.
- A black woman shopping in a department store that has had many robberies is watched more closely by the store detective than are the white women around her.
- A black child attends a school that has large classes, few books or study aids, and not nearly enough desks and chairs to go around.

- A teacher in that school says she is no longer as idealistic as she was when she began and that no matter how hard she tries, the kids don't seem to learn.
- A study reveals that garbage pickups in poor black neighborhoods are less frequent than in middle-class white neighborhoods.
- An activist for global environmental preservation advocates increasing efforts at promoting birth control in third world countries, where population increase is greatest.

These scenarios differ in a multitude of ways, but they have one significant thing in common: All have been labeled as instances of racism.

Do they all embody racism? Some of them seem to me clearly to merit the use of that term, but whether they all do is a virtually impossible question to answer. The platinum meter rod that lies in the International Bureau of Weights and Measures and defines for all of us just what a meter is has no real equivalent in the realm of language; no one owns a platinum dictionary that is the final arbiter of what the word "racism" should refer to. A word with such powerful emotional connotations, that is used to describe events and attitudes so close to the heart of our society's most basic afflictions, is bound to be a source of contention. "Looking it up in the dictionary" is utterly beside the point when a central issue is who gets to write the dictionary, who defines the terms of the debate. (Several of the black participants in our interracial dialogue groups contended that blacks cannot be racist "by definition" because the word racism means discrimination by the majority against an oppressed minority. Some of the whites, in turn, asked where they got that definition, and were convinced that most dictionaries did not define racism in that way — to which one black participant responded, "What color are the people who write the dictionaries?" This is at once a politically astute observation and an implicit acknowledgment that there is an element of arbitrariness that undermines *any* effort to assert in an absolute manner what racism "is.")[1]

But if we cannot really settle in any definitive or "objective" way what is and is not racism, we *can* ask what the *consequences* are of one or another way of using the term. Those consequences, I believe, point to the conclusion that we have seriously overused the words "racism" and "racist," to the detriment of the clarity and precision of our language and of our ability to overcome our racial divisions.

[1]On another occasion, a white participant pointed out that blacks are not a minority in South Africa and asked, "Does that mean that by definition South African whites can't be racist?" The black participant then amended her claim, saying that *any* oppressed group, even if a majority, could not be racist; only the oppressor could. This then led to a discussion about whether whites were in fact oppressors in American society (everyone in the group was in agreement about South Africa). Here the debate was not so much about definitions (though the contention about that remained) as about the facts. Was it so cut and dried that whites are oppressors and blacks oppressed? Not surprisingly, there were significant differences between whites and blacks with regard to this question. [All notes are author's, except 4.]

I make this suggestion not because I believe racism has disappeared in   5
American life, nor out of a view that our racial problems have become less
severe, therefore meriting our use of "milder" terms. Racism remains a central fact of our life together, and in certain respects our racial divisions have
become more rather than less intractable in recent years. What I wish to
introduce is not a "milder" vocabulary, not a list of euphemisms, but rather
a more *precise* and *differentiated* vocabulary. My aim is not to sweep racism
under the rug, but to understand more clearly the experiences and attitudes
to which the term is usually applied.

The terms racism and racist have been so stretched and extended in
contemporary dialogue on race and inequality that their usage has become a
serious impediment to our efforts to come to grips with problems that are
difficult enough to begin with. There are many instances in which words
like prejudice, bias, discrimination, stereotyping, ethnocentrism, insensitivity, inequality, injustice, indifference, and even ignorance, denote far more
accurately the social and psychological reality of events now depicted almost
reflexively as "racist." Moreover, not only does the use of these alternative
terms provide a sharper and more differentiated analytic tool for understanding our society's dilemmas, it also enables us to avoid falling into a
number of costly pitfalls embedded in our current linguistic habits.

One key problem is that the words "racism" and "racist" tend to be conversation stoppers. When "I disagree" or "You don't understand" or "You
don't know the facts" or even "You're wrong" becomes "You're racist," real
dialogue ceases. And it ceases regardless of whether what is evoked is an
angry retort or a deferential and ultimately insincere genuflection. When
whites walk on eggshells in their interactions with blacks, fearing that to
express their views in all their complexity would leave them open to the
accusation of being racists, all that results is a covering over of real issues
and feelings that are essential to address if any progress in race relations is
to be made. In this respect, blacks may actually not appreciate how guilty
many whites feel about the inequalities that exist in our society (even if that
guilt is frequently repressed or insufficiently a source of remedial action).
The use of a term that feels to blacks merely descriptive, simply an account
of what they encounter every day of their lives, can create in whites a defensive attitude that stifles honest communication. And while there may be
short-term advantage to blacks in being able to intimidate whites in this
way, and a kind of poetic justice in being able to turn the tables in certain
respects, there is, as I shall elaborate below, a high cost ultimately to be
paid for whatever satisfaction is thereby achieved.

Moreover, overextension of the terms "racism" and "racist" actually can
serve to obscure rather than make clearer the degree of racial injustice that
pervades our society. "Racism" is a strong word, and part of the rationale for
its use is that it takes a forceful message to break through strong denial:
euphemisms permit continuing evasion. But volume is not the only deter-
minant of what gets heard. After a while one habituates to — or "tunes

out" — even the loudest noise if it is unvarying. Indeed, at times a silence that replaces a steady noise is a more attention-getting stimulus than the noise itself. A varied vocabulary is not just an aesthetic virtue; it also counters the tendency to tune out. Conveying the message in a language about which the intended hearer is set to be defensive is likely to have less impact than doing so in a language that is straightforward and pulls no punches, but is not needlessly provocative.

In a 1992 panel discussion on the *MacNeil-Lehrer NewsHour,* black journalist Joseph Boyce lamented the fact that

> at one time the last thing anyone wanted to be called was a racist, whether they were or not. It was a mark to be avoided. And today I don't think people really care that much, some of them, you know. They'll say, "Yeah, I'm a racist, so what, so what are you going to do about it?"[2]

This is indeed a regrettable state of affairs, but I believe that one reason for it is that the word racist has been bandied about so much that for some people it has lost its impact, lost its power to shock, to evoke guilt or revulsion. A term that once referred to the most deplorable and shameful of traits and actions has been extended to include virtually universal human characteristics and to include within its purview practically everyone in our society.

It should *not* be easy and common to say with equanimity "Yes, I'm   10 a racist, so what?" But if we are told in essence that *every* white person is a racist,[3] then it *becomes* a matter to which a ho-hum response becomes possible. Racism *is* a strong word (or at least it *was* a strong word), and it should remain one. It should *not* be a word whose power habituates. We are much the worse off when people can acknowledge racism with impunity, as a simple, familiar fact of life rather than a terrible aberration.

Bull Connor or Joe Next Door?

The phenomenon painfully noted by Boyce was certainly not intended or expected by those whose rhetoric first created the expansion of the word's usage. In large measure the expansion developed as a response to the changing challenges of the civil rights movement as it moved from the South to the North. As long as the South persisted in a particularly explicit and ugly form of racial segregation and disparagement of blacks, the subtler, but often no less persistent or destructive segregation of the North was effectively shrouded. Especially combined with the earlier close association of the

---

[2]*The MacNeil-Lehrer NewsHour,* Thursday, June 11, 1992. Transcript provided by WNET and WETA. Page 14.

[3]See, among many examples, "Are you a racist?", by Peter Noel, *Village Voice,* February 11, 1992, pp. 34–35.

South with outright slavery, this pattern of difference between North and South enabled the rest of the country to externalize its own quite considerable racial prejudices by holding to a fantasy of the "bad" South and the "good" North. When the most egregious features of racial discrimination in the South gave way in the 1960s, it became increasingly apparent that the North differed much less from the South than it had thought. Workers for change were confronted with a set of prejudices and institutional constraints that were more difficult to confront than those of the South precisely because they were more subtle, disguised, and unacknowledged.

In response to this, and in an effort to communicate to whites in the North that "you're not as different as you think from the Southerners you have been smugly criticizing," writers and activists began increasingly to employ a term that had once stood in the national imagination for such violent acts of lynchings or the vicious use of police dogs by Birmingham police chief Bull Connor.[4] Their aim was to break through the numbing denial, to confront Northerners with the need for changes as radical in their own way as the opening of schools, lunch counters, and other public facilities to blacks in the South. But in the process, a term that had largely pointed toward the most serious and heinous offenses against human dignity began, in effect, to be watered down to stand for more common human foibles. As a consequence, subtle but powerful changes in connotation were set in motion: On the one hand, the special emotional impact of the word "racism" was diminished; if it is not a term referring to violence and the extremes of inhumanity, but rather to what the folks down the block do, then it's not really so bad. On the other hand, if the Bull Connors of the world are no different really from you or I or Joe next door, then an unfortunate covert link of solidarity is subtly fostered between flawed but decent people and people who deserve nothing but contempt.

The Paradoxes of Guilt

It may seem inconsistent to point out that "racist" is such a strong word that it stops meaningful dialogue and invokes defensiveness in whites, and simultaneously to contend that its overuse has desensitized us to the real horror the term should connote and enabled people to accept with equanimity the description of them as racist. The inconsistency, however, is more apparent than real. At the simplest level, we may note that different responses to the term can be manifested by different people; some may be intimidated or defensive while others are inured and desensitized. Moreover, even for the same person, the accusation of racism may sometimes be experienced as an intimidating conversation-stopper and sometimes as a tiresome harangue that has little real impact whatever formal obeisance may or may not be paid. Whether one or the other response is evoked will

---

[4]*Bull Connor:* T. Eugene "Bull" Connor directed police to use dogs and water hoses to quell antisegregation demonstrations in Birmingham, Alabama, in 1963. TV broadcasts of these violent images actually strengthened the civil rights movement.

depend on many factors: who is making the accusation; how it is presented; with what mood or set the accused enters the encounter; the number of people present and the ratio of blacks and whites among them; and a host of other aspects of context and personality.

Moreover, the two seemingly antithetical reactions can often be but two sides of the same response. Both the defiant embrace of the term referred to by Boyce ("Yeah, I'm racist. So what?") and the reaction of boredom or disinterest that mutes the impact of a message that needs to be heard ("Here we go again! More rhetoric!") can be defensive responses to having been made to feel guilty. In these instances, it is *because* the impact of the accusation is so strong that its conscious acknowledgment is so minimal.

Guilt is a complex emotion and does not always produce the response   15
we might wish or expect. Sometimes, to be sure, it leads to efforts to right the wrong one has done. But very often, especially if guilt threatens to be overwhelming, the response to guilt can be paradoxical: still *further* insensitivity to those we have harmed, and anger at them for confronting us with our inadequacies and iniquities. Conveying the bad news is a subtle art. Whether in a marriage or friendship or in a larger social context, it is far from universal that when we succeed in making the person we think has wronged us feel guilty we end up pleased with the results.

Salutary responses to feelings of guilt are most likely to occur when there is something productive and reparative the individual can do to relieve the guilt. Global and overextended depictions of white racism block this healthy and useful response. If whites are left feeling they are going to be seen as racist no matter what they do — "if I'm not an overt racist, I'm a covert one" — then the response is likely to be one of "why bother?" or some other defensive reaction. Ritualistic acknowledgments of "racism" may be offered, but they will be *in place of* effective action to heal our social wounds rather than a harbinger of such actions.

"Institutional Racism"

Different problems are introduced by another way in which the use of the term racism has been expanded over the years. Increasingly, discourse on racism has stressed its *institutional* nature rather than simply the attitudes of individuals, and the concept of "institutional racism" has become a central feature of contemporary dialogue on issues of race.

As James M. Jones, a leading African American writer on racism and prejudice, has delineated the distinction, "The critical aspect of institutional racism that distinguished it from prejudice and from individual racism was the notion that institutions can produce racist consequences *whether they do so intentionally or not*."[5] Robert Miles, a British sociologist who has written a comprehensive examination of the manifold ways in which the

[5]James M. Jones, Racism in black and white, in P. Katz & D. Taylor (Eds.), *Eliminating Racism: Profiles in Controversy*, New York: Plenum, 1986, p. 129. Emphasis added.

concept of racism is employed in contemporary discourse, offers a closely related definition of how the term is used — "all processes which, *intentionally or not,* result in the continued exclusion of a subordinated group."[6] In contrast with Jones, however, Miles sees serious difficulties with the concept. Although he views racism as indeed a central problem in contemporary society and regards the dissection of racism as a crucial task for social analysis, he decries the "conceptual inflation" that leads the term racism to be overused and overextended and its original sharp meaning to be significantly blurred. As the concept of racism is extended into the terminology of *institutional* racism the role of the motivations and attitudes of actual human beings becomes increasingly confused, and a highly abstract and impersonal conception becomes mischievously merged with one of the most emotionally charged words in our vocabulary.

The original use of the term institutional racism by Stokely Carmichael and Charles Hamilton in their influential book, *Black Power,*[7] was not as divorced from intentionality. They did depict two different kinds of racism — individual and institutional — and they noted how the latter, *seemingly* impersonal, can allow "respectable" individuals to dissociate themselves from the acts of those with the poor taste to be overtly racist, while continuing to benefit from the ways in which our institutions maintain the inequalities between blacks and whites. But Carmichael and Hamilton's conception of institutional racism does not eliminate motivation or intention. They state quite explicitly that

> Institutional racism relies on the active and pervasive operation of anti-black attitudes and practices. A sense of superior group position prevails: whites are "better" than blacks; therefore blacks should be subordinated to whites. This is a racist attitude and it permeates the society, on both the individual and institutional level, covertly and overtly.[8]

I believe that Carmichael and Hamilton accurately identified an attitude that continues to prevail in America to a disturbing degree, and I agree as well that it merits the description as racist. But as the idea of institutional racism evolved over the years, it has increasingly come to be evoked whenever differences between the races are found, *regardless* of whether there is any evidence of racist intent. The outcome itself is taken as proof that racism *must* underlie the differences.[9]

It is indeed crucially important to understand how our institutional

20

---

[6]Robert Miles, *Racism,* London: Routledge, 1989, p. 50.

[7]Stokely Carmichael and Charles V. Hamilton, *Black Power,* New York: Vintage, 1967.

[8]Carmichael & Hamilton, *Black Power,* p. 5.

[9]Many of these extensions of the meaning of racism are reviewed in Miles and depicted by him as an instance of "conceptual inflation." See also R. Blauner, *Racial Oppression in America,* New York: Harper & Row, 1972; D. Wellman, *Portraits of White Racism,* Cambridge: Cambridge University Press; and S. Steinberg, *The Ethnic Myth,* Boston: Beacon, 1989.

arrangements maintain inequalities and place continuing burdens on a people who already have a long history of oppression. But the labeling of these processes as institutional "racism" has muddled as much as it clarifies. The confusion arises because a term replete with connotations of intention is used to denote a process *outside* of specific intentions, a process almost mechanical in its impersonality and inexorability. To the white who says, "That's *not* how I feel; that's not what I want," the proponent of the concept of institutional racism can say, "You're misunderstanding what I'm saying. I'm not saying *you* want this to happen, I'm saying that the whole society is set up in such a way that certain outcomes inevitably result, and those outcomes are consistently to the detriment of people of color in comparison to whites."

This distinction is logically coherent (and, in my view, it is rooted in a largely accurate perception of how our society works). But it is couched in terms that fail to take into account how real people think and react. As a consequence, it injects into our public discourse a terminology that is misleading and inflammatory. No matter what disclaimers may be offered by the speaker, it is extremely difficult for whites (or blacks for that matter, though with a different set of reactions likely) to hear the term institutional *racism* without other, more sinister connotations of the word racism seeping in.

As a consequence, the concept of "institutional racism" can contribute to obscuring the very phenomenon it was designed to highlight. Because the terms "racism" and "racist" are likely to evoke in the hearer connotations of motivated rather than impersonal and systemic outcomes, whites who do not recognize racist *intent* in the operations of our dominant institutions or in the outcomes they yield are likely as a consequence to find claims of "institutional racism" implausible. In the process, they are enabled to avoid coming to grips with how the workings of our society do disadvantage blacks and other minorities even when there is no specific intention that that be the outcome.

As obvious as it ought to be that our social arrangements have a predictably differential overall impact on blacks and whites, it is easy not to see it, *and one need not be a racist not to.* For our society's customary way of thinking leads us to look away from predictable group differences and to emphasize instead individual choice and responsibility. This tendency is not limited to our perceptions with regard to minorities. It obscures as much about the differences in income and access among whites as it does about blacks. Part of the system we live under is that we are systematically trained not to see the system. That is, we are taught to understand the differences in income and influence that result from the way we organize our society as solely the result of individual choices and individual merit; and we are taught *not* to notice the statistical probabilities that make the bright child of a truck driver or a manual laborer less likely to go to college than the child of a doctor or lawyer.

Instead, we are trained to notice the *exceptions*. Since there are some   25
children of truck drivers and manual laborers who do go to college —
indeed, a sizable enough group to be noticeable — we affirm that we are a
"land of opportunity," and essentially ignore the fact that we can predict
with virtual statistical certainty the differential life courses of the children of
the two groups.[10]

In similar fashion, we may use the existence of a growing black middle
class to obscure the reality that blacks remain greatly overrepresented
among those who receive the least of our society's rewards. Here again, the
exceptions obscure the rule. The roots of the confusion lie in the fact that
the effects of institutional arrangements are statistical rather than universal.
That is, it is not the case that *no* blacks are able to succeed in our society or
that all whites do better than the average black. Rather, what is predictable
is that, all in all, the status and station of blacks is likely to be lower than that
of whites; or, put differently, that the circumstances most blacks encounter
from birth on are likely to make it harder for them to succeed than are the
circumstances most whites encounter. Since there are fairly numerous
exceptions — blacks who make it anyhow, through noteworthy talent, drive,
or persistence — it is easy to overlook the way the cards are stacked against
this happening. Instead, the very fact that *some* blacks have made it leads
many whites to conclude that those who haven't simply do not try hard
enough, are not sufficiently meritorious, or in some other way "deserve" the
deprivation they endure.

If we are to transcend this superficial and censorious way of understanding the disparities that haunt our society, we will indeed have to make
clearer the *institutional* aspects of what has been called institutional racism.
The rhetoric of institutional racism can impede such understanding, leading
people to focus on personal attitudes in a way that obscures precisely the
institutional dimension. What results are responses such as, "This talk about
institutional racism is nonsense. It's just an excuse. I'm not a racist. I judge
people as individuals. I don't care if they are black, white, green, or purple.
If they work hard and follow the rules, I respect them, and if they expect
special favors, I say 'life's hard for me too.' "

I've certainly had enough psychoanalytic training to know that such a
response *might* be covering over "unconscious racism." But I've also had
enough psychoanalytic training to know that such an automatic assumption
is a misuse of psychoanalysis. What is more obvious and definite is that such
a response reflects highly *individualistic* assumptions that obscure the way
social conditions influence people's behavior and aspirations. When people
believe that everyone makes his or her own fate, and ignore the role of

---

[10]A great deal of evidence demonstrating the powerful effects of parental income and
social class on children's prospects is reviewed by Richard Kahlenberg in *The Remedy: Class,
Race, and Affirmative Action,* New York: Basic Books, 1997. See especially pages 86–94.

circumstance, they are unlikely to be sympathetic to those who do not make it, regardless of race.

This is not to imply that racial feelings play no part in our society's readiness to accept institutional arrangements that leave so many people of color disadvantaged. Rather, the question is whether "racism" is the best way of understanding those racial feelings. I turn now to an alternative conceptualization that I believe is both more accurate and more likely to contribute to the sense of recognition that is an essential precursor of change.

"Otherness" and Indifference

A more useful way, I suggest, to conceptualize the broad commonality [30] among the diverse experiences typically labeled as "racist" is to focus our attention on the sense of "otherness" that is central to these experiences. "Otherness" is not as sexy a word as racism. It is unlikely to come into widespread use as a catch-all term, and indeed, that is one of its great advantages. It points us toward an understanding of the underlying foundations of these various problematic features of our life as a society without co-opting the differentiations.

There are subtle differences among the words that depict the attitudes increasingly lumped together under the global rubric of racism. Some whites, for example, may be able to hear and consider a claim that they have been *prejudiced* in some situation or other but will reject (or only give superficial lip service to) the claim that they were being racist. What is the difference? Prejudice implies jumping to a quick, and even unfair, conclusion, but for many people it does not imply hostility and brutality as does racism.[11] While it is not pleasant to acknowledge the former, it is still a far cry from being guilty of the latter.

In similar fashion, for a white to be confronted with having been *insensitive* in some remark he might have made can be a quite different experience from having the remark described as racist. Once again, although both are likely to be painful to acknowledge, the first characterization is much more likely to get through than the second.

What is perhaps most important of all for whites to acknowledge and understand is *indifference*. A great deal of what is often characterized as racism can be more precisely and usefully described as indifference. Perhaps no other feature of white attitudes, and of the underlying attitudinal structure of white society as a whole, is as cumulatively responsible for the pain and privation experienced by our nation's black minority at this point in our history as is indifference. At the same time, perhaps no feature is as misunderstood or overlooked.

---

[11]James M. Jones, for example, in a prominent textbook on racism and prejudice, depicts racism as something "far more sinister and deep" than prejudice (Jones, *Racism and Prejudice*, p. 196).

"Otherness" is at work in all of the destructive ways in which people of different groups interact. Prejudices, biases, stereotypes, and the like would have no objects were not some people experienced as "other." But "otherness" is perhaps especially germane to the role of indifference, which in a sense can be viewed as a pure culture of otherness. That is, in prejudice, stereotyping, ethnocentrism, and other such obviously problematic features of how groups of human beings interact, something is *added* to otherness. There is something more active in these behaviors and attitudes that makes them a bit more able to be detected. Indifference, in contrast, is a *quiet* toxin. It severs the sinews and nerves of society without announcing itself. Its effects are devastating, but its tracks are hidden in the overall attitude of "each man for himself" that is so prominent a part of our society's ethos.

Further obscuring the central role of indifference in our social problems is that highly immediate and visible tragedy can transcend the sense of otherness. Few white Americans would fail to rescue a black child trapped in a well or a black man pinned under the wreckage of a building collapse. At such moments the sense of human solidarity takes center stage, not the sense of differentness. And indeed, this is one of the reasons that most white Americans do not really believe in their heart of hearts that they are racist.

But when it comes to the slow bleeding that daily drains the spirit and hope from life in our nation's inner cities, indifference shows itself in full measure. We tolerate the misery in the midst of our affluent society because of the strong sense of "them" that attaches to the miserable, the sense that "they" are not like "us," that they are different. And so most whites, who are aware of little feeling of outright hostility, who believe in fair play and equal opportunity, see little that has to do with them in the painful realities of our inner cities. In both (ironically almost opposite) meanings of the phrase, what is happening there is "too bad." But for all too many whites, it is not perceived as their responsibility.

Of course, what I am describing comes very close in certain ways to what is often addressed under the rubric of institutional racism. Indifference, however, comes much closer to the unacknowledged core of truth in white America's guilty conscience. "Institutional racism" is unlikely to become a part of the phenomenological experience of white Americans; indifference can. It is indifference that whites can potentially recognize and acknowledge within themselves, and it is in combating indifference that the fulcrum of change may be most effectively placed.

Indifference and the sense of otherness are not experiences that are limited to issues of race. We may see them operating every time there is a plane crash abroad and the newscaster announces how many Americans are aboard. The likelihood, for any listener, that any American victim of the crash will be someone they actually know is exceedingly small; there are, after all, a quarter of a billion Americans. Yet this information is always supplied, for it defines whether the victim was "one of us," and, if truth be told, it defines to a significant degree whether we should *care*.[12]

This is precisely the issue that most burdens race relations in our society as well. The real meaning of race comes down largely to this: *Is this someone I should care about?* This is a terrible and shameful truth, and in its full impact it will not be easy for white America to face. But it points much more precisely, I believe, to the true source of white guilt than does the label of racism. As a consequence, it has a better chance both of leading us to examine what is in our hearts and of generating the concrete social and economic changes that are essential for real justice and equality to be achieved.

Summary and Conclusion

Accusing a guilty man of the wrong crime is one of the greatest gifts 40 one can bestow upon him. It fosters an orgy of self-righteous conviction of innocence, and conveniently diverts his attention from the offense of which he is truly guilty. In a similar fashion, the ubiquitous claim that racism is the cause of the grievous circumstances of life in our inner cities is, ironically, enabling white America to slough off its responsibility for the shameful neglect of the least privileged members of our society.

The real crime of which white America is now most guilty is not racism. It is indifference. Understanding the difference between the two is a crucial step in liberating ourselves from the sterile and unproductive impasse that has characterized the dialogue on race relations in recent years.

[12]I assume that something similar happens when a plane crash is announced on the news in other countries as well. The phenomenon I am describing is by no means uniquely American.

Distinguishing between racism and indifference is not a semantic quibble. The constant invocation of racism, often in ever more forced, abstract, and symbolic senses, can have the counterproductive effect of causing listeners to filter out potentially important arguments because they sound repetitive, rhetorical, and, most important, contrary to their experience. Racism is such a loaded word, so tinged with associations to lynchings and unprintable racial epithets, that many whites experience a sharp distinction between their own attitudes and what they believe is implied by such a word. As a consequence, accused of a crime of which their self-examination tells them they are innocent, they can go to bed with an undisturbed conscience.

But in fact there is little ground for a clear conscience in the relations of white America to its black minority. Many whites who can quite honestly claim that they hold no hatred for blacks, that they do not wish them harm or disparage them as a group — in short, that they are not "racist" — must acknowledge that it *is* true that almost daily news reports of the terrors and privations of growing up in the inner city leave them with the feeling, "That's not my problem." Such an attitude may be justified (or rationalized) by the claim that "Maybe there once were obstacles to blacks getting into college or getting good jobs, but times have changed. Now the opportunities are there if they'll only apply themselves."

And although there is a certain amount of truth in such a view, it fails not only to acknowledge the continuing discrimination that does still exist, but even more importantly, it fails to take into account how hard it is to *see* the new opportunities from the vantage point of the typical block in our poorest neighborhoods. Boarded-up buildings, drug pushers, gang members with guns, and the ubiquitous presence of unemployed men and women tend rather effectively to block the view of the wider world of opportunity readily visible from the suburbs. Few children, white or black, have the capacity to see past such a compellingly bleak immediate reality.

To some in the black community, describing the predominant white   45
attitude as indifference rather than racism may seem like a kind of plea-bargaining in which a lesser offense is acknowledged instead of the real crime. I disagree. For most white Americans the crime of which they are most guilty *is* indifference, *not* racism. Moreover, and even more important, indifference in the face of severe human suffering is not a minor offense.

Our society is deeply flawed by racial inequalities, but the unswerving emphasis on racism as the explanation has become part of the problem rather than part of the solution. It is time to retire the rhetoric of racism, not because white neglect has become benign, but because it is essential for the well-being of all of us, white *and* black, that that neglect be recognized and addressed.

ENGAGING THE TEXT

1. Wachtel proposes that "words like prejudice, bias, discrimination, stereotyping, ethnocentrism, insensitivity, inequality, injustice, indifference, and

even ignorance, denote far more accurately the social and psychological reality of events now depicted almost reflexively as 'racist'" (para. 6). How does each of these alternative terms differ in denotation or connotation from "racism"? Working in groups, draft definitions for these terms, and compare your results with those of your classmates.

2. Examine the scenarios at the beginning of this selection and discuss which ones illustrate true racism and which are instances of prejudice, insensitivity, indifference, ignorance, etc. How easy or difficult is it to agree on the interpretation of the scenarios?

3. Define "institutional racism." Why does Wachtel believe that the term is counterproductive although the concept itself is valid?

4. Define "otherness" and summarize the relationship Wachtel sees between otherness and indifference. Do you agree that white Americans, in general, are indifferent to the suffering of those they perceive as unlike themselves? If so, how might people in the United States behave differently if they cared deeply about the problems of "others," both within their own country and in the world? If not, what evidence do you see that contradicts Wachtel's claim?

5. In Wachtel's view, what role does the American ideal of individualism play in perpetuating racial misunderstanding and conflict?

EXPLORING CONNECTIONS

6. Write or act out imaginary dialogue between Ellis Cose (p. 492) and Wachtel on how best to achieve reparations for slavery.

7. Read the anecdote about the dinner party at the beginning of Shelby Steele's essay (p. 530). To what extent does Wachtel's analysis of cross-racial communication seem relevant or useful in understanding what happened? Could his advice about how to talk about racial issues have helped in the case of the stalled conversation Steele describes? Why or why not?

8. Review the racial encounters described by Stephen Cruz (p. 353), Cora Tucker (p. 358), and C. P. Ellis (p. 519). Which of these, if any, would you describe as instances of racism? Which would more accurately be defined by one of the alternative terms Wachtel proposes?

9. Compare Wachtel's discussion of individualism and race to Ken Hamblin's (p. 285). Which view do you find more compelling, and why?

10. What does the Ted Rall cartoon on page 552 suggest about whites' behavior and attitudes toward blacks? To what extent is the cartoonist's view of race relations consistent or inconsistent with Wachtel's?

EXTENDING THE CRITICAL CONTEXT

11. If you have witnessed or been involved in a confrontation about race, write a journal entry describing the conflict in detail. What was said and how did each participant react? Was the interaction productive? If so, for whom, and in what way(s)? If not, what made it frustrating or upsetting, and for whom? After reading Wachtel's analysis, do you understand the experience any differently? Why or why not?

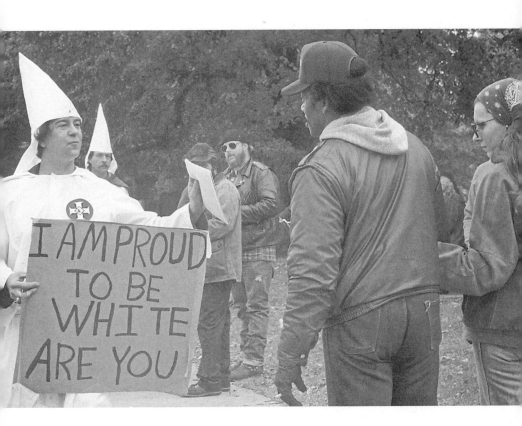

Visual Portfolio

READING IMAGES OF THE MELTING POT

1. What is the significance of making the ad for the American Civil Liberties Union look like a "Wanted" poster from the wild West? What is the purpose of pairing the photos of Dr. Martin Luther King Jr. and Charles Manson? What values does the ad associate with the ACLU, and how does it communicate those values? Do you find the ad effective? Why or why not?

2. Write a narrative that explains the situation pictured in the second image of the portfolio. What is happening and what led up to this scene? Who are these people and what are their relationships? Identify specific details of setting, dress, body language, and facial expression that support your interpretation. Compare narratives and discuss the assumptions that inform the stories as well as the persuasiveness of the evidence they are based on.

3. The image on page 558 depicts a section of the fence that divides the United States from Mexico. What sense does the picture give you of the photographer's views of immigration, the fence, the border, and the relationship between the two countries? What details of the picture itself — angle, lighting, proportion, position of the figures — suggest these views?

4. How do you think the people in the "Close the Border" photo (p. 559) would explain the motives for their protest? What motives might Parrillo (p. 504) or Fredrickson (below) attribute to them? Write an imaginary conversation among the protesters and the two writers.

5. How many different ways could you describe the ethnic or cultural identity of each of the four friends on page 560 based on the visual cues provided by the photo? What knowledge or assumptions about race, ethnicity, and culture underlie your interpretations?

Models of American Ethnic Relations: A Historical Perspective

GEORGE M. FREDRICKSON

Are Irish Americans white? The answer is so self-evident that the question seems absurd, but as historian George Fredrickson notes, the idea of "whiteness" has in the past excluded many Europeans, including the Irish. A survey of ethnic and racial categories in American history shows how much they change with the politics and prejudices of the time. Yet citizenship, civil rights, even human status have been granted or withheld on the basis of these

*shifting definitions. Fredrickson examines four models of ethnic relations —
hierarchy, assimilation, pluralism, and separatism — that have defined how
groups perceived as different from each other should interact. Fredrickson
(b. 1934) has written extensively about race in the history of the United
States and South Africa and is a past president of the Organization for American Historians.* His books include The Inner Civil War *(1965),* The Black
Image in the White Mind *(1972),* White Supremacy *(1981),* Black Liberation
(1995), and Racism: A Short History *(2002). He is the Edgar E. Robinson
Professor Emeritus of U.S. History at Stanford University.*

Throughout its history, the United States has been inhabited by a variety of interacting racial or ethnic groups. In addition to the obvious "color
line" structuring relationships between dominant whites and lower-status
blacks, Indians, and Asians, there have at times been important social distinctions among those of white or European ancestry. Today we think of the
differences between white Anglo-Saxon Protestants and Irish, Italian, Polish, and Jewish Americans as purely cultural or religious, but in earlier times
these groups were sometimes thought of as "races" or "subraces" — people
possessing innate or inborn characteristics and capabilities that affected
their fitness for American citizenship. Moreover, differences apparently
defined as cultural have sometimes been so reified[1] as to serve as the functional equivalent of physical distinctions. Indians, for example, were viewed
by most nineteenth-century missionaries and humanitarians as potentially
equal and similar to whites. Their status as noncitizens was not attributed to
skin color or physical appearance; it was only their obdurate adherence to
"savage ways" that allegedly stood in the way of their possessing equal rights
and being fully assimilated. Analogously, conservative opponents of affirmative action and other antiracist policies in the 1990s may provide a "rational"
basis for prejudice and discrimination by attributing the disadvantages and
alleged shortcomings of African Americans to persistent cultural "pathology" rather than to genetic deficiencies (D'Souza 1995).

It can therefore be misleading to make a sharp distinction between race
and ethnicity when considering intergroup relations in American history. As
I have argued extensively elsewhere, ethnicity is "racialized" whenever distinctive group characteristics, however defined or explained, are used as the
basis for a status hierarchy of groups who are thought to differ in ancestry or
descent (Fredrickson 1997, ch. 5).

Four basic conceptions of how ethnic or racial groups should relate to
each other have been predominant in the history of American thought
about group relations — ethnic hierarchy, one-way assimilation, cultural
pluralism, and group separatism. This [essay] provides a broad outline of
the historical career of each of these models of intergroup relations, noting

[1]*reified:* Treated as if real, concrete, but actually abstract.

some of the changes in how various groups have defined themselves or been defined by others.

Ethnic Hierarchy

Looking at the entire span of American history, we find that the most influential and durable conception of the relations among those American racial or ethnic groups viewed as significantly dissimilar has been hierarchical. A dominant group — conceiving of itself as society's charter membership — has claimed rights and privileges not to be fully shared with outsiders or "others," who have been characterized as unfit or unready for equal rights and full citizenship. The hierarchical model has its deepest roots and most enduring consequences in the conquest of Indians and the enslavement of blacks during the colonial period (Axtell 1981; Jordan 1968). But it was also applied in the nineteenth century to Asian immigrants and in a less severe and more open-ended way to European immigrants who differed in culture and religion from old-stock Americans of British origin (Higham 1968; Miller 1969). The sharpest and most consequential distinction was always between "white" and "nonwhite." The first immigration law passed by Congress in 1790 specified that only white immigrants were eligible for naturalization. This provision would create a crucial difference in the mid-nineteenth century between Chinese "sojourners," who could not become citizens and voters, and Irish immigrants, who could.

Nevertheless, the Irish who fled the potato famine of the 1840s by emigrating to the United States also encountered discrimination. Besides being Catholic and poor, the refugees from the Emerald Isle were Celts rather than Anglo-Saxons, and a racialized discourse,[2] drawing on British precedents, developed as an explanation for Irish inferiority to Americans of English ancestry (Knobel 1986). The dominant group during the nineteenth and early twentieth centuries was not simply white but also Protestant and Anglo-Saxon. Nevertheless, the Irish were able to use their right to vote and the patronage they received from the Democratic Party to improve their status, an option not open to the Chinese. Hence, they gradually gained the leverage and respectability necessary to win admission to the dominant caste, a process that culminated in Al Smith's nomination for the presidency in 1928 and John F. Kennedy's election in 1960.

The mass immigration of Europeans from eastern and southern Europe in the late nineteenth and early twentieth centuries inspired new concerns about the quality of the American stock. In an age of eugenics,[3]

5

---

[2]*racialized discourse:* Language that defines a group of people as a race and attributes distinctive "racial" characteristics to them.

[3]*eugenics:* Movement that advocated improving the human race by encouraging genetically "superior" people to reproduce and promoting the sterilization of "undesirables," including minorities, poor people, and those with mental and physical disorders.

scientific racism,[4] and social Darwinism,[5] the notion that northwestern Europeans were innately superior to those from the southern and eastern parts of the continent — to say nothing of those light-skinned people of actual or presumed west Asian origin (such as Jews, Syrians, and Armenians) — gained wide currency. A determined group of nativists, encouraged by the latest racial "science," fought for restrictive immigration policies that discriminated against those who were not of "Nordic" or "Aryan" descent (Higham 1968). In the 1920s the immigration laws were changed to reflect these prejudices. Low quotas were established for white people from nations or areas outside of those that had supplied the bulk of the American population before 1890. In the minds of many, true Americans were not merely white but also northern European. In fact, some harbored doubts about the full claim to "whiteness" of swarthy immigrants from southern Italy.

After immigration restriction had relieved ethnic and racial anxieties, the status of the new immigrants gradually improved as a result of their political involvement, their economic and professional achievement, and a decline in the respectability of the kind of scientific racism that had ranked some European groups below others. World War II brought revulsion against the genocidal anti-Semitism and eugenic experiments of the Nazis, dealing a coup de grâce to the de facto hierarchy that had placed Anglo-Saxons, Nordics, or Aryans at the apex of American society. All Americans of European origin were now unambiguously white and, for most purposes, ethnically equal to old-stock Americans of Anglo-Saxon, Celtic, and Germanic ancestry. Hierarchy was now based exclusively on color. Paradoxically, it might be argued, the removal of the burden of "otherness" from virtually all whites made more striking and salient than ever the otherness of people of color, especially African Americans.

The civil rights movement of the 1960s was directed primarily at the legalized racial hierarchy of the southern states. The Civil Rights Acts of 1964 and 1965 brought an end to government-enforced racial segregation and the denial of voting rights to blacks in that region. But the legacy of four centuries of white supremacy survives in the disadvantaged social and economic position of blacks and other people of color in the United States. The impoverished, socially deprived, and physically unsafe ghettos, barrios, and Indian reservations of this nation are evidence that ethnic hierarchy in a clearly racialized form persists in practice if not in law.

[4]*scientific racism:* Refers to various efforts to find some scientific basis for white superiority, the results of which were inevitably bad science.
[5]*social Darwinism:* The belief that Darwin's theory of evolution and natural selection applies to society; thus the existence of extreme wealth and poverty (whether of individuals or nations) is rationalized as a "natural" result of competition and the survival of the fittest.

One-Way Assimilation

Policies aimed at the assimilation of ethnic groups have usually assumed that there is a single and stable American culture of European, and especially English, origin to which minorities are expected to conform as the price of admission to full and equal participation in the society and polity of the United States (Gordon 1964, ch. 4). Assimilationist thinking is not racist in the classic sense: it does not deem the outgroups in question to be innately or biologically inferior to the ingroup. The professed goal is equality — but on terms that presume the superiority, purity, and unchanging character of the dominant culture. Little or nothing in the cultures of the groups being invited to join the American mainstream is presumed worthy of preserving. When carried to its logical conclusion, the assimilationist project demands what its critics have described — especially in reference to the coercive efforts to "civilize" Native Americans — as "cultural genocide."

Estimates of group potential and the resulting decisions as to which   10
groups are eligible for assimilation have varied in response to changing definitions of race. If an ethnic group is definitely racialized, the door is closed because its members are thought to possess ineradicable traits (biologically or culturally determined) that make them unfit for inclusion. At times there have been serious disagreements within the dominant group about the eligibility of particular minorities for initiation into the American club.

Although one-way assimilationism was mainly a twentieth-century ideology, it was anticipated in strains of nineteenth-century thinking about Irish immigrants, Native Americans, and even blacks. Radical white abolitionists and even some black antislavery activists argued that prejudice against African Americans was purely and simply a result of their peculiarly degraded and disadvantaged circumstances and that emancipation from slavery would make skin color irrelevant and open the way to their full equality and social acceptability (Fredrickson 1987, ch. 1). These abolitionists had little or no conception that there was a rich and distinctive black culture that could become the source of a positive group identity, and that African modes of thought and behavior had been adapted to the challenge of surviving under slavery.

threshold

If the hope of fully assimilating blacks into a color-blind society was held by only a small minority of whites, a majority probably supposed that the Irish immigrants of the 1840s and 1850s could become full-fledged Americans, if they chose to do so, simply by changing their behavior and beliefs. The doctrine of the innate inferiority of Celts to Anglo-Saxons was not even shared by all of the nativists who sought to slow down the process of Irish naturalization (Knobel 1986). A more serious problem for many of them was the fervent Catholicism of the Irish; Anglo-Protestant missionaries hoped to convert them en masse. The defenders of unrestricted Irish immigration came mostly from the ranks of the Democratic Party, which relied heavily on Irish votes. Among them were strong believers in religious toleration and a high wall of separation between church and state. They saw religious diversity as no obstacle to the full and rapid Americanization of all white-skinned immigrants.

The most sustained and serious nineteenth-century effort to assimilate people who differed both culturally and phenotypically[6] from the majority was aimed at American Indians. Frontier settlers, military men who fought Indians, and many other whites had no doubts that Indians were members of an inherently inferior race that was probably doomed to total extinction as a result of the conquest of the West. Their views were graphically expressed by General Philip Sheridan when he opined that "the only good Indian is a dead Indian." But an influential group of eastern philanthropists, humanitarian reformers, and government officials thought of the Indians as having been "noble savages" whose innate capacities were not inferior to those of whites. Thomas Jefferson, who had a much dimmer view of black potentialities, was one of the first to voice this opinion (Koch and Peden 1944, 210–11). For these ethnocentric humanitarians, the "Indian problem" was primarily cultural rather than racial, and its solution lay in civilizing the "savages" rather than exterminating them. Late in the century, the assimilationists adopted policies designed to force Indians to conform to Euro-American cultural norms; these included breaking up communally held reservations into privately owned family farms and sending Indian children to boarding schools where they were forbidden to speak their own languages and made to dress, cut their hair, and in every possible way act and look like white people. The policy was a colossal failure; most Native Americans refused to abandon key aspects of their traditional cultures, and venal whites took advantage of the land reforms to strip Indians of much of their remaining patrimony[7] (Berkhofer 1978; Hoxie 1984; Mardock 1971).

In the early twentieth century, the one-way assimilation model was applied to the southern and eastern European immigrants who had arrived in massive numbers before the discriminatory quota system of the 1920s was implemented. While some nativists called for their exclusion on the

[6]*phenotypically*: Physically.
[7]*patrimony*: Inheritance.

grounds of their innate deficiencies, other champions of Anglo-American cultural homogeneity hoped to assimilate those who had already arrived through education and indoctrination. The massive "Americanization" campaigns of the period just prior to World War I produced the concept of America as a "melting pot" in which cultural differences would be obliterated. The metaphor might have suggested that a new mixture would result — and occasionally it did have this meaning — but a more prevalent interpretation was that non-Anglo-American cultural traits and inclinations would simply disappear, making the final brew identical to the original one (Gordon 1964, ch. 5).

Before the 1940s, people of color, and especially African Americans, were generally deemed ineligible for assimilation because of their innate inferiority to white ethnics, who were now thought capable of being culturally reborn as Anglo-Americans. Such factors as the war-inspired reaction against scientific racism and the gain in black political power resulting from mass migration from the South (where blacks could not vote) to the urban North (where the franchise was again open to them) led to a significant reconsideration of the social position of African Americans and threw a spotlight on the flagrant denial in the southern states of the basic constitutional rights of African Americans. The struggle for black civil rights that emerged in the 1950s and came to fruition in the early 1960s was premised on a conviction that white supremacist laws and policies violated an egalitarian "American Creed" — as Gunnar Myrdal had argued in his influential wartime study *An American Dilemma* (1944). The war against Jim Crow[8] was fought under the banner of "integration," which, in the minds of white liberals at least, generally meant one-way assimilation. Blacks, deemed by Myrdal and others as having no culture worth saving, would achieve equal status by becoming just like white Americans in every respect except pigmentation.

When it became clear that the civil rights legislation of the 1960s had failed to improve significantly the social and economic position of blacks in the urban ghettos of the North, large numbers of African Americans rejected the integrationist ideal on the grounds that it had been not only a false promise but an insult to the culture of African Americans for ignoring or devaluing their distinctive experience as a people. The new emphasis on "black power" and "black consciousness" conveyed to those whites who were listening that integration had to mean something other than one-way assimilation to white middle-class norms if it was to be a solution to the problem of racial inequality in America (Marable 1991; Van Deburg 1992).

It should be obvious by now that the one-way assimilation model has not proved to be a viable or generally acceptable way of adjusting group differences in American society. It is based on an ethnocentric ideal of cultural homogeneity that has been rejected by Indians, blacks, Asians, Mexican

15

---

[8]*Jim Crow:* Collective term for southern segregation laws.

Americans, and even many white ethnics. It reifies and privileges one cultural strain in what is in fact a multicultural society. It should be possible to advocate the incorporation of all ethnic or racial groups into a common civic society without requiring the sacrifice of cultural distinctiveness and diversity.

Cultural Pluralism

Unlike assimilationists, cultural pluralists celebrate differences among groups rather than seek to obliterate them. They argue that cultural diversity is a healthy and normal condition that does not preclude equal rights and the mutual understandings about civic responsibilities needed to sustain a democratic nation-state. This model for American ethnic relations is a twentieth-century invention that would have been virtually inconceivable at an earlier time. The eighteenth and nineteenth centuries lacked the essential concept of the relativity of cultures. The model of cultural development during this period was evolutionary, progressive, and universalistic. People were either civilized or they were not. Mankind was seen as evolving from a state of "savagery" or "barbarism" to "civilization," and all cultures at a particular level were similar in every way that mattered. What differentiated nations and ethnic groups was their ranking on the scale of social evolution. Modern Western civilization stood at the apex of this universal historical process. Even nineteenth-century black nationalists accepted the notion that there were universal standards of civilization to which people of African descent should aspire. They differed from white supremacists in believing that blacks had the natural capability to reach the same heights as Caucasians if they were given a chance (Moses 1978).

The concept of cultural pluralism drew on the new cultural anthropology of the early twentieth century, as pioneered by Franz Boas. Boas and his disciples attempted to look at each culture they studied on its own terms and as an integrated whole. They rejected theories of social evolution that ranked cultures in relation to a universalist conception of "civilization." But relativistic cultural anthropologists were not necessarily cultural pluralists in their attitude toward group relations within American society. Since they generally believed that a given society or community functioned best with a single, integrated culture, they could favor greater autonomy for Indians on reservations but also call for the full assimilation of new immigrants or even African Americans. Boas himself was an early supporter of the National Association for the Advancement of Colored People (NAACP) and a pioneering advocate of what would later be called racial integration.

An effort to use the new concept of culture to validate ethnic diversity 20 within the United States arose from the negative reaction of some intellectuals to the campaign to "Americanize" the new immigrants from eastern and southern Europe in the period just before and after World War I. The inventors of cultural pluralism were cosmopolitan critics of American provincialism or representatives of immigrant communities, especially Jews, who valued their cultural distinctiveness and did not want to be melted down in an Americanizing crucible. The Greenwich Village intellectual Randolph Bourne described his ideal as a "transnational America" in which various ethnic cultures would interact in a tolerant atmosphere to create an enriching variety of ideas, values, and lifestyles (Bourne 1964, ch. 8). The Jewish philosopher Horace Kallen, who coined the phrase "cultural pluralism," compared the result to a symphony, with each immigrant group represented as a section of the orchestra (Higham 1984, ch. 9; Kallen 1924). From a different perspective, W. E. B. DuBois celebrated a distinctive black culture rooted in the African and slave experiences and heralded its unacknowledged contributions to American culture in general (Lewis 1993). But the dominant version advocated by Kallen and Bourne stopped, for all practical purposes, at the color line. Its focus was on making America safe for a variety of European cultures. As a Zionist, Kallen was especially concerned with the preservation of Jewish distinctiveness and identity.

Since it was mainly the viewpoint of ethnic intellectuals who resisted the assimilationism of the melting pot, cultural pluralism was a minority persuasion in the twenties, thirties, and forties. A modified version reemerged in the 1950s in Will Herberg's (1960) conception of a "triple melting pot" of Protestants, Catholics, and Jews. The revulsion against Nazi anti-Semitism and the upward mobility of American Jews and Catholics inspired a synthesis of cultural pluralism and assimilationism that made religious persuasion the only significant source of diversity among white Americans. Herberg conceded, however, that black Protestants constituted a separate group that was not likely to be included in the Protestant melting pot. He therefore sharpened the distinction between race or color and ethnicity that was central to postwar thinking about group differences. Nevertheless, Herberg's view that significant differences between, say, Irish and Italian Catholics were disappearing was challenged in the 1960s and later, especially in the "ethnic revival" of the 1970s, which proclaimed that differing national origins among Euro-Americans remained significant and a valuable source of cultural variations.

The "multiculturalism" of the 1980s operated on assumptions that were similar to those of the cultural pluralist tradition, except that the color line was breached and the focus was shifted from the cultures and contributions of diverse European ethnic groups to those of African Americans, Mexican Americans, Asian Americans, and Native Americans. Abandonment of the earlier term "multiracialism" signified a desire to escape from the legacy of biological or genetic determinism and to affirm that the differences among people who happened to differ in skin color or phenotype were the result of their varying cultural and historical experiences. Under attack was the doctrine, shared by assimilationists and most earlier proponents of cultural pluralism, that the cultural norm in the United States was inevitably European in origin and character. Parity was now sought for groups of Asian, African, and American Indian ancestry. This ideal of cultural diversity and democracy was viewed by some of its critics as an invitation to national disunity and ethnic conflict (Schlesinger 1992). But its most thoughtful proponents argued that it was simply a consistent application of American democratic values and did not preclude the interaction and cooperation of groups within a common civic society (Hollinger 1995). Nevertheless, the mutual understandings upon which national unity and cohesion could be based needed to be negotiated rather than simply imposed by a Euro-American majority.

Group Separatism

Sometimes confused with the broadened cultural pluralism described here is the advocacy of group separatism. It originates in the desire of a culturally distinctive or racialized group to withdraw as much as possible from American society and interaction with other groups. Its logical outcome, autonomy in a separate, self-governing community, might conceivably be achieved either in an ethnic confederation like Switzerland or in the dissolution of the United States into several ethnic nations. But such a general theory is a logical construction rather than a program that has been explicitly advocated. Group separatism emanates from ethnocentric concerns about the status and destiny of particular groups, and its advocates rarely if ever theorize about what is going to happen to other groups. Precedents for group separatism based on cultural differences can be found in American history in the toleration of virtually autonomous religious communities like the Amish and the Hutterites[9] and in the modicum of self-government and immunity from general laws accorded to Indian tribes and reservations since the 1930s.

The most significant and persistent assertion of group separatism in American history has come from African Americans disillusioned with the prospects for equality within American society. In the nineteenth century, several black leaders and intellectuals called on African Americans to emigrate from the United States in order to establish an independent black republic elsewhere; Africa was the most favored destination. In the 1920s, Marcus Garvey created a mass movement based on the presumption that blacks had no future in the United States and should identify with the independence and future greatness of Africa, ultimately by emigrating there. More recently, the Nation of Islam has proposed that several American states be set aside for an autonomous black nation (Fredrickson 1995, chs. 2, 4, 7). At the height of the black power movement of the 1960s and early 1970s, a few black nationalists even called for the establishment of a noncontiguous federation of black urban ghettos — a nation of islands like Indonesia or the Philippines, but surrounded by white populations rather than the Pacific Ocean.

---

[9]*the Amish and the Hutterites:* Religious groups that reject the values and technology of contemporary society, living in relatively isolated, self-sufficient farming communities.

The current version of black separatism — "Afrocentrism"[10] — has not   25
as yet produced a plan for political separation. Its aim is a cultural and spiritual secession from American society rather than the literal establishment of a black nation. Advocates of total separation could be found among other disadvantaged groups. In the late 1960s and 1970s Mexican American militants called for the establishment of the independent Chicano nation of Aztlán[11] in the American Southwest (Gutierrez 1995, 184–85) and some Native American radicals sought the reestablishment of truly independent tribal nations.

Group separatism might be viewed as a utopian vision or rhetorical device expressing the depths of alienation felt by the most disadvantaged racial or ethnic groups in American society. The extreme unlikelihood of realizing such visions has made their promulgation more cathartic than politically efficacious. Most members of groups exposed to such separatist appeals have recognized their impracticality, and the clash between the fixed and essentialist[12] view of identity that such projects entail and the fluid and hybrid quality of group cultures in the United States has become increasingly evident to many people of color, as shown most dramatically by the recent movement among those of mixed parentage to affirm a biracial identity. Few African Americans want to celebrate the greater or lesser degree of white ancestry most of them possess, but many have acknowledged not only their ancestral ties to Africa but their debt to Euro-American culture (and its debt to them). Most Mexican Americans value their cultural heritage but do not have the expectation or even the desire to establish an independent Chicano nation in the Southwest. Native Americans have authentic historical and legal claims to a high degree of autonomy but generally recognize that total independence on their current land base is impossible and would worsen rather than improve their circumstances. Asian Americans are proud of their various cultures and seek to preserve some of their traditions but have shown little or no inclination to separate themselves from other Americans in the civic, professional, and economic life of the nation. Afrocentrism raises troubling issues for American educational and cultural life but hardly represents a serious threat to national unity.

Ethnic separatism, in conclusion, is a symptom of racial injustice and a call to action against it, but there is little reason to believe that it portends "the disuniting of America." It is currently a source of great anxiety to many

---

[10]*Afrocentrism:* An academic movement intended to counter the dominant European bias of Western scholarship; Afrocentric scholars seek to show the influence of African cultures, languages, and history on human civilization.

[11]*Aztlán:* Includes those parts of the United States once governed by Mexico.

[12]*essentialist:* Refers to the idea that group characteristics are innate, or "essential," rather than cultural.

Euro-Americans primarily because covert defenders of ethnic hierarchy or one-way assimilation have tried to confuse the broad-based ideal of democratic multiculturalism with the demands of a relatively few militant ethnocentrists for thoroughgoing self-segregation and isolation from the rest of American society.

Of the four models of American ethnic relations, the one that I believe offers the best hope for a just and cohesive society is a cultural pluralism that is fully inclusive and based on the free choices of individuals to construct or reconstruct their own ethnic identities. We are still far from achieving the degree of racial and ethnic tolerance that realization of such an ideal requires. But with the demographic shift that is transforming the overwhelmingly Euro-American population of thirty or forty years ago into one that is much more culturally and phenotypically heterogeneous, a more democratic form of intergroup relations is a likely prospect, unless there is a desperate reversion to overt ethnic hierarchicalism by the shrinking Euro-American majority. It that were to happen, national unity and cohesion would indeed be hard to maintain. If current trends continue, minorities of non-European ancestry will constitute a new majority sometime in the next century. Well before that point is reached, they will have the numbers and the provocation to make the country virtually ungovernable if a resurgent racism brings serious efforts to revive the blatantly hierarchical policies that have prevailed in the past.

References

Axtell, James. (1981). *The European and the Indian: Essays in the Ethnohistory of Colonial North America.* New York: Oxford University Press.

Berkhofer, Robert F., Jr. (1978). *The White Man's Indian: Image of the American Indian from Columbus to the Present.* New York: Alfred A. Knopf.

Bourne, Randolph S. (1964). *War and the Intellectuals: Collected Essays, 1915–1919.* New York: Harper Torch.

D'Souza, Dinesh. (1995). *The End of Racism: Principles for a Multiracial Society.* New York: Free Press.

Fredrickson, George M. (1987). *The Black Image in the White Mind: The Debate on Afro-American Character and Destiny, 1817–1914.* Middletown, Conn.: Wesleyan University Press.

———. (1995). *Black Liberation: A Comparative History of Black Ideologies in the United States and South Africa.* New York: Oxford University Press.

———. (1997). *The Comparative Imagination: On the History of Racism, Nationalism, and Social Movements.* Berkeley: University of California Press.

Gordon, Milton M. (1964). *Assimilation in American Life: The Role of Race, Religion, and National Origins.* New York: Oxford University Press.

Gutierrez, David. (1995). *Walls and Mirrors: Mexican Americans, Mexican Immigrants, and the Politics of Ethnicity.* Berkeley: University of California Press.

Herberg, Will. (1960). *Protestant-Catholic-Jew: An Essay in American Religious Sociology.* Garden City, N.Y.: Anchor Books.

Higham, John. (1968). *Strangers in the Land: Patterns of American Nativism, 1860–1925.* New York: Atheneum.

———. (1984). *Send These to Me: Jews and Other Immigrants in Urban America.* Baltimore: Johns Hopkins University Press.

Hollinger, David. (1995). *Postethnic America: Beyond Multiculturalism.* New York: Basic Books.

Hoxie, Frederick E. (1984). A *Final Promise: The Campaign to Assimilate the Indians, 1880–1920.* Lincoln: University of Nebraska Press.

Jordan, Winthrop D. (1968). *White Over Black: American Attitudes Toward the Negro, 1550–1812.* New York: University of North Carolina Press.

Kallen, Horace. (1924). *Culture and Democracy in the United States: Studies in the Group Psychology of American Peoples.* New York: Boni & Liveright.

Koch, Adrienne, and Peden, William (eds.). (1944). *The Life and Selected Writings of Thomas Jefferson.* New York: Modern Library.

Knobel, Dale T. (1986). *Paddy and the Republic: Ethnicity and Nationality in Antebellum America.* Middletown, Conn.: Wesleyan University Press.

Lewis, David Levering. (1993). *W. E. B. DuBois: Biography of a Race, 1868–1919.* New York: Henry Holt.

Marable, Manning. (1991). *Race, Reform, and Rebellion: The Second Reconstruction in Black America.* Jackson, Miss.: University of Mississippi Press.

Mardock, Robert W. (1971). *The Reformers and the American Indian.* Columbia: University of Missouri Press.

Miller, Stuart Creighton. (1969). *The Unwelcome Immigrant: The American Image of the Chinese, 1785–1882.* Berkeley: University of California Press.

Moses, Wilson Jeremiah. (1978). *The Golden Age of Black Nationalism, 1850–1925.* Hamden, Conn.: Archon Books.

Myrdal, Gunnar. (1944). *An American Dilemma.* New York: Harper and Row.

Schlesinger, Arthur M., Jr. (1992). *The Disuniting of America.* New York: Norton.

Van Deburg, William L. (1992). *New Day in Babylon: The Black Power Movement and American Culture, 1965–1975.* Chicago: University of Chicago Press.

ENGAGING THE TEXT

1. How does Fredrickson distinguish between race and ethnicity? How and under what circumstances can ethnicity become "racialized" (para. 2)?

2. What does Fredrickson mean by "the burden of 'otherness' "? Summarize the ways in which racial categories and definitions of "whiteness" have changed during the course of American history.

3. What are some of the ways that ethnic hierarchy has been eliminated? In what ways does it persist, according to Fredrickson? What evidence can you think of that would support or challenge this contention?

4. Fredrickson writes that "assimilationist thinking is not racist in the classic sense" (para. 9) — thereby implying that such thinking may be racist in some other sense. What does he mean by this? Do you agree?

5. How does Fredrickson distinguish cultural pluralism from assimilation? How did earlier forms of pluralism differ from the current concept of multiculturalism?

6. Why does Fredrickson reject the claim that an emphasis on ethnic identity threatens the unity and stability of American society? Why does a Euro-American backlash against ethnic diversity pose a greater risk in his view? Have you observed any recent examples of either divisiveness or backlash? Compare your observations with those of classmates.

EXPLORING CONNECTIONS

7. Write an essay examining the ways in which various models of ethnic relations can be seen operating in one or more of the following selections:

> Richard Rodriguez, "The Achievement of Desire" (p. 193)
> Malcolm X, "Learning to Read" (p. 210)
> Studs Terkel, "Stephen Cruz" (p. 353)
> Judith Ortiz Cofer, "The Story of My Body" (p. 393)
> Thomas Jefferson, from "Notes on the State of Virginia" (p. 486)
> Studs Terkel, "C. P. Ellis" (p. 519)
> Sherman Alexie, "Assimilation" (p. 584)

8. What model or models of ethnic relations do you see represented in the cartoon by Lalo Alcaraz on page 565?
9. Examine the Visual Portfolio on pages 556–60. Identify the model of ethnic relations you see embodied in each image and explain your reasoning.

EXTENDING THE CRITICAL CONTEXT

10. If your campus or community is involved in a debate concerning affirmative action, immigration, bilingual education, multiculturalism, or ethnic studies, analyze several opinion pieces or position papers on the issue. What models of ethnic relations are expressed or assumed by each side of the debate?

The Crossing
RUBÉN MARTÍNEZ

Although the United States prides itself on being a nation of immigrants, Americans' attitudes toward immigrants can be complex and contradictory. One recent poll showed opinion evenly divided over whether immigration helps or hurts the country, and while Americans overwhelmingly oppose illegal immigration, a consistent majority believes that undocumented workers fill jobs that citizens don't want. In this essay, adapted from his book Burning Sand *(2006), Rubén Martínez explores the cultural contradic-*

tions that arise in our representations of the border and of those who cross it searching for a better life. Martínez is an award-winning journalist and associate professor of creative writing at the University of Houston. His earlier books include The Other Side: Notes from the New L.A., Mexico City and Beyond *(1993),* Crossing Over: A Mexican Family on the Migrant Trail *(2002), and* The New Americans *(2004).*

I am, again, on the line.

I've been drawn to it my entire life, beginning with frequent childhood jaunts across it to Tijuana and back — that leap from the monochrome suburban grids of Southern California to the Technicolor swirl of urban Baja California and back. I am an American today because of that line — and my parents' will to erase it with their desire.

I return to it again and again because I am from both sides. So for me, son of a mother who emigrated from El Salvador and a Mexican American father who spent his own childhood leaping back and forth, the line is a sieve. And it is a brick wall.

It defines me even as I defy it. It is a book without a clear beginning or end, and despite the fact that we refer to it as a "line," it is not even linear; to compare it to an actual book I'd have to invoke Cortázar's[1] *Hopscotch.* This line does and does not exist. It is a historical, political, economic, and cultural fact. It is a laughable, puny, meaningless thing. It is a matter of life and death. And it is a matter of representation. It is a very productive trope[2] in both American and Mexican pop.

The cowboy crosses the line to evade the law, because he imagines   5 there is no law in the South. The immigrant crosses the line to embrace the future because he imagines there is no past in the North. Usually rendered by the River (the Rio Grande/Río Bravo — its name changes from one shore to the other), the line appears again and again in film and literature and music from both sides.

Just a few: Cormac McCarthy and Carlos Fuentes, Marty Robbins and Los Tigres del Norte, Sam Peckinpah and Emilio "El Indio" Fernández, Charles Bowden and Gloria Anzaldúa.[3]

[1]*Cortázar:* Julio Florencio Cortázar (1914–1986), Argentine writer known for his short stories.

[2]*trope:* Figure of speech, such as metaphor.

[3]*Cormac McCarthy . . . Gloria Anzaldúa:* Cormac McCarthy (b. 1933), American novelist known for writing about the Southwest; Carlos Fuentes (b. 1928), Mexican essayist and fiction writer; Marty Robbins (1925–1982), American country-western singer; Los Tigres del Norte, Grammy-winning musical group formed in the late 1960s; Sam Peckinpah (1925–1984), American writer, director, and producer of western films and television series; Emilio Fernández (1903–1968), Mexican actor, writer, and director; Charles Bowden (b. 1945), American nonfiction writer and editor; Gloria Anzaldúa (1942–2004), Chicana writer and editor, best known for *Borderlands/La Frontera: The New Mestiza* (1987).

In the Western, the moment of the crossing (the lawless gang fleeing the lawmen, their horses' hooves muddying the muddy waters all the more) is heralded by a stirring musical figure, brassy and percussive, leaping several tonal steps with each note. Once we're safely on the other side, the melodic strings of Mexico take over. The swaggering American will have his way with a Mexican señorita. The post-colonial[4] representations of border-lands literature — produced by Mexicans and Americans alike — have yet to soften the edges of this Spring Break syndrome. The whorehouse-across-the-river is there for a spurned Jake Gyllenhaal to get off with smooth-skinned brown boys in an otherwise liberatory *Brokeback Mountain*. Americans fictional and real always fantasize remaining in that racy, lazy South, but business or vengeance or a respectable marriage (the señorita is a puta, and you can't marry a puto[5] on either side of the border) usually call the cowboy back home.

The Mexican or Chicano production is an inverted mirror of the same. The climax of Cheech Marin's *Born in East L.A.* (and dozens of Mexican B-movies) fulfills every migrant's fantasy of a joyous rush of brown humanity breaching a hapless Border Patrol, the victory of simple desire over military technology that occurs thousands of times a day on the border and feeds the paranoid vision of a reconquista[6] (which, a handful of crackpot Chicano nationalists notwithstanding, has been largely invented by the likes of the Minutemen,[7] white dudes with real economic insecurities unfortunately marinated in traditional borderlands racism).

Every step across the line is a breach of one code or another. Some of these laws are on the books; some have never been written down; some are matters more private than public.

I've been drawn to that line my whole life. Sometimes it's a metaphor.   10
Sometimes it's not.

This time, I am close to the line on the Buenos Aires National Wildlife Refuge in southern Arizona. It is a late August afternoon, a day that will not make headlines because there are no Minuteman patrols out hunting migrants, no Samaritans out seeking to save them. Nor is there, for the moment, any Border Patrol in the immediate vicinity. The land is as its public designation intended: a unique Sonoran desert habitat bizarrely and beautifully traversed by grasslands that are home to hundreds of unique species, including the endangered pronghorn antelope; it is also an outstanding birding location. But there are no birders in the dead of summer. The birders and the Minutemen have no wish to be out in temperatures

---

[4]*post-colonial:* Refers to the time following the independence of a colony; postcolonial literature often deals with the impact and legacy of colonial rule.

[5]*puta/puto:* Whore.

[6]*reconquista:* Reconquest; much of the American southwest once belonged to Mexico.

[7]*Minutemen:* Self-appointed anti-immigrant guardians of the U.S. borders, particularly in the southwest. This contemporary group has adopted the name of the well-known American military unit that fought in the Revolutionary War.

that often rise to more than 110 degrees. (Some Samaritans who belong to a group called No More Deaths are indeed in the area, but the day's final patrol is probably heading back to the church-based group's campground near the town of Arivaca, which borders the refuge.)

I park at the Arivaca Creek trailhead. The interpretive sign tells of the possibility of hearing the "snap of vermilion flycatchers snatching insects on the wing." It also tells of another species, a relative newcomer to this "riparian ribbon":

"Visitors to BANWR are advised to remain alert for illegal activity associated with the presence of undocumented aliens (UDAs). There is also increased law enforcement activity by several agencies & organizations."

The bulleted visitor guidelines advise not to let the "UDAs approach you or your vehicle," a Homeland Security variation of "do not feed the wildlife."

The humidity from recent monsoonal deluges is stifling, making 100   15
degrees feel much hotter — and wetter. The reed-like branches of ocotillos have sprouted their tiny lime-green leaves, hiding their terrifically sharp thorns. Moss flourishes on arroyo stones. Mosquitoes zip and whine through the thick air. The desert jungle.

I tell myself that I'll take a short stroll; it's getting late. I climb the trail from the creek bed, which is dominated by mammoth cottonwood trees, south toward the red dirt hills — a trail used by birders and "UDAs" alike. I can imagine an Audubon guide leading a gaggle of khaki-clad tourists peering through binoculars, first at a vermilion flycatcher and then at a Mexican rushing through a mesquite thicket, *Profugus mexicanus*. On the line everything seems to attract its opposite or, more accurately, everything seems to attract a thing that seems to have no relation to it, not parallel universes but saw-toothed eruptions, the crumpled metal of a collision. These pairings occur not just near the political border — I am about 11 miles from the boundary between the United States of America and the United States of Mexico — but throughout the West. The border is no longer a line. Its ink has diffused, an ambiguous veil across the entire territory.

Take the microcosm of the BANWR and its immediate vicinity. The birders and the migrants, the Samaritans and the Minutemen. Hunters and stoners. A "dude ranch" that charges city slickers up to $2,500 a week. Retirees of modest means. Hellfire Protestants and Catholic penitents and New Age vortex-seekers. Living here or passing through are Americans and Native Americans and Mexicans and Mexican Americans and Mexican Indians, all of varying shades and accents, and there are Iranians and Guatemalans and Chinese. This kind of situation was once affectionately referred to as the Melting Pot. But no, it is more like speaking in tongues, speaking in Babel.[8] The tower is crumbling. Melting pot meltdown.

---

[8]*Babel:* Refers to an ancient city whose inhabitants tried to build a tower to heaven, which God destroyed. He then made the people speak different languages so that they could no longer work together.

I climb into the red hills as the sun nears the horizon. The sky at the zenith is a stunning true blue. Reaching a saddle, I stumble on to a huge migrant encampment — water jugs and backpacks and soiled underwear and tubes of toothpaste and a brand-new denim jacket finely embroidered with the name of a car club, opened cans of refried beans, bottles of men's cologne, Tampax, tortillas curled hard in the heat. The things they carried and left behind because 11 miles into the 50-mile hike they'd begun to realize the weight of those things, and they'd resolved to travel lighter. If something was to go wrong and they got lost and hyperthermic, they might even begin stripping the clothes off their backs.

It is possible, too, that they've just broken camp; it is possible that they saw me coming and are hiding behind one of the saddle's humps. I call out: ¡No soy migra![9] This is a line from the script of the Samaritan Patrol, who, like the activists of No More Deaths, scour the desert searching for migrants in distress. They call out so that the fearful migrants might reveal themselves to receive food and water. It is a good line in the borderlands; I can't think of a better one. The real problem is, what am I going to say if someone actually responds? Buenas tardes señoras y señores, soy periodista y quería entervistarles, si es que no les es mucha molestia[10] . . . the journalist's lame introduction. Of course, they would have no reason to stop and speak to me — just the opposite. Indeed, why would they believe that I am not migra? And what if the smugglers are hauling a load of narcotics instead of humans? What if they are carrying weapons? This is not idle paranoia — this desert is armed with Mexican and American government-issue sidearms and the assault rifles of the paramilitary brigades on both sides. It is no surprise that there is bloodshed. Assault, rape, torture, and murder are common.

In any event, I have nothing to offer the trekkers; they have not run out of water yet (though by tomorrow, after 15 or 20 miles, they well might). I am suddenly ashamed, as if I've intruded on a tremendously private moment, as if I've stumbled upon a couple in erotic embrace, bodies vulnerable to the harshness of the landscape and my gaze. 20

The sun sets, a funnel of gold joining cerulean canopy to blood-red earth. The land is completely still. I hold my breath. I realize that I want them to appear. I want to join them on the journey. The Audubon birder needs the vermilion flycatcher; right now, the writer needs a mojado.[11]

The migrant stumbles through the desert and I after him — he's on a pilgrimage and I'm in pursuit of him. Thus I am the literary migra: I will trap the mojado within the distorting borders of representation — a

[9]*¡No soy migra!:* I'm not immigration ("la migra" refers generically to any branch or agent of the U.S. immigration authority, such as the Border Patrol).

[10]*Buenas tardes . . . mucha molestia:* Good afternoon, ladies and gentlemen, I'm a journalist and would like to interview you, if it's not too much trouble.

[11]*mojado:* Wetback.

U.S. immigration policy

problem no writer has ever resolved. But aren't I also representing the origins of my own family's journey? Don't I also return to the line because it was upon my parents and grandparents' crossing it that I became possible?

¡No soy migra! I call out again.

There is no response. I sweat profusely, soaking through my UNM[12] Lobos T-shirt. Even my jeans hang heavy with moisture. Swatting mosquitoes, I retrace my footsteps back to the car.

I drive west in the dimming light. There is no one on this road but me.   25

Suddenly, a flutter in my peripheral vision. And now a figure stumbles out of the desert green to remind me that the border is, above all else, a moral line. He crawls from the brush and waves to me from the south side of the road. I stop the truck and roll down my window. He is a plaintive-looking fellow in his 30s, with thick black curls, a sweaty and smudged moon of a face. He has large brown eyes ringed by reddened whites. He is wearing a black T-shirt, blue jeans, and white tennis shoes. He carries a small blue vinyl bag.

¿Qué pasó? I ask. What happened?

With the first syllables of his response I can tell that he is from El Salvador. It is an accent that splits the difference between the typically muted tones of the Latin American provinces and the urgent desire of urban

---

[12]*UNM:* University of New Mexico.

speech. It is the accent of my mother and her family; it is the Spanish accent I associate most with my childhood.

He says his name is Victor and that he had hiked about 12 miles into U.S. territory and could not make it any farther. His migrant crew had traveled all night and started up again late in the afternoon — just a couple of hours ago — but he'd become extremely fatigued and his vision began to blur.

Soy diabético,[13] says Victor.   30

Immediately I grab my phone to dial 911. It chirps a complaint: There is no signal. I think: Hypoglycemia, he needs something sweet. I think this because of the hundreds of plot lines in television dramas I've watched since I was a kid. In the backseat I have enough supplies to keep a dozen hikers going for at least a day in the desert — power bars, fruit cups, tins of Vienna sausages, peanut butter crackers, bags of trail mix, several bottles of Gatorade and gallon-jugs of drinking water. I expect him to tear ravenously into the strawberry-flavored bar I give him, but he eats it very slowly, taking modest sips of water between bites.

I flip open the cellphone again. Still no signal.

The particulars of a problem begin to form in my mind. Although I am not a medical expert, it is apparent that Victor needs urgent attention. But there is no way to contact medical personnel. The only option is to drive Victor to the nearest town, which is Arivaca, about 10 miles away. I become aware that by doing so, both Victor and I will be risking apprehension by the Border Patrol. More than one border denizen has told me that merely giving a migrant a ride can place one in a tenuous legal situation.

U.S. Code (Title 8, Chapter 12, Subchapter II, Part VIII, Section 1324) stipulates that an American citizen breaks the law when "knowing or in reckless disregard of the fact that an alien has come to, entered, or remains in the United States in violation of law, transports, or moves or attempts to transport or move such alien within the United States by means of trans-portation or otherwise, in furtherance of such violation of law."

The ethical calculation is simple enough. The law might contradict my   35
moral impulse, but the right thing to do is obvious. I also tell myself that in the event of apprehension by the Border Patrol, the truth of the situation will suffice. I am a Samaritan, after all, not a coyote. The truth will suffice at least for me, that is: I will go free, and Victor will be deported.

I tell Victor to get in the car.

The night falls fast. Soon the only things we can see through the bug-splattered windshield are the grainy blacktop ahead and the tangle of mesquites lining the road. I keep expecting more migrants to appear in the headlights and wave us down. At any given moment on this stretch of bor-derland there may be hundreds of migrants attempting passage.

It is a winding road and I'm a conservative driver, so there's time for small talk. Victor is much more animated now. He says he is feeling better.

---

[13]*Soy diabético:* I'm diabetic.

He is from Soyapango, a working-class suburb of San Salvador that I remember well from my time in the country during the civil war, when it had the reputation of being a rebel stronghold. Right now, Victor is 1,800 miles from Soyapango.

¿Y a qué se dedica usted? He asks what I do for a living.   40

I reply that I am a writer, and then there is silence for about a quarter of a mile.

The Border Patrol will appear any minute now, I think to myself.

His large round eyes glisten, reflecting the light from my dashboard. More questions. ¿Cómo se llama el pueblo al que vamos? ¿Qué lejos queda Phoenix? ¿Qué lejos queda Los Angeles? What's the name of the town we're heading to? How far is Phoenix? How far is Los Angeles? Phoenix: where the coyote told him he'd be dropped off at a safe house. Los Angeles: where his sister lives. He has memorized a phone number. It begins with the area code 818. Yes, he is feeling quite fine now, Victor says, and he realizes that I can't drive him all the way to L.A. But Phoenix is only 100 miles away. That's like from San Salvador to Guatemala City.

There is still no Border Patrol in sight. This does not make any sense. There are hundreds of agents on duty in what is called the Tucson Sector, the busiest and deadliest crossing along the U.S.–Mexico line. Is it the changing of the guard? Are the agents on dinner break? Are they tracking down Osama bin Laden, disguised as a Mexican day laborer?

Now, I realize, the problem is a bit different. Victor is apparently no   45
longer experiencing a medical emergency, although I cannot be absolutely certain of this. The law is ambiguous on the matter of Samaritan aid. I am aware of a pending federal court case against two young No More Deaths activists, Shanti Sellz and Daniel Strauss, who recently attempted to conduct a "medical evacuation" by taking two apparently ailing migrants directly to a hospital rather than handing them over to the BP. Federal prosecutors decided that the activists were transporting the migrants "in furtherance" of their illegal presence in the U.S. and indicted the pair on several felony charges. The activists and their supporters say that the ethical imperative of offering aid in the context of a medical emergency supersedes the letter of immigration law — a moral argument without juridical precedent on the border. The activists are clearly hoping to set one.

But the law is decidedly less ambiguous about what Victor is now asking me to do. If I drive him to Phoenix and put him in touch with his sister, I will clearly have provided transportation "in furtherance of" his illegal presence. He is no longer asking for medical aid.

The air-conditioning chills the sweat on the wet rag that my Lobos T-shirt has become. It seems that there are now several possibilities, several problems. It seems that there are many right and wrong things to do. The scenarios tumble through my mind.

Risk the trip to Phoenix. (Where is that BP checkpoint on I-19? Is it north or south of Arivaca Junction? I look into the sky — are there thunderheads? Checkpoints often close when it rains.) What if Victor is actually still sick and on the verge of a seizure — shouldn't I turn him over to the BP? But will the BP give him the medical care he needs? And, not least of all, what of Victor's human right to escape the living hell that is Soyapango (poverty and crime there today are taking nearly as much a toll as the civil war did)? If Victor has that essential human right to seek a better life for himself and his family, what is my moral duty when he literally stumbles into my life on the border? Am I willing to risk federal charges to fulfill an ethical responsibility that I decide trumps the laws of my country?

I slow down to a crawl as we near the outskirts of Arivaca, a town famed for a '60s-era commune and the weed-growing hippies that hung on long past the Summer of Love. It will all end here in Arivaca, I tell myself. The BP trucks will be lined up outside the one small grocery store in town, or maybe up at the Grubsteak, which is presided over by a gregarious Mexican who waits on the graying hippies and handful of outsider artists who arrived years ago thinking they'd found the grail of Western living, long before chaos came to the border.

But when I pull up to the store, there is only the heat of the night and a 50 flickering street lamp gathering a swarm of moths. I notice a few local kids — white, shaved heads — standing by a pay phone. Now it occurs to me that there is a possible solution to this mess. In the rush of events, I'd forgotten that No More Deaths had a camp about four miles east of town. Because it is a faith-based organization, the camp was baptized "Ark of the Covenant." Since 2004, No More Deaths had recruited student activists — like Sellz and Strauss, the pair under federal indictment — from around the country to come to southern Arizona and walk the lethal desert trails. There would be activists there with more experience than I in these matters. They could easily consult the doctors and lawyers supporting their cause to determine the right thing to do — or at least their version of the right thing.

I walk into the store. I tell Victor to stay inside the car. The clerk behind the counter is reading the newspaper, head cupped in her hands and elbows leaning on the food scale next to the cash register.

I briefly blurt out my story.

She asks me where Victor is. In the car, I say. Immediately she tells me that the BP can impound my vehicle, they can file charges. She tells me that she can call the Border Patrol for me. She seems to know exactly what the right thing to do is. The only thing to do. She places her hand on the phone.

A few seconds later I'm back in the heat of the night and I ask the first passerby, a young blond woman named Charity, for directions to the Ark of the Covenant. Do you have a map? She asks. She means a local map. No. Now she is drawing one on a page of my reporter's notebook. She draws many lines. Here there is a hill, she says; here, a llama ranch. She says a quarter of a mile, then a couple of miles, then three-quarters of a mile and left and right and across. It is a moonless night. Good luck, she says.

I climb back in the truck, I turn the ignition. I give Victor the notebook 55 with the map. In a minute we're out of town and on to the first dirt road of the route. Still no BP in sight. The map is accurate. I pass by the llama ranch, barely catching the sign in the dimness.

For several minutes I ride on impulse — no thoughts at all. But as I turn left just where Charity told me to, a thought powerful enough to take my foot off the gas seizes me.

I can't ride into the Ark of the Covenant with Victor in the truck. What I'd forgotten in my haste was the political reality of the moment: The feds had called No More Deaths' bluff and were going after them in court. I remembered hearing from a couple of activists that before and since the arrests of Sellz and Strauss, there had been constant BP surveillance on the encampment.

If the BP were to see me dropping off Victor at the camp now, would they, could they use this as more evidence of running a de facto smuggling operation? Perhaps this could strengthen the federal case against Sellz and Strauss. And what if there was a conviction? And what if a judge ordered the camp closed?

Now I was weighing Victor's singular rights and desire and the goals and strategy of an activist movement that had helped dozens of migrants in distress over the past two summers and that could continue to help many more. The problem was, my cellphone was dead. The problem was my desire to capture a mojado. The problem was, I didn't have enough information to know what the "right" decision was. I had placed myself on the line, and I wasn't ready for what it would ask of me.

I slow down, and the dust kicked up by the tires envelops the truck.   60
Victor and I turn to each other.

Fifteen minutes later, I pull up, for the second time, to the convenience store in Arivaca. The clerk is still reading the paper. I tell her to call the Border Patrol. I tell her that Victor has diabetes and symptoms of hypoglycemia.

She picks up the phone: "We've got a diabetic UDA."

I walk out to Victor, who is standing next to my truck, staring into the black desert night. He asks me again how far it is to Tucson. I tell him that he'll die if he tries to hike.

I tell myself that Victor is probably living and working somewhere in America now. It is quite possible that he attempted to cross over again after his apprehension by the Border Patrol, and that he succeeded. This thought does and does not comfort me.

I tell myself I did the right thing. I tell myself I did the wrong thing. I tell   65
myself that every decision on the line is like that, somewhere in between.

ENGAGING THE TEXT

1. What different meanings — personal, geographic, cultural, metaphoric — does Martínez associate with the border? Why does he emphasize this complexity? In what ways is he "on the line" (para. 1)?

2. How does Martínez's role as a journalist influence his decisions and actions? To what extent does his family history affect his thinking and behavior?

3. Martínez refers to trapping his subject "within the distorting borders of representation" (para. 22). How does he represent or misrepresent Victor? How might Victor represent himself differently?

4. What is the effect of Martínez's use of the derogatory word "mojado" in the passage describing his search for an undocumented immigrant to interview? Why do you think he chooses to use the term here and in paragraph 59 and not elsewhere in the essay?

5. Debate the ethical dilemma Martínez faces: Does the moral imperative to obtain medical assistance for Victor outweigh Martínez's legal obligation to turn him over to the Border Patrol? Write a journal entry explaining what you would have done in Martínez's place, and why. Share your responses in class.

EXPLORING CONNECTIONS

6. Which of George M. Fredrickson's models of ethnic relations (p. 561) appear to be operating along the U.S.–Mexican border as Martínez describes it? Do you see evidence of more than one model coexisting?

7. In "U.S. immigration policy" (p. 579) what is the cartoonist suggesting about American attitudes and laws regarding immigration? To what extent does Martínez share the cartoonist's view? How does his perspective differ?

EXTENDING THE CRITICAL CONTEXT

8. Write an essay comparing Martínez's representation of the U.S.–Mexican border to another depiction that you are familiar with in music, film, or literature.

9. Work in groups to research the Minutemen and No More Deaths. What is the history and purpose of each organization? What appear to be their primary values?

10. Examine the language used by news reporters, politicians, and pro- and anti-immigrant groups in discussing immigration issues: How are documented and undocumented immigrants portrayed? What metaphors are used to describe the number of immigrants entering the United States (e.g., flood) and what are their implications?

Assimilation

SHERMAN ALEXIE

Sherman Alexie won the 1999 World Heavyweight Championship Poetry Bout by improvising, in thirty seconds, a poetic riff on the word "dumbass." The poem, according to one reporter, was both humorous and poignant. Alexie's performance captured his sense of humor, his inventiveness, and his ability to wring insight from unlikely material. True to form, this story — about a Coeur d'Alene Indian woman who decides to cheat on her white husband — is a comedy that poses serious questions about race, class, culture, deception, and love. Alexie (b. 1966) grew up on the Spokane Indian Reservation in Washington State, but attended a high school where, in his words, he was "the only Indian . . . except the school mascot." He claims not to believe in writer's block, and has the publications to prove it: two novels, Reservation Blues *(1995) and* Indian Killer *(1996); twelve volumes of poems and short stories; many essays and reviews. He coauthored the script for the award-winning film* Smoke Signals *(1998) and both wrote and directed* The Business of Fancydancing *(2002). "Assimilation" comes from Alexie's short story collection,* The Toughest Indian in the World *(2000).*

Regarding love, marriage, and sex, both Shakespeare and Sitting Bull knew the only truth: treaties get broken. Therefore, Mary Lynn wanted to have sex with any man other than her husband. For the first time in her life, she wanted to go to bed with an Indian man only because he was Indian. She was a Coeur d'Alene Indian married to a white man; she was a wife who wanted to have sex with an indigenous stranger. She didn't care about the stranger's job or his hobbies, or whether he was due for a Cost of Living raise, or owned ten thousand miles of model railroad track. She didn't care if he was handsome or ugly, mostly because she wasn't sure exactly what those terms meant anymore and how much relevance they truly had when it came to choosing sexual partners. Oh, she'd married a very handsome man, there was no doubt about that, and she was still attracted to her husband, to his long, graceful fingers, to his arrogance and utter lack of fear in social situations — he'd say anything to anybody — but lately, she'd been forced to concentrate too hard when making love to him. If she didn't focus completely on him, on the smallest details of his body, then she would drift away from the bed and float around the room like a bored angel. Of course, all this made her feel like a failure, especially since it seemed that her husband had yet to notice her growing disinterest. She wanted to be a good lover, wife, and partner, but she'd obviously developed some form of sexual dyslexia or had picked up a mutant, contagious, and erotic strain of Attention Deficit Disorder. She felt baffled by the complications of sex. She haunted the aisles of bookstores and desperately paged through every book in the self-help section and studied every diagram and chart in the human sensuality encyclopedias. She wanted answers. She wanted to feel it again, whatever *it* was.

A few summers ago, during Crow Fair, Mary Lynn had been standing in a Montana supermarket, in the produce aisle, when a homely white woman, her spiky blond hair still wet from a trailer-house shower, walked by in a white t-shirt and blue jeans, and though Mary Lynn was straight — having politely declined all three lesbian overtures thrown at her in her life — she'd felt a warm breeze pass through her DNA in that ugly woman's wake, and had briefly wanted to knock her to the linoleum and do beautiful things to her. Mary Lynn had never before felt such lust — in Montana, of all places, for a white woman who was functionally illiterate and underemployed! — and had not since felt that sensually about any other woman or man.

Who could explain such things, these vagaries of love? There were many people who would blame Mary Lynn's unhappiness, her dissatisfaction, on her ethnicity. God, she thought, how simple and earnest was that particular bit of psychotherapy! Yes, she was most certainly a Coeur d'Alene — she'd grown up on the rez, had been very happy during her time there, and had left without serious regrets or full-time enemies — but that wasn't the only way to define her. She wished that she could be called Coeur d'Alene as a description, rather than as an excuse, reason, prescription, placebo, prediction, or diminutive. She only wanted to be understood as eccentric and complicated!

Her most cherished eccentricity: when she was feeling her most lonely, she'd put one of the Big Mom Singers' powwow CDs on the stereo (*I'm not afraid of death, hey, ya, hey, death is my cousin, hey, ya, ha, ha*) and read from Emily Dickinson's poetry (*Because I could not stop for Death — /He kindly stopped for me —).*

Her most important complication: she was a woman in a turbulent mar-   5
riage that was threatening to go bad, or had gone bad and might get worse.

Yes, she was a Coeur d'Alene woman, passionately and dispassionately, who wanted to cheat on her white husband because he was white. She wanted to find an anonymous lover, an Indian man who would fade away into the crowd when she was done with him, a man whose face could appear on the back of her milk carton. She didn't care if he was the kind of man who knew the punch lines to everybody's dirty jokes, or if he was the kind of man who read Zane Grey before he went to sleep, or if he was both of those men simultaneously. She simply wanted to find the darkest Indian in Seattle — the man with the greatest amount of melanin — and get naked with him in a cheap motel room. Therefore, she walked up to a flabby Lummi Indian man in a coffee shop and asked him to make love to her.

"Now," she said. "Before I change my mind."

He hesitated for a brief moment, wondering why he was the chosen one, and then took her by the hand. He decided to believe he was a handsome man.

"Don't you want to know my name?" he asked before she put her hand over his mouth.

"Don't talk to me," she said. "Don't say one word. Just take me to the   10
closest motel and fuck me."

The obscenity bothered her. It felt staged, forced, as if she were an actress in a three-in-the-morning cable-television movie. But she was acting, wasn't she? She was not an adulteress, was she?

Why exactly did she want to have sex with an Indian stranger? She told herself it was because of pessimism, existentialism, even nihilism, but those reasons — *those words* — were a function of her vocabulary and not of her motivations. If forced to admit the truth, or some version of the truth, she'd testify she was about to go to bed with an Indian stranger because she wanted to know how it would feel. After all, she'd slept with a white stranger in her life, so why not include a Native American? Why not practice a carnal form of affirmative action? By God, her infidelity was a political act! Rebellion, resistance, revolution!

In the motel room, Mary Lynn made the Indian take off his clothes first. Thirty pounds overweight, with purple scars crisscrossing his pale chest and belly, he trembled as he undressed. He wore a wedding ring on his right hand. She knew that some Europeans wore their wedding bands on the right hand — so maybe this Indian was married to a French woman — but Mary Lynn also knew that some divorced Americans wore rings on their right hands as symbols of pain, of mourning. Mary Lynn didn't care if he was married or not, or whether he shared custody of the sons and daughters, or whether he had any children at all. She was grateful that he was plain and desperate and lonely.

Mary Lynn stepped close to him, took his hand, and slid his thumb into her mouth. She sucked on it and felt ridiculous. His skin was salty and oily, the taste of a working man. She closed her eyes and thought about her husband, a professional who had his shirts laundered. In one hour, he was going to meet her at a new downtown restaurant.

She walked a slow, tight circle around the Indian. She stood behind him, reached around his thick waist, and held his erect penis. He moaned and she decided that she hated him. She decided to hate all men. Hate, hate, hate, she thought, and then let her hate go.   15

She was lovely and intelligent, and had grown up with Indian women who were more lovely and more intelligent, but who also had far less ambition and mendacity. She'd once read in a book, perhaps by Primo Levi or Elie Wiesel, that the survivors of the Nazi death camps were the Jews who lied, cheated, murdered, stole, and subverted. You must remember, said Levi or Wiesel, that the best of us did not survive the camps. Mary Lynn felt the same way about the reservation. Before she'd turned ten, she'd attended the funerals of seventeen good women — the best of the Coeur d'Alenes — and had read about the deaths of eighteen more good women since she'd left the rez. But what about the Coeur d'Alene men — those liars, cheats, and thieves — who'd survived, even thrived? Mary Lynn wanted nothing to do with them, then or now. As a teenager, she'd dated only white boys. As an adult, she'd only dated white men. God, she hated to admit it, but white men — her teachers, coaches, bosses, and lovers — had always been more dependable than the Indian men in her life. White men had rarely disappointed her, but they'd never surprised her either. White men were neutral, she thought, just like Belgium! And when has Belgium ever been sexy? When has Belgium caused a grown woman to shake with fear and guilt? She didn't want to feel Belgian; she wanted to feel dangerous.

In the cheap motel room, Mary Lynn breathed deeply. The Indian smelled of old sweat and a shirt worn twice before washing. She ran her finger along the ugly scars on his belly and chest. She wanted to know the scars' creation story — she hoped this Indian man was a warrior with a history of knife fighting — but she feared he was only carrying the transplanted heart and lungs of another man. She pushed him onto the bed, onto the scratchy comforter. She'd once read that scientists had examined a hotel-room comforter and discovered four hundred and thirty-two different samples of sperm. God, she thought, those scientists obviously had too much time on their hands and, in the end, had failed to ask the most important questions: Who left the samples? Spouses, strangers? Were these exchanges of money, tenderness, disease? Was there love?

"This has to be quick," she said to the stranger beside her.

Jeremiah, her husband, was already angry when Mary Lynn arrived thirty minutes late at the restaurant and he nearly lost all of his self-control when they were asked to wait for the next available table. He often raged at strangers, though he was incredibly patient and kind with their four children. Mary Lynn had seen that kind of rage in other white men when their wishes and desires were ignored. At ball games, in parking lots, and especially in airports, white men demanded to receive the privileges whose very existence they denied. White men could be so predictable, thought Mary Lynn. She thought: O, Jeremiah! O, season ticket holder! O, monthly parker! O, frequent flyer! She dreamed of him out there, sitting in the airplane with eighty-seven other white men wearing their second-best suits, all of them traveling toward small rooms in the Ramadas, Radissons, and sometimes the Hyatts, where they all separately watched the same pay-per-view porno that showed everything except penetration. What's the point of porno without graphic penetration? Mary Lynn knew it only made these lonely men feel all that more lonely. And didn't they deserve better, these white salesmen and middle managers, these twenty-first-century Willy Lomans,[1] who only wanted to be better men than their fathers had been? Of course, thought Mary Lynn, these sons definitely deserved better — they were smarter and more tender and generous than all previous generations of white American men — but they'd never receive their just rewards, and thus their anger was justified and banal.

"Calm down," Mary Lynn said to her husband as he continued to rage   20
at the restaurant hostess.

Mary Lynn said those two words to him more often in their marriage than any other combination of words.

"It could be twenty, thirty minutes," said the hostess. "Maybe longer."

"We'll wait outside," said Jeremiah. He breathed deeply, remembering some mantra that his therapist had taught him.

---

[1]*Willy Lomans:* Willy Loman, the protagonist of Arthur Miller's play *Death of a Salesman,* is an ordinary but driven man struggling to find meaning in his work and family life; he becomes a symbol of the problems and despair faced by the "little guy" in an increasingly impersonal world.

Mary Lynn's mantra: I cheated on my husband, I cheated on my husband.

"We'll call your name," said the hostess, a white woman who was tired   25
of men no matter what their color. "When."

Their backs pressed against the brick wall, their feet crossed on the
sidewalk, on a warm Seattle evening, Mary Lynn and Jeremiah smoked faux
cigarettes filled with some foul-tasting, overwhelmingly organic herb substance. For years they had smoked unfiltered Camels, but had quit after all
four of their parents had simultaneously suffered through at least one form
of cancer. Mary Lynn had called them the Mormon Tabernacle Goddamn
Cancer Choir, though none of them was Mormon and all of them were
altos. With and without grace, they had all survived the radiation,
chemotherapy, and in-hospital cable-television bingo games, with their bodies reasonably intact, only to resume their previously self-destructive habits.
After so many nights spent in hospital corridors, waiting rooms, and arm-
chairs, Mary Lynn and Jeremiah hated doctors, all doctors, even the ones on
television, especially the ones on television. United in their obsessive
hatred, Mary Lynn and Jeremiah resorted to taking vitamins, eating free-
range chicken, and smoking cigarettes rolled together and marketed by six
odoriferous white liberals in Northern California.

As they waited for a table, Mary Lynn and Jeremiah watched dozens of
people arrive and get seated immediately.

"I bet they don't have reservations," he said.

"I hate these cigarettes," she said.

"Why do you keep buying them?"   30

"Because the cashier at the health-food store is cute."

"You're shallow."

"Like a mud puddle."

Mary Lynn hated going out on weeknights. She hated driving into the
city. She hated waiting for a table. Standing outside the downtown restaurant, desperate to hear their names, she decided to hate Jeremiah for a few
seconds. Hate, hate, hate, she thought, and then she let her hate go. She
wondered if she smelled like sex, like indigenous sex, and if a white man
could recognize the scent of an enemy. She'd showered, but the water pressure had been weak and the soap bar too small.

"Let's go someplace else," she said.   35

"No. Five seconds after we leave, they'll call our names."

"But we won't know they called our names."

"But I'll feel it."

"It must be difficult to be psychic and insecure."

"I knew you were going to say that."   40

Clad in leather jackets and black jeans, standing inches apart but never
quite touching, both handsome to the point of distraction, smoking crappy
cigarettes that appeared to be real cigarettes, they could have been the subjects of a Schultz photograph or a Runnette poem.

The title of the photograph: "Infidelity."

The title of the poem: "More Infidelity."

Jeremiah's virtue was reasonably intact, though he'd recently been involved in a flirtatious near-affair with a coworker. At the crucial moment, when the last button was about to be unbuttoned, when consummation was just a fingertip away, Jeremiah had pushed his potential lover away and said I can't, I just can't, I love my marriage. He didn't admit to love for his spouse, partner, wife. No, he confessed his love for marriage, for the blessed union, for the legal document, for the shared mortgage payments, and for their four children.

Mary Lynn wondered what would happen if she grew pregnant with   45
the Lummi's baby. Would this full-blood baby look more Indian than her half-blood sons and daughters?

"Don't they know who I am?" she asked her husband as they waited outside the downtown restaurant. She wasn't pregnant; there would be no paternity tests, no revealing of great secrets. His secret: he was still in love with a white woman from high school he hadn't seen in decades. What Mary Lynn knew: he was truly in love with the idea of a white woman from a mythical high school, with a prom queen named *If Only* or a homecoming princess named *My Life Could Have Been Different.*

"I'm sure they know who you are," he said. "That's why we're on the wait list. Otherwise, we'd be heading for McDonald's or Denny's."

"Your kinds of places."

"Dependable. The Big Mac you eat in Hong Kong or Des Moines tastes just like the Big Mac in Seattle."

"Sounds like colonialism to me."   50

"Colonialism ain't all bad."

"Put that on a bumper sticker."

This place was called Tan Tan, though it would soon be trendy enough to go by a nickname: Tan's. Maybe Tan's would become T's, and then T's would be identified only by a slight turn of the head or a certain widening of the eyes. After that, the downhill slide in reputation would be inevitable, whether or not the culinary content and quality of the restaurant remained exactly the same or improved. As it was, Tan Tan was a pan-Asian restaurant whose ownership and chefs — head, sauce, and line — were white, though most of the wait staff appeared to be one form of Asian or another.

"Don't you hate it?" Jeremiah asked. "When they have Chinese waiters in sushi joints? Or Korean dishwashers in a Thai noodle house?"

"I hadn't really thought about it," she said.   55

"No, think about it, these restaurants, these Asian restaurants, they hire Asians indiscriminately because they think white people won't be able to tell the difference."

"White people can't tell the difference."

"I can."

"Hey, Geronimo, you've been hanging around Indians too long to be white."

"Fucking an Indian doesn't make me Indian."   60

"So, that's what we're doing now? Fucking?"

"You have a problem with fucking?"

"No, not with the act itself, but I do have a problem with your sexual thesaurus."

Mary Lynn and Jeremiah had met in college, when they were still called Mary and Jerry. After sleeping together for the first time, after her first orgasm and his third, Mary had turned to Jerry and said, with absolute seriousness: If this thing is going to last, we have to stop the end rhyme. She had majored in Milton and Blake. He'd been a chemical engineer since the age of seven, with the degree being only a matter of formality, so he'd had plenty of time to wonder how an Indian from the reservation could be so smart. He still wondered how it had happened, though he'd never had the courage to ask her.

Now, a little more than two decades after graduating with a useless   65
degree, Mary Lynn worked at Microsoft for a man named Dickinson. Jeremiah didn't know his first name, though he hoped it wasn't Emery, and had never met the guy, and didn't care if he ever did. Mary Lynn's job title and responsibilities were vague, so vague that Jeremiah had never asked her to elaborate. She often worked sixty-hour weeks and he didn't want to reward that behavior by expressing an interest in what specific tasks she performed for Bill Gates.

Waiting outside Tan Tan, he and she could smell ginger, burned rice, beer.

"Are they ever going to seat us?" she asked.

"Yeah, don't they know who you are?"

"I hear this place discriminates against white people."

"Really?"   70

"Yeah, I heard once, these lawyers, bunch of white guys in Nordstrom's suits, had to wait, like, two hours for a table."

"Were those billable hours?"

"It's getting hard for a white guy to find a place to eat."

"Damn affirmative action is what it is."

Their first child had been an accident, the result of a broken condom and   75
a missed birth control pill. They named her Antonya, Toni for short. The second and third children, Robert and Michael, had been on purpose, and the fourth, Ariel, came after Mary Lynn thought she could no longer get pregnant.

Toni was fourteen, immature for her age, quite beautiful and narcissistic, with her translucent skin, her long blond hair, and eight-ball eyes. Botticelli eyes, she bragged after taking an Introduction to Art class. She never bothered to tell anybody she was Indian, mostly because nobody asked.

Jeremiah was quite sure that his daughter, his Antonya, had lost her virginity to the pimply quarterback of the junior varsity football team. He found the thought of his daughter's adolescent sexuality both curious and disturbing. Above all else, he believed that she was far too special to sleep with a cliché, let alone a junior varsity cliché.

Three months out of every year, Robert and Michael were the same age. Currently, they were both eleven. Dark-skinned, with their mother's black hair, strong jawline, and endless nose, they looked Indian, very Indian. Robert, who had refused to be called anything other than Robert, was the smart boy, a math prodigy, while Mikey was the basketball player.

When Mary Lynn's parents called from the reservation, they always asked after the boys, always invited the boys out for the weekend, the holidays, and the summer, and always sent the boys more elaborate gifts than they sent the two girls.

When Jeremiah had pointed out this discrepancy to Mary Lynn, she   80
had readily agreed, but had made it clear that his parents also paid more attention to the boys. Jeremiah never mentioned it again, but had silently vowed to love the girls a little more than he loved the boys.

As if love were a thing that could be quantified, he thought.

He asked himself: What if I love the girls more because they look more like me, because they look more white than the boys?

Towheaded Ariel was two, and the clay of her personality was just beginning to harden, but she was certainly petulant and funny as hell, with the ability to sleep in sixteen-hour marathons that made her parents very nervous. She seemed to exist in her own world, enough so that she was periodically monitored for incipient autism. She treated her siblings as if they somehow bored her, and was the kind of kid who could stay alone in her crib for hours, amusing herself with all sorts of personal games and imaginary friends.

Mary Lynn insisted that her youngest daughter was going to be an artist, but Jeremiah didn't understand the child, and despite the fact that he was her father and forty-three years older, he felt inferior to Ariel.

He wondered if his wife was ever going to leave him because he was   85
white.

When Tan Tan's doors swung open, laughter and smoke rolled out together.

"You got another cigarette?" he asked.

"Quit calling them cigarettes. They're not cigarettes. They're more like rose bushes. Hell, they're more like the shit that rose bushes grow in."

"You think we're going to get a table?"

"By the time we get a table, this place is going to be very unpopular."   90

"Do you want to leave?"

"Do you?"

"If you do."

"We told the baby-sitter we'd be home by ten."

They both wished that Toni were responsible enough to baby-sit her   95
siblings, rather than needing to be sat along with them.

"What time is it?" she asked.

"Nine."

"Let's go home."

Last Christmas, when the kids had been splayed out all over the living room, buried to their shoulders in wrapping paper and expensive toys, Mary Lynn had studied her children's features, had recognized most of her face in her sons' faces and very little of it in her daughters', and had decided, quite facetiously, that the genetic score was tied.

We should have another kid, she'd said to Jeremiah, so we'll know if   100 this is a white family or an Indian family.

It's a family family, he'd said, without a trace of humor.

Only a white guy would say that, she'd said.

Well, he'd said, you married a white guy.

The space between them had grown very cold at that moment, in that silence, and perhaps one or both of them might have said something truly destructive, but Ariel had started crying then, for no obvious reason, relieving both parents of the responsibility of finishing that particular conversation. During the course of their relationship, Mary Lynn and Jeremiah had often discussed race as a concept, as a foreign country they occasionally visited, or as an enemy that existed outside their house, as a destructive force they could fight against as a couple, as a family. But race was also a constant presence, a houseguest and permanent tenant who crept around all the rooms in their shared lives, opening drawers, stealing utensils and small articles of clothing, changing the temperature.

Before he'd married Mary Lynn, Jeremiah had always believed there   105 was too much talk of race, that white people were all too willing to be racist and that brown people were just as willing and just as racist. As a rational scientist, he'd known that race was primarily a social construct, illusionary, but as the husband of an Indian woman and the father of Indian children, he'd since learned that race, whatever its construction, was real. Now, there were plenty of white people who wanted to eliminate the idea of race, to cast it aside as an unwanted invention, but it was far too late for that. If white people are the mad scientists who created race, thought Jeremiah, then we created race so we could enslave black people and kill Indians, and now race has become the Frankenstein monster that has grown beyond our control. Though he'd once been willfully blind, Jeremiah had learned how to recognize that monster in the faces of whites and Indians and in their eyes.

Long ago, Jeremiah and Mary Lynn had both decided to challenge those who stared by staring back, by flinging each other against walls and tongue-kissing with pornographic élan.

Long ago, they'd both decided to respond to any questions of why, how, what, who, or when by simply stating: Love is Love. They knew it was romantic bullshit, a simpleminded answer only satisfying for simpleminded people, but it was the best available defense.

Listen, Mary Lynn had once said to Jeremiah, asking somebody why they fall in love is like asking somebody why they believe in God.

You start asking questions like that, she had added, and you're either going to start a war or you're going to hear folk music.

You think too much, Jeremiah had said, rolling over and falling asleep.   110

Then, in the dark, as Jeremiah slept, Mary Lynn had masturbated while fantasizing about an Indian man with sundance scars on his chest.

After they left Tan Tan, they drove a sensible and indigenous Ford Taurus over the 520 bridge, back toward their house in Kirkland, a five-bedroom rancher only ten blocks away from the Microsoft campus. Mary Lynn walked to work. That made her feel privileged. She estimated there were twenty-two American Indians who had ever felt even a moment of privilege.

"We still have to eat," she said as she drove across the bridge. She felt strange. She wondered if she was ever going to feel normal again.

"How about Taco Bell drive-thru?" he asked.

"You devil, you're trying to get into my pants, aren't you?"   115

Impulsively, he dropped his head into her lap and pressed his lips against her black-jeaned crotch. She yelped and pushed him away. She wondered if he could smell her, if he could smell the Lummi Indian. Maybe he could, but he seemed to interpret it as something different, as something meant for him, as he pushed his head into her lap again. What was she supposed to do? She decided to laugh, so she did laugh as she pushed his face against her pubic bone. She loved the man for reasons she could not always explain. She closed her eyes, drove in that darkness, and felt dangerous.

Halfway across the bridge, Mary Lynn slammed on the brakes, not because she'd seen anything — her eyes were still closed — but because she'd felt something. The car skidded to a stop just inches from the bumper of a truck that had just missed sliding into the row of cars stopped ahead of it.

"What the hell is going on?" Jeremiah asked as he lifted his head from her lap.

"Traffic jam."

"Jesus, we'll never make it home by ten. We better call."   120

"The cell phone is in the glove."

Jeremiah dialed the home number but received only a busy signal.

"Toni must be talking to her boyfriend," she said.

"I don't like him."

"He doesn't like you."   125

"What the hell is going on? Why aren't we moving?"

"I don't know. Why don't you go check?"

Jeremiah climbed out of the car.

"I was kidding," she said as he closed the door behind him.

He walked up to the window of the truck ahead of him.   130

"You know what's going on?" Jeremiah asked the truck driver.

"Nope."

Jeremiah walked farther down the bridge. He wondered if there was a disabled car ahead, what the radio liked to call a "blocking accident." There was also the more serious "injury accident" and the deadly "accident with fatality involved." He had to drive this bridge ten times a week. The commute. White men had invented the commute, had deepened its meaning, had diversified its complications, and now spent most of the time trying to shorten it, reduce it, lessen it.

In the car, Mary Lynn wondered why Jeremiah always found it necessary to insert himself into every situation. He continually moved from the passive to the active. The man was kinetic. She wondered if it was a white thing. Possibly. But more likely, it was a Jeremiah thing. She remembered Mikey's third-grade-class's school play, an edited version of *Hamlet*. Jeremiah had walked onto the stage to help his son drag the unconscious Polonius, who had merely been clubbed over the head rather than stabbed to death, from the stage. Mortally embarrassed, Mikey had cried himself to sleep that night, positive that he was going to be an elementary-school pariah, while Jeremiah vainly tried to explain to the rest of the family why he had acted so impulsively.

I was just trying to be a good father, he had said.   135

Mary Lynn watched Jeremiah walk farther down the bridge. He was just a shadow, a silhouette. She was slapped by the brief, irrational fear that he would never return.

Husband, come back to me, she thought, and I will confess.

Impatient drivers honked their horns. Mary Lynn joined them. She hoped Jeremiah would recognize the specific sound of their horn and return to the car.

Listen to me, listen to me, listen to me, she thought as she pounded the steering wheel.

Jeremiah heard their car horn, but only as one note in the symphony of   140
noise playing on the bridge. He walked through that noise, through an ever-increasing amount of noise, until he pushed through a sudden crowd of people and found himself witnessing a suicide.

Illuminated by headlights, the jumper was a white woman, pretty, wearing a sundress and good shoes. Jeremiah could see that much as she stood on the bridge railing, forty feet above the cold water.

He could hear sirens approaching from both sides of the bridge, but they would never make it through the traffic in time to save this woman.

The jumper was screaming somebody's name.

Jeremiah stepped closer, wanting to hear the name, wanting to have that information so that he could use it later. To what use, he didn't know, but he knew that name had value, importance. That name, the owner of that name, was the reason why the jumper stood on the bridge.

"Aaron," she said. The jumper screamed, "Aaron."   145

In the car, Mary Lynn could not see either Jeremiah or the jumper, but she could see dozens of drivers leaving their cars and running ahead.

She was suddenly and impossibly sure that her husband was the reason for this commotion, this emergency. He's dying, thought Mary Lynn, he's dead. This is not what I wanted, she thought, this is not why I cheated on him, this is not what was supposed to happen.

As more drivers left their cars and ran ahead, Mary Lynn dialed 911 on the cell phone and received only a busy signal.

She opened her door and stepped out, placed one foot on the pavement, and stopped.

The jumper did not stop. She turned to look at the crowd watching her.   150 She looked into the anonymous faces, into the maw, and then looked back down at the black water.

Then she jumped.

Jeremiah rushed forward, along with a few others, and peered over the edge of the bridge. One brave man leapt off the bridge in a vain rescue attempt. Jeremiah stopped a redheaded young man from jumping.

"No," said Jeremiah. "It's too cold. You'll die too."

Jeremiah stared down into the black water, looking for the woman who'd jumped and the man who'd jumped after her.

In the car, or rather with one foot still in the car and one foot placed on   155 the pavement outside of the car, Mary Lynn wept. Oh, God, she loved him, sometimes because he was white and often despite his whiteness. In her fear, she found the one truth Sitting Bull never knew: there was at least one white man who could be trusted.

The black water was silent.

Jeremiah stared down into that silence.

"Jesus, Jesus," said a lovely woman next to him. "Who was she? Who was she?"

"I'm never leaving," Jeremiah said.

"What?" asked the lovely woman, quite confused.   160

"My wife," said Jeremiah, strangely joyous. "I'm never leaving her." Ever the scientist and mathematician, Jeremiah knew that his wife was a constant. In his relief, he found the one truth Shakespeare never knew: gravity is overrated.

Jeremiah looked up through the crossbeams above him, as he stared at the black sky, at the clouds that he could not see but knew were there, the invisible clouds that covered the stars. He shouted out his wife's name, shouted it so loud that he could not speak in the morning.

In the car, Mary Lynn pounded the steering wheel. With one foot in the car and one foot out, she honked and honked the horn. She wondered if this was how the world was supposed to end, with everybody trapped on a bridge, with the black water pushing against their foundations.

Out on the bridge, four paramedics arrived far too late. Out of breath, exhausted from running across the bridge with medical gear and stretchers, the paramedics could only join the onlookers at the railing.

A boat, a small boat, a miracle, floated through the black water. They   165 found the man, the would-be rescuer, who had jumped into the water after the young woman, but they could not find her.

Jeremiah pushed through the crowd, as he ran away from the place where the woman had jumped. Jeremiah ran across the bridge until he could see Mary Lynn. She and he loved each other across the distance.

ENGAGING THE TEXT

1. What is the significance of the title "Assimilation" in the context of this story? How do you interpret the "truths" that Mary Lynn and Jeremiah discover at the end of the story? Do you think that Alexie is endorsing assimilation in this story? Why or why not?

2. What is the purpose and effect of the paired cultural references — to Shakespeare and Sitting Bull, the Big Mom Singers and Emily Dickinson — that Alexie includes in the story?

3. What glimpses does Alexie give us of reservation life and of Indians less privileged than Mary Lynn? What do these allusions tell us about her character and motives? What do they suggest about the nature of the "white" culture she is immersed in?

4. Mary Lynn and the narrator make a number of observations about white men — that they are dependable but "neutral . . . like Belgium," that they invented the commute, and so forth. What overall portrait of white men emerges from these comments and from the character of Jeremiah? Explain why you think that Alexie is being fair or unfair in his characterization of white men.

5. What attitudes, behavior, and cultural phenomena does Alexie make fun of, and why? What values and ideas does he appear to take seriously? Are these categories mutually exclusive? Why or why not?

EXPLORING CONNECTIONS

6. Review the passages in the story that speak specifically about race. To what extent would Alexie endorse George Fredrickson's (p. 561) assertion that "ethnic hierarchy in a clearly racialized form persists in practice if not in law" in the United States?

7. Rubén Martínez (p. 574), like Mary Lynn, has a complex relationship to the dominant culture. What do they enjoy or value about mainstream American life? What do they dislike or distrust? To what extent are they assimilated, and how does that affect their relationship to their home cultures?

EXTENDING THE CRITICAL CONTEXT

8. Watch a film written and directed by Native American artists (e.g., *Smoke Signals*, *The Silent Runner*, *Skins*, *The Business of Fancydancing*) and compare it to any recent film that portrays, but was not created by, Indians (e.g., *Pocahontas*, *Apocalypto*, *Windtalkers*). What differences, if any, do you see in the way the films depict Indian and white cultures and relationships?

The Pressure to Cover

KENJI YOSHINO

An employee must choose between wearing her hair in cornrows or keeping her job. A Jewish soldier is discharged for refusing to remove his yarmulke. A lesbian loses custody of her adopted child because she "flaunts" her sexuality by holding hands with her partner in public. These scenarios, according to Kenji Yoshino, represent a new arena in the struggle for civil rights: forced assimilation, or "covering." As he explains on his Web site, his purpose is "to make 'covering' as much a part of our common vocabulary as 'passing' or 'the closet.' I want people to think about how and why they cover. And if they find the demand to cover to be oppressive, I want to encourage them to resist it, not just in the courts, but, perhaps more importantly, in their own lives." Yoshino, who specializes in constitutional and antidiscrimination law, teaches at Yale Law School, where he also serves as deputy dean for intellectual life. He has published extensively in academic journals such as the Stanford Law Review *and* Yale Law Journal *as well as in popular periodicals like* The Nation *and* The Village Voice. *This article originally appeared in* The New York Times Magazine *and is adapted from his 2006 book,* Covering: The Hidden Assault on Our Civil Rights.

When I began teaching at Yale Law School in 1998, a friend spoke to me frankly. "You'll have a better chance at tenure," he said, "if you're a homosexual professional than if you're a professional homosexual." Out of the closet for six years at the time, I knew what he meant. To be a "homosexual professional" was to be a professor of constitutional law who "happened" to be gay. To be a "professional homosexual" was to be a gay professor who made gay rights his work. Others echoed the sentiment in less elegant formulations. Be gay, my world seemed to say. Be openly gay, if you want. But don't flaunt.

I didn't experience the advice as antigay. The law school is a vigorously tolerant place, embedded in a university famous for its gay student population. (As the undergraduate jingle goes: "One in four, maybe more / One in three, maybe me / One in two, maybe you.") I took my colleague's words as generic counsel to leave my personal life at home. I could see that research related to one's identity — referred to in the academy as "mesearch" — could raise legitimate questions about scholarly objectivity.

I also saw others playing down their outsider identities to blend into the mainstream. Female colleagues confided that they would avoid references to their children at work, lest they be seen as mothers first and scholars second. Conservative students asked for advice about how open they could be about their politics without suffering repercussions at some imagined future confirmation hearing. A religious student said he feared coming out as a believer, as he thought his intellect would be placed on a 25 percent discount. Many of us, it seemed, had to work our identities as well as our jobs.

It wasn't long before I found myself resisting the demand to conform. What bothered me was not that I had to engage in straight-acting behavior, much of which felt natural to me. What bothered me was the felt need to mute my passion for gay subjects, people, culture. At a time when the law was transforming gay rights, it seemed ludicrous not to suit up and get in the game.

"Mesearch" being what it is, I soon turned my scholarly attention to the 5 pressure to conform. What puzzled me was that I felt that pressure so long after my emergence from the closet. When I stopped passing, I exulted that I could stop thinking about my sexuality. This proved naive. Long after I came out, I still experienced the need to assimilate to straight norms. But I didn't have a word for this demand to tone down my known gayness.

Then I found my word, in the sociologist Erving Goffman's book *Stigma*. Written in 1963, the book describes how various groups — including the disabled, the elderly and the obese — manage their "spoiled" identities. After discussing passing, Goffman observes that "persons who are ready to admit possession of a stigma . . . may nonetheless make a great effort to keep the stigma from looming large." He calls this behavior covering. He distinguishes passing from covering by noting that passing pertains to the visibility of a characteristic, while covering pertains to its obtrusiveness. He relates how F.D.R. stationed himself behind a desk before his advisers came in for meetings. Roosevelt was not passing, since everyone knew he used a wheelchair. He was covering, playing down his disability so people would focus on his more conventionally presidential qualities.

As is often the case when you learn a new idea, I began to perceive covering everywhere. Leafing through a magazine, I read that Helen Keller replaced her natural eyes (one of which protruded) with brilliant blue glass ones. On the radio, I heard that Margaret Thatcher went to a voice coach to lower the pitch of her voice. Friends began to send me e-mail. Did I know that Martin Sheen was Ramon Estevez on his birth certificate, that Ben Kingsley was Krishna Bhanji, that Kirk Douglas was Issur Danielovitch Demsky and that Jon Stewart was Jonathan Leibowitz?

In those days, spotting instances of covering felt like a parlor game. It's hard to get worked up about how celebrities and politicians have to manage their public images. Jon Stewart joked that he changed his name because Leibowitz was "too Hollywood," and that seemed to get it exactly right. My own experience with covering was also not particularly difficult — once I had the courage to write from my passions, I was immediately embraced.

It was only when I looked for instances of covering in the law that I saw how lucky I had been. Civil rights case law is peopled with plaintiffs who were severely punished for daring to be openly different. Workers were fired for lapsing into Spanish in English-only workplaces, women were fired for behaving in stereotypically "feminine" ways, and gay parents lost custody of their children for engaging in displays of same-sex affection. These cases revealed that far from being a parlor game, covering was the civil rights issue of our time.

The New Discrimination

In recent decades, discrimination in America has undergone a genera-   10
tional shift. Discrimination was once aimed at entire groups, resulting in the exclusion of all racial minorities, women, gays, religious minorities, and people with disabilities. A battery of civil rights laws — like the Civil Rights Act of 1964 and the Americans with Disabilities Act of 1990 — sought to combat these forms of discrimination. The triumph of American civil rights is that such categorical exclusions by the state or employers are now relatively rare.

Now a subtler form of discrimination has risen to take its place. This discrimination does not aim at groups as a whole. Rather, it aims at the subset of the group that refuses to cover, that is, to assimilate to dominant norms. And for the most part, existing civil rights laws do not protect individuals against such covering demands. The question of our time is whether we should understand this new discrimination to be a harm and, if so, whether the remedy is legal or social in nature.

Consider the following cases:

Renee Rogers, an African-American employee at American Airlines, wore cornrows to work. American had a grooming policy that prevented employees from wearing an all-braided hairstyle. When American sought to enforce this policy against Rogers, she filed suit, alleging race discrimination. In 1981, a federal district court rejected her argument. It first observed that cornrows were not distinctively associated with African-Americans, noting that Rogers had only adopted the hairstyle after it "had been popularized by a white actress in the film *10.*" As if recognizing the unpersuasiveness of what we might call the Bo Derek defense, the court further alleged that because hairstyle, unlike skin color, was a mutable characteristic, discrimination on the basis of grooming was not discrimination on the basis of race. Renee Rogers lost her case.

Lydia Mikus and Ismael Gonzalez were called for jury service in a case involving a defendant who was Latino. When the prosecutor asked them whether they could speak Spanish, they answered in the affirmative. The prosecutor struck them, and the defense attorney then brought suit on their behalf, claiming national-origin discrimination. The prosecutor responded that he had not removed the potential jurors for their ethnicity but for their ability to speak Spanish. His stated concern was that they would not defer to the court translator in listening to Spanish-language testimony. In 1991, the

Supreme Court credited this argument. Lydia Mikus and Ismael Gonzalez lost their case.

Diana Piantanida had a child and took a maternity leave from her job at   15
the Wyman Center, a charitable organization in Missouri. During her leave, she was demoted, supposedly for previously having handed in work late. The man who was then the Wyman Center's executive director, however, justified her demotion by saying the new position would be easier "for a new mom to handle." As it turned out, the new position had less responsibility and half the pay of the original one. But when Piantanida turned this position down, her successor was paid Piantanida's old salary. Piantanida brought suit, claiming she had been discharged as a "new mom." In 1997, a federal appellate court refused to analyze her claim as a sex-discrimination case, which would have led to comparing the treatment she received to the treatment of "new dads." Instead, it found that Piantanida's (admittedly vague) pleadings raised claims only under the Pregnancy Discrimination Act, which it correctly interpreted to protect women only while they are pregnant. Diana Piantanida lost her case.

Robin Shahar was a lesbian attorney who received a job offer from the Georgia Department of Law, where she had worked as a law student. The summer before she started her new job, Shahar had a religious same-sex commitment ceremony with her partner. She asked a supervisor for a late starting date because she was getting married and wanted to go on a celebratory trip to Greece. Believing Shahar was marrying a man, the supervisor offered his congratulations. Senior officials in the office soon learned, however, that Shahar's partner was a woman. This news caused a stir, reports of which reached Michael Bowers, the attorney general of Georgia who had successfully defended his state's prohibition of sodomy before the United States Supreme Court. After deliberating with his lawyers, Bowers rescinded her job offer. The staff member who informed her read from a script, concluding, "Thanks again for coming in, and have a nice day." Shahar brought suit, claiming discrimination on the basis of sexual orientation. In court, Bowers testified that he knew Shahar was gay when he hired her, and would never have terminated her for that reason. In 1997, a federal appellate court accepted that defense, maintaining that Bowers had terminated Shahar on the basis of her conduct, not her status. Robin Shahar lost her case.

Simcha Goldman, an Air Force officer who was also an ordained rabbi, wore a yarmulke at all times. Wearing a yarmulke is part of the Orthodox tradition of covering one's head out of deference to an omnipresent god. Goldman's religious observance ran afoul of an Air Force regulation that prohibited wearing headgear while indoors. When he refused his commanding officer's order to remove his yarmulke, Goldman was threatened with a court martial. He brought a First Amendment claim, alleging discrimination on the basis of religion. In 1986, the Supreme Court rejected his claim. It stated that the Air Force had drawn a reasonable line between "religious apparel that is visible and that which is not." Simcha Goldman lost his case.

These five cases represent only a fraction of those in which courts have refused to protect plaintiffs from covering demands. In such cases, the courts routinely distinguish between immutable and mutable traits, between being a member of a legally protected group and behavior associated with that group. Under this rule, African-Americans cannot be fired for their skin color, but they could be fired for wearing cornrows. Potential jurors cannot be struck for their ethnicity but can be struck for speaking (or even for admitting proficiency in) a foreign language. Women cannot be discharged for having two X chromosomes but can be penalized (in some jurisdictions) for becoming mothers. Although the weaker protections for sexual orientation mean gays can sometimes be fired for their status alone, they will be much more vulnerable if they are perceived to "flaunt" their sexuality. Jews cannot be separated from the military for being Jewish but can be discharged for wearing yarmulkes.

This distinction between being and doing reflects a bias toward assimilation. Courts will protect traits like skin color or chromosomes because such traits cannot be changed. In contrast, the courts will not protect mutable traits, because individuals can alter them to fade into the mainstream, thereby escaping discrimination. If individuals choose not to engage in that form of self-help, they must suffer the consequences.

The judicial bias toward assimilation will seem correct and just to many   20
Americans. Assimilation, after all, is a precondition of civilization — wearing clothes, having manners, and obeying the law are all acts of assimilation. Moreover, the tie between assimilation and American civilization may be particularly strong. At least since Hector St. John de Crèvecoeur's 1782 "Letters from an American Farmer," this country has promoted assimilation as the way Americans of different backgrounds would be "melted into a new race of men." By the time Israel Zangwill's play *The Melting Pot* made its debut in 1908, the term had acquired the burnish of an American ideal. Theodore Roosevelt, who believed hyphenations like "Polish-American" were a "moral treason," is reputed to have yelled, "That's a great play!" from his box when it was performed in Washington. (He was wrong — it's no accident the title has had a longer run than the play.) And notwithstanding challenges beginning in the 1960s to move "beyond the melting pot" and to "celebrate diversity," assimilation has never lost its grip on the American imagination.

If anything, recent years have seen a revival of the melting-pot ideal. We are currently experiencing a pluralism explosion in the United States. Patterns of immigration since the late 1960s have made the United States the most religiously various country in the history of the world. Even when the demographics of a group — like the number of individuals with disabilities — are presumably constant, the number of individuals claiming membership in that group may grow exponentially. In 1970, there were 9 disability-related associations listed in the Encyclopedia of Associations; in 1980, there were 16; in 1990, there were 211; and in 2000, there were 799. The boom in identity politics has led many thoughtful commentators to worry that we are losing our common culture as Americans. Fearful that we are breaking apart into balkanized fiefs, even liberal lions like Arthur Schlesinger have called for a recommitment to the ethic of assimilation.

Beyond keeping pace with the culture, the judiciary has institutional reasons for encouraging assimilation. In the yarmulke case, the government argued that ruling in favor of the rabbi's yarmulke would immediately invite suits concerning the Sikh's turban, the yogi's saffron robes and the Rastafarian's dreadlocks. Because the courts must articulate principled grounds for their decisions, they are particularly ill equipped to protect some groups but not others in an increasingly diverse society. Seeking to avoid judgments about the relative worth of groups, the judiciary has decided instead to rely on the relatively uncontroversial principle of protecting immutable traits.

Viewed in this light, the judiciary's failure to protect individuals against covering demands seems eminently reasonable. Unfortunately, it also represents an abdication of its responsibility to protect civil rights.

The Case Against Assimilation

The flaw in the judiciary's analysis is that it casts assimilation as an unadulterated good. Assimilation is implicitly characterized as the way in which groups can evade discrimination by fading into the mainstream — after all, the logic goes, if a bigot cannot discriminate between two individuals, he cannot discriminate against one of them. But sometimes assimilation is not an escape from discrimination, but precisely its effect. When a Jew is forced to convert to Protestantism, for instance, we do not celebrate that as an evasion of anti-Semitism. We should not blind ourselves to the dark underbelly of the American melting pot.

Take the cornrows case. Initially, this case appears to be an easy one for the employer, as hairstyle seems like such a trivial thing. But if hair is so trivial, we might ask why American Airlines made it a condition of Renee Rogers's employment. What's frustrating about the employment discrimination jurisprudence is that courts often don't force employers to answer the critical question of why they are requiring employees to cover. If we look to other sources, the answers can be troubling.

John T. Molloy's perennially popular self-help manual *New Dress for Success* also tells racial minorities to cover. Molloy advises African-Americans to avoid "Afro hairstyles" and to wear "conservative pinstripe suits, preferably with vests, accompanied by all the establishment symbols, including the Ivy League tie." He urges Latinos to "avoid pencil-line mustaches," "any hair tonic that tends to give a greasy or shiny look to the hair," "any articles of clothing that have Hispanic associations" and "anything that is very sharp or precise."

25

Molloy is equally frank about why covering is required. The "model of success," he says, is "white, Anglo-Saxon and Protestant." Those who do not possess these traits "will elicit a negative response to some degree, regardless of whether that response is conscious or subconscious." Indeed, Molloy says racial minorities must go "somewhat overboard" to compensate for immutable differences from the white mainstream. After conducting research on African-American corporate grooming, Molloy reports that "blacks had not only to dress more conservatively but also more expensively than their white counterparts if they wanted to have an equal impact."

Molloy's basic point is supported by social-science research. The economists Marianne Bertrand and Sendhil Mullainathan recently conducted a study in which they sent out resumes that were essentially identical except for the names at the top. They discovered that resumes with white-sounding names like Emily Walsh or Greg Baker drew 50 percent more callbacks than those with African-American-sounding names like Lakisha Washington or Jamal Jones. So it seems that even when Americans have collectively set our faces against racism, we still react negatively to cultural traits — like hairstyles, clothes, or names — that we associate with historically disfavored races.

We can see a similar dynamic in the termination of Robin Shahar. Michael Bowers, the state attorney general, disavowed engaging in first-generation discrimination when he said he had no problem with gay employees. This raises the question of why he fired Shahar for having a religious same-sex commitment ceremony. Unlike American Airlines, Bowers provided some answers. He argued that retaining Shahar would compromise the department's ability to deny same-sex couples marriage licenses and to enforce sodomy statutes.

Neither argument survives scrutiny. At no point did Shahar seek to   30
marry her partner legally, nor did she agitate for the legalization of same-sex marriage. The Georgia citizenry could not fairly have assumed that Shahar's religious ceremony would entitle the couple to a civil license. Bowers's claim that Shahar's wedding would compromise her ability to enforce sodomy statutes is also off the mark. Georgia's sodomy statute (which has since been struck down) punished cross-sex as well as same-sex sodomy, meaning that any heterosexual in the department who had ever had oral sex was as compromised as Shahar.

Stripped of these rationales, Bowers's termination of Shahar looks more sinister. When she told a supervisor she was getting married, he congratulated her. When he discovered she was marrying a woman, it wasn't long before she no longer had a job. Shahar's religious ceremony was not in itself indiscreet; cross-sex couples engage in such ceremonies all the time. If Shahar was flaunting anything, it was her belief in her own equality: her belief that she, and not the state, should determine what personal bonds are worthy of celebration.

The demand to cover is anything but trivial. It is the symbolic heartland of inequality — what reassures one group of its superiority to another.

When dominant groups ask subordinated groups to cover, they are asking them to be small in the world, to forgo prerogatives that the dominant group has and therefore to forgo equality. If courts make critical goods like employment dependent on covering, they are legitimizing second-class citizenship for the subordinated group. In doing so, they are failing to vindicate the promise of civil rights.

So the covering demand presents a conundrum. The courts are right to be leery of intervening in too brusque a manner here, as they cannot risk playing favorites among groups. Yet they also cannot ignore the fact that the covering demand is where many forms of inequality continue to have life. We need a paradigm that gives both these concerns their due, adapting the aspirations of the civil rights movement to an increasingly pluralistic society.

The New Civil Rights

The new civil rights begins with the observation that everyone covers. When I lecture on covering, I often encounter what I think of as the "angry straight white man" reaction. A member of the audience, almost invariably a white man, almost invariably angry, denies that covering is a civil rights issue. Why shouldn't racial minorities or women or gays have to cover? These groups should receive legal protection against discrimination for things they cannot help. But why should they receive protection for behaviors within their control — wearing cornrows, acting "feminine," or flaunting their sexuality? After all, the questioner says, I have to cover all the time. I have to mute my depression, or my obesity, or my alcoholism, or my shyness, or my working-class background, or my nameless anomie. I, too, am one of the mass of men leading lives of quiet desperation. Why should legally protected groups have a right to self-expression I do not? Why should my struggle for an authentic self matter less?

I surprise these individuals when I agree. Contemporary civil rights has   35 erred in focusing solely on traditional civil rights groups — racial minorities, women, gays, religious minorities, and people with disabilities. This assumes those in the so-called mainstream — those straight white men — do not also cover. They are understood only as obstacles, as people who prevent others from expressing themselves, rather than as individuals who are themselves struggling for self-definition. No wonder they often respond to civil rights advocates with hostility. They experience us as asking for an entitlement they themselves have been refused — an expression of their full humanity.

Civil rights must rise into a new, more inclusive register. That ascent makes use of the recognition that the mainstream is a myth. With respect to any particular identity, the word "mainstream" makes sense, as in the statement that straights are more mainstream than gays. Used generically, however, the word loses meaning. Because human beings hold many identities, the mainstream is a shifting coalition, and none of us are entirely within it. It is not normal to be completely normal.

This does not mean discrimination against racial minorities is the same as discrimination against poets. American civil rights law has correctly directed its concern toward certain groups and not others. But the aspiration of civil rights — the aspiration that we be free to develop our human capacities without the impediment of witless conformity — is an aspiration that extends beyond traditional civil rights groups.

To fulfill that aspiration, we must think differently both within the law and outside it. With respect to legal remedies, we must shift away from claims that demand equality for particular groups toward claims that demand liberty for us all. This is not an exhortation that we strip protections from currently recognized groups. Rather, it is a prediction that future courts will be unable to sustain a group-based vision of civil rights when faced with the broad and irreversible trend toward demographic pluralism. In an increasingly diverse society, the courts must look to what draws us together as citizens rather than to what drives us apart.

As if in recognition of that fact, the Supreme Court has moved in recent years away from extending protections on the basis of group membership and toward doing so on the basis of liberties we all possess. In 2003, the court struck down a Texas statute that prohibited same-sex sodomy. It did not, however, frame the case as one concerning the equality rights of gays. Instead, it cast the case as one concerning the interest we all — straight, gay, or otherwise — have in controlling our intimate lives. Similarly, in 2004, the court held that a state could be required by a Congressional statute to make its courthouses wheelchair accessible. Again, the court ruled in favor of the minority group without framing its analysis in group-based equality rhetoric. Rather, it held that all people — disabled or otherwise — have a "right of access to the courts," which had been denied in that instance.

In these cases, the court implicitly acknowledged the national exhaustion with group-based identity politics and quieted the anxiety about pluralism that is driving us back toward the assimilative ideal. By emphasizing the interest all individuals have in our own liberty, the court focused on what unites us rather than on what divides us. While preserving the distinction between being and doing, the court decided to protect doing in its own right.

If the Supreme Court protects individuals against covering demands in the future, I believe it will do so by invoking the universal rights of people. I predict that if the court ever recognizes the right to speak a native language, it will protect that right as a liberty to which we are all entitled, rather than as a remedial concession granted to a particular national-origin group. If the court recognizes rights to grooming, like the right to wear cornrows, I believe it will do so under something akin to the German Constitution's right to personality rather than as a right attached to racial minorities. And I hope that if the court protects the right of gays to marry, it will do so by framing it as the right we all have to marry the person we love, rather than defending "gay marriage" as if it were a separate institution.

A liberty-based approach to civil rights, of course, brings its own complications, beginning with the question of where my liberty ends and yours begins. But the ability of liberty analysis to illuminate our common humanity should not be underestimated. This virtue persuaded both Martin Luther King Jr. and Malcolm X to argue for the transition from civil rights to human rights at the ends of their lives. It is time for American law to follow suit.

While I have great hopes for this new legal paradigm, I also believe law will play a relatively small part in the new civil rights. A doctor friend told me that in his first year of medical school, his dean described how doctors were powerless to cure the vast majority of human ills. People would get better, or they would not, but it would not be doctors who would cure them. Part of becoming a doctor, the dean said, was to surrender a layperson's awe for medical authority. I wished then that someone would give an analogous lecture to law students and to Americans at large. My education in law has been in no small part an education in its limitations.

As an initial matter, many covering demands are made by actors the law does not — and in my view should not — hold accountable, like friends, family, neighbors, the "culture," or individuals themselves. When I think of the covering demands I have experienced, I can trace many of them only to my own censorious consciousness. And while I am often tempted to sue myself, I recognize this is not my healthiest impulse.

Law is also an incomplete solution to coerced assimilation because it 45 has yet to recognize the myriad groups that are subjected to covering demands even though these groups cannot be defined by traditional classifications like race, sex, orientation, religion, and disability. Whenever I speak about covering, I receive new instances of identities that can be covered. The law may someday move to protect some of these identities. But it will never protect them all.

For these and other reasons, I am troubled that Americans seem increasingly inclined to turn toward the law to do the work of civil rights precisely when they should be turning away from it. The primary solution lies in all of us as citizens, not in the tiny subset of us who are lawyers. People confronted with demands to cover should feel emboldened to seek a reason for that demand, even if the law does not reach the actors making the demand or recognize the group burdened by it. These reason-forcing conversations should happen outside courtrooms — in public squares and prayer circles, in workplaces and on playgrounds. They should occur informally and intimately, in the everyday places where tolerance is made and unmade.

What will constitute a good-enough reason to justify assimilation will obviously be controversial. We have come to some consensus that certain reasons are illegitimate — like racism, sexism, or religious intolerance. Beyond that, we should expect conversations rather than foreordained results — what reasons count, and for what purposes, will be for us all to decide by facing one another as citizens. My personal inclination is always to privilege the claims of the individual against countervailing interests like "neatness" or "workplace harmony." But we should have that conversation.

Such conversations are the best — and perhaps the only — way to give both assimilation and authenticity their due. They will help us alleviate conservative alarmists' fears of a balkanized America and radical multiculturalists' fears of a monocultural America. The aspiration of civil rights has always been to permit people to pursue their human flourishing without limitations based on bias. Focusing on law prevents us from seeing the revolutionary breadth of that aspiration. It is only when we leave the law that civil rights suddenly stops being about particular agents of oppression and particular victimized groups and starts to become a project of human flourishing in which we all have a stake.

I don't teach classes on gay rights any more. I suspect many of my students now experience me as a homosexual professional rather than as a professional homosexual, if they think of me in such terms at all. But I don't experience myself as covering. I've just moved on to other interests, in the way scholars do. So the same behavior — not teaching gay rights — has changed in meaning over time.

This just brings home to me that the only right I have wanted with any   50 consistency is the freedom to be who I am. I'll be the first to admit that I owe much of that freedom to group-based equality movements, like the gay rights movement. But it is now time for us as a nation to shift the emphasis away from equality and toward liberty in our debates about identity politics. Only through such freedom can we live our lives as works in progress, which is to say, as the complex, changeful, and contradictory creatures that we are.

ENGAGING THE TEXT

1. As Yoshino observes, "everyone covers" (para. 34). Write a journal entry recounting a time that you felt pressure to cover: What were the consequences of choosing or refusing to assimilate? In retrospect, do you feel that you made the right choice? Why or why not?

2. Summarize Yoshino's analysis of when and why the demand to cover is harmful. How does he distinguish between legitimate and discriminatory assimilation demands? Do you agree with his distinctions?

3. Examine the five cases Yoshino highlights: What would be the costs of "coerced assimilation" to each of the individuals involved? Does the employer (or the prosecutor in the jury selection case) seem to have a legitimate reason for demanding conformity or for penalizing the employee or potential juror?

4. What does Yoshino mean when he says that "the mainstream is a myth" (para. 36)? How persuasive is his reasoning? How would you define "mainstream"?

5. What are the legal and social rationales, according to Yoshino, for basing civil rights law on universal liberties rather than group rights? What are the drawbacks or difficulties?

6. Yoshino acknowledges that readers may distrust "mesearch" (para. 2), or research grounded in the writer's identity, because it doesn't appear objective. What strategies does Yoshino use in order to counter the appearance of bias in this essay? Do you think that his personal stake in the subject of this essay makes his argument weaker, stronger, or neither? Why?

EXPLORING CONNECTIONS

7. Yoshino points out that not only laws and regulations, but also "friends, family, neighbors, 'the culture,' or the individuals themselves" may pressure us to cover (para. 44). In what ways do Richard Rodriguez (p. 193), Stephen Cruz (p. 353), and Kathleen Boatwright (p. 676) feel pressured to cover? How do they respond to these pressures?

8. Examine Evan Wolfson's argument in favor of gay marriage (p. 98) and Deborah Rudacille's defense of transgender identities (p. 454): Do these writers appeal to readers on the basis of group rights, universal liberties, or both? How effective are their strategies?

EXTENDING THE CRITICAL CONTEXT

9. Research any one of the legal cases that Yoshino discusses and write an essay arguing why you think the court did or did not make the right decision. (You might begin your research by consulting www.findlaw.com.)

10. To what extent does your school, workplace, or community demand assimilation (dress or grooming codes, language restrictions, etc.)? Is there an explicit rationale for these covering requirements? Are they justified?

Child of the Americas
AURORA LEVINS MORALES

This poem concentrates on the positive aspects of a multicultural heritage, as Morales celebrates her uniqueness, her diversity, and her wholeness. It's an up-to-date and sophisticated reinterpretation of the melting pot myth. As this autobiographical poem states, Aurora Levins Morales (b. 1954) was the child of a Puerto Rican mother and a Jewish father. She moved to the United States when she was thirteen and now writes, performs, and teaches in the San Francisco Bay Area. "Child of the Americas" is from the collection Getting Home Alive *(1986), which she coauthored with her mother, Rosario Morales. Her mother has written that the book "began in long, budget-breaking telephone calls stretched across the width of this country . . . the phone line strung between us like a 3,000-mile umbilical cord from navel to navel, mine to hers, hers to mine, each of us mother and daughter by turns, feeding each other the substance of our dreams." Morales has taught Jewish studies and women's studies at Berkeley and lectures on a variety of issues, including Puerto Rican history and culture, Latina feminism, and community activism. She is the author of* Remedios: Stories of Earth and Iron from the History of Puertorriqueñas *(1998) and* Medicine Stories: History, Culture, and the Politics of Integrity *(1998).*

I am a child of the Americas,
a light-skinned mestiza of the Caribbean,
a child of many diaspora,[1] born into this continent at a crossroads.

I am a U.S. Puerto Rican Jew,
a product of the ghettos of New York I have never known.   5
An immigrant and the daughter and granddaughter of immigrants.
I speak English with passion: it's the tongue of my consciousness,
a flashing knife blade of crystal, my tool, my craft.

I am Caribeña,[2] island grown. Spanish is in my flesh,
ripples from my tongue, lodges in my hips: 10
the language of garlic and mangoes,
the singing in my poetry, the flying gestures of my hands.
I am of Latinoamerica, rooted in the history of my continent:
I speak from that body.

I am not african. Africa is in me, but I cannot return.   15
I am not taína.[3] Taíno is in me, but there is no way back.
I am not european. Europe lives in me, but I have no home there.

I am new. History made me. My first language was spanglish.[4]
I was born at the crossroads
and I am whole.   20

---

[1]*diaspora:* Scattered colonies. The word originally referred to Jews scattered outside Palestine after the Babylonian exile; it is now used to refer to African and other peoples scattered around the world.
[2]*Caribeña:* Caribbean woman.
[3]*taína:* Describing the Taíno, an aboriginal people of the Greater Antilles and Bahamas.
[4]*spanglish:* Spanish and English combined.

ENGAGING THE TEXT

1. Does this poem do more to challenge or to promote the myth of the melting pot? Explain.
2. Why does the poet list elements of her background that she scarcely knows ("the ghettos of New York" and Taíno)? How can they be part of her?
3. How do you interpret the last stanza? Rephrase its messages in more complete, more explicit statements.

EXPLORING CONNECTIONS

4. Many of the writers in this book express a sense of internal fragmentation or cultural conflict. How does the speaker of this poem avoid the feeling of cultural schizophrenia? How does her response compare to those of Richard Rodriguez (p. 193), Judith Ortiz Cofer (p. 393), Stephen Cruz (p. 353), Maysan Haydar (p. 402), and Rubén Martínez (p. 574). Which responses do you find most appealing or most realistic, and why?

EXTENDING THE CRITICAL CONTEXT

5. Write your own version of "Child of the Americas," following Morales's structure but substituting ideas and images from your own heritage. Read it to the class.

FURTHER CONNECTIONS

1. Research the history of the native peoples of your state. Learn as much as you can about a specific aspect or period of that history. What tribal groups inhabited the area before Europeans arrived? What is known about the cultures and languages of these tribes? How much and why did the native population decrease following European contact? What alliances and treaties were made between the tribes and the newcomers as non-natives began to occupy native lands? To what extent were treaties upheld or abandoned, and why? How were local native populations affected by relocation, the establishment of reservations, the creation of Indian boarding schools, the Dawes Act, or other legislation? What role has the Bureau of Indian Affairs played in protecting or failing to protect tribal interests? What issues are of greatest concern to the tribes in your area today? Write up the results of your research and present them to the class.

2. Some states and communities have responded to the rise in illegal immigration by enacting laws or ordinances that ban any language other than English, deny government services to undocumented immigrants, and penalize citizens (such as employers, landlords, and merchants) who "assist" them. Has your state or community adopted any such regulations? Research the arguments for and against such legislation and discuss your findings in class. Which arguments are the most compelling, and why?

3. Investigate a recent conflict between ethnic, racial, or cultural groups on your campus or in your community. Research the issue, and interview people on each side. What event triggered the conflict? How do the groups involved perceive the issue differently? What tension, prior conflict, or injustice has contributed to the conflict and to the perceptions of those affected by it? Has the conflict been resolved? If so, write a paper discussing why you feel that the resolution was appropriate or not. If the conflict is continuing, write a paper proposing how a fair resolution might be reached.

4. Contentious debates over issues like affirmative action often hinge on whether or not the debaters accept the idea of structural racism (also called systemic racism). Proponents argue that structural racism is largely responsible for persistent racial disparities in wealth, income, home ownership, education, health care, and life expectancy. Investigate the concept of structural racism: What is it? How does it differ from individual racism or intentional discrimination? What evidence and examples of systemic racism do proponents cite? How do opponents of the concept explain racial inequalities, and what supporting evidence do they offer? Argue a position: Is it necessary to address structural discrimination in order to achieve racial equality in the United States?

6

One Nation Under God

American Myths of Church and State

Madonna singing "Live to Tell" on her 2006 Confessions tour.

FAST FACTS

1. More than 87% of all Americans identify themselves as religious, and 57% claim to attend church regularly. The percentages of all citizens in the United Kingdom, France, and Israel who attend religious services regularly are, respectively, 10%, 15%, and 25%.

2. Some 73% of all Americans believe in miracles, 70% believe in the continued existence of the soul after death, 70% believe in heaven, and 59% believe in hell.

3. According to a 2005 CNN / USA Today Gallup poll, 53% of all Americans believe that God created human beings in their present form "exactly as the Bible describes it," while 31% of all Americans believe in Darwin's theory of evolution.

4. According to a 2005 Harris poll, 12% of all Americans think that only the theory of evolution should be taught in public schools to account for the development of human life, while 55% think that the theory of evolution should be taught along with the biblical account of creation and the theory of intelligent design.

5. According to a *Public Agenda* poll, 70% of Americans would like to see the influence of religion strengthen in American society while only 6% would like to see religion play a lesser role.

6. 66% of Americans believe that the government should support religious institutions that offer aid to the homeless and drug addicts, even if they promote religious beliefs while doing so.

Sources: (1) The Pew Forum on Religion and the Public Life (pewforum.org), *The American Religious Landscape and Politics, 2004;* (2) The Harris Poll (www.harrisinteractive.com), *The Religious and Other Beliefs of Americans 2005;* (3) PollingReport.com, "Science and Nature"; (4) The Harris Poll (www.harrisinteractive.com), Poll #52, July 6, 2005; (5) The Public Agenda (www.publicagenda.org), "For Goodness' Sake: Why So Many Want Religion to Play a Greater Role in American Life"; (6) The Pew Forum on Religion and the Public Life (pewforum.org), *Religion: A Strength and Weakness for Both Parties, 2005.*

The past few days when I've been at that window upstairs, I've thought a bit of the "shining city upon a hill." The phrase comes from John Winthrop, who wrote it to describe the America he imagined. What he imagined was important because he was an early Pilgrim, an early freedom man. He journeyed here on what today we'd call a little wooden boat; and like the other Pilgrims, he was looking for a home that would be free. I've spoken of the shining city all my political life, but I don't know if I ever quite communicated what I saw when I said it. But in my mind it was a tall, proud city built on rocks stronger than oceans, windswept, God-blessed, and teeming with people of all kinds living in harmony and peace. . . .

— RONALD REAGAN's farewell address, 1989

WHEN PRESIDENT REAGAN wanted to evoke the religious foundations of America during his final address to the country, he reached back nearly four hundred years to "A Model of Christian Charity," a speech delivered by John Winthrop on the eve of the Pilgrims' departure from England to create a new life in the "New World." According to the myth, and to President Reagan, the Pilgrims left Europe in pursuit of religious liberty. You know the old story: fleeing religious persecution, the "Pilgrim Fathers" cross the Atlantic in the *Mayflower* and found Plymouth Plantation in 1620. Ten years later, the Puritans make the same trip for the same reason and found the Massachusetts Bay Colony on the site of modern Boston. They all come seeking religious freedom and settle in nicely, but only after a couple of tough winters and a bountiful Thanksgiving dinner with the local Indians.

Of course, it wasn't really that simple. The Pilgrims and the Puritans did come to the New World seeking religious freedom, but this meant the freedom to practice what they deemed the one true faith. In the Puritan imagination, America was to be a sacred place, the site of the "New Jerusalem" where they, as God's chosen people, would create a "new world," a world free of the imperfections they left behind in Europe. The Puritans believed that they were "saints," holy people who had been "elected" by God before birth to restore Christian belief and practice to its original state. Once they arrived, they got busy setting up this Christian utopia. In 1630 they passed laws enforcing the public support of Puritan ministers. In 1631, they limited the right to vote and to hold political office to members of their church. In 1635, they required everyone, regardless of religious affiliation, to attend church services. In 1638, they forced nonbelievers to pay taxes in support of "preaching that might lead ultimately to their conversion." By 1692, Puritan political rule had led to the Salem witch trials and the eventual death of at least twenty colonists, women and men suspected of consorting with the devil.

As you might expect, the story of religion in America has always been more complicated, and more interesting, than politicians and religious leaders will ever admit. For example, one thing that's often left out of the Puritan saga is the simple fact that there was plenty of religion in the "New

World" before the "Pilgrim Fathers" got here. Every Native American tribal group had its own gods, goddesses, and holy spirits, complete with an elaborate accompaniment of rituals, sacraments, myths, and legends. Before the Puritans arrived with their Bibles, the Hopi worshipped Spider Woman, who, along with the Sky Spirit, sang humanity into being and taught us how to work, hunt, and cook. The Sioux had Old Man Coyote who created the first man from clay retrieved from below the eternal waters by some friendly red-eyed ducks. Long before the Puritans brought Christianity to what they mistook for a "new" world, Native Americans had worshipped the creator in their own way and had shaped a body of religious beliefs that have endured among tribal groups to this day.

It's also important to remember that the Puritans were neither the first nor the only colonists in the Americas. More than a decade before the Pilgrims arrived, King James I chartered an expedition to the territory now known as Virginia. Jamestown Colony, under the authority of Captain John Smith, was created primarily as a commercial enterprise to search for gold, silver, and copper. So the very first settlers in America came with no particular religious mission at all: like generations of immigrants after them, they came to make their fortune.

Other colonists besides the Pilgrims also ventured to the New World, bringing other — distinctly nonpuritanical — religions with them. In 1634, the *Ark* and the *Dove* sailed into Chesapeake Bay to establish the first Roman Catholic colony in what is now Maryland. Not long after in 1654, the first small contingent of Jews to settle North America took refuge in the Dutch colony of New Amsterdam, the site of present-day New York. In fact, even in New England it wasn't long before dissenters emerged among the Puritans. Within three years of the Puritans' arrival in 1630, Anne Hutchinson was tried for blasphemy because she opposed the mixing of church and state practiced in Massachusetts Bay Colony. In 1638, she and her family were banished. When she perished along with five of her children during an Indian raid in 1648, John Winthrop saw her death as confirmation of her guilt. Just a few years earlier, another famous dissenter named Roger Williams was also banished from Massachusetts. The first colonist to study and master a number of Native American languages, Williams eventually made his way to Rhode Island with the help of his Native American friends. There he founded his own colony based on the principle of "soul liberty" — the very American idea that all individuals should have the freedom to believe what they choose to believe according to the dictates of their own conscience.

Considering the record of violence that scarred the history of religion in the early colonies, it's little wonder that Revolutionary figures approached the idea of belief with a mixture of respect and suspicion. Figures like Ben Franklin, Thomas Paine, and James Madison identified themselves as "deists" — a term common in the eighteenth century that applied to anyone who believed in an impersonal creator who was knowable only through the laws of science or the beauties of the natural world. When challenged to describe his religion toward the end of his life, Ben Franklin expressed his view of the creator in the following terms:

> I believe in one God, creator of the universe. That he governs it by his Providence. That he ought to be worshipped. That the most acceptable service we can render to him is doing good to his other children. . . .
>
> As to Jesus of Nazareth . . . I think the system of morals and his religion as he left them to us, the best the world ever saw, or is likely to see; but I apprehend it has received various corrupting changes, and I have . . . some doubts as to his divinity; though it is a question I do not dogmatize upon, having never studied it, and think it needless to busy myself with it now, when I expect soon an opportunity of knowing the truth with less trouble.

American radical and revolutionary pamphleteer Tom Paine was more direct in his doubts about traditional forms of Christianity:

> I believe in one God, and no more, and I hope for happiness beyond this life. . . . I do not believe in the creed professed by the Jewish church, by the Roman church, by the Greek church, by the Turkish church, by the Protestant Church, nor by any church that I know of. My own mind is my own Church.

But of all early Americans, Thomas Jefferson clearly had the greatest impact on our views of church and state. The inscription on Jefferson's tombstone asks us to remember him for only three of his many accomplishments — for writing the Declaration of Independence, for founding the University of Virginia, and for drafting the "Virginia Statute on Religious Freedom." Ever mindful of the government's power to corrupt belief, Jefferson argues in this important document against the establishment of any one religion by the state. For Jefferson, there had to be a "wall of separation" between church and politics — a legal barrier that would shield the individual against the abuses of state power and that would guarantee the liberty of individual conscience.

Of course, this doesn't mean that America is a secular society. Far from it: as the Fast Facts at the beginning of this chapter demonstrate, America ranks among the most religious nations in the world. As a group, we attend church more regularly, put more faith in the power of prayer, and have greater trust in the literal truth of the Bible than do any other people on earth. Most Americans even think in religious terms when it comes to politics, with some 70 percent reporting that they prefer presidential candidates who have strong religious views.

And it's also important to remember that religion has always played an important role in shaping some of our most cherished values and principles. A dramatic revival of religious sentiment in the early 1800s, known as the Second Great Awakening, inspired American abolitionists to call for the end of slavery and set the stage for the Civil War. In the latter half of the nineteenth century, the Third Great Awakening laid the foundations of the social gospel movement, which led in turn to the creation of the first

social services for the poor, the battle against the abuse of industrial workers, and the struggle for women's rights. In the 1950s and 60s yet another
"great awakening" expressed itself most eloquently in the speeches of the
Reverend Martin Luther King Jr. and provided the moral purpose and
passion that sustained the American civil rights movement. Nearly half a
century later, we sometimes forget that the songs that accompanied the bus
boycotts and freedom marches in Alabama and Mississippi were *spirituals*
and that for many African Americans, the fight for civil rights was a struggle
of faith as much as it was a fight for equal treatment under the law.

Today, tensions between secular and religious values continue to play
themselves out in communities across America. Not a year goes by without a
case coming before the courts involving issues like prayer in school, the display of the Ten Commandments, the public celebration of religious holidays,
the teaching of evolution, or the inclusion of "God" in the Pledge of Allegiance. It's also clear that America today is in the grip of yet another great
religious revival, one that promises to have an indelible impact on our domestic affairs and our relationship with the rest of the world for decades to come.

In this chapter we'll explore the current resurgence of religion in the
United States and examine some of the myths of secularism and religious
belief that frame our thinking about the meaning of faith. We begin with
Anne Lamott's powerful account of her own awakening to faith, as she grew
up in a thoroughly secular household outside San Francisco in the 1960s.
Next, David Kupelian diagnoses the evils that infect America's contemporary "Killer Culture" and calls for a return to fundamental Christian values.
In "The Christian Paradox," environmentalist, essayist, and lay minister Bill
McKibben reconsiders the radical ethics of the Gospels and challenges us
to take the question "What would Jesus do?" in all its revolutionary seriousness. The first half of the chapter draws to a close with the story of Kathleen
Boatwright, a devout Christian who struggles to balance her life as a lesbian
with the demands of her faith.

The next section of the chapter expands on the theme of religion's
place in an ethnically diverse, ostensibly secular society. We begin with the
chapter's Visual Portfolio, which offers a pictorial meditation on the delicate
balance between belief and intolerance in American culture. In "Afraid of
Ourselves," professor of comparative religion and Indian studies Diana L.
Eck outlines the growing "religious diversity" that she sees in contemporary
America. Along the way Eck also raises questions about the role of religious
stereotypes and the limits of tolerance in an increasingly diverse society.
Next, Maria Poggi Johnson offers a personal reflection on what it's like to
live among neighbors whose faith builds a real wall of separation between
"Us and Them."

The chapter closes with three readings addressing the competing
claims of church and state. Composed less than ten years after the Revolutionary War, James Madison's "Memorial and Remonstrance Against Religious Assessments" makes the case against the public support of religious
institutions. Madison's eloquent argument for the division of church and
state makes it clear that secularism exists for the good of religion as much as

it does for the sake of individual liberty. Next, Noah Feldman's "Schools and Morals" invites us to rethink our preconceptions about religion and American education, and presents ample opportunity to explore questions about the proper place of religion in American public life. In "Reason in Exile," award-winning author Sam Harris closes the chapter with a trenchant attack on organized religion, which he sees as the greatest threat to the future of democracy and world peace.

Sources

Brooke Allen, "Our Godless Constitution." *The Nation*, February 21, 2005, p. 16.

Richard Erdos and Alfonso Ortiz, eds., *Native American Myths and Legends*. New York: Pantheon Books, 1985.

Donald A. Grinde and Bruce E. Johansen, *Exemplar of Liberty: Native America and the Evolution of Democracy*. Berkeley: University of California Press, 1991.

The Harris Poll, *The Religious and Other Beliefs of Americans 2005*. Harris Interactive, http://www.harrisinteractive.com.

Anne Hutchinson, "Biography." http://www.annehutchinson.com.

Jon Meacham, *American Gospel: God, the Founding Fathers and the Making of a Nation*. New York: Random House Publishers, 2006, p. 21.

The Pew Forum on Religion and the Public Life, *The American Religious Landscape and Politics, 2004.* http://pewforum.org.

PollingReport.com, "Science and Nature." http://www.pollingreport.com.

The Public Agenda, "For Goodness' Sake: Why So Many Want Religion to Play a Greater Role in American Life." http://www.publicagenda.org.

Ronald Reagan, "Farewell Address to the Nation" (1989). http://www.ronaldreagan.com.

Cornel West, *Democracy Matters: Winning the Fight Against Imperialism*. New York: Penguin Books, 2005.

BEFORE READING

- Write a journal entry about the role that religion has played in your life. How important do you think religion is in the experience of most Americans? Why? Share your results in small groups and discuss your perceptions of the role that religion plays in American culture.

- What does the image of Madonna on the cross (p. 613) suggest to you about American attitudes toward religion? In your view, is this image sacrilegious — or just another example of America's commercial culture?

- Do a brief freewrite on the topic of what you imagine America would be like today if the "Puritan Fathers" had succeeded in creating a true Christian theocracy — that is, a state that was controlled by Puritan values and beliefs. Discuss with your classmates your vision of what such a theocratic America would look like and how it might differ from the nation we live in today.

Overture: Lily Pads

ANNE LAMOTT

The idea of religious rebirth may be ancient, but it's also as American as apple pie. During the "Great Awakenings" of the 1800s — the nationwide religious revivals that preceded and followed the Civil War — the idea of being reborn assumed an importance in American culture that still resonates today. Next to the rags-to-riches myth of success, America loves a good story about personal redemption and having a second chance. In this selection, Anne Lamott traces the path that led her from the excesses of the 60s — alcohol, drugs, and sex — to redemption as a member of a small Oakland, California, church congregation. Lamott's personal quest for faith challenges stereotypes about "born-again" Christians and raises serious questions about whether secular culture is capable of sustaining the things that give life meaning. Anne Lamott (b. 1954) is the acclaimed author of the national nonfiction bestsellers Plan B: Further Thoughts on Faith *(2005),* Traveling Mercies: Some Thoughts on Faith *(1999),* Bird by Bird: Some Instructions on Writing and Life *(1994), and* Operating Instructions: A Journal of My Son's First Year *(1994), as well as five novels, including* Crooked Little Heart *(1997) and* Hard Laughter *(1988). She lives in Northern California with her son Sam.*

My coming to faith did not start with a leap but rather a series of staggers from what seemed like one safe place to another. Like lily pads, round and green, these places summoned and then held me up while I grew. Each prepared me for the next leaf on which I would land, and in this way I moved across the swamp of doubt and fear. When I look back at some of these early resting places — the boisterous home of the Catholics, the soft armchair of the Christian Science mom, adoption by ardent Jews — I can see how flimsy and indirect a path they made. Yet each step brought me closer to the verdant pad of faith on which I somehow stay afloat today.

That One Ridiculous Palm

The railroad yard below our house was ringed in green, in grass and weeds and blackberry bushes and shoulder-high anise plants that smelled and tasted of licorice; this wreath of green, like a cell membrane, contained the tracks and the trains and the roundhouse, where engines were repaired. The buildings rose up out of the water on the other side of the bay, past Angel Island, past Alcatraz. You could see the Golden Gate Bridge over to the right behind Belvedere, where the richer people lived;

the anise was said to have been brought over at the turn of the century by the Italians who gardened for the people of Belvedere.

Tiburon, where I grew up, used to be a working-class town where the trains still ran. Now mostly wealthy people live here. It means shark in Spanish, and there are small sharks in these parts. My father and shy Japanese fishermen used to catch leopard sharks in the cold green waters of the bay.

There was one palm tree at the western edge of the railroad yard, next to the stucco building of the superintendent — one tall incongruous palm tree that we kids thought was very glamorous but that the grown-ups referred to as "that ridiculous palm tree." It did not belong, was not in relationship to anything else in town. It was silent and comical, like Harpo Marx[1] with a crazy hat of fronds.

We took our underpants off for older boys behind the blackberry bushes. They'd give us things — baseball cards, Sugar Babies. We chewed the stems off the anise plants and sucked on them, bit the ends off nasturtiums and drank the nectar.   5

When I was five and six, my best friend was a Catholic girl who lived about fifteen minutes away, on foot, from our house — kids walked alone all over town back then. I loved the Catholic family desperately. There were dozens of children in that family, or maybe it just felt that way, babies everywhere, babies crawling out from under sofas like dust bunnies. We only had three kids in our family; my brother John, who is two years older than me and didn't like me very much back then, and my brother Stevo, who is five years younger than me, whom I always adored, and who always loved me. My mother nursed him discreetly, while the Catholic mother wore each new baby on her breasts like a brooch. The Catholic mama was tall and gorgeous and wore heels to church and lots of makeup, like Sophia Loren, and she had big bosoms that she showed off in stylish V-necked dresses from the Sears catalog. My mother was not much of a dresser. Also, she was short, and did not believe in God. She was very political, though; both she and Dad were active early on in the civil rights movement. My parents and all their friends were yellow-dog Democrats, which is to say that they would have voted for an old yellow dog before they would have voted for a Republican.

I was raised by my parents to believe that you had a moral obligation to try to save the world. You sent money to the Red Cross, you registered people to vote, you marched in rallies, stood in vigils, picked up litter. My mother used to take the Greyhound out to Marin City, which was a terrible ghetto then, and volunteer in an after-school program for boys and girls from impoverished families. She tutored kids in reading while other grown-ups worked with them in sports. My mother majored in the classics in college. She always brought along little paper candy cups filled with the

---

[1]*Harpo Marx:* One of the Marx brothers comedians, known for not speaking while in character (1888–1964).

fanciest candies from Blum's or the City of Paris to give to the children after their lessons. It used to make my father mad that she'd buy such expensive candies, but this didn't stop her.

My Catholic friend and I used to spend hours sitting on the couch with the latest Sears catalog spread across our knees, pretending that we got whatever was on our side of the page. I played this game with anxiety and grief, always thinking that the better dresses and shoes were on my friend's pages and that I would have been OK if they had just been on mine — *and* if I'd had her tall stylish mother, with the wonderful cleavage showing like the bottom of a baby in her low necklines. I knew I was not pretty because people were always making jokes about my looks. (Once, at a pizza joint, a stranger had included me in a collective reference to the Catholic children, and you would have thought from the parents' outrage that he had included a chimpanzee.) And I knew I was not OK because I got teased a lot by strangers or by big boys for having hair that was fuzzy and white. Also, I got migraines. I got my first one midway through kindergarten and had to lie down with my face on the cool linoleum in the back of the room until my father could come get me.

My friend and I gathered blackberries from the bushes in the train yard, and her mother made pies. She made apple pies too. We peeled each apple with precision, aiming for one long green spiral of peel, and my first memory of watching someone be beaten was on a night after we'd prepared apples for pie. My Catholic friend and I had been left with a baby-sitter and all those babies, and after we had sliced up and spiced the apples, we'd gone to bed without throwing out all those green snakes of peel, and I awoke with a start in the middle of the night because my friend's father was smacking her on the face and shoulders, fuming alcohol breath on the two of us in our one twin bed, raging that we were slobs, and I don't know how he knew to beat her instead of me because I don't remember there being any light on. We both cried in the dark, but then somehow we slept and in the morning when we woke the mother was frying up bacon, a baby slung over her shoulder, and the dad was happy and buoyant, thunderous in his praise of the pie now in the oven.

It was Sunday morning and I got to go to church with them. All the ⟨10⟩ children got dressed up. The parents looked like movie stars, so handsome and young, carrying babies, shepherding the bigger kids, smooching in the car.

I loved every second of Catholic church. I loved the sickly sweet rotting-pomegranate smells of the incense. I loved the overwrought altar, the birdbath of holy water, the votive candles; I loved that there was a poor box, and the stations of the cross rendered in stained glass on the windows. I loved the curlicue angels in gold paint on the ceiling; I loved the woman selling holy cards. I loved the slutty older Catholic girls with their mean names, the ones with white lipstick and ratted hair that reeked of Aqua Net. I loved the drone of the priest intoning Latin. All that life surrounding you on all four sides *plus* the ceiling — it was like a religious bus station. They had all that stuff holding them together, and they got to be so conceited because they were *Catholics.*

Looking back on the God my friend believed in, he seems a little erratic, not entirely unlike her father — God as borderline personality. It was like believing in the guy who ran the dime store, someone with a kind face but who was always running behind and had already heard every one of your lame excuses a dozen times before — why you didn't have a receipt, why you hadn't noticed the product's flaw before you bought it. This God could be loving and reassuring one minute, sure that you had potential, and then fiercely disappointed the next, noticing every little mistake and just in general what a fraud you really were. He was a God whom his children could talk to, confide in, and trust, unless his mood shifted suddenly and he decided instead to blow up Sodom and Gomorrah.[2]

My father's folks had been Presbyterian missionaries who raised their kids in Tokyo, and my father despised Christianity. He called Presbyterians "God's frozen people." My mother went to midnight mass on Christmas Eve at the Episcopal church in town, but no one in our family believed in God — it was like we'd all signed some sort of loyalty oath early on, agreeing not to believe in God in deference to the pain of my father's cold Christian childhood. I went to church with my grandparents sometimes and I loved it. It slaked my thirst. But I pretended to think it was foolish, because that pleased my father. I lived for him. He was my first god.

My mother and her twin sister had come over from Liverpool with their mother after their father died, when they were twelve. My mother had a lifelong compassion for immigrants; she used to find people waiting for boats to their homeland or waiting for money to be wired from the East so that they could catch a bus home, and she'd bring them to stay with us until everything was straightened out. She and my aunt Pat had been confirmed as Episcopalians in England — I have their confirmation picture on my mantel, two dark-haired beauties of twelve or so in long white baptismal-style dresses. But that was the last of their religious affiliation. My aunt Pat married a Jew, with a large Jewish family in tow, but they were not really into Moses Jews; they were bagelly Jews. My closest cousin was bar mitzvahed, but other than accusing you of anti-Semitism if you refused second helpings of my uncle Millard's food, they might as well have been Canadians.

None of the adults in our circle believed. Believing meant that you 15 were stupid. Ignorant people believed, uncouth people believed, and we were heavily couth. My dad was a writer, and my parents were intellectuals who went to the Newport Jazz festival every year for their vacation and listened to Monk[3] and Mozart and the Modern Jazz Quartet. Everyone read

---

[2]*Sodom and Gomorrah:* Biblical cities destroyed by God because of their immorality.
[3]*Monk:* Thelonious Sphere Monk (1917–1982), noted jazz composer and pianist.

all the time. Mt. Tamalpais loomed above us, and we hiked her windy trails many weekends, my dad with binoculars hanging around his neck because he was a serious bird-watcher. He worshiped in the church of Allen Ginsberg,[4] at the Roger Tory Peterson[5] Holiness Temple, the Tabernacle of Miles Davis.[6]

We were raised to believe in books and music and nature. My mother played the piano most weekend nights, and all of us kids knew the words to almost every song in the *Fireside Book of Folk Songs*. When my parents' friends came over on the weekends and everyone had a lot to drink, my mother played piano and everyone sang: English ballads, spirituals, union songs, "The Golden Vanity," "Joe Hill," "Bread and Roses."

Their friends, our family friends, were like us; they read as a vocation, worked for liberal causes, loved Dr. King and nature, smoked, drank a lot, liked jazz and gourmet food. They were fifties Cheever people,[7] with their cocktails and affairs. They thought practicing Catholics insane, ridiculous in their beliefs, and morally wrong to have so many children; also, the non-Italian Catholics were terrible cooks. My mother made curries surrounded by ten kinds of condiments, including chutney she and her friends made every year in our kitchen. I bowed my head in bed and prayed, because I believed — not in Jesus — but in someone listening, someone who heard. I do not understand how that came to be; I just know I always believed and that I did not tell a soul. I did not tell a soul that strange boys rode by on bikes shouting racist insults about my kinky hair, or that we showed our naked bodies to the big boys in exchange for baseball cards, or that the Catholic dad had beat his daughter, because I wanted to be loved, and so I stood around silently, bursting with hope and secrets and fear, all skin and bone and eyes, with a crazy hair crown like that one ridiculous palm.

Momcat

The Belvedere Lagoon was a body of green water surrounded on all sides by luxurious homes, each with a dock from which you might swim or launch a small Sunfish or rowboat. My best friend from second grade on was named Shelly. She was blonde, pretty, and had a sister one year younger, whose best friend was a girl named Pammy who lived at the other end of the lagoon.

Shelly's mother was a Christian Scientist. My father thought the Christian Scientists were so crazy that they actually made the Catholics look good.

---

[4]*Allen Ginsberg:* Beat poet (1926–1997) perhaps best known for his lengthy poem "Howl."

[5]*Roger Tory Peterson:* Artist and naturalist (1908–1996).

[6]*Miles Davis:* Jazz trumpeter and composer (1926–1991) whose album *Kind of Blue* is considered one of the greatest recordings of the twentieth century.

[7]*Cheever people:* Refers to novelist and short story writer John Cheever (1912–1982), known for his depictions of upper-middle-class suburban life.

I was no longer close to the Catholics, as we had moved by this time into an old stone castle on Raccoon Straits on the north shore of San Francisco Bay. The castle had been built a hundred years before by a German man who wanted to make his new bride feel at home in California. It had trapdoors, a dungeon, and two caves in the back. My parents had bought it for twenty thousand dollars the year John Kennedy became president. My parents campaigned for him, my father looked like him, my mother quivered for him. She was like the preacher in *Cold Comfort Farm* whenever she talked about either of the Kennedys, trembling with indignant passion — "I'm *quivering* for you, Jack" — as if the rest of us didn't also love him.

We lived in this marvelous castle, but things were not going well inside   20 its stone walls. My parents' marriage was not a very happy one, and everywhere you looked as the sixties traipsed along there was too much alcohol and pot and infidelity. But Shelly's parents did not drink at all, and their house was full of stability and warmth. Pammy and I were drawn to it like moths. Pammy's mother was an heiress and an alcoholic who weighed no more than eighty pounds and who had often passed out before breakfast. Her father was doing time in various California prisons for killing his mother's best friend.

So we came to this house on the lagoon where everyone looked so good and where the mother gathered her children (and any other loose kids who happened to be there) into an armchair, like Marmie in *Little Women*, and read to them from *Science and Health* or the Bible. She told you that you were a perfect child, that you were entirely good, and that everything was fine, all evidence to the contrary. She was kind, lovely, funny, an early feminist who wore huge Bermuda shorts and her husband's shirts and did not care what people thought of her. And she believed two of the most radical ideas I had ever heard: one, that God was both our Father *and* our Mother; and two, that I was beautiful. Not just in God's eyes, which didn't count — what's the point if Ed Sullivan[8] was considered just as beautiful as Julie Christie?[9] She meant physically, on the earth, a visibly pretty girl.

Now, I had skipped a grade, so I was a year younger than everyone else in my class, and at nine and ten and eleven was knee-knocking thin, with sharp wings for shoulder blades and wiry blonde hair that I wore short. All my life men had been nudging my dad and saying with great amusement that there must have been a nigger in the woodpile, I guess because of both the hair and my big heavy-lidded eyes. And my father, who never once in his life would have used the word *nigger*, would smile and give an almost imperceptible laugh — not a trace of rage on behalf of black people, not a trace of rage on behalf of me. I didn't even quite know what this phrase meant — I knew it meant that a black man must have been my father but I couldn't figure out how a woodpile figured in, since a woodpile housed only

[8]*Ed Sullivan:* Television host (1901–1974) of a variety show popular in the 1950s and '60s.
[9]*Julie Christie:* British actress (b. 1941).

the most terrible things: snakes, spiders, rats, vermin, grub. The one time my older brother used the word *nigger*, he was grounded for a week. But when men whispered it to my father, he let it go. Why was this? Why would old lefties make this joke, and why would my dad act amused? Was it like spitting, a bad-boy thing? Did it make them feel tough for the moment, like rednecks for a day, so they could briefly sport grossness and muscles?

Lee, the Christian Science mother, smoothed my hair with her grandmother's boar-bristle brush, instead of tearing at it with a comb. She said that half the women in Belvedere would pay their beauticians anything for my hair's platinum color, and the roses in my cheeks, and the long skinny brown legs that carried me and her daughter into endless victories on the tennis courts.

Shelly was my first doubles partner. We were tennis champs.

It was so strange to be with families who prayed before the children left   25 for school each day, before swim meets and work and tennis tournaments. Pammy would step over her mother on the way out the door and arrive at Shelly's house just as I did. At my house, no one had passed out on the floor, but my mom was scared and Dad was bored and my little brother was growing fat and my older brother was being called by the siren song of the counterculture. Pammy and I would walk in together and find Lee with her brood piled like puppies on top of her, in her armchair, reading the Bible. And she would pray for us all.

Shelly's house was the only place I could really sleep. At my own, I'd try to but would feel a threatening darkness hanging over the castle, as if my parents' bad marriage were casting shadows like giant wings — shadows of alcoholism, shadows of people at my parents' frequent parties who necked in our rooms with people who were married to somebody else. If I told my mom or dad, they said, Oh, honey, *stop*, that's ridiculous, or they explained that everyone had had a lot to drink, as if what I'd seen didn't count since it had sprung from a kind of accidental overdose. At Christmas there were Fishhouse punches so alcoholic you could have sterilized needles in them, and on hot summer nights, blenders full of frappéed whiskey sours. The kids were given sips of short glasses of drinks, and we helped ourselves to more. By the age of twelve, all three of us were drinking with some regularity. My mother did not drink very much and so was frappé herself a lot; she was trying to earn the money for law school, which was her dream, and trying to get my dad to want to stay, and she looked tired, scared, unhappy. But Pammy's mother made mine look like Julie Andrews in *The Sound of Music*.

Many of the houses on the lagoon held children who by thirteen were drinking and using pot, LSD, cocaine, and heroin. Five children I knew well from school or the tennis courts died in the sixties — three of overdose, one by hanging, and the boy who lived directly across the lagoon drowned in its cool waters.

I remember how disgusted my parents were whenever they heard that Lee had taken her kids in to see a practitioner, instead of an M.D., when they got sick, as if she had entrusted her kids to a leech specialist. They were hardly ever sick, though. I don't think they even got poison oak. I was sick much more often than Shelly was. My mother was always basting at least one of us kids with calamine lotion. I remember being sick with chest colds and croup, sitting on my mother's lap on the toilet seat while scalding water from the shower filled the room with steam, characters in a hot, misty fairy tale, breathing together till I was better.

Pammy and I basked in Lee's love like lizards on sunny rocks. Lee lay beside me in bed when I couldn't sleep and whispered the Twenty-third Psalm to me: "'The Lord is my shepherd, I shall not want' — I am not wanting for *anything*, Annie. Let's find a green pasture inside us to rest in. Let's find the still waters within." She'd lay beside me quietly for a while as we listened to the tide of the lagoon lap against the dock. Then she'd go on: "'Yea, though I walk *through* the valley of the shadow of death,' Annie, not 'Yea, as I end up living forever in the valley. . . .'" And she prayed for the Good Shepherd to gather my thoughts like sheep. I did not quite believe in the power of her Mother-Father God, because my frightened lamby thoughts seemed to be stampeding toward a wall, piling up on each other's backs, bleating plaintively while their wild eyes darted around frantically. But I believed in Lee, and I felt her arms around me. I could hear Shelly's even breathing in the next bed, sense Lee's younger daughter and Pammy asleep in the next room, and the whole house would be so quiet, no shadows at all, and Lee would whisper me to sleep.

B-plus

I was on tennis courts all over California the year we invaded Cambodia,[10] the year Janis Joplin[11] and Jimi Hendrix[12] died, the year the students were killed at Kent State.[13] I was at tournaments up and down the state with my doubles partner Bee. I was sixteen, a little bit fat in the can by now. Her mother Mimi drove us around the state in an old Country Squire station wagon. My own mother didn't know how to drive, and besides, she was putting herself through law school. We hardly saw her.

Mimi had prematurely white hair and a huge smile, sang songs from musicals as she drove along, and always reminded me of Carol Channing.[14] She used to say that I was the most "utterly marvelous girl." Bee and I had

30

---

[10]*the year we invaded Cambodia:* Refers to the 1970 incursion into Cambodia by the United States during the Vietnam War.

[11]*Janis Joplin:* Blues and rock singer (1943–1970).

[12]*Jimi Hendrix:* Innovative and influential blues and rock singer and guitarist (1942–1970).

[13]*Kent State:* Refers to the shooting by the Ohio National Guard on Monday, May 4, 1970, of students who were protesting the U.S. entrance into Cambodia during the Vietnam War. Four students were killed and nine others wounded.

[14]*Carol Channing:* American actress (b. 1921).

been ranked number one in the state the year before in sixteen-and-under doubles, but my game was beginning to fall apart. In singles, Bee was thriving, but I was no longer in the top ten and that was very painful. I had two lives now, one with Bee on the green hardcourts and occasional grass, and one with Pammy, with whom I now went to school. We attended a little hippie high school in San Francisco and were two of the best students. There were fifty kids in my graduating class, many of them troubled children from San Francisco's socialite families. It was 1970 and we were smoking a lot of dope, which we could buy upstairs on the second floor of the schoolhouse in the student lounge. Two kids overdosed on heroin that year, although only one died, and a sweet rich boy of fifteen, on LSD, ran into the surf at Ocean Beach and was never seen again. We could buy balls of hashish soaked in opium for five dollars each. Pammy and I were getting drunk whenever possible, and then I was showing up for tennis matches hungover and really uninterested, except that I loved Bee and Mimi so much and had spent the last four years practically living at their house. They were wealthy, and Mimi had exquisite taste. I rarely saw the Christian Scientists anymore, though Pammy was still close to them. We all went to different schools, and I did not live near them on the lagoon, as Pammy did, so although I still loved them, I was with Bee and Mimi now. Mimi was an artist, a painter, who claimed me as daughter number two. She and Bee fought; she and I didn't. Bee and I wore our hair in pigtails, tied in bright ribbons. Bee had brown hair, brown eyes, brown limbs, freckles.

Pammy looked like a Renaissance angel in tie-dye, with white-blonde electric hair the color of Maryiln Monroe's, angel hair like you put on Christmas trees, and her skin was as fair as a baby's. Her breasts were large, and she was always a little overweight; she refused for political reasons to be thin. We were high on the women's movement; the voices from New York[15] were like foghorns saving us in the night, but they also frightened us because they were so strident. I spent the night at Pammy's a lot; there we could swim in the lagoon, or sunbathe on the dock, and get away with almost anything, day or night. So Pammy and I sailed and swam and smoked dope and drank "spoolie-oolies," which were glasses of red wine and 7-Up. We listened to Stephane Grapelli,[16] because Pammy played flute, and we listened to Scott Joplin[17] before anyone else, because she also played classical piano. She took lessons from an old blind Russian named Lev Shore, who was the father she should have had. Her father was still in prison. She was a little in love with my father, who was so much hipper than most of the other dads. He still lived with my mother, although things had

---

[15]*the voices from New York:* An apparent allusion to pioneer east coast 1970s feminists, like Gloria Steinem (b. 1934) and Betty Friedan (1921–2006).

[16]*Stephane Grapelli:* Jazz violinist born in France (1908–1997).

[17]*Scott Joplin:* Composer and pianist (1867?–1917) known for a musical style known as ragtime.

continued to deteriorate around our house. But he took Pammy, my younger brother, and me to the beach on weekends, and his friends smoked dope with us and served us jug red wine.

I wasn't thinking about God that much, except that when I was stoned I felt a mystical sense of peace and expansion, and I secretly thought I might become a Buddhist one of these days. There were many Buddhists my father admired — Gary Snyder, Peter Matthiessen, Alan Watts.[18] My father by then was practicing transcendental meditation, which he'd first investigated for a book he wrote while Ronald Reagan was governor, called *Anti-California: Report from Our First Para-Fascist State.*

At any rate, Pammy and I had an English teacher our sophomore year whom we loved, a large long-haired woman named Sue who wore purple almost exclusively and was a friendly hippie sort. She was one of the best teachers I've ever had. Her hair fell to her chair like a puppet-show curtain. She made you want to be a teacher, to throw the lights on for children that way.

After school Pammy and I would drive home in her mother's car or   35 hitchhike if we'd ridden in on the ferry, and then she would go off to her music lessons, and I would go to practice with Bee at the courts by the deserted railroad tracks.

Pammy and I did really well in school, mostly A's and A-minuses, a few B-pluses. At Pammy's house, she and her three sisters forged their mother Mary's signature to their report cards, since Mary was such a mess she did not seem to be aware that report cards needed to be signed or, for that matter, were even given out. In a way life was easier there than over at my house, because at least it was consistent: Mary was *always* a drunken mess, Pammy's father was always in prison. Over at my house, things could go any number of ways. I have read since that this is how you induce psychosis in rats: you behave inconsistently with them; you keep changing the rules. One day when they press down the right lever, expecting a serving of grain like they've always gotten before, they instead get a shock. And eventually the switching back and forth drives them mad, while the rats who get shocked every time they press the lever figure it out right away and work around it. Pammy worked around it. She had other mothers, like I did, and inside herself she grew the mother she had needed all those years.

So I was doing well academically, and I was a well-ranked tennis player and was the apple of my handsome father's eye — and then I would bring home a report card with a B-plus on it, and my parents would look at the report card as if I'd flunked. "Uh, honey?" one of them would ask, looking perplexed. "Now, this isn't a criticism but, if you could get a B-plus in philosophy, how much harder would it have been to get an A-minus?"

---

[18]*Gary Snyder . . . Alan Watts:* Gary Snyder, Pulitzer Prize–winning poet (b. 1930); Peter Matthiessen, novelist and short story and fiction writer (b. 1927); Alan Watts, theologian (1915–1973).

It never once occurred to me to stare back at them and say, "What a *crock.*" I just felt shame that I had disappointed them again, and I felt that if I could do a little better, Mom and Dad would get along again, my big brother would come home more often, and neither my mom nor my brother Steve would be fat. Stevo was the only person in the family who loved and was loved by every other member of the family, but — or so — he was the sacrificial lamb, hiding politely upstairs in his room, watching our small TV, tending to his baseball-card collection. If I could just do a little better, I would finally have the things I longed for — a sense of OKness and connection and meaning and peace of mind, a sense that my family was OK and that we were good people. I would finally know that we were safe, and that my daddy wasn't going to leave us, and that I would be loved someday.

Drugs helped. More than anything else, they gave me the feeling that I was fine and life was good and something sacred shimmered at its edges.

Being sexual with boys helped, too. Being sexual with anybody helped — there was a girl named Deborah at our school, a full-tilt hippie who wore her long blonde hair up and antique lace blouses over Indian-print skirts and who looked like Liv Ullman.[19] She used to hold a Lifesaver between her teeth and have me close mine around the half that was showing so that our lips, our open mouths, met as I'd take the Lifesaver into my own mouth, and I would feel my insides grow hard and quivery. Being loved by my teachers helped, but then report cards would come out, and once again I would think I had fallen short.   40

I was thirty-five when I discovered that a B-plus was a really good grade.

I played tennis all that summer of 1970, sometimes hungover, always finding the kids at the tournament dances who had the beer or the Boone Farm strawberry wine, and I drank with them while Bee went to bed early. Someone would find me half passed out with boys on boats, or barfing in the girls' room, or smoking a joint in someone's car, and I would be delivered home. Once I played a finals match with a huge blister on my top lip, the kind nursing babies get, only I got mine from trying to get one more hit off a roach the size of a grain of rice. When I was with Pammy, between tournaments, tanning on the dock of her house, slathered in baby oil, listening to her mother rant around inside, I felt like I could breathe. When I spent the night there, we'd stay up watching Dick Cavett[20] with her older sister, and her mother would wake up long enough to come into the TV room and screech, "I hate you fucking goddamn shitfuck Lamotts, and your father's Commie bullshit," and we'd all say, "Hi, Mary," or "Hi, Mom," and she'd say, "OK, well, good night, girls, good night, Annie," and we'd all say liltingly, "Good niiiiight," without taking our eyes off the screen.

[19]*Liv Ullman:* Norwegian actress (b. 1938).
[20]*Dick Cavett:* Late-night television talk show host (b. 1936).

When I stayed at Bee's house, we went to bed early, giggled all night in the dark, then got up early, ate protein for breakfast, and headed to the courts.

When Pammy and I returned to school in the fall of my junior year, terrible news unfolded: our English teacher Sue had become a born-again Christian. And apparently all the students who were her friends, about a dozen or so, had been brought into the fold during the later summer, and now they all met in the courtyard during lunch to pray, to read from the Bible, and to beam at each other with amusement. Sue would still hand out the most wonderful poems in her class — Sylvia Plath and Auden, T. S. Eliot, Ferlinghetti[21] — but now she interpreted everything in Christian terms; it was all viewed through Christ's eyes and determined to be about resurrection or original sin. Ferlinghetti writing "I am waiting for the rebirth of wonder" opened the way for a short talk on the hunger of the unsaved person; Sylvia Plath's "Daddy" was about her father, of course, but it also referred to Jehovah.[22] I wept in Sue's class at the betrayal, and at her gentle patronizing efforts to console me.

Then Pammy and I fought back. We read the great atheists, studied   45 their reasoning, especially Bertrand Russell's[23] essay "Why I Am Not a Christian," which we basically memorized. We challenged Sue on everything, every assertion, even when she was right. When we studied the Dylan[24] song "Dear Landlord," I valiantly tried to convince the class that Dylan was actually peeved with the earthly and unjust owner of the house that he was renting. Sue and the saved students listened with great gentleness and then looked tenderly around the room at one another.

I realized for the first time in my life that I was capable of murder.

I told my father that night, and he was deeply sympathetic, since no one disliked Christians more than he. He offered me a glass of wine with dinner. My mother was in the city studying for a law school exam. My dad and I ended up getting drunk together for the first time. Emboldened by the wine, I asked him how he'd feel if I quit competitive tennis. He'd never been that keen on it to begin with, as he was not at all athletic, and he said I should do whatever my heart told me. When I went to bed that night, I knew my tennis days were over, and when I finished my last year as Bee's doubles partner in the girls sixteen and under, I gave my racket to the Goodwill, and I never got another migraine again.

---

[21]*Sylvia Plath . . . Ferlinghetti:* Sylvia Plath, American poet and novelist (1932–1963); W. H. Auden, English poet (1907–1973); T. S. Eliot, American-born Nobel Prize–winning poet (1888–1965); Lawrence Ferlinghetti, American Beat poet (b. 1919).

[22]*Jehovah:* The proper Hebrew name for God.

[23]*Bertrand Russell:* British philosopher (1872–1970).

[24]*Dylan:* Bob Dylan, American folk and rock composer and recording artist, born Robert Zimmerman in 1941.

Candle Salad

There were endless lawns, fields, and meadows on the grounds of the small women's college I attended in the East. I had already announced my plans to drop out at the end of my sophomore year to become a writer, so I just took English and philosophy; I didn't have to fulfill any of the requirements necessary to graduate. I was on the tennis team and played junior varsity basketball; I also took religion, in deference to this puzzling thing inside me that had begun to tug on my sleeve from time to time, trying to get my attention. I've read that Augustine[25] said that to look for God is to find him, but I was not looking for God, not really. Or at any rate I didn't know I was.

I also started getting laid with some regularity. I was spearheading the campus McGovern[26] movement and in love with a man who was running the entire Baltimore campaign. It was not at all convenient to fit classes and homework into this schedule.

I smoked a lot of dope that year and sat beneath the trees. There was a huge silver maple near my dormitory with big palmate leaves. In March you could look up through the branches and see puzzle pieces of blue sky. Then day by day the bright green leaves opened like fingers, until the canopy had filled in, like carpet in the sky.

I don't think I ever said the word *Jew* until college, although our house and town and tennis clubs had been filled with Jewish people — that's what we called them: "Jewish people." I believed you weren't supposed to call them Jews unless you were one. My aunt Pat's husband and kids were secular Jews, so I suppose they *could* have called themselves "Jews," but I don't think they did. Neither did my parents' Jewish friends. They just *were* Jewish, maybe a little more so than they were also Type AB or O positive, but not much more. In college, though, most of the smartest, funniest women in our dorm, the ones who always had the best dope, were Jews and referred endlessly to their Jewishness. It was exhilarating, and I wanted to be one of them. I'd thought for a while, and especially since Pammy and I had become strident atheists, that Jews were better, smarter, hipper than the rest of us. If you were Jewish, you were part of the tribe that included Lenny Bruce and Bette Midler.[27] Allen Ginsberg was one of you, and Mel Brooks, and Woody Allen.[28] The women we revered were Jews: Grace

50

[25]*Augustine:* Saint Augustine (354–430 C.E.), influential in the early Christian church; known for *The Confessions of St. Augustine*, the story of his sinful youth and conversion.

[26]*McGovern:* George McGovern (b. 1922) Democratic nominee for president in 1972; lost to Richard Nixon.

[27]*Lenny Bruce and Bette Midler:* Lenny Bruce, stand-up comedian and satirist (1925–1966) known in the 1960s for his then-shocking use of onstage profanity, for which he was convicted of obscenity; Bette Midler, Grammy Award–winning singer, actress, and comedienne (b. 1945).

[28]*Mel Brooks, and Woody Allen:* Brooks (b. 1926) and Allen (b. 1935) are comedic actors, writers, and film directors.

Paley, Hannah Arendt, Bella Abzug, Gloria Steinem.[29] Ram Dass,[30] who'd started out at Harvard as Richard Alpert but had just come back from India a Hindu convert, called himself a Hin-Jew. Most of the girls I wanted to be like were Jews, and in comparison, the rest of us looked like we'd come from Grand Rapids.[31]

One of my friends in college took me home to visit her mother one three-day weekend. Her mother Billie was big and fat and unbelievably beautiful, except that she sported a heavy beard — a real beard, like three-day stubble. She acted like she'd known me forever. When I woke up in her house that first morning, she had shaved for the occasion and put pancake makeup over the stubble. It looked like she had a thousand blackheads.

She was a Zionist[32] and convinced me that Israel should bomb the shit out of Syria, and by the time I'd finished my grapefruit, I too believed this to be obvious. I asked her if she went to temple, and she acted as if I'd asked if she frequently used an escort service.

"Of *course* not," she said. "What's there for me? You sit, they don't speak English, only the men count for much, you wait forever for a song you might understand, you check out what everyone is wearing? And what's the pitch — you're born, you die, you go into a box? What's so tempting there?"

"But, Mom," cried my friend, "you *never* let us go out on Friday   55
nights."

"You should be out gallivanting on the Sabbath?"

All my life people thought I looked Jewish — or rather, the ones who didn't think I was mulatto thought I might be a Jew. And when my friends in college said that I *felt* like a Jew to them, I understood this to be a great compliment.

They always threw their arms around me and hugged me while crying out Yiddish endearments. Yet none of them believed in God. They believed in social justice, good works, Israel, and Bette Midler. I was nearly thirty before I met a religious Jew. All these girls had been bat mitzvahed, but when I asked why they weren't religious, they shrugged. "Maybe," they said, "it's hard to believe in a God who would not stop the Holocaust."

I had established a bar in my dorm room with my roommate Amy, who was not a Jew or a believer. It was called the Roly-Poly Bar and Grill, because we had both gained so much weight our freshman years. It was open every weekend night, and there were always a number of friends who,

---

[29]*Grace Paley... Gloria Steinem:* Grace Paley, poet and short fiction writer (b. 1922); Hannah Arendt, political philosopher (1906–1975); Bella Abzug, women's rights activist and member of Congress from 1970 to 1976 (1920–1998); Gloria Steinem, noted feminist and journalist (b. 1934).

[30]*Ram Dass:* American psychologist (b. 1931).

[31]*Grand Rapids:* Second-largest city in Michigan.

[32]*Zionist:* One who supports a Jewish homeland in Israel.

like Amy, played great blues guitar and sang and knew all the words to those early Bonnie Raitt[33] albums and drank and smoked dope and sometimes took the Dexedrine the infirmary passed out. We talked all night. Everything felt so intense and coiled and Möbius strip–like, all those drinks and drugs and hormones making everything constantly double back over itself. There were lots of girls in love with lots of other girls, and all of us half in love with the lesbian radical wing of the faculty, because they were giving us our lives, giving us back the lives our mothers had lost, but I was seeing the McGovern man while in love with another man back home, and I felt like I'd always felt: the stranger in a strange land.[34] I was desperately homesick for my father and younger brother and Pammy. The times I felt most functional were when I was drinking at the Roly-Poly Bar and Grill or smoking pot under a tree with my friends.

The smell of the eastern spring was so different from spring in California.   60
Maybe it was the lack of marine smells, the salt, the algae. Maybe because everything was so cold and barren in the winter, the smell of spring greenness was much more acute. And there were so many different kinds of birds — mockingbirds, chickadee-dee-dees, and crows as big as cats. But the most amazing thing of all were the redbud trees. They would bud at the end of winter: in all that twiggy stick world of gray, buds bloomed pinker than cherry blossoms, Renoir-cheek pink.

I read Thomas Merton, Simone Weil, William Blake, Rumi.[35] I was thirsty for something that I will dare to call the truth, so I read a lot of East Indian poetry and sat in the little chapel on campus and tried to pray. In the spring of my sophomore year, I began a course with a tiny Czechoslovakian woman named Eva Gossman. I loved Mrs. Gossman in general and worked very hard in her class. Then one day she gave us Kierkegaard's[36] *Fear and Trembling*, and my life changed forever.

Eva Gossman loved Kierkegaard in the same way she loved Chekhov,[37] and she took us through *Fear and Trembling* slowly. We read a lot of it out loud in class. Kierkegaard retold the story of Abraham, who heard God's angels tell him to take his darling boy Isaac up to the mountain and offer him as a sacrifice. Now, this was exactly the sort of Old Testament behavior I had trouble with. It made me think that this God was about as kind and

---

[33]*Bonnie Raitt:* American blues singer-songwriter and guitarist (b. 1949); winner of nine Grammy Awards.

[34]*stranger in a strange land:* Refers to the title of a science fiction novel by Robert A. Heinlein published in 1961 about a Martian-born human who comes to Earth.

[35]*Thomas Merton . . . Rumi:* Thomas Merton (1915–1968), Trappist monk and prolific writer probably best known for his autobiography, *The Seven Storey Mountain*; Simone Weil, French philosopher (1909–1943); William Blake, British poet and artist (1757–1827); Mowlana Jalaluddin Rumi, Persian mystic poet (1207–1273).

[36]*Kierkegaard:* Danish existentialist philosopher Søren Kierkegaard (1813–1855).

[37]*Chekhov:* Anton Chekhov, Russian short story writer and dramatist (1860–1904).

stable as Judge Julius Hoffman of Chicago Seven fame.[38] But the way Kierkegaard wrote it, Abraham understood that all he really had in life was God's unimaginable goodness and love, God's promise of protection, God's paradoxical promise that Isaac would provide him with many descendants. He understood that without God's love and company, this life would be so empty and barbaric that it almost wouldn't matter whether his son was alive or not. And since this side of the grave you could never know for sure if there was a God, you had to make a leap of faith, if you could, leaping across the abyss of doubt with fear and trembling.

So Abraham walked to the mountaintop with his son. Isaac asked his father where they were going, and Abraham answered that they were going to the mountain to sacrifice a lamb, and Isaac, who was small but nobody's fool, said, Well, then, uh — where's that rascally lamb? Abraham answered that God would provide the lamb. They walked together up the mountain, Abraham grievous but trusting in his God. When they arrived, Abraham got his knife but *finally* an angel called to him from Heaven and told him that he had successfully shown his devotion to God. And the Lord had indeed provided a lamb, which was trapped in a thicket nearby.

In the interior silence that followed my understanding of this scene, I held my breath for as long as I could, sitting there under the fluorescent lights — and then I crossed over. I don't know how else to put it or how and why I actively made, if not exactly a *leap* of faith, a lurch of faith. It was like Jacques Tati — Mr. Hulot[39] — making his way across a rickety ladder that spanned a crevasse. I left class believing — accepting — that there was a God. I did not understand how this could have happened. It made no sense. It made no sense that what brought me to this conviction was the story of a God who would ask his beloved Abraham to sacrifice the child he loved more than life itself. It made no sense that Abraham could head for the mountain in Moriah still believing in God's goodness. It made no sense that even as he walked his son to the sacrificial altar, he still believed God's promise that Isaac would give him many descendants. It made no sense that he was willing to do the one thing in the world he could not do, just because God told him to. God told him to obey and to believe that he was a loving god and could be trusted. So Abraham did obey.

I felt changed, and a little crazy. But though I was still like a stained and slightly buckled jigsaw puzzle with some pieces missing, now there were at least a few border pieces in place. . . .

65

---

[38]*Judge Julius Hoffman of . . . :* Judge Hoffman presided over the 1969–1970 trial of the Chicago Seven, men accused of conspiring to incite a riot at the 1968 Democratic National Convention in Chicago. An appeals court subsequently found that Hoffman showed a "deprecatory and often antagonistic attitude toward the defense."

[39]*Jacques Tati — Mr. Hulot:* Tati, French filmmaker (1908–1982); Hulot was the comedic character he portrayed in almost all of his films.

Cracks

From the hills of Tiburon, Belvedere Island looks like a great green turtle with all of its parts pulled in. It's covered with eucalyptus, cedars, rhododendrons, manicured lawns.

I had come back to live in Tiburon. It was 1982, I was twenty-eight, and I had just broken up with a man in a neighboring county. He was the love of my life, and I of his, but things were a mess. We were taking a lot of cocaine and psychedelic mushrooms, and drinking way too much. When I moved out, he moved back in with his wife and son. My dad had been dead for three years. My mother still practiced law in Hawaii, my oldest brother John had moved even farther away, and my younger brother had, in the most incongruous act of our family's history, joined the army.

When my boyfriend and I split up, I had called a divorced friend named Pat who'd lived in Tiburon for twenty years; I had baby-sat for her kids when I was young. She had loved me since I was eleven. I said I needed a place to regroup for a couple of weeks. Then I stayed for a year and a half. (Let this be a lesson.)

She worked in the city all day so I had the house to myself. I woke up quite late every morning, always hungover, the shades drawn, the air reeking of cigarettes and booze. The whole time I stayed at her house, I kept drinking from her one bottle of Dewars. Most nights I'd sip wine or beer while she and I hung out, eating diet dinners together. Then after she'd gone to bed nice and early every night, I'd pour myself the first of sixteen ounces of Scotch. I'd put music on the stereo — Bruce Springsteen, Tom Petty — and dance. Sometimes I would dance around with a drink in my hand. Other times, I would toss down my drink and then sit on the couch in reveries — of romance, of seeing my dad again, of being on TV talk shows, chatting with Johnny Carson,[40] ducking my head down while the audience laughed at my wit, then reaching demurely for my glass of Scotch. My self-esteem soared, and when the talk show ended in my mind, I would dance.

I took a sleeping pill with the last glass of Scotch every night, woke up late, wrote for a couple of hours, and then walked to one of four local liquor stores to buy a pint of Dewars. Back at Pat's, I would pour the whiskey back into the big bottle, raising the level back to where it had been before I started the night before. Then I'd put the empty in a brown paper bag and take off for the bike path to dispose of it.

There were many benches along the way with beautiful views of Richardson Bay. Some of them had trash cans next to them, but others did not, and I'd be frantic to get rid of my empty bottles. Certainly someone might interpret them as a sign that I had developed some sort of drinking problem. But sometimes I'd be forced to leave the bag on a bench where there was no trash can, and I lived in terror of someone running up to me

70

[40]*Johnny Carson:* Longtime host of *The Tonight Show* (1925–2005).

holding out the paper bag, calling, "Oh, Misssss, you forgot something." Then they'd drop it, and it would shatter inside the brown bag, and the jig would be up.

I was scared much of the time. There were wonderful aspects to my life — I was writing, I loved my friends, I lived amidst all this beauty. I got to walk with Pammy several times a week, along the bike path or over in Mill Valley where she was living happily ever after with her husband. Every night I'd swear I wouldn't hit Pat's Scotch again, maybe instead just have a glass of wine or two. But then she'd go to bed, and without exactly meaning to, I'd find myself in the kitchen, quietly pouring a drink.

Life was utterly schizophrenic. I was loved and often seemed cheerful, but fear pulsed inside me. I was broke, clearly a drunk, and also bulimic. One night I went to bed so drunk and stuffed with food that I blacked out. When I awoke, feeling quite light, I got on the scale. Then I called Pat at work with my great news: "I lost five pounds last night!"

"And I found it," she said. It seemed she had cleaned up after me.

I made seven thousand dollars that year and could not afford therapy   75
or enough cocaine. Then my married man called again, and we took to meeting in X-rated motels with lots of coke, tasteful erotic romps on TV like *The Bitch of the Gestapo*. But it was hard for him to get away. I'd pine away at Pat's, waiting for her to go to sleep so I could dance.

I was cracking up. It was like a cartoon where something gets hit, and one crack appears, which spiderwebs outward until the whole pane or vase is cracked and hangs suspended for a moment before falling into a pile of powder on the floor. I had not yet heard the Leonard Cohen[41] song in which he sings, "There are cracks, cracks, in everything, that's how the light gets in." I had the cracks but not the hope.

In pictures of Pammy and me taken then, she weighs a lot more than I. I'm skinny, insubstantial, as if I want to disappear altogether and my body is already starting to, piece by piece like the Cheshire cat. Pammy looks expansive and buttery and smiling. I look furtive, like a deer surprised in a heinous act.

I'm always squinting in these pictures, too, baffled, suspicious — get this over with, my eyes say. Pammy's hair is no longer wild blonde hippie-girl hair. Now it falls in soft waves to her shoulders. My hair is in a long fuzzy Afro, a thicket behind which I'm trying to hide. Pammy gives off natural charm, like someone who is dangling a line with something lovely attached, saying, Come play with us — we're worth it! While I'm saying, Go away! Stop bothering me!

I kept the extent of my drinking a secret from her. And in a show of control, played to an often empty house, I'd try to wait until five for the first beer. But this other person inside me would start crying, Help me. So I'd get us a little something to tide us over.

[41]*Leonard Cohen:* Canadian-born singer-songwriter (b. 1934).

It was so frustrating to be in love with an unavailable married man that   80
of course I found a second one. He was a dentist, who met me in fancy
hotels, with lots of cocaine and always some Percodan to take the edge off.
He was also doing nitrous oxide after hours, but he wouldn't share. I tried
everything to get him to bring me a little soupçon of nitrous, but never got
it. When he reported one night that his wife had torn at one of her eyes in
despair over our affair and that he'd taken her to Emergency four days
before, I thought, "*God*, is your wife a mess."

But a feather of truth floated inside the door of my mind that night —
the truth that I was crossing over to the dark side. I still prayed but was no
longer sure anyone heard. I called a suicide hot line two days later, but hung
up when someone answered. Heaven forbid someone should think I
needed help. I was a Lamott — Lamotts *give* help.

I kept walking into town on the bike path to dispose of my bottle and
buy another; the path was where the railroad tracks used to be. I'd turn
right on Beach Road and walk along the west shore of Belvedere Island,
passing below the big concrete Episcopal church on the hill. I'd actually
spent some time at St. Stephen's as a child. My mother and I would go
there for Midnight Mass on Christmas Eve every year, and I went with
assorted friends every so often. It looked like a PG&E[42] substation. I'd
heard from family friends that there was a new guy preaching, named Bill
Rankin, an old civil rights priest who had gotten this stolid congregation
mobilized behind issues of peace and justice. I wasn't remotely ready for
Christianity, though — I mean, I wasn't *that* far gone.

Still, I had never stopped believing in God since that day in Eva Gossman's class. Mine was a patchwork God, sewn together from bits of rag
and ribbon, Eastern and Western, pagan and Hebrew, everything but the
kitchen sink and Jesus.

Then one afternoon in my dark bedroom, the cracks webbed all the
way through me. I believed that I would die soon, from a fall or an overdose. I knew there was an afterlife but felt that the odds of my living long
enough to get into heaven were almost nil. They couldn't possibly take you
in the shape I was in. I could no longer imagine how God could love me.

But in my dark bedroom at Pat's that afternoon, out of nowhere it   85
crossed my mind to call the new guy at St. Stephen's.

So I did. He was there, and I started to explain that I was losing my
mind, but he interrupted to say with real anguish that he was sorry but he
had to leave. He literally begged me to call back in the morning, but I
couldn't form any words in reply. It was like in the movies when the gang-
ster is blowing bubbles through the bullet hole in his neck. There was this
profound silence, except for my bubbling. Then he said, "Listen. Never
mind. I'll wait. Come on in."

---

[42]*PG&E:* Pacific Gas and Electric Company.

It took me forty-five minutes to walk there, but this skinny middle-aged guy was still in his office when I arrived. My first impression was that he was smart and profoundly tenderhearted. My next was that he was really listening, that he could hear what I was saying, and so I let it all tumble out — the X-rated motels, my father's death, a hint that maybe every so often I drank too much.

I don't remember much of his response, except that when I said I didn't think God could love me, he said, "God *has* to love you. That's God's job." Some years later I asked him to tell me about this first meeting. "I felt," he said, "that you had gotten yourself so tangled up in big God questions that it was suffocating you. Here you were in a rather desperate situation, suicidal, clearly alcoholic, going down the tubes. I thought the trick was to help you extricate yourself enough so you could breathe again. You said your prayers weren't working anymore, and I could see that in your desperation you were trying to save *yourself*: so I said you should stop praying for a while, and let me pray for you. And right away, you seemed to settle down inside."

"What did you hear in my voice when I called?"

"I just heard that you were in trouble."   90

He was about the first Christian I ever met whom I could stand to be in the same room with. Most Christians seemed almost hostile in their belief that they were saved and you weren't. Bill said it bothered him too, but you had to listen to what was underneath their words. What did it mean to be saved, I asked, although I knew the word smacked of Elmer Gantry[43] for both of us.

"You don't need to think about this," he said.

"Just tell me."

"I guess it's like discovering you're on the shelf of a pawnshop, dusty and forgotten and maybe not worth very much. But Jesus comes in and tells the pawnbroker, 'I'll take her place on the shelf. Let her go outside again.'"

When I met him for a second time in his office, he handed me a quote   95
of Dag Hammarskjöld's:[44] "I don't know Who or What put the question, I don't know when it was put. I don't even remember answering. But at some moment, I did answer Yes." I wanted to fall to my knees, newly born, but I didn't. I walked back home to Pat's and got out the Scotch. I was feeling better in general, less out of control, even though it would be four more years before I got sober. I was not willing to give up a life of shame and failure without a fight. Still, a few weeks later, when Bill and I met for our first walk, I had some progress to report: I had stopped meeting the love of my life at X-rated motels. I still met him at *motels*, but nicer ones. I had

---

[43]*Elmer Gantry:* 1927 novel by Sinclair Lewis about a coarse drunk turned hypocritical preacher.

[44]*Dag Hammarskjöld:* Swedish diplomat (1905–1961).

stopped seeing the man with the bleeding wife. I felt I had standards again — granted, they were very *low* standards, but still . . .

Slowly I came back to life. I'd been like one of the people Ezekiel comes upon in the valley of dry bones — people who had really given up, who were lifeless and without hope. But because of Ezekiel's[45] presence, breath comes upon them; spirit and kindness revive them. And by the time I was well enough for Bill even to *consider* tapering off our meetings, I had weaseled my way into his heart. I drank, he led a church, and together we went walking every week all over Belvedere Island, all over the back of that great green turtle.

Flea Market

In the dust of Marin City, a wartime settlement outside Sausalito where black shipyard workers lived during World War II, a flea market was held every weekend for years. In 1984 I was living in a mother-in-law unit on a houseboat berthed at the north end of Sausalito, on San Francisco Bay. I was almost thirty when I moved in, and I lived for the next four years in a space about ten feet square, with a sleeping loft. I had a view of the bay and of Angel Island. When it was foggy, San Francisco across the water looked like a city inside a snow globe.

I got pregnant in April, right around my thirtieth birthday, but was so loaded every night that the next morning's first urine was too diluted for a pregnancy test to prove positive. Every other day, Pammy, who still lived in Mill Valley with her husband, would come by and take a small bottle of pee to the lab that was near her home. I did not have a car. I had had a very stern conversation with myself a year before, in which I said that I had to either stop drinking or get rid of the car. This was a real no-brainer. I got around on foot, and by bus and friend.

The houseboat, on a concrete barge, barely moved even during the storms of winter. I was often sick in the mornings. On weekdays, I put coffee on, went for a run, took a shower, had coffee, maybe some speed, a thousand cigarettes, and then tried to write. On weekends, I went to the flea market.

Marin City is the ghetto in this luscious affluent county, built in a dusty   100 bowl surrounded by low green hills on the other side of the freeway from where my houseboat was. The town is filled with families — lots of little kids and powerful mothers. There are too many drugs and guns, there is the looming and crummy government housing called the Projects, and there are six churches in a town of two thousand people who are mostly black. On the weekends, the gigantic lot where the Greyhound bus depot used to be was transformed into one of the country's biggest flea markets. Many years before, I used to sit on my mother's lap on the exact same site

[45]*Ezekiel:* Biblical prophet. Lamott refers to Chapter 37 of the Book of Ezekiel.

and watch black men drink coffee at the counter while we waited for a bus into San Francisco. Now every square foot was taken up with booths and trucks and beach umbrellas and tables and blankets and racks displaying household wares and tools and crafts and clothes, much of it stolen, most of it going for a song — hundreds of sellers, thousands of buyers, children and dogs and all of us stirring up the dust.

You could buy the most wonderful ethnic food here, food from faraway places: Asia, India, Mexico, New York City. This is where I liked to be when I was hungover or coming down off a cocaine binge, here in the dust with all these dusty people, all this liveliness and clutter and color, things for sale to cheer me up, and greasy food that would slip down my throat.

If I happened to be there between eleven and one on Sundays, I could hear gospel music coming from a church right across the street. It was called St. Andrew Presbyterian, and it looked homely and impoverished, a ramshackle building with a cross on top, sitting on a small parcel of land with a few skinny pine trees. But the music wafting out was so pretty that I would stop and listen. I knew a lot of the hymns from the times I'd gone to church with my grandparents and from the albums we'd had of spirituals. Finally, I began stopping in at St. Andrew from to time, standing in the doorway to listen to the songs. I couldn't believe how run-down it was, with terrible linoleum that was brown and overshined, and plastic stained-glass windows. But it had a choir of five black women and one rather Amish-looking white man making all that glorious noise, and a congregation of thirty people or so, radiating kindness and warmth. During the time when people hugged and greeted each other, various people would come back to where I stood to shake my hand or try to hug me; I was as frozen and stiff as Richard Nixon. After this, Scripture was read, and then the minister named James Noel who was as tall and handsome as Marvin Gaye[46] would preach, and it would be all about social injustice — and Jesus, which would be enough to send me running back to the sanctuary of the flea market.

You'd always have to shower after you got home, you'd be so covered with dust, the soles of your shoes sticky with syrup from snow cones, or gum, or one of those small paper canoes that hot dogs are served in.

I went back to St. Andrew about once a month. No one tried to con me into sitting down or staying. I always left before the sermon. I loved singing, even about Jesus, but I just didn't want to be preached at about him. To me, Jesus made about as much sense as Scientology or dowsing.[47] But the church smelled wonderful, like the air had nourishment in it, or like it was composed of these people's exhalations, of warmth and faith and peace. There were always children running around or being embraced, and a gorgeous stick-thin deaf black girl signing to her mother, hearing the songs and

---

[46]*Marvin Gaye:* R&B and soul musician (1939–1984).

[47]*dowsing:* The unscientific act of using a stick or rod to locate such things as water or metal underground; also known as "water witching."

the Scripture through her mother's flashing fingers. The radical old women of the congregation were famous in these parts for having convinced the very conservative national Presbytery to donate ten thousand dollars to the Angela Davis[48] Defense Fund during her trial up at the Civic Center. And every other week they brought huge tubs of great food for the homeless families living at the shelter near the canal to the north. I loved this. But it was the singing that pulled me in and split me wide open.

I could sing better here than I ever had before. As part of these people,   105 even though I stayed in the doorway, I did not recognize my voice or know where it was coming from, but sometimes I felt like I could sing forever.

Eventually, a few months after I started coming, I took a seat in one of the folding chairs, off by myself. Then the singing enveloped me. It was furry and resonant, coming from everyone's very heart. There was no sense of performance or judgment, only that the music was breath and food.

Something inside me that was stiff and rotting would feel soft and tender. Somehow the singing wore down all the boundaries and distinctions that kept me so isolated. Sitting there, standing with them to sing, sometimes so shaky and sick that I felt like I might tip over, I felt bigger than myself, like I was being taken care of, tricked into coming back to life. But I had to leave before the sermon.

That April of 1984, in the midst of this experience, Pammy took a fourth urine sample to the lab, and it finally came back positive. I had published three books by then, but none of them had sold particularly well, and I did not have the money or wherewithal to have a baby. The father was someone I had just met, who was married, and no one I wanted a real life or baby with. So Pammy one evening took me in for the abortion, and I was sadder than I'd been since my father died, and when she brought me home that night, I went upstairs to my loft with a pint of Bushmills and some of the codeine a nurse had given me for pain. I drank until nearly dawn.

Then the next night I did it again, and the next night, although by then the pills were gone.

I didn't go to the flea market the week of my abortion. I stayed home,   110 and smoked dope and got drunk, and tried to write a little, and went for slow walks along the salt marsh with Pammy. On the seventh night, though, very drunk and just about to take a sleeping pill, I discovered that I was bleeding heavily. It did not stop over the next hour. I was going through a pad every fifteen minutes, and I thought I should call a doctor or Pammy, but I was so disgusted that I had gotten so drunk one week after an abortion that I just couldn't wake someone up and ask for help. I kept on changing Kotex, and I got very sober very quickly. Several hours later, the blood stopped flowing, and I got in bed, shaky and sad and too wild to have another drink or take a sleeping pill. I had a cigarette and turned off the

---

[48]*Angela Davis:* Radical activist and philosopher (b. 1944) tried and acquitted in 1970 for conspiracy; currently a professor at the University of California, Santa Cruz.

light. After a while, as I lay there, I became aware of someone with me, hunkered down in the corner, and I just assumed it was my father, whose presence I had felt over the years when I was frightened and alone. The feeling was so strong that I actually turned on the light for a moment to make sure no one was there — of course, there wasn't. But after a while, in the dark again, I knew beyond any doubt that it was Jesus. I felt him as surely as I feel my dog lying nearby as I write this.

And I was appalled. I thought about my life and my brilliant hilarious progressive friends, I thought about what everyone would think of me if I became a Christian, and it seemed an utterly impossible thing that simply could not be allowed to happen. I turned to the wall and said out loud, "I would rather die."

I felt him just sitting there on his haunches in the corner of my sleeping loft, watching me with patience and love, and I squinched my eyes shut, but that didn't help because that's not what I was seeing him with.

Finally I fell asleep, and in the morning, he was gone.

This experience spooked me badly, but I thought it was just an apparition, born of fear and self-loathing and booze and loss of blood. But then everywhere I went, I had the feeling that a little cat was following me, wanting me to reach down and pick it up, wanting me to open the door and let it in. But I knew what would happen: you let a cat in one time, give it a little milk, and then it stays forever. So I tried to keep one step ahead of it, slamming my houseboat door when I entered or left.

And one week later, when I went back to church, I was so hungover 115 that I couldn't stand up for the songs, and this time I stayed for the sermon, which I just thought was so ridiculous, like someone trying to convince me of the existence of extraterrestrials, but the last song was so deep and raw and pure that I could not escape. It was as if the people were singing in between the notes, weeping and joyful at the same time, and I felt like their voices or *something* was rocking me in its bosom, holding me like a scared kid, and I opened up to that feeling — and it washed over me.

I began to cry and left before the benediction, and I raced home and felt the little cat running along at my heels, and I walked down the dock past dozens of potted flowers, under a sky as blue as one of God's own dreams, and I opened the door to my houseboat, and I stood there a minute, and then I hung my head and said, "Fuck it: I quit." I took a long deep breath and said out loud, "All right. You can come in."

So this was my beautiful moment of conversion.

And here in dust and dirt, O here,
The lilies of his love appear.

I started to find these lines of George Herbert's[49] everywhere I turned — in Simone Weil, Malcolm Muggeridge,[50] books of English poetry.

---

[49]*George Herbert:* English poet and priest (1593–1633).
[50]*Malcolm Muggeridge:* British journalist and Christian scholar (1903–1990).

Meanwhile, I trooped back and forth through the dust and grime of the flea market every Sunday morning till eleven, when I crossed the street from the market to the church.

I was sitting through the sermon now every week and finding that I could not only bear the Jesus talk but was interested, searching for clues. I was more and more comfortable with the radical message of peace and equality, with the God in whom Dr. King believed. I had no big theological thoughts but had discovered that if I said, Hello?, to God, I could *feel* God say, Hello, back. It was like being in a relationship with Casper.[51] Sometimes I wadded up a Kleenex and held it tightly in one fist so that it felt like I was walking hand and hand with him.

Finally, one morning in July of 1986, I woke up so sick and in such   120
despair for the umpteenth day in a row that I knew that I was either going to die or have to quit drinking. I poured a bottle of pinot noir down the sink, and dumped a Nike box full of assorted pills off the side of my houseboat, and entered into recovery with fear and trembling. I was not sure that I could or even wanted to go one day without drinking or pills or cocaine. But it turned out that I could and that a whole lot of people were going to help me, with kind eyes and hot cups of bad coffee.

If I were to give a slide show of the next ten years, it would begin on the day I was baptized, one year after I got sober. I called Reverend Noel at eight that morning and told him that I really didn't think I was ready because I wasn't good enough yet. Also, I was insane. My heart was good, but my insides had gone bad. And he said, "You're putting the cart before the horse. So—honey? Come on *down*." My family and all my closest friends came to church that day to watch as James dipped his hand into the font, bathed my forehead with cool water, and spoke the words of Langston Hughes:

> Gather out of star-dust
> Earth-dust,
> Cloud-dust,
> Storm-dust,
> And splinters of hail,
> One handful of dream-dust
> Not for sale.

In the next slide, two years later, I'm pregnant by a man I was dating, who really didn't want to be a father at the time. I was still poor, but friends and the people at my church convinced me that if I decided to have a child, we would be provided for every step of the way. Pammy really wanted the kid. She had been both trying to conceive and waiting to adopt for years. She said, "Let me put it this way, Annie. We're going to have this baby."

---

[51]*Casper:* Casper the Friendly Ghost appeared in movies, comics, and an animated television show.

In the next slide, in August of 1989, my son is born. I named him Sam. He had huge eyes and his father's straight hair. Three months later he was baptized at St. Andrew.

Then, six months later, there would be a slide of me nursing Sam, holding the phone to my ear with a look of shock on my face, because Pammy had just been diagnosed with metastatic breast cancer. She had a lumpectomy and then aggressive chemotherapy. All that platinum hair fell out, and she took to wearing beautiful scarves and soft cotton caps. I would show you a slide of her dancing in a ballet group for breast cancer survivors. . . .

Meanwhile, Sam grew tall and thin and sweet, with huge brown eyes.   125

Then there would be thousands of slides of Sam and me at St. Andrew. I think we have missed church ten times in twelve years. Sam would be snuggled in people's arms in the earlier shots, shyly trying to wriggle free of hugs in the later ones. There would be different pastors along the way, none of them exactly right for us until a few years ago when a tall African-American woman named Veronica came to lead us. She has huge gentle doctor hands, with dimples where the knuckles should be, like a baby's fists. She stepped into us, the wonderful old worn pair of pants that is St. Andrew, and they fit. She sings to us sometimes from the pulpit and tells us stories of when she was a child. She told us this story just the other day: When she was about seven, her best friend got lost one day. The little girl ran up and down the streets of the big town where they lived, but she couldn't find a single landmark. She was very frightened. Finally a policeman stopped to help her. He put her in the passenger seat of his car, and they drove around until she finally saw her church. She pointed it out to the policeman, and then she told him firmly, "You could let me out now. This is my church, and I can always find my way home from here."

And that is why I have stayed so close to mine — because no matter how bad I am feeling, how lost or lonely or frightened, when I see the faces of the people at my church, and hear their tawny voices, I can always find my way home.

ENGAGING THE TEXT

1. What attracts Lamott to the various religions she encounters in her youth? What does she think about her Catholic, Christian Science, and Jewish friends and their faiths?

2. How does Lamott's family view religion? What are her parents' dominant values and beliefs? How does she seem to feel about her family and their values?

3. Why do you think the story of Abraham and Isaac has such a powerful effect on Lamott? Why might this particular tale, of all the stories in the Bible, be the one that she associates with her initial religious awakening?

4. How would you describe Lamott's evolving attitude toward God? What seems to trouble her about the very idea of godhood? How would you

describe her eventual understanding of the "patchwork God" she comes to accept into her life?

5. Working in small groups, develop an outline of the elements you would expect to find in typical stories of rebirth or religious conversion. Then compare your outline with the details of Lamott's account of her own spiritual awakening. How closely does Lamott's story fit the stereotypical story of spiritual rebirth? To what extent does it confirm or challenge the assumptions we have about what it means to be reborn?

EXPLORING CONNECTIONS

6. Compare Lamott's conversion experience and spiritual rebirth to the revolution of consciousness experienced by Malcolm X when he was in prison (p. 210). What similarities can you find between their experiences despite the obvious differences between them in terms of race, education, and family background?

7. What does the story of Lamott's spiritual rebirth suggest about Noah Feldman's claim that school represents our most important "common" experience (p. 724)? To what extent does school seem to have shaped Lamott's character? Do you think that going to a different kind of school — one with a more values-based curriculum — might have made a difference in her life? Why or why not?

EXTENDING THE CRITICAL CONTEXT

8. Research the values and attitudes associated with the 1960s counterculture. To what extent does Lamott's story of religious awakening confirm or challenge common criticisms of this American cultural period? What role do countercultural values and attitudes play in Lamott's search for faith?

9. View the 1997 film *The Apostle* and compare the story of personal rebirth it portrays with Lamott's story of religious awakening. How might Lamott explain the fact that the theme of religious conversion is rarely treated in popular culture?

Killer Culture

DAVID KUPELIAN

The first great preachers in the American colonies were men like Jonathan Edwards and Cotton Mather who hissed fire-and-brimstone warnings against the sinful ways of their congregants and exhorted them to follow the straight and narrow path prescribed in the Gospels. The dramatic sermons of these early Puritan preachers were called "jeremiads" because of their resemblance to the dark prophecies of the Old Testament's Book of Jeremiah. In recent years, the rebirth of Puritanical thought associated with Christian fundamentalism has brought with it a new wave of Jeremiahs — a new generation of religious commentators who damn the excesses of contemporary American society as they call for a return to basic Christian values. David Kupelian's "Killer Culture" offers a striking example of this age-old puritanical impulse. According to Kupelian, American teens have fallen "in love with death" under the influence of corporate culture and MTV. David Kupelian (b. 1949) began his adult life as a professional violinist. Today he is vice president and managing editor of WorldNetDaily.com and Whistleblower *magazine.*

A Scout is trustworthy . . . loyal . . . helpful . . . friendly . . . courteous . . . kind . . ."

I'm watching my twelve-year-old son, Joshua, and two dozen other Boy Scouts together recite the Scout Law at their weekly troop meeting. It's a refreshingly hopeful and manly vignette in an era of wall-to-wall teen confusion.

As I stand in rapt attention — my eyes exploring the boys' uniforms, searching out all the badges, patches, insignias, and other colorful signs of their allegiance to Scouting's high ideals — my mind wanders back a few years to a time when my son wanted to wear a different uniform.

Our family had traveled to Cape May, New Jersey, to vacation on a warm Atlantic beach with close relatives we hadn't seen in a long time. Joshua hit it off great with his cousin, a boy several years his senior. A fun-loving and thoroughly decent kid, the cousin didn't have a mean bone in his body. One little thing, though. He wore a choker around his neck. Of course, Joshua had always regarded necklaces, bracelets, earrings, and the like as strictly girls' stuff and wouldn't dream of donning such gear himself and "looking like a girl" (or a "weirdo").

You guessed it. By the end of one week, Joshua told me he really wanted to get a choker, like his cousin's. He just felt like wearing one, that's all. No big deal, Dad.

I took him for a walk on the jetty where we could be alone. Before long I discovered that not only had my son developed this powerful desire to wear a piece of punk jewelry around his neck — something he had formerly despised — but he was also noticeably hostile toward me for some strange reason, even though he admitted I had done nothing to offend him. As we talked, it dawned on me what was going on. Obviously he wanted to be like his older cousin, who he looked up to and had bonded with — hence the desire to wear a dumb-looking neck choker. But me? He now saw me in uncomfortable contrast to coolness, seeing as I represented his state of

5

mind *before* he was captivated by this alien desire. I was a threat to his new allegiance, so he was rejecting me along with his own previous viewpoint.

As it turned out, I didn't need to say too much. "Joshua, why are you mad at me? Is it because I don't think that deep down you really want to wear a necklace? Tell me something. What would you have thought if, two weeks ago, before we came to Cape May, I had asked you if you would like to wear a clunky wooden necklace. Would you have wanted to?"

"No way," he replied without hesitation. The trance was broken. Realization set in. He cried briefly, gave me a hug, and assured me manfully he did not want to look like a girl and wear a necklace. When we went into the little gift shop on that beach, he even pointed out the choker he had wanted, displayed there in the showcase, and let me know once again that he wasn't interested. So that was the end of it. But it sure illustrated to me just how sensitive children are to peer pressure.

Gangsta Generation

If Joshua felt the invisible pull of peer pressure to conform to his cousin's fashion preferences, what was influencing his cousin? Indeed, what is exerting this irresistible pressure to conform (by "rebelling") on most of today's youth?

Just as the military and private schools and Boy Scouts have uniforms, 10 so does the prevailing youth culture: baggy pants, backward hats, chokers and other jewelry, body piercings, tattoos, and the like. But if uniforms symbolize values and allegiance, a loyalty to a higher (or lower) order, then in this case it's an allegiance to an increasingly defiant musical, social, sexual, and cultural world, a mysterious (to parents) realm that seems magically to be drawing millions of children into it.

For three years, journalist Patricia Hersch journeyed into this exotic subculture. She observed, listened to, questioned, bonded with, and won the trust of eight teens in the posh, suburban American town of Reston, Virginia, ultimately producing her acclaimed portrait, *A Tribe Apart: A Journey into the Heart of American Adolescence.* The landscape she describes, as ubiquitous across America's fruited plain as McDonald's, is troubling indeed:

> It's hip-hop in suburbia, the culture of rap. Everywhere students wear baseball caps turned backwards or pulled down over their eyes, oversize T-shirts, ridiculously baggy jeans or shorts with dropped crotches that hang to mid-shin, and waists that sag to reveal the tops of brightly colored boxers. Expensive name-brand high-tops complete the outfit. Variations on the theme are hooded sweatshirts, with the hood worn during school, and "do rags," bandannas tied on the head, a style copied from street gangs. Just as ubiquitous are the free-flying swear words, sound bursts landing kamikaze-style, just out of reach of hall guards and teacher monitors. . . .

In the latest exasperating challenge to adult society, black rage is in as a cultural style for white middle-class kids. As in the sixties, when the sons and daughters of the middle class tossed out their tweed jackets and ladylike sheath dresses for the generational uniform of Levi's and work shirts and peacoats in their celebration of blue collar workers, "the Real Americans," so today's adolescents have co-opted inner-city black street-style as the authentic way to be. To act black, as the kids define it, is to be strong, confrontational, a little scary. . . .

"We are living in the gangsta generation," one white high school senior wearing his Malcolm X baseball cap turned backwards explains. "It is all about getting it. I look at what these cool dudes do and how it affects other people. These people are doing more than any faggoty white kid who plays basketball and gets accepted at Duke and has been rich his whole life and maybe gets drunk on the weekend. These kids put their ass on the line every day."

Hersch describes how hip-hop — a multimillion-dollar music industry filled with "the powerful political and sexual images of rap" — has captivated a generation with the drama of the ghetto and its daily struggle for survival:

> Hip-hop's in-your-face attitude looks strong and free to kids who feel constrained by expectations of the mundane middle-class world they have grown up in. Rappers have become the most popular attractions on MTV. In an interview on his album "Home Invasion," rapper Ice T refers to the "cultural invasion" that is occurring while unknowing adults sit around with their racist attitudes and their kids sit quietly in their bedrooms, his words pouring into their brains through their headphones: "Once I get 'em under my f — kin' spell / They may start giving you f — kin' hell," he raps. "Start changin' the way they walk, they talk, they act / Now whose fault is that?" The rap world of "hos and pimps, bitches, muthaf — kers, homeys and police" is an attractive diversion from the "ordinary" sphere of dental braces, college boards, and dating. The ghetto — experienced second-hand in movies and music and on the evening news, viewed from the comfort of nice suburban family rooms — holds enormous drama and appeal for young people.[1]

So is that it? Is today's bizarre youth subculture just the latest costume for adolescent rebellion, like the long hair of the 1960s and other, if less conspicuous, rebellious phases of previous generations of youngsters? Is adult concern over today's youth culture just the perennial hand-wringing of parents needlessly worried about their growing offspring's experiments with independence? Or is something else, something far more sinister at work?

---

[1]Patricia Hersch, *A Tribe Apart: A Journey into the Heart of American Adolescence* (New York: Ballantine, 1998), 82–83, 85. [All notes are author's, except 15, 16, 20, and 22.]

"Merchants of Cool"

"They want to be cool. They are impressionable, and they have the cash. They are corporate America's $150 billion dream."[2]

That's the opening statement in PBS's stunning 2001 *Frontline* docu-   15
mentary "The Merchants of Cool," narrated by author and media critic Douglas Rushkoff. What emerges in the following sixty minutes is a scandalous portrait of how major corporations — Viacom, Disney, AOL / Time Warner, and others — study America's children like laboratory rats in order to sell them billions of dollars in merchandise by tempting, degrading, and corrupting them.

Think that's a bit of an overstatement?

It's an understatement.

"When you've got a few gigantic transnational corporations, each one loaded down with debt, competing madly for as much shelf space and brain space as they can take," says NYU communications professor Mark Crispin Miller, "they're going to do whatever they think works the fastest and with the most people, which means that they will drag standards down."[3]

Let's see how far down.

"It's a blizzard of brands, all competing for the same kids," explains   20
Rushkoff. "To win teens' loyalty, marketers believe, they have to speak their language the best. So they study them carefully, as an anthropologist would an exotic native culture."

"Today," Rushkoff discloses, "five enormous companies are responsible for selling nearly all of youth culture. These are the true merchants of cool: Rupert Murdoch's Newscorp, Disney, Viacom, Universal Vivendi, and AOL/Time Warner."[4] The documentary demonstrates how big corporations literally send spies to infiltrate young people's social settings to gather intelligence on what they can induce these children to buy next.

"The entertainment companies, which are a handful of massive conglomerates that own four of the five music companies that sell 90 percent of the music in the United States — those same companies also own all the film studios, all the major TV networks, all the TV stations pretty much in the ten largest markets," University of Illinois communications professor Robert McChesney reveals in the documentary. "They own all or part of every single commercial cable channel.

"They look at the teen market as part of this massive empire that they're colonizing. You should look at it like the British Empire or the French Empire in the nineteenth century. Teens are like Africa. You know,

---

[2]"The Merchants of Cool," *Frontline*, PBS, February 27, 2001; see http://www.pbs.org/ wgbh/pages/frontline/shows/cool. By the way, I highly recommend you and your teenage children view "The Merchants of Cool," which is available at www.shoppbs.org.

[3]Ibid.

[4]Ibid.

that's this range that they're going to take over, and their weaponry are films, music, books, CDs, Internet access, clothing, amusement parks, sports teams. That's all this weaponry they have to make money off of this market."[5]

MTV

What about the cable channel that positions itself as champion of today's teens and preteens — champions of their music, their rebellious free spirit, and their genuine, if ever-changing, notions of what is "cool"? Whatever else MTV might be, at least it's interested in kids, right? Sure, just like the lion is interested in the gazelle.

"Everything on MTV is a commercial," explains McChesney. "That's   25 all that MTV is. Sometimes it's an explicit advertisement paid for by a company to sell a product. Sometimes it's going to be a video for a music company there to sell music. Sometimes it's going to be the set that's filled with trendy clothes and stuff there to sell a look that will include products on that set. Sometimes it will be a show about an upcoming movie paid for by the studio, though you don't know it, to hype a movie that's coming out from Hollywood. But everything's an infomercial. There is no non-commercial part of MTV."[6]

Rushkoff illustrates how the machine works by using the example of Sprite. What was once a struggling, second-string soft-drink company pulled off a brilliant marketing coup by underwriting major hip-hop music events and positioning itself as *the* cool soft drink for the vast MTV-generation market. Connecting the dots between Sprite, MTV, rap musicians, and other cross-promotion participants, Rushkoff lays out the behind-the-scenes game plan: "Sprite rents out the Roseland Ballroom and pays kids 50 bucks a pop to fill it up and look cool. The rap artists who perform for this paid audience get a plug on MTV's show, 'Direct Effects,' for which Sprite is a sponsor. MTV gobbles up the cheap programming, promoting the music of the record companies who advertise on their channel. Everybody's happy."[7]

"So what," you say? "What's wrong with that? Aren't MTV and rappers and clothing companies and others just giving kids what they want?"

That's what they say. But it's not what they do.

In reality, the companies are *creating* new and lower and more shocking — that's the key word, *shocking* — marketing campaigns, disguised as genuine, authentic expressions of youthful searching for identity and belonging, for the sole purpose of profiting financially from America's children.

They hold focus groups. They send out culture spies (which they call   30 "correspondents") to pretend to befriend and care about teens so they can

[5]Ibid.
[6]Ibid.
[7]Ibid.

study them — what they like, don't like, what's in, what's out, what's cool, and what's no longer cool. They engage in "buzz marketing" (where undercover agents talk up a new product). They hire shills to interact with young people in Internet chat rooms, and they engage "street snitches" to loudly talk up a band or other product to raise interest. They bring the entire machinery of modern market research and consumer psychology to bear on studying this gold mine of a market — to anticipate the next, and always weirder and more shocking, incarnation of "cool."

This would be bad enough — if corporate America were just following and marketing the basest instincts of confused, unsupervised teenagers. But they are not following, they are leading — downward. Exhibits A and B: the "mook" and the "midriff," two creations of this corporate youth-marketing consortium.

The mook is a marketing caricature of the wild, uninhibited, outrageous, and amoral male sex maniac. "Take Howard Stern," says Rushkoff, "perhaps the original and still king of all mooks. Look how Viacom leverages him across their properties. He is syndicated on fifty of Viacom's Infinity radio stations. His weekly TV show is broadcast on Viacom's CBS. His number one best-selling autobiography was published by Viacom's Simon and Schuster, then released as a major motion picture by Viacom's Paramount Pictures, grossing $40 million domestically and millions more on videos sold at Viacom's Blockbuster video." Rushkoff adds: "There is no mook in nature. He is a creation designed to capitalize on the testosterone-driven madness of adolescence. He grabs them below the belt and then reaches for their wallets."[8]

A great deal of MTV's programming features and markets to the mook in America's boys. For instance, a major venue of the mook is professional wrestling — one of the most-watched types of television among adolescent boys in America today.

Okay, what about the midriff?

Girls, says Rushkoff, "get dragged down there right along with boys.   35 The media machine has spit out a second caricature. . . . The midriff is no more true to life than the mook. If he is arrested in adolescence, she is prematurely adult. If he doesn't care what people think of him, she is consumed by appearances. If his thing is crudeness, hers is sex. The midriff is really just a collection of the same old sexual clichés, but repackaged as a new kind of female empowerment. 'I am midriff, hear me roar. I am a sexual object, but I'm proud of it.'"[9]

And what is the purpose of these debauched role models for America's future, fashioned out of market research compiled by culture spies hired by corporations to predict what the likely next step *down* — the next *shock wave* disguised as authentic "cool" — will be for the MTV generation? Why, to sell kids more stuff, of course.

[8]Ibid.
[9]Ibid.

"When corporate revenues depend on being ahead of the curve, you have to listen, you have to know exactly what they want and exactly what they're thinking so that you can give them what you want them to have," explains NYU's Crispin Miller. However, he adds, "the MTV machine doesn't listen to the young so it can make the young happier.... The MTV machine tunes in so it can figure out how to pitch what Viacom has to sell."[10]

And how do they manage to bond kids — imprint them — with the next round of musical, clothing, and lifestyle choices they should be buying into?

"Kids are invited to participate in sexual contests on stage or are followed by MTV cameras through their week of debauchery," says Rushkoff. "Sure, some kids have always acted wild, but never have these antics been so celebrated on TV. So of course kids take it as a cue, like here on the strip in Panama Beach, Florida, where high schoolers carry on in public as if they were on some MTV sound stage. Who is mirroring whom? Real life and TV life have begun to blur. Is the media really reflecting the world of kids, or is it the other way around? The answer is increasingly hard to make out."

Then the really devilish part of the marketers' modus operandi comes into view, as host Rushkoff relives his own epiphany: 40

> I'll never forget the moment that thirteen-year-old Barbara and her friends spotted our crew during a party between their auditions. They appeared to be dancing for us, for our camera, as if to sell back to us, the media, what we had sold to them.
>
> And that's when it hit me: It's a giant feedback loop. The media watches kids and then sells them an image of themselves. Then kids watch those images and aspire to be that mook or midriff in the TV set. And the media is there watching them do that in order to craft new images for them, and so on.[11]

"Is there any way to escape the feedback loop?" Rushkoff asks. Only in the kids' minds, he reveals, noting that "cool"-seeking youths continually reach downward to a new, raunchier, more outrageous expression — something, *anything*, as long as it hasn't been exploited and ripped off by the corporate world.

That said, Rushkoff rolls tape of a large, demonic-looking group of teens, faces painted, chanting and screaming obscenities in downtown Detroit on Halloween night. He explains:

> A few thousand mostly white young men have gathered to hear a concert by their favorite hometown band, Insane Clown Posse. ICP helped found a musical genre called rap metal or rage rock, which has created a stir across the country for its shock lyrics and ridicule of women and gays.... Rock music has always channeled rebellion, but

[10]Ibid.
[11]Ibid.

where it used to be directed against parents, teachers, or the government, today it is directed against slick commercialism itself, against MTV. These fans feel loyalty to this band and this music because they experience it as their own. It hasn't been processed by corporations, digested into popular culture and sold back to them at the mall.[12]

A member of Insane Clown Posse explains the group's attraction: "Everybody that likes our music feels a super connection. That's why all those juggaloes here, they feel so connected to it because it's — it's exclusively theirs. See, when something's on the radio, it's for everybody, you know what I mean? It's everybody's song. 'Oh, this is my song.' That ain't your song. It's on the radio. It's everybody's song. But to listen to ICP, you feel like you're the only one that knows about it."

"These are the extremes," intones Rushkoff, "to which teens are willing to go to ensure the authenticity of their own scene. It's the front line of teen cultural resistance: Become so crude, so intolerable, and break so many rules that you become indigestible." To complete the mood, in the background Insane Clown Posse is rapping "Bitch, you's a ho. And ho, you's a bitch. Come on!" and other uplifting lyrics.[13]

Then comes the betrayal. "The Merchants of Cool" shows how Insane Clown Posse and other "authentic" groups — untouched by commercialism — are ultimately bought off by the marketing machine, packaged, and sold back to the youth market. Of course, when the shock value wears off, and the mantle of cool — untouched and uncorrupted by corporate America — moves downward to the next, even more outrageous level of depravity — MTV, Viacom, and the other corporate giants will be there to package it and sell it, once again, to our children.

Oh, but don't bother trying to tell your kids about this fiendish game. You see, says Crispin Miller, "It's part of the official rock video world view, it's part of the official advertising world view, that your parents are creeps, teachers are nerds and idiots, authority figures are laughable, nobody can really understand kids except the corporate sponsor."[14]

Okay, so is that it? America's teens are in the grip of a malignant marketing campaign by big, greedy, uncaring corporations? And hopefully the kids will grow out of it and become normal sometime? End of story?

Not quite. To be sure, millions of youths are in the grip of something destructive, but the corporate aspect is just the visible part. *Behind* both the corporate manipulators and the youths caught in their selfish and shameful influence lurks another, much more formidable and all-pervasive marketing campaign — a malevolent dimension that has no one's best interests at heart and which is programmed to devour all in its path, from the highest to the lowest.

45

[12]Ibid.
[13]Ibid.
[14]Ibid.

That something, which we shall try to identify shortly, is intent on degrading this generation so totally that little hope would be left for the next generations of Americans.

No Limits

If you doubt there's anything more than youthful rebellion and soulless 50 marketing at work in today's youth culture, read on. But fasten your safety belt.

Remember how Sodom and Gomorrah[15] were portrayed in the classic biblical epic films of the 1950s? Drunken men with multiple piercings and bright red robes, one loose woman under each arm, cavorting in orgiastic revelry against a background of annoying, mosquito-like music? Maybe a bone through the nose as well? Hollywood took pains to depict these lost souls in the most debauched and irredeemable manner — to justify their subsequent destruction with fire and brimstone as punishment for their great sinfulness.

Guess what? Those Hollywood depictions don't even *begin* to capture the shocking reality of what is going on in America's culture today — they're not even close.

First of all, there's sex. Very simply, there seem to be neither boundaries nor taboos anymore when it comes to sex. Anything goes — from heterosexual to homosexual to bi-, trans-, poly-, and you-don't-want-to-know sexual experiences. Sex has become a ubiquitous, cheap, meaningless quest for ever-greater thrills. As Dr. Laura Schlessinger[16] quipped, "Men are astonished to discover they don't even need to court a woman, tell little romantic lies about love or the future. All they have to do is show up!"[17]

Moreover, with the evolution of online pornography, every type of sexual experience has literally been shoved under the noses of millions of Americans against their will. They find their e-mail filled with hardcore sexual images. As a result, many pastors are struggling with how to deal with large numbers of churchgoers reportedly caught up with Internet pornography.

What about body piercing? It has progressed from traditional earrings 55 for females, to earrings for males (eager to display their "feminine side" which the '60s "cultural revolution" sold them), to multiple piercings for both males and females in literally every part of the body — the tongue, nose, eyebrow, lip, cheek, navel, breasts, genitals — again, things you don't really want to know.

It's the same progression to extremes with tattooing. But why stop with conventional piercing and tattooing? Ritual scarification and 3D-art implants

---

[15]*Sodom and Gomorrah:* Biblical cities destroyed by God because of their immorality.

[16]*Dr. Laura Schlessinger:* Conservative talk-radio host.

[17]Dr. Laura Schlessinger, "Looking for Love," WorldNetDaily.com, July 1, 2002, online at http://www.wnd.com/news/article.asp?ARTICLE_ID=28138.

are big. So are genital beading, stretching and cutting, transdermal implants, scrotal implants, tooth art, and facial sculpture.

How about tongue splitting? How about branding? How about amputations? That's right — amputations. Some people find these activities a real turn on.

There are no bounds — no lower limits. Whatever you can imagine, even for a second in the darkest recesses of your mind, know that someone somewhere is doing it, praising it, and drawing others into it via the Internet.

Strangest of all is the fact that any behavior, any belief — no matter how obviously insane — is rationalized so it sounds reasonable, even spiritual. Satanism, and especially its variant, the worship of Lucifer (literally, "Angel of Light") can be made to sound almost enlightened — of course, only in a perverse way. But if you were sufficiently confused, rebellious, and full of rage — if you had been set up by cruelty or hypocrisy (or both) to rebel against everything good — the forbidden starts to be mysteriously attractive.

Let's pick just one of these bizarre behaviors. How about hanging by your skin from hooks? It's called suspension. In literally any other context, this would be considered a gruesome torture. But to many people who frequent suspension parties, it's a spiritual experience. Consider carefully what Body Modification Ezine (www.bmezine.com) — the Web's premiere site for body modification — says about suspension:

WHAT IS SUSPENSION?
The act of suspension is hanging the human body from (or partially from) hooks pierced through the flesh in various places around the body.

WHY WOULD SOMEONE WANT TO DO A SUSPENSION?
There are many different reasons to suspend, from pure adrenaline or endorphin rush, to conquering one's fears, to trying to reach a new level of spiritual consciousness and everything in between. In general, people suspend to attain some sort of "experience."
Some people are seeking the opportunity to discover a deeper sense of themselves and to challenge pre-determined belief systems which may not be true. Some are seeking a rite of passage or a spiritual encounter to let go of the fear of not being whole or complete inside their body.
Others are looking for control over their body, or seek to prove to themselves that they are more than their bodies, or are not their bodies at all. Others simply seek to explore the unknown.
Many people believe that learning how one lives inside one's body and seeing how that body adapts to stress — and passes through it — allows one to surrender to life and explore new realms of possibility.

Gosh — "control over their body," "discover a deeper sense of themselves," "conquering ones fears," "trying to reach a new level of spiritual consciousness." What could be wrong with that?

Or, how about tongue splitting — literally making yourself look like a human lizard — how could that be a positive, spiritual experience?

"The tongue," explains the BME Web site, "is one of the most immense nervous structures in your body. We have incredibly fine control over it and we receive massive feedback from it. When you dramatically alter its structure and free yourself of the physical boundaries your biology imposes, in some people it triggers a larger freeing on a spiritual level."

Here's one more experience I'll bet you didn't realize was so uplifting — getting AIDS.

Oh, you haven't heard about "bug-chasing"? *Rolling Stone* did a controversial exposé on this new underground movement. Very simply, bug-chasers are people for whom getting infected with the AIDS virus is the ultimate sexual experience. You heard it right: the main focus of their lives is to seek out sexual encounters that will infect them with HIV.

Reporter Gregory A. Freeman explained the phenomenon, focusing initially on a bug-chaser named Carlos:

> Carlos is part of an intricate underground world that has sprouted, driven almost completely by the Internet, in which men who want to be infected with HIV get together with those who are willing to infect them. The men who want the virus are called "bug chasers," and the men who freely give the virus to them are called "gift givers." While the rest of the world fights the AIDS epidemic and most people fear HIV infection, this subculture celebrates the virus and eroticizes it.
>
> HIV-infected semen is treated like liquid gold. Carlos has been chasing the bug for more than a year in a topsy-turvy world in which every convention about HIV is turned upside down. The virus isn't horrible and fearsome, it's beautiful and sexy — and delivered in the way that is most likely to result in infection. In this world, the men with HIV are the most desired, and the bug chasers will do anything to get the virus — to "get knocked up," to be "bred" or "initiated into the brotherhood."

And what, exactly, motivates Carlos and his bug-chasing colleagues?

> For Carlos, bug chasing is mostly about the excitement of doing something that everyone else sees as crazy and wrong. Keeping this part of his life secret is part of the turn-on for Carlos, which is not his real name. That forbidden aspect makes HIV infection incredibly exciting for him, so much so that he now seeks out sex exclusively with HIV-positive men. "This is something that no one knows about me," Carlos says. "It's mine. It's my dirty little secret."

Deliberately infecting themselves, explains Freeman, "is the ultimate taboo, the most extreme sex act left on the planet, and that has a strong erotic appeal for some men who have tried everything else."[18]

[18]Gregory A. Freeman, "Bug Chasers: The Men Who Long to Be HIV+," *Rolling Stone,* February 26, 2003.

No question about it: the forbidden is very attractive. As pop star Britney Spears admitted to an interviewer: "When someone tells me not to do something, I do it, that's just my rebellious nature." Similarly, Carlos's thrill at having a "dirty little secret" is a very common theme sounded by people explaining why they had some hidden body part pierced.

Why are so many attracted to the forbidden? Why is it so exciting?   70

In Love with Death

In the West we marvel at the death-oriented Islamic jihad subculture, which in some areas, particularly among the Palestinians, has become the dominant culture, a culture of death. We shake our heads sadly as we contemplate children growing up with the desire, above all else, to martyr themselves — which to them means blowing themselves up while killing as many Jews as possible and believing they're going to heaven.

These young people, caught up in the rage-fueled Islamist marketing campaign of global jihad, can look you right in the eye and express with great passion their conviction that committing mass murder is the mystical doorway to eternal life. Yet, in much the same way, bug-chasing men who seek AIDS, people suspending themselves from the ceiling by meat hooks, those who literally slice their own tongues in two — and even, albeit on a much more subtle level, "regular" people obsessed with the thought of getting their next piercing or tattoo — feel as though they, too, are moving, not toward death, but toward life and greater "spirituality," a more unique and authentic sense of self. Somehow the ritual of pain and mutilation or, in extreme cases, death drives out their awareness of inner conflict, replacing it with an illusion of freedom and selfhood.

Here's how psychotherapist Steven Levenkron, best-selling author and one of the nation's foremost experts on anorexia and other emotion-based illnesses, explains it in his landmark book *Cutting: Understanding and Overcoming Self-Mutilation:* "The self-mutilator is someone who has found that physical pain can be a cure for emotional pain."

After years of counseling patients, mostly young women, who purposely cut their bodies with razors and knives to obtain relief from emotional conflict, Levenkron concluded:

> Self-mutilators have many different reasons for their actions and are tormented by a spectrum of different feelings. Yet I consistently encounter two characteristics in all self-mutilators:
>
> 1. A feeling of mental disintegration, of inability to think.
> 2. A rage that can't be expressed, or even consciously perceived, toward a powerful figure (or figures) in their life, usually a parent.
>
> For the self-mutilator, the experience of one or both of these feelings is unbearable and must therefore be "drowned out," as they report, by some immediate method. Physical pain and the sight of oneself bleeding

become solutions because of their ability to overpower the strength of those feelings.

Usually, the first incident begins with strong feelings of anger, anxiety, or panic. If the feeling is not too intense, throwing an object, or breaking or knocking something over, may settle the person down. It's when the person becomes so overwhelmed that none of these "remedies" help that we may see them plunge a fist into a wall or through a window, bang their head against a wall, or finally take a weapon to use against themselves.

Someone who stumbles upon self-injury in this manner and discovers that it relieves one of the painful states listed above will be inclined to use this discovery again in the future. The individual who needs this kind of solution is a person who cannot redress the grievances she has with others, who is afraid to argue, to articulate what she is so angry about. The self-mutilator is ashamed of the mental pain that she experiences and has no language with which to describe it to others.

However they came to it, the self-mutilator is someone who has found that physical pain can be a cure for emotional pain. . . . When a person attacks his or her own body with an instrument that will wound the skin, and often worse, it means that the person feels helpless to use any other means to manage the mental anguish and chaos that is borne out of unmanageable feelings.[19]

Although Levenkron is describing a psychiatric syndrome afflicting young girls who ritualistically cut themselves to relieve inner pain, much of the same dynamic is at work to some degree in multitudes of people today finding solace and identity in self-destructive sexuality, pain, and disfigurement. For example, here's how one person explained her decision to have her tongue pierced, writing on the BME Web site: 75

I love piercings and wanted to do it but the guy that I'm interested in disapproved of it. So, I was reluctant to do the piercing seeing as I didn't want to start a relationship and having a piercing in an area that would affect our physical activities. Anyway, it turns out the bastard slept with my best friend the other night and I knew a new piercing had to take place. Weird, but getting a new piercing helps me to focus all my mental pain and then release it with the physical and also it leaves a nice looking piece of jewelry as well!

Her anger is extinguished, at least temporarily, by piercing her own body.

Piercing the Veil

"For we wrestle not against flesh and blood, but against principalities, against powers, against the rulers of the darkness of this world, against spiritual wickedness in high places" (Ephesians 6:12).

---

[19]Steven Levenkron, *Cutting: Understanding and Overcoming Self-Mutilation* (New York: Norton, 1998), 44–45.

Earlier in this exploration of youth culture we "pierced" the corporate veil, discovering the shameful marketing reality behind today's youth culture. Let's go the rest of the way now and pierce the spiritual veil.

History is full of times and places when *something* — call it a spirit if you wish — sweeps over a particular society. This something is drawn, as into a vacuum, into societies that have lost their way and have harkened to the voice of deceitful leaders and philosophies. During the mid-twentieth century a malevolent spirit swept over Germany, leading to unspeakable crimes being perpetrated against millions of Jews and other "undesirables" in the name of progress. In the late '70s the demonic spirit of Marxist "cleansing" swept through Cambodia[20] like a raging wildfire, resulting in the brutal deaths of perhaps two million. And today we see the worldwide spread of a maniacal jihad suicide cult that is attracting literally millions of Muslims.

But this phenomenon is evident not only in genocidal frenzies. The counterculture revolution of the 1960s was, to many, a spiritual phenomenon with profound reverberations to the present. Likewise, the New Age movement, the preoccupation with "channeling" and UFOs, and other similar movements have an uncanny spiritual, religious dimension that can't be ignored.

True, mass conformity even to bizarre beliefs and practices can be explained somewhat by the sheer power of peer pressure, but there is more to it. It's more akin to mass hypnosis, where large numbers of people simultaneously adopt the same bizarre mind-set, beliefs, and practices. Such instances of spiritual "possession" of a society, of a people made ripe for such a downward transformation by their sins and rebellion against God, are evident throughout history.

Well, now, is it just my imagination, or is there something about today's celebratory piercing and tattooing of the body and the free sex that permeates this culture that literally evokes the spirit of Sodom and Gomorrah? It's as though the rebellious spirit of reprobate, pagan civilizations of the past was being tapped into by today's pop culture.

"Oh, come on," you might say, dismissively. "They're just adorning the human body to make it more beautiful and unique. Let them have their fun. Who are they hurting?" Such mellifluous excuses spring up in our minds quite easily, as most certainly they did also in the time of Sodom, Gomorrah, and other perverse societies.

The fact is, what has risen "out of the pit" in today's world bears a striking resemblance to the ageless spirit of defiant paganism, a spirit now inhabiting millions of people "freed" by trauma (drugs, illicit sex, bodily mutilation, and so on) from the pain of their own conscience — which is to

---

[20]*Cambodia:* The Cambodian Khmer Rouge party ordered the deaths of between one and two million Cambodians in the late 1970s, supposedly because they were enemies of the state.

say, freed from God and the divine law written deep down in every person's heart. Why? Same reason as always: so they can be their own gods and make up their own rules.

Of course, in a very real sense they are also victims — they've been set up for all of this. For not only has today's popular culture — from its astonishing gender confusion to its perverse and powerful musical expression — become toxic virtually without precedent in modern history, but also most parents have not protected their own kids from it. 85

In past eras, if parents were very imperfect, even corrupt, children still had a reasonable chance of "growing up straight," since the rest of society more or less reflected Judeo-Christian values. The youngster could bond to a teacher, minister, mentor, or organization that could provide some healthy direction and stability. But today, because of the near-ubiquitous corruption "out there," if parents fail to properly guide and protect their children, the kids get swallowed whole by the culture. And as talk-show host Bob Just puts it so aptly, "Today's culture is a child molester."[21]

Let me make the point this way: Your being any way other than *genuinely virtuous* — not perfect, mind you, but honestly and diligently seeking to do the right thing at all times — will tend to drive your children crazy. Here's how the craziness unfolds. Children deserve and desperately need firmness, patience, fairness, limits, kindness, insight, and a good, non-hypocritical example. In other words, they need genuine parental love and guidance. If they don't get this, they will resent you. Even if you can't see it, even if they can't see it, and deny it, they will resent you for failing to give them real love.

And that resentment — which becomes suppressed rage — is a destructive, unpredictable, radioactive foreign element in their makeup, which then transmutes into every manner of problem, complex, and evil imaginable. It makes children feel compelled to rebel against you and against all authority out of revenge for your having failed them. And it makes everything forbidden — from sex to drugs to tongue studs to things worse — seem attractive, like a road to personal freedom. Rationalizations and philosophies that they would have once laughed at as ridiculous now make sense to them. Practices they would have shunned in more innocent times, they now not only embrace but celebrate. All of this usually occurs below the level of consciousness.

Today's youth rebellion is not only against failing parents but against the entire adult society — against the children of the 1960s cultural revolution who grew up to become their parents. Unfortunately, many of us never shook off the transforming effects of that national trauma, which birthed the "sex, drugs, and rock 'n' roll" youth counterculture, the leftist hate-America

---

[21]Bob Just, "Killer Culture: A Call to the Churches," WorldNetDaily.com, January 26, 2004, online at http://www.wnd.com/news/article.asp?ARTICLE_ID=36769.

movement, the women's liberation movement, and overriding all, of course, the sexual revolution.

So we grew up to elect one of our own — a traumatized, amoral baby 90 boomer named Bill Clinton. If you don't think Clinton's escapades[22] with Monica Lewinsky — covered by the media like the Super Bowl — had *everything* to do with the explosion of middle-school sexual adventures across America, then open your eyes. We, the parents of this generation, along with the degrading entertainment media, the biased news media, the lying politicians, the brainwashing government school system, and the rest of society's once-great institutions whose degradation we have tolerated, are responsible.

No wonder our children are rebelling. And today's insane Sodom-and-Gomorrah culture, which we have allowed and in many ways created, stands waiting in the wings to welcome them with open arms.

The Way Out

Today's culture is so poisonous that your only hope is to literally create (or plug into) another culture entirely — a subculture. Just as today's homosexual culture, for example, used to be a miserable subculture lurking in public toilets and seedy clubs, but today has become the sophisticated culture of the "beautiful people" and Hollywood, so must your true American culture — if it's ever to come back — begin again as a subculture.

The best solution I know of for accomplishing this is to homeschool your children and network with other like-minded parents in your area. Trust me, it's already being done, you're not reinventing the wheel. Sports, music, drama, Scouts, 4-H, whatever extracurricular activities you want are all available to homeschoolers. You can literally pick and choose the culture in which your children grow up, and you can actively participate in its creation. I believe homeschooling today represents the single most important and promising avenue for the true rebirth of American Judeo-Christian culture. The real America is now being reborn in families where children are raised with real understanding and insight and protected from the insanity of the popular culture until they're big enough and strong enough in their convictions to go out in the world and make their mark. May it only grow.

What if your children are already caught up in the youth subculture? Is it too late?

No, it's not. But it may be a difficult and long road back. It's a lot easier 95 to be corrupted than to become uncorrupted. Just know this: there is something almost magically liberating about confession. For parents to honestly confess their mistakes, regrets, failings, selfishness, and blindness to their

---

[22]*Clinton's escapades:* Refers to the Washington sex scandal involving then-President Bill Clinton and White House intern Monica Lewinsky in the late 1990s.

errant offspring is a spiritual experience for all involved. Of course, when youngsters have been "converted" to new loyalties and beliefs, maintained by unconscious rage and rebellion (and perhaps the desire for revenge), they may or may not right away want to come back over to your side. But by being truly repentant over your own culpability in their problem, and confessing this openly and genuinely — and from now on being the kind of person you always should have been — you are giving them the best chance possible to forgive you and find redemption themselves.

Even if they don't come around, or if it takes a long time, your honest self-examination and confession as a parent will free you from your own guilts and past sins. Beyond this, we need to have faith that, with God, all things are possible.

Following Higher Law

"A Scout is trustworthy . . . loyal . . . helpful . . . friendly . . . courteous . . . kind . . . obedient . . . cheerful . . . thrifty . . . brave . . . clean . . . and reverent."

As I stand there, listening to these boys recite the Scout law, I know what I'm looking at. These kids — young men, really — their afterburners roaring on a fabulous fuel mixture of youthful energy, playfulness, intelligence, testosterone, and dedication to higher things, are literally the future of America. I am grateful that at least a few institutions in today's world still exert a positive influence on children. I marvel at the powerful pull the Scout ethic has on them. It binds their lower impulses, hems them in, and appeals to the "better angels" of their nature.

Now they're reciting the Scout oath: "On my honor, I will do my best to do my duty to God and my Country, and to obey the Scout Law, to help other people at all times, to keep myself physically strong, mentally awake, and morally straight."

Or course — the Scouts, as well as other good institutions like our churches and even marriage itself — are torn at mercilessly from the outside by heartless activists. And they are torn at from within — by the occasional rotten Scout leader whose ultimate aim is to molest children. And yes, even within Scouts, the kids bring a bit of that *killer culture* in with them. Yet the Scout oath and law, the adult leaders, the time-tested-and-proven program, and the *positive* peer pressure — all of these beckon the boys to embrace a higher calling.

May we all do likewise. If we do, we can redeem our wretched culture one child, one family at a time. And those little swatches of the real American culture, the bits of heaven on earth residing in this home and that home and this church and that Scout troop will one day, please God, join together to form the fabric of a reborn American culture of virtue. Each of us must take that lonely high road. Otherwise, the marketers of evil will lead us all down to ever darker and lower levels of hell on earth.

ENGAGING THE TEXT

1. What are the hallmarks of America's "killer culture," according to Kupelian? What's wrong, in his view, with the marketing of "coolness" to kids? Would you agree that American teen culture is becoming increasingly "toxic"? Why or why not?

2. How accurate, in your estimation, is Kupelian's depiction of the "mook" and "midriff" as images of the ideal MTV generation male and female adolescent? Would you agree that there's a media conspiracy to promote these degraded forms of male and female identity?

3. Why are American teens so angry, in Kupelian's view? What other reasons might explain the grievances and anxieties of America's youth?

4. What, according to Kupelian, is the solution to the problem of our toxic culture? To what extent would you agree that parents can "pick and choose the culture in which [their] children grow up"?

EXPLORING CONNECTIONS

5. What do you think Kupelian would say about the image of Madonna on the cross (p. 613) that opens this chapter? Does this photo strike you as an example of "killer culture"? Why or why not?

6. How might Kupelian explain the difficulties Anne Lamott encountered in her personal search for faith (p. 620) How do you think Lamott would have reacted if her father had followed Kupelian's advice?

7. Write a dialogue between Kupelian and John Taylor Gatto (p. 152) on the influence of contemporary corporate culture on American children. Do you think that most American teens would be better off if they were home-schooled, as both Gatto and Kupelian suggest?

EXTENDING THE CRITICAL CONTEXT

8. Research the origins of some of the more extreme practices that Kupelian criticizes in this selection — activities like piercing, body modification, and "suspension." To what extent does your research indicate that people involved in these practices view them in "spiritual" terms?

9. Working in groups, tape and analyze a few hours of MTV programming and then conduct your own analysis to determine if there is such a thing as a "rock video world view," as Mark Crispin Miller claims (p. 654). How would you describe the worldview conveyed by MTV and other teen-oriented television programming?

10. Research the origins and philosophy of the American 1960s counterculture. How many different movements contributed to what we term the "counterculture"? How did these movements arise and what were their values and beliefs? Would you agree with Kupelian that the counterculture paved the way for the "downward transformation" of society?

The Christian Paradox: How a Faithful Nation Gets Jesus Wrong

BILL MCKIBBEN

What would Jesus do? According to Bill McKibben, the answer to this question depends a lot on which Jesus you believe in. One of the nation's leading environmentalists and advocates of rural life, McKibben feels that American Christianity is in danger of losing its way — and losing sight of the most fundamental teachings of the Gospels. Currently a scholar-in-residence at Middlebury College, McKibben (b. 1960) is the author of numerous books and articles, including The End of Nature *(1989),* The Age of Missing Information *(1992),* Wandering Home: A Long Walk Across America's Most Hopeful Landscape *(2005), and* The Comforting Whirlwind: God, Job, and the Scale of Creation *(2005).*

Only 40 percent of Americans can name more than four of the Ten Commandments, and a scant half can cite any of the four authors of the Gospels. Twelve percent believe Joan of Arc[1] was Noah's wife.[2] This failure to recall the specifics of our Christian heritage may be further evidence of our nation's educational decline, but it probably doesn't matter all that much in spiritual or political terms. Here is a statistic that does matter: Three quarters of Americans believe the Bible teaches that "God helps those who help themselves." That is, three out of four Americans believe that this uber-American idea, a notion at the core of our current individualist politics and culture, which was in fact uttered by Ben Franklin, actually appears in Holy Scripture. The thing is, not only is Franklin's wisdom not biblical; it's counter-biblical. Few ideas could be further from the gospel message, with its radical summons to love of neighbor. On this essential matter, most Americans — most American *Christians* — are simply wrong, as if 75 percent of American scientists believed that Newton[3] proved gravity causes apples to fly up.

Asking Christians what Christ taught isn't a trick. When we say we are a Christian nation — and, overwhelmingly, we do — it means something. People who go to church absorb lessons there and make real decisions based on those lessons; increasingly, these lessons inform their politics. (One poll found that 11 percent of U.S. churchgoers were urged by their

---

[1]*Joan of Arc:* At age seventeen, Joan (1412–1431) led French forces to the first of several important victories during the Hundred Years' War with England; she was canonized as a saint in 1920.

[2]*Noah's wife:* Wife of the famed ark builder in the Book of Genesis.

[3]*Newton:* Among other notable achievements, English mathematician and physicist Sir Isaac Newton (1643–1727) formulated key laws of motion that led to an understanding of gravity.

clergy to vote in a particular way in the 2004 election, up from 6 percent in 2000.) When George Bush says that Jesus Christ is his favorite philosopher, he may or may not be sincere, but he is reflecting the sincere beliefs of the vast majority of Americans.

And therein is the paradox. America is simultaneously the most professedly Christian of the developed nations and the least Christian in its behavior. That paradox — more important, perhaps, than the much touted ability of French women to stay thin on a diet of chocolate and cheese — illuminates the hollow at the core of our boastful, careening culture.

Ours is among the most spiritually homogenous rich nations on earth. Depending on which poll you look at and how the question is asked, somewhere around 85 percent of us call ourselves Christian. Israel, by way of comparison, is 77 percent Jewish. It is true that a smaller number of Americans — about 75 percent — claim they actually pray to God on a daily basis, and only 33 percent say they manage to get to church every week. Still, even if that 85 percent overstates actual practice, it clearly represents aspiration. In fact, there is nothing else that unites more than four-fifths of America. Every other statistic one can cite about American behavior is essentially also a measure of the behavior of professed Christians. That's what America is: a place saturated in Christian identity.

But is it *Christian?* This is not a matter of angels dancing on the heads   5 of pins.[4] Christ was pretty specific about what he had in mind for his followers. What if we chose some simple criterion — say, giving aid to the poorest people — as a reasonable proxy for Christian behavior? After all, in the days before his crucifixion, when Jesus summed up his message for his disciples, he said the way you could tell the righteous from the damned was by whether they'd fed the hungry, slaked the thirsty, clothed the naked, welcomed the stranger, and visited the prisoner. What would we find then?

In 2004, as a share of our economy, we ranked second to last, after Italy, among developed countries in government foreign aid. Per capita we each provide fifteen cents a day in official development assistance to poor countries. And it's not because we were giving to private charities for relief work instead. Such funding increases our average daily donation by just six pennies, to twenty-one cents. It's also not because Americans were too busy taking care of their own; nearly 18 percent of American children lived in poverty (compared with, say, 8 percent in Sweden). In fact, by pretty much any measure of caring for the least among us you want to propose — childhood nutrition, infant mortality, access to preschool — we come in nearly last among the rich nations, and often by a wide margin. The point is not just that (as everyone already knows) the American nation trails badly in

---

[4]*angels dancing . . . :* Medieval scholars were said to have argued over such topics as the number of angels who could dance on the head of a pin. In short, a useless or foolish matter.

all these categories; it's that the overwhelmingly *Christian* American nation trails badly in all these categories, categories to which Jesus paid particular attention. And it's not as if the numbers are getting better: the U.S. Department of Agriculture reported last year that the number of households that were "food insecure with hunger" had climbed more than 26 percent between 1999 and 2003.

This Christian nation also tends to make personal, as opposed to political, choices that the Bible would seem to frown upon. Despite the Sixth Commandment, we are, of course, the most violent rich nation on earth, with a murder rate four or five times that of our European peers. We have prison populations greater by a factor of six or seven than other rich nations (which at least should give us plenty of opportunity for visiting the prisoners). Having been told to turn the other cheek, we're the only Western democracy left that executes its citizens, mostly in those states where Christianity is theoretically strongest. Despite Jesus' strong declarations against divorce, our marriages break up at a rate — just over half — that compares poorly with the European Union's average of about four in ten. That average may be held down by the fact that Europeans marry less frequently, and by countries, like Italy, where divorce is difficult; still, compare our success with, say, that of the godless Dutch, whose divorce rate is just over 37 percent. Teenage pregnancy? We're at the top of the charts. Personal self-discipline — like, say, keeping your weight under control? Buying on credit? Running government deficits? Do you need to ask?

Are Americans hypocrites? Of course they are. But most people (me, for instance) are hypocrites. The more troubling explanation for this disconnect between belief and action, I think, is that most Americans — which means most believers — have replaced the Christianity of the Bible, with its call for deep sharing and personal sacrifice, with a competing creed.

In fact, there may be several competing creeds. For many Christians, deciphering a few passages of the Bible to figure out the schedule for the End Times has become a central task. You can log on to RaptureReady.com[5] for a taste of how some of these believers view the world — at this writing the Rapture Index had declined three points to 152 because, despite an increase in the number of U.S. pagans, "WalMart is falling behind in its plan to bar code all products with radio tags." Other End Timers are more interested in forcing the issue — they're convinced that the way to coax the Lord back to earth is to "Christianize" our nation and then the world. Consider House Majority Leader Tom DeLay. At church one day he listened as the

---

[5]*RaptureReady.com:* "The rapture" refers to a Biblical belief rooted in 1 Thessalonians 4:16–17: "For the Lord himself shall descend from heaven with a shout, with the voice of the archangel, and with the trump of God: and the dead in Christ shall rise first: Then we which are alive and remain shall be caught up together with them in the clouds, to meet the Lord in the air: and so shall we ever be with the Lord."

pastor, urging his flock to support the administration, declared that "the war between America and Iraq is the gateway to the Apocalypse." DeLay rose to speak, not only to the congregation but to 225 Christian TV and radio stations. "Ladies and gentlemen," he said, "what has been spoken here tonight is the truth of God."

The apocalyptics may not be wrong. One could make a perfectly serious   10 argument that the policies of Tom DeLay are in fact hastening the End Times. But there's nothing particularly Christian about this hastening. The creed of Tom DeLay — of Tim LaHaye and his *Left Behind* books, of Pat Robertson's "The Antichrist is probably a Jew alive in Israel today" — ripened out of the impossibly poetic imagery of the Book of Revelation. Imagine trying to build a theory of the Constitution by obsessively reading and rereading the Twenty-fifth Amendment, and you'll get an idea of what an odd approach this is. You might be able to spin elaborate fantasies about presidential succession, but you'd have a hard time working backwards to "We the People." This is the contemporary version of Archbishop Ussher's seventeenth-century calculation that the world had been created on October 23, 4004 B.C., and that the ark touched down on Mount Ararat on May 5, 2348 B.C., a Wednesday. Interesting, but a distant distraction from the gospel message.

The apocalyptics, however, are the lesser problem. It is another competing (though sometimes overlapping) creed, this one straight from the sprawling megachurches of the new exurbs, that frightens me most. Its deviation is less obvious precisely because it looks so much like the rest of the culture. In fact, most of what gets preached in these palaces isn't loony at all. It is disturbingly conventional. The pastors focus relentlessly on *you* and your individual needs. Their goal is to service consumers — not communities but individuals: "seekers" is the term of art, people who feel the need for some spirituality in their (or their children's) lives but who aren't tightly bound to any particular denomination or school of thought. The result is often a kind of soft-focus, comfortable, suburban faith.

A *New York Times* reporter visiting one booming megachurch outside Phoenix recently found the typical scene: a drive-through latte stand, Krispy Kreme doughnuts at every service, and sermons about "how to discipline your children, how to reach your professional goals, how to invest your money, how to reduce your debt." On Sundays children played with church-distributed Xboxes, and many congregants had signed up for a twice-weekly aerobics class called Firm Believers. A list of bestsellers compiled monthly by the Christian Booksellers Association illuminates the creed. It includes texts like *Your Best Life Now* by Joel Osteen — pastor of a church so mega it recently leased a 16,000-seat sports arena in Houston for its services — which even the normally tolerant *Publishers Weekly* dismissed as "a treatise on how to get God to serve the demands of self-centered individuals." Nearly as high is Beth Moore, with her *Believing God* — "Beth asks the tough questions concerning the fruit of our Christian lives," such as "are we

living as fully as we can?" Other titles include *Humor for a Woman's Heart,*
a collection of "humorous writings" designed to "lift a life above the
stresses and strains of the day"; *The Five Love Languages,* in which Dr. Gary
Chapman helps you figure out if you're speaking in the same emotional dialect as your significant other; and Karol Ladd's *The Power of a
Positive Woman.* Ladd is the co-founder of USA Sonshine Girls — the "Son"
in Sonshine, of course, is the son of God — and she is unremittingly
upbeat in presenting her five-part plan for creating a life with "more calm,
less stress."

   Not that any of this is so bad in itself. We *do* have stressful lives, humor
does help, and you *should* pay attention to your own needs. Comfortable
suburbanites watch their parents die, their kids implode. Clearly I need
help with being positive. And I have no doubt that such texts have turned
people into better parents, better spouses, better bosses. It's just that these
authors, in presenting their perfectly sensible advice, somehow manage to
ignore Jesus' radical and demanding focus on *others.* It may, in fact, be true
that "God helps those who help themselves," both financially and emotionally. (Certainly fortune does.) But if so it's still a subsidiary, secondary truth,
more Franklinity than Christianity. You could eliminate the scriptural references in most of these bestsellers and they would still make or not make the
same amount of sense. *Chicken Soup for the Zoroastrian Soul.* It is a perfect mirror of the secular bestseller lists, indeed of the secular culture, with
its American fixation on self-improvement, on self-esteem. On self. These
similarities make it difficult (although not impossible) for the televange-
lists to posit themselves as embattled figures in a "culture war" — they offer
too uncanny a reflection of the dominant culture, a culture of unrelenting
self-obsession.

   Who am I to criticize someone else's religion? After all, if there is anything Americans agree on, it's that we should tolerate everyone else's religious expression. As a *Newsweek* writer put it some years ago at the end of
his cover story on apocalyptic visions and the Book of Revelation,[6] "Who's
to say that John's mythic battle between Christ and Antichrist is not a valid
insight into what the history of humankind is all about?" (Not *Newsweek,*
that's for sure; their religious covers are guaranteed big sellers.) To that I
can only answer that I'm a . . . Christian.

   Not a professional one; I'm an environmental writer mostly. I've never   15
progressed further in the church hierarchy than Sunday school teacher at my
backwoods Methodist church. But I've spent most of my Sunday mornings in
a pew. I grew up in church youth groups and stayed active most of my adult
life — started homeless shelters in church basements, served soup at the

---

   [6]*the Book of Revelation:* Often attributed to John the Apostle, the last book in the New
Testament, which describes the apocalypse — the end of the world and second coming of Jesus
Christ.

church food pantry, climbed to the top of the rickety ladder to put the star on the church Christmas tree. My work has been, at times, influenced by all that — I've written extensively about the Book of Job,[7] which is to me the first great piece of nature writing in the Western tradition, and about the overlaps between Christianity and environmentalism. In fact, I imagine I'm one of a fairly small number of writers who have had cover stories in both the *Christian Century*, the magazine of liberal mainline Protestantism, and *Christianity Today*, which Billy Graham[8] founded, not to mention articles in *Sojourners*, the magazine of the progressive evangelical community co-founded by Jim Wallis.

Indeed, it was my work with religious environmentalists that first got me thinking along the lines of this essay. We were trying to get politicians to understand why the Bible actually mandated protecting the world around us (Noah: the first Green), work that I think is true and vital. But one day it occurred to me that the parts of the world where people actually had cut dramatically back on their carbon emissions, actually did live voluntarily in smaller homes and take public transit, were the same countries where people were giving aid to the poor and making sure everyone had health care — countries like Norway and Sweden, where religion was relatively unimportant. How could that be? For Christians there should be something at least a little scary in the notion that, absent the magical answers of religion, people might just get around to solving their problems and strengthening their communities in more straightforward ways.

But for me, in any event, the European success is less interesting than the American failure. Because we're not going to be like them. Maybe we'd be better off if we abandoned religion for secular rationality, but we're not going to; for the foreseeable future this will be a "Christian" nation. The question is, what kind of Christian nation?

The tendencies I've been describing — toward an apocalyptic End Times faith, toward a comfort-the-comfortable, personal-empowerment faith — veil the actual, and remarkable, message of the Gospels. When one of the Pharisees[9] asked Jesus what the core of the law was, Jesus replied:

> You shall love the Lord your God with all your heart, and with all your soul, and with all your mind. This is the greatest and first commandment. And a second is like it, You shall love your neighbor as yourself. On these two commandments hang all the law and the prophets.

---

[7]*the Book of Job:* Often considered one of the greatest and most challenging episodes in the Old Testament, the Book of Job describes how God allows Satan to subject the most righteous of men to repeated trials and tests, ending with Job's protest and God's assertion of his unquestionable authority as the creator of the natural world.

[8]*Billy Graham:* American evangelical preacher (b. 1918).

[9]*Pharisees:* Members of an ancient Jewish sect that emphasized strict interpretation and observance of religious law.

Love your neighbor as yourself: although its rhetorical power has been dimmed by repetition, that is a radical notion, perhaps the most radical notion possible. Especially since Jesus, in all his teachings, made it very clear who the neighbor you were supposed to love was: the poor person, the sick person, the naked person, the hungry person. The last shall be made first; turn the other cheek; a rich person aiming for heaven is like a camel trying to walk through the eye of a needle. On and on and on — a call for nothing less than a radical, voluntary, and effective reordering of power relationships, based on the principle of love.

I confess, even as I write these words, to a feeling close to embarrass- 20 ment. Because in public we tend not to talk about such things — my theory of what Jesus mostly meant seems like it should be left in church, or confined to some religious publication. But remember the overwhelming connection between America and Christianity; what Jesus meant is the most deeply potent political, cultural, social question. To ignore it, or leave it to the bullies and the salesmen of the televangelist sects, means to walk away from a central battle over American identity. At the moment, the idea of Jesus has been hijacked by people with a series of causes that do not reflect his teachings. The Bible is a long book, and even the Gospels have plenty in them, some of it seemingly contradictory and hard to puzzle out. But love your neighbor as yourself — not do unto others as you would have them do unto you, but *love your neighbor as yourself* — will suffice as a gloss. There is no disputing the centrality of this message, nor is there any disputing how easy it is to ignore that message. Because it is so counterintuitive, Christians have had to keep repeating it to themselves right from the start. Consider Paul, for instance, instructing the church at Galatea: "For the whole law is summed up in a single commandment," he wrote. " 'You shall love your neighbor as yourself.' "

American churches, by and large, have done a pretty good job of loving the neighbor in the next pew. A pastor can spend all Sunday talking about the Rapture Index, but if his congregation is thriving you can be assured he's spending the other six days visiting people in the hospital, counseling couples, and sitting up with grieving widows. All this human connection is important. But if the theology makes it harder to love the neighbor a little farther away — particularly the poor and the weak — then it's a problem. And the dominant theologies of the moment do just that. They undercut Jesus, muffle his hard words, deaden his call, and in the end silence him. In fact, the soft-focus consumer gospel of the suburban megachurches is a perfect match for emergent conservative economic notions about personal responsibility instead of collective action. Privatize Social Security? Keep health care for people who can afford it? File those under "God helps those who help themselves."

Take Alabama as an example. In 2002, Bob Riley was elected governor of the state, where 90 percent of residents identify themselves as Christians. Riley could safely be called a conservative — right-wing majordomo Grover

Norquist[10] gave him a Friend of the Taxpayer Award every year he was in Congress, where he'd never voted for a tax increase. But when he took over Alabama, he found himself administering a tax code that dated to 1901. The richest Alabamians paid 3 percent of their income in taxes, and the poorest paid up to 12 percent; income taxes kicked in if a family of four made $4,600 (even in Mississippi the threshold was $19,000), while out-of-state timber companies paid $1.25 an acre in property taxes. Alabama was forty-eighth in total state and local taxes, and the largest proportion of that income came from sales tax — a super-regressive tax that in some counties reached into double digits. So Riley proposed a tax hike, partly to dig the state out of a fiscal crisis and partly to put more money into the state's school system, routinely ranked near the worst in the nation. He argued that it was Christian duty to look after the poor more carefully.

Had the new law passed, the owner of a $250,000 home in Montgomery would have paid $1,432 in property taxes — we're not talking Sweden here. But it didn't pass. It was crushed by a factor of two to one. Sixty-eight percent of the state voted against it — meaning, of course, something like 68 percent of the Christians who voted. The opposition was led, in fact, not just by the state's wealthiest interests but also by the Christian Coalition of Alabama. "You'll find most Alabamians have got a charitable heart," said John Giles, the group's president. "They just don't want it coming out of their pockets." On its website, the group argued that taxing the rich at a higher rate than the poor "results in punishing success" and that "when an individual works for their income, that money belongs to the individual." You might as well just cite chapter and verse from *Poor Richard's Almanack.*[11] And whatever the ideology, the results are clear. "I'm tired of Alabama being first in things that are bad," said Governor Riley, "and last in things that are good."

A rich man came to Jesus one day and asked what he should do to get into heaven. Jesus did not say he should invest, spend, and let the benefits trickle down; he said sell what you have, give the money to the poor, and follow me. Few plainer words have been spoken. And yet, for some reason, the Christian Coalition of America — founded in 1989 in order to "preserve, protect and defend the Judeo-Christian values that made this the greatest country in history" — proclaimed last year that its top legislative priority would be "making permanent President Bush's 2001 federal tax cuts."

Similarly, a furor erupted last spring when it emerged that a Colorado 25 jury had consulted the Bible before sentencing a killer to death. Experts

[10]*Grover Norquist:* Conservative activist and antitax lobbyist (b. 1956).

[11]*Poor Richard's Almanack:* Yearly almanac published by Benjamin Franklin from 1733 to 1758 containing weather predictions and proverbs such as "Early to bed and early to rise, makes a man healthy, wealthy, and wise."

debated whether the (Christian) jurors should have used an outside authority in their deliberations, and of course the Christian right saw it as one more sign of a secular society devaluing religion. But a more interesting question would have been why the jurors fixated on Leviticus 24,[12] with its call for an eye for an eye and a tooth for a tooth. They had somehow missed Jesus' explicit refutation in the New Testament: "You have heard that it was said, 'an eye for an eye and a tooth for a tooth.' But I say to you, Do not resist an evildoer. But if anyone strikes you on the right cheek, turn the other also."

And on and on. The power of the Christian right rests largely in the fact that they boldly claim religious authority, and by their very boldness convince the rest of us that they must know what they're talking about. They're like the guy who gives you directions with such loud confidence that you drive on even though the road appears to be turning into a faint, rutted track. But their theology is appealing for another reason too: it coincides with what we want to believe. How nice it would be if Jesus had declared that our income was ours to keep, instead of insisting that we had to share. How satisfying it would be if we were supposed to hate our enemies. Religious conservatives will always have a comparatively easy sell.

But straight is the path and narrow is the way. The gospel is too radical for any culture larger than the Amish[13] to ever come close to realizing; in demanding a departure from selfishness it conflicts with all our current desires. Even the first time around, judging by the reaction, the Gospels were pretty unwelcome news to an awful lot of people. There is not going to be a modern-day return to the church of the early believers, holding all things in common — that's not what I'm talking about. Taking seriously the actual message of Jesus, though, should serve at least to moderate the greed and violence that mark this culture. It's hard to imagine a con much more audacious than making Christ the front man for a program of tax cuts for the rich or war in Iraq. If some modest part of the 85 percent of us who are Christians woke up to that fact, then the world might change.

It is possible, I think. Yes, the mainline Protestant churches that supported civil rights and opposed the war in Vietnam are mostly locked in a dreary decline as their congregations dwindle and their elders argue endlessly about gay clergy and same-sex unions. And the Catholic Church, for most of its American history a sturdy exponent of a "love your neighbor" theology, has been weakened, too, its hierarchy increasingly motivated by a single-issue focus on abortion. Plenty of vital congregations are doing great

[12]*Leviticus 24:* Biblical passage which includes verses 17–20, "And he that killeth any man shall surely be put to death. . . . And if a man cause a blemish in his neighbor; as he hath done, so shall it be done to him; breach for breach, eye for eye, tooth for tooth: as he hath caused a blemish in a man, so shall it be done to him *again.*"

[13]*Amish:* Religious group numbering about 200,000, found in Lancaster County, Pennsylvania, and throughout the United States and Canada, which embraces a strict interpretation of the Bible and traditional rather than modern technology and dress.

good works — they're the ones that have nurtured me — but they aren't where the challenge will arise; they've grown shy about talking about Jesus, more comfortable with the language of sociology and politics. More and more it's Bible-quoting Christians, like Wallis's *Sojourners* movement and that Baptist seminary graduate Bill Moyers[14] who are carrying the fight.

The best-selling of all Christian books in recent years, Rick Warren's *The Purpose-Driven Life,* illustrates the possibilities. It has all the hallmarks of self-absorption (in one five-page chapter, I counted sixty-five uses of the word "you"), but it also makes a powerful case that we're made for mission. What that mission is never becomes clear, but the thirst for it is real. And there's no great need for Warren to state that purpose anyhow. For Christians, the plainspoken message of the Gospels is clear enough. If you have any doubts, read the Sermon on the Mount.[15]

Admittedly, this is hope against hope; more likely the money changers   30 and power brokers will remain ascendant in our "spiritual" life. Since the days of Constantine,[16] emperors and rich men have sought to co-opt the

[14]*Bill Moyers:* Journalist and PBS television host (b. 1934).

[15]*the Sermon on the Mount:* Address by Jesus described in the Gospel of Matthew where Jesus praises the humble and downtrodden who will have a "reward in heaven"; rejects revenge, even for murder; and instructs his followers to love their enemies.

[16]*Constantine:* Flavius Valerius Constantinus (272?–337), known as Constantine I or Constantine the Great; first Roman emperor to legalize Christianity.

teachings of Jesus. As in so many areas of our increasingly market-tested lives, the co-opters — the TV men, the politicians, the Christian "interest groups" — have found a way to make each of us complicit in that travesty, too. They have invited us to subvert the church of Jesus even as we celebrate it. With their help we have made golden calves[17] of ourselves — become a nation of terrified, self-obsessed idols. It works, and it may well keep working for a long time to come. When Americans hunger for selfless love and are fed only love of self, they will remain hungry, and too often hungry people just come back for more of the same.

ENGAGING THE TEXT

1. Why does McKibben think the idea that God helps those who help themselves is "counter-biblical"? Would you agree? Why or why not?

2. What evidence does McKibben offer to support his claim that the United States does not live up to its professed Christian ideals? To what extent would you agree that America and Americans do not behave in a particularly Christian way?

3. How, in McKibben's view, have "competing creeds" undermined or displaced Jesus' original teachings? What evidence do you see that the idea of Jesus has been "hijacked" by people who use it to forward their own agendas? What's wrong, according to McKibben, with the approach to Christianity taken by the End-Timers or the new suburban megachurches?

4. What seems to be McKibben's view of Jesus and his teachings in the Gospels? How would American society have to change if this vision of Christianity actually did guide our domestic and foreign policies?

EXPLORING CONNECTIONS

5. How does McKibben's assessment of what's wrong with American culture compare with David Kupelian's (p. 646)? Which of these contrasting views of American society strikes you as more accurate? Which seems the more Christian? Why?

6. How might McKibben's account of the competing versions of Christianity in America help to explain the ambivalence that Anne Lamott (p. 620) initially feels toward religion? To what extent would you expect Lamott to agree with McKibben's view of Jesus and the Gospels?

7. Given McKibben's critique of current trends in American Christianity, compose your own version of the Ten Commandments, in the style of Horsey's cartoon on page 676. How might the "seekers" McKibben associates with the suburban megachurch movement rewrite the Ten Commandments?

8. How does Diana L. Eck's analysis of religious diversity in the United States (p. 693) complicate or challenge McKibben's assertion that American cul-

---

[17]*golden calves:* A reference to the statue created as an object of worship by Aaron for the Israelites. They were impatient for the return of Moses, who was receiving the Ten Commandments from God; see the Book of Exodus, Chapter 32.

ture is "saturated" with Christian identity? To what extent would you agree that, overall, America is a distinctly Christian nation?

EXTENDING THE CRITICAL CONTEXT

9. Working in groups, read selections from the Gospels to test McKibben's portrayal of Jesus and his teachings. To what extent does your reading support McKibben's view that Jesus is being misrepresented in many contemporary American churches?

10. Tour Web sites associated with some of the "competing creeds" that McKibben describes, including sites run by End-Times apocalyptic congregations and new suburban megachurches. What themes or ideas dominate these sites? To what extent does your research support or challenge McKibben's assessment of the agendas associated with these emerging forms of American Christianity?

11. As a class, view Paul Thomas Anderson's 1999 film *Magnolia* and reflect on its portrayal of American society and cultural values. To what extent does Anderson's film echo the concerns McKibben raises about America's increasing self-absorption and our collective lack of authentic spiritual values?

The Bridge Builder: Kathleen Boatwright
ERIC MARCUS

Is religious belief a preference? How about sexual orientation? There may be nothing more basic to personal identity than religious belief and sexuality, yet both seem beyond the scope of individual choice. The pain that results when these two imperatives come into conflict is the topic of this selection. "The Bridge Builder" tells the story of Kathleen Boatwright, devout Christian, mother of four, and lesbian activist, who struggles to reconcile her religious beliefs and values with the reality of her identity as a woman. This selection originally appeared in Making History: The Struggle for Gay and Lesbian Equal Rights 1945–1990 *(1992), a collection of oral histories edited by Eric Marcus. A former associate producer for CBS's* This Morning *and* Good Morning America, *Marcus (b. 1958) has written many books on gay and lesbian issues, including* Together Forever: Gay and Lesbian Marriage *(1998) and* What If Someone I Know Is Gay? Answers to Questions about Gay and Lesbian People *(2000). He has also co-authored two autobiographies:* Breaking the Surface *(1997) with Olympic diving champion Greg Louganis, and* Ice Breaker *(1997) with figure skater Rudy Galindo.*

Invariably wearing a sensible Sears dress or skirt and jacket, Kathleen Boatwright doesn't look the part of a social activist, as she describes herself. But as vice president of the Western Region of Integrity, the gay and lesbian Episcopal ministry, Kathleen uses her conventional appearance, her status as a mother of four, her Christian roots, her knowledge of the scriptures, and her disarming personal warmth to wage a gentle battle for reform in the church she loves — and to change the hearts and minds of individuals within the church. According to Kathleen, "I see myself uniquely gifted to show people what we do to each other in ignorance."

Kathleen Boatwright's very difficult and painful journey from fundamentalist Christian, director of the children's choir at her local church, and pillar of her community to Episcopal lesbian activist began one day in August 1984, when Jean, a veterinary student at Oregon State University, walked through the door of Kathleen's church in Corvallis, Oregon.

The first time I met Jean, she was having a nice conversation with my fifteen-year-old daughter at our church. I was very impressed by the mature way in which she spoke to my daughter. Then, during the service, I sat in the front row and watched Jean sing. I was so enamored by her presence that she stuck in my mind. But then she left town and was gone until January the following year.

Come January, I was sitting in church and I looked across the room, and there was Jean, carrying her guitar, walking down the aisle with such determination. I had this incredible lump in my throat, and I said to myself, *Jean's back.* After the service, and despite my difficulty talking to new people, I just had to ask Jean where she had been. I had to talk to her.

I found out that she was back in Corvallis for five months to finish her   5
degree. She didn't have a place to live. So I said to her, "Don't worry, my parents have always wanted to take in a college student. You're redheaded like Dad. They'll love it!" I went and dragged my mother away from where she was talking and I said, "You remember Jean, she's looking for a place to stay. Why don't you and Dad take her in and board her?"

From early on my parents encouraged the friendship because they saw how much Jean meant to me. Meeting her brought me to life in a way they hadn't seen before. They knew that I used to cry for hours on end when I was a child because no girls liked me at school. My mother would come in and rub my leg or pat my hand. I was extremely intelligent and bright, but I had low self-esteem because I wasn't able to find friendship. So my parents encouraged Jean to invite me to lunch or to take me for a drive or go horseback riding. They felt that her friendship was really wonderful for me. They were glad I was happy. For a while.

My husband didn't pay much attention — at first. He was a state policeman and had always been nonparticipatory, both as a parent and a spouse.

After four months of being friends, of having this wonderful platonic relationship, Jean had to go away for a month for her externship. While she was away she met a fundamentalist couple. Well, Jean sent me a postcard and said, "Something's going on. I'm playing with fire. I can't handle it. I've got to talk to you." My heart wrenched. What was going on?

When we were finally able to meet and talk, Jean explained to me how she and this fundamentalist woman started sharing in an intimate way. My response was to put my arm through hers and say, "Don't worry. We'll get it fixed." Jean couldn't be homosexual because it was wrong. Besides, if she was homosexual, then she would be leaving my life. And I think on a deeper level, I didn't want Jean exploring these things with anyone but me.

After her externship, Jean wanted to be more sensual with me. Her   10 attitude was, "Now I'm going to show *you*." She said, "I'll give you a back rub some night." So one night — after Bible study, no less — she was over at my house and said, "Why don't you lay down on the blanket on the floor and take off your blouse and bra and I'll rub your back?" And I was like, "Okaaay!" My husband was working all night, and this just seemed like a great setup. So this nice little Christian lady rubbed my back, and I said to myself, *Gee, this is it!*

All the little pieces, all the little feelings came together. Even comments my mother made to me over the years began to make sense. She'd say things like, "don't cut your hair too short." "You can't wear tailored clothes." It was then that I also realized that the neighbors I had grown up with were a lesbian couple, even though I had never thought about that before. I recalled the feeling of walking through the Waldenbooks bookstore, looking at *The Joy of Lesbian Sex* and longing for that kind of intimacy. It all came upon me at that moment, and I felt a real willingness to release myself to this person in a way I had never done before. Then the phone rang. It was my son from Bible college. I thought, *Oh, God, saved by the bell! I don't know where this would have gone.*

By the end of the month, Jean was graduating, taking her national boards, and trying to figure out what to do about her feelings toward me and what to do about the fundamentalist woman. It was Pentecostal hysteria.

Now don't forget, at this time I still had a husband and four kids. I had a nineteen-year-old son at a conservative Bible college. I had a sixteen-year-old daughter in the evangelical Christian high school, of which I was a board member. Two children were in parochial day school. My father was the worship leader at church. And I was still very bound to my parents for emotional support. I was the favorite child. And my grandparents lived in town.

Well, shit, I was in way over my head. I was really painted into a corner because there wasn't a single place I could turn for even questioning. So I started looking to some Christian sources. Some of the advice was so incredible, like, "If you feel homosexual tendencies, you can't have the person you have those feelings for over to your house in the evening." "You can never let a member of the same sex sit on your bed while you're chatting." "Meet only in a public place." I thought this advice was ridiculous, but I also thought it was my only option because my spiritual nature was more important than my physical nature. Intellectually and emotionally, I was so hungry and so turned on that I didn't know what to do with my feelings.

At this point, people pull the trigger, turn to the bottle, take drugs, leave town. But I didn't do any of those things because I was madly in love. If I had pulled the trigger, I wouldn't have been able to express the part of me I had discovered. I had found someone, someone who shared the same sort of values I had.   15

Everything reached a crisis point. I acknowledged to myself and to Jean that I was a lesbian and that I loved her. By this time we had already been sexually active. My husband began to get suspicious that something was going on, and he and I went into counseling. Jean was leaving for a job in Colorado and told me that I couldn't go with her because she was a responsible woman and didn't want to destroy my family. And I still hadn't yet found the spiritual guidance that I needed.

I had to get away and do some soul-searching. I needed to figure out if there was any Christian support somewhere that said I could reconcile my love for Jean and my love for my faith. I didn't feel I could build a life of love if I rejected my faith. So I packed my bags and told my parents that I was leaving to go to stay with my great-aunt in Los Angeles for ten days. I told my husband, "I am going to get away and I'm going to think about a bunch of issues, and then I'm coming back."

For the first time in my entire life, at the age of thirty-six, I was by myself with my own agenda. I had left my husband, my children, my parents, my support structures; got in a car; and started driving to West Hollywood, where I knew there was a lesbian mayor and a gay community. So surely, I thought, there had to be a spiritual gay community.

In West Hollywood I found Evangelicals Together. It's not a church, just a storefront ministry to the gay community for people coming out of an evangelical Christian background. It's led by a former American Baptist minister who talked my language. He said to me, "In order to deal with your dilemma, you have to take a step back from your relationship with Jean. Lay her aside and ask yourself, *Who did God create me to be?*"

Through our sharing, and by looking from a different perspective at the gospel and what Jesus had to say, I could embrace the theology that said, "God knew me before I was born. He accepted me as I was made to be, uniquely and wholly." Ultimately, in an obedience to God, you answer that call to be all that He has created you to be. I felt firmly and wholly that what I had experienced with Jean was no demonic possession, was not Satan tempting me with sins of lust, but an intimacy and a love that was beautiful and was God given. So now I had to figure out how to deal with it.   20

When you're my age, you're either going to go back to the way it's always been — go for the security you've always known — or take a chance.

I felt that for the love I felt for Jean I was willing to risk all. Of course, having Jean there, I was hedging my bet a bit. I was jumping off a cliff, but I was holding somebody's hand.

Jean flew down a few days later to join me in Los Angeles. She agreed to commit to me and I to her. The first Sunday after we affirmed our relationship, we worshiped at All Saints' Episcopal Church in Pasadena because I was told that the Episcopals had the framework of faith I loved, as well as an ability to use reason in light of tradition and scripture.

It was God answering the cry of my heart to send me to that worshiping place. Jean and I had never been to an Episcopal church before. We went into this beautiful place with the largest Episcopal congregation west of the Mississippi River. We sat in the fourth row. It was just this incredible Gothic wonderful place. It was All Saints' Day at All Saints' Church. They played the Mozart Requiem with a full choir and a chamber ensemble, and a female celebrant sang the liturgy. We held hands and wept and wept. We could go forward because in the Anglican tradition, the Eucharist is open for everyone. God extends himself. There are no outcasts in the Episcopal church.

When I got back to town, I met with my husband at a counselor's office. I said, "Yes, you're right. I am gay and I'm going to ask for a divorce. I'm going to take this stand. I want to meet with my older children and my parents to talk about the decisions I've made." I felt at least I had a right to make my own decisions. I went to pick up my two youngest girls at my father's house. I went to open the door and I heard a flurry of activity, and the children saw me. "Oh, Mommy's home! Mommy's home!" And my dad stepped out on the front porch and pushed the children away and slammed the door. He took me forcibly by the arm and led me down the stairs and said, "You're never seeing your children again without a court order! Just go shack up with your girlfriend!" And he forced me down to the street.

It took going to court to see my two youngest children. They hadn't 25 seen me for two weeks. They asked, "Mommy, Mommy, what's wrong?" I leaned over and whispered in their ears, "Mommy loves you." My husband wanted to know, "What are you telling the children?" I had only a minute with them, then went downstairs, and my husband told me that he wanted me to come back, that he would be my brother, not my husband.

I tell you, my whole world came down upon my ears. I wasn't allowed to see my children. I was denied access to my residence. The church had an open prayer meeting disclosing my relationship with Jean. They tried to get Jean fired from her job. And when that didn't work, they called Jean's parents, who then tried to have her committed or have me arrested. My family physically disinherited me and emotionally cut me off. My older daughter, upon the advice of her counselor-pastor, shook my hand and said, "Thank you for being my biological mother. I never want to have anything to do with you again." After that, whenever she saw me in town, she hid from me.

I saw her lay flat on the asphalt in the grocery store parking lot so I wouldn't see her. People I'd known all my life avoided me like I had the plague. I was surprised that Jean didn't just say, "Hey, lady, I'm out of here!"

Fortunately, I wasn't entirely without support. I went to Parents and Friends of Lesbians and Gays and I met some wonderful loving, Christian, supportive parents and gay children who said, "You're not sick. You're not weird. Everybody's hysterical." They offered any kind of assistance possible. Through their emotional support, I felt like it was possible to survive the crush.

Living in a small rural county in Oregon, I didn't know anything about women's rights, let alone gay rights. So it's not surprising that I bought into the lie that children of lesbians or gays are better off living with the custodial heterosexual parent. I believed my husband could provide a sense of normality that I could not. So I signed away my custodial rights and became a secondary parent. After being the primary-care parent for twenty devoted years, the judge only let me see the children two days a week.

By then I'd had enough. So I packed one suitcase and a few things in grocery sacks and left my family and children behind. Jean and I just rode quietly out of town in the sunset to her job in Denver, Colorado.

As you drive into Denver, you go over this big hill about fifteen miles 30 from town. We stopped at a phone booth and called the local Parents FLAG president to ask if there was a supportive Episcopal parish in town. She said, "Yes, go to this place, look up this person." It was getting to be evening. It was clear, and we were going over the mountain. It was a whole new adventure. It was real closure to my past and a real opening toward my future. Still, the guiding force in my life was, "The church has the answers."

Jean and I called the church and found out when services were and asked if they had an Integrity chapter. Integrity is the Episcopal ministry to the gay and lesbian community. There was one, so two nights later we walked into our first Integrity meeting. There were twelve attractive men in their thirties and the rector. They were shocked to see two women because it's unusual for women to be in Integrity. The only thing dirtier than being a lesbian in a Christian community is being a Christian in the lesbian community because it brings in so many other issues besides sexual orientation, like women's issues and patriarchy and all that stuff.

Denver Integrity was an affirming congregation. We were out as a couple. We were healed of so many things through the unconditional love and acceptance of this parish of eighty people. The rector there encouraged me to become involved. Out of his own pocket he sent me to the first regional convention I went to, in 1987 in San Francisco. Now, I'm vice president of the Western Region for Integrity, and I'm on the national board of directors, I'm one of only maybe 125 women in Integrity's membership of about 1,500.

Integrity gives me a forum for the things I want to say, both as a lesbian woman and as a committed Christian. And because of my background and experience, I can speak to the church I love on a variety of issues that others cannot. I can say, "I call you into accountability. You are bastardizing children raised in nontraditional households. You're not affirming the people that love and guide them. You say you welcome us, but on the other hand you don't affirm us. You don't give us rites of passage and ritual and celebration like you do for heterosexual families."

The church needs to change. What we're asking for are equal *rites*. We're asking the church to bless same-sex unions. I'm asking for canonical changes that affirm my wholeness as a child of Christ who is at the same time in a loving committed relationship with a woman. We're also challenging the church to make statements asking the government to legitimize our relationships and give us the same sorts of tax breaks, pension benefits, et cetera. But most importantly, we need the church to get off the dime and start affirming gay and lesbian children's lives. I never want a girl to go through what I went through. I want to spare everybody right up front.

To get my point across when I go out and talk to groups as a representa-   35
tive of Integrity, I personalize the issue. I personalize my political activism by speaking to people as a person, as Kathleen Boatwright. People don't need to hear dogma or doctrine or facts or theology. They need to meet people.

Here's a great example. For the first time, the women of Integrity got seated at Triennial, which is this gigantic group of very traditional women who have a convention every three years. It used to be that while the men were making the decisions, the women held their own convention. With women's issues having changed so dramatically in the Episcopal church, that's no longer true. Now that women are allowed to serve in the House of Deputies and can be ordained into the priesthood, we've become full team members in the canonical process.

Triennial was made for me. Everybody wears their Sears Roebuck dress. Everybody is a mom. Everybody lived like I had lived for twenty years. I know how to network and how to deal with those women. But I also have a new truth to tell them that will have an impact on their lives in very special ways. Gays and lesbians are 10 percent of the population. Everybody is personally affected by that issue, including these women at Triennial.

During the convention, I attended a seminar given by conservative Episcopals who said gays and lesbians have confused gender identity. Later, we had an open meeting in which we talked about human sexuality. But no one talked about sexuality. Instead, we only talked about information on biological reproduction. After about forty minutes of hearing these women drone on, I stood up in my Sears Roebuck dress and said, "OK ladies, put on your seat belts because you're going to take a trip into reality. You won't want to hear it, but I need to say it because you need to know what people's lives are really like."

I talked to them about my journey. I talked to them about the misnomers, about "confused gender identity." I was wearing this circle skirt and I said, "As you can see from my appearance," and I curtsied, "I do not have a 'confused gender identity.'" Everybody who had been really stiff started laughing — and they started listening. The key is that I take risks. I risk being vulnerable. I risk sharing the secrets of my heart. We already know what the straight people feel in their hearts. But no one talks about how the lesbian or gay person feels in his or her heart.

For the next hour and a half, people talked about where they really live.   40
They talked about their pregnant teenagers or the suicide attempts in their families. All those gut-level issues. But you have to have someone lead you to that. That's me — because I'm safe. I've also learned that instead of having all the answers, that God calls me to listen to people's pain, and not to judge it.

This one woman told me that she had been driving by her daughter's house for eight years and that her husband had never let her stop because her daughter was a lesbian. "But," she said, "I'm going to go home and I'm going to see her. My daughter's name is also Kathleen." Then she started to cry. She had never even told the women from her church about what had happened to her daughter. It's like the living dead for many Christian families. They just have a child who is lost prematurely in so many senses of the word.

Inevitably, everywhere I go I hear about parents who have made ultimatums. This one mother said, "I've never told anybody, but I said to my son, 'I wish you were dead.' And by forcing him into the closet, I fulfilled that prophecy. Three years later, he was dead." Then there was a woman who said to me, "Kathleen, I'm questioning my sexuality at seventy. Could you send me some information?"

I think in my heart that I represent the hidden majority of lesbian women because many, many are married or have been married, have children, and have too much to risk — like I've risked and lost — to come out. And those women who are out, who are much more political and aggressive, have seen enough successes happen, enough bridges built by my approach, that they're beginning to respect the fact that I can go through doors they never can.

The first time I spoke publicly to the leadership of the women of the church, I spoke along with another lesbian. She was politically correct and a strong feminist. *Feminist* was always a dirty word for me, so I've had to overcome a lot of my own bias. I said to her, "Please don't speak about politics. Don't browbeat these people. Stand up and say that you're a doctor, that you've never been in a committed relationship, that you're a feminist. Because I want to stand up and say, 'I've been a Blue Bird leader.' What that will say is that we represent the gamut of human experience, just like the heterosexual community. It's just our ability to develop intimate relationships with the same sex that makes us different."

People don't have to identify with my ideology. They identify with my   45
person, and then the questions come from them. We don't have to tell

them. They start asking us. People say to me, "What do you call your partner?" "You don't have any medical insurance?" To me that's the best sort of
teaching process: answering questions rather than giving information.

My husband remarried; he married the baby-sitter. At Easter of 1987, I
got a call informing me that he had removed my ten-year-old daughter from
his house, accusing her of using "inappropriate touch" with his new step-
sons. He wanted to unload the difficult child. Then he used that child as a
weapon to try and deny me visitation for the younger one. The end result
was that I had one child and he had one child. I filed suit against him without any hope or prayer of winning back custody of my other child.

I went to a lesbian minister to ask her about finding a lawyer to handle
my case, and she said to me, "The best attorney in this town is Hal Harding,
but he's your husband's attorney. Maybe that will prove to be a blessing." So
I had to find another attorney.

As part of the custody proceedings, Jean and I eventually met with my
husband's attorney. He took depositions and asked Jean and me really
heartfelt questions. Then he advised his client — my ex-husband — to go
ahead and have a psychological evaluation. The court had not ordered it
and, in fact, would not order it because there was no precedent in that
county. But my former husband agreed to go to the psychologist of his
choice. That psychologist, a woman, took the time and energy to interview
every person involved and recommended to the court that Jean and I
become custodial parents. We now have custody of both children, sole custody. It was indeed a blessing.

We just added Jean's ninety-one-year-old grandmother to our family.
So we are all-American lesbians living here in Greenacres, Washington. We
are Miss and Mrs. America living together. The thing that we need in our
life now that our faith doesn't give us is a community of supportive women.
We have yet to find that place.

Not long ago, I went to the National Organization for Women lesbian   50
rights agenda meeting and gave a workshop on spirituality for women, from
the Christian perspective. And I took a deep breath in my Betty Crocker
suit — if I ever write a book it's going to be *The Radicalization of Betty
Crocker* — and thought, *I wonder what the Assemblies of God girls would say
now? From their perspective, I'm walking into the total pit of hell, and I'm
bringing the very gift that they should be giving.* Who would have believed it?

ENGAGING THE TEXT

1. What family, religious, and cultural bonds initially restrained Boatwright
   from acknowledging her sexuality? What were her options? How do you
   think she should have reacted when she realized that she was attracted to
   Jean? Why?

2. In what different ways does Boatwright's emerging lesbian identity change her and her life? What price does she pay?

3. How do Boatwright's attitudes toward the church develop during her story? How does her self-image change?

4. How do you interpret the title of this oral history? In what different senses is Boatwright a "bridge builder"?

EXPLORING CONNECTIONS

5. To what extent does Boatwright's experience support Carmen Vázquez's (p. 472) assertion that "the straitjacket of gender roles suffocates many lesbians, gay men, and bisexuals, forcing them into closets without an exit and threatening our very existence when we tear the closet open" (para. 20)? What resources finally enable Boatwright to survive and thrive despite the open hostility of her family and community?

6. What advice do you think David Kupelian (p. 646) would have given Boatwright when she was first exploring her sexuality with her friend Jean? How do you think he would view the Integrity movement that she becomes involved with? How do you imagine she would respond?

7. Drawing on the experiences and ideas of Kathleen Boatwright, Anne Lamott (p. 620), and Bill McKibben (p. 665), write a brief essay or journal entry on the role that community plays in personal faith. How does the need to belong shape the spiritual life of each of these authors?

8. What flaws of logic does the cartoon on page 685 reveal in the speaker's antigay position? Why does the cartoonist depict both figures as relatively featureless?

EXTENDING THE CRITICAL CONTEXT

9. Browse the press releases and news postings about religion and lesbian/gay issues on one or more of the following Web sites:

> Parents and Friends of Lesbians and Gays (www.pflag.org)
>
> Integrity (www.integrityusa.org)
>
> Interfaith Working Group (www.iwgonline.org)
>
> Universal Fellowship of Metropolitan Community Churches (www.ufmcc.com)

Summarize your findings about how various religious groups are responding to questions about gay marriage, gay clergy, and violence against lesbians and gay men.

Visual Portfolio

READING IMAGES OF AMERICAN MYTHS OF CHURCH AND STATE

Visual Portfolio

READING IMAGES OF AMERICAN MYTHS OF CHURCH AND STATE

1. What does the 1802 depiction of George Washington's ascension into heaven (p. 687) say to you? How do you think Washington would have reacted to it? Why? If time permits, follow up by doing some Internet research to learn more about Washington's own religious views.

2. How does the image of "Buddy Christ" from the 1999 movie *Dogma* (p. 688) differ from more traditional depictions of Jesus? In your view, does this image convey an accurate, if exaggerated, view of the impact of contemporary American culture on Christian values? To what extent has contemporary American culture also shaped our views of other religions — such as Judaism, Buddhism, or Islam?

3. How does the fellow carrying the sign that reads "God Hates You Sodomites..." on page 689 know how God feels? Make a list of the other things you think God might hate. Compare these in small groups and discuss the images of God that emerge from them.

4. What is right — or wrong — with displaying the Ten Commandments in a public place like the Texas State Capitol, as pictured on page 690? What harm does it do to display religious images, symbols, or texts in schools or governmental offices?

5. What questions does the photo of Muslim protesters in Boston (p. 691) raise about God, religion, church, and state? How do you think the Founding Fathers would have responded to this image? Why?

6. What is your immediate reaction to the photo of children praying in school (p. 692)? What is right — or wrong — with the idea of introducing religious beliefs, practices, and values into public school settings?

Afraid of Ourselves

DIANA L. ECK

The idea of religious diversity isn't new in America. French Protestants — known as Huguenots — settled in New Jersey in 1624. Lord Baltimore secured the charter for the Maryland Colony, the first settlement for Roman Catholics, in 1632. The first Jewish settlers arrived in New York from South America in 1654. And in 1681 William Penn founded Pennsylvania for Quakers seeking sanctuary from religious persecution. Since the colonial era, the United States has also given birth to a number of "American-made" religions, including Christian Science, Mormonism, Pentecostalism, and the Jehovah's Witnesses. Today, perhaps more than ever, America has become a haven for people of nearly every religious persuasion — from Anglicans to Zoroastrians. In this selection, Professor Diana L. Eck explores some of the tensions that arise in a culture where Wicca co-exists with Christian fundamentalism and where communion and animal sacrifice are both seen as sacramental rites. Eck (b. 1945) teaches comparative religion and Indian studies at Harvard University, where she is director of the Pluralism Project, an effort to document the diversity of religion in America and its impact on American culture. She is the author of several highly regarded books on world religion, including a study of Hinduism's holiest city, Banaras: City of Light *(1982),* Encountering God: A Spiritual Journey from Bozeman to Banaras *(1993), and the source of this selection,* A New Religious America: How a "Christian Country" Has Become the World's Most Religiously Diverse Nation *(2001).*

"We the people of the United States of America" are now religiously diverse as never before, and some Americans do not like it. For the Fourth of July edition of the *Los Angeles Times* a few years ago, I wrote an op-ed piece on the many places we might find the American flag flying on the holiday — on the grand staircase of the Hsi Lai Buddhist Temple in Hacienda Heights, for example, or next to the blackboard in the fourth-grade classroom of an Islamic school in Orange County. A few weeks later I received a letter from a gentleman in Tampa, Florida, expressing astonishment at my article, which had been syndicated in a Florida newspaper. He was clearly upset by the piece and proffered his own conclusion: "If this is indeed the case, as you have alleged, then I wonder how all these people got here. Now is the time to close the doors. I suggest they go back where they came from." It is clear to me that the religious controversies of the American public square are just beginning.

I have often suspected that many Americans, like the man from Tampa, do not really know how much more complex our "sweet land of liberty" has become. When I read his letter, I thought of the days I had spent in another part of Florida, in the Miami area, visiting with Trinidadi immigrants at a Caribbean Hindu temple set in behind a shopping mall in Oakland Park, then finding my way to an Islamic center in a suburban area of Pompano Beach, and finally heading to a Thai Buddhist temple that translates its name as "Temple of the Good Lord" in the flats south of Miami. I had to go looking for these places, as did all of our Pluralism Project researchers. The new religious America did not simply present itself in a coherent group photo. Rather, we made it a point to search out its various expressions. So I often wondered as I drove America's highways from temple to mosque to gurdwara just how many people had any idea that this is all here and what they would think if they did. The man from Tampa gave it a voice. He did not know about all these new neighbors, and when he found out he did not like it. Alas, he is also not alone. The climate of suspicion created by a new spate of American xenophobia has given rise to a thousand stories of insult and insinuation, assault and hatred. . . .

A Visible Difference

Without question, some Americans are afraid of the changing face of our country. After all, the first response to difference is often suspicion and fear. Fear of the unknown is not so astonishing, especially in a country where we have done so little to make the cultural and religious traditions of the world better known and understood. Although some progress has been made in our public schools in recent years, most of us who are middle-aged know from experience how little we learned about the religious traditions of the world in junior high or high school. When I graduated in the top ten of my class from Bozeman Senior High School, I could not have provided even the most rudimentary account of the fundamentals of Islam or Hinduism, even though these constitute the faith and worldviews of nearly half the world's population. This is not unusual for people of my generation. Most of us simply do not know much about one another, and the images we may have of the strangers among us are transmitted through the shorthand of the media where the extreme too often becomes the norm.

Visible difference is the issue. People of many ideological, political, and religious persuasions may encounter one another without noticing, but when the difference is visible, we do take note. Surely the most visible difference in America's new multiethnic society is race. We are black and white and all the hues of Asia from Korea and Japan to Southeast Asia and South Asia. We are Latino and Hispanic. And we are increasingly multiracial as Latino and Euro-American, Native and African American, Asian and Latino become the components of our own racial *mestizaje*. It is difficult to underestimate just how prominently race figures in the perception of America by immigrants from other parts of the world. As Padma Rangaswamy put it in her book *Namaste America,* a study of Indian immigrants in Chicago, "Indians, because of their race and color, can never achieve total acceptance into a white American society that has race and color bias. It is difficult to envision a period in which race and color have not mattered in American history, or will not matter in the future."[1] This view of America's race consciousness stings on the page, but we must take it seriously if we are to create a multiracial and multireligious society that nurtures a sense of belonging — among all people.

---

[1]Padma Rangaswamy, *Namaste America* (University Park, PA: The Pennsylvania State University Press, 2000), 333. [All notes are the author's, except 2, 3, 5, 8, 9, 11–13, 15, 16, 20, and 23.]

After race, the most visible signal of difference is dress, and this is   5
where religious minorities become visible minorities. Many Muslim women
wear *hijab,* either a simple head scarf or a full outer garment. A few even
wear a face covering called *nikab.* Muslim men may wear a beard, and Sikh
men may wear not only a beard but also a turban wrapped around their
uncut hair. Jewish men may wear a yarmulke, or skullcap. Buddhist monks
may wear saffron, maroon, black, brown, or gray robes, depending upon
their culture of origin. In all these cases looking different may sometimes
trigger uneasiness and even fear — the fear that we do not know who "they"
are or perhaps that we do not know who "we" are. As Americans, we are literally afraid of ourselves.

Our visible differences are on the rise, not just in the building of
mosques and temples, but in the visible presence of people of many religious traditions. And this religious difference often has consequences. Just
ask the young Sikh man I sat next to at the *langar* meal in the Fremont gurdwara[2] in California. "You can't show up at a job interview wearing a turban
and beard," he said. He was clean-shaven and had a short haircut, but this
was the result of having spent five years in the U.S. and having experienced
discrimination because of his looks. To some Americans, turbaned Sikhs
look like what they imagine snake charmers or genies to be, he said. Others
associate the turbaned look with militancy and even terrorism. He found he
had no choice but to cut his hair. For observant Sikh women, the visibility
of not cutting their hair can also be a burden, as a young woman named
Kimpreet recalled when we interviewed her. Kimpreet had grown up in
New Jersey, and hers was the only Sikh family in town. She told us, "I was
the 'other.' I was the girl with the really, really super long hair who couldn't
cut it because of her religion." The thread worn by young Zoroastrians after
their *navjote* initiation also elicits this sense of the "other." A Zoroastrian
friend confided, "It's very common when young people are in gym class and
changing their clothes, someone will come up and say, 'What's that?' If they
say, 'This is part of my Zoroastrian custom,' the next line usually is 'Zoro-
what?' They want to know what kind of cult is that?"

The presence of Buddhist monks and nuns in America presents another
evidence of visible difference. We see fewer and fewer Catholic priests,
monks, and nuns on the streets of America these days. In the decades since
the Second Vatican Council[3] in the 1960s, most religious orders have moved
toward workaday nonreligious dress. Today, however, saffron-robed monks
from Laos are visible in Lowell, Massachusetts, and Cambodian monks are
found on the back roads of New England. When the Thai immigrant community built the Temple of the Good Lord in the flatlands south of Miami,
one of the lay members of the board told a reporter from the *Miami Herald,*

---

[2]*gurdwara:* Sikh place of worship.
[3]*the Second Vatican Council:* A meeting of bishops and other members of the Roman
Catholic Church on such topics as the role of the church in the modern world.

"The neighbors didn't know anything about Buddhism. They thought we were a cult."[4] And one of the monks added, "They thought we were Hare Krishnas."

The Hare Krishnas too have had their problems as a visible religious group. For a time, the young men in the order of celibate ascetics moved from their orange renouncers' robes, readily recognizable in the streets of Calcutta, to something that looks more the garb of Christian Franciscans. Though many Krishna devotees today wear ordinary Western dress, on the whole they dress in the dhotis and saris[5] of India, seeing this as a positive way of identifying themselves so that they may be approached by those interested in their spiritual movement.

Perhaps the most prominent icons of our new visible religious differences are the Muslim women wearing the head scarf. They are now visible almost everywhere, and every one of them has a story to tell. My friend Mary Lahaj is about my age, and our grandparents came to this country at about the same time, only hers came from Lebanon, whereas mine came from Sweden. Mary and I are both religious and both scholars as well. I am a Methodist and Mary a Muslim. But as third-generation Americans, our experience has been quite different in one respect. I have never experienced the discrimination that Mary has experienced just by being who she is, wearing a head scarf outside the home as part of her faith. Mary describes one incident when she experienced herself as the object of raw fear. She told us, "I was wearing my *hijab* in the toy store Child World, and I was buying some toy guns for my son and his two friends. As I turned the corner this young man about fourteen almost bumped into me. And when he saw me, he just got this awful expression on his face, like he was scared to death. You know, there was just this image of me with my head cover and these toy rifles in my arms, and he looked simply terrified."[6] The guns, of course, fit right into the prejudicial image of Muslims that this fourteen-year-old had already encountered, and then there she was — my friend Mary, the terrorist.

About the time Mary and I met in 1994, an article in the *Minneapolis*   10 *Star Tribune* told of a woman in full Islamic dress, including a partial face covering, being arrested in the Mall of America for wearing a disguise, which was banned by local ordinance. The police asked her to remove it, but she refused, arguing for the freedom of religious practice. Eventually a settlement was reached, but the issue of the *hijab* persists. A schoolgirl has her scarf pulled off by a classmate, for example, or a white American woman

---

[4]Peggy Landers, "Answer to a Prayer: Buddhists Break Ground on Controversial Temple," *The Miami Herald,* June 12, 1995.

[5]*dhotis and saris:* Types of Indian clothing. A *dhoti* is a cloth worn about the waist and legs by men; a *sari* is a length of cloth worn by women, wrapped around the waist and draped over the shoulder.

[6]Mary Lahaj, Pluralism Project interview, 1996.

wearing a head scarf in Tukwila, Washington, near Seattle, is accosted and chased through a parking lot by a group of young people yelling, "You Muslim! Go home!"[7] These are stories of harassment and incivility, and at the other end of the scale are stories of civil rights abuses and discrimination, especially in the workplace.

We should remember, however, that both sides experience the instability and fear generated by visible difference. Looking different comes with a price, as America's Amish and Hutterites[8] can testify and as people of racial minorities in the U.S. have experienced. Sister Aminah, a Euro-American Muslim who began wearing the Islamic head cover shortly after her conversion, testifies to this reality. Sister Aminah and I were on a panel together in an open forum of the President's Initiative on Race in June 1998 in Louisville, Kentucky. In her presentation she described the many ways in which she and her family had experienced the barbs of prejudice. "How much discrimination I have myself experienced!" she said. "I was in Oklahoma City after the bombing of the Federal Building, and my son begged me not to wear my head scarf in public. I was frightened, and our whole community was frightened." When she told her story, an African-American man in the audience spoke from the heart in response to her. He said that he had never heard a Muslim woman speak this way, and he had never imagined that Muslims, even Caucasian Muslims, might experience some of the overt discrimination and fear that he himself had lived with all his life.

Stereotypes: The Scratches on Our Minds

The newsman Walter Lippman[9] spoke of stereotypes as the "pictures in our heads," the sketchy and distorted images created by one group to describe, label, and caricature another. These pictures, shaped by media, reading, and hearsay, inevitably yield images that don't match the human being. They are stereotypes, some romantic and others denigrating. Harold Isaacs's book on American images of Asia first published in the 1950s was entitled *Scratches on Our Minds*. Some of the "scratchings" are not even full-blown images for, as Isaacs concludes, "Vagueness about Asia has been until now the natural condition even of the educated American."[10]

Prejudice is prejudging people and groups on the basis of these images, often half-formed caricatures. As the quip goes, prejudice is "being down

---

[7]Marc Ramirez, "Islam on the Rise — Muslim in America," *Seattle Times*, January 24, 1999.

[8]*Amish and Hutterites:* The Amish are a religious group numbering about 200,000, found in Lancaster County, Pennsylvania, and throughout the United States and Canada, which embraces a strict interpretation of the Bible and traditional rather than modern technology and dress. The Hutterites, also a religious group that disavows modern technology and dress, are found on the plains of the northern United States and Canada.

[9]*Walter Lippman:* American journalist (1889–1974).

[10]Harold Isaacs, 1958, *Scratches on Our Minds: American Images of China and India* (Armonk, New York: M. E. Sharpe, Inc. 1980), 37.

on something you're not up on." People "known" through stereotypes do not have the opportunity to tell us who they are. We do not let them get close enough to speak for themselves. We define them in their absence, on the basis of the images already present in our minds. Lata, a Boston Hindu friend, put it this way: "People have a prejudged opinion about you. Just seeing you, they already know who you are, even though they never want to take the time to really know who you are."

Stereotypes and prejudice have a long history in America. European settlers held negative racial stereotypes of the Native peoples and the Africans brought as slaves. We have been practicing our prejudices ever since, for these habits of the heart are very hard to change. Americans of Anglo-Saxon and northern European heritage held demeaning racial, religious, and cultural stereotypes of other European newcomers — especially the Irish, Poles, and Italians. Virtually all Europeans of Christian origin brought with them the bigotry and demeaning stereotypes of Jews they had come to know in Europe. As we have seen, prejudice also shaped European immigrants' attitudes toward newcomers from Asia — the Chinese and Japanese "yellow peril"[11] and the turbaned Sikh "ragheads."

Even today statistics reveal that the greatest percentage of hate crimes   15
is racially motivated, most against blacks, followed by whites, Hispanics, Asians, and Arabs. But religion is often conflated with race as a marker of the difference that generates fear or hate. An analysis of the politics of hatred, both historically and today, requires that we look at the ways in which religious symbols are manipulated and the ways in which demeaning a religion or defacing its place of worship targets the very soul of a community. The 1996 publication *Hate Crimes Statistics* reveals that most religiously motivated hate crimes are directed at property rather than people. But an American Muslim Council brochure provided to Muslim communities astutely explains, "Drawing graffiti on walls is designed to deface a structure; the same act done to a mosque is meant not only to deface the structure, but also to intimidate and invoke fear within the group."

Religious prejudice takes many forms, and among the most destructive is simply erasing a group's legitimacy as a religion. Anglo-Saxon newcomers to the continent did not see Native Americans as people with a "different" religious tradition but rather as "pagans" with no religion at all. Native peoples are sensitive to this negative image even today. Anne Marshall, a Muscogee Creek Indian and an executive in the United Methodist Church, says, "Our Native traditions are not pagan, they are sacramental. They have allowed our people to survive for five hundred years, no matter what was done to us. But people don't even classify our religion as a religion, along with Hinduism and Islam." Fellow citizens who identify religiously as Pagans also face an uphill climb toward recognition. Most people have no idea about

---

[11]"*yellow peril*": Phrase originating in the United States in the nineteenth century in reaction to the supposed threat of increased immigration from Asia.

the spiritual ecology of American Paganism, a path that emphasizes humans' intimate dependence upon the Earth and its ecosystems. They know little of Pagan ethics and the principle of the Threefold Return, reminding Pagans that every word and action directed outward, whether for good or ill, whether generous or miserly, will return to them threefold. Instead, people tend to identify Paganism with broad negative strokes, classifying it with Satanism and their worst stereotypes of witchcraft. Other religious communities have also felt the sting of being left out of majority consciousness, like the young Sikh college student who told us, "The thing that really bothered me about stereotyping and discrimination was just the fact that we're not really even recognized as a religion. You're Sikh? How do you spell that? You know, like, I've never heard of this before. I honestly feel I'm not accepted as fully having a religion here."

America's Catholics and Jews experienced not erasure but built-in tension with the vastly dominant Protestant mainstream. Catholics and Jews were pioneers, as we have seen, in dealing with the religious prejudices of America. Anti-Catholic prejudice began in the colonial period with the Puritans, who brought with them the anti-Catholic attitudes of the English Reformation. In the nineteenth century the growth of the American Catholic Church with immigration from Ireland, Italy, and Eastern Europe set in motion a new wave of anti-Catholic sentiment. Catholics were stereotyped as Romanists and Papists and were suspected of being incapable of participating in a Constitutional democracy. In 1834 a Protestant mob burned a Catholic convent school in Charlestown, Massachusetts, and in the 1850s the Know-Nothing party[12] with its virulent anti-Catholic rhetoric rose for a time to the public eye and elected candidates to office. Even during the campaign of John F. Kennedy for president in 1960, more than a hundred years later, the image of the American Catholic as subservient to the authority of the pope and potentially un-American lingered in the minds of some. Kennedy's election was a critical turning point in laying many of these stereotypes to rest.

Anti-Semitism also has a long American history. In colonial America Jews were warned out of town in Boston and after the Revolution were prohibited from voting and holding office in North Carolina and Maryland. The pervasive negative image of Jews was as Christ killers with the traits of Shylock[13] — wicked, greedy, unethical. The climate that permitted overt discrimination against Jews was based on the unquestioned assumption of Christian superiority and Jewish stubbornness and perfidy in rejecting Christ as Savior.

In the first decades of the twentieth century, Christian anti-Judaism gathered up the fears of a society convinced that not only were Jews a blight

---

[12]*the Know-Nothing party:* Anti-immigration, anti–Roman Catholic political organization active in the United States between 1852 and 1856.

[13]*Shylock:* A Jewish moneylender in William Shakespeare's play *The Merchant of Venice.*

on Christian America, but they were also gaining too much power. Of the more than sixteen million immigrants who came to the U.S. from 1890 to 1914, just over 10 percent were Jewish.[14] The rising concern about Jewish economic success compounded prejudice and suspicion. I have mentioned, for example, Harvard president Abbott Lawrence Lowell, who in the 1920s proposed a quota system to address the "Jewish problem," noting with alarm that the percentage of Jewish men at Harvard had risen from 6 percent in 1908 to 22 percent in 1922. The faculty rejected the plan but for many decades acquiesced in a de facto limitation on Jewish admissions.

The post–World War I xenophobia, spearheaded by the likes of Henry   20
Ford, his Dearborn, Michigan, newspaper, the *Dearborn Independent,* and the resurgence of the KKK,[15] linked anti-Catholicism and anti-Semitism. In the 1920s both Jews and Catholics were under attack by the newly reorganized Ku Klux Klan. In the 1930s and early 1940s hate organizations grew, and conspiracy theories about Jewish influence spread like wildfire. Despite reason for common cause, some American Catholics participated in anti-Semitism. Father Charles Coughlin[16] publicly articulated its propaganda through weekly radio programs that reached 3.5 million Americans. In 1939 he and his organization, called the Christian Front, filled Madison Square Garden with more than nineteen thousand people. The arena was draped with banners saying, "Wake Up America! Smash Jewish Communism!" and "Stop Jewish Domination of Christian America!"[17]

The experience of being the object of suspicion and distrust, of changing one's name to avoid being penalized for one's religion, of being called clannish and aloof if they kept to themselves and pushy and power hungry if they claimed a place in the public sphere; the experience of being seen as parasites on the economy if they were in need and taking jobs from others if they were successfully employed — all this is the texture of the immigrant experience pioneered by Jewish Americans. Unfortunately, Sikhs and Muslims, Hindus and Buddhists have now, in different ways, experienced it all for themselves.

The new immigrants of the late twentieth century faced denigrating stereotypes planted in the soil of ignorance and fed by a stream of negative media images. Terms like *Sikh militant* or *Islamic fundamentalist* express a shorthand version of complex political struggles abroad, and they shape in profound ways the mental images people hold of all Sikhs and Muslims. Muslims feel especially vulnerable to the stereotypes that so readily pair the word *Muslim* with *fundamentalist, terrorist,* or *holy war.*

---

[14]Leonard Dinnerstein, *Antisemitism in America* (New York: Oxford University Press, 1994), 58.

[15]*The KKK:* Ku Klux Klan, a white supremacist organization founded after the Civil War.

[16]*Charles Coughlin:* Roman Catholic priest whose weekly radio address was an extremely popular platform for his anti-Semitic views.

[17]Dinnerstein, *Antisemitism,* 122.

Mary Lahaj, my third-generation Muslim-American friend, told us, "Muslims are stereotyped as terrorists, fanatics. These kinds of labels, I would say, dehumanize the Muslim. This means that you literally don't look at the Muslim as another human being." Mary's words reminded me of the words of Nina Morais more than a century ago. Nina, a Philadelphia-born Sephardic Jew, lamented in 1881 in an article called "Jewish Ostracism in America," "In the popular mind, the Jew is never judged as an individual, but as a specimen of a whole race whose members are identically of the same kind."[18] Being judged as a group, not an individual, erases the human face and is the first step toward the dehumanization that gives rise to hate crimes. At the Islam Awareness Week I attended at Boston University, a Latino Muslim from Los Angeles spoke frankly about the stereotypes he encountered, and not the usual ones that associated Islam with violence. He told us, "When I first embraced Islam, I told my cousin. He said, 'How come your head's not shaved? Where's your ponytail? Your women wear a red dot, right?' He was unbelievably confused. Ladies and gentlemen, take a deep breath and relax. One of the reasons we are afraid of difference is because we know so little. But how are they going to understand unless we help them understand? I grew up in the USA, Chevrolet, mom and apple pie, and Little League baseball. The problem is most people just don't have an accurate knowledge of Islam!"

Couple a deep negativity toward religious difference with a deep ignorance of other religious traditions, and we have a recipe for prejudice. For example, in 1990 a small item in the *New York Times* caught my eye under the headline "Yoga and the Devil: Issue for Georgia Town."[19] The dateline was Toccoa, Georgia, and apparently officials barred a town-sponsored yoga class "because the relaxation of yoga exercises would open practitioners to the influence of the devil. 'The people who are signed up for the class are just walking into it like cattle to a slaughter,' said a leader of a local group comprised of Baptists, Lutherans, and other Christians." Defenders of the class insisted that the class was only for stretching and relaxing, not for promoting religion. Clearly what to many Americans has been a spiritual practice is perceived as threat in what must be a fairly homogeneous town. The small town of Winter, Wisconsin, was the scene of another such incident. A high school student found the computers of the school district blocked, preventing her from access to information on Wicca, and a member of the school board accused her of being a "devil worshiper" for seeking such information. The district had installed a computer filter system to restrict Internet access to subjects deemed controversial. The student complained, "I tried to look up Buddhism and it was blocked. Then, I tried to look up Wicca[20] and it was blocked. Then, I looked up Christian churches and you

---

[18]Cited in Dinnerstein, *Antisemitism*, 41.
[19]"Yoga and the Devil: Issue for Georgia Town," *New York Times*, September 7, 1990.
[20]*Wicca:* Neopagan religious and belief system based on northern European traditions.

could find anything you want."[21] The case attracted nationwide attention, and eventually the school district changed the system before the case reached the courts. But at the civic level, it is yet another example of the potent mixture of fear and ignorance that sparks so many incidents of outright discrimination.

In New Jersey in the late 1980s, the dot, or *bindi,* on the forehead worn   25 by many Hindu women stood for the strangeness of the whole Indian immigrant community in the eyes of a racist group calling themselves the Dot Busters. The attacks had nothing to do with Hinduism as a religion but were directed at all South Asian immigrants. In 1987 in Jersey City, a climate of constant low-level harassment turned to violence. A thirty-year-old Indian immigrant, Navroze Mody, was beaten to death by a gang chanting "Hindu, Hindu!" They conflated race, religion, and culture in one naked cry of hatred.

At that time, the Indian immigrant community was about fifteen thousand strong in Jersey City, and it was part of a much larger Indian community in northern New Jersey. Before the attack in the summer of 1987, a local newspaper had called attention to the rising number of incidents of harassment against South Asians. In response, it received a venomous letter signed by the "Jersey City Dot Busters":

> I hate [Indian people], if you had to live near them you would also. We are an organization called dot busters. We have been around for 2 years. We will go to any extreme to get Indians to move out of Jersey City. If I'm walking down the street and I see a Hindu and the setting is right, I will hit him or her. We plan some of our most extreme attacks such as breaking windows, breaking car windows, and crashing family parties. We use the phone books and look up the name Patel. Have you seen how many of them there are? . . . You said that they will have to start protecting themselves because the police cannot always be there. They will never do anything. They are a week race physically and mentally. We are going to continue our way. We will never be stopped.

The letter was published a month before the death of Navroze Mody. Then, a few weeks later, a young resident in medicine, Dr. Sharan, was assaulted by three young men with baseball bats as he walked home late one night in Jersey City. He was beaten severely and left unconscious with a fractured skull. Sharan was in a coma for a week and suffered severe neurological damage. He recalled that one of the young people yelled, "There's a dothead! Let's get him!" as they set out after him with their bats. . . .

---

[21]Doug Grow, "Wisconsin Teen Victorious in Her Free-Speech Fight," *Minneapolis Star Tribune,* March 31, 1999.

Working It Out: The Workplace and Religious Practice

One of the places we most commonly encounter religious difference in America today is the workplace. What religious attire may one wear? A cross? Yarmulke? Head scarf? Turban? Where and when is it appropriate to pray? What facilities do employers need to provide, and what policies do they need to implement? Religious difference is a question not just for theological schools and religious institutions but increasingly for businesses and corporations, offices and factories. These are the places where "we the people" most frequently meet, and how we manage our encounters here might be far more important than how we cope with imaginary encounters in the realm of theologies and beliefs.

The most common workplace issues have traditionally concerned working on the Sabbath, which is Saturday for Jews and Seventh-Day Adventists. Consider the case of a computer operator at a hospital in Fort Smith, Arkansas. Although he is a Seventh-Day Adventist and asked not to work on Saturdays, he was placed on call on Saturdays. When he refused to make himself available on his Sabbath, the hospital fired him. Title VII of the Civil Rights Act of 1964 prohibits discrimination on the basis of race, color, religion, national origin, or sex. In interpreting the act in relation to the religious practices of workers, the employer must try to make "reasonable accommodation" of religious practice, at least as long as it does not impose an "undue hardship" on the employer. In this case, the court ruled that the hospital was in violation of the Civil Rights Act. But just what constitutes "reasonable accommodation" and "undue hardship" is the thorny issue as each case comes forward.

In the past ten years the Equal Employment Opportunity Commission   30
(EEOC), which considers workplace complaints that may violate the Civil Rights Act, has reported a 31 percent rise in complaints of religious discrimination in the workplace. This is not surprising, given the number of new immigrants in the workforce and the range of questions their attire, their holidays, and their religious life bring to the workplace environment. We have already looked at the incivility and prejudice Muslim women wearing the *hijab* may encounter. But sometimes incivility slides up the scale toward discrimination. For example, in 1996 Rose Hamid, a twelve-year veteran flight attendant with U.S. Air, became increasingly serious about her faith in the wake of some health problems and made the decision to wear a head scarf. Her first day at work, she was ordered to take it off because it was not part of the uniform of a flight attendant, and when she refused she was put on unpaid leave. Rose filed a complaint with the Equal Employment Opportunity Commission. What is reasonable accommodation in Rose's case? Rose had modeled different ways in which the colors of her uniform would be duplicated in her scarf, and some would argue that reasonable accommodation would mean allowing some flexibility in the uniform as long as it was readily recognizable. But U.S. Air moved Rose to a job that did not require a uniform and hence put her out of public visibility. The issue was

resolved in a slightly different way by Domino's Pizza in 1998. That year, a convert to Islam who showed up at work wearing a head scarf was told by her employer at Domino's, "Unless you take that stupid thing off you have to leave."[22] The employer soon learned his response to her was more than just rude. It was against the law. Here, the Council on American Islamic Relations called attention to the case. The employers reached what they believed was a reasonable accommodation: wearing the signature Domino's baseball cap over a red and blue head scarf. . . .

Prayer in the workplace is another issue that has gained complexity with the new immigration. A Christian group might gather at 7:15 to pray together before work. A Buddhist meditation group might spend part of its lunch hour in sitting practice. In the spring of 1998 I received a CAIR bulletin with information on three similar cases of workplace prayer accommodation in manufacturing plants around Nashville. Whirlpool Corporation reportedly had refused to allow Muslim employees to offer obligatory prayers on the job. One Muslim employee quit, and the others continued to perform their obligatory midday prayer secretly during bathroom breaks. When CAIR intervened, contacted the managers, and began a dialogue, together they envisioned a solution: the Muslim employees could perhaps customize their coffee breaks so that they could fit an Islamic prayer schedule. Today, Muslim organizations, including CAIR, are taking the initiative in providing the kind of information that might head off the endless round of discrimination cases. They have published a booklet called *An Employer's Guide to Islamic Religious Practices,* detailing what employers might need to know about the obligations of Muslim workers. . . .

See You in Court

The American Constitution guarantees that there will be "no establishment" of religion and that the "free exercise" of religion will be protected. As we have seen, these twin principles have guided church-state relations in the United States for the past two hundred years. But the issues have become increasingly complex in a multireligious America, where the church in question may now be the mosque, the Buddhist temple, the Hindu temple, or the Sikh gurdwara. Every religious tradition has its own questions. Can a Muslim schoolteacher wear her head covering on the job as a public school teacher? Can a Sikh student wear the *kirpan,* the symbolic knife required of all initiated Sikhs, to school, or a Sikh worker wear a turban on a hard-hat job, in apparent violation of safety regulations? Should a crèche be displayed in the Christmas season on public property? Can the sanctity of Native lands be protected from road building? Should the taking of peyote[23] by Native Americans be protected as the free exercise of

---

[22]Katherine Roth, "God on the Job," *Working Woman,* February 1998, 65.

[23]*peyote:* Cactus that grows in the American Southwest and is used by some Native Americans in religious ceremonies because of its psychoactive effects.

religion? Can a city council pass an ordinance prohibiting the sacrifice of animals by the adherents of the Santería faith?

These difficult questions make clear that one vital arena of America's new pluralism is the courts. Since about 1960, church-state issues in America have been increasingly on court agendas. Just as the "church" is not a single entity in multireligious America, the "state" is multiple too, with zoning boards, city councils, state governments, and the federal government. At all levels, courts hear disputes and offer interpretations of laws and regulations and the constitutional principles that undergird them.

The First Amendment principles of nonestablishment of religion and the free exercise of religion sometimes almost seem to be in tension: the free exercise of religion calling for the protection of religious groups, while the nonestablishment of religion prohibiting any such special treatment. On the "no establishment" side, a landmark Supreme Court decision was made in the case of *Everson v. Board of Education* (1947) in which a school busing program in New Jersey was ruled to be accessible to students going to parochial schools. The Supreme Court's decision was clearly and narrowly defined: the busing program was a "generally available benefit" that should not be denied to children simply because their destination was a religious school. While the court has consistently ruled against state support of private religious schools, in this case, the benefit in question was not to the schools, but to the children. Justice Black wrote, "[T]he First Amendment requires the state to be neutral in its relations with groups of religious believers and non-believers; it does not require the state to be their adversary. State power is no more to be used so as to handicap religions than it is to favor them." The extended logic of this decision was that religious communities should have "equal access" to those benefits that are available to nonreligious communities. In other words, if a high school gymnasium in Bethesda, Maryland, can be used by the Girl Scouts or the Garden Club, its use cannot be denied to a Hindu temple community for its annual fall Diwali festival.

In "free exercise" cases, the *Sherbert v. Verner* decision in 1963 set 35 a precedent that guided religious liberty cases for thirty years. In South Carolina, Adell Sherbert, a Seventh-Day Adventist, was fired from her job because she refused to accept a schedule requiring her to work on Saturday, her Sabbath, and was then refused state unemployment compensation. In her case, the Supreme Court articulated three questions to guide its decision: Has the religious freedom of a person been infringed or burdened by some government action? If so, is there a "compelling state interest" that would nonetheless justify the government action? Finally, is there any other way the government interest can be satisfied without restricting religious liberty? In sum, religious liberty is the rule, any exception to the rule can be justified only by a "compelling state interest." This form of reasoning came to be called the "balancing test" — balancing state interest against the religious freedom of the individual.

In the Sherbert case, the court ruled that there was no state interest compelling enough to warrant the burden placed upon Sherbert's religious freedom. Similarly, when an Amish community in Wisconsin insisted on withdrawing its children from public schools after the eighth grade and the State of Wisconsin insisted the children comply with compulsory education laws, the Supreme Court applied the three-pronged test and ruled that the religious freedom of the Amish outweighed the state's interest in four years' more compulsory education (*Wisconsin v. Yoder*, 1972).

Beginning in the 1980s, however, a series of Supreme Court rulings gradually weakened the force of the Sherbert balancing test and, in the view of many, weakened the constitutional guarantee of the free exercise of religion. These rulings began to raise disturbing questions about the religious rights of minorities. In the case of *Lyng v. The Northwest Indian Cemetery Protective Association* (1988), the issue was whether the Native Americans' right to preserve intact their sacred sites outweighed the government's right to build roads through Forest Service land. The Yurok, Karok, and Tolowa Indians argued that building a logging road through the land would have "devastating effects" on their religious ways. A lower court acted to prevent the Forest Service from building the road, but the Forest Service appealed to the Supreme Court. In this case, the Supreme Court supported the Forest Service, saying,

> Incidental effects of government programs which may make it more difficult to practice certain religions, but which have no tendency to coerce individuals into acting contrary to their religious beliefs [do not] require government to bring forward a compelling justification for its otherwise lawful actions. . . . However much we might wish that it were otherwise, government simply could not operate if it were required to satisfy every citizen's religious needs and desires. . . . Whatever rights the Indians may have to the use of the area, however, those rights do not divest the government of its right to use what is, after all, its land.

Here, the balance tipped precipitously in favor of the government, whose policies, just incidentally, compromised Native religious practice.

For the Indians, one of the issues in this and other cases is whether the government recognizes the deeply held religious importance of preserving particular sacred sites undisturbed. A Hopi and Navajo case (*Wilson v. Block*, 1983) questioned whether a ski area could be built on a sacred mountain. The court ruled that the Forest Service had not infringed the religious rights of the Indians because it had not denied them access to the mountain. But the Navajo and Hopi argued that the mountain, the home of the Kachinas — divine messengers — would be desecrated by its commercial development. The court seemed to give little weight to the fact that the Native peoples considered the mountain to be inherently sacred, the very locus of the Divine, and not simply the place where they pray to the Divine. Here, the very nature of Native religious claims for the sanctity of the land seemed to be undermined, or perhaps not even understood, by the court's reasoning. . . .

These increasingly restrictive interpretations of the guarantees of the   40
First Amendment culminated in the controversial 1990 Supreme Court
decision about peyote use. In this case (*Employment Division, Department
of Human Resources of Oregon v. Smith*, 1990) two members of the Native
American church ingested peyote, as is common in the ceremonial life
of the church, and were subsequently fired from their jobs for "miscon-
duct." The state of Oregon denied them unemployment compensation
because they had been dismissed for the use of peyote, which was classified
as an illegal drug. The Supreme Court upheld Oregon's decision, arguing
that the state had a "generally applicable" law against drug use. The law did
not specifically target the Native American church or any other group, and
carving out exceptions to such laws would be impracticable, according to
the 5–4 majority of the court. Justice Antonin Scalia argued that to require
the government to demonstrate a "compelling state interest" in enforcing
generally applicable laws would be "courting anarchy."

The Smith decision thus reversed many years of court precedent, which
presumed that religious freedom would be the rule, with any infringement
requiring the demonstration of a compelling state interest. Many critics
insisted that for the court to refuse to apply the balancing test to "generally
applicable laws" would seriously damage the first-amendment protection of
religious freedom. The Smith decision, critics argued, would be especially
hard on minority religions, since generally applicable laws are passed by the
majority. Freedom of religion, on the other hand, is not subject to majority
rule. The purpose of the Bill of Rights was precisely to limit the power of
the majority in areas of fundamental rights, such as the freedom of conscience and speech.

The Santería Church of the Lukumi Babalu Aye in Hialeah, Florida,
was a minority group in danger of losing its freedom of religious practice
due to its unpopular and widely misunderstood practice of animal sacrifice.
An estimated fifty thousand practitioners of the Afro-Caribbean Santería
religion now live in South Florida, and their ceremonial life includes the
sacrifice of chickens, pigeons, or other small animals to the *orisha*, their
gods. The case that came to the Supreme Court (*Church of the Lukumi
Babalu Aye v. City of Hialeah*, 1993) began in 1987 when Ernesto Pichardo,
a priest of the Santería religion, purchased a building and a former used car
lot to open a place of worship. The city council of Hialeah met to consider
the matter, and many voices hostile to Santería were raised. The council
passed three ordinances that effectively prohibited animal sacrifice within
the city limits. As the city attorney explained, "This community will not tolerate religious practices which are abhorrent to its citizens."

Ernesto Pichardo and his community protested, insisting that the ordinances specifically targeted Santería, as they did not prohibit the killing of
animals within city limits for secular reasons but only for religious ones and
only, seemingly, for those of the Santería religion. Indeed, the ordinances
specifically excluded Jewish kosher slaughter practices. Animals could be
killed in butcher shops and restaurants but not in the religious context of

Santería. Many quipped that the Church of Lukumi Babalu Aye was being persecuted for killing a few chickens with a prayer, while Frank Perdue and Colonel Sanders kill tens of thousands without one. The question before the Supreme Court was whether the three ordinances passed by the city council were constitutional or whether they violated the constitutional rights of the practitioners of Santería by specifically legislating against their religious practices. The judges unanimously struck down the ordinances, stating that they were not generally applicable laws at all but specifically aimed at the Santería religion. As Justice Anthony M. Kennedy wrote, "Although the practice of animal sacrifice may seem abhorrent to some, 'religious beliefs need not be acceptable, logical, consistent, or comprehensible to others in order to merit First Amendment protection.'"

The Santería case was an easy one, resting on the principle that "government may not enact laws that suppress religious belief or practice." However, many people, including Justice David Souter, were still disquieted about the merits and the precedent of the Smith decision. By this time, legislation called the Religious Freedom Restoration Act had been introduced in Congress precisely to restore the religious freedom many people in public life felt had been eroded with the Smith decision. This act, passed in 1995, stated simply, "The government cannot burden a person's free exercise of religion, even if the burden results from a rule of general applicability, unless the burden is essential to further a compelling governmental interest and is the least restrictive means of furthering that interest." In effect, it reinstituted the balancing test of the Sherbert case, this time in law. The legislation was eventually ruled unconstitutional by the Supreme Court in 1997, in part because it was a legislative maneuver to reestablish a form of judicial reasoning. This, the court believed, was the prerogative of the judiciary.

Questions of religious freedom lie at the heart of some of America's   45 most hotly contested cases. The courts are one site of the encounter and disputation that are endemic to America's new pluralism. They represent the difficult places where we the people do not seem to be able to resolve our differences on our own. Cases involving America's newer religious communities have gradually made their way into the court system and into case law. The willingness to take advantage of access to the courts is itself a signal of the Americanization process. . . .

ENGAGING THE TEXT

1. How much have you learned in school about world religions like Islam, Buddhism, and Hinduism? Does your own experience support or challenge Eck's assertion that "some progress has been made in recent years" in the way that America's schools deal with issues of religious diversity?

2. Would you agree that clear stereotypes exist for all major religious groups? What stereotypes, if any, are associated with Unitarians, Lutherans, Southern Baptists, Roman Catholics, Jews, Muslims, Buddhists, and Hindus? To

what extent, if any, are such stereotypes distinguishable from simple racist thinking?

3. Do you agree with Eck that we can defeat religious prejudice and over-come intolerance and xenophobia by learning more about other religions? What evidence supports the idea that greater understanding leads to peaceful coexistence between different religious groups?

4. Do you think that employees and students should have the right to express their religious identities in the workplace or at school? For example, should students be free to wear yarmulkes, crosses, hijabs, ceremonial knives, chadors, or other forms of religious dress while at school? Should employ-ees have the right to pray during working hours or to refuse to work on their Sabbath days? Why might schools or employers want to limit such practices?

5. What difficulties arise, according to Eck, when attempting to determine the constitutionality of certain unusual religious practices? Do you think, for example, that members of the Native American Church should have the right to use peyote to induce visionary experiences as part of their sacred rites — or that people who believe in Santería should be allowed to prac-tice animal sacrifice? Why or why not?

EXPLORING CONNECTIONS

6. How might Anne Lamott's account of her religious conversion (p. 620) illustrate Eck's assertion that greater contact with people of other faiths leads to acceptance and appreciation? To what extent do Lamott's experi-ences reflect common religious stereotypes? Why do you think Lamott was so open to different religious points of view?

7. How might Eck respond to David Kupelian's (p. 646) assessment of people who practice "suspension" and his condemnation of paganism? How do you think Kupelian might view many of the religions that Eck describes in this selection? Would you consider paganism, Wicca, and Santería to be religions on equal footing with Christianity or Islam? Why or why not?

8. How might Sam Harris (p. 738) respond to the growing religious diversity that Eck sees in America today? How might he explain the source of the prejudice and intergroup conflict that Eck attributes to ignorance? Which of these explanations of religious intolerance do you find more persuasive, and why?

EXTENDING THE CRITICAL CONTEXT

9. Working in groups, research one of the lesser-known religions that Eck discusses. What are the central ideas, values, and beliefs associated with this religion? Share your findings in class and discuss whether your new knowledge has changed the way you think about this particular religious group.

10. Do some Web-based research on recent hate crimes in the United States that have involved violence against religious groups. What do your findings suggest about the state of tolerance in a religiously diverse America?

Us and Them
MARIA POGGI JOHNSON

Over the past two hundred years, Americans have made remarkable strides when it comes to issues of tolerance and diversity. Today, it's cool to be different, to mix cultural styles, and to get along with everyone, regardless of upbringing or background. Unless, that is, you're sure your neighbors are unredeemed sinners, doomed to burn for eternity because of their beliefs. In America, tolerance requires toleration of the intolerant. And that's a paradox that leaves many of us scratching our heads about what it means to share our daily existence with religious "others." Maria Poggi Johnson got to experience this peculiarly American situation herself when she and her Catholic family moved into an Orthodox Jewish neighborhood in New York. A professor of comparative religion, Johnson reflects in this selection on the limits and virtues of religious tolerance and on what it means to live next door to "Them." Johnson (b. 1967) is currently an associate professor of theology at the University of Scranton in northeastern Pennsylvania. She is the editor of Sermons of the Christian Year, *a compilation of works by John Keble (2004), and* Strangers and Neighbors: What I Have Learned about Christianity by Living Among Orthodox Jews *(2006). This selection appeared in* The Best American Spiritual Writing 2005, *edited by Philip Zaleski.*

Six months out of grad school and into our first jobs, my husband and I fell in love with a house, a beautiful, eccentric Victorian. It was, of course, a fixer-upper, with a few caved-in ceilings, and it stood on a block that might be called borderline — there were some neglected houses nearby with bad landlords and worse tenants, a certain amount of drug activity, and there had been a shooting across the road the month before. This was why we could afford the house. On the plus side, there were a number of long-established stable families, and on the next block was a synagogue that was the center of a growing community of strictly observant Orthodox Jews. We persuaded ourselves that things couldn't get too bad, took a gamble, and bought the house.

Not only did things not get bad, they got very good indeed. Seven years later, the fixing-up is far from complete, but we have welcomed four babies into our home among the paint pots and half-built bookcases, and the block, now free of trouble spots, has welcomed four new Orthodox Jewish families with twenty-three children among them. There is a thriving and cohesive community on our street, and to our surprise we have been cheerfully welcomed into many aspects of its life. We've been invited to numerous festive meals (of course, we could not return the favor, although my husband's single-malt scotch has been enthusiastically pronounced kosher), we have joined in neighborhood patrols when there was a spate of vandalism against the *succahs*,[1] we have performed the office of what I believe is called a *Shabbos goy*, which involves setting the timer on an Orthodox family's heat and lights for the Sabbath when they forget to do so. We have taken our turn with the scissors when Binyomin had his first haircut at his third birthday party, and we have spent many hours sitting on doorsteps chatting idly and watching children practice riding tricycles. Having become good friends with a couple of families has made us automatically acquaintances of all the Orthodox in the neighborhood: children wave to me and mothers greet me when I walk past the Hebrew day school on my way to the office. We only wish that the sense of community among the Christians we know could rival what we have experienced among Orthodox Jews.

Living on the fringes of such a strong community is intriguing and deeply appealing in itself, and, of course, for us as Christians the fact that it is a Jewish community, intensely and vividly Jewish, is particularly meaningful. My theological views are much what they were — I'm a theologian by profession and had a pretty good handle on the whole law/gospel/covenant thing at a theoretical level — but my grasp of and relation to my own faith has been altered profoundly by living on familiar terms with a religious reality that precedes and underpins my own, even as it differs dramatically. The imaginative and emotional resonances of the Holy Week[2] liturgies and the

---

[1]*succah:* Also spelled *sukkah*, a temporary structure built as part of the Jewish holiday Sukkot, or "Feast of the Tabernacles."

[2]*Holy Week:* The week before Easter, which is the holiest day of the Christian calendar.

Eucharist, to give just two examples, are deepened by the fact that I have friends for whom the phrase "paschal lamb"[3] refers to what one eats on Passover.

Another effect has been the way I teach the introductory Bible course that all students at my university are required to take. When teaching about Mount Sinai,[4] the law, and the covenant,[5] for instance, I can fulfill my responsibilities as a Catholic and a scholar, be faithful to the teaching of *Dei Verbum*,[6] and meet the departmental objectives for the course if I (attempt to) help my students to understand the law both as an ancient Near Eastern legal, social, and ritual code and as a revelation of the character and will of God and a key stage in the salvation history that culminates in the coming of Christ. And before living in this neighborhood I might have felt that that was plenty. But now I feel I have not told my students the whole story unless I can get them to see a little of what I have learned from living in a place where the law is not a historical relic or a preliminary stage in the plot of a larger story but something vividly and vigorously alive in every aspect of life.

When possible, I invite a good friend to talk to my students about the   5
law in her daily life. Initially she talked mainly about kosher laws and the Sabbath, but after coming to class a few times she got the measure of the students' reaction and now mischievously enjoys watching their jaws drop in disbelief as she describes dating and marriage, sex and modesty in Orthodox communities. They are fascinated and bewildered by the notion of according such deep and demanding seriousness to such things as time, food, and sex — things that they are used to handling with an eye to speedy self-fulfillment. Some of them would doubtless like to dismiss the whole thing as weirdness or fanaticism, but it is impossible to do that with my friend, who is a thoroughly appealing person — warm, clever, funny, and very obviously sane and happy. "Who's got it right?" she says. "Well, when Moshiach[7] comes, we'll just have to ask him, 'Well then, have you been here before, or is this your first time?' "

My attempt to put my students in touch with the Jewishness of the scriptures is not limited to those scriptures that Christians share with Jews. It is hard enough when we read the Old Testament to keep some students from throwing into their essays wildly anachronistic (rather than properly typological,[8] which is way beyond most of them) references to Jesus and the Church. When we turn to the New Testament and meet the baby Jesus

---

[3]*"paschal lamb"*: Refers to Biblical instruction given by God to the Israelites to put the blood of a lamb on their doorposts to mark the people inside as believers.

[4]*Mount Sinai*: Biblical name of the peak on which Moses received the Ten Commandments.

[5]*the covenant*: Agreement related in the Old Testament between God and the Israelites regarding their behavior and mutual obligations.

[6]*Dei Verbum*: Document of the Second Vatican Council (Latin for "Word of God").

[7]*Moshiach*: Hebrew for "anointed one" or messiah.

[8]*typological*: Method of interpreting Biblical people or events in the Old Testament as prefiguring those in the New Testament.

in the manger, they imagine themselves on home ground and they can become lazy. I have to remind them energetically that this is still a book largely by and about Jews; that although we are reading about the roots of the Church to which they belong, the world of the New Testament is very different from the novenas,[9] CCD classes,[10] and parish raffles of our area's deep-rooted Catholic culture. I find that the more I succeed in getting them to "think Jewish," the better readers of the text they become and the more attuned they are to the intense drama of the New Testament. If I can help them to grasp that the apostles[11] and the Pharisees[12] are as passionate about the law and about their Jewishness as that lady in the hat who came to class to talk to us, then Jesus starts to look a lot more exciting and troubling. They can better appreciate what is at stake in the story of Cornelius's conversion[13] if they can identify with Peter, who, tossed a few cryptic clues and forced to think on his feet, must rethink hundreds of years of religious tradition in the course of an afternoon. They must learn to side with the conservatives at the Jerusalem conference in the Acts of the Apostles[14] in order to understand the depth of the debate about whether gentiles must be circumcised in order to become Christians.

If I have to remind my students to think Jewish, I have also to remind myself to think Christian. In my eagerness to help my students see that the decision at Jerusalem against circumcision was a difficult one to make, and in my fascination with the lives of my neighbors (a fascination in part foolish and romantic, I admit), I become half a Judaizer myself, and occasionally find myself musing about how it might be nice to do something with candles on Friday evenings or even keep just a very little bit kosher. When Paul bellows, "You foolish Galatians! Who has bewitched you?"[15] I have to shake myself and remember that this question has already been dealt with, and an answer has been given, with a clarity that it would be more than foolish to second-guess.

What precisely my students make of the heavily Jewish emphasis of my Bible courses or whether they will remember anything at all in the long term I cannot say. But at home the main day-to-day contact with Orthodox Jewish life is still through the children, and I can confidently say that these friendships will have a long-lasting impact. The neighborhood children live, like ours, in homes without video games or cable TV. Our tree house with a

---

[9]*novenas:* Set of prayers said by a Catholic over the course of nine days.

[10]*CCD classes:* Religious instruction provided prior to confirmation in the Catholic Chuch.

[11]*apostles:* A group of twelve men chosen by Jesus to preach the Gospel.

[12]*Pharisees:* Members of an ancient Jewish sect that emphasized strict interpretation and observance of religious law.

[13]*Cornelius's conversion:* As described in the Bible, Cornelius was a Roman who was the first non-Jew to convert to Christianity.

[14]*The Acts of the Apostles:* Fifth book of the New Testament in the Bible.

[15]*"You foolish Galatians! . . .":* Remark made by Saint Paul to the Galatians (inhabitants of present-day Turkey) in the Bible.

slide and our big box of dress-up clothes are enough to render our house a highly desirable venue, and some collection of neighborhood children is at our home most days. They are all a mother could desire in her children's friends — they are friendly, polite, good at sharing, and they are unlikely ever to set undesirable examples with regard to skimpy T-shirts and obnoxious music, or to share unhelpful stories about Mom's new boyfriend.

The religious and cultural difference is always present and often hilarious. Our Adam, blessed with three sisters and quick to latch onto anything male that comes through the door and identify with it for all he is worth, has decided that Real Men wear yarmulkes.[16] We have had to get him his own to stop him from constantly stealing Binyomin's. The occasional rainy-day movie on the VCR is considerably enlivened by Chaya Sara's emphatic editorial comments to the effect that Sleeping Beauty's dress is not *tznius*[17] or that the best part of *Prince of Egypt* is "the bit where Ha-Shem saves the yids[18] and drowns all the goys."[19] This necessitated a stern lecture to my children as soon as their friends had gone home: "Listen, *yid* is a very special word that only Jews are allowed to use, and you must never, ever say it, do you understand?"

The children are allowed in our house because their parents trust that I "get it." I think I do, but still, some amount of vigilance on my part is necessary to ensure that their trust is not betrayed. Batsheva has a liking for rosary beads and has to be routinely frisked before she goes home. I have had to deflect endless arguments along the lines of "Catherine had a banana at my house yesterday so our food is kosher for you, so your food must be kosher for us, so can I have a sandwich, please?" The idea that our food isn't kosher, period, not even for us, is rejected as obviously absurd. The only effective explanation on these occasions, I have reluctantly learned from the children themselves, is to say, "That's not for Jews." This is not a phrase that trips easily off the tongue, as may well be imagined, but it is promptly and cheerfully accepted as permitting no appeal.

Besides having the sort of peer group that many modern parents can only dream of, our children are learning all sorts of things from their familiarity with Jewish life. Some of the lessons are essentially the same as those I try to communicate to my students — Abraham, Isaac, and Jacob[20] are rendered much more interesting than they would be otherwise by virtue of being Moshe Yehuda's great-great-great-great-grandfathers. Our children are bright and curious and very interested in the differences between their lives and their friends' lives, the relationship between church and *shul*,[21]

10

---

[16]*yarmulkes:* Small, circular head coverings worn by Jewish men and boys.
[17]*tznius:* Adhering to religious law governing dress and behavior.
[18]*yids:* Jews.
[19]*goys:* Non-Jews.
[20]*Abraham, Isaac, and Jacob:* Figures from the Old Testament.
[21]*shul:* Synagogue.

between Jesus and Ha-Shem,[22] between Sunday and Shabbos.[23] They discuss it among themselves from time to time and come to us for clarification when necessary. Having learned Christianity as a story rather than as a series of propositions, they have no trouble understanding that "they have different rules from us because it reminds us that they were God's friends first. The law is how they are friends with God, and Jesus is how we and everybody else can be his friends." Sometimes they push the point a little: If we are friends of the same God after all, and if Jesus really is God's son, then why can't we make them Christmas cards? They are contented for the present with a simple, and truthful, "because they would think it was rude," but it's only a matter of time before that is subjected to the inevitable "why?" When that happens, we will have to decide whether to tackle the question historically or philosophically. Even when one has a Ph.D. in theology, it requires a certain amount of delicacy to maintain the finality of God's self-revelation in Christ while at the same time eschewing supersessionism;[24] it is naturally much harder when one is only eight. On the other hand, I'm in no hurry to explain to my open-hearted innocents the historical reasons that anything remotely like proselytism[25] would be offensive to their friends.

However complex the questions and answers may become, they will arise, if they do arise, among friends who have already dealt with heated debates over whose turn it is to go down the slide and who gets to wear the sparkly shoes. There is a great deal of nonsense written, to be sure, on the subject of diversity and multiculturalism, but the fact remains that the great challenge facing our world is that of maintaining clear convictions and strong commitments while living in peaceful proximity with people with different convictions and commitments, avoiding brittle bigotry on the one hand and soggy relativism on the other. If we are to make it into the next century, we need to figure out how to do this, and I cannot imagine a stronger foundation for doing so than the negotiations that are second nature to our children and their friends: "We've got to have lunch now so you have to go home, but can we come to yours after?" "My mom says I have to have a shower now — I'll come back later, but I'll have my Shabbos clothes on so we'll have to play inside." "We call it a creche[26] — I don't think you're supposed to play with the baby because it's Jesus, but the camels and the sheep are probably OK. Are Jews allowed angels?"

For our part, my husband and I feel at home in the Jewish life around us in large part precisely because there is no attempt to deny the extent of

[22]*Ha-Shem:* Term used when referring to God.

[23]*Shabbos:* Saturday, the special day of religious observance for Jews; the Sabbath.

[24]*supersessionism:* Belief that Christianity is the fulfillment of the Old Testament (and thus that Jewish religious beliefs are mistaken).

[25]*proselytism:* Practice of trying to convert people.

[26]*creche:* Representation of the newborn Jesus surrounded by Mary, Joseph, shepherds, wise men, and animals.

the gulf between us and our neighbors, to pretend that we and they are really all the same. Our neighbors are infinitely tolerant of my no doubt tedious fascination with the details of Torah[27] observance, but they have never attempted to feign interest in what Catholics believe and do. They are both warmly generous in their hospitality and unapologetically clear that all they will accept from us is tap water in a paper cup. My friend cheerfully welcomes my children, who are constantly banging on her door, and openly discusses with me her acute distress about her sister, who is dating a Gentile[28] and whom she will no longer allow in her home. There is none of the painful embarrassment that attends deliberate attempts at cultural sensitivity; nor, ironically, is there any of the suspicion or tension that can mar relationships among our Catholic colleagues, some of whom are inclined to keep a sharp eye on those whom they suspect of being not quite Catholic enough, or altogether too Catholic. Because the boundaries between us and our Orthodox neighbors are so unequivocally clear, they do not spill over into the rest of our dealings; I would no more waste my time with "Are you sure I can't get you a cup of tea?" than they would in trying to gauge my level of loyalty to the Church's magisterium.[29]

The image of Christians as an alien branch engrafted, by the grace of God, into the vine of the covenant and thus truly of the Chosen People would probably sound thoroughly absurd, at best, to our Jewish friends. For us the image expresses not only a theological proposition subject to analysis and interpretation but also a simple fact of daily life, and as such it makes perfect sense.

ENGAGING THE TEXT

1. How would you describe Johnson's relationship with her Orthodox Jewish neighbors? To what extent do you think her academic background influenced her attitudes toward them?

2. Would you agree with Johnson that "the great challenge facing our world today" is that of holding on to strong personal beliefs while living at peace with people who are different? How strong do Johnson's own religious beliefs seem to be?

3. How do your own interactions with people of different faiths compare with Johnson's encounters with her neighbors? Have your own experiences affected you as deeply and as meaningfully as hers?

4. What meaning do you see in the title that Johnson chose for this selection? How accurately does the phrase "Us and Them" capture the essence of Johnson's relationship with her neighbors? What does it suggest about the quality and intensity of this relationship?

[27]*Torah:* The first five books of the Hebrew scriptures.
[28]*Gentile:* A non-Jew.
[29]*magisterium:* In the Roman Catholic Church, the authority to teach religious doctrine.

EXPLORING CONNECTIONS

5. To what extent does Johnson's account of living among "Them" support or complicate Diana L. Eck's (p. 693) claim that greater knowledge is the key to dispelling religious bigotry? Who seems more tolerant, Johnson or her neighbors? Why?

6. How does Johnson's story of her relationship with her Orthodox neighbors compare with Anne Lamott's account (p. 620) of her contact with different religious groups? Which of the two accounts seems to depend more heavily on stereotypical ideas or thinking? Which of the two authors seems more profoundly affected by their respective experiences?

EXTENDING THE CRITICAL CONTEXT

8. Divide into groups by faith, and prepare a brief introduction to the most distinctive features, values, and beliefs of your own religious group. Share these with the entire class and then discuss the differences and similarities you discover.

9. Interview one or more people you know from a religious background that is significantly different from yours. What do they consider to be the most important ideas or values associated with their faith? In what ways do they see their own beliefs as differing from those of nonbelievers? How do they view people outside their faith? Compare notes and discuss your findings with your classmates.

Memorial and Remonstrance Against Religious Assessments

JAMES MADISON

> *"Congress shall make no law respecting an establishment of religion, or prohibiting the free exercise thereof . . ."*

Long before the famous "establishment clause" was included in the U.S. Constitution, questions about the proper relationship of church and state divided America. We've grown so used to Thomas Jefferson's notion of a "wall of separation" between the realms of church and state, we often forget that in 1776 strong support remained for the idea of state-supported religion. In Virginia, Thomas Jefferson and James Madison worked for more than a decade against multiple attempts to re-establish Anglicanism as the state's official faith. In 1784, fellow Virginian and Revolutionary-era hero Patrick

Henry proposed an "Assessment Bill" that would have provided public support for Anglican ministers at the expense of non-Anglican congregations. Madison reacted by publishing his "Memorial and Remonstrance Against Religious Assessments," which expressed his thoughts on the dangers of state-supported religion. Two years later in 1786, Madison succeeded in orchestrating passage of Jefferson's "Virginia Statute for Religious Freedom," which set the pattern for our modern concept of church-state relations. James Madison (1751–1836) was the fourth president of the United States (1809–1817). He is often called the "Father of the Constitution" because of his role in drafting and securing passage of many of its key provisions — including the Bill of Rights. Between 1787 and 1788, he, along with coauthors Alexander Hamilton and John Jay, published the Federalist Papers, *a series of eighty-five articles that argued in favor of the Constitution's ratification. Madison's "Memorial and Remonstrance" is widely viewed as his most eloquent statement in support of freedom of conscience and one of the nation's most important documents in the debate about the relationship between church and state.*

To the Honorable the General Assembly of the Commonwealth of Virginia
A Memorial and Remonstrance Against Religious Assessments

We the subscribers, citizens of the said Commonwealth, having taken into serious consideration, a Bill printed by order of the last Session of General Assembly, entitled "A Bill establishing a provision for Teachers of the Christian Religion," and conceiving that the same if finally armed with the sanctions of a law, will be a dangerous abuse of power, are bound as faithful members of a free State to remonstrate against it, and to declare the reasons by which we are determined. We remonstrate against the said Bill,

1. *Because* we hold it for a fundamental and undeniable truth, "that religion or the duty which we owe to our Creator and the manner of discharging it, can be directed only by reason and conviction, not by force or violence." The Religion then of every man must be left to the conviction and conscience of every man; and it is the right of every man to exercise it as these may dictate. This right is in its nature an unalienable right. It is unalienable, because the opinions of men, depending only on the evidence contemplated by their own minds cannot follow the dictates of other men: It is unalienable also, because what is here a right towards men, is a duty towards the Creator. It is the duty of every man to render to the Creator such homage and such only as he believes to be acceptable to him. This duty is precedent, both in order of time and in degree of obligation, to the claims of Civil Society. Before any man can be considered as a member of Civil Society, he must be considered as a subject of the Governour of the Universe: And if a member of Civil Society, do it with a saving of his allegiance to the Universal Sovereign. We maintain therefore that in matters of Religion, no man's right is abridged by the institution of Civil Society and that Religion is wholly

exempt from its cognizance. True it is, that no other rule exists, by which any question which may divide a Society, can be ultimately determined, but the will of the majority; but it is also true that the majority may trespass on the rights of the minority.

2. *Because* Religion be exempt from the authority of the Society at large, still less can it be subject to that of the Legislative Body. The latter are but the creatures and viceregents of the former. Their jurisdiction is both derivative and limited: it is limited with regard to the co-ordinate departments, more necessarily is it limited with regard to the constituents. The preservation of a free Government requires not merely, that the metes[1] and bounds which separate each department of power be invariably maintained; but more especially that neither of them be suffered to overleap the great Barrier which defends the rights of the people. The Rulers who are guilty of such an encroachment, exceed the commission from which they derive their authority, and are Tyrants. The People who submit to it are governed by laws made neither by themselves nor by an authority derived from them, and are slaves.

3. *Because* it is proper to take alarm at the first experiment on our liberties. We hold this prudent jealousy to be the first duty of Citizens, and one of the noblest characteristics of the late Revolution. The free men of America did not wait till usurped power had strengthened itself by exercise, and entangled the question in precedents. They saw all the consequences in the principle, and they avoided the consequences by denying the principle. We revere this lesson too much soon to forget it. Who does not see that the same authority which can establish Christianity, in exclusion of all other Religions, may establish with the same ease any particular sect of Christians, in exclusion of all other Sects? that the same authority which can force a citizen to contribute three pence only of his property for the support of any one establishment, may force him to conform to any other establishment in all cases whatsoever?

4. *Because* the Bill violates the equality which ought to be the basis of every law, and which is more indispensible, in proportion as the validity or expediency of any law is more liable to be impeached. If "all men are by nature equally free and independent," all men are to be considered as entering into Society on equal conditions; as relinquishing no more, and therefore retaining no less, one than another, of their natural rights. Above all are they to be considered as retaining an "equal title to the free exercise of Religion according to the dictates of Conscience." Whilst we assert for ourselves a freedom to embrace, to profess, and to observe the Religion which we believe to be of divine origin, we cannot deny an equal freedom to those whose minds have not yet yielded to the evidence which has con-

[1]*metes:* Boundaries or limits.

vinced us. If this freedom be abused, it is an offence against God, not against man: To God, therefore, not to man, must an account of it be rendered. As the Bill violates equality by subjecting some to peculiar burdens, so it violates the same principle, by granting to others peculiar exemptions. Are the Quakers and Menonists[2] the only sects who think a compulsive support of their Religions unnecessary and unwarrantable? Can their piety alone be entrusted with the care of public worship? Ought their Religions to be endowed above all others with extraordinary privileges by which proselytes may be enticed from all others? We think too favorably of the justice and good sense of these denominations to believe that they either covet pre-eminences over their fellow citizens or that they will be seduced by them from the common opposition to the measure.

5. *Because* the Bill implies either that the Civil Magistrate is a competent Judge of Religious Truth; or that he may employ Religion as an engine of Civil policy. The first is an arrogant pretension falsified by the contradictory opinions of Rulers in all ages, and throughout the world; the second an unhallowed perversion of the means of salvation.

6. *Because* the establishment proposed by the Bill is not requisite for the support of the Christian Religion. To say that it is, is a contradiction to the Christian Religion itself, for every page of it disavows a dependence on the powers of this world: it is a contradiction to fact; for it is known that this Religion both existed and flourished, not only without the support of human laws, but in spite of every opposition from them, and not only during the period of miraculous aid, but long after it had been left to its own evidence and the ordinary care of Providence. Nay, it is a contradiction in terms; for a Religion not invented by human policy, must have pre-existed and been supported, before it was established by human policy. It is moreover to weaken in those who profess this Religion a pious confidence in its innate excellence and the patronage of its Author; and to foster in those who still reject it, a suspicion that its friends are too conscious of its fallacies to trust it to its own merits.

7. *Because* experience witnesseth that ecclesiastical establishments, instead of maintaining the purity and efficacy of Religion, have had a contrary operation. During almost fifteen centuries has the legal establishment of Christianity been on trial. What have been its fruits? More or less in all places, pride and indolence in the Clergy, ignorance and servility in the laity, in both, superstition, bigotry, and persecution. Enquire of the Teachers of Christianity for the ages in which it appeared in its greatest lustre; those of every sect, point to the ages prior to its incorporation

---

[2]*Menonists:* Religious group, also known as Mennonites, related to the Amish. They settled in Pennsylvania and Ohio in the seventeenth and eighteenth centuries and were committed to pacifism.

with Civil policy. Propose a restoration of this primitive State in which its Teachers depended on the voluntary rewards of their flocks, many of them predict its downfall. On which Side ought their testimony to have greatest weight, when for or when against their interest?

8. *Because* the establishment in question is not necessary for the support of Civil Government. If it be urged as necessary for the support of Civil Government only as it is a means of supporting Religion, and it be not necessary for the latter purpose, it cannot be necessary for the former. If Religion be not within the cognizance of Civil Government how can its legal establishment be necessary to Civil Government? What influence in fact have ecclesiastical establishments had on Civil Society? In some instances they have been seen to erect a spiritual tyranny on the ruins of the Civil authority; in many instances they have been seen upholding the thrones of political tyranny: in no instance have they been seen the guardians of the liberties of the people. Rulers who wished to subvert the public liberty, may have found an established Clergy convenient auxiliaries. A just Government instituted to secure and perpetuate it needs them not. Such a Government will be best supported by protecting every Citizen in the enjoyment of his Religion with the same equal hand which protects his person and his property; by neither invading the equal rights of any Sect, nor suffering any Sect to invade those of another.

9. *Because* the proposed establishment is a departure from the generous policy, which, offering an Asylum to the persecuted and oppressed of every Nation and Religion, promised a lustre to our country, and an accession to the number of its citizens. What a melancholy mark is the Bill of sudden degeneracy? Instead of holding forth an Asylum to the persecuted, it is itself a signal of persecution. It degrades from the equal rank of Citizens all those whose opinions in Religion do not bend to those of the Legislative authority. Distant as it may be in its present form from the Inquisition,[3] it differs from it only in degree. The one is the first step, the other the last in the career of intolerance. The magnanimous sufferer under this cruel scourge in foreign Regions, must view the Bill as a Beacon on our Coast, warning him to seek some other haven, where liberty and philanthropy in their due extent, may offer a more certain repose from his Troubles.

10. *Because* it will have a like tendency to banish our Citizens. The allurements presented by other situations are every day thinning their number. To superadd a fresh motive to emigration by revoking the liberty which they now enjoy, would be the same species of folly which has dishonoured and depopulated flourishing kingdoms.

---

[3]*Inquisition:* Formal judicial procedure by which the Catholic Church charged heretics; during the Middle Ages, thousands of those accused were tortured and killed.

11. *Because* it will destroy that moderation and harmony which the forbearance of our laws to intermeddle with Religion has produced among its several sects. Torrents of blood have been spilt in the old world, by vain attempts of the secular arm, to extinguish Religious discord, by proscribing all difference in Religious opinion. Time has at length revealed the true remedy. Every relaxation of narrow and rigorous policy, wherever it has been tried, has been found to assuage the disease. The American Theatre has exhibited proofs that equal and compleat liberty, if it does not wholly eradicate it, sufficiently destroys its malignant influence on the health and prosperity of the State. If with the salutary effects of this system under our own eyes, we begin to contract the bounds of Religious freedom, we know no name that will too severely reproach our folly. At least let warning be taken at the first fruits of the threatened innovation. The very appearance of the Bill has transformed "that Christian forbearance, love and charity," which of late mutually prevailed, into animosities and jealousies, which may not soon be appeased. What mischiefs may not be dreaded, should this enemy to the public quiet be armed with the force of a law?

Engaging the Text

1. Working in groups, make a list of the primary reasons Madison offers against the use of tax dollars in support of religious schools. Which of these reasons strike you as the most important or persuasive and why?

2. How would you characterize Madison's view of established — or state-supported — religion? To what extent do you agree with Madison's claim that when religions are aligned with government, they have never been "the guardians of the liberties of the people"?

3. Why does Madison view the idea of providing governmental support to religious institutions as a "contradiction to the Christian religion itself"? Why would Christians be particularly opposed to the notion of accepting financial support from the state? Would you agree?

4. What, in your opinion, are the major civic or democratic virtues that Madison celebrates in this selection?

Exploring Connections

5. How do you think Madison would react to the picture of George Washington's ascension into heaven on page 687? Do you feel that this mixing of religious and public themes, figures, and ideas is inappropriate? Why or why not?

6. To what extent does Bill McKibben's "radical" view of the Gospels (p. 665) help to clarify Madison's assertion that Christianity, of all religions, should be opposed to state support?

7. How do you think Madison would view the variety of religions in contemporary American culture, as described by Diana L. Eck (p. 693)? Why?

EXTENDING THE CRITICAL CONTEXT

8. Working in groups, research the attitudes of other important Revolutionary War figures toward state-supported religion. How did thinkers like Jefferson, Franklin, and Thomas Paine view the role that state-supported religions had played in Europe before the founding of the colonies? How would you describe their attitudes toward religion and religious belief?

9. Read more about recent proposals to provide state funding, in the form of vouchers, to religious schools. What arguments are advanced, for example, in favor of a voucher system to pay parochial school tuition? In your view, would the use of vouchers violate the principles Madison establishes in this selection? Why or why not?

Schools and Morals

NOAH FELDMAN

America's schools have often served as a flashpoint in the debate over the relationship between church and state. Since the 1950s, conflicts over the proper role of faith in a secular society have erupted in classrooms across the country. Communities have been torn apart over issues like school prayer,

*the display of the Ten Commandments, religious holiday celebrations, Bible
reading, the teaching of evolution, the direct instruction of moral values, and
federal support of parochial schools. Religious conservatives argue that
schooling should be about moral as well as intellectual development, and that
the moral foundation of the nation and the nation's schools is founded on the
Judeo-Christian tradition. Secularists counter that U.S. public schools have
never endorsed a particular religion or supported a single religious point of
view. As you might expect — and as Noah Feldman demonstrates in this
selection — both of these views simplify the complex interaction of belief and
secularism in American public education. A graduate of Harvard University,
Oxford University, and Yale Law School, Noah Feldman (b. 1970) is a professor of law at New York University and a regular contributor to the* New York
Times Magazine. *In 2003, he served as senior advisor on constitutional law
to the Coalition Provisional Authority in Iraq. His publications include* After
Jihad: America and the Struggle for Islamic Democracy *(2003),* What We
Owe Iraq: War and the Ethics of Nation Building *(2004), and* Divided by
God: America's Church-State Problem *(2005), the source of this selection.*

Public schools are quintessentially American. Attending public school is
probably the most important common experience undergone by people all
over our diverse country. Some forty-eight million children attend today, and
the roughly five million[1] who are educated in parochial or private schools can
take in the public school experience vicariously through countless movies,
television shows, and books. Yet at the time of the American Revolution,
there were no public schools in the modern sense anywhere in the United
States — or anywhere else, for that matter. When the Constitution was
drafted a decade later, not much had changed in this respect. The Northwest
Ordinance of 1789 proclaimed that "religion, morality, and knowledge, being
necessary to good government and the happiness of mankind, schools and
the means of education shall forever be encouraged,"[2] but did not allocate
funds for schools in the federally administered territories, and government-
supported education in the territories was limited to some scattered Indian
schools. Anyone bothering to check again during the War of 1812 would
have found a single school built by the Free School Society of New York
three years earlier[3] but little formal public primary education elsewhere. Not
until the 1820s did so-called common or public schools begin to be founded

[1]National Center for Education Statistics, U.S. Department of Education, Projection of
Education Statistics to 2012 (2002), 13. [All notes are author's, except 4, 7, 8, 11, 13, 18–20, 26,
30, 31, 34, and 35.]

[2]An Act to Provide for the Government of the Territory Northwest of the River Ohio,
chap. 8, 1 Stat. 50 (1789).

[3]Diane Ravitch, *The Great School Wars: A History of the New York City Public Schools*
(Baltimore: Johns Hopkins University Press, 2000), 8–12.

in big cities, promoted by old elites reacting to the gradual urbanization that accompanied industrial growth.

The well-off gentlemen in New York or Boston who took an interest in public schooling had different motivations from those of the patrons of the boarding schools and colleges — such as Philips Andover and Exeter,[4] Harvard and Yale — that until then represented the most important vectors of formal education in America. These elite institutions had at first trained ministers and were now slowly shifting their mission to educating lawyers, political leaders, and businessmen.[5] By contrast, the new public schools aimed to educate ordinary working people, who might in the past have lived in the countryside and deferred to large landowners when it came to politics but who increasingly demanded a voice in public affairs as they began to make their way to the growing cities of the North. The unwelcome prospect of living alongside large numbers of uneducated workingmen in what was becoming a more broadly based democracy encouraged the educated class to think about preserving the republican character of their society.

Education was the answer. For men (still the only bearers of political rights) to deliberate about public affairs and vote responsibly, they must be educated enough to read about the issues of the day, and they must be committed to the unifying process of debating and voting, not to mob rule. Jefferson had earlier argued for the necessity of education to maintain republican government, and he had founded the University of Virginia to that end, but the new theorists of public education cared more about primary school than about college. The common purpose necessary to sustain a republic called for shared knowledge and common moral values, neither of which could be taken for granted in a changing America.

Today education advocates often argue that good schools enable us to compete globally; in his day, Benjamin Franklin also thought that education should prepare students for business and the professions.[6] In the 1820s and '30s, though, political concerns drove the common school movement more than economic ones. Newly emerging factory jobs did not necessarily

---

[4]*Andover and Exeter:* Phillips Academy Andover and Phillips Exeter Academy are prestigious Eastern college preparatory schools.

[5]The story of the rise of the common school has been told and retold. One thoughtful treatment of the subject is Charles Leslie Glenn Jr., *The Myth of the Common School* (Amherst: University of Massachusetts Press, 1988). An influential book in the field is Lawrence A. Cremin, *American Education: The National Experience, 1783–1876* (New York: Harper, 1980). For a still-valuable introduction to the earlier history of education, especially on the difficulty of comparing what came before the common schools movement and after, see Bernard Bailyn, *Education in the Forming of American Society: Needs and Opportunities for Study* (New York: Norton, 1960), especially 9–15. An excellent theoretical treatment of the schools question — and of Catholic objections — is Macedo, *Diversity and Distrust,* 44–87.

[6]Benjamin Franklin, *Idea of the English School* (Philadelphia: B. Franklin, 1751) ("Thus instructed, Youth will come out of this School fitted for learning any Business, Calling or Profession"), available at www.historycarper.com/resources/twobf2/school.htm; cf. Bailyn, *Education,* 35.

require literacy; that would soon be demonstrated by the influx of unskilled workers who would be hired to operate those factories as the demand for labor grew. The reason to educate the workers was primarily to domesticate them for participation in the civic life of the American republic. The election of the unpolished frontiersman Andrew Jackson[7] in 1820 heralded the expanded political influence of nonelites. Only education, it was thought, could save the republic from collapsing into a mere popular democracy in which competing social forces fought for the resources of the state, with the more numerous poorer classes inevitably victorious.

From the very start, the common school movement had to confront the question of religion. The older, private schools in America had uniformly incorporated religious instruction. Formal education — as opposed to basic reading and writing, taught informally in a range of contexts — had long been seen as a social function belonging to the sphere of religion, with schools founded by and for ministers. Not only did religious education seem like a familiar component of education more generally, it served the all-important purpose of teaching moral values to the young. If the point of the common schools was to gentle the unlettered and the ill-bred, so that they would participate in the republican project instead of subverting it, then surely the schools must give children the solid morals that they might not get at home. Teaching them to read and write without inculcating proper moral values would have been, on this theory, worse than irresponsible — it would have been a waste of money.

The notion of teaching children morality by some means that did not involve religion would hardly have entered the American mind. Morality, it was understood, derived from religion, and for even the most liberal of the Protestants who made up the northeastern elite in the 1820s and '30s, that meant morality came from the Bible, especially the Gospels. Without religion there could be no foundation stone on which to rest basic values of honesty and rule following. None of the theorists of the new common schools advocated keeping religion out of the classroom. No religion would have meant no morality, and no morality would have meant that the schools could not achieve their society-shaping function.

Yet the impulse to teach religion in the new common schools faced a major practical obstacle: by the 1830s, Americans were hopelessly divided on which version of Christianity was right. The Second Great Awakening[8] of the previous decades had seen extraordinary, unprecedented multiplication of new sects. Established denominations like Congregationalism were splitting up, to be replaced, in New England, by two offshoots: an old-line Trinitarian church that carried the Congregationalist banner, and a liberal, even radical

5

---

[7]*Andrew Jackson:* Seventh president of the United States (1767–1845).

[8]*The Second Great Awakening:* The second great renewal of religious interest in the United States, which took place in the early to mid-1800s. (The first was in the 1730s and 1740s.)

Unitarianism.[9] Meanwhile, Baptists and Methodists were growing by leaps and bounds in the most "dramatic rise in religious adherence and corresponding religious influence on the broader national culture" in American history.[10] Catholic immigration from Ireland was also increasing, although it had not yet become a preoccupation of domestic politics as it would in a few short years.

This drastically increased religious diversity resulted in a paradox. The new common schools must teach religion yet must appeal to parents across the spectrum of denominations. If religion were not taught, morality would disappear and the schools would fail; if religion were introduced into the curriculum, many parents would object that it was not the right religion and might pull their children out, causing the schools to fail for a different reason. The common school movement could have been stillborn if its theorists had not come up with a creative solution to the problem.

The Nonsectarian Solution

The solution lay in what was coming to be called "nonsectarianism": the claim that there were moral principles shared in common by all Christian sects, independent of their particular theological beliefs. Nonsectarianism would turn out to be among the most powerful — and controversial — ideas in American public life in the nineteenth century and beyond, an idea whose resonances are still felt in our own contemporary debates over religion and values. It promised to unite Americans behind common, identifiable moral commitments, transcending their religious differences and engendering unity of purpose. It also seemed to have a basis in observed social reality. Visiting America in 1830, Alexis de Tocqueville[11] put the point this way: "There is an innumerable multitude of sects in the United States. All differ in the worship one must render to the Creator, but all agree on the duties of man toward one another. Each sect therefore adores God in its manner, but all sects preach the same morality in the name of God."[12] Tocqueville, himself a liberal Catholic, offered this comment as an observation of American mores, but for advocates of nonsectarianism, the argument had a practical cast: if moral beliefs were truly held in common, they could be shared by all Christians and taught in the common schools without fear of offending any sect in particular.

---

[9]For a detailed account of this process, see McLoughlin, *New England Dissent;* see also Sydney E. Ahlstrom and Jonathan S. Carey, *An American Reformation: A Documentary History of Unitarian Christianity* (Middletown, CT: Wesleyan University Press, 1985), 164.

[10]Mark A. Noll, *America's God: From Jonathan Edwards to Abraham Lincoln* (New York: Oxford University Press, 2002), 166.

[11]*Alexis de Tocqueville:* Frenchman (1805–1859) whose visit took him throughout the United States; his resultant book *Democracy in America* is still widely read today. See an excerpt on p. 376.

[12]Alexis de Tocqueville, *Democracy in America*, eds. and trans. Harvey C. Mansfield and Delba Winthrop (Chicago: University of Chicago Press, 2000), 278. I first discussed many of the texts in this section in Noah Feldman, "Non-sectarianism Reconsidered," *The Journal of Law and Politics* 18 (2002): 65–117, and I draw on that analysis here.

To compound the usefulness of the nonsectarian idea, the font of com-   10
mon morality was said to be the Bible, which — Protestants had long
held — could be interpreted by the individual and so did not need to be
interpreted by the school. When Horace Mann,[13] the great theorist of education and for a dozen years secretary of the Massachusetts Board of Education, addressed the question, he explained that, in Massachusetts schools,
the Bible was allowed to do "what it is allowed to do in no other system —
to speak for itself." By reading the Bible in an unmediated fashion, with no
comment from the teacher, the student would be enabled "to judge for
himself according to the dictates of his own reason and conscience."[14]

The invocation of the liberty of conscience was no coincidence. It tied
nonsectarianism to what had been, since the founding, the dominant American principle regarding the relation of church and state. In Mann's view,
the individual freedom to make decisions in matters of religion ran parallel
to the individual freedom to make political choices. Nonsectarianism in the
schools was therefore presented as fully compatible with the distinctive
American experiment in protecting religious liberty and separating church
and state, even as it promised to unite Americans in a common morality
derived from religion itself. Outside the schools, liberty of conscience was
also said to be essential to nonsectarian Christianity, which was by extension
itself indispensable to free government.[15] The ideal American citizen, then,
enjoyed dual manifestations of the voluntary principle: to choose freely in
politics — the principle of republicanism; and in religion — the principle of
Protestantism.

On a practical level, invoking nonsectarianism seems to have forestalled
the very real concern that too much sectarian religious instruction would
scare parents away from the public schools. With Bible reading a daily
staple, the common schools grew, attracting students with the promise of
free education. Yet nonsectarianism from the start attracted critics who
alleged that it was nothing more than a cover for a highly attenuated liberal
Protestantism. The cart of morality, said the critics, was being put before
the horse of true faith.

Some of this criticism came from committed Protestants, like the old-
fashioned Congregationalist minister Matthew Hale Smith of Massachusetts, who believed that nonsectarianism offered watered-down religion,

[13]*Horace Mann:* See p. 121.

[14]Horace Mann, "Twelfth Annual Report to the Massachusetts Board of Education"
(1848), in *Life and Works of Horace Mann,* 5 vols. (Boston: Lee and Shepard, 1891), 4:222,
311–13.

[15]See, e.g., *Updegraph v. Commonwealth,* 11 Serg. and Rawle 394 (Pa. 1824). In this
decision upholding a blasphemy conviction, the Pennsylvania Supreme Court declared that the
Christianity that constituted a part of the common law was "not Christianity founded on particular religious tenets . . . but Christianity with liberty of conscience for all" (400). It went on to
assert that "no free government now exists in the world, unless where Christianity is acknowledged, and is the religion of the country" (406–7).

which was worse than no religion at all. Smith argued that the decision not to teach basic Christian doctrine like the Trinity amounted to a sectarian religious preference for Unitarianism, the dangerous new heresy shared by many elite New England liberals, Horace Mann among them. Moral decline, Smith suggested, resulted precisely from treating religious morality as separate from religious doctrine. To make such a separation was "to elevate the intellectual over the moral, and man above God."[16]

Smith struck close to home with his argument that nonsectarian teaching of basic morality elevated human-focused preferences and judgments above a commitment to the divine. Nonsectarian moral education indeed operated on the presumption that religion was valuable because it inculcated morals, not that morality was desirable because God commanded it — a hierarchy that always tends to crop up in arguments for the value of public religion. By implication, then, the state's need to maintain a moral populace to keep republicanism alive weighed more heavily than any inherent love of godly morals. Nonsectarian moral teaching functioned as religion in the service of the state, not the other way around.

Even as Smith and other orthodox Protestants objected to nonsectarian   15
moral teaching as essentially irreligious, there emerged a more powerful and lasting critique that characterized nonsectarian teaching as sectarian Protestantism in disguise. The Roman Catholic leaders who developed this line of attack spoke on behalf of a Catholic population that began growing seriously in the middle of the 1820s and amounted to some 341,000 during the 1830s. Ultimately, in the years from 1847 to 1854, it would rise to 1.3 million in the wake of the Great Famine in Ireland.[17] The wave of immigration corresponded, in other words, to the growth years of the public schools in America.

From the perspective of the new immigrants, the idea that the Bible would be read, in the Protestant King James Version,[18] and that children

---

[16]Elwood P. Cubberley, ed., *Readings in Public Education in the United States: A Collection of Sources and Readings to Illustrate the History of Educational Practice and Progress in the United States* (1934) (Westport, CT: Greenwood, 1970), 207.

[17]See George W. Potter, *To the Golden Door: The Story of the Irish in Ireland and America* (Boston: Little, Brown, 1960), 133–34 (calling the year 1846 "the vanguard" of an "emigration phenomenon not paralleled until the population uprootings of the two world wars of the twentieth century," and citing Irish immigration to the United States as 341,000 from 1831 to 1840; 1,321,725 from 1847 to 1854); see also Arnold Schrier, *Ireland and the American Emigration 1850–1900* (Minneapolis: University of Minnesota Press, 1958), 157 (noting that Irish immigration to the United States surpassed 100,000 annually only during the years 1846–54); Noel Ignatiev, *How the Irish Became White* (New York: Routledge, 1995), 38 (calculating Irish immigration to the United States as 800,000–1,000,000 between 1815 and 1845, but 1,800,000 in the decade 1845–55); Thomas T. McAvoy, *A History of the Catholic Church in the United States* (South Bend, IN: University of Notre Dame Press, 1969), 137–38 (places Irish immigration into the United States at 207,381 from 1830 to 1840, 780,719 from 1841 to 1850, and 914,119 from 1851 to 1860).

[18]*King James Version:* English translation of the Bible created under King James I of England, completed in 1611 and noted for its graceful language.

would be encouraged to decide on the meaning of the Bible for themselves, ran headlong into Catholic teaching that conferred the authority for biblical interpretation on the church's priests and saw the church-sanctioned Douay-Reims translation, based on the Latin Vulgate,[19] as the only legitimate English version of the Bible. The Catholic church had never embraced Luther's position[20] that his individual conscience came before the judgment of the church on the meaning of Scripture, and the question of who was entitled to find the true meaning of the Bible represented a crucial point of departure between Catholics and Protestants. By emphasizing individual choice in matters of faith, the common schools were revealing themselves to be Protestant. Dr. John Power, a Catholic vicar general in New York, summed up the problem succinctly in 1840: "The Catholic Church tells her children that they must be taught their religion by AUTHORITY. The Sects [i.e., Protestants] say, read the bible, judge for yourselves. The bible is read in public schools, the children are allowed to judge for themselves. The Protestant principle is therefore acted upon, slily inculcated, and the schools are Sectarian."[21] In a sense, Power was right. The theory of nonsectarianism that underlay Bible reading in the public schools was thoroughly Protestant, and liberal Protestant at that, committed to the possibility of establishing common morality without delving too deeply into religious doctrine. The emphasis on students' choice in the interpretation of the Bible did reflect a peculiarly Protestant "voluntary principle" in religion, which had come to be associated with individual choice in republican politics.

In 1840, however, this Protestant aspect of common school education was still largely unconscious from the perspective of the Protestants who had deployed the idea of nonsectarianism to deal with religious diversity, hardly taking note that, in their minds, the relevant diversity was among different kinds of Protestants, not between Protestants and Catholics. The King James Version of the Bible was read in the schools — complete with its original seventeenth-century introduction describing the pope as "that man of sin"[22] — not to score points against the Catholic Douay-Reims translation but because the King James Bible had been the reigning Bible translation in the mostly Protestant English-speaking world for two hundred years and had acquired the air of sacred inspiration. The association of voluntary choice in religion with voluntary choice in politics had also come

---

[19]*Latin Vulgate:* Early version of the Bible in Latin translation.

[20]*Luther's Position:* Refers to Martin Luther (1483–1546), a German monk whose attack on papal corruption inspired the Reformation and who felt that salvation required faith alone.

[21]Ravitch, *Great School Wars,* 45 (quoting Power in *The Freeman's Journal,* July 11, 1840). Notice that in Power's formulation, the very word "sect" is associated with Protestantism.

[22]Epistle and Dedicatorie, King James Version (1611, spelling modernized); for the text, see Alfred W. Pollard, ed., *Records of the English Bible: The Documents Relating to the Translation and Publication of the Bible in English, 1525–1611* (New York: Oxford University Press, 1911), 340–77.

naturally to Protestants and had not been dreamed up in a fit of anti-Catholicism. After all, Tocqueville, himself a Catholic highly attuned to the subtleties of Catholic-Protestant differences, had described both the non-sectarian argument and the voluntary principle in 1830, and he had not seen either as anti-Catholic. The common schools were effectively nonsectarian Protestant — but until Catholics began to say so, no one had noticed it.

When they did raise the subject, Catholics ran into extraordinarily rigid opposition. Initially, they tried to remedy the problem of having their children taught Protestant ideology by founding Catholic schools. To pay for the Catholic education system that was emerging in areas of heavy Catholic concentration, they sought state funding. Starting with a letter circulated in 1829, the Catholic bishops in America had called for parents to send their children to Catholic schools that would inculcate Catholic values and teach church doctrine.[23] Now, beginning in New York in 1840, Catholics argued that the same government support available to the essentially Protestant common schools should be made available to support Catholic schools.[24]

At first the argument was pressed on the basis of plain fairness: If effectively Protestant schools received funding, why shouldn't Catholic schools receive the same? Soon, however, Catholics began to say that supporting public schools that their children could not in good conscience attend amounted to a violation of their religious liberty, and (an argument still heard today) that they were being taxed unfairly for schools they did not use. An 1853 petition submitted by Michigan Catholics to the state legislature put it this way: "our Public School Laws compel us to violate our conscience, or deprive us unjustly of our share of the Public School funds, and also impose on us taxes for the support of schools which, as a matter of conscience, we cannot allow our children to attend."[25]

When this petition was composed, the Catholic church was more than a century away from officially embracing the idea that liberty of conscience was a basic right. Indeed, the church was undergoing a period of antiliberal "ultramontane"[26] reaction to the European revolutions of 1848,[27] and in 1864, the papal encyclical *Quanta Cura* would condemn as "insanity" (*deliramentum*)

20

[23]Ravitch, *Great School Wars*, 34.

[24]See E. R. Dille, *Rome's Assault on Our Public Schools* (Oakland, CA: Carruth and Carruth, 1889), 10 (quoting one Father Gleeson, who said, "We Catholics call for a reformation of the public school system of education, because it is dangerous to the well-being of the community, because it is the parent of infidelity, an abridgement of our Constitutional rights and destructive of parental authority." Dille retorted that "there is an irreconcilable and irrepressible conflict between the Roman Catholic and American theories of education, and it is for the American people to say which of them shall go to the wall, for it is war to the death between them"); see also Ray Allen Billington, *The Protestant Crusade: 1800–1860* (New York: Macmillan, 1938).

[25]Cubberley, *Readings*, 212.

[26]"*ultramontane*": Supporting the policies of the pope over other authorities.

[27]See John T. McGreevy, *Catholicism and American Freedom* (New York: Norton, 2003), 19–42.

the view that liberty of conscience was a universal right that ought to exist in every well-governed state.[28] American Catholics, then, were not relying on Catholic sources for their argument. Instead, they were using the distinctly American Protestant-origin argument for liberty of conscience and voluntarism in religion to make their case.

Framed in terms of the American notion that paying taxes to support religious teachings with which one disagrees violates the liberty of conscience — an idea developed, widely embraced, and constitutionalized at the federal level by the framers' generation — the Catholics' argument seemed almost airtight. By using the voluntary principle against the common schools, Catholics had painted American Protestants into a corner. Of course it was possible for Protestants to respond, in an inclusive vein, that the public schools should make a serious effort to be not Protestant but Christian and to do all they could to accommodate Catholics. Horace Bushnell, a nationally influential Protestant minister, called for this approach in 1853.[29] But Catholics could respond that inclusiveness was precisely what they rejected as a matter of conscience. Professing faith in the truth as taught by their church, not in Christianity in general, they needed Catholic schools, and any generic Christian compromise would not satisfy their religious beliefs.

So Protestants responded in the time-honored fashion of the intolerant when faced with a claim of conscience: instead of offering an accommodation, they simply refused to acknowledge Catholics' concern and used their legislative majorities to refuse the funding of Catholic schools. At this juncture, the previously unacknowledged Protestantism of the common schools became an overt rallying cry. Catholic schools were depicted as potential agents of separatism and the subversion of republican politics. The argument against Catholic schools became part of the nativist argument[30] against the transformation of America through the immigration of Irish Catholics. If Protestantism was associated with republicanism through the association of liberty of conscience in religion and free choice in politics, then Catholicism could be associated with despotism through its insistence on authority. If Catholics were unprepared for republican political participation, then they needed the Protestant-inflected education of the common schools all the more.

To republicans, the patterns of Irish Catholic bloc voting that began changing politics in the urban centers of the Northeast in the 1840s and '50s

---

[28]*Quanta Cura*, encyclical of Pope Pius IX, promulgated December 8, 1864, ¶3 (the modern translation differs only in trivial detail). See Anne Fremantle, ed., *The Papal Encyclicals in Their Historical Context* (New York: Putnam, 1956), 137.

[29]Horace Bushnell, *Common Schools: A Discourse on the Modifications Demanded by the Roman Catholics Delivered in the North Church, Hartford, on the Day of Late Fast, March 25, 1853* (Hartford, CT: Tiffany and Co., 1853), 6, 7, 24.

[30]*the nativist argument:* Opposition to immigration, particularly in response to an influx of Irish Catholics in the early 1800s.

were also cause for concern. By voting in concert, Catholics appeared to the native-born to be complying with authority. Instead of integrating into pre-existing political patterns, Catholic interests and their votes could be described as separate and distinct. When combined with Catholic leaders' own insistence on the importance of church authority, the immigrant response of group solidarity looked like a threat to the American way in politics as well as religion. Today, ethnic or racial interest-group voting is considered the very essence of urban politics, not a transformative challenge to our democracy — and Madison,[31] had he lived, might have urged that diversity only secured religious liberty. But from the perspective of 1840, the combination of a sudden change in the nature of American religious diversity and an emerging new trend in group political action seemed radically new and seriously threatening.

Nativists were responding to the social dislocation of urbanization and industrialization, and Irish Catholic immigrants represented a symbol of these changes more easily attacked than the factories or the cities themselves. At the same time, the fact that the immigrants were Catholic enabled the nativists to tap into a centuries-old tradition of Protestant-Catholic polemic. Catholics unwittingly walked into the trap of this rhetorical tradition when, having been rebuffed in their call for public funding for their schools, they adopted the alternative tack of demanding that the common schools give up the offensive practice of reading from the King James Bible or reciting the Ten Commandments in their Protestant enumeration rather than the slightly different Catholic count.[32]

From the Catholic perspective, eliminating Bible reading in the common schools seemed like a sensible compromise to the problem of their religious objection. If they could not get funding for their own schools, they could at least send their children to the public schools without having them subjected to an unconscionable religious practice. Again, their argument resonated with the voluntary principle that no one should be coerced against the liberty of conscience.

But in calling for the removal of the Bible from the schools, Catholics misunderstood both the initial purpose of the common schools and the depth of Protestant commitment to the Bible as a symbol. The common schools had been founded as much to teach morals to the new urban workers as to teach them to read and write. According to the emerging nonsectarian

25

---

[31]*Madison:* James Madison (1751–1836), fourth president of the United States, elected 1809. See headnote on p. 718.

[32]Catholic and Protestant versions of the Ten Commandments differ; McGreevy, *Catholicism,* begins with an account of a ten-year-old Catholic student refusing to recite the Protestant version of the commandments in Massachusetts in 1859 (8). See also Richard W. Garnett, "American Conversations Within Catholicism," *Michigan Law Review* 102 (2004): 1191, 1198, and n. 34. McGreevy emphasizes the intentional anti–public school activism of ultramontane priests, but in picking a fight on the ground of the Bible, these recent immigrant priests were getting much more than they bargained for.

theory of education, the Bible was the central means of moral education. Taking the Bible out of the schools would therefore, in the view of the Protestants who had created those schools in the first place, defeat their very purpose. In this sense, Catholics were unintentionally calling for the undermining of the unifying mission of public education. The increased presence of religious diversity in the schools was, not for the last time, challenging the premise that public schools were places for the inculcation of common values.

Protestants — even moderate Protestants — defended the use of the Bible in the schools on the ground that it did not serve the forbidden purpose of sectarian theological instruction but only contained a message of pure morality, with which even Catholics who objected to the King James translation could not disagree. That morality was necessary to make good citizens out of Catholic immigrants. When a Catholic public school pupil went all the way to the Maine Supreme Court to argue that her liberty of conscience was violated by a school board regulation that required reading the King James Bible in her public school, the court insisted, on the one hand, that the Bible was used "merely as a reading book," and on the other, that the complaining young woman could hardly object to the Bible itself, which was "consonant to the soundest principles of morality." The court also argued that the curriculum could not be made subject to the objections of the Catholic church, which, it said rhetorically, might seek the exclusion of other books that appeared on its official prohibited index. The court concluded that it was up to the school board to train the "large masses of foreign population [who] are among us," Catholics who must "become citizens in fact as well as in name . . . through the medium of the public schools, which are alike open to the children of the rich and poor, of the stranger and the citizen."[33] Urging the school board to follow the Golden Rule (which it pointed out was almost the same in every English Bible translation), the court nonetheless refused to require the board to allow other versions of the Bible in the schools. The Catholic bid for a constitutional right to liberty of conscience foundered on the Protestant perception that an exemption from Bible reading would undermine the schools' project of teaching a shared republican, Christian morality.

Far worse from a practical perspective, the Catholic call against reading the Bible in the public schools could be depicted by nativists as a Catholic attack on the Bible itself. Here the polemical tradition came fully into play. Historically, Protestantism, including English evangelical Protestantism, condemned the Catholic church for keeping the Bible from the masses and interposing the priesthood between God's word and man. The church had, before the Reformation,[34] opposed translating the Bible into English; John

---

[33]*Donahoe v. Richards*, 38 Me. 379, 398, 400, 413 (1854).

[34]*the Reformation:* Sixteenth-century religious movement inspired by Martin Luther, aimed at reforming the Roman Catholic Church and resulting in the establishment of Protestantism.

Wycliffe's[35] pre-Protestant reform movement in England had made his New Testament translation into a staple of popular, individual resistance to the Catholic church. The nativists, of course, did not have the fourteenth century in mind when they took to the streets in support of the Bible in the schools. But they did know one crudely stated formula that would have been familiar to their ancestors in England: the Catholic church was against the Bible, and they were for it.

Where the Catholic request to stop Bible reading in schools met strong nativist sentiment, rioting followed. In 1844, over the course of several days, nativists in Philadelphia claiming that Catholics wanted the Bible out of the schools killed thirteen people and burned a Catholic church to the ground.[36] The so-called Bible riots in Philadelphia constituted one of the worst instances of nativist violence touched off by the controversy over the Bible, but they were not the only ones. Rioting in dozens of cities in the 1840s and '50s could be connected to the fight over the Bible in the schools.

The Bible wars of the mid-nineteenth century did not reflect any par-   30
ticularly deep religious faith on the part of the nativists who took to the streets. The Bible mattered as a symbol of American Protestantism and the republican ideology connected with it. The nativists' anti-Catholicism was more political, economic, and cultural than religious. Yet unquestionably the fight over the curriculum in the public schools mattered so centrally because those schools, still in their infancy, were already understood as sites for the creation of American identity, with which nativists were obsessed. This was true as a practical matter, since compulsory public schooling was the only time in an American's life when one was subjected, like it or not, to the propaganda of the state. But the public schools were also centrally important symbolically, because there the government revealed what values it intended to support. Loss of control over what was taught in the schools would be evidence of lost control over the public meaning of American life.

ENGAGING THE TEXT

1. What, according to Feldman, was the original mission of the public school in the United States? Based on your own experience, what would you say was the mission — or missions — of the elementary school you attended?

2. What part did religious instruction play in America's earliest public schools? Why do you think direct religious instruction eventually disappeared from U.S. schools?

3. How did the concept of nonsectarianism rescue early U.S. public schools from the problems posed by religious diversity? Why did the notion of nonsectarianism seem so appealing in the early 1800s? What objections were

---

[35]*John Wycliffe:* English theologian and church reformer (1320?–1384).
[36]*A Full and Complete Account of the Late Awful Riots in Philadelphia* (Philadelphia: J. B. Perry, 1844).

eventually leveled against this approach for reconciling conflicts between church and state?

4. Feldman argues that the task of teaching "common values" was an essential aspect of U.S. public education in the early 1800s. Do you think it's possible or even advisable to teach common values in public schools today, without reference to religious beliefs? What values, if any, can't be taught in a secular context?

EXPLORING CONNECTIONS

5. How might John Taylor Gatto (p. 152) or Jonathan Kozol (p. 239) respond to Feldman's claims that public schools are "quintessentially American" and that they represent "the most important common experience undergone by people in our diverse country"? In your view, are today's public schools still as central to the American experience as Feldman suggests? Why or why not?

6. What objections might James Madison (p. 718) raise against the idea that public schools can fulfill their central mission only by means of religious instruction or that there exists a set of "common values" that can be taught in public school?

7. How does Diana L. Eck's account of the growing religious diversity in American culture (p. 693) complicate the idea of teaching common values in the schools?

8. How would a public school in Maria Poggi Johnson's neighborhood (p. 711) probably deal with the issue of teaching values? How do you think Johnson's neighbors would be likely to view public education? In your opinion, would they be right?

EXTENDING THE CRITICAL CONTEXT

9. Working in groups, research one of the current church-state debates associated with public schooling, including those involving prayer in schools, Bible reading, the Pledge of Allegiance, display of the Ten Commandments, the celebration of religious holidays, and the teaching of evolution and intelligent design. How have public schools across the country dealt with these issues? How successful have we been as a nation in reconciling liberty of conscience with the claims of personal belief?

10. As Feldman indicates, the idea of public support for parochial education inspired some of the earliest conflicts of church and state. Recently, this issue has re-emerged as the call for tax-supported vouchers, which can be used to pay for private as well as public schooling. Research the arguments offered for and against the use of vouchers and write a paper in which you offer your own position on the issue.

11. Feldman suggests that the basic values of Protestantism harmonized particularly well with the central principles of a democratic state — principles like liberty of conscience, suspicion of authority, and voluntary action. As a class, discuss whether you believe any one religion is better suited than others to the nurturing of democratic values.

Reason in Exile

SAM HARRIS

    Since 9/11, Americans have begun to see danger in extreme religious views and radical cults and sects. Religious extremists—whether they are associated with the Taliban or the right-to-life movement—are frequently associated in the common imagination with terrorist acts that contradict the most sacred values of religious faith. But to a radical secularist like Sam

Harris, all religions are potential sources of irrationality and violence. According to Harris, even religious moderates pose a serious threat to the future existence of democracy and democratic institutions. Harris (b. 1967) studied philosophy and neuroscience at Stanford University and currently lives in New York, where he is pursuing research on the neural basis of religious belief. The source of this selection, The End of Faith *(2005), won the PEN/Martha Albrand Award for First Nonfiction. Harris's essays have also appeared in the* Los Angeles Times, The Times *(London),* Free Inquiry *magazine, and* Playboy.

The young man boards the bus as it leaves the terminal. He wears an overcoat. Beneath his overcoat, he is wearing a bomb. His pockets are filled with nails, ball bearings, and rat poison.

The bus is crowded and headed for the heart of the city. The young man takes his seat beside a middle-aged couple. He will wait for the bus to reach its next stop. The couple at his side appears to be shopping for a new refrigerator. The woman has decided on a model, but her husband worries that it will be too expensive. He indicates another one in a brochure that lies open on her lap. The next stop comes into view. The bus doors swing. The woman observes that the model her husband has selected will not fit in the space underneath their cabinets. New passengers have taken the last remaining seats and begun gathering in the aisle. The bus is now full. The young man smiles. With the press of a button he destroys himself, the couple at his side, and twenty others on the bus. The nails, ball bearings, and rat poison ensure further casualties on the street and in the surrounding cars. All has gone according to plan.

The young man's parents soon learn of his fate. Although saddened to have lost a son, they feel tremendous pride at his accomplishment. They know that he has gone to heaven and prepared the way for them to follow. He has also sent his victims to hell for eternity. It is a double victory. The neighbors find the event a great cause for celebration and honor the young man's parents by giving them gifts of food and money.

These are the facts. This is all we know for certain about the young man. Is there anything else that we can infer about him on the basis of his behavior? Was he popular in school? Was he rich or was he poor? Was he of low or high intelligence? His actions leave no clue at all. Did he have a college education? Did he have a bright future as a mechanical engineer? His behavior is simply mute on questions of this sort, and hundreds like them.[1] Why is it

---

[1] ... the chances are decidedly *against* the possibility that he comes from the lowest strata of society. [All notes are author's, except 3–6, 8, 10–12, 14–16, 19, and 21–26.]

so easy, then, so trivially easy — you-could-almost-bet-your-life-on-it easy —
to guess the young man's religion.[2]

A belief is a lever that, once pulled, moves almost everything else in a   5
person's life. Are you a scientist? A liberal? A racist? These are merely
species of belief in action. Your beliefs define your vision of the world; they
dictate your behavior; they determine your emotional responses to other
human beings. If you doubt this, consider how your experience would suddenly change if you came to believe one of the following propositions:

1. You have only two weeks to live.
2. You've just won a lottery prize of one hundred million dollars.
3. Aliens have implanted a receiver in your skull and are manip-
   ulating your thoughts.

These are mere words — until you believe them. Once believed, they become part of the very apparatus of your mind, determining your desires,
fears, expectations, and subsequent behavior.

There seems, however, to be a problem with some of our most cherished beliefs about the world: they are leading us, inexorably, to kill one
another. A glance at history, or at the pages of any newspaper, reveals that
ideas which divide one group of human beings from another, only to unite
them in slaughter, generally have their roots in religion. It seems that if our
species ever eradicates itself through war, it will not be because it was written in the stars but because it was written in our books; it is what we do with
words like "God" and "paradise" and "sin" in the present that will determine
our future.

Our situation is this: most of the people in this world believe that the
Creator of the universe has written a book. We have the misfortune of having many such books on hand, each making an exclusive claim as to its infal-
libility. People tend to organize themselves into factions according to which
of these incompatible claims they accept — rather than on the basis of lan-

[2]Some readers may object that the bomber in question is most likely to be a member of
the Liberation Tigers of Tamil Eelam — the Sri Lankan separatist organization that has perpetrated more acts of suicidal terrororism than any other group. Indeed, the "Tamil Tigers" are
often offered as a counterexample to any claim that suicidal terrorism is a product of religion.
But to describe the Tamil Tigers as "secular" — as R. A. Pape, "The Strategic Logic of Suicide
Terrorism," *American Political Science Review* 97, no. 3 (2003): 20–32, and others have — is
misleading. While the motivations of the Tigers are not explicitly religious, they are Hindus
who undoubtedly believe many improbable things about the nature of life and death. The cult
of martyr worship that they have nurtured for decades has many of the features of religiosity
that one would expect in people who give their lives so easily for a cause. Secular Westerners
often underestimate the degree to which certain cultures, steeped as they are in otherworldli-
ness, look upon death with less alarm than seems strictly rational. I was once traveling in India
when the government rescheduled the exams for students who were preparing to enter the
civil service: what appeared to me to be the least of bureaucratic inconveniences precipitated a
wave of teenage *self-immolations* in protest. Hindus, even those whose preoccupations appear
to be basically secular, often harbor potent religious beliefs.

guage, skin color, location of birth, or any other criterion of tribalism. Each of these texts urges its readers to adopt a variety of beliefs and practices, some of which are benign, many of which are not. All are in perverse agreement on one point of fundamental importance, however: "respect" for other faiths, or for the views of unbelievers, is not an attitude that God endorses. While all faiths have been touched, here and there, by the spirit of ecumenicalism[3] the central tenet of every religious tradition is that all others are mere repositories of error or, at best, dangerously incomplete. Intolerance is thus intrinsic to every creed. Once a person believes — *really* believes — that certain ideas can lead to eternal happiness, or to its antithesis, he cannot tolerate the possibility that the people he loves might be led astray by the blandishments of unbelievers. Certainty about the next life is simply incompatible with tolerance in this one.

Observations of this sort pose an immediate problem for us, however, because criticizing a person's faith is currently taboo in every corner of our culture. On this subject, liberals and conservatives have reached a rare consensus: religious beliefs are simply beyond the scope of rational discourse. Criticizing a person's ideas about God and the afterlife is thought to be impolitic in a way that criticizing his ideas about physics or history is not. And so it is that when a Muslim suicide bomber obliterates himself along with a score of innocents on a Jerusalem street, the role that faith played in his actions is invariably discounted. His motives must have been political, economic, or entirely personal. Without faith, desperate people would still do terrible things. Faith itself is always, and everywhere, exonerated.

But technology has a way of creating fresh moral imperatives. Our technical advances in the art of war have finally rendered our religious differences — and hence our religious *beliefs* — antithetical to our survival. We can no longer ignore the fact that billions of our neighbors believe in the metaphysics of martyrdom, or in the literal truth of the book of Revelation,[4] or any of the other fantastical notions that have lurked in the minds of the faithful for millennia — because our neighbors are now armed with chemical, biological, and nuclear weapons. There is no doubt that these developments mark the terminal phase of our credulity. Words like "God" and "Allah" must go the way of "Apollo" and "Baal,"[5] or they will unmake our world.

A few minutes spent wandering the graveyard of bad ideas suggests that   10
such conceptual revolutions are possible. Consider the case of alchemy:[6] it fascinated human beings for over a thousand years, and yet anyone who seriously claims to be a practicing alchemist today will have disqualified himself

---

[3]*ecumenicalism:* The promotion of unity among churches and religious groups.

[4]*the book of Revelation:* The last book of the New Testament in the Bible; it has been the subject of a wide variety of interpretations.

[5]*"Apollo" and "Baal":* In ancient Greek and Roman mythology, Apollo is the sun god. Baal is a god who was worshipped by ancient Semitic people.

[6]*alchemy:* A nonscientific practice, dating from medieval times or earlier, by which people sought to transform base metals into gold.

for most positions of responsibility in our society. Faith-based religion must suffer the same slide into obsolescence.

What is the alternative to religion as we know it? As it turns out, this is the wrong question to ask. Chemistry was not an "alternative" to alchemy; it was a wholesale exchange of ignorance at its most rococo for genuine knowledge.[7] We will find that, as with alchemy, to speak of "alternatives" to religious faith is to miss the point.

Of course, people of faith fall on a continuum: some draw solace and inspiration from a specific spiritual tradition, and yet remain fully committed to tolerance and diversity, while others would burn the earth to cinders if it would put an end to heresy. There are, in other words, religious *moderates* and religious *extremists*, and their various passions and projects should not be confused. . . . [But] religious moderates are themselves the bearers of a terrible dogma: they imagine that the path to peace will be paved once each of us has learned to respect the unjustified beliefs of others. I hope to show that the very ideal of religious tolerance — born of the notion that every human being should be free to believe whatever he wants about God — is one of the principal forces driving us toward the abyss.

We have been slow to recognize the degree to which religious faith perpetuates man's inhumanity to man. This is not surprising, since many of us still believe that faith is an essential component of human life. Two myths now keep faith beyond the fray of rational criticism, and they seem to foster religious extremism and religious moderation equally: (1) most of us believe that there are good things that people get from religious faith (e.g., strong communities, ethical behavior, spiritual experience) that cannot be had elsewhere; (2) many of us also believe that the terrible things that are sometimes done in the name of religion are the products not of *faith* per se but of our baser natures — forces like greed, hatred, and fear — for which religious beliefs are themselves the best (or even the only) remedy. Taken together, these myths seem to have granted us perfect immunity to outbreaks of reasonableness in our public discourse.

Many religious moderates have taken the apparent high road of pluralism, asserting the equal validity of all faiths, but in doing so they neglect to notice the irredeemably sectarian truth claims of each. As long as a Christian believes that only his baptized brethren will be saved on the Day of Judgment, he cannot possibly "respect" the beliefs of others, for he knows

---

[7]I am speaking here of "alchemy" as that body of ancient and ultimately fanciful metallurgic and chemical techniques whose purpose was to transmute base metals into gold and mundane materials into an "elixir of life." It is true that there are people who claim to find the alchemical literature prescient with the most contemporary truths of pharmacology, solid-state physics, and a variety of other disciplines. I find the results of such Rorschach readings less than inspiring, however. See T. McKenna, *The Archaic Revival* ([San Francisco]: Harper San Francisco, 1991), *Food of the Gods: The Search for the Original Tree of Knowledge* (New York: Bantam Books, 1992), and *True Hallucinations* ([San Francisco]: Harper San Francisco, 1993), for an example of a bright and beautiful mind that takes such revaluations of alchemy seriously, however.

that the flames of hell have been stoked by these very ideas and await their adherents even now. Muslims and Jews generally take the same arrogant view of their own enterprises and have spent millennia passionately reiterating the errors of other faiths. It should go without saying that these rival belief systems are all equally uncontaminated by evidence.

And yet, intellectuals as diverse as H. G. Wells, Albert Einstein, Carl Jung, Max Planck, Freeman Dyson, and Stephen Jay Gould[8] have declared the war between reason and faith to be long over. On this view, there is no need to have all of our beliefs about the universe cohere. A person can be a God-fearing Christian on Sunday and a working scientist come Monday morning, without ever having to account for the partition that seems to have erected itself in his head while he slept. He can, as it were, have his reason and eat it too. [But] it is only because the church has been politically hobbled in the West that anyone can afford to think this way. In places where scholars can still be stoned to death for doubting the veracity of the Koran, Gould's notion of a "loving concordat" between faith and reason would be perfectly delusional.[9]

This is not to say that the deepest concerns of the faithful, whether moderate or extreme, are trivial or even misguided. There is no denying that most of us have emotional and spiritual needs that are now addressed — however obliquely and at a terrible price — by mainstream religion. And these are needs that a mere *understanding* of our world, scientific or otherwise, will never fulfill. There is clearly a sacred dimension to our existence, and coming to terms with it could well be the highest purpose of human life. But we will find that it requires no faith in untestable propositions — Jesus was born of a virgin; the Koran is the word of God — for us to do this.

The Myth of "Moderation" in Religion

The idea that any one of our religions represents the infallible word of the One True God requires an encyclopedic ignorance of history, mythology, and art even to be entertained — as the beliefs, rituals, and iconography of each of our religions attest to centuries of cross-pollination among them. Whatever their imagined source, the doctrines of modern religions are no more tenable than those which, for lack of adherents, were cast upon the scrap heap of mythology millennia ago; for there is no more evidence to justify a belief in the literal existence of Yahweh[10] and Satan than there was to keep Zeus perched upon his mountain throne or Poseidon[11] churning the seas.

---

[8]*H. G. Wells . . . Gould:* H. G. Wells (1866–1946), English writer known for his science fiction novels, such as *The War of the Worlds;* Albert Einstein, Nobel Prize–winning German physicist (1879–1955); Carl Jung, Swiss psychiatrist (1875–1961); Max Planck, Nobel Prize–winning German physicist (1858–1947); Freeman Dyson, English-born physicist (b. 1923); Stephen Jay Gould, American paleontologist and prolific writer (1941–2002).

[9]S. J. Gould, "Nonoverlapping Magisteria," *Natural History,* March 1997.

[10]*Yahweh:* God's Hebrew name.

[11]*Poseidon:* In Greek mythology, god of the sea.

According to Gallup,[12] 35 percent of Americans believe that the Bible is the literal and inerrant word of the Creator of the universe.[13] Another 48 percent believe that it is the "inspired" word of the same — still inerrant, though certain of its passages must be interpreted symbolically before their truth can be brought to light. Only 17 percent of us remain to doubt that a personal God, in his infinite wisdom, is likely to have authored this text — or, for that matter, to have created the earth with its 250,000 species of beetles. Some 46 percent of Americans take a literalist view of creation (40 percent believe that God has guided creation over the course of millions of years). This means that 120 million of us place the big bang 2,500 years *after* the Babylonians and Sumerians learned to brew beer. If our polls are to be trusted, nearly 230 million Americans believe that a book showing neither unity of style nor internal consistency was authored by an omniscient, omnipotent, and omnipresent deity. A survey of Hindus, Muslims, and Jews around the world would surely yield similar results, revealing that we, as a species, have grown almost perfectly intoxicated by our myths. How is it that, in this one area of our lives, we have convinced ourselves that our beliefs about the world can float entirely free of reason and evidence?

It is with respect to this rather surprising cognitive scenery that we must decide what it means to be a religious "moderate" in the twenty-first century. Moderates in every faith are obliged to loosely interpret (or simply ignore) much of their canons in the interests of living in the modern world. No doubt an obscure truth of economics is at work here: societies appear to become considerably less productive whenever large numbers of people stop making widgets and begin killing their customers and creditors for heresy. The first thing to observe about the moderate's retreat from scriptural literalism is that it draws its inspiration not from scripture but from cultural developments that have rendered many of God's utterances difficult to accept as written. In America, religious moderation is further enforced by the fact that most Christians and Jews do not read the Bible in its entirety and consequently have no idea just how vigorously the God of Abraham[14] wants heresy expunged. One look at the book of Deuteronomy[15] reveals that he has something very specific in mind should your son or daughter return from yoga class advocating the worship of Krishna.[16]

> If your brother, the son of your father or of your mother, or your son or daughter, or the spouse whom you embrace, or your most intimate friend, tries to secretly seduce you, saying, "Let us go and serve other gods," unknown to you or your ancestors before you, gods of the peoples surrounding you, whether near you or far away, anywhere throughout

[12]*Gallup:* Organization that conducts polls.

[13]G. H. Gallup Jr., *Religion in America 1996* (Princeton: Princeton Religion Research Center, 1996).

[14]*God of Abraham:* God of the Old Testament of the Bible.

[15]*Deuteronomy:* The Fifth Book of the Old Testament. It includes the Ten Commandments.

[16]*Krishna:* Hindu deity.

the world, you must not consent, you must not listen to him; you must show him no pity, you must not spare him or conceal his guilt. No, you must kill him, your hand must strike the first blow in putting him to death and the hands of the rest of the people following. You must stone him to death, since he has tried to divert you from Yahweh your God . . . (Deuteronomy 13:7–11)

While the stoning of children for heresy has fallen out of fashion in our country, you will not hear a moderate Christian or Jew arguing for a "symbolic" reading of passages of this sort. (In fact, one seems to be explicitly blocked by God himself in Deuteronomy 13:1 — "Whatever I am now commanding you, you must keep and observe, adding nothing to it, taking nothing away.") The above passage is as canonical as any in the Bible, and it is only by ignoring such barbarisms that the Good Book can be reconciled with life in the modern world. This is a problem for "moderation" in religion: it has nothing underwriting it other than the unacknowledged neglect of the letter of the divine law.

The only reason anyone is "moderate" in matters of faith these days is that he has assimilated some of the fruits of the last two thousand years of human thought (democratic politics,[17] scientific advancement on every front, concern for human rights, an end to cultural and geographic isolation, etc.). The doors leading out of scriptural literalism do not open from the *inside.* The moderation we see among nonfundamentalists is not some sign that faith itself has evolved; it is, rather, the product of the many hammer blows of modernity that have exposed certain tenets of faith to doubt. Not the least among these developments has been the emergence of our tendency to value evidence and to be convinced by a proposition to the degree that there is evidence for it. Even most fundamentalists live by the lights of reason in this regard; it is just that their minds seem to have been partitioned to accommodate the profligate truth claims of their faith. Tell a devout Christian that his wife is cheating on him, or that frozen yogurt can make a man invisible, and he is likely to require as much evidence as anyone else, and to be persuaded only to the extent that you give it. Tell him that the book he keeps by his bed was written by an invisible deity who will punish him with fire for eternity if he fails to accept its every incredible claim about the universe, and he seems to require no evidence whatsoever.

Religious moderation springs from the fact that even the least educated person among us simply *knows* more about certain matters than anyone did two thousand years ago — and much of this knowledge is incompatible with

[17]This is not to deny that there are problems with democracy, particularly when it is imposed prematurely on societies that have high birthrates, low levels of literacy, profound ethnic and religious factionalism, and unstable economies. There is clearly such a thing as a benevolent despotism, and it may be a necessary stage in the political development of many societies. See R. D. Kaplan, "Was Democracy Just a Moment?," *Atlantic Monthly,* Dec. 1997, pp. 55–80, and F. Zakaria, *The Future of Freedom: Illiberal Democracy at Home and Abroad* (New York: W. W. Norton, 2003).

scripture. Having heard something about the medical discoveries of the last hundred years, most of us no longer equate disease processes with sin or demonic possession. Having learned about the known distances between objects in our universe, most of us (about half of us, actually) find the idea that the whole works was created six thousand years ago (with light from distant stars already in transit toward the earth) impossible to take seriously. Such concessions to modernity do not in the least suggest that faith is compatible with reason, or that our religious traditions are in principle open to new learning: it is just that the utility of ignoring (or "reinterpreting") certain articles of faith is now overwhelming. Anyone being flown to a distant city for heart-bypass surgery has conceded, tacitly at least, that we have learned a few things about physics, geography, engineering, and medicine since the time of Moses.

So it is not that these texts have maintained their integrity over time (they haven't); it is just that they have been effectively edited by our neglect of certain of their passages. Most of what remains — the "good parts" — has been spared the same winnowing because we do not yet have a truly modern understanding of our ethical intuitions and our capacity for spiritual experience. If we better understood the workings of the human brain, we would undoubtedly discover lawful connections between our states of consciousness, our modes of conduct, and the various ways we use our attention. What makes one person happier than another? Why is love more conducive to happiness than hate? Why do we generally prefer beauty to ugliness and order to chaos? Why does it feel so good to smile and laugh, and why do these shared experiences generally bring people closer together? Is the ego an illusion, and, if so, what implications does this have for human life? Is there life after death? These are ultimately questions for a mature science of the mind. If we ever develop such a science, most of our religious texts will be no more useful to mystics than they now are to astronomers.

While moderation in religion may seem a reasonable position to stake out, in light of all that we have (and have not) learned about the universe, it offers no bulwark against religious extremism and religious violence. From the perspective of those seeking to live by the letter of the texts, the religious moderate is nothing more than a failed fundamentalist. He is, in all likelihood, going to wind up in hell with the rest of the unbelievers. The problem that religious moderation poses for all of us is that it does not permit anything very critical to be said about religious literalism. We cannot say that fundamentalists are crazy, because they are merely practicing their freedom of belief; we cannot even say that they are mistaken in *religious* terms, because their knowledge of scripture is generally unrivaled. All we can say, as religious moderates, is that we don't like the personal and social costs that a full embrace of scripture imposes on us. This is not a new form of faith, or even a new species of scriptural exegesis; it is simply a capitulation to a variety of all-too-human interests that have nothing, in principle, to do with God. Religious moderation is the product of *secular* knowledge and scriptural *ignorance* — and it has no bona fides, in religious terms, to put it on a par with fundamentalism.[18] The texts themselves are unequivocal: they are perfect in all their parts. By their light, religious moderation appears to be nothing more than an unwillingness to fully submit to God's law. By failing to live by the letter of the texts, while tolerating the irrationality of those who do, religious moderates betray faith and reason equally. Unless the core dogmas of faith are called into question — i.e., that we know there is a God, and that we know what he wants from us — religious moderation will do nothing to lead us out of the wilderness.

The benignity of most religious moderates does not suggest that religious faith is anything more sublime than a desperate marriage of hope and ignorance, nor does it guarantee that there is not a terrible price to be paid for limiting the scope of reason in our dealings with other human beings. Religious moderation, insofar as it represents an attempt to hold on to what is still serviceable in orthodox religion, closes the door to more sophisticated approaches to spirituality, ethics, and the building of strong communities. Religious moderates seem to believe that what we need is not radical insight and innovation in these areas but a mere dilution of Iron Age[19] philosophy. Rather than bring the full force of our creativity and rationality to bear on the problems of ethics, social cohesion, and even spiritual experience, moderates merely ask that we relax our standards of adherence to ancient superstitions and taboos, while otherwise maintaining a belief system that was passed down to us from men and women whose lives were simply ravaged by their basic ignorance about the world. In what other sphere of life is such subservience to tradition acceptable? Medicine? Engineering? Not even politics suffers the anachronism that still dominates our thinking about ethical values and spiritual experience.

Imagine that we could revive a well-educated Christian of the fourteenth   25
century. The man would prove to be a total ignoramus, except on matters of faith. His beliefs about geography, astronomy, and medicine would embarrass even a child, but he would know more or less everything there is to know about God. Though he would be considered a fool to think that the earth is the center of the cosmos, or that trepanning[20] constitutes a wise medical intervention, his religious ideas would still be beyond reproach. There are two

[18]Bernard Lewis, in "The Revolt of Islam," *New Yorker,* Nov. 19, 2001, pp. 50–63, and *The Crisis of Islam: Holy War and Unholy Terror* (New York: Modern Library, 2003), has pointed out that the term "fundamentalist" was coined by American Protestants and can be misleading when applied to other faiths. It seems to me that the term has escaped into general usage, however, and that it now signifies any sort of scriptural literalism. I use it only in this general sense.

[19]*Iron Age:* Time during which technology permitted the use of iron tools and weapons (rather than less advanced bronze), starting from around the twelfth century B.C.E. in Greece and the sixth century B.C.E. in northern Europe and ending with the early part of the first millennium.

[20]Trepanning (or trephining) is the practice of boring holes in the human skull. Archaeological evidence suggests that it is one of the oldest surgical procedures. It was presumably performed on epileptics and the mentally ill as an attempt at exorcism. While there are still many reasons to open a person's skull nowadays, the hope that an evil spirit will use the hole as a point of egress is not among them.

explanations for this: either we perfected our religious understanding of the world a millennium ago — while our knowledge on all other fronts was still hopelessly inchoate — or religion, being the mere maintenance of dogma, is one area of discourse that does not admit of progress. . . .

With each passing year, do our religious beliefs conserve more and more of the data of human experience? If religion addresses a genuine sphere of understanding and human necessity, then it should be susceptible to *progress*; its doctrines should become more useful, rather than less. Progress in religion, as in other fields, would have to be a matter of *present* inquiry, not the mere reiteration of past doctrine. Whatever is true now should be *discoverable* now, and describable in terms that are not an outright affront to the rest of what we know about the world. By this measure, the entire project of religion seems perfectly backward. It cannot survive the changes that have come over us — culturally, technologically, and even ethically. Otherwise, there are few reasons to believe that we will survive *it*.

Moderates do not want to kill anyone in the name of God, but they want us to keep using the word "God" as though we knew what we were talking about. And they do not want anything too critical said about people who *really* believe in the God of their fathers, because tolerance, perhaps above all else, is sacred. To speak plainly and truthfully about the state of our world — to say, for instance, that the Bible and the Koran both contain mountains of life-destroying gibberish — is antithetical to tolerance as moderates currently conceive it. But we can no longer afford the luxury of such political correctness. We must finally recognize the price we are paying to maintain the iconography of our ignorance.

The Shadow of the Past

Finding ourselves in a universe that seems bent upon destroying us, we quickly discover, both as individuals and as societies, that it is a good thing to understand the forces arrayed against us. And so it is that every human being comes to desire genuine knowledge about the world. This has always posed a special problem for religion, because every religion preaches the truth of propositions for which it has no evidence. In fact, every religion preaches the truth of propositions for which no evidence is even *conceivable*. This put the "leap" in Kierkegaard's[21] leap of faith.

What if all our knowledge about the world were suddenly to disappear? Imagine that six billion of us wake up tomorrow morning in a state of utter ignorance and confusion. Our books and computers are still here, but we can't make heads or tails of their contents. We have even forgotten how to drive our cars and brush our teeth. What knowledge would we want to reclaim first? Well, there's that business about growing food and building shelter that we would want to get reacquainted with. We would want to relearn how to use and repair many of our machines. Learning to under-

---

[21]*Kierkegaard:* Danish existentialist philosopher Søren Kierkegaard (1813–1855).

stand spoken and written language would also be a top priority, given that these skills are necessary for acquiring most others. When in this process of reclaiming our humanity will it be important to know that Jesus was born of a virgin? Or that he was resurrected? And how would we relearn these truths, if they are indeed *true*? By reading the Bible? Our tour of the shelves will deliver similar pearls from antiquity — like the "fact" that Isis,[22] the goddess of fertility, sports an impressive pair of cow horns. Reading further, we will learn that Thor carries a hammer and that Marduk's[23] sacred animals are horses, dogs, and a dragon with a forked tongue. Whom shall we give top billing in our resurrected world? Yahweh or Shiva?[24] And when will we want to relearn that premarital sex is a sin? Or that adulteresses should be stoned to death? Or that the soul enters the zygote at the moment of conception? And what will we think of those curious people who begin proclaiming that one of our books is distinct from all others in that it was actually written by the Creator of the universe?

There are undoubtedly spiritual truths that we would want to   30
relearn — once we manage to feed and clothe ourselves — and these are truths that we have learned imperfectly in our present state. How is it possible, for instance, to overcome one's fear and inwardness and simply love other human beings? Assume, for the moment, that such a process of personal transformation exists and that there is something worth knowing about it; there is, in other words, some skill, or discipline, or conceptual understanding, or dietary supplement that allows for the reliable transformation of fearful, hateful, or indifferent persons into loving ones. If so, we should be positively desperate to know about it. There may even be a few biblical passages that would be useful in this regard — but as for whole rafts of untestable doctrines, clearly there would be no reasonable basis to take them up again. The Bible and Koran, it seems certain, would find themselves respectfully shelved next to Ovid's *Metamorphoses*[25] and the *Egyptian Book of the Dead*.[26]

The point is that most of what we currently hold sacred is not sacred for any reason other than that it was thought sacred *yesterday*. Surely, if we could create the world anew, the practice of organizing our lives around untestable propositions found in ancient literature — to say nothing of killing and dying for them — would be impossible to justify. What stops us from finding it impossible *now*?

Many have observed that religion, by lending meaning to human life, permits communities (at least those united under a single faith) to cohere. Historically this is true, and on this score religion is to be credited as

[22]*Isis:* Ancient Egyptian deity.

[23]*Marduk:* Ancient Mesopotamian deity.

[24]*Shiva:* Hindu deity.

[25]*Ovid's Metamorphoses:* Ovid was a Roman poet (43 B.C.E.–17 C.E.); his poem *The Metamorphoses* describes the creation of the world according to Greco-Roman mythology.

[26]*the Egyptian Book of the Dead:* Ancient Egyptian writing providing instruction and guidance for resurrection in the after life.

much for wars of conquest as for feast days and brotherly love. But in its effect upon the *modern* world — a world already united, at least potentially, by economic, environmental, political, and epidemiological necessity — religious ideology is dangerously retrograde. Our past is not sacred for being *past,* and there is much that is behind us that we are struggling to *keep* behind us, and to which, it is to be hoped, we could never return with a clear conscience: the divine right of kings, feudalism, the caste system, slavery, political executions, forced castration, vivisection, bearbaiting, honorable duels, chastity belts, trial by ordeal, child labor, human and animal sacrifice, the stoning of heretics, cannibalism, sodomy laws, taboos against contraception, human radiation experiments — the list is nearly endless, and if it were extended indefinitely, the proportion of abuses for which religion could be found directly responsible is likely to remain undiminished. In fact, almost every indignity just mentioned can be attributed to an insufficient taste for evidence, to an uncritical faith in one dogma or another. The idea, therefore, that religious faith is somehow a *sacred* human convention — distinguished, as it is, both by the extravagance of its claims and by the paucity of its evidence — is really too great a monstrosity to be appreciated in all its glory. Religious faith represents so uncompromising a misuse of the power of our minds that it forms a kind of perverse, cultural singularity — a vanishing point beyond which rational discourse proves impossible. When foisted upon each generation anew, it renders us incapable of realizing just how much of our world has been unnecessarily ceded to a dark and barbarous past.

ENGAGING THE TEXT

1. How does Harris portray religion and religious belief? Do you think most religions are as divisive and intolerant as he claims?

2. What evidence does Harris offer to support his assertion that ideas rooted in religious thinking pose a serious threat to the survival of the world today? Would you agree that religions will inevitably become obsolete? Why or why not?

3. Do you think it would be possible for most people to live without some kind of religion? How might people in a secular society satisfy what Harris terms the "sacred dimension" of human existence? How are many Americans fulfilling their need for the "sacred" today?

4. Why are religious moderates even more dangerous, according to Harris, than religious fundamentalists and extremists? In his view, how do moderates make the continuation of religious extremism possible? Would you agree?

5. To what extent might the case that Harris presents against religion also be true of other forms of extreme belief? For example, what difference do you see between religious belief and scientific certitude, political conviction, philosophical principle, or simple, everyday common sense? Is it possible that Harris himself is just an intolerant secularist?

EXPLORING CONNECTIONS

6. How might the story of Anne Lamott's religious conversion (p. 620) challenge Harris's claims about the inherent divisiveness of religion and secular society's ability to satisfy the individual's need for "the sacred"? How do you think Lamott would view Harris's arguments against even moderate forms of religious belief?

7. Write a brief dialogue between Harris and David Kupelian (p. 646) on the value of religion. What would the ideal society probably be like for Kupelian? For Harris? Which would you prefer to live in and why?

8. Do you think that Harris would view Bill McKibben (p. 665) as a religious moderate or as a fundamentalist? How might McKibben respond to Harris's claim that all religions are inherently intolerant, divisive, and potentially violent?

9. How might Harris interpret Maria Poggi Johnson's relationship with her Orthodox neighbors (p. 711)? Would he be likely to see this experience as evidence of tolerance among religious fundamentalists?

10. Compare Harris's attitude toward religion with that offered by James Madison in "Memorial and Remonstrance Against Religious Assessments" (p. 718). To what extent do Madison's ideas about liberty of conscience and the separation of church and state address the concerns that Harris raises in this selection?

EXTENDING THE CRITICAL CONTEXT

11. Working in groups, research the role that religion has played in major world conflicts over the past century. How many wars have been caused by clashing religious beliefs? To what extent would you agree that the current War on Terror is itself a religious conflict?

12. View Mel Gibson's film *The Passion of the Christ* (2004) and discuss the messages you think it was meant to convey to an audience of Christian believers. To what extent do you think it expresses the kind of intolerance that Harris associates with all forms of organized religion?

13. Working in groups, brainstorm a list of the "spiritual truths" you think people would want to relearn if the human race actually did wake up one day with collective amnesia. Which biblical stories or teachings, if any, would you deem crucial to human survival? Why?

FURTHER CONNECTIONS

1. Research any one of the following figures from colonial and Revolutionary era American history to learn more about their personal religious beliefs: John Winthrop, William Bradford, Jonathan Edwards, Cotton Mather, Anne Hutchinson, Roger Williams, William Penn, Thomas Jefferson, Thomas Paine, Benjamin Franklin, and James Madison. How would you describe the personal religious beliefs of the famous American you chose to study? What was this figure's attitude about the relationship of religion and state power? Based on your findings, write a brief profile of the figure you chose and present and discuss these profiles in class.

2. Do additional research on the role that religion played in any one of the following social movements in American history: the abolition movement, the early women's liberation movement, the Social Gospel movement, and the American civil rights movement. What religious groups were important in relation to the movement you chose to study? Which of the leaders in this movement were particularly inspired by principles of religious faith? How did religious beliefs and values influence the movement's goals? Based on your research, to what extent would you agree that religion has had a serious impact on social issues and social reform in America?

3. Working as a class, and using the "Fast Facts" at the beginning of the chapter as a model, develop your own survey of the religious attitudes and beliefs of the students at your college. As you construct your survey, plan your questions carefully so that they will be as objective and unbiased as possible. After working together to sample the opinions of as many students as you can, tabulate and discuss your results. In general, do the students at your college appear to be as religious as the average American? How might you account for any major differences that you note?

4. Using library and Internet resources, survey how the image of Jesus has changed over the past two hundred years. How did painters and sculptors portray Jesus before the twentieth century? How do contemporary portrayals compare with these earlier views of Jesus? To what extent do you think recent representations of Jesus have been influenced by contemporary American values and attitudes?

5. Do some Internet and newspaper research on recent disputes associated with the teaching of evolution and the theory of intelligent design. What arguments are offered for and against the teaching of intelligent design in public schools? Drawing on what you learn, hold your own debate on the issue in class. Overall, do you think that religious "theories" should ever be taught in public school classrooms? Why or why not?

6. Do some additional reading about any of the religions or religious movements that originated in America after the Revolutionary War,

such as the Church of Christ, Scientist (Christian Science), the Church of Jesus Christ of Latter-Day Saints (Mormonism), the Jehovah's Witnesses, Pentecostalism, charismatic Christianity, and the Church of Scientology. What is the history of the religion you chose to focus on? What are its central beliefs and values? What, if anything, strikes you as being particularly American about the ideas or principles of this faith?

7. Working in groups, track every reference to religion you can find in contemporary popular culture, including those that appear in song lyrics, films, television shows, and video games. To what extent is religion addressed in the mass media? When religious themes or ideas do come up in films, television shows, song lyrics, or video games, how are they portrayed or treated? Overall, how would you characterize the relationship between organized religion and the pop culture industry?

8. Learn more about the religious beliefs and practices of American tribal groups or about the original religious beliefs of some of the Africans who were brought to America as slaves. What were the central tenets and values associated with the beliefs of these groups? How do they differ from the central beliefs and values of Christianity? How were these other religions viewed by European Americans?

7

Land of Liberty

The Myth of Freedom in a "New World Order"

FAST FACTS

1. In 2005, U.S. military spending accounted for 48% of total world military expenditures, with China and Russia each accounting for about 6%, the United Kingdom for 5%, France for 4%, Germany for 3%, and Iran and North Korea for about .5% each.

2. In 2006, 51% of all Americans believed that the Iraq War had made the world a safer place, while the percentage of the population that agreed with this idea in Germany, France, Russia, Pakistan, Egypt, China, and Spain was, respectively, 21%, 20%, 17%, 11%, 10%, 8%, and 7%.

3. Between 2000 and 2006, the percentage of those who held a "favorable opinion" of the United States dropped from 83% to 56% in Great Britain, from 62% to 39% in France, from 78% to 37% in Germany, from 50% to 23% in Spain, from 75% to 30% in Indonesia, and from 52% to 12% in Turkey.

4. According to the White House, President Bush ordered more than thirty unauthorized wiretaps between 2002 and 2005.

5. Between 2001 and 2006, the number of inmates imprisoned indefinitely, without charges, at the Guantánamo Bay Naval Base in Cuba is estimated to have ranged between 450 and 759.

6. On an average day, McDonald's opens a new restaurant every three hours, a rate that equals 2,500 restaurants per year, two-thirds of which will be located in foreign countries.

7. All but one of the top 200 highest-grossing movies in the history of cinema were produced by American film companies.

Sources: (1) The Center for Arms Control and Non-Proliferation (www.arms controlcenter.org); (2, 3) The Pew Global Attitudes Project (www.pewglobal.org), "America's Image Slips ..." (June 13, 2006); (4) CNN.com, "Bush Says He Signed NSA Wire Tap Order" (December 17, 2005); (5) *The Washington Post*, "Three Detainees Commit Suicide at Guantanamo" (Sunday, June 11, 2006), p. A01; (6) McDonald's PR Newswire (www.licenseenews.com); (7) The Internet Movie Database.

 T HE EVENTS OF SEPTEMBER 11, 2001, came as a shock to most Americans. As a nation, we were stunned by the violence of the assaults on New York's World Trade Center and the Pentagon, and appalled by the senseless loss of life. But what confounded so many Americans was the fact that we, as a nation, could inspire the kind of insane rage that motivated our attackers. As observers across the country were quick to point out, America lost its innocence on 9/11 — as if overnight we found ourselves the object of hatred in a world teeming with potential enemies.

The idea of our essential "innocence" in relation to other nations is a central feature of America's cultural mythology. It has played an important role in shaping our national identity, and it is inextricably bound up with another powerful cultural myth — the notion of American freedom. Even before Columbus sailed for India in 1492, Europeans had long idealized the mythic lands they believed lay beyond the western horizon. In the Classical era, Greeks and Romans had envisioned a utopian realm to the west inhabited by "fabulous races" unlike any other people in the known world. Trying to describe the promise of this uncharted land, the poet and orator Horace encouraged his fellow Romans to

> See, see before us the distant glow,
> Through the thin dawn-mists of the West,
> Rich sunlit plains and hilltops gemmed with snow,
> The islands of the Blest!

To European minds straining to imagine what eyes could not see, the world beyond the curve of the Atlantic was an enchanted place. It was Atlantis, Avalon, the Garden of the Hesperides, the Seven Cities of Antillia, the New Eden, the promised land of Canaan. It was Elysium, the "happy land," where the weather was always gentle and people lived forever "untouched by sorrow." It was Eldorado, the mythic city where the streets were paved with gold, and precious jewels littered the earth like stones.

The Puritans who founded Plymouth Plantation in 1620 spiritualized this mythic vision of the meaning of the New World. Puritan fantasies of America were shaped by the stories that dominated the Protestant imagination — the legends of suffering and redemption related in the Bible. Persecuted by what they saw as a corrupt and authoritarian church in Europe, the Pilgrims viewed America through Old Testament stories of exile, enslavement, and salvation. They came to see themselves as the new "children of Israel," a "chosen people" destined to embark on an "errand in the wilderness" in search of the New Jerusalem, a new Promised Land. From the start, European colonizers were convinced that America was a place apart, a land that was sanctified by God and preordained to fulfill a special destiny in the history of the world. Colonial poets Philip Freneau and Hugh Brackenridge celebrated this biblical vision of America's destiny in their "Poem on the Rising Glory of America":

A new Jerusalem, sent down from heaven
Shall grace our happy earth. . . .
Paradise anew
Shall flourish, by no second Adam lost . . .
Another Canaan shall excel the old . . .

In the space of two generations, the Puritan fantasy of America as the cradle of the world's spiritual rebirth would collapse into the mass hysteria of the Salem witch trials and genocidal warfare against the same Native Americans who helped the original Pilgrims survive their first winter. But the Puritan contribution to America's cultural mythology would live on. From the founding of the Massachusetts Bay Colony to the present day, America has seen itself as a nation with a special role to play on the stage of world history. The New World has long dreamed itself the home of the "New Adam," a new kind of human being, capable of rising above the sins and weaknesses of the old "fallen" world of Europe. Growing directly from the Puritan religious vision of the New World as a place of personal rebirth, this belief in America's "exceptionalism" would become one of the central tenets in our national ideology.

By 1776, the Puritan vision of American exceptionalism had been thoroughly secularized. Americans no longer expected to create, in literal terms, a "New Jerusalem" on earth, but we hadn't given up on the idea that America itself was a place with a special meaning and destiny in the world. For the Founders of the Republic, freedom is what made America special, and the love of freedom is what distinguished America from all previous civilizations. Writing in 1769, the French immigrant farmer and social observer J. Hector St. John de Crèvecoeur celebrated this special commitment to the spirit of liberty in his *Letters from an American Farmer.* American society, according to Crèvecoeur, was difficult to describe because it differed so radically from the authoritarian societies of Europe:

> It is not composed, as in Europe, of great lords, who possess every thing, and of a herd of people who have nothing. Here are no aristo-cratical families, no courts, no kings, no bishops, no ecclesiastical dominion, no invincible power. . . . The rich and the poor are not so far removed from each other as they are in Europe. . . . We have no princes, for whom we toil, starve, and bleed: we are the most perfect society now existing in the world. Here man is free as he ought to be. . . .

This vision of a new race of free human beings, liberated from the shackles of government, aristocracy, and religious domination, fueled the American Revolution. It found expression in the Declaration of Independence, which proclaims "that all men are created equal, that they are endowed by their Creator with certain unalienable Rights, that among these are Life, Liberty, and the pursuit of Happiness." And it is similarly enshrined in the Constitution — both in the preamble, which asserts that the Constitution itself was framed in order "to secure the blessings of liberty to ourselves and our posterity," and of course in the Bill of Rights.

Little wonder then that Americans were shocked by 9/11. After all, who would lash out against the country that symbolizes liberty and freedom to the rest of the world? And little wonder, too, that the president of the United States would respond to 9/11 by invoking the myth of freedom. As President Bush reminded us in his 2002 State of the Union address, America is synonymous with the ideal of liberty, and Americans, unlike the terrorists who attacked us, are a proud and free people:

> Our enemies send other people's children on missions of suicide and murder. They embrace tyranny and death as a cause and a creed. We stand for a different choice, made long ago, on the day of our founding. We affirm it again today. We choose freedom and the dignity of every life.
>
> Steadfast in our purpose, we now press on. We have known freedom's price. We have shown freedom's power. And in this great conflict, my fellow Americans, we will see freedom's victory.

From the perspective of American mythology, the events of 9/11 may be tragic and shocking, but they are easily explained. The United States stands for freedom in the world, and because we're a good and free people we inspire hatred among those who are either "evil," as the president has put it, or so backward as to oppose civilization's inevitable march toward liberty. Seen in this light, we're a peace-loving nation, whose only interest is to spread the gospel of democracy and respect for human rights. The problem, of course, is that a good deal of American history seems to challenge this glowing self-estimate. The principles of "Life, Liberty, and the pursuit of Happiness" that we as a nation extolled in the Declaration of Independence clearly didn't apply to the Native Americans who were systematically deprived of all three of these benefits during the first three hundred years of the American experiment. Nor did the rights guaranteed under the Constitution extend to all Americans. Indeed, the Constitution itself didn't ban the practice of slavery until the Fourteenth Amendment was adopted at the end of the Civil War, and another century would pass before equal treatment under the law was extended to African Americans during the civil rights movement of the 1960s.

Unfortunately, the American record on freedom abroad is even more problematic. Yes, the United States supported the cause of world freedom in World Wars I and II, but did we make the world a safer and more democratic place by allying ourselves with well-known tyrants like Francisco Franco in Spain, Ferdinand Marcos in the Philippines, Augusto Pinochet in Chili, Reza Shah Pahlavi in Iran, Roberto D'Aubuisson in El Salvador, and Suharto in Indonesia? Moreover, as critics of American foreign policy have repeatedly pointed out, we've made a habit of demonizing tyrants who were once ardent American allies. After all, we trained Manuel Noriega at our CIA-sponsored School of the Americas and helped him rise to power in Panama before deciding that he represented such a threat to liberty that he had to be driven by force from his country. In similar fashion, before we declared Iraq's Saddam Hussein an enemy of democratic values, we provided him and his Baathist followers both monetary and military assistance in abundance. Most astonishingly, we were even once the principal ally of Osama bin Laden — back in the days when the U.S. government portrayed him as a freedom fighter, and not as the embodiment of evil.

And since 9/11, our relation to the principle of liberty has become increasingly ambiguous, as well. As we send U.S. troops off to fight the enemies of freedom abroad, our leaders have begun to restrict American liberties at home. Arab Americans, Arab immigrants, and anyone who looks even vaguely "Middle Eastern" are now fair game at American airports as we embrace a campaign of ethnic profiling that echoes the anti-Japanese excesses of World War II. In the name of "homeland security" we've passed legislation that threatens to undermine the most fundamental of our civil liberties, including the right to privacy, the right of free speech, and the right to due process. It's even become acceptable today to debate whether torture or state-sponsored assassination are reasonable weapons in the war against terror.

Perhaps even more amazing is the fact that little more than two centuries after winning our own freedom from the British Empire, the prospect of an "American Empire" has moved to the forefront of U.S. foreign policy. The original founders of the United States took pains to warn against the temptations of empire building. In his farewell address of 1797, George Washington cautioned his countrymen against becoming enmeshed in the intrigues and entanglements of foreign governments. In 1812, John Quincy Adams echoed Washington when he warned that if America were to "become the dictatress of the world, she would be no longer the ruler of her own spirit." Yet today the prospect of an American empire is no longer unthinkable. In an age of unilateral invasions, preemptive first strikes, regime change, and U.S.-sponsored "nation building," the idea that America might someday rule the world seems more and more like a real possibility.

But can the United States dominate world affairs and still lay claim to innocence? Can we pursue a policy of empire building and still take pride in the fact that we represent freedom to the rest of the world? These are just a few of the questions you'll encounter in this chapter. Our exploration of America's meaning in the new world order begins with two examples of the myth of freedom at work in the service of U.S. foreign policy. Written on the brink of America's war with Spain in 1898, Albert J. Beveridge's "The March of the Flag" is one of the best examples of modern American colonialist thinking. Published a little more than a century later, Dinesh D'Souza's "America the Beautiful" demonstrates just how powerful the ideology of American freedom continues to be as a justification for our attitudes toward the rest of the world.

The next two selections challenge the notion of American innocence. In "The Oblivious Empire," journalist Mark Hertsgaard offers a critical perspective on why America fascinates and infuriates the world as he explores the contradictions of events in recent U.S. foreign relations. Joel Andreas's graphic exposé "The War on Terrorism" complements Hertsgaard by raising questions about how the United States has responded to the events of September 11, 2001, and how these responses relate to the role we've played in the Middle East.

The Visual Portfolio that follows offers the chance to explore images that comment on the myth of freedom and America's meaning in the world. The photographs you'll find in this section challenge some of our most deeply held assumptions about the way America is perceived by peoples in other nations. Eyal Press next urges us to consider what it means to use torture as a means of preserving national security and the implications of practices like "extraordinary rendition" and detention without trial in a free society. Todd Gitlin rounds off this section by offering an analysis of the meaning of America's "fun" culture in "Under the Sign of Mickey Mouse & Co."

The chapter and the book close with two readings that invite us to reflect on the promise of freedom in American society. In "Resistance to Civil Government," Henry David Thoreau muses on what the individual owes the state when the state itself has betrayed its own fundamental values in a time of crisis. Thoreau's declaration of the individual's right to defy governmental authority in the name of liberty remains as timely and powerful today as it was during the Mexican-American War. The chapter concludes with Langston Hughes's impassioned appeal to make America a land that lives up to its most fundamental ideal:

> The land that never has been yet —
> And yet must be — the land where *every* man is free.

Sources

George W. Bush, 2002 State of the Union Address, available at www. whitehouse.gov/news/releases/2002/01/20020129-11.html.

Noam Chomsky, *9-11.* New York: Seven Stories Press, 2002.

J. Hector St. John de Crèvecoeur, *Letters from an American Farmer.* New York: Dolphin Books, 1961. First published in London, 1782.

Anne Taylor Fleming, "Aftermath: Innocence Lost; A Tragedy for an Optimistic Land." *New York Times,* September 23, 2001, Section 4, p. 4.

Michael Ignatieff, "The American Empire." *New York Times,* January 5, 2003, Section 6, p. 22.

Krishan Kumar, *Utopia and Anti-Utopia in Modern Times.* Oxford: Basil Blackwell, 1987.

Howard Zinn, *A People's History of the United States.* New York: Harper and Row, 1980.

Howard Zinn, *Terrorism and War.* New York: Seven Stories Press, 2002.

BEFORE READING

- Using the picture at the beginning of this chapter as a point of departure, write about how you think America has changed since September 11, 2001. In what ways have American freedoms been restricted since 9/11? How has the threat of terrorism changed the way we see ourselves? How has it changed our way of life?

- Working in small groups, discuss what you think America represents to people in other countries. What values, ideas, and attitudes do you think America represents abroad? What misconceptions might people in other lands have about life in the United States? Why?

- Compare notes with your classmates about how well your own education has prepared you to cope with issues like U.S. foreign policy, globalization, and terrorism. How were these topics addressed in your prior educational experience? Test your own international literacy by working in pairs to sketch a rough map of the world with as many countries and capitals filled in as possible. How well do your results compare with those of your fellow students?

The March of the Flag

ALBERT J. BEVERIDGE

On September 16, 1898, during a political rally in Indianapolis, Indiana, a relatively unknown twenty-five-year-old lawyer offered a spirited defense of the United States in relation to the impending Spanish-American War. In "The March of the Flag," Albert Jeremiah Beveridge (1862–1927) argued for America's right to seize and maintain possession of the Philippines — a radical idea for a nation that had, until then, resisted the idea of meddling in the affairs of other countries. Within months, Beveridge's speech sold more than 300,000 copies and was well on its way to becoming one of the most important documents in twentieth-century American foreign policy. Beveridge himself was elected to the U.S. Senate a year later, where he served until 1911. In addition to his career in politics, Beveridge was a trained historian who published biographies of Abraham Lincoln and John Marshall, fourth chief justice of the United States.

It is a noble land that God has given us; a land that can feed and clothe the world; a land whose coastlines would inclose half the countries of Europe;

a land set like a sentinel between the two imperial oceans of the globe, a greater England with a nobler destiny.

It is a mighty people that He has planted on this soil; a people sprung from the most masterful blood of history; a people perpetually revitalized by the virile, man-producing working-folk of all the earth; a people imperial by virtue of their power, by right of their institutions, by authority of their Heaven-directed purposes — the propagandists and not the misers of liberty.

It is a glorious history our God has bestowed upon His chosen people; a history heroic with faith in our mission and our future; a history of states-men who flung the boundaries of the Republic out into unexplored lands and savage wilderness; a history of soldiers who carried the flag across blazing deserts and through the ranks of hostile mountains, even to the gates of sunset; a history of a multiplying people who overran a continent in half a century; a history of prophets who saw the consequences of evils inherited from the past and of martyrs who died to save us from them; a history divinely logical, in the process of whose tremendous reasoning we find ourselves to-day.

Therefore, in this campaign,[1] the question is larger than a party question. It is an American question. It is a world question. Shall the American people continue their march toward the commercial supremacy of the world? Shall free institutions broaden their blessed reign as the children of liberty wax in strength, until the empire of our principles is established over the hearts of all mankind?

Have we no mission to perform, no duty to discharge to our fellowman?   5 Has God endowed us with gifts beyond our deserts and marked us as the people of His peculiar favor, merely to rot in our own selfishness, as men and nations must, who take cowardice for their companion and self for their deity — as China has, as India has, as Egypt has?

Shall we be as the man who had one talent and hid it, or as he who had ten talents and used them until they grew to riches? And shall we reap the reward that waits on our discharge of our high duty; shall we occupy new markets for what our farmers raise, our factories make, our merchants sell — aye, and, please God, new markets for what our ships shall carry?

Hawaii is ours; Porto Rico is to be ours; at the prayer of her people Cuba finally will be ours; in the islands of the East, even to the gates of Asia, coaling stations are to be ours at the very least; the flag of a liberal government is to float over the Philippines, and may it be the banner that Taylor[2] unfurled in Texas and Fremont[3] carried to the coast.

---

[1]*this campaign:* This may refer to the Spanish-American War of 1898.

[2]*Taylor:* Zachary Taylor (1784–1850), twelfth president of the United States, famous for the role he played in the U.S. war against Mexico (1846–1848), which led to the annexation of Texas and other western states.

[3]*Fremont:* John Charles Frémont (1813–1890), U.S. explorer, soldier, and politician who sparked a revolt against Mexican authorities in California in 1846.

The Opposition tells us that we ought not to govern a people without their consent. I answer, The rule of liberty that all just government derives its authority from the consent of the governed, applies only to those who are capable of self-government. We govern the Indians without their consent, we govern our territories without their consent, we govern our children without their consent. How do they know that our government would be without their consent? Would not the people of the Philippines prefer the just, humane, civilizing government of this Republic to the savage, bloody rule of pillage and extortion from which we have rescued them?

And, regardless of this formula of words made only for enlightened, self-governing people, do we owe no duty to the world? Shall we turn these peoples back to the reeking hands from which we have taken them? Shall we abandon them, with Germany, England, Japan, hungering for them? Shall we save them from those nations, to give them a self-rule of tragedy?

They ask us how we shall govern these new possessions. I answer: Out   10
of local conditions and the necessities of the case methods of government will grow. If England can govern foreign lands, so can America. If Germany can govern foreign lands, so can America. If they can supervise protectorates, so can America. Why is it more difficult to administer Hawaii than New Mexico or California? Both had a savage and an alien population; both were more remote from the seat of government when they came under our dominion than the Philippines are to-day.

Will you say by your vote that American ability to govern has decayed; that a century's experience in self-rule has failed of a result? Will you affirm by your vote that you are an infidel to American power and practical sense? Or will you say that ours is the blood of government; ours the heart of dominion; ours the brain and genius of administration? Will you remember that we do but what our fathers did — we but pitch the tents of liberty farther westward, farther southward — we only continue the march of the flag?

The march of the flag! In 1789 the flag of the Republic waved over 4,000,000 souls in thirteen states, and their savage territory which stretched to the Mississippi, to Canada, to the Floridas. The timid minds of that day said that no new territory was needed, and, for the hour, they were right. But Jefferson, through whose intellect the centuries marched; Jefferson, who dreamed of Cuba as an American state; Jefferson, the first Imperialist of the Republic — Jefferson acquired that imperial territory which swept from the Mississippi to the mountains, from Texas to the British possessions, and the march of the flag began!

The infidels to the gospel of liberty raved, but the flag swept on! The title to that noble land out of which Oregon, Washington, Idaho, and Montana have been carved was uncertain; Jefferson, strict constructionist of constitutional power though he was, obeyed the Anglo-Saxon impulse within him, whose watchword then and whose watchword throughout the world to-day is, "Forward!": another empire was added to the Republic, and the march of the flag went on!

Those who deny the power of free institutions to expand urged every argument, and more, that we hear, to-day; but the people's judgment approved the command of their blood, and the march of the flag went on!

A screen of land from New Orleans to Florida shut us from the Gulf, 15 and over this and the Everglade Peninsula[4] waved the saffron flag of Spain; Andrew Jackson[5] seized both, the American people stood at his back, and, under Monroe,[6] the Floridas came under the dominion of the Republic, and the march of the flag went on! The Cassandras[7] prophesied every prophecy of despair we hear, to-day, but the march of the flag went on!

Then Texas responded to the bugle calls of liberty, and the march of the flag went on! And, at last, we waged war with Mexico, and the flag swept over the southwest, over peerless California, past the Gate of Gold to Oregon on the north, and from ocean to ocean its folds of glory blazed.

And, now, obeying the same voice that Jefferson heard and obeyed, that Jackson heard and obeyed, that Monroe heard and obeyed, that Seward[8] heard and obeyed, that Grant[9] heard and obeyed, that Harrison[10] heard and obeyed, our President[11] to-day plants the flag over the islands of the seas, outposts of commerce, citadels of national security, and the march of the flag goes on!

Distance and oceans are no arguments. The fact that all the territory our fathers bought and seized is contiguous, is no argument. In 1819 Florida was farther from New York than Porto Rico is from Chicago today; Texas, farther from Washington in 1845 than Hawaii is from Boston in 1898; California, more inaccessible in 1847 than the Philippines are now. Gibraltar is farther from London than Havana is from Washington; Melbourne is farther from Liverpool than Manila is from San Francisco.

The ocean does not separate us from lands of our duty and desire — the oceans join us, rivers never to be dredged, canals never to be repaired. Steam joins us; electricity joins us — the very elements are in league with

[4]*the Everglade Peninsula:* Florida.

[5]*Andrew Jackson:* Jackson (1767–1845), seventh president of the United States, extended U.S. claims to Florida in 1818 by crossing into Spanish territory and seizing Pensacola while carrying out reprisals against Seminole Indians.

[6]*Monroe:* James Monroe (1758–1831), fifth president of the United States and author of the Monroe Doctrine of 1823, which laid the groundwork for later U.S. imperialism in the Caribbean and Latin America by asserting that the United States has a special interest in maintaining the independence of all nations in the Americas.

[7]*the Cassandras:* In Greek legend, Cassandra is given the power of prophecy but is also cursed so that all of her prophesies remain unbelieved.

[8]*Seward:* William Henry Seward (1801–1872), American statesman and secretary of state under the administration of Abraham Lincoln.

[9]*Grant:* Ulysses Simpson Grant (1822–1885), eighteenth president of the United States.

[10]*Harrison:* William Henry Harrison (1773–1841), ninth president of the United States.

[11]*our President:* William McKinley (1843–1901), twenty-fifth president of the United States, who oversaw the expansion of American interests during the Spanish-American War (1898) and the Philippine Insurrection (1899–1901).

our destiny. Cuba not contiguous! Porto Rico not contiguous! Hawaii and the Philippines not contiguous! The oceans make them contiguous. And our navy will make them contiguous.

But the Opposition is right — there is a difference. We did not need the western Mississippi Valley when we acquired it, nor Florida, nor Texas, nor California, nor the royal provinces of the far northwest. We had no emigrants to people this imperial wilderness, no money to develop it, even no highways to cover it. No trade awaited us in its savage vastnesses. Our productions were not greater than our trade. There was not one reason for the land-lust of our statesmen from Jefferson to Grant, other than the prophet and the Saxon within them. But, to-day, we are raising more than we can consume, making more than we can use. Therefore we must find new markets for our produce.   20

And so, while we did not need the territory taken during the past century at the time it was acquired, we do need what we have taken in 1898, and we need it now. The resources and the commerce of these immensely rich dominions will be increased as much as American energy is greater than Spanish sloth. In Cuba, alone, there are 15,000,000 acres of forest unacquainted with the ax, exhaustless mines of iron, priceless deposits of manganese, millions of dollars' worth of which we must buy, to-day, from the Black Sea districts. There are millions of acres yet unexplored.

The resources of Porto Rico have only been trifled with. The riches of the Philippines have hardly been touched by the finger-tips of modern methods. And they produce what we consume, and consume what we produce — the very predestination of reciprocity — a reciprocity "not made with hands, eternal in the heavens." They sell hemp, sugar, cocoanuts, fruits of the tropics, timber of price like mahogany; they buy flour, clothing, tools, implements, machinery, and all that we can raise and make. Their trade will be ours in time. Do you indorse that policy with your vote?

Cuba is as large as Pennsylvania, and is the richest spot on the globe. Hawaii is as large as New Jersey; Porto Rico half as large as Hawaii; the Philippines larger than all New England, New York, New Jersey and Delaware combined. Together they are larger than the British Isles, larger than France, larger than Germany, larger than Japan.

If any man tells you that trade depends on cheapness and not on government influence, ask him why England does not abandon South Africa, Egypt, India. Why does France seize South China, Germany the vast region whose port is Kaouchou?

Our trade with Porto Rico, Hawaii, and the Philippines must be as free   25 as between the states of the Union, because they are American territory, while every other nation on earth must pay our tariff before they can compete with us. Until Cuba shall ask for annexation, our trade with her will, at the very least, be like the preferential trade of Canada with England. That, and the excellence of our goods and products; that, and the convenience of traffic; that, and the kinship of interests and destiny, will give the monopoly of these markets to the American people.

The commercial supremacy of the Republic means that this Nation is to be the sovereign factor in the peace of the world. For the conflicts of the future are to be conflicts of trade — struggles for markets — commercial wars for existence. And the golden rule of peace is impregnability of position and invincibility of preparedness. So, we see England, the greatest strategist of history, plant her flag and her cannon on Gibraltar, at Quebec, in the Bermudas, at Vancouver, everywhere.

So Hawaii furnished us a naval base in the heart of the Pacific; the Ladrones another, a voyage further on; Manila another, at the gates of Asia — Asia, to the trade of whose hundreds of millions American merchants, manufacturers, farmers, have as good right as those of Germany or France or Russia or England; Asia, whose commerce with the United Kingdom alone amounts to hundreds of millions of dollars every year; Asia, to whom Germany looks to take her surplus products; Asia, whose doors must not be shut against American trade. Within five decades the bulk of Oriental commerce will be ours.

Wonderfully has God guided us. Yonder at Bunker Hill[12] and Yorktown[13] His providence was above us. At New Orleans[14] and on ensanguined seas His hand sustained us. Abraham Lincoln was His minister and His was the altar of freedom the Nation's soldiers set up on a hundred battle-fields. His power directed Dewey[15] in the East and delivered the Spanish fleet into our hands, as He delivered the elder Armada into the hands of our English sires two centuries ago. . . . We can not fly from our world duties; it is ours to execute the purpose of a fate that has driven us to be greater than our small intentions. We can not retreat from any soil where Providence has unfurled our banner; it is ours to save that soil for liberty and civilization.

ENGAGING THE TEXT

1. What is America's mission, according to Beveridge? What assumptions are embedded in this notion of a national "mission"? How, for example, does the idea of a national mission differ from a strategic goal or national interest? What is the source of this sense of mission?

2. How does Beveridge view America and Americans in relation to other peoples and nations? How would you describe his attitude toward other cultures and countries?

---

[12]*Bunker Hill:* Site of the first successful colonial resistance against British forces at the outbreak of the American Revolution in 1775.

[13]*Yorktown:* Site of the British surrender to American forces at the end of the American Revolution in 1781.

[14]*New Orleans:* Site of Andrew Jackson's decisive defeat of British forces at the end of the War of 1812 (1812–1815).

[15]*Dewey:* George Dewey (1837–1917), American admiral, who defeated the Spanish fleet at Manila at the outbreak of the Spanish-American War.

3. What arguments, stated or implied, does Beveridge offer to justify American imperialism? What role do history, economic forces, and American ideology play in this justification?

EXPLORING CONNECTIONS

4. To what extent do the images in the Visual Portfolio for this chapter (p. 806) support Beveridge's claim that American society has a special destiny to fulfill in the world?

EXTENDING THE CRITICAL CONTEXT

5. Research the history of any of the U.S. territories or protectorates that Beveridge mentions in this selection. How have the original inhabitants of these nations fared under America's influence? To what extent has history borne out Beveridge's claims about the benefits of American civilization and administration?

6. Research statements made by contemporary U.S. politicians and foreign policy experts about America's role in relation to the rest of the world to see how they compare with Beveridge's view of America's international mission. To what extent does Beveridge's early argument for imperialism prefigure current trends in U.S. foreign policy?

America the Beautiful: What We're Fighting For
DINESH D'SOUZA

Before 9/11, most Americans probably hadn't given a lot of thought to how we, as a people, are viewed by the rest of the world. Of course, many of us were aware of the negative image of "the ugly American" that developed as the power and prestige of the United States grew after World War II. But nothing had prepared us for the idea that others hated the United States so much they'd gladly die to do us damage. In this selection, conservative thinker Dinesh D'Souza suggests that we're despised by much of the rest of the world precisely because we're so good: our freedom itself, according to D'Souza, lies at the root of the most toxic forms of anti-Americanism in the world today. The Robert and Karen Rishwain Fellow at the Stanford-based Hoover Institution, D'Souza (b. 1961) served as senior domestic policy analyst at the White House during the Reagan administration, has written extensively for the Wall Street Journal, *the* New York Times, *the* Boston Globe, *and the* Washington Post, *and appears regularly on news programs like* Nightline, Crossfire, Firing Line, *and* Good Morning America. *He has also written a number of best-selling books on politics and current events, including* Illiberal Education *(1991),* The End of Racism *(1995), and the source of this selection,* What's So Great About America? *(2002).*

> We have it in our power to begin the world all over again.
> — THOMAS PAINE

America represents a new way of being human and thus presents a radical challenge to the world. On the one hand, Americans have throughout their history held that they are special: that their country has been blessed by God, that the American system is unique, that Americans are not like people everywhere else. This set of beliefs is called "American exceptionalism." At the same time, Americans have also traditionally insisted that they provide a model for the world, that theirs is a formula that others can follow, and that there is no better life available elsewhere. Paradoxically enough, American exceptionalism leads to American universalism.

Both American exceptionalism and American universalism have come under fierce attack from the enemies of America, both at home and abroad. The critics of America deny that there is anything unique about America, and they ridicule the notion that the American model is one that others should seek to follow. Indeed, by chronicling the past and present crimes of America, they hope to extract apologies and financial reparations out of Americans. Some even seek to justify murderous attacks against America on the grounds that what America does, and what she stands for, invites such attacks.

These critics are aiming their assault on America's greatest weakness: her lack of moral self-confidence. Americans cannot effectively fight a war without believing that it is a just war. That's why America has only lost once, in Vietnam, and that was because most Americans did not know what they were fighting for. The enemies of America understand this vulnerability. At the deepest level their assault is moral: they seek to destroy America's belief in herself, knowing that if this happens, America is finished. By the same token, when Americans rally behind a good cause, as in World War II, they are invincible. The outcome of America's engagements abroad is usually determined by a single factor: America's will to prevail. In order to win, Americans need to believe that they are on the side of the angels. The good news is that they usually are.

The triumph of American ideas and culture in the global marketplace, and the fact that most immigrants from around the world choose to come to the United States, would seem to be sufficient grounds for establishing the superiority of American civilization. But this is not entirely so, because we have not shown that the people of the world are *justified* in preferring the American way of life to any other. We must contend with the Islamic fundamentalists' argument that their societies are based on high principles while America is based on low principles. The Islamic critics are happy to concede the attractions of America, but they insist that these attractions are base. America, they say, appeals to what is most degraded about human nature; by contrast, Islamic societies may be poor and "backward," but they at least aspire to virtue. Even if they fall short, they are trying to live by God's law.

Americans usually have a hard time answering this argument, in part   5 because they are bewildered by its theological cadences. The usual tendency is to lapse into a kind of unwitting relativism. "You are following what you believe is right, and we are living by the values that we think are best." This pious buncombe usually concludes with a Rodney King–style[1] plea for tolerance, "So why don't we learn to appreciate our differences? Why don't we just get along?" To see why this argument fails completely, imagine that you are living during the time of the Spanish Inquisition.[2] The Grand Inquisitor is just starting to pull out your fingernails. You make the Rodney King move on him. "Torquemada,[3] please stop pulling out my fingernails. Why don't we learn to appreciate our differences?" Most of us probably realize that Torquemada would not find this persuasive. But it is less obvious why he would not. Let me paraphrase Torquemada's argument: "You think I am taking away your freedom, but I am concerned with your immortal soul. Ultimately virtue is far more important than freedom. Our lives last for a mere second in the long expanse of eternity. What measure of pleasure or pain we experience in our short life is trivial compared to our fate in the never ending life to come. I am trying to save your soul from damnation. Who cares if you have to let out a few screams in the process? My actions are entirely for your own benefit. You should be *thanking me* for pulling out your fingernails."

I have recalled the Spanish Inquisition to make the point that the Islamic argument is one that we have heard before. We should not find it so strange that people think this way; it is the way that many in our own civilization used to think not so very long ago. The reason that most of us do not think this way now is that Western history has taught us a hard lesson. That lesson is that when the institutions of religion and government are one, and the secular authority is given the power to be the interpreter and enforcer

---

[1]*Rodney King:* Los Angeles resident whose apparently unprovoked beating by police was videotaped and televised, sparking riots across the city in 1992. [Notes 9, 12, and 13 are D'Souza's.]

[2]*Spanish Inquisition:* Tribunal of the Roman Catholic Church in Spain from 1478 until 1510, famous for its cruelty and intolerance.

[3]*Torquemada:* Tomás de Torquemada (1420–1498), Spanish churchman who led the Inquisition and earned infamy for his brutal persecution of Spanish Jews.

of God's law, then horrible abuses of power are perpetrated in God's name. This is just what we saw in Afghanistan with the Taliban,[4] and what we see now in places like Iran. This is not to suggest that Islam's historical abuses are worse than those of the West. But the West, as a consequence of its experience, learned to disentangle the institutions of religion and government — a separation that was most completely achieved in the United States. As we have seen, the West also devised a new way of organizing society around the institutions of science, democracy, and capitalism. The Renaissance, the Reformation, the Enlightenment, and the Scientific Revolution were some of the major signposts on Western civilization's road to modernity.

By contrast, the Islamic world did not have a Renaissance or a Reformation. No Enlightenment or Scientific Revolution either. Incredible though it may seem to many in the West, Islamic societies today are in some respects not very different from how they were a thousand years ago. Islam has been around for a long time. This brings us to a critical question: why are we seeing this upsurge of Islamic fundamentalism and Islamic fanaticism now?

To answer this question, we should recall that Islam was once one of the greatest and most powerful civilizations in the world. Indeed, there was a time when it seemed as if the whole world would fall under Islamic rule. Within a century of the prophet Muhammad's[5] death, his converts had overthrown the Sassanid dynasty in Iran and conquered large tracts of territory from the Byzantine dynasty. Soon the Muslims had established an empire greater than that of Rome at its zenith. Over the next several centuries, Islam made deep inroads into Africa, Southeast Asia, and southern Europe. The crusades were launched to repel the forces of Islam, but the crusades ended in failure. By the sixteenth century, there were no fewer than five Islamic empires, unified by political ties, a common religion, and a common culture: the Mamluk sultans in Egypt, the Safavid dynasty in Iran, the Mughal empire in India, the empire of the Great Khans in Russia and Central Asia, and the Ottoman Empire based in Turkey. Of these, the Ottomans were by far the most formidable. They ruled most of North Africa, and threatened Mediterranean Europe and Austria. Europe was terrified that they might take over all the lands of Christendom. In all of history, Islam is the only non-Western civilization to pose a mortal threat to the West.

Then it all went wrong. Starting in the late seventeenth century, when the West was able to repel the Ottoman siege of Vienna, the power of Islam began a slow but steady decline. By the nineteenth century the Ottoman Empire was known as the "sick man of Europe," and it collapsed completely after World War I, when the victorious European powers carved it up and

---

[4]*the Taliban:* Radical Islamic sect that came to power in Afghanistan in 1996.

[5]*Muhammad:* The prophet of Islam (570?–632), whose collected visions and revelations compose the Koran.

parceled out the pieces. Not only did the Muslims lose most of the territory they had conquered, but they also found themselves being ruled, either directly or indirectly, by the West. Today, even though colonialism has ended, the Islamic world is in a miserable state. Basically all that it has to offer is oil, and as technology opens up alternative sources of energy, even that will not amount to much. Without its oil revenues, the Islamic world will find itself in the position of sub-Saharan Africa: it will cease to matter. Even now it does not matter very much. The only reason it makes the news is by killing people. When is the last time you opened the newspaper to read about a great Islamic discovery or invention? While China and India, two other empires that were eclipsed by the West, have embraced Western technology and even assumed a leadership role in some areas, Islam's contribution to modern science and technology is negligible.

In addition to these embarrassments, the Islamic world faces a for-   10
midable threat from the United States. This is not the threat of American force or of American support for Israel. Israel is an irritant, but it does not threaten the existence of Islamic society. By contrast, America stands for an idea that is fully capable of transforming the Islamic world by winning the hearts of Muslims. The subversive American idea is one of shaping your own life, of making your own destiny, of following a path illumined not by external authorities but by your inner self. This American idea endangers the sanctity of the Muslim home, as well as the authority of Islamic society. It empowers women and children to assert their prerogatives against the male head of the household. It also undermines political and religious hier-archies. Of all American ideas, the "inner voice" is the most dangerous because it rivals the voice of Allah as a source of moral allegiance. So Islam is indeed, as bin Laden[6] warned, facing the greatest threat to its survival since the days of Muhammad.

In recent decades, a great debate has broken out in the Muslim world to account for Islamic decline and to formulate a response to it. One response — let us call it the reformist or classical liberal response — is to acknowledge that the Islamic world has been left behind by modernity. The reformers' solution is to embrace science, democracy, and capitalism. This would mean adaptation — at least selective adaptation — to the ways of the West. The liberal reformers have an honorable intellectual tradition, associ-ated with such names as Muhammad Abduh, Jamal al-Afghani, Muhammad Iqbal, and Taha Husayn. This group also enjoys a fairly strong base of sup-port in the Muslim middle class. In the past two decades, however, the reformers have been losing the argument in the Islamic world to their rival group, the fundamentalists.

---

[6]*bin Laden:* Osama bin Laden (b. 1957), son of one of Saudi Arabia's wealthiest families and founder of the international terrorist organization al-Qaeda, which has been linked to numerous attacks on U.S. targets around the world, including the attacks of September 11, 2001.

Here, in short, is the fundamentalist argument. The Koran promises that if Muslims are faithful to Allah, they will enjoy prosperity in this life and paradise in the next life. According to the fundamentalists, the Muslims were doing this for centuries, and they were invincible. But now, the fundamentalists point out, Islam is not winning any more; in fact, it is losing. What could be the reason for this? From the fundamentalist point of view, the answer is obvious: Muslims are not following the true teaching of Allah! The fundamentalists allege that Muslims have fallen away from the true faith and are mindlessly pursuing the ways of the infidel. The fundamentalists also charge that Islamic countries are now ruled by self-serving despots who serve as puppets for America and the West. The solution, the fundamentalists say, is to purge American troops and Western influence from the Middle East; to overthrow corrupt, pro-Western regimes like ones in Pakistan, Egypt, and Saudi Arabia; and to return to the pure, original teachings of the Koran. Only then, the fundamentalists insist, can Islam recover its lost glory.

One can see, from this portrait, that the fundamentalists are a humiliated people who are seeking to recover ancestral greatness. They are not complete "losers": they are driven by an awareness of moral superiority, combined with political, economic, and military inferiority. Their argument has a powerful appeal to proud Muslims who find it hard to come to terms with their contemporary irrelevance. And so the desert wind of fundamentalism has spread throughout the Middle East. It has replaced Arab nationalism as the most powerful political force in the region.

The success of the fundamentalists in the Muslim world should not blind us from recognizing that their counterattack against America and the West is fundamentally defensive. The fundamentalists know that their civilization does not have the appeal to expand outside its precinct. It's not as if the Muslims were plotting to take, say, Australia. It is the West that is making incursions into Islamic territory, winning converts, and threatening to subvert ancient loyalties and transform a very old way of life. So the fundamentalists are lashing out against this new, largely secular, Western "crusade." Terrorism, their weapon of counterinsurgency, is the weapon of the weak. Terrorism is the international equivalent of that domestic weapon of discontent: the riot. Political scientist Edward Banfield once observed that a riot is a failed revolution. People who know how to take over the government don't throw stones at a bus. Similarly terrorism of the bin Laden variety is a desperate strike against a civilization that the fundamentalists know they have no power to conquer.

But they do have the power to disrupt and terrify the people of America 15 and the West. This is one of their goals, and their attack on September 11, 2001, was quite successful in this regard. But there is a second goal: to unify the Muslim world behind the fundamentalist banner and to foment uprisings against pro-Western regimes. Thus the bin Ladens of the world are waging a two-front war: against Western influence in the Middle East and against pro-Western governments and liberal influences within the Islamic world. So the West is not faced with a pure "clash of civilizations."[7] It is not "the West" against "Islam." It is a clash of civilizations within the Muslim world. One side or the other will prevail.

So what should American policy be toward the region? It is a great mistake for Americans to believe that their country is hated because it is misunderstood. It is hated because it is understood only too well. Sometimes people say to me, "But the mullahs have a point about American culture. They are right about Jerry Springer."[8] Yes, they are right about Springer. If we could get them to agree to stop bombing our facilities in return for us shipping them Jerry Springer to do with as they like, we should make the deal tomorrow, and throw in some of Springer's guests. But the Islamic fundamentalists don't just object to the excesses of American liberty: they object to liberty itself. Nor can we appease them by staying out of their world. We live in an age in which the flow of information is virtually unstoppable. We do not have the power to keep our ideals and our culture out of their lives.

Thus there is no alternative to facing their hostility. First, we need to destroy their terrorist training camps and networks. This is not easy to do, because some of these facilities are in countries like Iraq, Iran, Libya, and the Sudan. The U.S. should demand that those countries dismantle their terror networks and stop being incubators of terrorism. If they do not, we should work to get rid of their governments. How this is done is a matter of prudence. In some cases, such as Iraq, the direct use of force might be the answer. In others, such as Iran, the U.S. can capitalize on widespread popular dissatisfaction with the government.[9] Iran has a large middle class, with strong democratic and pro-American elements. But the dissenters are sorely in need of leadership, resources, and an effective strategy to defeat the ruling theocracy.

The U.S. also has to confront the fact that regimes allied with America, such as Pakistan, Egypt, and Saudi Arabia, are undemocratic, corrupt, and repressive. Indeed, the misdoings and tyranny of these regimes strengthen the cause of the fundamentalists, who are able to tap deep veins of popular discontent. How do the regimes deal with this fundamentalist resistance? They subsidize various religious and educational programs administered by the fundamentalists that teach terrorism and hatred of America. By focusing the people's discontent against a foreign target, the United States, the

---

[7]*"clash of civilizations":* The title of Samuel P. Huntington's controversial 1996 book, based on a 1993 article published in *Foreign Affairs* magazine, which argues that the culture of the Western democracies, founded on "individualism, liberalism, constitutionalism, human rights, equality, liberty, [and] the rule of law," will inevitably come into conflict with the non-Western cultures across the globe.

[8]*Jerry Springer:* Talk show host known for featuring sexually explicit and violent themes and for instigating brawls among his guests.

[9]See, for example, Amy Waldman, "In Iran, an Angry Generation Longs for Jobs, More Freedom, and Power," *New York Times,* 7 December 2001.

regimes of Saudi Arabia, Egypt, and Pakistan hope to divert attention from their own failings. The United States must make it clear to its Muslim allies that this "solution" is unacceptable. If they want American aid and American support, they must stop funding mosques and schools that promote terrorism and anti-Americanism. Moreover, they must take steps to reduce corruption, expand civil liberties, and enfranchise their people.

In the long term, America's goal is a large and difficult one: to turn Muslim fundamentalists into classical liberals. This does not mean that we want them to stop being Muslims. It does mean, however, that we want them to practice their religion *in the liberal way.* Go to a Promise Keepers[10] meeting in Washington, D.C., or another of America's big cities. You will see tens of thousands of men singing, praying, hugging, and pledging chastity to their wives. A remarkable sight. These people are mostly evangelical and fundamentalist Christians. They are apt to approach you with the greeting, "Let me tell you what Jesus Christ has meant to my life." They want you to accept Christ, but their appeal is not to force but to consent. They do not say, "Accept Christ or I am going to plunge a dagger into your chest." Even the fundamentalist Christians in the West are liberals: they are practicing Christianity "in the liberal way."

The task of transforming Muslim fundamentalists into classical liberals   20 will not be an easy one to perform in the Islamic world, where there is no tradition of separating religion and government. We need not require that Islamic countries adopt America's strict form of separation, which prohibits any government involvement in religion. But it is indispensable that Muslim fundamentalists relinquish the use of force for the purpose of spreading Islam. They, too, should appeal to consent. If this seems like a ridiculous thing to ask of Muslims, let us remember that millions of Muslims are already living this way. These are, of course, the Muslim immigrants to Europe and the United States. They are following the teachings of their faith, but most of them understand that they must respect the equal rights of others. They have renounced the *jihad*[11] of the sword and confine themselves to the *jihad* of the pen and the *jihad* of the heart. In general, the immigrants are showing the way for Islam to change in the same way that Christianity changed in order to survive and flourish in the modern world.

Whether America can succeed in the mammoth enterprises of stopping terrorism and liberalizing the Islamic world depends a good deal on the people in the Middle East and a great deal on us. Fundamentalist Islam has now succeeded Soviet communism as the organizing theme of American foreign policy. Thus our newest challenge comes from a very old

---

[10]*Promise Keepers:* Nationwide organization of Christian men.

[11]*jihad:* Arabic for "struggle," denoting the kind of spiritual effort required of Muslims by the teachings of the Koran, and today frequently misinterpreted as being synonymous with the notion of holy war.

adversary. The West has been battling Islam for more than a thousand years. It is possible that this great battle has now been resumed, and that over time we will come to see the seventy-year battle against communism as a short detour.

But are we up to the challenge? There are some who think we are not. They believe that Americans are a divided people: not even a nation, but a collection of separate tribes. The multiculturalists actually proclaim this to be a good thing, and they strive to encourage people to affirm their differences. If, however, the multiculturalists are right in saying that "all we have in common is our diversity," then it follows that we have *nothing* in common. This does not bode well for the national unity that is a prerequisite to fighting against a determined foe. If the ethnic group is the primary unit of allegiance, why should we make sacrifices for people who come from ethnic groups other than our own? Doesn't a nation require a loyalty that transcends ethnic particularity?

Of course it does. And fortunately America does command such a loyalty. The multiculturalists are simply wrong about America, and despite their best efforts to promote a politics of difference, Americans remain a united people with shared values and a common way of life. There are numerous surveys of national attitudes that confirm this,[12] but it is most easily seen when Americans are abroad. Hang out at a Parisian café, for instance, and you can easily pick out the Americans: they dress the same way, eat the same food, listen to the same music, and laugh at the same jokes. However different their personalities, Americans who run into each other in remote places always become fast friends. And even the most jaded Americans who spend time in other countries typically return home with an intense feeling of relief and a newfound appreciation for the routine satisfactions of American life.

It is easy to forget the cohesiveness of a free people in times of peace and prosperity. New York is an extreme example of the great pandemonium that results when countless individuals and groups pursue their diverse interests in the normal course of life. In a crisis, however, the national tribe comes together, and this is exactly what happened in New York and the rest of America following the terrorist attack. Suddenly political, regional, and racial differences evaporated; suddenly Americans stood as one. This surprised many people, including many Americans, who did not realize that, despite the centrifugal forces that pull us in different directions, there is a deep national unity that holds us together.

Unity, however, is not sufficient for the challenges ahead. America also needs the moral self-confidence to meet its adversary. This is the true   25

---

[12]See, for example, John Fetto and Rebecca Gardyn, "An All-American Melting Pot," *American Demographics,* July 2001, 8. The survey was conducted by Maritz Marketing Research.

lesson of Vietnam: Americans cannot succeed unless they are convinced that they are fighting on behalf of the good. There are some, as we have seen, who fear that America no longer stands for what is good. They allege that American freedom produces a licentious, degenerate society that is scarcely worth defending. We return, therefore, to the question of what America is all about, and whether this country, in its dedication to the principle of freedom, subverts the higher principle of virtue.

So what about virtue? The fundamental difference between the society that the Islamic fundamentalists want and the society that Americans have is that the Islamic activists seek a country where the life of the citizens is *directed by others,* while Americans live in a nation where the life of the citizens is largely *self-directed.* The central goal of American freedom is self-reliance: the individual is placed in the driver's seat of his own life. The Islamic fundamentalists presume the moral superiority of the externally directed life on the grounds that it is aimed at virtue. The self-directed life, however, also seeks virtue — virtue realized not through external command but, as it were, "from within." The real question is: which type of society is more successful in achieving the goal of virtue?

Let us concede at the outset that, in a free society, freedom will frequently be used badly. Freedom, by definition, includes freedom to do good or evil, to act nobly or basely. Thus we should not be surprised that there is a considerable amount of vice, licentiousness, and vulgarity in a free society. Given the warped timber of humanity, freedom is simply an expression of human flaws and weaknesses. But if freedom brings out the worst in people, it also brings out the best. The millions of Americans who live decent, praiseworthy lives deserve our highest admiration because they have opted for the good when the good is not the only available option. Even amidst the temptations that a rich and free society offers, they have remained on the straight path. Their virtue has special luster because it is freely chosen. The free society does not guarantee virtue any more than it guarantees happiness. But it allows for the pursuit of both, a pursuit rendered all the more meaningful and profound because success is not guaranteed: it has to be won through personal striving.

By contrast, the externally directed life that Islamic fundamentalists seek undermines the possibility of virtue. If the supply of virtue is insufficient in self-directed societies, it is almost nonexistent in externally directed societies because coerced virtues are not virtues at all. Consider the woman who is required to wear a veil. There is no modesty in this, because the woman is being compelled. Compulsion cannot produce virtue: it can only produce the outward semblance of virtue. And once the reins of coercion are released, as they were for the terrorists who lived in the United States, the worst impulses of human nature break loose. Sure enough, the deeply religious terrorists spent their last days in gambling dens, bars, and strip clubs, sampling the licentious lifestyle they were about to strike out against.[13] In this respect they were like the Spartans,[14] who — Plutarch[15] tells us — were abstemious in public but privately coveted wealth and luxury. In externally directed societies, the absence of freedom signals the absence of virtue. Thus the free society is not simply richer, more varied, and more fun: it is also morally superior to the externally directed society. There is no reason for anyone, least of all the cultural conservatives, to feel hesitant about rising to the defense of our free society.

Even if Americans possess the necessary unity and self-confidence, there is also the question of nerve. Some people, at home and abroad, are skeptical that America can endure a long war against Islamic fundamentalism because they consider Americans to be, well, a little bit soft. As one of bin Laden's lieutenants put it, "Americans love life, and we love death." His implication was that Americans do not have the stomach for the kind of deadly, drawn-out battle that the militant Muslims are ready to fight. This was also the attitude of the Taliban. "Come and get us," they taunted America. "We are ready for *jihad*. Come on, you bunch of weenies." And then the Taliban was hit by a juggernaut of American firepower that caused their regime to disintegrate within a couple of weeks. Soon the Taliban leadership had headed for the caves, or for Pakistan, leaving their captured soldiers to beg for their lives. Even the call of *jihad* and the promise of martyrdom could not stop these hard men from — in the words of Mullah Omar[16] himself — "running like chickens with their heads cut off." This is not to say that Americans should expect all its battles against terrorism and Islamic fundamentalism to be so short and so conclusive. But neither should America's enemies expect Americans to show any less firmness or fierceness than they themselves possess.

... The firefighters and policemen who raced into the burning towers of   30 the World Trade Center showed that their lives were dedicated to something higher than "self-fulfillment." The same can be said of Todd Beamer and his fellow passengers who forced the terrorists to crash United Airlines Flight 93 in the woods of western Pennsylvania rather than flying on to Camp David or the White House.... The military has its own culture, which is closer to that of the firefighters and policemen, and also bears an affinity with the culture of the "greatest generation."[17] Only now are those Americans who grew up during the 1960s coming to appreciate the virtues — indeed the indispensability — of this older, sturdier culture of courage, nobility, and sacrifice. It is this culture that will protect the liberties of all Americans....

[13]Diane McWhorter, "Terrorists Tasted Lusty Lifestyle They So Despised," *USA Today*, 26 September 2001, 11-A.

[14]*Spartans:* In Classical Greece, the nondemocratic adversaries of the Athenians.

[15]*Plutarch:* Greek essayist and biographer (46–119).

[16]*Mullah Omar:* Leader of the Taliban (b. 1959).

[17]*the "greatest generation":* Refers to the generation that fought in World War II, supposedly distinguished from following generations by their spirit of service and self-sacrifice.

As the American founders knew, America is a new kind of society that produces a new kind of human being. That human being — confident, self-reliant, tolerant, generous, future oriented — is a vast improvement over the wretched, servile, fatalistic, and intolerant human being that traditional societies have always produced, and that Islamic societies produce now. In America, the life we are given is not as important as the life we make. Ultimately, America is worthy of our love and sacrifice because, more than any other society, it makes possible the good life, and the life that is good.

American is the greatest, freest, and most decent society in existence. It is an oasis of goodness in a desert of cynicism and barbarism. This country, once an experiment unique in the world, is now the last best hope for the world. By making sacrifices for America, and by our willingness to die for her, we bind ourselves by invisible cords to those great patriots who fought at Yorktown, Gettysburg, and Iwo Jima,[18] and we prove ourselves worthy of the blessings of freedom. By defeating the terrorist threat posed by Islamic fundamentalism, we can protect the American way of life while once again redeeming humanity from a global menace. History will view America as a great gift to the world, a gift that Americans today must preserve and cherish.

ENGAGING THE TEXT

1. What, according to D'Souza, is meant by the terms American "exceptionalism" and American "universalism"? What makes the United States "exceptional" in his view? To what extent do you agree with the contention that our civilization is superior to the cultures of other countries?

2. Would you agree with D'Souza's claim that America's greatest weakness is "her lack of moral self-confidence"? Why, in his view, is it so important for Americans to believe in the moral superiority of our way of life? Do most Americans strike you as lacking this kind of self-confidence?

3. Why do Islamic peoples "hate" the United States, in D'Souza's view? What other possible reasons might be offered to explain the antipathy that some Islamic groups feel toward America? How does D'Souza view the criticisms that Islamic fundamentalists level at American society and American values? To what extent do you believe that we "don't have the power to keep our ideals and our culture out of their lives"?

4. Would you agree that Christian fundamentalism is more "liberal" than its Islamic counterpart? In what sense can Christian fundamentalist attitudes toward issues like gay marriage, censorship, abortion, and the relationship between church and state be viewed as liberal?

---

[18]*Yorktown, Gettysburg, and Iwo Jima:* Sites of famous American victories during the American Revolution, the Civil War, and World War II, respectively.

EXPLORING CONNECTIONS

5. Compare D'Souza's view of America's relation to other nations and cultures with that expressed by Albert J. Beveridge in "The March of the Flag" (p. 762). Is D'Souza, like Beveridge, arguing for the establishment of a worldwide empire? What differences do you see between these two articulations of the myth of American exceptionalism?

6. How might Paul L. Wachtel (p. 541) interpret D'Souza's depictions of "other" cultures and civilizations? To what extent, if any, do D'Souza's views of Islamic nations echo racist stereotypes? Is it possible to move beyond such stereotypes while still acknowledging the differences between different world cultures? Why or why not?

7. Write a brief imaginary dialogue between D'Souza, John Taylor Gatto (p. 152), and/or Michael Moore (p. 132) on the importance of freedom in American culture. Would these critics of the American educational system be likely to agree that American civilization has created a "new way of being human" that is essentially superior to and more free than the ways of human beings found in "traditional societies"? Why or why not?

EXTENDING THE CRITICAL CONTEXT

8. Locate and examine statements made by political leaders or members of the Bush administration justifying the U.S. invasion of Afghanistan and Iraq or any other relatively unilateral U.S. military action. To what extent do such statements echo ideas expressed in D'Souza's assessment of the United States and our meaning in the world?

9. Working in groups, debate whether or not you agree with the notion of U.S. exceptionalism. Do you believe, as D'Souza does, that the United States is "an oasis of goodness in a desert of cynicism and barbarism" — or that "America is a new kind of society that produces a new kind of human being"? Is there a basis in fact for such claims, or are they simply a matter of nationalism or prejudice?

10. Research the traditions, values, and attitudes associated with Islam. How does the information you gather substantiate or challenge D'Souza's depiction of Islamic cultures and their attitudes toward the West?

The Oblivious Empire
MARK HERTSGAARD

The idea that America is an exceptional country that produces a unique kind of human being is as old as the concept of America itself. Belief in American "exceptionalism" goes all the way back to the Pilgrims, who came to the "New World" to liberate themselves from what they saw as the decadent civilizations of old Europe. During the colonial period and the nineteenth century, this belief in the uniqueness of the American mission was repeatedly invoked to justify the destruction of Native American tribes and military interventions against other sovereign nations in the Western Hemisphere. Today, political observers note the emergence of a "new exceptionalism" — the rebirth of the conviction that America has a special mission and meaning in world affairs. But as Mark Hertsgaard suggests in this selection, America's sense of superiority may well be the very thing that's feeding the flames of anti-Americanism around the world. A broadcaster and journalist who contributes regularly to The New Yorker, The Atlantic, Vanity Fair, Harper's, *the* New York Times, *and the* Washington Post, *Hertsgaard has also authored five*

books, including Earth Odyssey: Around the World in Search of Our Environmental Future *(1999) and the source of this selection,* The Eagle's Shadow:
Why America Fascinates and Infuriates the World *(2001).*

"Texans are the worst," said the London cabbie. It was a fine late summer morning and we were waiting for the light to change so we could cross
the Thames.[1] "I had one in the cab a few weeks ago, must have been in his
thirties. We were driving past the London Eye[2] and he says, 'What's 'at?' I
tell him it's the London Eye, the tallest Ferris wheel in the world. He says,
'We got one bigger than that.' I thought, 'Uh-oh, one of those.' I mean, I
don't care if the Eye is the tallest in the world or not, maybe there is a bigger one in Texas for all I know. It's the bragging and the arrogance that put
me off. No matter what he saw, Texas had more. I forget what we passed
next, a double-decker bus, maybe, or Big Ben[3] — something totally unique
to London. He says, 'What's 'at?' I tell him. He says, 'We got one bigger
than that.' After that I couldn't be bothered."

The light went green, the cabbie hit the accelerator. "I like most Americans," he added, "but it is quite amazing how they don't know anything
about other places in the world" — he shot me a sly glance through the
rearview mirror — "unless they're invading them."

The cabbie delivered that little jab on September 10, 2001, but I doubt
he would have repeated it two days later. In the immediate aftermath of
September 11, the mood in Europe was one of shock and deep sympathy for
Americans. "We are very sorry," friends in Paris told me, as if I myself had
been attacked. A couple of days later, in Prague, I happened to walk by the
United States embassy one night on the way to dinner. The entire block was
softly lit by candles well-wishers had left, along with hundreds of flowers and
notes of condolence and encouragement. I found more flowers and notes at
one of Prague's most revered public places: the monument on Wenceslas
Square where the student Jan Palach set himself on fire to protest the Soviet
crackdown of 1968. "No Terrorism" read one message spray-painted onto
the concrete. Newspapers across the Continent ran articles reporting similar
acts of solidarity in Japan, Russia, and elsewhere, as well as commentaries
declaring, "We are all Americans now."

The sympathy was genuine and genuinely touching, but as I continued
in the following weeks to talk with people across Europe and to survey the
local media, it was also clear that the terror attacks had not caused Euro-

[1]*Thames:* River running through central London. [All notes are author's, except 1–3, 7, 8,
11, 15–18, 23–26, and 30.]

[2]*London Eye:* Gigantic Ferris wheel built on the south bank of the Thames as part of the
millennial celebrations in 2002.

[3]*Big Ben:* London landmark clock located on the main tower of Parliament.

peans to forget whatever they had once believed about the United States. Good manners might have restrained the London cabbie from repeating his remark, but it didn't mean he'd stopped thinking Americans were arrogant know-nothings. History did not begin on September 11.

Horrified as they were by the tragedy in the United States, many foreigners were not exactly surprised. Most of them knew the reasons why the United States was resented, even hated, in parts of the world, and they usually had complaints of their own. A high school teacher in Spain offered condolences for the September 11 victims and their families, but he told me he hoped Americans would recognize that the tragedy was "a consequence of U.S. foreign policy," especially its one-sided approach to the Israeli-Palestinian conflict. Some Europeans went so far as to cite America's conduct overseas as a virtual justification for the attacks. Even those who rejected the argument that the United States had brought September 11 on itself admitted that America could be infuriating at times.

Perhaps nothing irritates foreigners more than America's habit of thinking it has all the answers, and the right to impose them on everyone else. An outstanding example was President Bush's first major speech after the terror attacks. Speaking before Congress on September 20, Bush declared that foreign nations had to understand that, in the impending U.S.-led war against terrorism, "either you are with us, or you are with the terrorists." Like Bush's declaration that he wanted bin Laden "dead or alive," this was more cowboy talk, the Wild West sheriff warning, "Do as I say or get out of town" — the very attitude that had irritated America's friends and enemies alike for decades. Never mind that many nations already had their own painful experiences with terrorism; they would follow Washington's orders or else.

The United States would never accept such ultimatums itself, yet the arrogance of Bush's remark went unnoticed by America's political and journalistic elite. The *International Herald Tribune,* the overseas daily published by the *New York Times* and the *Washington Post,* did not even mention Bush's statement until the twentieth paragraph of its story, deep inside the paper. By contrast, the French daily *Le Monde* highlighted it three times on its front page, including in the headline and first paragraph. If opinion polls can be trusted, ordinary Americans also saw nothing wrong with their president's stance toward the rest of the world. Throughout the autumn of 2001, Bush's approval rating remained at above 75 percent.[4]

But I would plead ignorance rather than venality on behalf of my fellow Americans. The embarrassing truth is that most of us know little about the outside world, and we are particularly ill-informed about what our government is doing in our name overseas. For example, Americans are ceaselessly, and accurately, reminded that Saddam Hussein is an evil man, but not that American-enforced economic sanctions have, since 1991, caused the deaths

[4]Bush's 77 percent approval rating was reported in *Time,* February 4, 2002.

of at least 350,000[5] Iraqi children and impoverished a once prosperous Iraqi middle class. The bloody violence between Israelis and Palestinians that raged throughout March and April of 2002 got plenty of media coverage in the United States. Nevertheless, many Americans remained uninformed about basic aspects of the conflict. A poll conducted in early May by the University of Maryland's Program on International Policy Attitudes revealed, for example, that only 32 percent of Americans were aware that more Palestinians than Israelis had died in the fighting; only 43 percent knew that most other countries in the world disapproved of America's Middle East policies; and a mere 27 percent knew that most countries were more sympathetic to the Palestinian than to the Israeli side of the dispute.[6]

In the wake of September 11, the question obsessing Americans about the Muslim world was "Why do they hate us?" But Muslims had long wondered the same about Americans. In a sparkling exception to most American news coverage, Sandy Tolan reported on National Public Radio in January 2002 that nearly everyone he had interviewed during six weeks of recent travel through the Middle East resented the negative stereotypes attached to Muslims and Arabs by American movies, television, and news coverage. In Europe, stretching back to the novels of Goethe[7] and the operas of Mozart,[8] there had long been respect for the great achievements of Islamic civilization in culture, astronomy, architecture, and more. America, by contrast, regarded Muslims as primitive, untrustworthy fanatics, worth dealing with only because they had oil.

"You are dealing here with people who are almost childlike in their   10 understanding of what is going on in the world," Gerald Celente, director of the Trends Research Institute in Rhinebeck, New York, told the *Financial Times* shortly after September 11.[9] "It's all: 'We never did anything to anybody, so why are they doing this to us?'"

Some Americans have taken refuge in the obvious answer: they envy our wealth and resent our power. There is truth in this, as I'll discuss, but it barely scratches the surface. The reason many foreigners don't share Americans' high opinion of themselves is simple: they dislike both how America behaves overseas and its attitude about that behavior.

America, foreigners say, is a trigger-happy bully that is both out for itself and full of itself. It feels no obligation to obey international law; it often

---

[5]The justification for the 350,000 figure, which is considerably lower than some frequently cited estimates, is discussed in "A Hard Look at Iraq Sanctions," by David Cortright, *The Nation*, December 3, 2001.
[6]Americans' views of the Middle East conflict were examined in a poll conducted by the Program on International Policy Attitudes of the University of Maryland, released to the media on May 8, 2002, and available via the program's web site at www.pipa.org.
[7]*Goethe:* Johann Wolfgang von Goethe (1749–1832), German poet, novelist, and dramatist.
[8]*Mozart:* Wolfgang Amadeus Mozart (1756–1791), Austrian composer.
[9]Gerald Celente's quote appeared in the *Financial Times* of September 29–30, 2001.

pushes other countries around, forcing on them policies and sometimes tyrannical leaders that serve only American interests, and then, if they resist too much, it may bomb obedience into them with cruise missiles. Only an American would blink to hear the United States called the most bellicose major power in the world; to foreigners, the observation is obvious to the point of banality. America's high-handed behavior puzzles admirers of its domestic freedoms: how to explain the inconsistency? Less sentimental observers point out that this is how the strong have treated the weak throughout history. But, they add, what makes the United States uniquely annoying is its self-righteous insistence that it does nothing of the kind, that it is the epitome of evenhanded virtue and selfless generosity — the Beacon of Democracy that other nations should thank and emulate.

On November 10, 2001, President Bush made his first appearance before the United Nations General Assembly and, in a speech praised by the *New York Times* for its "plain-spoken eloquence,"[10] told the rest of the world it wasn't doing enough to help the United States fight terrorism. "Every nation in the world has a stake in this cause," declared Bush before lecturing his audience that the responsibility to fight terrorism was "binding on every nation with a place in this chamber." Yet on the same day — indeed, at the very moment — that Bush was admonishing others about their international responsibilities, his own administration was shunning negotiations in Morocco to finalize the Kyoto protocol[11] on global warming. Talk about an issue that every nation has a stake in! Already the earth's glaciers are melting, sea levels are rising, and catastrophic storms are becoming more severe and frequent — this after a mere 1 degree Fahrenheit increase in temperatures over the past century. The scientific consensus predicts 3 to 10.5 degrees of additional warming by 2100, bringing more violent weather, flooded coastlines, and social havoc. Yet the Bush administration insists on doing nothing to lower U.S. greenhouse gas emissions. No wonder foreigners resent us.

American elites sometimes talk of our nation's isolationist tendencies, but the correct adjective is unilateralist. The United States has hardly shunned overseas involvement over the years; we simply insist on setting our own terms. This tendency has become especially pronounced since victory in the Cold War left us the only remaining superpower. Determined to keep it that way, senior officials in the first Bush administration drafted a grand strategy for the new era (which got leaked to the *New York Times*):[12] henceforth the goal of American foreign policy would be to prevent any

---

[10]Bush's speech was reported, and praised, in the November 11 edition of the *New York Times.*

[11]*Kyoto protocol:* U.S. refusal to ratify the 1997 United Nations–sponsored Kyoto protocol, which aimed at reducing greenhouse gas emissions below 1990 levels worldwide, has been seen as an example of American arrogance and unilateralism.

[12]The first Bush administration's grand strategy is described in *The New Yorker* of April 1, 2002.

other nation or alliance from becoming a superpower; the United States would rule supreme. This strategy lives on under George W. Bush — which is no surprise, since Vice President Dick Cheney and other key advisers were the ones who devised the strategy for Bush's father. Shortly after taking office, the administration of Bush II announced it was going to withdraw from the Anti-Ballistic Missile Treaty, a cornerstone of nuclear arms control for the past thirty years, in an assertion of unilateralism that evoked dismay not just from treaty partner Russia but from the entire global community. Bush's oddest rejection of global cooperation was his refusal to join, even retroactively, the accord against bioterrorism reached in July 2001 that could hinder future anthrax attacks. The United States delegation walked out of the negotiations because the Bush administration refused to accept the same rules it demands for Iraq and other "rogue states": international inspections of potential weapons production sites.[13]

I don't mean to pick on Mr. Bush. Double standards have a long bipartisan pedigree in American foreign policy. Bush's father uttered one of the most feverish declarations of American prerogative in 1988, while serving as Ronald Reagan's vice president. Five years earlier, when the Soviet Union shot down a Korean Airlines passenger jet over the Pacific, killing all 276 people on board, the United States had condemned the attack as further evidence of the "evil empire's" true nature, rejecting the Soviet explanation that the jet was acting like a military aircraft. Now the tables were turned: the United States had shot down an Iranian civilian jet it mistakenly believed was a military craft. All 290 passengers died. When Bush senior was asked if an apology was in order, he replied, "I will never apologize for the United States. I don't care what the facts are."   15

Democrats have been just as bad about this kind of thing. In 1998 critics at home and abroad were condemning the Clinton administration's launch of cruise missiles against Iraq as at best unnecessary and at worst a self-serving ploy to weaken impeachment proceedings against the president. But no, Secretary of State Madeleine Albright modestly explained, "if we have to use force, it is because we are America. We are the indispensable nation. . . . We see farther into the future." As Rupert Cornwell, the Washington correspondent for the British newspaper *The Independent,* observed on another occasion, "No one wraps self-interest in moral superiority quite like the Americans do."[14]

Americans are a fair-minded people, however, and I doubt that a majority of us would support such hypocrisy if we were truly aware of it. I believe most of us would instead urge that the United States bring its global behavior into accord with its domestic principles. But that might threaten

---

[13]Bush's rejection of the verification protocol for biological weapons was analyzed by Milton Leitenberg in the *Los Angeles Times Book Review,* October 28, 2001.

[14]Rupert Cornwell's remark appeared in *The Independent* on July 27, 2001.

what Washington considers vital national interests, so the powers that be resist. Since America is the land of both Hollywood and Madison Avenue, our official response has instead been to hire public relations experts to do a better job of "getting our message out" overseas. Brilliant touch, no? After all, the problem couldn't possibly be our policies themselves.

Americans will continue to misunderstand the world, and our place within it, until we face the full truth of how our government has acted overseas — a fact made powerfully clear to me in South Africa, where . . . enthusiasm for America . . . is balanced by the anger of those who recall that the United States was a firm, long-standing supporter of apartheid.[15]

Why Don't They Love Us?

The ferry from Cape Town takes forty minutes to reach Robben Island, the notorious prison where Nelson Mandela[16] and other South African freedom fighters were jailed during their struggle for freedom. The ferry lands at a jetty two hundred yards from a complex of low buildings with corrugated tin roofs that is the prison proper. A sign retained from apartheid days reads, in English and Afrikaans, "Robben Island. Welcome. We Serve with Pride."

There are now guided tours of the island, and what makes them especially compelling is that they are conducted by a thin man in a white windbreaker named Siphiwo Sobuwa. Speaking in a flat, deliberate tone, Sobuwa said he had been imprisoned at age seventeen after being captured smuggling arms for the ANC's[17] military wing. Interrogated, beaten, denied a lawyer, he was sentenced to forty-eight years in jail. He served fifteen years, all on Robben Island, before the crumbling of apartheid enabled his release in 1991.

As he ushered us into the prison's entry hall, Sobuwa recalled how he spent his first two years in solitary confinement because he didn't speak Afrikaans. A warden told his group of arriving prisoners that no talking was allowed, but since Sobuwa didn't understand Afrikaans, he asked another inmate what was going on. The warden decided to make an example of Sobuwa. "I was sent to A section, the torture section," he told us. "I could not write or receive letters. I could not speak, sing, or whistle. Food was slipped underneath the grille of my cell. Those two years were the hardest."

We pushed through a door into an open-air courtyard, where we listened to Sobuwa recount other punishments common on Robben Island. Most humiliating was the guards' game of ordering an inmate buried in the

20

---

[15]*apartheid:* The South African government policy of racial segregation, abolished in 1992.

[16]*Nelson Mandela:* Nelson Rolihlahla Mandela (b. 1918), South African political leader, elected president in the nation's first post-apartheid multiracial elections in 1994.

[17]*ANC:* The African National Congress, a South African political organization, led by Nelson Mandela from 1991 until 1994, prominent for its opposition to apartheid.

ground up to his neck and then leaving him there all day to roast in the sun while guards took turns urinating on him. More gruesome was the practice of hanging a prisoner upside down from a tree and waiting as the hours passed for him to pass out and, in one case, to perish as the body's blood supply gradually accumulated in the brain, starving it of oxygen. But of all the deprivations — punishing physical labor, numbing boredom, inedible food, lack of heat — Sobuwa said the blackout on news was the hardest to bear. Inmates did their best to compensate. "The guard towers had no toilets," he explained, "so guards would relieve themselves in newspapers, then throw the papers down to the ground. We would retrieve those papers, scrape them off, and read the news they contained. We didn't care what kind of mess was inside, we wanted that news."

Hearing about such abominations firsthand makes visiting Robben Island as unforgettable as a pilgrimage to Dachau or Hiroshima.[18] And talking with a man like Sobuwa rescues foreign policy from its usual abstractions, making concrete the implications of such diplomatic double-talk as "constructive engagement," the Reagan administration's justification for its unswerving support for apartheid. When I interviewed Sobuwa at his cinder-block house in a Cape Town township, he said his work had taught him to distinguish between Americans as people and the American government. He had little good to say about the latter. Washington, he pointed out, as well as Israel, had supported apartheid — and thus the oppression on Robben Island — until the very end. Furthermore, he said, "it is a trend among United States presidents that so-called Third World countries must be destabilized. America believes in solving problems not by negotiations but through military pressure."

But his tour guide conversations had made Sobuwa realize that not all Americans supported their government's policy. He was grateful for those who had joined the protests that eventually forced Western governments, including that of the United States, to endorse apartheid's demise. He was unaware that America's new vice president had, as a U.S. congressman in 1985, voted against urging Mandela's release from jail,[19] but then neither were most Americans aware of this aspect of Dick Cheney's past. What Sobuwa did know was that Bill Clinton had a lot of nerve. "He came here a couple years ago to visit Mandela and speak to our Parliament, and he told us South Africa should cut its ties to Cuba because Cuba was a bad government. Well, when we needed help during our liberation struggle, Cuba gave it.

---

[18]*Dachau or Hiroshima:* Respectively, the site of a World War II–era Nazi "death camp" and the Japanese city that, along with Nagasaki, was the first populated area to be targeted by nuclear weapons.

[19]Dick Cheney was one of only eight members of Congress who voted against the resolution urging the government of South Africa to release Mandela from jail and initiate negotiations with the African National Congress. See Joe Conason's story in Salon.com., August 1, 2000.

When we needed food, Cuba provided it. For someone who did not help our struggle to come now and ask us to distance ourselves from someone who did, that is very arrogant behavior."

Arrogant but, alas, not atypical. The United States has long pressed South American nations to cut ties with the Castro government. Likewise, in June 2002 George W. Bush announced that Yasir Arafat had to go as the Palestinian leader. Free elections had to be held, said Bush, but Washington would push for a Palestinian state only if those "free" elections got rid of Arafat.

Washington's might-makes-right view of such matters was succinctly expressed by Henry Kissinger when, as President Richard Nixon's national security adviser, he privately defended overthrowing the elected government of Chile by saying he saw no reason why the United States had to allow Chile to "go Marxist" simply because "its people are irresponsible."[20] Testifying before the U.S. Senate on the day of the coup, Kissinger claimed the United States had played no role in the 1973 coup that toppled Allende. But voluminous government documents show that Kissinger, as head of the so-called Forty Committee that supervised U.S. covert actions between 1969 and 1976, was well-informed about how the CIA had ordered a coup in 1970 that had failed to thwart Allende and, in 1973, had at least condoned if not actively aided the Chilean military men who, under future dictator General Augusto Pinochet, imposed martial law and eventually killed 3,197 Chilean citizens.[21]

Note the date of the U.S.–sponsored assault on democratic government in Chile: September 11, 1973. Note the estimated Chilean death toll — executions plus military casualties — of 3,197 people. Is not the congruence between that coup and the World Trade Center attack striking? True, one was authored by religious fanatics and the other by a state, and the events were separated in time by twenty-eight years, yet both took place on the same date and caused comparable numbers of deaths. Nevertheless, this eerie coincidence passed virtually unremarked in the United States.

This is self-defeating. It's no secret to Chileans that the United States helped bring to power the dictatorship that ruled them for seventeen years. Nor are the people of El Salvador and Guatemala unaware that the United States gave money, weapons, and training to the military governments that killed so many of their fellow citizens in recent decades. In Guatemala, a truth commission sponsored by the United Nations concluded in 1999 that "American training of the officer corps in counterinsurgency

[20]Kissinger's quote about Chile and his activities with the Forty Committee are described in "The Case Against Henry Kissinger," by Christopher Hitchens, in *Harper's Magazine*, February and March 2001.

[21]The death toll resulting from the 1973 coup in Chile is documented by John Dinges in *The Condor Years: How Pinochet and His Allies Brought Terrorism to Three Continents* (New York: New Press, 2003), chapter 1.

techniques" was a "key factor" in a "genocide" that included the killing of 200,000 peasants.

Switch to Asia[22] or the Middle East and the same point applies. Virtually every one of Washington's allies in the Middle East is an absolute monarchy where democracy and human rights are foreign concepts and women in particular are second-class citizens. But they have oil, so all is forgiven. Likewise, in South Korea everyone knows that the United States chose the generals that ruled their country from the end of World War II until 1993; the facts came out during a trial that found two of the surviving dictators guilty of state terrorism. Ferdinand Marcos of the Philippines, General Suharto of Indonesia, General Lon Nol of Cambodia — the list of tyrants that Washington has supported in Asia is widely known, except in the United States.

Again, what offends is not simply the ruthlessness of American policies   30
but their hypocrisy. The United States insists on the sanctity of United Nations resolutions when they punish enemies like Iraq with arms inspections, but not when they oblige its number-one foreign aid recipient, Israel, to withdraw from occupation of Palestinian territories in the West Bank and Gaza. On trade policy, Washington demands that poor countries honor World Trade Organization rules against subsiding domestic farmers or industries because these rules enable U.S.–based multinational firms to invade those countries' economies. Without blushing, Washington then lavishes billions of dollars in subsidies on our own agriculture sector (dominated, by the way, by those same multinationals) and imposes tariffs against foreign steel imports. Why do we violate fair play so brazenly? Because we can. "The United States can hurt us a lot worse than we can hurt them," grumbled one Canadian trade official.

Then there is our self-serving definition of "terrorism," a concept America's political and media elites never apply to the United States or its allies, only to enemies or third parties. No one disputes that the September 11 attacks against the United States were acts of terrorism; that is, they targeted innocent civilians to advance a political or military agenda. When the Irish Republican Army exploded bombs inside London subway stations and department stores in the mid-1990s, that, too, was terrorism. So were the Palestinian suicide bombings in Israel in early 2002, and Saddam Hussein's use of poison gas against Kurds in Iraq in 1988. But when Israel attacked Palestinian refugee camps in April 2002, demolishing buildings and killing or wounding many civilians, was that not also terrorism? When the United States lobbed Volkswagen-sized shells into Lebanese villages in 1983 and

---

[22]The findings of the United Nations–sponsored Commission for Historical Clarification, as well as American support for Asian dictators, were summarized in *Blowback: The Costs and Consequences of American Empire,* by Chalmers Johnson (New York: Henry Holt, Owl Books, 2001), pages 14 and 25–27, respectively.

dropped "smart bombs" on Baghdad in 1991, many innocent civilians perished while Washington sent its geopolitical message. The napalm dropped during the Vietnam War, the bombing of Dresden,[23] and the annihilation of Hiroshima and Nagasaki in World War II — these acts all pursued military or political objectives by killing vast numbers of civilians, just as the September 11 attacks did. Yet in mainstream American discourse, the United States is never the perpetrator of terrorism, only its victim and implacable foe.

These and other unsavory aspects of America's overseas dealings are not completely unknown in the United States. Academic specialists, human rights activists, and partisans of the political left are familiar with this history. Glimpses of the truth appear (very) occasionally in mainstream press coverage, and the CIA's role in subverting democracies and overthrowing governments was documented by congressional investigations in 1975. In 2002 Samantha Powers published a book, *A Problem from Hell*, that meticulously documented how Washington deliberately chose not to intervene against some of the worst acts of genocide in the twentieth century, including Pol Pot's[24] rampages in Cambodia, ethnic cleansing in Bosnia,[25] and tribal slaughter in Rwanda.[26] The book received considerable attention within media circles; its message got out. But in general, critical perspectives on American actions are given nowhere near the same prominence or repetition in government, media, and public discussion as is the conventional view of the United States as an evenhanded champion of democracy and freedom. Thus the basic direction of American foreign policy rarely shifts, and Washington creates for itself what the late *Wall Street Journal* reporter Jonathan Kwitny called "endless enemies"[27] around the world. Worse, average Americans are left unaware that this is happening, and so are shocked when foreigners don't love us as much as we think they should.

Ignorance is an excuse, but it is no shield. "Although most Americans may be largely ignorant of what was, and still is, being done in their names,

[23]*Dresden:* One of the world's most beautiful cities before World War II, Dresden, Germany, was the site of a particularly violent attack by Allied bombers in 1945 that resulted in 35,000 to 135,000 casualties and destroyed many of the city's original buildings.

[24]*Pol Pot:* Communist leader (1925–1998) who seized the government of Cambodia in 1975 and instituted a repressive regime that became infamous for its policy of systematic murder of rival groups and forced labor in the "killing fields" until Vietnam invaded in 1979. Pol Pot retired in 1985.

[25]*ethnic cleansing in Bosnia:* After Bosnia and Herzegovina declared their independence from Yugoslavia in 1992, Serbian and Croat Christian forces in Bosnia began a systematic campaign of "ethnic cleansing" to exterminate the majority Muslim population.

[26]*Rwanda:* In 1994, the Hutu tribe joined Rwandan government troops in a genocidal attack on their longtime rivals, the Tutsi clan, that resulted in between 500,000 and 800,000 casualties.

[27]Kwitny's phrase was the title of his illuminating and comprehensive book *Endless Enemies: The Making of an Unfriendly World* (New York: Congdon & Weed, 1984).

all are likely to pay a steep price . . . for their nation's continued efforts to dominate the global scene," veteran Asian affairs analyst Chalmers Johnson wrote in his fierce book, *Blowback*. America's tendency to bully, warns Johnson, will "build up reservoirs of resentment against all Americans — tourists, students, and businessmen, as well as members of the armed forces — that can have lethal results."

"Blowback" is a CIA term for how foreign policy can come back to haunt a country years later in unforeseen ways, especially after cases of secret operations. Thus Johnson quotes a 1997 report by the Pentagon's Defense Science Board: "Historical data show a strong correlation between U.S. involvement in international situations and an increase in terrorist attacks against the United States." A glaring example is the Iranian hostage crisis of 1979. To protect American oil interests, the CIA in 1953 overthrew the elected government of Iran and installed Shah Reza Pahlavi (an act a subsequent CIA director, William Colby, described as the CIA's "proudest moment").[28] The shah ruled with an iron hand, murdered thousands, duly became widely hated, and was forced from power in 1979. Residual Iranian anger led to an attack on the United States embassy in Tehran and seizure of fifty-four hostages, a crisis that doomed Jimmy Carter's presidency.[29]

Because Johnson's book was published in 2000, it was unable to address   35 the most spectacular of all cases of blowback: the September 11 terror attacks. But in the October 15 and December 10, 2001, issues of *The Nation*, Johnson explained how the CIA supported Osama bin Laden[30] from at least 1984 as part of its funding of the mujahideen, the Islamic resistance to the Soviet Union's occupation of Afghanistan. The CIA funneled its support for bin Laden and other mujahideen, including building the complex where bin Laden trained some thirty-five thousand followers, through Pakistan's intelligence service. But bin Laden turned against the United States after the 1991 Persian Gulf War, when "infidel" American troops were stationed on the Islamic holy ground of Saudi Arabia to prop up its authoritarian regime. The September 11 attacks, Johnson concludes, were the blowback from America's covert action in Afghanistan in the 1970s, and the cycle is probably not over: "The Pentagon's current response of 'bouncing the rubble' in Afghanistan [is] setting the stage for more rounds to come."

[28]The quotes from Johnson, *Blowback*, are from pages 33 and 4, respectively.

[29]The definitive account of America's actions in Iran, including the help that the local *New York Times* correspondent gave to the coup plotters, is found in Kwitny, *Endless Enemies*, pages 161–78.

[30]*Osama bin Laden:* Son of one of Saudi Arabia's wealthiest families, Osama bin Laden (b. 1957) founded the international terrorist organization al-Qaeda in 1988, which has since been linked to numerous attacks on U.S. targets around the world, including the attacks of September 11, 2001.

ENGAGING THE TEXT

1. How does the rest of the world view America, according to Hertsgaard? To what extent would you agree that we are a particularly "oblivious" nation when it comes to our relationships with other peoples?

2. What is the difference between American "isolationism" and what Hertsgaard terms American "unilateralism"? What examples does he offer of the new American unilateral approach to world affairs? How might recent events support or challenge this view?

3. Why does Hertsgaard object to the way our government defines terrorism? Does the idea of terrorism have a clear definition, or is it a purely political term used to demonize our enemies and justify our own national policies?

4. What is "blowback," and how does it account, in Hertsgaard's view, for much of the anti-American feeling in the world today? Do you think it's appropriate to speculate about the motives of terrorists, or does this kind of analysis amount to sympathizing with the enemy?

5. What would be required for the United States to "bring its global behavior into accord with its domestic principles" (para. 17)? How would the U.S. have to change its current approach to foreign affairs to do this?

EXPLORING CONNECTIONS

6. How does the historical context provided by Albert J. Beveridge's "The March of the Flag" (p. 762) help account for current American attitudes toward other nations, as described by Hertsgaard? How does it complicate Hertsgaard's claim that American unilateralism is a relatively recent development?

7. Compare Hertsgaard's analysis of anti-Americanism with that offered by Dinesh D'Souza (p. 768). Which strikes you as the more plausible? Why? Are these conflicting explanations mutually exclusive, or might they both have some merit?

8. To what extent might Michael Moore (p. 132) agree with Hertsgaard about the "obliviousness" of most Americans? Would you agree with Moore that most Americans are woefully uninformed when it comes to basic world knowledge?

EXTENDING THE CRITICAL CONTEXT

9. Working in small groups, research the history of any of the examples Hertsgaard offers of U.S. "unilateralism," including American involvement in South Africa, Chile, El Salvador, Guatemala, the Philippines, Indonesia, Cambodia, Bosnia, Rwanda, Iran, and any other nation you might think a good candidate. Report your findings in class and discuss how the results

of your research confirm or challenge Hertsgaard's view of American attitudes toward the rest of the world.

10. Test Hertsgaard's belief in our national ignorance by creating a survey of five to ten questions based on facts he provides in this selection or on your own knowledge of U.S. foreign policy. Administer the survey to fellow students, friends, relatives, or members of your local community, and report your results in class. Do your findings suggest that we are, in fact, as "oblivious" as Hertsgaard suggests?

11. Since the formulation of the Defense Planning Guidance draft in 1992, which first articulated the case for American military domination in the post–Cold War era, the idea of a new American "empire" has been growing in popularity. Research the idea of American empire and related concepts like "the Bush Doctrine" to learn more about what Hertsgaard terms the new "grand strategy of American foreign policy." What, if anything, might be wrong with the idea of establishing an "empire" as a goal for America in its dealings with the rest of the world?

The War on Terrorism

JOEL ANDREAS

You might think that comics are all about teenage superheroes or ducks in short jackets, but not if you've ever encountered the source of this selection. Joel Andreas's Addicted to War: Why the U.S. Can't Kick Militarism *(2002) is a cultural phenomenon — a comic book with a deadly serious subject that, in an era of ever-increasing international tensions, has emerged as a nationwide best-seller. Joel Andreas (b. 1956) became a committed political activist while attending antiwar demonstrations with his parents in Vietnam-era Detroit. He completed his Ph.D. in sociology at UCLA and now teaches at Johns Hopkins University. In addition to* Addicted to War, *Andreas has published two other "illustrated exposés":* The Incredible Rocky, *an unauthorized biography of the Rockefeller family and* Made with Pure Rocky Mountain Scab Labor *(1977), a comic broadside in support of a strike by Coors Brewery workers.*

[1]Bin Laden cited in *Wall Street Journal* online, October 7, 2001.

Few people anywhere in the world, including the Middle East, support bin Laden's terrorist methods. But most people in the Middle East **share his anger** at the United States. They are angry at the U.S. for supporting **corrupt** and **dictatorial regimes** in the region, for **supporting Israel** at the expense of the Palestinians and for imposing **U.S. dictates** on the Middle East through **military might** and **brutal economic sanctions**.

The Bush Administration immediately instructed U.S. television networks to **"exercise caution"** in airing bin Laden's taped messages. The official reason?

The tapes may contain **secret coded messages** for terrorist operatives

But were **covert messages** the Administration's main concern? Perhaps it was more worried about the impact of bin Laden's **overt message** - that the **September 11** attacks were carried out in **retaliation** for U.S. foreign policy and particularly **U.S. military intervention** in the Middle East.

If Americans realized that U.S. military intervention abroad brought retaliation - causing **death and destruction at home** — we might **think twice** about whether the U.S. should be so **eager to go to war** overseas

The Pentagon has demonstrated time and again that its advanced weaponry can **devastate countries** targeted for attack, **leveling** basic **infrastructure** and **killing thousands,** even hundreds of thousands of people.

It would be **naive** to think there would be **no retaliation**

Over the last several decades the **true costs** of the wars the U.S. has waged overseas have been largely **hidden**. We have had to **pay the military bills** but few Americans have died. The **death and destruction** was all **overseas**. That changed on **September 11**.

The **violence reached the United States**

The September 11 attacks, however, were not simply acts of **retribution**. They were also **provocation**. Bin Laden expected the U.S. to respond with **massive violence**, knowing this would bring him **new recruits**. Ultimately, he hoped to win the majority of the Muslim world to support his **holy war on the U.S.**

More **martyrs**, more **recruits**.

The Bush Administration responded according to **bin Laden's script**. George W. Bush declared a "**War on Terrorism**," using "good vs. evil" rhetoric that mirrored bin Laden's. Bush and his advisors were ready, **even eager**, for the war bin Laden wanted. They saw the September 11 attacks as a **grand opportunity** to boost military spending and demonstrate U.S. military power.

"This will be a monumental struggle of **good versus evil**... This **crusade**, this **war on terrorism**, is going to take a while"

G.W. Bush, Sept. 12 and 16, 2001

Bush's "**War on Terrorism**" began with U.S. warplanes **bombing Afghanistan**. The Bush Administration refused to negotiate or consider any **alternatives to war**. When the Afghan government asked for evidence against bin Laden, a reasonable request that might have made it possible to cooperate with the U.S., Bush replied:

I said—**no negotiations!** Cough up bin Laden now or die along with him!

Relatives prepare the bodies of four small children for burial after a U.S. airstrike. Kabul, October 2001.

The people of Afghanistan **suffered the consequences**. **U.S. bombing** killed many civilians and the war cut off relief supplies to millions already **facing starvation**. The total number of deaths will never be known, but it's likely there will be many times more **civilian deaths** in Afghanistan than in the World Trade Center.

[2] Bush cited in "The President's Words," *Los Angeles Times*, September 22, 2001.

[3] Millions were endangered because the war cut off relief supplies (http://www/observer .co.uk/afghanistan/story/0,1501,577996,00.html). Analyzing media reports, Marc Herold of the University of New Hampshire estimated that U.S. bombs killed 3100 to 3700 Afghan civilians (http://www.pubpages.unh.edu/~mwherold). The *New York Times* estimated that 3086 people died in the Sept. 11 terrorist attacks (February 9, 2002, p. A7).

As warplanes of the world's **richest and most powerful** country bombed people in one of the **poorest and most miserable** countries on earth, the streets of cities throughout the Muslim world filled with **angry demonstrations**. Not only religious radicals were angry. Almost everybody in the Muslim world **opposed the war.**

The war **added fuel** to simmering anti-American sentiments in the Middle East. Bombing Muslim countries and sending U.S. troops into this volatile region will only inspire more hatred for the United States and **more terrorist attacks** on Americans. Bush surely knows this, yet he decided to go ahead and **place us in greater danger** anyway.

We **never said** this war was not going to have **costs!**

The War on Terrorism **cannot possibly end terrorism**. Even if bin Laden is killed, **new converts will rally** to join his war to drive the U.S. out of the Middle East. The **spiral of violence** is escalating dangerously.

And the warmakers on both sides are **itching to escalate!**

The self-righteous "**good vs. evil**" rhetoric of the War on Terrorism sharpens ironies that have long shadowed U.S. pronouncements against **state-sponsored terrorism**. President Bush, for instance, promises to scour the globe in search of **states** that **harbor terrorists**.

He could start in the **State of Florida**

What do you mean?

For over forty years, **Miami** has served as the base of operations for well-financed groups of **Cuban exiles** that have carried out violent **terrorist attacks on Cuba**.

Most recently, they **bombed** a number of Havana tourist spots in 1997, killing an Italian tourist, and they tried to **assassinate** Fidel Castro in Panama in 2000.

[4]Bosch cited in Alexander Cockburn, "The Tribulations of Joe Doherty," *Wall Street Journal*, reprinted in the *Congressional Record*, page E2639.

[5]Cockburn; John Rice, "Man with CIA Links Accused of Plotting to Kill Castro," Associated Press, November 18, 2000; Frances Robles and Glenn Garvin, "Four Held in Plot Against Castro," *Miami Herald*, November 19, 2000; Jill Mullin, "The Burden of a Violent History," *Miami New Times*, April 20, 2000.

[6]Joe Conason, "The Bush Pardons," http://www.salon.com/news/col/cona/2001/02/27/
pardons/print.html.

[7]Bosch cited in Cockburn.

[8]William Blum, *Killing Hope: U.S. Military and CIA Interventions Since World War II*
(Monroe, Maine: Common Courage Press, 1995).

[9]Post–9/11 restrictions on civil liberties: American Civil Liberties Union, http://www.aclu.org/safeandfree.

[10]Joshua Cohen, "An Interview with Ted Postol: What's Wrong with Missile Defense," *Boston Review*, October/November 2001; David E. Sanger, "Washington's New Freedom, and New Worries, in the Post-ABM-Treaty Era," *New York Times*, December 15, 2001.

[11]Submarine-based missiles: http://no-nukes.org/nukewatch/.

[12]R. Jeffrey Smith, "U.S. Urged to Cut 50% of A-Arms: Soviet Breakup Is Said to Allow Radical Shift in Strategic Targeting," *Washington Post,* January 6, 1991, p. A1.

[13]Judith Miller, "U.S. Seeks Changes in Germ War Pact," *New York Times,* November 1, 2001; William Broad and Judith Miller, "U.S. Recently Produced Anthrax in a Highly Lethal Powder Form," *New York Times,* December 13, 2001.

[14]William Broad, Judith Miller, *Germs: Biological Weapons and America's Secret War,* (New York: Simon & Schuster, 2001); William Blum.

[15]Center for Defense Information, http://www.cdi.organization/issues/wme/.

ENGAGING THE TEXT

1. How does Andreas explain the motives behind the 9/11 attacks? Why, in his view, is it crucial to understand that these were acts of provocation and not merely acts of retribution or revenge?

2. How does Andreas view the Bush administration's response to September 11? What does he see as the real motive behind the war on terrorism? What problems does he see with the notion of the United States declaring a war against terror?

3. Why, according to Andreas, would strengthening the U.S. military actually make us less safe? To what extent would you agree that the war on terror will actually end by making the world more dangerous? Who, from Andreas's perspective, is the greater threat to the world — terrorists like Osama bin Laden, or militaristic superpowers like the United States? Why?

4. Why do you think Andreas chose to present his views in comic book form? How do the images work here to support his argument? How, for example, does he portray military and political figures, and how do these portrayals compare with the mother and son figures who clearly speak for Andreas? Would Andreas's ideas and claims have been less persuasive if presented in the form of a traditional essay? Why or why not?

EXPLORING CONNECTIONS

5. How might Dinesh D'Souza (p. 768) respond to Andreas's depiction of American foreign policy? According to D'Souza, what does such thinking do to the United States? To what extent would you agree with him?

6. How does the information provided by Andreas challenge or support Mark Hertsgaard's claims about recent directions in U.S. foreign policy (p. 781)? Would Andreas be likely to agree with Hertsgaard that America is an "oblivious empire"? Which of these selections did you find the more persuasive? The more informative? Why?

EXTENDING THE CRITICAL CONTEXT

7. Do some research to test Andreas's depiction of the U.S. military. How has the size of the armed forces varied over the past 100 years? How has the level of military spending changed over the same period? How have the functions of the armed services evolved? To what extent do the results of your research support or challenge Andreas's depiction of the United States as an aggressively militaristic nation?

8. Research the accuracy of Andreas's claims about Afghanistan. How many military and civilian casualties resulted from the U.S.-led "liberation" of this country? What were the economic, cultural, and political impacts of military intervention? Overall, would you say that the United States achieved its goals in Afghanistan? How has "liberation" affected the lives of the Afghan people? If you wish, you might extend your research to Iraq as well.

9. Research the claim that our government has frequently been involved in acts of state terrorism. What can you learn about the "covert operations" engaged in by the CIA over the past fifty years? What role, for example, did the U.S. play in the early careers of Osama bin Laden and Saddam Hussein? To what extent do you feel it is justifiable for the United States to engage in activities like assassinations, illegal traffic in weapons, sabotage, and support for paramilitary groups, in pursuit of its foreign policy goals?

Visual Portfolio

READING IMAGES OF AMERICA'S MEANING IN A "NEW WORLD ORDER"

Visual Portfolio

READING IMAGES OF AMERICA'S MEANING IN A "NEW WORLD ORDER"

1. What do you think the images of Rambo and Colonel Sanders mean to the people in the first two photos in this Visual Portfolio? What do you think such advertising images say to people in other lands about America and American society?

2. How might the image of Afghan prisoners at Guantánamo Bay, Cuba, challenge the myth of the United States as the land of the free? How would you feel if you saw a photo that showed American prisoners of war held by another country in similar circumstances?

3. What does the photo of the American Marine Corps doctor comforting an Iraqi girl during "Operation Iraqi Freedom" suggest about Americans and the values of the United States? Why do you think it was featured so prominently in major U.S. newspapers and magazines at the beginning of the war?

4. In what countries might you expect to see the kind of anti-American protest that is represented on page 810? Why might South Koreans feel negatively toward the United States? What aspects of U.S. culture seem to be singled out for criticism in this protest?

5. Freewrite for a few minutes on what you think the pictures of Iraqi prisoners being abused by U.S. troops at Baghdad's Abu Ghraib detention center (pp. 811–12) say to most Americans. How do you think they are viewed by people in other countries around the world?

6. Why do you think the government tried to block publication in 2004 of photos showing coffins of American soldiers being returned from Iraq for burial (p. 813)? Do you consider such photos "news" that should be published for the American people? Why or why not?

In Torture We Trust?

EYAL PRESS

You've seen the pictures. Beaming GIs pose over stacked naked bodies. A young woman in fatigues tugs at a man on a leash. A figure on a stool balances precariously, arms outstretched, in a pointed hood and robe that conjure collective nightmares of Jim Crow–era brutality. When photos of U.S. troops torturing prisoners at Baghdad's Abu Ghraib prison first surfaced in

2004, *Americans were stunned. We were supposed to be the good guys, the liberators who entered Iraq to make the world a safer place. But as the War on Terror grinds on, it's becoming increasingly clear that we, as a nation, have participated in a number of practices that contradict our loftiest cultural ideals. At Camp X-ray in Guantánamo Bay, Cuba, we've imprisoned hundreds of detainees without charges or hearings for years. Around the world, it's rumored that we've engaged in "extraordinary rendition"—the practice of kidnapping individuals and then shipping them off to countries where they can be interrogated without the interference of constitutional protections. In secret prisons across the globe, we're alleged to have "broken" suspects using techniques that range from sleep deprivation to electric shock. How far would you go to protect America? In this selection, Eyal Press (b. 1970) suggests that it's time for the government to acknowledge the commonplace use of torture in the national interest and that it's also time we begin discussing what it means to kill for the common good. Press is a journalist and a contributing editor of* The Nation *magazine, whose articles and essays have appeared in the* Los Angeles Times, *the* New York Times Magazine, Mother Jones, *and the* Atlantic Monthly. *He has also published two books on social issues in the United States:* Uncivil War: Race, Civil Rights, & the Nation *(1995) and* Absolute Convictions: My Father, a City, and the Conflict that Divided America *(2006).*

The recent capture of Al Qaeda leader Khalid Shaikh Mohammed[1] is the latest indication that the taboo on torture has been broken. In the days after Mohammed's arrest, an unnamed official told the *Wall Street Journal* that U.S. interrogators may authorize "a little bit of smacky-face" while questioning captives in the war on terrorism. Others proposed that the United States ship Mohammed off to a country where laxer rules apply. "There's a reason why [Mohammed] isn't going to be near a place where he has Miranda rights[2] or the equivalent," a senior federal law enforcer told the *Journal.* "You go to some other country that'll let us pistol-whip this guy."

Asked about this by CNN's Wolf Blitzer, Senator Jay Rockefeller IV, a Democrat from West Virginia and vice chairman of the Senate Select Committee on Intelligence, replied, "I wouldn't take anything off the table where he is concerned, because this is the man who has killed hundreds and hundreds of Americans over the last ten years." (An aide to Rockefeller subsequently insisted that the senator did not condone turning Mohammed over to a regime that tortures.) In fact, sending U.S. captives to abusive

---

[1]*Khalid Shaikh Mohammed:* Planner of the September 11, 2001, attacks (b. 1964 or 1965); linked to several other terrorist plots. Captured in Pakistan in March 2003.

[2]*Miranda rights:* Rights to an attorney and to remain silent during police questioning; silence cannot be used as evidence of guilt. From the 1966 U.S. Supreme Court case *Miranda v. Arizona.*

allies, and other policies that potentially implicate America in torture, have been in use for months.

On December 26 [,2002], the *Washington Post* published a front-page story detailing allegations of torture and inhumane treatment involving thousands of suspects apprehended since the September 11 terrorist attacks. Al Qaeda captives held at overseas CIA interrogation centers, which are completely off-limits to reporters, lawyers, and outside agencies, are routinely "softened up" — that is, beaten — by U.S. Army Special Forces before interrogation, as well as thrown against walls, hooded, deprived of sleep, bombarded with light, and bound in painful positions with duct tape. "If you don't violate someone's human rights some of the time, you probably aren't doing your job," one official said to the *Post* of these methods, which at the very least constitute cruel and inhumane treatment and may rise to the level of "severe pain or suffering, whether physical or mental," the benchmark of torture.

The same article reported that approximately 100 suspects have been transferred to U.S. allies, including Saudi Arabia and Morocco, whose brutal torture methods have been amply documented in the State Department's own annual human rights reports. "We don't kick the [expletive] out of them," one official told the *Post*. "We send them to other countries so they can kick the [expletive] out of them." Many captives have been sent to Egypt, where, according to the State Department, suspects are routinely "stripped and blindfolded; suspended from a ceiling or doorframe with feet just touching the floor; beaten with fists, whips, metal rods, or other objects; subjected to electric shocks." In at least one case, a suspect was sent to Syria, where, the State Department says, torture methods include "pulling out fingernails; forcing objects into the rectum . . . using a chair that bends backwards to asphyxiate the victim or fracture the spine." A story in *Newsday* published just after Mohammed's arrest quoted a former CIA official who, describing a detainee transferred from Guantánamo Bay to Egypt, said, "They promptly tore his fingernails out and he started telling things."

Just as pundits debated Mohammed's possible transfer, evidence   5
emerged that remaining in U.S. custody might not be any safer: Death certificates released for two Al Qaeda suspects who died while in U.S. custody at the Bagram base in Afghanistan showed that both were killed by "blunt force injuries." Other detainees told of being hung from the ceiling by chains.

The Bush Administration insists that the United States has not violated the UN Convention Against Torture, which the Senate ratified in 1994. But the cascade of recent revelations has left human rights groups understandably alarmed. Shortly after the *Washington Post* article appeared, a coalition of organizations, including Amnesty International and Human Rights Watch, fired off a letter to Deputy Defense Secretary Paul Wolfowitz calling upon the Bush Administration to unequivocally denounce torture and clarify that the United States will "neither seek nor rely upon intelligence obtained" through such practices. But few have echoed their call. "There's been a painful silence about this," says Human Rights Watch executive director Ken Roth. "I haven't heard anyone in Congress call for hearings or even speak out publicly." The silence extends to the media, where, until Mohammed's capture, no follow-up investigations and few editorials had appeared — not even in the *New York Times*.

The absence of debate may simply reflect a preoccupation with Iraq, but it may also signal that in these jittery times, many people see torture as justified. In the aftermath of the World Trade Center attack, numerous commentators did suggest that the absolute prohibition on torture should be reconsidered. Harvard law professor Alan Dershowitz famously proposed allowing U.S. judges to issue "torture warrants" to prevent potentially catastrophic terrorist attacks. Writing in *The New Republic* last fall, Richard Posner, a judge on the U.S. Court of Appeals for the Seventh Circuit, expressed reservations about Dershowitz's proposal but argued that "if the stakes are high enough, torture is permissible. No one who doubts that this is the case should be in a position of responsibility."

Lurking behind such comments is the specter of the so-called "ticking bomb": the captive who knows of an imminent attack that will cost thousands of lives, imagined vividly on February 4 in the hit Fox series *24*, in which U.S. agents used electroshock to extract a confession about an impending nuclear attack.

Should an exceptional captive such as Mohammed be tortured to extract potentially lifesaving information? *The Nation*[3] spoke with several prominent theorists of ethics, human rights and the law, all of whom acknowledged that this is very difficult emotional terrain, even if there is, in the end, only one truly ethical answer. Martha Nussbaum, a professor at the University of Chicago who has written several books on ethics and human rights, offered a frank — and somewhat jarring — admission. "I don't think any sensible moral position would deny that there might be some imaginable situations in which torture [of a particular individual] is justified," Nussbaum wrote in an e-mail to *The Nation*.

But as Nussbaum went on to note, in the real world, governments don't just torture ticking time bombs: They torture their enemies, under circumstances that routinely stray from the isolated, extreme scenario. Even the most scrupulous regime is bound to do so, for the simple reason that nobody can know for certain whether a suspect really is a ticking bomb. "There's an inevitable uncertainty," explains Georgetown law professor David Cole, the author of *Terrorism and the Constitution* and a forthcoming book on September 11 and civil liberties. "You can't know whether a person knows where the bomb is, or even if they're telling the truth.   10

---

[3]*The Nation:* A publication describing itself as "America's oldest and most widely read journal of progressive political and cultural news, opinion, and analysis." Founded 1865.

Because of this, you end up going down a slippery slope and sanctioning torture in general." So while Cole and Nussbaum can imagine scenarios where torture might constitute a lesser evil, both favor a "bright line," in Cole's words, banning the practice.

Henry Shue, a professor of politics and international relations at Oxford who has published an influential academic article on torture, points out that the French experience in Algeria is illustrative. Though justified as a rare measure to prevent imminent assaults on civilians, says Shue, torture quickly spread through the French security apparatus "like a cancer." "The problem is that torture is a shortcut, and everybody loves a shortcut," Shue says. "I think it's a fantasy to believe that the United States is that much better than anybody else in this respect."

The Algerian experience recurred in Israel, where, until the Israeli Supreme Court formally banned the practice in 1999, preventing "ticking bombs" from carrying out suicide attacks served as the justification for hooding, beating, and abusing hundreds of Palestinians. "Very quickly, from a rare exception torture in Israel became standard practice, in part because the ticking bomb metaphor is infinitely expandable," says Human Rights Watch's Roth. "Why stop with the bomber? Why not torture the person who could introduce you to the cousin who knows someone who planted the bomb? Why not torture the wife and kids? Friends? All of this becomes justified."

And once torture becomes common practice, it severely undermines a society's democratic norms. As Shibley Telhami, a professor at the University of Maryland and an expert on the Middle East, writes in his new book, *The Stakes,* "We cannot defend what we stand for by subverting our own values in the process." In the current climate, conservatives may dismiss such talk as soft-minded idealism. In fact, nobody has more adamantly insisted that the war on terrorism is, at root, a conflict about values than George W. Bush. In his recent State of the Union address, the president catalogued the torture methods administered to prisoners in Iraq. "Electric shock, burning with hot irons, dripping acid on the skin, mutilation with electric drills," Bush said. "If this is not evil, then evil has no meaning."

For the same government that denounces such practices to soften the rules when its own interests are at stake sends a disturbing message: that American moralizing is meaningless. That the United States is willing to dehumanize its enemies in much the way that it complains Islamic terrorists dehumanize theirs.

The parallel between terrorism and torture is instructive. Proponents of   15 each practice maintain that the ends justify the means. They explain away violence by framing it as a necessary "last resort." And they obscure the human impact of that violence by refusing to register the humanity of their victims.

For torture is — and has always been — a function not of brute sadism but of the willingness to view one's enemies as something less than human.

As Edward Peters, a professor of history at the University of Pennsylvania, has shown in his authoritative history of the subject, in ancient Greece only slaves and foreigners were subjected to *basanos* (torture). During the late eighteenth and early nineteenth centuries, as the Enlightenment swept across Europe, one nation after another abolished the practice, to the point where, by 1874, Victor Hugo could proclaim that "torture has ceased to exist." Yet torture was reinstated during the decades that followed — just as the European powers established colonial empires. It became acceptable to treat "natives" in ways that were unacceptable for "the civilized." In more recent decades, when torture has been employed — South Africa, Cambodia, Tibet — it has often been meted out to members of groups so demonized that their individual identities were erased. In this context, it is chilling that the names and identities of the captives in the war on terrorism are as unknown to us as the methods being used against them.

"For the torturers, the sheer and simple fact of human agony is made invisible, and the moral fact of inflicting that agony is made neutral," writes Elaine Scarry in her powerful book *The Body in Pain*. But those facts are neither invisible nor neutral to the victims. "Whoever has succumbed to torture can no longer feel at home in the world," the Holocaust survivor (and torture victim) Jean Améry observed in his searing memoir *At the Mind's Limits*. "It is fear that henceforth reigns. . . . Fear — and also what is called resentments. They remain, and have scarcely a chance to concentrate into a seething, purifying thirst for revenge." In a recent article in the London *Guardian*, Hafiz Abu Sa'eda, head of the Egyptian Organization for Human Rights, described how the experience of being tortured by Egyptian authorities has played a role in radicalizing members of Islamist groups such as the Muslim Brotherhood.

"Torture demonstrates that the regime deserves destroying because it does not respect the dignity of the people," Sa'eda explains. "[The Muslim Brotherhood[4]] began to argue that society should be destroyed and rebuilt again on the basis of an Islamic state." Among those who have been transformed from relative moderates into hard-line fanatics through such a process, the *Guardian* noted, is Dr. Ayman al-Zawahiri, a surgeon who, after being tortured in Egypt, fled to Afghanistan to join the mujahedeen and eventually became Osama bin Laden's deputy. It's possible that Zawahiri would have followed this path independently, of course. But no regime has ever quelled the hatred of its enemies by engaging in torture. The abuses instead fuel this hatred and indelibly transform not only the victims but the torturers themselves. "The screaming I heard on Saturday morning . . . those were screams which until today, when I sleep at night, I hear them inside my ears all the time," an Israeli soldier who stood guard

---

[4]*the Muslim Brotherhood:* Religious and political group founded in Egypt in 1928 that opposes Western intervention in Muslim nations and supports the re-establishment of a united, worldwide Islamic state.

over tortured prisoners said in an oral history published in 1990. "It doesn't leave me, I can't get rid of it."

To insist that the ban on torture should be absolute ought not to lead one to deny that this position comes with certain costs. It is probable that Israeli security forces have prevented some suicide bombings over the years by subjecting Palestinians to beatings and shakings, just as the French crushed the National Liberation Front[5] during the Battle of Algiers partly by torturing (and killing) many of its members. In democratic societies, however, it is understood that, as the Israeli Supreme Court noted in its 1999 decision banning torture, "not all means are acceptable." Torture, in this sense, is hardly unique: Most rights — free speech, privacy, freedom of assembly — entail potential costs by limiting what governments can do to insure order. Holding the line on torture should thus be viewed in the context of a broad debate about where to draw the line between liberty and security, and whether, in the aftermath of September 11, America is willing to stand by its professed values.

Those who advocate crossing the line frequently invoke the famous   20
warning from Supreme Court Justice Robert Jackson that, however much we value our liberties, the Bill of Rights should not become "a suicide pact." But as real as the danger of Al Qaeda may be, few would argue that it constitutes an existential threat to the nation. As the world's wealthiest and most powerful country, the United States has enormous resources at its disposal and countless tools with which to wage its war on terror. In this respect, it's worth asking why brutal CIA interrogation methods could be considered necessary for our security — while adequately funding homeland security is not.

As a tool for collecting information, moreover, torture is notoriously ineffective (since people in pain have the unfortunate habit of lying to make it stop) and has done little to solve long-term security threats. Witness modern Israel — or for that matter France in Algeria.

A deeper problem is that, all too often, even the absolutist position goes unenforced. No government on earth admits to practicing torture, yet each year Amnesty International documents countless states that do. The disparity stems from the fact that torture nearly always takes place in private settings, and in societies loath to discuss the subject openly. In a forthcoming article, Sanford Levinson, a professor at the University of Texas Law School and a noted legal realist, argues that this gap between rhetoric and reality may bolster [the] proposal that torture should be brought out into the open and regulated.

---

[5]*the National Liberation Front:* Group in Algeria that fought for independence from France. Algeria, a country in northwest Africa, was invaded by France in 1830 and gained independence in 1962.

As William Schulz has argued . . . , there are many reasons why, far from limiting torture, such a policy would end up making the practice more ubiquitous than ever. Any country in the world, Schulz points out, would henceforth be able to issue similar warrants and torture at will, free of criticism from the nation that pioneered the practice.

Levinson is right that it won't do simply to pretend that torture is not being perpetrated, as CNBC news anchor Brian Williams did the day after Mohammed's capture, saying to his guest, "Now, the United States says it does not engage in torture, and certainly for the purposes of this conversation and beyond we will take the government at its word." What's needed instead are scholars, reporters, politicians, and citizens who are willing both to hold democracies such as the United States to their stated ideals, and to ask hard questions about what, in a democratic society, should constitute permissible methods of interrogation during wartime. If violence and the threat of violence are out, should prolonged interrogations be permitted? (The Supreme Court has ruled that any confession obtained after thirty-six hours of questioning is by definition coerced.) Should captives have access to lawyers? Should solitary confinement be allowed? This entire area of the law, says David Cole, remains nebulous, perhaps because it is an unpleasant topic to discuss.

Accompanying this discussion should be an equally frank dialogue 25 about the safeguards we need to insure that rampant violations don't occur. For torture, like all governmental abuses, thrives in the absence of openness and accountability. In January the International Secretariat of the World Organisation Against Torture (OMCT), a coalition of nongovernmental organizations from more than sixty-five different countries, issued a press release urging Washington to allow the United Nations Special Rapporteur on Torture to visit the Bagram base in Afghanistan, where the practices the *Washington Post* described are taking place. The OMCT's recommendation was met with stony silence, not only in Washington but by the U.S. media.

The chilled atmosphere is reminiscent of the cold war, when discussion of U.S. support for regimes that engaged in torture (Pinochet's Chile, Suharto's Indonesia)[6] was likewise swept beneath the rug of national security. A language of euphemism and evasion emerged that became so ingrained as to go unnoticed. On February 6, in a disturbing sign that the pattern is being repeated, the *New York Times* published a front-page story detailing the intelligence breakthrough that led U.S. officials to connect the recent murder of a diplomat to an Al Qaeda cell in Baghdad. "Critical information about the network emerged from interrogations of captured cell members conducted under *unspecified circumstances of psychological*

---

[6]*Pinochet's Chile, Suharto's Indonesia:* Dictator Augusto Pinochet (b. 1915) ruled Chile from 1973 to 1990. Mohamed Suharto (b. 1921) ruled Indonesia from 1967 to 1998. Both became infamous for their brutality.

pressure [emphasis added]," the *Times* reported, a phrase you would expect to find in the training manual of a South American police state, not the world's leading newspaper. In the days following Mohammed's arrest, the U.S. media uncritically accepted the Bush Administration's vow not to violate the UN Convention Against Torture, while casually mentioning (sometimes in the same article) that America could persuade Mohammed to talk by reminding him that it has access to his two young children. (Any threat to physically harm a captive's children would constitute torture.) London's *Economist*, by contrast, has questioned whether the United States is "quietly sanctioning the use of some forms of torture" and called on Bush to stop "handing prisoners over to less scrupulous allies."

In early March, the same week that news broke of the cause of the captives' deaths in Afghanistan, the *Post* reported that some nineteen detainees have attempted suicide at the U.S. Navy Prison at Guantánamo Bay, which Michael Ratner, president of the Center for Constitutional Rights, says "begs the question of the long-term psychological effects of the techniques that are being employed there." For Americans to accept their government's assurances in light of these and other recent disclosures is deeply disquieting. For, as historian Peters has noted, the source of torture throughout history has always been the same: not the depraved prison guard who relishes inflicting pain but the society that agrees to tolerate, or even encourage, his actions. "It is still civil society," Peters writes, "that tortures or authorizes torture or is indifferent to those wielding it on civil society's behalf."

America's unique stature encumbers it with a special responsibility in this regard. "For better or worse, the United States sets precedents and examples," Henry Shue says. "We're very visible. If the most powerful country in the world has to torture, how are we supposed to convince anyone else that they shouldn't torture?" In Iran, a group of reformists in Parliament recently submitted a bill calling on their country to sign the UN Convention Against Torture. One can only hope that Teheran's hard-line clerics haven't been reading the *Washington Post*.

ENGAGING THE TEXT

1. Would you agree that it may be necessary to resort to torture to keep America safe? Under what circumstances, if any, would you condone the use of torture, and why?

2. What specific reasons does Press offer against the use of torture? Why, according to Press, might torture be ineffective or counterproductive in even the most extreme scenarios? In his view, how might the use of torture and other extreme measures in the name of national security undermine the virtues and freedoms it is meant to preserve?

3. What does the state-sanctioned use of torture have in common with terrorism, according to Press? Would you agree that there is little difference between those who torture and those who commit terrorist acts? Why or why not?

4. Do you think it might actually be better to acknowledge the use of torture so that it can be defined and regulated by international law? How might such regulation work? What moral or ethical impact, if any, might this open acknowledgment of torture have on society?

EXPLORING CONNECTIONS

5. What role might American obliviousness, as described by Mark Hertsgaard (p. 781), play in supporting the use of torture by the United States? What might Hertsgaard think about the idea of tolerating practices like torture or extraordinary rendition?

6. How might Press's discussion of the use of torture as a tool in support of national security challenge Dinesh D'Souza's claim that America is an exceptional nation (p. 768)? Can the United States offer a model of freedom and liberty to the world if it engages in such activities?

7. Drawing on ideas you encounter in D'Souza (p. 768), Hertsgaard (p. 781), Andreas (p. 794), and Press, write an essay on the moral health of American society. How might each of these writers assess America's spiritual state since 9/11? In general, do you think the United States is ethically stronger or weaker since the attacks on the World Trade Center and the War on Terror?

EXTENDING THE CRITICAL CONTEXT

8. Working in groups, research abuses of power by U.S. agents, authorities, and troops since 9/11 and the beginning of the War on Terror. What evidence is there to suggest that Americans have engaged in torture, extraordinary rendition, and war crimes against civilians or prisoners of war? To what extent might these activities challenge the notion of American innocence?

9. Do some additional reading about the detention of suspected al-Qaeda supporters at Guantánamo. Would you agree that the United States has the right to hold suspected terrorists without trial, or does such open-ended detainment amount to a form of torture? What do you think should be done with the 400-plus inmates who remain incarcerated at Guantánamo?

Under the Sign of Mickey Mouse & Co.
TODD GITLIN

Walt Disney's "Magic Kingdom" bills itself as the "Happiest Place on Earth," and that's exactly the way America's mass media present the United States, according to Todd Gitlin. Over the past twenty years American culture has been infiltrating nations all over the world, homogenizing traditional cultures into the kind of global "fun" culture that Disney is famous for. The question, of course, is whether it's good for Uzbek kids to spurn their parents' ways for Western styles or for American teens to groove to the beat of Third World music as they "shimmy" through the local mall. A nationally recognized authority on mass media, Todd Gitlin (b. 1943) has authored a novel and five works of nonfiction on popular culture and American society, including Inside Prime Time *(1983),* The Twilight of Common Dreams: Why America is Wracked by Culture Wars *(1995), and* Media Unlimited: How the Torrent of Images and Sounds Overwhelms Our Lives *(2001), the source of this selection. He is also the North American editor of* openDemocracy, *a member of the editorial board of* Dissent *magazine, and a faculty member of Columbia University's Graduate School of Journalism.*

Everywhere, the media flow defies national boundaries. This is one of its obvious, but at the same time amazing, features. A global torrent is not, of course, the master metaphor to which we have grown accustomed. We're more accustomed to Marshall McLuhan's *global village*.[1] Those who resort to this metaphor casually often forget that if the world is a global village, some live in mansions on the hill, others in huts. Some dispatch images and sounds around town at the touch of a button; others collect them at the touch of *their* buttons. Yet McLuhan's image reveals an indispensable half-truth. If there is a village, it speaks American. It wears jeans, drinks Coke, eats at the golden arches, walks on swooshed shoes, plays electric guitars, recognizes Mickey Mouse, James Dean, E.T., Bart Simpson, R2-D2, and Pamela Anderson.

At the entrance to the champagne cellar of Piper-Heidsieck[2] in Reims, in eastern France, a plaque declares that the cellar was dedicated by Marie Antoinette. The tour is narrated in six languages, and at the end you walk back upstairs into a museum featuring photographs of famous people drinking champagne. And who are they? Perhaps members of today's royal houses, presidents or prime ministers, economic titans or Nobel Prize winners? Of course not. They are movie stars, almost all of them American — Marilyn Monroe to Clint Eastwood. The symmetry of the exhibition is obvious, the premise unmistakable: Hollywood stars, champions of consumption, are the royalty of this century, more popular by far than poor doomed Marie.

Hollywood is the global cultural capital — capital in both senses. The United States presides over a sort of World Bank of styles and symbols, an International Cultural Fund of images, sounds, and celebrities. The goods may be distributed by American-, Canadian-, European-, Japanese-, or Australian-owned multinational corporations, but their styles, themes, and images do not detectably change when a new board of directors takes over. Entertainment is one of America's top exports.[3] In 1999, in fact, film, television, music, radio, advertising, print publishing, and computer software together *were* the top export, almost $80 billion worth, and while software alone accounted for $50 billion of the total, some of that category also qualifies as entertainment — video games and pornography, for example. Hardly anyone is exempt from the force of American images and sounds. French resentment of Mickey Mouse, Bruce Willis, and the rest of American civilization is well known. Less well known, and rarely acknowledged by the French, is the fact that *Terminator 2* sold 5 million tickets in France during the month it opened — with no submachine guns at the heads of the

---

[1]*Marshall McLuhan's global village:* Canadian communications theorist and educator, Herbert Marshall McLuhan (1911–1980) believed that the modern electronic media would eventually blur regional and cultural differences and unite the world in a single global culture or community. [All notes are author's, except 1, 2, 5, 15, 18, 20, 29, and 30.]

[2]*Piper-Heidsieck:* Brand of French champagne.

[3]*America's top exports:* Economists Incorporated for the International Intellectual Property Alliance, Executive Summary, 2000_SIWEK_EXEC.pdf. Thanks to Siva Vaidhyanathan for his discerning analysis of these statistics.

customers. The same culture minister, Jack Lang, who in 1982 achieved a moment of predictable notoriety in the United States for declaring that *Dallas* amounted to cultural imperialism, also conferred France's highest honor in the arts on Elizabeth Taylor and Sylvester Stallone. The point is not hypocrisy pure and simple but something deeper, something obscured by a single-minded emphasis on American power: dependency. American popular culture is the nemesis that hundreds of millions — perhaps billions — of people love, and love to hate. The antagonism and the dependency are inseparable, for the media flood — essentially American in its origin, but virtually unlimited in its reach — represents, like it or not, a common imagination.

How shall we understand the Hong Kong T-shirt that says "I Feel Coke"? Or the little Japanese girl who asks an American visitor in all innocence, "Is there really a Disneyland in America?" (She knows the one in Tokyo.) Or the experience of a German television reporter[4] sent to Siberia to film indigenous life, who after flying out of Moscow and then traveling for days by boat, bus, and jeep, arrives near the Arctic Sea where live a tribe of Tungusians known to ethnologists for their bearskin rituals. In the community store sits a grandfather with his grandchild on his knee. Grandfather is dressed in traditional Tungusian clothing. Grandson has on his head a reversed baseball cap.

American popular culture is the closest approximation today to a global lingua franca,[5] drawing the urban and young in particular into a common cultural zone where they share some dreams of freedom, wealth, comfort, innocence, and power — and perhaps most of all, youth as a state of mind. In general, despite the rhetoric of "identity," young people do not live in monocultures. They are not monocular. They are both local and cosmopolitan. Cultural bilingualism is routine. Just as their "cultures"[6] are neither hard-wired nor uniform, so there is no simple way in which they are "Americanized," though there are American tags on their experience — low-cost links to status and fun. Everywhere, fun lovers, efficiency seekers, Americaphiles, and Americaphobes alike pass through the portals of Disney and the arches of McDonald's wearing Levi's jeans and Gap jackets. Mickey Mouse and Donald Duck, John Wayne, Marilyn Monroe, James Dean, Bob Dylan, Michael Jackson, Madonna, Clint Eastwood, Bruce Willis, the multicolor chorus of Coca-Cola, and the next flavor of the month or the universe are the icons of a curious sort of one-world sensibility, a global semiculture. America's bid for global unification surpasses in reach that of the Romans,

5

---

[4]*a German television reporter:* This story is told by Berndt Ostendorf in "What Makes American Popular Culture So Popular: A View from Europe" (Odense, Denmark: Oasis, 2000).

[5]*lingua franca:* The commonly used language of trade or business.

[6]*Just as their "cultures":* I benefited from a discussion about the overuse of the term *culture* with Kevin Robins, March 2, 2001.

the British, the Catholic, or Islam; though without either an army or a God, it requires less. The Tungusian boy with the reversed cap on his head does not automatically think of it as "American," let alone side with the U.S. Army.

The misleadingly easy answer to the question of how American images and sounds became omnipresent is: American imperialism. But the images are not even faintly force-fed by American corporate, political, or military power. The empire strikes from inside the spectator as well as from outside. This is a conundrum that deserves to be approached with respect if we are to grasp the fact that Mickey Mouse and Coke are everywhere recognized and often enough *enjoyed.* In the peculiar unification at work throughout the world, there is surely a supply side, but there is not only a supply side. Some things are true even if multinational corporations claim so: there is demand.

What do American icons and styles mean to those who are not American? We can only imagine — but let us try. What young people graced with disposable income encounter in American television shows, movies, soft drinks, theme parks, and American-labeled (though not American-manufactured) running shoes, T-shirts, baggy pants, ragged jeans, and so on, is a way of being in the world, the experience of a flow of ready feelings and sensations bobbing up, disposable, dissolving, segueing to the next and the next after that. . . . It is a quality of immediacy and casualness not so different from what Americans desire. But what the young experience in the video game arcade or the music megastore is more than the flux of sensation. They flirt with a loose sort of social membership that requires little but a momentary (and monetary) surrender. Sampling American goods, images, and sounds, they affiliate with an empire of informality. Consuming a commodity, wearing a slogan or a logo, you affiliate with disaffiliation. You make a limited-liability connection, a virtual one. You borrow some of the effervescence that is supposed to emanate from this American staple, and hope to be recognized as one of the elect. When you wear the Israeli version that spells *Coca-Cola* in Hebrew, you express some worldwide connection with unknown peers, or a sense of irony, or both — in any event, a marker of membership. In a world of ubiquitous images, of easy mobility and casual tourism, you get to feel not only local or national but global — without locking yourself in a box so confining as to deserve the name "identity."

We are seeing on a world scale the familiar infectious rhythm of modernity. The money economy extends its reach, bringing with it a calculating mentality. Even in the poor countries it stirs the same hunger for private feeling, the same taste for disposable labels and sensations on demand, the same attention to fashion, the new and the now, that cropped up earlier in the West. Income beckons; income rewards. The taste for the marketed spectacle and the media-soaked way of life spreads. The culture consumer may not like the American goods in particular but still acquires a taste for the media's speed, formulas, and frivolity. Indeed, the lightness of

American-sponsored "identity" is central to its appeal. It imposes few burdens. Attachments and affiliations coexist, overlap, melt together, form, and re-form.

Marketers, like nationalists and fundamentalists, promote "identities," but for most people, the mélange is the message. Traditional bonds bend under pressure from imports. Media from beyond help you have your "roots" and eat them, too. You can watch Mexican television in the morning and American in the afternoon, or graze between Kurdish and English. You can consolidate family ties with joint visits to Disney World — making Orlando, Florida, the major tourist destination in the United States, and the Tokyo and Marne-la-Vallée spin-offs massive attractions in Japan and France. You can attach to your parents, or children, by playing oldie music and exchanging sports statistics. You plunge back into the media flux, looking for — what? Excitement? Some low-cost variation on known themes? Some next new thing? You don't know just what, but you will when you see it — or if not, you'll change channels.

As devotees of Japanese video games, Hong Kong movies, and Mexican   10
telenovelas would quickly remind us, the blends, juxtapositions, and recombinations of popular culture are not just American. American and American-based models, styles, and symbols are simply the most far-flung, successful, and consequential. In the course of a century, America's entertainment corporations succeeded brilliantly in cultivating popular expectations for entertainment — indeed, the sense of a *right* to be entertained, a right that belongs to the history of modernity, the rise of market economies, and individualism. The United States, which began as Europe's collective fantasy, built a civilization to deliver the goods for playing, feeling, and meaning. Competitors ignore its success at their own peril, financial and otherwise.

The Supply Side

About the outward thrust of the American culture industry there is no mystery. The mainspring is the classic drive to expand markets. In the latter half of the 1980s,[7] with worldwide deregulation, export sales increased from 30 percent to 40 percent of Hollywood's total revenue for television and film. Since then, the percentages have stabilized. In 2000,[8] total foreign revenues for all film and video revenue streams averaged 37 percent — for theatrical releases, 51 percent; for television, 41 percent; and for video, 27 percent.

Exporters benefit from the economies of scale afforded by serial production. American industrialists have long excelled at efficiencies, first

[7]*In the latter half of the 1980s:* National Technical Information Service, *Globalization of the Mass Media* (Washington, D.C.: Department of Commerce, 1993), pp. 1–2, cited in Edward S. Herman and Robert W. McChesney, *The Global Media: The New Missionaries of Corporate Capitalism* (London: Cassell, 1997), p. 39.

[8]*In 2000:* Calculated from *Schroder's International Media and Entertainment Report 2000*, p. 37. Courtesy of David Lieberman, media business editor of *USA Today.*

anticipating and later developing the standardized production techniques of Henry Ford's assembly line. Early in the nineteenth century, minstrel shows[9] were already being assembled from standardized components. Such efficiencies were later applied to burlesque, melodrama, vaudeville, radio soap opera, comic books, genre literature, musical comedy, and Hollywood studio productions. Cultural formula is not unique to the United States, but Americans were particularly adept at mass-producing it, using centralized management to organize road shows and coordinate local replicas.

If the American culture industry has long depended on foreign markets, foreign markets now also depend on American formulas: Westerns, action heroes, rock music, hip-hop. Globalized distribution expedites imitation. The American way generates proven results. Little imagination is required to understand why global entertainment conglomerates copy proven recipes or why theater owners outside the United States (many of whom are themselves American) want to screen them, even if they exaggerate the degree to which formula guarantees success. In a business freighted with uncertainty, the easiest decision is to copy. Individuals making careers also want to increase their odds of success.

It's a mistake to exaggerate the power of central supply to generate audiences, but the financial rewards of imitation are potentially so great, legions of entrepreneurs everywhere make the effort. All over the world, young filmmakers aspire to become the next Steven Spielberg or George Lucas, with their blatant emotional payoffs and predictable lines.

Around the world, as in the United States itself, America fabricated the 15 templates, first, for Italian and Spanish Westerns, later for Hong Kong kung fu and "action," Europop, French soap operas, and so on. The Hollywood star system also came in for imitation everywhere. Even if, when faced with a choice,[10] people tend to prefer domestically produced television to Hollywood goods, competitors in television, as in film and music, are pulled[11] into America's gravitational field.

The Demand Side

But the supply-side argument won't suffice to explain global cultural dominance. American popular culture is not uniquely formulaic or

[9]*minstrel shows:* Ostendorf, "What Makes American Popular Culture So Popular?" pp. 16–18, 47.

[10]*when faced with a choice:* Herman and McChesney, *Global Media,* p. 42. See also Tapio Varis, "Values and the Limits of the Global Media in the Age of Cyberspace," in Michael Prosser and K. S. Sitaram, eds., *Civic Discourse: Intercultural, International, and Global Media* (Stamford, CT: Ablex, 1999), vol. 2, pp. 5–17. During one week in the spring of 2001, not one of the fifty top-rated British TV shows was American.

[11]*competitors . . . are pulled:* Jeremy Tunstall, *The Media Are American: Anglo-American Media in the World* (New York: Columbia University Press, 1977), pp. 50–51.

transportable. (Indeed, in 1900, 142 special trains[12] transported touring companies of actors and musicians throughout England and Wales every Sunday.) Moreover, availability is not popularity. No one forced Danes to watch *Dallas*, however cheaply purchased. In fact, when a new television entertainment chief took charge in 1981–82 and proceeded to cancel the show, thirty thousand protest letters[13] poured in, and hundreds of Danes (mostly women, many rural) demonstrated in Copenhagen. When the chief's superiors told him he had better rethink his decision, he passed a sleepless night, bowed, and reversed himself. The dominance of American popular culture is a soft dominance — a collaboration. In the words of media analyst James Monaco, "American movies and TV are popular because they're *popular.*"[14]

That popularity has much to do with the fusion of market-mindedness and cultural diversity. The United States has the advantages of a polyglot, multirooted (or rather, uprooted) society that celebrates its compound nature and common virtues (and sins) with remarkable energy. Popular culture, by the time it ships from American shores, has already been "pretested" on a heterogeneous public — a huge internal market with variegated tastes. American popular culture is, after all, the rambunctious child of Europe and Africa. Our popular music and dance derive from the descendants of African slaves, among others. Our comic sense derives principally from the English, East European Jews, and, again, African-Americans, with growing Hispanic infusions. Our stories come from everywhere; consider Ralph Waldo Ellison's *Invisible Man*, inspired jointly by Dostoyevsky,[15] African-American folktales, and jazz. American culture is spongy, or in James Monaco's happy term, *promiscuous.*[16] He adds, "American culture simply doesn't exist without its African and European progenitors, and despite occasional outbursts of 'Americanism' it continues to accept almost any input."

To expand in the United States, popular culture had a clear avenue. It did not have to squeeze up against an aristocratic model, there being no wealthy landowning class to nourish one except in the plantation South — and there, slaves were the population that produced the most influential popular culture. Outside the South, from the early nineteenth century on, the market enjoyed prestige; it was no dishonor to produce culture for popular purposes. Ecclesiastical rivals were relatively weak. From the early

---

[12]*142 special trains:* Cyril Ehrlich, *The Music Profession in Britain Since the Eighteenth Century* (London: Oxford University Press, 1985), p. 56. Thanks to Peter Mandler for this reference.

[13]*thirty thousand protest letters:* Personal communication, Henrik Christiansen, former chief of entertainment for Danish television (and previously head of news), September 1998.

[14]*James Monaco:* "Images and Sounds as Cultural Commodities," p. 231, from an article I clipped a long time ago but without noting from which magazine I'd clipped it.

[15]*Dostoyevsky:* Fyoder Michaylovich Dostoyevsky (1821–1881), Russian novelist.

[16]*Monaco's happy term:* Monaco, p. 231.

years of the Republic, American culture was driven[17] by a single overriding purpose: to entertain the common man and woman. Hence Tocqueville's[18] recognition that American artists cultivated popularity, not elevation; fun, not refinement. As Daniel Dayan[19] has put it with only slight exaggeration, European (and traditional) cultures have a superego,[20] American culture does not. What is the market for entertainment if not a market for id?

Think about possible sources of competition, and the American advantage stands out. In the global market, bottom-up outsells top-down. Despite a tradition of popular culture, the main British model was classbound — culture as cultivation, culture as good for you. The head of the BBC's General Overseas Service[21] complained in 1944 that "if any hundred British troops are invited to choose their own records 90 per cent of the choice will be of American stuff," and from then onward Americanization came in for much high-minded abuse. As for Soviet Russia, when it was a major world power, its culture was mainly didactic. (In 1972, Soviet film exports[22] to its captive market in eastern and central Europe were still weaker, proportionately, than Hollywood's exports everywhere else in the world.) Who could produce fun like Americans? Who believed so fervently in colorful spectacle? In 1992, as France debated the establishment of Euro Disneyland outside Paris, as the theatrical director Arianne Mnouchkin denounced this "cultural Chernobyl" and French intellectuals joined her protest, it was not completely disingenuous for a Disney official[23] to deny the charge of American cultural imperialism by saying: "It's not America, it's Disney. . . . We're not trying to sell anything but fun, entertainment."

It is to America's advantage as well that commercial work emerges from   20

[17]*American culture was driven:* Library shelves groan with histories of popular American culture, but fundamental works worth singling out include Henry Nash Smith, *Virgin Land: The American West as Symbol and Myth* (Cambridge, Mass.: Harvard University Press, 1950); Richard Slotkin, *Regeneration Through Violence: The Mythology of the American Frontier, 1600–1860* (Middletown, Conn.: Wesleyan University Press, 1973); John G. Cawelti, *Adventure, Mystery, and Romance: Formula Stories as Art and Popular Culture* (Chicago: University of Chicago Press, 1976); and Michael Denning, *Mechanic Accents: Dime Novels and Working-Class Culture in America* (London: Verso, 1987).

[18]*Tocqueville:* Alexis de Tocqueville (1805–1859), French politician and writer, renowned for his observations on U.S. society and culture in *Democracy in America* (1835–40).

[19]*Daniel Dayan:* Personal communication, July 20, 2000.

[20]*superego:* Austrian psychiatrist Sigmund Freud (1856–1939) divided the human personality into three functional parts: the id, which is dominated by the pleasure principle and the quest for immediate gratification; the superego, which internalizes the role of the parent and thus embodies social expectations that "censor" the urges of the id; and the ego, which results from the interaction of id and superego with the external world.

[21]*The head of the BBC's General Overseas Service:* Quoted in Asa Briggs, *The War of Words* (London: Oxford University Press, 1970), pp. 567–68. *Americanization:* Dick Hebdige, *Hiding in the Light* (London: Routledge/Comedia, 1988), pp. 52–76. There were exceptions, however. In the Noel Coward/David Lean film *Brief Encounter* (1946), the Trevor Howard character raves about the merits of Donald Duck as a distraction from the war.

[22]*Soviet film exports:* Tunstall, *Media Are American,* p. 62.

[23]*a Disney official:* Quoted in Todd Gitlin, "World Leaders: Mickey, et al." *New York Times,* Arts and Leisure Section, May 3, 1992, p. 1.

Hollywood, New York, and Nashville in the principal world language. Thanks to the British Empire-cum-Commonwealth, English is the second most commonly spoken native language in the world, and the most international. (The vast majority of those who speak the leading language, Chinese, live in a single country, and their language, tonal in speech and ideographic on paper, is not well adapted for export.) English is spoken and read as a second language more commonly than any other. Increasingly, the English that is taught and learned, the language in demand, is American, not British. It is the language of business and has acquired the cachet of international media. Of the major world languages, English is the most compressed; partly because of its Anglo-Saxon origins, the English version of any text is almost always shorter than translations in other languages. English is grammatically simple. American English in particular[24] is pungent, informal, absorptive, evolving, precise when called upon to be precise, transferable between written and verbal forms, lacking in sharp distinctions between "high" and "low" forms, and all in all, well adapted for slogans, headlines, comic strips, song lyrics, jingles, slang, dubbing, and other standard features of popular culture. English is, in a word, the most torrential language.

Moreover, the American language of images is even more accessible than the American language of words. The global popularity of Hollywood product often depends less on the spoken word, even when kept elementary (non-English-speakers everywhere could understand Arnold Schwarzenegger without difficulty), than on crackling edits, bright smiles, the camera tracking and swooping, the cars crashing off cliffs or smashing into other cars, the asteroids plunging dramatically toward earth. In action movies, as in the Westerns that preceded them, speech is a secondary mode of expression. European competitors cannot make this claim, though Hong Kong can.

It is also an export advantage that "American" popular culture is frequently not so American at all. "Hollywood" is an export platform that happens to be located on the Pacific coast of the United States but uses capital, hires personnel, and depicts sites from many countries. Disney casually borrows mythologies from Britain, Germany, France, Italy, Denmark, China, colonial America, the Old Testament, anywhere. Any myth can get the Disney treatment: simplified, smoothed down, prettified. Pavilions as emblems of foreign countries, sites as replicas of sites, *Fantasia, Pinocchio, Song of the South, Pocahontas, Mulan* — Disney takes material where it can, as long as it comes out Disney's industrialized fun.

Moreover, to sustain market advantages, the Hollywood multinationals, ever thirsting for novelty, eagerly import, process, and export styles and practitioners from abroad. Consider, among directors, Alfred Hitchcock, Charlie Chaplin, Douglas Sirk, Michael Curtiz, Billy Wilder, Otto Preminger, Ridley Scott, Peter Weir, Bruce Beresford, Paul Verhoeven, John Woo, Ang Lee. (The big Hollywood movie of 1996, *Independence Day,* with its rousing nationalist features, was directed by the German Roland Emmerich — a

[24]*American English in particular:* Tunstall, *Media Are American,* pp. 127–8.

Hollywood fact reminiscent of Louis B. Mayer's decision[25] to celebrate his birthday on July 4.) Consider, among stars, Greta Garbo, Ingrid Bergman, Cary Grant, Anthony Quinn, Sean Connery, Arnold Schwarzenegger, Jean-Claude Van Damme, Mel Gibson, Hugh Grant, Jackie Chan, Kate Winslet, Michelle Yeoh, Chow Yun-Fat, Catherine Zeta-Jones, Antonio Banderas, Penelope Cruz. Hollywood is the global magnet — and (to mix metaphors) the acid bath into which, often enough, talent dissolves. Even the locales come from everywhere, or nowhere. It is striking how many blockbusters take place in outer space (the *Star Wars, Alien*, and *Star Trek* series), in the prenational past (the *Jurassic Park* series), in the post-national future (the *Planet of the Apes* series, the two *Terminator* films, *The Matrix*), at sea (*Titanic, The Perfect Storm* — the latter also directed by a German, Wolfgang Petersen), or on an extended hop-skip-and-jump around the world (the James Bond series, *Mission: Impossible*).

In music, cultural import-export relations can be intricate. What exactly is an "American" style anyway? In the art critic Harold Rosenberg's phrase, the great American tradition is "the tradition of the new."[26] The cultural gates are poorly guarded and swing both ways. American rhythm and blues influenced Jamaican ska, which evolved into reggae, which in turn was imported to the United States, mainly via Britain. "Musicians in the Kingston tenement yards[27] picked up poor reception of New Orleans radio stations," writes music journalist Vivien Goldman, "and retransmitted boogie woogie piano, horn sections, and strolling, striding bass into Jamaica's insidious one drop groove and scratchy skanga-skanga guitar." The Jamaican custom of "toasting," with the disc jockey talking over prerecorded rhythm tracks (a style that in turn derived from African griot "chats"), led to "dub," in which the DJ remixed the song, which in turn evolved into American rap. The "trance-like quality" of dub's "thudding bass" led to "the incantatory, undulating repetitions of ambient and rave music." American punks[28] who imported ska from London in the 1990s were not necessarily aware that it was Jamaican. Mambo, tango, bossa nova, techno — dancing America puts up no obstacles to imported energies. The result is not an American equivalent of France's *mission civilisatrice;*[29] arguably it is the opposite, in which

[25]*Louis B. Mayer's decision:* Neal Gabler, *An Empire of Their Own: How the Jews Invented Hollywood* (New York: Crown, 1988), p. 3.

[26]*Harold Rosenberg: The Tradition of the New* (New York; Grove, 1961). Rosenberg was referring to modernism in the arts, but he might equally well have meant popular culture.

[27]*"Musicians in the Kingston tenement yards":* Vivien Goldman, "One Drop of Mighty Dread: How Jamaica Changed the World's Music," *CommonQuest* 4, no. 3 (2000), pp. 23, 22, 25.

[28]*American punks:* Ibid., p. 27. American food has been and continues to be shaped by a similar hybridization, which is the point of the joke about the tourist who walks up to a stranger in New York and asks where he can get a pizza. The stranger points to a Chinese restaurant. Perplexed, the tourist walks into the restaurant and says hesitantly to a waiter, "Is it really true that you serve pizza?" "Of course," is the answer, "what size would you like, and what topping? We have mushroom, pepperoni — " "Excuse me," says the tourist, "but I don't understand why a Chinese restaurant serves pizza." The waiter replies, "For all our Jewish customers!"

[29]*mission civilisatrice:* French for "civilizing mission."

American teenagers shimmy through the malls to the rhythms of the wretched of the earth.

No matter. Of Americanized popular culture, nothing more or less is asked but that it be *interesting,* a portal into the pleasure dome. In the main, an all-too-bearable lightness[30] is what the traffic will bear. Not for American culture the televisual intricacies of Rainer Werner Fassbinder's   25 *Berlin Alexanderplatz* or Dennis Potter's *The Singing Detective,* or the subtlety and inwardness of the great European filmmakers, or the historical scale of Latin Americans, Japanese, and Chinese. Not for American popular culture the presumption of Art with a capital *A,* known colloquially as *artiness.* Playful, expressive, comfortably uplifting — a host of styles and themes converge in what the psychologist Martha Wolfenstein called a *fun morality:* Thou Shalt Have Fun.[31]

ENGAGING THE TEXT

1. What specific qualities, values, and attitudes does Gitlin identify with American culture? Why, in his view, are these aspects of American culture so attractive to people in other countries? To what extent do these qualities and attitudes strike you as particularly "American"? Are there any others that you would add to Gitlin's list?

2. What does American global media do to local cultures and regional identities, according to Gitlin? What takes the place of local identity in the media-dominated world that Gitlin describes? What, in your estimation, is gained or lost in this transaction?

3. What is Gitlin suggesting when he says that American culture is "spongy" or "promiscuous" — or when he says that American popular culture produces entertainment for the "id" and not for the "superego"? What does he mean when he claims that, unlike traditional cultures, American culture is "bottom-up" instead of "top-down"? To what extent would you agree with these depictions of U.S. popular culture? Why?

4. In what way has the English language itself contributed to the worldwide dominance of American culture, according to Gitlin? Why, in this view, is English particularly well suited to a commercial culture built on advertising, slogans, headlines, and comic strips?

5. Overall, how would you characterize Gitlin's attitude toward American popular culture? Does he see it as a threat to the rest of the world, as an invitation to freedom, or simply as a source of pleasure? What concerns or limitations do you see in the "fun morality" that Gitlin identifies with America's cultural influence across the world? Is it in any way distasteful, for example, for American teens to "shimmy through the malls to the rhythms of the wretched of the earth" (para. 24)?

[30]*all-too-bearable lightness:* An allusion to the title of Czech author Milan Kundera's (b. 1929) novel *The Unbearable Lightness of Being* (1984).
[31]*Martha Wolfenstein:* "The Emergence of Fun Morality," in Eric Larrabee, ed., *Mass Leisure* (Glencoe, IL: Free Press, 1958), p. 86.

EXPLORING CONNECTIONS

6. To what extent might Gitlin's analysis of American culture be seen as supporting Dinesh D'Souza's view of what America represents to the rest of the world (p. 768)? How would you expect people who live in "traditional" Middle Eastern, Asian, or African societies to respond to a foreign culture that respects only "the tradition of the new"?

7. How might David Kupelian (p. 646) respond to Gitlin's analysis of America's "fun culture"? How might Kupelian view the impact of American popular culture on other, more traditional societies?

EXTENDING THE CRITICAL CONTEXT

8. Pool your knowledge of American pop music to test Gitlin's claims about how it has been influenced by other cultures from around the world. What specific "foreign" influences can you identify in recent pop music hits? What types or styles of popular music seem to be most open to non-American influences? Would you agree, as Gitlin suggests, that it's difficult to define what "American style" amounts to in relation to contemporary music?

This Modern World by Tom Tomorrow. © Dan Perkins. All rights reserved. Used with permission.

Resistance to Civil Government
(Civil Disobedience)

HENRY DAVID THOREAU

Henry David Thoreau has long been considered a model of American freedom. Born in Concord, Massachusetts, in 1817, Thoreau was a tutor, teacher, philosopher, pacifist, naturalist, and early environmentalist. After graduating from Harvard University with a degree in English, Thoreau met Ralph Waldo Emerson, one of the nation's leading authors and founder of the American transcendentalist movement. In his youth, Thoreau was strongly attracted to the tenets of transcendentalism, which stressed the uniqueness of the individual spirit and the individual's duty to search for universal truth. Inspired by the transcendental ideal of harmony with nature, in 1845 Thoreau went to live in a hand-built one-room cabin near Walden Pond outside Concord. The record of his experiences over the next two years of living as simply and as close to nature as possible became the substance of Walden *(1854), which remains a landmark in American literary history. According to one of many legends told about Thoreau, while walking into town from Walden Pond one day in 1846, he encountered the local tax collector who demanded that he pay six years of back poll taxes. Thoreau refused in protest of the federal government's continuing support of slavery and its invasion of Mexico at the onset of the Mexican-American War. After spending a night in jail, Thoreau was released against his will, thanks to the intervention of his aunt, who paid his debt to the state. Written to explain this act of civil disobedience, "Resistance to Civil Government" records Thoreau's reflections on the limits of state power and the principle of majority rule when issues of human rights and individual conscience are at stake. It also represents one of the nation's greatest contributions to the philosophy of liberty — one, in fact, that has inspired visionaries and world leaders like Leo Tolstoy, Mohandas Gandhi, and Martin Luther King Jr. Before his death in 1869 at the early age of forty-four, Thoreau published a number of memorable reflections on nature and philosophy, including* A Week on the Concord and Merrimack Rivers *(1849) and* The Maine Woods *(1864).*

I heartily accept the motto — "That government is best which governs least"; and I should like to see it acted up to more rapidly and systematically. Carried out, it finally amounts to this, which also I believe, — "That government is best which governs not at all"; and when men are prepared for it, that will be the kind of government which they will have. Government is at best but an expedient; but most governments are usually, and all governments are sometimes, inexpedient. The objections which have been brought against a standing army, and they are many and weighty, and deserve to prevail, may also at last be brought against a standing government. The standing army is only an arm of the standing government. The government itself, which is only the mode which the people have chosen to execute their will, is equally liable to be abused and perverted before the people can act through it. Witness the present Mexican war,[1] the work of comparatively a few individuals using the standing government as their tool; for, in the outset, the people would not have consented to this measure.

This American government, — what is it but a tradition, though a recent one, endeavoring to transmit itself unimpaired to posterity, but each instant losing some of its integrity? It has not the vitality and force of a single living man; for a single man can bend it to his will. It is a sort of wooden gun to the people themselves; and, if ever they should use it in earnest as a real one against each other, it will surely split. But it is not the less necessary for this; for the people must have some complicated machinery or other, and hear its din, to satisfy that idea of government which they have. Governments show thus how successfully men can be imposed on, even impose on themselves, for their own advantage. It is excellent, we must all allow; yet this government never of itself furthered any enterprise, but by the alacrity with which it got out of its way. *It* does not keep the country free. *It* does not settle the West. *It* does not educate. The character inherent in the American people has done all that has been accomplished; and it would have done somewhat more, if the government had not sometimes got in its way. For government is an expedient by which men would fain succeed in letting one another alone; and, as has been said, when it is most expedient, the governed are most let alone by it. Trade and commerce, if they were not made of india rubber, would never manage to bounce over the obstacles which legislators are continually putting in their way; and, if one were to judge these men wholly by the effects of their actions, and not partly by their intentions, they would deserve to be classed and punished with those mischievous persons who put obstructions on the railroads.

But, to speak practically and as a citizen, unlike those who call themselves no-government men, I ask for, not at once no government, but *at once a better government*. Let every man make known what kind of government would command his respect, and that will be one step toward obtaining it.

After all, the practical reason why, when the power is once in the hands of the people, a majority are permitted, and for a long period continue, to rule, is not because they are most likely to be in the right, nor because this seems fairest to the minority, but because they are physically the strongest. But a government in which the majority rule in all cases cannot be based on justice, even as far as men understand it. Can there not be a

[1]*Mexican war:* Conflict between the United States and Mexico from 1846 to 1848, which led to the United States obtaining much territory in what is now the American southwest.

government in which majorities do not virtually decide right and wrong, but conscience? — in which majorities decide only those questions to which the rule of expediency is applicable? Must the citizen ever for a moment, or in the least degree, resign his conscience to the legislator? Why has every man a conscience, then? I think that we should be men first, and subjects afterward. It is not desirable to cultivate a respect for the law, so much as for the right. The only obligation which I have a right to assume, is to do at any time what I think right. It is truly enough said, that a corporation has no conscience; but a corporation of conscientious men is a corporation *with* a conscience. Law never made men a whit more just; and, by means of their respect for it, even the well-disposed are daily made the agents of injustice. A common and natural result of an undue respect for law is, that you may see a file of soldiers, colonel, captain, corporal, privates, powder-monkeys and all, marching in admirable order over hill and dale to the wars, against their wills, aye, against their common sense and consciences, which makes it very steep marching indeed, and produces a palpitation of the heart. They have no doubt that it is a damnable business in which they are concerned; they are all peaceably inclined. Now, what are they? Men at all? or small moveable forts and magazines, at the service of some unscrupulous man in power? Visit the Navy Yard, and behold a marine, such a man as an American government can make, or such as it can make a man with its black arts, a mere shadow and reminiscence of humanity, a man laid out alive and standing, and already, as one may say, buried under arms with funeral accompaniments, though it may be

"Not a drum was heard, nor a funeral note,
    As his corse to the ramparts we hurried;
Not a soldier discharged his farewell shot
    O'er the grave where our hero we buried."[2]

The mass of men serve the State thus, not as men mainly, but as   5
machines, with their bodies. They are the standing army, and the militia, jailers, constables, *posse comitatus,* &c. In most cases there is no free exercise whatever of the judgment or of the moral sense; but they put themselves on a level with wood and earth and stones; and wooden men can perhaps be manufactured that will serve the purpose as well. Such command no more respect than men of straw, or a lump of dirt. They have the same sort of worth only as horses and dogs. Yet such as these even are commonly esteemed good citizens. Others, as most legislators, politicians, lawyers, ministers, and office-holders, serve the State chiefly with their heads; and, as they rarely make any moral distinctions, they are as likely to serve the devil,

---

[2]*"Not a drum was heard..."*: From "The Burial of Sir John Moore at Corunna" by Charles Wolfe (1791–1823).

without intending it, as God. A very few, as heroes, patriots, martyrs, reformers in the great sense, and *men* serve the State with their consciences also, and so necessarily resist it for the most part; and they are commonly treated by it as enemies. A wise man will only be useful as a man, and will not submit to be "clay," and "stop a hole to keep the wind away," but leave that office to his dust at least: —

> "I am too high-born to be propertied,
>   To be a secondary at control,
>   Or useful serving-man and instrument
>   To any sovereign state throughout the world."[3]

He who gives himself entirely to his fellow-men appears to them useless and selfish; but he who gives himself partially to them is pronounced a benefactor and philanthropist.

How does it become a man to behave toward this American government to-day? I answer that he cannot without disgrace be associated with it. I cannot for an instant recognize that political organization as *my* government which is the *slave's* government also.

All men recognize the right of revolution; that is, the right to refuse allegiance to and to resist the government, when its tyranny or its inefficiency are great and unendurable. But almost all say that such is not the case now. But such was the case, they think, in the Revolution of '75. If one were to tell me that this was a bad government because it taxed certain foreign commodities brought to its ports, it is most probable that I should not make an ado about it, for I can do without them: all machines have their friction; and possibly this does enough good to counterbalance the evil. At any rate, it is a great evil to make a stir about it. But when the friction comes to have its machine, and oppression and robbery are organized, I say, let us not have such a machine any longer. In other words, when a sixth of the population of a nation which has undertaken to be the refuge of liberty are slaves, and a whole country is unjustly overrun and conquered by a foreign army, and subjected to military law, I think that it is not too soon for honest men to rebel and revolutionize. What makes this duty the more urgent is the fact, that the country so overrun is not our own, but ours is the invading army. . . .

Practically speaking, the opponents to . . . reform . . . are not a hundred thousand politicians at the South, but a hundred thousand merchants and farmers here, who are more interested in commerce and agriculture than they are in humanity, and are not prepared to do justice to the slave and to Mexico, *cost what it may.* I quarrel not with far-off foes, but with those who, near at home, co-operate with, and do the bidding of those far away,

---

[3]"*I am too high-born . . .*": From *The Tragedy of Hamlet, Prince of Denmark*, by William Shakespeare (1564–1616).

and without whom the latter would be harmless. We are accustomed to say, that the mass of men are unprepared; but improvement is slow, because the few are not materially wiser or better than the many. It is not so important that many should be as good as you, as that there be some absolute goodness somewhere; for that will leaven the whole lump. There are thousands who are *in opinion* opposed to slavery and to the war, who yet in effect do nothing to put an end to them; who, esteeming themselves children of Washington and Franklin, sit down with their hands in their pockets, and say that they know not what to do, and do nothing; who even postpone the question of freedom to the question of free-trade, and quietly read the prices-current along with the latest advices from Mexico, after dinner, and, it may be, fall asleep over them both. What is the price-current of an honest man and patriot to-day? They hesitate, and they regret, and sometimes they petition; but they do nothing in earnest and with effect. They will wait, well disposed, for others to remedy the evil, that they may no longer have it to regret. At most, they give only a cheap vote, and a feeble countenance and God-speed, to the right, as it goes by them. There are nine hundred and ninety-nine patrons of virtue to one virtuous man; but it is easier to deal with the real possessor of a thing than with the temporary guardian of it.

All voting is a sort of gaming, like chequers or backgammon, with a   10
slight moral tinge to it, a playing with right and wrong, with moral questions; and betting naturally accompanies it. The character of the voters is not staked. I cast my vote, perchance, as I think right; but I am not vitally concerned that that right should prevail. I am willing to leave it to the majority. Its obligation, therefore, never exceeds that of expediency. Even voting *for the right* is *doing* nothing for it. It is only expressing to men feebly your desire that it should prevail. A wise man will not leave the right to the mercy of chance, nor wish it to prevail through the power of the majority. There is but little virtue in the action of masses of men. When the majority shall at length vote for the abolition of slavery, it will be because they are indifferent to slavery, or because there is but little slavery left to be abolished by their vote. *They* will then be the only slaves. Only *his* vote can hasten the abolition of slavery who asserts his own freedom by his vote.

I hear of a convention to be held at Baltimore, or elsewhere, for the selection of a candidate for the Presidency, made up chiefly of editors, and men who are politicians by profession; but I think, what is it to any independent, intelligent, and respectable man what decision they may come to, shall we not have the advantage of his wisdom and honesty, nevertheless? Can we not count upon some independent votes? Are there not many individuals in the country who do not attend conventions? But no: I find that the respectable man, so called, has immediately drifted from his position, and despairs of his country, when his country has more reason to despair of him. He forthwith adopts one of the candidates thus selected as the only *available* one, thus proving that he is himself *available* for any purposes of the demagogue. His vote is of no more worth than that of any unprincipled foreigner or hireling native, who may have been bought. Oh for a man who is a *man,* and, as my neighbor says, has a bone in his back which you cannot pass your hand through! Our statistics are at fault: the population has been returned too large. How many *men* are there to a square thousand miles in this country? Hardly one. Does not America offer any inducement for men to settle here? The American has dwindled into an Odd Fellow,[4] — one who may be known by the development of his organ of gregariousness, and a manifest lack of intellect and cheerful self-reliance; whose first and chief concern, on coming into the world, is to see that the alms-houses are in good repair; and, before yet he has lawfully donned the virile garb, to collect a fund for the support of the widows and orphans that may be; who, in short, ventures to live only by the aid of the mutual insurance company, which has promised to bury him decently.

It is not a man's duty, as a matter of course, to devote himself to the eradication of any, even the most enormous wrong; he may still properly have other concerns to engage him; but it is his duty, at least, to wash his hands of it, and, if he gives it no thought longer, not to give it practically his support. If I devote myself to other pursuits and contemplations, I must first see, at least, that I do not pursue them sitting upon another man's shoulders. I must get off him first, that he may pursue his contemplations too. See what gross inconsistency is tolerated. I have heard some of my townsmen say, "I should like to have them order me out to help put down an insurrection of the slaves, or to march to Mexico, — see if I would go;" and yet these very men have each, directly by their allegiance, and so indirectly, at least, by their money, furnished a substitute. The soldier is applauded who refuses to serve in an unjust war by those who do not refuse to sustain the unjust government which makes the war; is applauded by those whose own act and authority he disregards and sets at naught; as if the State were penitent to that degree that it hired one to scourge it while it sinned, but not to that degree that it left off sinning for a moment. Thus, under the name of order and civil government, we are all made at last to pay homage to and support our own meanness. After the first blush of sin, comes its indifference; and from immoral it becomes, as it were, unmoral, and not quite unnecessary to that life which we have made.

The broadest and most prevalent error requires the most disinterested virtue to sustain it. The slight reproach to which the virtue of patriotism is commonly liable, the noble are most likely to incur. Those who, while they disapprove of the character and measures of a government, yield to it their allegiance and support are undoubtedly its most conscientious supporters, and so frequently the most serious obstacles to reform. Some are petitioning the State to dissolve the Union, to disregard the requisitions of the

---

[4]*an Odd Fellow:* Independent Order of Odd Fellows is a worldwide fraternal organization dating from the mid-1700s in England.

President. Why do they not dissolve it themselves, — the union between themselves and the State, — and refuse to pay their quota into its treasury? Do not they stand in the same relation to the State that the State does to the Union? And have not the same reasons prevented the State from resisting the Union, which have prevented them from resisting the State?

How can a man be satisfied to entertain an opinion merely, and enjoy *it?* Is there any enjoyment in it, if his opinion is that he is aggrieved? If you are cheated out of a single dollar by your neighbor, you do not rest satisfied with knowing that you are cheated, or with saying that you are cheated, or even with petitioning him to pay you your due; but you take effectual steps at once to obtain the full amount, and see that you are never cheated again. Action from principle, — the perception and the performance of right, — changes things and relations; it is essentially revolutionary, and does not consist wholly with any thing which was. It not only divides states and churches, it divides families; aye, it divides the *individual,* separating the diabolical in him from the divine.

Unjust laws exist: shall we be content to obey them, or shall we endeavor   15
to amend them, and obey them until we have succeeded, or shall we transgress them at once? Men generally, under such a government as this, think that they ought to wait until they have persuaded the majority to alter them. They think that, if they should resist, the remedy would be worse than the evil. But it is the fault of the government itself that the remedy *is* worse than the evil. *It* makes it worse. Why is it not more apt to anticipate and provide for reform? Why does it not cherish its wise minority? Why does it cry and resist before it is hurt? Why does it not encourage its citizens to be on the alert to point out its faults, and *do* better than it would have them? Why does it always crucify Christ, and excommunicate Copernicus and Luther, and pronounce Washington and Franklin rebels?

One would think, that a deliberate and practical denial of its authority was the only offence never contemplated by government; else, why has it not assigned its definite, its suitable and proportionate penalty? If a man who has no property refuses but once to earn nine shillings for the State, he is put in prison for a period unlimited by any law that I know, and determined only by the discretion of those who placed him there; but if he should steal ninety times nine shillings from the State, he is soon permitted to go at large again.

If the injustice is part of the necessary friction of the machine of government, let it go, let it go: perchance it will wear smooth — certainly the machine will wear out. If the injustice has a spring, or a pulley, or a rope, or a crank, exclusively for itself, then perhaps you may consider whether the remedy will not be worse than the evil; but if it is of such a nature that it requires you to be the agent of injustice to another, then, I say, break the law. Let your life be a counter friction to stop the machine. What I have to do is to see, at any rate, that I do not lend myself to the wrong which I condemn.

As for adopting the ways which the State has provided for remedying the evil, I know not of such ways. They take too much time, and a man's life will be gone. I have other affairs to attend to. I came into this world, not chiefly to make this a good place to live in, but to live in it, be it good or bad. A man has not every thing to do, but something; and because he cannot do *every thing*, it is not necessary that he should do *something* wrong. It is not my business to be petitioning the governor or the legislature any more than it is theirs to petition me; and if they should not hear my petition, what should I do then? But in this case the State has provided no way: its very Constitution is the evil. This may seem to be harsh and stubborn and unconciliatory; but it is to treat with the utmost kindness and consideration the only spirit that can appreciate or deserves it. So is all change for the better, like birth and death which convulse the body.

I do not hesitate to say, that those who call themselves abolitionists should at once effectually withdraw their support, both in person and property, from the government of Massachusetts, and not wait till they constitute a majority of one, before they suffer the right to prevail through them. I think that it is enough if they have God on their side, without waiting for that other one. Moreover, any man more right than his neighbors constitutes a majority of one already.

I meet this American government, or its representative the State government, directly, and face to face, once a year, no more, in the person of its tax-gatherer; this is the only mode in which a man situated as I am necessarily meets it; and it then says distinctly, Recognize me; and the simplest, the most effectual, and, in the present posture of affairs, the indispensablest mode of treating with it on this head, of expressing your little satisfaction with and love for it, is to deny it then. My civil neighbor, the tax-gatherer, is the very man I have to deal with, — for it is, after all, with men and not with parchment that I quarrel, — and he has voluntarily chosen to be an agent of the government. How shall he ever know well what he is and does as an officer of the government, or as a man, until he is obliged to consider whether he shall treat me, his neighbor, for whom he has respect, as a neighbor and well-disposed man, or as a maniac and disturber of the peace, and see if he can get over this obstruction to his neighborliness without a ruder and more impetuous thought or speech corresponding with his action? I know this well, that if one thousand, if one hundred, if ten men whom I could name, — if ten *honest* men only, — aye, if *one* HONEST man, in this State of Massachusetts, *ceasing to hold slaves,* were actually to withdraw from his copartnership, and be locked up in the county jail therefor, it would be the abolition of slavery in America. For it matters not how small the beginning may seem to be: what is once well done is done for ever. But we love better to talk about it: that we say is our mission. Reform keeps many scores of newspapers in its service, but not one man. If my esteemed neighbor, the State's ambassador, who will devote his days to the settlement of the question of human rights in the Council Chamber, instead of being threatened

20

with the prisons of Carolina, were to sit down the prisoner of Massachusetts, that State which is so anxious to foist the sin of slavery upon her sister, — though at present she can discover only an act of inhospitality to be the ground of a quarrel with her, — the Legislature would not wholly waive the subject the following winter.

Under a government which imprisons any unjustly, the true place for a just man is also in prison. The proper place to-day, the only place which Massachusetts has provided for her freer and less desponding spirits, is in her prisons, to be put out and locked out of the State by her own act, as they have already put themselves out by their principles. It is there that the fugitive slave, and the Mexican prisoner on parole, and the Indian come to plead the wrongs of his race, should find them; on that separate, but more free and honorable ground, where the State places those who are not *with* her, but *against* her, — the only house in a slave-state in which a free man can abide with honor. If any think that their influence would be lost there, and their voices no longer afflict the ear of the State, that they would not be as an enemy within its walls, they do not know by how much truth is stronger than error, nor how much more eloquently and effectively he can combat injustice who has experienced a little in his own person. Cast your whole vote, not a strip of paper merely, but your whole influence. A minority is powerless while it conforms to the majority; it is not even a minority then; but it is irresistible when it clogs by its whole weight. If the alternative is to keep all just men in prison, or give up war and slavery, the State will not hesitate which to choose. If a thousand men were not to pay their tax-bills this year, that would not be a violent and bloody measure, as it would be to pay them, and enable the State to commit violence and shed innocent blood. This is, in fact, the definition of a peaceable revolution, if any such is possible. If the tax-gatherer, or any other public officer, asks me, as one has done, "But what shall I do?" my answer is, "If you really wish to do any thing, resign your office." When the subject has refused allegiance, and the officer has resigned his office, then the revolution is accomplished. But even suppose blood should flow. Is there not a sort of blood shed when the conscience is wounded? Through this wound a man's real manhood and immortality flow out, and he bleeds to an everlasting death. I see this blood flowing now.

I have contemplated the imprisonment of the offender, rather than the seizure of his goods, — though both will serve the same purpose, — because they who assert the purest right, and consequently are most dangerous to a corrupt State, commonly have not spent much time in accumulating property. To such the State renders comparatively small service, and a slight tax is wont to appear exorbitant, particularly if they are obliged to earn it by special labor with their hands. If there were one who lived wholly without the use of money, the State itself would hesitate to demand it of him. But the rich man — not to make any invidious comparison — is always sold to the institution which makes him rich. Absolutely speaking, the more money, the less virtue; for money comes between a man and his objects, and obtains them for him; and it was certainly no great virtue to obtain it. It puts to rest many questions which he would otherwise be taxed to answer; while the only new question which it puts is the hard but superfluous one, how to spend it. Thus his moral ground is taken from under his feet. The opportunities of living are diminished in proportion as what are called the "means" are increased. The best thing a man can do for his culture when he is rich is to endeavour to carry out those schemes which he entertained when he was poor. Christ answered the Herodians according to their condition. "Show me the tribute-money," said he; — and one took a penny out of his pocket; — if you use money which has the image of Caesar on it, and which he has made current and valuable, that is, *if you are men of the State,* and gladly enjoy the advantages of Caesar's government, then pay him back some of his own when he demands it. "Render therefore to Caesar that which is Caesar's, and to God those things which are God's," — leaving them no wiser than before as to which was which; for they did not wish to know.

When I converse with the freest of my neighbors, I perceive that, whatever they may say about the magnitude and seriousness of the question, and their regard for the public tranquillity, the long and the short of the matter is, that they cannot spare the protection of the existing government, and they dread the consequences of disobedience to it to their property and families. For my own part, I should not like to think that I ever rely on the protection of the State. But, if I deny the authority of the State when it presents its tax-bill, it will soon take and waste all my property, and so harass me and my children without end. This is hard. This makes it impossible for a man to live honestly, and at the same time comfortably in outward respects. It will not be worth the while to accumulate property; that would be sure to go again. You must hire or squat somewhere, and raise but a small crop, and eat that soon. You must live within yourself, and depend upon yourself, always tucked up and ready for a start, and not have many affairs. A man may grow rich in Turkey even, if he will be in all respects a good subject of the Turkish government. Confucius said, — "If a State is governed by the principles of reason, poverty and misery are subjects of shame; if a State is not governed by the principles of reason, riches and honors are the subjects of shame." No: until I want the protection of Massachusetts to be extended to me in some distant southern port, where my liberty is endangered, or until I am bent solely on building up an estate at home by peaceful enterprise, I can afford to refuse allegiance to Massachusetts, and her right to my property and life. It costs me less in every sense to incur the penalty of disobedience to the State than it would to obey. I should feel as if I were worth less in that case.

Some years ago, the State met me in behalf of the church, and commanded me to pay a certain sum toward the support of a clergyman whose preaching my father attended, but never I myself. "Pay it," it said, "or be locked up in the jail." I declined to pay. But, unfortunately, another man saw fit to pay it. I did not see why the schoolmaster should be taxed to support the priest, and not the priest the schoolmaster; for I was not the State's schoolmaster, but I supported myself by voluntary subscription. I did not see why the lyceum should not present its tax-bill, and have the State to back its demand, as well as the church. However, at the request of the selectmen, I condescended to make some such statement as this in writing: — "Know all men by these presents, that I, Henry Thoreau, do not wish to be regarded as a member of any incorporated society which I have not joined." This I gave to the town-clerk; and he has it. The State, having thus learned that I did not wish to be regarded as a member of that church, has never made a like demand on me since; though it said that it must adhere to its original presumption that time. If I had known how to name them, I should then have signed off in detail from all the societies which I never signed on to; but I did not know where to find a complete list.

I have paid no poll-tax for six years. I was put into a jail once on this 25 account, for one night; and, as I stood considering the walls of solid stone, two or three feet thick, the door of wood and iron, a foot thick, and the iron grating which strained the light, I could not help being struck with the foolishness of that institution which treated me as if I were mere flesh and blood and bones, to be locked up. I wondered that it should have concluded at length that this was the best use it could put me to, and had never thought to avail itself of my services in some way. I saw that, if there was a wall of stone between me and my townsmen, there was a still more difficult one to climb or break through, before they could get to be as free as I was. I did not for a moment feel confined, and the walls seemed a great waste of stone and mortar. I felt as if I alone of all my townsmen had paid my tax. They plainly did not know how to treat me, but behaved like persons who are underbred. In every threat and in every compliment there was a blunder; for they thought that my chief desire was to stand the other side of that stone wall. I could not but smile to see how industriously they locked the door on my meditations, which followed them out again without let or hinderance, and *they* were really all that was dangerous. As they could not reach me, they had resolved to punish my body; just as boys, if they cannot come at some person against whom they have a spite, will abuse his dog. I saw that the State was half-witted, that it was timid as a lone woman with her silver spoons, and that it did not know its friends from its foes, and I lost all my remaining respect for it, and pitied it.

Thus the State never intentionally confronts a man's sense, intellectual or moral, but only his body, his senses. It is not armed with superior wit or honesty, but with superior physical strength. I was not born to be forced. I will breathe after my own fashion. Let us see who is the strongest. What force has a multitude? They only can force me who obey a higher law than I. They force me to become like themselves. I do not hear of *men* being *forced* to live this way or that by masses of men. What sort of life were that to live? When I meet a government which says to me, "Your money or your life," why should I be in haste to give it my money? It may be in a great strait, and not know what to do: I cannot help that. It must help itself; do as I do. It is not worth the while to snivel about it. I am not responsible for the successful working of the machinery of society. I am not the son of the engineer. I perceive that, when an acorn and a chestnut fall side by side, the one does not remain inert to make way for the other, but both obey their own laws, and spring and grow and flourish as best they can, till one, perchance, overshadows and destroys the other. If a plant cannot live according to its nature, it dies; and so a man. . . .

The authority of government, even such as I am willing to submit to, — for I will cheerfully obey those who know and can do better than I, and in many things even those who neither know nor can do so well, — is still an impure one: to be strictly just, it must have the sanction and consent of the governed. It can have no pure right over my person and property but what I concede to it. The progress from an absolute to a limited monarchy, from a limited monarchy to a democracy, is a progress toward a true respect for the individual. Even the Chinese philosopher was wise enough to regard the individual as the basis of the empire. Is a democracy, such as we know it, the last improvement possible in government? Is it not possible to take a step further towards recognizing and organizing the rights of man? There will never be a really free and enlightened State, until the State comes to recognize the individual as a higher and independent power, from which all its own power and authority are derived, and treats him accordingly. I please myself with imagining a State at last which can afford to be just to all men, and to treat the individual with respect as a neighbor; which even would not think it inconsistent with its own repose, if a few were to live aloof from it, not meddling with it, nor embraced by it, who fulfilled all the duties of neighbors and fellowmen. A State which bore this kind of fruit, and suffered it to drop off as fast as it ripened, would prepare the way for a still more perfect and glorious State, which also I have imagined, but not yet anywhere seen.

ENGAGING THE TEXT

1. How does Thoreau view government? What, in his view, are its proper functions? What kinds of things should governments not do? To what extent would you agree? Why?
2. What are Thoreau's complaints against the United States? How do you think he would respond to slogans like "Support our troops"? Why?
3. Why does Thoreau dislike the idea of voting? How should a democracy function, in his view, if it doesn't rely on majority rule?
4. How would you characterize Thoreau's view of his fellow Americans? Do you think that we, as a people, have changed much since the 1840s?
5. What, exactly, is Thoreau suggesting that citizens do when they feel their principles are being violated by the state? How does this form of "peaceable revolution" differ from simple lawlessness? When does he feel that acts of civil disobedience are justified?

6. Freewrite for a few minutes about what you think the United States would be like if it were organized according to Thoreau's theory of radical individualism. How would American government and society function if the United States were structured around Thoreau's vision of absolute independence?

EXPLORING CONNECTIONS

7. How would Thoreau be likely to respond to the depiction of America's role in world affairs, as presented by Albert J. Beveridge (p. 762) and Joel Andreas (p. 794)?

8. Compare Thoreau's notion of freedom with that of Dinesh D'Souza (p. 768). To what extent might Thoreau agree with D'Souza's claim that America, as the home of the free, has as its goal "transforming Muslim fundamentalists into classical liberals" or that "America is worthy of our love and sacrifice because . . . it makes possible the good life, and the life that is good"?

9. Who, among all the authors and characters you've encountered in this book, do you think Thoreau would most admire? Why?

EXTENDING THE CRITICAL CONTEXT

10. To test Thoreau's notion of resistance to government authority, hold a class debate on whether Americans would be justified in refusing to serve in the military if "universal conscription" were reinstated for all residents between the ages of eighteen and twenty-six. Given what's happening in the world today, would you personally refuse to serve if the draft were reinstated? Why or why not?

11. Research the concept of civil disobedience, including its association with historical figures like Leo Tolstoy, Mohandas Gandhi, Martin Luther King Jr., and Nelson Mandela. When, in your view, is the individual citizen justified in resisting governmental authority?

12. Research the historical background of Thoreau's essay, including the debates surrounding the Mexican-American War and the abolition movement in the 1840s. What parallels do you see between America's situation then and now?

Let America Be America Again

LANGSTON HUGHES

Our survey of American culture closes with a reflection on the power that the myth of freedom has to inspire hope, even in the face of despair. Written nine years into the great Depression, "Let America Be America Again" (1938) offers a stinging indictment of the hypocrisy that Langston Hughes perceived everywhere in American life. Yet Hughes transcends his rage and dares to hope for America's future; in so doing he pays homage to ideals that retain their potency even in the twenty-first century. James Langston Hughes (1902–1967) was a major figure in the Harlem Renaissance — a flowering of African American artists, musicians, and writers in New York City in the 1920s. His poems, often examining the experiences of urban African American life, use the rhythms of jazz, spirituals, and the blues. Among the most popular of his works today are The Ways of White Folks *(1934), a collection of short stories, and* Montage of a Dream Deferred *(1951), a selection of his poetry.*

Let America be America again.
Let it be the dream it used to be.
Let it be the pioneer on the plain
Seeking a home where he himself is free.

(America never was America to me.)   5

Let America be the dream the dreamers dreamed —
Let it be that great strong land of love
Where never kings connive nor tyrants scheme
That any man be crushed by one above.

(It never was America to me.)   10

O, let my land be a land where Liberty
Is crowned with no false patriotic wreath,
But opportunity is real, and life is free,
Equality is in the air we breathe.

(There's never been equality for me,   15
Nor freedom in this "homeland of the free.")

Say who are you that mumbles in the dark?
And who are you that draws your veil across the stars?

I am the poor white, fooled and pushed apart,
I am the red man driven from the land.   20
I am the refugee clutching the hope I seek —
But finding only the same old stupid plan
Of dog eat dog, of mighty crush the weak.
I am the Negro, "problem" to you all.
I am the people, humble, hungry, mean —   25
Hungry yet today despite the dream.
Beaten yet today — O, Pioneers!
I am the man who never got ahead.
The poorest worker bartered through the years.

Yet I'm the one who dreamt our basic dream 30
In that Old World while still a serf of kings,
Who dreamt a dream so strong, so brave, so true,
That even yet its mighty daring sings
In every brick and stone, in every furrow turned
That's made America the land it has become. 35
O, I'm the man who sailed those early seas
In search of what I meant to be my home —
For I'm the one who left dark Ireland's shore,
And Poland's plain, and England's grassy lea,
And torn from Black Africa's strand I came 40
To build a "homeland of the free."

The free?
Who said the free? Not me?
Surely not me? The millions on relief today?
The millions who have nothing for our pay 45
For all the dreams we've dreamed
And all the songs we sung
And all the hopes we've held
And all the flags we've hung,
The millions who have nothing for our pay — 50
Except the dream we keep alive today.

O, let America be America again —
The land that never has been yet —
And yet must be — the land where *every* man is free.
The land that's mine — the poor man's, Indian's, Negro's, ME — 55
Who made America,
Whose sweat and blood, whose faith and pain,
Whose hand at the foundry, whose plow in the rain,
Must bring back our mighty dream again.

O, yes, 60
I say it plain,
America never was America to me,
And yet I swear this oath —
America will be!

ENGAGING THE TEXT

1. Explain the two senses of the word "America" as Hughes uses it in the title and refrain of the poem.
2. According to Hughes, who must rebuild the dream, and why?
3. Why does Hughes reaffirm the dream of an ideal America in the face of so much evidence to the contrary?

4. Explain the irony of lines 40–41 ("And torn from Black Africa's strand I came / To build a 'homeland of the free' ").
5. Examine the way Hughes uses line length, repetition, stanza breaks, typography, and indentation to call attention to particular lines of the poem. Why does he emphasize these passages?

EXPLORING CONNECTIONS

6. Write an imaginary dialogue between Hughes, Dinesh D'Souza (p. 768), Todd Gitlin (p. 823), and Henry David Thoreau (p. 836) on the state of freedom in America. What does freedom mean to each of these writers? Which conveys the most optimistic view of the future of freedom in America?
7. Review some or all of the poems in *Rereading America:*

Melvin Dixon, "Aunt Ida Pieces a Quilt" (p. 48)

Sharon Olds, "From Seven Floors Up" (p. 332)

Dana Gioia, "Money" (p. 330)

Aurora Levins Morales, "Child of the Americas" (p. 609)

Inés Hernández-Ávila, "Para Teresa" (p. 206)

Langston Hughes, "Let America Be America Again" (p. 848)

Then discuss the role of poetry as a form of social action. What are the characteristics of this type of poetry? How does it differ from the poetry you have read before in school?

EXTENDING THE CRITICAL CONTEXT

8. Working in groups, "stage" a reading of the poem, using multiple speakers. Consider carefully how to divide up the lines for the most effective presentation. After the readings, discuss the choices made by the different groups in the class.
9. Working in pairs or in small groups, write prose descriptions of the two versions of America Hughes evokes. Read these aloud and discuss which description more closely matches your own view of the United States.

FURTHER CONNECTIONS

1. Survey the contents of several online foreign newspapers and news services available in English to assess how other nations view America. To make this task easier, you may want to work in groups that focus on papers from a specific region (for example, Europe, the Middle East, or Asia). To what extent do foreign news sources support or challenge the mythic view of America as the land of liberty?

2. Working in groups, assemble a collage of quotations, words, and images, from magazines, newspapers, books, or Web sites, that evoke the idea of American freedom. Try to make your collage as rich and as complicated as possible, without worrying about coherence or about focusing it on a particular theme or message. After you're done, share the results of your work in class and discuss what these collages say about the meaning of freedom in America.

3. Since 9/11, many groups, including the American Library Association and the American Civil Liberties Union, have complained that domestic surveillance provisions in the 2001 USA PATRIOT Act (Senate Bill 3162) have infringed on individual rights. Do some online research to learn more about the controversy surrounding the Patriot Act. How might extreme antiterrorism measures, such as the use of warrantless wiretaps, the surveillance of Internet searches, and the subpoenaing of library records, jeopardize freedom of thought in the United States? How far do you think we can go as a nation to protect national security without giving up essential individual freedoms?

4. Do additional research on the impact of American popular culture abroad. How popular are American films, television shows, and music in countries around the world? What concerns do foreign cultural and political leaders raise about the spread of American cultural influences? To what extent does your research confirm or challenge the idea that American culture continues to be the dominant world culture in an era of increasing globalization?

5. Choose a contemporary or historical American figure who represents the spirit of American freedom for you, and do additional research to learn more about this person's life and values. Once you've completed your research, write a brief profile of this person, detailing his or her beliefs, values, and accomplishments. Later, share these profiles in class, and discuss what they suggest about the way you view the idea of freedom in America.

Text Acknowledgments

Sherman Alexie. "Assimilation." From *The Toughest Indian in the World* by Sherman Alexie. Copyright © 2000 by Sherman Alexie. Used by permission of Grove/Atlantic, Inc.

Horatio Alger. "Assimilation." From *Ragged Dick and Mark the Match Boy* by Horatio Alger. Copyright © 1962 by Macmillan Publishing Company. Reprinted with the permission of Scribner, a Division of Simon & Schuster Adult Publishing Group. All rights reserved.

Joel Andreas. "The War on Terrorism." Reprinted with the permission of the author.

Jean Anyon. "Social Class and the Hidden Curriculum of Work." From *Journal of Education*, Boston University School of Education (1980), Volume 162, No. 1. Copyright © 1980 by the Trustees of Boston University. Reprinted with permission from the Trustees of Boston University and the author.

Judy Root Aulette. Excerpt from *Changing American Families* by Judy Root Aulette. Copyright © 2002 by Pearson Education. Published by Allyn and Bacon, Boston, MA. Reprinted by permission of the publisher.

Toni Cade Bambara. "The Lesson." From *Gorilla, My Love* by Toni Cade Bambara. Copyright © 1972 by Toni Cade Bambara. Used by permission of Random House, Inc.

Stephanie Coontz. "What We Really Miss About the 1950s." From *The Way We Really Are* by Stephanie Coontz. Copyright © 1997 by Basic Books, a division of HarperCollins Publishers, Inc. Reprinted by permission of Basic Books, a member of Perseus Books Group.

Ellis Cose. "Discharging a Debt." From *Bone to Pick: Of Forgiveness, Reconciliation, Reparation, and Revenge* by Ellis Cose. Copyright © 2004 by Ellis Cose. Reprinted and edited with the permission of Atria Books, an imprint of Simon & Schuster Adult Publishing Group. All rights reserved.

Harlon L. Dalton. "Horatio Alger." From *Racial Healing* by Harlon L. Dalton. Copyright © 1995 by Harlon L. Dalton. Used by permission of Doubleday, a division of Random House, Inc.

Aaron H. Devor. "Becoming Members of Society: Learning the Social Meanings of Gender." From *Gender Blending: Confronting the Limits of Duality* by Holly Devor. Copyright © 1998 by Indiana University Press. Reprinted with the permission of the publisher.

Melvin Dixon. "Aunt Ida Pieces a Quilt." From *Love's Instruments* by Melvin Dixon. Originally published by Tia Churcha Press. Reprinted with permission of the Estate of Melvin Dixon.

Dinesh D'Souza. "America the Beautiful: What We're Fighting For." From *What's So Great About America* by Dinesh D'Souza. Copyright © 2002 by Dinesh D'Souza. Reprinted with permission of Regnery Publishing.

Diana L. Eck. "Afraid of Ourselves." From *A New Religious America* by Diana L. Eck. Copyright © 2001 by Diana L. Eck. Reprinted by permission of HarperCollins Publishers.

Barbara Ehrenreich. "Serving in Florida." From *Nickel and Dimed* by Barbara Ehrenreich. Copyright © 2001 by Barbara Ehrenreich. Reprinted by permission of Henry Holt and Company, LLC.

Noah Feldman. "Schools and Morals." From *Divided by God: America's Church-State Problem* by Noah Feldman. Copyright © 2005 by Noah Feldman. Copyright © 2005 by Noah Feldman. Reprinted with permission of Farrar, Straus and Giroux, LLC.

George M. Fredrickson. "Models of American Ethnic Relations: A Historical Perspective." From *Cultural Divides: Understanding and Overcoming Group Conflict*, edited by Deborah A. Prentice and Dale T. Miller. Copyright © 1999 Russell Sage Foundation. Reprinted with the permission of the Russell Sage Foundation.

558, Todd Bigelow/Aurora Photos.

559, © A. Ramey/PhotoEdit.

560, Photograph by Roland Charles © Roland Charles Fine Art Collection & Black Photographers of California/Corbis.Used with permission of Deborah Charles.

565, *La Cucaracha* © 2003 Lalo Alcaraz. Distributed by Universal Press Syndicate. All rights reserved.

579, © Christophe Vorlet. Used with permission.

CHAPTER 6: ONE NATION UNDER GOD
613, David Hogan/Getty Images.

674, David Horsey. © Tribune Media Services, Inc. Reprinted with permission. All rights reserved.

685, *TOLES* © 2000 The Buffalo News. Reprinted with permission of Universal Press Syndicate. All rights reserved.

687, *Apotheosis of George Washington.* Jack Smith Lincoln Collection. Collection number P 0406. Digital image © 2003 Indiana Historical Society. All rights reserved.

688, *Buddy Christ,* © Kevin Smith/View Askew. All rights reserved. Used with permission. Photo courtesy of Shooting Star.

689, © Sonda Dawes/The Image Works.

690, © Bob Daemmrich/Corbis.

691, Marilyn Humphries/The Image Works.

692, © Bettmann/Corbis.

710, Rob Rogers © The Pittsburgh Post-Gazette/Dist. By United Feature Syndicate, Inc.

724, © Sargent. © 2001 Austin American-Statesman. Reproduced with permission of Universal Press Syndicate. All rights reserved.

738, *Non Sequitur* © 2006 Wiley Miller. Dist. By Universal Press Syndicate. All rights reserved.

CHAPTER 7: LAND OF LIBERTY
755, Mel Levine/Time Life Pictures/Getty Images.

780, © 2001 Matt Groening. All rights reserved. Reprinted by permission of Acme Features Syndicate.

806, © Michael Fairbanks, photographer.

807, Jimin Lai/AFP/ © Getty Images.

808, Shane McCoy/Mai/AFP/ © Getty Images.

809, © Damir Sagolj/© Getty Images.

810, Chung Sung-Jun/AFP/ © Getty Images.

811–12, Associated Press Photo.

813, © 2004 Getty Images/ Photo by Brian Davidson/U.S. Air Force via Getty Images.

823, *TOLES* © 2006 The Washington Post. Reproduced with permission of Universal Press Syndicate. All rights reserved.

835, *This Modern World* by Tom Tomorrow. © Dan Perkins. All rights reserved. Used with permission.

Index of Authors and Titles

Visit the RE: WRITING Web Site
for Help with Writing and Research

bedfordstmartins.com/rewriting

RE: WRITING is a comprehensive Web site designed to help students with the most common writing concerns. You'll find advice from experts, models you can rely on, and exercises that will tell you right away how you're doing. And it's all free and available any hour of the day.

RE: WRITING includes help for all of the following situations:

Need help with grammar problems?
    Exercise Central

Want to see what papers for your other courses look like?
    Model Documents Gallery

Stuck somewhere in the research process? (Maybe at the beginning?)
    The Bedford Research Room

Wondering whether a Web site is good enough to use in your paper?
    Evaluating Online Sources Tutorial

Having trouble figuring out how to cite a source?
    Research and Documentation Online

Confused about plagiarism?
    Avoiding Plagiarism Tutorial

Want to get more out of your word processor?
    Using Your Word Processor

Trying to improve the look of your paper?
    Designing Documents with a Word Processor

Need to create slides for a presentation?
    Preparing Presentation Slides Tutorial

Interested in creating a Web site?
    Mike Markel's Web Design Tutorial